AutoCAD® 2010 in 2D and 3D

AutoCAD® 2010 in 2D and 3D
A Modern Perspective

Paul Richard

Frank E. Puerta

Jim Fitzgerald

Prentice Hall

Boston   Columbus   Indianapolis   New York   San Francisco   Upper Saddle River
Amsterdam   Cape Town   Dubai   London   Madrid   Milan   Munich   Paris   Montreal   Toronto
Delhi   Mexico City   Sao Paulo   Sydney   Hong Kong   Seoul   Singapore   Taipei   Tokyo

Editor in Chief: Vernon R. Anthony
Acquisitions Editor: Jill Jones-Renger
Editorial Assistant: Doug Greive
Director of Marketing: David Gesell
Marketing Manager: Kara Clark
Senior Marketing Coordinator:
   Alicia Wozniak
Senior Managing Editor: JoEllen Gohr
Associate Managing Editor: Alexandrina Wolf
Project Manager: Louise Sette
Senior Operations Supervisor: Pat Tonneman

Operations Specialist: Deidra Schwartz
Senior Art Director: Diane Y. Ernsberger
Cover Designer: Jason Moore
Cover Image: Super Stock
AV Project Manager: Janet Portisch
Full-Service Project Management:
   Lisa Garboski, bookworks publishing services
Composition: Aptara®, Inc.
Printer/Binder: Edwards Brothers, Inc.
Cover Printer: Coral Graphic Services, Inc.
Text Font: Times New Roman

Certain images and materials contained in this publication were reproduced with the permission of Autodesk, Inc. © 2010. All rights reserved. Autodesk, AutoCAD, DWG, and the DWG logo are registered trademarks of Autodesk, Inc., in the U.S.A. and certain other countries.

Disclaimer:

The publication is designed to provide tutorial information about AutoCAD® and/or other Autodesk computer programs. Every effort has been made to make this publication complete and as accurate as possible. The reader is expressly cautioned to use any and all precautions necessary, and to take appropriate steps to avoid hazards, when engaging in the activities described herein.

Neither the author nor the publisher makes any representations or warranties of any kind, with respect to the materials set forth in this publication, express or implied, including without limitation any warranties of fitness for a particular purpose or merchantability. Nor shall the author or the publisher be liable for any special, consequential or exemplary damages resulting, in whole or in part, directly or indirectly, from the reader's use of, or reliance upon, this material or subsequent revisions of this material.

Library of Congress Cataloging-in-Publication Data: 2009925834

10 9 8 7 6 5 4 3 2

Prentice Hall
is an imprint of

www.pearsonhighered.com

ISBN-10:   0-13-507931-4
ISBN-13: 978-0-13-507931-7

THE NEW AUTODESK EDUCATION PRESS SERIES

Pearson/Prentice Hall has formed an alliance with Autodesk® to develop textbooks and other course materials that address the skills, methodology, and learning pedagogy for the industries that are supported by the Autodesk® Education software offerings that assist educators in teaching design.

Features of the New Autodesk Education Press Series

Job Skills—Coverage of computer-aided drafting job skills, compiled through research of industry associations, job websites, college course descriptions, and the Occupational Information Network database, has been integrated throughout the AEP books.

Professional and Industry Association Involvement—These books are written in consultation with and reviewed by professional associations to ensure they meet the needs of industry employers.

Autodesk Learning Licenses Available—Many students ask how they can get a copy of the AutoCAD® software for their home computer. Through a recent agreement with Autodesk®, Prentice Hall now offers the option of purchasing textbooks with a 1-year student software license agreement for AutoCAD. This provides adequate time for a student to complete all the activities in the book. The software is functionally identical to the professional license, but is intended for student personal use only. It is not for professional use.

Learning licenses may be purchased for an additional fee only by ordering a special textbook package ISBN. Instructors should contact their local Pearson Professional and Career sales representative. For the name and number of your sales representative, please contact Pearson Faculty Services at 1-800-526-0485.

Autodesk Student Engineering and Design Community—The Autodesk Student Engineering and Design Community provides free Autodesk design software for download and learning resources to help you get started in your academic career. Join today; go to **www.autodesk.com/edcommunity**.

This text presents a modern approach to using AutoCAD. That is, it addresses advances in technology and software evolution and introduces commands and procedures that reflect a modern, efficient use of AutoCAD 2010. Features include:

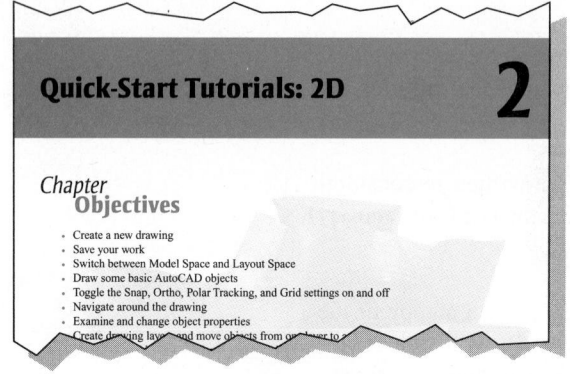

Quick-Start Tutorials Chapters 2 and 20 allow users to get up to speed in no time to create and even plot AutoCAD drawings. Quick Start topics and concepts are linked to corresponding chapters later in the book, providing a motivational preview and allowing the user to delve into detailed topics of instruction as they choose, at their own pace.

Chapter Objectives, a bulleted list of learning objectives for each chapter, provide users with a roadmap of important concepts and practices that will be introduced in the chapter.

Key Terms are boldfaced and italicized within the running text, briefly defined in the margin, and defined in more detail in the Glossary at the end of the book to help students understand and use the language of the computer-aided drafting world.

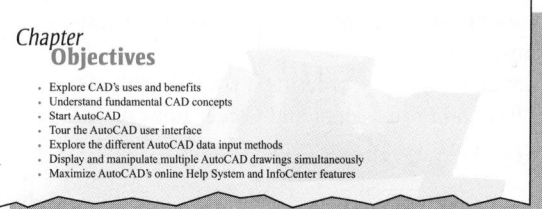

Command Grids appear in the margin, alongside the discussion of the command. These grids provide a visual of the action options using the Standard Toolbar, Menu, Command Line, or Command Alias, ensuring that the student is in the right place at the right time and correctly following the authors' direction.

Discipline Icons are placed in the margin alongside each project and identify the discipline to which each project applies: General, Mechanical, Architectural, Electrical, Plumbing/HVAC, or Civil. These icons allow instructors to quickly identify homework assignments that will appeal to the varying interests of their students and allow students to work on projects that have the most interest and relevance depending on their course of study.

The AutoCAD User Interface

Because AutoCAD is a program for drawing, the focal po
the drawing window. This is where you create your draw
Everything else surrounding the drawing window helps
accomplish this task. The ribbons, panels, menus, toolb
and other tools that you interact with to create your dra

A **New to AutoCAD 2010** icon flags features that are new to the 2010 version of the AutoCAD software, creating a quick "study guide" for instructors who need to familiarize themselves with the newest features of the software to prepare for teaching the course. Additional details about these new features can be found in the Online Instructor's Manual.

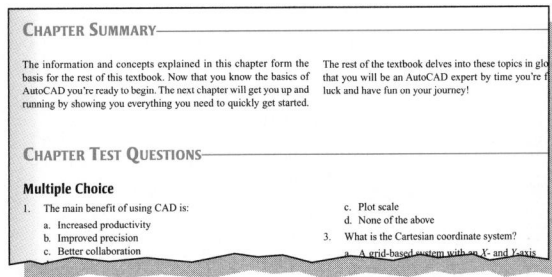

Exercise 2-2: Switching Between Model and Layout Space

1. Click on the **Model** tab. AutoCAD switches to model space
   icon is displayed (see Figure 2-5).
2. Click on the **ANSI A Title Block** tab. AutoCAD switches back
3. Save your drawing as **EX2-2**.

AutoCAD's model space looks distinctively different from layout
to the space as there is in layout space. The **XY** icon (called the **UCS** ic
In contrast, layout space looks like a piece of paper. The space has ed
a shadow along the edges), and the **UCS** icon looks like a page corner

Exercises throughout the chapters provide step-by-step walk-through activities for the student, allowing immediate practice and reinforcement of newly learned skills.

FOR MORE DETAILS AutoCAD's display tools are described in detail in Chapter 3.

The Cartesian Coordinate System

The primary means of locating information in an AutoCAD drawing is the Cartesian coordinate system. The Cartesian coordinate system is a grid-based system where points are represented by their X and Y coordinate values separated by a comma as follows:

X,Y

TIP, NOTE, FOR MORE DETAILS, and **JOB SKILLS** highlight additional helpful information for the student.

CHAPTER SUMMARY

The information and concepts explained in this chapter form the basis for the rest of this textbook. Now that you know the basics of AutoCAD you're ready to begin. The next chapter will get you up and running by showing you everything you need to quickly get started.

The rest of the textbook delves into these topics in glo
that you will be an AutoCAD expert by time you're f
luck and have fun on your journey!

CHAPTER TEST QUESTIONS

Multiple Choice

1. The main benefit of using CAD is:
   a. Increased productivity
   b. Improved precision
   c. Better collaboration
   c. Plot scale
   d. None of the above
3. What is the Cartesian coordinate system?
   a. A grid-based system with an X- and Y-axis

End-of-Chapter material, easily located by shading on page edges, provides:

- Summaries
- Test Questions
- Projects and Tutorials

to help students check their own understanding of important chapter concepts.

CHAPTER PROJECTS

Project 4-1: Lines, Circle, and Arcs

1. Start a new drawing using the acad.dwt template.
2. Draw the lines, circle, and arcs shown in Figure P4-1 to the best of your ability.
   Do not draw dimensions. *Hint:* Use the **Tan, Tan, Tan** circle option to place the corner circles.
3. Save the drawing as **P4-1**.

6.0

Projects and **Tutorials** are organized by discipline to allow for application of skills to various fields, and numbered consistently among the chapters for easy back-and-forth reference. The end-of-chapter projects require students to use all the commands and skills they have learned cumulatively. Project types include:

- Mechanical B-Size Title Borders/Annotation symbols
- Architectural D-Size Title Borders/Annotation symbols
- Electrical schematics
- Plumbing/HVAC schematics
- Architectural plans
- Architectural details
- Mechanical—English
- Mechanical—Metric
- Civil plans
- Civil details

Project 23-4: Creating a Bolt 3D Model with Real Thread

OPEN the drawing *Project 23-4* in the student data files. It contains the objects shown in Figure 23-228. You will use these objects to create the 3D model of the bolt with real thread shown in Figure 23-229.

To access student data files, go to www.pearsondesigncentral.com.

URLs in the margin direct students to the online student data files.

INSTRUCTOR RESOURCES

The Online Instructor's Manual provides answers to chapter exercises and tests and solutions to end-of-chapter problems and drawing files to get users started.

To access supplementary materials online, instructors need to request an instructor access code. Go to **www.prenhall.com**, click the **Instructor Resource Center** link, and then click **Register Today** for an instructor access code. Within 48 hours after registering you will receive a confirming e-mail including an instructor access code. Once you have received your code, go to the site and log on for full instructions on downloading the materials you wish to use.

STUDENT RESOURCES

Pearson Design Central—Pearson has created an online community where students can share examples of their drawings and obtain resources for their drawing projects. Student data files needed for certain projects in this book can be obtained at **www.pearsondesigncentral.com**. **URLs** in the margin direct students to the online student data files.

Preface

We live in a digital world where the trend in technology is to duplicate reality as much as possible. As time goes on, more and more industries and fields require the use of AutoCAD drafting and design software and 3D CAD files. AutoCAD has long been, and will remain, the industry standard for generating top-of-the-line CAD drawings in the least amount of time possible as well as excellent 3D work.

AutoCAD® 2010 in 2D and 3D: A Modern Perspective offers a complete guide for students and professionals who want to enter the interesting world of computer-aided drafting using AutoCAD. This book covers all aspects of the AutoCAD program's 2D and 3D tools, from the basic concepts to the most powerful tools used in design and engineering.

In this book, readers will find an interesting combination of theory and many complex projects and exercises, as well as many clear and descriptive illustrations. Real design problems starting from scratch will be solved throughout the projects. In addition, many other short exercise sections are included to ensure full comprehension of the commands.

Concepts are explained clearly in easy-to-understand language and are accompanied by descriptive illustrations, which will help the reader understand each topic and speed up the learning process. By following the steps in each project, readers will see results immediately and will understand the development process as they go along, rather than just entering instructions.

After using this book, readers will realize that AutoCAD is the premier software for generating 2D drawings and 3D models. Its ease of use, combined with its ability to create complex drawings, makes it the first choice among many design and drafting professionals.

About This Book

This book can serve as a reference for designers, draftspersons, or anyone with a basic knowledge of technical drawing who wants to learn how to use the AutoCAD program to create their work and to enter the interesting world of 3D modeling. The projects and the exercise sections are designed to enhance and help the reader retain the content learned in each chapter.

You do not need to be an expert draftsperson to use this book, but you should have some drafting background. Parts One through Seven focus more on using AutoCAD as a tool for creating 2D CAD drawings. Occasionally, industry standards are referenced as they relate to a topic. Unfortunately, it is impossible to address standards thoroughly because each industry and discipline is different. Parts Eight through Eleven address concepts such as paper space and tracking methods, however, as well as commands related to 3D work, such as **SPLINE, FILLET**, and **CHAMFER**. The main purpose is to make you understand that 3D modeling is, above all else, the combination of the way you look at the objects and the way the working plane is set.

It is also assumed that you have some knowledge of computers and basic file management. Because some of the topics in the later chapters are rather technically advanced, having some computer background is helpful. A basic technical background is required because AutoCAD has many Internet and network-enabled features that facilitate the sharing of electronic information.

In addition to learning the basic AutoCAD tools, you will also learn to recognize and use these tools to achieve specific goals. A number of challenging end-of-chapter projects from varying disciplines progress through multiple chapters so you can see how a drawing is put together from beginning until end. Brief definitions of the commands involved, as well as notes containing tips and warnings, will give you extra help in understanding the commands.

Chapter Organization

The book is organized into eleven parts that advance in complexity as you go through each chapter. Each subsequent chapter is meant to build on the preceding chapters so you can see the steps typically taken to create a set of drawings from start to finish.

PART ONE – An Introduction to AutoCAD

Chapter 1: Introduction to AutoCAD introduces you to fundamental CAD concepts and the AutoCAD interface.

Chapter 2: Quick-Start Tutorials: 2D allows you to hit the ground running so that you learn the basics necessary to start a new drawing, create and modify some objects, add annotation features, and print out your work. All topics are then explained in detail in the subsequent chapters.

PART TWO – Drafting Skills: Drawing with AutoCAD

Chapter 3: Controlling the Drawing Display shows you how to move around in a drawing by panning and zooming. It also introduces some different display performance settings.

Chapter 4: Basic Drawing Commands provides an overview of the basic drawing commands such as **LINE** and **CIRCLE** so you can create a simple drawing.

Chapter 5: Drawing Tools and Drafting Settings explains the different drawing tools and settings available to help you create and modify your work.

Chapter 6: Managing Object Properties shows how to set up and apply different layer systems and manage other object properties.

PART THREE – Understanding Editing Techniques: Basics Through Advanced

Chapter 7: Basic Editing Techniques explains how to select groups of AutoCAD objects that can be modified as a single unit. Grips are introduced to teach you how to modify objects directly by simply selecting them in your drawing.

Chapter 8: Advanced Editing Techniques introduces some of the more advanced modify commands that allow you to perform complex operations.

PART FOUR – Working with Complex Objects

Chapter 9: Drawing and Editing Complex Objects looks at creating and editing complex polyline-based objects with multiple line segments.

Chapter 10: Pattern Fills and Hatching provides information about incorporating different predefined pattern fills and hatch patterns into your drawings to create filled areas.

PART FIVE – Annotating Drawings

Chapter 11: Adding Text shows the different ways to manage and create text in a drawing.

Chapter 12: Working with Tables explains how to insert and modify different types of tables in a drawing, including those linked to Microsoft Excel spreadsheets and those extracted from object information in a drawing.

Chapter 13: Dimensioning Drawings outlines the different dimensioning tools and shows how to manage their appearance using dimension styles.

PART SIX – Outputting Your Work

Chapter 14: Managing Paper Space Layouts shows you step by step how to set up paper space layouts for plotting using industry standard techniques, including multiple layouts and multiple scaled viewports.

Chapter 15: Plotting and Publishing provides an overview of the different plotting tools and settings, including how to batch plot a group of drawings using the **PUBLISH** command.

PART SEVEN – Advanced Drawing and Construction Methods

Chapter 16: Blocks and Block Attributes explains how to create complex named symbols that can be inserted anywhere in a drawing or drawings. Dynamic block attribute text examples are explained to show how to update individual blocks quickly, as well as extract alphanumeric information to a table or external file.

Chapter 17: Working with External References shows you how to reference external files (drawings, images, DWF, and DGN files) into your current drawing so that you can coordinate and communicate work without having to open the referenced file.

Chapter 18: File Management and Object Linking and Embedding provides an overview of AutoCAD's Drawing Utilities for fixing and/or restoring drawings. Object linking and embedding is explained so that you can share information with other Windows programs.

PART EIGHT – An Introduction to 3D Modeling with AutoCAD

Chapter 19: Introduction to 3D in the AutoCAD® Program introduces the theory needed to begin your journey into the 3D modeling world, equipping you with a solid background. Here you will be given the most important tools for success, such as controlling the point from where you look at the 3D model, managing the User Coordinate System (UCS), and many more.

Chapter 20: Quick-Start Tutorials: 3D challenges you to create two different 3D models by following step-by-step instructions, without going through the theory behind it beforehand. The commands introduced in this chapter will be further discussed in subsequent chapters. This chapter has been intentionally designed to stimulate your interest in 3D modeling with AutoCAD, walking you through the entire process of creating 3D objects that are common to you.

Even though the modeling techniques used in the AutoCAD program have much in common, this chapter treats the three methods separately for better organization as well as understanding. In everyday real usage, different disciplines tend to use one of these methods specifically.

PART NINE – Creating 3D Models

Chapter 21: Wireframe Modeling describes the curves used in the AutoCAD program, including the most complex ones (splines and spline-fit polylines), as well as other wireframe-type objects. You will also learn the importance of using such objects for 3D work and how to control them properly.

Chapter 22: Creating and Modifying Meshes allows you to discover and practice specific tools used to create and modify meshes or faceted surfaces. You will also learn how to use these tools on other objects that are suitable for this particular method of representing 3D models.

Faceted surfaces are the oldest type of 3D object used in the AutoCAD program. In fact, no tools are available that make this particular type of object interact with any other object. The use of faceted surfaces in the AutoCAD program persists, however, due to their very specific uses.

Chapter 23: Creating 3D Solids and Surfaces introduces you to the two most important objects in the creation of 3D models: surfaces and 3D solids. In this chapter you will learn aspects of the AutoCAD software that are particularly related to the creation of these two types of objects.

An AutoCAD file or drawing file (DWG) can contain any kind of object. You can actually create a 3D model that is a combination of meshes, 3D solids, and surfaces. The AutoCAD program, however, provides specific tools that allow 3D solids and surfaces to interact, so studying these two objects separately will deepen your understanding of them.

Surfaces and 3D solids are the most useful objects in the development of 3D models. In fact, short courses could use only this chapter along with specific material selected from Chapter 1. Such content will provide you with the knowledge needed to start generating 3D models and to understand the construction process.

PART TEN – Advanced 3D Models

Unlike with faceted surfaces or meshes, a wide set of tools allows you to edit surfaces and 3D solids after they have been created. All these tools, as well as their practical uses, are presented in *Chapter 24: Editing 3D Solids and Surfaces.*

Chapter 25: Advanced Tutorials walks you from scratch through the complete design process of a bench vise. This 3D project allows you to review and put into practice most of the knowledge you have acquired in Chapters 5 and 6.

PART ELEVEN – Important Uses of 3D Models

Chapter 26: Generating Drawings and DWF Files instructs you on some of the advantages of creating 3D models. Here you will learn different procedures to generate drawings and other documents from existing 3D models and to create DWF files. This knowledge will allow you to generate high-quality technical documentation.

Chapter 27: Rendering and Other Presentations demonstrates more of the many advantages of generating 3D models. This chapter provides you with sufficient knowledge to generate artistic presentations from your 3D models. Here you will learn how to control the effect of light, shadows, and materials on 3D objects, and use these objects to generate rendered images and animations.

Acknowledgments

We would like to thank the following individuals, who reviewed this book:

Reviewers

Scott Anthony Boudreau
Joliet Junior College

Jon Bridges
Lane Community College, OR

Joel Robert Brodeur
Montana State University—Northern

Paul Clarke
MiraCosta College, CA

Dr. Robert Cobb, Jr.
North Carolina A&T State University

Michael B. Daniels
Western Piedmont Community
College, NC

Gene Fosheim
Lake Washington Technical College,
WA

James Freygang
Ivy Tech Community College, IN

Howard M. Fulmer
Villanova University

Richard Garthe
Kalamazoo Valley Community College,
MI

George Gibson
Athens Technical College

Dr. Tony E. Graham
North Carolina A&T State University

Dennis Hughes
CS Mott Community College, MI

John L. Irwin, EdD
Michigan Technological University

Dr. Beverly K. Jaeger
Northeastern University College of
Engineering

Dimitrios Karamanlidis
University of Rhode Island

Charles Kimball
City College of San Francisco, CA

John Knapp
Metro Community College, NE

Harold S. Lamm
San Antonio College, TX

Lloyd W. Lunde
Southeast Technical Institute

Randal Reid
Chattahoochee Technical College

Leland Scott
Baker College of Owosso, MI

Mohd Fairuz Shiratuddin
The University of Southern Mississippi

Walter John Smith
Southwestern Community College

Ron Sorensen
Southeast Technical Institute

Tony Thomas
Amarillo College

Mary Tolle
South Dakota State University, SD

Marsha Walton
Finger Lakes Community College, NY

Content Contributors

Chapter 17: Working with External References
Craig Stinchcomb
Terra Community College, OH

Chapter 18: File Management and Object Linking and Embedding
Kelly Keala
Clackamas Community College, OR

Appendix A
Dr. Gerald L. Bacza
Coordinator and Professor: Drafting/Design/CAD
Engineering Technology
Fairmont State Community and Technical College

Appendices B through E
Marsha Walton
Finger Lakes Community College, NY

Drawings and Drawing Expertise
Hennebery Eddy Architects, Inc.

Kimi Barham
Student, Clackamas Community College, OR

Jason Lee Strother
Student, Clackamas Community College, OR

Text Element	Example
Key terms—Boldface and *italic* on first mention (first letter lowercase, as it appears in the body of the text). Brief definition in margin alongside first mention. Full definition in Glossary at back of book.	Views are created by placing ***viewport*** objects in the paper space layout.
AutoCAD commands—Bold and uppercase.	Start the **LINE** command.
Ribbon and panel names, palette names, toolbar names, menu items, and dialog box names—Bold and follow capitalization convention in AutoCAD toolbar or pull-down menu (generally first letter cap).	The **Layer Properties Manager** palette The **File** menu
Panel tools, toolbar buttons and dialog box controls/buttons/input items—Bold and follow the name of the item or the name shown in the AutoCAD tooltip.	Choose the **Line** tool from the **Draw** panel. Choose the **Symbols and Arrows** tab in the **Modify Dimension Style** dialog box. Choose the **New Layer** button in the **Layer Properties Manager** palette. In the **Lines and Arrows** tab, set the **Arrow size:** to **.125**.
AutoCAD prompts—Dynamic input prompts are italic. Command window prompts use a different font (Courier New) and are not italicized. This makes them look like the text in the command window. Prompts follow capitalization convention in AutoCAD prompt (generally first letter cap).	AutoCAD prompts you to *Specify first point:* AutoCAD prompts you to *Specify next point or ↓.* Specify center point for circle or [3P/2P/Ttr (tan tan radius)]:
Keyboard input—Bold with special keys in brackets.	Type **3.5 <Enter ↵>**

Contents

Chapter 4   Basic Drawing Commands

Chapter 5   Drawing Tools
            and Drafting Settings

Chapter 6   Managing Object Properties

Chapter 27   Rendering and Other Presentations

Appendix A

Appendix B

Appendix C

Appendix D

Appendix E

Glossary   1355

Index   1359

New to AutoCAD 2010

AutoCAD® 2010 in 2D and 3D

Introduction to AutoCAD

1

Chapter Objectives

- Explore CAD's uses and benefits
- Understand fundamental CAD concepts
- Start AutoCAD
- Tour the AutoCAD user interface
- Explore the different AutoCAD data input methods
- Display and manipulate multiple AutoCAD drawings simultaneously
- Maximize AutoCAD's online Help System and InfoCenter features

INTRODUCTION

This textbook is designed to allow you to "hit the ground running" using AutoCAD so that you can quickly start creating accurate technical drawings using accepted industry drafting standards. The next chapter (Chapter 2, Quick Start) shows you the minimum you need to know in order to create and plot an AutoCAD drawing starting from scratch. These introductory concepts and techniques are then linked to detailed information about each topic so you can explore them at your own pace.

    Before you can do any of that though, we need to cover some basics. This chapter introduces you to some fundamental CAD concepts and the AutoCAD *user interface* so you are prepared to hit the ground running in Chapter 2.

user interface: The commands and mechanisms the user interacts with to control a program's operation and input data.

WHAT IS CAD?

In a little over a generation's time the methods used to create technical drawings have fundamentally changed from using pencil and paper to the use of Computer Aided Drafting, better known as CAD. The analog world of drafting boards, T squares, triangles, and even the romantic french curve (see Figure 1-1) has given way to the brave new digital world of computers. No longer must you refill your mechanical pencil when you run out of lead, find your eraser when you make a mistake, or walk across the room to share a design with another person.

    Using CAD, you can draw something once and copy it hundreds, or even thousands, of times. Changing a design can be as simple as pushing a button. Drawings can be shared instantaneously across the room or even around the world over a computer network. These and the other benefits of CAD include the following:

- Increased productivity
  - Drawing content can be continuously reused.
  - Text and dimensions can be created and updated automatically.
  - Hatch and pattern fills can be placed with a single pick of the mouse.
  - Revising and editing drawings can be done quickly with minimum effort.

Triangle

T-Square

French Curve

Figure 1-1   A T square, a triangle, and a french curve

- Improved precision
  - Digital information is accurate to 14 decimal places.
  - Geometry is precisely located using the Cartesian coordinate system.
  - It is possible to snap to control points and features on existing drawing geometry to accurately locate drawing information.
  - Polar and object tracking features can be utilized for precise angular measurements.
- Better collaboration
  - Drawings can be shared across a network (locally and globally).
  - Drawings can be referenced and updated in real time with notification.
  - Revisions and markups can be managed electronically via email and Internet-based document management systems.
- 3D visualization and analysis (see Figure 1-2).

Figure 1-2   Sample 3D rendering created in AutoCAD

- 3D animations and walk-throughs can be easily generated to allow you and potential clients to visualize a design before it is constructed.
- Interference checking can be done to ensure that parts do not run into each other before they are created.
- Engineering calculations such as Finite Element Analysis (FEA) and other structural calculations can be performed automatically.
- Computer prototypes can be created and tested, eliminating the time and materials needed to manufacture a real-world prototype.

All these benefits are explored in this textbook, except for 3D visualization and analysis, which is beyond the scope of this text. The following chapters explain how to utilize the tools provided in AutoCAD to create and share the most accurate technical drawings in the quickest and most efficient manner. Using AutoCAD you will learn how to do the following:

- Set up and lay out different types of AutoCAD 2D drawings using AutoCAD model space and paper space techniques.
- Quickly create accurate 2D drawing information using AutoCAD's precision drafting aids.
- Edit and modify 2D drawing information in a productive fashion.
- Annotate and dimension drawings using AutoCAD's automated annotation and dimensioning features.
- Create section views utilizing AutoCAD's predefined and custom hatch and pattern fills.
- Utilize and manage CAD standards including:
  - Layers
  - Linetypes
  - Text styles
  - Dimension styles
- Coordinate drawing information with other team members using external reference files.
- Create and manage symbol libraries using AutoCAD's DesignCenter and Tool Palettes.
- Output your drawings to different plotting devices with specific colors and lineweights.
- Share information with other Windows Office applications using Object Linking and Embedding (OLE).

FUNDAMENTAL CAD CONCEPTS

Because CAD-based drafting is a digital pursuit, some of the concepts that apply to its analog "on the board" cousin are a bit different. It is important that you are aware of and understand these concepts before we begin any drawing.

Drawing Actual Size

Board drafting requires that you select a scale before you begin a drawing. This is to ensure that whatever it is that you are drawing fits properly on the selected paper, or *sheet size*.

    Large objects are scaled down so that you can see the complete design on the sheet while smaller objects are scaled up so that you can clearly discern finer details.

    Unlike drawing on the board, CAD-based drafting does not require design information to be scaled as it is drawn. Everything is drawn actual size as it exists in the real world. This means that the layout of a floor plan that is $100'-0'' \times 50'-0''$ is actually drawn $100'-0''$ long $\times$ $50'-0''$ wide in AutoCAD. The scaling process occurs when the drawing is being set up to be printed or plotted to ensure that your drawing fits properly on the desired sheet size.

sheet size: The size of the paper on which a drawing is printed or plotted.

FOR MORE DETAILS   See Appendix A for detailed information about standard sheet sizes.

Using CAD, you have a theoretically infinite amount of space within your CAD drawing file to create your design. A drawing can be as large as our entire solar system or small enough to fit on the head of a pin. To help navigate within this infinite drawing space, AutoCAD provides a number of display tools that allow you to zoom and pan around a drawing similar to the zoom and pan functions found on a camera. This allows you to zoom up close to your drawing for detailed work or zoom out so that you can view the complete drawing.

Note:

Annotation features like text and dimensions have their own unique scaling issues. You must typically scale annotation features so that they appear at the correct size in relation to the actual size drawing you are creating. For instance, 1/8"-high text appears as a tiny speck next to a 100'-0"-long wall. AutoCAD provides an **Annotation Scale** feature that helps automate the process. This feature is explained later in the "Annotation Scale" section.

FOR MORE DETAILS   AutoCAD's display tools are described in detail in Chapter 3.

The Cartesian Coordinate System

The primary means of locating information in an AutoCAD drawing is the Cartesian coordinate system. The Cartesian coordinate system is a grid-based system where points are represented by their X and Y coordinate values separated by a comma as follows:

X,Y

For example, a point located at $X = 4$ and $Y = 2$ is represented as follows:

4,2

There is also a Z coordinate, but we'll talk about that later. For now, think of your computer screen as a 2D sheet of paper where the origin of the coordinate system (0,0) is in the lower left-hand corner of your screen as shown in Figure 1-3.

Positive X and Y coordinate values are represented in the upper right quadrant of the grid. Because it is easiest to work with positive coordinates exclusively, this is where most of your drawings will be created.

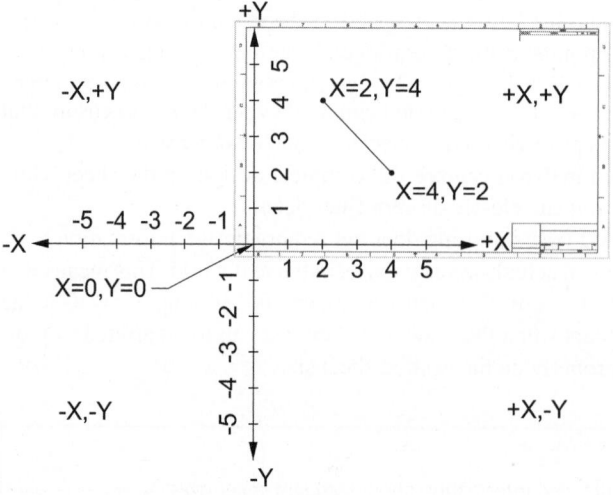

Figure 1-3   The Cartesian coordinate system

Right-Hand Rule

As alluded to earlier, the Cartesian coordinate system also has a Z coordinate that is used to locate points in 3D space. The Z-axis runs perpendicular to the XY plane shown in Figure 1-3.

The easiest way to represent this concept is to rely on what is known as the **right-hand rule**—it's as easy as 1-2-3.

To start, clench your right hand into a fist with your palm facing toward you.

1. Extend your thumb to the right.
2. Uncurl your pointer finger so that it points straight up.
3. Uncurl your middle finger so that it points toward you.

Your hand should now look similar to the one shown in Figure 1-4. Using the right-hand rule, your thumb represents the positive X-axis, your pointer finger represents the positive Y-axis, and your middle finger represents the positive Z-axis.

right-hand rule: Easy-to-understand reference that can be used to determine the positive and negative direction of the X-, Y-, and Z-axes.

Figure 1-4　The right-hand rule

Your palm, and by extension, your computer screen, represents the 2D XY plane where $Z = 0$. Using this analogy, positive Z values are toward you, or above the screen, while negative Z values are away from you, or into the screen.

By default, the Z coordinate value is set to 0. Because of this, there is no need to specify a Z coordinate value when you locate 2D points. If the Z coordinate is omitted, it is interpreted as 0. For instance, to locate a 2D point where $X = 4$ and $Y = 2$, you can enter either of the following:

4,2,0　or　4,2

Of course, it makes sense to type the least amount as possible, so all examples in this book rely on the shorthand version.

TIP　In AutoCAD, the default Cartesian coordinate system explained in this section is referred to as the **World Coordinate System**, or **WCS**. It is possible to change the origin and orientation of the X-, Y-, and Z-axes for high-level drawing operations by creating your own temporary **User Coordinate System**, or **UCS**. Creating and modifying User Coordinate Systems are beyond the scope of this book. For more information, please consult the AutoCAD help.

World Coordinate System (WCS): The default coordinate system in AutoCAD upon which all objects and user coordinate systems are based.

User Coordinate System (UCS): A user-defined variation of the World Coordinate System.

Grid Units

In AutoCAD, one unit on the Cartesian coordinate grid system can represent whatever you want it to represent. A unit can be 1 inch, 1 foot, 1 millimeter, 1 meter, 1 nautical league, or even 1 *parsec*.

Fortunately for us, the majority of the drafting and design world works in either inches (Imperial) or millimeters (Metric) where the following applies:

Imperial:

1 grid unit = 1 inch

Metric:

1 grid unit = 1 millimeter

There are of course exceptions to this unwritten rule, most notably the civil design field. Because civil engineers work with drawings that cover large areas (parcel plans, highway plans, etc.), it is common for them to work in decimal feet or decimal meters where the following applies:

Imperial:

1 grid unit = 1 foot

Metric:

1 grid unit = 1 meter

Unless otherwise noted, most of the examples and drawing problems in this book will rely on 1 unit = 1 inch for Imperial type drawings and 1 unit = 1 millimeter for Metric type drawings.

TIP   The default drawing setup in AutoCAD is an Imperial-type drawing where 1 grid unit = 1 inch. Setting a drawing up for the Metric system where 1 grid unit = 1 millimeter is described in Chapter 4.

Angle Measurement

By default, angles in AutoCAD are measured counterclockwise from 0°, which is due east, or right, on the positive *X*-axis as shown in Figure 1-5. Using this system of angle measurement, 90° is north, 180° is west, and 270° is south. It is possible to change the default 0° base angle to any

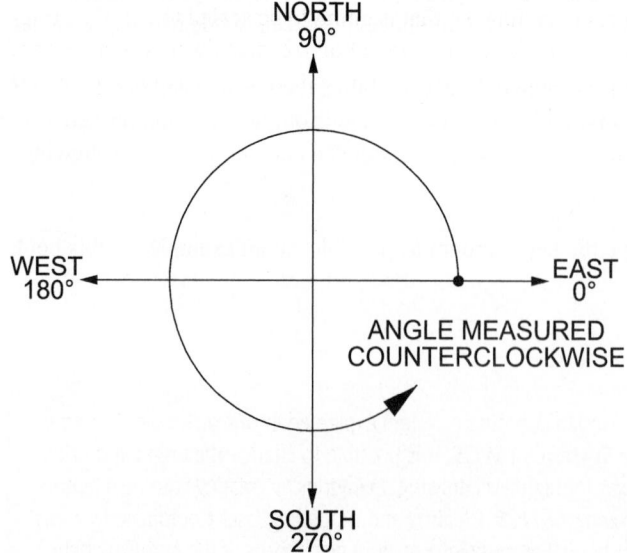

Figure 1-5   AutoCAD base angle and direction

of the other three compass directions, or a custom angle, as well as change the default angle measurement direction from counterclockwise to clockwise.

AutoCAD provides five different types of angle unit settings so you can enter angles in a format that applies to the type of work you are doing. Most architects and engineers prefer angles in decimal units (i.e., 45.00°), or degrees, minutes, and seconds (i.e., 45°00′00″), while those in the civil engineering world rely on surveyor units (i.e., N45°0′0″E).

FOR MORE DETAILS   Setting different angle unit settings as well as setting a different base angle and angle direction is described in Chapter 4.

TIP   You can also enter negative angle measurements when working in AutoCAD to input an angle that is measured in the clockwise direction. For example, an angle of 315° can also be entered as −45°.

Exercise 1-1: Using Cartesian Coordinates

1. Using pencil and paper, lay out a Cartesian coordinate grid system similar to the one shown in Figure 1-3.
2. Draw a line from the coordinate point (2,1) to the coordinate point (4,5).
3. Draw a line from the origin (0,0) at an approximate angle of 135° to the edge of the grid.
4. Draw a line from the coordinate point (−2,−1) to the origin (0,0).
5. Draw a line from the origin at an approximate angle of −30° to the edge of the grid.

Annotation Scale

As mentioned earlier in the section "Drawing Actual Size," the lines, circles, and other geometry that represent your design are drawn to their exact "real-world" specifications; the scaling occurs when you set your drawing up to plot on the desired sheet size.

To accommodate this scaling process, the size of annotation features such as text and dimensions must be adjusted accordingly when they are added to your drawing. This ensures that they print out at the correct size after they are scaled up or scaled down. Most organizations rely on drafting standards that define specific text heights, arrowhead sizes, and other annotation specifications so that drawings maintain a consistent appearance. The proper scaling of annotation features is very important so that drafting standards are always maintained.

As an example, annotation features on a drawing that is going to be scaled to 1/2 of its original size when it is printed must be scaled up by the reciprocal of 1/2, or 2 times, when they are created. With this in mind, if your drafting standards require that text print out 1/8″ high, you must apply the following formula:

$$1/8″ \times 2 = 1/4″ \text{ high text}$$

When the drawing is then plotted, the 1/4″-high text is scaled by 1/2 and prints out at the correct standard text height of 1/8″. See Figure 1-6. In this example, 2 is considered the scale factor. The *scale factor* is the reciprocal of the plotted scale. Calculating the scale factor in the preceding example is easy because the plotted scale is a simple ratio of 1:2. It's obvious that the reciprocal of 1:2 is 2.

scale factor: Multiplier that determines the size of annotation features when a drawing is plotted or printed.

FOR MORE DETAILS   See Appendix A for more information about standard annotation specifications and the steps necessary to calculate other scale factors, based on standard drawing scales. Appendix A also contains a list of the most common standard drawing scales, their corresponding scale factor, and even suggested text sizes and dimension scales.

Figure 1-6   1/4″ text scaled to 1/8″ at plot time

Calculating, *and applying,* scale factors for all the different annotation-type objects can be a tedious, time-consuming process. Fortunately, it is possible to automate the process using the AutoCAD **Annotation Scale** feature. Annotation objects such as text and dimensions have an **Annotative** property that, when enabled, automatically scales the objects according to the scale selected. The **Annotation Scale** is controlled via an easily accessible list of the same standard drawing scales found in Appendix A. Annotation objects can even have more than one **Annotation Scale** so that they are displayed at the correct size on multiple different scale drawings!

Note:
There are other things in a drawing that are affected by the **Annotation Scale** besides just text and dimensions. Special linetype definitions and hatch patterns can also be affected.

FOR MORE DETAILS	See Chapter 6 for details regarding scaling linetype definitions. See Chapter 10 for more information about scaling hatch patterns. See Chapter 11 for more information about the **Annotation Scale** feature.

Object Properties

In AutoCAD, the lines, circles, text, dimensions, and just about everything else that make up a drawing are commonly referred to as *objects.* All these drawing objects have properties associated with them that control their appearance and behavior. Some properties are unique to a particular type of object, especially properties that relate to an object's geometry. For example, a circle object has a radius, whereas text has a height. Other object properties are shared by all the objects in a drawing. These general object properties are introduced in the following sections.

Layers.   Before the advent of CAD, drafters and designers coordinated their drawings by physically overlaying them on top of each other. The paper, known as *vellum,* was translucent so that as you layered each drawing on top of the previous one, the drawing(s) underneath were still visible. This allowed the drafters and designers to compare the work on each individual drawing and coordinate them as a complete system. See Figure 1-7.

Flash forward to the digital world of the twenty-first century. Using CAD, this concept of physically "layering" multiple drawings one on top of another has morphed into the ability to separate distinct drawing information using named layers. Typically, the name of the layer reflects the type of information that resides on it. For instance, a layer named **WALL** might contain drawing information that relates to the walls of a floor plan, while a layer named **DOOR** might contain the lines and arcs that represent the doors. In fact, numerous standard layer-naming conventions and guidelines have been created that allow people to share CAD drawings and understand what type of drawing information resides on each layer.

CAD-based layers provide much more functionality and control than their analog vellum-based cousins. Layers in CAD can be turned off and on so that you can create multiple views of

Furniture Plan

Mechanical Plan

Floor Plan

Figure 1-7   Overlay drafting

your drawing information. For instance, text and dimensions can be put on their own unique layers so that they can be turned off when you want to concentrate on your design. Similar drawing information can be grouped on specific layers so that you can coordinate between different disciplines. The electrical wiring might be located on a layer named **ELEC** while the mechanical heating ductwork might be located on a layer named **HVAC**. Basically, layers give your drawings a level of intelligence that allows you to indicate what objects in a CAD drawing represent in the real world.

Besides controlling the visibility of drawing information, layers also can be used to control the color, linetype, and lineweight of an object. You can even use layers to determine whether an object is plotted or not.

FOR MORE DETAILS   Layer property management is discussed in greater detail in Chapter 6.

Colors

Colors serve two purposes in an AutoCAD drawing:

1. They separate drawing information so that it is easily identifiable on the computer screen.
2. They allow printing and plotting with specific line thicknesses.

The first use of colors is fairly obvious. One of the easiest ways to differentiate between different drawing information on the computer screen is by using color. You might set up your drawing so that all the walls are green, the doors are blue, and the text is yellow. This color coding makes your drawing easier to comprehend and work with.

The second use of colors might seem a bit obscure to many new AutoCAD users—to control line thicknesses when plotting. This use of colors was introduced very early on in AutoCAD's life as one of the only means of plotting a drawing with varying line thicknesses, a necessity for most organizations. This color-based approach to controlling lineweights is still in use today because of the time and effort necessary to update legacy systems. For this reason, it is a good idea to at least have a basic understanding of how the color-based approach works.

Without getting into too much detail, color-based plotting is based on the fact that each color in AutoCAD is associated with an integer value. This relationship is referred to as the *AutoCAD Color Index,* or *ACI.* The ACI consists of 255 colors numbered from 1 to 255, with the first seven colors represented as follows:

1 = Red

2 = Yellow

3 = Green

4 = Cyan

5 = Blue

6 = Magenta

7 = White

plot style: A collection of property settings that is applied when the drawing is plotted to control the appearance of the drawing objects on the printed drawing.

In the early days, plotting was done on pen plotters using numbered ink pens with varying pen tip sizes that created different line thicknesses. The numbered plotter pens were associated with the information in the drawing via the object's color. For example, red drawing objects plot with pen #1 because the color red = 1 in AutoCAD's Color Index. This color–to–plot pen relationship is referred to as a plotter's "pen mapping." Thankfully, this antiquated approach to controlling plotter pens is quickly being heaped on the trash bin of history as the much simpler approach of using AutoCAD's lineweight property becomes more popular.

Note:
There is another approach to controlling line thicknesses on a plot using *plot styles.* It is possible to assign a unique plot style directly to an object that will control the object's appearance on the printed page.

> **FOR MORE DETAILS**   See Appendix A for detailed information about standard line thicknesses. Plotting with lineweights and plot styles is discussed in detail in Chapter 15.

Linetypes

Manually drawing objects with different linetypes on the board is a very tedious process, if not an art form. A mechanical pencil and a scale must be utilized so that you can accurately measure out the dashes, dots, and/or gaps over the distance of a line.

Fortunately, AutoCAD provides more than 40 different predefined linetypes that can be applied directly to your line work with a click of a button. Figure 1-8 shows examples of linetypes that come with AutoCAD.

> **TIP**   The dashes, dots, and gaps that make up a linetype definition are also affected by the scale factor described earlier. Their size must be adjusted to accommodate the plot scale in the same fashion as the other annotation features in order for them to print out at the right size.

> **FOR MORE DETAILS**   See Appendix A for a detailed description of different linetype standards. Linetypes and linetype scaling are explained in detail in Chapter 6.

Figure 1-8   Examples of default AutoCAD linetypes

Lineweights

In AutoCAD, the term *lineweight* is used to refer to a line's thickness. Different drafting standards dictate how line thicknesses should be applied in technical drawings.

Drawing different line thicknesses on the board requires that you use different pencils with different lead thicknesses. AutoCAD provides graphical lineweights that you can assign to your line work, which allows you to see different line thicknesses on the screen *before* you plot your drawing. There are more than 20 different lineweights available in both Imperial (inches) and Metric (millimeters) format.

FOR MORE DETAILS	See Appendix A for detailed information regarding line thickness drafting standards. AutoCAD lineweights are discussed in detail in Chapter 6.

Controlling Object Properties.   The common approach to controlling the general object properties discussed in the previous sections is to set the desired object property active, or current, before drawing an object. An object assumes the current object properties when it is drawn. This does not mean you cannot change an object's properties after it is drawn. In fact, there are a multitude of tools in AutoCAD to help you accomplish this.

FOR MORE DETAILS	Controlling AutoCAD object properties is discussed in detail in Chapter 6.

Exercise 1-2: Researching CAD Layer Guidelines

1. Using the Internet, search for Websites with information about the "AIA layer guidelines."
   (Note: AIA is the abbreviation for the American Institute of Architects.)

2. Describe the AIA layer-naming scheme and how it is organized.
3. Find an example of at least one other layer standard or guideline.

Model Space and Paper Space

AutoCAD has two distinct drawing environments: model space and paper space. Model space is the 3D drawing environment described in "The Cartesian Coordinate System" section earlier that is used for the drawing *model*, or 3D representation of your design. Model space contains most of the line work, text, and dimensions that make up a drawing.

model: The geometry (lines, circles, etc.) created in a drawing that defines the object or objects drawn.

Paper space is the 2D environment used for laying out different views of the model space information on a standard sheet size and scale for plotting purposes. This 2D page setup is known as a *layout* in AutoCAD and typically consists of one or more views of your drawing along with a border and title block.

layout: 2D page setup created in paper space that represents the paper size and what the drawing will look like when it is printed.

Metaphorically speaking, an AutoCAD paper space layout can be thought of as a 2D sheet of paper that hovers over your 3D model space drawing. Scaled views are created by cutting holes in the paper so you can see the 3D drawing model below. See Figure 1-9.

Figure 1-9   Model space and paper space

TIP   It is possible to have multiple layouts in an AutoCAD drawing. Each layout can be a different sheet size and can also contain multiple scaled views.

FOR MORE DETAILS   Layouts and views are discussed in detail in Chapter 14.

A FIRST LOOK AT AutoCAD

Now that we have the preliminaries out of the way, it's time to start AutoCAD so we can take the grand tour. AutoCAD is one of the more complex Windows programs. There are a myriad of commands, menus, toolbars, palettes, and dialog boxes. The following sections explain all these features and how they work so you can get the most out of the AutoCAD user interface.

Starting AutoCAD

Like most Windows programs, there are multiple ways to start AutoCAD. The three most popular methods are explained next.

Using the Start Menu.   The traditional method of starting a Windows program is to rely on the **Start** menu.

To start AutoCAD via the **Start** menu, select the **Start** button on the Windows taskbar and select **All Programs** so that all the programs installed on your computer are displayed. Open the Autodesk folder to see all your installed Autodesk programs and then select the **AutoCAD 2010** icon as shown in Figure 1-10 in the **AutoCAD 2010** folder.

Figure 1-10   Starting AutoCAD via the **Start** menu

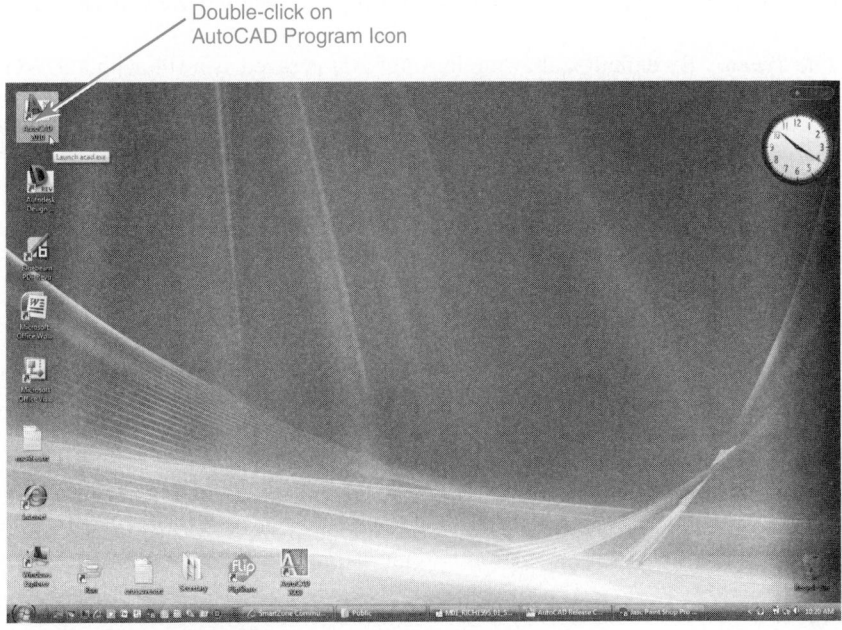

Figure 1-11   Starting AutoCAD via its program icon

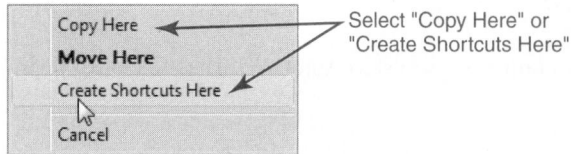

Figure 1-12   Shortcut menu

Using the AutoCAD Program Icon.   One of the quickest and most convenient ways to start AutoCAD, or most Windows programs for that matter, is to click on a program icon on your Windows desktop. Typically, when you install a program it will create a program icon on your desktop as well as add it to the **Start** menu. The standard **AutoCAD 2010** icon is shown in Figure 1-11.

If you do not have an **AutoCAD** program icon on your desktop, you can easily create one from the **Start** menu by right-clicking on the **AutoCAD** icon shown in Figure 1-10 and dragging and dropping it on your desktop. When you release the right mouse button, the shortcut menu shown in Figure 1-12 is displayed. Make sure you select **Copy Here** or **Create Shortcuts Here** from the shortcut menu; otherwise, the original program shortcut will be removed from the AutoCAD folder and put on your desktop.

Double-Clicking on a Drawing File.   When you install a new program, Windows associates the program's three-letter file extension (i.e., .DWG) with the program so that you can double-click on a file in Windows Explorer and the program will automatically start and open the file.

Double-clicking on a .DWG file in Explorer will start AutoCAD and open the drawing. Double-clicking on a .DOC file starts Microsoft Word, while double-clicking on a file with an .XLS extension starts Excel. There are literally thousands of different file extensions and associations. You can typically discern what program is associated with a file by looking at the Type column in Windows Explorer when files are displayed using the detailed view as shown in Figure 1-13.

AutoCAD File Types.   By default, a drawing in AutoCAD is saved as a file with a .DWG file extension. For example, a floor plan drawing might be saved with the file name

`Floor Plan.dwg`

A file name can be up to 256 characters long and can include most of the alphanumeric characters, including spaces ( ), dashes (-), and underscores (_). A file name **CANNOT** include any of the following special characters:

`\ / | : " * ? > <`

Windows is not case sensitive, so you can mix uppercase and lowercase letters when naming a file and Windows will not distinguish between them. For instance, the file name in the example above:

`Floor Plan.dwg`

is the same as

`FLOOR PLAN.DWG`

Double-click Drawing File
to Start AutoCAD

Type Column Indicates
Program Association

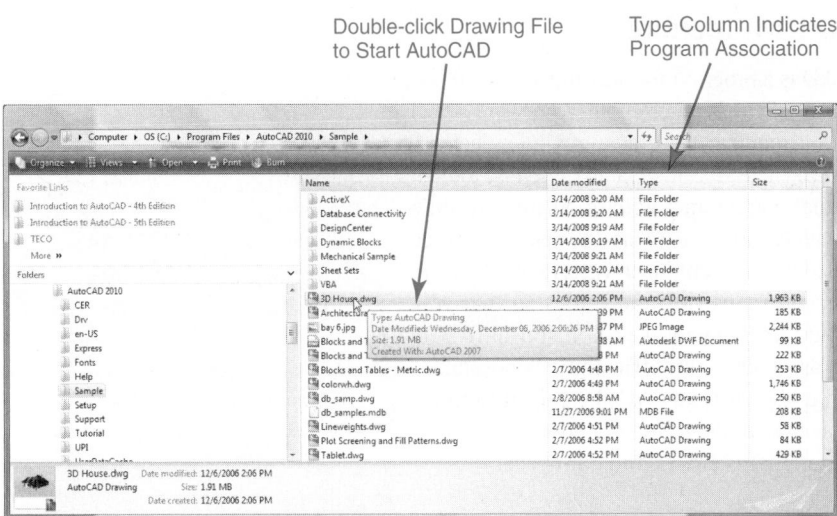

Figure 1-13   Starting AutoCAD by double-clicking on a file

Proper file naming, and by extension, proper file management, is one of the most important aspects of using CAD effectively.

TIP   By default, every time you save a drawing in AutoCAD, a backup file with the .BAK file extension is created. The backup file is the last saved version of the .DWG drawing file. This allows you to always have the last saved version of your drawing to "roll back" to if something happens to the current .DWG file.

Some of the other common file types and extensions used by AutoCAD are listed in the following table.

AutoCAD File Types	
File Extension	**Description**
AC$	Temporary AutoCAD file. Created automatically by AutoCAD
BAK	AutoCAD drawing backup file. Created automatically when a drawing is saved
DWG	AutoCAD drawing file
DWF	AutoCAD Design Web Format file
DWL	AutoCAD drawing lock file. Created automatically by AutoCAD
DWS	AutoCAD Drawing Standards file
DWT	AutoCAD drawing template
DXB	Binary AutoCAD drawing exchange format file
DXF	ASCII AutoCAD drawing exchange format file
PLT	AutoCAD plot file
SV$	AutoCAD automatic save file

If you are unsure of a file type, consult the Windows Help and Support Center.

The AutoCAD User Interface

Because AutoCAD is a program for drawing, the focal point is the drawing window. This is where you create your drawing. Everything else surrounding the drawing window helps you accomplish this task. The ribbons, panels, menus, toolbars, and other tools that you interact with to create your drawings are collectively referred to as the user interface. AutoCAD provides different user interfaces that are tailored for specific industries and trades so that you have the tools that **YOU** need at your disposal to get your work done as quickly and efficiently as possible. The first time you launch AutoCAD the **Initial Setup** window is displayed with the following options so you can select the setup that is closest to your needs:

> **Note:**
> You can access **Initial Setup** anytime later and change your setup via the **User Preferences** tab in the **Options** dialog box described later in this section.

- Architectural
- Civil Engineering
- Electrical Engineering
- Manufacturing
- Mechanical, Electrical, and Plumbing (MEP)
- Structural Engineering
- Other (General Design and Documentation)

workspace: A named configuration of menus, toolbars, and palettes that are grouped and organized so that you can work in a custom, task-oriented drawing environment.

Most of the features that define the user interface for a particular setup (i.e., ribbons, panels, menus, toolbars, etc.) are managed using what are referred to as AutoCAD *workspaces*.

The workspace created when you go through the **Initial Setup** process described above is named **Initial Setup Workspace** and it is the default current workspace when you start AutoCAD. AutoCAD comes with three other standard workspaces that you can switch to at any time by selecting the **Workspace Switching** button on the right side of the AutoCAD status bar at the bottom of the AutoCAD drawing window to display a list of workspaces, as shown in Figure 1-14.

Figure 1-14   **Workspace Switching** button

Switching to the **AutoCAD Classic** workspace turns off the ribbon at the top of the AutoCAD drawing window and turns on the traditional pull-down menus and toolbars found in earlier releases of AutoCAD. The **3D Modeling** workspace turns off most of the 2D AutoCAD tools and replaces them with AutoCAD's advanced 3D tools and features. The **2D Drafting & Annotation** workspace, shown in Figure 1-15, turns off all of AutoCAD's 3D tools and features so that you have quick and easy access to all of the 2D tools required for this textbook.

> **Note:**
> The **2D Drafting & Annotation** workspace is the default workspace used for all of the exercises in this textbook. If it is not your current workspace, you should set it current now.

Figure 1-15   The AutoCAD **2D Drafting & Annotation** user interface

The major interface features provided in the **2D Drafting & Annotation** workspace are as follows:

- **Quick Access** toolbar   Provides easy access to all the most commonly used tools such as **New, Open, Save, Undo, Redo**, and **Plot**.

- **Application Menu**   Clicking on the **Application Menu** button displays a menu of commonly used AutoCAD file tools and drawing utilities, as well as quick access to open or recently opened drawings

- **Ribbon**   Provides easy access to most of the AutoCAD tools via task specific tabs and panels. Each tab has multiple panels containing related tools. Panels with a black arrow on the bottom center can be expanded to access additional tools

- **Drawing Window**   The theoretically infinite space where you create the lines, circles, text, and so on that make up your drawing using the Cartesian coordinate system explained earlier

- **Mouse Crosshairs**   Used for locating points and selecting objects when working in a drawing. The crosshairs switch back to a pointer when the mouse is outside of the drawing window

- **UCS Icon**   Represents the current User Coordinate System (UCS); by default, this is set to the World Coordinate System (WCS) explained earlier in this chapter where the X-axis is aligned horizontally and the Y-axis is aligned vertically

- **Command Line Window**   Provides access to the AutoCAD command line where it is possible to enter commands and their options by typing them at the keyboard. The command line window is also where AutoCAD displays many default command settings and other important messages

- **Model/Layout Tabs**   The **Model** and **Layout** tabs allow you to quickly switch between model space and different paper space layouts.

- **Status Bar**   Mini-dashboard for AutoCAD that does many things, including interactively displaying the current mouse crosshair coordinate location, toggling different drawing tools on and off, switching between model space and paper space layouts, panning and zooming the display, setting the scale factor, managing workspaces, and more

- **InfoCenter**   Allows you to search for useful information about a topic by entering key words or phrases, provides access to the Internet-enabled **Communication Center** for product updates and announcements, and displays a list of Favorites so you can access saved topics

Figure 1-16   **Quick Access** toolbar

Quick Access Toolbar

The **Quick Access** toolbar shown in Figure 1-16 provides quick and easy access to the following commonly used AutoCAD tools so that they are always available:

- **New**   Creates a new drawing file based on the selected AutoCAD template file
- **Open**   Opens an existing AutoCAD drawing or template file
- **Save**   Saves the drawing in its current location if it has been saved previously. Otherwise, performs a "Save As" the first time so that the drawing file name and location can be specified
- **Undo**   Allows you to undo one or more recent commands
- **Redo**   Allows you to reverse the effect of the last undo command
- **Plot**   Prints a drawing to the specified printing device or file type with the settings specified

Clicking on the down arrow on the right side of the **Quick Access** toolbar displays the menu shown in Figure 1-17 so you can add or remove common tools.

Selecting **More Commands...** from the menu allows you to add additional commands via the **Customize User Interface** (CUI) dialog box.

In addition, the **Show Menu Bar** option allows you to turn on the pull-down menus traditionally located across the top in previous releases of AutoCAD. The **Show Below the Ribbon** option moves the **Quick Access** toolbar below the ribbon.

Right-clicking on the **Quick Access** toolbar displays the shortcut menu shown in Figure 1-18 that provides some of the same options as the flyout menu discussed above plus a few more. Using the right-click menu you can remove tools, add separators between tools, add additional commands via the **Customize User Interface** (CUI) dialog box, or move the toolbar below the ribbon.

Figure 1-17   **Quick Access** toolbar flyout menu

Figure 1-18   **Quick Access** toolbar shortcut menu

Application Menu

Clicking on the big "A" button at the top left of the AutoCAD window displays the **Application Menu** shown in Figure 1-19.

The **Application Menu** provides easy access to commonly used AutoCAD file tools and drawing utilities via a menu that is split into a left pane and a right pane so that placing your mouse pointer over the main menu item on the left automatically displays a submenu list of

Figure 1-19   Displaying the **Application Menu**

related tools on the right as shown in Figure 1-20. If the submenu list is longer than can be displayed, you must use the arrow at the bottom of the right pane to scroll down so that you see the desired menu item.

The search tool at the top right of the **Application Menu** allows you to search through all of the AutoCAD tools by specifying key terms. For example, if you start typing L-I-N-E in the search field, AutoCAD dynamically displays all the tools that include the word LINE, as shown in Figure 1-21. Click on an item in the list to initiate the associated AutoCAD tool.

Additional Timesaving Application Menu Features.   In addition to easy access to AutoCAD file tools and drawing utilities, it is also possible to view and access recently opened drawings or drawings that are currently open in other windows via the two buttons at the top of the **Application Menu** shown in Figure 1-19. For example, selecting the **Recent Documents** button displays a list of recently opened drawings, as shown in Figure 1-22.

By default, recent drawings are displayed in an ordered list of when they were last accessed. It is possible to group drawings by access date, size, or file type via the **By Ordered List** drop-down menu at the top left.

The **View icon** button directly to the right of the **By Ordered List** drop-down menu allows you to change the file display from icons to small, medium, or large preview images. Additionally, briefly hovering the cursor over the drawing name displays a preview image. If you do not move your cursor for a few split seconds, the preview is expanded to include other important file information as shown in Figure 1-23.

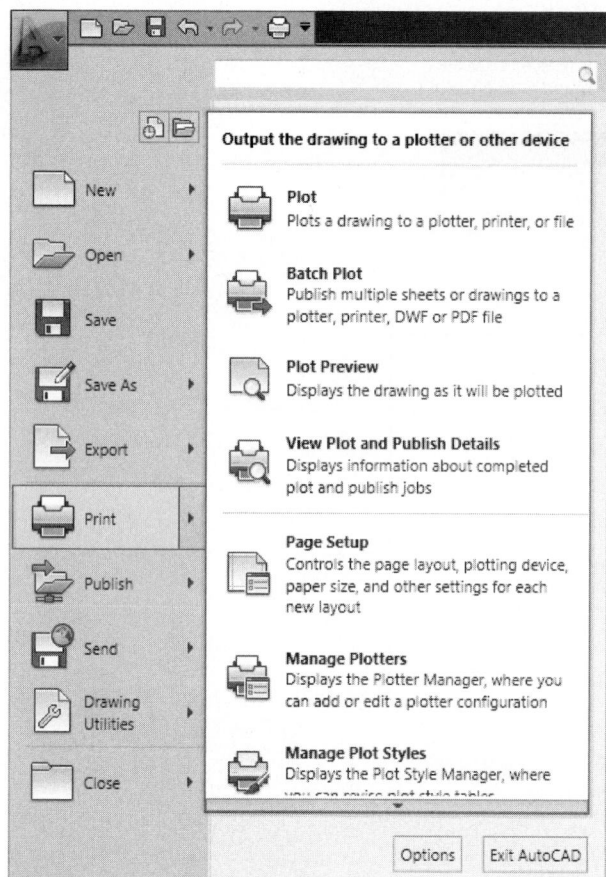

Figure 1-20 The **Print** submenu

Figure 1-21 Using the **Application Menu** search tool

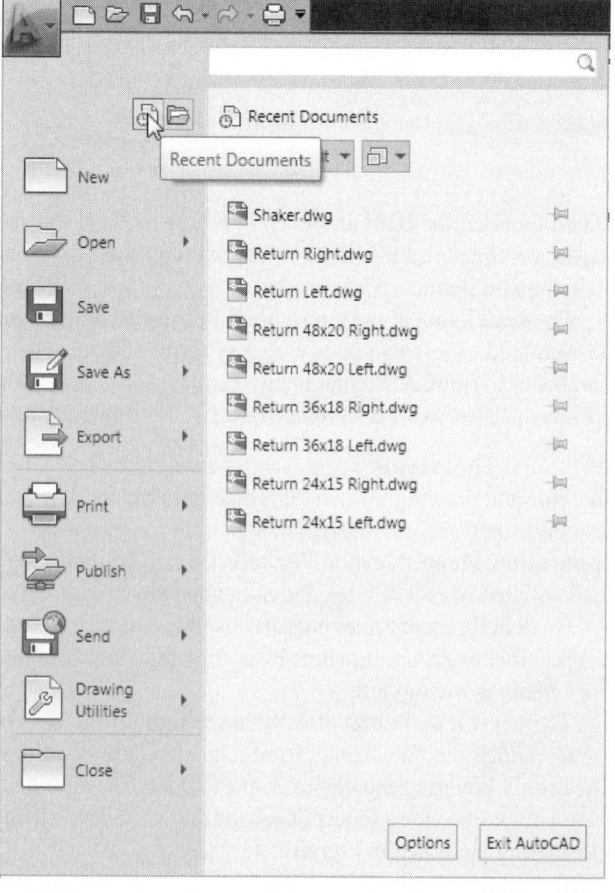

Figure 1-22 Viewing
recently opened drawings

Figure 1-23   Displaying a preview image

AutoCAD Options.   The **Options** button at the bottom right of the **Application Menu** displays the AutoCAD **Options** dialog box shown in Figure 1-24. The **Options** dialog box is your one-stop shop for controlling and maintaining most AutoCAD features and settings such as the color of different window elements, size of the cursor crosshairs, default print settings, and so on. Because it is accessed so often, it is located on the **Application Menu** for easy access. It can also be found at the bottom of most AutoCAD right-click shortcut menus discussed later in the chapter. You'll want to remember this because accessing and using the **Options** dialog box is discussed often throughout the rest of the textbook.

Ribbon

The ribbon at the top of the AutoCAD window shown in Figure 1-25 provides quick and easy access to the most used AutoCAD tools and features via a variety of task-specific tabs and panels.

Each task-specific tab contains multiple panels that, in turn, contain related tools. In addition, panels with a black arrow next to the panel name can be expanded to access additional tools as shown in Figure 1-26.

The default tab is the **Home** tab shown in Figure 1-25, which provides access to the most commonly used AutoCAD tools and features. The other tabs and their associated ribbons are as follows:

- **Insert**   Tools for working with blocks and block attributes, external references, importing different file formats, and managing drawing data

Figure 1-24   The AutoCAD **Options** dialog box

Figure 1-25   Ribbon

Figure 1-26   The **Draw** ribbon panel with additional tools displayed

- **Annotate**   Tools for creating and modifying text and dimensions, creating leader notes and tables, marking up and revising drawings, and managing **Annotation Scaling** features
- **Parametric**   Tools for establishing and maintaining geometric constraints and dimensional relationships
- **View**   Tools for managing the User Coordinate System (UCS), navigating in a drawing, managing viewports, turning different palettes on and off, viewing and switching multiple open drawings, controlling the display of different AutoCAD interface features, and managing named views
- **Manage**   Tools for recording and playing command macros, customizing the AutoCAD interface, loading and running custom programs, and managing CAD standards
- **Output**   Tools for plotting and publishing drawings, creating DWF and PDF files, and changing a drawing so that it looks hand-drawn
- **Express Tools**   Variety of productivity tools that allow you to perform a number of different useful tasks and operations. Technically not supported by Autodesk because they were originally developed by outside users.

Clicking on another tab swaps the current ribbon displayed with the ribbon selected so that a minimum amount of space is required for the tools you need and the drawing space is always maximized. In Figure 1-27 the **Annotate** tab has been selected so that the ribbon for adding text, dimensions, and other annotation features is now displayed.

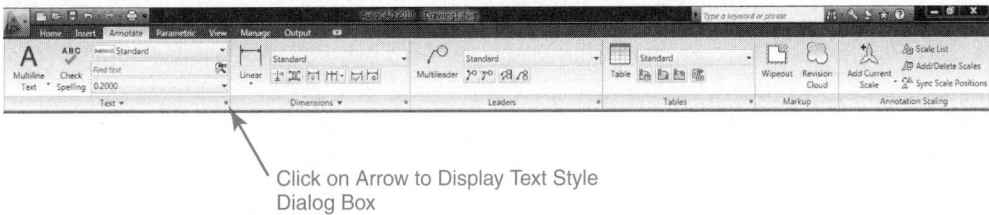

Click on Arrow to Display Text Style
Dialog Box

Figure 1-27   **Annotate** ribbon

TIP   The small arrows pointing down on the right side of some panel title bars shown in Figure 1-27 are buttons that when clicked display the style dialog box for the corresponding panel. For instance, clicking on the down arrow button on the right side of the **Text** panel displays the **Text Style** dialog box.

FOR MORE DETAILS   See Chapter 11 for more information about creating and managing text styles.

Controlling the Ribbon Display.   The ribbon has a number of different display features and options. You can control the majority of them by right-clicking on a panel tab to display the shortcut menu shown in Figure 1-28.

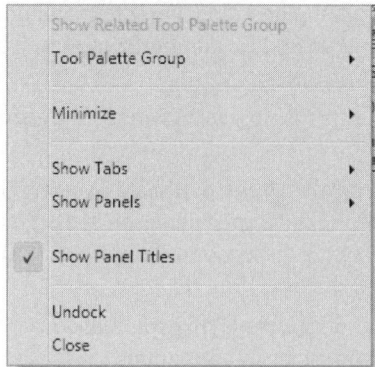

Figure 1-28   The **Ribbon** right-click menu

Using the right-click menu, you can turn different ribbon tabs and panels on and off by selecting them from their corresponding submenus. You can turn off all of the panel titles at the bottom of the ribbon by deselecting the **Show Panel Titles** option.

The **Minimize** submenu allows you to maximize the size of the drawing display window even further. Selecting the **Minimize to Panel Titles** option collapses all of the panels so that only the ribbon tabs and panel titles are displayed as shown in Figure 1-29.

Figure 1-29   **Minimize to Panel Titles** ribbon display

Placing your mouse pointer over a panel title temporarily displays the panel so that you can select the desired tool as shown in Figure 1-30. The panel then collapses back to the title only display when you move your mouse pointer back over the drawing window.

Figure 1-30   Single ribbon panel temporarily displayed

Selecting the **Minimize to Tabs** option collapses all of the panels and their titles so that all that is visible are the ribbon tabs across the top. You must click on the tab to display its respective ribbon temporarily while you choose the desired tool. The ribbon then disappears when you move your cursor back over the drawing window.

The down arrow button at the right of the **Output** tab shown in Figure 1-25 provides a shortcut to the **Minimize to Panel Titles** and **Minimize to Tabs** options described above. Clicking on the button once turns off the ribbon and displays only the panel titles. Clicking on it twice turns off everything except the ribbon tabs. Clicking on it again turns everything back on so that the ribbon is displayed normally.

You can reorganize ribbon tabs, or panels within individual tabs, by simply dragging and dropping them to a different location on the ribbon using your mouse. It is even possible to drag panels completely off the ribbon and create separate, what are called "sticky," panels, which float above your drawing window.

Note:
The ribbon is actually an AutoCAD palette, so it has a number of special properties and features. For instance, palettes can be attached to either side of the Auto-CAD window (docked) by dragging them with your mouse. All of the properties and features of palettes are described in detail later in this chapter.

Tooltips

You may have already noticed that information about a tool automatically appears directly at your mouse pointer if you hover the pointer over a tool for a short period of time. This useful feature is commonly referred to as a *tooltip*. The tooltip for the **Line** tool is shown in Figure 1-31.

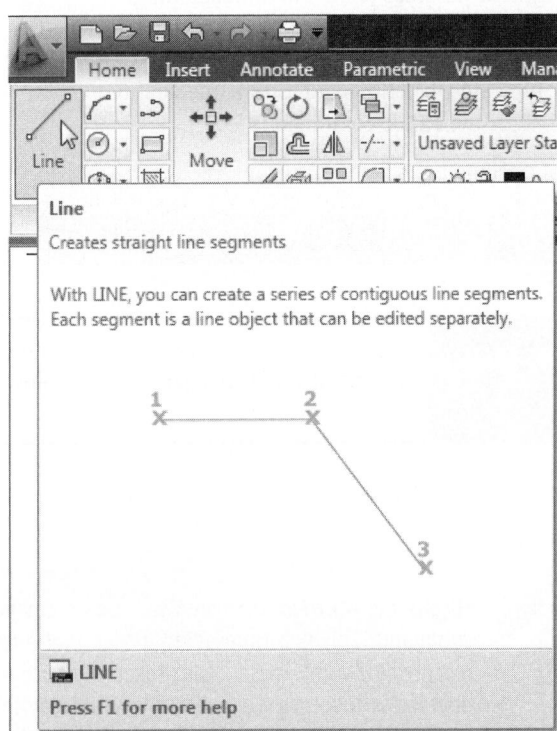

Figure 1-32   **Line** tooltip with additional information displayed

Figure 1-31   **Line** tooltip

Command Line Grab Bar

Figure 1-33   The command line window

The best part is that if you hover the mouse pointer for a split second more without moving, the tooltip expands to display additional information if it is available, sometimes even including helpful graphics as shown in Figure 1-32.

In addition, pressing the **<F1>** function key on your keyboard will display the complete AutoCAD online help topic for the current tool for even more detailed information. The AutoCAD online help system is discussed in detail at the end of this chapter.

The Command Line Window

The **command line** window provides access to the AutoCAD command line. See Figure 1-33. The AutoCAD command line allows you to enter AutoCAD commands by typing them on the keyboard. It is also one of the ways AutoCAD communicates with you via command prompts and messages.

Entering Commands via the Keyboard.   AutoCAD commands can also be entered by typing them at the keyboard. For instance, the command to draw a line can be entered by typing **Line<Enter ↵>** at the command line as follows:

Command: **Line<Enter ↵>**

AutoCAD commands are not case sensitive so you can enter any combination of uppercase and lowercase characters with the same result.

AutoCAD also provides a feature called **AutoComplete** that allows you to begin typing a command and then press the **<Tab>** key to cycle through all the commands and *system variables* that start with the letters you typed.

system variable: A named setting maintained by AutoCAD that controls an aspect of a drawing or the drawing environment.

For example, type **DIM<Tab>** at the command prompt to cycle through all the commands and system variables related to dimensioning.

Most commands can also be abbreviated to speed up their entry. The abbreviated version of a command is known as a *command alias*.

command alias: An abbreviated definition of a command name that enables you to enter commands faster at the keyboard by typing the first one or two letters of the command.

Typically, the command alias is the first one or two letters of the full command. The abbreviation for the **LINE** command is **L**:

Command: **L<Enter ↵>**

FOR MORE DETAILS   A complete list of command aliases is provided in Appendix C.

TIP   Hitting the **<Enter ↵>** key when no command has been typed will reenter the last command. This is a timesaving device that allows you to enter the same command repeatedly. For this reason, the most productive way to work in AutoCAD is to group like operations together. This allows you to "stay in the command" without losing focus jumping around to other menus, toolbars, and commands. Always try to focus on one operation.

Entering Command Options at the Command Line.   Many commands have options that the user can select by entering a designated response using the keyboard. Options are always displayed as a list in square brackets with each option separated with a forward slash. The ZOOM command prompts you with the following options at the command line:

```
Specify corner of window, enter a scale factor (nX or nXP),
or [All/Center/Dynamic/Extents/Previous/Scale/Window/Object] <real
time>:
```

Options can be entered by typing in the complete option keyword or, more simply, by typing in whatever letter is capitalized in the option keyword. For example, to use the **ZOOM** command with the **Window** option, you can enter either **Window** or **W** in response to the **ZOOM** command prompt. The **Previous** option can be entered as **P,** the **Extents** option as **E,** and so on. Obviously, typing a shortened abbreviation is faster than typing the complete word so their liberal use is suggested.

Default Command Options.   Sometimes a command will display a default option indicated with the option displayed between angle brackets. The default can be selected by simply hitting the **<Enter ⏎>** key. For instance, the default option for the **ZOOM** command is always **<real time>**. This means if you simply hit the **<Enter ⏎>** key in response to the **ZOOM** options prompt, you will be automatically placed in the **Zoom Realtime** mode.

Note:
The space bar at the bottom of the keyboard works exactly the same as the **<Enter ⏎>** key in Auto-CAD. Because it is larger, some people prefer using it over the **<Enter ⏎>** key because it is easier and faster to get to. The space bar is especially helpful when used as described in the preceding **TIP** to repeat commands!

AutoCAD remembers some command options so you don't have to type them the next time you use the command. For example, the default radius for a circle always reflects the radius you entered the last time you created a circle. The following is a **CIRCLE** command prompt with the default set to 2.0000 units.

```
Specify radius of circle or [Diameter] <2.0000>: <Enter ⏎>
```

If you are creating another circle with a radius of 2.0000 units, hit the **<Enter ⏎>** key, and voilà!

Canceling a Command with the <Esc> Key.   The **<Esc>** key at the top left of the keyboard cancels, or aborts, an active command. It is probably the most used keyboard key in AutoCAD! When you hit the **<Esc>** key, the current command is immediately aborted, and the word *Cancel* is displayed at the command line as follows:

```
Command: *Cancel*
```

Hitting the **<Esc>** key will also "unselect" any objects that are currently selected in the drawing window.

FOR MORE DETAILS   How to select objects in the drawing window is explained in detail in Chapter 7.

The Command History.   AutoCAD remembers every command entered in an AutoCAD session from the time you start AutoCAD up until the very last command you enter. This is known as the command history. You can scroll backward and forward through the command history using the arrow keys on your keyboard. The up arrow scrolls backward through the command history, while the down arrow scrolls forward. You can scroll backward or forward to any command in the history and run it again by hitting the **<Enter⏎>** key.

Resizing and Moving the Command Line Window.   The command line window can be resized, moved, and even made to float. To resize the command line window so you can see more lines of text, place your mouse pointer over the horizontal lines that separate the command line window from the drawing window so that the pointer switches into a double arrow. Hold down your left mouse button and drag up or down, and the window size changes accordingly.

To move the command line window, place your mouse point over the grab bar on the far left, then pick and drag the window out into the drawing window. See Figure 1-34. The command line window can also be docked on any of the four sides of the drawing window. It is typical to dock it at either the top or the bottom of the drawing window.

Figure 1-34 Floating command line window

Turning the Command Line Window Off.   The command line window can be turned off and on via the **Tools** menu or the **<Ctrl>+9** keyboard combination. When the command line window is turned off, commands can still be entered with the keyboard using **Dynamic Input** explained in the next section.

The Full Text Window.   It is possible to switch to a larger separate command line window known as the **Text** window by hitting the **<F2>** function key at the top of your keyboard. All the function key toggles are explained later in this chapter. Hitting **<F2>** once will display the **Text** window as shown in Figure 1-35. The **Text** window can be minimized, maximized, and resized using standard Windows techniques. Hitting the **<F2>** key again toggles the window off.

You'll notice that there is an **Edit** pull-down menu in the **Text** window. Selecting it displays the menu shown in Figure 1-36.

Figure 1-35 The **Text** window

Figure 1-36   **Text** window menu

This menu gives you even more command line options. You can run recent commands, select old commands and paste them to the command line to repeat them, and even copy the complete command history.

Dynamic Input

Dynamic Input is a set of related input display features that allows you to enter information near the mouse cursor so you can focus on your drawing instead of constantly switching focus to the command line.

Viewing and Entering Data Near the Mouse Cursor.   When **Dynamic Input** is on, data input occurs at the cursor by toggling between different input fields. Figure 1-37 shows the **Pointer Input** feature, which allows you to enter X and Y coordinate values right at the cursor. Coordinates are entered by typing the X coordinate value and the Y coordinate value separated by a comma. When you enter the comma, the X value is locked, and input changes to the Y value. You can also use the **<Tab>** key to switch between the X and Y values. Hitting **<Enter ↵>** accepts both values.

Dynamic Input also provides a **Dimension Input** feature that displays temporary dimensions as you draw that you can dynamically update to create objects ***parametrically***. The values that you enter in the Dimension Input fields are the values used to create the object. See Figure 1-38.

parametric: Automated creation of a drawing based on a given set of dimensions referred to as parameters.

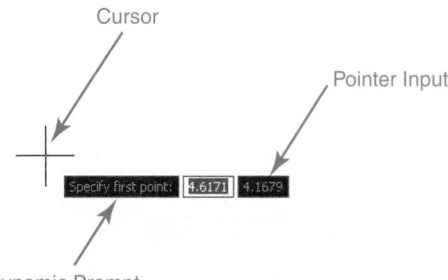

Figure 1-37   Viewing and entering data near the mouse cursor

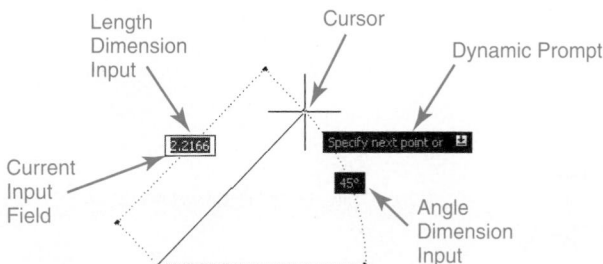

Figure 1-38   Using dynamic dimensions to create a line

The **<Tab>** key allows you to toggle between the different input fields. For instance, pressing the **<Tab>** key in the example shown in Figure 1-38 switches the input field from the dynamic length dimension to the dynamic angle dimension as shown in Figure 1-39.

Selecting Command Options Near the Mouse Cursor.   Earlier we saw that command options can be specified by typing all or part of them at the AutoCAD command line. Using the **Dynamic Prompt** feature you can select command options using your mouse! If you press the down arrow key on your keyboard, a list of the valid command options is displayed near the cursor as shown in Figure 1-40. You can either use your mouse to select the desired option or navigate up and down the list using the arrow keys on your keyboard. Using this method, you must press **<Enter ↵>** when the desired option is indicated.

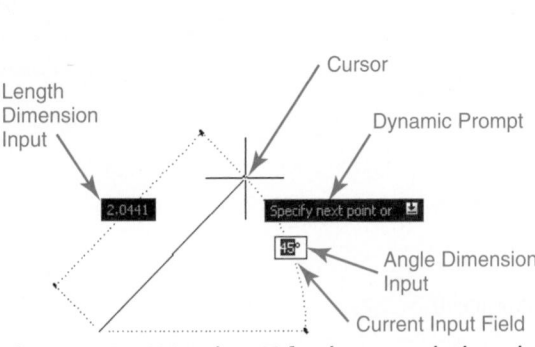

Figure 1-39   Using the **<Tab>** key to toggle through input fields

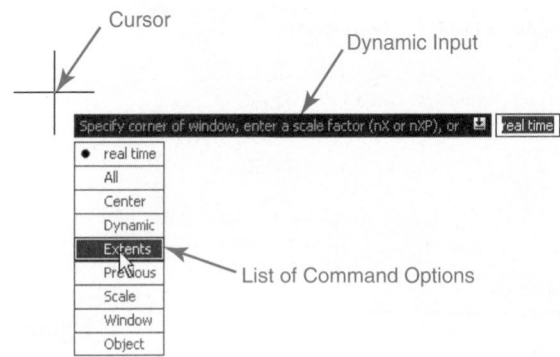

Figure 1-40   Selecting **ZOOM** command options using **Dynamic Input**

FOR MORE DETAILS   See Chapter 6 for more information about **Dynamic Input** features and settings.

Right-Click Shortcut Menus

AutoCAD is chock-full of right-click shortcut menus. They're everywhere. If you're ever in doubt, right-click with your mouse, and you are bound to find something useful. Some of the more prominent right-click menus are introduced below.

If you right-click with your mouse over the drawing window when no drawing objects are selected, the **Default** shortcut menu shown in Figure 1-41 is displayed.

If you right-click when objects are selected in the drawing window, the **Edit** shortcut menu shown in Figure 1-42 is displayed so that you can modify the selected object(s).

If you right-click when a command is active, the **Command** shortcut menu shown in Figure 1-43 is displayed, providing access to different command options, etc.

Figure 1-41   **Default** shortcut menu

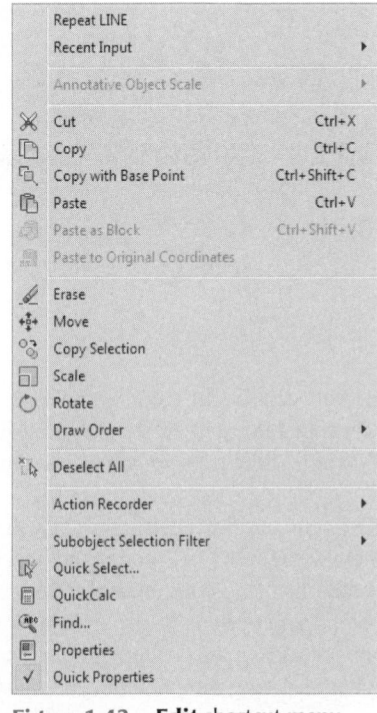

Figure 1-42   **Edit** shortcut menu

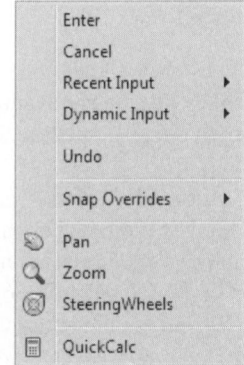

Figure 1-43   **Command** shortcut menu

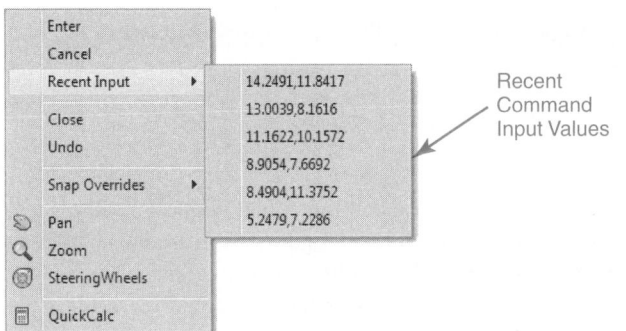

Figure 1-44   Accessing recent input

Accessing Recent Input.   It is possible to access recent command input using the keyboard up and down arrow keys or the right-click shortcut menu shown in Figure 1-44.

Using the **Recent Input** feature is a timesaving feature that allows you to recall recently entered data values so you don't have to type them again regardless if the values were entered via the keyboard in the first place. AutoCAD remembers all the input values from all the input methods.

TIP   If you use the right-click menu to list the recent input when no command is active, AutoCAD will display a list of recently used commands.

Status Bars

There are two different status bars in AutoCAD: the Drawing Status Bar, which is at the bottom of every individual drawing window, and the Application Status Bar, which is located at the very bottom of the AutoCAD window shown earlier in Figure 1-15.

The Drawing Status Bar is used primarily for controlling the Annotation and Viewport Scale in each drawing and is explained in detail in Chapter 14. It is turned off by default.

The Application Status Bar, on the other hand, is always on because it controls so many different things. It is like a mini-dashboard for AutoCAD. See Figure 1-45.

Figure 1-45   The Application Status Bar

Like your car's dashboard, the Application Status Bar provides a myriad of different features and functionality:

Coordinate Display.   The Coordinate display keeps track of where your mouse crosshairs are located by interactively displaying their coordinates as you move your mouse.

You can disable the Coordinate display by double-clicking on it with your mouse. Right-clicking on the Coordinate display button displays a shortcut menu that allows you to switch between relative, absolute, and geographic coordinate display. The difference between absolute and relative coordinates is explained in Chapter 4.

Drawing Tool Buttons.   The **Drawing Tool** buttons allow you to toggle different drawing tools on and off interactively as you work in your drawing. The majority of the tools are explained in detail in Chapter 5.

| 18.9961, 2.0700 , 0.0000 | SNAP | GRID | ORTHO | POLAR | OSNAP | OTRACK | DUCS | DYN | LWT | QP |

Figure 1-46   Drawing Tool buttons in text-only mode

Each **Drawing Tool** button has its own unique right-click menu that allows you to control that tool's specific settings and features. In addition, each tool's right-click menu has a **Display** submenu that allows you to remove any of the **Drawing Tool** buttons from the Status Bar, as well as switch from the icon-type buttons that have pictures back to the traditional text-only style shown in Figure 1-46 that was used in earlier releases of AutoCAD.

Quick Properties Button.   The **Quick Properties** button toggles on and off the **Quick Properties** feature that allows you to quickly view and modify object properties directly where the objects are located on your screen via a trimmed down **Properties** palette like the one shown in Figure 1-47.

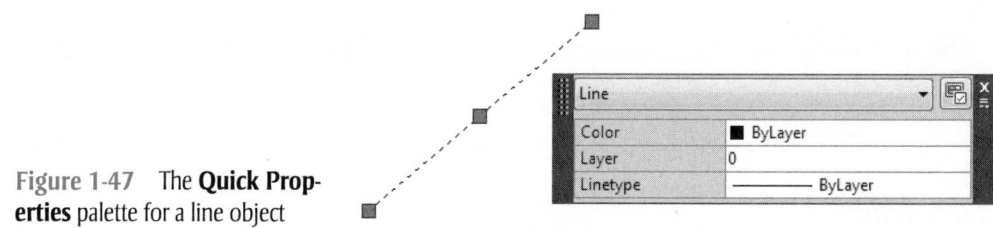

Figure 1-47   The Quick Properties palette for a line object

When **Quick Properties** is on, the **Properties** palette is automatically displayed near your mouse pointer whenever you select one or more objects in your drawing, saving both time and valuable screen real estate! The **Quick Properties** feature and the **Properties** palette are explained in detail in Chapter 6.

Model or Paper Space Button.   The **Model or Paper Space** button switches the drawing environment to the last active paper space layout if you are currently in model space. Select it so it switches to PAPER. If you are in paper space and select the button and change it to MODEL, the last viewport will become active so you can work "through" the viewport (same as double-clicking on a viewport).

Quick View Drawings and Layouts Tools.   The **Quick View Drawings** and **Quick View Layouts** tools allow you to visually switch between open drawings or layouts via a horizontal row of preview images. The **Quick View Drawings** tool is explained later in this chapter. See Chapter 14 for more information about the **Quick View Layouts** tool.

Pan and Zoom Tools.   The **Pan** and **Zoom** tools allow you to navigate the drawing display window so that you can view all the information in your drawing at the scale necessary to do your work.

Clicking on the **Pan** tool changes your mouse pointer to a hand icon that indicates that you can click and hold you left mouse button down to drag your drawing around the drawing display. You can hit **<Enter ↵>** or **<Esc>** to close the **Pan** tool. Right-clicking will display a handy shortcut menu that also allows you to exit, or switch to a few useful **Zoom** tools.

The **Zoom** tool allows you to zoom in on your drawing by picking two points to define a rectangular window that is zoomed in to fill the drawing display. Pressing the **<Enter ↵>** key instead of picking a point changes your mouse pointer to a small magnifying glass icon that indicates that you are in the interactive **Zoom** "realtime" mode. If you click and hold your left mouse button down and drag the icon up the screen you will zoom in on the drawing. Dragging the mouse down will zoom out on the drawing. The **Pan** and **Zoom** tools are explained in detail in Chapter 3.

SteeringWheel and Show Motion 3D Navigation Tools. The **SteeringWheel** and **Show Motion** navigation tools are primarily for navigating around in a 3D drawing. The **SteeringWheel** combines a variety of display navigation tools like **Pan** and **Zoom** with other complex view manipulation features into one centralized tool. The **Show Motion** tool allows you to easily create 3D animations and walk-throughs. Both tools are beyond the scope of this textbook. For further information about either tool, consult the AutoCAD online help discussed at the end of the chapter.

Annotation Scale Tools. As mentioned earlier in the "Fundamental CAD Concepts" section, it is now possible to automate the process of creating annotation objects such as text and dimensions at the correct size for the final plotted drawing scale using the **Annotation Scale** feature located on the right side of the Status Bar. See Figure 1-45. Clicking on the **Annotation Scale** button displays a menu with a list of predefined scales as shown in Figure 1-48.

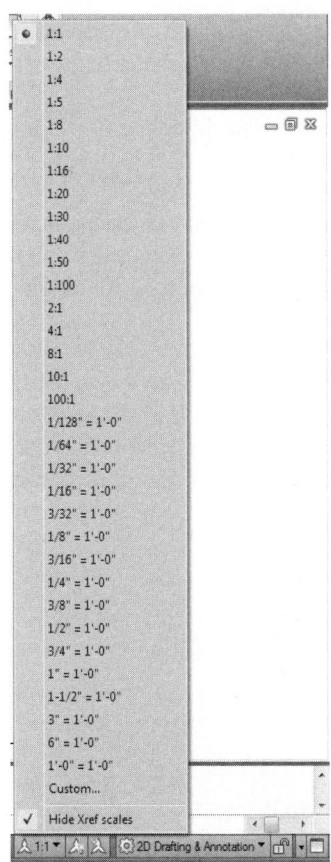

Figure 1-48   The **Annotation Scale** menu

When annotation objects that have their **Annotative** property enabled are added to the drawing they will automatically scale up or down by the current **Annotation Scale** so that you do not have to scale them manually.

The two buttons to the right of the **Annotation Scale** allow you to add and view annotation objects at multiple scales so that it is possible to reduce redundant annotation information in your drawings.

In the past, drawings that had multiple scales had to have separate copies of all the annotation objects like text and dimensions at different scales to account for each drawing scale factor. Typically, different scale representations of the annotation objects were located on separate layers so that they could be turned on and off for each scale as needed. It was a very complex process, and because it required redundant information, it was prone to errors and omissions.

Chapters 11 through 14 discuss in detail how to utilize the AutoCAD **Annotation Scale** features to add and manage different annotation objects.

Workspace Switching Button.   The **Workspace Switching** button allows you to switch between AutoCAD's default workspaces, save a custom workspace, control workspace settings, and customize workspaces.

Workspaces allow you to save and restore the on/off status and positions of the ribbon, palettes, pull-down menus, and toolbars so that you can set up different work environments for different tasks. For instance, you might set up a dimensioning environment that has all the AutoCAD dimension tools turned on while most of the other AutoCAD tools are turned off so that you can focus strictly on the task of dimensioning.

To save your own custom workspace, you first set up the AutoCAD environment in the way you wish to save it by turning on and off the features you want and positioning them accordingly. Click on the **Workspace Switching** button and select **Save Current As...** from the menu and then enter a workspace name.

To restore a saved workspace, click on the **Workspace Switching** button and select it from the list.

The **Workplace Settings...** menu item allows you to control which workspaces are displayed, the menu order, and whether workspace changes are automatically saved when switching workspaces.

The **Customize...** menu item displays the AutoCAD Customize User Interface (CUI) for more high-level-type customization tasks.

Toolbar/Window Locking.   The **Toolbar/Window Locking** tool allows you to lock toolbars, palettes, and other AutoCAD features so you do not accidently move them. Locking the various AutoCAD user interface features is discussed later in this chapter after most of the different interface features have been covered.

Status Tray.   On the far right of the Status Bar is the Status Tray. The Status Tray dynamically updates with different icons that are used for notification features and different task-specific settings depending on what you're doing. For instance, after a plot is complete a notification balloon is displayed in the Status Tray with information about whether the plot was successful as shown in Figure 1-49.

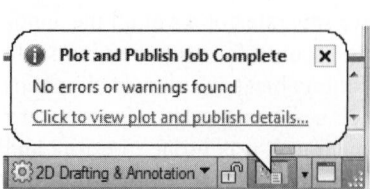

Figure 1-49   Plot status notification balloon

Figure 1-50   The **Status Bar** menu

Clean Screen Toggle. The **Clean Screen** toggle temporarily turns off most of AutoCAD's graphical interface features like the ribbon, palettes, and toolbars and maximizes your drawing area so that you have more room to draw. Clicking on the **Clean Screen** toggle again turns everything back on again. The **Clean Screen** toggle is explained in detail in Chapter 3.

 TIP   It is possible to turn the Application Status Bar features on and off as well as manage the Status Tray settings by clicking on the arrow at the far right of the Application Status Bar to display the **Status Bar** menu shown in Figure 1-50.

Dialog Boxes

Dialog box is the term used to describe any of the graphical windows displayed in response to a command that allows you to select and specify various command options. AutoCAD has many different dialog boxes. Selecting the **Open** tool from the **Quick Access** toolbar displays the **Select File** dialog box shown in Figure 1-51. This dialog box is common to many file-related commands. The common file dialog boxes work very similarly to Windows Explorer as explained earlier.

Figure 1-51   Select File dialog box

 TIP   The common file dialog boxes contain a right-click shortcut menu that provides the same commands and options found in Windows Explorer so that you can perform different file operations without leaving AutoCAD.

Palettes

Palettes are separate windows that provide additional AutoCAD functionality. The cool thing is that palettes can be continuously displayed so that you can work between the palette and your drawing, like an artist creating a painting. Because of this capability, palettes have a special feature called *Auto-hide* that can be set to automatically hide a palette when you are not using it, freeing up your drawing window for actual drawing.

The easiest way to turn palettes on and off is via the **Palettes** panel on the **View** ribbon shown in Figure 1-52.

Figure 1-52   Palettes panel buttons

Tool Palettes.   **Tool** palettes provide easy access to commands, hatch patterns, and blocks via a series of tabbed palettes as shown in Figure 1-53. To switch to a palette, select the corresponding tab. You can select a **Tool** palette item either by clicking on its icon or by dragging an icon into your drawing window.

Tool palettes are meant to be customized, allowing you to add and organize your own commands, blocks, and hatch patterns. The default content is provided as a sample of what you can do. Creating custom **Tool** palettes with your own blocks, hatch patterns, and commands is discussed later in the book.

Properties Palette.   The **Properties** palette is your one-stop shop for managing the drawing object properties explained earlier. In Figure 1-54, the properties of a line are displayed in the **Properties** palette.

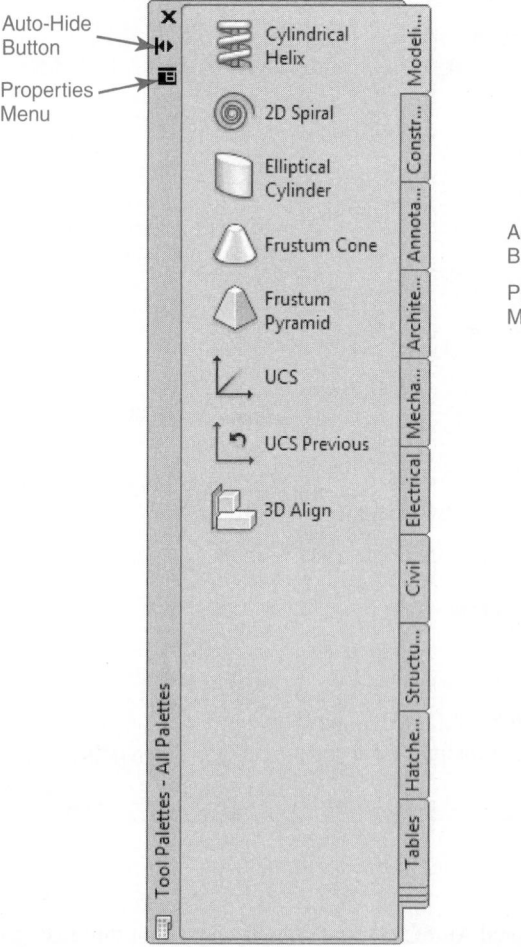

Figure 1-53   The **Tool** palette

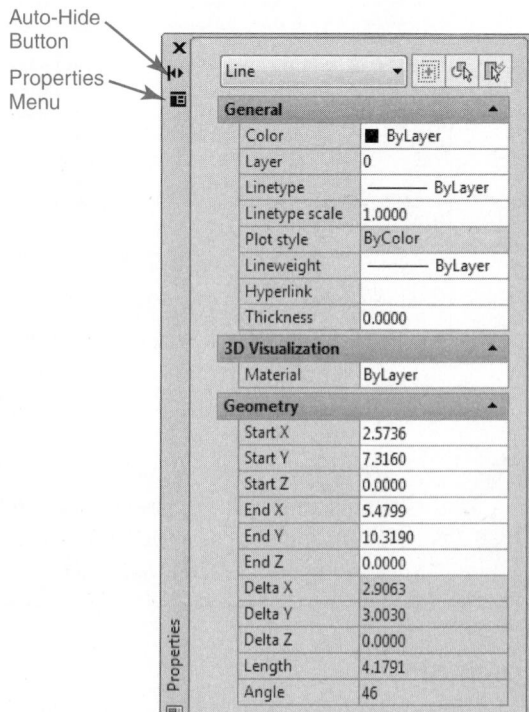

Figure 1-54   The **Properties** palette

Sheet Set Manager Palette.   The **Sheet Set Manager** is used to create and manage AutoCAD *sheet sets*. For further information about the **Sheet Set Manager**, please consult AutoCAD Help.

sheet set: An organized and named collection of sheets created from multiple AutoCAD drawing files.

> **FOR MORE DETAILS**   Using the **Properties** palette is thoroughly detailed in Chapter 6.

Auto-hide Feature.   As mentioned, it is possible to "hide" a palette using the **Auto-hide** feature. When Auto-hide is on, the palette collapses so only the title bar is visible when your mouse is not over the palette. When you move your mouse back over the palette's title bar, the palette expands so it is completely visible again.

The easiest way to turn the **Auto-hide** feature on and off is by clicking on the **Auto-hide** arrow icon on the palette's title bar. Auto-hide can also be turned on and off using the palette **Properties** shortcut menu explained in the next section.

Note: The **Auto-hide** feature can be used when a palette is docked by selecting the "⌄" button on the right side of the title bar.

Palette Properties.   Each of the palettes introduced above have similar properties that are controlled by clicking on the **Properties** icon on the palette's title bar. Selecting the **Properties** icon on any palette displays a **Properties** shortcut menu similar to the one shown in Figure 1-55. Using the **Properties** menu, you can turn the **Auto-hide** feature on and off and indicate whether a palette can be docked or not. A palette can be docked on either the left or right side of your drawing window. The **Properties** palette is shown docked on the right side of the screen in Figure 1-56.

Figure 1-55   Palette Properties menu

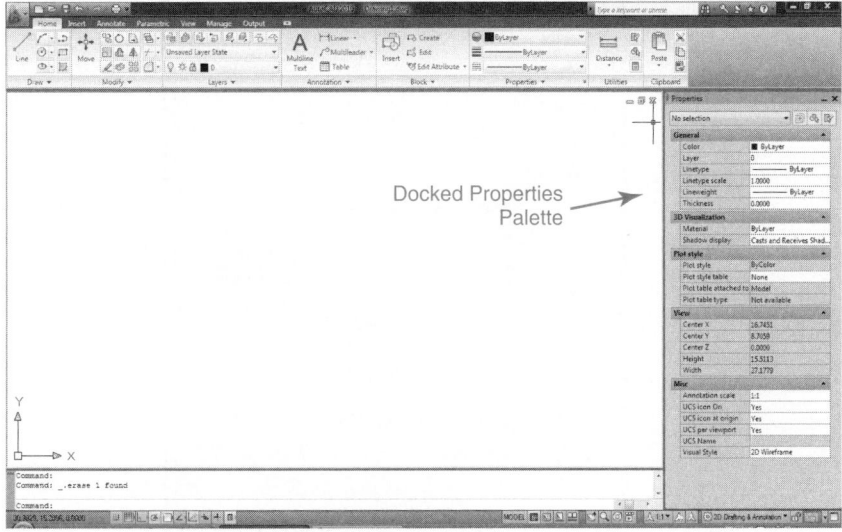

Figure 1-56   Docking the **Properties** palette

The **Anchor Left** and **Anchor Right** options on the **Palette Properties** menu allows you to dock a palette on the left or right of the AutoCAD window with the **Auto-hide** feature on so that the palette is reduced to a thin strip represented by the palette title bar as shown in Figure 1-57.

Figure 1-57   **Properties** palette anchored on the right

Placing your mouse pointer over the title bar displays the palette temporarily so that you can make any changes or updates. Turning the **Auto-hide** feature off when a palette is anchored will change it back to the docked mode shown earlier.

Transparency.   It is possible to make palettes transparent so that you can see the drawing under, or through, the palette. The **Transparency...** menu item on the **Palette Properties** menu displays the **Transparency** dialog box shown in Figure 1-58.

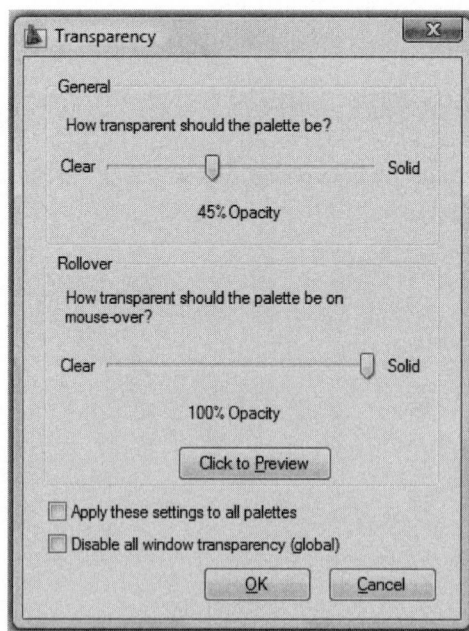

Figure 1-58   The **Transparency** dialog box

The slider bar at the top in the **General** area controls the overall transparency of palettes. By default, palettes are set to 100% opacity so that you cannot see through them. Sliding the bar to the left makes the palettes more transparent.

By default, palettes that are transparent will change back to 100% opacity when your mouse pointer is above them so that you can see them. The slider bar on the bottom in the **Rollover** area allows you to change it so the palette will stay transparent.

It is possible to apply any changes to all the palettes in AutoCAD by selecting the **Apply these settings to all palettes** check box at the bottom of the dialog box. To make all palettes 100% opaque and turn off transparency throughout AutoCAD, select the **Disable all window transparency (global)** check box.

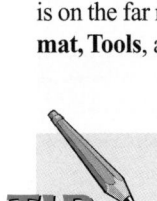

Note: Select the **AutoCAD Classic** workspace to set the AutoCAD interface back to the traditional environment where pull-down menus and toolbars are turned on and the ribbon is turned off.

Pull-Down Menus

The pull-down menus across the top of the AutoCAD window provide access to most of the AutoCAD commands. You'll notice that the menus are organized in the same order from left to right as other Windows programs like Word and Excel. The **File** menu is on the far left and the **Help** menu is on the far right, with many of the same menus in between (**Edit, View, Insert, Format, Tools**, and **Window**). Most of these menus contain similar commands and behavior.

TIP You can also turn on the pull-down menus by selecting **Show Menu Bar** from the **Quick Access** toolbar right-click shortcut menu shown in Figure 1-17.

Putting your mouse pointer over a pull-down menu heading and clicking the mouse will display the pull-down menu. The **File** pull-down menu is shown in Figure 1-59. To select a menu item on a pull-down menu, position your mouse over the desired menu item so it is highlighted and then click with your mouse.

Figure 1-59   The **File** pull-down menu

TIP   It is also possible to select a menu item via the keyboard by selecting the **<Alt>** key on your keyboard in combination with the underlined character on the pull-down menu. For instance, the **File** pull-down menu can be displayed by holding down the **<Alt>** key in combination with the **F** key on your keyboard. You can then select the desired menu item by hitting the key for the underlined letter in the menu label. Hitting the **N** key while the **File** pull-down menu is displayed selects the **New...** menu item.

Cascading Menus.   Menu items with an arrow on the right indicate a cascading submenu. Simply placing your cursor over a menu item with an arrow will display the cascade menu. The **Drawing Utilities** cascade menu from the **File** pull-down menu is shown in Figure 1-60. The three dots, or ellipses, next to a menu item indicate that a dialog box is displayed when that menu item is selected. Dialog boxes are explained in the next section.

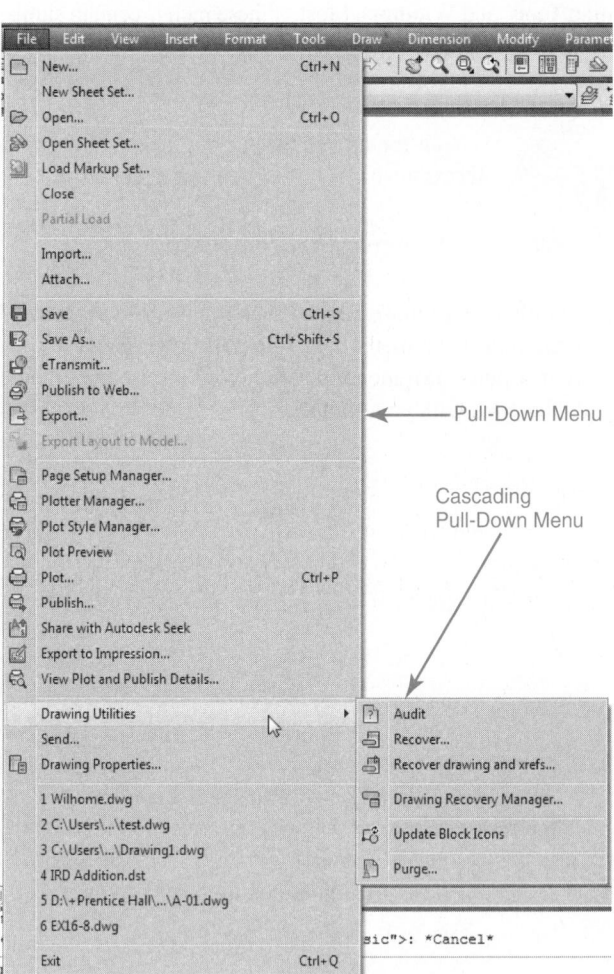

Figure 1-60   Cascading pull-down menu

Toolbars

They say a picture is worth a thousand words. Toolbars provide an easy-to-use graphical interface to most of the AutoCAD commands by using pictures called *toolbar icons* to represent different commands. The **Standard** toolbar is shown in Figure 1-61. You will probably recognize some of the icons from other Windows programs. Toolbar buttons provide quick access to a command because they require only one click of the mouse.

Figure 1-61   The **Standard** toolbar

Toolbar Flyouts.   A toolbar button with a small arrow indicates that it is a toolbar flyout. A toolbar flyout button displays a subtoolbar with additional buttons when it is selected. It is the toolbar equivalent of a cascading menu. Figure 1-62 shows the **Zoom** toolbar flyout.

Toolbar Flyout Menu

Figure 1-62   **Zoom** toolbar flyout menu

TIP   The last toolbar button selected on a toolbar flyout menu will become the button shown on the main toolbar after it is selected. This means that the next time you need the command you don't have to display the flyout menu; you can select it from the main toolbar.

Turning Toolbars On and Off.   AutoCAD has over 30 toolbars that can be turned on and off as needed. By default, the **AutoCAD Classic** workspace has the following toolbars turned on:

- **Standard** toolbar   Contains standard commands
- **Layers** toolbar   Used to manage layers in a drawing
- **Properties** toolbar   Used to manage object properties
- **Styles** toolbar   Used to manage styles in a drawing
- **Draw** toolbar   Contains drawing commands
- **Modify** toolbar   Contains modify commands
- **Draw order** toolbar   Controls stacking order of objects

The easiest way to turn toolbars on and off is to simply right-click with your mouse when the mouse pointer is over a toolbar button. This displays the **Toolbar** shortcut menu shown in Figure 1-63 that lists all the toolbars with a check mark next to those that are currently on.

Selecting a toolbar that is not currently checked will turn it on and place it on the screen wherever it was located when it was last displayed. You can then move it and place it where you want using the techniques explained in the next section.

Moving and Placing Toolbars.   Toolbars can exist in two states—floating and docked. Floating means that the toolbar is located somewhere (floating) over your drawing window with the title shown at the top and the window-close "X" visible in the upper right corner. The **Dimension** toolbar is shown floating in Figure 1-64. When a toolbar is floating, you can move it by placing your mouse pointer over the title bar on top, clicking with your left mouse button, and dragging the toolbar where you want it.

You can dock a toolbar by dragging it to any side of the drawing window. In Figure 1-64 the **Draw** and **Modify** toolbars are docked. To dock a toolbar, simply drag it to any of the four sides of the drawing window until the shadow line changes shape, indicating it is ready to be docked, and then release the mouse button. In Figure 1-65 the **Dimension** toolbar has been docked on the left side of the screen. To float a toolbar that has been docked, select the grab bars (Figure 1-65) at the top or left side of the toolbar with your mouse pointer and drag the toolbar into the drawing window to the desired location.

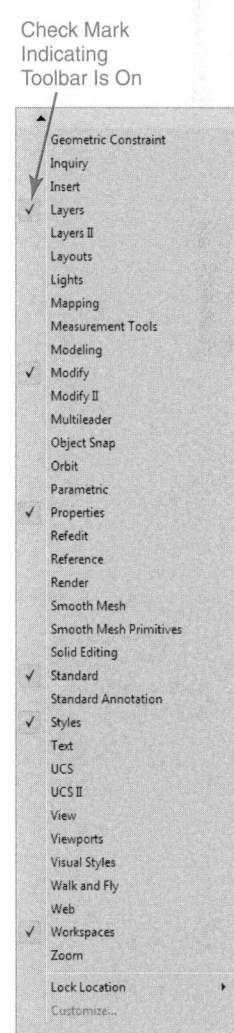

Check Mark Indicating Toolbar Is On

Figure 1-63   Turning toolbars on and off

Toolbar
Grab
Bars

Draw
Toolbar

Floating Toolbar

Modify
Toolbar

Figure 1-64 Floating
toolbar

Toolbar
Grab
Bars

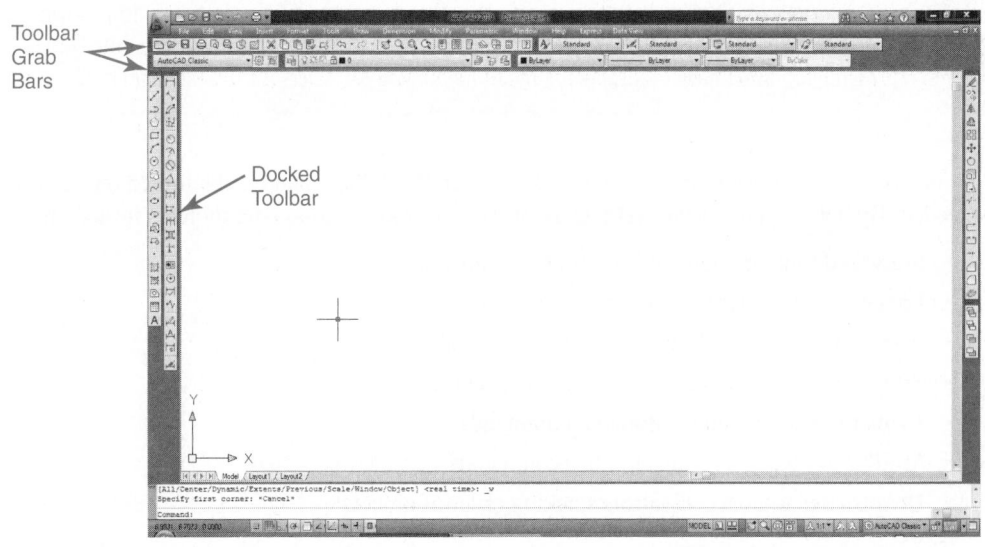

Docked
Toolbar

Figure 1-65 Docking a
toolbar

Floating Toolbars/Panels
Docked Toolbars/Panels
Floating Windows
Docked Windows
All ▸
Help

Figure 1-66 The **Lock**
shortcut menu

Locking Toolbars and Windows.   As you can see, manipulating toolbars and windows is easy—almost too easy. To eliminate any accidental changes, AutoCAD provides the ability to lock them.

The **Lock** icon on the far right of the Status Bar indicates the current lock status. Select it with your mouse to display the **Lock** shortcut menu shown in Figure 1-66.

Click on the desired menu item to lock that feature. Once any feature is locked, the **Lock** icon changes to the locked status on the Status Bar.

You can also lock toolbars and windows via the **Locking** tool located on the **Windows Elements** panel on the **View** ribbon.

TIP

You can override toolbar and palette locking by holding down the **<Ctrl>** key while you select the toolbar or palette with your mouse.

Multiple Drawing Interface

AutoCAD has what is known as a *Multiple Drawing Interface*, or *MDI*. This just means you can open more than one drawing at a time. This allows you to do things like compare multiple related drawings simultaneously so you can coordinate your work and, even better, copy drawing information between drawings using *drag and drop* techniques. In order to facilitate these features, you must be able to quickly switch between open drawings as well as organize your open drawing windows on your screen.

Switching Between Open Drawings.   The **Quick View Drawings** tool located on the right side of the Status Bar shown earlier in Figure 1-45 is the best way to switch between open drawings because it provides preview images of the drawings; plus, you can also preview and switch to any layout within a drawing.

Clicking on the **Quick View Drawings** tool on the Status Bar displays a horizontal row of drawing preview images at the bottom of the AutoCAD window of all drawings that are currently open and a toolbar displayed underneath with a few tools, explained later. See Figure 1-67.

Quick View
Preview Images   Quick View Toolbar

Figure 1-67   The **Quick View Drawings** tool

TIP   You can move the mouse past the edge of the image strip to view drawing images that extend beyond the screen. You can increase or decrease the size of the drawing preview images by pressing the **<Ctrl>** key while rolling the mouse wheel up or down.

When you move your mouse pointer over a **Quick View Drawing** preview, preview images of all the layouts in that drawing, including model space, display above the **Drawing** preview images as a separate image bar as shown in Figure 1-68.

Clicking a preview image will switch AutoCAD's focus to that drawing. It is also possible to save or close a drawing via its preview image by clicking on the corresponding **Save** and **Close** icons in the upper corners of the preview window.

To see a larger view of the layouts, simply move your mouse pointer over a layout preview image. AutoCAD enlarges the size of all the layout images and reduces the size of the drawing images. **Plot** and **Publish** icons are also displayed in the upper corners of the current **Layout** preview making it possible to print directly from the preview. See Figure 1-69.

Figure 1-68 The **Quick View Drawings** tool with a drawing selected

Model/Layout Previews

Selected Drawing Preview

Figure 1-69 The **Quick View Drawings** tool with a layout selected

Enlarged Model/Layout Previews

Reduced Drawing Preview

Moving the cursor back over a drawing preview reverses the process and returns the drawing preview images back to their larger size and the layout preview images back to their smaller size.

Additional tools are provided via the **Quick View Drawings** toolbar, which is automatically displayed below the **Quick View Drawings** preview images as shown in Figure 1-67. Using these tools you can pin **Quick View Drawings** open so that it remains visible while you work in the drawing editor. You can use the **Close** tool to turn off **Quick View Drawings** when you no longer want it displayed. The **New** button creates a new drawing and displays the preview at the end of the **Quick View** toolbar. You can easily open existing drawings using the **Open** tool.

The Windows Panel on the View Ribbon. The **Windows** panel on the **View** ribbon also allows you to quickly switch between open drawings and provides a number of window display options for viewing multiple drawings.

Figure 1-70   Cascading drawing windows

Figure 1-71   Tiling windows horizontally

Cascading Windows.   The **Cascade** option displays all open drawings stacked in a tiered fashion so that you can see all open drawings one on top of another as shown in Figure 1-70. You can then switch to another drawing by simply clicking on the desired drawing's title bar.

Tiling Windows Horizontally.   The **Tile Horizontally** option fills the drawing window with all the open drawings tiled in a horizontal fashion as shown in Figure 1-71.

Tiling Windows Vertically.   The **Tile Vertically** option fills the drawing window with all the open drawings tiled in a vertical fashion as shown in Figure 1-72.

TIP   Tiling the open drawings either horizontally or vertically is best when you need to share information between drawings. With the drawings tiled, you can use drag and drop techniques to copy information from one drawing to another!

FOR MORE DETAILS   Copying information between drawings is discussed in Chapter 7.

Vertically Tiled Drawing Windows

Figure 1-72 Tiling
windows vertically

Keyboard Commands

AutoCAD has a number of other keyboard commands besides the **<Esc>** key that cancels a command in progress and the **<F2>** function key that displays the **Text** window. Keyboard commands provide quick access to a number of commands and options already available on a pull-down menu, a toolbar, or the status bar.

Function Keys.   Function keys are the keys at the top of most keyboards that are labeled **<F1>** through **<F12>**. The most famous function key is **<F1>**, which is used to display the **Help** window in almost every Windows program. We have already seen the **<F2>** key, which toggles the AutoCAD **Text** window on and off. The other function keys also work as toggles, mostly as alternates for the drafting aids found on the AutoCAD Status Bar. A complete list of function keys and their associated functions is provided in the following table.

AutoCAD Function Keys	
Function Key	**Description**
F1	AutoCAD online Help system
F2	Text screen toggle
F3	Object snap toggle
F4	Tablet mode toggle
F5	Isoplane toggle
F6	Dynamic UCS toggle
F7	Grid mode toggle
F8	Ortho mode toggle
F9	Snap mode toggle
F10	Polar mode toggle
F11	Object snap tracking toggle
F12	Dynamic Input toggle

Control Key Combinations.   Control key combinations are created by holding down the <**Ctrl**> key, typically located on the bottom row of your keyboard, while selecting some other key on the keyboard. For example, holding down the <**Ctrl**> key and selecting the **C** key at the same time copies information to the Windows clipboard. A control key combination is typically expressed as <**Ctrl**>+**Key**. The copy example above is expressed as <**Ctrl**>+**C**.

Like the function keys, control key combinations are provided as a quick alternative to commands found elsewhere in AutoCAD. Some control key combinations are common to many Windows programs, while some are exclusive to AutoCAD. A complete list is provided in the following table.

AutoCAD Control Key Combinations	
Combination	**Description**
Ctrl+A	Select all
Ctrl+B	**Snap Mode** toggle
Ctrl+C	**COPYCLIP** command
Ctrl+D	**Dynamic UCS** command
Ctrl+E	**Isoplane** toggle
Ctrl+F	**Osnap** toggle
Ctrl+G	**Grid mode** toggle
Ctrl+H	**Pickstyle** toggle
Ctrl+I	**Coordinate display** toggle
Ctrl+J	Repeats last command
Ctrl+K	**HYPERLINK** command
Ctrl+L	**Ortho Mode** toggle
Ctrl+M	Repeats last command
Ctrl+N	**NEW** command
Ctrl+O	**OPEN** command
Ctrl+P	**PLOT** command
Ctrl+Q	**QUIT** command
Ctrl+R	**Viewport** toggle
Ctrl+S	**SAVE** command
Ctrl+T	**Tablet Mode** toggle
Ctrl+U	**Polar Mode** toggle
Ctrl+V	**PASTECLIP** command
Ctrl+W	**Object Snap Tracking** toggle
Ctrl+X	**CUTCLIP** command
Ctrl+Y	**REDO** command
Ctrl+Z	**UNDO** command

Ctrl+0	**Clean Screen** toggle
Ctrl+1	**Properties Manager** toggle
Ctrl+2	**DesignCenter** toggle
Ctrl+3	**Tool Palettes** toggle
Ctrl+4	**Sheet Set Manager** toggle
Ctrl+5	Not Used
Ctrl+6	**dbConnect Manager** toggle
Ctrl+7	**Markup Set Manager**
Ctrl+8	Quick Calculator
Ctrl+9	**Command Line** toggle

TIP   The **<Ctrl+Alt>** keyboard combination allows you to cycle through all your open drawings so that you can quickly switch the active drawing window.

The Online Help System

AutoCAD provides substantial online help via the standard Windows Help system. You are probably familiar with the standard Windows Help system from using other Microsoft Windows programs. Most Windows programs share the same Help interface to make it easier to find help when you need it most.

As mentioned in the "Keyboard Commands" section, the quickest way to activate the Windows Help system is by hitting the **<F1>** function key. You can also access Windows Help via the **Help** menu, by clicking on the **Question Mark** at the top right of the AutoCAD window, or by entering a question mark **<?>** at the keyboard. Using any of these methods displays the dialog box shown in Figure 1-73.

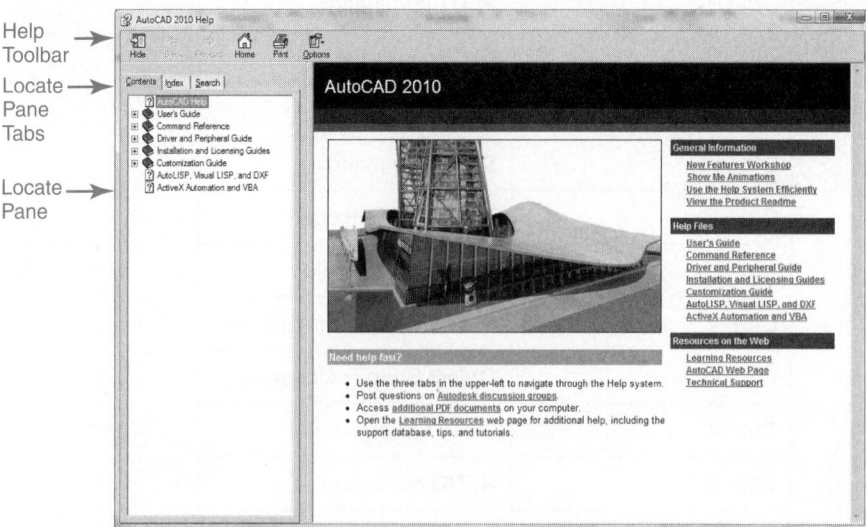

Figure 1-73   AutoCAD **Help** window

The **Help** dialog box is split into two panes. The left side of the dialog box is used to locate different help topics, and the right side of the dialog box displays information about the current topic. The toolbar at the top of the dialog box provides the following features:

- **Hide**   Toggles the locate pane on the left on and off so you have more space to display the current topic on the right

- **Back Arrow**   Works like the **Back** button in your Internet browser so that you can display topic information that you previously viewed

- **Forward Arrow**   Works like the **Forward** button in your Internet browser to allow you to move forward again after using the **Back Arrow** button

- **Home**   Immediately displays the Help welcome page that is always displayed when you first start the Help system

- **Print**   Allows you to print the topic displayed in the **Contents** pane on the right or the topic selected on the left including all its subtopics

- **Options**   Provides most of the same functionality of the other buttons on the toolbar, including Hide, Back, Forward, Home, and Print. Additional Internet browserlike functionality includes the ability to stop the **Contents** pane from loading, refresh the **Contents** pane, and bring up the **Internet Options** dialog box. You can also turn search text highlighting on and off.

Locating Information on a Help Topic.   The tabs at the top of the **Locate** pane on the left allow you to locate information about a topic using a variety of different techniques. How the different tabs are utilized is explained in the following sections.

Utilizing the Contents Tab.   The **Contents** tab organizes help information such as topics, guides, and reference manuals using a Windows Explorer–type interface. Topics are represented with an icon that looks like a sheet of paper with a question mark; guides and references are represented with icons that look like books. See Figure 1-73.

Similar to Windows Explorer, if you click on the (+) symbol to the left of a book icon, a tree is expanded to display the chapters and topics in the book in hierarchical format. Using this method, you locate information about a topic in the same manner you locate information in a book. Decide which guide or reference manual contains the info you need, then *drill down* through the chapters and their associated topics until you find what you're looking for.

For example, information about how to draw lines is found in the User's Guide by navigating to the "Draw Lines" topic in the chapter titled "Create and Modify Objects" as shown in Figure 1-74.

Figure 1-74   The Draw Lines help topic

AutoCAD provides the following top-level topics, guides, and reference manuals:

- **AutoCAD Help**   The default Help topic. Provides help on using the Help system with links to General Information topics, other Help files, and resources on the Web

- **User's Guide**   The online AutoCAD user's guide with information organized in chapter and topic form

- **Command Reference**   Reference guide that includes all the AutoCAD commands and system variables listed in alphabetical format. Also includes information about command modifiers and various AutoCAD utilities

- **Driver and Peripheral Guides**   Guides to attaching and setting up various hardware devices such as digitizer tablets, printers, and plotters

- **Installation and Licensing Guide**   Information about installing and licensing Auto-CAD in a stand-alone or network environment

- **Customization Guide**   Guide for experienced users that provides information about customizing AutoCAD

- **AutoLISP, VisualLISP, and DXF**   Documentation for AutoCAD's AutoLISP and VisualLISP programming languages along with the DXF file format reference guide

- **ActiveX Automation and VBA**   ActiveX and VBA developer's guide and reference

Utilizing the Index Tab.   The **Index** tab allows you to locate information by typing in a keyword. For instance, to find information about drawing lines you could type **line** in the **Type in the keyword to find:** text edit box on the **Index** tab as shown in Figure 1-75.

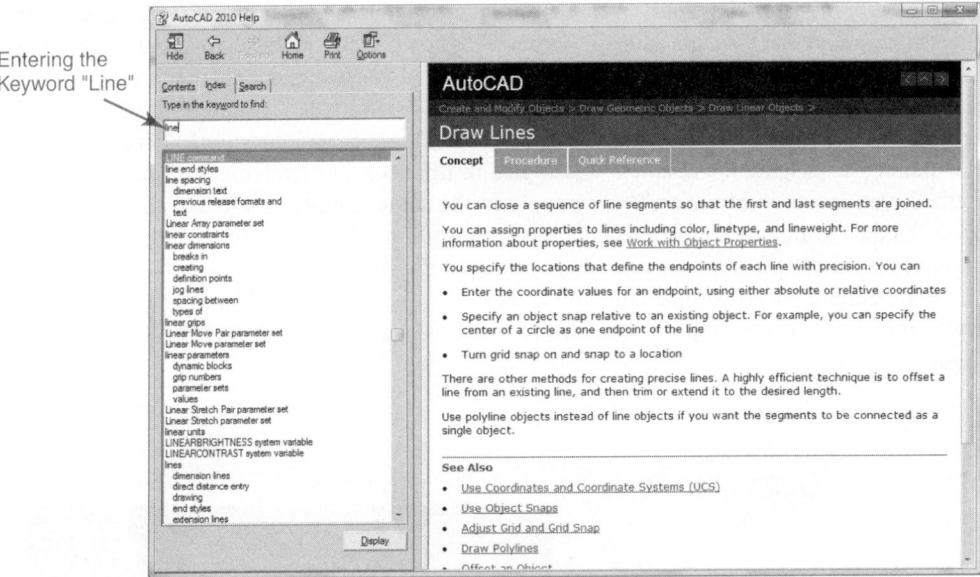

Figure 1-75   The **Index** tab

As you type, every topic that starts with the keyword "line" is displayed in the list box below the keyword. Selecting a topic from the list will usually display information in the **Contents** pane on the right unless multiple rated topics are found. If this is the case, then a **Topics Found** dialog box is displayed so you can further refine your selection.

Utilizing the Search Tab.   The **Search** tab allows you to Search Help system for information by asking a question in normal human terms. All you have to do is enter your question or phrase in the **Type in a question and press Enter** text edit box as shown in Figure 1-76.

Selecting the **Ask** button returns a list of topics that should answer your question. Select the desired topic to display it in the **Contents** pane on the right.

Displaying Information about a Help Topic.   When the information you need is located using one of the tabbed methods provided, it is always displayed in the **Contents** pane, regardless of the technique you used to locate the topic.

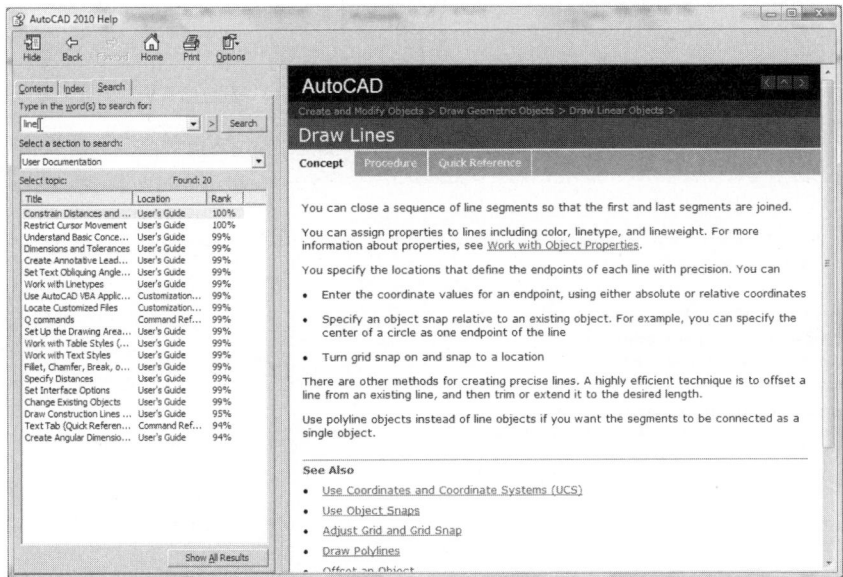

Figure 1-76   The **Search** tab

The Concept Tab.   The **Concept** tab provides detailed information about the selected topic in conceptual format. In Figure 1-77, detailed information about drawing lines in AutoCAD is displayed, including an explanation of what a line is and how it is drawn. Text that is underlined is a hyperlink to related information that when clicked on will take you to that topic.

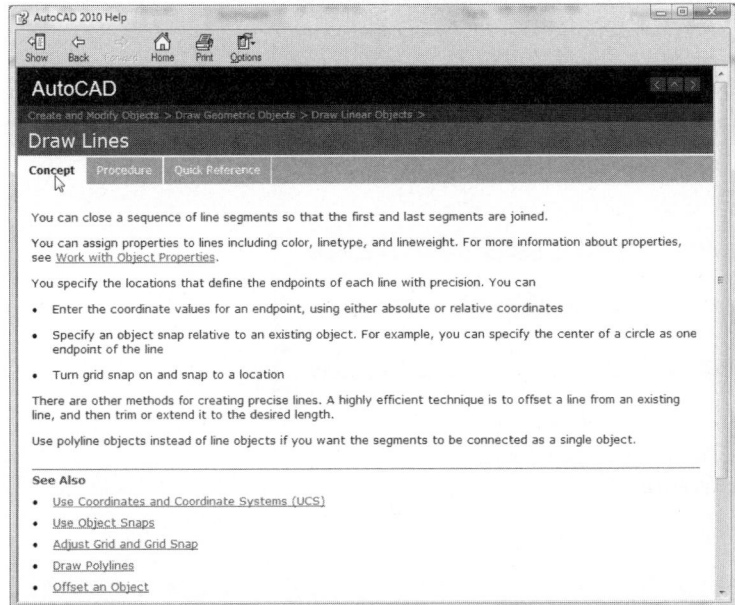

Figure 1-77   The **Concept** tab

The Procedure Tab.   The **Procedure** tab provides step-by-step instructions, or procedures, related to the current topic. In Figure 1-78, the steps necessary to create a line are shown. If there are no procedures related to the current topic, the **Procedure** tab will be disabled so it cannot be selected.

The Quick Reference Tab.   The **Quick Reference** tab lists any AutoCAD commands and AutoCAD system variables related to the current topic. In Figure 1-79, the commands used to draw different linear objects are shown along with a brief description.

Because it is hyperlinked, you can click on the command name to go to the topic page for that command.

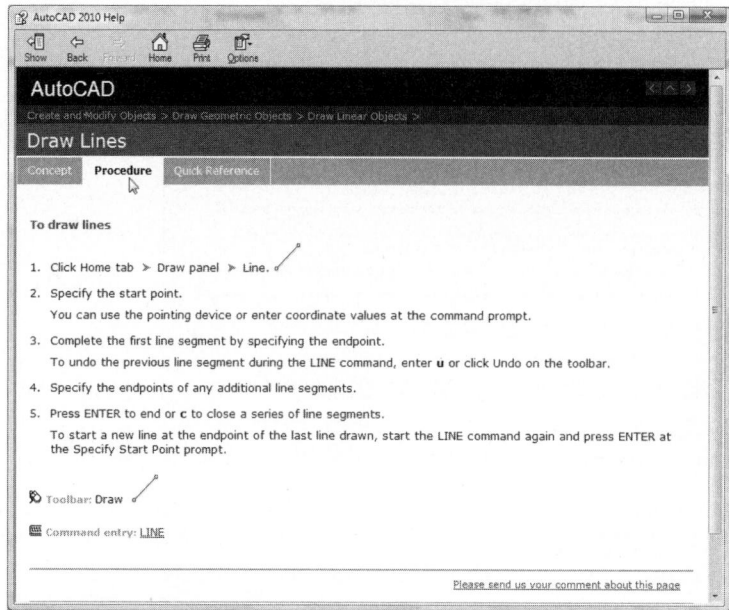

Figure 1-78   The **Procedure** tab

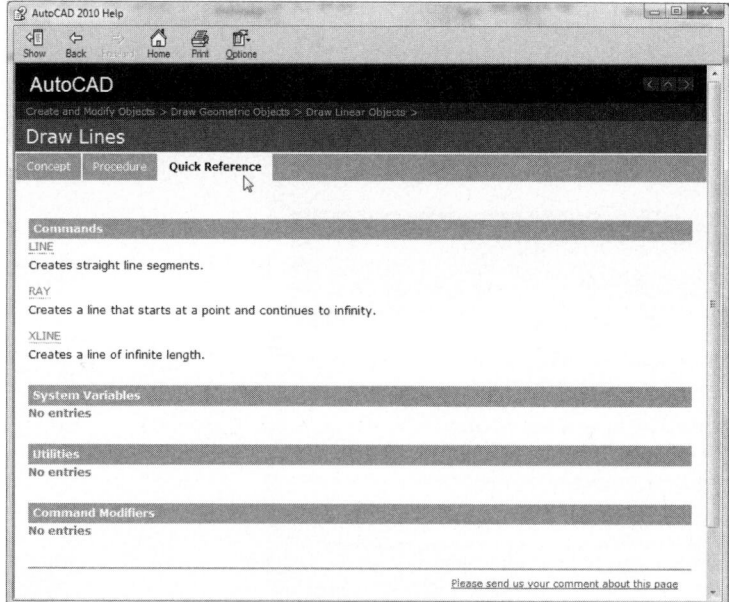

Figure 1-79   The **Quick Reference** tab

TIP

If you are not familiar with the standard Windows Help system, the Help welcome page provides detailed information about how to use help by clicking on the "Using the Help System Efficiently" link in the "General Information" section.

The New Features Workshop

The New Features Workshop is a multimedia presentation that provides a series of animated demonstrations, tutorials, and new feature overviews so that you can quickly get up to speed with all the latest and greatest features in the most recent version of AutoCAD. By default, the New Features Workshop is automatically displayed the first time you start AutoCAD. To start the New Features Workshop manually, you must select it from the **Help** menu.

Utilizing Online Resources

AutoCAD provides direct links to a number of helpful Internet Websites on the **Additional Resources** cascading submenu located on the **Help** menu. Selecting any of the menu items on this menu will start your Internet browser and display one of the following Web pages:

- **Support Knowledge Base**   Link to the AutoCAD Support Website. Features include the ability to search the vast Support Knowledge Base and links to Hot Issues
- **Online Training Resources**   Link to the AutoCAD Training Website. Features include links to information about instructor-led training, self-paced training, how-to articles, and various AutoCAD tips
- **Online Developer Center**   Link to the AutoCAD Developer Center that provides information about customizing AutoCAD using the various programming tools provided in AutoCAD
- **Autodesk User's Group International**   Link to the AUGI Website

The beauty of utilizing the Online Resources is that it provides you with real-time information. You will want to make a habit of checking your Online Resources frequently!

Customer Involvement Program

The Customer Involvement Program is an Internet-enabled feature that automatically sends Autodesk information about the commands and features you use most, any errors or problems that you encounter, and other information helpful to the future development of AutoCAD.

Some types of information that are automatically sent to Autodesk include the following:

- Name and version of AutoCAD
- AutoCAD commands used and frequency of use
- Errors encountered
- File formats imported or exported
- Operating system name and version
- System configuration information such as processor, memory, and graphics card
- IP address

In order to protect your privacy, the Customer Involvement Program cannot do any of the following:

- Collect any drawing or design data
- Collect any identity information such as name, address, or phone number
- Send you email or contact you in any other way

The Customer Involvement Program is a useful feature because it involves you directly in informing Autodesk about the following:

- The commands and features on which Autodesk should focus
- Rarely used commands and features
- The most common types of errors
- The computer hardware typically used with AutoCAD

You can start or stop your participation in the Customer Involvement Program at any time via the **Help** menu.

Exercise 1-3: Exploring the AutoCAD User Interface

1. Start AutoCAD using one of the three different methods explained in this chapter.
2. Click on the **Application Menu** button (big "A") on the upper left of the AutoCAD window to display the list of AutoCAD menus.
3. Select each menu to display its contents.

4. Select the **Home** tab on top of the AutoCAD window to display the **Home** ribbon.
5. Click on the black arrow in the middle of the **Draw** panel title to display the expanded panel and all the **Draw** tools.
6. Click on the black arrow on the right of the **Circle** tool to display the **Circle** subpanel with all the **Circle** options.
7. Click on the **3-Point Circle** tool to start the **CIRCLE** command.
8. Hit the **<Esc>** key to cancel.
9. Notice that the **3-Point Circle** tool is now the default **Circle** tool option displayed on the **Draw** panel.
10. Right-click with your mouse on any ribbon tab to display the shortcut menu and click on the **Show Panel Titles** option to unselect it (unchecked) so all panel titles are turned off.
11. Right-click with your mouse on any ribbon tab to display the shortcut menu and click on the **Show Panel Titles** option again to select it (checked) so all panel titles are turned back on.
12. Click on the **Minimize to Panels Titles** button to the right of the **Output** tab on the top right to turn off the panels and display only the panel titles.
13. Put your mouse pointer over the **Modify** panel title to display the full **Modify** panel.
14. Click on what is now the **Minimize to Tabs** button to the right of the **Output** tab on the top right to turn off the panel titles and display only the tabs.
15. Click on the **Annotate** tab to display the **Annotate** ribbon.
16. Click on what is now the **Show Full Ribbon** button to the right of the **Output** tab on the top right to turn the ribbon back on again.
17. Resize the command line window so it displays six lines.
18. Hit the **<F1>** function key to display the **AutoCAD 2010 Help** window.
19. Locate the "Draw Lines" topic using any of the methods explained in this chapter.
20. Switch between the **Concept, Procedure**, and **Quick Reference** tabs in the **Contents** pane on the right side of the **Help** window.
21. Exit AutoCAD.

InfoCenter

InfoCenter is your one-stop shop for AutoCAD information and help. Conspicuously located at the top far right of the AutoCAD window (see Figure 1-80), InfoCenter allows you to:

- Search multiple sources simultaneously for AutoCAD information using keywords and phrases
- Access subscription services
- Receive product updates and announcements
- Save searched topics in a list of Favorites for later
- Access AutoCAD help

Figure 1-80   InfoCenter

Searching for Information.   To search for information, enter a keyword or phrase in the **InfoCenter** box on the left of the InfoCenter bar and either press **<Enter ⏎>** or click on the **Search** icon directly on the right. By default, AutoCAD searches through the contents of most of the pertinent AutoCAD help documentation, as well as additional online resources. The search results are displayed as links on a drop-down panel as shown in Figure 1-81.

The results are categorized by the AutoCAD resource where the topic was found. Click on a link to display the topic. The **Display More Results** and **Display Previous Results** arrow buttons at the right of the title bar of each category allow you to navigate back and forth between topics.

Clicking on the white star icon to the right of a topic adds the topic to your list of favorites so that you can display the topic later via the **InfoCenter Favorites** button.

You can limit your search to a single source by clicking on the down arrow to the right of the **Search** icon and selecting the desired location to search. You can also add documents to search by selecting **Add Search Location...** and specifying a file location.

Figure 1-81   Search results drop-down panel

Figure 1-82   Communication Center

Selecting **Search Settings** from the bottom of the list displays the **InfoCenter Settings** dialog box so that you can add or remove default search locations, as well as specify the total number of results to display. The **InfoCenter Settings** dialog box is discussed later in this section.

Subscription Center.   Selecting the **Subscription Center** icon displays a drop-down panel with links to information about different Autodesk subscription services that include product updates and enhancements, personalized web support, and self-paced e-learning. You can learn more about Autodesk subscriptions at www.autodesk.com/subscriptioncenter.

Communication Center.   Selecting the **Communication Center** icon displays a drop-down panel like the one shown in Figure 1-82 with links to product updates, RSS feeds, and the following announcement types:

- **Autodesk Channels**   Receive support information, product updates, and other announcements
- **CAD Manager Channel:**   Receive RSS feeds published by your CAD manager
- **RSS Feeds**   Automatically receive information from RSS feeds to which you subscribe

Clicking on the white star icon to the right of a topic adds the topic to your list of favorites so that you can display the topic later via the **InfoCenter Favorites** button.

Which channels and RSS feeds you subscribe to and all of the **Communication Center** settings are managed using the **InfoCenter Settings** described later in this section. You are automatically subscribed to several default RSS feeds when you install AutoCAD.

Favorites. Selecting the **Favorites** button displays a drop-down panel of saved topics and links locations. Select a topic or link to display it. You can use the **Next** and **Previous** buttons to browse search results. It is also possible to click and drag categories or groups and rearrange them.

InfoCenter Settings. The **InfoCenter Settings** button located on the top right next to the **Close** button of all the **InfoCenter** panels allows you to manage different **InfoCenter** settings via the **InfoCenter Settings** dialog box shown in Figure 1-83.

Figure 1-83   The **InfoCenter Settings** dialog box

The different **InfoCenter** settings include:

- **General**   Your current geographic location, how often to check for new online content, and whether to use animated transition effects for panels.
- **Search Locations**   Locations to search for information and the number of results to display for each. You can also add or remove search locations.
- **Communication Center**   The maximum age of articles displayed on the **Communication Center** panel and the location and name of the **CAD Manager Channel** if any.
- **Autodesk Channels**   Channels to display in the **Communication Center** panel.
- **Balloon Notification**   Control notifications for software updates, product support announcements, CAD Manager channel, RSS feeds, and Did You Know messages. You can also control the display time of balloons as well as increase or decrease balloon transparency.
- **RSS Feeds**   RSS feed subscriptions. Several default RSS feeds are automatically subscribed to when you install the program. You can also add or remove RSS feeds.

CHAPTER SUMMARY

The information and concepts explained in this chapter form the basis for the rest of this textbook. Now that you know the basics of AutoCAD you're ready to begin. The next chapter will get you up and running by showing you everything you need to quickly get started.

The rest of the textbook delves into these topics in glorious detail so that you will be an AutoCAD expert by time you're finished. Good luck and have fun on your journey!

CHAPTER TEST QUESTIONS

Multiple Choice

1. The main benefit of using CAD is:
   a. Increased productivity
   b. Improved precision
   c. Better collaboration
   d. All of the above

2. When you create a drawing using AutoCAD, most of the information that makes up your design should be drawn at what scale?
   a. 1:1
   b. Half scale

   c. Plot scale
   d. None of the above

3. What is the Cartesian coordinate system?
   a. A grid-based system with an X- and Y-axis
   b. A grid-based system with an X-, Y-, and Z-axis
   c. A system for coordinating your work
   d. None of the above

4. The default units in AutoCAD are:
   a. Millimeters
   b. Inches
   c. Feet
   d. Meters

5. By default, angles in AutoCAD are measured:
   a. Clockwise
   b. Counterclockwise
   c. Using radians
   d. Using a protractor

6. How high should text be if it needs to plot at 1/8″ high on a drawing that is plotted at a scale ratio of 2:1?
   a. 1/4″
   b. 1/2″
   c. 1/16″
   d. 12″

7. Layers in AutoCAD are used for the following:
   a. Controlling object colors
   b. Organizing drawing information
   c. Controlling an object's visibility
   d. All of the above

8. The AutoCAD Color Index consists of how many colors?
   a. 7
   b. 256
   c. 255
   d. None of the above

9. Paper space is primarily used for:
   a. Creating 3D models for visualization
   b. Laying out multiple 2D sheets for plotting purposes
   c. Storing extra copy paper
   d. All of the above

10. AutoCAD can be started by:
    a. Using the **Start** button to navigate to and start AutoCAD
    b. Double-clicking on the **AutoCAD** program icon
    c. Double-clicking on an AutoCAD drawing file
    d. All of the above

11. The default three-letter file extension for AutoCAD is:
    a. DWL
    b. DWT
    c. DWG
    d. BAK

12. The large window in AutoCAD where you do most of your drawing is known as the:
    a. Graphics display
    b. Drawing window
    c. Command window
    d. Layout

13. To turn off the tool ribbon at the top of the AutoCAD window so that only the panel titles are displayed, you should:
    a. Right-click with your mouse while it is over any ribbon panel
    b. Click on the arrow in the middle of a panel title
    c. Click on the button to the right of the **Output** tab near the top of the AutoCAD window
    d. None of the above

14. The abbreviated version of a command is referred to as a:
    a. Command accelerator
    b. Command shortcut
    c. Command control
    d. Command alias

15. What keyboard key cancels any active command?
    a. **\<Tab\>** key
    b. **\<F1\>** key
    c. **\<F2\>** key
    d. **\<Esc\>** key

16. What keyboard key toggles the full text command window on and off?
    a. **\<F1\>** key
    b. **\<Esc\>** key
    c. **\<F2\>** key
    d. **\<Tab\>** key

17. What keyboard key toggles between input fields when using the **Dynamic Input** feature?
    a. **\<F2\>** key
    b. **\<F1\>** key
    c. **\<Tab\>** key
    d. **\<Esc\>** key

Matching

a. Cartesian coordinate system

b. Right-hand rule

c. Scale factor

d. Layer

e. Model space

f. Paper space

g. Drawing window

h. Command window

i. Dynamic Input

j. Status Bar

1. 3D drawing environment where most of a drawing's linework and text reside

2. Main window in AutoCAD where you create and modify drawing object

3. Grid-based system where points are represented by their X and Y coordinate values

4. 2D environment used to layout a drawing for plotting

5. Technique for visualizing the X-, Y-, and Z-axes

6. Multiplier applied to annotation features like text and dimensions

7. Window that provides access to the AutoCAD command line

8. Feature that allows you to enter input information near the mouse cursor

9. AutoCAD mini-dashboard at the bottom of the AutoCAD window

10. Object property used to organize drawing information

Quick-Start Tutorials: 2D

2

Chapter Objectives

- Create a new drawing
- Save your work
- Switch between model space and layout space
- Draw some basic AutoCAD objects
- Toggle the Snap, Ortho, Polar Tracking, and Grid settings on and off
- Navigate around the drawing
- Examine and change object properties
- Create drawing layers and move objects from one layer to another
- Make some basic modifications to the drawing
- Add basic dimensions and annotation to your drawing
- Plot your drawing

INTRODUCTION

This chapter will give you an overview of a typical AutoCAD drawing session. You will examine some of the basic operations you will do on a day-to-day basis when using AutoCAD, including starting an AutoCAD session, drawing and modifying some objects, and saving and plotting your drawing. All the topics touched on in this chapter will be explained in greater detail in the following chapters. Let's start by creating a new drawing.

CREATING A NEW DRAWING

When AutoCAD starts, it places you in a blank drawing by default. This blank drawing is based on a number of default AutoCAD settings, which are stored in a ***drawing template***. In addition to this default template, AutoCAD gives you other templates to choose from, which can save you time setting up your drawing.

Using a Template

AutoCAD provides a number of predefined templates with default settings for various drawing disciplines. These drawing templates typically have title blocks in them and predefined settings for text, dimensioning, and plotting. You can also create your own templates or save any drawing as a template.

You can create a new drawing by selecting **New** from the **Quick Access** toolbar. This displays the **Select template** dialog box (see Figure 2-1), which allows you to select one of these predefined templates as a starting point.

drawing template: A drawing used as a starting point when creating a new drawing. Drawing templates can contain page layouts, borders, title blocks, layer settings, and any other settings or drawing objects you use on a regular basis.

Figure 2-1   The **Select template** dialog box

Saving Your Work

When you create a new drawing using a template, it is initially named "Drawing" followed by an incremental number (Drawing1.dwg, Drawing2.dwg, Drawing3.dwg, etc.) indicating its place in the series when it was created. The drawing does not exist as a file on your computer or network until you save it at least once by selecting **Save** from the **Quick Access** toolbar, which runs the **QSAVE** command.

The **QSAVE** command is short for "Quick Save," although it is not so quick the first time you use it. The first time you use **QSAVE**, the standard Windows **Save Drawing As** file dialog box shown in Figure 2-2 is displayed so that you can give the drawing a file name and folder location to store the file on your computer or network. Subsequent use of the **QSAVE** command simply updates the file in its specified location, hence the "Quick" part.

> **Note:**
> The template files that contain "ISO" in the file name are set up for metric units. In fact, the acadiso.dwt template is the default metric template.

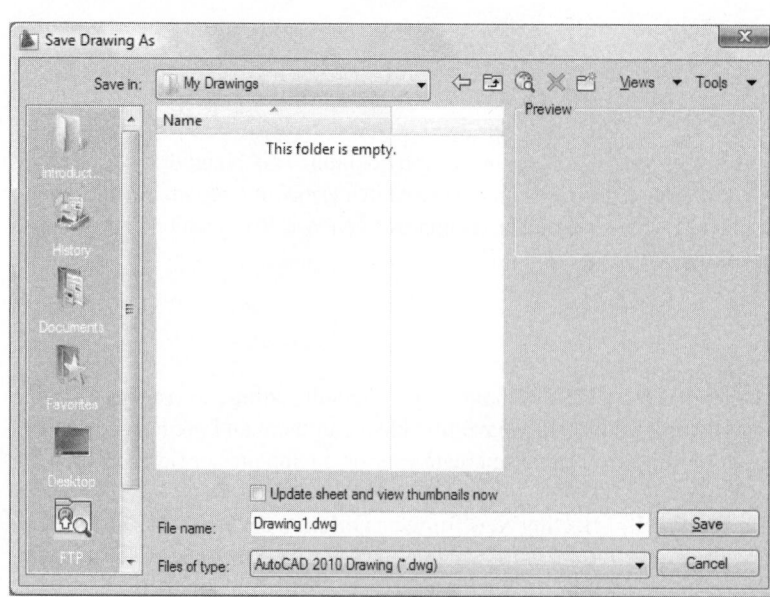

Figure 2-2   The **Save Drawing As** file dialog box

Select the drive or device where you want to save the file by selecting it from the **Save in:** drop-down list at the top and navigate to the desired folder using the Explorer-type interface in the middle. Enter the drawing name in the **File name:** list box or select a previous name from the drop-down list. Select the **Save** button to save the drawing in the specified folder and close the dialog box.

TIP   You can use the **SAVEAS** command to save your drawing to a new location or to change the file name. You can access the **SAVEAS** command by choosing **Save As** from the **Application Menu** (the big red A). In addition to changing the location and name of your file, the **SAVEAS** command allows you to save your drawing to a previous version of AutoCAD or to convert it to a DXF (Drawing eXchange Format) file. This allows you to share your drawing data with earlier versions of AutoCAD or with other CAD packages. You can also use the **SAVEAS** command to save your drawing as a drawing template. See Chapter 18 for more on file formats and exchanging drawing data.

FOR MORE DETAILS   See Chapter 1 for more information about naming drawing files and the other AutoCAD file types.

Now that the drawing is named, each time you use the **QSAVE** command from now on, by clicking on the **Save** icon on the **Quick Access** toolbar, AutoCAD will update the file in the specified location and overwrite the last saved version. You should save your drawing often using the **QSAVE** command to ensure that you don't lose too much work if an unexpected and/or catastrophic failure occurs. A good rule of thumb is to save your drawing every 10 to 15 minutes. Get in the habit of choosing **Save** from the **Quick Access** toolbar or by using the **<Ctrl>+S** keyboard combination.

Note: By default, the current file name and path is always displayed in the blue title bar at the top of the AutoCAD window. Keeping your eye on the title bar after a drawing is saved is a good way to keep track of the file you're currently working on.

File Safety Precautions

After you save a drawing once, every time you use the **QSAVE** command thereafter, a backup of the previous saved version of the drawing is saved in the same location with the same name as the drawing, except with a .BAK file extension. This feature allows you to recover drawing information up until the last time you saved if for some reason this is necessary. In order to open the backup file you must either rename the .BAK extension to .DWG or use the **Drawing Recovery Manager**.

As double insurance, AutoCAD automatically saves your drawing at preset intervals to the Windows Temporary folder using a file name that consists of the drawing name followed by six numbers generated by AutoCAD and the file extension .SV$. The default interval between saves is 10 minutes. In order to restore an automatically saved file with the .SV$ extension, you must either rename the extension to .DWG or use the **Drawing Recovery Manager**.

Note: The automatic save feature is meant to be used as a failsafe so that you can recover drawing information when things go wrong. It should not be relied on as a primary means of saving your work. In fact, because the automatic save files (.SV$) are saved to the Windows Temporary folder, their life span is unpredictable, and they may be deleted at any time.

TIP The **Options** command is your one-stop shop for controlling most of the user settings that affect the AutoCAD environment. You can access the **Options** command by selecting **Options** from the **Application Menu**, or by right-clicking anywhere in the drawing area and choosing **Options** from the right-click menu. You can also type **OPTIONS** or **OP** at the AutoCAD command line.

Exercise 2-1: Setting Up a Drawing

1. Choose **New** from the **Quick Access** toolbar to display the **Select template** dialog box shown in Figure 2-1. The **Select template** dialog box opens in the default AutoCAD **Template** folder.

To access student data files, go to www.pearsondesigncentral.com.

2. Select the **Look in:** list at the top of the dialog box, and open the **Chapter 2** folder in the student data files.
3. Select the **ANSI-A.dwt** template file and select the **Open** button to start a new drawing with the predefined **ANSI-A** title block shown in Figure 2-3.
4. Choose the **Save** button from the **Quick Access** toolbar, and save your drawing as **EX2-1** using the **Save Drawing As** file dialog box shown in Figure 2-2.

Figure 2-3   A new drawing created from a template

MODEL SPACE AND LAYOUT SPACE

Chapter 1 discussed AutoCAD's two distinct drawing environments, model space and layout space. Generally speaking, model space is used for creating the geometry of your drawing. Objects that exist in the physical world (walls, doors, mechanical parts, etc.) are generally drawn in model space. Objects that exist only on a piece of paper (annotation, dimensions, notes, title blocks, etc.) are generally placed in layout space. Each drawing has only one model space but can have multiple layout spaces, each with its own name.

The drawing template used in this chapter has one layout named **ANSI A Title Block**. You can switch between model space and the layout using the tabs at the bottom of the drawing window shown in Figure 2-4.

Model Tab ⟋   ⟍ Layout Tab   **Figure 2-4**   The **Model** and **Layout** tabs

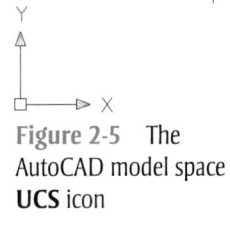

Figure 2-5   The AutoCAD model space **UCS** icon

Exercise 2-2: Switching Between Model and Layout Space

1. Click on the **Model** tab. AutoCAD switches to model space and the model space **UCS** icon is displayed (see Figure 2-5).
2. Click on the **ANSI A Title Block** tab. AutoCAD switches back to layout space.
3. Save your drawing as **EX2-2**.

AutoCAD's model space looks distinctively different from layout space. There is no "edge" to the space as there is in layout space. The **XY** icon (called the **UCS** icon) looks different as well. In contrast, layout space looks like a piece of paper. The space has edges (and the appearance of a shadow along the edges), and the **UCS** icon looks like a page corner. See Figure 2-6.

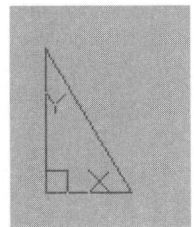

Figure 2-6   The AutoCAD paper space **UCS** icon

Viewports

An AutoCAD layout can be thought of as a sheet of paper with scaled views or pictures of the AutoCAD model placed on it. These views are created by creating *viewports* in the paper space layout. Viewports are holes or windows in the paper that look into the model space environment. You can activate viewports and make changes directly to the model space environment through the viewport.

    The **ANSI A Title Block** layout contains a single viewport. In the following exercise, you'll examine this viewport.

viewport: A window in the paper space environment that shows the view of the model space environment.

Exercise 2-3: Activating a Viewport

1. Double-click with your mouse near the center of the drawing within the border outline. AutoCAD outlines the viewport so it becomes bold (see Figure 2-7).
2. Drag your mouse around the screen. Notice that the crosshair appears only inside the viewport. When you drag the cursor outside the viewport, the crosshair turns into a pointer.
3. Double-click outside the viewport to close the viewport and return to layout space.
4. Save your drawing as **EX2-3**.

> **Note:**
> You can also use the MODEL/PAPER button on the Status Bar (see Figure 2-4) to activate a single viewport. Switching from PAPER to MODEL makes a viewport active. Switching back to PAPER returns you to layout space.

The drawing template used in this chapter contains a single viewport; however, you can create multiple viewports in each layout.

| **FOR MORE DETAILS** | Chapter 14 provides detailed information about model space, paper space, layouts, and how to create and control viewports. |

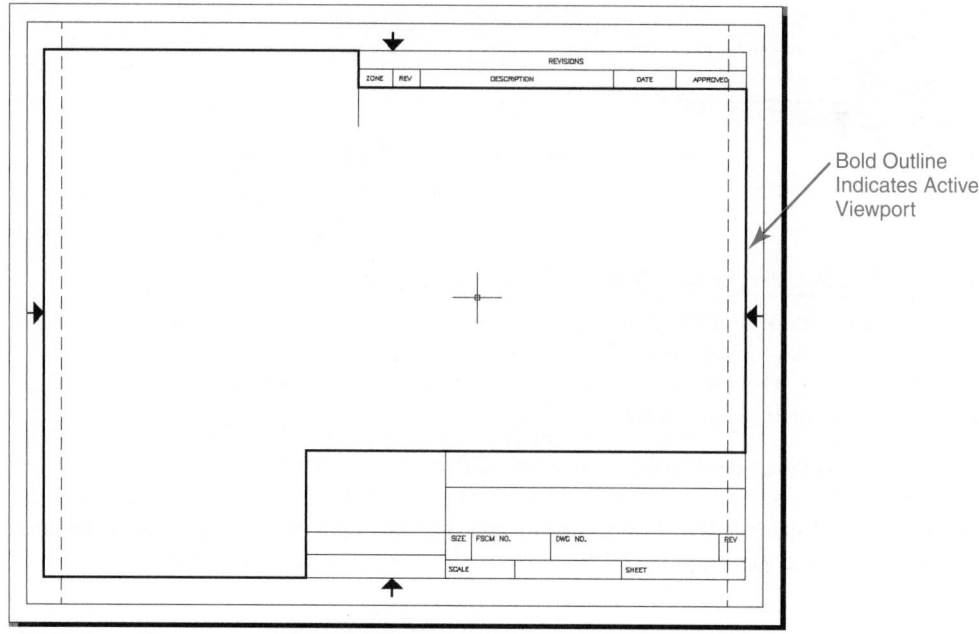

Figure 2-7   The active model space viewport

COMMUNICATING WITH AUTOCAD

objects: Graphical drawing elements, such as lines, arcs, circles, polylines, and text.

When you create a drawing, you are placing AutoCAD **objects** in the drawing. There are different types of objects (lines, arcs, circles, text, etc.) Each type of object has a unique set of properties. When you create an object, AutoCAD will ask you to specify the various aspects of that object. This is done primarily through prompts. AutoCAD will prompt you for information at both the cursor and the command line window.

The Command Line

The command line window is docked at the bottom of the drawing area by default (see Figure 2-8). This is one place where AutoCAD communicates with you. When you select a tool, AutoCAD will display the command name in the command line window and then prompt you for more information. The command line window can be undocked and moved. It can also be turned off completely, but it is not recommended.

Figure 2-8   The command line window

FOR MORE DETAILS	Chapter 1 provides detailed information about the command line window and how to move it, dock and undock it, and turn it on and off.

Dynamic Input

Dynamic Input (see Figure 2-9) uses a floating command prompt that moves with your cursor and provides instant, dynamic feedback as you move around the drawing. Dynamic Input provides you with active, heads-up feedback that allows you to read and respond to AutoCAD's prompts

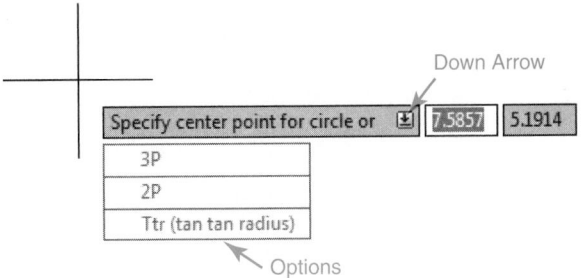

Figure 2-9   Dynamic Input

without changing focus away from your drawing. Dynamic Input can be turned on and off by toggling the **Dynamic Input** button on the Status Bar.

Whether using Dynamic Input, the command window, or both, the general process you'll follow when creating drawing objects is:

1. Start a command.
2. Read AutoCAD's prompt.
3. Pick points and/or respond to prompts.
4. Press **<Enter ↵>** or **<Esc>** to end the command.

Sometimes the AutoCAD prompts can be difficult to decipher. There are some general conventions that AutoCAD uses.

- AutoCAD will ask you to *specify* a placement point (for example, the start point of a line or arc or the center point of a circle). You can specify a placement point by picking a point on the screen, typing in a coordinate, or using an object snap.

- When there are multiple ways to create an object, AutoCAD will display a down arrow next to the Dynamic Input prompt (see Figure 2-9). Press the down arrow key to see the list of command options.

- In the command window, options are enclosed in square brackets [] and are separated by a slash mark (/). You specify an option by typing in the capital letter(s) shown for that option. For example, when drawing a circle, AutoCAD gives you the following prompt and options:

      Specify center point for circle or [3P/2P/Ttr (tan tan radius)].

In this example, AutoCAD is asking you either to specify the center point of the circle or to select one of three options (3P, 2P, or TTR). To specify the TTR option, you would type **T** and press **<Enter ↵>**.

FOR MORE DETAILS	See Chapter 4 for more on coordinate entry methods and all the specifics on the **CIRCLE** command and its options.

Keep in mind that when you specify a point or select an option, AutoCAD will continue to ask you for more information until it has everything it needs to create that object.

Exercise 2-4: Draw a Line

1. Select the **Model** tab from the Status Bar to switch to model space.
2. Choose the **Line** tool from the **Draw** panel (see Figure 2-10). AutoCAD prompts you to *Specify first point:*.

Figure 2-10 The **Line** tool on the **Draw** panel

3. Look in the command window. AutoCAD shows the following:

   Command: _line Specify first point:

   _line is the command you started when you chose the **Line** tool. AutoCAD is asking where you want to start the line.

rubber band: A live preview of a drawing object as it is being drawn. The rubber-band preview allows you to see objects as they are being created.

4. Pick anywhere on the screen to start the line. You should now have a ***rubber-band*** line extending from the first point you specified along with dynamic information about the length and direction of the rubber-band line (see Figure 2-11).

5. AutoCAD prompts you to *Specify next point or* ↓. The down arrow indicates that a command option is available. Press the down arrow key, and you'll see the **Undo** option appear (see Figure 2-12).

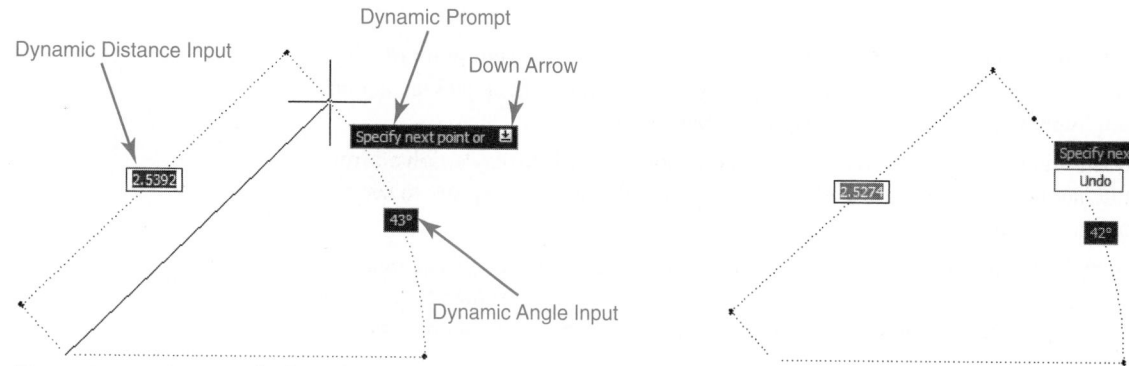

Figure 2-11 Dynamic display information

Figure 2-12 Dynamic display options

6. Look again at the command window. It shows:

   Specify next point or [Undo]:

   You can now either specify the next point on the line, choose the **Undo** option from the dynamic display, or type **U<Enter ↵>** to undo that point.

7. Pick another point anywhere on the screen. AutoCAD will draw a single line segment and automatically start drawing another line segment. AutoCAD again prompts you to *Specify next point or* ↓.

8. Press the down arrow and select **Undo** from the option list. The second point you specified is "undone," and the rubber-band line is now extending from the first point you selected.

9. AutoCAD again prompts you to *Specify next point or* ↓. Pick another point on the screen. AutoCAD draws that line segment and repeats the prompt.

10. Press **<Esc>** to end the **LINE** command.

11. Save your drawing as **EX2-4**.

Your drawing may look different from Figure 2-13 since you specified different points, but it should be similar. The Dynamic Input at the cursor should disappear and you should now see the *Command:* prompt in the command window. This is AutoCAD's way of letting you know that it is idle and ready for the next command.

Figure 2-13   Drawing some lines

TIP You can repeat the last command you used by pressing either **<Enter ↵>** or **<Space>** at the command prompt. In most cases, AutoCAD interprets pressing **<Space>** the same as pressing **<Enter ↵>**. The exception to this is when you are typing in a line of text where spaces are expected.

OBJECT SNAPS, ORTHO, AND POLAR TRACKING

Because precision is important, AutoCAD can look for key points on objects and select those points automatically. These key points are known as *object snaps* or *osnaps*.

By default, AutoCAD will look for the endpoints of lines and arcs and the center points of circles. You can turn object snapping on and off by selecting the **Object Snap** button on the Status Bar.

object snaps/osnaps: Geometric points on objects such as the endpoints or mid-point of a line or the center of an arc or circle.

TIP Right-click on the **Object Snap** button in the Status Bar and choose **Settings...** to change the default object snap setting.

AutoCAD can help you draw perfectly vertical or horizontal lines. AutoCAD does this with both the **Ortho Mode** and **Polar Tracking** buttons. When turned on, **Ortho Mode** (which stands for *orthographic*) will restrict the crosshair movement to either horizontal or vertical movement. **Ortho Mode** takes effect only when you are specifying a point relative to another point (when specifying the second point of a line, for example).

orthographic: 90° increments.

TIP The **<F8>** key will toggle **Ortho Mode** on and off.

polar tracking: A process in which AutoCAD will lock the cursor movement to predefined angles.

The *Polar Tracking* button is similar to **Ortho Mode** except it simply indicates when your crosshair is close to a vertical or horizontal angle. When you get close to these directions, AutoCAD will display an alignment path and a tooltip showing you how far and in what direction you have dragged your crosshair (see Figure 2-14). When the alignment path is visible, the point you pick will be placed along that alignment path at the distance indicated.

Figure 2-14   Polar tracking

 TIP   By default, polar tracking is set to select angles in increments of 90°. Right-click on the **Polar Tracking** button in the Status Bar and choose **Settings…** to change the default increment angle and to detect specific angles to track.

FOR MORE DETAILS   See Chapter 5 for a complete list of object snaps and how to use them and for more on using the **Ortho Mode** and **Polar Tracking** buttons.

Exercise 2-5: Object Snaps, Ortho, and Polar Tracking

1. Toggle the **Object Snap** button on.
2. Select the **Line** tool from the **Draw** panel.
3. Move your crosshair close to the start of the first line and let it sit there for a moment. A square will appear at the end of the line along with a tooltip that says *Endpoint* (see Figure 2-15).

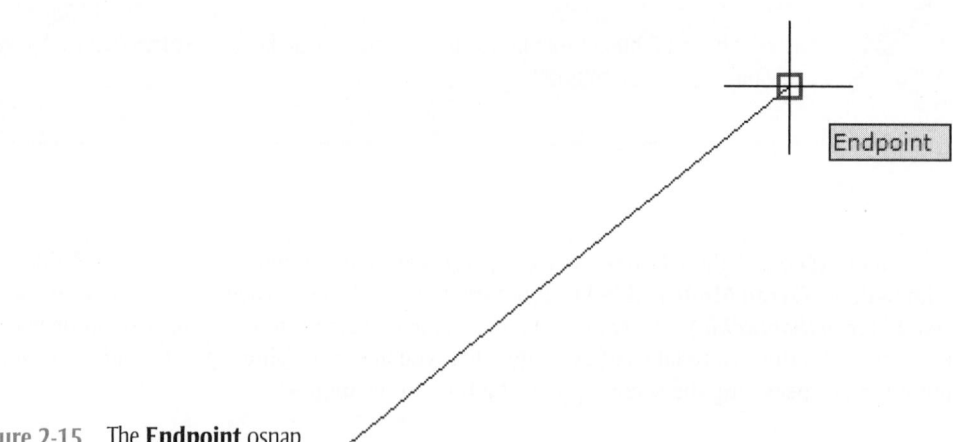

Figure 2-15   The **Endpoint** osnap

4. Pick near the end of the line. AutoCAD will automatically select the endpoint of that line.
5. Toggle the **Polar Tracking** button to the **ON** position.
6. Drag your crosshair straight up until the polar tracking appears. Notice the polar tracking shows a distance and direction (90°).
7. Pick a point approximately 1 inch 90° above the end of the line.

8. Toggle the **Polar Tracking** button **OFF** and the **Ortho Mode** button **ON**.

9. Drag your crosshair around the screen. The crosshair is now restricted to horizontal and vertical movement only.

10. Drag the cursor to the right and type **3<Enter ↵>**. AutoCAD draws a line, 3 units long to the right.

11. Press **<Esc>** to end the **LINE** command.

12. Save your drawing as **EX2-5**.

Note:
The last line you drew was done using a method called *direct distance entry*. This is a combination of cursor movement and keyboard input in which you drag your cursor to indicate direction and use the keyboard to type in the distance. Direct distance input can be used anytime you need to specify a coordinate location. Used with the **Ortho Mode** and **Polar Tracking** controls, it can greatly simplify coordinate entry. See Chapter 5 for more on various coordinate entry methods.

direct distance entry: The process of specifying a point by dragging the AutoCAD cursor to specify direction and typing in a distance.

UNDO/REDO

AutoCAD keeps a running history of all the commands you've issued within a single drawing session. This allows you to back up to any point in the drawing session. The **UNDO** command will take you back through your drawing session, one command at a time, all the way back to the start of your drawing session. If you go back too far, the **REDO** command will move you forward, one command at a time, until you've restored everything.

Exercise 2-6: Undo/Redo

1. From the **Quick Access** toolbar, choose **Undo** (or press **<Ctrl> + Z**). The lines created with the previous **LINE** command will disappear. Look at the *Command:* prompt and see that the lines were undone. The **Redo** button is now active in the **Quick Access** toolbar.

2. Choose the **Redo** tool. The lines will reappear.

3. Choose the **Undo** tool until all the lines are gone (model space is empty). If you go back too far (for example, back into paper space), use the **Redo** tool to get back to an empty model space.

4. Save your drawing as **EX2-6**.

Note:
The **REDO** command can be used only immediately after using the **UNDO** command. Once you use **REDO** and resume drawing, you cannot use the **REDO** command again until you use the **UNDO** tool.

GRID AND SNAP

In addition to polar tracking and object snaps, you can also control the crosshair movement by turning on **Snap Mode**. **Snap Mode** simply locks your crosshair movement to a predefined increment.

Along with **Snap Mode**, you can also display a visual grid of dots on the screen. The **Grid Display** button toggles the display grid **ON** and **OFF**. The grid is simply a visual display; it does not print and does not control the cursor movement. The grid and snap settings are not the same thing and are set separately.

TIP The **<F7>** key toggles **Grid Display ON** and **OFF**. **<F9>** toggles **Snap Mode ON** and **OFF**.

Exercise 2-7: Using **Grid Display** and **Snap Mode**

1. Toggle the **Grid Display** button **OFF** and toggle the **Snap Mode** button **ON**.
2. Move the cursor around and notice how it jumps from one point to another. The coordinate readout is locked into .5 unit increments (see Figure 2-16).

Coordinate Display

Figure 2-16   Coordinate readout

3. Toggle the **Grid Mode** button **ON** and toggle the **Snap Mode** button **OFF**. Now move your cursor around the screen and look at the coordinate readout on the cursor. Notice that the cursor is no longer jumping from point to point and the coordinate readout is no longer locked to .5 unit increments.
4. Toggle the **Snap Mode** button **ON** and pick the **Line** tool from the **Draw** panel.
5. Move your cursor to the coordinate 4,2 and pick that point. Continue picking to draw the outline shown in Figure 2-17.
6. Choose the down arrow to display the options list and choose the **Close** option. AutoCAD will close the figure and end the **LINE** command.
7. Save your drawing as **EX2-7**.

Figure 2-17   Drawing with **Snap Mode**

DRAW A CIRCLE

Let's add a hole to our drawing. To do that, we'll place a circle on the drawing using the **CIRCLE** command.

Exercise 2-8: Drawing a Circle

1. Toggle the **Grid Mode** and **Snap Mode** buttons **OFF**.
2. Choose the **Center, Radius** tool from the **Draw** panel. AutoCAD prompts you: *Specify center point for circle or* ↓. AutoCAD is asking you to either specify a center point location or choose an option.

3. Type **9,5<Enter ↵>**. AutoCAD places the center of the circle at the coordinate 9,5 and starts dragging a preview of the circle.
4. AutoCAD prompts you to *Specify radius of circle or [Diameter]:*. It is asking you to either specify the radius of the circle or choose an option.
5. Type **3/8<Enter ↵>** to specify a radius of 3/8″. The circle is drawn, and AutoCAD ends the **CIRCLE** command.
6. Save your drawing as **EX2-8**. Your drawing should now resemble Figure 2-18.

In the previous exercise, there were a couple of things to notice. First, when you specified the center point of the circle, you typed the coordinate instead of picking it on the screen. This is an example of ***absolute coordinate entry***.

The second thing to note is that when you specified the radius of the circle you typed in a fraction (3/8) instead of the decimal number (.375). AutoCAD will accept fractions and mixed numbers (for example, 1-3/8) as well as decimal numbers.

Note:
You must use a hyphen (-) to separate whole numbers and fractions as shown because the keyboard space bar works as an **<Enter ↵>** key in AutoCAD. Pressing the space bar will simply enter the whole number value, making it impossible to enter the fractional portion.

absolute coordinate entry: The process of specifying a point by typing in a coordinate. The coordinate is measured from the origin or 0,0 point in the drawing.

FOR MORE DETAILS	See Chapter 4 to learn more about coordinate input methods.

Figure 2-18   Drawing a circle

NAVIGATING AROUND THE DRAWING

In order to work effectively, you must be able to navigate around the drawing by controlling what is displayed on your screen. Sometimes it is necessary to zoom in close to your drawing to do detailed work, while at other times, you might need to zoom out to see the big picture. If you are zoomed in close, but the portion of the drawing you need to work on next is off the edge of the screen so it is not visible, you need to be able to shift the display to view that area of the drawing. In AutoCAD this is referred to as ***panning***.

The easiest way to navigate around the drawing is using the **Pan** and **Zoom** tools located on the right side of the Status Bar shown in Figure 2-19.

panning: The process of moving around the drawing by shifting the display.

Figure 2-19   The **Pan** and **Zoom** tools on the Status Bar

Pan Tool   Zoom Tool

Selecting the **Pan** tool changes the cursor to a little hand icon that you click and drag in the drawing window to shift your display. If necessary, you can click and drag repeatedly until you reach the desired location in the drawing. When you reach the area of the drawing you want to display, press the **<Enter ↵>** or **<Esc>** key to exit.

By default, selecting the **Zoom** tool allows you to zoom up on an area of the drawing by selecting two corner points to define a rectangular window area to zoom in on. When you click on the **Zoom** tool AutoCAD prompts you to *Specify corner of window, enter a scale factor (nX or nXP), or ↓*. Pick the first corner. A preview window is displayed so you can draw a rectangle around the area you want to zoom and pick the other corner point. After you pick a point the drawing is immediately zoomed.

If you press **<Enter ↵>** before picking the first corner point, AutoCAD defaults to the **Zoom Realtime** tool and the cursor changes to a magnifying glass icon with a plus/minus sign. The plus/minus sign indicates that clicking and dragging the mouse up the screen will zoom in closer to the drawing, while clicking and dragging the mouse down the screen will zoom out farther from the drawing. If necessary, you can click and drag repeatedly until you zoom in or out to the desired location in the drawing. When you reach the area of the drawing you want to display, press the **<Enter ↵>** or **<Esc>** key to exit.

The **Pan** and **Zoom** tools, as well as other useful navigation tools, are also available on the **Navigate** panel located on the **View** ribbon shown in Figure 2-20.

Pan Tool

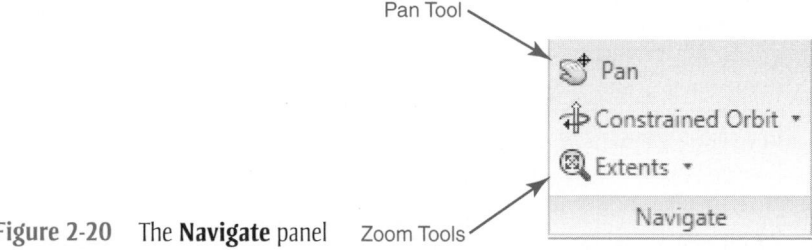

Figure 2-20   The **Navigate** panel   Zoom Tools

Some of the more useful **Zoom** tools include:

- **Zoom Extents**   Displays everything visible in your drawing by fitting the outermost extents of your drawing information within the AutoCAD drawing window. Good command to use if you "lose" your work off the screen and you want to get it back!
- **Zoom Window**   Allows you to define a rectangular window area to zoom up on by specifying two corner points of a boundary area.
- **Zoom Previous**   Restores the previous pan/zoom display so you can back up through your pan/zoom history. It does NOT undo any other commands; it affects only the display. AutoCAD keeps track of up to 10 previous views.

Exercise 2-9: Navigating Around the Drawing

1. Select the **Zoom** tool from the Status Bar. AutoCAD prompts you to *Specify corner of window, enter a scale factor (nX or nXP), or ↓*.
2. Pick a point slightly below and to the left of the circle. AutoCAD prompts you to *Specify opposite corner:*.
3. Pick a point slightly above and to the right of the circle. AutoCAD will zoom into the area you selected.
4. Select the **Zoom Previous** tool from the **Navigate** panel on the **View** ribbon. AutoCAD switches back to the previous view.

5. Select the **Zoom Extents** tool from the **Navigate** panel on the **View** ribbon. AutoCAD fills the display with the drawing.
6. Select the **Zoom Previous** tool again to return to the original display.
7. Select the **Zoom** tool from the Status Bar and press the **<Enter ↵>** key without picking a point to start the **Zoom Realtime** tool.
8. Hold down the mouse button and drag your mouse up and down the screen. AutoCAD zooms in and out accordingly. Press **<Esc>** to exit the command.
9. Select the **Pan** tool from the Status Bar.
10. Hold down the mouse button and drag your mouse back and forth across the screen. AutoCAD pans the display accordingly. Press **<Esc>** to exit the command.
11. Using the **Pan** and **Zoom** tools, pan and zoom your drawing as needed so it resembles Figure 2-21.
12. Save your drawing as **EX2-9**.

Figure 2-21   The zoomed drawing

Zooming with a Wheel Mouse

If you use a wheel mouse with your computer, AutoCAD will make use of the scroll wheel. When you scroll the wheel up and down, AutoCAD will zoom in and out, respectively. The zoom will be centered about the location of the cursor.

Pressing and holding down the scroll wheel allows you to dynamically pan around the drawing.

TIP   Using the scroll wheel is a system behavior and not technically a command. Because of this, you can use the dynamic zoom and pan of the scroll wheel at any time during the drawing process, even while in the middle of a command.

OBJECT PROPERTIES

As mentioned earlier in this chapter, when you create a drawing, you are placing AutoCAD objects in the drawing. When you create an object, AutoCAD will ask you to specify the various aspects or *properties* of that object. Chapter 1 described how some properties are common to all objects (for example, layer, color, etc.) and other properties are unique to a given type of object (for example, the radius of a circle or the height of text).

When you select an object, AutoCAD displays the **Quick Properties** panel. This panel displays the layer, color, and linetype of the selected object. It also displays other object properties depending on the type of object selected. Figure 2-22 shows the **Quick Properties** panel for a line segment. If more than one object is selected, AutoCAD will show only common properties of all the selected objects. You can change the properties of any selected object by changing their values in the **Quick Properties** panel.

properties: The settings that control how and where a drawing object is shown in the drawing.

Figure 2-22   The Quick Properties panel

Exercise 2-10: Using the Quick Properties panel

1. Drag your cursor over the circle in the drawing. The circle will highlight when the cursor hovers over it.
2. Select the circle in your drawing. The circle will change to a dashed line to indicate that it has been selected. Blue boxes will also appear on the circle. The **Quick Properties** panel will display the object properties for that circle.
3. Move you cursor over the blue bar on the left of the **Quick Properties** panel to expand the list of properties. Select the **Diameter** box and type **1<Enter ↲>**. The circle will immediately change its size. Notice that the values for radius, circumference, and area update as well.
4. Change the **Center X** value to **5**.
5. Change the **Center Y** value to **3**.
6. Press **<Esc>** to deselect the circle.
7. Select the line on the far right of the drawing. The **Quick Properties** panel now shows the properties for that object.
8. While the line is still selected, select the circle. AutoCAD now shows only the properties that are common to those two objects.
9. Press **<Esc>** to clear the selection. Your drawing should resemble Figure 2-23.
10. Save your drawing as **EX2-10**.

Figure 2-23   The modified circle

LAYERS

As you saw in the previous exercise, some properties are common to all objects. These include color, linetype, lineweight, and layer. Color is fairly obvious; it is the display color of the object on the screen. Linetype refers to how the line is displayed—for example, a dashed line, dotted line, continuous line, etc. Lineweight is the plotted width of the object (think of it as pen width).

You can assign a color, linetype, and lineweight to each object individually; however, when your drawing grows in complexity, you can quickly find it difficult to manage each object individually. This is where layers come to the rescue.

> **FOR MORE DETAILS**   Chapter 1 provides a brief description of how layering is used in CAD. Chapter 6 provides a complete description of layers and other object properties.

Layers give you a way to group objects together logically. The objects are still separate but share common properties and can be manipulated as a group.

Each layer consists of a name, color, linetype, lineweight, and a number of on/off settings. When you draw an object, the properties of the current layer are applied to that object. The **Layer** pull-down list allows you to set the current drawing layer. The **Layer Properties Manager** palette allows you to create and manage drawing layers.

Exercise 2-11: Creating New Layers

1. Choose the **Layer Properties** tool from the **Layers** panel. The **Layer Properties Manager** palette appears (see Figure 2-24). There are three layers currently defined. Layer **0** is the default layer included in every drawing. The **Title** and **Viewport** layers came from the drawing template.
2. Choose the **New Layer** button at the top of the palette (see Figure 2-24). Type **Dim<Enter ↵>** for the name.
3. Press **<Enter ↵>** again. AutoCAD will create another new layer. Type **Object <Enter ↵>** for the name.
4. Choose the color setting for the **Object** layer you just created. This will display the **Select Color** dialog box (see Figure 2-25). Choose the color red (Index color 1) and choose **OK** to close the dialog box.
5. Choose the **New Layer** button and create a layer named **Center**.
6. Select the color setting for the **Center** layer. Set the color to blue (Index color 5) and choose **OK** to close the **Select Color** dialog box.

Figure 2-24   The **Layer Properties Manager** palette

Figure 2-25   The **Select Color** dialog box

7. Choose the linetype setting for the **Center** layer. This displays the **Select Linetype** dialog box (see Figure 2-26).
8. Choose the **Load** button. This displays the **Load or Reload Linetypes** dialog box (see Figure 2-27).

Figure 2-26   The **Select Linetype** dialog box

Figure 2-27   The **Load or Reload Linetypes** dialog box

9. Scroll down through the list to see the available linetypes. Next to each line is a text representation of what the linetype looks like. Select the **CENTER2** linetype and choose **OK**. This loads this linetype definition into the drawing and returns you to the **Select Linetype** dialog box.

10. In the **Select Linetype** dialog box, select the **CENTER2** linetype you just loaded and choose **OK**. This assigns the linetype you just loaded to the layer and returns you to the **Layers Properties Manager** palette.

11. Choose the **Layer Properties** button to close the **Layer Properties Manager** palette.

12. Save your drawing as **EX2-11**.

So far, the appearance of your drawing hasn't changed. All you have done at this point is to define some new layers.

Exercise 2-12: Drawing on a Layer

1. From the **Layers** panel, choose **Center** from the **Layer** drop-down list (see Figure 2-28). This sets the layer **Center** as the current drawing layer.

Figure 2-28   The **Layer** drop-down list

2. Toggle the **Ortho Mode** button to **ON** and choose the **Line** tool. Type **4.25,3<Enter ↵>** to specify the starting point.

3. Drag your cursor to the right and type **1.5<Enter ↵>** to specify the length and direction of the line segment.

4. Press **<Esc>** to end the **LINE** command.

5. Press **<Space>** to restart the **LINE** command. Type **5,2.25<Enter ↵>** to specify the starting point.

6. Drag the cursor up and type **1.5<Enter ↵>** to specify the length and direction of the line segment.

7. Press **<Esc>** to end the **LINE** command. Your drawing should now resemble Figure 2-29.

8. Save your drawing as **EX2-12**.

Figure 2-29   Adding centerlines to the drawing

The new lines have the color and linetype of the **Center** layer. The rest of the drawing was created on layer **0**. In the next exercise, you'll move those objects from layer **0** to the **Object** layer.

Exercise 2-13: Moving Objects to Another Layer

1. In the drawing area, pick a point below and to the left of your figure. AutoCAD prompts you to *Specify opposite corner:*. A blue selection window will drag from the point you picked.
2. Pick a point above and to the right of your figure. This will select all the objects inside the box you just specified. The **Quick Properties** panel appears.
3. Hold down the **<Shift>** key and pick the two centerlines you just drew. This removes those lines from the selection.
4. Select the **Layer** property from the **Quick Properties** panel and select **Object** from the drop-down list. The objects "move" to the **Object** layer and take on the properties of that layer.
5. Press **<Esc>** to clear the selection.
6. Save your drawing as **EX2-13**.

Of course, the objects didn't actually move. Their layer property was simply changed from **0** to **Object**. However, you can think of this as the objects "floating" from one layer to another or (in the pin-board drafting world) moving the objects from one overlay sheet to another.

Freeze and Thaw a Layer

Your drawing objects are now organized into a few logical layers. Next we'll look at some methods of manipulating layers in your drawing.

Exercise 2-14: Freezing and Thawing Layers

1. Select layer **0** from the **Layer** drop-down list. This sets layer **0** as the current layer.
2. From the **Layer** drop-down list, click on the sun icon next to layer **Center** (see Figure 2-30). The sun icon will change to a snowflake. Now pick anywhere in your drawing to close the **Layer** drop-down list. This *freezes* the **Center** layer and hides it from view.
3. From the **Layer** drop-down list, click on the snowflake icon next to layer **Center**. The snowflake now turns back to a sun. Pick anywhere in the drawing area to close the **Layer** drop-down list. This *thaws* the **Center** layer, making it visible again.
4. Save your drawing as **EX2-14**.

freeze/thaw: Hiding or displaying the contents of a drawing layer. Objects on a frozen layer are ignored by AutoCAD, are not shown in the drawing, and cannot be edited.

Figure 2-30   The **Layer** drop-down list

When layers are frozen, AutoCAD acts as if the objects on those layers don't exist. Objects on frozen layers are hidden from view and cannot be changed while the layer is frozen. The current drawing layer cannot be frozen.

AutoCAD also has an ON/OFF setting for layers (represented by the lightbulb in the **Layer** drop-down list). While turning layers off will hide them from view, objects on those layers can still be modified (i.e., erased). For this reason, freezing and thawing layers is generally preferred to turning layers on and off.

Lock and Unlock a Layer

While the **Freeze** option will prevent objects from being modified, it also hides them from view. The **Lock/Unlock** setting allows you to prevent objects from being modified while still keeping them displayed on screen.

Figure 2-31   Locking the **Object** layer

Figure 2-32   The AutoCAD alert box

Exercise 2-15: Locking and Unlocking Layers

1. From the **Layer** drop-down list, click on the **Open lock** icon next to layer **Object** (see Figure 2-31). The **Open lock** icon will change to a closed lock. Pick anywhere in your drawing to close the **Layer** drop-down list.
2. Select the circle. The **Quick Properties** panel opens.
3. Change the **Radius** property of the circle to **1**. AutoCAD responds with an alert box stating: *one or more selected objects is on a locked layer and cannot be updated.* (see Figure 2-32). The circle is now deselected, and the **Quick Properties** panel is hidden.
4. Choose **Close** to close the alert box.
5. From the **Layer** drop-down list, click on the **Lock** icon next to layer **Object** and pick anywhere in the drawing to close the **Layer** drop-down list. The **Object** layer is now unlocked.
6. Save your drawing as **EX2-15**.

This section has touched on only a few key elements of layering and AutoCAD's layer management tools. Layer management is a crucial element of using AutoCAD effectively.

FOR MORE DETAILS	Chapter 6 explains how to use AutoCAD's layer management tools and describes some of the issues involved in layer management.

DIMENSION STYLES

dimension style: A collection of dimension settings that control how dimension objects act and are displayed.

Now that you have created a basic drawing, it's time to dimension it. Before we start dimensioning, we need to set up the appearance of the dimensions to reflect industry standards. The look and behavior of dimensions are controlled through *dimension styles*. A dimension style is simply a collection of dimension settings saved with a certain name. A dimension object takes on the look and behavior of its dimension style. AutoCAD uses a dimension style called *Standard* as a default, but you can modify the Standard dimension style or create new ones as needed. In the following exercise, you'll take a quick tour through all the various dimension style settings.

FOR MORE DETAILS	There are a lot of settings, and the following exercise goes through them quickly: don't get overwhelmed. Chapter 13 gives a detailed description of dimensioning and dimension style settings.

Exercise 2-16: Changing Dimension Styles

1. Choose the **Dimension Style** tool from the **Dimension** panel on the **Annotate** ribbon by selecting the down arrow on the right side of the panel title bar. The **Dimension Style Manager** dialog box appears (see Figure 2-33).

Figure 2-33   The **Dimension Style Manager** dialog box

Figure 2-34   The **Modify Dimension Style** dialog box

Figure 2-35   The **Symbols and Arrows** tab

Figure 2-36   The **Text** tab

2. Choose the **Modify...** button to modify the **Standard** dimension style. The **Modify Dimension Style** dialog box appears (see Figure 2-34).

3. Choose the **Symbols and Arrows** tab and change the **Arrow Size** value to **.125**. In the **Center marks** area, change the type to **None** (see Figure 2-35).

4. Choose the **Text** tab and change the **Text height:** value to **.125** (see Figure 2-36).

5. Click on the down arrow to the right of the **Text style**: drop-down list and select the **Roman** text style (see Figure 2-37).

6. Choose the **Fit** tab and turn on the **Annotative** option (see Figure 2-38).

7. Choose the **Primary Units** tab and select **0.00** from the **Precision** drop-down list (see Figure 2-39).

8. Choose **OK** to close the **Modify Dimension Style** dialog box.

9. Choose **Close** to close the **Dimension Style Manager** dialog box.

10. Save your drawing as **EX2-16**.

Due to the sheer number of options, modifying and managing dimension styles can be one of the more challenging aspects of AutoCAD. As with layers, managing dimensions and dimension styles is a crucial element of using AutoCAD effectively.

Figure 2-37   The **Text style**: drop-down list

Figure 2-38   The **Fit** tab

Figure 2-39   The **Primary Units** tab

Figure 2-40   The **Dimensions** panel

DIMENSIONING

AutoCAD's dimensioning tools can easily measure distances and place dimensions on your drawing. You tell AutoCAD what type of dimension you want to place and what object or points you wish to dimension, and AutoCAD will measure and place the dimension on the drawing. You can access the dimension tools from the **Dimensions** panel on the **Annotate** ribbon shown in Figure 2-40.

Exercise 2-17: Placing Dimensions

1. In the **Layer** drop-down list, set the **Dim** layer current.
2. Choose the **Linear** tool from the **Dimensions** panel on the **Annotate** ribbon to start the **DIMLINEAR** command. AutoCAD prompts you to *Specify first extension line origin or <select object>:*.
3. Press **<Enter ↵>** to select an object. AutoCAD prompts you to *Select object to dimension:*.
4. Pick the line at the bottom of the drawing (point 1 in Figure 2-41). AutoCAD starts dragging a dimension from that line and prompts you *Specify dimension line location or ↓*.

Figure 2-41 Adding dimensions

5. Pick a point below the line. The dimension is placed, and the **DIMLINEAR** command ends.
6. Press **<Enter ↵>** to restart the **DIMLINEAR** command.
7. Press **<Enter ↵>** to select an object and pick the line at the right side of the drawing (point 2 in Figure 2-41).
8. Drag the dimension to the right and pick a point to place it. The **DIMLINEAR** command ends.
9. From the **Dimensions** panel, choose **Diameter** to start the **DIMDIAMETER** command. AutoCAD prompts you to *Select arc or circle:*.
10. Select the circle and pick a point above and to the left of the circle (point 3 in Figure 2-41). The **DIMDIAMETER** command ends.
11. Choose the **Baseline** tool to start the **DIMBASELINE** command. AutoCAD starts dragging a dimension from the end of the last linear dimension. AutoCAD prompts you to *Specify a second extension line origin or ↓*.
12. Press the down arrow and choose the **Select** option from the menu. AutoCAD prompts you to *Select base dimension:*.
13. Pick the left dimension line of the first dimension you created (point 1 in Figure 2-42). A dimension line rubber-bands from the dimension you selected.

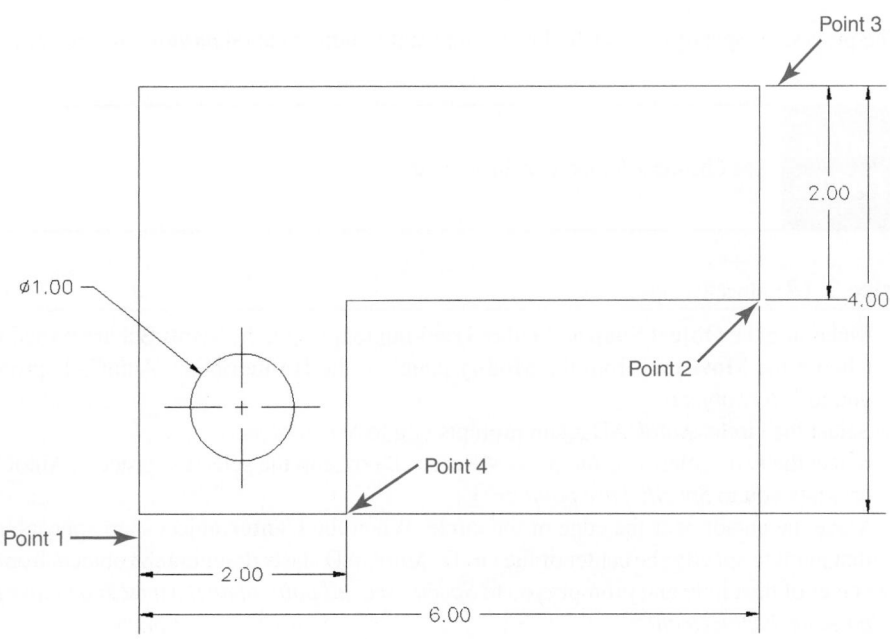

Figure 2-42 Adding baseline dimensions

14. Make sure your **Object Snap** toggle is turned **ON** on the Status Bar and move your cursor near point 2 shown in Figure 2-42. When the **Endpoint** object snap appears, pick that point to select the endpoint of that line. AutoCAD will place the dimension and start dragging a new dimension.

15. AutoCAD again prompts you to *Specify a second extension line origin or* ↓. Press the down arrow and choose the **Select** option from the menu. AutoCAD prompts you to *Select base dimension:.*

16. Pick the upper dimension line of the vertical dimension (point 3 in Figure 2-42).

17. Move your cursor near point 4 shown in Figure 2-42. When the **Endpoint** object snap appears, pick that point to select the endpoint of that line. AutoCAD will place the dimension and start dragging a new dimension.

18. Press **<Esc>** to end the **DIMBASELINE** command.

19. Save your drawing as **EX2-17**.

You now have some basic dimensions on your drawing. The look and orientation of the dimensions are controlled by the dimension style.

One of the unique aspects of dimensions is their ability to update automatically as the drawing changes. This feature is called ***associativity***, which means that dimensions are associated with the geometry and will automatically update when the geometry changes. In the next section, we'll look at some ways to modify your drawing and see how the associative dimensions follow along.

associativity: A link between drawing objects and dimension objects. Associative dimensions will update and follow the drawing objects to which they are linked.

MODIFYING DRAWING OBJECTS

So far, we've looked at modifying object properties through the **Quick Properties** panel. One of the most powerful benefits of CAD systems is their unique ability to make changes to your drawing. This section introduces you to some of the basic tools used to modify your drawing.

Selection Sets

As with the drawing tools, AutoCAD has a general process for modifying objects, which is to:

1. Select an editing tool.
2. Specify which object(s) you want to modify.
3. Read the prompt.
4. Specify points and answer prompts.
5. Press **<Enter ↵>** or **<Esc>** to end the command.

building a selection set: The process of specifying the objects you wish to edit.

The process of specifying which objects you want to edit is called ***building a selection set***.

FOR MORE DETAILS	See Chapter 7 for more on building selection sets.

Exercise 2-18: Moving Objects

1. Make sure the **Object Snap** and **Polar Tracking** toggles on the Status Bar are turned **ON**.

2. Choose the **Move** tool from the **Modify** panel on the **Home** ribbon. AutoCAD prompts you to *Select objects:.*

3. Select the circle. AutoCAD again prompts you to *Select objects:.*

4. Select the two centerlines and press **<Enter ↵>** to stop the selection process. AutoCAD prompts you to *Specify base point or* ↓.

5. Move the cursor near the edge of the circle. When the **Center** object snap appears, pick that point to specify the center of the circle. AutoCAD starts dragging the objects from the center of the circle and prompts you to *Specify second point of displacement or <use first point as displacement>:.*

6. Drag the object straight up until the 90° polar tracking alignment path appears (see Figure 2-43). Once it appears, type **2<Enter ↵>**. The circle, lines, and dimensions move up 2″.
7. Save your drawing as **EX2-18**.

Figure 2-43   Moving objects

When you started the **MOVE** command, AutoCAD needed to know which objects you wanted to move. The *Select objects:* prompt repeated until you pressed **<Enter ↵>**, telling AutoCAD you had finished selecting objects. Once you finished selecting objects, AutoCAD then went on to complete the command. It asked you to specify where you wanted to move the objects from (the base point) and where you wanted to drag the objects (the second point).

Notice that even though you didn't select the dimension, it moved as well. This is because of the associativity of the dimension with the circle.

It is possible to preselect the objects you want to modify. If any objects are selected prior to starting a command, AutoCAD will use these objects as the selection set and will skip the *Select objects:* prompt.

Exercise 2-19: Selecting First

1. Pick a point on the screen above and to the right of the circle (point 1 in Figure 2-44). AutoCAD will prompt you: *Specify opposite corner:*.

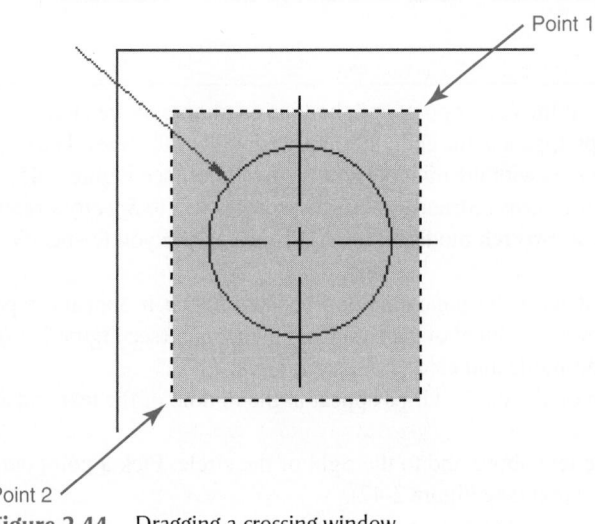

Figure 2-44   Dragging a crossing window

crossing window: A method of selecting objects in a selection set by specifying a rectangular area. Anything that touches the crossing window area is selected.

2. Drag the cursor down and to the left of the circle. AutoCAD will drag a dotted rectangle from the first point you picked (see Figure 2-44). This is called a *crossing window*.
3. Pick a point below and to the left of the circle (point 2 in Figure 2-44). AutoCAD will select all the objects that are inside or touch the edge of the crossing window you picked.
4. Choose the **Erase** tool from the **Modify** panel. AutoCAD immediately erases the selected objects.
5. Choose the **Undo** tool from the **Quick Access** toolbar to bring the objects back.
6. Save your drawing as **EX2-19**.

FOR MORE DETAILS   The crossing window is one of a number of ways to select objects. Chapter 7 discusses crossing windows and other ways to select objects.

Notice that AutoCAD did not prompt you to select objects. Because you selected the objects before you started the command, AutoCAD assumed that those were the objects you wanted to erase. AutoCAD doesn't care whether you select the objects before or after you start the command. If no objects are selected, AutoCAD will simply ask you to select them before it continues with the command.

GRIP EDITING

grips: Editing points that appear at key locations on drawing objects.

You may have noticed in previous exercises that when you preselect objects, the objects highlight and little squares show up on them. These squares are known as *grips*. Grips appear when you select objects when there is no active command. Grips are located at strategic points on an object. For example, on a circle, grips appear at the center and the four quadrants of the circle. On lines, grips appear at the end and midpoints of the line. On dimensions, they appear on the dimension text and the ends of the dimension lines and arrows.

Grips give you a quick way to modify objects by giving you access to commonly used editing commands and commonly used object points. There are five grip editing modes: stretch, move, rotate, scale, and mirror. When you select a grip, AutoCAD starts the grip editing command and places you in stretch mode. You can toggle between the different editing modes by pressing **<Enter ↵>**. Like other commands, the grip editing modes have prompts and options.

FOR MORE DETAILS   See Chapter 7 for more on grip editing.

Exercise 2-20: Editing with Grips

1. Select the circle. Grips appear at the center point and the four quadrants of the circle.
2. Select the two centerlines. Grips appear at the endpoints and midpoint of the lines. The grip at the center of the circle coincides with the midpoints of the two lines (see Figure 2-45).
3. Click on the center grip. The grip turns red, and AutoCAD prompts you to *Specify stretch point or ↓*. AutoCAD is now in **Stretch** mode. AutoCAD is prompting you to specify a stretch point.
4. Move your cursor to the right until the polar tracking appears. Once it appears, type **3.5<Enter ↵>**. AutoCAD moves the center of the circle 3.5″ to the right (see Figure 2-46).
5. Press **<Esc>** to exit **Grip Edit** mode and clear the selection set.
6. Select the diameter dimension on the circle. Grips appear at the middle of the text and at two points on the circle.
7. Pick the text grip and drag the text above and to the right of the circle. Pick a point outside of the drawing to place the text (see Figure 2-47).
8. Press **<Esc>** to exit **Grip Edit** mode and clear the selection set.
9. Save your drawing as **EX2-20**.

Figure 2-45   Grips

Figure 2-46   The modified circle

Notice that when you *stretched* the center and midpoints of the objects, the end result was that the objects moved. It's a subtle distinction but worth noting. AutoCAD defines circles by a center point (the center grip) and a radius (the quadrant grips). Since you stretched only the center point, only the location of the circle changed, not its size. The same thing applies to the line; because you stretched just the midpoint of the line, the size and direction of the line didn't change, only its location.

In the previous example, once you selected a grip, AutoCAD immediately switched to **Grip Edit** mode. It is possible to select multiple grips and modify them as a group. To do this, you simply hold down the **<Shift>** key while selecting the grips. Once you're finished selecting grips, release the **<Shift>** key and then pick one of the grips to start the editing process.

Exercise 2-21: Editing with Multiple Grips

1. Press **<Esc>** to cancel any active commands and clear any selections.
2. Select the three lines on the right side of the drawing (see Figure 2-48). Select the top line first.
3. Hold down the **<Shift>** key and select the two grips at the corners of the selected lines (see Figure 2-48). The two grips are highlighted, but grip editing has not started.

Figure 2-47   The modified dimension

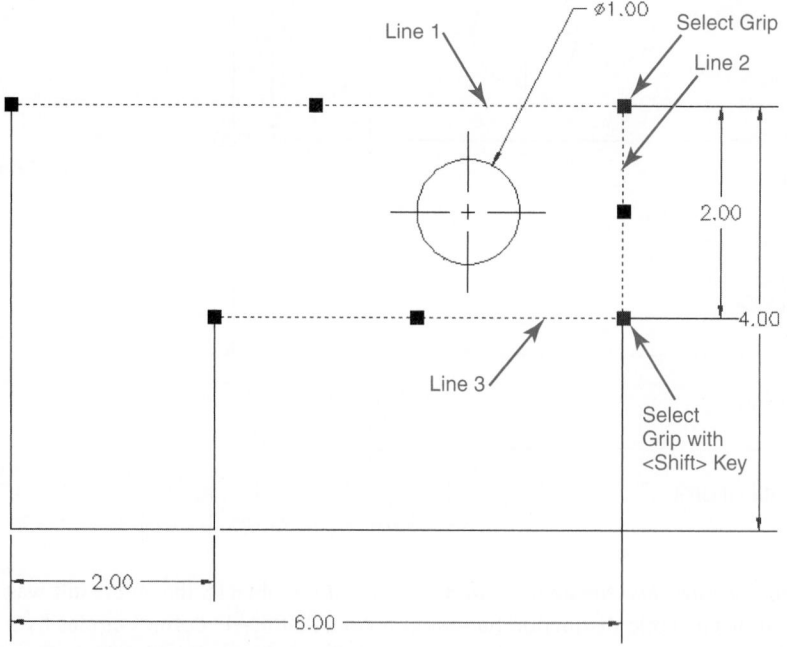

Figure 2-48   Selecting multiple grips

4. Release the **<Shift>** key and select either one of the highlighted grips. AutoCAD now enters **Grip Edit** mode.
5. Drag the grip to the left until the polar tracking appears. Once the polar tracking appears, type **.5<Enter ↵>** into the **Dynamic Input** box (see Figure 2-49).
6. AutoCAD stretches the longest line to a length of 5.5 (see Figure 2-50).
7. Press **<Esc>** to exit **Grip Edit** mode and clear the selection set.
8. Save your drawing as **EX2-21**.

The order in which you select the lines is important. The first line you selected determined which dimension would appear in the **Dynamic Input** box. You should have also seen the associative dimensions in action again. The dimensions updated to follow the changes in the geometry.

Figure 2-49   Grips and Dynamic Input

Figure 2-50   The stretched objects

INTRODUCTION TO ADVANCED EDITING TECHNIQUES

A few of the advanced editing techniques are indispensable in AutoCAD. In fact, these commands and techniques are used extensively when creating AutoCAD drawings, which may seem counterintuitive. Using CAD, it is not uncommon to create a drawing by drawing more than you need and then editing and refining information to make the final product. This section introduces you to a few of these techniques.

FOR MORE DETAILS   See Chapter 8 for more information regarding different advanced editing techniques.

Making Parallel Copies

Sometimes it is necessary to make an exact copy of a line or circle that is a specific distance from the original. This is referred to as an *offset* in AutoCAD. It is possible to offset a specific distance or even through a point that you specify while maintaining a copy of the original object. It is even possible to make multiple copies.

Exercise 2-22: Offsetting Objects

1. Choose the **Offset** tool from the **Modify** panel. AutoCAD prompts you to *Specify offset distance or* ↓.
2. Type **.125<Enter ↵>**. AutoCAD prompts you to *Select object to offset or* ↓.
3. Pick the horizontal line at the top of the drawing (point 1 in Figure 2-51). AutoCAD prompts you to *Specify point on side to offset or* ↓.
4. Pick a point below that line (point 2 in Figure 2-51). AutoCAD places a copy of the line .125″ below the original. AutoCAD prompts you again to *Select object to offset or* ↓.

Figure 2-51   Offsetting lines

5. Pick the next horizontal line down from the top of the drawing (point 3 in Figure 2-51). AutoCAD prompts you to *Specify point on side to offset or* ↓.

6. Pick a point above that line (point 4 in Figure 2-51). AutoCAD places a copy of the line .125″ above the original. AutoCAD prompts you again to *Select object to offset or* ↓.

7. Pick the vertical line on the left side of the drawing (point 5 in Figure 2-51). AutoCAD prompts you to *Specify point on side to offset or* ↓.

8. Pick a point to the right of that line (point 6 in Figure 2-51). AutoCAD places a copy of the line .125″ to right of the original and prompts you again to *Select object to offset or* ↓.

9. Pick the next vertical line to the right of the drawing (point 7 in Figure 2-51). AutoCAD prompts you to *Specify point on side to offset or* ↓.

10. Pick a point to the left of that line (point 8 in Figure 2-51). AutoCAD places a copy of the line .125″ to the left of the original and prompts you again to *Select object to offset or* ↓.

11. Save your drawing as **EX2-22**.

Fixing Overlapping Lines and Closing Gaps

Often it is necessary to "clean up" lines that overlap and/or do not meet exactly so that there is a gap. Remember that the key to using AutoCAD effectively is to draw everything as precisely as possible. There is no room for even the tiniest overlap or gap. These small errors can propagate larger errors when dimensions are added or parts are mated together. AutoCAD provides a number of methods for cleaning up your drawings quickly.

Exercise 2-23: Trimming and Extending Objects

1. Choose the **Trim** tool from the **Modify** panel. The current command settings are displayed in the command window, and AutoCAD prompts you:

```
Current settings: Projection=UCS, Edge=None
Select cutting edges...
Select objects or <select all>:
```

2. Select lines 1–4 shown in Figure 2-52 and press **<Enter ↵>**. AutoCAD prompts you to *Select object to trim or shift-select to extend or* ↓.

Figure 2-52   Trimming and extending lines

3. Pick a point on the short line segment shown at point 1 in Figure 2-52. The vertical line is trimmed, and AutoCAD prompts you again to *Select object to trim or shift-select to extend or* ↓.
4. Pick the line segments shown at points 2, 3, and 4 in Figure 2-52. The lines are trimmed.
5. Press **<Enter ↵>** to exit the **Trim** tool. Notice that the dimensions automatically update to reflect the new sizes.
6. Choose the **Extend** tool from the **Modify** panel. The current command settings are displayed in the command window, and AutoCAD prompts you:

```
Current settings: Projection=UCS, Edge=None
Select boundary edges...
Select objects or <select all>:
```

7. Select lines 3 and 4 in Figure 2-52 and press **<Enter ↵>**. AutoCAD prompts you to *Select object to extend or shift-select to trim or* ↓.
8. Press the down arrow on your keyboard or type **E<Enter ↵>** and select the **Extend** option.
9. Pick a point toward the top of line 3 in Figure 2-52. The vertical line is extended, and AutoCAD prompts you again to *Select object to extend or shift-select to trim or* ↓.
10. Pick a point on the left of line 4 in Figure 2-52. The line is extended.
11. Press **<Enter ↵>** to exit the **Extend** tool.
12. Choose the **Fillet** tool from the **Modify** panel. The current command settings are displayed in the command window, and AutoCAD prompts you:

```
Current settings: Mode = TRIM, Radius = 0.0000
Select first object or ↓.
```

13. Select lines 1 and 2 near the upper left corner in Figure 2-52. Both lines are trimmed to form a closed corner by creating a fillet with a radius of 0.0″.
14. Choose the **Erase** tool from the **Modify** panel and erase lines 5, 6, 7, and 8 (see Figure 2-52).
15. Your drawing should now look like Figure 2-53. Use grips to select the dimension extension line origin as shown and attach it back to the corner of the drawing using an **Endpoint** object snap. Make sure the **Object Snap** button is **ON**.
16. Save your drawing as **EX2-23**.

Figure 2-53   The updated drawing

CLEANING UP LAYOUT SPACE

Now that we have some basic dimensions on the drawing, let's go back to the layout space and make some adjustments to the viewport and the title block.

Setting the Viewport Scale

Remember that in layout space (paper space), viewports are simply holes or windows into the model space environment. You can open up that viewport to zoom and pan around model space and can even make changes to your model. You can also assign a viewport scale to each viewport. By setting this viewport scale, you are telling AutoCAD to display the model at a certain scale (full-scale, half-scale, 1/8″ = 1′-0″, etc.) within that viewport. The viewport in the **ANSI A Title Block** layout was part of the template file used to create the drawing. In the next exercise, you'll set the scale of the viewport and adjust the position of the model within the title block.

Exercise 2-24: Setting the Viewport Scale

1. Choose the **ANSI A Title Block** tab at the bottom of the drawing to switch to layout space. The geometry from model space will show up in the viewport.
2. Choose the **Zoom Extents** tool from the **Zoom** tools on the **Navigate** panel on the **View** ribbon. This will fill the drawing area with your layout sheet.
3. Double-click inside the viewport to activate it. The viewport will highlight, and the crosshair will appear only inside the viewport.
4. Click on the **Automatically Add Scales** icon with the lightbulb at the far right of the **Viewport Scale** on the Status Bar shown in Figure 2-54, and turn it on so that the dimensions automatically scale in the next step.

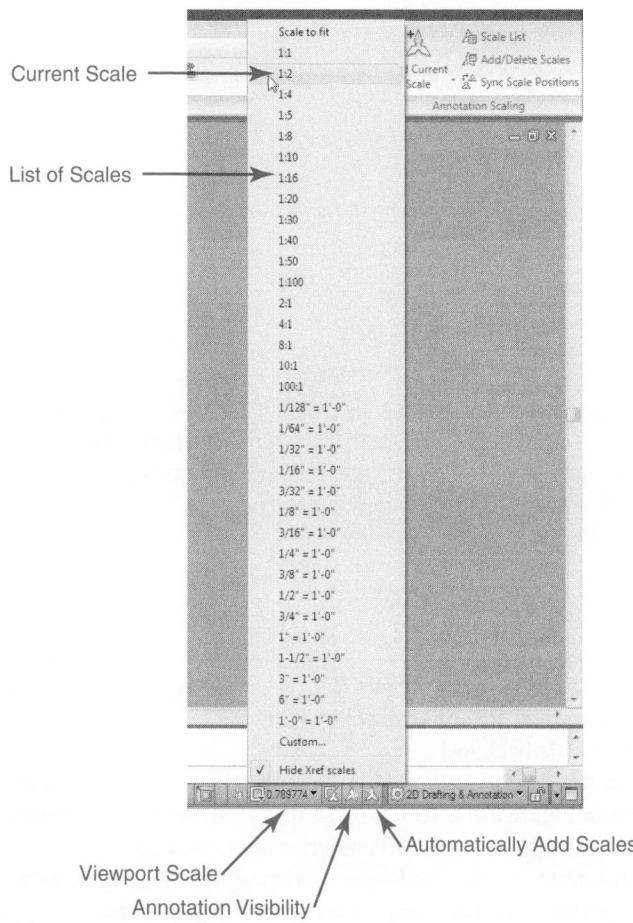

Figure 2-54   Setting the viewport scale

5. Click on the down arrow to the right of the **Viewport Scale** on the Status Bar shown in Figure 2-54 and choose **1:2**. Your drawing will zoom so that your model is half-scale (1:2) on your layout (paper).
6. Choose **Pan** from the Status Bar and pan your drawing so that it looks like Figure 2-55.
7. Save your drawing as **EX2-24**.

Notice that the dimension features are now twice as large as they were before you set the viewport scale. This is because the dimension style was set up earlier with the **Annotative** feature turned on (see Figure 2-38). When combined with turning on the feature that automatically scales annotative objects, as done in step 4 of Exercise 2-24, this setting actually creates another

Figure 2-55   The scaled viewport

set of dimensions for the new viewport/annotation scale so that you can view your drawing at different scales and have all the annotation objects display at the correct size.

TIP   It is possible to display all of an annotation object's scale representations when you select it so that each size is visible. You can grip edit the current scale's representation without affecting any of the other scale representations. For instance, by using grips, you can relocate one scale representation while leaving the others in their current locations.

Exercise 2-25: Adjusting Dimensions

1. Change the **Viewport Scale** back to 1:1 on the Status Bar. The view is zoomed in at a scale of 1:1, and the dimension features are scaled down by half.
2. Choose the **Undo** tool to set the scale back to 1:2.
3. Click on the **Annotation visibility** icon with the lightbulb to the right of the **Viewport Scale** on the Status Bar shown in Figure 2-54. Turn it on so that all scale representations of an annotation object are shown when it is selected and grips are turned on.
4. Use grips to relocate the dimensions so that they no longer overlap as shown in Figure 2-56.
5. Double-click outside the viewport to close the viewport and switch to paper space.
6. Save your drawing as **EX2-25**.

Figure 2-56   The adjusted dimensions

Text

Let's update the title block and place some text. When placing text in a drawing, AutoCAD will ask you to define a box in which to place the text. Once that text box is defined, a miniature text editor appears where you specified, and you can start typing your text. The text editor has a number of formatting features found in many text editors (fonts, bold, justification, etc.). You can insert predefined text fields (like the file name, date, plot scale, etc.) and can also import text from an external text file.

FOR MORE DETAILS	Chapter 11 describes the various options for placing and formatting text.

Exercise 2-26: Placing Text

1. Set the **Title Block** layer current by selecting it from the **Layer** drop-down list.
2. Choose **Zoom** from the Status Bar and zoom up on the lower right corner of the title block as shown in Figure 2-57.

Point 1

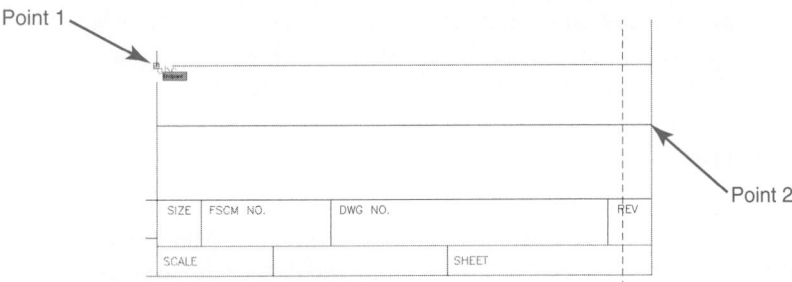
Point 2

Figure 2-57   Defining a text box

3. Choose the **Multiline Text** tool from the **Annotate** panel. AutoCAD prompts you to *Specify first corner:*.
4. Pick the endpoints at point 1 and point 2 shown in Figure 2-57. The **Multiline Text** ribbon will appear. A flashing text cursor will appear at the upper left corner of the text box. This indicates where the text will appear when you type.
5. In the **Style** panel, set the text height to **.125** and the style to **Roman**.

6. Choose the **Justification** button in the **Paragraph** panel and choose **Middle Center MC** from the menu. The flashing cursor will move to the middle of the text box.
7. In the text box, type **Introduction to AutoCAD** and choose **Close Text Editor** from the **Close** panel. AutoCAD places the text centered in the text box you specified.
8. Press **<Enter ↵>** to repeat the **MTEXT** command.
9. Pick the endpoints at point 1 and point 2 shown in Figure 2-58. The **Multiline Text** ribbon reappears along with the flashing text cursor.
10. Set the text height to **.250** and choose **Middle Center MC** from the **Justification** menu. Set the style to **Roman**.
11. Type **Angle Bracket** in the text box and then choose **Close Text Editor** to end the command.
12. Save your drawing as **EX2-26**.

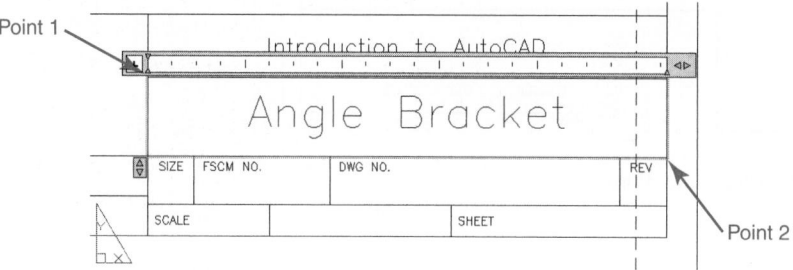

Figure 2-58   Placing more text

So far, you've simply typed in the text you want to display. You may want to place text that is specific to the drawing (like the drawing file name) or that is dynamic (for example, the plot time or date the drawing was last revised). AutoCAD provides you with a number of predefined text fields that will display various drawing or system information. In the following exercise, you'll use a text field to create the text.

Exercise 2-27: Using a Text Field

1. Choose the **Multiline Text** tool from the **Annotate** panel and select the endpoints at point 1 and point 2 shown in Figure 2-59.

Figure 2-59   Placing a text field

2. Set the text height to **.125**, the style to **Roman**, and the justification to **Middle Center MC**.
3. Choose **Field** from the **Insert** panel. This displays the **Field** dialog box (see Figure 2-60).
4. From the **Field names**: list, choose **Filename**.
5. In the **Format**: area, choose **Uppercase**.
6. Select the **Filename only** option and put a check in the box on the **Display file extension** setting (see Figure 2-60).
7. Choose **OK** to insert the field into the drawing. The **Field** dialog box will close.
8. Choose **Close Text Editor** to end the command. The drawing file name **EX2-26** appears in the title block (see Figure 2-61). The field text is highlighted to indicate that it is a field value.

Figure 2-60   The **Field** dialog box

Figure 2-61   The **Filename** text field

9. Choose **Zoom Extents** from the **Navigate** panel on the **View** ribbon.
10. Save your drawing as **EX2-27**.

As you can see from the **Field** dialog box (see Figure 2-60), there are a number of predefined fields. Using field names is a great timesaver. Because the field is updated every time you regenerate, any changes to the drawing file information (such as the file name) will automatically update the text.

FOR MORE DETAILS	Chapter 11 covers text fields and how to use them.

PLOTTING AND PAGE SETUPS

When you plot a drawing, AutoCAD needs to know a number of different settings (printer, paper size, orientation, margins, color settings, plot scale, etc.). You can specify these settings each time you plot, but for consistency, AutoCAD allows you to save all these settings to a ***page setup***. A page setup is simply a group of plot settings saved to a user-specified name. In the following exercise, you will make changes to the page setup associated with the **ANSI A Title Block** layout.

page setup: A collection of plot settings that are applied to a drawing layout.

Exercise 2-28: Page Setup

1. Choose **Page Setup Manager** from the **Plot** panel on the **Output** ribbon. This displays the **Page Setup Manager** dialog box shown in Figure 2-62.
2. Choose **New** to display the **New Page Setup** dialog box (see Figure 2-63).
3. Enter **ANSI A Title Block—Windows System Printer** as the new page setup name and choose **OK**. This displays the **Page Setup** dialog box (see Figure 2-64).
4. From the **Printer/plotter** list, select **Default Windows System Printer.pc3**. This is your default Windows printer.
5. From the **Paper size** list, choose **Letter**.
6. Choose **Extents** from the **What to plot**: list. This tells AutoCAD to plot everything currently shown in the drawing.
7. Check the **Center the plot** option in the **Plot offset** area.
8. If checked, clear the check from the **Fit to paper** box.
9. Choose **1:1** from the **Scale** drop-down list.

Figure 2-62   The **Page Setup Manager** dialog box

Figure 2-63   The **New Page Setup** dialog box

Figure 2-64   The **Page Setup** dialog box

10. Choose **Landscape** in the **Drawing orientation** area. Your selections should be the same as those shown in Figure 2-64.
11. Choose **Preview** to see how your drawing will look when it is printed. AutoCAD will switch to a print preview view (see Figure 2-65). The buttons at the top of the print preview window allow you to pan and zoom around the preview.
12. Choose the **Close** button to close the preview window.
13. Choose **OK** to save the page setup. The **Page Setup Manager** dialog box returns with the new page setup listed.
14. Select the page setup you just created and then choose **Set Current**. This applies the page setup settings to the current layout.

Plot Button

Pan and Zoom Tools

Close Button

Figure 2-65   The **Print Preview** window

15. Choose **Close** to close the **Page Setup Manager** dialog box.
16. Save your drawing as **EX2-28**.

Notice the dashed line that appears around the edge of the layout (see Figure 2-66). This dashed line represents the printable area on your drawing. It's not an actual drawing object (you can't select it), but only a visual indication of what part of your drawing will be printed. If any part of your drawing extends outside this dashed line, those parts will be clipped from the final print. To fix this, you can adjust the plot scale of your drawing, move or adjust the geometry within your drawing, or adjust the margins of your printer.

Note:

Many times a page setup has the same name as the layout space; however, they are not the same thing. Be careful not to confuse the page setup with the drawing layout. The layout is a drawing space where your drawing objects (title blocks, viewports, etc.) reside. The page setup is a collection of plot settings that are applied to the layout when you plot the drawing.

Printable Area Outline

Figure 2-66   The printable drawing area

FOR MORE DETAILS   See Chapter 14 for more on page setups.

Plotting

When you plot a drawing in AutoCAD, you are presented with the **Plot** dialog box (see Figure 2-67). The **Plot** dialog box has all the same settings as the **Page Setup** dialog box (in fact, you can use the **PLOT** command to create page setups). These options allow you to make last-minute changes to your page setup or temporarily override settings contained in the page setup. For example, your page setup may be defined for a C- or D-size plot, but you may want to create a quick check plot on an A-size sheet. The **PLOT** command allows you to change your plot setting without going through the process of creating a new page setup.

Figure 2-67   The Plot dialog box

In the following exercise, you'll do a plot using the page setup you just created.

Note: In the following exercise, your printer features and settings may differ from those shown here.

Exercise 2-29: Plotting

1. Choose the **Plot** tool from the **Plot** panel on the **Output** ribbon. The **Plot** dialog box appears (see Figure 2-67). If your dialog box looks different, choose the arrow next to the **Help** button to expand the dialog box and see all options.
2. From the **Page setup** list, choose **ANSI A Title Block – Windows System Printer**.
3. Verify that all the settings are correct and choose **Preview**. The plot preview displays.
4. Choose the **Plot** button to plot your drawing to your default Windows system printer. A plot progress bar will appear briefly, and AutoCAD will return to the command prompt when the plot is complete.
5. Save your drawing as **EX2-29**.

Once the plot is complete, AutoCAD will display a balloon in the lower right corner of the Status Bar (see Figure 2-68). This indicates the results of the **PLOT** command and reports any errors that may have occurred. To view the plot results, click on the indicated link to display the **Plot and Publish** details box. Here you can view the results of all plots submitted during the current AutoCAD session.

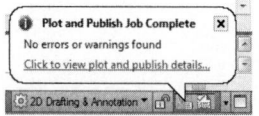

Figure 2-68   The Plot and Publish balloon

CHAPTER SUMMARY

You have now walked through a typical AutoCAD drawing session. Although your drawing sessions will no doubt be different and most likely involve a variety of more complex tasks, the exercises in this chapter give you an idea of what is involved in working with Auto-CAD. The tasks you completed in this chapter will be built on and expanded in the rest of the text. You should now feel fairly comfortable navigating the AutoCAD workspace and drawing some basic objects.

CHAPTER TEST QUESTIONS

Multiple Choice

1. Model space is:
   a. Only for three-dimensional objects
   b. Limited in size so you must scale your model appropriately
   c. Generally used to draw objects that exist in the real world
   d. Generally used to draw objects that exist only on paper

2. In the following command window prompt, what would you type to use the TTR option?

   `Specify center point for circle or [3P/2P/Ttr (tan tan radius)]:`

   a. **3P<Enter ↵>**
   b. **(tan tan radius)<Enter ↵>**
   c. **2P<Enter ↵>**
   d. **T<Enter ↵>**

3. Which of the following settings do NOT allow you to control point specifications?
   a. Grid
   b. Snap
   c. Ortho
   d. Polar

4. The command window:
   a. Cannot be moved
   b. Can be turned off
   c. Is the only way to communicate with AutoCAD
   d. Cannot be undocked

5. Scrolling the wheel of a wheel mouse will:
   a. Scroll the text in the command window
   b. Do nothing
   c. Pan the drawing up and down
   d. Zoom the drawing in and out

6. Which of the following is NOT a property common to all objects?
   a. Length
   b. Layer
   c. Color
   d. Lineweight

7. Dimensions:
   a. Can be placed only in model space
   b. Can be placed only in paper space
   c. Must be erased and redrawn if the model changes
   d. Are controlled by their associated dimension style

8. Grips appear:
   a. At key points on drawing objects
   b. On a separate layer
   c. Every time you click on the screen
   d. Only in model space

9. A page setup:
   a. Is the same thing as a paper space layout
   b. Can be defined only in a drawing template
   c. Is a collection of plot settings
   d. Must have the same name as a paper space layout

10. The dashed line that appears around the edge of a layout:
    a. Can be erased if needed
    b. Is on its own layer and can be turned off if desired
    c. Shows a visual indication of the area that will be printed
    d. Shows up on the printed drawing

Matching

a. Drawing template

b. Objects

c. Dimension style

d. Page setup

e. Grips

f. Object snaps

g. Object properties

1. The process of moving around the drawing by shifting the display

2. The settings that control how and where a drawing object is shown in the drawing

3. A link between drawing objects and dimension objects

4. The process of specifying the objects you wish to edit

5. A collection of plot settings that are applied to a drawing layout

6. A drawing file used as a starting point when creating new drawings

7. Editing points that appear at key locations on drawing objects when they are selected

h. Panning

i. Associativity

j. Building a selection set

8. Graphical drawing elements, such as lines, arcs, circles, polylines, and text

9. Geometric points on objects such as the endpoints or midpoint of a line or the center of an arc or circle

10. A collection of dimension settings that control how dimension objects act and are displayed

Controlling the Drawing Display

3

Chapter Objectives

- Zoom in and out of a drawing
- Pan around a drawing
- Create and restore named views
- Split the drawing display into multiple viewports
- Refresh the drawing display
- Toggle all the ribbons, toolbars, and palettes off and on
- Make arcs and circles appear smoother
- Increase drawing display regeneration speed by turning off text and solid fill areas

INTRODUCTION

The AutoCAD drawing display window is one of the most important features of the AutoCAD user interface. It is here where you do most of your work creating and modifying the objects that make up your drawing. AutoCAD provides a number of tools and settings that allow you to control how and what drawing information is displayed in the drawing display window. The drawing display tools and their settings are explained in detail in this chapter.

ZOOMING IN AND OUT OF A DRAWING

The AutoCAD drawing display window is like a camera lens. You control what's displayed in your drawing by zooming in to get a closer look and by zooming out to see the big picture, similar to a camera.

Unlike most cameras, AutoCAD provides a number of different ways to control the zooming process. The **Zoom** tools are located on the **Navigate** panel found on the **View** ribbon as shown in Figure 3-1.

All of the **Zoom** tools can be displayed by selecting the **Zoom Extents** tool to display the **Zoom** flyout menu shown in Figure 3-2. As you can see, there are many different **Zoom** tools available. Some of the tools are holdovers from early releases of AutoCAD and are beginning to show their age. They still exist in AutoCAD for legacy reasons, for the most part. You will need to refer to the AutoCAD Help for information regarding the legacy **Zoom** tools. The next section covers most of the **Zoom** tools that are still relevant today.

TIP The **Zoom** tool on the right side of the Status Bar introduced in Chapter 1 defaults to the **Zoom Window** tool. The **Zoom Window** tool is explained in detail later in this chapter.

Zoom Flyout
Menu →

Figure 3-1   The **Navi-
gate** panel **Zoom** tools

Figure 3-2   The **Zoom** flyout menu

Zoom Tools

The following **Zoom** tools are the easiest to use and provide the most "bang for the buck" when you need to zoom in and out of your drawing quickly. You will likely find yourself using the **Zoom** tools explained in this section most often out of the many different **Zoom** tools provided by AutoCAD.

Zoom Extents.   The **Zoom Extents** tool is very useful because it allows you to view everything in your drawing on your screen quickly. AutoCAD calculates the extents of the outermost objects in your drawing that are not on a frozen layer and then zooms out so that everything is visible. This is especially helpful when you are zoomed in to a small area of your drawing and you draw an object that goes off the screen. Using **Zoom Extents** allows you to see the complete object.

Zoom Extents	
Ribbon & Panel:	View | Navigate 🔍Extents
Zoom Toolbar:	🔍
Menu:	View| Zoom| Extents
Command Line:	ZOOM
Command Alias:	Z

TIP
Sometimes when you use the **Zoom Extents** tool, it might appear that there is nothing in your drawing—don't panic. Usually this means that there is some rogue object out in the nether regions of your drawing. If you zoom out just a little, you can usually find the object and determine its identity so that it might be moved or deleted.

To access student data files, go to www.pearsondesigncentral.com.

Exercise 3-1: Using the Zoom Extents Tool

1. Open the drawing **Willhome** located in the student data files.
2. Select the **Model** tab so that model space is active.
3. Select the **Zoom Extents** tool on the **Navigate** panel and zoom to the extents of the drawing.
4. Zoom in on an area of the drawing using your mouse wheel or any of the techniques introduced in Chapter 2.
5. Select the **Zoom Extents** tool again.
6. All the drawing information is now displayed in the drawing display window.

Note:
If there are no objects in your drawing or everything is on layers that are currently frozen. The **Zoom Extents** tool will zoom to the limits of your drawing. See Chapter 4 for more information about controlling drawing limits.

Figure 3-3   Defining the **Zoom Window** area

Zoom Window.   The **Zoom Window** tool allows you to define a rectangular area, or window, using two mouse pick points so that you can quickly zoom in on a specific area of your drawing. The windowed area is zoomed *and* centered at a scale that fills your drawing display area.

After selecting the **Zoom Window** tool, you are prompted to select the two corner points of the window. Select two points in your drawing to define the rectangular area you wish to zoom as shown in Figure 3-3.

The display is zoomed immediately after selecting the second corner point as shown in Figure 3-4.

Zoom Window	
Ribbon & Panel:	View | Navigate Window
Zoom Toolbar:	
Menu:	View| Zoom| Window
Command Line:	ZOOM
Command Alias:	Z

Figure 3-4   Display after second window corner point is selected

Exercise 3-2: Using the Zoom Window Tool

To access student data
files, go to
www.pearsondesigncentral.com.

1. Open the drawing **Willhome** located in the student data files.
2. Select the **Model** tab so that model space is active.
3. Select the **Zoom Extents** tool on the **Navigate** panel and zoom to the extents of the drawing.
4. Select the **Zoom Window** tool on the **Zoom** flyout menu on the **Navigate** panel. AutoCAD prompts you to *Specify first corner:*.
5. Pick a point in your drawing. AutoCAD places the first point and drags a rectangular rubber-band line from that point and prompts you to *Specify opposite corner:*.
6. Size the rectangle so that the information you want to zoom in on is within the windowed area and pick another point in your drawing (see Figure 3-3).
7. After picking the second point, the windowed area is zoomed to fill the drawing display window (see Figure 3-4).

TIP It is also possible to zoom using a window by selecting the **Zoom** button on the right side of the Status Bar introduced in Chapter 1.

Zoom Previous	
Ribbon & Panel:	View | Navigate ⊘Previous
Standard Toolbar:	⊘
Menu:	View| Zoom| Previous
Command Line:	ZOOM
Command Alias:	Z

Zoom Previous. The **Zoom Previous** tool is probably the most popular of the zoom tools because it allows you to restore the previous drawing display. In fact, you can restore up to 10 previous views, so that you can step back in time. This capability allows you to zoom in on an area of your drawing to get close to your work (see Figure 3-4) and then quickly return to the previous overall view (see Figure 3-3). From there you can zoom in on other areas and then zoom back out again. The combination of the **Zoom Window** tool and the **Zoom Previous** tool provides one of the easiest, most efficient ways to navigate around your drawing.

AutoCAD stores up to 10 previous views. The following message is displayed at the command line if there is no previous view to display:

```
Command: No previous view saved.
```

Exercise 3-3: Using the Zoom Previous Tool

To access student data
files, go to
www.pearsondesigncentral.com.

1. Open the drawing **Willhome** located in the student data files.
2. Select the **Model** tab so that model space is active.
3. Select the **Zoom Extents** tool and zoom to the extents of the drawing.
4. Follow the steps shown in Exercise 3-2 and zoom in on an area of the drawing so that the drawing display looks similar to Figure 3-4.
5. Select the **Zoom Previous** tool on the **Navigate** panel.
6. The drawing information displayed in the drawing display window returns to the previous view.
7. Continue selecting the **Zoom Previous** tool until AutoCAD displays the following prompt at the command line:

```
No previous view saved.
```

Note: The **Zoom Previous** tool does not undo any drawing or editing commands and affects the display only.

Zoom Realtime	
Ribbon & Panel:	View | Navigate 🔍Realtime
Standard Toolbar:	🔍
Menu:	View| Zoom| Realtime
Command Line:	ZOOM
Command Alias:	Z

Zoom Realtime. Zooming in "realtime" simply means that the zooming process is interactive. As you zoom in, objects grow larger on the screen; as you zoom out, objects grow smaller.

Selecting the **Zoom Realtime** tool causes the mouse pointer to change to the magnifying glass icon shown in Figure 3-5.

Figure 3-5   The Zoom Realtime mouse pointer icon

Notice that there is a plus sign at the top right of the magnifying glass and a minus sign at the bottom left. Holding your mouse button down and moving the magnifying glass toward the top of the screen zooms in and increases the display magnification (+). See Figures 3-6A and 3-6B. Holding the button down and moving the magnifying glass toward the bottom of the screen zooms out and decreases the display magnification (−).

If you run out of mouse pad during the process of moving your mouse up or down the screen, just pick up your mouse, reposition it, and repeat the process. When you are finished zooming and the drawing display appears at the desired magnification factor, press **<Enter ↵>** or **<Esc>** to complete the zoom process.

TIP If you reach a point in zooming in or out when the display will not zoom any farther and appears stuck, don't worry. This just means that you need to regenerate your display using the **REGEN** command. The **REGEN** and **REGENALL** commands are discussed in detail later in the section "Cleaning Up the Drawing Display."

Figure 3-6A   Original **Zoom Realtime** mouse pointer position (bottom of screen)

Figure 3-6B   New **Zoom Realtime** mouse pointer position (top of screen)

Exercise 3-4: Using the Zoom Realtime Tool

1. Open the drawing **Willhome** located in the student data files.
2. Select the **Model** tab so that model space is active.
3. Select the **Zoom Extents** tool on the **Navigate** panel.
4. Select the **Zoom Realtime** tool on the **Navigate** panel.
5. Notice that your mouse pointer changes to a magnifying glass (see Figure 3-5).
6. Click with your mouse at the bottom of the drawing display window and hold the mouse button down (see Figure 3-6A).
7. Drag your mouse to the top of the drawing display window while continuing to hold the mouse button down.
8. Release the mouse button when the mouse pointer reaches the top of the drawing display window (see Figure 3-6B).
9. Click with your mouse at the top of the drawing display window and hold the mouse button down.
10. Drag your mouse to the bottom of the drawing display window while continuing to hold the mouse button down.
11. Release the mouse button when the mouse pointer reaches the bottom of the drawing display window.
12. Press **<Enter ↵>** or **<Esc>** to complete the zoom process.

Zoom Object	
Ribbon & Panel:	View | Navigate 🔍 Object
Zoom Toolbar:	🔍
Menu:	View| Zoom| Object
Command Line:	ZOOM
Command Alias:	Z

Zoom Object.   The **Zoom Object** tool allows you to zoom up on a selected object, or objects, so that it fills the entire drawing display area.

After selecting the **Zoom Object** tool, AutoCAD prompts you to select the object to zoom in on. Select the objects you want to zoom in on and press **<Enter↵>** to accept the selection. AutoCAD then zooms up on the object to fill the display as shown in Figure 3-7.

This **Zoom Object** tool is especially useful for updating text in a drawing. In this example, the section cut bubble was selected in the windowed view shown in Figure 3-3. You can now update the text and then select the **Zoom Previous** tool to return to the previous view.

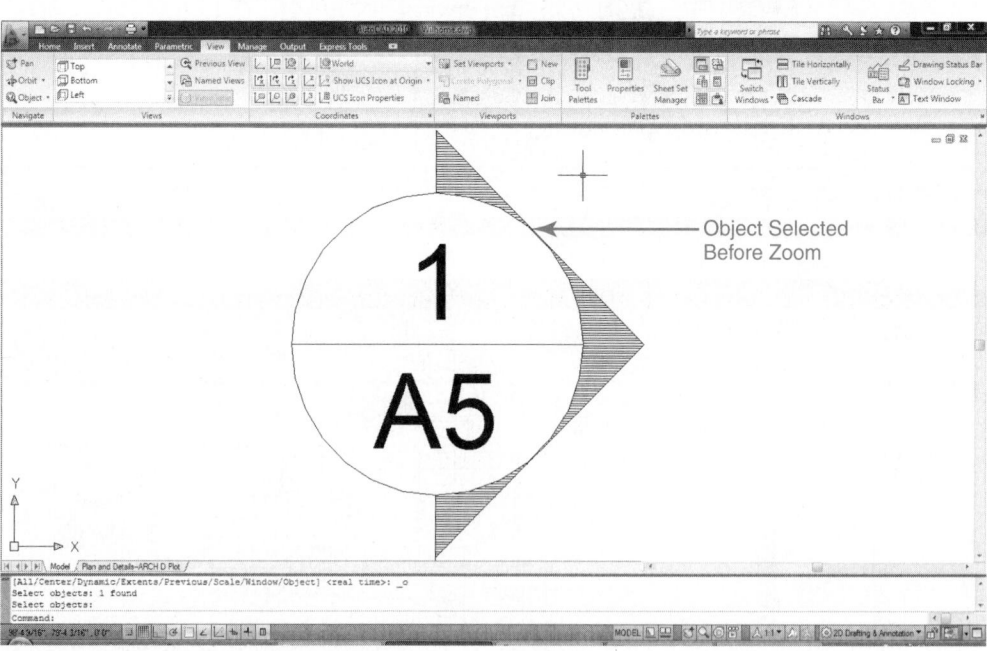

Figure 3-7   Display after object is zoomed

Exercise 3-5: Using the Zoom Object Tool

1. Open the drawing **Willhome** located in the student data files.
2. Select the **Model** tab so that model space is active.
3. Select the **Zoom Extents** tool and zoom to the extents of the drawing.

4. Follow the steps shown in Exercise 3-2 and zoom in on an area of the drawing so that the drawing display looks similar to Figure 3-3.
5. Select the **Zoom Object** tool on the **Navigate** panel. AutoCAD prompts you to *Select objects:*.
6. Select the section cut bubble labeled "1/A5" and press **<Enter↵>**.
7. The section cut bubble is zoomed so that it fills the whole drawing display (see Figure 3-7).
8. Double-click with your cursor on the "1/A5" text to display the **Enhanced Attribute Editor** dialog box.
9. Type **2** in the **Value:** text box and then select **OK** at the bottom of the dialog box.
10. Select the **Zoom Previous** tool so that the drawing display returns to the view shown in Figure 3-4.

Using the Mouse Wheel

If you have a wheel mouse, you can use the wheel to zoom in and out. Rolling the wheel toward the computer (away from you) zooms in to your drawing. Rolling the wheel away from the computer (toward you) will zoom out of your drawing.

Each click of the mouse wheel zooms in or out by 10 percent. You can change this zoom scale factor via the **ZOOMFACTOR** system variable. The **ZOOMFACTOR** default value is 60 and can be set to a value of between 3 and 100.

TIP   The mouse wheel also acts as a mouse button. In fact, it can be used to either pan your drawing display or display the **Object Snap** shortcut menu (see the next section, "Panning Around a Drawing"). It's also a little-known fact that double-clicking the wheel button will zoom to the extents of your drawing just like the **Zoom Extents** tool!

Exercise 3-6: Using the Mouse Wheel to Zoom In and Out

1. Open the drawing **Willhome** located in the student data files.
2. Select the **Model** tab so that model space is active.
3. Select the **Zoom Extents** tool and zoom to the extents of the drawing.
4. Roll the mouse wheel forward toward your computer screen.
5. The drawing display zooms in as you roll the mouse wheel forward.
6. Roll the mouse wheel away from the computer screen or toward yourself.
7. The drawing display zooms out as you roll the mouse wheel backward.
8. Double-click the mouse wheel button.
9. The drawing display is zoomed to the extents of the drawing.

To access student data files, go to www.pearsondesigncentral.com.

Note: In order to do this exercise, you must have a mouse with a thumb wheel.

PANNING AROUND A DRAWING

When you move a camera from side to side to change the subject matter displayed in the camera lens, it is referred to as *panning*. Borrowing yet another term from the world of photography, AutoCAD uses the term **pan** to describe the process of moving your drawing from side to side in the drawing display window.

Just as the subject matter doesn't move when you pan a camera, your drawing doesn't actually move, just what's shown in the display window so that you can view another area.

The different methods used to pan around your drawing are explained in the following sections.

pan: The process of moving your drawing from side to side in the display window so the location of the view changes without affecting the zoom scale

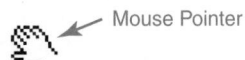

Figure 3-8 The **Pan** mouse pointer icon

Pan	
Ribbon & Panel:	View | Navigate
Standard Toolbar:	
Menu:	View| Pan| Realtime
Command Line:	PAN
Command Alias:	P

The Pan Tool

The **Pan** tool allows you to pan your drawing so that you can recenter it in the drawing display without affecting the current zoom display scale factor. This allows you to view drawing information quickly that might not be visible because it is off the side of the drawing display.

After you select the **Pan** tool, your mouse pointer changes to the hand icon shown in Figure 3-8.

Using the **Pan** tool, you simply grab on to the drawing with your "hand" by clicking with your mouse and then drag the drawing across the drawing display window by holding the mouse button down. See Figures 3-9A and 3-9B.

Like the **Zoom Realtime** tool, if you run out of mouse pad during the process of moving your mouse across the screen, just pick up your mouse, reposition it, and repeat the process. When you are finished panning and the drawing display contains the desired drawing information, press **<Enter ↵>** or **<Esc>** to complete the panning process.

> **TIP** You can quickly switch between the **Pan** tool and the **Zoom Realtime** tool by right-clicking to display the shortcut menu shown in Figure 3-10.

Figure 3-9A Original **Pan** mouse pointer position (right side of screen)

Mouse Pointer Position Before Pan

Mouse Pointer Position After Pan

Figure 3-9B New **Pan** mouse pointer position (left side of screen)

Exercise 3-7: Using the Pan Tool

1. Open the drawing **Willhome** located in the student data files.
2. Select the **Model** tab so that model space is active.
3. Select the **Zoom Extents** tool and zoom to the extents of the drawing.
4. Select the **Zoom In** tool to zoom in by a scale factor of 2.
5. Select the **Pan** tool on the **Navigate** panel.
6. The mouse pointer changes to a hand icon (see Figure 3-8), and AutoCAD prompts you at the command line:

   Press ESC or ENTER to exit, or right-click to display shortcut menu.

7. Place your mouse pointer at the right edge of the drawing display window (see Figure 3-9A).
8. Click with your mouse and drag the drawing display to the left by holding down the mouse button (see Figure 3-9B).
9. Release the left mouse button and then click the right mouse button to display the **Pan/Zoom** shortcut menu (see Figure 3-10).
10. Select **Zoom** from the menu to switch to the **Zoom Realtime** tool.
11. Zoom in and out of the drawing a few times using the **Zoom Realtime** tool.
12. Right-click with the mouse to display the **Pan/Zoom** shortcut menu again.
13. Select **Exit** from the menu to end the command.

To access student data files, go to www.pearsondesigncentral.com.

Figure 3-10   Pan/Zoom shortcut menu

TIP It is also possible to select the **Pan** tool via the **Pan** button on the right side of the Status Bar introduced in Chapter 1.

Using the Middle Mouse Button

As alluded to earlier in the section "Zooming In and Out of a Drawing," you can also use the wheel on a mouse as a button to either activate the **Pan** tool or display the **Object Snap** shortcut menu. The **MBUTTONPAN** system variable determines whether the **Pan** tool is activated or the **Object Snap** shortcut menu is displayed. It has the following settings:

MBUTTONPAN = 0: **Object Snap** shortcut menu displayed
MBUTTONPAN = 1: **Pan** tool activated (Default)

TIP Holding down the **<Ctrl>** key when you use the middle button of your mouse to activate the **Pan** tool will put you in "joystick" mode (see Figure 3-11) so that the mouse pointer acts like a game joystick.

Figure 3-11   Pan tool in "joystick" mode

Exercise 3-8: Using the Middle Mouse Button to Pan

1. Open the drawing **Willhome** located in the student data files.
2. Select the **Model** tab so that model space is active.
3. Select the **Zoom Extents** tool and zoom to the extents of the drawing.
4. Select the **Zoom In** tool to zoom in by a scale factor of 2.
5. Click the center mouse button or mouse wheel and hold it down. The mouse pointer changes to the hand icon (see Figure 3-8).
6. Hold the button down and pan back and forth in your drawing.

Note:
In order to do this exercise you must have a mouse with a center button or a thumb wheel, and the **MBUTTONPAN** system variable must be set to 1.

To access student data files, go to www.pearsondesigncentral.com.

7. Release the button.
8. Hold down the **<Ctrl>** key on your keyboard.
9. Click the center mouse button or mouse wheel and hold it down. The mouse pointer changes to the joystick icon (see Figure 3-11).
10. Hold the button down and pan around in your drawing.

PANNING AND ZOOMING TRANSPARENTLY

One of best things about the **Pan** and **Zoom** display tools is that you can use them *transparently*. Select the **Zoom Window** tool and check out the command line window (see Figure 3-12).

Notice that the **ZOOM** command is preceded by an apostrophe ('). The apostrophe is the flag that indicates that the **ZOOM** command can be run while another command is still active, hence the term *transparent*.

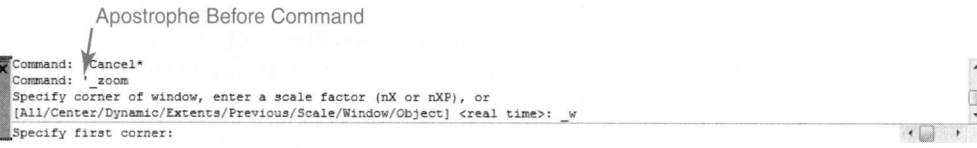

Apostrophe Before Command

```
Command: Cancel*
Command: '_zoom
Specify corner of window, enter a scale factor (nX or nXP), or
[All/Center/Dynamic/Extents/Previous/Scale/Window/Object] <real time>: _w
Specify first corner:
```

Figure 3-12   A transparent **Zoom** command

This ability allows you to pan and zoom in the middle of drawing or editing. For instance, you can begin drawing a line by selecting the first point in an overall view (see Figure 3-13A), use the **Zoom Window** tool to zoom closer to your work, and select the endpoint (see Figure 3-13B).

Check out the command line window in Figure 3-13B. When you are prompted for the corner points to define the window area, both prompts are preceded with double arrows (>>) to indicate the command is transparent. After the zoom process is complete and control passes back to the **LINE** command, AutoCAD displays the following prompt at the command line:

Resuming the LINE command.

The transparent display commands can be used in conjunction with almost every draw or modify command and can substantially increase both your precision and productivity.

Line Start Point   Cursor

Figure 3-13A   A transparent **Zoom** command

Line End Point

Transparent
Prefix (>>)

Figure 3-13B   A transparent **Zoom** command (continued)

Exercise 3-9: Panning and Zooming Transparently

1. Open the drawing **Willhome** located in the student data files.
2. Select the **Model** tab so that model space is active.
3. Select the **Zoom Extents** tool and zoom to the extents of the drawing.
4. Select the **Line** tool from the **Draw** panel. Auto-CAD prompts you:

   ```
   Specify first point:
   ```

5. Pick a point in your drawing to begin the line (see Figure 3-13A).
6. Select any of the **Zoom** or **Pan** tools explained so far in this chapter.
7. Zoom and pan around your drawing and change the drawing display.
8. Exit out of the **Zoom** or **Pan** command. Auto-CAD prompts you to select the next point of the line (see Figure 3-13B):

   ```
   Resuming LINE command.
   Specify next point or [Undo]:
   ```

9. Pick the next point for the line and press **<Enter ⏎>** to end the **LINE** command.

To access student data
files, go to
www.pearsondesigncentral.com.

Note:
The wheel mouse **Pan** and **Zoom Realtime** tools described earlier also work transparently, although there is no feedback at the command line in the form of an apostrophe.

GROUPING PAN AND ZOOM COMMANDS TOGETHER

It is possible to group consecutive zoom and pan operations into a single operation. Grouping consecutive zoom and pan operations together minimizes the steps required to return to previous views, saving time and increasing productivity. You can turn this feature on and off via the **Combine zoom and pan commands** check box in the **Undo/Redo** area at the bottom right of the **User Preferences** tab in the **Options** dialog box. It is on by default.

SPLITTING YOUR SCREEN INTO TILED VIEWPORTS

floating viewport: Paper space viewport created in a drawing layout tab that can have almost any size and shape and can also be modified using standard AutoCAD commands

tiled viewport: Rectangular model space viewport

isometric view: A pseudo-3D pictorial drawing in which three axes represent accurate measurements of the drawing model in order to show three sides of an object.

There are two distinctly different types of viewports in AutoCAD: *floating* and *tiled*. Floating viewports exist *only* in paper space and were first introduced in Chapter 2. Tiled viewports exist *only* in model space and are discussed next. Why the two different types, you might ask? The answer requires a little AutoCAD history lesson.

Before the paper space environment was introduced, all that existed in AutoCAD was the 3D model space environment. Multiple viewports were provided primarily to make it possible to view and work on different views of a 3D model simultaneously. See Figure 3-14.

The screen in Figure 3-14 has been split into four tiled viewports: a front view, a top view, a right-side view, and even an *isometric view*.

Each viewport can be panned and zoomed separately. Using tiled viewports, it is possible to work in any viewport and update all of the other viewports simultaneously. It is even possible to work between multiple viewports so that you can start a line in one viewport and end it in another. You can even move and copy selected objects between viewports.

The term *tiled* is used because model space viewports must abut each other with no space between them and no overlapping edges. These limitations stand in stark contrast to paper space floating viewports, which do not have to adhere to any of these requirements. Paper space viewports can be any shape or size, have space between them, and even overlap if necessary. Paper space viewports can also be edited using standard AutoCAD modify commands so that they can be moved and resized.

FOR MORE DETAILS Floating paper space viewports are discussed in detail in Chapter 14.

Figure 3-14   Four viewports shown tiled in model space

Viewports	
Ribbon & Panel:	View | Viewports
	New **New**
Viewports Toolbar:	
Menu:	View| Viewports| New Viewports... or View| Viewports| Named Viewports...
Command Line:	VPORTS
Command Alias:	None

Creating Viewports in Model Space

Both model space and paper space viewports are created using the same tool. The type of viewport(s) created depends on your current drawing environment. If you are in model space, tiled viewports are created. If you are in paper space, floating viewports are created.

To split your drawing display screen up into multiple tiled viewports, switch to model space and select the **Viewports** tool.

Figure 3-15 The **Viewports** dialog box

Selecting the **Viewports** tool displays the **Viewports** dialog box shown in Figure 3-15.

The **Viewports** dialog box provides a number of different viewport configurations that vary between one and four total viewports. Selecting a configuration on the left previews it in the **Preview** pane on the right.

You can apply the configuration to the current display screen, which is the default, or to the current viewport via the **Apply to:** list.

The **Setup:** list allows you to set up standard viewport configurations for 2D or 3D drawings.

After selecting the desired settings, select **OK** to display the viewport configuration on your screen.

Tiled viewports aren't just for working in 3D; they can also be utilized when creating 2D drawings. For example, you might have one viewport with an overall view of the drawing along with a few other viewports that are zoomed in on specific areas as shown in Figure 3-16.

The viewport setup shown in Figure 3-16 allows you to coordinate four different areas of a drawing at the same time.

Figure 3-16 2D application of tiled viewports

Saving and Restoring a Viewport Configuration

It is possible to save a tiled viewport configuration with a user-defined name so that it can be recalled later.

Saving a viewport configuration requires that you type in a name when you create the viewports in the **Viewports** dialog box as shown in Figure 3-17 and then select **OK**.

The **Named Viewports** tab of the **Viewports** dialog box allows you to restore a saved viewport configuration. See Figure 3-18. Highlight the configuration you want to restore and select **OK** to restore the viewport configuration on your screen.

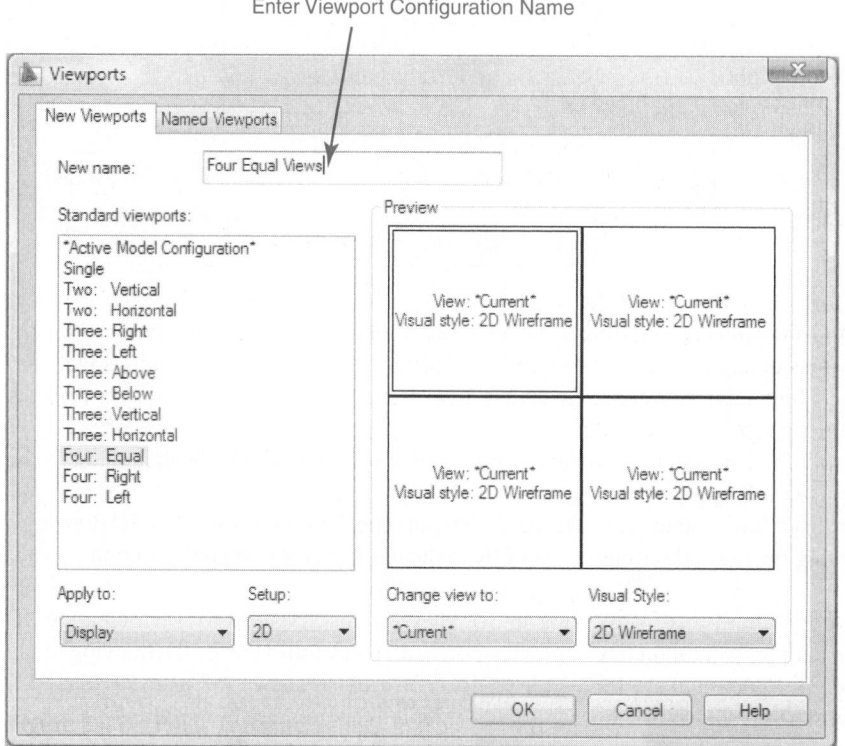

Figure 3-17   Saving a viewport configuration

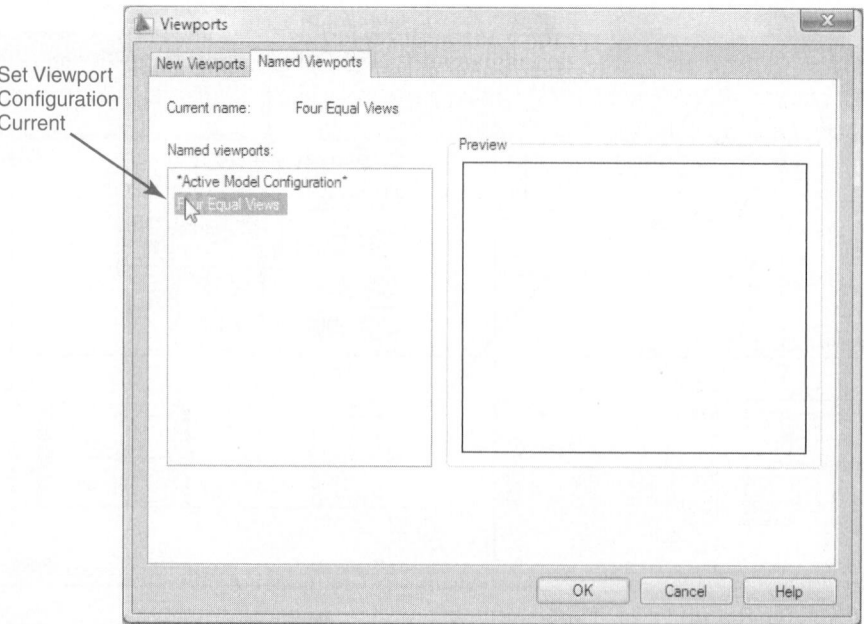

Figure 3-18   The **Named Viewports** tab of the **Viewports** dialog box

Exercise 3-10: Working with Tiled Viewports

1. Open the drawing **Willhome** located in the student data files.
2. Select the **Model** tab so that model space is active.
3. Select the **Zoom Extents** tool and zoom to the extents of the drawing.
4. Select the **New** tool from the **Viewports** panel on the **View** ribbon to display the **Viewports** dialog box (see Figure 3-15).
5. Select the **Four: Equal** viewport configuration from the **Standard viewports:** list box.
6. Type **Four Equal** in the **New name:** text box.
7. Select **OK** to close the **Viewports** dialog box and return to the drawing.
8. The drawing display changes to four equal tiled viewports (see Figure 3-16).
9. Click with the mouse pointer in the upper left viewport to make it active.
10. Change the view in the upper left viewport to the Powder Room elevations using the pan and zoom techniques explained in this chapter.
11. Click with the mouse pointer in the lower left viewport to make it active.
12. Change the view to display the Kitchen elevations using the pan and zoom techniques explained in this chapter.
13. Click with the mouse pointer in the lower right viewport to make it active.
14. Change the view to display the Fireplace elevations using the pan and zoom techniques explained in this chapter.
15. Click with the mouse pointer in the upper right viewport to make it active.
16. Use the **Zoom Extents** tool to zoom to the extents of the drawing.
17. Save the drawing as **EX3-10**.

To access student data files, go to www.pearsondesigncentral.com.

CLEANING UP THE DRAWING DISPLAY

Occasionally it is necessary to "clean up" the drawing display area. This can range from removing the blip marks left on the screen when the **BLIPMODE** system variable is turned on (see below) to recalculating the entire display because information on a layer that was frozen does not redisplay when it is thawed (see Chapter 6). AutoCAD provides a few commands that serve this cleanup purpose. They are explained in the following sections.

The REDRAW Command

The **REDRAW** command is primarily used to remove the small crosses, known as *blips,* that appear on your screen when the system variable **BLIPMODE** has been turned on. By default, **BLIPMODE** is turned off. Turning **BLIPMODE** on displays the blips shown on the screen every time you pick a point in your drawing (see Figure 3-19).

Blips appear for any action that requires a pick point, from drawing lines to selecting existing objects for modification. You can see how quickly your drawing can get cluttered. To clean up the screen, enter **REDRAW** at the AutoCAD command line, or even easier, simply enter **R<Enter ⏎>**, the command alias for the **REDRAW** command. Entering either the command or its alias will instantly clean up the screen and remove all the blips.

The REGEN and REGENALL Commands

The **REGEN** and **REGENALL** commands are like the **REDRAW** command on steroids. Unlike the **REDRAW** command, the **REGEN** commands completely recalculate, or regenerate, your drawing display, updating all drawing objects. So not only are blips cleaned up, but information that is on layers that did not reappear after a layer was thawed is redisplayed and all curved objects such as circles, arcs, and splines are recalculated so that they appear much smoother.

Figure 3-20 shows what occasionally happens when you zoom in on a circle after being zoomed out in a drawing.

Blips

Figure 3-19 Blips created when **BLIPMODE** system variable is turned on

Jagged Straight
Chord Segments

Figure 3-20 Zoomed circle before the **REGEN** command is used

AutoCAD approximates the curve using straight chord segments. This approximation is done primarily to accelerate display performance. To smooth out the curve, you can enter **REGEN<Enter ⏎>**, or **RE<Enter ⏎>**, at the AutoCAD command line. Entering either will totally recalculate the display so that the curve is smoothed out as shown in Figure 3-21.

The **REGENALL** command allows you to regenerate multiple viewports at the same time if you have split up your display using the techniques shown in the previous section, "Splitting Your Screen into Tiled Viewports." The command alias for the **REGENALL** command is **REA**. The **REGENALL** command works for both tiled viewports (model space) and floating viewports (paper space).

Smoothed Curve

Figure 3-21   Zoomed circle after the **REGEN** command is used

Exercise 3-11: Regenerating the Drawing Display

1. Start a new drawing using the acad.dwt drawing template.
2. Type **BLIPMODE<Enter ⏎>**.
3. AutoCAD prompts you to turn the **BLIPMODE** system variable on or off:

   Enter mode [ON/OFF] <OFF>:

4. To turn **BLIPMODE** on, either select **On** from the command option list or type **ON<Enter ⏎>**.
5. Pick a bunch of points in the drawing display area with the mouse.
6. Small crosses, or blips, are located at every pick point (see Figure 3-19).
7. Type **R<Enter ⏎>** at the AutoCAD command line to run the **REDRAW** command.
8. The drawing display is refreshed so that all the small crosses disappear.
9. Select the **Zoom All** tool to zoom to the limits of the drawing.
10. Draw a tiny circle at the center of the drawing display using the **CIRCLE** command introduced in Chapter 2.
11. Select the **Zoom Window** tool and zoom in so the circle fills the drawing display.
12. The perimeter of the circle should appear jagged (see Figure 3-20).
13. Type **RE<Enter ⏎>** at the AutoCAD command line to run the **REGEN** command.
14. The drawing display is regenerated so that the perimeter of the circle is now smooth (see Figure 3-21).
15. Open the drawing **EX3-10.DWG** if it is not open already.
16. Select the **Model** tab so that model space is active.
17. Type **REA<Enter ⏎>** at the AutoCAD command line to run the **REGENALL** command.
18. All four viewports are regenerated.
19. Turn **BLIPMODE** off by typing **BLIPMODE <Enter.⏎>** and typing or selecting **Off**.

The Clean Screen Toggle

The **Clean Screen** toggle temporarily turns off the ribbon and any toolbars and palettes so that you have more room to draw because sometimes the screen can get a bit cluttered. See Figure 3-22.

Figure 3-22 is an extreme example of what your screen might look like if you turned on every AutoCAD toolbar and palette. Fortunately, AutoCAD provides a way out of this mess.

Drawing Window

Figure 3-22   Where's my drawing?

Clean Screen
Toggle Button

The **CLEANSCREENON** command turns the ribbon, toolbars, and palettes off while the **CLEANSCREENOFF** command turns them back on. You can toggle **Clean Screen** on and off by clicking on the button on the right side of the Status Bar as shown in Figure 3-22.

Selecting **Clean Screen** will turn off the ribbon, toolbars, and palettes and maximize your drawing area as shown in Figure 3-23.

When **Clean Screen** is turned on, your drawing display is maximized to completely fill your Windows desktop so that the Windows taskbar is no longer available. You must turn **Clean Screen** off in order to access the Windows taskbar again.

TIP   You can also use the **<Ctrl>+0** keyboard combination to toggle **Clean Screen** on and off.

Figure 3-23   Drawing display with **Clean Screen** turned on

Exercise 3-12: Toggling Clean Screen On and Off

1. Start a new drawing using the acad.dwt drawing template.
2. Select the **Clean Screen** button on the right side of the Status Bar.
3. The ribbon and any toolbars are temporarily turned off, and the drawing display area is increased.
4. Select the **Clean Screen** button on the Status Bar again.
5. The ribbon and any toolbars that were turned off are turned back on again, and the drawing display returns to its previous size.
6. Use the **<Ctrl>+0** keyboard combination to turn **Clean Screen** on and off again.

DRAWING DISPLAY RESOLUTION AND PERFORMANCE

There are a number of AutoCAD settings that can be used to control the resolution of drawing objects on your screen and, in turn, enhance your computer's performance when regenerating the drawing display. With the advent of high-performance computers and workstations, some of the settings described in this section have lost a little significance.

All the display settings can be managed on the **Display** tab of the **Options** dialog box. See Figure 3-24.

Figure 3-24   **Display** tab of **Options** dialog box

Controlling Arc and Circle Smoothness

AutoCAD uses short vectors, or chords, to represent radial geometry such as arcs, circles, ellipses, and splines on the drawing display. These chords are not typically noticeable until you zoom in on a curved surface like a circle without regenerating your drawing (see Figure 3-20).

The number of chords used to represent a curve and determine its smoothness is controlled via the **Arc and circle smoothness** setting in the **Display** tab of the **Options** dialog box shown in Figure 3-24. Settings can range from 1 to 20,000. The default setting is 1000. Setting this number higher makes curved surfaces appear smoother by increasing the number of vectors used to represent each curve. This increased resolution does come at a cost in performance, however. The higher the number, the longer it takes to regenerate your drawing.

Exercise 3-13: Controlling Arc and Circle Smoothness

1. Start a new drawing using the acad.dwt drawing template.
2. Select the **Options** button from the bottom of the **Application Menu** list to display the **Options** dialog box.
3. Select the **Display** tab.
4. Increase the **Arc and circle smoothness** setting in the **Display resolution** area at the top right of the dialog box from the default value of **1000** to **10,000**.
5. Select **OK** to close the **Options** dialog box and return to the drawing.
6. Select the **Zoom Extents** tool to zoom to the limits of the drawing.
7. Draw a tiny circle at the center of the drawing display using the **CIRCLE** command introduced in Chapter 2.
8. Select the **Zoom Window** tool and zoom in so the circle fills the drawing display (see Figure 3-20).
9. The perimeter of the circle should appear smooth (see Figure 3-21).

> **Note:** The Arc and circle smoothness setting can also be controlled via the VIEWRES command. Type VIEWRES at the AutoCAD command line and enter a value between 1 and 20,000. This VIEWRES setting is saved with the drawing.

Turning Text Display On and Off

Text is one of the most resource-intensive object types in an AutoCAD drawing because of its detail. If you have a large drawing with lots of text (see Figure 3-25A), regenerating a drawing can become a time-consuming task. To help, AutoCAD provides a way to turn text off in a drawing so that only a boundary frame outline of the text is visible (see Figure 3-25B).

This allows you to still locate each text object in a drawing but not have to regenerate it in finite detail. To turn off text display in a drawing, select the **Show text boundary frame only** check box on the **Display** tab of the **Options** dialog box shown in Figure 3-24. After turning the text display off, you must regenerate the drawing in order to see the results.

Text Boundary Frames Off

Figure 3-25A Text display on

Text Boundary Frames On

Figure 3-25B   Text display off

Exercise 3-14: Turning Text Display On and Off

1. Open the drawing **Willhome** located in the student data files.
2. Select the **Model** tab so that model space is active.
3. Select the **Zoom Extents** tool and zoom to the extents of the drawing.
4. Select the **Options** button from the bottom of the **Application Menu** to display the **Options** dialog box.
5. Select the **Display** tab.
6. Select the **Show text boundary frame only** option in the **Display performance** area at the middle right of the dialog box so it is turned on (checked).
7. Select **OK** to close the **Options** dialog box and return to the drawing.
8. Zoom in on an area of the drawing that contains text.
9. Type **RE<Enter ↵>** to run the **REGEN** command.
10. All text is turned off so only the rectangular boundary frames are visible.
11. Select the **Options** button from the bottom of the **Application Menu** to display the **Options** dialog box.
12. Select the **Display** tab.
13. Select the **Show text boundary frame only** option in the **Display performance** area at the middle right of the dialog box so it is turned off (unchecked).
14. Select **OK** to close the **Options** dialog box and return to the drawing.
15. Select the **Zoom Extents** tool and zoom to the extents of the drawing.
16. Type **RE<Enter ↵>** at the AutoCAD command line to run the **REGEN** command.
17. All text is turned back on so it is visible.

To access student data files, go to www.pearsondesigncentral.com.

> **Note:**
> The **Show text boundary frame only** setting can also be controlled via the **QTEXTMODE** system variable. Setting **QTEXTMODE = 1** turns off text display and turns on text boundary frames. Setting **QTEXTMODE = 0** will turn text back on in a drawing. This **QTEXTMODE** setting is saved with the drawing.

Turning Fills On and Off

Like text, hatch patterns and solid filled areas are also very resource-intensive. Many hatched and/or solid filled areas in a drawing can significantly increase the time it takes to regenerate the drawing display. Fortunately, you can turn off hatch patterns and solid fills by deselecting (unchecking) the **Apply solid fill** check box on the **Display** tab in the **Options** dialog box shown in Figure 3-24. After turning solid fill areas off you must regenerate the drawing in order to see the results.

Exercise 3-15: Turning Fill Areas On and Off

To access student data files, go to www.pearsondesigncentral.com.

1. Open the drawing **Plot Screening and Fill Areas** located in the student data files.
2. Select the **Model** tab so that model space is active.
3. Select the **Zoom Extents** tool and zoom to the extents of the drawing.
4. Select the **Option** button from the bottom of the **Application Menu** to display the **Options** dialog box.
5. Select the **Display** tab.
6. Select the **Apply solid fill** option in the **Display performance** area at middle right of the dialog box so that it is turned off (unchecked).
7. Select **OK** to close the **Options** dialog box and return to the drawing.
8. Type **RE<Enter ↵>** at the AutoCAD command line to run the **REGEN** command.
9. All filled areas are now turned off.
10. Select the **Options** button from the bottom of the **Application Menu** again to display the **Options** dialog box.
11. Select the **Display** tab.
12. Select the **Apply solid fill** option in the **Display performance** area at the middle right of the dialog box so that it is turned on (checked).
13. Select **OK** to close the **Options** dialog box and return to the drawing.
14. Type **RE<Enter ↵>** at the AutoCAD command line to run the **REGEN** command.
15. All filled areas are now turned back on.

Note:
The **Apply solid fill** setting can also be controlled via the **FILLMODE** system variable. Setting **FILLMODE** = 0 turns off hatching, solid fills, gradient fills, and wide polylines. Setting **FILLMODE** = 1 turns hatching, solid fills, gradient fills, and wide polylines back on in a drawing. This **FILLMODE** setting is saved with the drawing.

Chapter Summary

Mastering the drawing display tools and settings explained in this chapter will help to make you a more productive and precise drafter. Because there is not one display tool that provides all the ideal functionality, practice using a combination of tools to navigate around your drawing as you are working. Experiment with the different display settings and see how they affect your drawing display and performance. Eventually, you will settle on the tools and settings with which you are most comfortable.

Chapter Test Questions

Multiple Choice

1. The AutoCAD drawing display is similar to a:
   a. Telescope
   b. TV screen
   c. Mirror
   d. Camera lens

2. To make drawing objects appear larger on the screen, you should:
   a. Zoom out
   b. Zoom in
   c. Get a bigger computer monitor
   d. Pan

3. Almost all the **Zoom** tools are available on what ribbon?
   a. **View**
   b. **Input**
   c. **Output**
   d. **Home**

4. The **Zoom Realtime** tool allows you to:
   a. Zoom in and zoom out
   b. Zoom interactively
   c. Draw faster
   d. All of the above

5. The **Zoom Window** tool zooms in your drawing when you:
   a. Choose a view
   b. Pick two points
   c. Pick one point
   d. Specify a scale factor

6. The **Zoom Object** tool will zoom in on:
   a. Text
   b. Circles
   c. Lines
   d. All of the above

7. To move the drawing display area back and forth without changing the drawing's zoom scale factor, you should use:
   a. **Pan** tool
   b. Middle mouse button
   c. Scroll bars
   d. All of the above

8. The system variable that controls whether the middle mouse button activates the **Pan** tool is:
   a. **MOUSEPANBUTTON**
   b. **MIDDLEBUTTONPAN**
   c. **MBUTTONPAN**
   d. **MPAN**

9. Entering a command transparently allows you to:
   a. Not see the command at the command line window
   b. Use the command while another command is already active

   c. Temporarily turn off the drawing display
   d. All of the above

10. Double-clicking the mouse wheel will:
    a. Display the **Object Snap** shortcut menu
    b. Put the mouse in joystick mode
    c. Pan the display
    d. **Zoom Extents**

11. Viewports that are created in model space are referred to as:
    a. Floating viewports
    b. Stacked viewports
    c. Cascading viewports
    d. Tiled viewports

12. Which command will clean up and refresh the drawing display?
    a. **REDRAW**
    b. **REGEN**
    c. **REGENALL**
    d. All of the above

13. The **Clean Screen** toggle allows you to:
    a. Clean up blips created when **BLIPMODE** is turned on
    b. Turn off the ribbon, toolbars, and palettes
    c. Erase all objects displayed on the screen
    d. Clear smudge marks off your screen

Matching

a. **Zoom Realtime** tool
b. **Zoom Window** tool
c. **Zoom Previous** tool
d. **Zoom Extents** tool
e. **ZOOMFACTOR** system variable
f. **Zoom Object** tool
g. **Pan** tool
h. **VIEWRES** system variable
i. Tiled viewport

1. Zooms to the outermost visible drawing objects
2. Returns to the previously zoomed view
3. Zooms in on an object or objects
4. Zooms interactively
5. Controls mouse thumbwheel zoom increment
6. Controls arc and circle smoothness
7. Viewport created in model space
8. Pans interactively
9. Zooms to a user-defined rectangular area

CHAPTER PROJECTS

Project 3-1: Using the Zoom Tools

1. Open the drawing **Willhome** located in the student data files.
2. Select the **Model** tab so that model space is active.
3. Select the **Zoom Extents** tool and zoom to the extents of the drawing.
4. Use the **Zoom Object** tool to zoom in on the "Breakfast" room label text at the top of the floor plan.
5. Double-click on the text and change it to "Breakfast Nook" using the **Edit Text** dialog box.
6. Zoom to the extents of the drawing.
7. Save the drawing as **P3-1**.

To access student data files, go to www.pearsondesigncentral.com.

Project 3-2: Creating Tiled Viewports

1. Open drawing **P3-1**.
2. Create the four tiled model space viewports using the **Four: Left** standard viewport option.
3. Use the **Zoom** and **Pan** tools to set up each viewport so that the drawing areas listed in the following table are displayed in the corresponding viewport:

Viewport	View Area
Top Left	Kitchen Area
Middle Left	Breakfast Area
Bottom Left	Laundry Area
Right	Floor Plan

4. Save the drawing as **P3-2**.

Project 3-3: Changing Display Resolution and Performance Settings

1. Open drawing **P3-2**.
2. Turn off the text display so only the text boundary boxes are visible.
3. Regenerate all the viewports.
4. Turn off all solid fill areas.
5. Regenerate all the viewports.
6. Increase the arc and circle smoothness factor to 10,000.
7. Regenerate all the viewports.
8. Change the drawing display from four viewports to a default single viewport.
9. Save the drawing as **P3-3**.

Basic Drawing Commands

4

Chapter Objectives

- Create a new drawing
- Establish the drawing units
- Set the drawing limits
- Create lines, circles, and arcs
- Create ellipses and elliptical arcs
- Create point objects and control their size and appearance
- Divide and measure using point objects

INTRODUCTION

The vast majority of drawings are comprised of three basic drawing elements: lines, circles, and arcs. The size, location, color, line width, and linetype may vary. They may even be combined or joined together to create more complex objects. But most drawings can be broken down to these three basic elements. Chapter 2 gave you a quick introduction to these basic drawing objects. In this chapter, we'll take a closer look at these basic drawing commands as well as ellipses and points. We'll also examine some ways to control precisely the placement of AutoCAD objects and take a closer look at the various ways to create new drawings.

DRAWING SETUP

AutoCAD provides a number of ways to get started in a drawing. In Chapter 2, you used a drawing template to quickly start a new drawing with a number of preconfigured settings. Templates make starting a drawing quick and easy.

Templates

Drawing templates are simply drawings that have been set up and saved as templates with the file extension *dwt*. AutoCAD comes with a number of predefined templates for various page sizes and industry standards. They typically have specific unit settings, title blocks, layer definitions, page layouts, dimension styles, and so on. The template acad.dwt is the default template. When you start a new session of AutoCAD, the blank drawing you see is created from the acad.dwt drawing template.

Any drawing can be saved as a template. To save a drawing as a template, choose **Save as** from the **Application Menu** and choose **AutoCAD Drawing Template** to display the **Save Drawing As** dialog box (see Figure 4-1).

By default, drawing templates are stored in a folder named **Template** that is created by AutoCAD.

Figure 4-1   Creating a drawing template

You can specify a different default template folder by changing the **Default Template File Location** setting under **Template settings** on the **Files** tab of the AutoCAD **Options** dialog box.

Units	
Application Menu:	Drawing Units
Toolbar:	None
Menu:	Format| Units...
Command Line:	UNITS
Command Alias:	UN

Units

Typically, the first step in setting up your drawing is to set the drawing units. Chapter 1 discussed the fact that AutoCAD is, for the most part, a unitless environment. One unit in AutoCAD can represent any measurement you want (1 inch, 1 foot, 1 millimeter, 1 meter, 1 nautical league, or even 1 parsec). The **UNITS** command allows you to control how AutoCAD displays units. It is located on the **Drawing Utilities** menu on the **Application Menu** (big "A").

The **UNITS** command displays the **Drawing Units** dialog box (see Figure 4-2).

The **Drawing Units** dialog box allows you to set how both linear and angular measurements are displayed.

Note:
The **UNITS** command controls only how units are displayed in the drawing. It does not control how geometry is stored nor does it control the precision of the geometry.

Linear Units.   The **Length** settings control how linear units are displayed. You can choose from among five different linear unit display options: **Decimal, Engineering, Architectural, Fractional**, and **Scientific**. They are described in the following table.

Figure 4-2   The **Drawing Units** dialog box

Decimal	This is the default format for displaying units. The **Decimal** setting is unitless in that decimal units can represent any unit of measurement. In general, you should note on your drawing which drawing units you are using.
Engineering	Engineering units are based on Imperial feet-inch units. 1 unit is 1″ and 12 units are 1′. Inches are displayed in decimal units. For example, 15½″ would be displayed as 1′-3.5″.
Architectural	Architectural units are similar to engineering units except inches are displayed as fractions. For example, 15½″ would be displayed as 1′-3½″.
Fractional	Fractional units are similar to decimal units except that numbers are represented as fractions. For example, 15.5 units would display as 15½. Like the **Decimal** setting, the fractional setting is unitless.
Scientific	Scientific unit display uses exponential notation. For example, 15.5 would display as 1.5500E+01 (1.55×10^1). Like the decimal and fractional unit displays, scientific unit display is unitless.

There is also a **Precision** drop-down list that allows you to set the round-off setting for each unit type. The precision setting controls how precisely the number is displayed. The units are rounded off to the specified level of precision. It is important to note that this affects only how units are displayed on the screen. AutoCAD still stores numbers accurately; the numbers are simply rounded off when displayed on screen.

Angular Units. The **Angular** area controls how angles are input and displayed.

Note:
You can enter feet (′) and inches (″) only when drawing units are set to either **Architectural** or **Engineering**. If you try to enter either unit designation when drawing units are set to anything else, AutoCAD will reject the entry and display the following ambiguous message at the command line: Point or option keyword required. If you are using Dynamic Input, a bright red border is displayed around the distance input box and you are forced to reenter a valid input value.

Decimal Degrees	This is the default format for displaying angular measurements. 1 unit equals 1 degree.
Deg/Min/Sec	Degrees Minutes and Seconds. With this format, there are 360 degrees in a full circle, 60 minutes in 1 degree, and 60 seconds in 1 minute. A 30-degree angle would display as 30d0′0″ where d denotes degrees, ′ denotes minutes, and ″ denotes seconds. Latitude and longitude are typically displayed using Deg/Min/Sec.
Grads	400 grads = 360 degrees. 1 grad is roughly 0.9 degree.
Radians	Radians are measured as multiples of pi (Π). 2pi radians (~6.28r) equals 360 degrees. Pi radians (3.14r) is 180 degrees.
Surveyor's Units	Surveyor's units show angles as bearings, using N or S for north or south, degrees/minutes/seconds to denote how far east or west the angle is from direct north or south, and E or W for east or west. For example, N 45d0′0″ E represents 45 degrees from north in the east direction (45 degrees in decimal units). Angles are always less than 90 degrees and are displayed in the Deg/Min/Sec format. You can simply use E, N, W, and S to represent 0, 90, 180, and 270 degrees, respectively.

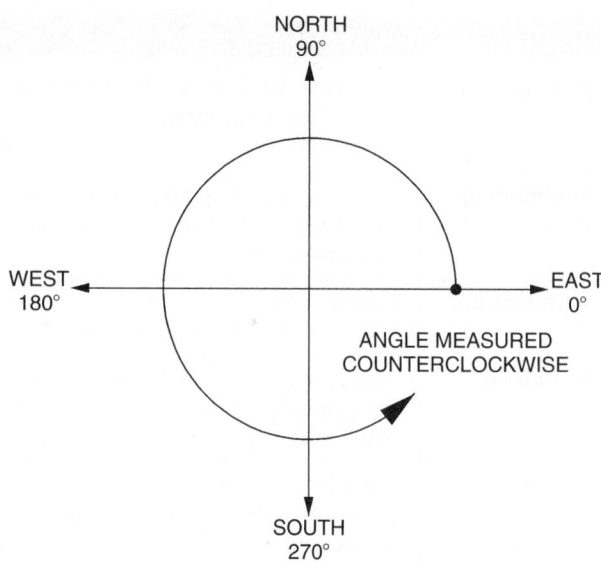

Figure 4-3 Angular measurements

The **Precision** drop-down list works the same for angular units as it does for linear units. The **Clockwise** check box allows you to change the direction that angles are measured. By default, angles are measured in a counterclockwise direction (see Figure 4-3).

Putting a check in the **Clockwise** box changes the direction of angular measurement so that 90 degrees is south, and 270 degrees is north.

Exercise 4-1: Setting the Drawing Units

1. Start a new drawing using the acad.dwt drawing template.
2. On the **Application Menu**, choose **Units** from the **Drawing Utilities** menu. The **Drawing Units** dialog box is displayed.
3. In the **Length** area, choose **Decimal** from the **Type** drop-down list and set the **Precision** to **0.00** (2 decimal places).
4. In the **Angle** area, choose **Decimal Degrees** from the **Type** drop-down list and set the **Precision** to **0.0** (1 decimal place).
5. Make sure there is no check in the **Clockwise** box and the **Insertion scale** is set to **Inches**. Choose **OK** to close the dialog box.
6. Save your drawing as **EX4-1**.

Setting the Drawing Area

AutoCAD provides an unlimited space for you to create your drawing. Chapter 1 discussed the concept of drawing objects their actual size. You'll want to set up a large drawing area to draw large objects and a small drawing area to draw small ones. In model space, the drawing area is not critical and can be changed at any time. In layout (paper) space, the drawing area determines the paper size. The drawing area is set up using the **LIMITS** command in model space.

When you start the **LIMITS** command, AutoCAD will ask you to specify two points: the lower left corner and the upper right corner. These two corners determine the drawing area.

Note: The **ZOOM ALL** command will zoom your drawing to fit the drawing area to your screen.

Limits	
Ribbon & Panel:	None
Toolbar:	None
Menu:	F̲ormat| Dra̲wing Limits...
Command Line:	LIMITS
Command Alias:	None

Exercise 4-2: Setting the Drawing Limits

1. Continue from Exercise 4-1.
2. Type **limits <Enter ↲>**. AutoCAD prompts you to *Specify lower left corner or ↓*.
3. Press **<Enter ↲>** to accept the default setting of 0,0. AutoCAD then prompts you to *Specify upper right corner <12.00,9.00>:*.

4. Type **11,8.5<Enter ↵>** to set the upper right corner. You now have an 11 × 8.5 drawing area.
5. Save your drawing as **EX4-2**.

DRAWING LINES

In Chapter 2, we used the **LINE** command to create some simple geometric shapes. Lines are one of the fundamental drawing objects in AutoCAD. As you've seen, when you start the **LINE** command, AutoCAD prompts you for the first (or start) point and then prompts you for the next point. AutoCAD then simply draws a straight line segment between those two points. AutoCAD will continue to prompt you for the next point and continue to draw line segments until you either press **<Enter ↵>** or cancel the command by pressing **<Esc>**.

While drawing line segments, you have two options available: **Undo** and **Close**. The **Undo** option will delete the last line segment and resume drawing from the end of the previous line segment.

The **Close** option will draw a line segment from the last specified point to the point specified at the start of the **LINE** command. For example, in Figure 4-4, if you draw line segments from point A to B to C and to D, selecting the **Close** option would draw a line segment from point D to A. The **Close** option is available only after three points are specified.

Line	
Ribbon & Panel:	Home| Draw
Draw Toolbar:	
Menu:	Draw|Line
Command Line:	LINE
Command Alias:	L

D _____ C

A   B

Figure 4-4   Using the **Close** option

Exercise 4-3: Drawing Lines

1. Continue from Exercise 4-2. Toggle the **Dynamic Input** setting **OFF** on the Status Bar.
2. Start the **LINE** command. AutoCAD prompts you to:

   `Specify first point:`

3. Type **2,2<Enter ↵>**. AutoCAD places the first point and drags a rubber-band line from that point. AutoCAD then prompts you to:

   `Specify next point or [Undo]:`

4. Type **10,2<Enter ↵>**. AutoCAD places the second point and draws a line segment from the first point to the second. AutoCAD then drags a rubber-band line from the second point and prompts you to:

   `Specify next point or [Undo]:`

5. Type **16,3<Enter ↵>**. AutoCAD places the third point and prompts you to:

   `Specify next point or [Close/Undo]:`

   Since you have specified three points, the **Close** option is now available.

6. Type **U<Enter ↵>** to undo the third point. AutoCAD now drags a rubber-band line from the second point and prompts you to:

   `Specify next point or [Undo]:`

   Since you have now specified only two points, the **Close** option is no longer available.

7. Type **6,10<Enter ↵>**. AutoCAD places the new third point and prompts you to:

   `Specify next point or [Close/Undo]:`

   Since you have specified three points, the **Close** option is available again.

8. Type **C<Enter ↵>** to close the shape. AutoCAD draws a line from the third point back to the first point and ends the **LINE** command. Your drawing should now resemble Figure 4-5.

9. Save your drawing as **EX4-3**.

Figure 4-5   Drawing lines

COORDINATE ENTRY METHODS

As you've seen, to place objects in AutoCAD, you need to specify where in the drawing you want to place them. For example, when drawing a line, AutoCAD prompts you to *Specify first point:* and to *Specify next point:*. This process of specifying point locations is called ***coordinate entry***. Auto-CAD uses two basic types of coordinate systems: Cartesian coordinates and polar coordinates.

coordinate entry: The process of specifying point locations

Cartesian Coordinates

In Chapter 1, we discussed the Cartesian coordinate system, where 0,0 is the origin and a point location is described as an *X* and *Y* coordinate (see Figure 4-6).

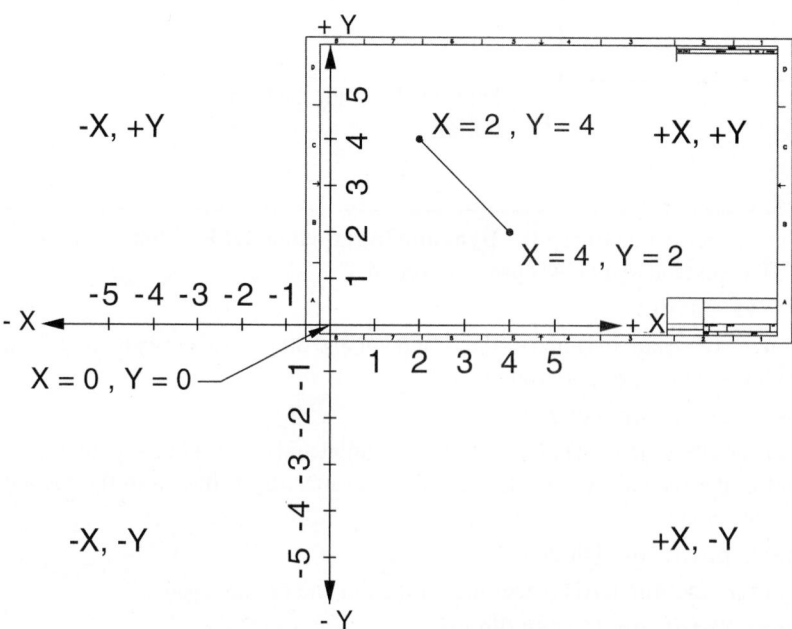

Figure 4-6   The Cartesian coordinate system

Using this system, it's possible to describe accurately any position on a two-dimensional plane. However, while it is possible to use basic Cartesian coordinates all the time, it is not always practical or efficient to do so. For example, let's look at a 2 × 2 square with its lower left corner located at the coordinate 3,2. To describe this square using Cartesian coordinates, you would need to calculate the location of each corner by taking the starting coordinate (3,2) and adding the dimensions to the respective *X* and *Y* coordinates (see Figure 4-7).

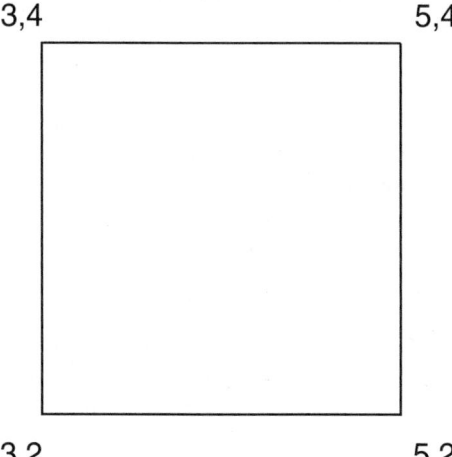

3,4   5,4

3,2   5,2

Figure 4-7   2 × 2 square coordinates

Exercise 4-4: Drawing with Cartesian Coordinates

1. Open the drawing **EX4-2**. Toggle the **Dynamic Input** setting **OFF**.
2. Start the **LINE** command. AutoCAD prompts you to:

   `Specify first point:`
3. Type **3,2<Enter ↵>**. AutoCAD places the first point and prompts you to:

   `Specify next point or [Undo]:`
4. Type **5,2<Enter ↵>**. AutoCAD places the second point and prompts you to:

   `Specify next point or [Undo]:`
5. Type **5,4<Enter ↵>**. AutoCAD places the third point and prompts you to:

   `Specify next point or [Close/Undo]:`
6. Type **3,4<Enter ↵>**. AutoCAD places the fourth point and prompts you to:

   `Specify next point or [Close/Undo]:`
7. Type **C<Enter ↵>** to close the square and end the **LINE** command. Your drawing should now resemble Figure 4-8.
8. Save your drawing as **EX4-4**.

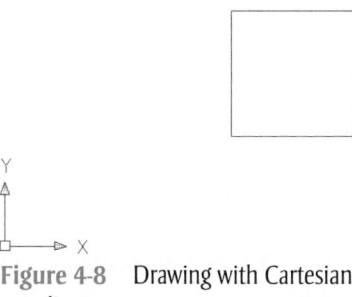

Figure 4-8   Drawing with Cartesian coordinates

Although drawing using only Cartesian coordinates is possible, it's not an efficient way to draw. The coordinates in the previous exercise are fairly simple, but the problem is made more difficult if the square is rotated or the points do not lie on easily determined coordinates.

To address these issues, AutoCAD gives you some additional ways of specifying coordinates.

Absolute Versus Relative Coordinate Entry

When specifying Cartesian coordinates, you are telling AutoCAD to measure from the absolute origin of the drawing (0,0). For example, if you specified the point 4,2, you are telling AutoCAD to start at the origin and go to the point measured 4 units in the positive X direction and 2 units in the positive Y direction (see Figure 4-6). This is known as *absolute coordinate entry*.

You can tell AutoCAD to measure coordinates from the last specified point by simply placing the @ character in front of the coordinate—for example, @4,2. By using the @ symbol, you are telling AutoCAD to measure 4 units in the positive X direction and 2 units in the positive Y direction from your current position, or from where you are. This is known as *relative coordinate entry*.

Let's redraw the 2 × 2 square, this time using relative coordinate entry.

Exercise 4-5: Drawing with Relative Coordinates

1. Continue from Exercise 4-4. Toggle the **Dynamic Input** setting back ON.
2. Start the **LINE** command. AutoCAD prompts you to:

   `Specify first point:`
3. Type **6,2<Enter ↵>**. AutoCAD places the first point and prompts you to:

   `Specify next point or [Undo]:`
4. Type **@2,0<Enter ↵>**. AutoCAD places a point 2 units to the right of the first point and prompts you to:

   `Specify next point or [Undo]:`
5. Type **@0,2<Enter ↵>**. AutoCAD places a point 2 units above the second point and prompts you to:

   `Specify next point or [Close/Undo]:`
6. Type **@-2,0<Enter ↵>**. AutoCAD places a point 2 units to the left of the third point and prompts you to:

   `Specify next point or [Close/Undo]:`
7. Type **C<Enter ↵>** to close the square and end the **LINE** command. Your drawing should now resemble Figure 4-9.
8. Save your drawing as **EX-4-5**.

Figure 4-9   Drawing with relative coordinates

You used absolute coordinate entry to place the first point (6,2), but each subsequent point was measured from the last placed point—i.e., from where you were.

Polar Coordinates

Cartesian coordinates work well when drawing objects with right angles or when coordinates lie on a well-defined grid. However, when drawing objects that have angles other than 90°, calculating coordinate locations is quite a bit more difficult. Let's take our 2 × 2 square and rotate it 45° (see Figure 4-10).

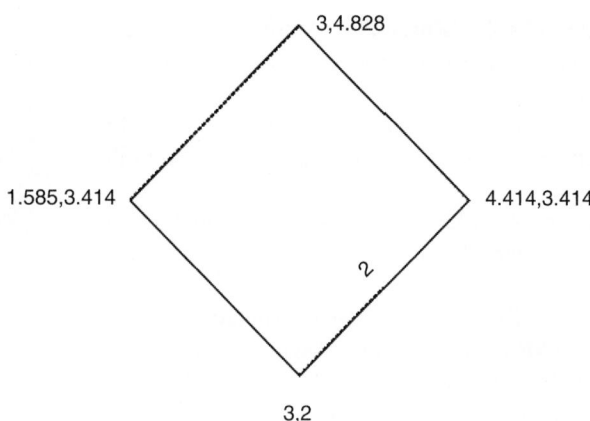

Figure 4-10   The rotated
2 × 2 square

To calculate the location of these coordinates, you'll need to either use the Pythagorean the-orem ($x^2 + y^2 = z^2$) or use AutoCAD's polar coordinates.

Polar coordinates use distance and direction to specify locations. For example, if you spec-ify a location of 2<0, 2 is the distance, < is the angle indicator, and 0 is the direction in degrees. The coordinate 2<0 tells AutoCAD to measure 2 units in the 0° direction from the origin (0,0). Remember from Chapter 1 that in AutoCAD, angles are measured counterclockwise from 0°, which is east, or to the right, of the origin along the positive X-axis.

Like Cartesian coordinates, polar coordinates can be either absolute (measured from 0,0) or relative (measured from the last specified point). Also, angles can be positive (counterclockwise) or negative (clockwise). Figure 4-11 shows some examples of polar coordinate entry and the re-sulting point locations.

Let's draw the rotated 2 × 2 square using polar coordinate entry.

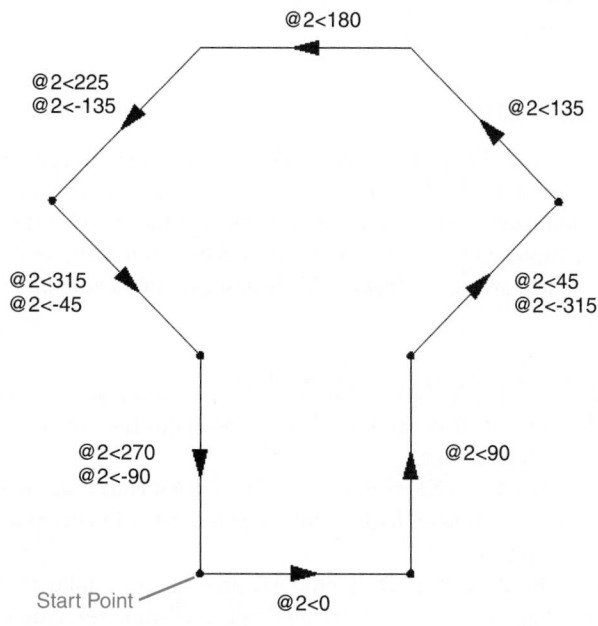

Figure 4-11   The polar coordi-nate examples

Exercise 4-6: Drawing with Polar Coordinates

1. Continue from Exercise 4-5.
2. Start the **LINE** command. Type **4,5<Enter ↵>** to specify the first point. AutoCAD starts drawing the line and prompts you for the second point.

3. Type **@2<45<Enter ⏎>**. AutoCAD draws a line segment 2 units long at an angle of 45° from the first point.
4. Type **@2<135<Enter ⏎>**. AutoCAD draws a line segment 2 units long at an angle of 135° from the second point.
5. Type **@2<−135<Enter ⏎>**. AutoCAD draws a line segment 2 units long at an angle of −135° from the third point.
6. Type **C<Enter ⏎>** to close the square and end the **LINE** command. Your drawing should now resemble Figure 4-12.
7. Save your drawing as **EX4-6**.

Note: Absolute coordinate entry, whether Cartesian or polar coordinates, is rarely used. The majority of points are specified using either Object Snaps (see Chapter 5) or some form of relative coordinate entry.

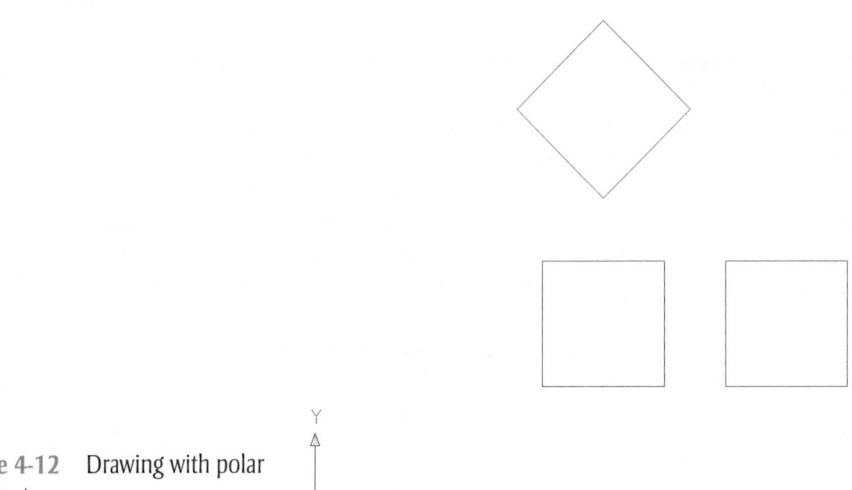

Figure 4-12   Drawing with polar coordinates

Dynamic Input

As you saw in Chapter 2, AutoCAD's dynamic floating prompt moves with your cursor and provides instant feedback as you move around the drawing. One of the advantages of **Dynamic Input** is the immediate coordinate and dimensional information it provides while drawing. Using **Dynamic Input**, you can use the cursor location to determine the angle and dimensions of the objects as they are being drawn. This is best explained with an example.

Exercise 4-7: Drawing with Dynamic Input

1. Continue from Exercise 4-6. On the Status Bar, turn on both the **Ortho Mode** and **Dynamic Input** settings.
2. Start the **LINE** command and type **6,5<Enter ⏎>** to specify the first point.
3. Drag the cursor to the right. The **Ortho Mode** setting will lock the cursor movement to the 0° direction.
4. Type **2<Enter ⏎>**. AutoCAD draws a line 2 units to the right (angle of 0°).
5. Drag the cursor up (90°) and type **2<Enter ⏎>**. AutoCAD draws a line 2 units up (angle of 90°).
6. Drag the cursor to the left (180°) and type **2<Enter ⏎>**. AutoCAD draws a line 2 units to the left (angle of 180°).
7. Press the down arrow and choose **Close** from the list of options. AutoCAD closes the square and ends the **LINE** command. Your drawing should now resemble Figure 4-13.
8. Save your drawing as **EX4-7**.

Figure 4-13 Drawing with **Dynamic Input**

Dynamic Input automates the process of specifying relative coordinates. When **Dynamic Input** is turned on, all dimensions and coordinates you type are measured from the last specified point. **Dynamic Input** also allows you to see the length and direction visually without having to calculate the direction angles. You simply point the way and tell AutoCAD how far to go.

FOR MORE DETAILS	Chapter 5 covers more ways of specifying coordinate locations and demonstrates how to combine Cartesian, polar, and direct distance coordinate entry methods with Object Snaps and Polar Tracking.

We've seen that AutoCAD remembers the last specified coordinate. When inputting relative coordinates, AutoCAD will measure coordinates from the last specified point. The **LINE** command can also make use of the last point. When you start the **LINE** command, AutoCAD prompts you to specify the first point. If you simply press **<Enter ↵>**, AutoCAD will start the line from the last specified point.

DRAWING CIRCLES

A circle is another basic AutoCAD drawing object. By default, AutoCAD asks for a center coordinate and a radius distance. However, there are a number of other ways to draw a circle. When you start the **CIRCLE** command, AutoCAD prompts you to *Specify center point for circle or ↓*. If you choose the down arrow, you'll see that you have three other options for drawing a circle.

Altogether, there are six different options for creating a circle: **Center Radius, Center Diameter, 2 Point, 3 Point, Tangent Tangent Radius**, or **Tangent Tangent Tangent**.

Center Radius

This is AutoCAD's default method for creating a circle. You can specify the center point using any of the coordinate entry methods. Once you have the center point placed, AutoCAD will then display a rubber-band line and drag a circle from the center point. You can specify the radius either by picking a point on the screen or by typing in a radius value.

Exercise 4-8: Drawing a Circle

1. Continue from Exercise 4-7. Toggle the **Ortho Mode** setting **OFF**.
2. Start the **CIRCLE** command. AutoCAD prompts you to *Specify center point for circle or ↓*.
3. Type **1,3<Enter ↵>**. AutoCAD places the center of the circle and starts dragging the radius. A preview image of the circle appears (see Figure 4-14). AutoCAD prompts you to *Specify radius of circle or ↓*.

Circle	
Ribbon & Panel:	Home| Draw
Draw Toolbar:	
Menu:	Draw| Circle
Command Line:	CIRCLE
Command Alias:	C

Figure 4-14   The preview image of the circle

4. Type **1<Enter ↵>** to specify a radius of 1. AutoCAD creates the circle and ends the **CIRCLE** command. Your drawing should now look like Figure 4-15.
5. Save your drawing as **EX4-8**.

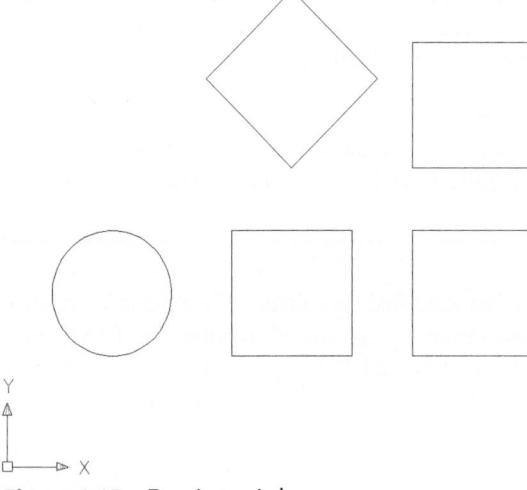

Figure 4-15   Drawing a circle

Center Diameter

This is similar to the **Center Radius** option. Once you specify a center point, AutoCAD prompts you to *Specify radius of circle or* ↓.

You can then type **D<Enter ↵>** or press the down arrow and choose **Diameter**. AutoCAD will then prompt you for the diameter or the circle. The rubber-band line will now stretch out twice the radius of the circle, and the Dynamic Input will be located at the center of the circle. You can specify the diameter either by picking a point on the screen or by typing in a diameter.

Exercise 4-9: Drawing a Circle Using Center Diameter

1. Continue from Exercise 4-8.
2. Start the **CIRCLE** command. AutoCAD prompts you to *Specify center point for circle or* ↓.
3. Type **4,3<Enter ↵>**. AutoCAD places the center of the circle and starts dragging the radius. AutoCAD prompts you to *Specify radius of circle or* ↓.
4. Choose **Diameter** from the options list. AutoCAD prompts you to *Specify diameter of circle:*. Notice that the default value is the diameter of the last circle drawn (**2.00**).
5. Press **<Enter ↵>** to accept the default diameter value. AutoCAD places the circle and ends the **CIRCLE** command. Your drawing should resemble Figure 4-16.
6. Save your drawing as **EX4-9**.

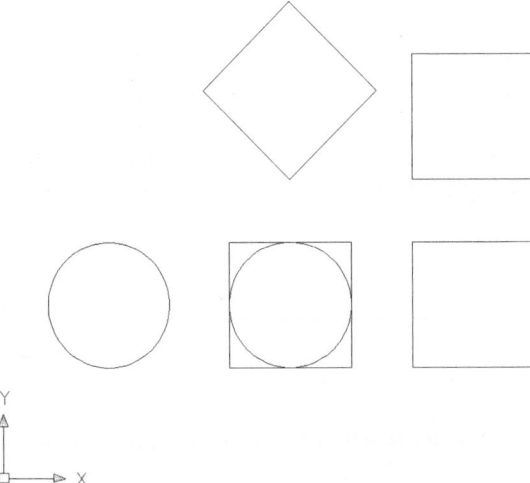

Figure 4-16 Drawing a diameter circle

2 Point Circle

A 2 point circle is defined by specifying two points on the diameter of the circle. To use this option, start the **CIRCLE** command and either type **2P<Enter ↵>** at the prompt or choose **2P** from the options list. AutoCAD then asks you to specify the first point of the circle's diameter and the second point and will draw a circle whose diameter passes through the two points.

Exercise 4-10: Drawing a 2 Point Circle

1. Continue from Exercise 4-9. Toggle the **Ortho Mode** setting on.
2. Start the **CIRCLE** command. AutoCAD prompts you to *Specify center point for circle or ↓*.
3. Select **2P** from the options list. AutoCAD prompts you to *Specify first endpoint of circle's diameter:*.
4. Type **7,2<Enter ↵>** to specify the first point on the circle's diameter. AutoCAD prompts you to *Specify second endpoint of circle's diameter:*.
5. Drag the cursor up and type **2<Enter ↵>** to place the second point on the circle's diameter. AutoCAD draws the circle and ends the **CIRCLE** command.
6. Save your drawing as **EX4-10**. Your drawing should resemble Figure 4-17.

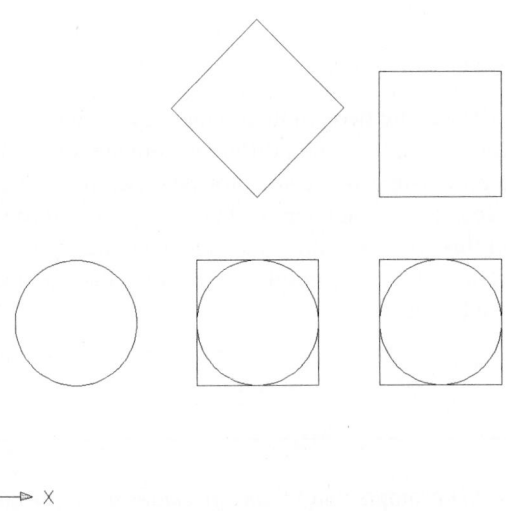

Figure 4-17 Drawing a 2 point circle

3 Point Circle

A 3 point circle is defined by specifying three points on the circle's circumference. To use this option, start the **CIRCLE** command and type **3P<Enter ↵>** or choose **3P** from the options list. AutoCAD asks you to specify the first point on the circle, then the second point. Once you specify the second point, AutoCAD will prompt you for the third and will drag a circle that passes through the first two points. AutoCAD will not display the preview circle until the first two points are specified.

Exercise 4-11: Drawing a 3 Point Circle

1. Continue from Exercise 4-10.
2. Start the **CIRCLE** command. AutoCAD prompts you to *Specify center point for circle or ↓*.
3. Select **3P** from the options list. AutoCAD prompts you to *Specify first point on circle:*.
4. Type **7,5<Enter ↵>** to specify the first point on the circle.
5. Type **1,1<Enter ↵>** to specify the second point on the circle. The Dynamic Input places the point at the middle of the right side of the square. AutoCAD now displays the preview circle. AutoCAD prompts you to *Specify third point on circle:*.
6. Drag your cursor to the left and type **2<Enter ↵>** to place the last point on the circle. AutoCAD creates the circle and ends the **CIRCLE** command.
7. Save your drawing as **EX4-11**. Your drawing should resemble Figure 4-18.

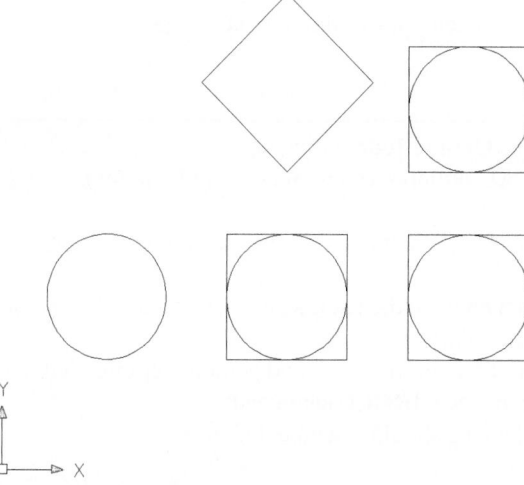

Figure 4-18   Drawing a 3 point circle

Tangent Tangent Radius

A tangent tangent radius, or TTR, circle is defined by two points of tangency on existing objects and a radius value. This method of creating a circle is a bit different from the other methods. First, the points of tangency must be on existing objects. AutoCAD uses the **Tangent** Object Snap to get the points of tangency. Second, the exact points of tangency are determined only after you specify the radius. Because of this, you can't drag and pick the radius of the circle. Last, it is possible to specify a combination of tangent points and a radius that cannot be created. In this case, AutoCAD will simply tell you:

```
Circle does not exist.
```

Exercise 4-12: Drawing a TTR Circle

1. Continue from Exercise 4-11.
2. Start the **CIRCLE** command. AutoCAD prompts you to *Specify center point for circle or ↓*.

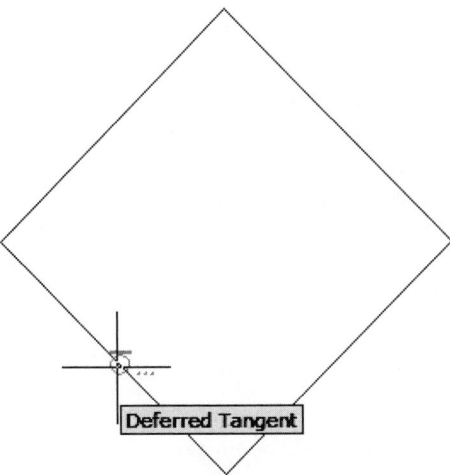

Figure 4-19   The **Deferred Tangent** Object Snap

3. Select **Ttr** from the options list. AutoCAD prompts you to *Specify point on object for first tangent of circle:*.
4. Drag your cursor over the lower left side of the rotated box (see Figure 4-19). AutoCAD will display the **Deferred Tangent** Object Snap.
5. Pick anywhere along the line to select the first tangent point. AutoCAD prompts you to *Specify point on object for second tangent of circle:*.
6. Pick anywhere along the lower right line to select the second tangent point. AutoCAD prompts you to *Specify radius of circle <1.00>:*.
7. Press **<Enter ↵>** to accept the default circle radius (**1.00**). AutoCAD creates the circle and ends the **CIRCLE** command.
8. Save your drawing as **EX4-12**. Your drawing should resemble Figure 4-20.

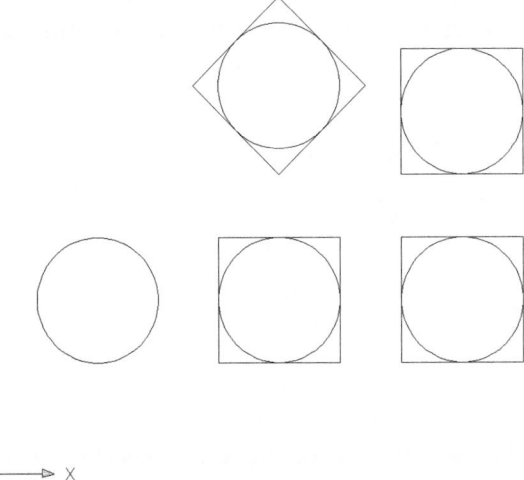

Figure 4-20   Drawing a **TTR** circle

Tan, Tan, Tan.   When choosing the **CIRCLE** command from the **Draw** panel, you'll notice that there is yet another option listed: **Tan, Tan, Tan**. This is technically *not* an option of the **CIRCLE** command. It is simply a method of constructing a circle using the **3P** option of the **CIRCLE** command along with AutoCAD's **Tangent** Object Snap.

DRAWING ARCS

Arcs are another type of basic drawing object. An arc is simply a segment of a circle. Like circles, arcs are defined by a center point and radius, but they also include a starting angle and an ending angle (see Figure 4-21). The part of the circle between the start and end angles defines the arc segment. Keep in mind that, by default, AutoCAD measures angles in a counterclockwise direction, with 0 along the positive portion of the X-axis. Likewise, arcs are also drawn in a counterclockwise direction. This means that by default, AutoCAD will draw the arc segment from the starting angle in a counterclockwise direction toward the ending angle.

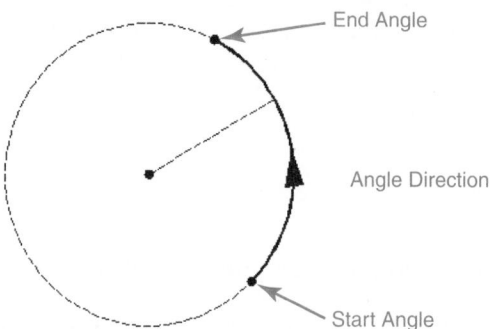

Figure 4-21   How arcs are defined

Arc	
Ribbon & Panel:	Home|Draw
Draw Toolbar:	
Menu:	Draw|Arc
Command Line:	ARC
Command Alias:	A

The ARC Command

Arcs are created with the **ARC** command.

3 Point Arc

By default, AutoCAD prompts you to pick three points: a start point, a second point along the arc, and the endpoint of the arc. From these three points, AutoCAD will calculate the center point and radius of the arc as well as the starting and ending angles. AutoCAD draws an arc segment through the three points you specify. Direction is not important when picking points for a 3 point arc. AutoCAD will draw the arc through the three points in the order they are specified (see Figure 4-22).

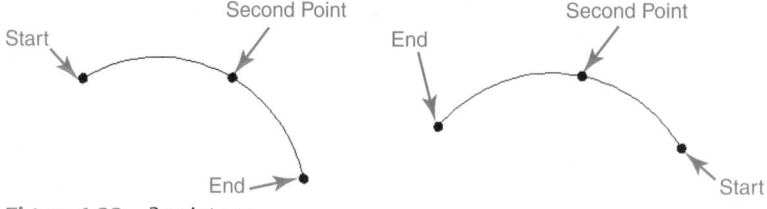

Figure 4-22   3 point arcs

You may find that while easy to use, the 3 point method of drawing an arc is not always practical. You may not know the exact location of a second point on the arc, or even the start or endpoint of the arc. You might know the radius of the arc, the center point, the included angle, or some combination of these properties.

Arc Options

AutoCAD provides a number of options for constructing arcs. These options can be used in various combinations, depending on what information you know. The options are described below.

Start	The **Start** option defines the start point of the arc.
End	The **End** option defines the endpoint of the arc.
Center	The **Center** option defines the center point of the arc.
Radius	The **Radius** option defines the radius of the arc. This option can be used only after the start point and endpoint of the arc are defined.
Angle	The **Angle** option defines the included angle of the arc. This is the difference between the starting angle and the ending angle. The **Angle** option is available only after the start point and either the endpoint or the center point have been picked.
Length	The **Length** option defines the length of the chord between the start point and endpoint of the arc (see Figure 4-23).
Direction	The **Direction** option defines the direction of a line tangent to the starting point of the arc (see Figure 4-23). The direction option can be used only after the start and endpoints of the arc have been defined.
Continue	This is not technically an option, but a behavior of the **ARC** command. When you start the **ARC** command, if you press <**Enter** ↵> at the first prompt, AutoCAD will start drawing an arc segment tangent to the previous line or arc segment drawn. AutoCAD uses the last specified point as the start point and determines the tangent direction from the previous line or arc segment. AutoCAD then prompts you for the endpoint of the arc (see Figure 4-23).

Figure 4-23   Arc options

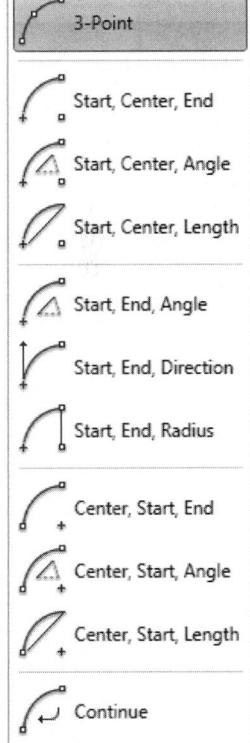

Figure 4-24   The **Home|Draw|Arc** menu

Using the ARC Command

When you start the **ARC** command, AutoCAD will prompt you to *Specify start point of arc or* ↓. You can specify the start point, choose the **Center** option, or press <**Enter** ↵> to create an arc tangent to the previous line or arc segment. Depending on the options you choose, AutoCAD will present you with other options. There are 10 different combinations of options for drawing an arc.

When accessing the **ARC** command from the **Draw** panel, you'll see the 10 different combinations of options used to draw arcs (see Figure 4-24). When using these menu options, AutoCAD will automatically type the options for you after each point selection.

TIP
Before drawing an arc, take a moment to consider what information you know about the arc. This will help you decide which **ARC** command options to use.

Let's look at some examples of drawing arcs.

Exercise 4-13: Drawing Arcs

1. Continue from Exercise 4-12.
2. Choose **Start, End, Radius** from the **Draw** panel. AutoCAD prompts you to *Specify start point of arc or* ↓.
3. Type **8,7<Enter ↵>** to start the arc at the top right corner of the upper right box. A rubber-band line stretches from the point. AutoCAD prompts you to *Specify end point of arc:.* Notice that AutoCAD has specified the **End** option for you.
4. Type **6,7<Enter ↵>** to specify the upper left corner of the square. A preview image of the arc appears, and a rubber-band line stretches from the end of the arc. AutoCAD has also specified the **Radius** option for you. AutoCAD prompts you to *Specify radius of arc:.*
5. Type **1<Enter ↵>** to specify a radius of 1. AutoCAD draws the arc. Your drawing should look like Figure 4-25.

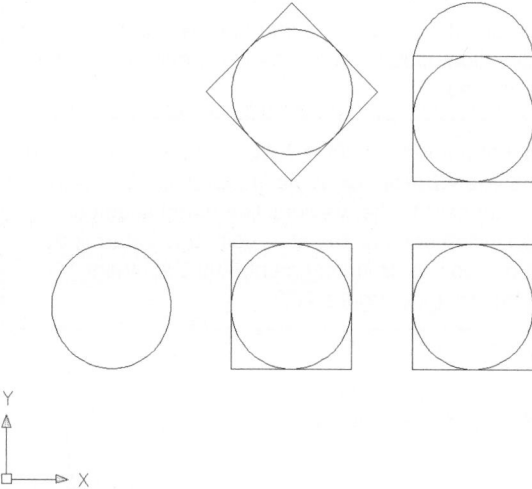

Figure 4-25   Start, End, Radius arc

6. Choose **Start, End, Angle** from the **Draw** panel. AutoCAD prompts you to *Specify start point of arc or* ↓.
7. Type **0,3<Enter ↵>** to start the arc at the left quadrant of the circle on the left of your drawing. A rubber-band line stretches from the point. AutoCAD prompts you to *Specify end point of arc:.*
8. Type **1,3<Enter ↵>** to specify the center of the circle. A preview image of the arc appears, and a rubber-band line stretches from the start of the arc. AutoCAD prompts you to *Specify included angle:.*
9. Drag the cursor up and type **180<Enter ↵>**. AutoCAD draws an arc with an 180° included angle from the start point to the endpoint in a counterclockwise direction. Your drawing should look like Figure 4-26.
10. Press **<Enter ↵>** to repeat the **ARC** command. AutoCAD prompts you to *Specify start point of arc or* ↓.
11. Press **<Enter ↵>** to continue an arc from the end of the last arc. AutoCAD stretches a tangent arc from the end of the last arc and prompts you to *Specify endpoint of arc:.*
12. Drag the cursor to the right and type **1<Enter ↵>** to specify the right quadrant of the circle. AutoCAD places the arc tangent to the first arc. Your drawing should look like Figure 4-27.
13. Save your drawing as **EX4-13**.

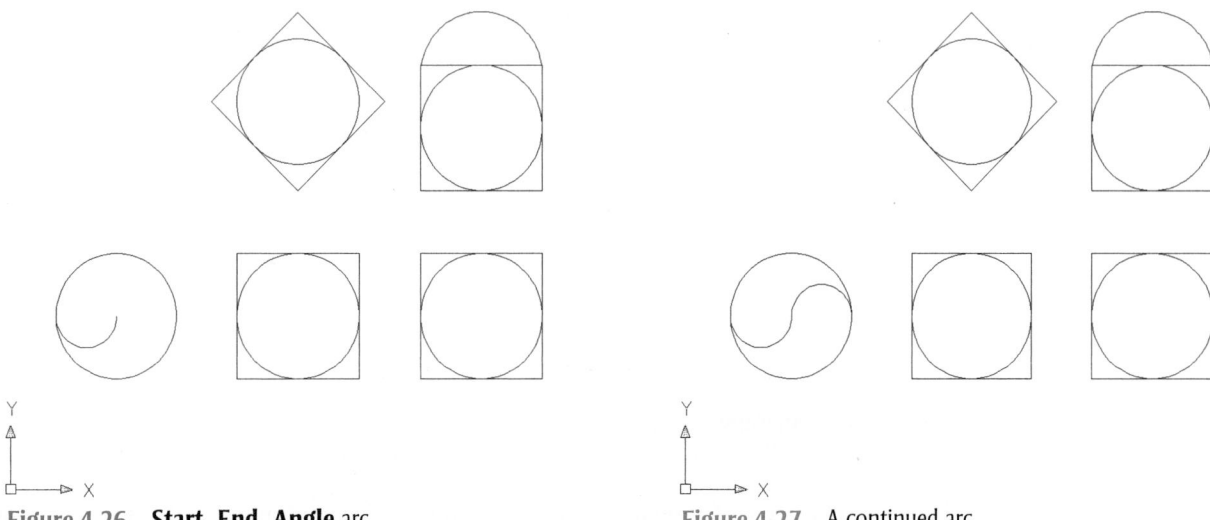

Figure 4-26   Start, End, Angle arc   **Figure 4-27**   A continued arc

DRAWING ELLIPSES

An ellipse (or oval) is similar in definition to a circle except that it has both a major and a minor radius (see Figure 4-28).

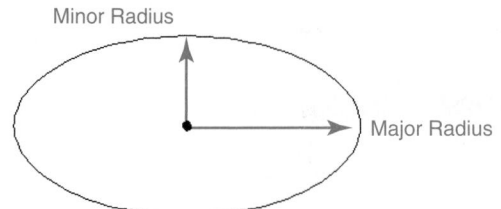

Figure 4-28   An ellipse

Ellipse	
Ribbon & Panel:	Home| Draw
Draw Toolbar:	
Menu:	Draw| Ellipse
Command Line:	ELLIPSE
Command Alias:	EL

An ellipse is created with the **ELLIPSE** command.

You can construct an ellipse either by specifying the center point and points on the major and minor radii or by picking points on the major and minor axes.

Let's draw an ellipse.

Exercise 4-14: Drawing an Ellipse

1. Start a new drawing using the acad.dwt drawing template.
2. Toggle the **Ortho Mode** setting to **ON** and start the **ELLIPSE** command. AutoCAD prompts you to *Specify axis endpoint of ellipse or ↓*.
3. Pick a point on the screen to select the first axis endpoint. AutoCAD drags a rubber-band line from the point. AutoCAD prompts you to *Specify other endpoint of axis:*.
4. Pick a point to the right of the first point. AutoCAD will calculate the midpoint of that line and use it as the center of the ellipse. A rubber-band line stretches from this center point. AutoCAD prompts you to *Specify distance to other axis or ↓*.
5. Drag the mouse around to see how the shape of the ellipse changes as you move it. Pick a point above the center point to create the ellipse. Your drawing should look something like Figure 4-29.
6. Save your drawing as **EX4-14**.

When drawing an ellipse, once you specify the major axis (by picking either a center and major radius or two points on the major axis), you'll have a **Rotation** option available. The **Rotation** option allows you to draw the ellipse as though it is a circle being viewed from an angle. Imagine holding a hula hoop directly in front of you so it looks like a circle. Now imagine tilting the hula

Figure 4-29   An ellipse

hoop away from you. The outline of the tilted circle is now an ellipse. When using the **Rotation** option, you are specifying that tilt angle. A tilt angle of 0 will draw a circular ellipse (the major and minor axes are equal). You can specify a maximum tilt angle of 89.4°. Figure 4-30 shows the results of different rotation angles.

0°   30°   45°   60°   89.4°

Figure 4-30   The **Rotation** option values of the **ELLIPSE** command

Elliptical Arcs

Unlike circular arcs, elliptical arcs are drawn with the **ELLIPSE** command. In fact, AutoCAD considers an ellipse and an elliptical arc as the same type of object. An ellipse has an included angle of 360, while an elliptical arc has an included angle less than 360.

To create an elliptical arc, start the **ELLIPSE** command and select the **Arc** option or choose the **Ellipse Arc** tool from the **Draw** panel. Once you have defined the ellipse, you are prompted for the start angle and end angle. Like circular arcs, AutoCAD draws the elliptical arcs from the start angle to the end angle in a counterclockwise direction.

Exercise 4-15: Drawing an Elliptical Arc

1. Start a new drawing using the acad.dwt template.
2. Toggle the **Ortho Mode** setting to **ON** and choose the **Ellipse Arc** tool from the **Draw** panel. AutoCAD prompts you to *Specify axis endpoint of ellipse or ↓*.
3. Pick a point on the screen to select the first axis endpoint. AutoCAD drags a rubber-band line from the point. AutoCAD prompts you to *Specify other endpoint of axis:*.
4. Pick a point to the right of the first point. AutoCAD will calculate the midpoint of that line and use it for the center of the ellipse. A rubber-band line stretches from this center point. AutoCAD prompts you to *Specify distance to other axis or ↓*.
5. Pick a point above the center point to create the ellipse. AutoCAD prompts you to *Specify start angle or ↓*.
6. Toggle the **Ortho** setting off and pick a point along the ellipse to specify the start angle. AutoCAD prompts you to *Specify end angle or ↓*.
7. Pick a second point along the ellipse to specify the end angle. The elliptical arc is created between the start and end angles. Your drawing should look something like Figure 4-31.
8. Save your drawing as **EX4-15**.

Figure 4-31   The **Angle** option of the **ELLIPSE** command

The Parameter Option.   When drawing elliptical arcs, the **Parameter** option is available when specifying the start and end angles of the elliptical arc. The **Parameter** option uses the same input as start angle but creates the elliptical arc using the parametric vector equation

$$p(u) = c + a* \cos(u) + b* \sin(u)$$

where *c* is the center of the ellipse and *a* and *b* are its major and minor axes, respectively.

FOR MORE DETAILS	See the AutoCAD **Help** file for more detailed information on using the **Parameter** option.

point: A one-dimensional object that is defined as a single coordinate in space. Points have no length or width, only a coordinate location

Point	
Ribbon & Panel:	Home| Draw
Draw Toolbar:	
Menu:	D̲raw| P̲oint
Command Line:	POINT
Command Alias:	PO

POINTS

Another basic drawing object is the ***point***. To draw a point, AutoCAD simply prompts you to specify a point.

Exercise 4-16: Drawing a Point

1. Start a new drawing using the acad.dwt template.
2. Start the **POINT** command. AutoCAD prompts you to *Specify a point:*.
3. Pick a point on the screen. AutoCAD will place a point object.

Points can be difficult to see. By default, points appear as dots with no real size or shape. When you zoom in on a point, it does not get larger. If you place a point directly on top of another object, you might not see it at all. However, you can change the appearance of points to make them easier to spot.

Point Styles

When you start the **POINT** command, AutoCAD shows you the current value of the **PDMODE** and **PDSIZE** system variables in the command window.

```
Current point modes: PDMODE=0
PDSIZE=0.0000
```

These variables control the look (style) and size of points in your drawing. The **DDPTYPE** command allows you to set the **PDMODE** and **PDSIZE** system variables.

When you start the **DDPTYPE** command, the **Point Style** dialog box appears (see Figure 4-32).

You can choose the desired point style as well as specify a display size for the points. Point size can be entered as an absolute size (for example, 0.1″) or as a relative size (a percentage of the display height). When using a relative point size, AutoCAD will recalculate the point size every time the drawing regenerates.

Note:
Keep in mind that the point style and the point size are global settings, meaning that all the points in the drawing are affected by these settings. You cannot have one point displayed using one point style and another point with a different style.

Point Style	
Ribbon & Panel:	None
Toolbar:	None
Menu:	F̲ormat| Point Style...
Command Line:	DDPTYPE
Command Alias:	None

Note:
You can choose a point style that will make all points invisible (**PDMODE** = 1). When this point style is selected, points in your drawing will not be displayed on your screen but can still be moved, copied, erased, etc.

Exercise 4-17: Changing the Point Style

1. Continue from Exercise 4-16.
2. Type **DDPTYPE <Enter ↵>**. The **Point Style** dialog box is displayed.

Figure 4-32   The **Point Style** dialog box

Figure 4-33   Choosing a point style

3. Choose the point style shown in Figure 4-33 and choose **OK** to close the dialog box.
4. Type **REGEN<Enter ↵>** to regenerate your drawing. AutoCAD updates the point display.

The values for **PDMODE** and their associated shapes are shown in Figure 4-34.

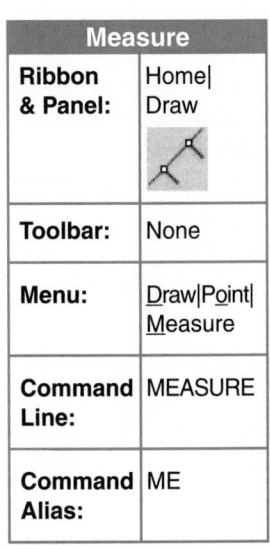

Figure 4-34 PDMODE values and their associated point styles

When using the **POINT** command, the values shown for **PDSIZE** will be either positive numbers or negative numbers. Positive numbers indicate an absolute size, and negative numbers indicate a percentage of the viewport height. For example, a **PDSIZE** value of −10.0 would make points 10% of the current display area. A value of (+) 10 would create points that were 10 units tall. A **PDSIZE** value of 0.0 will default the point size to 5% of the current display height. The **PDSIZE** variable has no effect when **PDMODE** is set to 0 (a dot) or 1 (blank).

Points can be used for a number of things, including simple markers, and AutoCAD uses them when dimensioning. Points are also used as measurement indicators in the **DIVIDE** and **MEASURE** commands.

Measure and Divide

The **MEASURE** and **DIVIDE** commands are used to automatically place point objects at regular intervals along an existing object. The **MEASURE** command places points at a specified distance along an object, whereas the **DIVIDE** command places points so that the object is divided into a specified number of segments.

Measure	
Ribbon & Panel:	Home|Draw
Toolbar:	None
Menu:	Draw|Point|Measure
Command Line:	MEASURE
Command Alias:	ME

Figure 4-35   Selecting the object to be measured

Divide	
Ribbon & Panel:	Home| Draw
Toolbar:	None
Menu:	Draw|P<u>o</u>int| <u>D</u>ivide
Command Line:	DIVIDE
Command Alias:	DIV

MEASURE.   The **MEASURE** command will prompt you to select an object and then ask you to specify a length. AutoCAD will then place points along the object at the specified interval, starting at the end closest to where you selected the object. For example, in Figure 4-35, if you selected the arc near point 1, Auto-CAD would measure the distances from endpoint 1. If you selected the arc near point 2, AutoCAD would measure the distances starting at endpoint 2.

> **Note:**
> Although the command names imply otherwise, the **MEASURE** and **DIVIDE** commands are simply methods of placing point objects. The **DISTANCE** command allows you to measure distances, and the **BREAK** command (Chapter 8) allows you to break an object into multiple pieces.

Points are not placed on the endpoints of objects and points are placed until the remaining distance is less than the specified distance.

Exercise 4-18: Measuring with Points

1. Start a new drawing using the acad.dwt template.
2. Draw a line and an arc in your drawing similar to what is shown in Figure 4-36. Do not draw the dimension.
3. Type **DDPTYPE <Enter ⏎>**. Select the point style that corresponds to **PDMODE 3** (see Figure 4-34) and choose **OK**.
4. Start the **MEASURE** command. AutoCAD prompts you to *Select object to measure:*.
5. Select the arc near the left endpoint. AutoCAD prompts you to *Specify length of segment or ↓*.
6. Type **.5<Enter ⏎>**. AutoCAD places points every .5 unit along the arc starting at the end closest to where you picked. Your drawing should look similar to Figure 4-36.
7. Save your drawing as **EX4-18**.

Figure 4-36   Measuring objects

DIVIDE.   The **DIVIDE** command prompts you to select an object and then asks for the number of segments. The number must be an integer between 2 and 32767; decimals or fractions are not allowed. AutoCAD will then place points along the object at equal intervals that divide the object into the specified number of segments.

Exercise 4-19: Dividing Objects with Points

1. Continue from Exercise 4-18.
2. Start the **DIVIDE** command. AutoCAD prompts you to *Select object to divide:*.
3. Pick anywhere along the line object. AutoCAD prompts you to *Enter the number of segments or ↓*.
4. Type **5<Enter ⏎>**. AutoCAD places 4 points along the line that divide the line into 5 equal pieces. The line object has not been changed or broken. Points have just been placed on top of the line. Your drawing should now look like Figure 4-37.
5. Save your drawing as **EX4-19**.

Figure 4-37   Placing points with **DIVIDE**

Like the **MEASURE** command, the **DIVIDE** command does not place points at the end-points of objects. It will always place one point less than the number of segments you specify (for example, specifying 5 segments creates 4 points, 10 segments will create 9 points, etc.).

Both the **MEASURE** and **DIVIDE** commands have a **Block** option. This option allows you to substitute a block reference for the point objects.

FOR MORE DETAILS	See Chapter 16 for more detailed information about blocks.

CHAPTER SUMMARY

You have now covered some of the basic drawing objects in Auto-CAD. Lines, circles, and arcs are the building blocks of all drawings. The majority of AutoCAD drawing objects are variations of these basic objects. Learning how to create and modify these objects effectively is key to becoming proficient with AutoCAD.

CHAPTER TEST QUESTIONS

Multiple Choice

1. The @ symbol is used to denote:
   a. Relative coordinate entry
   b. Polar coordinate systems
   c. Cartesian coordinate systems
   d. Absolute coordinate entry

2. Drawing templates have the file extension:
   a. DWF
   b. DWT
   c. DXF
   d. DWG

3. Which drawing units are specifically based on Imperial (feet-inches) units?
   a. Decimal and Engineering
   b. Engineering and Architectural
   c. Architectural and Fractional
   d. Fractional and Scientific

4. Which of the following is an example of polar coordinate entry?
   a. 3,0
   b. 3>90
   c. 3<90
   d. 90<3

5. Which of the following is an example of relative coordinate entry?
   a. 3<4
   b. 3<90
   c. 3d90
   d. @3,4

6. By default, in which direction are positive angles measured in AutoCAD?
   a. 90°
   b. Clockwise
   c. Counterclockwise
   d. Depends on where you pick

7. Which of the following is NOT a valid method of drawing a circle?
   a. Center Radius
   b. 2 Points on the Diameter
   c. Tangent Tangent Radius
   d. Center Circumference

8. Which of the following is NOT a valid method for constructing an arc?
   a. Start, End, Length
   b. Start, End, Radius
   c. Start, Center, Length
   d. 3 Points on the Arc

9. Drawing templates:
   a. Cannot be created in AutoCAD
   b. Cannot contain geometry; only drawing settings are stored
   c. Can contain both geometry and drawing settings
   d. Can be stored only in a specific folder on your computer

10. Points:
    a. Do not plot
    b. Cannot be erased or modified
    c. Cannot change their appearance
    d. Are stored as a single coordinate in space

Matching

a. Drawing template

b. Cartesian coordinate system

c. Scientific unit display

d. **DIVIDE**

e. Circle

f. **MEASURE**

g. Point objects

h. Architectural units

i. Drawing limits

j. Surveyor's units

1. A system of locating points using an X- and Y-axis

2. N32d8′26″E

3. Command used to place points at a specified interval along an object

4. The active drawing area. In layout space, it determines the size of your paper

5. A drawing object defined by a center point and a radius length

6. A drawing file used as a starting point when creating new drawings

7. 1.4200E+01

8. Command used to place points at equal distances along an object

9. 4′ 8 3/16″

10. A system of locating points using distance and direction

CHAPTER PROJECTS

Project 4-1: Lines, Circle, and Arcs

1. Start a new drawing using the acad.dwt template.
2. Draw the lines, circle, and arcs shown in Figure P4-1 to the best of your ability. **Do not** draw dimensions. *Hint:* Use the **Tan, Tan, Tan** circle option to place the corner circles.
3. Save the drawing as **P4-1**.

Figure P4-1

Project 4-2: B-Size Mechanical Border

1. Start a new drawing using the acad.dwt template.
2. Set the **LIMITS** for a 17″ × 11″ drawing area.
3. Draw the border as shown in Figure P4-2 to the best of your ability. **Do not** draw the dimensions.
4. Zoom to the drawing extents.
5. Save the drawing to a template file as **Mechanical B-Size.DWT**.

Figure P4-2

Project 4-3: Architectural D-Size Border (36 × 24)

1. Start a new drawing using the acad.dwt template.
2. Set linear **UNITS** to **Architectural** with precision set to **1/16″**.
3. Set angular **UNITS** to **Deg/Min/Sec** with precision set to **0d00′00″**.

4. Set **LIMITS** to 36″ × 24″ for a D-size drawing.
5. Draw the border as shown in Figure P4-3 to the best of your ability. **Do not** draw the dimensions.
6. Zoom to the drawing extents.
7. Save the drawing to a template file as **Architectural D-Size.DWT**.

Figure P4-3

Project 4-4: Electrical Schematic

1. Start a new drawing using the acad.dwt template.
2. Draw the electrical symbols shown in Figure P4-4 to the best of your ability at the sizes shown using the **LINE, CIRCLE,** and **ARC** commands. *Hint:* Each grid square is equal to 1/8″.
3. Save the drawing as **P4-4**.

Figure P4-4

Project 4-5: Residential Architectural Plan

1. Start a new drawing using the acad.dwt template.
2. Set linear **UNITS** to **Architectural** with precision set to **1/16″**.
3. Draw the building outline as shown in Figure P4-5 to the best of your ability. Place the corner of the building at 0,0 as shown. Draw the North arrow to the best of your abilities. **Do not** include dimensions. *Hint:* The North arrow is pointing at an angle of 247°.
4. Save the drawing as **P4-5**.

Figure P4-5

Project 4-6: Support Plate—English Units

1. Start a new drawing using the acad.dwt template.
2. Create the geometry shown in Figure P4-6. **Do not** include dimensions.
3. Save the drawing as **P4-6**.

Project 4-7: Gasket—Metric

1. Start a new drawing using the acadiso.dwt template.
2. Draw the gasket as shown in Figure P4-7 to the best of your ability. **Do not** include dimensions.
3. Save the drawing as **P4-7**.

Figure P4-6

Figure P4-7

Project 4-8: Civil Site Plan

1. Start a new drawing using the acad.dwt template. Set the linear drawing units to **Architectural** with **1/16″** precision. Set the angular units to **Surveyor's Units** with a precision of **N0d00′00″E**.
2. Draw the site outline, elevation lines, and building site as shown in Figure P4-8 to the best of your ability. Place the corner of the site at **0,0** as shown. Draw the elevation lines approximately where shown. Do **not** include dimensions or text.
3. Save the drawing as **P4-8**.

Figure P4-8

Drawing Tools and Drafting Settings

5

Chapter
Objectives

- Use the **Grid Display** and **Snap Mode** drawing tools to locate points quickly and precisely
- Draw orthogonally using the **Ortho Mode** drawing tool
- Draw at angles using the **Polar Tracking** drawing tool
- Use basic Object Snaps to locate points precisely relative to existing objects
- Defer Object Snaps to locate complex points
- Use advanced Object Snaps to locate points using acquired points and alignment paths
- Locate points relative to multiple objects by using the **Object Snap Tracking** feature to display multiple intersecting alignment path tracking vectors
- Control **Dynamic Input** settings
- Use construction lines to increase productivity and precision when creating multiple view drawings

INTRODUCTION

Remember from Chapter 1 that two of the most important benefits of using CAD to create technical drawings are increased productivity and improved precision.

These benefits are achieved in AutoCAD primarily through the use of the drawing tools and drafting settings explained in this chapter.

Drawing tools are toggles that can be turned on and off as needed by clicking on the appropriate Status Bar buttons located at the bottom of the AutoCAD display window shown in Figure 5-1.

Drawing Aid Buttons

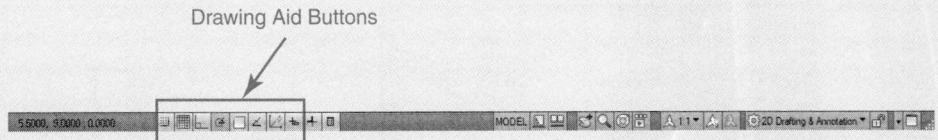

Figure 5-1 The AutoCAD Status Bar

Right-clicking with your mouse over a drawing tool button allows you to switch the Status Bar button display from icons to the traditional text-only label display by unchecking the **Use Icons** menu item as shown in Figure 5-2.

Additional button-specific menu items are also included on each button's right-click shortcut menu so that you can quickly access the selected drawing tool's settings and features. The shortcut menu for the **Snap Mode** tool is shown in Figure 5-2.

Drawing tools can also be turned on and off using the function keys at the top of your keyboard, or they can be typed in at the AutoCAD command line. Each method is listed with the corresponding drawing tool throughout this chapter.

Figure 5-2   The Status Bar with traditional text-only buttons displayed

Drafting Settings	
Menu:	<u>T</u>ools| Dr<u>a</u>fting Settings...
Command Line:	DSETTINGS
Command Alias:	DS or SE

Most of the drawing tools work in conjunction with different drafting settings. For instance, the **Grid Display** button turns a grid display on and off, whereas the grid spacing (X and Y distance between grid dots) is controlled via the drafting settings. The grid spacing and other drafting settings are managed using the **Drafting Settings** dialog box shown in Figure 5-3.

Note:
Any of the drawing tool buttons discussed in this chapter can be removed from the Status Bar via the **Status Bar** menu. To display the **Status Bar** menu, click on the down arrow at the far right of the Status Bar.

FOR MORE DETAILS	See the section "Keyboard Commands" in Chapter 1 for a complete list of function keys. See the "Status Bars" section in Chapter 1 for more information about turning Status Bar features on and off.

Figure 5-3   The **Drafting Settings** dialog box

The **Drafting Settings** dialog box can be displayed by selecting **Drafting Settings...** from the **Tools** menu or typing **DSETTINGS**. Even easier, you can right-click on any of the drawing tool buttons on the Status Bar to display a shortcut menu like the one shown in Figure 5-4 and select the **Settings...** menu item.

Figure 5-4   **Drawing Tools** right-click short-cut menu

TIP   All the drawing tools and drafting settings can be accessed when a command is active. This means that you can turn drawing tools on or off or change your drafting settings in the middle of most commands on an as-needed basis.

GRID DISPLAY

The **Grid Display** is a rectangular pattern of evenly spaced dots you can turn on in your drawing to help you visually locate points. It is similar to using a sheet of graph paper when drawing with pencil and paper, except that you can control the distance between the dots and can change them at any time using the **Drafting Settings** dialog box. The **Grid Display** does not plot and is provided strictly as a visual aid. *The Grid Display does not affect the cursor movement—*this feature is controlled by the **Snap Mode** explained in the next section.

By default, the rectangular **Grid Display** area is determined by the current drawing limits setting. The drawing limits for the default acad.dwt template are set to a rectangular area defined by the lower left coordinate value of (0.0,0.0) and an upper right corner coordinate value of (12.0,9.0).

Note:
It is possible to display the grid beyond the drawing limits by selecting the **Display grid beyond Limits** check box on the **Drafting Settings** dialog box.

Grid Display	
Status Bar:	⊞ or GRID
Function Key:	F7
Command Line:	GRID
Keyboard Combo:	Ctrl+G

FOR MORE DETAILS   See Chapter 4 for information about changing the drawing limits.

Figure 5-5 shows a drawing with the **Grid Display** turned on with the default spacing of 0.50″ between the dots in both the horizontal and vertical axes.

Setting the Grid Spacing

The horizontal and vertical spacing between the grid dots is controlled on the **Snap and Grid** tab of the **Drafting Settings** dialog box shown in Figure 5-6. You can change the distance between

Figure 5-5   **Grid Display** turned on

Figure 5-6   **Grid Display** settings

the dots by specifying the **Grid X spacing** for the horizontal distance and the **Grid Y spacing** for the vertical distance. The X and Y distances are typically set to an equal value. In fact, when you try to change one distance, the other distance is updated automatically.

The **Major line every:** setting specifies the frequency of major grid lines compared to minor grid lines when the visual style is set to anything other than 2D Wireframe. The other 3D visual styles display grid lines rather than grid dots. Primarily a 3D tool, the current visual style is controlled by the **VSCURRENT** command.

When the visual style is set to 2D Wireframe and the **Adaptive grid** setting is turned on in the **Grid behavior** section (explained below), the **Major line every:** setting controls the grid dot display when you zoom out. If the grid spacing is too dense to display, the minor grid dots are turned off.

Controlling Grid Display Behavior

The settings in the **Grid behavior** section of the **Drafting Settings** dialog box are primarily used to control the appearance of the grid lines that are displayed when the current visual style is set to any visual style except 2D Wireframe.

The **Adaptive grid** setting limits the density of the grid when the drawing is zoomed out using the **Major line every:** setting introduced earlier to turn minor grid lines/dots off.

The **Allow subdivision below grid spacing** setting generates additional, more closely spaced grid lines/dots when zoomed in. The spacing and frequency of these minor grid lines/dots is determined by the frequency of the major grid lines.

The **Display grid beyond Limits** setting allows you to display the grid beyond the area specified by the **LIMITS** command as mentioned earlier.

The **Follow Dynamic UCS** setting is a 3D tool that allows you to automatically update the grid plane to follow the *XY* plane of the dynamic UCS.

SNAP MODE

The **Snap Mode** drawing tool controls the movement of your cursor so that you can select points in your drawing only at specific X and Y increments. It is typically used in conjunction with the **Grid Display** explained in the previous section. The **Grid Display** provides the visual reference, whereas the **Snap Mode** forces your pick points to be located precisely at specific coordinate locations.

By default, the X and Y spacing for both tools are set the same so that your cursor "snaps" directly to the **Grid Display** dots when both drawing tools are turned on at the same time. It is possible to set the X and Y spacing for **Grid** and **Snap** to different values, although it is recommended that they relate to each other to avoid confusion.

Setting the Snap Spacing

The horizontal and vertical spacing between the snap points is controlled on the **Snap and Grid** tab of the **Drafting Settings** dialog box shown in Figure 5-7. You can change the distance between the snap points by specifying the **Snap X spacing** for the horizontal distance and the **Snap Y spacing** for the vertical distance. The X and Y distances are typically set to an equal value. By default, when you try to change one distance the other distance is updated automatically. You must uncheck the **Equal X and Y spacing** check box shown in Figure 5-7 before setting values that are not the same.

As mentioned, it is possible to set the **Snap** X and Y spacing to different values than the **Grid** X and Y spacing, but it is suggested that one is an increment of the other. For instance, you might set the **Snap** X and Y spacing to 0.25″, while the **Grid** X and Y spacing remains at 0.50″. With these settings, your cursor will still snap to each grid and halfway between each grid dot.

Snap Mode	
Status Bar:	or SNAP
Function Key:	F9
Command Line:	SNAP
Keyboard Combo:	Ctrl+B

Snap Settings

Figure 5-7   **Snap Mode** settings

Setting the Snap Type and Style

There are two major types of **Snap Modes: Grid Snap** and **Polar Snap**. You can switch between the different types using the option buttons in the **Snap type** section of the **Drafting Settings** dialog box shown in Figure 5-7. The default mode is **Grid snap**, which has two different styles:

- **Rectangular snap (default)**   Traditional orthogonal snap pattern with rows and columns of snap points at the specified X and Y spacing
- **Isometric snap**   Angled snap pattern where snap points are aligned at 30°, 90°, and 150° angles at the specified spacing so you can create isometric drawings

Polar Snap mode is used with the **Polar Tracking** drawing tool so that you can snap to points along **Polar Tracking** vectors at the specified spacing. **Polar Tracking** and the **Polar Snap** mode are explained later in this chapter.

Exercise 5-1: Creating a Drawing Using Snap Mode and Grid Display

1. Start a new drawing using the acad.dwt drawing template.
2. Turn off all the drawing tool buttons on the Status Bar.
3. Turn on the **Grid Display** button on the Status Bar.
4. Select the **Zoom Extents** tool to zoom to the limits of the drawing. You should now be able to see the whole grid on the drawing display.
5. Start the **LINE** command.
6. Draw a rectangle by picking points in the drawing.
7. Exit the **LINE** command.
8. Turn on the **Snap Mode** button on the Status Bar.
9. Start the **LINE** command.
10. Draw another rectangle similar to the first by picking points in the drawing. The cursor now snaps to the grid dots on the screen.
11. Exit the **LINE** command.
12. Right-click on the **Snap Mode** button on the Status Bar and select **Settings...** from the shortcut menu. The **Snap and Grid** tab of the **Drafting Settings** dialog box is displayed. See Figure 5-6.
13. Change the **Snap X spacing** to **0.25**. The **Snap Y spacing** will change to match. Exit the **Drafting Settings** dialog box by selecting **OK**.
14. Start the **LINE** command.
15. Draw another rectangle by picking points in the drawing. The cursor now snaps both to the grid dots and to points halfway between the grid marks.
16. Exit the **LINE** command.
17. Save your drawing as **EX5-1**.

ORTHO MODE

Ortho Mode	
Status Bar:	or ORTHO
Function Key:	F8
Command Line:	ORTHO
Keyboard Combo:	Ctrl+L

The **Ortho Mode** drawing tool restricts your cursor movement to the horizontal (*X*) and vertical (*Y*) axes so you can quickly draw horizontal and vertical lines at right angles (90°) to each other. This right-angle approach to drafting is often referred to as drawing "orthogonally," hence the term *Ortho*. Drawing with **Ortho Mode** turned on allows you to draw rectangular objects quickly and be assured that all the angles are square.

When **Ortho Mode** is turned off, the rubber-band line that indicates the cursor movement points at any angle you move your cursor, as shown in Figure 5-8A. When **Ortho Mode** is turned on, the rubber-band line that indicates the cursor direction follows the horizontal or vertical axis, depending on which axis is nearer to the cursor at the time, as shown in Figure 5-8B.

Note: Ortho Mode and the Polar Tracking drawing tools described later in this chapter cannot be on at the same time. Turning Ortho Mode on immediately turns Polar Tracking off, and vice versa.

Rubber-Band Line at Any Angle

Cursor

Rubber-Band Line Only Points 0°, 90°, 180°, 270°

Cursor

Cursor

Figure 5-8A Ortho mode turned off **B** Ortho mode turned on

AutoCAD overrides **Ortho Mode** when you enter coordinates on the command line or use any of the Object Snaps explained later in this chapter.

Exercise 5-2: Creating a Drawing Using Ortho Mode

1. Start a new drawing using the acad.dwt drawing template.
2. Turn off all the drawing tool buttons on the Status Bar.
3. Select the **Zoom Extents** tool to zoom to the limits of the drawing.
4. Turn the **Ortho Mode** button on.
5. Start the **LINE** command.
6. Type **2,2<Enter ↵>** to specify the first point.
7. Drag the cursor to the right. The **Ortho Mode** setting will lock the cursor movement to the 0° direction.
8. Type **2<Enter ↵>**. AutoCAD draws a line 2 units to the right (angle of 0°).
9. Drag the cursor up (90°) and type **2<Enter ↵>**. AutoCAD draws a line 2 units up (angle of 90°).
10. Drag the cursor to the left (180°) and type **2<Enter ↵>**. AutoCAD draws a line 2 units to the left (angle of 180°).
11. Type **C<Enter ↵>**. AutoCAD closes the square and exits the **LINE** command.
12. Save your drawing as **EX5-2**. Your drawing should look like Figure 5-9.

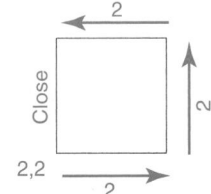

Figure 5-9   Drawing using **Ortho Mode**

POLAR TRACKING

AutoCAD provides a feature called *AutoTracking*™ that helps you to draw objects at specific angles using dashed lines known as *alignment paths*.

The **Polar Tracking** drawing tool utilizes **AutoTracking** so you can quickly draw and modify objects using preset polar angles. **Polar Tracking** works by displaying a dashed alignment path and a **Polar Tracking** tooltip as you move your cursor around in a drawing that temporarily restricts your cursor movement to preset angle increments.

By default, the increment angle is set at 90° so that an alignment path is displayed at every 90° (0°, 90°, 180°, 270°, and 360°) when the **Polar Tracking** button is turned on. This provides the same basic functionality of the **Ortho Mode** drawing tool explained earlier in the chapter. As noted earlier, when you turn the **Polar Tracking** button on, the **Ortho Mode** button gets turned off automatically and vice versa. Both drawing tools cannot be on at the same time. Figure 5-10 shows an alignment path displayed at 0°.

AutoTracking: AutoCAD feature that helps you to draw objects at specific angles or in specific relationships to other objects

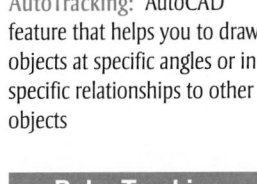

Polar Tracking	
Status Bar:	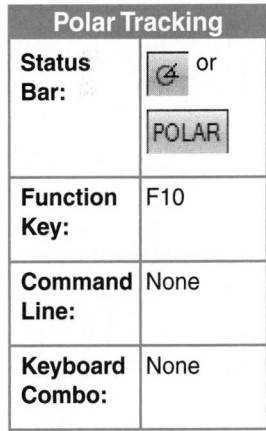
Function Key:	F10
Command Line:	None
Keyboard Combo:	None

Figure 5-10   **Polar Tracking** alignment path

If you pick a point when an alignment path is displayed, the point is located at the distance and angle displayed in the **Polar Tracking** tooltip. Even better, it is possible to use the direct distance coordinate entry method explained in Chapter 4 to locate a point at a specified distance along an alignment path. Any time an alignment path is displayed, you can enter a distance, and AutoCAD will follow the alignment path the distance specified. For example, if you enter **2** in response to the *Specify next point or [Undo]:* prompt while the 0° alignment path is displayed as shown in Figure 5-10, a horizontal line segment 2 units long is created. Combining **Polar Tracking** with direct distance coordinate entry is one of the fastest and easiest ways to locate points in your drawings.

TIP   **Polar Tracking** is not just for drawing objects. It also works with AutoCAD's modify tools. For example, using **Polar Tracking**, you can move objects at a specific angle and distance.

FOR MORE DETAILS   Using the AutoCAD **MOVE** command is explained in Chapter 7.

Setting the Polar Tracking Angle and Measurement Method

The **Polar Tracking** settings are controlled on the **Polar Tracking** tab of the **Drafting Settings** dialog box shown in Figure 5-11.

Polar Tracking Settings

Figure 5-11   Polar Tracking settings

The **Polar Tracking** angle is set in the **Polar Angle Settings** area on the **Polar Tracking** tab. There are two **Polar Angle** settings:

- **Increment angle**   A list of default preset angles ranging from 5° through 90° that controls the increment angle that **Polar Tracking** alignment paths are displayed. In Figure 5-11, a default increment angle of 45° has been selected so that a **Polar Tracking** alignment path will be displayed at every increment of 45° (0°, 45°, 90°, 135°, 180°, 225°, 270°, and 315°).

- **Additional angles**   Additional angles that can be added using the **New** button. *These angles are not incremental.* **Polar Tracking** alignment paths will be displayed only at each additional angle specified.

The **Polar Tracking** measurement method is set in the **Polar Angle measurement** area on the right side of the **Polar Tracking** tab. There are two **Polar Angle measurement** options:

- **Absolute**   All **Polar Tracking** angles are measured from the current AutoCAD base angle setting. The default base angle setting is 0° due east or to the right.

- **Relative to last segment**   **Polar Tracking** angles are measured relative to the last segment, and the absolute angle is ignored.

Figures 5-12A through D show a square that is rotated at 45° being drawn with **Polar Tracking** turned on with an increment angle setting of 45° using the absolute method of angle measurement.

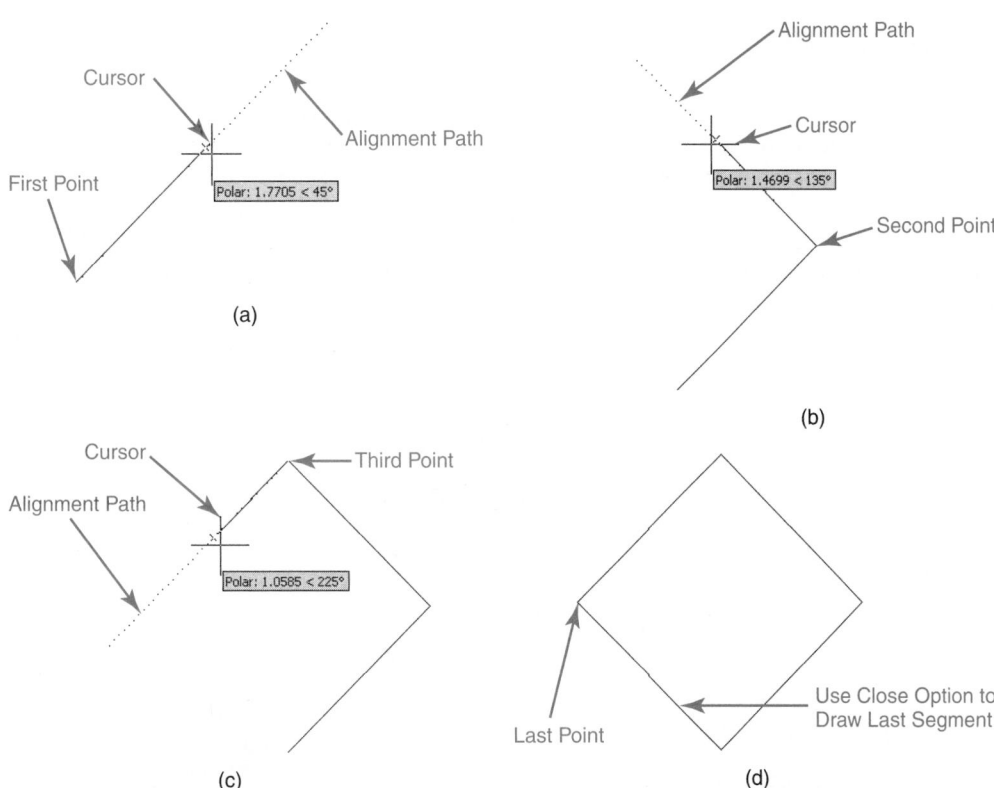

Figure 5-12A **Polar Tracking** alignment path at 45° **B Polar Tracking** alignment path at 135°
C Polar Tracking alignment path at 225° **D** Completed 45° square

> **TIP** The **AutoTrack** settings are controlled via the **Drafting** tab of the **Options** dialog box. You can toggle on and off the following features: **Polar Tracking** alignment vectors, **AutoTrack** tooltips, and full-screen tracking vectors.

Exercise 5-3: Creating a Drawing Using Polar Tracking

1. Continue from Exercise 5-2.
2. Turn off all the drawing tool buttons on the Status Bar.
3. Right-click on the **Polar Tracking** button on the Status Bar and select **Settings...** from the shortcut menu. The **Polar Tracking** tab of the **Drafting Settings** dialog box is displayed. See Figure 5-11.
4. Change the **Increment Angle** list box setting to 45°. Make sure that the **Polar Angle measurement** setting is set to **Absolute**. Exit the **Drafting Settings** dialog box by selecting **OK**.
5. Turn the **Polar Tracking** button on.
6. Start the **LINE** command.
7. Type **3,5.5<Enter ↵>** to specify the first point.
8. Drag the cursor up to the right until a **Polar Tracking** alignment path is displayed at 45°.
9. Type **2<Enter ↵>** while the alignment path is displayed. AutoCAD draws a line 2 units at the angle of 45°.
10. Drag the cursor up to the left until a **Polar Tracking** alignment path is displayed at 135°.
11. Type **2<Enter ↵>** while the alignment path is displayed. AutoCAD draws a line 2 units at the angle of 135°.
12. Drag the cursor down to the left until **Polar Tracking** alignment path is displayed at 225°.
13. Type **2<Enter ↵>** while the alignment path is displayed. AutoCAD draws a line 2 units at the angle of 225°.
14. Type **C<Enter ↵>**. AutoCAD closes the square and exits the command.
15. Save your drawing as **EX5-3**. Your drawing should look like Figure 5-13.

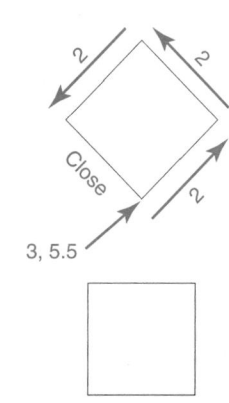

Figure 5-13   Drawing using **Polar Tracking**

OBJECT SNAPS

Object Snaps, or OSNAPS as they are sometimes called, are among the most essential features available in AutoCAD. Object Snaps allow your cursor to snap to exact locations relative to existing objects in your drawing so that you can locate points precisely when you are drawing or editing. Using Object Snaps, you can snap to the endpoint of a line (Figure 5-14A), the center point of a circle (Figure 5-14B), or if a line and circle overlap, their point of intersection (Figure 5-14C), just to name a few. There are more than 15 different types of Object Snaps ranging from the basic to the advanced.

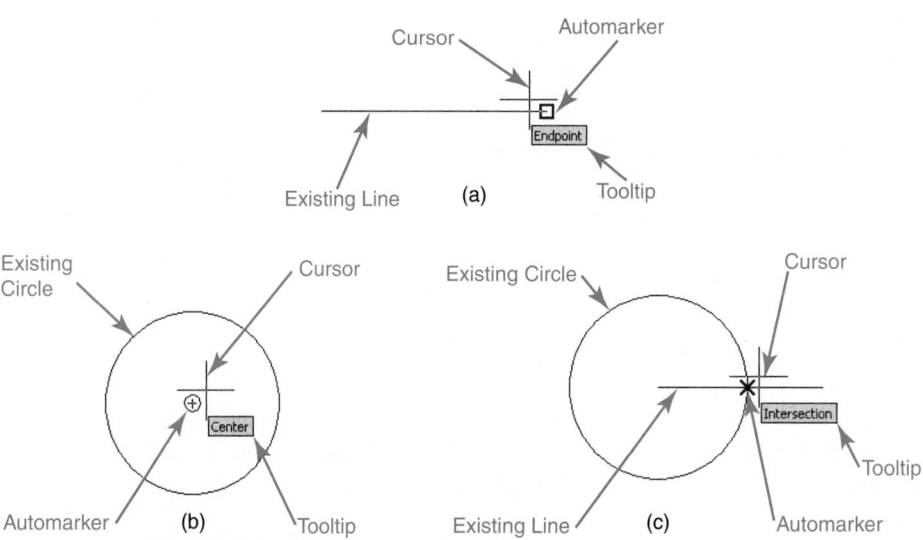

Figure 5-14A Endpoint Object Snap **B Center** Object Snap **C Intersection** Object Snap

In order to help you use Object Snaps most effectively, a visual aid called **AutoSnap** is provided. **AutoSnap** provides the following features, most of which are on by default:

- **Marker**   Displays the Object Snap type and location when the cursor moves over or near an object
- **Tooltip**   Text description of the type of Object Snap you are snapping to in a small box at the cursor location
- **Magnet**   Feature that attracts and locks the cursor onto the Object Snap point when your cursor gets near an AutoSnap Marker
- **Aperture box**   Boxed area that defines how close you need to be to an object in order to snap to an Object Snap point. The aperture box can be resized and turned on or off

All these settings, and a few others explained later, can be controlled on the **Drafting** tab of the **Options** dialog box shown in Figure 5-15.

TIP   Object Snaps work only when you are prompted for a point. If you try to use an Object Snap alone when no command is active, the error message *Unknown command* is displayed.

Object Snap Modes

There are two different ways you can utilize Object Snaps:

- They can be used individually in response to each prompt for point coordinate information.
- You can turn on one or more Object Snaps on the **Object Snap** tab of the **Drafting Settings** dialog box so that they are automatically active each time you are prompted to select a point.

Auto Snap Settings

Figure 5-15   AutoSnap Settings on **Drafting** tab of the **Options** dialog box

Figure 5-16   Right-click Object Snap shortcut menu

Entering an Object Snap individually in response to a request for point information makes the Object Snap active for only one cursor pick point. *Each time AutoCAD prompts for a point you must respond with another Object Snap.* There are a couple of ways to enter an Object Snap using this approach:

- Select the Object Snap from the **Object Snap** right-click shortcut menu (see Figure 5-16). The **Object Snap** shortcut menu is displayed by holding down the **<Shift>** key on your keyboard while right-clicking with your mouse.

- Type the desired Object Snap at the command line in response to a point request. The following is an example of activating the **Endpoint** Object Snap by typing **end** at the command line in response to a prompt for a point:

```
Specify first point: end
```

Most Object Snaps can be specified by entering the first three or four characters of the Object Snap name. In fact, if you observe the command line while selecting an Object Snap using the right-click shortcut menu, you can glean what is being entered at the command line so you can type it in the next time.

The second approach to using Object Snaps is to turn on a select number of Object Snaps via the **Object Snap** tab of the **Drafting Settings** dialog box (see Figure 5-17) so that they are automatically activated each time you are prompted for a point location.

This technique is typically referred to as *setting running Object Snaps* because the selected Object Snaps are always running in the background as you draw.

When your cursor gets close to any running Object Snap feature when you are selecting points in your drawing, an AutoSnap Marker is automatically displayed so you can quickly snap to the corresponding feature.

You can also set running Object Snaps by right-clicking on the **Object Snap** button and selecting the desired Object Snap from the shortcut menu.

TIP

Figure 5-17   Setting running
Object Snaps

Using running Object Snaps is typically considered the most efficient approach because it allows you to quickly locate objects precisely in your drawing without having to activate an Object Snap each time you need it. If you do need a particular Object Snap that is not currently active, you can always fall back on one of the individual Object Snap selection approaches explained earlier:

- Use the **<Shift>** key and the right-click shortcut menu.
- Type the Object Snap name at the command line.

When you activate an individual Object Snap this way, it is considered an override because you are temporarily suppressing any active running Object Snaps for a single point selection using the currently selected Object Snap. After a point is selected, all the running Object Snaps are active again until another Object Snap override is selected or Object Snaps are turned off using the **Object Snap** button on the Status Bar.

Sometimes when using running Object Snaps, you might need to select a point in your drawing without using any of the active running Object Snaps. The easiest thing to do is to disable running Object Snaps by turning off the **Object Snap** button on the Status Bar. It is also possible to activate the **None** Object Snap using one of the individual override methods. The **None** Object Snap turns Object Snaps off temporarily.

TIP

As you will discover in this chapter, there are many different Object Snaps that provide a wide array of features and functionality. You will want to be judicious as you start exploring and turning on different running Object Snaps. You definitely don't want to turn them all on at the same time. This will create confusion as you try to select points in your drawing. Select a few you use most often as running Object Snaps and then select others on an as-needed basis using the override approach.

deferred point: Object Snap feature that allows you to "build" the Object Snap point using multiple point selection input by deferring the first point selected

Basic Object Snaps

The following Object Snaps are basic in nature and require minimal user interaction. Most involve a single point selection near the feature you want to snap to—end of a line, center of a circle, intersecting objects, and so on. Some of the Object Snaps in this section provide an additional feature, known as a ***deferred point***.

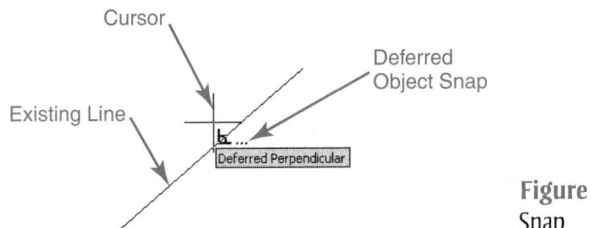

Figure 5-18   **Deferred** Object Snap

Deferred Object Snaps allow you to "build" the Object Snap point by selecting additional points and/or objects. When an Object Snap is deferred, there is an ellipsis (...) displayed after the Object Snap AutoSnap Marker, indicating that there are more selections required (see Figure 5-18).

Endpoint.   **Endpoint** is easily the most used Object Snap. The **Endpoint** Object Snap snaps to the closest endpoint of an arc, elliptical arc, line, multiline, polyline, spline, region, or ray. The **Endpoint** Object Snap will also snap to the closest corner of a trace, solid, or 3D face. Figures 5-19A and B show how to snap to the endpoint of a line using the **Endpoint** Object Snap when drawing a line.

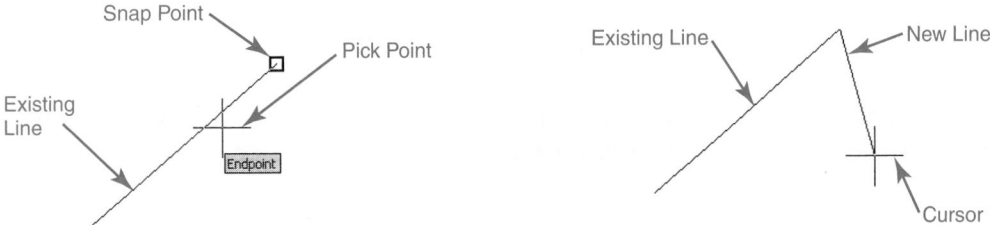

Figure 5-19A Using the **Endpoint** Object Snap—Step 1 **B** Using the **Endpoint** Object Snap—Step 2

Midpoint.   The **Midpoint** Object Snap snaps to the midway point of an arc, ellipse, elliptical arc, line, multiline, polyline, region, solid, spline, or Xline. The selected object is bisected exactly at the halfway point. Figures 5-20A and B show how to snap to the midpoint of a line using the **Midpoint** Object Snap when drawing a line.

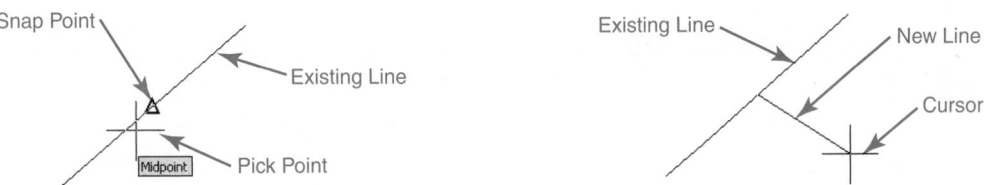

Figure 5-20A Using the **Midpoint** Object Snap—Step 1 **B** Using the **Midpoint** Object Snap—Step 2

Intersection.   The **Intersection** Object Snap snaps to the intersection of two objects. The two objects can be any combination of the following: arc, circle, ellipse, elliptical arc, line, multiline, polyline, ray, region, spline, or Xline. Figures 5-21A and B show how to snap to the intersection of two lines using the **Intersection** Object Snap when drawing a line.

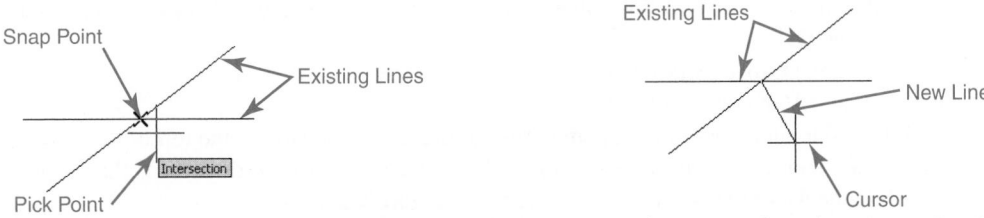

Figure 5-21A Using the **Intersection** Object Snap—Step 1 **B** Using the **Intersection** Object Snap—Step 2

It is also possible to snap to the intersection of two objects that do not physically cross in your drawing but would intersect if either of them, or both, were extended. The **Extended Intersection** Object Snap snaps to the implied intersection of two objects. The extension mode occurs automatically through the deferred pick point process explained earlier. If you do not pick close to the physical intersection of two objects when using the **Intersection** Object Snap, AutoCAD automatically puts you in **Extended Intersection** mode and displays the **Extended Intersection** AutoSnap Marker (Figure 5-22A).

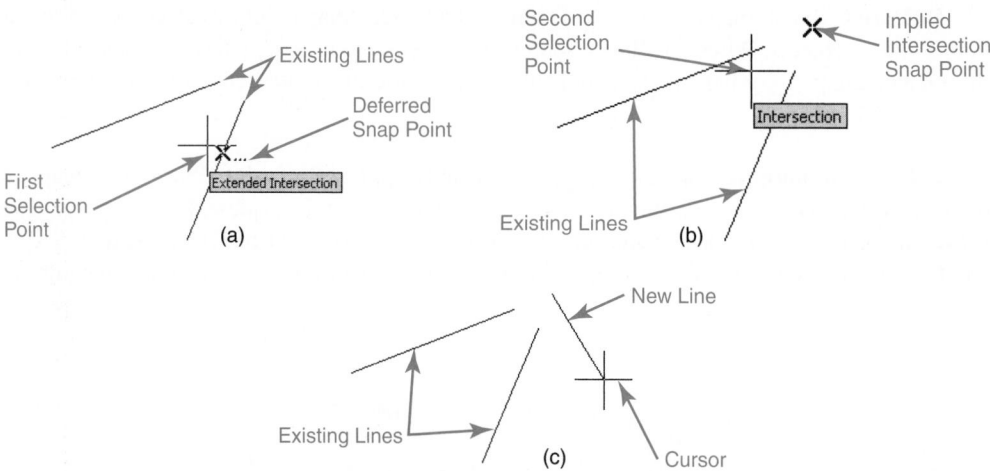

Figure 5-22A Using the **Extended Intersection** Object Snap—Step 1 **B** Using the **Extended Intersection** Object Snap—Step 2 **C** Using the **Extended Intersection** Object Snap—Step 3

Remember that any time you see the ellipsis (...) next to an AutoSnap Marker it means AutoCAD is waiting for more input. If you move your cursor over the other object that would intersect if it were extended, the typical **Intersection** AutoSnap Marker is displayed (Figure 5-22B).

As soon as the **Intersection** AutoSnap Marker is displayed, you can pick a point, and it will snap to the implied intersection (Figure 5-22C).

Extended Intersection is not available as a running Object Snap.

Exercise 5-4: Using the Endpoint, Midpoint, and Intersection Object Snaps

1. Continue from Exercise 5-3.
2. Turn off all the drawing tool buttons on the Status Bar.
3. Right-click on the **Object Snap** button on the Status Bar and select **Settings...** from the shortcut menu. The **Object Snap** tab of the **Drafting Settings** dialog box is displayed. See Figure 5-17.
4. Select the **Clear All** button to clear any running Object Snaps. Turn on the **Endpoint, Midpoint**, and **Intersection** Object Snaps. Exit the **Drafting Settings** dialog box by selecting **OK**.
5. Turn on the **Object Snap** button on the Status Bar.
6. Start the **LINE** command.
7. Place your cursor over the bottom corner of the rotated square on the top of the drawing and wait until the **Endpoint** AutoSnap Marker and tooltip are displayed. Pick a point while the AutoSnap Marker is displayed. See Figure 5-23.

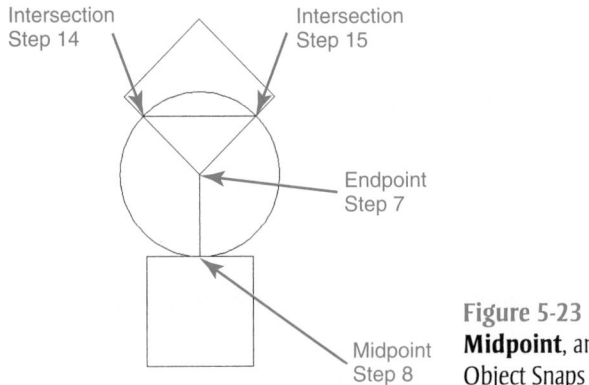

Figure 5-23   Using **Endpoint**, **Midpoint**, and **Intersection** Object Snaps

8. Place your cursor over the middle of the top line of the square on the bottom of the drawing and wait until the **Midpoint** AutoSnap Marker and tooltip are displayed. Pick a point while the AutoSnap Marker is displayed. See Figure 5-23.
9. Press **<Enter ↵>** to end the **LINE** command.
10. Start the **CIRCLE** command.
11. Choose the same point selected in step 7 to locate the circle center point.
12. Choose the same point selected in step 8 to indicate the circle radius.
13. Start the **LINE** command.
14. Place your cursor over the intersection on the left side of the circle and bottom left angled line of the rotated square and wait until the **Intersection** AutoSnap Marker and tooltip are displayed. Pick a point while the AutoSnap Marker is displayed. See Figure 5-23.
15. Place your cursor over the intersection on the right side of the circle and bottom right angled line of the rotated square and wait until the **Intersection** AutoSnap Marker and tooltip are displayed. Pick a point while the AutoSnap Marker is displayed. See Figure 5-23.
16. Hit **<Enter ↵>** to end the **LINE** command.
17. Save your drawing as **EX5-4**. Your drawing should look like Figure 5-23.

Apparent Intersection.   The **Apparent Intersection** Object Snap snaps to the visual intersection of two objects that are not in the same plane in 3D space so they don't physically intersect but appear to intersect when viewed from certain angles. Its use is reserved for working in 3D drawings.

Center.   The **Center** Object Snap snaps to the center of an arc, circle, ellipse, or elliptical arc. Figures 5-24A and B show how to snap to the center of a circle using the **Center** Object Snap when drawing a line.

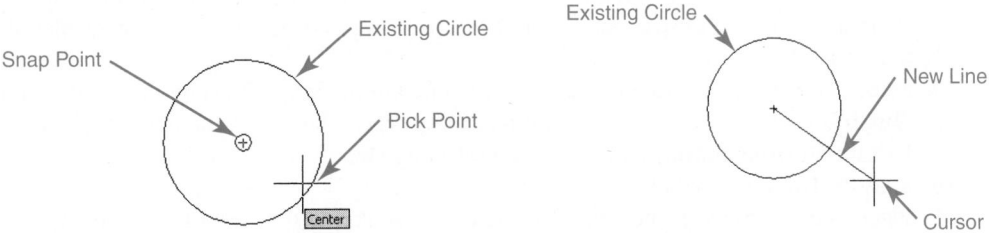

Figure 5-24A Using the **Center** Object Snap—Step 1 B Using the **Center** Object Snap—Step 2

Quadrant.   The **Quadrant** Object Snap snaps to one of the four quadrant points (0°, 90°, 180°, or 270°) of an arc, circle, ellipse, or elliptical arc. The quadrant point selected is the one closest to where you select the object. Figures 5-25A and B show how to snap to the 0° quadrant point of a circle using the **Quadrant** Object Snap when drawing a line.

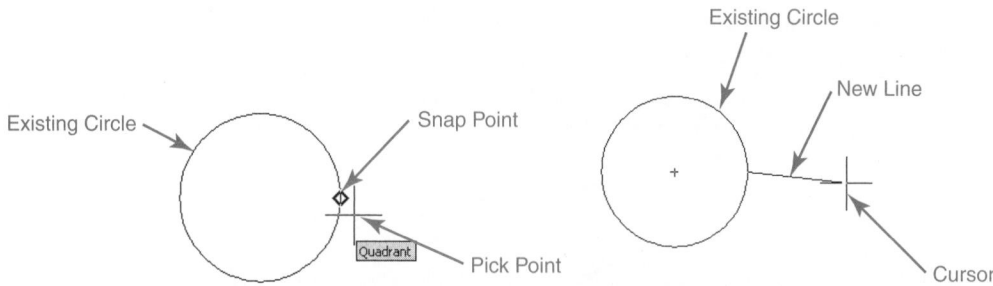

Figure 5-25A Using the **Quadrant** Object Snap—Step 1 **B** Using the **Quadrant** Object Snap—Step 2

Exercise 5-5: Using the Center and Quadrant Object Snaps

1. Start a new drawing using the acad.dwt drawing template.
2. Select **Zoom Extents** to zoom to the limits of the drawing.
3. Start the **CIRCLE** command. AutoCAD prompts you to *Specify center point for circle or* ↓.
4. Type **2,2<Enter ↵>**. AutoCAD prompts you to *Specify radius of circle or* ↓.
5. Type **1<Enter ↵>** to specify a radius of 1″.
6. Repeat Steps 4 and 5 to create two more 1″-radius circles at the coordinate locations of **(4,5)** and **(6,2)**. See Figure 5-26.

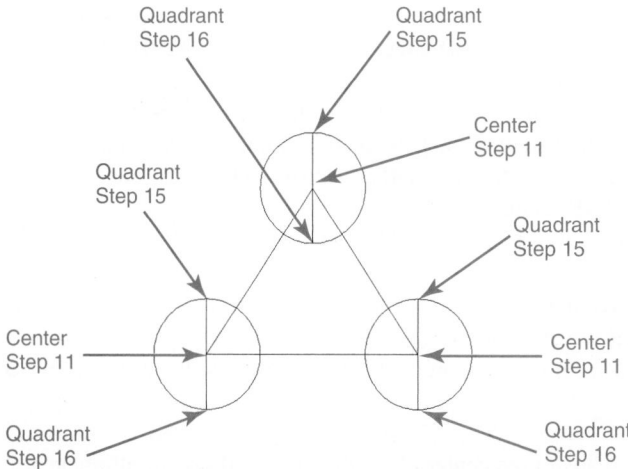

Figure 5-26   Using the **Center** and **Quadrant** Object Snaps

7. Turn *off* all the drawing tool buttons on the Status Bar.
8. Right-click on the **Object Snap** button on the Status Bar and select **Settings...** from the shortcut menu. The **Object Snap** tab of the **Drafting Settings** dialog box is displayed. See Figure 5-17.
9. Select the **Clear All** button to clear any running Object Snaps. Turn on the **Center** and **Quadrant** Object Snaps. Turn the **Object Snaps** check box on in the upper left corner. Exit the **Drafting Settings** dialog box by selecting **OK**.
10. Start the **LINE** command.
11. Place your cursor over the center of the circle on the bottom left of the drawing and wait until the **Center** AutoSnap Marker and tooltip are displayed. Pick a point while the AutoSnap Marker is displayed. See Figure 5-26.
12. Repeat step 11 for the other two circles and draw three lines to create a triangle. See Figure 5-26.
13. Type **C<Enter ↵>**. AutoCAD closes the triangle and exits the **LINE** command.
14. Start the **LINE** command.
15. Place your cursor over the top quadrant point (90°) of the circle on the bottom left of the drawing drand wait until the **Quadrant** AutoSnap Marker and tooltip are displayed. Pick a point while the AutoSnap Marker is displayed. See Figure 5-26.

16. Place your cursor over the bottom quadrant point (270°) of the circle on the bottom left of the drawing and wait until the **Quadrant** AutoSnap Marker and tooltip are displayed. Pick a point while the AutoSnap Marker is displayed. See Figure 5-26.

17. Repeat steps 14 though 16 to create vertical lines from quadrant to quadrant on the other two circles.

18. Save your drawing as **EX5-5**. Your drawing should look like Figure 5-26.

Tangent.   The **Tangent** Object Snap snaps to the tangent of an arc, circle, ellipse, elliptical arc, or spline. Figures 5-27A and B show how to snap to the tangent of a circle using the **Tangent** Object Snap when drawing a line.

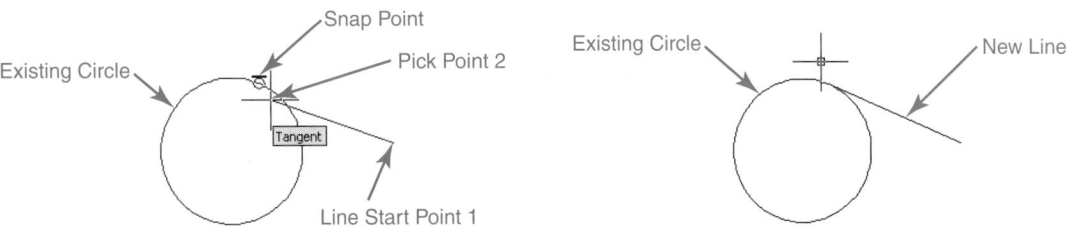

Figure 5-27A Using the **Tangent** Object Snap—Step 1

Figure 5-27B Using the **Tangent** Object Snap—Step 2

It is possible to defer a tangent point by first selecting the object you want to be tangent to before picking any other points. Picking a circle first displays the **Deferred Tangent** AutoSnap Marker (Figure 5-28A).

Again, the ellipsis (...) next to an AutoSnap Marker means AutoCAD is waiting for more input. Pick another point to locate the end of the line (Figure 5-28B).

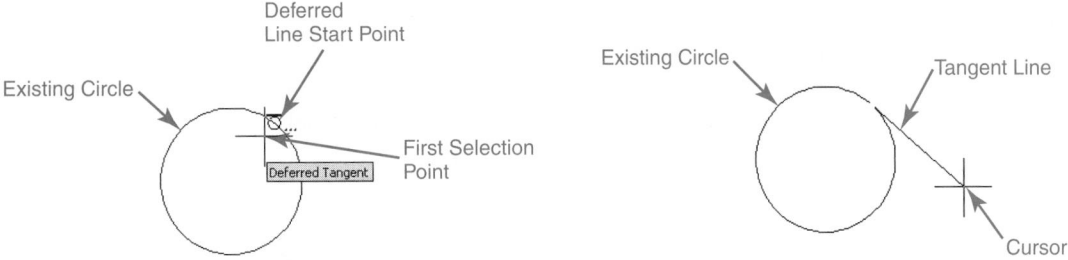

Figure 5-28A Using the **Deferred Tangent** Object Snap—Step 1 **B** Using the **Deferred Tangent** Object Snap—Step 2

Exercise 5-6: Using the Tangent Object Snap

1. Continue from Exercise 5-5.
2. Start the **LINE** command.
3. Hold down the **<Shift>** key on your keyboard while right-clicking with your mouse to display the **Object Snap** shortcut menu. See Figure 5-16.
4. Select the **Tangent** Object Snap from the menu.
5. Place your cursor over the left side of the circle on the bottom left of the drawing and wait until the **Deferred Tangent** AutoSnap Marker and tooltip are displayed. Pick a point while the AutoSnap Marker is displayed. See Figure 5-29.
6. Repeat steps 3 and 4 to select the **Tangent** Object Snap again.
7. Place your cursor over the left side of the circle on the top middle of the drawing and wait until the **Deferred Tangent** AutoSnap Marker and tooltip are displayed. Pick a point while the AutoSnap Marker is displayed. See Figure 5-29.
8. There should now be a line segment tangent to both circles.
9. Repeat steps 2 through 7 and create two more line segments tangent to the other two circles. See Figure 5-29.
10. Save your drawing as **EX5-6**. Your drawing should look like Figure 5-29.

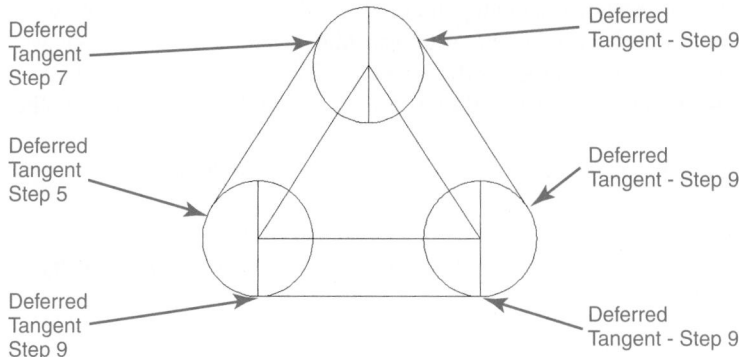

Figure 5-29 Using the **Tangent** Object Snap

Perpendicular. The **Perpendicular** Object Snap snaps to a point perpendicular to an arc, circle, ellipse, elliptical arc, line, multiline, polyline, ray, region, solid, spline, or Xline. Figures 5-30A and B show how to draw a line perpendicular to another line using the **Perpendicular** Object Snap.

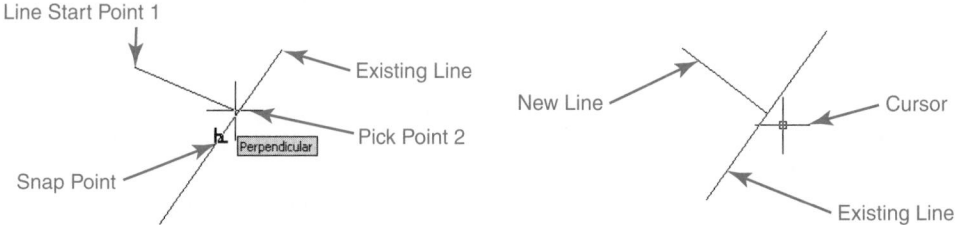

Figure 5-30A Using the **Perpendicular** Object Snap—Step 1 **B** Using the **Perpendicular** Object Snap—Step 2

It is possible to defer a perpendicular point by first selecting the object you want to be perpendicular to before picking any other points. Picking a line first displays the **Deferred Perpendicular** AutoSnap Marker (Figure 5-31A).

Again, the ellipsis (...) next to an AutoSnap Marker means AutoCAD is waiting for more input. Pick another point to locate the end of the line, which in turn determines where the new line attaches to the existing line (Figure 5-31B).

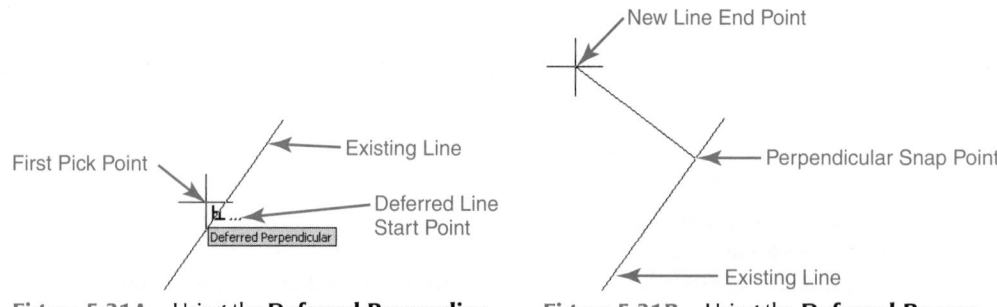

Figure 5-31A Using the **Deferred Perpendicular** Object Snap—Step 1

Figure 5-31B Using the **Deferred Perpendicular** Object Snap—Step 2

Exercise 5-7: Using the Perpendicular Object Snap

1. Continue from Exercise 5-6.
2. Turn off all the drawing tool buttons on the Status Bar.
3. Right-click on the **Object Snap** button on the Status Bar and select **Settings...** from the shortcut menu. The **Object Snap** tab of the **Drafting Settings** dialog box is displayed. See Figure 5-17.
4. Select the **Clear All** button to clear any running Object Snaps. Turn on the **Perpendicular** Object Snap. Turn **Object Snaps** on in the upper left corner. Exit the **Drafting Settings** dialog box by selecting **OK**.

5. Start the **LINE** command. AutoCAD prompts you to *Specify first point:*.
6. Type **8,6<Enter ↵>**. AutoCAD prompts you to *Specify next point or ↓*.
7. Place your cursor over the angled line on the right side of the triangle and wait until the **Perpendicular** AutoSnap Marker and tooltip are displayed. Pick a point while the AutoSnap Marker is displayed. See Figure 5-32.

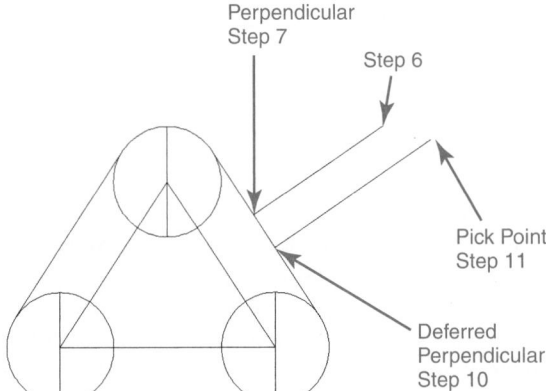

Figure 5-32   Using the **Perpendicular** Object Snap

8. Type **<Enter ↵>** to end the **LINE** command.
9. Start the **LINE** command again.
10. Place your cursor over the angled line on the right side of the triangle and wait until the **Deferred Perpendicular** AutoSnap Marker and tooltip are displayed. Pick a point while the AutoSnap Marker is displayed. See Figure 5-32.
11. Move your cursor up to the right and pick another point to create a perpendicular line segment. See Figure 5-32.
12. Type **<Enter ↵>** to end the **LINE** command.
13. Save your drawing as **EX5-7**. Your drawing should look like Figure 5-32.

Insert.   The **Insert** Object Snap snaps to the insertion point of an attribute, block, shape, or text. Figure 5-33 shows how to snap to the insertion point of a text object using the **Insert** Object Snap.

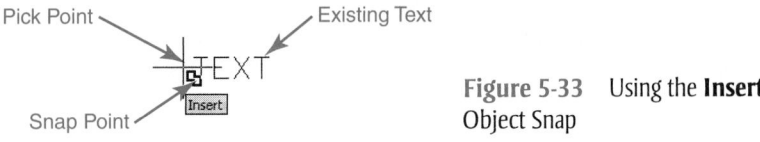

Figure 5-33   Using the **Insert** Object Snap

Node.   The **Node** Object Snap snaps to a point object, dimension definition point, or dimension text origin. Figures 5-34A and B show how to snap to a point created using the **DIVIDE** or **MEASURE** command and the **Node** Object Snap when drawing a line.

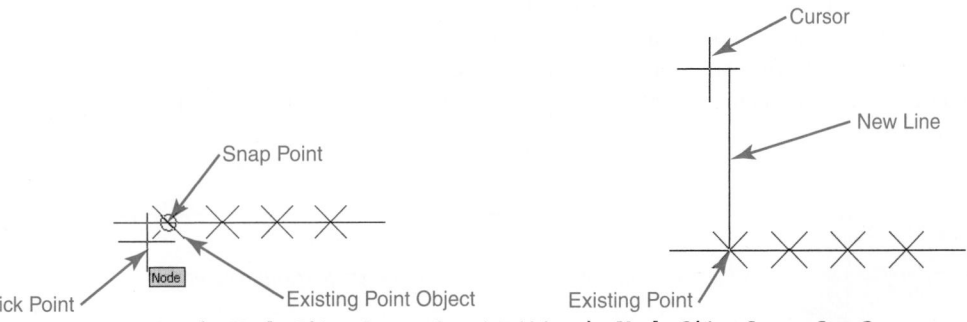

Figure 5-34A Using the **Node** Object Snap—Step 1 **B** Using the **Node** Object Snap—Step 2

Nearest. The **Nearest** Object Snap snaps to the nearest point on an arc, circle, ellipse, elliptical arc, line, multiline, point, polyline, ray, spline, or Xline. This allows you to pick a point near an object and be assured that it snaps directly on the object. Figures 5-35A and B show how to snap to a point exactly on a line using the **Nearest** Object Snap when drawing a line.

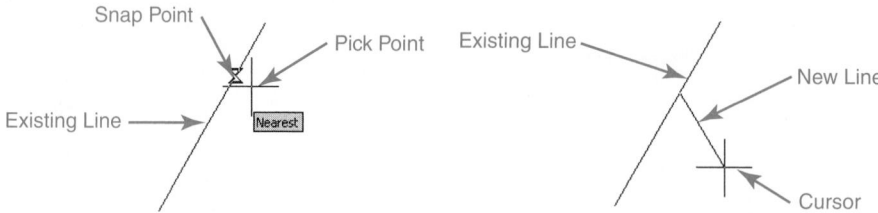

Figure 5-35A Using the **Nearest** Object Snap—Step 1 **B** Using the **Nearest** Object Snap—Step 2

None. The **None** Object Snap allows you to snap to nothing... literally. The **None** Object Snap temporarily disables any running Object Snaps set on the **Object Snaps** tab of the **Drafting Settings** dialog box for the next picked point. This makes it possible to pick a point in your drawing that doesn't snap to any objects that might be nearby, particularly when you are working in close quarters. You can always turn the **Object Snap** button off on the Status Bar at any time as well, but then you have to turn it back on when you need Object Snaps enabled again.

Advanced Object Snap Modes

The following Object Snaps are more advanced than those introduced in the previous section. The Object Snaps in this section require additional information to build the snap point based on the geometry of an existing object, or even objects. This can range from entering an offset distance to acquiring points that are used to display alignment paths (see Figure 5-36).

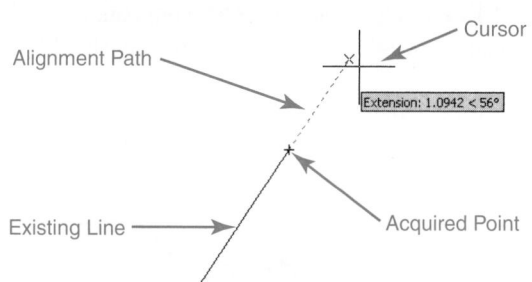

Figure 5-36 Acquired point and alignment path

acquired point: Object tracking feature used to locate a point as an intermediate location in order to locate temporary alignment paths

Some *acquired points* are selected automatically by simply moving your cursor over an object, whereas others require that you explicitly pick a point in the drawing.

The difference between the two methods of acquiring points is highlighted in the following sections to help reduce any confusion.

From. The **From** Object Snap allows you to specify a relative distance from a selected point and is typically used in conjunction with other Object Snaps. The distance can be entered either as a relative Cartesian coordinate using the format @X,Y (for example, @2,2) or as a polar coordinate using the distance and angle format (for example, @2<45). Figures 5-37A and B show how to snap to a point that is 0.5″ to the right and 0.5″ above the endpoint of a line using the **From** Object Snap.

FOR MORE DETAILS See Chapter 4 for more information about relative coordinate entry.

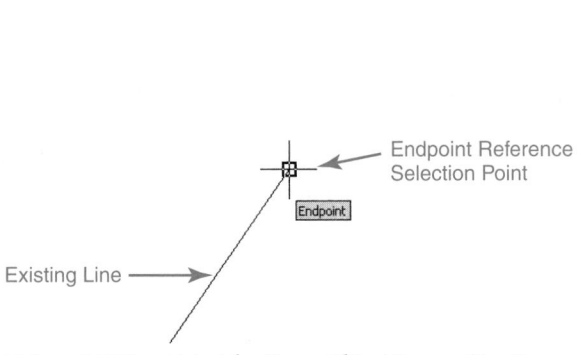

Endpoint Reference
Selection Point

Endpoint

Existing Line ———→

Figure 5-37A   Using the **From** Object Snap—Step 1

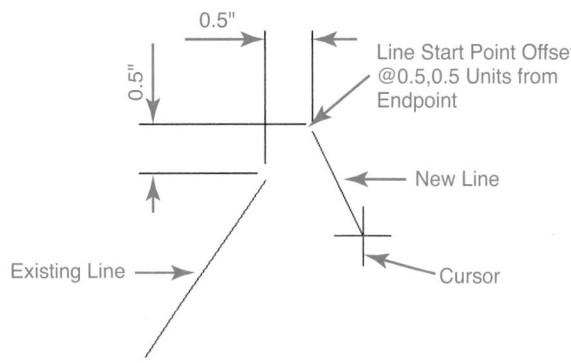

0.5"

0.5"

Line Start Point Offset
@0.5,0.5 Units from
Endpoint

New Line

Existing Line ———→

Cursor

Figure 5-37B   Using the **From** Object Snap—Step 2

Exercise 5-8: Using the From Object Snap

1. Open drawing **EX5-2.dwg**.
2. Turn off all the drawing tool buttons on the Status Bar.
3. Right-click on the **Object Snap** button on the Status Bar and select **Settings...** from the shortcut menu. The **Object Snap** tab of the **Drafting Settings** dialog box is displayed. See Figure 5-17.
4. Select the **Clear All** button to clear any running Object Snaps. Turn on the **Endpoint** Object Snap. Turn **Object Snaps** on in the upper left corner. Exit the **Drafting Settings** dialog box by selecting **OK**.
5. Start the **CIRCLE** command. AutoCAD prompts you to *Specify center point for circle or ↓.*
6. Hold down the **<Shift>** key on your keyboard while right-clicking with your mouse to display the **Object Snap** shortcut menu. See Figure 5-16.
7. Select the **From** Object Snap from the menu. AutoCAD prompts you for a base point:

    `Base point:`

8. Place your cursor over the endpoints on the bottom left corner of the square and wait until the **Endpoint** AutoSnap Marker and tooltip are displayed. Pick a point while the AutoSnap Marker is displayed. See Figure 5-38.

Note:
Specifying an absolute coordinate without the symbol will simply locate the point at the coordinate specified.

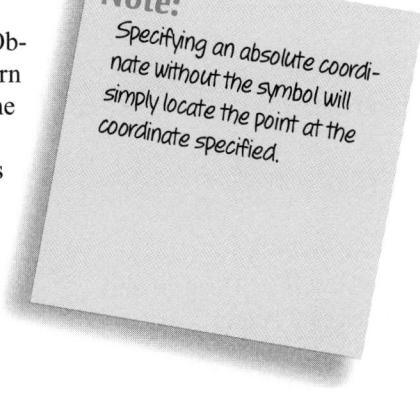

Endpoint
Reference
Step 12

Endpoint
Reference
Step 12

0.5"

Endpoint
Reference
Step 8

0.5"

Endpoint
Reference
Step 12

Figure 5-38   Using the **From** Object Snap

9. AutoCAD then prompts you for an offset distance:

    `<Offset>:`

10. Type **@.5,.5<Enter ↵>**. AutoCAD locates the center point of the circle and prompts you for a radius:

    `Specify radius of circle or ↓.`

11. Type **.25<Enter ↵>**.
12. Repeat steps 5 through 11 to locate three more circles with a 0.25 radius a half inch in from each corner. See Figure 5-38.
13. Save your drawing as **EX5-8**. Your drawing should look like Figure 5-38.

Mid Between 2 Points.   The **Mid Between 2 Points** Object Snap allows you to locate a snap point midway between two points and is typically used in conjunction with other Object Snaps so that you can locate the point precisely. Figures 5-39A through C show how to snap midway between the endpoints of two lines using the **Mid Between 2 Points** Object Snap when drawing a circle.

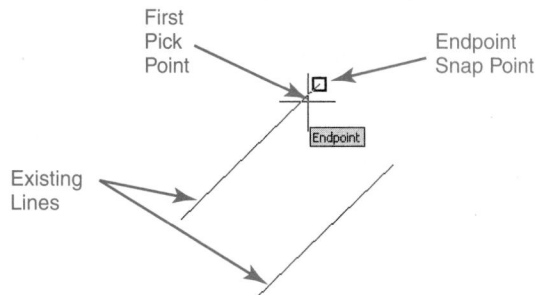

Figure 5-39A   Using the **Mid Between 2 Points** Object Snap—Step 1

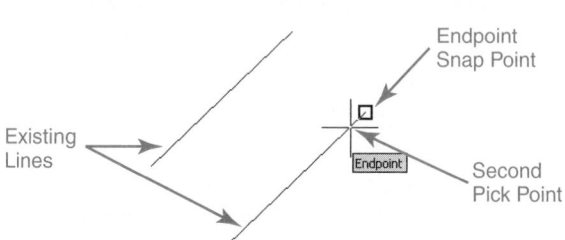

Figure 5-39B   Using the **Mid Between 2 Points** Object Snap— Step 2

Figure 5-39C   Using the **Mid Between 2 Points** Object Snap—Step 3

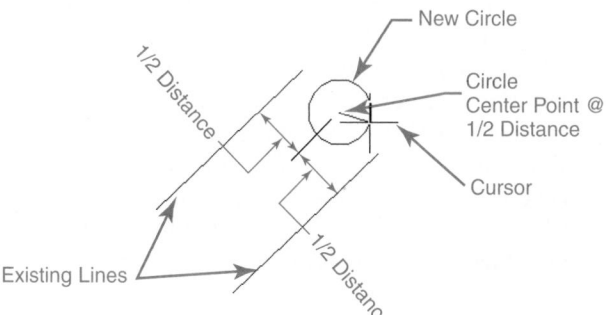

Extension.   The **Extension** Object Snap allows you to display an alignment path along the extension of an arc, elliptical arc, line, multiline, polyline, region, or ray by acquiring an endpoint on one or more objects.

A point is acquired by simply moving your cursor over an endpoint of a valid object type. You *do not* need to pick a point to acquire it when using the **Extension** Object Snap. A small cross is displayed after a point is acquired. You can deselect an acquired point by moving your cursor back over the acquired point so the cross disappears.

After a point is acquired, you display an alignment path by moving your cursor in the object's extension direction. Once the alignment path is displayed, you can locate a point by picking a point on the path or by using direct distance entry to specify a distance to travel along the vector. Figures 5-40A and B show how to locate a line start point on the extension alignment path of a line using the **Extension** Object Snap.

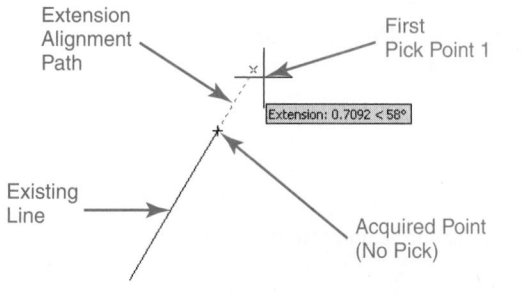

Figure 5-40A   Using the **Extension** Object Snap—Step 1

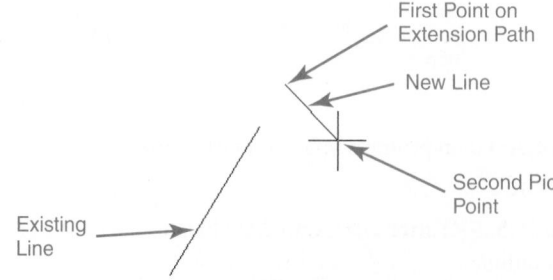

Figure 5-40B   Using the **Extension** Object Snap—Step 2

Exercise 5-9: Using the Extension Object Snap

1. Continue from Exercise 5-8.
2. Turn on the **Ortho Mode** button on the Status Bar.
3. Right-click on the **Object Snap** button on the Status Bar and select **Settings...** from the shortcut menu. The **Object Snap** tab of the **Drafting Settings** dialog box is displayed. See Figure 5-17.
4. Select the **Clear All** button to clear any running Object Snaps. Turn on the **Extension** Object Snap. Turn **Object Snaps** on in the upper left corner. Exit the **Drafting Settings** dialog box by selecting **OK**.
5. Start the **LINE** command.
6. Place your cursor over the endpoints on the bottom left corner of the square to acquire a point. See Figure 5-41.

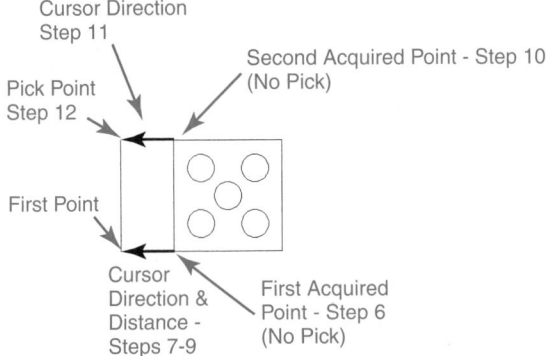

Figure 5-41   Using the **Extension** Object Snap

7. Move your cursor to the left of the corner to display a horizontal alignment path and tooltip indicating you are pointing at 180°. See Figure 5-41.
8. Type **1<Enter ↵>**.
9. AutoCAD uses direct distance entry to place a point 1 unit from the lower left corner along the 180° horizontal extension alignment path. See Figure 5-41.
10. Place your cursor over the endpoints on the top left corner of the square to acquire another point. See Figure 5-41.
11. Move your cursor to the left to display a horizontal alignment path and tooltip indicating you are pointing at 180°. See Figure 5-41.
12. Use **Ortho Mode** to pick a point on the alignment path 90° from the first point. See Figure 5-41.
13. Save your drawing as **EX5-9**. Your drawing should look like Figure 5-41.

Parallel.   The **Parallel** Object Snap allows you to draw a parallel line using a parallel alignment path. The alignment path is displayed by acquiring a point on the line segment to which you want to draw a parallel line when AutoCAD prompts you for the second point of a line.

A **Parallel** Object Snap point is acquired by moving your cursor over the desired line segment. You *do not* need to pick a point to acquire it when using the **Parallel** Object Snap. When you move your cursor over a line segment after selecting the **Parallel** Object Snap, the **Parallel** AutoSnap Marker is displayed, and a point is acquired showing a small cross. You can deselect an acquired point by moving your cursor back over the acquired point so the cross disappears.

After a point is acquired, you display a parallel alignment path by moving your cursor in the parallel direction. Once the alignment path is displayed, you can locate a point by picking a point on the path or by using direct distance entry to specify a distance to travel along the vector. Figures 5-42A and B show how to draw a line parallel to another line using the **Parallel** Object Snap when drawing a line.

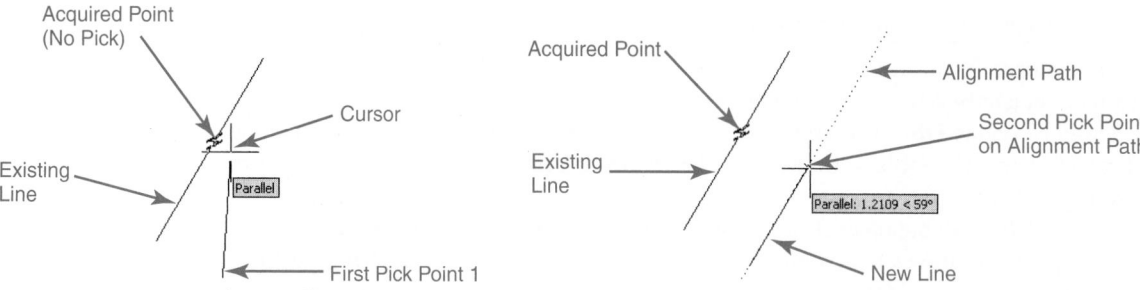

Figure 5-42A Using the **Parallel** Object Snap—Step 1

Figure 5-42B Using the **Parallel** Object Snap—Step 2

OBJECT SNAP TRACKING

Object Snap Tracking relies on the **AutoTracking** feature (explained earlier in the "Polar Tracking" section) to display alignment paths at orthogonal or polar angle settings using points you select in your drawing using Object Snaps. The angle settings used, polar or orthogonal, are controlled in the **Object Snap Tracking Settings** section on the **Polar Tracking** tab of the **Drafting Settings** dialog box shown in Figure 5-43.

Figure 5-43   Object Snap Tracking Settings

By default, **Object Snap Tracking** is set to track orthogonally at horizontal and vertical angles. There are two types of **Object Snap Tracking**:

- **Temporary Tracking**
- **Object Snap Tracking** mode

Temporary Tracking works like an Object Snap override to display tracking alignment paths on an as-needed basis at picked points. The **Object Snap Tracking** mode works with running Object Snaps so that when it is turned on, tracking alignment paths are automatically displayed at all the currently running Object Snap points. Both types of tracking are explained in detail in the following sections.

Temporary Tracking

Temporary Tracking is used on an as-needed basis to display **AutoTracking** alignment paths at acquired points and is typically used in conjunction with Object Snaps.

You must pick a point in your drawing to acquire a point when using **Temporary Tracking**. A small cross is displayed after a point is acquired. You can deselect an acquired point by moving your cursor back over the acquired point so the cross disappears.

After a point is acquired, **AutoTracking** alignment paths are displayed at the angles specified on the **Polar Tracking** tab of the **Drafting Settings** dialog box. Once the alignment path is displayed, you can locate a point by picking a point on the path or by using direct distance entry to specify a distance to travel along the alignment vector. Figures 5-44A through C show how to locate the center point of a circle by tracking horizontally from the midpoint of a vertical line.

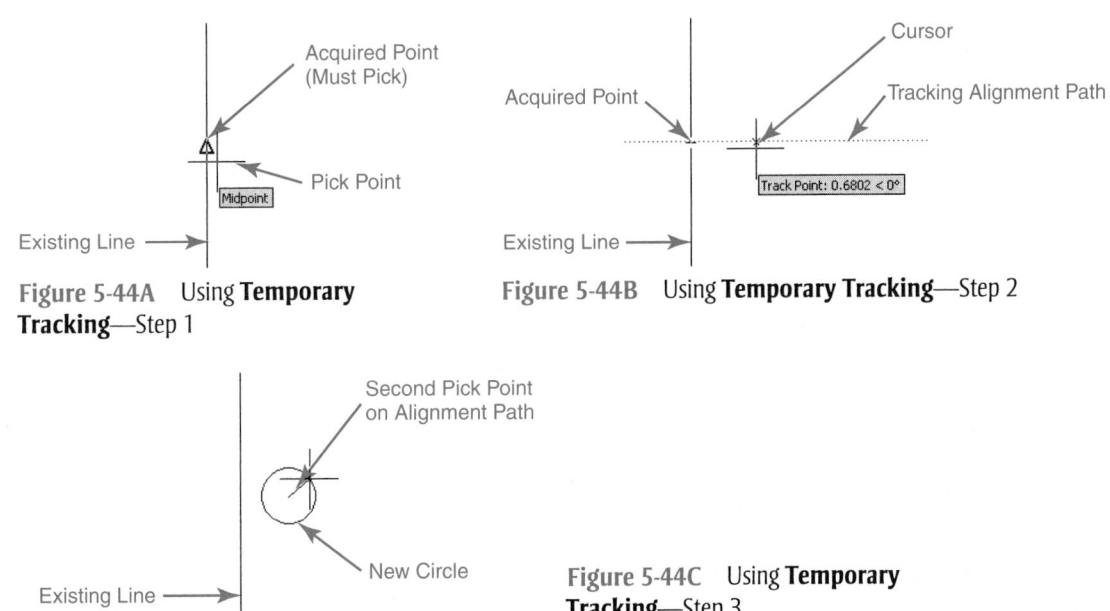

Figure 5-44A   Using **Temporary Tracking**—Step 1

Figure 5-44B   Using **Temporary Tracking**—Step 2

Figure 5-44C   Using **Temporary Tracking**—Step 3

Object Snap Tracking

Object Snap Tracking	
Status Bar:	∠ or OTRACK
Function Key:	F11
Command Line:	None
Keyboard Combo:	None

The **Object Snap Tracking** drawing tool works with running Object Snaps so that when **Object Snap Tracking** mode is turned on **AutoTracking** alignment paths can be displayed by acquiring a point at any currently running Object Snap point.

Unlike **Temporary Tracking**, when **Object Snap Tracking** mode is on, you *do not* have to pick a point to acquire it. You just move your cursor over an Object Snap point, and a small cross (+) is displayed, indicating the point is acquired. You can deselect an acquired point by moving your cursor back over the acquired point so the cross disappears.

After a point is acquired, **AutoTracking** alignment paths are displayed at the angle specified on the **Polar Tracking** tab of the **Drafting Settings** dialog box. Once the alignment path is displayed, you can locate a point by picking a point on the path or by using direct distance entry to specify a distance to travel along the alignment vector.

Intersecting Alignment Paths

Both **Temporary Tracking** and **Object Snap Tracking** allow you to display multiple **AutoTracking** alignment paths so that you can locate points relative to multiple objects in your drawing. When you use **AutoTracking**, each point you snap to displays its own alignment path. If multiple alignment paths cross, it is possible to snap to their point of intersection by putting your cursor over the intersection until a small cross appears that looks similar to an acquired point and then picking a point. Figures 5-45A through C show how to locate the center of a circle using the intersection point of vertical and horizontal **AutoTracking** alignment paths.

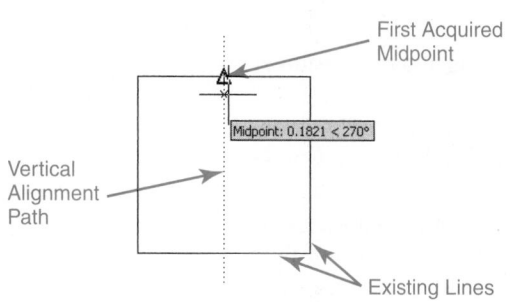

Figure 5-45A   Intersecting alignment paths—Step 1

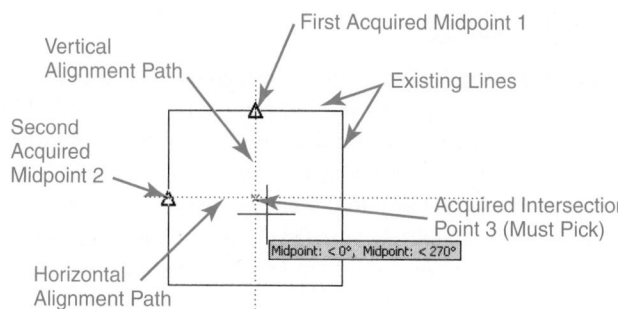

Figure 5-45B   Intersecting alignment paths—Step 2

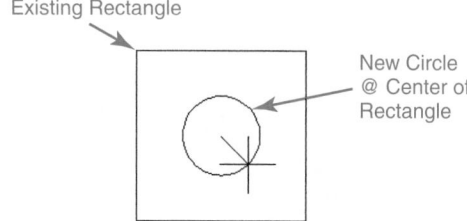

Figure 5-45C   Intersecting
alignment paths—Step 3

Exercise 5-10: Using Object Snap Tracking

1. Continue from Exercise 5-9.
2. Turn off all the drawing tool buttons on the Status Bar.
3. Right-click on the **Object Snap** button on the Status Bar and select **Settings...** from the shortcut menu. The **Object Snap** tab of the **Drafting Settings** dialog box is displayed. See Figure 5-17.
4. Select the **Clear All** button to clear any running Object Snaps. Turn on the **Midpoint** Object Snap. Turn **Object Snaps** on in the upper left corner. Exit the **Drafting Settings** dialog box by selecting the **OK** button.
5. Turn on the **Object Snap Tracking** button on the Status Bar.
6. Start the **CIRCLE** command. AutoCAD prompts you to *Specify center point for circle or* ↓.
7. Acquire a point at the middle point of the horizontal line on the top of the square by placing your cursor over the horizontal line so the **Midpoint** AutoSnap Marker and tooltip are displayed. *Do not* pick a point. See Figure 5-46.

Figure 5-46   Using
Object Snap Tracking

8. Acquire a point at the middle point of the vertical line on the left of the square by placing your cursor over the vertical line so the **Midpoint** AutoSnap Marker and tooltip are displayed. *Do not* pick a point. See Figure 5-46.
9. Move your cursor to the middle of the rectangle to display both a horizontal alignment path with tooltip and a vertical alignment path with tooltip.
10. Pick a point when the two alignment paths cross and the small acquired intersection point marker (x) is displayed. See Figure 5-46.
11. AutoCAD locates the center point of the circle at the center of the rectangle and prompts you for a radius:

   Specify radius of circle or ↓.

12. Type **.25<Enter ↵>**.
13. Save your drawing as **EX5-10**. Your drawing should look like Figure 5-46.

DYNAMIC INPUT

As mentioned in Chapter 1, **Dynamic Input** is a set of related input and display features that allows you to enter information near the mouse cursor so you can focus on your drawing instead of constantly switching focus to the command line for command prompts and data entry.

The **Dynamic Input** interface consists of three different components:

- **Pointer Input**
- **Dimension Input**
- **Dynamic Prompts**

Each of these different components is explained in the following sections.

Dynamic Input	
Status Bar:	⊹ or DYN
Function Key:	F12
Command Line:	None
Keyboard Combo:	None

Pointer Input

When **Pointer Input** is on, the coordinate location of the mouse crosshairs is displayed as *X* and *Y* values in a tooltip near the cursor. As you move your mouse the coordinate values are dynamically updated to reflect the cursor's new location. The **Pointer Input** for the first point of a line is shown in Figure 5-47.

Figure 5-47   Using **Pointer Input**

The **Pointer Input** tooltip consists of *X* and *Y* input fields that you can update with a coordinate value of your choice via the keyboard using the same comma-delimited format used for entering coordinates at the command line by typing **X,Y<Enter ↵>**. Entering the comma after the *X* value locks the input field for *X* and shifts focus to the *Y* input field. Entering the desired *Y* value and hitting **<Enter ↵>** accepts the coordinate value.

TIP   It is also possible to use the **<Tab>** key to switch between the *X* and *Y* coordinate input fields.

Dimension Input

When **Dimension Input** is on, distance and angle values are displayed in multiple tooltips near the cursor when a command prompts for a second point. The values in the dimension tooltips change as you move the cursor. The **Dimension Input** for the second point of a line is shown in Figure 5-48.

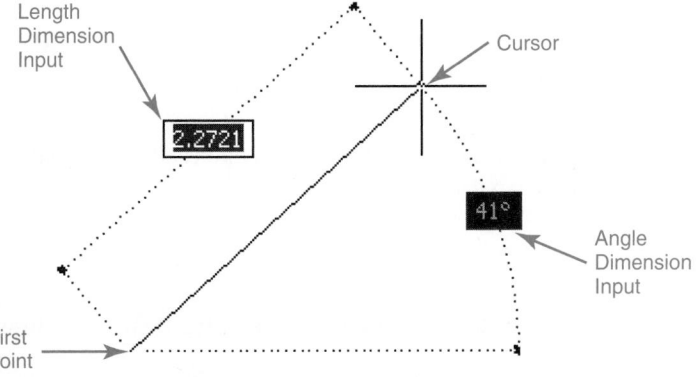

Figure 5-48   Using **Dimension Input**

You can use the **<Tab>** key to switch between the different length and angle **Dimension Input** fields. When you use the **<Tab>** key, focus switches to another **Dimension Input** field while locking the previous field. Using this feature, you can input a length for a line and then press the **<Tab>** key to switch to the angle field to specify the angle. Any angle you input will create a line at that angle with the length previously entered in the length field. This process also works in reverse so that you can press the **<Tab>** key to enter the angle first and then press the **<Tab>** key again to enter the length. Now a line will be created at the preset input angle at any length specified.

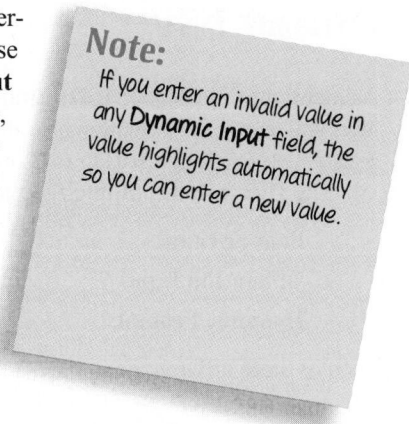

Note:
If you enter an invalid value in any **Dynamic Input** field, the value highlights automatically so you can enter a new value.

Dynamic Prompts

When **Dynamic Prompts** are on, command prompts and options are displayed in a tooltip near the cursor. You can type a response in the **Dynamic Prompt** input field instead of on the command line. The **Dynamic Prompt** for the **POLYGON** command is shown in Figure 5-49.

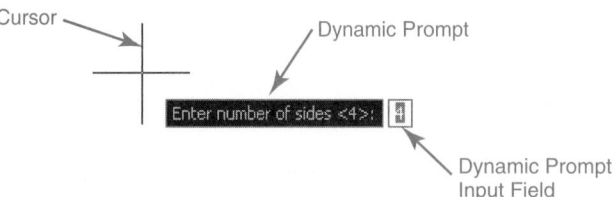

Figure 5-49   Using **Dynamic Prompts**

Dynamic Prompts also allow you to select command options near the cursor using the arrow keys on your keyboard. If a command has options, a down arrow is displayed in the **Dynamic Prompt** tooltip. Pressing the down arrow key displays the command options in a shortcut menu near the cursor. The **ZOOM** command options are shown in Figure 5-50.

Figure 5-50   Selecting **Dynamic Prompt** options

You can use your up and down arrow keys to navigate to the desired option and hit **<Enter ↵>**, or you can select an option with your mouse pointer.

Dynamic Input Settings

The **Dynamic Input** settings are managed on the **Dynamic Input** tab of the **Drafting Settings** dialog box shown in Figure 5-51.

Pointer
Input
Settings

Dimension
Input
Settings

Tooltip Appearance
Settings

Figure 5-51   Dynamic Input settings

The following sections explain the different dynamic input settings.

Pointer Input Settings.   You can turn **Pointer Input** on and off via the **Enable Pointer Input** check box. The **Settings...** button displays the **Pointer Input Settings** dialog box shown in Figure 5-52. This dialog box allows you to control the format and visibility of the **Pointer Input** coordinate tooltips.

The different format settings are as follows:

- **Polar format**   Enter the second or next point in polar coordinate format. Enter a comma (,) to change to Cartesian format.

- **Cartesian format**   Enter the second or next point in Cartesian coordinate format. You can enter an angle symbol (**<**) to change to polar format.

Figure 5-52   The **Pointer Input Settings** dialog box

- **Relative coordinates**   Enter the second or next point in relative coordinate format. Enter a pound sign (**#**) to change to absolute format.
- **Absolute coordinates**   Enter the second or next point in absolute coordinate format. Enter an at sign (**@**) to change to polar format.

The different visibility settings are as follows:

- **As soon as I type coordinate data**   Displays tooltips only when you start to enter coordinate data
- **When a command asks for a point**   Displays tooltips whenever a command prompts for a point
- **Always—even when not in command**   Always displays tooltips when **Pointer Input** is turned on

Dimension Input Settings.   You can turn **Dimension Input** on and off via the **Enable Dimension Input where possible** check box. The **Settings...** button displays the **Dimension Input Settings** dialog box shown in Figure 5-53. This dialog box allows you to control the visibility of the **Dimension Input** coordinate tooltips when you are editing using grips.

Figure 5-53   The **Dimension Input Settings** dialog box

The different visibility settings are as follows:

- **Show only 1 dimension input field at a time**   Displays only the distance **Dimension Input** tooltip when you are using grips
- **Show 2 dimension input fields at a time**   Displays the distance and angle **Dimension Input** tooltips when you are using grips
- **Show the following dimension input fields simultaneously**   Displays the selected **Dimension Input** tooltips when you are using grips. You can select one or more of the check boxes

Dynamic Prompts.   You can turn **Dynamic Prompts** on and off via the **Show command prompting and command input near the crosshairs** check box (see Figure 5-51).

Controlling the Drafting Tooltip Appearance.   The **Drafting Tooltip Appearance...** button displays the **Tooltip Appearance** dialog box shown in Figure 5-54. This dialog box allows you to control the color, size, and transparency of the **Dynamic Input** tooltips.

To change the color of the tooltip in model space, select the **Model Color** button. To change the color of the tooltip in paper space, select the **Layout color** button. Both buttons display the

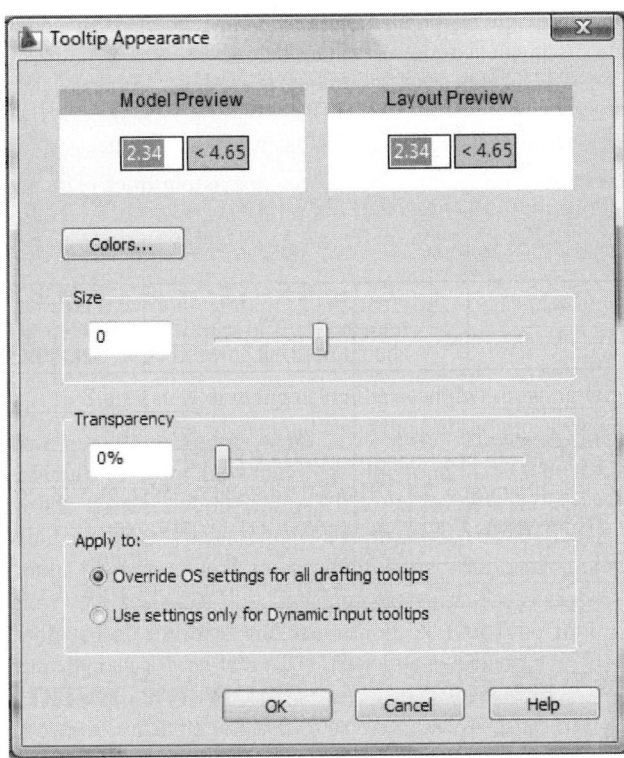

Figure 5-54 The **Tooltip Appearance** dialog box

AutoCAD **Select Color** dialog box where you can specify a color for the tooltips in the space you selected.

To change the size of tooltips, you can either move the slider to the right to make tooltips bigger or move it to the left to make tooltips smaller. The default size is 0.

To change the transparency of tooltips, you can either move the slider to the right to make tooltips more transparent or move it to the left to make them less transparent. A value of 0 makes the tooltips opaque.

You can choose to apply your changes using the following:

- **Override OS settings for all drafting tooltips** Applies the settings to all tooltips, overriding the settings in the operating system

- **Use settings only for Dynamic Input tooltips** Applies the settings only to the drafting tooltips used in **Dynamic Input**

USING CONSTRUCTION LINES

Construction lines are temporary lines that are used to help you lay out, or construct, a drawing. Using construction lines to create drawings is a technique that has been around since the early days of drafting. On the board, construction lines were typically drawn with very light lines that could be erased after the final drawing was created. Using AutoCAD, construction lines are typically created on a separate layer so you can control their visibility by turning them on and off.

| **FOR MORE DETAILS** | See Chapter 6 for detailed information on using layers to separate drawing information to control the visibility of objects. |

Construction lines serve many purposes. Some of the more common uses of construction lines are:

- Creating multiple views of a mechanical drawing using ***orthographic projection***
- Temporary locating of geometric features using Object Snaps and offset distances
- Creating architectural elevations based on features located on an existing floor plan, and vice versa
- Bisecting an angle

One of the classic uses of construction lines is in the creation of multiple views of a mechanical drawing using orthographic projection. See Figure 5-55.

orthographic projection:
The two-dimensional graphic representation of an object formed by the perpendicular intersections of lines drawn from points on the object to a plane of projection

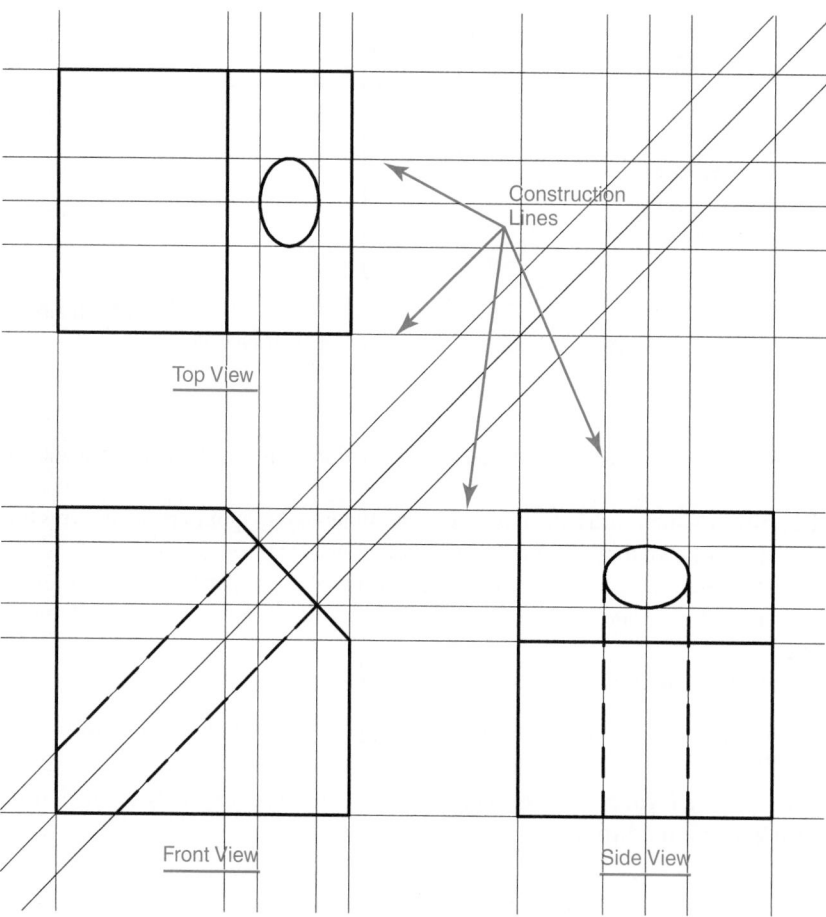

Figure 5-55   Multiview drawing using orthographic projection

Using construction lines, you can create one view of a part (i.e., Front, Top, Side) and then locate horizontal and vertical (orthographic) construction lines on key points of the part using the Object Snaps explained earlier in the chapter to project the points as construction lines in other views. You can then create the other views by drawing directly over the top of the construction lines using the **Intersection** Object Snap introduced earlier. Once you complete all the necessary views to describe the part, you can erase or turn off the construction line layer, and you have a finished drawing.

Using the construction line approach, you have to measure distances only once when you create the first view of the part. Most, if not all, of the other views can then be created by projecting construction lines from the original view, which you know is accurate. Theoretically, if you draw the part correctly in the first view, all the other views that are based on it should also be correct. Using construction lines is a great timesaving technique that increases production and promotes precision.

The XLINE Command

In AutoCAD, construction lines are referred to as *Xlines* and extend infinitely in both directions. This infinite property allows you to zoom or pan as far as necessary and always have the construction lines visible so you can reference them. Construction lines are created using the **XLINE** command.

There are a number of different ways to create construction lines using the **XLINE** command:

- Using two pick points
- Horizontally
- Vertically
- Offset from an existing line
- Specified angle
- Bisected angle

The **XLINE** command options are explained in the following sections.

Note: The **Zoom Extents** tool is unaffected by Xline objects. Any Xlines that exist in a drawing are ignored when zooming to the drawing extents.

Construction Line	
Ribbon & Panel:	Home|Draw 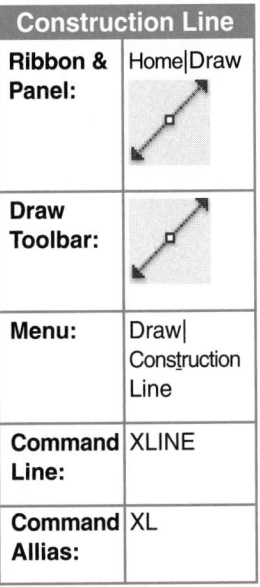
Draw Toolbar:	
Menu:	Draw| Construction Line
Command Line:	XLINE
Command Allias:	XL

FOR MORE DETAILS   See Chapter 3 for more information about using the **Zoom Extents** tool.

Drawing a Construction Line Using Two Points.   This is the default option for creating construction lines. To create an Xline using two points, select the **XLINE** command and pick two points. The first point locates the Xline, and the second point determines its angle. Typically you select points using the Object Snaps explained earlier in the chapter when creating construction lines so that the construction line is drawn relative to an existing object. See Figure 5-56.

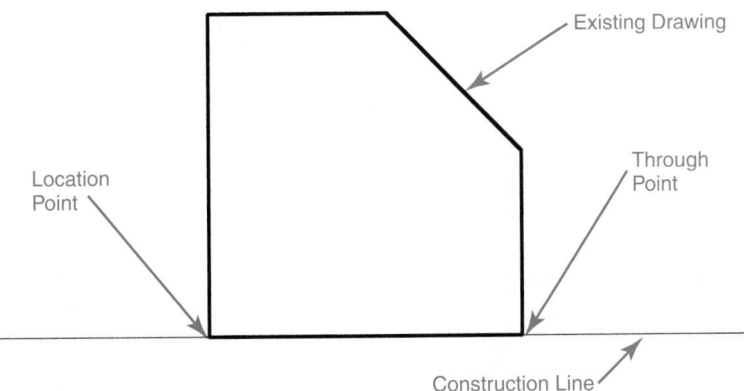

Existing Drawing

Through Point

Location Point

Construction Line

Figure 5-56   Drawing a construction line using two points

TIP   The first point you select to create a construction line using two points becomes the midpoint of the construction line so that you can snap to it using the **Midpoint** Object Snap later.

Drawing Horizontal and Vertical Construction Lines.   Horizontal and vertical construction lines are the two most popular **XLINE** command options because they help facilitate the creation of multiview drawings using orthographic projection.

To create a horizontal construction line, select the **XLINE** command and type **H<Enter ↵>** at the command line or select **Hor** from the list of **Dynamic Input** command options. To create a vertical construction line, select the **XLINE** command and type **V<Enter ↵>** at the command line or select **Ver** from the list of **Dynamic Input** command options. You then select a single point to locate the horizontal or vertical construction line in your drawing. AutoCAD continues to prompt for points until you type **<Enter ↵>** so you can create as many construction lines as needed. See Figures 5-57A and B.

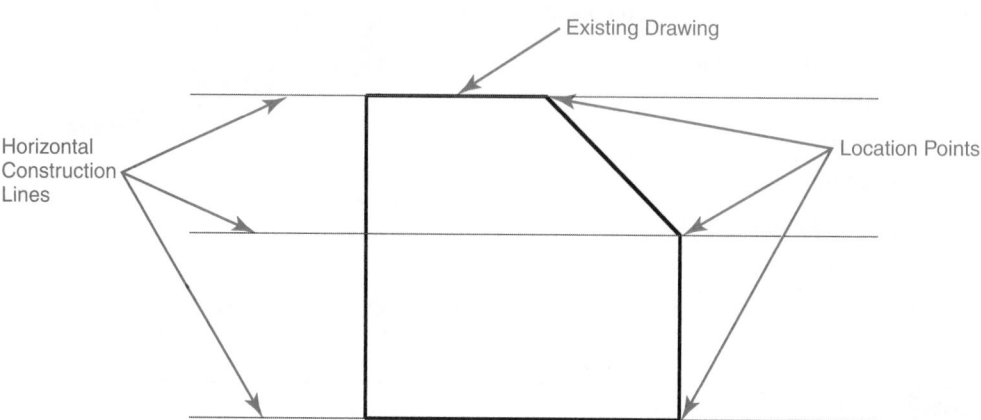

Figure 5-57A   Drawing horizontal construction lines

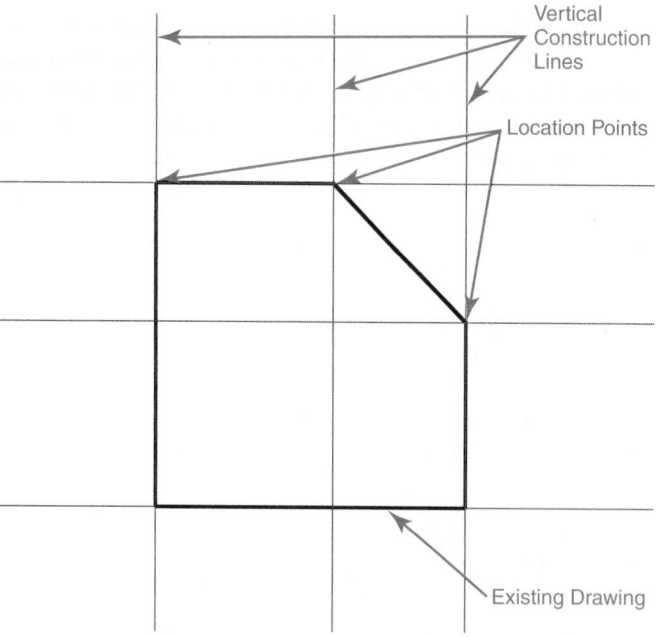

Figure 5-57B   Drawing vertical construction lines

Exercise 5-11: Drawing Horizontal and Vertical Construction Lines

1. Start a new drawing using the acad.dwt drawing template.
2. Create the drawing shown in Figure 5-58.
3. Turn off all the drawing tool buttons on the Status Bar.
4. Right-click on the **Object Snap** button on the Status Bar and select **Settings...** from the shortcut menu. The **Object Snap** tab of the **Drafting Settings** dialog box is displayed. See Figure 5-17.

Figure 5-58   Front view of part

5. Select the **Clear All** button to clear any running Object Snaps. Turn on the **Endpoint, Midpoint,** and **Intersection** Object Snaps. Exit the **Drafting Settings** dialog box by selecting **OK**.
6. Turn on the **Object Snap** button on the Status Bar.
7. Start the **XLINE** command.
8. Type **H<Enter ↵>** or select **Hor** from the **Dynamic Input** command options. AutoCAD prompts you for a through point:

   `Specify through point:`

9. Create three horizontal construction lines by snapping to the three endpoints using the **Endpoint** Object Snap as shown in Figure 5-57A.
10. Type **<Enter ↵>** to end the **XLINE** command.
11. Start the **XLINE** command again.
12. Type **V<Enter ↵>** or select **Ver** from the **Dynamic Input** command options. AutoCAD prompts you for a through point:

    `Specify through point:`

13. Create three vertical construction lines by snapping to the three endpoints using the **Endpoint** Object Snap as shown in Figure 5-57B.
14. Type **<Enter ↵>** to end the **XLINE** command.
15. Save your drawing as **EX5-11**. Your drawing should look like Figure 5-59.

Offsetting Objects with Construction Lines.   To further facilitate the layout and construction of a drawing, you can offset an existing line object (Line, Polyline, etc.) with a parallel construction line by either specifying a distance or picking a through point.

To offset an object, select the **XLINE** command and type **O<Enter ↵>** at the command line or select **Offset** from the list of **Dynamic Input** command options. The offset distance can either be entered via the keyboard, or it can be indicated by selecting the point in the drawing you want to offset through. The default is to enter the distance at the keyboard.

Both options require that you select the line object you want to offset (see Figure 5-60A) and then pick a point on either side of the selected line object to indicate the direction you want to

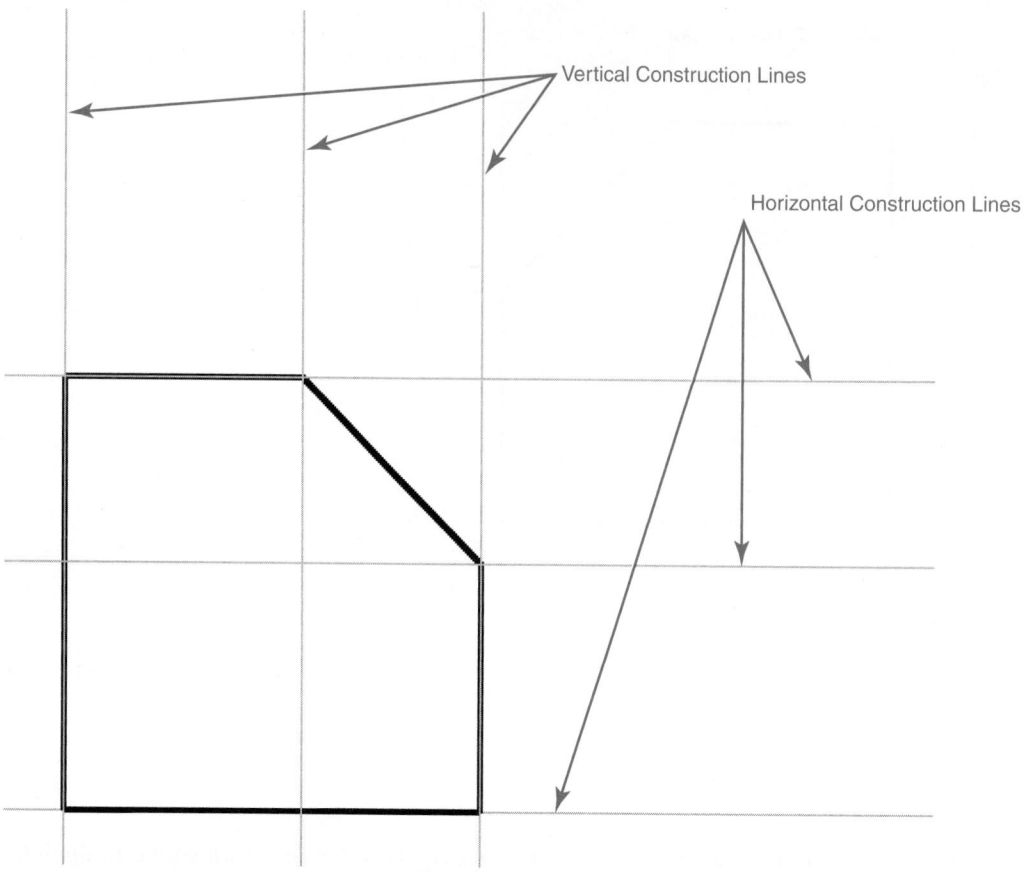

Figure 5-59   Drawing horizontal and vertical construction lines

offset (see Figure 5-60B). If you are using the **Through** option, the pick point is also used to locate the line.

AutoCAD will continue to prompt you to select objects to offset until you press **<Enter ↵>** so that it is possible to offset multiple objects at a time.

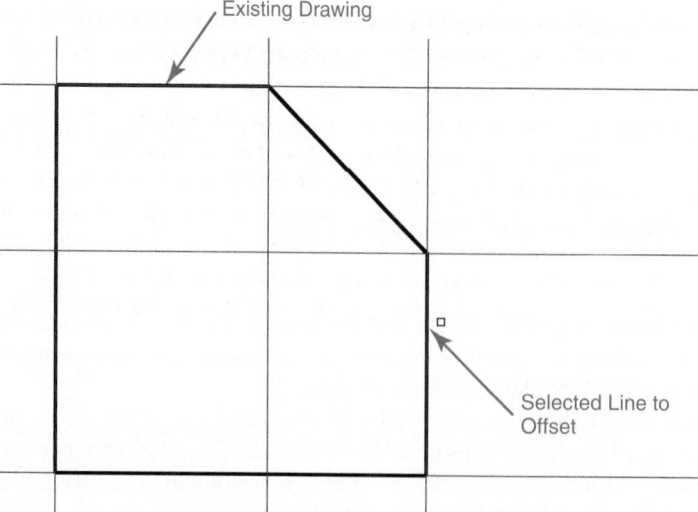

Figure 5-60A   Offsetting an object with a construction line

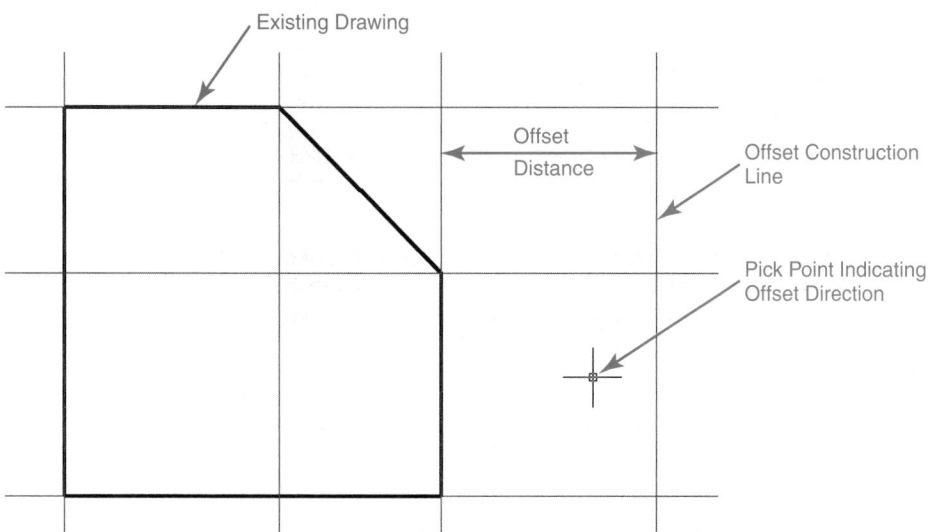

Figure 5-60B   Offsetting an object with a construction line

Exercise 5-12: Offsetting Objects with Construction Lines

1. Continue from Exercise 5-11.
2. Select the **XLINE** command from the **Draw** panel.
3. Type **O<Enter ↵>** or select **Offset** from the **Dynamic Input** command options.
4. AutoCAD prompts you for an offset distance or through point:

   Specify offset distance or ↓.

5. Type **2<Enter ↵>**. AutoCAD prompts you to select the object you want to offset:

   Select a line object:

6. Select the vertical line as shown in Figure 5-60A. AutoCAD then prompts you for the side you wish to offset:

   Specify side to offset:

7. Pick a point on the right side of the object as shown in Figure 5-60B to indicate that you want to create a vertical construction line offset on the right-hand side of the line.
8. AutoCAD continues to prompt you to select line objects.
9. Repeat Steps 6 and 7 to create a horizontal construction line offset 2 units up from the horizontal line on top of the part as shown in Figure 5-61.
10. Type **<Enter ↵>** to end the **XLINE** command.
11. Repeat steps 2 through 9 to create vertical and horizontal construction lines offset 3 units from the construction lines you just created so your drawing looks like Figure 5-61.
12. Save your drawing as **EX5-12**.

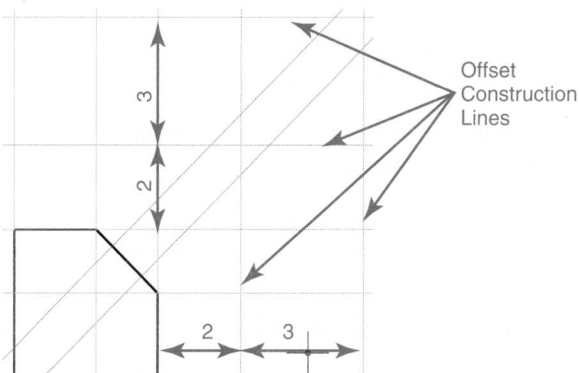

Figure 5-61   Offsetting objects with construction lines

Figure 5-62 Drawing a construction line at an angle

Drawing Angular Construction Lines.   Construction lines can be created at an angle by either specifying an angle from the horizontal axis 0° or referencing an angle from an existing line.

To create a construction line at an angle, select the **XLINE** command and type **A<Enter ↵>** at the command line or select **Angle** from the list of **Dynamic Input** command options. By default, AutoCAD prompts you for an angle. Enter the desired angle and locate the construction line by selecting a point. Figure 5-62 shows a 45° construction line located at the **Midpoint** Object Snap of an angled line.

Using the **Reference** option allows you to select a line object and use its existing angle as a base angle. You can then enter the angle relative to the selected line object. For instance, to create the 45° construction line shown in Figure 5-62 using the **Reference** option, you would first select the existing angled line and then input the desired angle relative to the selected line. Inputting 90° creates a construction line perpendicular to the angled line, which just so happens to also be 45° from the *X*-axis.

Exercise 5-13: Drawing Angular Construction Lines

1. Continue from Exercise 5-12.
2. Start the **XLINE** command.
3. Type **A<Enter ↵>** or select **Angle** from the **Dynamic Input** command options.
4. AutoCAD prompts you to enter an angle:

   `Enter angle of xline (0) or ↓.`

5. Type **45<Enter ↵>**. AutoCAD prompts you for a through point:

   `Specify through point:`

6. Select the **Midpoint** Object Snap of the angled line as shown in Figure 5-62.
7. Type **<Enter ↵>** to end the **XLINE** command.
8. Start the **XLINE** command again.
9. Type **O<Enter ↵>** or select **Offset** from the **Dynamic Input** command options.
10. AutoCAD prompts you to specify an offset distance:

    `Specify offset distance or ↓.`

11. Type **.5<Enter ↵>**. AutoCAD prompts you to select the object you want to offset:

    `Select a line object:`

12. Select the angled construction line you just created. AutoCAD then prompts you for the side you wish to offset:

    `Specify side to offset:`

13. Pick a point on the bottom right side of the angled construction line.
14. Select the angled construction line again. AutoCAD then prompts you for the side you wish to offset:

    `Specify side to offset:`

15. Pick a point on the top left side of the angled construction line.
16. Type **<Enter ⏎>** to end the **XLINE** command.
17. Save your drawing as **EX5-13**. Your drawing should look like Figure 5-63.

Figure 5-63   Drawing angular construction lines

Bisecting an Angle with a Construction Line.   You can split an angle into two equal parts by creating a construction line at the bisector of an existing angle using the **XLINE** command's **Bisect** option.

To create a construction line at the bisector of an angle, select the **XLINE** command and type **B<Enter ⏎>** at the command line or select **Bisect** from the list of **Dynamic Input** command options. AutoCAD prompts you to select a vertex point, an angle start point, and an angle endpoint as shown in Figure 5-64.

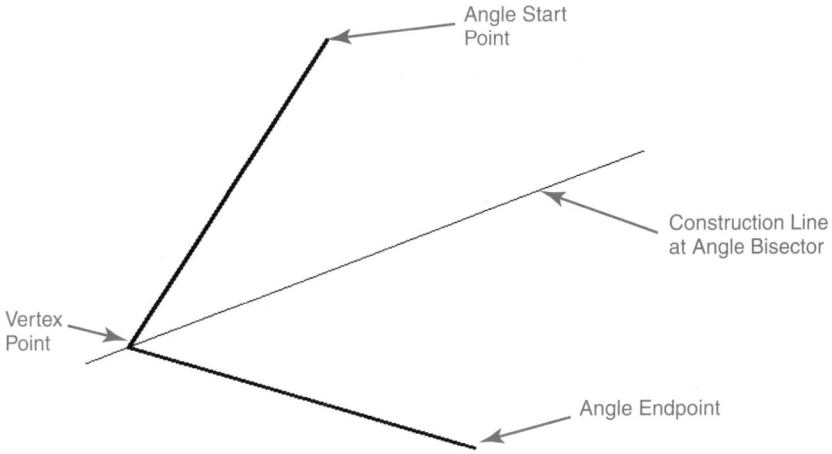

Figure 5-64   Drawing a construction line at an angle

AutoCAD will continue to prompt you to select angle endpoints until you press **<Enter ⏎>** so that it is possible to bisect multiple related angles at the same time.

Exercise 5-14: Creating the Final Drawing Using Construction Lines

1. Continue from Exercise 5-13.
2. Create the remaining horizontal and vertical construction lines shown in Figure 5-65.
3. Use the **Intersection** Object Snap with the **LINE** and **ELLIPSE** commands to create the final drawing shown in Figure 5-65. Hidden lines are not required.

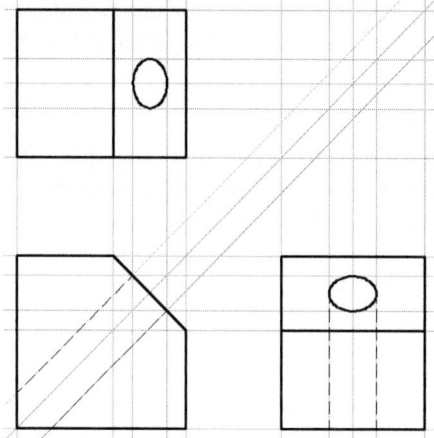

Figure 5-65   Creating the final
drawing using construction lines

4. Erase all the construction lines using the **ERASE** command.
5. Save your drawing as **EX5-14**.

Ray	
Ribbon & Panel:	Home|Draw
Toolbar:	None
Menu:	Draw|Ray
Command Line:	RAY
Command Allias:	None

The RAY Command

It is also possible to create a special construction line known as a *ray* that is like an Xline except that, unlike an Xline, it extends to infinity in only one direction. Rays are created using the **RAY** command.

After selecting the **RAY** command, AutoCAD prompts you to pick a start point and a through point to indicate the direction and angle of the ray as shown in Figure 5-66.

AutoCAD will continue to prompt you for through points until you press **<Enter ↵>** so that it is possible to create multiple rays that share the same start point.

Note:
Similar to Xlines, the **Zoom Extents** tool is unaffected by ray objects. Any rays that exist in a drawing are ignored when zooming to the drawing extents.

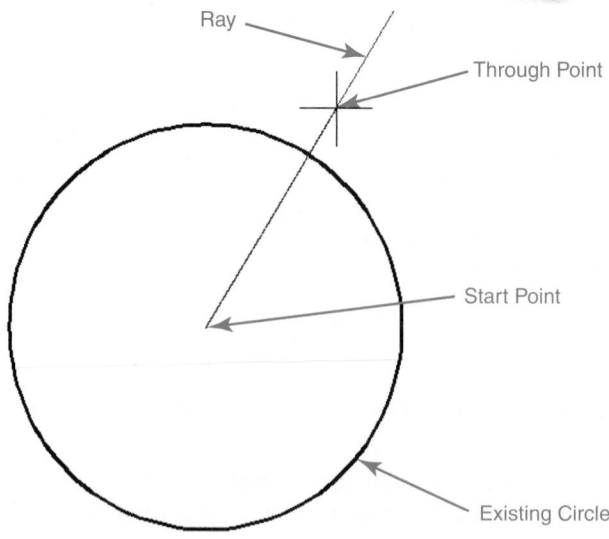

Figure 5-66   Drawing a ray

FOR MORE DETAILS   See Chapter 3 for more information about using the **Zoom Extents** tool.

TIP It is possible to trim and break Xlines and rays using the advanced editing commands introduced in Chapter 8 so that they can be converted into regular AutoCAD lines. When you trim or break the infinite end of a ray, it changes into a line with two endpoints. You must trim or break both infinite ends of an Xline to change it into a line. Using this approach, you can convert your construction lines directly into the final drawing geometry, thus reducing the time it takes to create a drawing.

CHAPTER SUMMARY

Mastering the drawing aids and drafting settings explained in this chapter will increase your drafting productivity exponentially. Being able to locate points quickly and accurately is one of the main keys to being productive. Knowing that a point is located exactly where you intend it makes you a more confident, assured drafter. It's these qualities that help you to succeed in creating quality CAD drawings.

CHAPTER TEST QUESTIONS

Multiple Choice

1. Most of AutoCAD's drawing tools can be toggled on and off by:
   a. Selecting the buttons on the Status Bar
   b. Using keyboard function keys
   c. Typing them at the command line
   d. All of the above

2. The **Drafting Settings** dialog box can be displayed by:
   a. Typing **DS** at the command line
   b. Right-clicking with your mouse on a drawing tool button
   c. Selecting **Drafting Settings...** from the **Tools** menu
   d. All of the above

3. The rectangular **Grid Display** area is determined by the:
   a. Units setting
   b. Drawing limits
   c. Zoom scale factor
   d. Size of your computer monitor

4. The two major different **Snap** styles are:
   a. Rectangular and polar
   b. Rotated and isometric
   c. Horizontal and vertical
   d. Rows and columns

5. The **Ortho Mode** drawing tool restricts your cursor movement to:
   a. 45° angles
   b. 90° angles
   c. Horizontal axis
   d. Vertical axis

6. **Polar Tracking** works by displaying a dashed line referred to as:
   a. Construction line
   b. Vector path
   c. Alignment path
   d. Tracking path

7. Object Snaps can be selected by:
   a. Right-clicking on the **Object Snap** button on the Status Bar
   b. Using the right-click shortcut menu
   c. Typing them at the command line
   d. All of the above

8. Turning an Object Snap on via the **Object Snap** tab of the **Drafting Settings** dialog box is referred to as:
   a. Making an Object Snap permanent
   b. Setting a running Object Snap
   c. Creating an Object Snap override
   d. Setting the default Object Snap

9. An ellipsis (...) next to an Object Snap AutoSnap Marker indicates the Object Snap is:
   a. Implied
   b. Delayed
   c. Waiting for AutoCAD to regen
   d. Deferred

10. The correct format for entering the offset distance when using the **From** Object Snap is:
    a. @2<45
    b. @2,2
    c. All of the above
    d. None of the above

11. **Object Snap Tracking** can display alignment paths:
    a. At all polar increment angles
    b. Horizontally
    c. Vertically
    d. Horizontally and vertically

12. Construction lines are used for:
    a. Laying out your drawing
    b. Creating different views using orthographic projection
    c. Bisecting angles
    d. All of the above

13. The special construction line type that extends infinitely in only one direction is:
    a. Xline
    b. Leader
    c. Ray
    d. Mline

Matching

a. **Grid Display**

b. **Snap Mode**

c. **Ortho Mode**

d. **Polar Tracking**

e. Running Object Snap

f. Object Snap override

g. Acquired point

h. Alignment path

i. **Object Snap Tracking**

j. Construction line

1. Displays dashed alignment paths that temporarily restrict cursor to preset angle increments
2. Object Snap tracking vector used to locate a point
3. Temporary Object Snap that can be used for one pick point
4. Rectangular pattern of evenly spaced dots displayed on the screen
5. Controls movement of cursor to specific X and Y increments
6. Restricts cursor movement to the horizontal (X) and vertical (Y) axes
7. Displays dashed alignment paths at Object Snap points
8. Temporary lines used to lay out a drawing
9. Object Snaps that are on continuously
10. Selected point used to create complex Object Snaps

CHAPTER PROJECTS

Project 5-1: Calculator

1. Start a new drawing using the acad.dwt template.
2. Draw the figure shown in Figure P5-1 using the appropriate grid and snap settings. Toggle the **Object Snap** button **ON** and **OFF** as needed. The borders around the perimeter and around the screen area are 1/16″. The spacing between the buttons is 1/8″. Do **not** draw the dimensions.
3. Save the drawing as **P5-1**.

Figure P5-1

Project 5-2: B-Size Mechanical Border—Continued from Chapter 4

1. Open the template file **Mechanical B-Size.DWT** from Chapter 4.
2. Add the line work shown in Figure P5-2. Do **not** include dimensions.
3. Save the drawing to a template file as **Mechanical B-Size.DWT**.

Figure P5-2

Project 5-3: Architectural D-Size Border—Continued from Chapter 4

1. Open the template file **Architectural D-Size.DWT**.
2. Add the line work as shown to the border as shown in Figure P5-3 using construction lines and object snaps to your advantage. *Hint:* You can use the **DIVIDE** command to lay out the equally spaced title block lines.
3. Save the drawing to a template file as **Architectural D-Size.DWT**.

Project 5-4: Electrical Schematic—Continued from Chapter 4

1. Open drawing **P4-4** from Chapter 4.
2. Set the **Grid Display** and **Snap Mode** drawing tools to **0.125**.
3. Draw the electrical schematic shown in Figure P5-4. *Hint:* Use **Grid Display** and **Snap Mode** to draw the lines and Object Snaps to locate the electrical symbols.
4. Save the drawing as **P5-4**.

Figure P5-3

Figure P5-4

Project 5-5: Residential Architectural Plan—Continued from Chapter 4

1. Open drawing **P4-5** from Chapter 4.
2. Draw the interior and exterior walls as shown in Figure P5-5. The exterior walls are 6″ thick; interior walls are 4″ thick. Use the appropriate Object Snap, **Ortho**, and **Polar Tracking** settings to ensure there are no gaps in the geometry and the

walls are at the correct angle and location. **Do not** draw dimensions or text.
Hint: Use the **Offset** option of the **XLINE** command to locate walls.

3. Save the drawing as **P5-5**.

Figure P5-5

Project 5-6: Support Plate—English Units—Continued from Chapter 4

1. Open drawing **P4-6** from Chapter 4.
2. Create the projected front and right views as shown in Figure P5-6. **Do not** draw dimensions.
3. Save the drawing as **P5-6**.

Figure P5-6

Project 5-7: Widget—Metric

1. Start a new drawing using the acadiso.dwt template.
2. Draw the front and right side views of the part shown in Figure P5-7. **Do not** include dimensions. *Hint:* Draw the front view on the left first and then use construction lines and Object Snaps to draw the right side view using orthographic projection.
3. Save the drawing as **P5-7**.

Figure P5-7

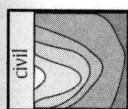

Project 5-8: Civil Site Plan—Continued from Chapter 4

1. Open drawing **P4-8** from Chapter 4.
2. Draw the plant symbols shown in Figure P5-8 to the best of your ability. Use Object Snaps where appropriate. The scale and grid lines are for reference only; do **not** draw the dimensions or reference lines.
3. Save the drawing as **P5-8**.

Figure P5-8

Managing Object Properties

6

Chapter Objectives

- Create layers
- Set layer properties
- Load linetypes
- Modify the properties of drawing objects
- Use DesignCenter to import layers from other drawings
- Create layer filters and groups
- Manage layer states

INTRODUCTION

Precise, accurate, and clear drawings are a primary goal of any drafter. However, equally important in CAD is creating a well-organized drawing. Chapter 2 gave you a brief overview of object properties and layering. In this chapter, we'll take a closer look at object properties, how to effectively use layers to organize your drawing, and how to control the look and final output of your drawing.

COMMON OBJECT PROPERTIES

Every object in AutoCAD has four primary properties associated with it: Color, Linetype, Lineweight, and Layer. These properties control how objects are displayed in your drawing and also control how objects are plotted. Color controls the color of an object and can also be used to control the plotted lineweight of an object, Linetype controls the line pattern (dashed, dotted, etc.) used to display objects, and Lineweight (or pen width) controls the width of objects when plotted.

A *layer* is a collection of color, linetype, and lineweight properties that can be used to organize the objects in your drawing. Layers are the primary way in which drawing information is organized.

The concept of layering goes back to the days of manual drafting in which transparent overlays were used to control the content of a blueprint. For example, an architect might create an architectural base print showing the location of walls, doors, windows, and so on. An electrical engineer might then create a transparent overlay showing the location of the electrical equipment, outlets, and such. To create the electrical plan blueprint, you would take the architectural base print, place the electrical overlay on top of it, and run the stack of drawings through the blueprint machine. The resulting print would show the electrical drawing layer over the top of the architectural base drawing.

Layering in AutoCAD works in a similar way. By assigning a layer to an AutoCAD object, you are, in effect, putting those objects on a transparent overlay. You can then turn these layers on and off and control which objects are shown in the drawing.

layer: A collection of object properties and display settings that are applied to objects

LAYERS

When you create a layer, you provide a name for that layer and then assign it a color, linetype, and lineweight. Any objects placed on that layer will then, by default, take on the color, linetype, and lineweight associated with that layer.

AutoCAD comes with a predefined layer, called layer **0**. By default, everything on layer 0 is drawn with color 7 (white/black), has a continuous linetype, and uses the default lineweight (.25 mm or .01 inch) for plotting. You can change the color, linetype, and lineweight settings for layer **0**, but you cannot delete or rename layer **0**.

Layers are created with the **LAYER** command.

Layer	
Ribbon & Panel:	Home| Layers
Layers Toolbars:	
Menu:	Format| Layer...
Command Line:	LAYER
Command Alias:	LA

The LAYER Command

When you start the **LAYER** command, AutoCAD displays the **Layer Properties Manager** palette (see Figure 6-1). The **Layer Properties Manager** palette works like all other palettes. It can be docked, hidden, or closed as needed.

Figure 6-1   The **Layer Properties Manager** palette

The **Layer Properties Manager** palette allows you to create and control all aspects of your layers. The palette is divided into two main areas; the layer filters are listed on the left, and the list of layers is shown on the right.

Layer filters allow you to show only layers that match a certain criterion—for example, all the layers that start with the letter "E" or all the layers that are red. The list of layers shows the layers currently defined in your drawing along with their current settings.

Layer Name List

The list of layers is divided into columns with each column representing a layer setting. The column headings can be resized by dragging the divider bar between each column. You can also sort the layers by any of the columns by clicking on the column heading. To change a setting for a layer, simply click on the setting. To change the settings for multiple layers, first select the layers by holding down either the **<Shift>** or **<Ctrl>** key and selecting the layers, then click on the setting you want to change. The change will be applied to all the selected layers.

Layer Names.   The layer name is the primary means of identifying a layer. Layer names can have up to 255 characters and can include letters and numbers as well as other special characters, including spaces. Layer names should convey the contents of that layer. Layer names can be based on part numbers, project names, design discipline (civil, architectural, etc.), or any other agreed-upon standard.

Layer Naming Standards.   Many companies create layering standards based on their own experience and practices, or they may adopt or adapt a national or industry CAD standard. A good standard will be well documented, showing the appropriate settings and the type of drawing content that belongs on each layer.

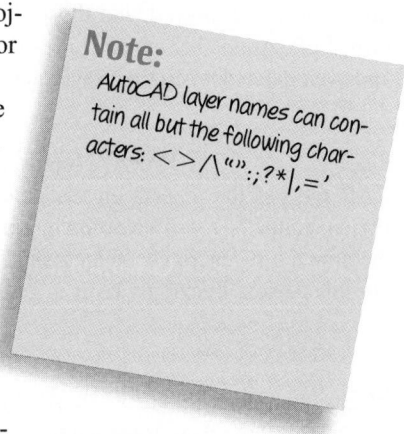

Note:
AutoCAD layer names can contain all but the following characters: <>/\"":;?*|,='

The American Institute of Architects (AIA) has published the CAD Layer Guidelines for the building industry that has been adopted by the National CAD Standards organization (*http://nationalcadstandard. org*). This layering standard describes a method of organizing layers based on a series of prefixes and descriptors that are easy to understand. Each discipline has a prefix; for example, all architectural layers start with A, electrical layers start with E, civil layers start with C, etc. Following the prefix is an abbreviation for the content of that layer, such as A-WALL for architectural walls or E-DEMO for electrical demolition.

The student data files included with this book contain standard drawings for both Architectural and Mechanical Design disciplines. The drawings contain layers set up in accordance with common industry standards.

To access student data files, go to www.pearsondesigncentral.com.

Creating New Layers.   To create a new layer, choose the **New Layer** button on the **Layer Properties Manager** palette. AutoCAD will create a new layer and automatically call it **Layer1**. The layer name is highlighted, so to rename the layer, simply type in the new name and press **<Enter ↵>**. You can press **<Enter ↵>** again to create another new layer.

TIP   You can also create multiple layers by typing the layer names separated by a comma. When you press the comma key, AutoCAD will end the first layer and create a new layer. This method allows you to create multiple layers easily.

Exercise 6-1: Creating Layers

1. Start a new drawing using the acad.dwt drawing template.
2. Start the **LAYER** command to display the **Layer Properties Manager** palette.
3. Choose the **New Layer** button. AutoCAD will create a layer called **Layer1**.
4. Type **Object<Enter ↵>** to rename the new layer.
5. Press **<Enter ↵>** to create another new layer.
6. Type **Hidden<Enter ↵>** to rename the new layer.
7. Press **<Enter ↵>** to create another new layer.
8. Type **Center,Dim,Title<Enter ↵>** to create three new layers. Notice how every time you type the comma key, AutoCAD creates a new layer. You should now have a total of six layers (including layer **0**) in your drawing.
9. Close the **Layer Properties Manager** palette.
10. Save your drawing as **EX6-1**.

Setting the Current Layer.   To set a layer current, select the layer and choose the **Set Current** button (or press **<Alt>+C**). The current layer is the default layer for new drawing objects. Any new object will be placed on the current layer.

On/Off.   The **On/Off** settings control the visibility of the layers in the drawing. Layers that are turned on are displayed, and those that are turned off do not display. However, when a layer is turned off, AutoCAD simply hides the layer from view. Objects can still be selected, modified, and even deleted when their layer is turned off.

Freeze/Thaw.   The **Freeze/Thaw** settings are similar to **On/Off**. When a layer is frozen, Auto-CAD ignores the objects on that layer and does not display them on screen. When a layer is frozen, AutoCAD will completely ignore the objects on that layer until that layer is thawed and the drawing regenerates. Objects on frozen layers cannot be modified until that layer is thawed. For this reason, freezing a layer is generally preferred to turning a layer off.

Exercise 6-2: Freeze and Thaw Versus On and Off

1. Continue from Exercise 6-1.
2. Draw a line anywhere on the screen. Since layer **0** is current, the new line is drawn on layer **0**.
3. Start the **LAYER** command.
4. Select the **Object** layer and choose the **Set Current** button. The **Object** layer is now the current layer.
5. Select layer **0** and choose the sun icon in the **Freeze** column. The sun icon will change to a snowflake, indicating that the layer is frozen. Close or hide the **Layer Properties Manager** palette. The line will disappear because layer **0** is frozen.
6. Choose the **Erase** tool from the **Modify** panel. AutoCAD prompts you to *Select objects:*.
7. Type **All<Enter ↵>**. This tells AutoCAD to select all the objects in the drawing. In the command window, AutoCAD responds 0 found. This tells you that AutoCAD ignored the line on the frozen layer **0**. Press **<Esc>** to end the **ERASE** command.
8. Start the **LAYER** command again and thaw layer **0** by selecting the snowflake in the layer **0 Freeze** column. Select the lightbulb in the **On** column to turn off layer **0**. Close or hide the **Layer Properties Manager** palette.
9. Choose the **Erase** tool again from the **Modify** panel and type **All<Enter ↵>** at the *Select objects:* prompt. In the command window, AutoCAD responds 1 found. This tells you that AutoCAD has selected the line on layer **0**, even though the layer is turned off. Press **<Enter ↵>** to finish the **ERASE** command. AutoCAD will erase the line.
10. Start the **LAYER** command and select the lightbulb to turn layer **0** on. Close the palette to verify that the line was erased.

You can see that although the **On/Off** and **Freeze/Thaw** settings are similar, AutoCAD treats them very differently.

Lock/Unlock.   The **Lock/Unlock** setting controls whether objects on a layer can be modified. Objects on a locked layer can be seen but not modified. To lock a layer, choose the icon in the **Lock** column for the layer you wish to lock.

olor.   The color property is the default display color for objects on a layer. To assign a color to ayer, pick the color swatch for the layer you wish to change. AutoCAD will display the **Select lor** dialog box (Figure 6-2). The **Select Color** dialog box has three tabs: **Index Color, True lor**, and **Color Books**. The three tabs provide different ways to specify colors.

The AutoCAD Color Index (ACI).   The **Index Color** tab shows the **AutoCAD Color** x (ACI), which is the primary way colors are assigned in AutoCAD. The ACI consists of 255 s (numbered 1–255). Colors 1–9 are called the *standard colors* and are shown below the color palette. Grayscale colors are shown below the standard colors.

Colors 1–7 have names assigned to them. The names are shown in the following table:

ACI Number	Color
1	Red
2	Yellow
3	Green
4	Cyan
5	Blue
6	Magenta
7	White

The remaining colors are shown in the large color palette (see Figure 6-2). As you drag your cursor over the various color patches, AutoCAD will display the color number as well as the red, green, and blue components of each color. To select a color, simply click on a color patch. AutoCAD will display the color name or number in the **Color** box. AutoCAD will also show you a preview of the selected color. If you know the color name or number you wish to use, you can simply type it into the **Color** text area.

Note:
Color 7 shows up as black on a white background and white on a black background.

True Color.   The **True Color** tab allows you to select colors based on either the RGB (Red, Green, Blue) or HSL (Hue, Saturation, Luminance) color model (see Figure 6-3). You can select the color model you wish to use from the **Color model**: drop-down list.

The HSL color model allows you to control color properties in three ways. The **Hue** setting refers to a color in the visible spectrum, from 0 to 360. On the color chart, a **Hue** setting goes from 0 on the left of the chart to 360 on the right.

Figure 6-2   The **Select Color** dialog box

Figure 6-3   The HSL color mo

The **Saturation** setting refers to the purity of that color on a scale of 0 to 100 percent. On the color chart, saturation values go from 0 (gray) at the bottom of the chart to 100 (the pure color) at the top of the chart.

The **Luminance** setting represents the brightness of the color on a scale of 0 to 100 percent. The **Luminance** setting is represented in the bar to the right of the color chart. A luminance value of 0 (the bottom of the bar) gives you black, a value of 100 (the top of the bar) gives you white, and a setting of 50 represents the brightest value of the color.

When you select a color on the chart, its color is displayed in the preview area, and its RGB color values are displayed in both the color box and below the **Color model**: drop-down list.

The RGB color model (see Figure 6-4) allows you to mix colors based on the red, green, and blue components. An RGB number is a set of three numbers representing the red, green, and blue color components, respectively. Each component can have a value from 0 to 255 with 0 representing black, or no color, and 255 representing the pure color component. For example, a color setting of 255,0,0 represents red, 0,255,0 represents green, and 0,0,255 represents blue. White has an RGB value of 255,255,255, and black has an RGB value of 0,0,0.

When you select the RGB color model, AutoCAD gives you three sliders to control the RGB components. You can type in a value, pick a point on each slider, or drag the indicator to a location on the slider to specify the value for each component.

Color Books. The **Color Books** tab allows you to select colors based on various color matching standards, such as Pantone, DIC, or RAL. When you select the **Color Books** tab, AutoCAD provides you with a list of available color books and a list of colors in each book (see Figure 6-5). Once you select a color, AutoCAD displays its RGB color value on the right side of the dialog box and shows the color in the preview area.

Figure 6-4   The RGB color model

Figure 6-5   The **Color Books** tab

Exercise 6-3: Setting Layer Colors

1. Continue from Exercise 6-2.
2. Start the **LAYER** command.
3. Choose the color box in the **Color** column of the **Object** layer. The **Select Color** dialog box will appear.
4. In the **Index Color** tab, select the color red (color index 1) and choose **OK** to close the dialog box.
5. Continue setting colors for the layers as follows:
   Center—Blue (color 5)
   Dim—Color 8
   Hidden—Green (color 3)
   Title—White (color 7)

6. Close the **Layer Properties Manager** palette.

7. Save your drawing as **EX6-3**.

Linetypes.   *Linetype* refers to the pattern (continuous, dashed, dotted, etc.) of a line. Linetypes are generally a series of lines, spaces, dots, and symbols (circles, squares, text, etc.) at preset intervals. Linetypes are used to designate a particular type of object (fence line, railroad tracks, hot water line, etc.) or a feature of an object (the hidden edge of an object, centerline of a circle or arc, etc.).

To assign a linetype to a layer, choose the **Linetype** setting for the layer you want to change. The **Select Linetype** dialog box will appear (see Figure 6-6). The **Select Linetype** dialog box shows all the currently available linetypes in your drawing. Before you can use a linetype, it must first be loaded into your drawing.

Figure 6-6   The **Select Linetype** dialog box

Standard Linetypes.   AutoCAD comes with a large selection of standard linetypes. These linetype definitions are stored in linetype files. AutoCAD comes with two standard linetype files, ACAD.LIN and ACADISO.LIN. The standard AutoCAD linetypes are shown in the following table. You can also create and modify linetypes to meet your needs.

Linetype	Description
ACAD_ISO02W100	ISO dash __ __ __ __ __ __ __ __ __ __ __ __ __
ACAD_ISO03W100	ISO dash space __ __ __ __ __ __
ACAD_ISO04W100	ISO long-dash dot ____ . ____ . ____ . ____ . _
ACAD_ISO05W100	ISO long-dash double-dot ____ .. ____ .. ____ .
ACAD_ISO06W100	ISO long-dash triple-dot ____ ... ____ ... ____
ACAD_ISO07W100	ISO dot . . . .
ACAD_ISO08W100	ISO long-dash short-dash ____ __ ____ __ ____ _
ACAD_ISO09W100	ISO long-dash double-short-dash ____ __ __ ____
ACAD_ISO10W100	ISO dash dot __ . __ . __ . __ . __ . __ .
ACAD_ISO11W100	ISO double-dash dot __ __ . __ __ . __ __ . __ _
ACAD_ISO12W100	ISO dash double-dot __ .. __ .. __ .. __ ..

(*continued*)

ACAD_ISO13W100	ISO double-dash double-dot __ __ .. __ __ .. _
ACAD_ISO14W100	ISO dash triple-dot __ ... __ ... __ ... _
ACAD_ISO15W100	ISO double-dash triple-dot __ __ ... __ __ ..
BATTING	Batting SSSSSSSSSSSSSSSSSSSSSSSSSSSSSSSSSSSSSSSS
BORDER	Border __ __ . __ __ . __ __ . __ __ . __ __ .
BORDER2	Border (.5x) __.__.__.__.__.__.__.__.__.
BORDERX2	Border (2x) ____ ____ . ____ ____ . ____
DASHDOT	Dash dot __ . __ . __ . __ . __ . __ . __
DASHDOT2	Dash dot (.5x) __._._._._._._._._._._._.
DASHDOTX2	Dash dot (2x) ____ . ____ . ____ . ___
DIVIDE	Divide ____ .. ____ .. ____ .. ____ .. ____
DIVIDE2	Divide (.5x) __.__.._.__.__._.__._.__._.__
DIVIDEX2	Divide (2x) _____ .. _____ .. _
FENCELINE1	Fenceline circle ----O-----O----O-----O----O-----O--
FENCELINE2	Fenceline square ----[]-----[]----[]-----[]----[]--
GAS_LINE	Gas line ----GAS----GAS----GAS----GAS----GAS----GAS--
HIDDEN	Hidden __ __ __ __ __ __ __ __ __ __ __ __ __
HIDDEN2	Hidden (.5x) _ _ _ _ _ _ _ _ _ _ _ _ _ _ _
HIDDENX2	Hidden (2x) ____ ____ ____ ____ ____ ____ ____
HOT_WATER_SUPPLY	Hot water supply ---- HW ---- HW ---- HW ----
TRACKS	Tracks -|-|-|-|-|-|-|-|-|-|-|-|-|-|-|-|-|-|-|-
ZIGZAG	Zigzag /\/\/\/\/\/\/\/\/\/\/\/\/\

AutoCAD's linetype files, along with the ability to create your own linetypes, means there is a potentially unlimited number of linetypes available. In any given drawing, you will use only a limited number of these linetypes so linetypes are loaded into your drawing on an as-needed basis. To load linetypes into your drawing, choose the **Load...** button in the **Select Linetype** dialog box. This will display the **Load or Reload Linetypes** dialog box (see Figure 6-7).

The **Load or Reload Linetypes** dialog box shows the current linetype file and displays all the linetypes defined within that file. You can specify a different file by choosing the **File...** button and selecting the linetype file you wish to use.

To load a linetype, select a linetype from the list of available linetypes and choose **OK**. You can select multiple linetypes by holding down either the **<Shift>** or **<Ctrl>** key while selecting linetypes. Once you choose **OK**, you are returned to the **Select Linetype** dialog box.

Note:
The ACADISO.LIN file contains all the linetypes included in the ACAD.LIN file but also contains linetypes that support the Japanese Industrial Standard (JIS Z 8312).

Figure 6-7   The **Load or Reload Linetypes** dialog box

Once the linetypes are loaded into your drawing, you can assign a linetype to a layer by selecting a linetype in the **Select Linetype** dialog box and choosing **OK**. The selected linetype will be assigned to the layer.

Exercise 6-4: Setting the Layer Linetype

1. Continue from Exercise 6-3.
2. Start the **LAYER** command.
3. Choose **Continuous** in the **Linetype** column of layer **Center**. This displays the **Select Linetype** dialog box.
4. Choose the **Load...** button. This displays the **Load or Reload Linetypes** dialog box.
5. Hold down the **<Ctrl>** key and select the **CENTER** and **HIDDEN** linetypes. Choose **OK** to return to the **Select Linetype** dialog box. The linetypes have now been loaded into your drawing.
6. Choose the **CENTER** linetype and choose **OK** to assign the linetype to layer **Center**.
7. Choose **Continuous** in the **Linetype** column of layer **Hidden**. This displays the **Select Linetypes** dialog box.
8. Choose the **HIDDEN** linetype and choose **OK** to assign the linetype to layer **Hidden**.
9. Choose **OK** to close the **Layer Properties Manager** palette.
10. Save your drawing as **EX6-4**.

Lineweights. *Lineweight* refers to the printed width of a line. The ANSI (American National Standards Institute) standard Y14.2 recommends using two lineweights (thick and thin) to differentiate contrasting lines. The actual values you use will depend on your particular CAD standards. AutoCAD's default lineweight is .25 mm (.010″).

> **Note:**
> Some linetypes have multiple versions of each linetype defined in the .LIN file. Generally, these linetypes have lines and spaces that are either half or twice the size of the original. For example, in addition to the CENTER linetype, there are also CENTER2 and CENTERX2 linetypes. The CENTER2 linetype has lines and spaces that are half (.5x) the size of the CENTER linetype. The CENTERX2 linetype has lines and spaces that are twice (2x) the size of the CENTER linetype.

> **Note:**
> Before the lineweight setting was introduced in AutoCAD, pen tables were used to map AutoCAD colors to plotted lineweights. For example, all red objects are plotted with a .35 mm pen, yellow objects with a .15 mm pen, etc. AutoCAD still supports pen tables and gives you a number of options for creating and managing pen tables.

Figure 6-8   The **Lineweight** dialog box

FOR MORE DETAILS   See Chapter 15 for more on plotting and the use of pen tables.

To assign a lineweight to a layer, choose the value in the **Lineweight** column for that layer. This will bring up the **Lineweight** dialog box (see Figure 6-8). Select the lineweight you wish to use and choose **OK** to assign the lineweight to the layer.

Exercise 6-5: Setting the Layer Lineweight

1. Continue from Exercise 6-4 and start the **LAYER** command.
2. Choose **Default** in the **Lineweight** column of layer **Object**. This displays the **Lineweight** dialog box.
3. Choose **0.60 mm** from the list and choose **OK**. This sets the lineweight for layer **Object**.
4. Hold down the **<Ctrl>** key and select the **Center, Hidden**, and **Dim** layer names. The layers will highlight.
5. Choose the **Default** icon in the **Lineweight** column of the **Center** layer, and choose **0.30 mm** from the lineweight list. Choose **OK** to set the lineweight for all the selected layers.
6. Choose **OK** to close the **Layer Properties Manager** palette.
7. Save your drawing as **EX6-5**.

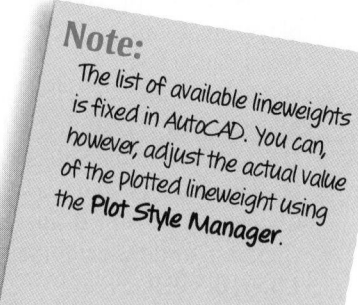

Note:
The list of available lineweights is fixed in AutoCAD. You can, however, adjust the actual value of the plotted lineweight using the **Plot Style Manager.**

You can choose whether or not to display lineweights in your drawing by toggling the **Show/Hide Lineweight** button in the AutoCAD Status Bar.

le.   The **Plot Style** setting is used when a drawing is set up to use color-dependent plot
his is a drawing setting that allows you to use AutoCAD object colors to control the plot-
eight. Chapter 15 describes how to set up and manage color-dependent drawings.

FOR MORE DETAILS   See Chapter 15 for more on plotting and the **Plot Style Manager**.

Plot/Noplot.   The **Plot/Noplot** setting controls whether the contents of a layer will appear on a print of the drawing. This setting allows you to create objects in AutoCAD that will appear only in the drawing file, but not on any of the printed output of the drawing. For example, you may wish to create layers for construction lines, internal design notes, or drafting markups. To toggle the **Plot/Noplot** setting, choose the **Plot** setting for that layer. Plotting layers will show a printer icon, and nonplotting layers will have a red line through the printer icon.

New VP Freeze.   The **New VP Freeze** setting freezes the selected layer in any new viewports that are subsequently created in a paper space layout. It is possible to control layer visibility per individual viewport in paper space so that you can set up multiple views in one or more layouts that each show different drawing information.

In fact, if you are in a paper space layout and start the **LAYER** command to display the **Layers Properties Manager** palette, four columns are added to the right of the **New VP Freeze** column so that you can control all aspects of a layer's appearance per viewport using the following Viewport Overrides:

Note:
In order to take advantage of Viewport Overrides, all drawing objects should be created using the **ByLayer** property discussed later in this chapter in the "Hard-Coded Versus Soft-Coded Properties" section.

- **VP Color**   Controls the layer color per viewport
- **VP Linetype**   Controls the layer linetype per viewport
- **VP Lineweight**   Controls the layer lineweight per viewport
- **VP Plot Style**   Controls the layer plot style per viewport

---

FOR MORE DETAILS   See Chapter 14 for more information on controlling layer properties per paper space viewport using Viewport Overrides.

Description.   The **Description** setting allows you to add a brief description of the layer. For example, a layer named **A-Wall** might have a description of "Architectural walls." To change the description of a layer, select the layer and then single-click inside the **Description** field. A flashing text cursor will appear, allowing you to change the layer description.

Controlling the Column Display.   Clicking on a column heading at the top of the layer list in the **Layer Properties Manager** will toggle the display order of the layers in ascending or descending order using the information in the column header you click on.

You can resize a column by dragging the vertical bar between columns with your mouse, as well as rearrange the display order of the columns by dragging and dropping the column headings to different locations.

Right-clicking on a column heading displays a shortcut menu that allows you to turn different property columns on and off, maximize column widths, or reset everything back to the default. You can also display the **Customize Layer Columns** dialog box to turn multiple columns off simultaneously and rearrange the column order via the **Customize...** menu item.

Layer List Right-Click Shortcut Menu.   Right-clicking anywhere in the layer list in the **Layer Properties Manager** displays the shortcut menu shown in Figure 6-9.

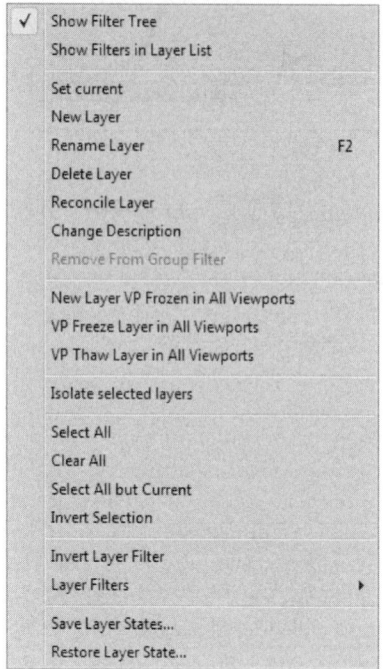

Figure 6-9 Layer list right-click shortcut menu

This shortcut menu provides a number of handy, timesaving features and capabilities. Many of the features and capabilities can be found elsewhere in the **Layer Properties Manager**, but a few are unique to the right-click menu. Some of the things you can do include:

- Turn the **Layer Filter** list on the left off and on
- Show any layer filters in the **layer name** list on the right so you can manage them as a unit
- Remove viewport property overrides
- Select all/deselect all layers for mass property updates

You can also create and restore layer states, which allow you to manage different saved layer settings. Layer states are discussed in detail later in this chapter.

Deleting a Layer

To delete a layer from your drawing, select the layer(s) from the layer list and choose the **Delete Layer** button (or choose <**Alt**>+**D**). A layer can be deleted only if it is not used in the drawing or if it is not the current layer. If the layer is not used and is not the current layer, AutoCAD will delete the layer. You can use ～do in the **Quick Access** toolbar to bring back a ～eted layer.

If the layer is used in the drawing, or if it is the ～ent layer, AutoCAD will display an error mes-～ (see Figure 6-10).

Note:
Sometimes a layer may appear empty or unused in your drawing but you are still unable to delete it. Many times this is due to a layer being used in a block or xref. Even though the layer is currently empty, you cannot delete that layer until the block or xref that uses that layer is also deleted.

MORE
AILS   See Chapter 16 for more on deleting block and xrefs from your drawing.

Figure 6-10   The **Delete Layer** error message

Figure 6-11   The **Layer Settings** dialog box

Layer Settings

Selecting the **Setting** button in the **Layer Properties Manager** displays the **Layer Settings** dialog box shown in Figure 6-11.

The **Layer Settings** dialog box allows you to control the **New Layer Notification** feature, apply a layer filter to the **Layer** toolbar so only filtered layers are displayed, and change the background color for Viewport Overrides, introduced earlier in the chapter.

The **New Layer Notification** feature prevents new layers from being added to your drawing without your knowledge by creating a list of what are referred to as *reconciled* layers, using all the existing layer names the first time you save or plot a drawing.

When the **Evaluate new layers added to drawing** check box is turned on, a **Notification** icon is displayed in the Status Tray at the bottom right of the AutoCAD window when a new layer is added to your drawing that does not match the reconciled layer list. Clicking on the **Notification** icon will display a list of unreconciled layers in the **Layer Properties Manager**.

TIP   A layer filter of unreconciled layers is automatically created in the **Layer Properties Manager** so that you can review them. You can select and reconcile layers in the **Layer Properties Manager** using the **Reconcile Layer** option from the right-click menu explained earlier.

You can choose to evaluate only new layers that are added when an external refererence (xref) drawing is attached or to evaluate all new layers that are added to your drawing, regardless of the source.

FOR MORE DETAILS	See Chapter 14 for more information on controlling layer properties per paper space viewport using Viewport Overrides.

You can control when layer evaluation and notification is performed when the **Notify when new layers are present** check box is selected. Layer evaluation can be performed when the **OPEN, SAVE, ATTACH/RELOAD XREFS, INSERT**, or **RESTORE LAYER STATE** commands are activated.

The **Display alert for plot when new layers are present** check box allows you to control separately whether layer evaluation and notification is performed when a plot is created.

The **Isolate Layer Settings** area allows you to control how layers are isolated using the **LAYISO** command. The **LAYISO** command allows you to work only on a selected group of layers. Nonselected layers are either locked and faded or turned off. The **Isolate Layer Settings** area of the **Layer Settings** dialog box allows you to select which method to use as well as set the amount of fading that occurs.

USING LAYERS

In AutoCAD, the current layer is shown in the **Layer Control** drop-down list in the **Layers** panel (see Figure 6-12). This drop-down list shows you the current settings for your layers. You can change the active layer by selecting a new layer from the drop-down list. You can also toggle layer settings from this list by selecting the icon for that setting. For example, to freeze a layer, choose the drop-down list and select the **Freeze/Thaw** icon next to the layer you wish to freeze. The icon will change from a sun to a snowflake, indicating the layer has been frozen. You can use this list to toggle the **On/Off, Freeze/Thaw**, and **Lock/Unlock** settings.

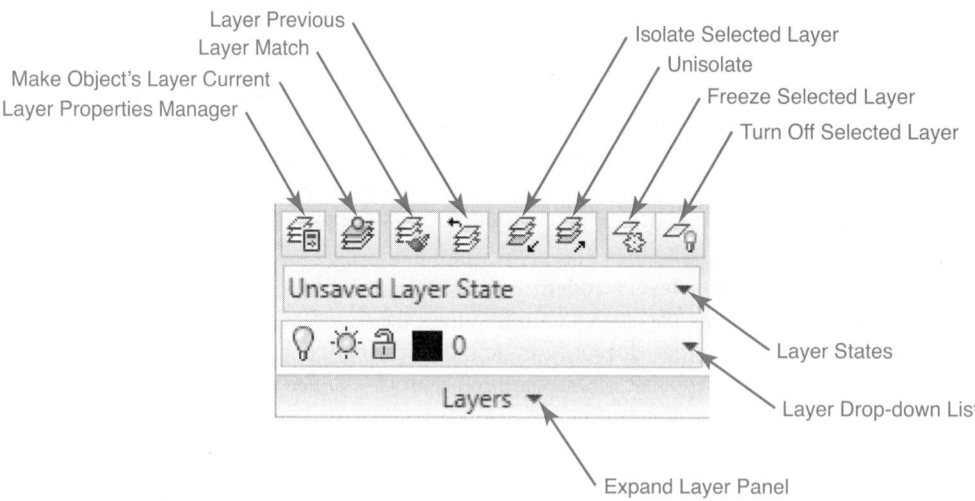

Figure 6-12   The **Layers** panel

The **Layers** panel has some additional buttons. The **Make Object's Layer Current** button allows you to select an object in your drawing and have that object's layer become the current drawing layer.

The **Match** button changes the layer of one or more selected objects to match the destination layer of another object that you select in the drawing.

The **Layer Previous** button will switch the current layer back to its previous setting. For example, if you were to change the current layer from **Object** to **Hidden**, the **Layer Previous** button would reset the current layer to **Object**.

Selecting the **Layer Previous** button undoes the most recent change, or set of changes, made using either the **Layer Properties Manager** or the **Layer Control** drop-down list on the **Layers** toolbar. Every change you make to the layer settings is tracked and can be undone with **Layer Previous** with the following special exceptions:

- Deleted layers **Layer Previous** does not restore deleted and/or purged layers
- New layers **Layer Previous** does not remove any newly added layers
- Renamed layers **Layer Previous** does not restore the original layer name

The **Layer States Manager** button displays the **Layer States Manager** dialog box discussed later in this chapter.

The **Isolate** button hides or locks all the objects in the drawing except for the ones you select. This allows you to work on a selected layer without worrying about accidentally modifying objects. The **Isolate Layer Settings** discussed above allows you to control how objects are isolated and displayed.

The **Unisolate** button simply undoes the **Isolate** tool. Selecting this button reverts all layers to their state prior to using the **Isolate** tool.

The **Freeze** button freezes the layer of a selected object whereas the **Off** button turns a layer off instead. Both commands have settings for how to handle viewports and block definitions that persist from session to session.

Exercise 6-6: Using the Layers Panel

1. Continue from Exercise 6-5.
2. In the **Layer Control** drop-down list, choose **Hidden** to set that layer current.
3. Draw a line anywhere on the screen. The line will have the color and linetype of layer **Hidden**.
4. In the **Layer Control** drop-down list, set the layer **Object** current. Draw a line anywhere in the drawing. The line will have the color and linetype of the **Object** layer.
5. In the Status Bar, toggle the **Show/Hide Lineweight** button **On**. The line on the **Object** layer should now show the **.60 mm** lineweight.
6. Set the **Center** layer current and draw a circle anywhere on the drawing. The line will have the color and linetype of the **Center** layer. Your drawing should resemble Figure 6-13.
7. Save your drawing as **EX6-6**.

Figure 6-13   Drawing with layers

LINETYPE SCALE

The linetypes displayed in the drawing are defined by the linetype definitions that were loaded from the .lin file. The linetype is defined by the length of the dashes and spaces in the line and uses the drawing units to define those lengths. For example, say a linetype is defined as a line segment .5 unit long followed by a space of .25 unit and then repeated. When drawn in a metric drawing using mm as the base unit, that linetype would be a series of .5 mm lines and .25 mm spaces.

The **LTSCALE** command allows you to set a global scaling factor for all linetypes. The **LTSCALE** command prompts you for a new linetype scale factor. The linetypes of all objects are multiplied by this scaling factor. For example, an **LTSCALE** setting of **2** would make each line segment and space twice its defined size. An **LTSCALE** of **.5** would make each linetype half its defined size.

It is also possible to set the LTSCALE via the **Linetype Manager** dialog box shown in Figure 6-18, although it is not obvious where it is set. In order to access any of the linetype scaling options you must select the **Show details** button on the top right to display the details at the bottom of the dialog box (Figure 6-19). The **Global scale factor:** setting updates the LTSCALE. See the "Linetype Property Override" section later in this chapter for more information about the **Linetype Manager** dialog box.

Linetype Scale	
Ribbon & Panel:	None
Properties Toolbar:	Other...
Menu:	Format| Linetype
Command Line:	LTSCALE
Command Alias:	LTS

Exercise 6-7: Setting the LTSCALE

1. Continue from Exercise 6-6.
2. Type **LTSCALE<Enter ↵>**. AutoCAD prompts you to *Enter new linetype scale factor <1.0000>:*.
3. Type **.5<Enter ↵>** to set the linetype scale. The linetype pattern of the objects on the **Hidden** and **Center** layers will scale down by 50 percent.
4. Save your drawing as **EX6-7**.

HARD-CODED VERSUS SOFT-CODED PROPERTIES

Note:
The **MSLTSCALE** system variable allows you to scale linetype definitions by the current **Annotation Scale**. Setting **MSLTSCALE** to 1 turns on automatic linetype scaling. It is on by default.

By default, when an object is created in a drawing, it takes on the color, linetype, and lineweight settings of the current layer. When this happens, its properties are defined as *Bylayer*. This means that the color, linetype, and lineweight of an object are defined by the layer on which the object resides. For example, say your drawing has a layer called **Object**, which is red, and has a continuous linetype and a lineweight of .6 mm. If you draw a line on that layer, by default it would show up as a red, continuous, .6 mm-wide line. This line is considered to have soft-coded properties in that its properties are defined indirectly by the layer on which it resides. If you were to change the layer color to blue, the object would update to reflect the changes to its layer.

It is possible to override these soft-coded properties and define the color, linetype, and lineweight directly. These are called *hard-coded* properties because the properties are assigned directly to the object, regardless of which layer it resides on.

Setting the Default Object Properties

The current settings for the Color, Linetype, and Lineweight properties are shown in the **Properties** panel (see Figure 6-14). AutoCAD applies these current property settings to all new objects. By default, these are all set to **ByLayer**.

To change the current setting, select the setting from its respective drop-down list. Any new objects you create will take on these properties.

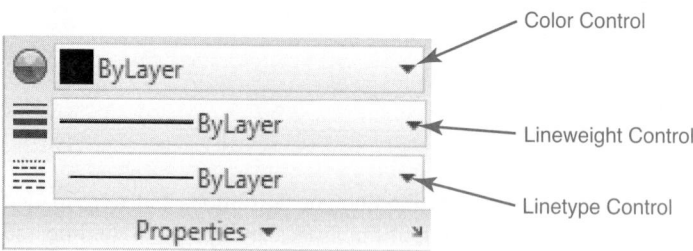

Figure 6-14   The **Properties** panel

Color Property Override

In the **Color Control** drop-down list, you see a list consisting of **ByLayer, ByBlock,** color numbers 1–7, and a **Select Colors...** item (see Figure 6-15). The **Select Colors...** item starts the **COLOR** command and displays the **Select Color** dialog box (see Figure 6-16). This is the same dialog box used to select colors within the **LAYER** command. To set the current drawing color, select the color from the **Color Control** drop-down list or choose the **Select Colors...** item and select the color from the **Select Color** dialog box.

Color	
Ribbon & Panel:	Home| Properties
Select Color...	
Properties Toolbar:	
Red	
Menu:	Format| Color...
Command Line:	COLOR
Command Alias:	COL

FOR MORE DETAILS   See Chapter 16 for more on blocks and the **ByBlock** setting.

Figure 6-15 The **Color Control** drop-down list

Figure 6-16 The **Select Color** dialog box

Linetype	
Ribbon & Panel:	Home| Properties
	Other...
Properties Toolbar:	
	——— – · CENTER
Menu:	Format| Linetype...
Command Line:	LINETYPE
Command Alias:	LT

Linetype Property Override

In the **Linetype Control** drop-down list (see Figure 6-17), you are shown a list of all the currently loaded linetypes in the drawing as well as the **ByLayer** and **ByBlock** settings and an **Others...** item. The **Others...** item starts the **LINETYPE** command, which displays the **Linetype Manager** dialog box (see Figure 6-18).

The **Linetype Manager** dialog box is similar to the **Select Linetype** dialog box within the **LAYER** command (see Figure 6-6) but with a few added features. The **Linetype Manager** dialog box shows you all the currently loaded linetypes but also includes a filter that allows you to show all the linetypes loaded into the drawing, only the linetypes currently in use, or all that are used in any xref files. You can also invert the filter to show you only linetypes that are *not* in use or *not* used in xref files.

Note:
In the LAYER command, the Select Color dialog box has the ByLayer and ByBlock buttons disabled. In the COLOR command, these buttons are enabled. These choices are also available in the Color Control drop-down list in the Properties toolbar. The ByLayer setting resets the color to its layer-defined, soft-coded color property. The ByBlock setting creates everything using color 7 until the objects are grouped into a block.

Figure 6-17 The **Linetype Control** drop-down list

Figure 6-18 The **Linetype Manager** dialog box

> **FOR MORE DETAILS** *Xref* stands for Externally Referenced Files. Xrefs allow you to display the contents of other drawing files overlaid onto your current drawing. Chapter 17 describes how to use and manage xrefs.

The **Load...** button displays the **Load or Reload Linetypes** dialog box. This is the same dialog box used within the **LAYER** command and allows you to load linetypes from .LIN files.

The **Delete** button allows you to delete unused linetypes from the drawing. Only linetypes that are not currently used can be deleted.

The **Show details** button displays an additional area of the dialog box that shows additional information about each linetype and also allows you to set the linetype scale for all objects (the **Global scale factor**) or newly created objects (the **Current object scale**) (see Figure 6-19).

Figure 6-19   The **Linetype Manager** details

Lineweight Property Override

Lineweight	
Ribbon & Panel:	Home|Properties
	——— ByLayer ▾
Properties Toolbar:	
	▐ ——— 0.60 mm ▾
Pull-down Menu:	Format|Lineweight...
Command Line:	LINEWEIGHT or LWEIGHT
Command Alias:	LW

The **Lineweight Control** drop-down list shows you a list of all available lineweights. These lineweights are shown as millimeter (mm) units by default. You can change these units and control other aspects of lineweight setting with the **LINEWEIGHT** command.

The **LINEWEIGHT** command displays the **Lineweight Settings** dialog box (see Figure 6-20), which includes controls to turn the lineweight display on and off, set the default lineweight, and switch the units from millimeters to inches. The **Adjust Display Scale** slider allows you to control the relative thickness of the lineweight display on your screen. It does not affect the plotted width of the lineweight.

Figure 6-20   The **Lineweight Settings** dialog box

Exercise 6-8: Setting Hard-Coded Properties

1. Continue from Exercise 6-7.
2. From the **Layer Control** drop-down list, set the **Object** layer current.
3. From the **Color Control** drop-down list, set the current color to **Magenta** (color 6).
4. From the **Linetype Control** drop-down list, choose **Others...** to display the **Linetype Manager** dialog box.
5. Load the **ZIGZAG** linetype from the acad.lin linetype file and set it to be the current linetype. Choose **OK** to close the **Linetype Manager** dialog box.
6. From the **Lineweight Control** drop-down list, set the current lineweight to **0.80 mm**.
7. Draw a line anywhere on the screen. The new line will have the current color, linetype, and lineweight settings even though the **Object** layer has different properties. Your drawing should resemble Figure 6-21.
8. Save your drawing as **EX6-8**.

Figure 6-21   Hard-coded object properties

Hard-coded object properties can be useful in certain situations but can lead to confusion as your drawing complexity grows. In general, objects are identified by the color and linetype associated with their layer. For this reason, soft-coded, **ByLayer** properties are generally preferred.

TIP   The **SETBYLAYER** command allows you to quickly update the color, linetype, and lineweight of objects to the **ByLayer** property.

CHANGING THE PROPERTIES OF OBJECTS

There are a number of ways to change the properties of existing objects. In Chapter 2, you were introduced to the **Properties** palette, which provides an easy way to change the properties of any object. The **Properties** palette is accessed through the **PROPERTIES** command.

The Properties Palette

As stated at the beginning of the chapter, there are four properties that are common to all objects: Layer, Color, Linetype, and Lineweight. These are shown in the **General** area of the **Properties** palette (see Figure 6-22). You can change any of the properties by selecting the value from the palette and choosing a new value.

The **Linetype scale** option in the **Properties** palette allows you to change the linetype scale of individual objects. This object linetype scale factor is applied in addition to the global linetype scale set by the **LTSCALE** command. For example, a line created with an object linetype of 2 in a drawing with **LTSCALE** set to **0.5** would appear the same as a line created with an object linetype of 1 in a drawing with a **LTSCALE** set to **1**.

The **Hyperlink** property allows you to assign an Internet URL or email address to an object.

Note:
The **Thickness** property shown in the **Properties** palette is used to assign a three-dimensional "thickness" to AutoCAD objects. Although it is a common property of all objects, it is rarely used in 2D drawings and is beyond the scope of this book.

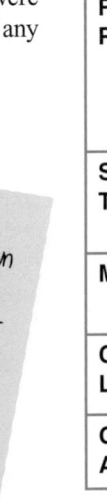

Properties	
Ribbon & Panel:	View|Palettes
Standard Toolbar:	
Menu:	Modify|Properties
Command Line:	PROPERTIES
Command Alias:	PR

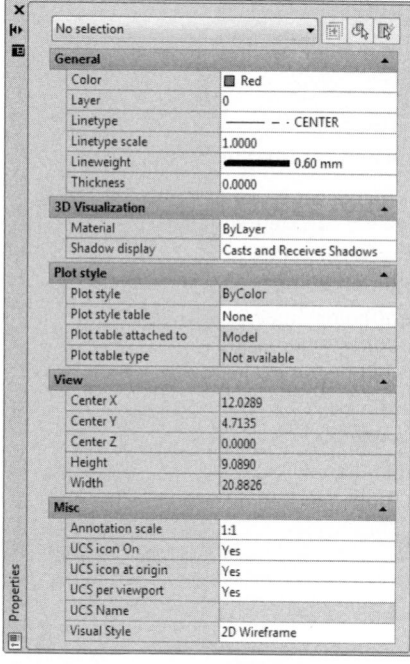

Figure 6-22   The **Properties** palette

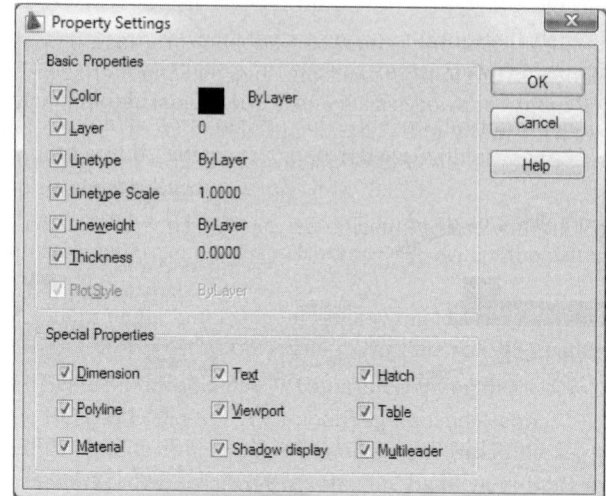

Figure 6-23   The **Properties Settings** dialog box

FOR MORE DETAILS   See the online AutoCAD documentation for more on using the **Thickness** setting.

The Properties Panel

Another way to change object properties is through the **Properties** drop-down menus. To change an object's property, select the object and then choose the property you wish to change from its drop-down menu.

Copying Properties Between Objects

AutoCAD gives you a way to copy the properties from one object to another. This is done through the **MATCHPROP** or **PAINTER** command.

The **MATCHPROP** command prompts you to select a source object and a destination object. The properties from the source object are then applied to the destination object. There is a **Settings** option that allows you to control which object properties are applied to the destination object. When you choose the **Settings** option, AutoCAD shows you the **Property Settings** dialog box (see Figure 6-23). This shows you the properties of the source object and allows you to specify which property settings to apply to the destination object.

> **Note:**
> The **MATCHPROP** and **PAINTER** commands are identical. AutoCAD simply has two names for the same command.

In the following exercise, you'll examine some of the different ways of changing object properties.

Exercise 6-9: Changing Object Properties

1. Continue from Exercise 6-8. Set the **Object** layer current.
2. Select the circle in your drawing. Notice that values in the **Layer, Color, Linetype**, and **Lineweight Control** drop-down lists all change to show you the property settings for the selected circle.

3. Open the **Properties** palette.
4. Change the **Linetype scale** value to **2**. The linetype scale of the circle will double. Press **<Esc>** to clear the circle selection and close the **Properties** palette.
5. Select the line on layer **Hidden**. Again, the **Properties** drop-down lists show the values of the selected object.
6. Select the **Object** layer in the **Layer Control** drop-down list. The line is changed to the **Object** layer. Since the linetype, color, and lineweight properties of the line were all set to **ByLayer**, those properties were updated as well. Press **<Esc>** to clear line selection.
7. Start the **MATCHPROP** command. AutoCAD prompts you to *Select source object:*. Select one of the lines on the **Object** layer.
8. AutoCAD prompts you to *Select destination objects(s) or ↓*. Select the zigzag line. All the properties of the zigzag line are changed to match the properties of the **Object** line. Press **<Enter ↵>** or **<Esc>** to end the **MATCHPROP** command.
9. Save your drawing as **EX6-9**.

Using DesignCenter to Import Layers

In many cases, drawing information such as layers, linetypes, symbols, text styles, and dimension settings are common across multiple drawings. The layers you use in one drawing might be part of a company or project standard that are used over and over. AutoCAD's DesignCenter is a tool that allows you to share common information and settings between multiple drawings.

The **DesignCenter** palette (see Figure 6-24) is arranged in tabs that show drawings you currently have open, drawings in other local or network folders, and drawings you've recently accessed.

DesignCenter	
Ribbon & Panel:	View|Palettes
Standard Toolbar:	
Menu:	Tools|Palettes|Design Center
Command Line:	ADCENTER
Command Alias:	DC

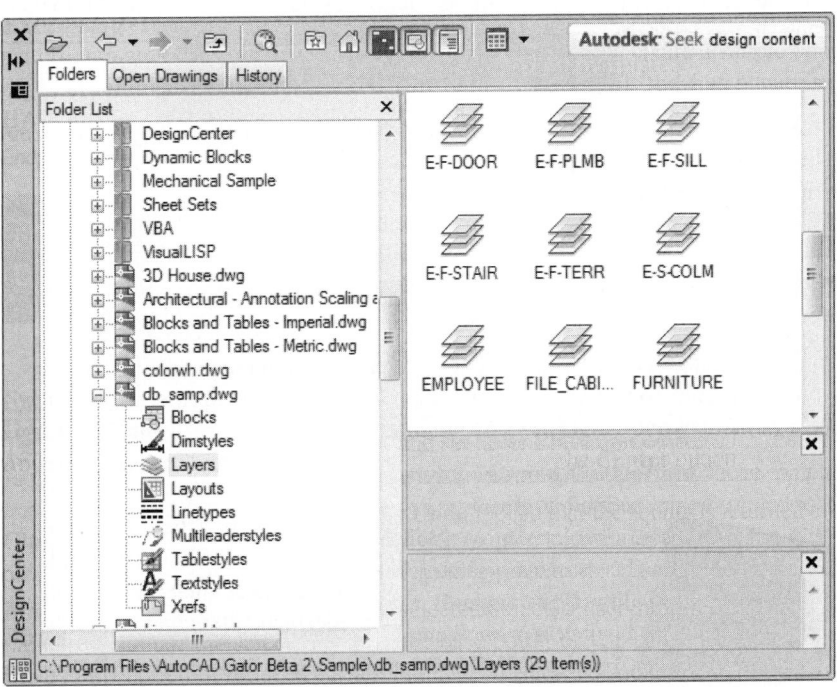

Figure 6-24   The **DesignCenter** palette

The **Folders** tab shows you a directory tree similar to what you might see in Windows Explorer. With the **Folders** tab, you can navigate to drawing files in any accessible local or network folder. The **Open Drawings** and **History** tabs show you a list of currently or recently open drawing files.

When you select a drawing file in DesignCenter, AutoCAD shows you a list of drawing information contained in that drawing. The drawing information is divided into categories (Blocks, Dimstyles, Layers, Layouts, Linetypes, Multileaderstyles, Tablestyles, Textstyles, and Xrefs), and within each category are the specific objects and settings contained within that drawing. These objects and settings can be copied into your current drawing by selecting them from the list on the right and then dragging them into the drawing area of your current drawing. The settings and objects are then copied into your drawing.

Note:
When drawing objects such as blocks and xrefs are placed in the drawing, the objects are placed on the current layer. For settings, such as layer definitions, dimension styles, and other nongraphical information, only the settings are loaded into the drawing. If an object or setting with the same name already exists in your drawing, DesignCenter will simply ignore duplicate items and not import them.

Exercise 6-10: Using DesignCenter to Import Layers

1. Start a new drawing using the acad.dwt drawing template.
2. Choose the **DesignCenter** button from the **Palettes** panel on the **View** ribbon. This opens the **DesignCenter** palette. Position the palette on your screen anywhere you like.
3. In the **Folders** tab, navigate to the **\AutoCAD 2010\Samples** folder and select the + box next to the **db_samp.dwg** file. This will show the objects and settings available in this drawing.
4. Select the **Layers** item in the list. A list of available layers will appear in the right-hand pane.
5. Select the **E-B-CORE** layer, hold down the **<Shift>** key, and select the **E-S-COLM** layer. AutoCAD will select all the layers between these two layers.
6. Press and hold your mouse button on one of the selected layers and drag the layers into your drawing area. When you release the mouse button, the layers will be copied into your new drawing. In the command window, AutoCAD will respond with

```
Layer(s) added. Duplicate definitions will be ignored.
```

7. Start the **LAYER** command to verify that the layers have been imported into your drawing.
8. Close or hide the **DesignCenter** palette.
9. Save the drawing as **EX6-10**.

LAYER FILTERS

When working in drawings that have a large number of layers, managing layer settings in a long list of layers can prove difficult. To help manage this, AutoCAD allows you to filter the list of layers. This allows you to display only the layers you are interested in or will be using. The **Layer Filter** list of the **Layer Properties Manager** palette allows you to create and manage these filters (see Figure 6-25).

The filter tree shows you a hierarchy of layers, starting with all layers. Clicking on the **All** level will list all the layers in the drawing in the layer list area. Below the **All** filter is the **All Used Layers** filter. Selecting this will filter the layer list to show only the layers that are currently in use in the drawing. The **All** and **All Used Layers** filters are predefined filters that cannot be renamed or deleted. You can create your own custom layer filters.

The Filter Tree

To activate a layer filter, simply select it from the filter tree. The filter tree is hierarchical, which means that the filter is applied to the layers on the level above it in the tree.

Below the filter tree are two boxes: **Invert filter** and **Indicate layers in use**. Putting a check in the **Invert filter** box will reverse the effects of the filter. For example, if you choose

Figure 6-25   The **Layer Filters** area of the **Layer Properties Manager** palette

the **All Used Layers** filter, putting a check in the **Invert filter** box will show you all the unused layers.

Checking the **Indicate layers in use** option will indicate which layers have drawing information on them by making the icon in the **Status** column darker for referenced layers and lighter for layers that do not have anything on them. This is a good way to determine which layers can be deleted and which layers cannot.

Property Filters

Property filters will filter your layer list based upon certain matching criteria. For example, you might create a filter that shows you only layers that start with characters "C-," or a filter that shows only thawed layers, or only locked layers. You can also combine criteria. For example, you can create a filter that shows all layers that are both frozen and locked and contain the letter X in their name.

To create a property filter, choose the **New Property Filter** button. The **Layer Filter Properties** dialog box will appear (see Figure 6-26).

Figure 6-26   The **Layer Filter Properties** dialog box

The **Filter name** area allows you to change the name of your filter. You create a filter by selecting criteria in the **Filter definition** area. You can select multiple criteria on a single row. As you specify filter criteria, the **Filter preview** area shows you all the layers that match your filter. The various filter criteria are defined in the following table:

Status	Shows only layers that are used in the drawing or only layers that are not used in the drawing.
Name	Shows only layer names that match the criteria. You can specify a full layer name or a partial name with wildcards. For example, **W*** will show only layers that start with the letter W. A name filter of ***C*** will show you all the layer names containing the letter C. The **Layer Name** filter is not case sensitive.
On	Shows only layers that are turned on or only layers that are turned off.
Freeze	Shows only layers that are frozen or only layers that are thawed.
Lock	Shows only layers that are locked or only layers that are unlocked.
Color	Shows only layers that match the color specified. You can either specify a color name or number or choose the **...** box to select from the **Select Color** dialog box. Like the layer name, you can specify a partial color number with wildcards. For example, specifying **4*** for the color will show color 4 and colors 40–49.
Linetype	Shows only layers that match the specified linetype. You can type in the linetype name or choose **...** to select the linetype from the **Select Linetype** dialog box. Partial names with wildcards are allowed.
Lineweight	Shows only layers that are a specified lineweight.
Plot Style	Shows only layers that match a specific plot style. This option is available only in drawings where named plot styles are used. Partial names with wildcards are allowed.
Plot	Shows only layers that are set to either **Plot** or **Noplot**.
New VP Freeze	Shows only layers that are either frozen in new viewports or thawed in new viewports. This option is available only when accessed from a drawing layout (paper space).

All the criteria you specify in a row are applied to the layer list. For example, a filter row with the name criteria of "A-" and "Frozen" will show only layers that both start with "A-" *and* are frozen.

Once you specify some criteria, a new row is added to the **Filter definition** list. Each row is applied separately to the filter. For example, if you have one row that has a name criterion of "E-" and another row that has a name criterion of "Wall," all layers that start with "E-" will be shown *and* all the layers that contain the word "WALL" will also be shown.

Note:
Criteria within a single row are the equivalent of an AND search query. AutoCAD will show all the layers that meet all the criteria in that row (the first criterion AND the second criterion, etc.).

Criteria listed on separate rows are the equivalent of an OR search query. AutoCAD will show all the layers that match the criteria of any row (the first row OR the second row, etc.).

Exercise 6-11: Creating a Layer Property Filter

1. Continue from Exercise 6-10.
2. Start the **LAYER** command and choose the **New Property Filter** button. The **Layer Filter Properties** dialog box will appear (see Figure 6-27).
3. Change the **Filter name** to **E-B** and click inside the **Name** criteria column. An asterisk (*) will appear in the **Name** column and all the layers will appear in the **Filter preview** area.
4. Type **E-B*** in the **Name** column. The **Filter preview** area will update to show you only layer names that start with E-B.
5. Choose **OK** to save the filter and close the dialog box. The **E-B** filter will now appear in the **Layer Filter** area. The filter is applied to the layer list so only the **E-B** layers are shown.
6. Select the **Invert filter** box. The filter is reversed and all layers except the **E-B** layers are shown.
7. Remove the check from the **Invert filter** box. Choose **OK** to end the **LAYER** command.
8. Select the **Layer Control** drop-down list. Notice that only layers that match the **E-B** filter are shown.
9. Save the drawing as **EX6-11**.

Figure 6-27   The **Layer Filter Properties** dialog box

Group Filters

A group filter allows you to filter your layer list to show only layers you select. The layers do not need to match any particular criteria; you simply select the layers you want to include in your filter. To create a group filter, choose the **New Group Filter** button in the **Layer Properties Manager** palette. AutoCAD will create a new group filter called **Group Filter1** and highlight the name. You can then type a new name for the filter. To add layers to the filter, select the layers from the layer list on the right side and drag them onto the group filter name on the left side.

Exercise 6-12: Creating a Group Filter

1. Continue from Exercise 6-11.
2. Start the **LAYER** command and choose the **New Group Filter** button. AutoCAD creates a new group filter called **Group Filter1** and highlights the name. Type **Misc** for the group filter name. The layer list is now empty since the new group filter is active and has no layers in it.

Figure 6-28   Creating a group filter

3. Select **All** in the **Layer Filter** area to show all the layers. Hold down the **<Ctrl>** key and select the **E-C-HEAD, E-S-COLM**, and **EMPLOYEE** layers from the layer list. Click and drag the layers onto the **Misc** filter and release the mouse button (see Figure 6-28). The selected layers are added to the group filter.
4. Select the **All** filter and choose **OK** to end the **LAYER** command.
5. Save the drawing as **EX6-12**.

Search Filter

In the top right corner of the **Layer Properties Manager** palette is a box that says **Search for layer**. This is a layer search filter that allows you to do a temporary name filter on the current list of layers. You can type in a layer name (including wildcards) to show a list of layers that match that name. The search filter cannot be saved; it works only while the dialog box is open or until you select another filter. The search filter applies only to the list of layers shown in the layer list at the time the search is done.

Layer States Manager	
Ribbon & Panel:	Home| Layers
Standard Toolbar:	
Menu:	Format| Layer States Manager
Command Line:	LAYERSTATE
Command Alias:	LAS

LAYER STATES MANAGER

There may be times when you have a set of layer settings that you use or need to restore at certain times. For example, you might want to freeze a set of layers before you plot, or you might want to lock certain layers before you share them with others. The **Layer States Manager** will save a snapshot of layer settings that you can then recall at any time. To create a layer state, set the layers to the setting you want to save, and then start the **LAYERSTATE** command to display the **Layer States Manager** dialog box (see Figure 6-29) either by selecting the **Layer States Manager** button in the **Layer Properties Manager** palette or by selecting **Manage Layer States...** on the **Layers** panel on the **Home** ribbon.

Choose the **New...** button to create a new layer state. The **New Layer State to Save** dialog box appears (see Figure 6-30), and you are asked for a layer state name. You can also provide an optional description for the layer state. Once you've supplied a name, choose **OK**, and you'll be returned to the **Layer States Manager** dialog box.

It is possible to edit a layer state directly by selecting the **Edit** button so that the layer state does not need to be deleted and re-created. Selecting the **Edit** button displays the **Edit Layer State** dialog box so that you can update any of the standard layer properties, add new layers, or delete existing layers from the currently selected layer state.

Figure 6-29   The **Layer States Manager** dialog box

Figure 6-30   The **New Layer State to Save** dialog box

Selecting the **More Restore Options** arrow button at the bottom right of the dialog box displays the **Layer properties to restore** options on the right of the dialog box so you can control which layer properties you wish to save and restore. Simply select which properties you wish to maintain.

Layer states can be exported to a file. This allows you to create standard layer settings that can be shared among multiple drawings in a project or used within a company standard. Use the **Export** and **Import** buttons in the **Layer States Manager** dialog box to export a layer state setting or to import an existing layer state file with an LAS extension. It is also possible to import layer states directly from DWG, DWT, or DWS files.

To restore a layer state, choose the **Layer States Manager** button on the **Layer Properties Manager** palette, select the layer state you wish to restore, and then choose the **Restore** button. All the settings for that layer state will be restored.

Exercise 6-13: Creating and Restoring Layer States
_____

1. Continue from Exercise 6-12.
2. Start the **LAYER** command and select the **All** filter from the filter tree.
3. Choose the **Layer States Manager** button to display the **Layer States Manager** dialog box.
4. Choose the **New...** button to display the **New Layer State to Save** dialog box. Type **Default** in the **New layer state name** area and choose **OK** to close the dialog box. You are returned to the **Layer States Manager** dialog box.
5. Select the **More Restore Options** arrow button at the bottom right of the dialog box to display more options. Choose the **Select All** button and put a check in the **Turn off layers not found in layer state** box. Choose **Restore** to save the layer state and close the dialog box. You are now returned to the **Layer Properties Manager** palette.
6. Select the **E-B** filter to filter the layer list. Select all the layers in the list and select the sun icon in the **Freeze** column to freeze all the layers.
7. Select the **Misc** group filter to refilter the layer list. Select all the layers and set the color to white (color 7). Choose the **All** filter to see all layers. Notice the changes you made to the layer settings.

8. Select the **Layer States Manager** button. The **Default** layer state is highlighted. Choose **Restore** to restore the layer settings. The layer settings should now be restored to their previous state.
9. Save the drawing as **EX6-13**.

Layer Tools

The popular Express **Layer Tools** commands and utilities have been integrated into AutoCAD so that you can access them via the **Layers** panel shown in Figure 6-31 and the **Layer Tools** cascade menu found on the **Format** menu shown in Figure 6-32 or via the **Layers II** toolbar shown in Figure 6-33.

Layer Tools

Figure 6-31   The **Layers** panel

Figure 6-32   The **Layer Tools** cascade menu

Figure 6-33   The **Layers II** tool-bar menu

The **Layer** tools and their usages are listed in the following table.

	Layer Tools		
	Layer Tool	**Command**	**Description**
	Make Object's Layer Current	**LAYMCUR**	Changes the current layer to match the selected object.
	Layer Previous	**LAYERP**	Undoes the last change or set of changes made to layer settings
	Layer Walk	**LAYWALK**	Dynamically displays objects on selected layers.
	Layer Match	**LAYMCH** or **-LAYMCH**	Changes the layer(s) of selected objects to match the layer of a selected destination object.
	Change to Current Layer	**LAYCUR**	Moves selected objects to the current layer.
	Copy Objects to New Layer	**COPYTOLAYER** or **-COPYTOLAYER**	Copies selected objects to another layer, leaving the original objects intact.
	Layer Isolate	**LAYISO**	Isolates the layer of the selected object(s) so that all other layers are turned off.
	Isolate Layer to Current Viewport	**LAYVPI**	Isolates an object's layer to the current viewport.
	Layer Unisolate	**LAYUNISO**	Turns on layers that were turned off with the **LAYISO** command.
	Layer Off	**LAYOFF**	Turns off the layer of the selected object(s).
	Turn All Layers On	**LAYON**	Turns on all layers.
	Layer Freeze	**LAYFRZ**	Freezes the layer of selected objects.
	Thaw All Layers	**LAYTHW**	Thaws all layers.
	Layer Lock	**LAYLCK**	Locks the layer of a selected object.

(continued)

	Layer Unlock	**LAYULK**	Unlocks the layer of a selected object.
	Layer Merge	**LAYMRG** or **-LAYMRG**	Moves all objects from the first selected layer to the second selected layer and deletes the first layer.
	Layer Delete	**LAYDEL** or **-LAYDEL**	Deletes all objects from the specified layer and purges the layer from the drawing.

CHAPTER SUMMARY

A well-organized drawing is something to which every CAD user should strive. Clear and concise CAD standards and drawing objects placed on their proper layers can make the difference between a drawing that is easy to read and understand and one that is confusing.

Good layer management practices are critical in group settings in which multiple people will be accessing and editing your drawings. This chapter has given you an in-depth look at how to use layers effectively to organize your drawing.

CHAPTER TEST QUESTIONS

Multiple Choice

1. A layer is:
   a. A separate drawing that you merge into your drawing
   b. The only way to control the color of drawing objects
   c. A collection of color, linetype, lineweight, and other display settings
   d. A 3D setting

2. Turning a layer off:
   a. Prevents objects on that layer from being seen
   b. Prevents objects on that layer from being edited
   c. Deletes all the objects on a layer
   d. Is the same as freezing a layer

3. The color blue is AutoCAD Color Index number:
   a. 3
   b. 4
   c. 5
   d. 6

4. An RGB color number of 0,255,0 is what color?
   a. Red
   b. Green
   c. Blue
   d. Black
   e. White

5. AutoCAD linetypes:
   a. Consist of only lines and spaces
   b. Are loaded automatically when you assign them to a layer
   c. Cannot be modified
   d. Must be loaded into the drawing before they can be used

6. Deleting a layer:
   a. Deletes the layer and all the objects on the layer
   b. Deletes all the objects on a layer but keeps the layer name in the drawing

   c. Can be done only when a layer is unused
   d. Can be done at any time regardless of whether the layer is used or not

7. The **LTSCALE** setting:
   a. Is a global scale factor applied to all objects' linetypes
   b. Affects the lineweight of all objects
   c. Affects the plot scale of layout viewports
   d. Does not affect objects that have an individual object linetype scale

8. An object with a color of **ByLayer**:
   a. Gets its color setting from its layer
   b. Is white
   c. Is white until a hard-coded color is assigned to it
   d. Is always the same color regardless of its layer color setting

9. Property filters:
   a. Are case sensitive
   b. Can filter only layers based on a single criterion
   c. Can use wildcards
   d. Are not based on any specific criteria

10. Group filters:
    a. Are case sensitive
    b. Can filter only layers based on a single criterion
    c. Can use wildcards
    d. Are not based on any specific criteria

Matching

a. Layer
b. Property filter
c. Linetype
d. LTSCALE
e. RGB

f. Lineweight

g. Hard-coded object properties
h. DesignCenter
i. Group layer filter
j. Layer state

1. A layer filter based on user-selected layer names
2. The pattern of a line
3. A color model based on red, green, and blue color components
4. Object properties set independently of an object's layer
5. A collection of Color, Linetype, Lineweight, and Display settings
6. A tool used to share design information between AutoCAD drawings
7. The printed width of a line
8. A saved collection of layer settings
9. A global scale factor applied to all linetypes
10. A layer filter based on matching criteria

CHAPTER PROJECTS

Project 6-1: Classroom Plan

1. Start a new drawing using the acad.dwt template. Set the **UNITS** to **Architectural** with **1/16″** precision. Set the **LTSCALE** to **6**.
2. Create the following layers:

Name	Color	Linetype	Lineweight	Description
A-Anno-Note	7	Continuous	Default	Notes
A-Door	4	Continuous	Default	Doors
A-Eqpm	6	Continuous	Default	Equipment
A-Furn	7	Continuous	Default	Furniture
A-Furn-Char	7	Continuous	Default	Chairs
A-Glaz	4	Continuous	Default	Windows
A-Wall	7	Continuous	Default	Walls

3. Draw the desk, monitor, computer tower, mouse, chair, and keyboard shown in Figure P6-1. Draw the desk on the **A-Furn** layer. Place all other objects on the **A-Eqpm** layer.
4. Do **not** draw dimensions or text.
5. Save the drawing as **P6-1**.

Figure P6-1

Project 6-2: B-Size Mechanical Border—Continued from Chapter 5

1. Open the template file **Mechanical B-Size.DWT** from Chapter 5.
2. Create the following layers:

Name	Color	Linetype	Lineweight	Plot/Noplot	Description
Title	7	Continuous	Default	Plot	Title border and text
Logo	7	Continuous	Default	Plot	Logo
Notes	7	Continuous	Default	Plot	Notes
Viewport	9	Continuous	Default	Noplot	Viewports

3. Place the existing geometry on layer **Title**.
4. Add the line work shown in Figure P6-2 to the drawing. Use the **Title** layer for all geometry. **Do not** draw dimensions.
5. Save the drawing to a template file as **Mechanical B-Size.DWT**.

Figure P6-2

Project 6-3: Architectural D-Size Border—Continued from Chapter 5

1. Open the template file **Architectural D-Size.DWT** from Chapter 5.
2. Create the following layers:

Name	Color	Linetype	Lineweight	Plot/Noplot	Description
A-Anno-Ttlb	7	Continuous	Default	Plot	Title block/ border lines
A-Anno-Ttlb-Text	1	Continuous	Default	Plot	Title block text
A-Anno-Ttlb-Logo	3	Continuous	Default	Plot	Logo
A-Anno-Vprt	7	Continuous	Default	Noplot	Viewport lines

3. Put all the existing line work on layer **A-Anno-Ttlb**.
4. Save the drawing to a template file as **Architectural D-Size.DWT**.

Project 6-4: Electrical Schematic—Continued from Chapter 5

1. Open drawing **P5-4** from Chapter 5.
2. Create the following layers:

Name	Color	Linetype	Lineweight	Description
E-Anno	7	Continuous	Default	Title border and text
E-Risr	7	Continuous	Default	Schematic lines

3. Add the geometry shown in Figure P6-4 to the schematic using the **E-Risr** layer. Use the hard-coded **Hidden** linetype as needed. Do **not** draw dimensions.
4. Save the drawing as **P6-4**.

Figure P6-4

Project 6-5: Residential Architectural Plan—Continued from Chapter 5

1. Open drawing **P5-5** from Chapter 5.
2. Create the following layers:

Name	Color	Linetype	Description
A-Anno-Symb	7	Continuous	Misc. symbols, north arrow
A-Flor-Ovhd	3	Dashed	Overhead skylights and overhangs
A-Door	5	Continuous	Doors
A-Glaz	5	Continuous	Windows
A-Wall	7	Continuous	Walls
A-Wall-Pat	7	Continuous	Wall hatch patterns and fills

3. Set the **LTSCALE** to **6**.
4. Place all existing walls on the **A-Wall** layer and the north arrow on the **A-Anno-Symb** layer.
5. Draw the geometry shown in Figure P6-5 on the appropriate layer.
6. Save the drawing as **P6-5**.

Figure P6-5

Project 6-6: Support Plate—English Units—Continued from Chapter 5

1. Open drawing **P5-6** from Chapter 5.
2. Create the following layers:

Name	Color	Linetype	Lineweight	Description
Object	7	Continuous	0.35 mm	Object lines
Hidden	7	Hidden	Default	Hidden lines
Center	7	Center	Default	Centerlines

3. Set the **LTSCALE** to **.25**.
4. Place the existing geometry on the **Object** layer. Project the hidden lines and draw the centerlines on all views as shown in Figure P6-6.
5. Save the drawing as **P6-6**.

Figure P6-6

Project 6-7: Hex Head Bolts and Nuts—Metric

1. Start a new drawing using the acadiso.dwt template.
2. Create the following layers:

Name	Color	Linetype	Lineweight	Description
Object	7	Continuous	0.35 mm	Object lines
Hidden	7	Hidden	Default	Hidden lines
Center	7	Center	Default	Centerlines

3. Draw object lines as shown in Figure P6-7 on layer **Object**.
4. Draw hidden lines as shown in Figure P6-7 on layer **Hidden**.
5. Draw centerlines as shown in Figure P6-7 on layer **Center**.
6. Adjust the **LTSCALE** system variable so linetypes appear properly.
7. Do **not** include text or dimensions.
8. Save the drawing as **P6-7**.

Figure P6-7

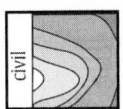

Project 6-8: Civil Site Plan—Continued from Chapter 5

1. Open the drawing **P5-8** from Chapter 5.
2. Create the following layers:

Name	Color	Linetype	Description
C-Anno-Note	7	Continuous	Notes
C-Road-Cntr	4	Center	Road centerlines
C-Topo	6	Hidden	Proposed contour lines and elevations
C-Bldg	7	Continuous	Building footprints
C-Prop	7	Phantom	Property lines and survey benchmarks
C-Watr	4	Continuous	Domestic water
C-Sswr	5	Dashed	Sanitary sewer

C-Ngas-Undr	6	Gas_Line	Natural gas underground
L-Plnt	3	Continuous	Plant and landscape materials
L-Walk	7	Continuous	Driveway, walks, and steps
L-Site-Fenc	7	Fenceline1	Fencing

3. Place the existing geometry on the appropriate layers. Draw the cut and fill lines on the **C-Topo** layer, approximately where shown in Figure P6-8. Add the water, sewer, and gas utility lines where shown. Do **not** draw text.
4. Save the drawing as **P6-8**.

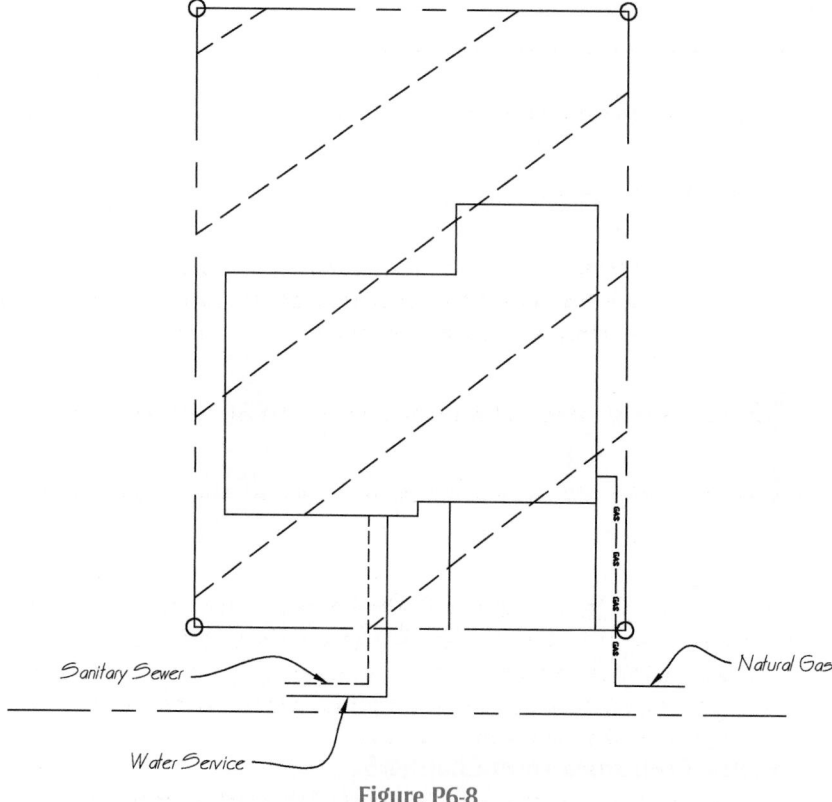

Figure P6-8

Basic Editing Techniques

Chapter Objectives

- Understand the difference between editing objects using the verb/noun technique and editing objects using the noun/verb technique
- Use the **ERASE** command to remove objects from a drawing
- Learn different ways to select one or more objects so that they can be modified
- Move objects
- Copy objects
- Mirror objects
- Rotate objects
- Scale objects
- Stretch objects
- Use grips to modify objects

INTRODUCTION

The ability to edit and modify objects quickly and with minimum effort is one of the keys to increasing your productivity when using AutoCAD. On the board, if a line is drawn in the wrong location, you must erase it and then redraw it in the correct location. In fact, most on-the-board changes require this same process—erase and redraw, erase and redraw, erase and redraw. . . . Using AutoCAD, a drawing can be edited and revised countless times without worry of burning a hole in your drawing with an electric eraser.

In AutoCAD you simply edit the existing drawing information. If a line is in the wrong location, you can just move it. You do not need to erase it and draw it again, although you can if you want. Most of the time, you will want to take advantage of the edit and modify tools provided by AutoCAD. Most of the basic editing tools can be found on the **Modify** menu or the **Modify** panel on the **Home** ribbon. See Figure 7-1.

In this chapter, you'll learn how to modify an object, or a group of objects, using two different approaches:

- Activating a modify command and then selecting the object(s) you want to modify (verb/noun)
- Selecting the object(s) to modify and then activating a modify command (noun/verb)

The noun/verb terminology might seem a little confusing at first, but if you consider that nouns represent objects (lines, circles, text, etc.) and that verbs represent actions (move, copy, rotate, etc.) it makes sense:

- Noun = Drawing object
- Verb = AutoCAD command

The traditional approach to editing in AutoCAD is verb/noun—activate the command first and then select the object(s). The alternative noun/verb approach to editing can actually be disabled—it

ROTATE command

COPY command

MOVE command

STRETCH command

MIRROR command

SCALE command

ERASE command

Figure 7-1 The **Modify** panel

is on by default. The noun/verb selection mode and other object selection features are controlled on the **Selection** tab of the **Options** dialog box shown in Figure 7-2.

Many of the settings located on the **Selection** tab are explained throughout this chapter. For now, make sure that your **Selection modes** settings match those shown in Figure 7-2. Failure to do so can cause some of the examples and exercises in this chapter to behave differently than anticipated.

Note:
You can display the **Options** dialog box using the following techniques:
- Select **Options** from the bottom of the **Application Menu**.
- Select **Options...** from the **Tools** menu.
- Right-click with your mouse in the command line window and select **Options...** from the **Command Line** shortcut menu.
- Right-click with your mouse when nothing is selected in the drawing window and select **Options...** from the **Default** shortcut menu.
- Type **OP** or **Options**.

Selection Settings

Figure 7-2 **Selection** settings on the **Selection** tab of the **Options** dialog box

THE ERASE COMMAND

In order to explain the different ways to select objects using either the verb/noun approach or the noun/verb approach, we first need a verb, or command. The **ERASE** command is a good candidate, considering it is probably the most used of all the modify commands. The **ERASE** command removes, or erases, the selected objects from a drawing.

	Erase
Ribbon & Panel:	Home| Modify
Modify Toolbar:	
Menu:	Modify| Erase
Command Line:	ERASE
Command Alias:	E

> **TIP** If you erase something by accident, remember that you can always use the **UNDO** command to bring it back. You can either select the **Undo** tool from the **Quick Access** toolbar or simply type **U<Enter ↵>** at the AutoCAD command line. Entering **U** repeatedly at the command line will undo commands one at a time until you reach the beginning of your drawing session.

SELECTING OBJECTS FOR EDITING

As described in the introduction, there are two ways to edit information in AutoCAD—verb/noun and noun/verb. The beginning of this chapter concentrates on the traditional verb/noun approach of activating the command first and then selecting the object(s). Once we understand this approach, we can explore the noun/verb way of doing things. The basics of the modify commands remain the same.

All modify commands work by modifying objects contained in what is referred to as a *selection set* in AutoCAD.

A selection set is simply the object, or objects, that you select to be modified. Any time you activate an AutoCAD modify command, and no objects are already selected, AutoCAD prompts you to create a selection set as follows:

selection set: One or more selected objects that are treated as one unit by an AutoCAD command

```
Select objects:
```

This is your cue to start selecting the object(s) in your drawing that you want to modify. AutoCAD repeats the *Select objects:* prompt until you "accept" the selection set by pressing **<Enter ↵>** without selecting anything. This approach allows you to build a selection set using multiple selection techniques ranging from picking objects individually with your mouse to selecting multiple objects using the different selection set options explained in this chapter.

Selecting Objects Individually

Selecting objects individually is the default selection mode. Any time AutoCAD prompts you to *Select objects:* to create a selection set, the cursor crosshairs change to what is referred to as the *pickbox*.

The size of the pickbox is used to determine how close you need to be to an object in order to select it. To select an object, it must be within or touching the pickbox. By default, objects that are within the pickbox are previewed by highlighting the objects so that they become dashed *and* thicker. (See Figure 7-3.) This **Selection Preview** feature provides you feedback regarding what object will be selected before you pick with your mouse so that you don't pick the wrong object unintentionally.

pickbox: Square box that replaces the cursor crosshairs whenever AutoCAD prompts you to *Select objects:*. It is used to pick objects in a drawing to create a selection set

> **TIP** You can control the size of the pickbox and turn the **Selection Preview** feature on and off via the **Selection** tab of the **Options** dialog box shown in Figure 7-2. Other **Selection Preview** features are controlled via the **Visual Effect Settings** dialog box, which can be displayed by selecting the **Visual Effect Settings...** button in the **Selection preview** area.

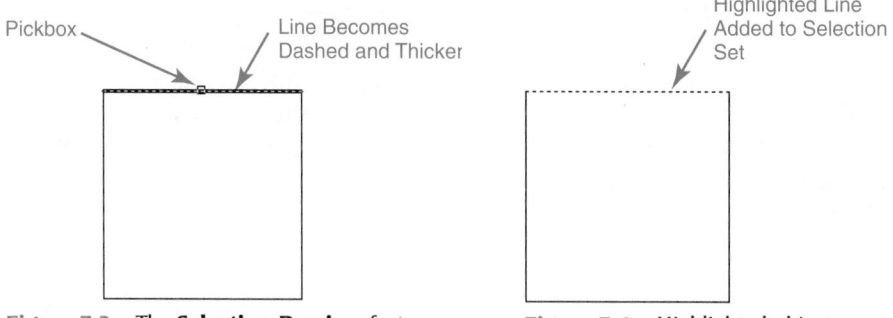

Pickbox

Line Becomes
Dashed and Thicker

Highlighted Line
Added to Selection
Set

Figure 7-3   The **Selection Preview** feature   **Figure 7-4**   Highlighted object

Picking an object adds it to the current selection set and highlights it so it is dashed. See Figure 7-4.

You also get feedback at the command line informing you that one object was found:

```
Select objects: 1 found
Select objects:
```

AutoCAD stays in the selection mode until you press the **<Enter ↵>** key without selecting anything to accept the selection set. This allows you to continue to add to the selection set by selecting more objects. As objects are selected, AutoCAD prompts you if the object was found and keeps a running tally of how many total objects are part of the current selection set:

```
Select objects: 1 found, 2 total
Select objects:
```

You can enter **U<Enter ↵>** in response to the *Select objects:* prompt to undo, or deselect, the last object selected. If you have more than one object selected, you can enter **U<Enter ↵>** repeatedly to deselect multiple objects in the order they were selected.

 TIP   You can also remove selected objects from the selection set by holding down the **<Shift>** key and selecting the object you want to remove.

implied windowing: Feature that allows you to create a **Window** or a **Crossing** selection automatically by picking an empty space in a drawing to define the first corner point

If you try to select an object and you miss because the object isn't within the pickbox, you may automatically be put in what is known as ***implied windowing*** mode, depending on whether it is turned on or not.

Implied windowing is turned on and off on the **Selection** tab of the **Options** dialog box shown in Figure 7-2. If implied windowing mode is on, AutoCAD automatically initiates the **Window** selection option. The **Window** selection option is discussed in detail a little later in this section. For the time being, you can hit the **<Esc>** key to exit out of the **Window** selection mode and return to selecting objects individually.

Toggling Between Adding and Removing Objects from a Selection Set.   It is possible to toggle between adding and removing objects from a selection set using the **A** (Add) and **R** (Remove) selection set options. If you type **R<Enter ↵>** in response to the *Select objects:* prompt, AutoCAD enters the **Remove** object mode and the prompt changes to *Remove objects:*. Objects you then select are removed from the selection set so that they are no longer highlighted. AutoCAD stays in the **Remove** object mode until you enter **A<Enter ↵>** in response to the *Remove objects:* prompt to switch back to **Add** mode.

Switching to **Add** mode changes the prompt back to the familiar *Select objects:* prompt.

Note: The **Add** and **Remove** toggle also works with all the multiple object selection modes described later in this chapter.

Using the <Shift> Key to Add to a Selection Set.   When selecting objects individually, it is possible to change the selection mode so that you must use the **<Shift>** key when adding objects to the current selection set. If you select the **Use Shift to add to selection** check box in the **Selection modes** area on the **Selection** tab of the **Options** dialog box (see Figure 7-2) so that it is turned on, you must hold down the **<Shift>** key when selecting more than one object. When the **Use Shift to add to selection** mode is on and you try to select more than one object *without* using the **<Shift>** key, the first object is deselected so it is no longer highlighted. By default, the **Use Shift to add to selection** mode is off.

Selecting Stacked and Overlaid Objects Using <Shift> + Space Bar.   You can select objects that are overlaid on top of each other by holding down **<Shift> + space bar** on your keyboard before you pick an object in response to a *Select objects:* prompt. After you select one object, you release **<Shift> + space bar** and enter into a cycle mode that allows you to pick repeatedly in the same spot to cycle through the different objects that are overlaid on top of each other, highlighting each one individually. See Figures 7-5A through C. While you are in cycle mode, AutoCAD prompts you at the command line as follows:

> **Note:** The **LEGACYCTRL PICK** system variable controls whether the legacy **<Ctrl>** key method of selecting stacked options is used instead of **<Shift>** + space bar.

        Select objects: <Cycle on>

When the object you want to select is highlighted, press **<Enter ↵>** to exit out of the cycle mode. AutoCAD prompts you as follows:

        Select objects: <Cycle off>

This puts you back in the regular selection mode so that you must press **<Enter ↵>** one additional time to accept the selection set.

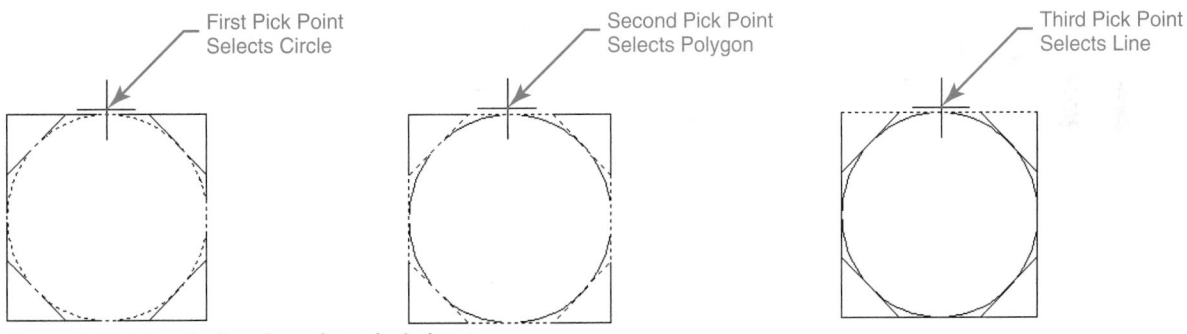

First Pick Point
Selects Circle

Second Pick Point
Selects Polygon

Third Pick Point
Selects Line

Figure 7-5ABC   Cycling through stacked objects

Exercise 7-1: Selecting Objects Individually

1. Start a new drawing using the acad.dwt drawing template.
2. Make sure that your **Selection modes** settings on the **Selection** tab of the **Options** dialog box match those shown in Figure 7-2.
3. Draw a rectangle similar to one shown in Figure 7-3 using the **LINE** command so that the rectangle consists of four separate line segments. *Do not use the RECTANGLE command!*
4. Start the **ERASE** command.
5. Select the top line as shown in Figure 7-4 and press **<Enter ↵>**. The line is erased.
6. Type **U<Enter ↵>** or select the **Undo** tool so that the line is undeleted.
7. Start the **ERASE** command again.
8. Select the top line as shown in Figure 7-4.
9. Select the other three lines in a clockwise direction using your cursor so that all the rectangle lines are highlighted.

10. Type **U<Enter ⏎>** three times so that only the top line is highlighted as shown in Figure 7-4.
11. Select the other three lines again in a clockwise direction using your cursor so that all the rectangle lines are highlighted.
12. Hold down the **<Shift>** key and select the vertical line on the left side of the rectangle so it is no longer highlighted.
13. Type **R<Enter ⏎>**.
14. Select the remaining three highlighted lines so that all the rectangle lines are no longer highlighted.
15. Type **A<Enter ⏎>**.
16. Select all four lines so that the entire rectangle is highlighted again and press **<Enter ⏎>** so that the rectangle is erased.
17. Type **U<Enter ⏎>** or select the **Undo** tool so that the rectangle is undeleted.
18. Save the drawing as **EX7-1**.

Selecting Multiple Objects

Oftentimes, you need to select more than one object when modifying a drawing. Suppose you need to erase a large portion of your drawing—you don't want to have to pick each object individually. Doing so would be very time-consuming. Fortunately, AutoCAD provides a number of selection set options that expedite the process of selecting multiple objects. All these options are entered via the keyboard in response to the *Select objects:* prompt. The following sections explain each of these selection set options.

W—Window Option.   To use the **Window** option, type **W<Enter ⏎>** in response to the *Select objects:* prompt. The **Window** option allows you to define a rectangular window selection area by prompting you to pick two corner points as shown in Figure 7-6.

By default, the windowed area is shaded a semitransparent blue color to make it obvious which objects will be selected before the second corner point is picked. This **Selection Preview** feature helps you to avoid the unintentional selection of objects.

Using the **Window** option, only objects that are *completely within* the window boundary area are selected. Objects that cross the window boundary are ignored. See Figure 7-7.

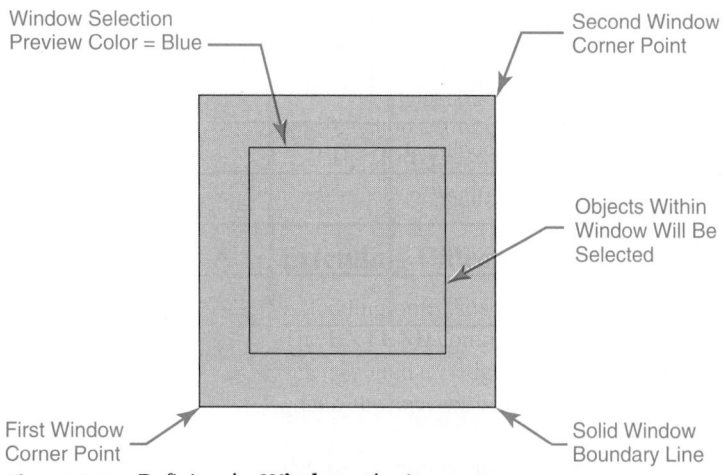

Window Selection Preview Color = Blue

Second Window Corner Point

Objects Within Window Will Be Selected

First Window Corner Point

Solid Window Boundary Line

Figure 7-6   Defining the **Window** selection area

All Four Lines Selected

Figure 7-7   Objects selected using the **Window** option

TIP   Remember from Chapter 6 that objects on frozen or locked layers are not affected by any of the selection methods explained in the chapter. You can use this to your advantage when selecting multiple objects so that you can select a large group of objects but filter out the objects you don't want to be part of the selection set.

Exercise 7-2: Selecting Multiple Objects with the Window Option

1. Continue from Exercise 7-1.
2. Start the **ERASE** command.
3. Type **W<Enter ↵>**
4. Create a **Window** selection similar to the one shown in Figure 7-6 and press **<Enter ↵>** twice. The four lines of the rectangle are erased.
5. Type **U<Enter ↵>** or select the **Undo** tool so that the rectangle is undeleted.
6. Save the drawing as **EX7-2**.

C—Crossing Option.   To use the **Crossing** option, type **C<Enter ↵>** in response to the *Select objects:* prompt. The **Crossing** option allows you to define a rectangular window selection area by picking two corner points similar to the **Window** option as shown in Figure 7-8.

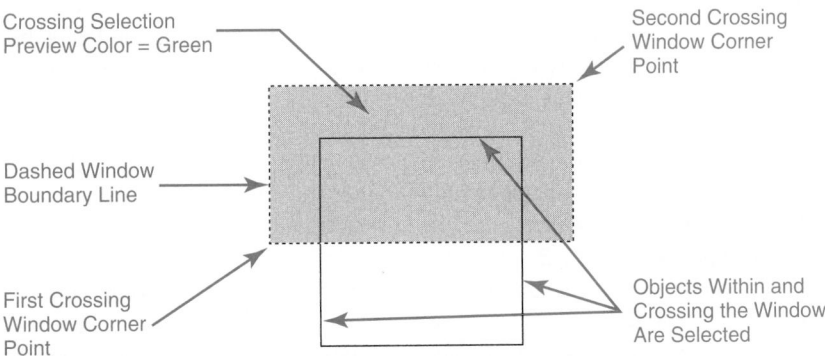

Figure 7-8   Defining the **Crossing** selection area

In order to distinguish between the **Window** option and the **Crossing** option, the **Crossing** option window boundary is dashed (see Figure 7-8), whereas the **Window** option window boundary is solid (see Figure 7-6). In addition, the **Crossing** option windowed area is, by default, shaded a semitransparent green color (see Figure 7-8) instead of the default blue color used with the **Window** option (see Figure 7-6).

The major difference between the **Crossing** option and the **Window** option is that the **Crossing** option will select objects that *cross over* the rectangular window boundary in addition to the objects that lie completely within the window boundary area. See Figure 7-9.

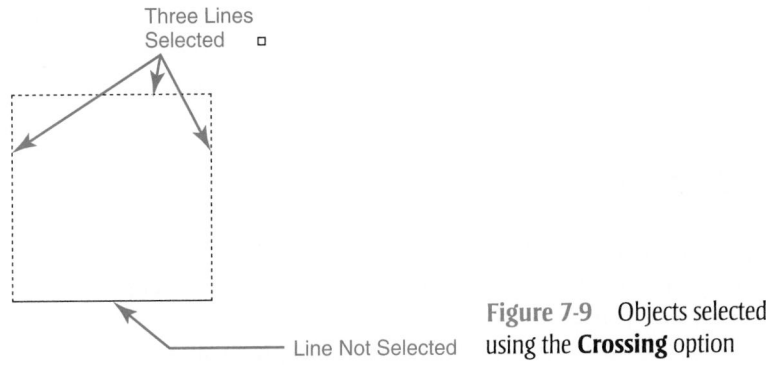

Figure 7-9   Objects selected using the **Crossing** option

TIP   You can control the window selection shading features via the **Visual Effect Settings** dialog box, which can be displayed by selecting the **Visual Effect Settings...** button in the **Selection preview** area on the **Selection** tab of the **Options** dialog box shown in Figure 7-2.

Exercise 7-3: Selecting Multiple Objects with the Crossing Option

1. Continue from Exercise 7-2.
2. Start the **ERASE** command.
3. Type **C<Enter ↵>**.
4. Create a **Crossing** selection similar to the one shown in Figure 7-8 and press **<Enter ↵>** twice. The top horizontal line and the two vertical lines of the rectangle are erased. The bottom horizontal line remains in the drawing.
5. Type **U<Enter ↵>** or select the **Undo** tool so that the three lines are undeleted.
6. Save the drawing as **EX7-3**.

Press and Drag Window Mode. It is possible to change the window selection mode so that you can define the window area for both the **Window** and **Crossing** options by picking the first window corner point and then, instead of picking the opposite corner point, simply dragging your mouse to the opposite corner location and releasing the button—eliminating the need to pick a second point. This semiautomated window creation mode is enabled by selecting the **Press and drag** check box in the **Selection modes** area on the **Selection** tab of the **Options** dialog box (see Figure 7-2). By default, the **Press and drag** window selection mode is turned off.

Implied Windowing. As mentioned earlier in the section "Selecting Objects Individually," it is possible to initiate the **Window** *or* the **Crossing** option automatically by relying on a feature called **Implied windowing. Implied windowing** can be turned on and off on the **Selection** tab of the **Options** dialog box shown in Figure 7-2.

When **Implied windowing** is on, you can initiate either the **Window** or **Crossing** option by picking an empty space in your drawing so that no objects fall within your pickbox in response to the *Select objects:* prompt. When you pick and no objects are found, AutoCAD interprets the pick point as the first corner point of a rectangular window area and prompts you to select the second corner point as follows:

```
Specify opposite corner:
```

This is where it gets interesting. If you move your cursor to the *right* of the first pick point, you initiate the **Window** option—the window boundary outline is solid, and the default shade color is blue (see Figure 7-6).

If you move your cursor to the *left* of the first pick point, you initiate the **Crossing** option—the window boundary outline is dashed, and the default shade color is green (see Figure 7-8).

The **Implied windowing** option can be a real timesaving device when selecting objects. Its use basically eliminates the need to enter either the **W** or the **C** option at the keyboard. The key is placing the first point in the correct location in response to the *Select objects:* prompt. If you know you want to use the **Crossing** option, place the first point to the right of the objects you want to select and move your cursor to the left to pick the second point. If it's the **Window** option you desire, pick to the left and move your cursor to the right.

Exercise 7-4: Selecting Multiple Objects with an Implied Window

1. Continue from Exercise 7-3.
2. Start the **ERASE** command.
3. Pick a point to the lower left of the rectangle so that no objects are within your pickbox and pick a point.
4. Drag your cursor up to the right of the rectangle so that an implied window similar to the **Window** selection shown in Figure 7-6 is created.
5. Press **<Enter ↵>**. The four lines of the rectangle are erased.
6. Type **U<Enter ↵>** or select the **Undo** tool so that the four lines are undeleted.
7. Start the **ERASE** command again.
8. Pick a point to the upper right of the rectangle so that no objects are within your pickbox and pick a point.
9. Drag your cursor down and to the left of the rectangle so that an implied window similar to the **Crossing** selection shown in Figure 7-8 is created.

10. Press **<Enter ↵>**. The top horizontal line and the two vertical lines of the rectangle are erased. The bottom horizontal line remains in the drawing.
11. Type **U<Enter ↵>** or select the **Undo** tool so that the three lines are undeleted.
12. Save the drawing as **EX7-4**.

WP—Window Polygon Option. To use the **Window Polygon** option, type **WP<Enter ↵>** in response to the *Select objects:* prompt. The **Window Polygon** option allows you to define a polygonal window area using multiple pick points so that you can select multiple objects in a complex drawing that you might not be able to select using a simple rectangular window. When you enter the **WP** option, AutoCAD prompts you for the first polygon point and then prompts you for line endpoints until you press **<Enter ↵>** as shown in Figure 7-10.

Similar to the **Window** option, the **Window Polygon** option selects only objects that are completely within the window boundary area. Objects that cross the window boundary are ignored. See Figure 7-11.

Figure 7-10   Defining the **Window Polygon** selection area

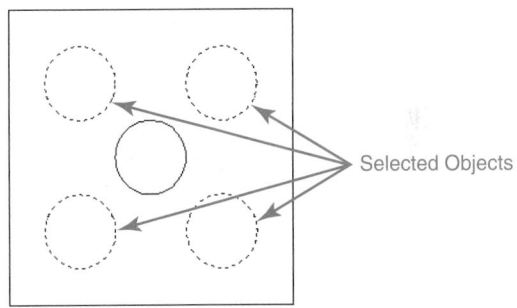

Figure 7-11   Objects selected using the **Window Polygon** option

TIP

All the multiple selection options that rely on more than two pick points have an **Undo** option that allows you to "unpick" points you have already selected so that you can relocate an errant pick point without canceling and starting over. To use the **Undo** option, type **U<Enter ↵>** in response to a prompt for the next point, and the last point will be erased.

Exercise 7-5: Selecting Multiple Objects with a Window Polygon

1. Continue from Exercise 7-4.
2. Add five circles so your drawing looks as shown in Figure 7-10.
3. Start the **ERASE** command.
4. Type **WP<Enter ↵>**.
5. Create a **Window Polygon** selection similar to the one shown in Figure 7-10 and press **<Enter ↵>** twice. The four circles at the corners of the rectangle are erased.
6. Type **U<Enter ↵>** or select the **Undo** tool so that the four circles are undeleted.
7. Save the drawing as **EX7-5**.

CP—Crossing Polygon Option. To use the **Crossing Polygon** option, type **CP<Enter ↵>** in response to the *Select objects:* prompt. The **Crossing Polygon** option works similarly to the **Window Polygon** option. It also allows you to define a polygonal window area using multiple pick points except that, like the **Crossing** option, objects that cross the polygon window are also selected. When you enter the **CP** option, AutoCAD prompts you for the first polygon point and then prompts you for line endpoints until you press **<Enter ↵>** as shown in Figure 7-12.

As noted, the **Crossing Polygon** option selects objects that *cross over* the polygon window boundary in addition to the objects that lie completely within the window boundary area. See Figure 7-13.

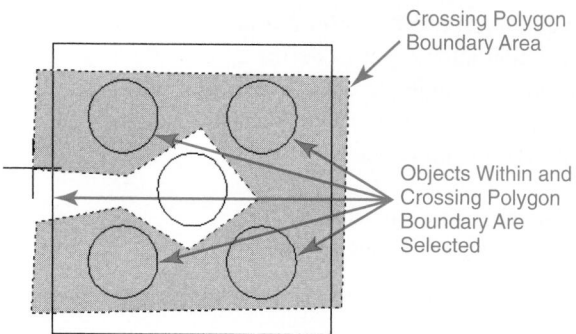

Figure 7-12   Defining the **Crossing Polygon** selection area

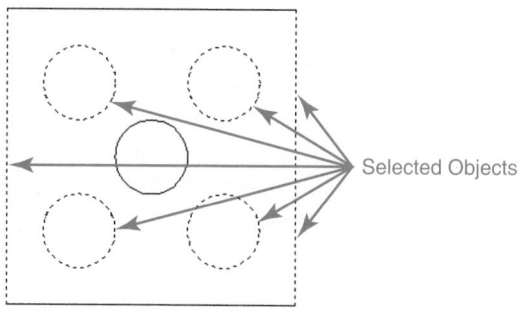

Figure 7-13   Objects selected using the **Crossing Polygon** option

Exercise 7-6: Selecting Multiple Objects with a Crossing Polygon

1. Continue from Exercise 7-5.
2. Start the **ERASE** command.
3. Type **CP<Enter ↵>**.
4. Create a **Crossing Polygon** selection similar to the one shown in Figure 7-12 and press **<Enter ↵>** twice. The four circles at the corners and the two vertical lines of the rectangle are erased.
5. Type **U<Enter ↵>** or select the **Undo** tool so that the four circles and two lines are undeleted.
6. Save the drawing as **EX7-6**.

Note:
Both the **Window Polygon** and **Crossing Polygon** options interact the same as their **Window** and **Crossing** counterparts so that a solid window boundary is used for the **Window Polygon** option and a dashed window boundary is used for the **Window Crossing** option. The window selection shading feature settings are also shared between the corresponding options.

F—Fence Option.   To use the **Fence** option, type **F<Enter ↵>** in response to the *Select objects:* prompt. The **Fence** option allows you to define a multisegmented fence line that selects everything it crosses similar to the **Crossing** option. When you enter the **F** option, AutoCAD prompts you for the first fence point and then prompts you for additional fence endpoints until you press **<Enter ↵>** as shown in Figure 7-14.

The **Fence** option selects all objects that the fence line crosses over or touches. See Figure 7-15.

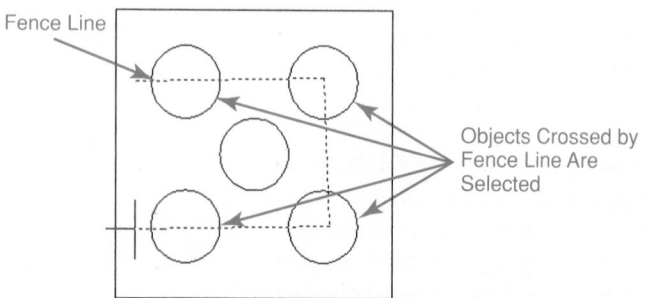

Figure 7-14   Defining the **Fence** selection line

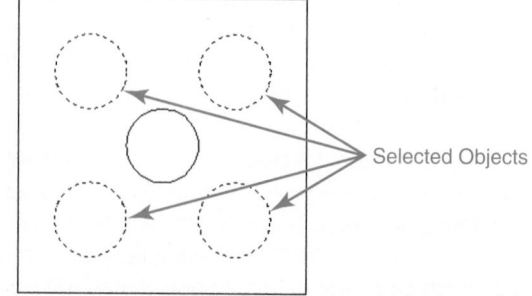

Figure 7-15   Objects selected using the **Fence** option

Exercise 7-7: Selecting Multiple Objects with a Fence

1. Continue from Exercise 7-6.
2. Start the **ERASE** command.
3. Type **F<Enter ⏎>**.
4. Create a **Fence** selection similar to the one shown in Figure 7-14 and press **<Enter ⏎>** twice. The four circles at the corners of the rectangle are erased.
5. Type **U<Enter ⏎>** or select the **Undo** tool so that the four circles are undeleted.
6. Save the drawing as **EX7-7**.

Advanced Selection Techniques

The following selection set options provide additional ways to select objects without having to pick any points in your drawing.

All—All Option.   To use the **All** option, type **All<Enter ⏎>** in response to the *Select objects:* prompt. The **All** option selects *all* the objects in a drawing—even those objects that lie outside the visible drawing window! Because of this, care should be taken when using it. When used properly, it can be a handy way to modify everything in a drawing.

TIP Objects that are on frozen or locked layers are protected when using the **All** option so that they are not selected.

L—Last Option.   To use the **Last** option, type **L<Enter ⏎>** in response to the *Select objects:* prompt. The **Last** option selects the last object created in a drawing. For instance, if you draw a line in a drawing and then enter the **ERASE** command, entering **L** in response to the *Select objects:* prompt highlights and selects the line you just drew.

P—Previous Option.   To use the **Previous** option, type **P<Enter ⏎>** in response to the *Select objects:* prompt. The **Previous** option recalls the last selection set created so that you can modify the same objects again. If no previous selection set exists, AutoCAD displays the following at the command line:

```
No previous selection set.
```

Exercise 7-8: Using Advanced Selection Techniques

1. Continue from Exercise 7-7.
2. Start the **ERASE** command.
3. Type **All<Enter ⏎>**.
4. Press **<Enter ⏎>** again. All the drawing objects are erased.
5. Type **U<Enter ⏎>** or select the **Undo** tool so that everything is undeleted.
6. Start the **ERASE** command again.
7. Type **L<Enter ⏎>**.
8. Press **<Enter ⏎>** again. The last object added to the drawing is erased.
9. Type **U<Enter ⏎>** or select the **Undo** tool so that the object is undeleted.
10. Save the drawing as **EX7-8**.

MOVING OBJECTS

Now that you are familiar with all the different ways to select objects, it's time for some action. The **MOVE** command moves objects a user-supplied distance and angle.

Move	
Ribbon & Panel:	Home | Modify Move
Modify Toolbar:	
Menu:	Modify | Move
Command Line:	MOVE
Command Alias:	M

When you start the **MOVE** command, AutoCAD prompts you to *Select objects:*. Select the object(s) you want to move and press **<Enter ↵>** to accept the selection set. AutoCAD then prompts you to *Specify base point or ↓*. You have three options:

1. Specify a base point.
2. Select the **Displacement** option either by using your arrow keys or by typing **D<Enter ↵>**.
3. Enter a displacement distance using Cartesian coordinates.

Note:
It is also possible to type a base point as a Cartesian coordinate value at the cursor or the command line. You can then specify a destination point either by using your mouse or by entering an absolute, relative, or polar coordinate value.

Using the first option, you typically pick a base (*from*) point by snapping to a key object feature using an Object Snap. AutoCAD then prompts you to *Specify second point or <use first point as displacement>:*. You can then pick a destination (*to*) point, and the selected objects are moved to the new location. See Figure 7-16.

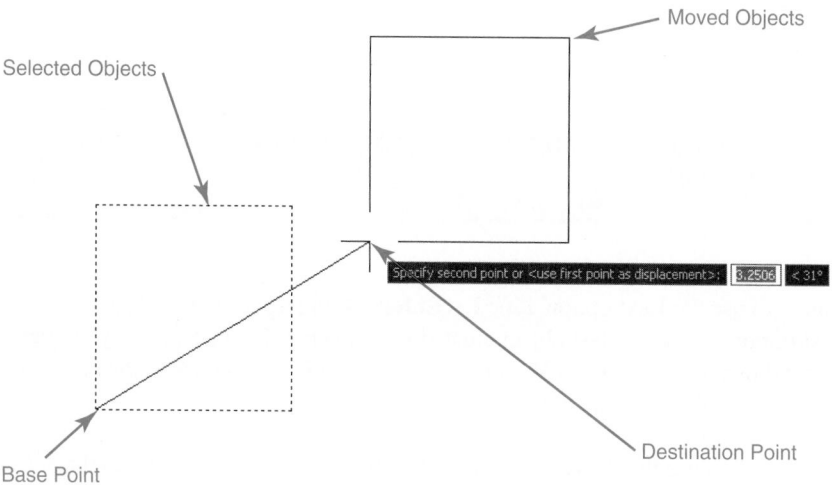

Figure 7-16   Moving objects using mouse pick points

You can also use direct distance entry to locate the second point. Using direct distance, you simply point the direction you want to move the selected object(s) and type in the distance you want to travel. See Figure 7-17.

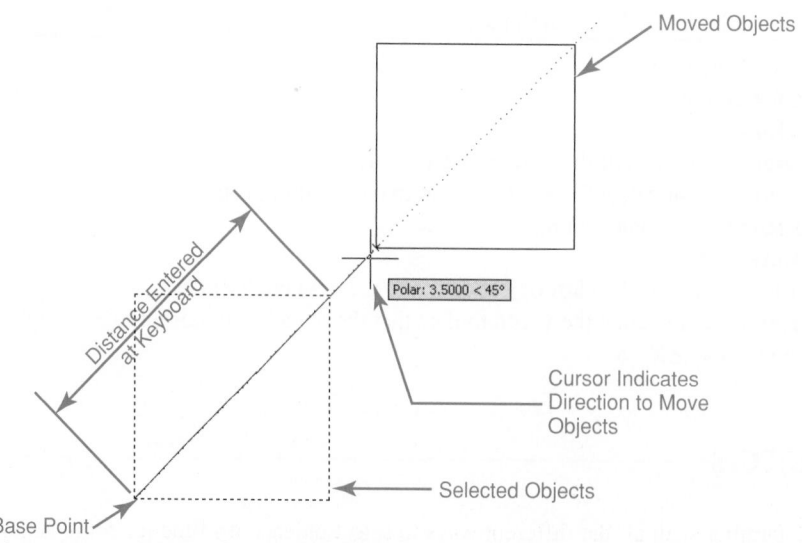

Figure 7-17   Moving objects using direct distance

TIP Remember that the best way to utilize direct distance entry is to use it in conjunction with either **Polar Tracking** or **Ortho Mode**. Using either of these drawing tools allows you to lock in an angle and enter a distance for precise movement.

FOR MORE DETAILS See Chapter 5 for detailed information about using the **Polar Tracking** and **Ortho Mode** drawing tools.

The **Displacement** option allows you to specify a displacement distance using rectangular or polar coordinates. The coordinate value you enter is *always* the relative distance the selected object(s) will be moved, even if you omit the @ sign.

To use the **Displacement** option, you can either select the option using your arrow keys or type **D<Enter ↵>**. AutoCAD prompts you to *Specify displacement <2.0000, 2.0000, 0.0000>:*. You can then enter the displacement distance using either rectangular (*X,Y*) or polar coordinates (@Distance<Angle). Entering **3,3<Enter ↵>** results in the move operation shown in Figure 7-18.

Moved Objects

Selected Objects

3.000

3.000

Figure 7-18 Moving objects using the **Displacement** option

TIP AutoCAD remembers the displacement distance entered so that it is now the default distance. The next time you use the **MOVE** command, you can just press **<Enter ↵>** to move the same distance again.

The third option is basically a shortcut to the **Displacement** option explained above. It is possible to enter a Cartesian coordinate displacement distance directly in response to the first *Specify base point or ↓* prompt explained earlier. Entering an *X,Y* distance and pressing **<Enter ↵>** displays the standard prompt *Specify second point or <use first point as displacement>:*. Pressing **<Enter ↵>** selects the default **<use first point as displacement>** option so that the *X,Y* distance entered is used as the displacement distance.

Exercise 7-9: Moving Objects

1. Start a new drawing using the acad.dwt drawing template.
2. Draw a 2″ × 2″ square similar to one shown in Figure 7-16.
3. Start the **MOVE** command and select the square using your preferred selection method so that AutoCAD prompts *Specify base point or ↓*.
4. Snap to the lower left corner of the square using the **Endpoint** Object Snap as shown in Figure 7-16.
5. Move the square using a second pick point as shown in Figure 7-16.
6. Type **U<Enter ↵>** or select the **Undo** tool so that the square is in its original location.
7. Start the **MOVE** command again and select the square using your preferred selection method so that AutoCAD prompts *Specify base point or ↓*.
8. Snap to the lower left corner of the square using the **Endpoint** Object Snap as shown in Figure 7-17.
9. Move your cursor so the rubber-band line points to the right as shown in Figure 7-17 and type **3<Enter ↵>**. The square moves 3 units along the rubber-band line.
10. Type **U<Enter ↵>** or select the **Undo** tool so that the square is in its original location.
11. Start the **MOVE** command again and select the square using your preferred selection method so that AutoCAD prompts *Specify base point or ↓*.
12. Type **3,3<Enter↵>**. AutoCAD prompts *Specify second point or <use first point as displacement>:*.
13. Press **<Enter ↵>** again to use the first point entered as the displacement distance. The square moves +3 units on the *X*-axis and +3 units on the *Y*-axis as shown in Figure 7-18.
14. Type **U<Enter ↵>** or select the **Undo** tool so that the square is in its original location.
15. Save the drawing as **EX7-9**.

> **Note:**
> It is possible, and quite common, to use Object Snaps when modifying objects, especially when selecting a base point.

COPYING OBJECTS

Copy	
Ribbon & Panel:	Home | Modify
Modify Toolbar:	
Menu:	Modify | Copy
Command Line:	COPY
Command Alias:	CO

The **COPY** command copies objects a user-supplied distance and angle. Its usage is similar to the **MOVE** command except that the **COPY** command maintains the selected objects in their original location. It is possible to make multiple copies if you specify a base point.

When you start the **COPY** command, AutoCAD prompts you to *Select objects:*. Select the object(s) you want to copy and press **<Enter ↵>** to accept the selection set. AutoCAD then prompts you to *Specify base point or ↓*. Similar to the **MOVE** command, you have three options:

1. Specify a base point.
2. Select the **Displacement** option either by using your arrow keys or by typing **D<Enter ↵>**.
3. Enter a displacement distance using Cartesian coordinates.

Using the first option, you typically pick a base (*from*) point by snapping to a key object feature using an Object Snap. AutoCAD then prompts you to *Specify second point or <use first point as displacement>:*. You can then pick a destination (*to*) point, and the selected objects are copied to the new location as shown in Figure 7-19.

Just like the **MOVE** command, you can also rely on direct distance entry to locate the second point. Using direct distance, you simply point the direction you want to copy the selected object(s) and type in the distance you want to travel.

If you use the first option and specify a base point, AutoCAD remains in the **COPY** command after the first copy is created so that it is possible to make multiple copies by specifying multiple destination points. After making the first copy, AutoCAD repeatedly prompts you to

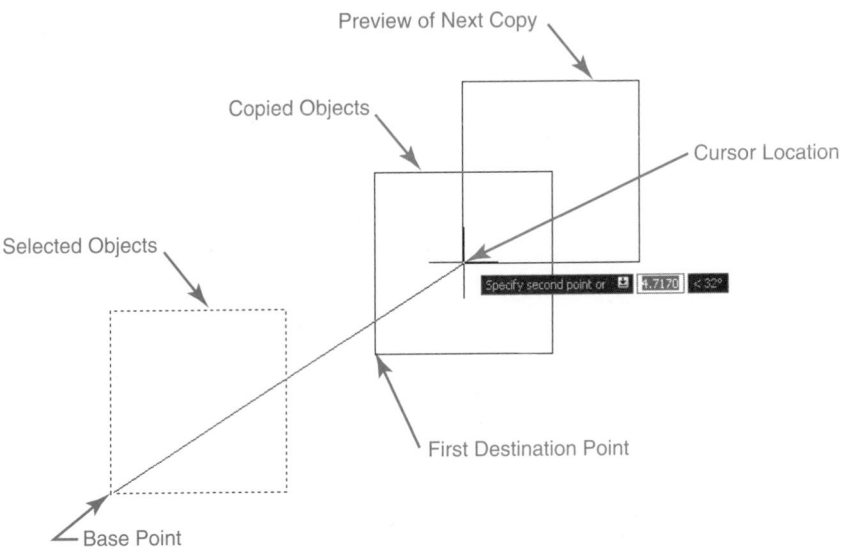

Figure 7-19   Copying objects using mouse pick points

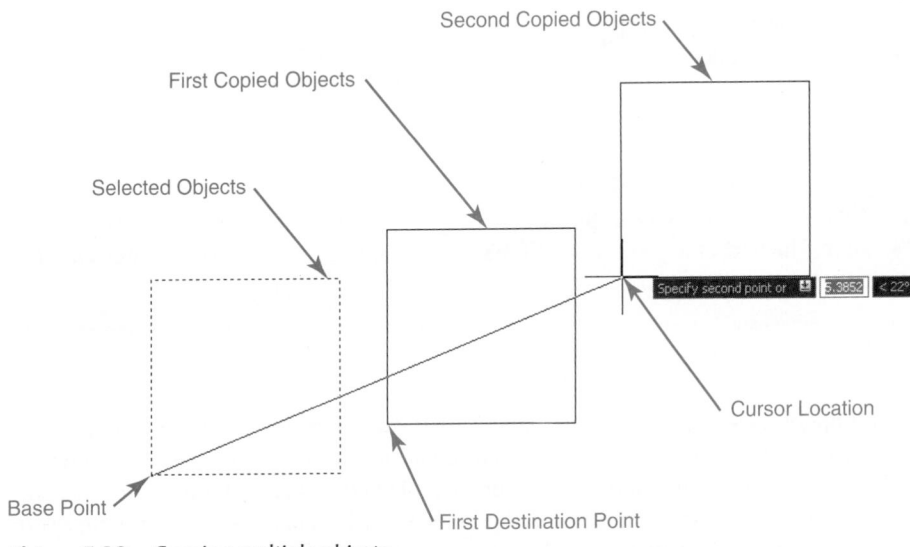

Figure 7-20   Copying multiple objects

Specify second point or ↓ until you select the **Exit** option or type **E<Enter** ↲**>** to end the command as shown in Figure 7-20.

> **TIP**
> The **COPY** command has an **Undo** option when you are making multiple copies so that you can undo a copy operation if it is the wrong location. To use the **Undo** option, you can either select the option using your arrow keys or type **U<Enter** ↲**>**.

The **Displacement** option allows you to specify a displacement distance using rectangular or polar coordinates. The coordinate value you enter is *always* the relative distance the selected object(s) will be copied, even if you omit the @ sign.

To use the **Displacement** option, you can either select the option using your arrow keys or type **D<Enter** ↲**>**. AutoCAD prompts you to *Specify displacement <3.0000, 3.0000, 0.0000>:*. You can then enter the displacement distance using either rectangular (*X,Y*) or polar coordinates (@Distance<Angle). Entering **3,3<Enter** ↲**>** results in the copy operation shown in Figure 7-21.

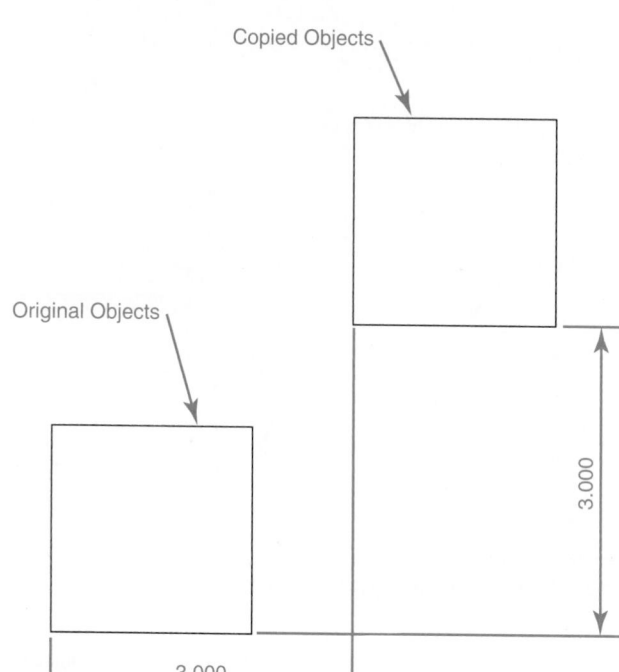

Figure 7-21 Copying objects
using the **Displacement** option

TIP

AutoCAD remembers the displacement distance entered so that it is now the default distance. The next time you use the **COPY** command, you can just press **<Enter ⏎>** to copy the same distance again.

The third option is a shortcut to the **Displacement** option explained above, similar to the **MOVE** command. It is possible to enter a Cartesian coordinate displacement distance directly in response to the first *Specify base point or ↓* prompt explained earlier. Entering an *X,Y* distance and pressing **<Enter ⏎>** displays the standard prompt *Specify second point or <use first point as displacement>:*. Hitting **<Enter ⏎>** selects the default **<use first point as displacement>** option so that the *X,Y* distance entered is used as the displacement distance.

Exercise 7-10: Copying Objects

1. Continue from Exercise 7-9.
2. Start the **COPY** command and select the square using your preferred selection method so that AutoCAD prompts *Specify base point or ↓*.
3. Snap to the lower left corner of the square using the **Endpoint** Object Snap as shown in Figure 7-19. AutoCAD prompts *Specify second point or <use first point as displacement>:*.
4. Copy the square using a second pick point as shown in Figure 7-19. AutoCAD repeatedly prompts *Specify second point or ↓*.
5. Continue to pick points to make multiple copies as shown in Figure 7-20.
6. Press **<Enter ⏎>**, select the **Exit** option, or type **E<Enter ⏎>** to end the **COPY** command.
7. Type **U<Enter ⏎>** or select the **Undo** tool so that only one square is left in its original location.
8. Start the **COPY** command and select the square using your preferred selection method so that AutoCAD prompts *Specify second point or ↓*.
9. Type **3,3<Enter ⏎>**. AutoCAD prompts *Specify second point or <use first point as displacement>:*.

10. Press **<Enter ↵>** again to use the first point entered as the displacement distance. The square is copied +3 units on the *X*-axis and +3 units on the *Y*-axis as shown in Figure 7-21.
11. Type **U<Enter ↵>** or select the **Undo** tool so that only one square is left in its original location.
12. Save the drawing as **EX7-10**.

MIRRORING OBJECTS

The **MIRROR** command creates a mirror image of objects about a mirror axis line defined by two user-supplied line endpoints.

When you start the **MIRROR** command, AutoCAD prompts you to *Select objects:*. Select the object(s) you want to mirror and press **<Enter ↵>** to accept the selection set. AutoCAD then prompts you to specify the two endpoints of a line about which to mirror the selected objects as shown in Figure 7-22, while maintaining a ghost image of the original objects and displaying a preview of the mirrored objects.

Mirror	
Ribbon & Panel:	Home | Modify
Modify Toolbar:	
Menu:	Modify | Mirror
Command Line:	MIRROR
Command Alias:	MI

TIP You can use either **Ortho Mode** or **Polar Tracking** to create either a horizontal or vertical mirror axis line quickly by simply picking two points.

FOR MORE DETAILS See Chapter 5 for more information about using the **Ortho Mode** and **Polar Tracking** drawing tools.

After selecting the second point, AutoCAD prompts you to *Erase source objects? ↓*. You have the option of either erasing the originally selected objects, so only the mirrored copies remain, or leaving them in the drawing. The default is *not* to erase the original objects so that you can just press **<Enter ↵>**. Of course, you can also select the **No** option using your arrow keys. Either response to the *Erase source objects? ↓* prompt results with the mirrored object *and* the original as shown in Figure 7-23.

Figure 7-22   Mirroring objects

Figure 7-23   Mirrored objects with original objects maintained

To erase the original objects, you can either select the **Yes** option using your arrow keys or type **Y<Enter ↵>** in response to the *Erase source objects? ↓* prompt. The result of erasing the original objects is shown in Figure 7-24.

Figure 7-24 Mirrored objects with original objects erased

Original Objects Erased ⟶   Mirrored Objects

Mirroring Text

Usually, when you mirror text you want it to retain its original left-to-right orientation so that the text isn't reversed as shown in Figure 7-25.

The AutoCAD **MIRRTEXT** system variable controls whether or not text is reversed when it is mirrored. Setting **MIRRTEXT** to **1** (on) will cause text to be reversed when it is mirrored as shown in Figure 7-25. Setting **MIRRTEXT** to **0** (off) retains the text's original orientation as shown in Figure 7-26.

By default, the **MIRRTEXT** system variable is set to **0** (off).

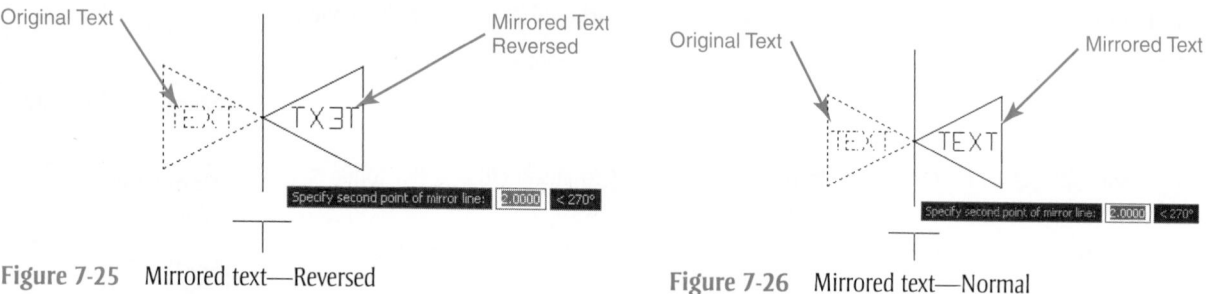

Original Text   Mirrored Text Reversed

Original Text   Mirrored Text

Figure 7-25 Mirrored text—Reversed   **Figure 7-26** Mirrored text—Normal

Exercise 7-11: Mirroring Objects

1. Start a new drawing using the acad.dwt drawing template.
2. Draw a triangle similar to the one shown in Figure 7-22.
3. Start the **MIRROR** command and select the triangle using your preferred selection method so that AutoCAD prompts *Specify first point of mirror line:*.
4. Pick a point above the right side vertex as shown in Figure 7-22. AutoCAD prompts you to *Specify second point of mirror line:*.
5. Turn on the **Ortho Mode** drawing tool if it is not already on.
6. Pick a point directly below the first point at 270° using the **Ortho Mode** drawing tool as shown in Figure 7-22. AutoCAD mirrors the triangle and prompts *Erase source objects?* ↓.
7. Press **<Enter ↵>** to accept the default and retain the original triangle so that the drawing looks similar to Figure 7-23.
8. Save the drawing as **EX7-11**.

Rotate	
Ribbon & Panel:	Home | Modify ↻
Modify Toolbar:	↻
Menu:	Modify | Rotate
Command Line:	ROTATE
Command Alias:	RO

ROTATING OBJECTS

The **ROTATE** command rotates objects a user-specified rotation angle around a user-specified base point.

When you start the **ROTATE** command, AutoCAD prompts you to *Select objects:*. Select the object(s) you want to rotate and press **<Enter ↵>** to accept the selection set. AutoCAD then prompts you to *Specify base point:*. The base point is the axis of rotation about which the selected object(s) are rotated. Typically you pick a base point by snapping to a key object feature using an Object Snap.

After specifying the base point, AutoCAD then prompts you to *Specify rotation angle or* ↓. You have three different ways you can enter the rotation angle:

1. Pick a point with your mouse that defines the rotation angle using the base point as the vertex.

Note:
It is also possible to type in a base point as a Cartesian coordinate value at the cursor or the command line. For instance, to rotate an object using the drawing origin as the base point, you can enter **0,0 <Enter ↵>** in response to the *Specify base point:* prompt.

2. Enter the angle at the keyboard.

3. Use the **Reference** option to reference a start angle and then enter a new angle either at the keyboard or by picking points.

Using the first option, you simply move your cursor and pick a point in your drawing to indicate the desired rotation angle. AutoCAD provides a preview of the rotation as shown in Figure 7-27.

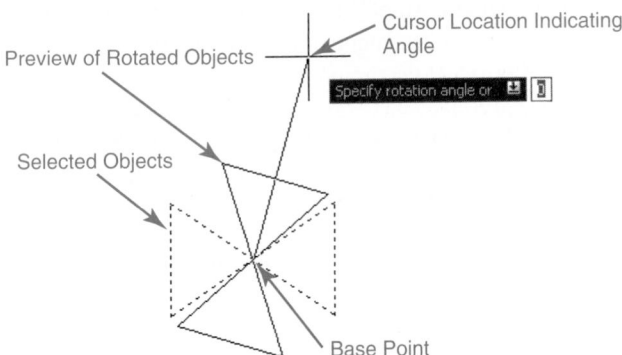

Figure 7-27   Rotating objects using your mouse

TIP   You can use either **Ortho Mode** or **Polar Tracking** to quickly rotate object(s) at predefined angles.

FOR MORE DETAILS   See Chapter 5 for more information about using the **Ortho Mode** and **Polar Tracking** drawing tools.

The second option is to enter the rotation angle at the keyboard. Angles are measured using the current base angle and direction. The default base angle is 0°=East with angles measured counterclockwise. The current direction and base angle are displayed at the command line when you use the **ROTATE** command for an easy reference as follows:

```
Current positive angle in UCS: ANGDIR=clockwise ANGBASE=0
```

Entering **45<Enter ↵>** with the settings above rotates the selected objects as shown in Figures 7-28A and B.

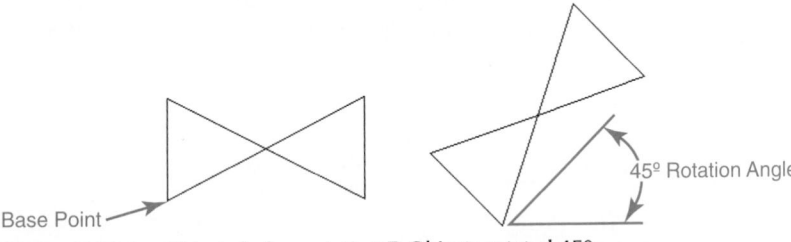

Figure 7-28A   Objects before rotating **B** Objects rotated 45°

TIP   It is also possible to enter a negative angle and rotate objects in the opposite direction of the current angle direction setting. For example, entering **−45°** is equal to entering **315°**.

FOR MORE DETAILS   See Chapter 4 for more information about setting the base angle and direction.

The **Reference** option allows you to rotate object(s) by specifying a reference, or start angle, and then specifying a new, absolute angle to rotate to. AutoCAD determines the necessary rotation angle by calculating the difference from the reference angle to the new angle.

To use the **Reference** option, you can either select the option using your arrow keys or type **R<Enter ⏎>** at the command line. AutoCAD prompts you to *Specify the reference angle <0>:*. You can either type in an angle via the keyboard, or you can select two points in your drawing that define the reference angle. The **Reference** option is invaluable if you don't know the angle of an existing object. Using Object Snaps, you can snap to two points on the object(s) that define its current angle as shown in Figure 7-29.

AutoCAD then prompts you to *Specify the new angle or ↓*. You can either type in an angle via the keyboard, or you can use the **Points** option to select two points in the drawing to define the new angle as shown in Figure 7-30.

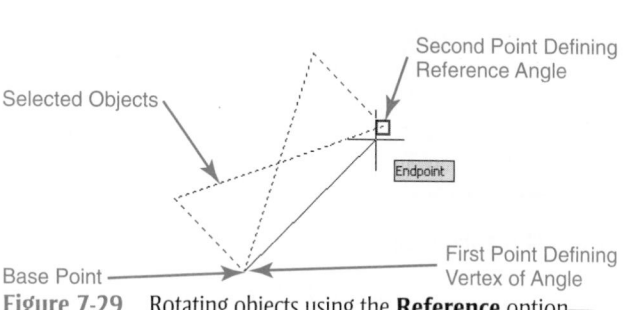

Figure 7-29   Rotating objects using the **Reference** option— Start angle

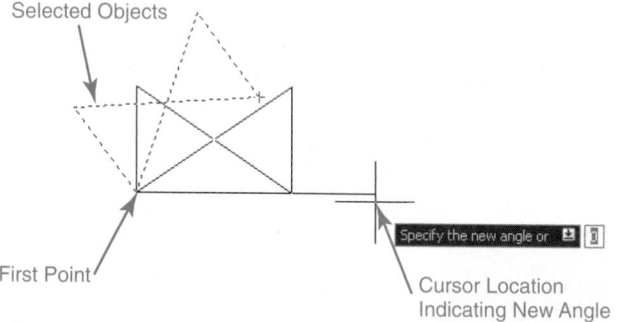

Figure 7-30   Rotating objects using the **Reference** option— New angle

Rotating and Copying Objects

It is possible to rotate and copy objects using the **Copy** option. To use the **Copy** option, you can either select the option using your arrow keys or type **C<Enter ⏎>** at the command line when AutoCAD prompts you to *Specify rotation angle or ↓*. When you select the **Copy** option, AutoCAD displays the following at the command line:

```
Rotating a copy of the selected objects.
```

You can use any of the methods explained earlier to specify a rotation angle. Figure 7-31 shows the results of using the **Copy** option and rotating the objects shown in Figure 7-28A 90° from horizontal.

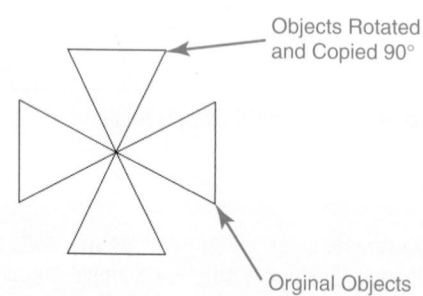

Figure 7-31   Rotating and copying objects

TIP AutoCAD remembers the angle entered using any of the **ROTATE** command options so that it is now the default angle. The next time you use the **ROTATE** command, you can press **<Enter ↵>** to rotate the same angle again.

Exercise 7-12: Rotating Objects

1. Continue from Exercise 7-11.
2. Start the **ROTATE** command and select both triangles using your preferred selection method so that AutoCAD prompts *Specify base point or ↓*.
3. Snap to the intersection of both triangles using the **Intersection** Object Snap as shown in Figure 7-27. AutoCAD prompts *Specify rotation angle or ↓*.
4. Rotate the triangles to any angle using a cursor pick point as shown in Figure 7-27.
5. Type **U<Enter ↵>** or select the **Undo** tool so that the triangles are oriented horizontally again as shown in Figure 7-28A.
6. Start the **ROTATE** command again and select the triangles using your preferred selection method so that AutoCAD prompts *Specify base point or ↓*.
7. Snap to the intersection of both triangles using the **Intersection** Object Snap as shown in Figure 7-27. AutoCAD prompts *Specify rotation angle or ↓*.
8. Type **45<Enter ↵>**. The triangles are rotated 45° as shown in Figure 7-28B.
9. Type **U<Enter ↵>** or select the **Undo** tool so that the triangles are oriented horizontally again as shown in Figure 7-28A.
10. Start the **ROTATE** command again and select the triangles using your preferred selection method so that AutoCAD prompts *Specify base point or ↓*.
11. Snap to the intersection of both triangles using the **Intersection** Object Snap as shown in Figure 7-27. AutoCAD prompts *Specify rotation angle or ↓*.
12. Select the **Copy** option either by selecting the option using your arrow keys or by typing **C<Enter ↵>** at the command line.
13. Type **90<Enter ↵>**. The triangles are copied and rotated 90° as shown in Figure 7-31.
14. Type **U<Enter ↵>** or select the **Undo** tool so that only two triangles are left at their original horizontal orientation.
15. Save the drawing as **EX7-12**.

SCALING OBJECTS

The **SCALE** command scales objects a user-specified scale factor about a user-specified base point.

When you start the **SCALE** command, AutoCAD prompts you to *Select objects:*. Select the object(s) you want to scale and press **<Enter ↵>** to accept the selection set. AutoCAD then prompts you to *Specify base point:*. The base point is the point about which the selected object(s) are scaled. Typically you pick a base point by snapping to a key object feature using an Object Snap.

After specifying the base point, AutoCAD then prompts you to *Specify scale factor or ↓*. You have three different ways you can enter the scale factor:

Note:
It is also possible to type in a base point as a Cartesian coordinate value at the cursor or the command line. For instance, to scale an object using the drawing origin as the base point, you can enter **0,0 <Enter ↵>** in response to the *Specify base point:* prompt.

Scale	
Ribbon & Panel:	Home | Modify
Modify Toolbar:	
Menu:	Modify | Scale
Command Line:	SCALE
Command Alias:	SC

1. Pick a point with your mouse that defines the scale factor.
2. Enter the scale factor at the keyboard.
3. Use the **Reference** option to reference a starting size/length and then enter a new size/length either at the keyboard or by picking points.

Using the first option you simply move your cursor and pick a point in your drawing to indicate the desired scale factor. AutoCAD provides a preview of the scaling process as shown in Figure 7-32.

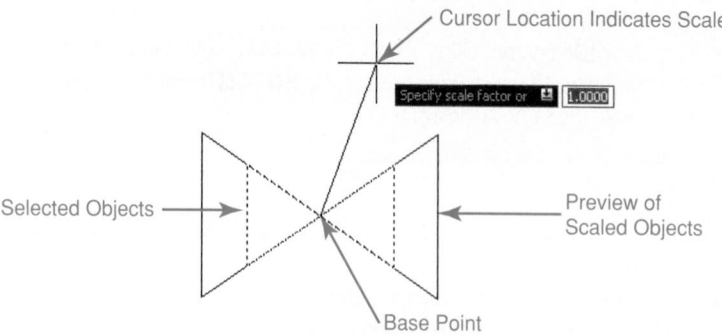

Figure 7-32   Scaling objects using your mouse

The second option is to enter the scale factor at the keyboard. A scale factor greater than 1 makes objects larger, and a scale factor less than 1 makes objects smaller. Scale factors must always be greater than zero. Entering **2<Enter ↵>** in response to the *Specify scale factor or* ↓ prompt scales the selected objects up by a factor of 2 so that they are twice as large, as shown in Figures 7-33A and B.

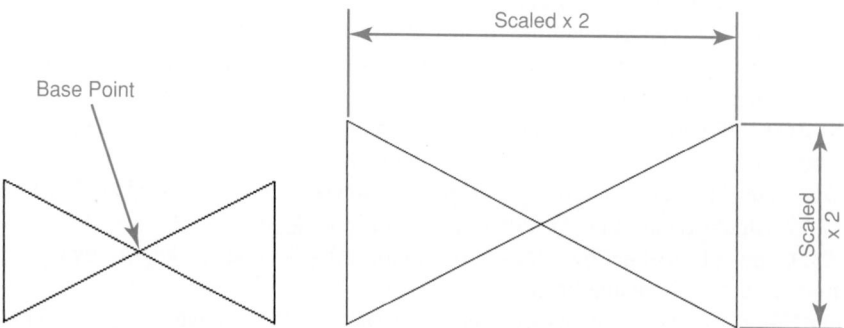

Figure 7-33A   Objects before scaling **B** Objects scaled by a factor of 2

The **Reference** option allows you to scale objects by specifying a reference, or start, length and then a new, absolute length to scale to. AutoCAD determines the necessary scale factor by calculating the difference between the reference length and the new length.

To use the **Reference** option, you can either select the option using your arrow keys or type **R<Enter ↵>**. AutoCAD prompts you to *Specify reference length <1.0000>:*. You can either type in a length via the keyboard, or you can select two points in your drawing that define the reference length. The **Reference** option is invaluable if you don't know the length of an existing object but you do know the length it needs to be. Using Object Snaps, you can snap to two points on the object(s) that define its current length as shown in Figure 7-34.

Figure 7-34   Scaling objects using the **Reference** option—
Start length

AutoCAD then prompts you to *Specify new length or* ↓. You can either type in a length via the keyboard, or you can use the **Points** option to select two points in the drawing to define the new length as shown in Figure 7-35.

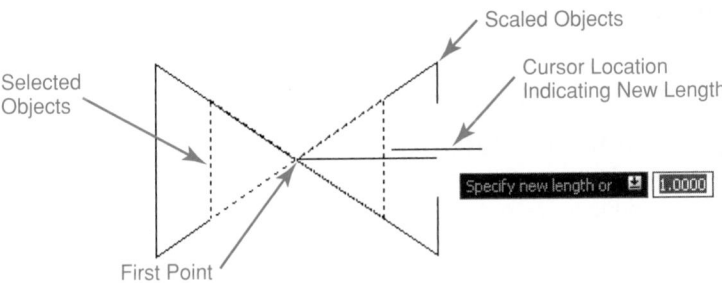

Figure 7-35   Scaling objects using the **Reference** option—New length

Scaling and Copying Objects

It is possible to scale and copy object(s) using the **Copy** option. To use the **Copy** option, you can either select the option using your arrow keys or type **C<Enter ↵>** when AutoCAD prompts you to *Specify scale factor or* ↓. Using the **Copy** option, AutoCAD displays the following at the command line:

```
Scaling a copy of the selected objects.
```

You can use any of the methods explained earlier to specify a scale factor.

TIP   AutoCAD remembers the scale factor entered using any of the **SCALE** command options so that it is now the default scale factor. The next time you use the **SCALE** command, you can press **<Enter ↵>** and scale by the same factor again.

Exercise 7-13: Scaling Objects

1. Continue from Exercise 7-12.
2. Start the **SCALE** command and select both triangles using your preferred selection method so that AutoCAD prompts *Specify base point or* ↓.
3. Snap to the intersection of both triangles using the **Intersection** Object Snap as shown in Figure 7-32. AutoCAD prompts *Specify scale factor or* ↓.
4. Scale the triangles to any scale using a cursor pick point as shown in Figure 7-32.
5. Type **U<Enter ↵>** or select the **Undo** tool so that the triangles are scaled to their original size again as shown in Figure 7-33A.
6. Start the **SCALE** command again and select the triangles using your preferred selection method so that AutoCAD prompts *Specify base point or* ↓.
7. Snap to the intersection of both triangles using the **Intersection** Object Snap as shown in Figure 7-32. AutoCAD prompts *Specify scale factor or* ↓.
8. Type **2<Enter ↵>**. The triangles are scaled up by a factor of 2 as shown in Figure 7-33B.
9. Type **U<Enter ↵>** or select the **Undo** tool so that the triangles are scaled to their original size again as shown in Figure 7-33A.
10. Save the drawing as **EX7-13**.

STRETCHING OBJECTS

The **STRETCH** command moves or stretches objects a user-supplied distance and angle using the **Crossing Window** or **Crossing Polygon** selection option. The key to the **STRETCH** command is that it moves only endpoints and vertices that lie inside the crossing selection, leaving those outside unchanged.

Stretch	
Ribbon & Panel:	Home| Modify
Modify Toolbar:	
Menu:	Modify| Stretch
Command Line:	STRETCH
Command Alias:	S

When you start the **STRETCH** command, AutoCAD displays the following at the command line:

```
Select objects to stretch by crossing-window or crossing-polygon...
```

AutoCAD also prompts you to *Select objects:*. You *must* select the object(s) you want to stretch using either the **Crossing** or **Crossing Polygon** selection option and press **<Enter ↵>** to accept the selection set as shown in Figure 7-36.

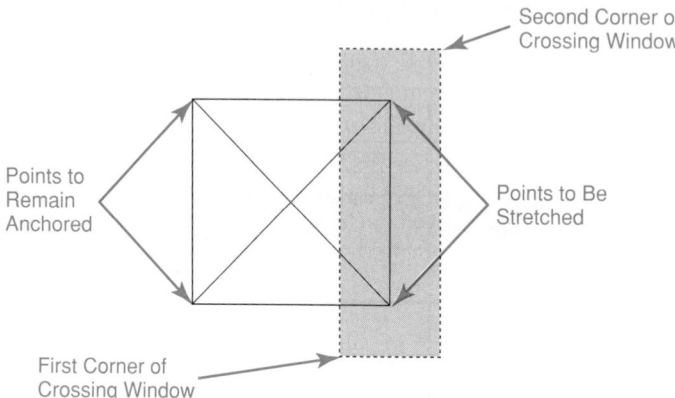

Figure 7-36   Selecting objects to stretch using a **Crossing** selection

AutoCAD then prompts you to *Specify base point or* ↓. You have three options:

1. Specify a base point.
2. Select the **Displacement** option either by using your arrow keys or by typing **D<Enter ↵>**.
3. Enter a displacement distance using Cartesian coordinates.

TIP   You can use standard object selection methods such as picking on the object, and Auto-CAD automatically treats those objects with a **MOVE** operation. You can also apply multiple crossing selections within a single **STRETCH** operation to stretch multiple object selections simultaneously.

Using the first option, you typically pick a base (*from*) point by snapping to a key object feature using an Object Snap. AutoCAD then prompts you to *Specify second point or <use first point as displacement>:*. You can then pick a destination (*to*) point, and the selected objects are stretched or moved to the new location as shown in Figure 7-37.

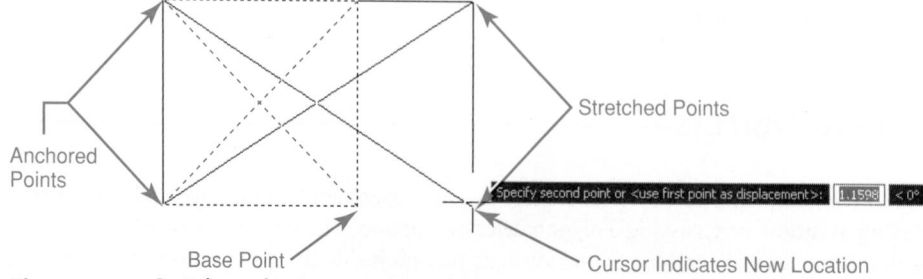

Figure 7-37   Stretching objects using mouse pick points

Notice in Figure 7-37 that the **STRETCH** command leaves any points or vertices outside the crossing selection anchored in place so that they are unaffected by the move. This is useful when you need to move or stretch part of a drawing but leave other portions of the drawing intact.

In the example above, you can also rely on direct distance entry to locate the second point. Using direct distance you simply point the direction you want to stretch the selected object(s) and type in the distance you want to travel.

Note:
It is also possible to type a base point as a Cartesian coordinate value at the cursor or the command line. You can then specify a destination point either by using your mouse or by entering an absolute, relative, or polar coordinate value.

TIP Remember that the best way to utilize direct distance entry is to use it in conjunction with either **Polar Tracking** or **Ortho Mode**. Using either of these drawing tools allows you to lock in an angle and enter a distance for precise movement.

FOR MORE DETAILS See Chapter 5 for detailed information about using the **Polar Tracking** and **Ortho Mode** drawing tools.

The **Displacement** option allows you to specify a displacement distance using rectangular or polar coordinates. The coordinate value you enter is *always* the relative distance the selected object(s) will be stretched, even if you omit the @ sign.

To use the **Displacement** option, you can either select the option using your arrow keys or type **D<Enter ↵>**. AutoCAD prompts you to *Specify displacement <2.0000, 2.0000, 0.0000>:*. You can then enter the displacement distance using either rectangular (*X,Y*) or polar coordinates (@Distance<Angle). Entering **2,0<Enter ↵>** results in the stretch operation shown in Figure 7-38.

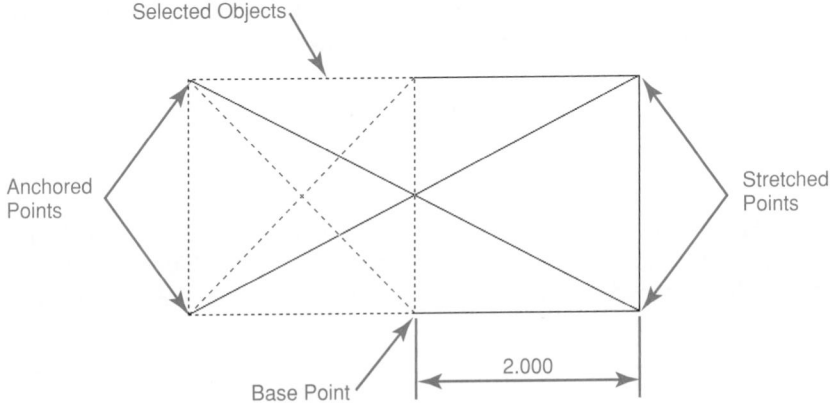

Figure 7-38   Stretching objects using the **Displacement** option

TIP AutoCAD remembers the displacement distance entered so that it is now the default distance. The next time you use the **STRETCH** command, you can just press **<Enter ↵>** to stretch the same distance again.

The third option is a shortcut to the **Displacement** option explained above. It is possible to enter a Cartesian coordinate displacement distance directly in response to the first *Specify base point or* ↓ prompt explained earlier. Entering an *X,Y* distance and pressing **<Enter ↵>** displays the standard prompt *Specify second point or <use first point as displacement>:.* Pressing **<Enter ↵>** selects the default **<use first point as displacement>** option so that the *X,Y* distance entered is used as the displacement distance.

Exercise 7-14: Stretching Objects

1. Start a new drawing using the acad.dwt drawing template.
2. Draw a 2″ × 2″ square with a cross similar to the one shown in Figure 7-36.
3. Start the **STRETCH** command and select the line endpoints on the right side of the square using the **Crossing** selection method shown in Figure 7-36 so that AutoCAD prompts *Specify base point or* ↓.
4. Snap to the lower right corner of the square using the **Endpoint** Object Snap as shown in Figure 7-37. AutoCAD prompts *Specify second point or <use first point as displacement>:.*
5. Stretch the line endpoints to the right using a second pick point as shown in Figure 7-37.
6. Type **U<Enter ↵>** or select the **Undo** tool so that the square is its original size.
7. Start the **STRETCH** command and select the line endpoints on the right side of the square using the **Crossing** selection method shown in Figure 7-36 so that AutoCAD prompts *Specify base point or* ↓.
8. Type **2,0<Enter ↵>.** AutoCAD prompts *Specify second point or <use first point as displacement>:.*
9. Press **<Enter ↵>** again to use the first point entered as the displacement distance. The square is stretched +2 units on the *X*-axis as shown in Figure 7-38.
10. Type **U<Enter ↵>** or select the **Undo** tool so that only one square is left in its original location.
11. Save the drawing as **EX7-14**.

SELECTING OBJECTS FIRST

Now that you have seen how to modify objects using the traditional verb/noun approach of selecting a modify command and then the objects to modify, let's look at the noun/verb approach of selecting objects first and *then* selecting a modify command. First, make sure that the **Noun/verb selection** check box is selected on the **Selection** tab of the **Options** dialog box as shown in Figure 7-2. It is on by default.

TIP   The **PICKFIRST** system variable can also be used to control the noun/verb selection setting. Setting **PICKFIRST** to **1** (on) is the same as selecting the **Noun/verb selection** check box. Setting **PICKFIRST** to **0** (off) turns off the **Noun/verb selection** check box.

Using noun/verb selection, you can select objects either by using your cursor or by using implied windowing to create a **Window** or **Crossing** selection. Selected objects are highlighted, and if grips are enabled, their grips are turned on as shown later in Figure 7-39. Grips are explained in detail in the next section. If you now select any of the modify commands introduced in this chapter, the selected objects become the default selection set for the modify command, and you are *not* prompted to select any objects. You can then use the command and any command options by applying the same techniques explained in the previous sections.

Exercise 7-15: Selecting Objects First for Editing

1. Continue from Exercise 7-14.
2. Select all the objects in the drawing either by selecting objects individually with your mouse or by using implied windowing.
3. Select the **ERASE** command. All the objects are erased.
4. Type **U<Enter ↵>** or select the **Undo** tool so that all the objects are undeleted.
5. Save the drawing as **EX7-15**.

USING GRIPS TO EDIT

Grips are the small colored squares (default=blue) that appear at key object definition points when an object is selected as shown in Figure 7-39.

Grips act as object handles and when selected provide quick, easy access to the five basic modify commands explained earlier in this chapter so that you can maintain your focus on your drawing. The five grip commands, or modes, are as follows:

1. **Stretch**
2. **Move**
3. **Rotate**
4. **Scale**
5. **Mirror**

Selecting grips and using the different grip modes is explained in detail a little later in this section. First we need to make sure grips are enabled, as well as look at some of the different grip settings such as size and color.

Controlling Grips

Grips are controlled on the **Selection** tab of the **Options** dialog box shown in Figure 7-40.

The different grip features and their settings are as follows:

- **Grip size**   Controls the display size of grips
- **Unselected grip color**   Determines the color of an unselected grip
- **Selected grip color**   Determines the color of a selected grip

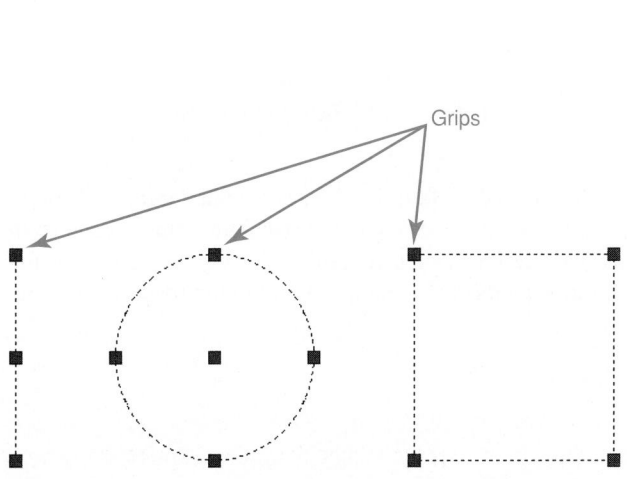

Figure 7-39   Grips displayed for a line, circle, and rectangle

Figure 7-40   **Grip** settings on the **Selection** tab of the **Options** dialog box

- **Hover grip color**   Determines the color a grip displays when the cursor hovers over the grip
- **Enable grips**   Displays grips on an object when it is selected
- **Enable grips within blocks**   Controls how grips are displayed on a block after you select it. If this option is selected, AutoCAD displays all grips for each object in the block. If this option is cleared, AutoCAD displays one grip located at the insertion point of the block
- **Enable grip tips**   Displays grip-specific tips when the cursor hovers over a grip on a custom object that supports grip tips. This option has no effect on standard AutoCAD objects
- **Object selection limit for display of grips**   Suppresses the display of grips when the initial selection set includes more than the specified number of objects. The valid range is 1 to 32,767. The default setting is 100.

FOR MORE DETAILS   See Chapter 16 for more information about blocks.

For the best results, make sure that your **Grip** settings closely match those shown in Figure 7-40. Failure to do so can cause some of the examples and exercises in the following sections to behave differently than anticipated.

Selecting Grips

To select a grip, you must place your cursor within the grip box and pick with your mouse. When a grip is selected, it changes color (default=red), and you are placed in grid edit mode as shown in Figure 7-41.

It is possible to select multiple grips by holding down the **<Shift>** key before selecting the first grip. You can continue to select grips until you release the **<Shift>** key. In Figure 7-42, two grips have been selected.

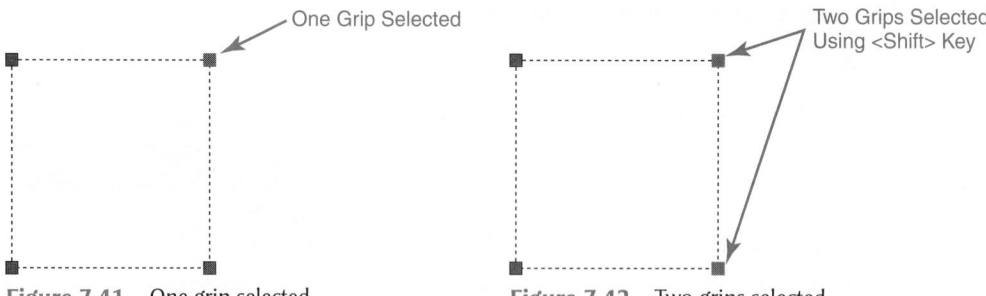

Figure 7-41   One grip selected   **Figure 7-42**   Two grips selected

To "unselect" all grips that have been selected (default=red) as shown in Figure 7-41, press the **<Esc>** key once. This changes the grips to the unselected mode (default=blue) as shown in Figure 7-41. To turn off all the grips that are unselected (default=blue), you must press the **<Esc>** key again. This will result in the object(s) being simply highlighted (dashed) with no grips displayed.

TIP   You can remove objects from the selection set by holding down the **<Shift>** key and selecting the object you want to remove.

Grip Modes

After at least one grip is selected (default=red) and you are in grip edit mode as shown in Figure 7-42, the desired grip mode can be selected either at the command line or via the right-click **Grip** shortcut menu.

The command line approach allows you to cycle through the five different grip modes starting with **Stretch** mode by pressing the space bar or the **<Enter ↵>** key as follows:

```
** STRETCH **
Specify stretch point or [Base point/Copy/Undo/eXit]:
** MOVE **
Specify move point or [Base point/Copy/Undo/eXit]:
** ROTATE **
Specify rotation angle or [Base point/Copy/Undo/Reference/eXit]:
** SCALE **
Specify scale factor or [Base point/Copy/Undo/Reference/eXit]:
** MIRROR **
Specify second point or [Base point/Copy/Undo/eXit]:
```

Each time you press the space bar or **<Enter ↵>**, AutoCAD cycles to the next grip mode in the order shown above, repeating the modes again when it gets back to **Stretch** mode.

TIP   You can also type keyboard shortcuts to go directly to the desired grip mode option at the command line. The shortcuts are **ST** for **Stretch**, **MO** for **Move**, **RO** for **Rotate**, **SC** for **Scale**, and **MI** for **Mirror**.

The other option is to right-click with your mouse to display the **Grip** shortcut menu shown in Figure 7-43.

Figure 7-43   **Grip** shortcut menu

This approach allows you to go directly to the desired grip mode option without having to hit your space bar or the **<Enter ↵>** key multiple times.

> The **Grip** shortcut menu provides a quick way to edit the properties of the selected object using the **Properties** palette by selecting the **Properties** menu item.

Using either approach, the different grip modes work similarly to their traditional modify command counterparts explained earlier in the chapter and share most of the same options. Each grip mode shares the following options:

- **Base Point**   Allows you to specify a new base point to use with current grip mode. By default, the base point is set to the selected grip
- **Copy**   Allows you to create a copy of the selected object(s) to use with the current grip mode
- **Undo**   Undoes the last grip mode operation
- **Exit**   Exits the current grip mode and leaves grips on but unselected

In addition, the **Rotate** and **Scale** modes also have a **Reference** option that works exactly the same as described earlier in the **ROTATE** and **SCALE** modify command sections.

After selecting the desired grip mode either at the command line or via the **Grip** shortcut menu, the different grip mode options can be selected by typing the first letter of the option at the command line, by selecting the option from the right-click shortcut menu, or by using your arrow keys if you are using **Dynamic Input**.

Stretch Mode.   **Stretch** mode stretches the selected grip(s) while leaving unselected grips anchored in their current location. **Stretch** mode is the default mode. Figure 7-44 shows the corner point of a square being stretched using grips.

Remember that you can select multiple grip points by holding down the **<Shift>** key before selecting the first grip. Figure 7-45 shows two corner points being stretched using grips.

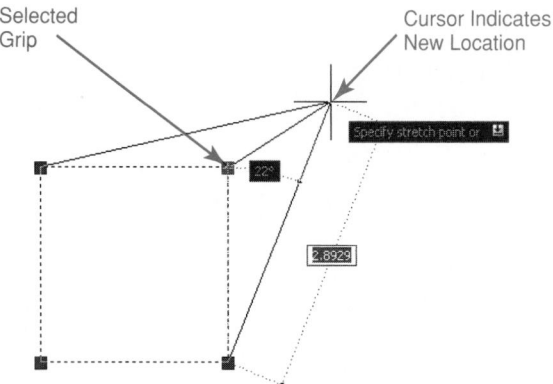

Figure 7-44   Stretching a corner point using grips

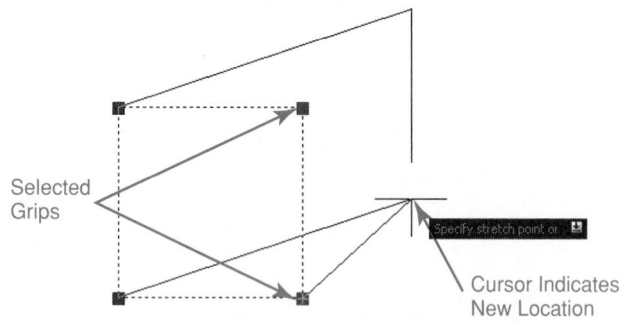

Figure 7-45   Stretching two corner points using grips

> You can rely on any of the coordinate entry methods explained earlier to relocate grip points, including absolute coordinates (*X,Y*), relative coordinates (@*X,Y*), polar coordinates (@Distance<Angle), and even direct distance using the **Ortho Mode** and **Polar Tracking** drawing tools. It is also possible to tab between the different **Dimension Input** fields if **Dynamic Input** is on so that you can enter lengths and/or angles for any input field.

If you stretch a line using grips when **Dynamic Input** is on, the default dimension input field is a "delta," or change, distance as shown in Figure 7-46.

Remember that you can switch between the different dimension input fields using the <**Tab**> key so that you can also enter the overall length dimension and/or the angle.

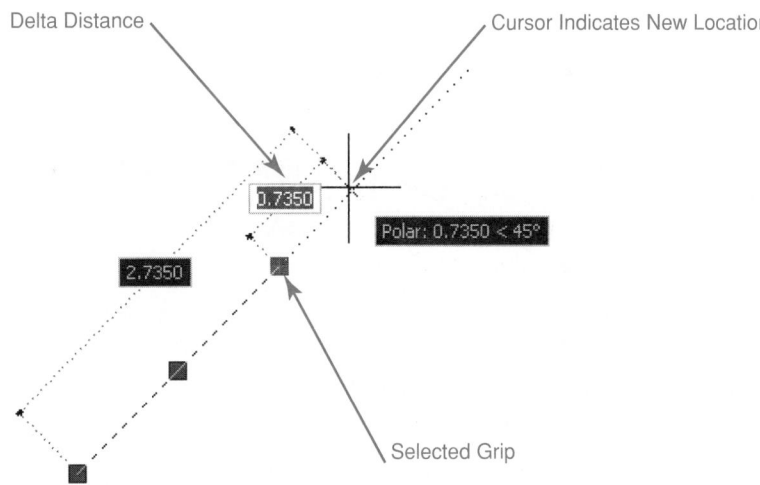

Figure 7-46 Stretching a line segment using the delta dimension input field

TIP You can change the angle and lock it in by tabbing to the angle input field, entering a new angle value, and tabbing back to the overall dimension or the delta distance dimension. Any distance you input will stretch the line using the locked-in angle.

Exercise 7-16: Stretching Objects Using Grips

1. Start a new drawing using the acad.dwt drawing template.
2. Make sure that your **Grip** settings on the **Selection** tab of the **Options** dialog box match those shown in Figure 7-40.
3. Draw a 2″ × 2″ square similar to the one shown in Figure 7-44 using the **LINE** command.
4. Select all four lines either by selecting them with your mouse or by using implied windowing so that grips are displayed.
5. Select the grip at the upper right corner and stretch the objects as shown in Figure 7-44.
6. Press <**Esc**> to turn grips off.
7. Type **U**<**Enter ↵**> or select the **Undo** tool so that the square is returned to its original size.
8. Select all four lines again either by selecting them with your mouse or by using implied windowing so that the grips are displayed.
9. Select both grips on the right side of the square using the <**Shift**> key and stretch the objects as shown in Figure 7-45.
10. Press <**Esc**> to turn grips off.
11. Type **U**<**Enter ↵**> or select the **Undo** tool so that the square is returned to its original size.
12. Save the drawing as **EX7-16**.

Move Mode.   **Move** mode moves the selected objects a user-supplied distance and angle. By default, you can use the selected grip as the base point, or you can select a new base point via the **Base Point** option introduced earlier. Figure 7-47 shows a square being moved using grips.

TIP Picking a grip at a midpoint or a center point automatically puts you in **Move** mode.

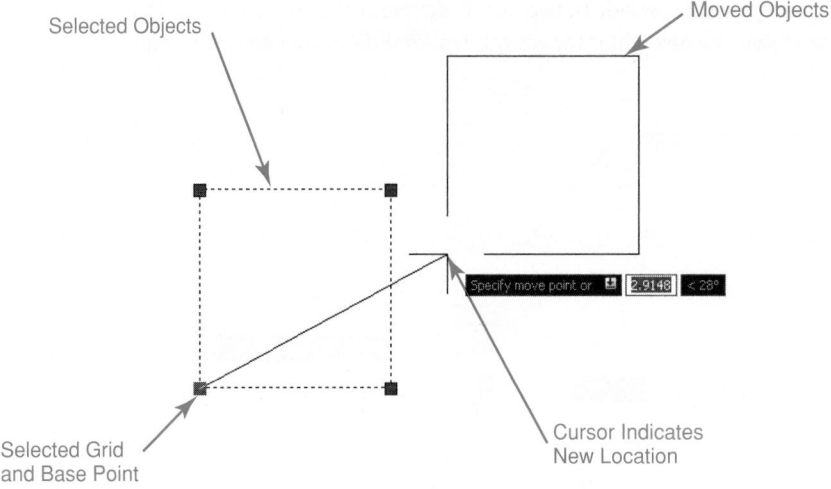

Figure 7-47   Moving objects using grips

You can move and copy the selected objects by using the **Copy** option introduced earlier. You can select the **Copy** option by typing **C<Enter ↵>**, by selecting **Copy** from the right-click shortcut menu, or by using the arrow keys with **Dynamic Input** when AutoCAD prompts you to *Specify move point or ↓*. Figure 7-48 shows a square being copied using grips.

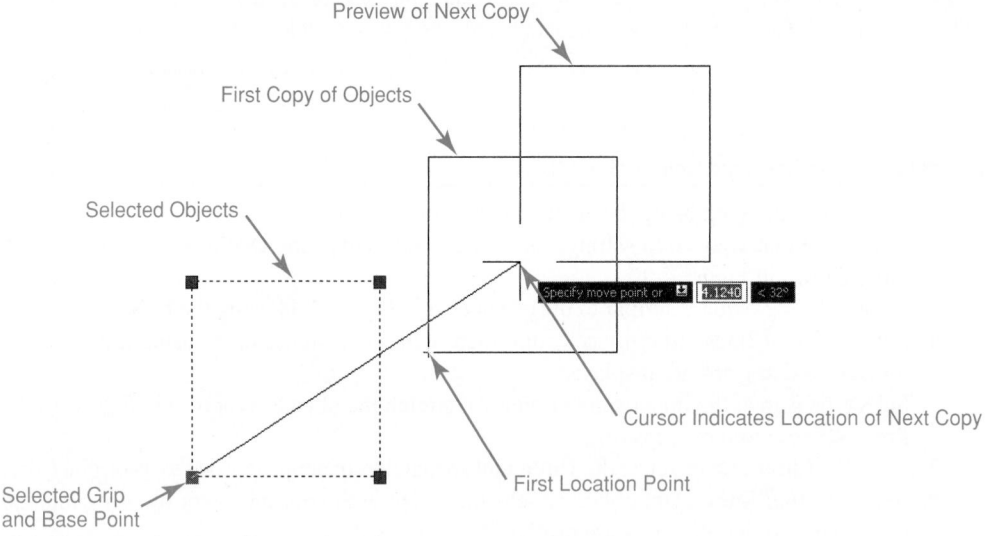

Figure 7-48   Copying objects using grips

Exercise 7-17: Moving Objects Using Grips

1. Continue from Exercise 7-16.
2. Select all four lines either by using your mouse or by using implied windowing so that the grips are displayed.
3. Select the grip at the lower left corner as shown in Figure 7-47.
4. Select the **Move** grip mode by right-clicking and selecting **Move** from the **Grip** shortcut menu or by pressing the space bar once.
5. Move the objects as shown in Figure 7-47.
6. Press **<Esc>** to turn grips off.
7. Type **U<Enter ↵>** or select the **Undo** tool so that the square is returned to its original location.
8. Select all four lines again either by selecting them with your mouse or by using implied windowing so that the grips are displayed.

9. Select the grip at the lower left corner as shown in Figure 7-48.
10. Select the **Move** grip mode by right-clicking and selecting **Move** from the **Grip** shortcut menu or by pressing the spacebar once.
11. Select the **Copy** option by right-clicking and selecting **Copy** from the **Grip** shortcut menu or by typing **C<Enter ↵>**.
12. Move and copy the objects multiple times as shown in Figure 7-48.
13. Press **<Esc>** to turn grips off.
14. Type **U<Enter ↵>** or select the **Undo** tool so that all copies of the square are undone.
15. Save the drawing as **EX7-17**.

Rotate Mode.   The **Rotate** mode rotates the selected objects a user-specified rotation angle around a user-specified base point. By default, you can use the selected grip as the base point, or you can select a new base point via the **Base Point** option introduced earlier. Figure 7-49 shows a square being rotated using grips.

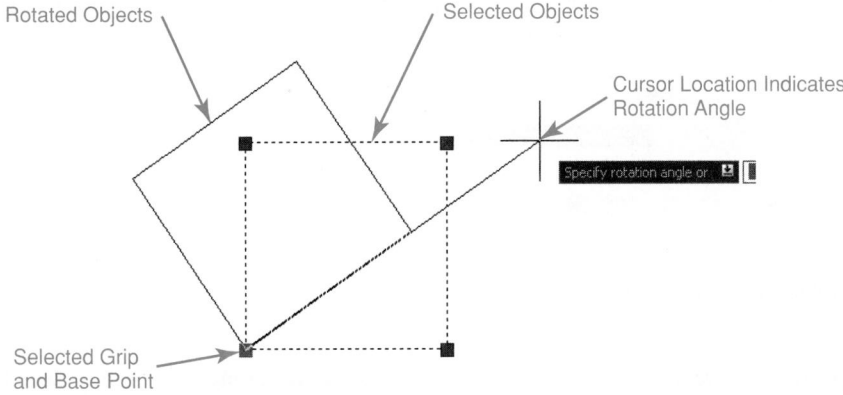

Figure 7-49   Rotating objects using grips

You can specify a reference, or start angle, by selecting the **Reference** option introduced earlier. The **Reference** option allows you to rotate object(s) by specifying a reference, or start angle, and then specifying a new, absolute angle to rotate to. You can select the **Reference** option by typing **R<Enter ↵>**, by selecting **Reference** from the right-click shortcut menu, or by using the arrow keys with **Dynamic Input** when AutoCAD prompts you to *Specify rotation angle or ↓*.

You can rotate and copy the selected objects using the **Copy** option introduced earlier. You can select the **Copy** option by typing **C<Enter ↵>**, by selecting **Copy** from the right-click shortcut menu, or by using the arrow keys with **Dynamic Input** when AutoCAD prompts you to *Specify rotation angle or ↓*.

TIP   You can rotate and copy multiple objects by entering successive angle measurements or by picking points with your mouse. Note that each angle is measured from the 0° base angle so that angle measurements must be cumulative. For example, to rotate and copy at 45° increments, you need to enter 45°, 90°, 135°, and so on.

Exercise 7-18: Rotating Objects Using Grips

1. Continue from Exercise 7-17.
2. Select all four lines either by selecting them with your mouse or by using implied windowing so that the grips are displayed.
3. Select the grip at the lower left corner as shown in Figure 7-49.

4. Select the **Rotate** grip mode by right-clicking and selecting **Rotate** from the **Grip** shortcut menu or by pressing the spacebar twice.
5. Rotate the objects as shown in Figure 7-49.
6. Press **<Esc>** to turn grips off.
7. Type **U<Enter ↵>** or select the **Undo** tool so that the square is rotated back to 0°.
8. Save the drawing as **EX7-18**.

Scale Mode.   The **Scale** mode scales the selected objects a user-specified scale factor using a user-specified base point. By default, you can use the selected grip as the base point, or you can select a new base point via the **Base Point** option introduced earlier. Figure 7-50 shows a square being scaled using grips.

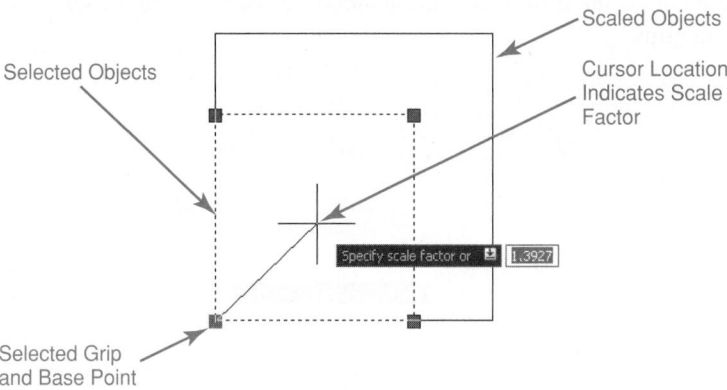

Figure 7-50   Scaling objects using grips

You can specify a reference, or start length, by selecting the **Reference** option introduced earlier. The **Reference** option allows you to scale object(s) by specifying a reference, or start length, and then specifying a new, absolute length to scale to. You can select the **Reference** option by typing **R<Enter ↵>**, by selecting **Reference** from the right-click shortcut menu, or by using the arrow keys with **Dynamic Input** when AutoCAD prompts you to *Specify scale factor or ↓*.

Exercise 7-19: Scaling Objects Using Grips

1. Continue from Exercise 7-18.
2. Select all four lines either by selecting them with your mouse or by using implied windowing so that the grips are displayed.
3. Select the grip at the lower left corner as shown in Figure 7-50.
4. Select the **Scale** grip mode by right-clicking and selecting **Scale** from the **Grip** shortcut menu or by pressing the space bar three times.
5. Scale the objects as shown in Figure 7-50.
6. Press **<Esc>** to turn grips off.
7. Type **U<Enter ↵>** or select the **Undo** tool so that the square is returned to its original size.
8. Save the drawing as **EX7-19**.

Mirror Mode.   The **Mirror** mode creates a mirror image of the selected objects about a mirror axis line defined by two user-supplied line endpoints. By default, you can use the selected grip as the first point of the mirror axis line, or you can select a different axis line location via the **Base Point** option introduced earlier. Figure 7-51 shows a triangle being mirrored vertically by picking a point 90° above the base point in response to the *Specify second point or ↓* prompt.

TIP   Remember that you can use the **Ortho Mode** or the **Polar Tracking** drawing tool to create horizontal and vertical mirror axis lines quickly.

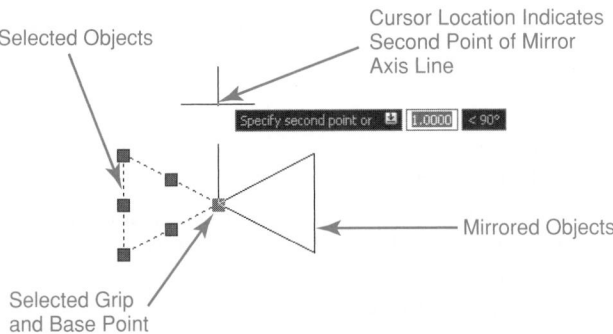

Figure 7-51   Mirroring objects using grips

Unlike the **MIRROR** command explained earlier, when you use grips to mirror objects, the original objects are erased by default. To maintain the original objects, you must use the **Copy** option introduced earlier. You can select the **Copy** option by typing **C<Enter ↵>**, by selecting **Copy** from the right-click shortcut menu, or by using the arrow keys with **Dynamic Input** when AutoCAD prompts you to *Specify second point or ↓*.

Exercise 7-20: Mirroring Objects Using Grips

1. Start a new drawing using the acad.dwt drawing template.
2. Draw a triangle similar to the one shown in Figure 7-51.
3. Select all three lines either by selecting them with your mouse or by using implied windowing so that the grips are displayed.
4. Select the grip at the vertex of the triangle on the right as shown in Figure 7-51.
5. Select the **Mirror** grip mode by right-clicking and selecting **Mirror** from the **Grip** shortcut menu or by pressing the spacebar four times.
6. Turn on the **Ortho Mode** drawing tool if it is not already on.
7. Mirror the objects by picking a point 90° above the selected grip as shown in Figure 7-51.
8. Press **<Esc>** to turn grips off.
9. Type **U<Enter ↵>** or select the **Undo** tool so that the triangle is mirrored back to its original location and orientation.
10. Select all three lines again either by selecting them with your mouse or by using implied windowing so that the grips are displayed.
11. Select the grip at the vertex of the triangle on the right as shown in Figure 7-51.
12. Select the **Mirror** grip mode by right-clicking and selecting **Mirror** from the **Grip** shortcut menu or by pressing the space bar once.
13. Select the **Copy** option by right-clicking and selecting **Copy** from the **Grip** shortcut menu or by typing **C<Enter ↵>**.
14. Mirror and copy the objects by picking a point 90° above the selected grip as shown in Figure 7-51.
15. Press **<Esc>** to turn grips off.
16. Save the drawing as **EX7-20**.

CHAPTER SUMMARY

This chapter presents the basics of selecting and modifying objects in an AutoCAD drawing. The different object selection techniques explored in this chapter can be applied throughout the rest of the textbook. As you can see, there are many different ways to go about creating and modifying a selection set. Practice using, and even combining, the different selection and editing techniques and try to think "outside of the box." Sometimes you may want to pick objects first and then select a modify command; other times it makes sense to pick the command first and *then* the object(s) to modify. Find which approach to editing your drawings you are most comfortable with, but don't be afraid to experiment!

CHAPTER TEST QUESTIONS

Multiple Choice

1. Selecting objects first and then selecting a modify command is referred to as what type of editing process?

   a. Noun/verb
   b. Verb/noun
   c. Grip mode
   d. Cut and paste

2. A selection set is:

   a. Set of commands used to select objects
   b. All currently selected objects
   c. Group of similar objects
   d. None of the above

3. The box that appears at the mouse crosshairs when you are prompted to select objects is called:

   a. Grip
   b. Aperture
   c. Pickbox
   d. Window area

4. When you are creating a selection set, you can remove objects by:

   a. Typing **U<Enter ↵>**
   b. Holding down the **<Shift>** key while selecting objects
   c. Entering **Remove Objects** mode by typing **R<Enter ↵>**
   d. All of the above

5. The special keyboard key that allows you to select objects that are overlaid on top of each other when creating a selection set is:

   a. **<Shift>**
   b. **<Esc>**
   c. **<Alt>**
   d. **<Ctrl>**

6. The difference between the **Window** selection method and the **Crossing** selection method is:

   a. A **Window** boundary is a solid line, and a **Crossing** boundary is a dashed line
   b. The **Window** method selects only objects inside the boundary, and the **Crossing** method selects objects inside *and* objects that cross the boundary
   c. By default, the **Window** area preview is blue, and the **Crossing** area preview is green
   d. All of the above

7. Implied windowing allows you to:

   a. Automatically create a **Window** or **Crossing** selection
   b. Turn off **Window** and **Crossing** selection options
   c. Pick one corner point to define a window and drag your mouse and release to create the other corner point
   d. Select objects with your mind

8. The selection set option that allows you to select the last object created in a drawing is:

   a. **Previous**
   b. **All**

   c. **Last**
   d. All of the above

9. The proper format for entering a displacement distance for the **MOVE, COPY**, and **STRETCH** commands is:

   a. Absolute coordinates (ex. 2,2)
   b. Relative coordinates (ex. @2,2)
   c. Polar coordinates (ex. @2<45)
   d. All of the above

10. The system variable that controls whether text is reversed when it is mirrored is:

    a. **MIRRORTEXT**
    b. **MIRRTEXT**
    c. **TEXTMIRROR**
    d. **MTEXT**

11. The **ROTATE** command option that allows to you specify a start angle and then an absolute, new angle to rotate to is:

    a. **Base Point**
    b. **Reference**
    c. **Copy**
    d. **Displacement**

12. The system variable that allows you to select objects first and *then* a modify command is:

    a. **FIRSTPICK**
    b. **PICKFIRST**
    c. **SELFIRST**
    d. **PICKAUTO**

13. To select multiple grips, you must hold down what key when picking the first grip?

    a. **<Ctrl>**
    b. **<Shift>**
    c. **<Esc>**
    d. Space bar

14. Grip modes can be selected via:

    a. Command line
    b. Right-click shortcut menu
    c. Keyboard shortcuts
    d. All of the above

15. The keyboard key that turns off (deselects) grips is:

    a. **<Ctrl>**
    b. **<Enter ↵>**
    c. **<Esc>**
    d. **<Alt>**

Matching

a. **ERASE** command

b. Selection set

c. Implied window

d. Grips

e. **MOVE** command

f. **COPY** command

g. **MIRROR** command

h. **ROTATE** command

i. **SCALE** command

j. **STRETCH** command

1. Automated **Window** and **Crossing** selection option

2. Moves objects a user-supplied distance and angle

3. Creates a mirror image of objects about a mirror axis line

4. Small squares that appear when an object is selected

5. Removes objects from a drawing

6. Rotates objects a user-specified rotation angle around a user-specified base point

7. Moves or stretches objects a user-supplied distance and angle

8. Scales objects a user-specified scale factor about a user-specified base point

9. Copies objects a user-supplied distance and angle

10. Group of one or more objects selected in a drawing

CHAPTER PROJECTS

Project 7-1: Classroom Plan—Continued from Chapter 6

1. Open drawing **P6-1** from Chapter 6.
2. Draw the floor plan shown in Figure P7-1 using the **A-Door** and **A-Wall** layers for the doors and walls. Place the heater on the **A-Eqpm** layer. The wall next to the heater is 8″ thick; all other walls are 4″ thick. The doors are each 3′-0″ wide and the heater is 1′-0″ wide. **Do not** draw dimensions or text.
3. Use the **MOVE, COPY**, and **MIRROR** commands to place the desks in the configuration shown. Use Object Snaps and the **Polar Tracking** and/or **Ortho Mode** settings to ensure the desks are aligned.
4. Save the drawing as **P7-1**.

Figure P7-1

Project 7-2: C-Size Mechanical Border

1. Start a new drawing using the acad.dwt template.
2. Set the **LIMITS** for a 22.0 × 17.0 drawing area.
3. Create the following layers:

Name	Color	Linetype	Lineweight	Plot/Noplot	Description
Title	7	Continuous	Default	Plot	Title border and text
Logo	7	Continuous	Default	Plot	Logo
Notes	7	Continuous	Default	Plot	Notes
Viewport	9	Continuous	Default	Noplot	Viewports

4. Draw the C-size title block as shown in Figure P7-2. Use the **Title** layer for all geometry. Use appropriate **Grid, Snap** and, **Object Snap** settings. **Do not** draw dimensions.
5. Save the drawing to a template file as **Mechanical C-Size.DWT**.

Figure P7-2

Project 7-3: Architectural B-Size Border (17 × 11)

1. Start a new drawing using the acad.dwt template.
2. Set linear **UNITS** to **Architectural** with precision set to **1/16″**.
3. Set angular **UNITS** to **Deg/Min/Sec** with precision set to **0d00′00″**.

4. Set the drawing **LIMITS** to 17″ × 11″ for a B-size drawing.
5. Create the following layers:

Name	Color	Linetype	Lineweight	Plot/Noplot	Description
A-Anno-Ttlb	7	Continuous	Default	Plot	Title block/ border lines
A-Anno-Ttlb-Text	1	Continuous	Default	Plot	Title block text
A-Anno-Ttlb-Logo	3	Continuous	Default	Plot	Logo
A-Anno-Vprt	7	Continuous	Default	Noplot	Viewport lines

6. Draw the border as shown in Figure P7-3 on layer **A-Anno-Ttlb**. Do **not** include dimensions.
7. Zoom to the drawing extents.
8. Save the drawing to a template file as **Architectural B-Size.DWT**.

Figure P7-3

Project 7-4: Electrical Distribution Panel

1. Start a new drawing using the acad.dwt template.
2. Create the following layer:

Name	Color	Linetype	Lineweight	Plot/Noplot	Description
E-Powr-Panl	7	Continuous	Default	Plot	Electrical power panels

3. Set the **GRID** to **.5** and the **SNAP** to **.25** and draw the electrical distribution panel shown in Figure P7-4. Do **not** draw text or dimensions. *Hint:* The grid lines shown are spaced at .5 intervals.
4. Save the drawing as **P7-4**.

Figure P7-4

Project 7-5: Residential Architectural Plan—Continued from Chapter 6

1. Open drawing **P6-5** from Chapter 6.
2. Draw the door and window symbols shown in Figure P7-5A using the **A-Door** and **A-Glaz** layers.

SYM.	SIZE	TYPE	QTY.
A	3'-0" X 3'-6"	S.H.	10
B	2'-0" X 3'-6"	S.H./FROSTED	1
C	2'-0" X 3'-0"	S.H.	4
D	3'-0" X 3'-0"	PCT.	2
E	5'-0" X 5"-0"	TEMP. PCT.	3
F	1'-0" X 3'-0"	S.H.	2
G	2'-0" X 6'-0"	GLASS SKY.	2

WINDOW SCHEDULE

SYM.	SIZE	TYPE	QTY.
1	3'-0" X 6'-8"	M.I./R.P.	1
2	2'-8" X 6'-8"	M.I./S.C.	2
3	2'-8" X 6'-8"	H.C.	8
4	2'-6" X 6'-8"	POCKET/H.C.	2
5	2'-6" X 6'-8"	H.C./BI-FOLD	2
6	6'-0" X 6'-8"	TEMP. SLIDER	2
7	8'-0" X 6'-8"	GARAGE	2

DOOR SCHEDULE

Figure P7-5A

3. Add the walls and place the doors and windows as shown in Figure P7-5B according to the schedules. Use appropriate Object Snaps to ensure the proper placement of the symbols. Doors and windows that are not dimensioned are either centered on the interior wall or located 3″ from the nearest wall. *Hint:* Use the **Offset** option of the **XLINE** command to locate the door and window symbols.
4. Do **not** draw the door schedule or identifier symbols. Do **not** draw dimensions or text.
5. Save the drawing as **P7-5**.

Figure P7-5B

Project 7-6: Socket Head Cap Screws—English Units

1. Start a new drawing using the acad.dwt template.
2. Create the two socket head cap screws described in the table shown in Figure P7-6. **Do not** draw dimensions or table.
3. Save the drawing as **P7-6**.

Socket Head Cap Screw					
Nominal Size (D)	Thread/In	A	B	C	L
10 (.190)	24	.312	5/32	.171	.500
¼ (.250)	20	.375	3/16	.225	.750

Figure P7-6

Project 7-7: Motorcycle Head Gasket—Metric

1. Start a new drawing using the acadiso.dwt template.
2. Create the following layers:

Name	Color	Linetype	Lineweight	Description
Object	7	Continuous	0.35 mm	Object lines
Hidden	1	Hidden	Default	Hidden lines
Center	2	Center	Default	Centerlines
Hatch	4	Continuous	Default	Hatch patterns and fills
Notes	3	Continuous	Default	Text and notes
Dims	2	Continuous	Default	Dimensions

3. Draw object lines as shown in Figure P7-7 on layer **Object**.
4. Draw hidden lines as shown in Figure P7-7 on layer **Hidden**.
5. Draw centerlines as shown in Figure P7-7 on layer **Center**.
6. Adjust the **LTSCALE** system so linetypes appear properly.
7. Do **not** include dimensions.
8. Save the drawing as **P7-7**.

Figure P7-7

Project 7-8: Civil Site Plan—Continued from Chapter 6

1. Open drawing **P6-8** from Chapter 6.
2. Move the house forward 5′. Add the swimming pool and shed shown in Figure P7-8.
3. Use the **MOVE** and **COPY** commands to place the landscaping as shown.
4. Save the drawing as **P7-8**.

Figure P7-8

Advanced Editing Techniques

8

Chapter Objectives

- Offset objects through a specified distance
- Create rectangular and polar arrays
- Trim and extend objects
- Use the **FILLET** and **CHAMFER** commands to modify intersecting objects
- Break single objects into multiple objects
- Join separate objects into a single object
- Use the **LENGTHEN** command to modify the length of an object

INTRODUCTION

As you've seen, there is usually more than one way to accomplish a given task in AutoCAD. For example, to create multiple line segments, you could simply draw multiple lines using the **LINE** command, or you could create a single line segment and copy it using grips or the **COPY** command. There are multiple ways to create arcs and circles as well as different methods for creating layers and changing object properties.

offset: To create a parallel copy of an object

In Chapter 7, you used basic editing commands such as **MOVE**, **COPY**, and **ROTATE** to modify objects. In this chapter, you'll examine some editing tools that provide additional functionality.

Offset	
Ribbon & Panel:	Home| Modify
Modify Toolbar:	
Menu:	Modify| Offset
Command Line:	OFFSET
Command Alias:	O

OFFSETTING OBJECTS

To *offset* an object is to make a copy of an object parallel to the original. This is similar to the **COPY** command but allows you to make parallel copies at a specified distance from the original. This can be used to make concentric arcs and circles as well as parallel lines (such as roads, walls, etc.). Offsetting is done with the **OFFSET** command.

The **OFFSET** command works by copying an object a specified distance away from the original or source object. When using the **OFFSET** command, you specify a distance, select an object to offset, and tell AutoCAD on which side of the original object you want to place the new object. To provide the offset distance, you can either specify the distance or pick a point that the new object will pass through. The **OFFSET** command has three options: **Through**, **Erase**, and **Layer**.

Through	Allows you to pick a point that the new object will pass through. AutoCAD measures the distance from the point to the source object.
Erase	Controls whether the source object is kept or deleted after the offset is complete. You can answer **Yes** (erase the source object) or **No** (keep the source object).
Layer	Allows you to control the layer of the new object. You can choose to have the new object take on the current layer setting or retain the layer setting of the source object.

Offsetting an Object a Specified Distance

Specifying a distance is the default method and the most commonly used. When specifying a distance, you can simply type in the distance or pick two points. If you pick two points, AutoCAD will measure the distance between the two points and use that as the offset distance.

> Whenever AutoCAD asks you to provide a numeric value such as a length or distance, you can usually pick two points and have AutoCAD measure the distance.

Offsetting Through a Point

It is also possible to offset objects through a point that you pick in the drawing using the **Through** option. Typically, this is done in conjunction with Object Snaps so that you can snap to specific key features in your drawing. The easiest way to specify the **Through** options is to press **<Enter ↵>** when AutoCAD prompts you to *Select object to offset or* ↓.

Offset Options

By default, the **OFFSET** command will copy the selected object on the same layer as the original, or source, object. The **Layer** option allows you to offset an object on the current layer. The **Erase** option allows you to erase the original object. The current settings are displayed in the command window each time you select the **OFFSET** command.

> The **OFFSET** command continues to prompt you to *Select object to offset or* ↓ until you press **<Enter ↵>** so that is possible to offset multiple objects without exiting the command. Even better, after you select an object to offset, the **Multiple** option is available so that you can make multiple copies the same distance apart by continuing to click with your mouse.

Exercise 8-1: Offsetting Objects

1. Start a new drawing using the acad.dwt drawing template.
2. Create two layers with the following settings:
   C-ROAD, Continuous, Color 7 (White)
   C-ROAD-CNTR, Center, Color 5 (Blue)
   Set layer **C-ROAD-CNTR** as the current layer.
3. Set the **LTSCALE** system variable to **12**.
4. Draw a line from the coordinates **100,100** to **100,250**. Zoom out until the line is somewhat centered in the screen.
5. Set the **C-ROAD** layer current and draw a circle centered at **100,250** with a radius of **35**.
6. Start the **OFFSET** command. AutoCAD prompts you to *Specify offset distance or* ↓.

7. Press **<Enter ↵>** to select the **Through** option. AutoCAD prompts you to *Select object to offset or ↓*.

8. Select the centerline. AutoCAD prompts you to *Specify point on side to offset or ↓*.

9. Type **QUA<Enter ↵>** to activate the **Quadrant** Object Snap.

10. Move your cursor to the right side quadrant point on the circle and pick a point when the **Quadrant** Object Snap AutoSnap Marker is displayed. The centerline is offset through the circle quadrant point on the same layer and linetype as the original centerline.

11. Type **U<Enter ↵>** to undo the offset line and press **<Enter ↵>** to exit the **OFFSET** command.

12. Press **<Enter ↵>** to run the **OFFSET** command again. AutoCAD prompts you to *Select object to offset or ↓*.

13. Choose the **Layer** option and choose **Current**. The new objects will be placed on the current drawing layer. AutoCAD again prompts you to *Specify offset distance or ↓*.

14. Type **25<Enter ↵>** to set the offset distance. AutoCAD prompts you to *Select object to offset or ↓*.

15. Select the centerline. AutoCAD prompts you to *Specify point on side to offset or ↓*. Pick anywhere off to the left of the centerline. AutoCAD will create a new line 25 units to the left of the centerline. AutoCAD again prompts you to *Select object to offset or ↓*.

16. Select the centerline again and pick anywhere off to the right of the line. AutoCAD places a new line 25 units to the right of the original. Both of the new lines are on the current layer (**C-ROAD**).

17. Press **<Enter ↵>** or **<Esc>** to exit the **OFFSET** command.

18. Save your drawing as **EX8-1**. Your drawing should resemble Figure 8-1.

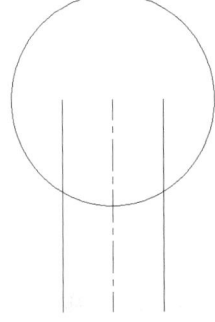

Figure 8-1   Offsetting objects

ARRAYING OBJECTS

An **array** of objects is multiple objects copied in a regular pattern. In AutoCAD there are two types of arrays: rectangular and polar. A rectangular array is a pattern of rows and columns at predefined distances. A polar array is a circular pattern of objects copied around a center point. Arrays are created with the **ARRAY** command. The **ARRAY** command displays the **Array** dialog box (see Figure 8-2).

array: A circular or rectangular pattern of objects

Array	
Ribbon & Panel:	Home| Modify
Modify Toolbar:	
Menu:	Modify| Array…
Command Line:	ARRAY
Command Alias:	AR

Array dialog box

◉ Rectangular Array   ○ Polar Array   Select objects

1 objects selected

⊞ Rows: [4]   ▥ Columns: [4]

Offset distance and direction

Row offset: [1.0000]

Column offset: [1.0000]

Angle of array: [0]

💡 Tip   By default, if the row offset is negative, rows are added downward. If the column offset is negative, columns are added to the left.

[OK]
[Cancel]
[Preview <]
[Help]

Figure 8-2   The **Array** dialog box

The **Array** dialog box is divided into two sections. The left side allows you to choose either a rectangular or polar array and allows you to control the settings for each type of array. The right-hand side allows you to select objects and displays a preview of what the array will look like.

Creating a Rectangular Array

To create a rectangular array, choose the **Rectangular Array** button at the top of the **Array** dialog box (see Figure 8-2). A rectangular array consists of rows and columns, a distance between the rows and columns, and a rotation angle. The **Rows** and **Columns** controls allow you to specify the number of rows and columns. As you change the number of rows and columns, the preview image will update.

Selecting Objects to Array.   The **Select objects** button will temporarily hide the **Array** dialog box and allow you to select the objects you wish to array. You can select objects using any of the normal object selection methods.

FOR MORE DETAILS	See Chapter 7 for more on building selection sets.

Specifying Distance Between Rows and Columns.   The **Row offset** controls the distance between the rows (the vertical pitch of the objects). A positive offset distance will create rows in the positive *Y* direction (up). A negative offset distance creates rows in the negative *Y* direction (down). The **Column offset** controls the distance between the columns (the horizontal pitch of the objects). A positive offset distance creates columns to the right (positive *X* direction). A negative value creates columns to the left (negative *X* direction). (See Figure 8-3.)

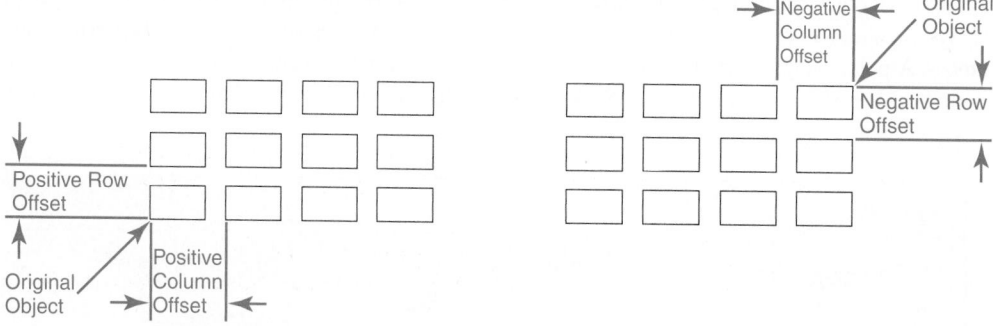

Figure 8-3   Row and **Column offsets**

You can specify the **Row** and **Column offsets** independently either by typing the values into the boxes or by choosing the cursor buttons. There is also a combination button that allows you to pick both the **Row** and **Column offsets** by specifying two opposite corners of a rectangle. The length (*X*) of the rectangle is the **Column offset** and the width (*Y*) is the **Row offset** (see Figure 8-4).

Arraying at an Angle.   You can control the overall angle of the rectangular array (see Figure 8-5) by changing the **Angle of array**. This setting determines the rotation angle of the first row of the

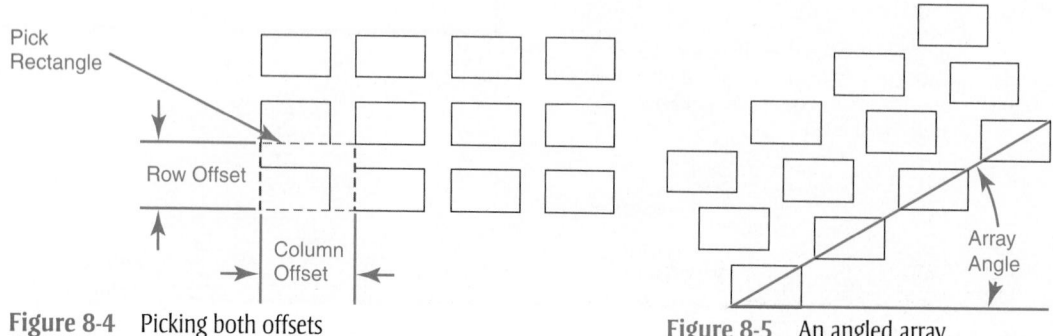

Figure 8-4   Picking both offsets

Figure 8-5   An angled array

array. You can either specify an angle or choose the cursor button to pick points in your drawing. When you choose the cursor button, you are asked to specify two points. AutoCAD will measure the angle of the line between these two points and use it for the angular measurement. By default, the angle is measured from 0 degrees (Figure 8-5).

TIP As with distance measurements, whenever AutoCAD requires you to provide an angular measurement, you can typically either type in the angular value or pick points to have AutoCAD measure the angle for you.

Previewing the Array.   As you change each of these values, the preview image will update to show you a representation of what the final array will look like. The preview image uses boxes to represent your actual objects. To see what your final array will look like, choose the **Preview** button. AutoCAD will temporarily hide the **Array** dialog box and show you a preview of what the actual array will look like using the objects you selected. The **Preview** button will be available only after you've selected objects. Press **<Esc>** or pick anywhere on the screen to end the preview and return to the dialog box.

Exercise 8-2: Creating a Rectangular Array

1. Start a new drawing using the acad.dwt drawing template.
2. Use the **LINE** command to draw the geometry shown in Figure 8-6.
3. Start the **ARRAY** command. AutoCAD displays the **Array** dialog box.
4. Select **Rectangular Array** and then choose the **Select objects** button. AutoCAD hides the dialog box and prompts you to *Select objects:*. Select the circle and press **<Enter ↵>** to return to the **Array** dialog box.
5. Set the **Rows** to **3** and **Columns** to **3**. Set the **Row offset** to **5.25** and the **Column offset** to **3.25**.
6. Choose the **Preview** button. AutoCAD will show you a preview of the array.
7. Right-click anywhere to accept the array and end the command.
8. Use the **ERASE** command to delete the hole in the center of the part.
9. Save your drawing as **EX8-2**. Your drawing should look like Figure 8-7.

Figure 8-6   A rectangle and circle

Figure 8-7   A rectangular array

Creating a Polar Array

To create a polar array, choose the **Polar Array** button at the top of the **Array** dialog box (see Figure 8-8). When creating a polar array, AutoCAD will copy objects in a circular pattern. You must specify the center point of that circle, as well as the number of items you want to create and the angle between the objects.

Specifying Center Point of Polar Array.   To specify the **Center point**, you can either type the *X* and *Y* values into the boxes or pick the cursor button to temporarily hide the dialog box and select the center point in the drawing.

Figure 8-8   The **Polar Array** settings

Choosing a Polar Array Method.   AutoCAD can determine the total number of objects using one of three methods. AutoCAD is looking for three values: the total number of items to create, the total angle to fill with the polar array, and the angle between each item in the array (see Figure 8-9). You can specify any two of those values, and AutoCAD will calculate the third. The **Method** drop-down list allows you to choose which two values you are going to provide.

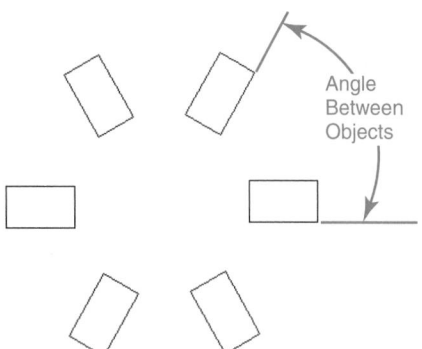

Figure 8-9   Polar Array methods

Total Number of Items and Angle to Fill.   Using this method, AutoCAD will take the **Angle to fill** value, divide it by the **Total number of items**, and calculate the angle between each of the items. When you select this method, the **Total number of items** box and the **Angle to fill** box are enabled, and the **Angle between items** box is disabled. To specify the **Angle to fill**, you can either type in a value or choose the cursor button to temporarily hide the dialog box and pick the angle from the drawing.

Total Number of Items and Angle Between Items.   Using this method, AutoCAD will take the **Total number of items** and multiply it by the **Angle between items** to calculate the **Angle to fill**. When you select this method, the **Angle to fill** box is disabled. As before, you can either type in an angle or choose the cursor button to specify an angle within the drawing.

Angle to Fill and Angle Between Items.   Using this method, you provide both the angle to fill and the angle between items, and AutoCAD will calculate the total number of items to create. When you choose this method, the **Total number of items** box is disabled.

TIP When specifying either the **Angle to fill** or the **Angle between items**, a positive value will copy items in a counterclockwise direction, and a negative value will copy items in a clockwise direction.

Rotating Objects as They Are Arrayed.   At the bottom of the **Polar Array** settings is a check box that allows you to control whether individual objects are rotated as they are arrayed. Removing the check from this box will keep objects at their original angle, and placing a check in this box will rotate each item around its base point as it is arrayed around the circle.

Note:
If you are unsure of the effect of any of these settings, the best approach is to simply modify the settings and keep an eye on the preview image.

Selecting the **More** button will display additional options for controlling how various objects are rotated as they are arrayed. By default, objects are rotated based on the type of object they are. Linear objects (lines, polylines, rays, etc.) are rotated about their start point. Circles, arcs, and ellipses are rotated about their center points. Blocks and text are rotated about their insertion point, and construction lines are rotated about their midpoint. You can override these defaults by removing the check from the **Set to objects default** box, and specifying a rotation base point.

Exercise 8-3: Creating a Polar Array

1. Start a new drawing using the acad.dwt drawing template.
2. Use the **LINE** command to draw the geometry shown in Figure 8-10.
3. Start the **ARRAY** command. AutoCAD displays the **Array** dialog box.
4. Select **Polar Array** and then choose the **Select objects** button. AutoCAD hides the dialog box and prompts you to *Select objects:*. Select the two angled lines and press **<Enter ↵>** to return to the **Array** dialog box.
5. Choose the **Center point** button and select the bottom endpoint of the middle line for the center of the array.
6. In the **Method** drop-down list, choose **Total number of items and Angle to fill**. Set the **Total number of items** to **16** and the **Angle to fill** to **360**.
7. Choose the **Preview** button. AutoCAD will show you a preview of the array. Right-click anywhere to accept the array and end the command.
8. Save your drawing as **EX8-3**. Your drawing should look like Figure 8-11.

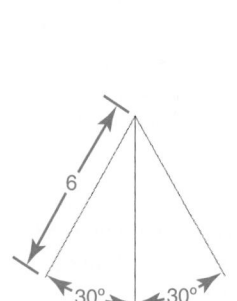

Figure 8-10   The starting geometry

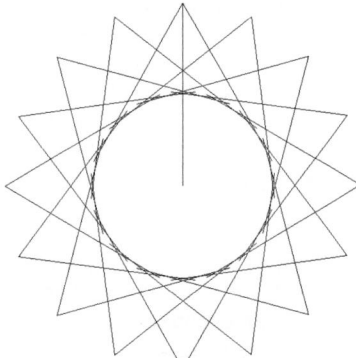

Figure 8-11   A polar array

TRIMMING AND EXTENDING OBJECTS

Trimming and extending is the process of lengthening or shortening objects using AutoCAD objects as the boundaries. When you trim or extend, you use existing AutoCAD objects as the boundary edges, and AutoCAD either lengthens or shortens your objects to touch those edges.

Trim	
Ribbon & Panel:	Home| Modify
Modify Toolbar:	
Menu:	<u>M</u>odify| <u>T</u>rim
Command Line:	TRIM
Command Alias:	TR

Trimming Objects

Objects are trimmed using the **TRIM** command. When you start the **TRIM** command, AutoCAD prompts you to select your cutting edges. These cutting edges determine the stopping boundaries of the trimmed objects. Select the cutting edges using AutoCAD's standard selection methods. Once you've selected the cutting edges, press **<Enter ↵>**, and AutoCAD will prompt you to select the object to trim. As you pick each object, AutoCAD will trim the object back to the cutting edge. The portion of the object you select is the part that is deleted. In order for an object to be trimmed, it must cross one of the cutting edges. If AutoCAD cannot detect an intersection between the cutting edges and the object to be trimmed, it displays a message: *Object does not intersect an edge.*

Selecting Cutting Edges.   In some cases, the cutting edges and the objects to be trimmed may be the same objects. AutoCAD does not distinguish between the cutting edges and the objects to be trimmed. You can select a cutting edge as an object to be trimmed.

> **TIP** Sometimes determining the cutting edges can be a difficult task. If there's ever any doubt if an object should be chosen as a cutting edge, your best bet is to go ahead and select it. If you select an extra cutting edge, you may end up "nibbling away" at the object, but that is better than having to start over and reselect cutting edges.

AutoCAD will allow you to select all the drawing objects as cutting edges. To do this, simply press **<Enter ↵>** when prompted to select the cutting edges. When you do this, AutoCAD will use all the objects in the drawing as cutting edges and simply trim an object to the closest intersecting edge.

Trim Options.   After you select the cutting edges, the **TRIM** command has a number of options. They are listed in the following table.

Fence	This option allows you to select multiple objects to trim by drawing a fence line. Anything that touches the fence line will be trimmed back to the nearest cutting edge.
Crossing	Like the **Fence** option, this allows you to select multiple objects to trim by drawing a crossing box. Anything that touches the edge of the crossing box is trimmed to its nearest cutting edge.
Project	This option is for objects located in different three-dimensional planes. It allows you to trim objects that appear to intersect even though they are in different 3D planes.
Edge	The **Edge** option allows you to trim objects based on an implied intersection with a cutting edge. When this option is selected, you can set the edge mode to **Extend** or **No extend**. In **No extend** mode, an object must actually intersect with a cutting edge in order to be trimmed. With **Extend** mode, an object will be trimmed as if the cutting edge extended out to infinity (see Figure 8-12). **No extend** mode is the default setting.
Erase	The **Erase** option allows you to erase objects instead of trimming them. You may find that once you start trimming an object, you simply want to trim it all away. The **Erase** option allows you to do that within the **TRIM** command instead of exiting the command and starting the **ERASE** command.
Undo	**Undo** will undo the last trim action. If you selected a single object to trim, the **Undo** option will undo that trim. If you used either the **Fence** or **Crossing** option to select multiple objects, AutoCAD will undo all the trims done with that selection.

Some closed objects such as circles or ellipses require that the object intersect a cutting edge in at least two places. This is because these objects have no endpoints and must therefore be trimmed between two edges. If you attempt to trim one of these objects with only one cutting edge, AutoCAD will display the message: *Object must intersect twice.* Some objects cannot be trimmed, such as text and blocks.

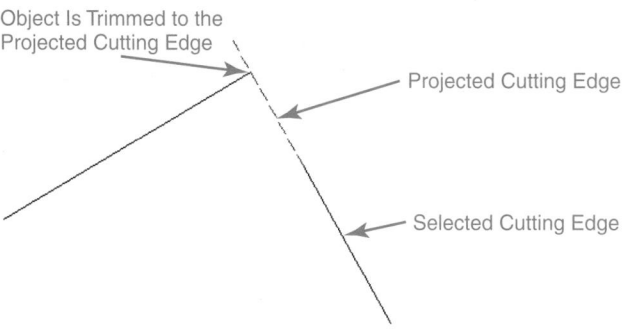

Object Is Trimmed to the
Projected Cutting Edge

Projected Cutting Edge

Selected Cutting Edge

Figure 8-12   Extend mode settings

Exercise 8-4: Trimming

1. Start a new drawing using the acad.dwt drawing template.
2. Draw a circle with a radius of **5**. Draw three lines that are **6** units long, starting at the center of the circle at an angle of **80°**, **90°**, and **100°**, respectively. Use the **OFFSET** command and offset each line **.5** unit as shown in Figure 8-13.
3. Start the **TRIM** command. AutoCAD prompts you to *Select objects or <select all>:*.
4. Press **<Enter ↵>** to select all the objects as cutting edges. AutoCAD prompts you: *Select object to trim or shift-select to extend or ↓*.
5. Pick the points shown in Figure 8-13 to trim the objects so that all overlapping lines at the corners are cleaned up. AutoCAD continues to prompt you: *Select object to trim or shift-select to extend or ↓*.
6. Select the **eRase** option. AutoCAD prompts you to *Select objects to erase:*. Select the three vertical lines, the 80° line, and the 100° line that start at the circle center point as shown in Figure 8-13. Press **<Enter ↵>** to erase the selected objects. Your drawing should look like Figure 8-14.

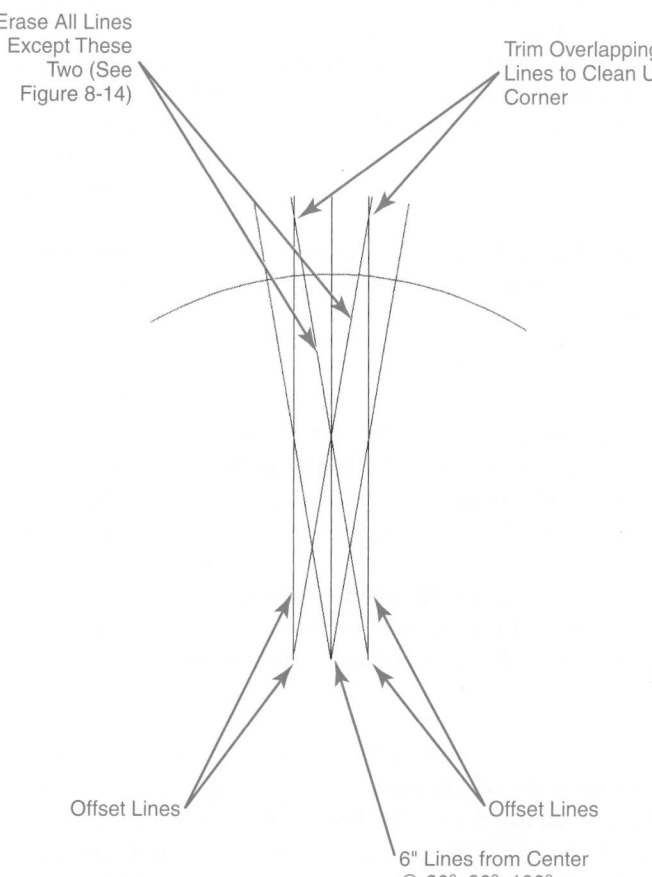

Erase All Lines
Except These
Two (See
Figure 8-14)

Trim Overlapping
Lines to Clean Up
Corner

Offset Lines

Offset Lines

6" Lines from Center
@ 80°, 90°, 100°

Figure 8-13   Cleaning up corners using the **TRIM command**

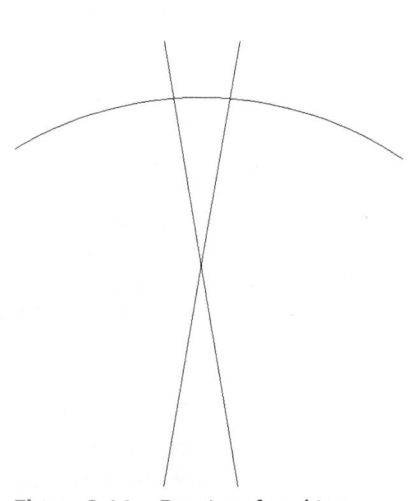

Figure 8-14   Drawing after objects trimmed and erased

Figure 8-15 Offsetting and trimming the circles

Figure 8-16 Erasing the remaining objects

7. AutoCAD again prompts you to: *Select object to trim or shift-select to extend or* ↓. Press **<Enter ↵>** or **<Esc>** to exit the **TRIM** command.
8. Draw two circles with a diameter of **0.3125** by snapping to the endpoints of the angled lines as shown in Figure 8-15. Start the **OFFSET** command and offset each of these circles **0.6875** toward the outside of each circle as shown in Figure 8-15.
9. Zoom in to the two circles at the top of the drawing. Start the **TRIM** command and press **<Enter ↵>** to select all the objects as cutting edges, then select the six trim points shown in Figure 8-15.
10. Choose the **eRase** option and select the objects shown in Figure 8-16 to erase. Press **<Enter ↵>** to erase the objects. Press **<Enter ↵>** again to end the **TRIM** command.
11. Save your drawing as **EX8-4**.

Extending Objects

Extending objects is similar to trimming them; the objects simply get longer instead of shorter. The **EXTEND** command has options similar to the **TRIM** command except you are prompted to select boundary edges instead of cutting edges. Whether they are called boundary or cutting edges, the concept is the same; the edge determines the edge where the object is extended.

Extend Options.   The options for the **EXTEND** command are identical to those for the **TRIM** command with the exception of the **Erase** option. Because extending is an additive process (you are adding length to objects) and the **Erase** option is a subtractive process, this option is omitted from the **EXTEND** command.

Using the <Shift> Key to Switch Between Trim and Extend.   Because the **EXTEND** and **TRIM** commands are so similar, AutoCAD provides an easy way to switch back and forth between them. You may have noticed that in the **TRIM** command, after you select the cutting edges, AutoCAD prompts you to *Select object to trim or shift-select to extend or* ↓. By holding down the **<Shift>** key while selecting the objects to extend, you can use the **TRIM** command to trim objects. The same is true for the **EXTEND** command. After you select the boundary edges, Auto-CAD prompts you to *Select object to extend or shift-select to trim or ↓*. While the **<Shift>** key is depressed, the **EXTEND** command will trim objects, using the boundary edges as the cutting edges.

Extend	
Ribbon & Panel:	Home|Modify
Modify Toolbar:	
Menu:	M̲odify|Exten̲d
Command Line:	EXTEND
Command Alias:	EX

Exercise 8-5: Extending Objects

1. Continue from Exercise 8-4.
2. Start the **OFFSET** command and offset the large circle **3.5** units toward the center of the circle. Repeat the **OFFSET** command and offset the new circle **.5** unit toward the center.
3. Draw two lines, each **8** units long, from the center of the circle at an angle of **85°** and **95°**, respectively.
4. Draw two more short lines, each **3** units long, from the center of the circle at an angle of **60°** and **120°**, respectively.
5. Start the **OFFSET** command, set the **Erase** option to **Yes** so the original lines are erased, and set the offset distance to **.25**. Offset the two short lines. Offset the left-hand line to the right, and the right-hand line to the left. Your drawing should look like Figure 8-17.
6. Zoom in to the top of the drawing and start the **EXTEND** command. AutoCAD prompts you to *Select objects or <select all>:*. Select the two 8″ long angled lines and press **<Enter ↓>** to make them the boundary edges.
7. AutoCAD prompts you to *Select object to extend or shift-select to trim or ↓*. Pick the two small arc segments nearest to the angled lines selected in step 6 as shown in Figure 8-18 so that the arcs extend out to meet the boundary edges.

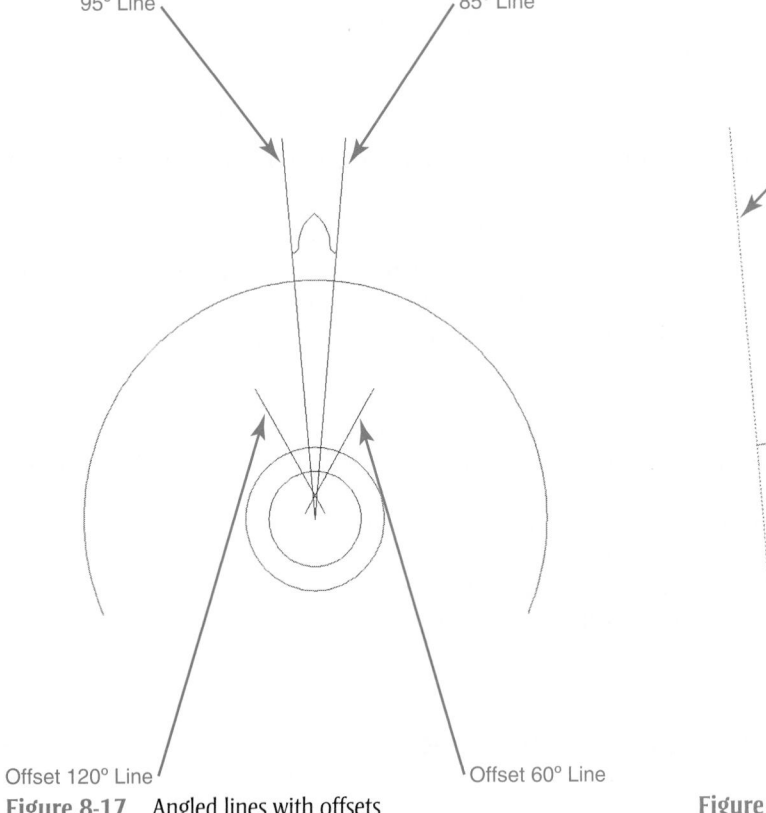

Figure 8-17   Angled lines with offsets

Figure 8-18   Extending the arcs

8. Select the **ERASE** command and delete the two 8″ long angled lines used as boundary edges in step 7.
9. Zoom out to see the entire drawing and select the **EXTEND** command again. Select the two outer circles and the two angled lines as boundary edges as shown in Figure 8-19 and press **<Enter ↓>**.
10. Pick near the ends of the two angled lines using the pick points shown in Figure 8-19 to extend the lines to meet the outer circle.

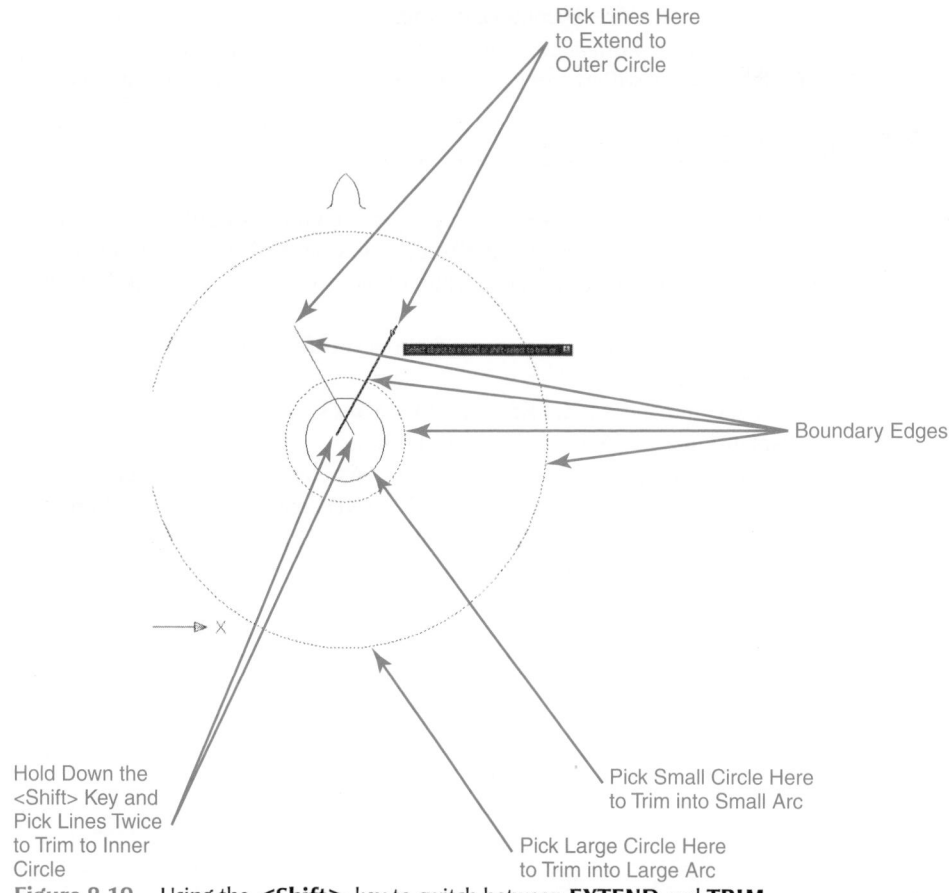

Boundary Edges

Hold Down the
<Shift> Key and
Pick Lines Twice
to Trim to Inner
Circle

Pick Small Circle Here
to Trim into Small Arc

Pick Large Circle Here
to Trim into Large Arc

Figure 8-19   Using the **<Shift>** key to switch between **EXTEND** and **TRIM**

Figure 8-20   Drawing after trimming/extending lines and arcs

11. Hold down the **<Shift>** key to enter **Trim** mode. Select the inner circle using the pick points shown in Figure 8-19 and trim it into the small arc segment shown in Figure 8-20.
12. Hold down the **<Shift>** key to enter **Trim** mode. Select the two angled lines using the pick points shown in Figure 8-19 and trim them to meet the small arc segment created in step 11 as shown in Figure 8-20.
13. Press **<Enter ↵>** to end the **EXTEND** command.
14. Start the **TRIM** command and select the two angled lines as cutting edges as shown in Figure 8-19 and press **<Enter ↵>**.
15. Pick the outer circle near the bottom as shown in Figure 8-19 to trim it into the large arc segment shown at the top in Figure 8-20.
16. Press **<Enter ↵>** to end the **TRIM** command.
17. Save your drawing as **EX8-5**. Your drawing should look like Figure 8-20.

CREATING FILLETS AND CHAMFERS

Fillets and chamfers are rounded and angled corners, respectively. To create a fillet or a chamfer using basic drawing and editing commands would be a difficult task. The process of rounding a simple right-angle corner would involve shortening each leg by the radius of the round, and then creating an arc segment between the two shortened ends. Using **TRIM** and **EXTEND** might make the process easier, but you would still need to draw an arc or circle and use a combination of **TRIM** and/or **EXTEND** to clean up the intersections. Creating a chamfered or angled corner might prove easier but would still involve drawing new objects and cleaning up their intersections. The **FILLET** and **CHAMFER** commands allow you to easily add rounds and angled lines at the corner of two intersecting objects.

Fillet	
Ribbon & Panel:	Home| Modify
Modify Toolbar:	
Menu:	Modify| Fillet
Command Line:	FILLET
Command Alias:	F

Creating Fillets

To create a fillet, you specify a fillet radius and select two objects. AutoCAD will place an arc between the two objects and trim and extend the objects as needed. The point where you select the objects determines where the arc is placed. AutoCAD will place the fillet so that the selected portions will remain (see Figure 8-21).

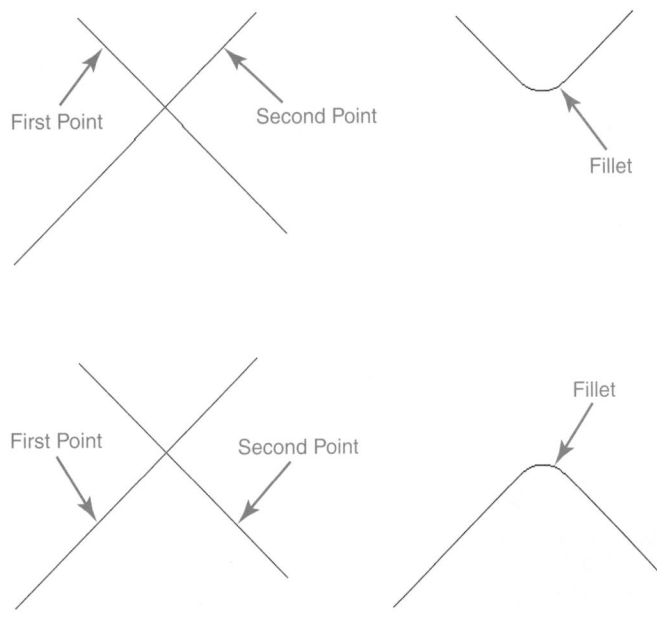

Figure 8-21   Fillet selections

Radius Option.   When you start the **FILLET** command, the current radius setting is listed in the command window. The **Radius** option allows you to set the fillet radius. The fillet radius is stored in the **FILLETRAD** system variable and once set, AutoCAD will retain the setting until you change it. Setting the **Radius** option to **0** will result in AutoCAD squaring off a corner.

You can create a fillet between open objects (lines, arcs, and elliptical arcs) as well as closed objects (circles and ellipses). When you select a closed object, AutoCAD doesn't actually trim the closed object but simply draws the fillet arc. (See Figure 8-22.)

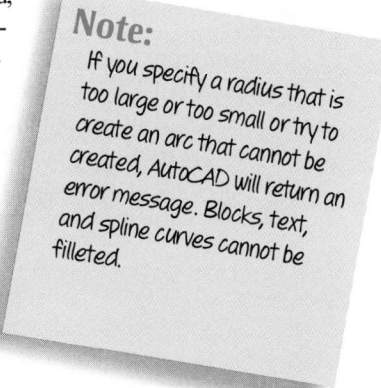

Note:
If you specify a radius that is too large or too small or try to create an arc that cannot be created, AutoCAD will return an error message. Blocks, text, and spline curves cannot be filleted.

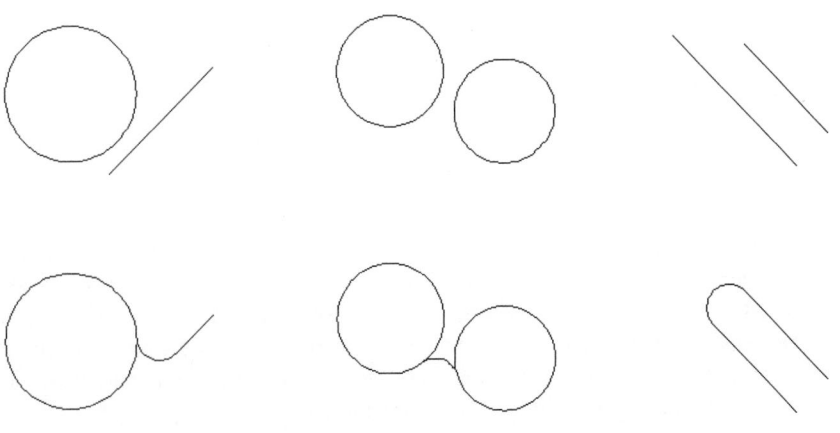

Figure 8-22   Some sample fillets

Multiple Mode.   The **Multiple** option puts you into **Multiple** mode and allows you to create multiple fillets in a single command. In **Multiple** mode, the **FILLET** command simply repeats until you press **<Enter ↵>** or **<Esc>**. The **Undo** option allows you to undo the last fillet while in **Multiple** mode.

Trim Mode.   The **Trim** option allows you to turn **Trim** mode on and off. With **Trim** mode turned on, objects are trimmed or extended to the fillet arc. With **Trim** mode turned off, Auto-CAD creates the fillet arc but leaves the source objects unchanged. Like the **Radius** option, the **Trim** setting is retained after the **FILLET** command is complete until you change it.

The Polyline Option.   The **Polyline** option allows you to add a fillet radius to all the intersections in a polyline object.

Capping Two Parallel Lines Using the Fillet Tool

If you fillet two parallel lines, AutoCAD will create a rounded end cap between the two lines. In this case, AutoCAD will ignore the **Radius** setting and create a 180° arc using half the distance between the lines as the radius. If the lines are different lengths, the first object you select will determine the start point of the arc. The other line will be trimmed or extended to match the first selected object (see Figure 8-22).

FOR MORE DETAILS	See Chapter 9 for more on creating and editing polylines.

Exercise 8-6: Creating a Fillet

1. Continue from Exercise 8-5.
2. Start the **FILLET** command. AutoCAD prompts you to *Select first object or ↓*.
3. Choose the **Multiple** option to turn on **Multiple** mode.
4. Choose the **Radius** option and type **.5<Enter ↵>** to set the fillet radius.
5. Pick the lines and arc shown in Figure 8-23 to round the outer corners. AutoCAD will round the corners and continue prompting you to select objects.

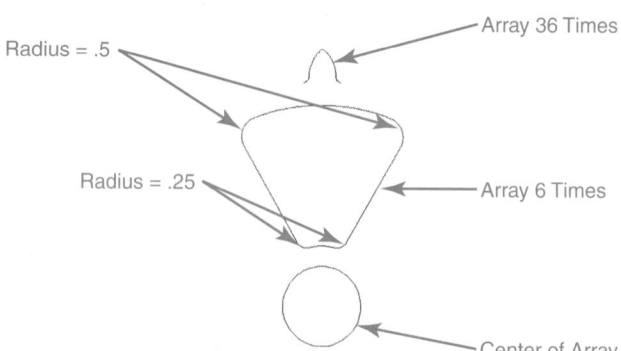

Figure 8-23   Creating fillets

6. Choose the **Radius** option and type **.25<Enter ↵>** to set the fillet radius.
7. Pick the lines and arc shown in Figure 8-23 to round the inner corners. When you've finished rounding the four corners, press **<Esc>** to end the **FILLET** command.
8. Start the **ARRAY** command and create a polar array of the pointed geometry at the top of the drawing. Center the array about the center of the circle and create **36** items through **360°**, rotating the objects as they are copied.

9. Repeat the **ARRAY** command and create a polar array of the rounded wedge. Center the array about the center of the circle and create **6** items through **360°**, rotating the objects as they are copied. Your drawing should look like Figure 8-24.

10. Save your drawing as **EX8-6**.

Figure 8-24   The finished drawing

Creating Chamfers

The **CHAMFER** command is used to create angled corners between two intersecting objects. Drawing a chamfer between intersecting objects is similar to drawing a fillet. However, instead of a fillet radius, you need to provide two distances from the intersection along each object, or a distance and an angle for the chamfer (see Figure 8-25).

The **CHAMFER** command has two methods for creating chamfers: distance and angle. The **mEthod** option allows you to select which chamfer method to use.

Chamfer	
Ribbon & Panel:	Home| Modify
Modify Toolbar:	
Menu:	Modify| Chamfer
Command Line:	CHAMFER
Command Alias:	CHA

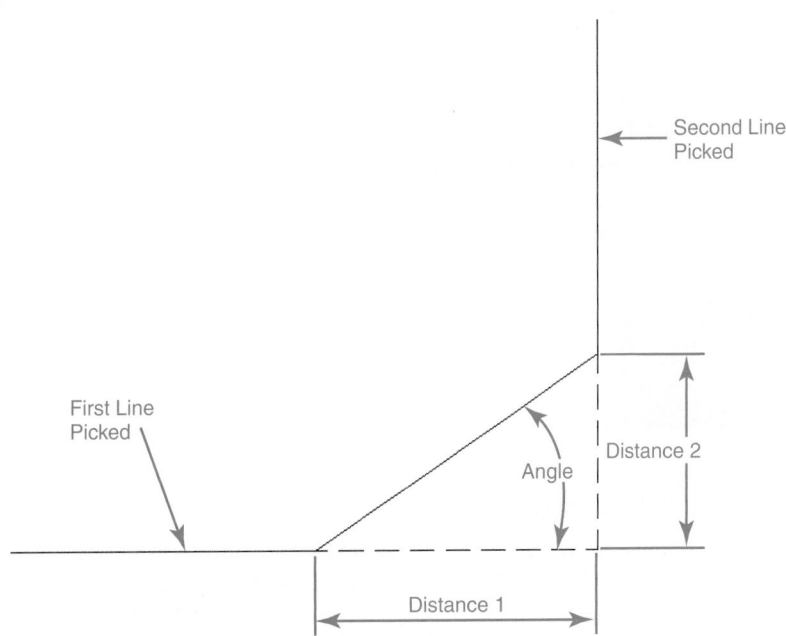

Figure 8-25   Creating a chamfer

Distance Method.   With the **Distance** method, you specify the distance from the intersection along each line. From the intersection, AutoCAD subtracts the first chamfer distance from the first object and the second chamfer distance from the second object and then draws a line between these two points. The **Distance** option allows you to set the chamfer distances. The first distance is applied to the first object you select, and the second distance is applied to the second object.

If the chamfer distances are equal, a 45° chamfer is drawn. When you set the first distance, AutoCAD sets the default value of the second distance to the first distance. To accept this default, just press **<Enter ↵>** when prompted for the second chamfer distance.

Note: Whereas the **FILLET** command allows you to create arcs between both straight and curved objects, the **CHAM-FER** command works only on straight, linear objects (lines, straight polyline segments, Xlines, and rays).

Angle Method. The **Angle** method uses a distance and angle to determine the chamfer line. The distance is subtracted from the first object selected to determine the starting point and the chamfer line is drawn at the specified angle until it intersects with the second object. By default, the angle is measured in a counterclockwise direction from the first object (see Figure 8-26).

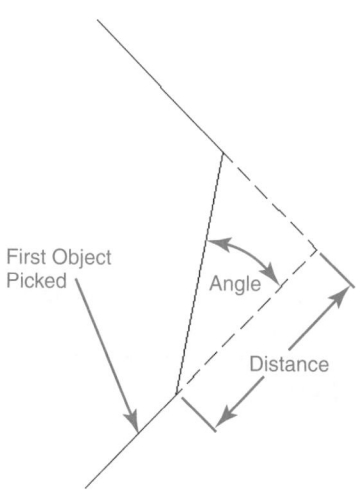

Figure 8-26 The **Angle** chamfer method

The Polyline Option. The **Undo, Polyline, Trim,** and **Multiple** options work the same way as on the **FILLET** command. When chamfering a polyline with the **Polyline** option, the first and second objects are determined by the order in which the polyline was drawn. When in doubt, or if you are not getting the results you're expecting, your best bet may be to not use the **Polyline** option and just chamfer the polyline segments individually.

FOR MORE DETAILS See Chapter 9 for more on creating and editing polylines.

Exercise 8-7: Creating a Chamfer

1. Continue from Exercise 8-2. If you've closed the drawing, open the drawing **EX8-2**.
2. Start the **CHAMFER** command and select the **Angle** option. AutoCAD prompts you to *Specify chamfer length on the first line:*. Type **.75<Enter ↵>** to set the length.
3. AutoCAD prompts you to *Specify chamfer angle from the first line:*. Type **60<Enter ↵>** to set the chamfer angle.
4. AutoCAD prompts you to *Select first line or* ↓. Pick the objects shown in Figure 8-27. AutoCAD chamfers the corner. Note that the .75 distance is taken off of the first line you selected.

Figure 8-27   Using the **Angle** method

5. Because this chamfer comes very close to the hole, type **U<Enter ↵>** to undo the last chamfer.
6. Restart the **CHAMFER** command and select the **Distance** option. Set the first distance to **.5**. AutoCAD sets the default value of the second distance to match the first. Press **<Enter ↵>** to accept the default. AutoCAD prompts you to *Select first line or ↓*.
7. Select the **Multiple** option and chamfer the four corners of the part. Your drawing should look like Figure 8-28.
8. Save your drawing as **EX8-7**.

Figure 8-28   Creating chamfers

BREAKING AN OBJECT

The **BREAK** command allows you to remove portions of an object or to break a single object into two separate objects. The **BREAK** command requires you to select an object and then select two points on the object. The portion of the object between the two points is then removed.

Creating a Gap in an Object

When you start the **BREAK** command, AutoCAD prompts you to select an object. By default, when you select the object, the point you pick on the object becomes the first break point, and AutoCAD will prompt you to select the second break point. If the point you select is not the point you want, you can use the **First** option to repick the first break point on the selected object.

Once you specify the first break point, AutoCAD prompts you for the second break point and breaks the object between the two points.

Breaking an Object Exactly at a Point

There may be times when you want to break the object in two without creating a physical gap. To break an object without creating an opening, simply use the @ symbol to specify the second point. When you use the @ symbol, AutoCAD will place the second point at the same coordinate as the first point. The end result is the object is broken in two without creating a gap.

Break	
Ribbon & Panel:	Home| Modify
Modify Toolbar:	
Menu:	Modify| Brea<u>k</u>
Command Line:	BREAK
Command Alias:	BR

Breaking Circles, Xlines, and Rays

Depending on the type of object you select, the **BREAK** command will create new objects. When you break a line, AutoCAD simply creates two lines. However, when you break a circle, Xline, or ray, AutoCAD will create different types of objects.

Note: Circles and ellipses must be broken in two distinct locations. Using @ when specifying the second break point is not allowed.

Circle. When you break a circle, AutoCAD converts the circle to an arc. The order in which you select the points will determine which portion of the circle is kept. AutoCAD will remove the portion of the circle starting at the first in a counterclockwise direction. Figure 8-29 shows the results of selecting different points along a circle.

Xlines and Rays. When you break an Xline, AutoCAD will create two rays with the starting points of the rays located at the first and second break points. Breaking a ray will result in a line and a ray.

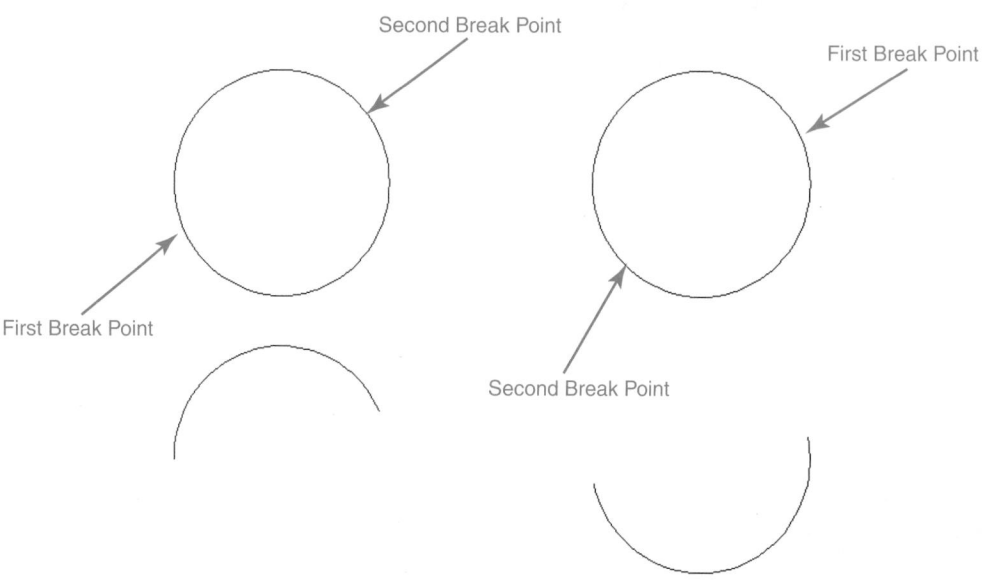

Figure 8-29 Breaking a circle

Selecting the Second Points

When you select the second break point, there are a couple of things to keep in mind. First, if you select the second point somewhere away from the object, AutoCAD will project a break point along a line perpendicular to the object passing through the selected point. Second, if the second break point lies past the end of the object, AutoCAD will simply remove everything between the first point and the end of the object. Figure 8-30 shows examples of these.

Exercise 8-8: Breaking Objects

1. Continue from Exercise 8-1. If you've closed the drawing, open the drawing **EX8-1**.
2. Start the **BREAK** command and select the circle near the bottom quadrant, between the two vertical lines. AutoCAD prompts you to *Specify second break point or* ↓. Pick anywhere near the arc to break the circle into an arc segment. Don't worry about the final length of the arc segment.
3. Restart the **BREAK** command. AutoCAD prompts you to *Select object:*. Hold down the **<Shift>** key and right-click to bring up the **Object Snap** menu. Choose **Midpoint** and select the centerline. This selects the line and places the first break point at the midpoint of the line. AutoCAD prompts you to *Specify second break point or* ↓.

Figure 8-30   Breaking objects

Figure 8-31   Breaking objects

4. Type **@<Enter ↵>** to break the line at the midpoint. Drag your cursor over a portion of the centerline. AutoCAD will highlight half of the centerline.
5. Start the **FILLET** command and set the radius to **25**. Turn on **Multiple** mode and add fillets between the arc and line segments. Your drawing should look like Figure 8-31.
6. Save your drawing as **EX8-8**.

JOINING MULTIPLE OBJECTS

The **JOIN** command does the opposite of the **BREAK** command by closing the gap between objects and converting multiple objects into a single object. The **JOIN** command starts by asking you to select a source object and then prompts you to select the objects to join to the source. The objects you want to join must match the source object and have different rules depending on the type of source object you choose.

Lines.   When joining lines, all the lines must lie in the same plane and must be collinear. The line segments can overlap or there can be gaps between the line segments, but the end result must be a single, continuous line. Joining multiple line segments results in a single line object.

Arcs.   Arcs must lie in the same circular path, meaning they must have the same center point and radius. Like lines, the arcs can overlap or have gaps between them. The end result should be a single continuous arc segment. If the arcs overlap to form a complete circle, AutoCAD will ask you if you want to convert the arcs into a circle.

You can also use the **JOIN** command to convert an arc into a circle. When you select an arc as the source object, AutoCAD provides a **cLose** option. Choosing this option will close the arc and convert it to a circle.

Elliptical Arcs.   Elliptical arcs behave the same as circular arcs. The elliptical arcs must lie on the same elliptical path. Gaps and overlaps are allowed, and the **cLose** option is available to convert an elliptical arc into an ellipse.

Polylines.   The objects must be lines, arcs, or open polylines. Gaps and overlapping are not allowed when joining polylines. All the segments must lie end-to-end in the same plane.

Spline Curves.   Spline curves behave similarly to polylines. All the objects must be spline curves that lie in the same plane. Gaps and overlapping are not allowed; all the segments must lie end-to-end.

Join	
Ribbon & Panel:	Home| Modify
Modify Toolbar:	
Menu:	Modify| Join
Command Line:	JOIN
Command Alias:	J

FOR MORE DETAILS	See Chapter 9 for more on creating polylines and editing polylines and spline curves.

Exercise 8-9: Joining Objects

1. Continue from Exercise 8-8.
2. Start the **JOIN** command. AutoCAD prompts you to *Select source object:*.
3. Select one portion of the centerline. AutoCAD prompts you to *Select lines to join to source:*. Pick the other half of the centerline and press **<Enter ↵>**. AutoCAD joins the two lines together.
4. Drag your cursor over the centerline to verify it is a single object. Save your drawing as **EX8-9**.

LENGTHENING AN OBJECT

Lengthen	
Ribbon & Panel:	Home| Modify
Toolbar:	None
Menu:	Modify| Lengthen
Command Line:	LENGTHEN
Command Alias:	LEN

The **LENGTHEN** command allows you to lengthen or shorten drawing objects as well as get information about the length of selected objects. When you start the **LENGTHEN** command, you are asked to select an object and are given four options, **DElta, Percent, Total,** and **DYnamic**. When you select an object, the **LENGTHEN** command displays the length of the object in the command line window. If the object is an arc, the included angle of the arc is also displayed.

> **TIP** The length information for most objects is displayed in the **Properties** palette. However, for some objects such as spline curves, ellipses, and elliptical arcs, the **Properties** palette doesn't display total length information. The **LENGTHEN** command is an easy way to display this information for these complex curves.

The LENGTHEN Command Options

When lengthening an object, AutoCAD must know how much length to add or subtract from the object. Once it knows what changes to make, the **LENGTHEN** command will prompt you to select an object to lengthen. You can either select a single object or use the **Fence** selection method to drag a fence crossing line across the items you wish to lengthen. AutoCAD will keep prompting you to select objects, allowing you to lengthen multiple objects within a single command.

The **LENGTHEN** command options provide four different methods for altering the length of an object.

DElta Option.   The **DElta** option allows you to specify a discreet length to add or subtract from the object. When you choose the **DElta** option, AutoCAD asks you to enter a delta length and then prompts you to select an object. The length you specify is then added to the object at the end closest to where you select. A positive delta value will increase the length, and a negative delta will shorten the object.

The **DElta** option also includes an **Angle** option. This allows you to modify the included angle of an arc. By default, positive angles add length in the counterclockwise direction, and negative angles subtract length in the clockwise direction.

Percent Option.   The **Percent** option allows you to scale the line by a percentage value. A percent value of 200 will make an object twice as long. A value of 50 will make it half as long. A value of 110 will add 10 percent to the length of the object. A value of 100 will leave the object unchanged.

Total Option.   The **Total** option allows you to set the total length of an object. If the value is greater than the current length of the object, the object will increase in length. If the value is smaller, the object will shorten.

DYnamic Option.   The **DYnamic** option allows you to specify the length of an object by dragging it around the screen. When you use this option, you are asked to select an object. AutoCAD will then ask you to specify a new endpoint for the object. You can then drag your cursor around the drawing and dynamically see the length change. To set the length, simply pick a point.

Invalid Objects

When using the **LENGTHEN** command, it's possible to ask AutoCAD to create objects that can't exist or to lengthen objects that cannot be lengthened. For example, although AutoCAD will tell you the length of a closed object like a circle or an ellipse, you can't add length to a closed object. Another example would be to try to increase the included angle of a line, or to increase the included angle of an arc beyond 360°. In cases like these, AutoCAD will simply display a message stating that it cannot lengthen the object, and it will ignore the selected object.

Exercise 8-10: Lengthening an Object

1. Continue from Exercise 8-9.
2. Start the **LENGTHEN** command and select the centerline. AutoCAD replies *Current length: 100.0000* and prompts you to *Select an object or ↓*.
3. Select the **DElta** option and enter a value of **25**. AutoCAD prompts you to *Select an object to change or ↓*. Select the bottom portion of each of the vertical lines. Each line is lengthened by 25 units. AutoCAD continues to prompt you to *Select an object to change or ↓*.
4. Type **F<Enter ↵>** to specify a **Fence** selection. Draw a fence through the three bottom lines (see Figure 8-32) and press **<Enter ↵>** to end the selection process. AutoCAD will lengthen the three lines by another 25 units.
5. Save your drawing as **EX8-10**. Your drawing should resemble Figure 8-33.

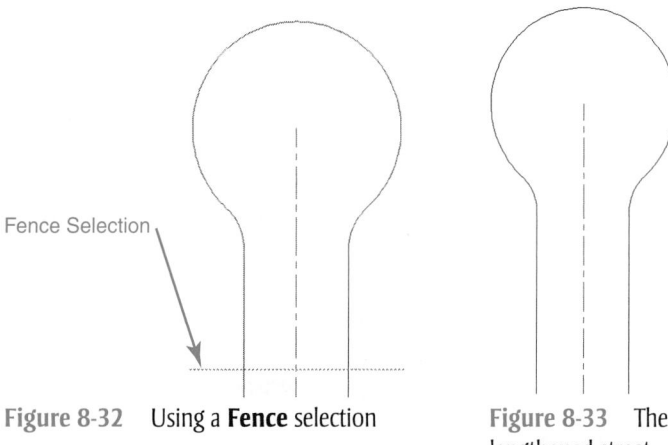

Fence Selection

Figure 8-32   Using a **Fence** selection

Figure 8-33   The lengthened street

CHAPTER SUMMARY

In this chapter you've explored some additional methods of editing geometry. The editing techniques covered here add to the basic edit- ing commands and provide additional methods of accomplishing some potentially tedious tasks.

CHAPTER TEST QUESTIONS

Multiple Choice

1. Copying an object parallel to an existing object is called:
   a. Filleting
   b. Chamfering
   c. Offsetting
   d. Extending

2. In a rectangular array, the row offset represents:
   a. The horizontal (X) spacing of the arrayed objects
   b. The vertical (Y) spacing of the arrayed objects
   c. The number of rows in the array
   d. None of the above

3. In the **TRIM** command, when selecting objects to trim, holding down the **<Shift>** key:
   a. Allows you to remove objects from the selection set
   b. Puts a 0 radius corner at the intersection of the two objects
   c. Allows you to select additional cutting edges
   d. Allows you to extend objects to the cutting edges

4. In the **FILLET** command, when selecting the objects to fillet, holding down the **<Shift>** key:
   a. Allows you to remove objects from the selection set
   b. Puts a 0 radius corner at the intersection of the two objects
   c. Allows you to select additional cutting edges
   d. Allows you to extend objects to the cutting edges

5. In the **TRIM** command, when asked to select cutting edges, pressing **<Enter ↵>**:
   a. Ends the **TRIM** command
   b. Switches between **EXTEND** and **TRIM**
   c. Selects all the objects in the drawing as cutting edges
   d. None of the above

6. While creating a rectangular array, the array angle:
   a. Rotates the array
   b. Changes your rectangular array to a polar array
   c. Sets the polar array fill angle
   d. None of the above

7. When creating a polar array, entering a negative angle to fill:
   a. Will copy objects in a clockwise direction
   b. Will copy objects in a counterclockwise direction
   c. Is not allowed
   d. None of the above

8. The **BREAK** command:
   a. Will work on lines and arcs
   b. Will work on closed objects
   c. Can have the same first and second break point
   d. All of the above

9. To convert an arc to a circle:
   a. Use the **FILLET** command with a 0 radius
   b. Use the **EXTEND** command
   c. Use the **LENGTHEN** command
   d. Use the **JOIN** command

10. Breaking an Xline:
    a. Creates a line and a ray
    b. Creates two rays
    c. Converts the Xline to polyline
    d. Is not allowed

Matching

a. **ARRAY** command
b. Polar array
c. Fillet radius
d. Rectangular array
e. **JOIN** command
f. **BREAK** command
g. **LENGTHEN** command
h. **Extend** mode
i. **Erase** mode
j. **CHAMFER** command

1. Items copied in a circular pattern
2. Moves objects a user-supplied distance and angle
3. Can convert an arc into a full circle
4. The radius of a rounded intersection
5. Copies objects in rectangular or circular patterns
6. Can convert a circle into an arc and turn a single object into multiple objects
7. A mode of the **OFFSET** command that deletes the source object after it is offset
8. Items copied in a rectangular pattern of rows and columns
9. A mode of the **TRIM** and **EXTEND** commands that allows you to trim or extend to implied intersections
10. Allows you to display and modify the length of objects

CHAPTER PROJECTS

Project 8-1: Classroom Plan—Continued from Chapter 7

1. Open drawing **P7-1** from Chapter 7.
2. Draw the remaining equipment and windows shown in Figure P8-1A using the appropriate layers. The windows are all 4′-6″ wide. Do **not** draw dimensions or text.

3. Locate the chairs and windows as shown in Figure P8-1B. Trim the walls as necessary to allow for the window openings. Change the layout of the desks to reflect the updated plan.
4. Save your drawing as **P8-1**.

Figure P8-1A

Figure P8-1B

Project 8-2: A-Size Portrait Mechanical Border

1. Start a new drawing using the acad.dwt template.
2. Set the **LIMITS** for an 8.5 × 11.0 drawing area.
3. Create the following layers:

Name	Color	Linetype	Lineweight	Plot/Noplot	Description
Title	7	Continuous	Default	Plot	Title border and text
Logo	7	Continuous	Default	Plot	Logo
Notes	7	Continuous	Default	Plot	Notes
Viewport	9	Continuous	Default	Noplot	Viewports

4. Draw the A-size title block as shown in Figure P8-2. Use the **Title** layer for all geometry. **Do not** draw dimensions.
5. Save the drawing to a template file as **Mechanical A-Size-Portrait.DWT**.

Figure P8-2

Project 8-3: Architectural A-Size Border (8½ × 11)

1. Start a new drawing using the acad.dwt template.
2. Set linear **UNITS** to **Architectural** with precision set to **1/16″**.
3. Set angular **UNITS** to **Deg/Min/Sec** with precision set to **0d00′00″**.
4. Set the drawing **LIMITS** to **8½″ × 11″** for an A-size drawing.

5. Create the following layers:

Name	Color	Linetype	Lineweight	Plot/Noplot	Description
A-Anno-Ttlb	7	Continuous	Default	Plot	Title block/ border lines
A-Anno-Ttlb-Text	1	Continuous	Default	Plot	Title block text
A-Anno-Ttlb-Logo	3	Continuous	Default	Plot	Logo
A-Anno-Vprt	7	Continuous	Default	Noplot	Viewport lines

6. Draw the border as shown in Figure P8-3 on layer **A-Anno-Ttlb**. **Do not** include dimensions.
7. Zoom to the drawing extents.
8. Save the drawing to a template file as **Architectural A-Size.DWT**.

Figure P8-3

Project 8-4: Residential Electrical Plan—Continued from Chapter 7, Problem 7

1. Open drawing **P7-5** from Chapter 7.
2. Add the following layers:

Name	Color	Linetype	Lineweight	Plot/Noplot	Description
E-Lite	7	Continuous	Default	Plot	Lighting
E-Lite-Circ	7	Continuous	Default	Plot	Lighting circuiting
E-Powr	7	Continuous	Default	Plot	Power
E-Powr-Circ	9	Continuous	Default	Plot	Power circuiting
E-Anno	7	Continuous	Default	Plot	Electrical annotation

3. Create the symbols shown in Figure P8-4A. Place the symbols on the floor plan
   as shown in Figure P8-4B.
4. Save the drawing as **P8-4**.

φ   110 CONVENIENCE OUTLET   ○   CEILING MOUNTED LITE FIXTURE

φ   220 OUTLET   ⊙   CAN CEILING LITE FIXTURE

φ   SINGLE POLE SWITCH   -φ-   WALL MOUNTED LITE

                                         ▢   RECESSED LITE FIXTURE

♤   LITE, HEATER, & FAN   ⊖   FLOOR OUTLET

                                    ▭▭▭▭▭▭   48" SURFACE MOUNTED
                                                  FLOURESCANT LITE FIXTURE

Figure P8-4A

Figure P8-4B

Project 8-5: Residential Architectural Plan—Continued from Chapter 8, Problem 4

1. Open drawing **P8-4** from Chapter 8, Problem 4. If you are not completing Problem 4, open **P7-5** from Chapter 7.
2. Modify the floor plan as shown in Figure P8-5. Use the **TRIM, EXTEND**, and **FILLET** commands to clean up wall intersections and door/window openings. Do **not** draw dimensions or text.
3. Save your drawing as **P8-5**.

Note:
This problem continues from Problem 4–Residential Electrical Plan, presented earlier. If you are not completing Problem 5, continue from Problem 5 in Chapter 7.

Figure P8-5

Project 8-6: Optical Mount—English Units

1. Start a new drawing using the acad.dwt template.
2. Create the following layers:

Name	Color	Linetype	Lineweight	Description
Object	7	Continuous	0.35 mm	Object lines
Hidden	1	Hidden	Default	Hidden lines
Center	2	Center	Default	Centerlines
Hatch	4	Continuous	Default	Hatch patterns and fills
Notes	3	Continuous	Default	Text and notes
Dims	2	Continuous	Default	Dimensions

3. Create the three-view drawing as shown in Figure P8-6. *Hint:* Use the **FILLET** command to create the round ends of the slots.
4. Adjust the **LTSCALE** system so linetypes appear properly.
5. Do **not** include notes or dimensions.
6. Save your drawing as **P8-6**.

Figure P8-6

Project 8-7: 68-Tooth Rear Sprocket—Metric

1. Start a new drawing using the acadiso.dwt template.
2. Create the following layers:

Name	Color	Linetype	Lineweight	Description
Object	7	Continuous	0.35 mm	Object lines
Hidden	1	Hidden	Default	Hidden lines
Center	2	Center	Default	Centerlines
Hatch	4	Continuous	Default	Hatch patterns and fills
Notes	3	Continuous	Default	Text and notes
0 Dims	2	Continuous	Default	Dimensions

3. Draw object lines as shown in Figure P8-7 on layer **Object**.
4. Draw centerlines as shown in Figure P8-7 on layer **Center**. *Hint:* Draw one sprocket tooth as indicated in Detail A and array it using the **ARRAY** command with the **Polar** option. You can use the same technique to create the holes.
5. Adjust the **LTSCALE** system so linetypes appear properly.
6. Do **not** include notes or dimensions.
7. Save the drawing as **P8-7**.

Figure P8-7

Project 8-8: Civil Site Plan—Continued from Chapter 7

1. Open drawing **P7-8** from Chapter 7.
2. Round the corners of the pool as shown in Figure P8-8. Add the garden beds and plants as shown.
3. Save the drawing as **P8-8**.

Figure P8-8

Drawing and Editing Complex Objects

9

Chapter Objectives

- Draw polylines with straight line segments
- Draw polyline arcs
- Create rectangles using two points
- Make multisided polygons
- Create solid and hollow donuts
- Draw revision clouds
- Edit polylines as a unit
- Explode complex objects

INTRODUCTION

AutoCAD provides a number of complex line objects that consist of multiple segments but are treated as a single line with multiple points:

- Polyline
- Rectangle
- Polygon
- Donut
- Revision cloud

Complex line objects serve many different purposes and needs. Polylines allow you to define a closed boundary that can be used to calculate an enclosed area. Polylines are also used extensively to create *contour lines* on civil engineering maps.

In fact, AutoCAD uses polylines to create the rectangles, polygons, donuts, and revision clouds described in this chapter. This chapter explores the commands used to create and edit these different complex line objects. Also covered is the ability to break complex line objects down into their individual line and arc segments using the **EXPLODE** command.

contour line: A line on a map that joins points of equal elevation

Polyline	
Ribbon & Panel:	Home| Draw
Draw Toolbar:	
Menu:	Draw| Polyline
Command Line:	PLINE
Command Alias:	PL

DRAWING POLYLINES

A polyline is a complex line object made up of one or more connected line segments and/or arcs that are treated as a single line. See Figure 9-1.

Polylines are created using the **PLINE** command.

When you start the **PLINE** command, AutoCAD prompts you to *Specify start point:*. You can either type in a coordinate value or pick a point in your drawing similar to the **LINE** command. After you specify the first point, AutoCAD will continue to prompt you to *Specify next point or ↓* until you press **<Enter ↵>** without specifying a point as shown in Figure 9-2.

Figure 9-1   Examples of polylines

Figure 9-2   Drawing a polyline

You can specify points when drawing a polyline using absolute, relative, or polar coordinate entry methods. It is also possible to use direct distance entry with either the **Ortho Mode** or **Polar Tracking** drawing tool.

You can create a closed polyline line using the **Close** option just like the **LINE** command, except that the closed polyline creates a true closed polygon, unlike the **LINE** command, which creates individual line segments. The **Close** option will draw a line segment from the last point back to the start point. Figure 9-3 shows the result of selecting the **Close** option after drawing two line segments.

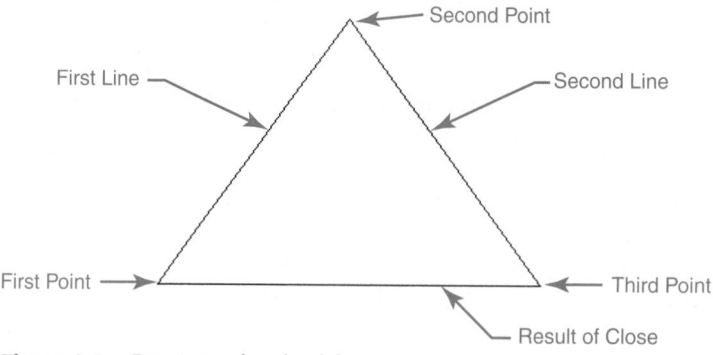

Figure 9-3   Drawing a closed polyline

It is possible to get the area and perimeter of a closed polyline using the **LIST** command. To use the **LIST** command type **LIST** or **LI**, select the polyline, and press **<Enter ↵>**. AutoCAD switches to the full text window and lists the area, perimeter, vertex point information, and a few other properties. You can also retrieve the same information using the **Properties** palette.

The **PLINE** command also has a built-in **Undo** option that allows you to undo points as you draw. Using the **Undo** option repeatedly will undo all the polyline points back to the first point.

Note:
By default, AutoCAD creates what's referred to as an optimized polyline that has the object name LWPOLYLINE. The *LW* stands for lightweight because the method in which polylines store vertex point information has been optimized. The old unoptimized polyline format still exists for legacy reasons and is referred to simply as a POLYLINE object.

TIP

You can control the type of polyline used via the **PLINETYPE** system variable. **PLINETYPE** controls both the creation of new polylines and the conversion of existing polylines in drawings from previous releases of AutoCAD. **PLINETYPE** has three settings.

0 Polylines in older drawings are not converted when opened; **PLINE** command creates old-format polylines.

1 Polylines in older drawings are not converted when opened; **PLINE** command creates optimized polylines.

2 Polylines in AutoCAD Release 14 or older drawings are converted when opened; **PLINE** creates optimized polylines.

The default setting is **2**.

Exercise 9-1: Drawing a Polyline

1. Start a new drawing using the acad.dwt drawing template.
2. Create the drawing shown in Figure 9-4 using the **PLINE** command. **Do not** draw dimensions.
3. The polyline should be closed using the **Close** option.
4. Save the drawing as **EX9-1**.

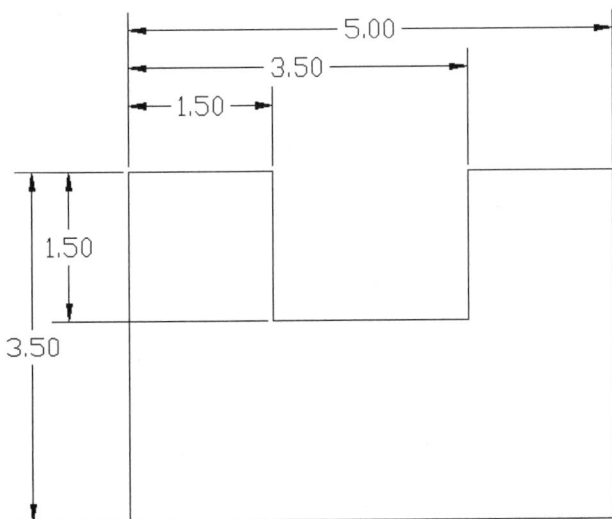

Figure 9-4   Drawing a polyline

Drawing Polyline Arcs

It is possible to switch from drawing line segments to drawing arcs when creating a polyline using the **Arc** option. After selecting the **Arc** option, AutoCAD prompts you to *Specify endpoint of arc or* ↓. By default, specifying an arc endpoint creates an arc that is tangent to the last line or arc segment as shown in Figure 9-5.

The direction of the arc is determined by where the arc endpoint is located relative to the current polyline point. If you continue to specify points in response to the *Specify endpoint of arc or* ↓ prompt, AutoCAD will create multiple tangent arc segments as shown in Figure 9-6.

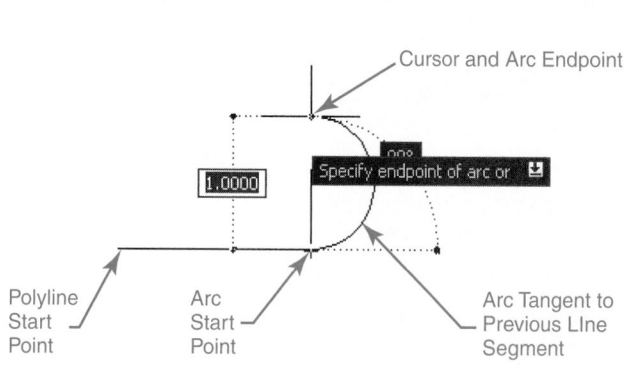

Figure 9-5   Drawing a tangent polyline arc

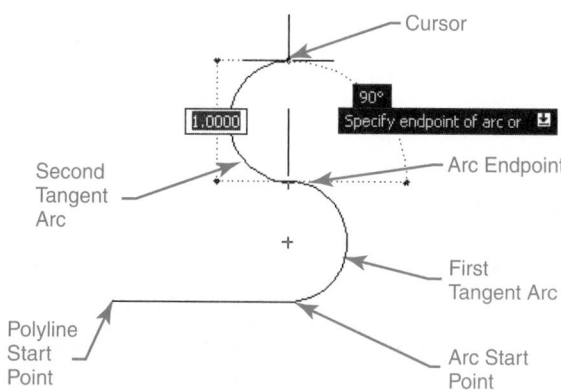

Figure 9-6   Drawing multiple tangent polyline arcs

You can switch back to drawing straight line segments using the **Line** option by either typing **L<Enter ↵>** or using the arrow keys if you're using **Dynamic Input** in response to the *Specify endpoint of arc or* ↓ prompt as shown in Figure 9-7.

There are a number of other options for creating polyline arcs, which are explained in the following sections.

Exercise 9-2: Drawing Tangent Polyline Arcs

1. Start a new drawing using the acad.dwt drawing template.
2. Create the drawing shown in Figure 9-8 using the **PLINE** command and the default tangent **Arc** option.
3. Save the drawing as **EX9-2**.

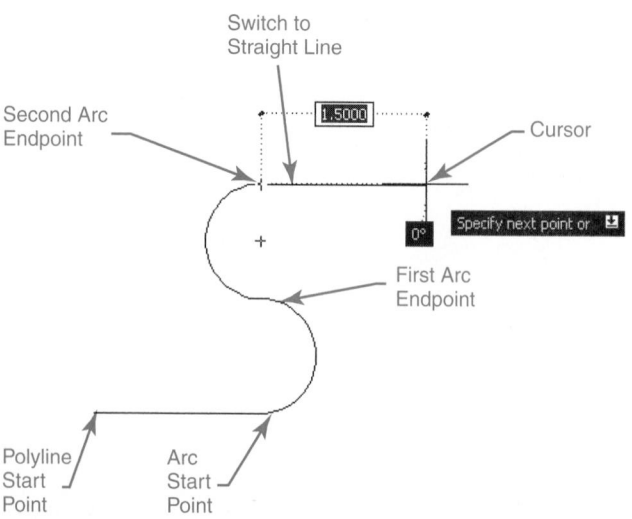

Figure 9-7   Switch from a polyline arc to a straight line segment

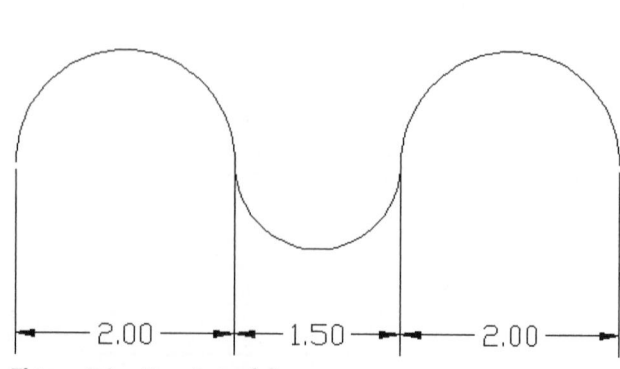

Figure 9-8   Drawing polyline arcs

Angle Option.   The **Angle** option allows you to specify the included angle of the arc segment from the start point. After you select the **Angle** option, AutoCAD prompts you to *Specify included angle:*. Enter the desired angle and press **<Enter ↵>**.

After you enter the angle, AutoCAD prompts you to *Specify endpoint of arc or ↓*. You can specify an endpoint or enter one of the following options:

CEnter: Allows you to specify the center of the arc segment

Radius: Allows you to specify the radius of the arc segment. After you enter the radius, AutoCAD prompts you to *Specify direction of chord for arc <45>:*. You can pick a point to indicate the direction or enter an angle at the keyboard

Figure 9-9 shows the results of drawing a polyline arc using the **Angle** option.

Note:
Entering a positive number creates counterclockwise arc segments. Entering a negative number creates clockwise arc segments.

CEnter Option.   The **CEnter** option allows you to specify the center of the arc segment. After you select the **CEnter** option, AutoCAD prompts you to *Specify center point of arc:*. You can pick a point or enter a coordinate value at the keyboard.

After you enter the point, AutoCAD prompts you to *Specify endpoint of arc or ↓*. You can specify an endpoint or enter one of the following options:

Angle: Allows you to enter the included angle of the arc segment from the start point

Length: Allows you to specify the chord length of the arc segment

Figure 9-10 shows the results of drawing a polyline arc using the **CEnter** option.

Note:
AutoCAD draws the new arc segment tangent to the previous arc segment if the previous segment is an arc.

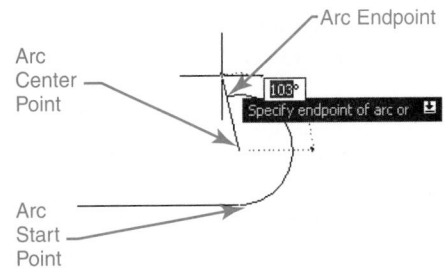

Figure 9-9   Drawing a polyline arc using the **Angle** option

Figure 9-10   Drawing a polyline arc using the **CEnter** option

Close Option.   The **Close** option allows you to close a polyline with an arc segment.

Direction Option.   The **Direction** option allows you to indicate the starting direction for the arc segment. After you select the **Direction** option, AutoCAD prompts you to *Specify the tangent direction from the start point of arc:*. You can pick a point or enter a coordinate value at the keyboard.

After you enter the angle, AutoCAD prompts you to *Specify endpoint of arc:*. You can pick a point or enter a coordinate value at the keyboard.

Figure 9-11 shows the results of drawing a polyline arc using the **Direction** option.

Note:
The ending half-width becomes the uniform half-width for all new segments until you change the half-width again.

Halfwidth Option.   The **Halfwidth** option allows you to specify the width from the center of a wide polyline segment to one of its edges. After you select the **Halfwidth** option, AutoCAD prompts you to *Specify starting half-width <current>:*. Enter a value or press **<Enter ⏎>** to use the current half-width. AutoCAD then prompts you to *Specify ending half-width <starting width>:*. You can either enter a different half-width value to create a tapered arc or press **<Enter ⏎>** for a uniform width.

Figure 9-12 shows the results of drawing a polyline arc using the **Halfwidth** option.

Figure 9-11   Drawing a polyline arc using the **Direction** option

Figure 9-12   Drawing a polyline arc using the **Halfwidth** option

Line Option.   The **Line** option exits the **Arc** option and returns to the initial **PLINE** command prompt so you can draw straight line segments. Input at the *Specify endpoint of arc or ↓* prompt.

Radius Option.   The **Radius** option allows you to specify the radius of the arc segment. After you select the **Radius** option, AutoCAD prompts you to *Specify radius of arc:*. Enter the desired radius and press **<Enter ⏎>**.

After you enter the radius, AutoCAD prompts you to *Specify endpoint of arc or ↓*. You can specify an endpoint or select the **Angle** option. The **Angle** option allows you to enter the included angle of the arc segment from the start point. After you enter the angle, AutoCAD prompts you to *Specify direction of chord for arc <45>:*. You can pick a point to indicate the direction or enter an angle at the keyboard.

Figure 9-13 shows the results of drawing a polyline arc using the **Radius** option.

Second Pt Option.   The **Second Pt** option allows you to specify the second point and the endpoint of a three-point arc. After you select the **Second Pt** option, AutoCAD prompts you to *Specify second point on arc:*. You can pick a point or enter a coordinate value at the keyboard.

After you specify the second point, AutoCAD prompts you to *Specify endpoint of arc ↓*. You can pick a point or enter a coordinate value at the keyboard.

Figure 9-14 shows the results of drawing a polyline arc using the **Second Pt** option.

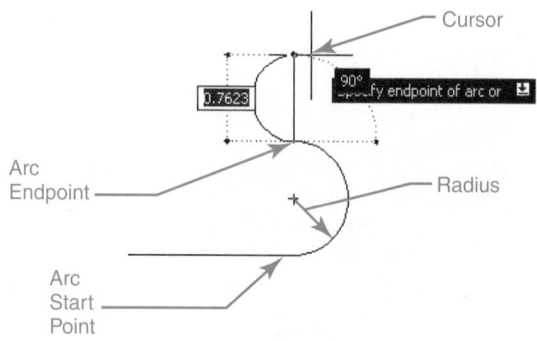

Figure 9-13   Drawing a polyline arc using the **Radius** option

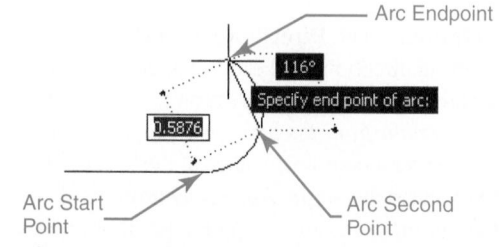

Figure 9-14   Drawing a polyline arc using the **Second Pt** option

Undo Option.   The **Undo** option allows you to undo the most recent arc segment added to the polyline.

Width Option.   The **Width** option allows you to change the width of the next arc segment. After you select the **Width** option, AutoCAD prompts you to *Specify starting width <current>:.* Enter a value or press **<Enter ↵>** to use the current width. AutoCAD then prompts you to *Specify ending width <starting width>:.* You can either enter a different width value to create a tapered arc or press **<Enter ↵>** for a uniform width.

Figure 9-15 shows the results of drawing a polyline arc using the **Width** option.

> **Note:**
> The ending width becomes the uniform width for all new segments until you change the width again.

Exercise 9-3: Drawing Complex Polyline Arcs

1. Start a new drawing using the acad.dwt drawing template.
2. Create the drawing shown in Figure 9-16 using the **PLINE** command and the **Arc** options covered in this section. **Do not** draw dimensions.
3. Close the polyline using the **PLINE** command's **Close** option.
4. Save the drawing as **EX9-3**.

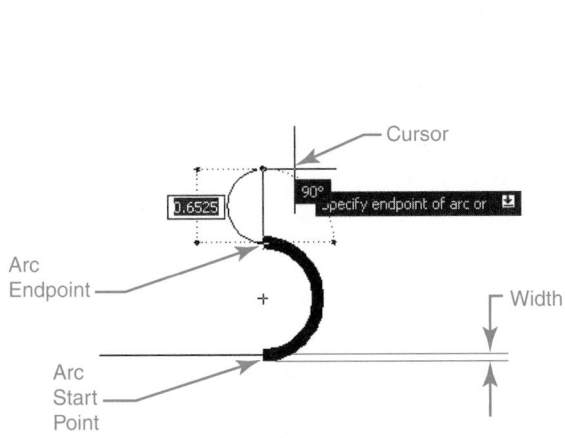

Figure 9-15   Drawing a polyline arc using the **Width** option

Figure 9-16   Drawing complex polyline arcs

Drawing Polylines with a Width

It is possible to assign a physical width to a polyline using the **Width** option. In fact, it is possible to vary a polyline's width between vertex points using the **Width** option so that a polyline segment can be tapered.

After you select the **Width** option, AutoCAD prompts you for a starting width and an ending width. This allows you to vary the width from point to point. To apply a width to all the line segments of a polyline, you simply specify an equal starting and ending width. For instance, to draw a polyline with a constant width of 0.100″, you type **.1<Enter ↵>** when AutoCAD prompts you to *Specify starting width <0.0000>:.* AutoCAD then prompts you for the ending width of the polyline segment

> **Note:**
> Polyline width is not related to the lineweight property discussed in Chapter 6. Polyline width is a unique property that is assigned directly to the polyline. Because it is unrelated to the lineweight property, it is not affected by the **Show/Hide Lineweight** lineweight toggle on the Status Bar.

using the starting width as the default by prompting *Specify ending width <0.1000>:*. This allows you to simply press the **<Enter ↵>** key to create a constant width. Figure 9-17 shows a polyline drawn with a constant width of 0.100″.

Varying a polyline width provides many unique possibilities. For instance, you can use a polyline with varying widths to create an arrow by specifying a starting width of 0.000″ to create the point, or tip, and then specifying an ending width greater than zero for the next point so the line is tapered. For instance, to create an arrow that tapers from a point to a base width of 0.25″, you would type **0<Enter ↵>** when AutoCAD prompts *Specify starting width <0.0000>:* to create the arrow point and then type **.25<Enter ↵>** when AutoCAD prompts *Specify ending width <0.1000>:* to indicate the base width as shown in Figure 9-18.

You can even combine these varying width techniques with polyline arcs to create curved arrows that can be used for signage on parking lot plans and roadways as shown in Figure 9-19.

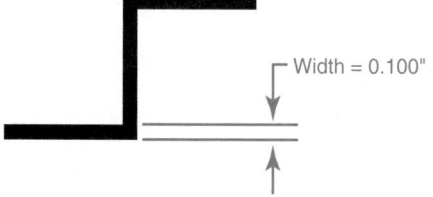

Figure 9-17   A polyline drawn with a constant width of 0.100″

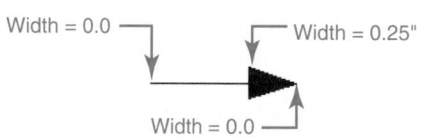

Figure 9-18   A polyline arrow created by varying the polyline width

Figure 9-19   A curved polyline arrow created using polyline arcs

Exercise 9-4: Drawing Polylines with a Width

1. Start a new drawing using the acad.dwt drawing template.
2. Create a polyline with a uniform width of 0.100″ similar to the polyline shown in Figure 9-17 using the **PLINE** command and the **Width** option.
3. Create a polyline arrow that tapers from a point to a base width of 0.25″ similar to the polyline shown in Figure 9-18 using the **PLINE** command and the **Width** option.
4. Create a curved polyline arrow similar to the polyline shown in Figure 9-19 using the **PLINE** command and the **Width** and **Arc** options.
5. Save the drawing as **EX9-4**.

DRAWING RECTANGLES

Rectangle	
Ribbon & Panel:	Home|Draw
Draw Toolbar:	
Menu:	Draw|Rectangle
Command Line:	RECTANGLE or RECTANG
Command Alias:	None

The **RECTANGLE** or **RECTANG** command draws a polyline rectangle using two user-supplied corner points.

When you start the **RECTANG** command, AutoCAD prompts you to *Specify first corner point or ↓*. You can either type in a coordinate value, or you can pick a point in your drawing. After you specify the first point, AutoCAD prompts you to *Specify other corner point or ↓* so you can locate the other corner point as shown in Figure 9-20.

Figure 9-20   Drawing a 3 × 2 rectangle

Remember that it always possible to enter a coordinate value any time AutoCAD prompts you for a point. In fact, if you know the length and width of the rectangle, you can enter a relative coordinate where *X* is the length and *Y* is the width. For instance, to draw a 3.000″ × 2.000″ rectangle, you can type **@3,2<Enter ↵>** when AutoCAD prompts you to *Specify other corner point or ↓*.

TIP If you are using **Dynamic Input**, you do not need to use the @ prefix. The second pick point is relative by default.

Entering the Length and Width. The **Dimensions** option allows you to draw a rectangle by entering the length and width in response to AutoCAD prompts. To use the **Dimensions** option, you must pick the first corner point. After you select the **Dimensions** option, AutoCAD prompts you to *Specify length for rectangles <3.0000>:*. Enter the desired length and press **<Enter ↵>**. AutoCAD then prompts you to *Specify width for rectangles <2.0000>:* so you can enter the width. After you enter a length and width, AutoCAD prompts you for a direction point by prompting *Specify other corner point or ↓*. The point you pick determines the rectangle's orientation as shown in Figure 9-21.

Note: AutoCAD remembers the length and width dimensions you enter so the next time you draw a rectangle using the **Dimensions** option you can simply press **<Enter↵>** to draw a rectangle the same size.

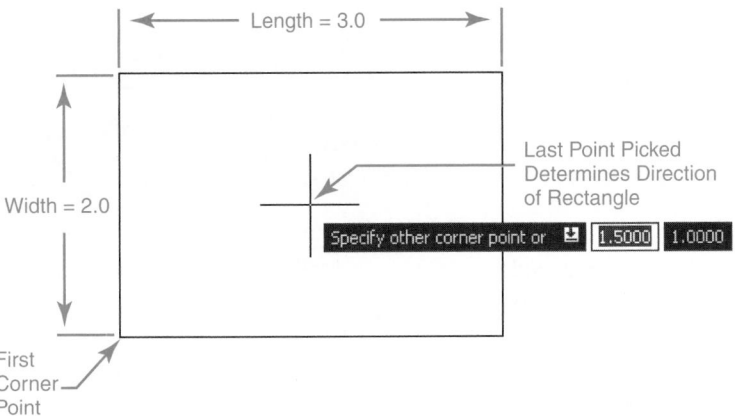

Figure 9-21   Drawing a rectangle by entering the length and width

Drawing a Rectangle at an Angle. The **Rotation** option allows you to draw a rectangle at a user-specified angle. To use the **Rotation** option, you must pick the first corner point. After you select the **Rotation** option, AutoCAD prompts you to *Specify rotation angle or ↓*. You have three possible ways to input the rotation angle:

- Type the angle at the keyboard.
- Pick a point to define the angle using the first corner point as the base point.
- Use the **Points** option to pick two separate points to define the angle.

The first option requires that you enter the angle by typing it at the keyboard. For instance, to create a rectangle that is rotated 45°, you enter **45<Enter ↵>**. After you enter the angle, the rectangle preview changes to the input angle, and AutoCAD again prompts you to *Specify other corner point or ↓*. You can locate the second corner point using any of the techniques explained in this section, including using the **Dimensions** and **Area** options as shown in Figure 9-22.

You can also pick a point to define the angle using the first corner point as the base point, or vertex. When picking a point to define the angle, it is usually beneficial to use either the **Ortho Mode** or **Polar Tracking** drawing tool.

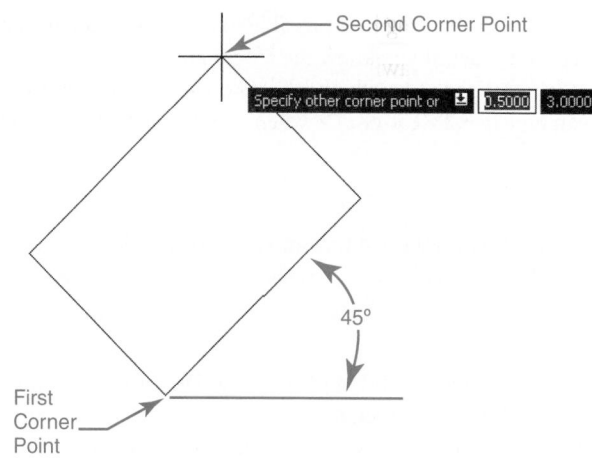

Figure 9-22 Drawing a rectangle at a 45° angle

FOR MORE DETAILS   See Chapter 5 for more information about using the **Ortho Mode** and **Polar Tracking** drawing tools.

The **Pick points** option gives you the ability to define the rotation angle using two *separate* points instead of using the first corner point as the default base point. After you select the **Pick points** option, AutoCAD prompts you for two pick points. After you pick the two points, the rectangle preview changes to the input angle, and AutoCAD again prompts you to *Specify other corner point or ↓*. You can locate the second corner point using any of the techniques explained in this section.

Note:
AutoCAD remembers the last rotation angle used so that it becomes the default the next time you use the **RECTANG** command. AutoCAD defaults to creating a rectangle at the same rotation angle the next time you use the command by displaying the current rotation angle at the command line:

Current rectangle modes:
Rotation=45

Drawing a Rectangle by Specifying the Area. The **Area** option allows you to draw a rectangle by specifying its area and either the length or the width. To use the **Area** option, you must pick the first corner point. After you select the **Area** option, AutoCAD prompts you to *Enter area of rectangle in current units <100.0000>:*. Enter the desired area and press **<Enter ↵>**. AutoCAD then asks you if you want to specify the length or width by prompting *Calculate rectangle dimensions based on [Length/Width]*. AutoCAD will prompt you for the length or width accordingly. After you enter the distance, AutoCAD draws the rectangle automatically at the first corner point location as shown in Figure 9-23.

Figure 9-23 Drawing a rectangle by specifying the area

Exercise 9-5: Drawing Rectangles

1. Start a new drawing using the acad.dwt drawing template.
2. Create a 3.000″ × 2.000″ rectangle similar to the rectangle shown in Figure 9-20 using the **RECTANG** command and relative coordinate entry.
3. Create a 3.000″ × 2.000″ rectangle similar to the rectangle shown in Figure 9-21 in another location using the **RECTANG** command and the **Dimensions** option to input the length and width.
4. Create a 3.000″ × 2.000″ rectangle at a 45° angle similar to the rectangle shown in Figure 9-22 in another location using the **RECTANG** command and the **Angle** option to input the 45° angle.
5. Save the drawing as **EX9-5**.

Chamfering Corners. The **Chamfer** option allows you to draw a rectangle with four beveled, or *chamfered*, corners using the specified distance from the corner point to the beginning of each chamfer.

After you select the **Chamfer** option, Auto-CAD prompts you to *Specify first chamfer distance for rectangles <0.0000>:*. Enter the distance for the first leg of the chamfer and press **<Enter ↵>**. AutoCAD then prompts you to *Specify second chamfer distance for rectangles <0.2500>:* using the first distance as the default. Typically, you want to simply press **<Enter ↵>** to accept the default and create a rectangle with 45° chamfers, although you can specify a different distance. After entering the chamfer distances, you can create a rectangle with chamfered corners using any of the techniques already explained. Figure 9-24 shows a 3.000″ × 2.000″ rectangle drawn with 0.250″ × 0.250″ chamfered corners.

> **Note:**
> AutoCAD remembers the last chamfer distances used so that they become the default the next time you use the **RECTANG** command. AutoCAD defaults to creating a rectangle with chamfered corners the next time you use the command by displaying the current chamfer distances at the command line:
>
> Current rectangle modes:
> Chamfer=0.2500 x 0.2500

chamfer: To cut off a corner with a slight angle or bevel

Rounding Corners. The **Fillet** option allows you to draw a rectangle with four rounded, or *filleted*, corners using the specified radius from the corner point.

After you select the **Fillet** option, Auto-CAD prompts you to *Specify fillet radius for rectangles <0.2500>:*. Enter the radius and press **<Enter ↵>**. After entering the radius, you can create a rectangle using any of the techniques explained above. Figure 9-25 shows a 3.000″ × 2.000″ rectangle drawn with 0.250″ filleted corners.

> **Note:**
> AutoCAD remembers the last radius used so that it becomes the default the next time you use the **RECTANG** command. AutoCAD defaults to creating a rectangle with filleted corners the next time you use the command by displaying the current fillet radius at the command line:
>
> Current rectangle modes:
> Fillet=0.2500

fillet: To round off an inside or outside corner at a specific radius

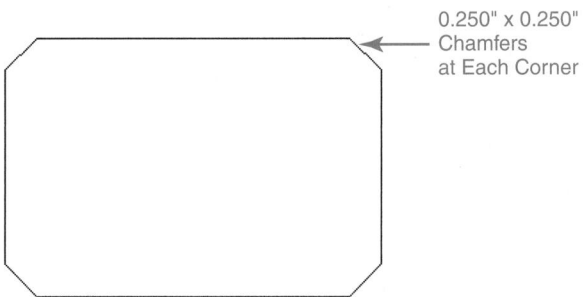
0.250" x 0.250"
Chamfers
at Each Corner

Figure 9-24 Drawing a rectangle with chamfered corners

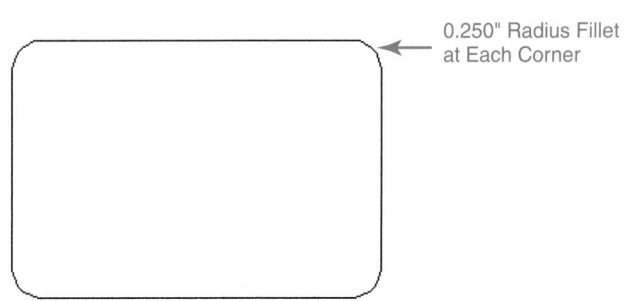
0.250" Radius Fillet
at Each Corner

Figure 9-25 Drawing a rectangle with filleted corners

Drawing a Rectangle with a Width.   The **Width** option allows you to draw a rectangle with a user-specified polyline width as explained earlier in the section "Drawing Polylines with a Width."

After you select the **Width** option, AutoCAD prompts you to *Specify line width for rectangles <0.0000>:*. Enter the line width and press **<Enter ↵>**. After entering the width, you can create a rectangle using any of the techniques explained above. Figure 9-26 shows a 3.000″ × 2.000″ rectangle drawn with a 0.100″ uniform line width.

Note:
AutoCAD remembers the last line width used so that it becomes the default the next time you use the **RECTANG** command. AutoCAD defaults to creating a rectangle with a width the next time you use the command by displaying the current line width at the command line:

```
Current rectangle modes:
Width=0.1000
```

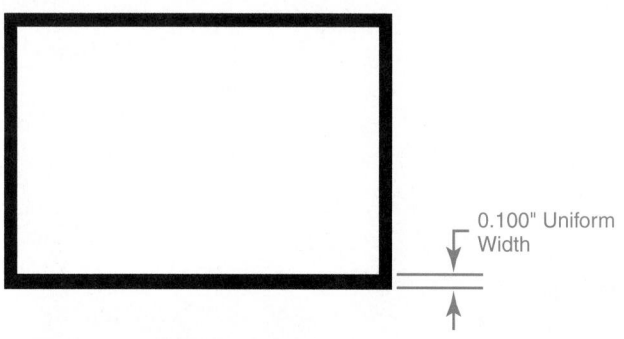

0.100" Uniform
Width

Figure 9-26   Drawing a rectangle with a uniform line width

Exercise 9-6: Drawing Rectangles with Chamfered and Rounded Corners

1. Start a new drawing using the acad.dwt drawing template.
2. Draw a 3.000″ × 2.000″ rectangle with 0.250″ × 0.250″ chamfered corners similar to the rectangle shown in Figure 9-24 using the **RECTANG** command and the **Chamfer** option.
3. Draw a 3.000″ × 2.000″ rectangle in another location with 0.250″ rounded corners similar to the rectangle shown in Figure 9-25 using the **RECTANG** command and the **Fillet** option.
4. Draw a 3.000″ × 2.000″ rectangle with a 0.100″ uniform width similar to the rectangle shown in Figure 9-26 using the **RECTANG** command and the **Width** option.
5. Save the drawing as **EX9-6**.

Polygon	
Ribbon & Panel:	Home| Draw
Draw Toolbar:	
Menu:	Draw| Polygon
Command Line:	POLYGON
Command Alias:	POL

DRAWING POLYGONS

The **POLYGON** command draws a polyline polygon with a user-supplied number of sides. See Figure 9-27.

Diamond   Hexagon   Octagon

Figure 9-27   Examples of polygons

When you start the **POLYGON** command, AutoCAD prompts you to *Enter number of sides <4>:*. You can enter a number between 3 and 1024. The length of the sides is determined either by specifying a center point and a radius or by indicating the length of a typical side, called the *edge*. The default is to specify a center point and radius; the radius indicates a circle that either inscribes or circumscribes the polygon, and the length of the sides is generated automatically.

After you specify the number of sides, AutoCAD prompts you to *Specify center of polygon or ↓*. The default is to locate a center point either by picking a point or by typing in a coordinate value. AutoCAD then asks you if you want to create the polygon inscribed inside a circle (see Figure 9-28A) with the specified radius or circumscribed on the outside of the circle (see Figure 9-28B) by prompting *Enter an option ↓*. You can type either **I<Enter ↵>** for inscribed or **C<Enter ↵>** for circumscribed or use the arrow keys to select either option if you are using **Dynamic Input**. AutoCAD then prompts you to *Specify radius of circle:*. You can either type a radius at the keyboard or pick a point as shown in Figures 9-28A and B.

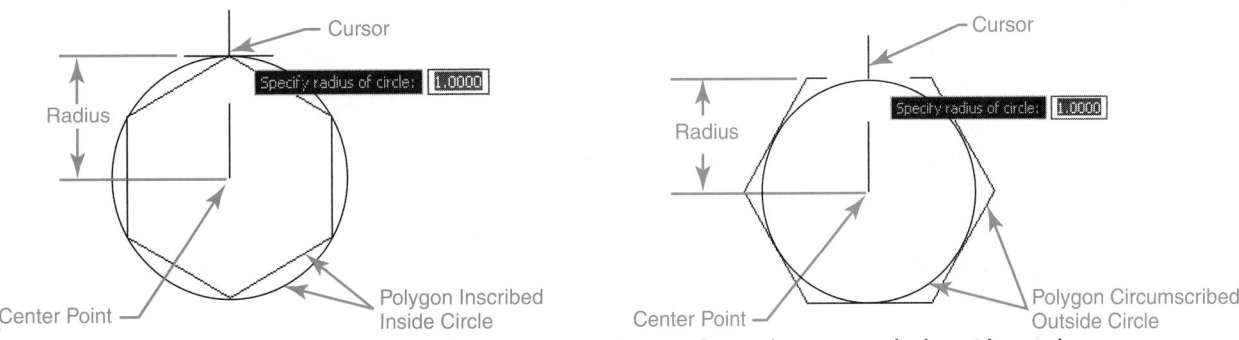

Figure 9-28A   Polygon with six sides inscribed in a circle **B** Polygon with six sides circumscribed outside a circle

Specifying the Length of a Side.   The **Edge** option allows you to create a polygon by specifying the location and length of a side. AutoCAD uses the input length to automatically create the remaining specified number of sides.

After you select the **Edge** option, AutoCAD prompts you to *Specify first endpoint of edge:*. You can either pick a point or type in a coordinate value to locate the starting point of one of the sides. AutoCAD then prompts *Specify second endpoint of edge:*. The second point determines the length for all the sides specified *and* the rotation angle of the finished polygon as shown in Figure 9-29.

Note:
AutoCAD remembers the number of sides you enter so the next time you draw a polygon you can simply press **<Enter ↵>** to draw a polygon with the same number of sides.

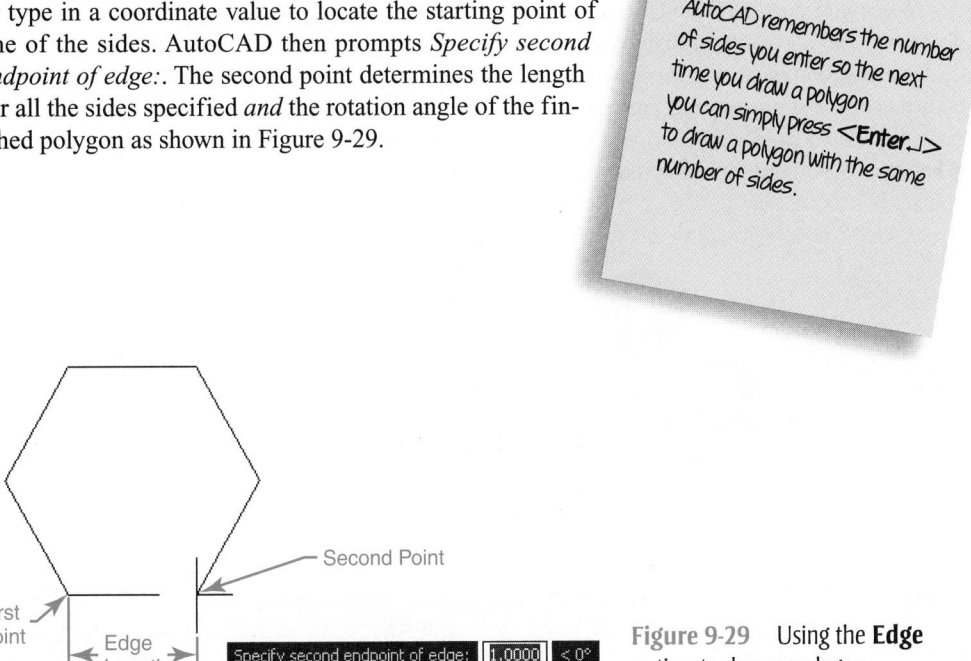

Figure 9-29   Using the **Edge** option to draw a polygon

TIP You can specify the second edge point using absolute, relative, or polar coordinate entry methods. It is also possible to use direct distance entry with either the **Ortho Mode** or **Polar Tracking** drawing tool.

Exercise 9-7: Drawing Polygons

1. Start a new drawing using the acad.dwt drawing template.
2. Draw a six-sided polygon *inscribed inside* a circle with a radius of 1.000″ similar to the polygon shown in Figure 9-28A using the **POLYGON** command.
3. Next to the polygon created in step 2, draw a six-sided polygon *circumscribed outside* a circle with a radius of 1.000″ similar to the polygon shown in Figure 9-28B using the **POLYGON** command.
4. Next to the polygon created in step 3, draw a six-sided polygon with an edge length of 0.500″ similar to the polygon shown in Figure 9-29 using the **POLYGON** command and the **Edge** option.
5. Save the drawing as **EX9-7**.

DRAWING DONUTS

Donut	
Ribbon & Panel:	Home| Draw
Toolbar:	None
Menu:	Draw| Donut
Command Line:	DONUT
Command Alias:	DO

The **DONUT** command draws a ring, or donut, with a user-specified inside diameter and outside diameter. The ring thickness equals the outside diameter minus the inside diameter. See Figure 9-30.

Figure 9-30   Examples of donuts

When you start the **DONUT** command, AutoCAD prompts you to *Specify inside diameter of donut <0.5000>:*. Enter a diameter greater than or equal to zero and press **<Enter ↵>**. AutoCAD then prompts you to *Specify outside diameter of donut <1.0000>:*. Enter a value greater than the inside diameter and press **<Enter ↵>**. AutoCAD repeatedly prompts you to *Specify center of donut or <exit>:* so you can locate multiple donuts as shown in Figure 9-31. Press **<Enter ↵>** without inputting a point to exit the command.

Figure 9-31   Drawing donuts

TIP Specifying an inside diameter equal to 0 creates a solid filled circle with the specified outside diameter.

Exercise 9-8: Drawing Donuts

1. Start a new drawing using the acad.dwt drawing template.
2. Create some donuts with an inside diameter of 0.500″ and an outside diameter of 1.000″ using the **DONUT** command.
3. Create some *solid* donuts with an inside diameter of 0.000″ and an outside diameter of 1.000″ using the **DONUT** command.
4. Save the drawing as **EX9-8**.

DRAWING REVISION CLOUDS

The **REVCLOUD** command draws a polyline of sequential arcs to form a cloud shape that can be used as a ***revision cloud*** on a drawing to highlight markups and changes. See Figure 9-32.

revision cloud: Continuous line made from arcs to resemble a cloud that is used to highlight markups and changes

Figure 9-32 Example of revision cloud

There are two different styles for a revision cloud: Normal or Calligraphy. The default style, Normal, draws the revision cloud using regular polyline arcs with no thickness. The Calligraphy style tapers the polyline arc thickness so the revision cloud looks as if it were drawn with a calligraphy pen.

When you start the **REVCLOUD** command, AutoCAD displays the default settings at the command line as follows:

```
Minimum arc length: 0.5000    Maximum arc length: 0.5000
Style: Normal
```

To create a revision cloud using the default settings, pick a point with your mouse and guide your mouse along the desired revision cloud path when AutoCAD prompts you to *Specify start point or ↓*. You *do not* need to hold the mouse button down. Simply drag the mouse to create the clouded area. When your cursor position returns to the beginning point of the first arc, the revision cloud is closed automatically as shown in Figure 9-33.

Revision Cloud	
Ribbon & Panel:	Home| Draw
Draw Toolbar:	
Menu:	Draw| Revision Cloud
Command Line:	REVCLOUD
Command Alias:	None

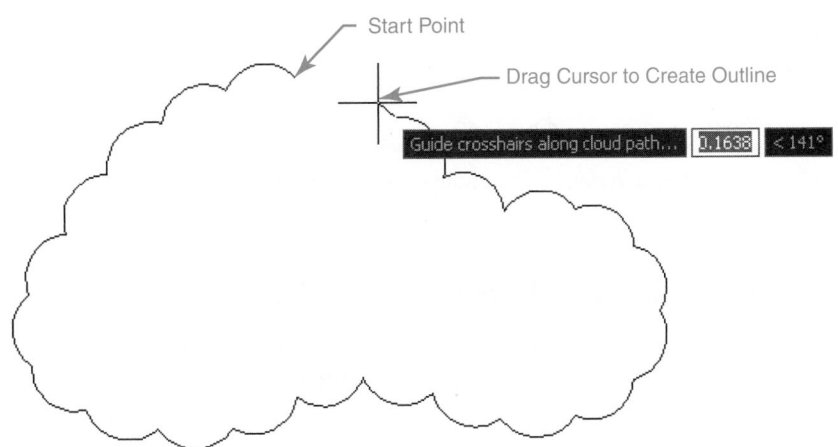

Figure 9-33 Drawing a revision cloud

AutoCAD interactively flips the arc direction based on the direction you drag your mouse after specifying the start point so that the arc bulge faces the proper way.

Changing the Arc Length

The **Arc length** option allows you to change the minimum and maximum arc length used to create the polyline arcs when the revision cloud is being drawn so that you can make them bigger or smaller.

After you select the **Arc length** option, AutoCAD prompts you to *Specify minimum length of arc <0.5000>:.* Enter the desired minimum length and press **<Enter ↵>**. AutoCAD prompts you to *Specify maximum length of arc <0.5000>:.* Enter the desired maximum length and press **<Enter ↵>**. The values become the default the next time you use the **REVCLOUD** command.

Note:
AutoCAD accounts for the drawing scale factor by multiplying the minimum and maximum arc lengths by the current dimension scale factor, which is set via the **Dimension Style Manager** or the **DIMSCALE** system variable.

FOR MORE DETAILS See Chapter 13 for more information about setting the dimension scale factor. See Chapter 1 for more information about the drawing scale factor.

Switching Styles

The **Style** option allows you to switch between the Normal style and the Calligraphy style. After you select the **Style** option, AutoCAD prompts you to *Select arc style ↓.* You can type **C<Enter ↵>** for the Calligraphy style or **N<Enter ↵>** for the Normal style or use the arrow keys to select the desired style if you're using **Dynamic Input**. Figure 9-34 shows a revision cloud drawn using the Calligraphy style.

Tapered arcs

Figure 9-34   Revision cloud drawn using the Calligraphy style

Creating Revision Clouds from Existing Objects

You can convert existing objects such as a circles, ellipses, and polylines into a revision cloud using the **Object** option. After selecting the **Object** option, AutoCAD prompts you to *Select object:.* Select the object you want to convert. After converting the object, AutoCAD allows you to change the direction of the arcs so they face in or out by prompting you if you want to *Reverse direction* ↓.

TIP

You can control whether the existing object is deleted after it is converted into a revision cloud via the **DELOBJ** system variable. Setting **DELOBJ** to **1** deletes the original object and setting **DELOBJ** to **0** maintains the original object.

Exercise 9-9: Drawing Revision Clouds

1. Start a new drawing using the acad.dwt drawing template.
2. Create a revision cloud using the Calligraphy style similar to the one shown in Figure 9-34 using the **REVCLOUD** command and the **Style** option.
3. Create a circle using the **CIRCLE** command.
4. Convert the circle to a revision cloud using the **REVCLOUD** command and the **Object** option.
5. Save the drawing as **EX9-9**.

EDITING POLYLINES

You can edit polylines after they are created using the **PEDIT** command. The **PEDIT** command allows you to:

- Convert lines and arcs to polylines
- Close and open polylines
- Join multiple polylines together
- Change a polyline's width
- Edit polyline vertices so that you can move, add, and remove points
- Curve fit a polyline
- Control a polyline's linetype generation

When you start the **PEDIT** command, AutoCAD prompts you to *Select polyline or* ↓. You can then select a polyline, a line, or an arc. If you select an object that is not a polyline, AutoCAD displays the following at the command line so you can convert it:

```
Object selected is not a polyline
```

AutoCAD allows you to convert the object by prompting *Do you want to turn it into one?* ↓. The default is **Yes** so you can simply press **<Enter ↵>** to convert the selected line or arc.

Edit Polyline	
Ribbon & Panel:	Home|Modify
Modify II Toolbar:	
Menu:	Modify|Object|Polyline
Command Line:	PEDIT
Command Alias:	PE

TIP

The **PEDITACCEPT** system variable allows you to suppress display of the `Object selected is not a polyline` prompt so that objects are automatically converted. Setting the **PEDITACCEPT** to **1** (on) suppresses the prompt. Setting **PEDITACCEPT** to **0** (off) turns the prompt back on.

You can edit multiple polylines using the **Multiple** option. To select multiple objects, either type **M<Enter ↵>** or use the arrow keys to select the option if you are using **Dynamic Input** after starting the **PEDIT** command and AutoCAD prompts you to *Select polyline or* ↓. You can then use any of the selection options to select multiple objects. If any of the objects are not polylines, AutoCAD allows you to convert them using the same approach mentioned earlier.

After a polyline is selected, or converted, AutoCAD prompts you to *Enter an option* ↓ to allow you to select an editing option. All the **PEDIT** options are explored in the following sections.

Note: You **cannot** edit polyline vertices if you select multiple polylines.

Closing and Opening Polylines

You can close or open a polyline using either the **Close** or **Open** option. The **PEDIT** command provides one option or the other depending on the polyline's current open or closed status.

To close an open polyline so that a polyline segment is created between the first and last point, you can either type **C<Enter ↓>** or use the arrow keys if you are using **Dynamic Input** in response to the **PEDIT** command *Enter an option* ↓ prompt. Figure 9-35 shows the result of selecting the **Close** option.

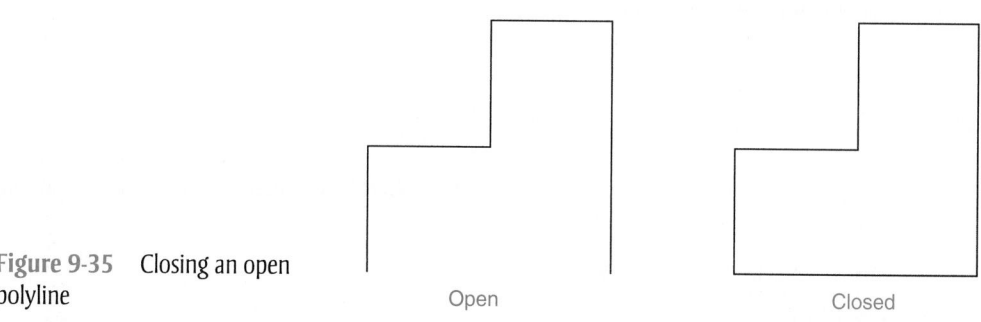

Figure 9-35   Closing an open polyline

Open   Closed

To open a closed polyline so that the polyline segment between the first and last point is removed, you can either type **O<Enter ↓>** or use the arrow keys if you are using **Dynamic Input** in response to the *Enter an option* ↓ prompt.

Note: A polyline is considered open until it has been closed using the **Close** option either when it was created or using the **PEDIT** command.

Exercise 9-10: Opening and Closing a Polyline Using PEDIT

1. Open drawing **EX9-1**.
2. Open the polyline using the **PEDIT** command and the **Open** option.
3. Close the polyline using the **PEDIT** command and the **Close** option.
4. Save the drawing as **EX9-10**.

Joining Polylines

The **Join** option allows you to join a polyline, line, or arc to one or more open polylines if their ends either connect or if they are within a specified *fuzz distance* of each other.

Applying a fuzz distance is available only when you use the **Multiple** option and is explained in detail in the following section. After you select the **Join** option, AutoCAD prompts you to *Select objects:*. You can then use any of the selection options to select one or more connected objects and press **<Enter ↓>** as shown in Figure 9-36.

Note: When you join objects using the **Join** option, the properties of the polyline selected first, including the polyline's ending width, are inherited by all the objects that are successfully joined.

fuzz distance: Distance used to determine if polyline end points that are not connected can be connected by extending them or trimming them, or connecting them with a new polyline segment

Line to Join

All Objects
Joined

Arc to Join

Polyline Before Join

Polyline After Join

Figure 9-36   Joining an open polyline

AutoCAD reports the success or failure of the join attempt by displaying how many objects were added to the original polyline at the command line:

`2 segments added to polyline`

It is your job to determine if all the objects were joined based on how many objects you originally selected. For instance, if you selected three objects and AutoCAD says that only two segments were added, you have a problem. You then have to inspect visually the endpoints of each object that was not joined and connect any points that are not connected. This can become a very tedious process with a complex join operation that consists of many objects. Luckily, we can use the fuzz distance mentioned earlier.

Joining Polylines That Do Not Meet.   As mentioned earlier, you can join polylines, lines, and arcs whose endpoints are not connected but are within a specified fuzz distance of each other. AutoCAD will either extend, trim, or insert a line segment in order to create the connection. To enter a fuzz distance, you *must* use the **Multiple** option explained earlier to select the objects you want to join first. If you then select the **Join** option using the same methods explained earlier, AutoCAD prompts you to *Enter fuzz distance or* ↓ after you select the objects to join. You can then enter the distance you want to close and press **<Enter ↵>**. AutoCAD displays how many segments were added at the command line in the same fashion as a regular join operation so you can determine if all the objects were joined successfully.

You can set the method that AutoCAD uses to join polylines via the **Jointype** option. After selecting the **Jointype** option, you can choose one of the following options:

- **Extend**   Joins by extending or trimming the segments to the nearest endpoints.
- **Add**   Joins by adding a straight segment between the nearest endpoints.
- **Both**   Joins by extending or trimming if possible. Otherwise joins by adding a straight segment between the nearest endpoints.

TIP

Joining a polyline removes the curve fitting from a curve fit polyline. Curve fitting polylines are explained later in this section.

Exercise 9-11: Joining Polylines Using PEDIT

1. Start a new drawing using the acad.dwt drawing template.
2. Create the drawing shown in Figure 9-37 using only the **LINE** and **ARC** commands, making sure to connect all the line and arc segments.
3. Join all the line and arc segments using the **PEDIT** command and the **Join** option.
4. Save the drawing as **EX9-11**.

Changing the Polyline Width

The **Width** option allows you to specify a new uniform width for all the polyline segments. After you select the **Width** option, AutoCAD prompts you to *Specify new width for all segments:*. Enter the new uniform width and press **<Enter ↵>** to change the width as shown in Figure 9-38.

Figure 9-37   Joining polylines using **PEDIT**

Figure 9-38   Changing the polyline width

TIP

You can vary the width from point to point by either using the **Edit vertex** option explained later or, even easier yet, using the **Properties** palette. The **Properties** palette allows you to step through each vertex of a polyline and set its width property individually.

Exercise 9-12: Changing Polyline Width Using PEDIT

1. Open drawing **EX9-11**.
2. Change the polyline width to a uniform width of **0.100″** using the **PEDIT** command and the **Width** option.
3. Save the drawing as **EX9-12**.

Editing Polyline Vertices

The **Edit vertex** option allows you to edit a polyline's vertex points individually so you can:

- Break one or more polyline segments
- Insert a vertex point
- Move a vertex point
- Regenerate the polyline
- Straighten two more polyline segments
- Attach a tangent direction
- Change the starting and ending width of a polyline segment

> **Note:**
> The **X** marker stops when you get to the last polyline point. It does not skip back to the first point.

After you select the **Edit vertex** option, AutoCAD marks the first vertex of the polyline with an **X** and prompts you to *Enter a vertex editing option:*. Pressing **<Enter ↵>** will select the default **Next** or **Previous** option. These and all the other **Edit vertex** options are explained in the following sections.

Next Option.   The **Next** option moves the **X** marker to the next polyline vertex point. To use the **Next** option, you can either type **N<Enter ↵>** or you can use the arrow keys to select the **Next**

option if you're using **Dynamic Input** at the *Enter a vertex editing option:* prompt as shown in Figure 9-39.

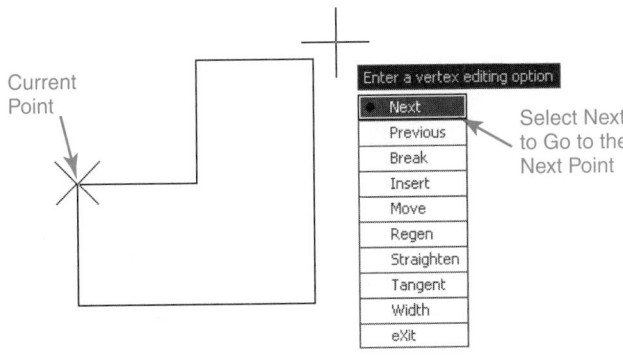

Figure 9-39   Using the **Next** option to move the current point

TIP

You can simply press the **<Enter ↵>** key if **Next** or **Previous** is the default option.

Previous Option.   The **Previous** option moves the **X** marker to the previous polyline vertex point.

Break Option.   The **Break** option allows you to break one or more polyline segments and create a gap from the current vertex point to the polyline vertex point you specify by stepping through the points using the **Next** and **Previous** options. After you select the **Break** option, AutoCAD prompts you to *Enter an option ↓*. You can press **<Enter ↵>** to select the default option or choose one of the following:

Note:
You cannot break a polyline at an endpoint.

Next: Moves the **X** marker to the next point

Previous: Moves the **X** marker to the previous point

Go: Deletes any segments and vertices between the two points you specify and returns to **Edit vertex** mode

Exit: Exits **Break** mode and returns to **Edit vertex** mode

The key to breaking a polyline is to start the break by selecting the **Break** option when the **X** marker is at the desired start point and then use the **Next** and **Previous** options to indicate where you want the break to end. When the **X** marker is on the desired endpoint, select the **Go** option by typing **G<Enter ↵>** or select the **Go** option using the arrow keys if you are using **Dynamic Input** to break the polyline as shown in Figure 9-40.

TIP

You can break a polyline at a point by simply using the **Go** option without using the **Next** or **Previous** option to move the **X** marker.

Figure 9-40 Using the **Break** option to break a polyline

Insert Option. The **Insert** option adds a new vertex point to a polyline after the current point with the **X** marker. After you select the **Insert** option, AutoCAD prompts you to *Specify location for new vertex:*. You can either pick a point or enter a coordinate value at the keyboard and press **<Enter ↵>** as shown in Figure 9-41.

Figure 9-41 Using the **Insert** option to insert a polyline vertex point

Move Option. The **Move** option moves the marked vertex. After you select the **Move** option, AutoCAD prompts you to *Specify new location for marked vertex:*. You can either pick a point or enter a coordinate value at the keyboard and press **<Enter ↵>** as shown in Figure 9-42.

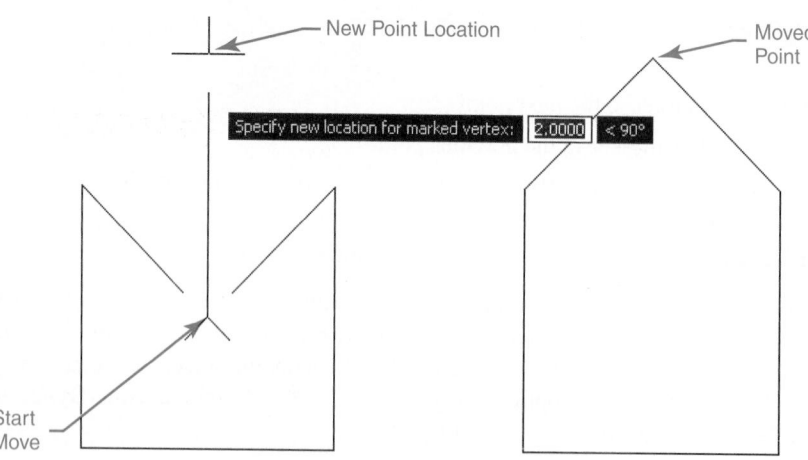

Figure 9-42 Using the **Move** option to move a polyline vertex point

Regen Option. The **Regen** option regenerates a polyline so any jagged curved segments are smoothed out.

Straighten Option. The **Straighten** option allows you to remove one or more polyline vertex points and create a straight polyline segment from the current vertex point to the polyline vertex point you specify by stepping through the points using the **Next** and **Previous** options. After you select the **Straighten** option, AutoCAD prompts you to *Enter an option* ↓. You can press **<Enter.↵>** to select the default option or choose one of the following:

Next: Moves the **X** marker to the next point

Previous: Moves the **X** marker to the previous point

Go: Deletes any polyline segments and vertices between the two points you specify, replaces them with a single straight line segment, and returns to **Edit vertex** mode

Exit: Exits **Straighten** mode and returns to **Edit vertex** mode

The **Straighten** option works similarly to the **Break** option. Select the **Straighten** option when the **X** marker is at the desired start point and then use the **Next** and **Previous** options to indicate where you want the straight segment to end. When the **X** marker is on the desired endpoint, select the **Go** option by typing **G<Enter ↵>** or select the **Go** option using the arrow keys if you are using **Dynamic Input** to delete any vertices and create a straight polyline segment as shown in Figure 9-43.

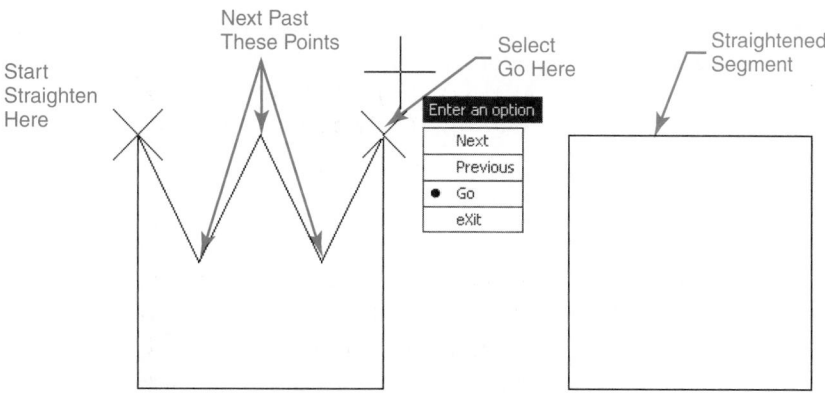

Figure 9-43   Using the **Straighten** option to straighten a polyline

Tangent Option.   The **Tangent** option attaches a tangent direction to the current vertex point for use in curve fitting. Curve fitting is explained in detail in the next section. After you select the **Tangent** option, AutoCAD prompts you to *Specify direction of vertex tangent:*. You can either pick a point or enter a tangent angle at the keyboard and press **<Enter ↵>**.

Note:
You must regenerate the polyline in order to display the new width.

Width Option.   The **Width** option changes the starting and ending widths for the segment that immediately follows the marked vertex. Press **<Enter ↵>** to use the current width. AutoCAD then prompts you to *Specify ending width <starting width>:*. You can enter a different width value to create a tapered polyline segment as shown in Figure 9-44.

eXit.   The **eXit** option exits **Edit vertex** mode. AutoCAD returns you to the **PEDIT** command *Enter an option* ↓ prompt.

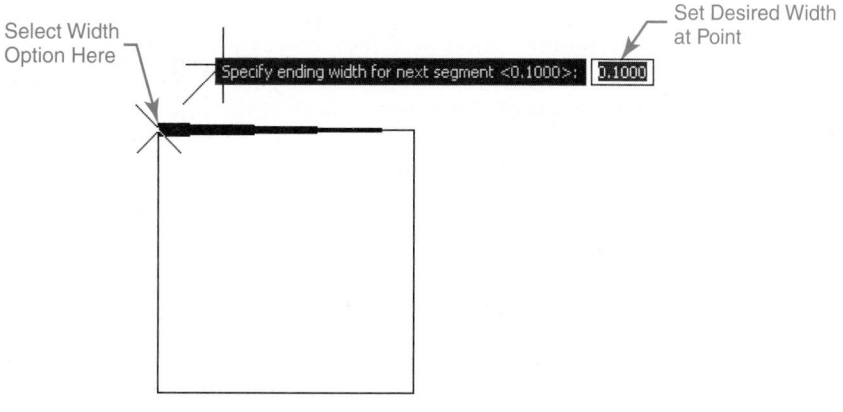

Figure 9-44   Using the **Width** option to change a polyline segment width

Exercise 9-13: Editing Polyline Vertices Using PEDIT

1. Open drawing **EX9-11**.
2. Change the polyline to look like the polyline shown in Figure 9-45 using the **PEDIT** command and the **Edit vertex** options.
3. Save the drawing as **EX9-13**.

Converting Polylines into Smooth Curves

curve fit: The process of adding vertex points to a straight line segment polyline in order to create a smooth curve

You can transform a polyline that is made up of straight line segments into a polyline with smooth curves using the **Fit** and **Spline** options. Both options allow you to *curve fit* a polyline with very different results.

After a polyline is curve fit using either option, it is possible to convert it back to straight polyline segments using the **Decurve** option. All the curve fit options are explained in detail in the following sections.

Fit Option.   The **Fit** option creates an arc fit polyline. An arc fit polyline is a smooth curve consisting of arcs joining each pair of vertex points with the curve passing through all vertices of the polyline as shown in Figure 9-46.

Figure 9-45   Editing polyline vertices using **PEDIT**

Figure 9-46   Arc fit polyline created using the **Fit** option

 TIP   You can adjust how the arcs are fit by editing the tangency direction of the polyline vertex points *before* you use the **Fit** option. See the preceding section for information about how to change a vertex point's tangency direction using the **PEDIT** command's **Tangent** option.

B-spline: An approximate spline curve also referred to as a nonuniform rational B-spline, or NURBS, curve

Spline Option.   The **Spline** option uses the vertices of the selected polyline as the control points to create a curve approximating a *B-spline* but is not as accurate as a true spline.

A spline fit polyline passes through the first and last polyline vertex points unless the original polyline was closed. The curve is pulled toward the other vertex points but does not pass through them as shown in Figure 9-47. The more control points you specify, the more pull they exert on the curve.

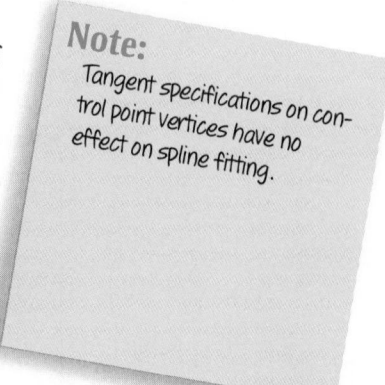

Note: Tangent specifications on control point vertices have no effect on spline fitting.

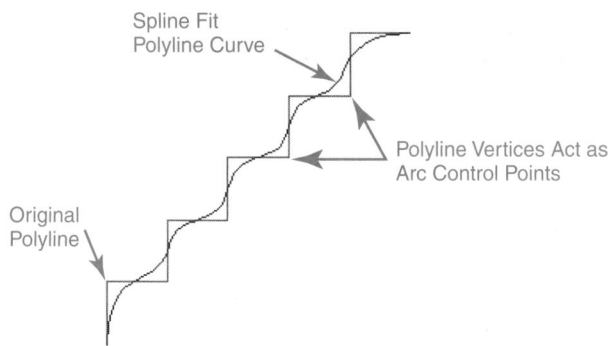

Figure 9-47   Spline fit polyline created using the **Spline** option

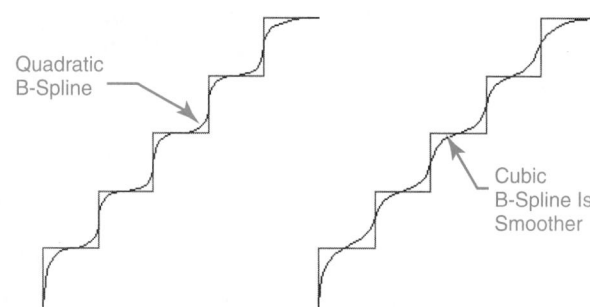

Figure 9-48   Quadratic and cubic B-splines compared

TIP

Setting the **SPLFRAME** system variable to **1** (on) turns on the spline curve control point frame the next time the drawing is regenerated. AutoCAD draws both the frame and the spline curve. Set **SPLFRAME** to **0** (off) to turn the spline curve control frame off.

AutoCAD can generate either quadratic or cubic spline fit polylines. A cubic B-spline is very smooth, much smoother than a quadratic B-spline as shown in Figure 9-48.

The default spline curve type is the smoother cubic B-spline. The **SPLINETYPE** system variable controls the type of spline curve created. Setting **SPLINETYPE** to **5** creates a quadratic B-spline. Setting **SPLINETYPE** to **6** creates a cubic B-spline.

TIP

You can also control the smoothness of a spline approximation via the **Segments in a polyline curve** setting in the **Display Resolution** area on the **Display** tab of the **Options** dialog box. This setting controls the number of line segments generated for each polyline curve. Setting this value higher means a greater number of line segments are drawn to create a more precise spline curve. The default value is 8. The maximum setting is 32767.

Decurve Option.   The **Decurve** option removes extra points inserted by an arc fit or spline fit curve and straightens all the polyline segments back to their original straight line segments as shown in Figure 9-49.

Note:
Any tangent information assigned to the polyline vertices is maintained.

Figure 9-49   Curve fit polyline decurved using the **Decurve** option

TIP You cannot use the **Decurve** option after you edit a spline fit polyline with either the **BREAK** or **TRIM** command.

Exercise 9-14: Converting Polylines into Smooth Curves

1. Start a new drawing using the acad.dwt drawing template.
2. Create an arc fit polyline similar to the polyline shown in Figure 9-46 using the **PEDIT** command and the **Fit** option.
3. Create a cubic spline fit polyline in another location similar to the polyline shown in Figure 9-48 using the **PEDIT** command and the **Spline** option.
4. Convert both curve fit polylines created in steps 2 and 3 back into straight line segments similar to those shown in Figure 9-49 using the **PEDIT** command and the **Decurve** option.
5. Save the drawing as **EX9-14**.

Controlling Polyline Linetype Generation

The **Ltype gen** option allows you to generate the polyline's linetype definition in a continuous pattern through all the vertices of the polyline. When polyline linetype generation is turned off, the linetype definition is applied to each individual polyline segment so dashes, gaps, etc. are sometimes not displayed. Figure 9-50 shows a polyline with a CENTER linetype with linetype generation turned on and off.

Note: The **Ltype gen** option does not apply to polylines with tapered segments.

Linetype Generation Off

Linetype Generation On

Figure 9-50 Polyline linetype generation turned on and turned off

EXPLODING COMPLEX OBJECTS

Explode	
Ribbon & Panel:	Home| Modify
Modify Toolbar:	
Pull-down Menu:	Modify| Explode
Command Line:	EXPLODE
Command Alias:	X

You can explode any of the complex line objects discussed in this chapter and convert them into multiple individual line and arc segments using the **EXPLODE** command.

When you start the **EXPLODE** command, AutoCAD prompts you to *Select objects:* so that you can select one or more complex objects.

If you select one or more objects that cannot be exploded, AutoCAD displays how many objects could not be exploded at the command line:

```
1 was not able to be exploded.
```

Note: When you explode a polyline with a width, all the associated width information is discarded, and the resulting lines and arcs follow the polyline's centerline.

TIP You can also explode other complex AutoCAD objects such as hatch objects, multiline text, dimensions, and blocks into their individual subobjects. These and other complex objects are discussed later in the textbook.

CHAPTER SUMMARY

This chapter showed you how to create and edit the different complex polyline objects in AutoCAD. Remember that rectangles, polygons, donuts, and revision clouds are all constructed with polylines. This means that you can use the **PEDIT** command to edit any of these objects so you can add and remove points, add or change the width, and so on.

The **EXPLODE** command can be used to explode any of the complex object types introduced in this chapter into individual line and arc segments. This can have a negative effect because it adds more information to your drawing. The complex line objects store point information in the most efficient manner. Because of this, you should use the **EXPLODE** command only when absolutely necessary.

CHAPTER TEST QUESTIONS

Multiple Choice

1. Complex line objects can be used for which of the following purposes?
    a. Drawing contour lines
    b. Calculating areas
    c. Drawing roadways
    d. All of the above

2. The command that breaks a complex line object down into individual lines and arcs is:
    a. **ERASE**
    b. **EXPLODE**
    c. **EXTEND**
    d. None of the above

3. The default polyline type that is created by the **PLINE** command is called a:
    a. POLYLINE
    b. LWPOLYLINE
    c. LIGHTPOLYLINE
    d. POLYLINELW

4. The system variable that controls whether an old format polyline is created or a new optimized polyline is created when you use the **PLINE** command is named:
    a. **PLTYPE**
    b. **PLINEWID**
    c. **PLINETYPE**
    d. **PTYPE**

5. By default, the polyline arcs created using the **PLINE** command's **Arc** option are:
    a. Created using three points
    b. Created using two points
    c. Tangent
    d. b and c

6. To create a clockwise polyline arc using the **Angle** option, you can:
    a. Enter an angle greater than 360°
    b. Enter an angle less than 0°
    c. Pick a point
    d. Change the base angle

7. You can use polyline widths to create:
    a. Arrowheads
    b. Road signs
    c. Border lines
    d. All of the above

8. You can draw a polyline rectangle with the **RECTANG** command by:
    a. Picking points
    b. Entering a length and width
    c. Specifying the total area and one side length
    d. All of the above

9. A polygon can have up to how many sides?
    a. 100
    b. 1024
    c. 2048
    d. None of the above

10. To draw a solid donut when using the **DONUT** command, specify an inside diameter:
    a. Greater than the outside diameter
    b. That is negative
    c. Of 0.000″
    d. Of 1.000″

11. The system variable that allows you to suppress the *Object selected is not a polyline* prompt when converting an arc or line into a polyline using the **PEDIT** command is named:
    a. **PEDITACCEPT**   c. **PLINEDIT**
    b. **ACCEPTPEDIT**   d. **APEDIT**

12. The maximum gap size that objects can be apart and still be joined using the **PEDIT** command's **Join** option is called:
    a. Join distance   c. Max gap
    b. Fuzz distance   d. Join gap

13. The system variable that allows you to control the type of spline fit polyline that is created is named:
    a. **SPLINEFIT**
    b. **SPLINESEGS**
    c. **SPLINETYPE**
    d. **SPLFRAME**

Matching

a. Polyline

b. Rectangle

c. Polygon

d. Donut

e. Revision cloud

f. Arc fit polyline

g. Spline fit polyline

h. Quadratic B-spline

i. Cubic B-spline

1. Multisided polyline object created by inputting the number of sides

2. Smooth polyline curve that uses the vertices of the selected polyline as the control points to create an approximate B-spline

3. Polyline object with four sides that can be created with two points

4. Smooth polyline curve consisting of arcs joining each pair of vertex points with the curve passing through all vertices

5. Complex line object made up of one or more connected line segments

6. Smoother of the B-spline curves

7. Continuous line made of arcs that resembles a cloud, used to highlight markups and changes

8. Rougher of the B-spline curves

9. Round polyline object that can be a ring or a solid circle

CHAPTER PROJECTS

Project 9-1: Circuit Board

1. Start a new drawing using the acad.dwt template. Set the **GRID** spacing to **.1**, the **SNAP** spacing to **.025**, and turn both **Grid Display** and **Snap Mode** on.
2. Create the following layers:

Name	Color	Linetype	Lineweight	Description
Fab	7	Continuous	Default	Fabrication drawing
Top	5	Continuous	Default	Top layer of metal
Bottom	6	Continuous	Default	Bottom layer of metal
Drill	7	Continuous	Default	Via drill locations
Smask	3	Continuous	Default	Top layer solder mask
Silkscreen	7	Continuous	Default	Top layer silkscreen

3. With **Snap Mode** turned on, draw the parts shown in Figure P9-1A. Each round pad consists of a 0.060″-diameter circle on the **Top** layer, a 0.020″-diameter circle on the **Drill** layer, and another 0.060″-diameter circle on the **Bottom** layer. The center of each pad should be placed on a grid point.
4. Create the board outline and move and copy the parts to arrange them as shown in Figure P9-1B.
5. Using polylines, draw the wiring on the **Top** layer as shown in Figure P9-1C. Use a polyline width of 0.006″. All points should be placed on snap coordinates.
6. Do **not** draw text or dimensions.
7. Save your drawing as **P9-1**.

Figure P9-1A

Figure P9-1B

Figure P9-1C

Project 9-2: Logo

1. Start a new drawing using the acad.dwt template.
2. Create the logo shown in Figure P9-2 using polyline objects. Do **not** draw dimensions.
3. Save your drawing as **P9-2**.

Figure P9-2

Project 9-3a: Architectural D-Size Border—Continued from Chapter 6

1. Open the template file **Architectural D-Size.DWT**.
2. Create the logo outline and graphic scale outlines as shown in Figure P9-3A using polylines and a circle on the layer **A-Anno-Ttlb-Logo**. **Do not** draw dimensions.
3. Save the drawing to a template file as **Architectural D-Size.DWT**.

Figure P9-3A

Project 9-3b: Architectural B-Size Border—Continued from Chapter 7

1. Open the template file **Architectural B-Size.DWT**.
2. Create the logo outline with the same dimensions shown in Figure P9-3A on the left side of the title block on the bottom of the border using polylines and a circle on the layer **A-Anno-Ttlb-Logo**.
3. Save the drawing to a template file as **Architectural B-Size.DWT**.

Project 9-4: Residential Electrical Plan—Continued from Chapter 8, Problem 5

1. Open drawing **P8-5** from Chapter 8.
2. Modify the drawing to match Figure P9-4. Draw the wiring using polyline objects.
3. Save the drawing as **P9-4**.

Figure P9-4

Project 9-5: Residential Architectural Plan—Continued from Chapter 9, Problem 4

1. Open drawing **P9-4** from Chapter 9, Problem 4. If you are not completing Problem 4, open **P8-5** from Chapter 8.
2. Create the following layers:

Note:
This problem continues from Problem 4—Residential Electrical Plan, presented earlier. If you are not completing Problem 4, continue from the Problem 5 drawing in Chapter 8.

Name	Color	Linetype	Lineweight	Plot/Noplot	Description
A-Eqpm-Fixd	White	Continuous	Default	Plot	Fixed equipment (fireplaces)
L-Walk	8	Continuous	Default	Plot	Driveway, patio, walkways, and steps
L-Walk-Pat	8	Continuous	Default	Plot	Cross-hatch patterns for driveway, patio, walkways, and steps

3. Draw the fireplace, patio, and driveway as shown in Figure P9-5. Use spline fit polylines to create the driveway and patio lines. Do **not** draw dimensions or text. Use appropriate layers for all objects.
4. Save your drawing as **P9-5**.

Figure P9-5

Project 9-6: Bearing—English Units

1. Start a new drawing using the acad.dwt template.
2. Create the following layers:

Name	Color	Linetype	Lineweight	Description
Object	7	Continuous	0.60 mm	Object lines
Hidden	1	Hidden	Default	Hidden lines
Center	2	Center	Default	Centerlines
Hatch	4	Continuous	Default	Hatch patterns and fills
Notes	3	Continuous	Default	Text and notes
Dims	2	Continuous	Default	Dimensions

3. Create the front and section views shown in Figure P9-6. Use appropriate layers for all objects. Create the section line as a single polyline. Do **not** draw dimensions or text. *Hint:* Use polyline segments with different starting and ending widths for the arrowhead.
4. Save the drawing as **P9-6**.

Figure P9-6

Project 9-7: Window Extrusion—Metric

1. Start a new drawing using the acadiso.dwt template.
2. Create the following layers:

Name	Color	Linetype	Lineweight	Description
Object	7	Continuous	0.60 mm	Object lines
Hidden	1	Hidden	Default	Hidden lines
Center	2	Center	Default	Centerlines
Hatch	4	Continuous	Default	Hatch patterns and fills
Notes	3	Continuous	Default	Text and notes
Dims	2	Continuous	Default	Dimensions

3. Draw the window extrusion as shown in Figure P9-7 using a single polyline on layer **Object**.
4. Draw the 150-mm-diameter aluminum billet so that the window extrusion is contained completely within as shown in Figure P9-7.
5. Do **not** draw Detail A.
6. Do **not** include notes or dimensions.
7. Save the drawing as **P9-7**.

Figure P9-7

Project 9-8: Civil Site Plan—Continued from Chapter 8

1. Open drawing **P8-8** from Chapter 8.
2. Use the **PEDIT** command to join the property boundary into a single closed polyline. Join the house outline into a single closed polyline as well.
3. Add the patio around the swimming pool and modify the driveway as shown. Join the patio lines into a single closed polyline as well as the modified driveway.
4. Save the drawing as **P9-8**.

R 15'-0"

Join Property
Boundary into a
Single Polyline

Join House
Outline into a
Single Polyline

35'-0"

48'-0"

R6'-0"

R5'-0"

Figure P9-8

Chapter Objectives

- Select a hatch boundary area
- Select and create hatch objects
- Modify hatched areas
- Match the settings of existing hatched areas
- Create solid and gradient fills
- Edit hatched areas
- Use DesignCenter to create hatch objects

INTRODUCTION

Hatching is the process of filling in a closed area with a pattern. This is typically used in cross-section or elevation drawings to denote different material usage. Hatch patterns can consist of lines and dots as well as solid colors and gradient fill patterns. Hatching must be placed within a closed area, which means that the edges of the hatch area cannot contain any gaps or openings. AutoCAD provides a couple of different ways to create and select hatch boundaries. In this chapter, you'll look at how hatch patterns are created, controlled, and modified.

hatching: The process of filling in a closed area with a pattern

HATCHING

Figure 10-1 shows some different hatched areas. The *hatch boundary* defines the area of the hatch. *Hatch islands* are closed areas inside the outer hatch boundary. When you hatch an area, you can control how island areas are dealt with. The *hatch pattern* is the pattern used to fill in the boundary. The hatch pattern has a scale, rotation angle, and origin associated with it as well.

The **HATCH** command is used to place hatch patterns. When you start the **HATCH** command, AutoCAD displays the **Hatch and Gradient** dialog box (Figure 10-2).

The **Hatch and Gradient** dialog box is divided into three general sections. The **Hatch** and **Gradient** tabs on the left side of the dialog box allow you to control how the hatch looks. The **Boundaries** area in the center of the dialog box allows you to select or create a hatch area and controls how the hatch will behave. The right side of the dialog box allows you to control how hatch boundaries are created and how island areas are treated.

hatch boundary: The edges of a hatched area

hatch islands: Closed areas within a hatch boundary

hatch pattern: The pattern used to fill a hatch boundary

> **Note:**
> If your **Hatch and Gradient** dialog box doesn't show all the options, select the arrow in the lower right corner of the dialog box. This will expand the dialog box to show all the options for the **HATCH** command.

Hatch	
Ribbon & Panel:	Home| Draw
Draw Toolbar:	
Menu:	Draw| Hatch…
Command Line:	HATCH / BHATCH
Command Alias:	H

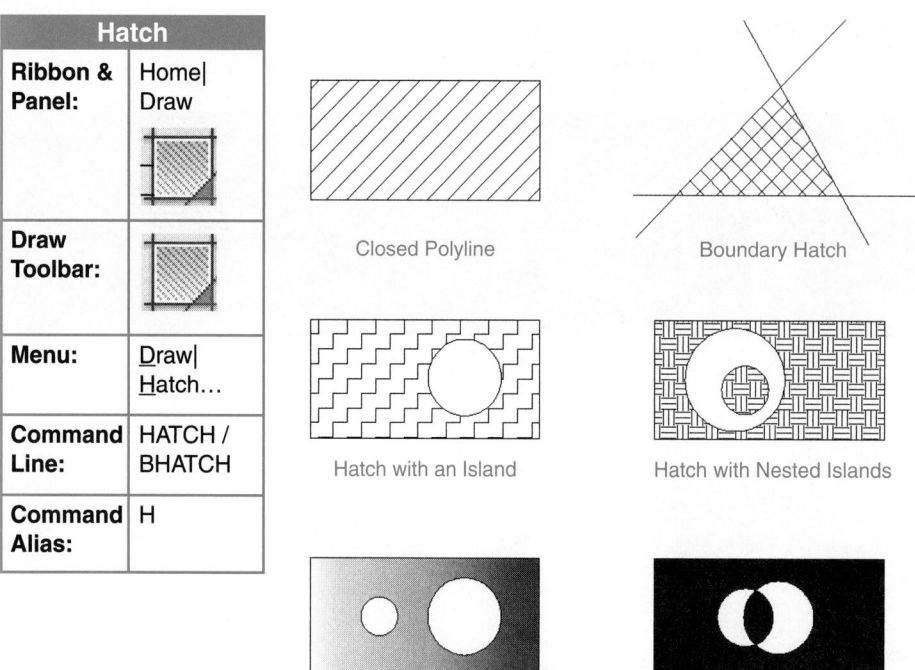

Closed Polyline   Boundary Hatch

Hatch with an Island   Hatch with Nested Islands

Gradient Fill   Solid Fill

Figure 10-1   Hatch and gradient fill examples

Figure 10-2   The **Hatch and Gradient** dialog box

Before you can create a hatch, you must specify the boundaries of the hatch area. This is done with the **Boundaries** area of the **Hatch and Gradient** dialog box.

Selecting a Hatch Area

There are two ways to select hatch boundaries. One is to select objects to use as boundaries; the other is to pick points inside closed areas of your drawing.

Selecting Objects.   If you select closed areas (such as circles or closed polylines) AutoCAD will simply hatch inside those closed areas. If you select open objects (such as lines, arcs, and open polylines), AutoCAD will attempt to calculate a hatch area. If the open objects are placed end to end and clearly define a closed area, then the results are predictable. However, if you choose overlapping objects, or if the objects don't clearly define a closed area, then your hatch area may not turn out the way you intend. Figure 10-3 shows some examples of selecting open and closed objects for hatch boundaries.

Previewing the Pattern.   Once you have defined the boundaries, you can preview how the hatch will look by choosing the **Preview** button. When you select the **Preview** button, AutoCAD will close the **Hatch and Gradient** dialog box and temporarily hatch the selected boundaries. If you're happy with the results, you can right-click or press **<Enter ↵>** to accept the hatch or press **<Esc>** to cancel the preview and return to the **Hatch and Gradient** dialog box. From there, you can modify the hatch settings and redefine the boundaries.

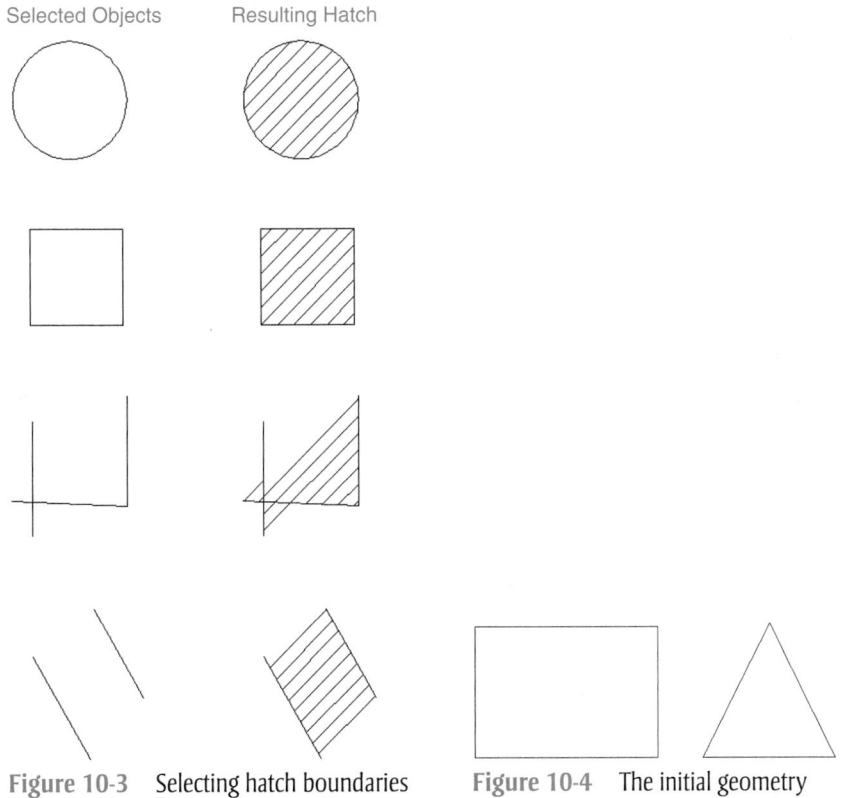

Figure 10-3   Selecting hatch boundaries   Figure 10-4   The initial geometry

Exercise 10-1: Selecting Hatch Boundaries

1. Start a new drawing using the acad.dwt drawing template.
2. Create the geometry shown in Figure 10-4. Dimensions are not important; create the rectangle using the **RECTANGLE** command, and the triangle with the **LINE** command. Make sure the lines are touching end to end.
3. Start the **HATCH** command and pick the **Add: Select objects** button. Select the rectangle and press **<Enter ↵>** to end the selection process. AutoCAD will return you to the **Hatch and Gradient** dialog box.
4. Keep all the default hatch settings and choose the **Preview** button to see a preview of the hatch pattern. Press **<Enter ↵>** to accept the hatch pattern and end the **HATCH** command. Because the rectangle was a single, closed polyline, the hatch boundary was completely defined. Your drawing should look like Figure 10-5.
5. Restart the **HATCH** command and pick the **Add: Select objects** button. Select the bottom and right legs of the triangle and press **<Enter ↵>** to end the selection process. AutoCAD will return you to the **Hatch and Gradient** dialog box.

Figure 10-5   Hatching the rectangle

Figure 10-6   An open boundary selection

6. Choose the **Preview** button to see a preview of the hatch pattern (see Figure 10-6). Because the two lines you selected don't fully define a closed area, AutoCAD creates a pattern that doesn't extend beyond the endpoint of either boundary object. Press **<Esc>** to cancel the preview and return to the dialog box.
7. Choose the **Add: Select objects** button and select the left leg of the triangle. Press **<Enter ↵>** to end the selection process. This object is added to the previously selected lines.
8. Choose the **Preview** button to see a preview of the hatch pattern. Because the triangle boundary is fully defined, the hatch pattern completely fills the hatch area. Press **<Enter ↵>** to accept the hatch pattern and end the **HATCH** command.
9. Save your drawing as **EX10-1**. Your drawing should resemble Figure 10-7.

Picking Points.   When you pick points, AutoCAD will search out from the point you pick and attempt to trace a closed area around the point you selected. If it's successful, AutoCAD will highlight the closed area and allow you to select additional points. This is a quick and easy way to create hatch areas.

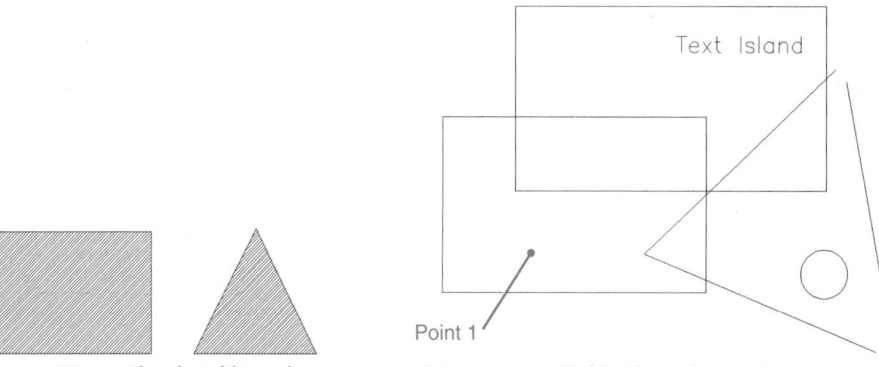

Figure 10-7   The closed boundary selection

Figure 10-8   Picking boundary points

Exercise 10-2: Picking Boundary Points

To access student data files, go to www.pearsondesigncentral.com.

1. Open drawing **EX10-2** located in the student data files.
2. Start the **HATCH** command and choose the **Add: Pick points** button. Pick point 1 shown in Figure 10-8. AutoCAD will detect the boundary and highlight the boundary area. Press **<Enter ↵>** to end the boundary detection process.
3. Choose the **Preview** button to see a preview of the hatch pattern. Press **<Enter ↵>** to accept the hatch pattern and end the **HATCH** command.
4. Save the drawing as **EX10-2**. Your drawing should look like Figure 10-9.

Figure 10-9   The hatched area

Advanced Options.   When picking points, AutoCAD provides different options that control the generation of the hatch boundaries. These advanced options allow you to control island detection, retain the hatch boundaries, and heal or ignore gaps in the boundary edge.

Island Detection.   The **Islands** area of the **Hatch and Gradient** dialog box allows you to turn island detection on and off and tells AutoCAD how to deal with island areas when placing the hatch. The **Island detection** box allows you to turn island detection on and off. When turned off, AutoCAD will ignore any island areas and create a single boundary around the point you pick.

> **Note:**
> Text objects (text, mtext, and dimension text) are treated as though a closed box were drawn around the text. Selecting text inside a closed shape will result in the text being treated as an island within the boundary.

The **Island display style** area controls how island areas are treated when the hatch pattern is applied. The **Normal** setting applies the hatch pattern to every other nesting level starting with the outer boundary. The **Outer** setting applies the hatch pattern between the outer boundary and the first nesting level. All further nesting levels are ignored. The **Ignore** setting simply ignores all internal islands and fills the entire outer boundary with the hatch pattern. Figure 10-10 shows the effect of the different **Island display style** settings.

Figure 10-10   Island display styles

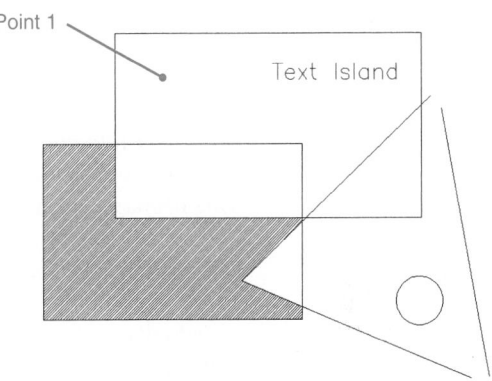

Figure 10-11   The boundary pick point

Exercise 10-3: Island Detection

1. Continue from Exercise 10-2.
2. Start the **HATCH** command and make sure the **Island detection** is enabled and the **Island display style** is set to **Normal**. **Choose** the **Add: Pick points** button and pick point 1 shown in Figure 10-11. AutoCAD will detect the boundary along with the text island. Press **<Enter ↵>** to end the boundary detection process.
3. Choose the **Preview** button to see a preview of the hatch pattern. The hatch pattern will fill around the text island. Press **<Esc>** to cancel the preview and return to the dialog box.
4. Set the **Island display style** to **Ignore** and choose **Preview** to see a preview of the hatch pattern. The hatch pattern should now fill over the top of the text island. Press **<Esc>** to cancel the preview and return to the dialog box.
5. Set the **Island display style** back to **Normal** and choose **OK** to create the hatch pattern and end the **HATCH** command.
6. Save your drawing as **EX10-3**. Your drawing should resemble Figure 10-12.

Retaining the Boundary.   When you create a boundary hatch, you have the option of keeping the boundary as either a polyline or a region. When the **Retain boundaries** option is selected, AutoCAD will create the boundary as a polyline by default. The polyline is created on the same layer as the hatch pattern.

If your drawing has a lot of hatching or contains complex boundaries, you may wish to retain your hatch boundaries and place the boundaries and hatch patterns on a separate layer. This allows you to make changes easily to the hatch patterns and boundaries and also allows you to turn off complex patterns that can sometimes get in the way when editing your drawing.

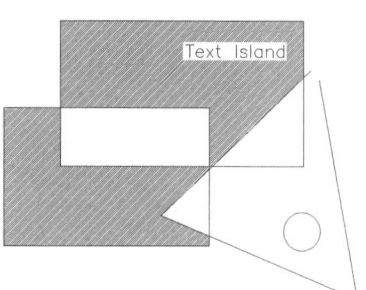

Figure 10-12   The completed hatch

Figure 10-13   The **Open Boundary Warning** box

Gap Tolerance.   The **Gap tolerance** setting allows you to heal any gaps in a boundary. When the gap tolerance is set to 0, the boundary must be completely closed in order for a valid boundary to be created. When the gap tolerance is set greater than 0, AutoCAD will attempt to determine a boundary and will ignore any gaps that are smaller than or equal to the specified tolerance. When it finds a valid boundary with gaps smaller than the specified tolerance, AutoCAD will display the **Open Boundary Warning** box (see Figure 10-13) asking if you'd like to proceed with the hatch.

When AutoCAD detects a boundary with gaps, it will project the objects out to their intersection and use this point as the corner of the boundary.

Boundary Set.   The **Boundary set** area allows you to control which objects are used when detecting a boundary. The boundary set is a set of objects used to determine boundaries when picking points. By default, everything that is visible in the current viewport is used as the boundary set. If there are objects you wish to ignore or only certain objects you wish to use, select the **New** button to create a new boundary set. The boundary set is reset to all objects upon the completion of the **HATCH** command.

Note:
If a boundary area contains gaps and is therefore not closed, AutoCAD displays a message warning **Boundary Not Closed** and displays red circles showing where the gaps are located on the drawing. You can either fix them or adjust the **Gap tolerance**.

With large drawings, AutoCAD can sometimes take a while to calculate boundary areas. If this is the case, you may want to create a new boundary set or consider turning off or freezing layers to reduce the number of calculations needed to determine the boundary.

Adding and Removing Boundaries.   Once you have selected a hatch area, you can add additional boundaries by either selecting objects or picking additional points. You can also remove boundaries using the **Remove boundaries** button. When you choose this button, AutoCAD hides the dialog box and highlights the existing boundary edges. You can simply select an edge to remove the boundary from the selection.

Creating Separate Hatches.   When you select or create more than one boundary, you have the option of creating a single hatch object that spans all the boundaries, or you can create separate hatch objects in each hatch area. The **Create separate hatches** option allows you to control this. Placing a check in the **Create separate hatches** box will create one hatch object for each closed boundary.

> **Note:**
> Hatch boundaries don't have to touch in order to create hatch objects. You can create a single hatch object that spans multiple boundaries that don't physically overlap.

Exercise 10-4: Boundary Gaps

1. Continue from Exercise 10-3.
2. Start the **HATCH** command and make sure the **Island detection** is enabled and the **Island display style** is set to **Normal**.
3. Choose the **Add: Pick points** button and pick point 1 as shown in Figure 10-14. AutoCAD will display the **Boundary Not Closed** dialog box and place red circles on the drawing where the gaps are located. Select the **Close** button to close the dialog box.
4. Press **<Enter ↵>** to display the **Hatch and Gradient** dialog box again. Set the **Gap Tolerance** to **2.00** and choose the **Add: Pick points** button and pick point 1 again. AutoCAD will display the **Open Boundary Warning** box. Choose **OK** to close the warning box. AutoCAD will create a closed boundary along with the circle island. Press **<Enter ↵>** to end the boundary detection process.
5. Choose the **Preview** button to see a preview of the hatch pattern. Press **<Enter ↵>** to accept the pattern and end the **HATCH** command.
6. Save your drawing as **EX10-4**. Your drawing should resemble Figure 10-15.

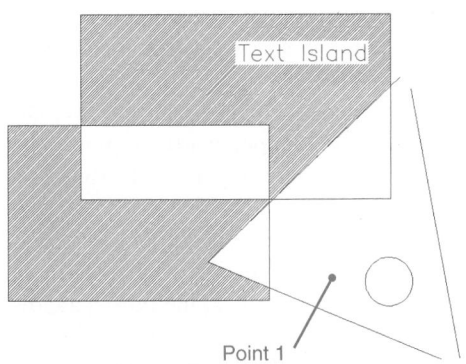

Figure 10-14   The boundary pick point

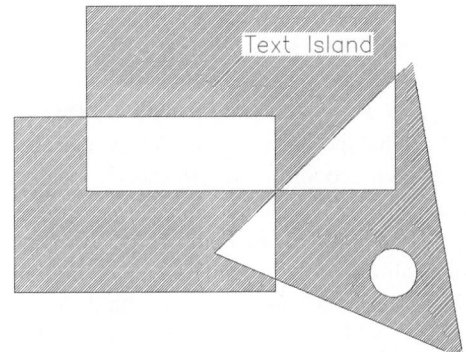

Figure 10-15   The completed hatch

Hatch Patterns

In addition to defining the boundary of the hatch area, you need to specify how the hatch pattern should look. This includes specifying the particular pattern you wish to use as well as the size or scale of the pattern, the angle of the pattern, and the hatch origin.

> **Note:**
> The acadiso.pat file contains all the pattern definitions as acad.pat but also includes support for the JIS A 0150 standard.

Specifying a Pattern.   AutoCAD hatch patterns are similar to AutoCAD linetypes. Hatch patterns are stored in external .pat files that can be modified. You can also create your own custom .pat files.

Predefined Patterns.   AutoCAD comes with a set of predefined hatch patterns (acad.pat and acadiso.pat) that contain a number of different hatch pattern definitions. To select a predefined hatch pattern, select the **Hatch** tab of the **Hatch and Gradient** dialog box and set the **Type** to **Predefined**. A list of all predefined hatch patterns will appear in the **Pattern** drop-down list. When you select a pattern from the list, the **Swatch** setting will display a small preview of the pattern.

Figure 10-16   The ANSI hatch patterns

Figure 10-17   The ISO hatch patterns

Next to the **Pattern** drop-down list is a **...** button. When you select this button, AutoCAD displays the **Hatch Pattern Palette** dialog box, which allows you to see a small preview of each pattern. The patterns are divided into four tabs: **ANSI, ISO, Other Predefined**, and **Custom** (see Figure 10-16). Simply click on the pattern you wish to use and choose **OK** (or double-click a pattern) to select it.

ANSI Patterns.   Figure 10-16 shows the **ANSI** hatch patterns. These patterns are generally used to denote materials in mechanical drawings.

ISO Patterns.   AutoCAD's 14 **ISO** patterns are designed to comply with the ISO/DIS 12011 linetype specification. When you select an ISO pattern, the **ISO pen width** drop-down list is enabled and allows you to specify a pen width for the hatch pattern. Figure 10-17 shows the predefined ISO patterns.

Other Predefined Patterns.   The **Other Predefined** patterns are designed for a variety of applications. Included in this selection of hatch patterns are a number of patterns that start with AR-. These patterns are architectural in nature and are larger in scale than the other patterns. Figure 10-18 shows the **Other Predefined** patterns.

Specifying an Angle and Scale.   Like linetypes, .pat files describe the length, spacing, and angles of the lines within the pattern. For example, the ANSI31 pattern is defined as a continuous line segment, rotated 45° with 0.125 unit between each parallel line. The **Angle and scale** area of the **Hatch and Gradient** dialog box allows you to add additional rotation and a scaling factor to your hatch pattern. The **Angle** drop-down list contains a number of common rotation angle values. You can select a value from the list or simply type in the rotation angle.

The **Scale** drop-down list contains a list of commonly used scales. Like the **Angle** list, you can select one of the listed scales or simply type in a scale factor. The **Angle** and **Scale** values are applied to the defined scale of the selected pattern. For example, using the ANSI31 pattern already described, specifying a scale factor of **2** and a rotation angle of **45°** would result in a pattern of 90° lines (45° + 45°) with a spacing of 0.25 unit (0.125 × 2).

When working in paper space, you can also choose the **Relative to paper space** option. This will add an additional scale factor to the hatch that will adjust the hatch pattern scale according to the viewport scale factor.

Annotative Scale.   As mentioned in Chapter 1, you can automatically scale annotation objects such as text, dimension, and hatching using the AutoCAD **Annotation Scale** feature on the right side of the Status Bar at the bottom of the AutoCAD window. To enable the **Annotation Scale** feature, select the **Annotative** option in the **Options** area of the **Hatch and Gradient** dialog box. The hatch pattern will now scale automatically based on the current **Annotation Scale** when it is created.

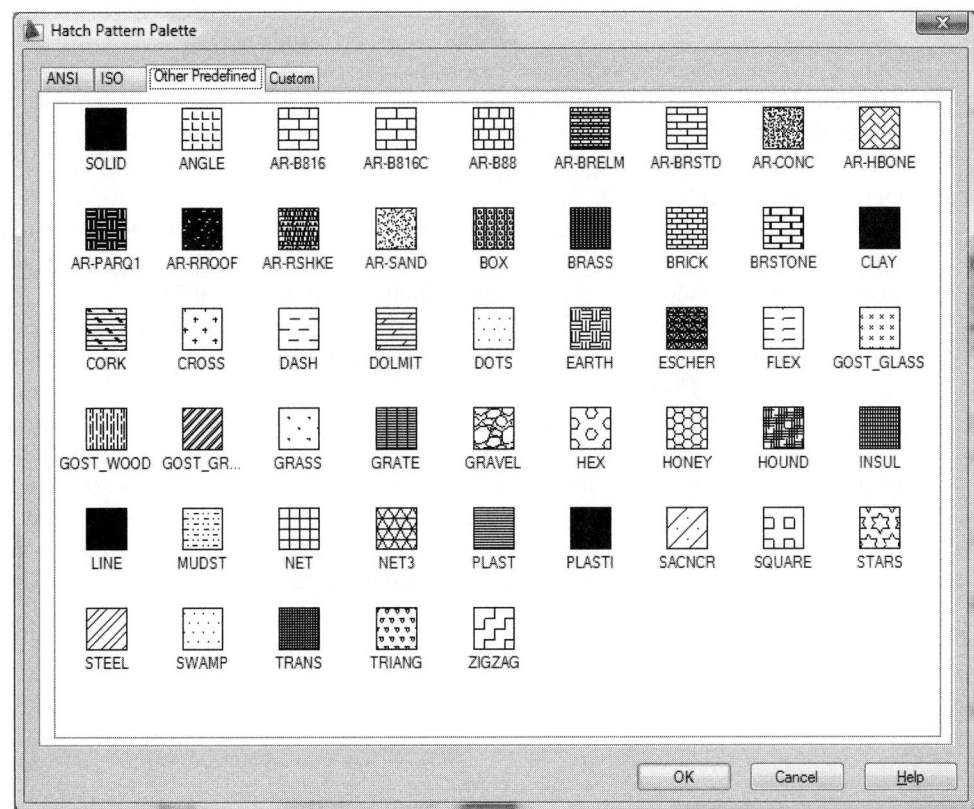

Figure 10-18 Other predefined hatch patterns

FOR MORE DETAILS See Chapter 14 for more on setting viewport scale factors and controlling the **Annotation Scale**.

Associative Hatching. In AutoCAD, associativity means a link between one drawing object and another. In Chapter 2, you saw an example of associative dimensioning. When you placed a dimension object, it was associated with the points on the objects you dimensioned. If those points moved, the dimension object moved along with it.

Associativity can also occur between a hatch object and its boundary. If the boundary edge is modified, its associated hatch objects will update and fill in the changed boundary. The **Associative** option in the **Hatch and Gradient** dialog box turns associativity on and off.

Note:
Hatch pattern associativity can be a fleeting thing. Associativity can be lost if the boundary edges change significantly. For example, if two overlapping objects were used to create a hatch boundary, modifying the objects so that they no longer overlap will cause the hatch associativity to be lost. When hatch associativity is lost, AutoCAD will display a message in the command line window: **Hatch boundary associativity removed.**

TIP If hatch associativity is removed, it is still possible to dynamically change the hatch boundary area by selecting it and using special intuitive grips. See Chapter 7 for information about using grips.

Exercise 10-5: Hatch Patterns

To access student data
files, go to
www.pearsondesigncentral.com.

1. Open drawing **EX10-5** located in the student data files.
2. Start the **HATCH** command and make sure the **Island detection** is enabled and the **Island display style** is set to **Normal**. Set the **Gap Tolerance** to **0.00**. Choose the **Add: Pick points** button and pick points 1 and 2 shown in Figure 10-19. Press **<Enter ↵>** to end the boundary selection.
3. In the **Type and pattern** area, set the **Type** to **Predefined** and select **EARTH** from the **Pattern** list.
4. In the **Angle and scale** area, set the **Angle** to **0.00** and the **Scale** to **0.50**.
5. Make sure the **Associative** and **Create separate hatches** options are checked and choose the **Preview** button to see a preview of the hatch pattern. Press **<Enter ↵>** to accept the pattern and end the **HATCH** command.
6. Zoom into the hatch boundary around the **EARTH** hatch you just created. Select the diagonal edge to activate the grips and experiment with moving the vertices of the polyline boundary around. The hatch pattern will update each time you move a vertex. When you are satisfied with the boundary changes, use the **ERASE** command to delete the diagonal **EARTH** hatch boundary lines. In the command window, AutoCAD displays the message: *Hatch boundary associativity removed*. Your drawing should look similar to Figure 10-20.

Figure 10-19   The boundary pick point   **Figure 10-20**   The **EARTH** hatch pattern

7. Restart the **HATCH** command. Choose the **Add: Pick points** button and pick points 3 and 4 shown in Figure 10-19. Press **<Enter ↵>** to end the boundary selection.
8. Select the **AR-CONC** pattern and set the **Scale** to **0.10**. Choose the **Preview** button to see a preview of the hatch pattern.
9. The pattern is a little large for the area so press **<Esc>** to cancel the preview and change the **Scale** to **0.05**. Choose the **Preview** button to see a preview of the hatch pattern and then press **<Enter ↵>** to accept the pattern and end the **HATCH** command.
10. Save your drawing as **EX10-5**. Your drawing should resemble Figure 10-21.

Solid Pattern.   Included in the **Other Predefined** patterns is a **Solid** pattern. This is not a pattern, but rather a fill color. When you specify a **Solid** pattern, the **Swatch** display changes to a color selection list that allows you to set the color for the solid fill. Choosing **Select Color...** from the drop-down list will display AutoCAD's **Select Color** dialog box, which allows you to choose colors using the ACI, True Color, or Color Book color definitions. The **Angle** and **Scale** options are also disabled because these settings are irrelevant with a solid fill.

User-Defined Patterns.   A user-defined pattern allows you to define a hatch pattern consisting of straight lines at a defined angle and spacing. The user pattern can have either a single set of parallel lines or a double set of perpendicular lines. The current linetype is used to draw the hatch pattern.

Figure 10-21   The completed hatch

Figure 10-22   User-defined hatch patterns

When specifying a user-defined hatch pattern, only the **Angle** and **Spacing** options are enabled. The **Angle** represents the angle of the lines (a setting of 0 would produce horizontal lines, 90 would produce vertical lines). The **Spacing** is the spacing between the parallel lines. When the **Double** option is checked, an additional set of lines will be drawn perpendicular to the first set of hatch lines. The perpendicular hatch lines will have the same spacing as the parallel hatch lines. Figure 10-22 shows some examples of user-defined patterns.

Custom Patterns.   When you create a custom .pat file, AutoCAD makes those patterns available in the **Custom** tab of the **Hatch Pattern Palette** dialog box. These custom patterns can be used along with all the other predefined hatch patterns.

Setting the Hatch Origin.   The **Hatch origin** area allows you to control the starting point of the hatch pattern. By default, all hatch patterns are drawn using 0,0 as a base point. This means that AutoCAD calculates where the hatch pattern will be drawn based on the hatch pattern definition starting at the 0,0 coordinate. Typically that is what you want; however, there may be times when you want the hatch pattern to start at a specific coordinate. For example, if you are using a brick or tile pattern, you may want the pattern to start with a full brick or tile in the corner of the boundary. To do this, you select the hatch origin to be the corner of the hatch boundary. Figure 10-23 shows some examples of setting the hatch origin.

Figure 10-23   Selecting a hatch origin

The **Hatch origin** area has two options. The **Use current origin** option simply uses the default hatch origin. By default this origin is 0,0 until you change it. The **Specified origin** option allows you to either select an origin point in your drawing or use a predefined point along the boundary edge. Once you specify a new origin, placing a check in the **Store as default origin** box will retain that point at the new default hatch origin.

Exercise 10-6: Creating a Solid Fill

1. Open drawing **EX10-6** located in the student data files.
2. Start the **HATCH** command and make sure the **Island detection** is enabled and the **Island display style** is set to **Normal**. Set the **Gap Tolerance** to **0.00**, choose the **Add: Pick points** button, and pick the three points shown in Figure 10-24. Press **<Enter ↵>** to end the boundary selection.

To access student data files, go to www.pearsondesigncentral.com.

Figure 10-24   The
boundary pick points

Figure 10-25   Solid fills

3. In the **Type and pattern** area, set the **Type** to **Predefined** and select **Solid** from the **Pattern** list. Select **Blue** from the **Swatch** list.
4. Choose the **Preview** button to see a preview of the hatch pattern. Press **<Enter ↵>** to accept the pattern and end the **HATCH** command.
5. Save your drawing as **EX10-6a**. Your drawing should look like Figure 10-25.

Matching Existing Hatch Patterns

If you have an existing hatch pattern in your drawing, AutoCAD can read the properties of the hatch pattern and use those settings to create a new hatch pattern. The **Inherit Properties** button in the **Hatch and Gradient** dialog box allows you to select an existing hatch pattern from your drawing and will use the properties of the selected hatch as the default values in the dialog box.

Inherit Hatch Origin.   When you inherit hatch pattern properties, you have the option of inheriting the hatch origin of the selected hatch pattern or using the currently defined hatch origin. The **Inherit options** area of the **Hatch and Gradient** dialog box allows you to choose which origin to use. The **Use source hatch origin** option will use the hatch origin of the selected hatch pattern.

Exercise 10-7: Inheriting Hatch Patterns

To access student data
files, go to
www.pearsondesigncentral.com.

1. Open drawing **EX10-7** located in the student data files. Set the layer **Fence** current.
2. Start the **HATCH** command and choose the **Inherit Properties** button. AutoCAD hides the **Hatch and Gradient** dialog box and prompts you to *Select hatch object:*.
3. Pick the brick wall pattern on the left side of the drawing. AutoCAD now prompts you to *Pick internal point or ↓*. Pick the two points shown in Figure 10-26 and press **<Enter ↵>** to return to the **Hatch and Gradient** dialog box. All the settings for the selected hatch are now the default options for your new hatch.
4. Choose the **Preview** button to see a preview of the hatch pattern. Press **<Enter ↵>** to accept the pattern and end the **HATCH** command.
5. Save your drawing as **EX10-7a**. Your drawing should look like Figure 10-27.

Draw Order

The **Draw order** setting in the **Hatch and Gradient** dialog box allows you to control the order in which the hatch pattern is drawn with respect to the boundary. The default option is to send the

Figure 10-26   The boundary pick points

Pick Points

Figure 10-27   Inheriting hatch properties

hatch pattern behind the boundary, which means that the boundary will be drawn on top of the hatch pattern. In most cases, the draw order doesn't matter; however, in cases where the boundary is on a different layer or is a different color from the hatch pattern, the draw order can affect the look of your drawing.

TIP The draw order can also affect the ability to select easily either the hatch or the boundary, especially with solid fill or gradient patterns. The object drawn on top will be selected first when you pick along a common edge.

The DRAWORDER Command.   The **Draw order** setting in the **Hatch and Gradient** dialog box affects hatch patterns only at the time it is created. Subsequent editing of the boundary edges can result in the display order being changed. In this case, you can reassign the draw order with the **DRAWORDER** command.

The **DRAWORDER** command allows you to take a selection set and either draw it on top (in front) of other objects or draw it below (behind) other objects. When you start the **DRAWORDER** command, you are prompted to build a selection set. Once you've selected the objects, you have four options: **Above objects, Under objects, Front**, or **Back**. The **Front** and **Back** options send the selected objects to either the top or the bottom of the drawing order. Objects in the front are drawn last and are therefore drawn on top of other objects. Objects in the back are drawn first and are therefore drawn behind other objects.

The **Above objects** and **Under objects** options prompt you to select a second set of objects. With the **Above objects** option, the objects in the first selection set are drawn in front of or above the objects in the second selection set. With the **Under objects** option, objects in the first selection set are drawn in back of or under the objects in the second selection set.

The drawing order affects how overlapping objects are selected. Objects on top or in front are selected before objects in back of or under other objects. This can also affect the order in which things are plotted.

GRADIENT FILLS

In addition to solid fills and hatch patterns, AutoCAD can also create gradient fills. Gradient fills create a smooth color transformation from either one color to light (or dark) or between two selected colors. Gradient fills can be created with the **Gradient** tab of the **HATCH** command or with the **GRADIENT** command.

The **GRADIENT** command displays the **Gradient** tab of the **Hatch and Gradient** dialog box. The **Gradient** options are similar to a solid hatch fill with two noticeable differences: the number of colors and the gradient pattern.

Draw Order	
Ribbon & Panel:	Home|Modify
Draw Order Toolbar:	
Menu:	Tools|Draw Order
Command Line:	DRAWORDER
Command Alias:	DR

Gradient	
Ribbon & Panel:	Home|Draw
Draw Toolbar:	
Menu:	Draw|Gradient...
Command Line:	GRADIENT
Command Alias:	None

One-Color Gradient

A one-color gradient fill creates a smooth color transition from a selected color to another shade of that color. You can select the base color you wish to use with the **...** button located under the **One color** radio button. Selecting this button brings up AutoCAD's standard **Select Color** dialog box.

Next to the color patch is a **Shade/Tint** slider bar. This slider bar controls the shade of the transition color. With the slider at the left-hand side, the transition color is black. With the slider all the way to the right, the transition color is white.

Note:
The **GRADIENT** command is actually the same command as the **HATCH** command. The only difference is that the **HATCH** command displays the **Hatch** tab by default, whereas the **GRADIENT** command displays the **Gradient** tab. Access the command by whichever name and method works best for you.

Two-Color Gradient

A two-color gradient fill transitions between two selected colors. When the **Two color** option is selected, the **Shade/Tint** slider bar is replaced with a second color patch. You can select the second transition color by picking the **...** button and selecting a color from the **Select Color** dialog box.

Gradient Pattern

There are nine predefined gradient fill patterns to choose from. You choose the pattern you want and then optionally choose a rotation angle. You can also choose to have the fill centered within the boundary or generated from the edge of the boundary. With the **Centered** option turned off, you can use the **Angle** setting to control which side the pattern generated from. Figure 10-28 shows some combinations of gradient patterns and rotation angles.

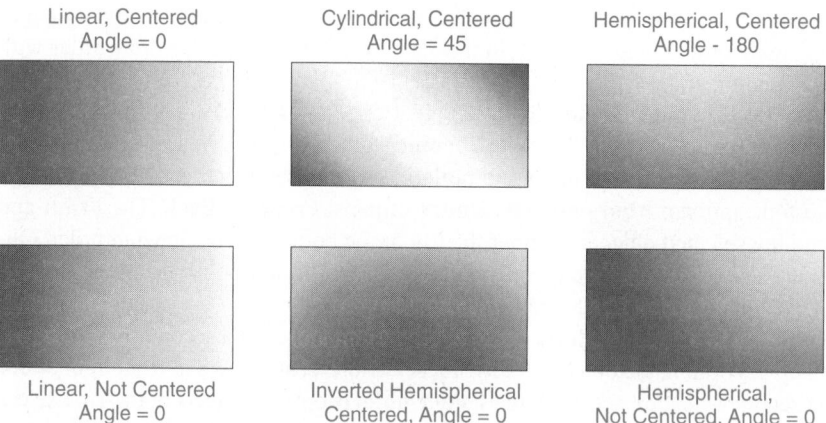

Figure 10-28 Gradient fill patterns

Linear, Centered Angle = 0

Cylindrical, Centered Angle = 45

Hemispherical, Centered Angle - 180

Linear, Not Centered Angle = 0

Inverted Hemispherical Centered, Angle = 0

Hemispherical, Not Centered, Angle = 0

Exercise 10-8: Creating a Gradient Fill

1. Continue from Exercise 10-7 and set layer **Window** current.
2. Start the **GRADIENT** command (or start the **HATCH** command and choose the **Gradient** tab). Choose **Add: Pick Points** and pick the points inside the eight window panes shown in Figure 10-29. Press **<Enter ↵>** to return to the **Hatch and Gradient** dialog box.

Pick Points

Figure 10-29 The boundary pick points

3. On the **Gradient** tab, select the **One color** option. Select the **...** button next to the color swatch and specify **ACI color 142** as the base color for the gradient fill. Choose **OK** to close the **Select Color** dialog box.

4. In the **Shade/Tint** slider, move the slider so it is almost to the right end of the bar, near the **Tint** end.

5. Select the linear pattern (the first pattern in the upper left corner) and set the **Angle** to **270**.

6. Choose the **Preview** button to see a preview of the hatch pattern and press **<Enter ⏎>** to accept the pattern and end the **HATCH** command.

7. Save your drawing as **EX10-8**. Your drawing should look like Figure 10-30.

Figure 10-30   A gradient fill

EDITING HATCH PATTERNS

Once a hatch object is created, there are a number of ways to modify it. You can change the hatch pattern along with any of the hatch options. You can even change a hatch pattern to a solid or gradient fill. This is done with the **HATCHEDIT** command.

The HATCHEDIT Command

The **HATCHEDIT** command allows you to modify any aspect of a hatch pattern. When you start the **HATCHEDIT** command, you are asked to select a hatch pattern. Once you select a hatch pattern (or a solid or gradient fill), AutoCAD displays the **Hatch Edit** dialog box (see Figure 10-31).

Edit Hatch	
Ribbon & Panel:	Home| Modify
Modify II Toolbar:	
Menu:	Modify| Object| Hatch...
Command Line:	HATCHEDIT
Command Alias:	HE

Figure 10-31   The **Hatch Edit** dialog box

TIP You can double-click on a hatch object to access the **HATCHEDIT** command quickly.

This dialog box is identical to the **Hatch and Gradient** dialog box used to create hatch objects. When you select a hatch object, all of that object's settings are shown as the default values in the **Hatch Edit** dialog box. From this dialog box, you can change any aspect of the hatch object.

One option that is available in the **Hatch Edit** dialog box that is not available in the **HATCH** command is the **Recreate boundary** button. When you select this button, AutoCAD will create a new boundary for the hatch. If the hatch is associative, you have the option of keeping the association with the original boundary or reassociating the hatch with the new boundary. The **Recreate boundary** button always retains the new boundary as a new drawing object.

Exercise 10-9: Using HATCHEDIT

1. Continue from Exercise 10-8.
2. Double-click the fence hatch pattern on the left side of the building to start the **HATCHEDIT** command. AutoCAD displays the **Hatch Edit** dialog box with the setting for the fence hatch loaded as default.
3. Select the **ANSI37** pattern from the **Pattern** list and set the **Scale** to **30**. Choose **Preview** to see a preview of the hatch pattern and press **<Enter ↵>** to accept the pattern and end the **HATCH** command.
4. Double-click the brick pattern on the right side of the drawing to start the **HATCHEDIT** command. Choose the **Inherit Properties** button and select the **ANSI37** pattern you just created. AutoCAD returns to the **Hatch Edit** dialog box with the setting for the **ANSI37** pattern loaded.
5. Choose the **Preview** button to see a preview of the hatch pattern and press **<Enter ↵>** to accept the pattern and end the **HATCH** command.
6. Save your drawing as **EX10-9**. Your drawing should look like Figure 10-32.

Figure 10-32   The modified hatch patterns

Using the Properties Palette

The **Properties** palette is another easy way to make changes to hatch objects. Although you can't make changes to the hatch boundaries, you can change the hatch pattern, scale, rotation angle, and hatch origin. You can also turn off the associativity and change the island detection method.

Trimming Hatches

When using the **TRIM** and **EXTEND** commands, you can select hatch objects as cutting/boundary edges. The edges of the individual hatch pattern lines will be used as stopping points. Only hatch patterns can be used in this manner; gradient and solid fill patterns will be ignored.

When using the **TRIM** command, you can trim hatch patterns back to selected cutting edges. When trimmed, the boundary edge of the hatch is trimmed back to the cutting edge, and the boundary is recalculated and reassociated if necessary. You cannot extend a hatch pattern out to a boundary edge.

Exercise 10-10: Trimming Hatch Patterns

1. Continue from Exercise 10-9 and thaw layer **Fence2**. Two new fence posts are displayed on the left and right sides of the drawing.
2. Zoom into the fence post on the left side and start the **TRIM** command. Select the new fence post as the cutting edge and press **<Enter ↵>** to end the edge selection.
3. Pick the fence pattern in the middle of the post to trim the hatch pattern back to the new post. You can also select the boundary line near the top of the fence post to clean up the fence post. Repeat this process on the right-hand fence post.
4. Save your drawing as **EX10-10**. Your drawing should resemble Figure 10-33.

Figure 10-33   Trimming hatch objects

Exploding Hatches

There may be times when you need to modify the individual lines within a hatch pattern. To do this, you can use the **EXPLODE** command on hatch patterns. The **EXPLODE** command will convert hatch patterns to individual line segments.

You must take care when deciding to explode a hatch pattern. Exploding a hatch pattern can create a large number of individual objects and can greatly increase the size of your drawing. You may also have a hard time finding and cleaning up all the little line objects that the **EXPLODE** command creates.

Using DesignCenter with Hatch Patterns

AutoCAD's DesignCenter can also be used to create hatch patterns. When using DesignCenter, you can find and select .pat files on your hard drive or any accessible network drive. When you select a .pat file, DesignCenter will read the file and display a list of all hatch patterns defined within that file.

To create a hatch object with **DesignCenter**, you can simply drag and drop the desired hatch pattern into any closed area on your drawing. AutoCAD will create a simple boundary hatch using the default hatch settings. You can then double-click the hatch pattern to access the **HATCHEDIT** command and make any desired changes.

> **FOR MORE DETAILS**   See Chapter 16 for more information about DesignCenter.

Exercise 10-11: Hatching with DesignCenter

1. Continue from Exercise 10-10 and set layer **Elevation** current.
2. Start the **ADCENTER** command to display the **DesignCenter** palette. Position the **DesignCenter** palette at a convenient location on your screen.
3. In **DesignCenter**, choose the **Folders** palette and navigate to the **C:\Program Files\ AutoCAD 2010\User Data Cache\Support** folder. Double-click on the acad.pat hatch pattern file. After a few moments, **DesignCenter** will show a list of all the hatch patterns defined in this file.
4. Scroll down the list and select **AR-BRELM** pattern. Drag this hatch pattern onto your drawing and release it within the boundary of the building wall. AutoCAD will fill the building wall with this pattern. Close or hide the **DesignCenter** palette.
5. Double-click the pattern you just created to start the **HATCHEDIT** command. Change the **Scale** to **2.0** and set the **Island display style** to **Outer**.
6. Choose the **Preview** button to see a preview of the hatch pattern and press **<Enter ↵>** to accept the pattern and end the **HATCH** command.
7. Save your drawing as **EX10-11**. Your drawing should resemble Figure 10-34.

Figure 10-34   Hatching
with DesignCenter

CHAPTER SUMMARY

Hatching is an integral part of drafting and design. What was once a tedious process in manual drafting is easily accomplished in Auto-CAD. AutoCAD's boundary detection and creation makes defining a hatch area a very simple process.

In this chapter you've seen how to select hatch boundary areas, specify hatch patterns and creation options, and how to preview, create, and modify hatch and fill patterns.

CHAPTER TEST QUESTIONS

Multiple Choice

1. Which of the following is *not* a way to specify hatch boundaries in the **HATCH** command?
   a. Choose the **Add: Draw boundary** button and draw a closed shape
   b. Choose the **Add: Select objects** button and select existing drawing objects
   c. Choose the **Add: Pick points** button and pick points within closed areas of the drawing
   d. Choose the **Remove Boundaries** button and select existing boundary edges to delete

2. A hatch boundary:
   a. Must consist of drawing objects connected end to end
   b. Cannot contain any islands
   c. Can consist of only straight line segments; curved boundaries are not allowed
   d. None of the above

3. The **Island display style** setting:
   a. Controls how island areas are hatched
   b. Allows you to ignore all island areas
   c. Allows you to hatch every other nested island area
   d. All of the above

4. A solid fill pattern:
   a. Can use only ACI color numbers
   b. Does not work with Color Book defined colors
   c. Can use any valid AutoCAD color
   d. Can use only RGB or HLS defined colors

5. The boundary set is:
   a. The set of objects used when detecting boundary edges
   b. The boundary edge of a hatched area

   c. Created when associative hatching is turned on
   d. None of the above

6. The **HATCHEDIT** command:
   a. Is used to explode hatch objects
   b. Is used to modify hatch patterns
   c. Does not work on gradient fills
   d. All of the above

7. If a predefined hatch pattern is defined as a set of parallel lines .5 unit apart at a 45° angle, applying a hatch scale of 2 and a hatch angle of 180° will result in an area hatch consisting of lines:
   a. 2 units apart at an angle of 45°
   b. 1 unit apart at an angle of 225°
   c. .5 unit apart at an angle of 180°
   d. 2 units apart at an angle of 180°

8. The **DRAWORDER** command allows you to move objects:
   a. To the back of all other objects
   b. To the front of all other objects
   c. To the back of selected objects
   d. All of the above

9. A one-color gradient fill transitions only between:
   a. Black and white
   b. A selected color and white
   c. A selected color and black
   d. None of the above

10. Hatch patterns can be:
    a. Exploded
    b. Used as edges in the **TRIM** and **EXTEND** commands
    c. Modified with the **TRIM** command
    d. All of the above

Matching

a. Hatching

b. Gradient fill

c. Hatch boundary

d. Associativity

e. Hatch islands

f. Gap tolerance

g. Boundary set

1. A file that contains hatch pattern definitions

2. A link between two drawing objects so that when one changes, the other updates

3. Used to place overlapping objects on top of one another

4. A solid pattern with a smooth transition from one color to another

5. The allowable open area allowed when detecting boundary edges

6. Closed areas within a hatch boundary

7. The process of filling in a closed area with a pattern

h. Hatch pattern

i. ACAD.PAT

j. **DRAWORDER**

8. The set of objects used when detecting boundary edges

9. The edges of a hatched area

10. The pattern used to fill a hatched area

CHAPTER PROJECTS

Project 10-1a: Calculator—Continued from Chapter 5

1. Open the drawing **P5-1** from Chapter 5.
2. Create the solid and gradient fill areas shown in Figure P10-1A. Experiment with different gradient settings to achieve the desired effect.
3. Save your drawing as **P10-1A**.

Figure P10-1A

Project 10-1b: Circuit Board—Continued from Chapter 9

1. Open drawing **P9-1** from Chapter 9.
2. Using polylines, draw the wiring shown in Figure P10-1B on the **Bottom** layer.
3. Create the solid fill areas shown in Figure P10-1C on the **Smask** layer. Use the **ANSI31** pattern with a scale of **.25**. *Hint:* Draw the outer boundary and then freeze the **Silkscreen, Top,** and **Bottom** layers before hatching.
4. Save your drawing as **P10-1B**.

Figure P10-1B

Figure P10-1C

Project 10-2: Logo—Continued from Chapter 9

1. Open drawing **P9-2** from Chapter 9.
2. Create the solid fill areas shown in Figure P10-2.
3. Save your drawing as **P10-2**.

Figure P10-2

Project 10-3a: Architectural D-Size Border—Continued from Chapter 9

1. Open the template file **Architectural D-Size.DWT**.
2. Hatch the logo outline as shown in Figure P10-3A using a two-color gradient hatch on the layer **A-Anno-Ttlb-Logo**.
3. Hatch the graphic scale outline as shown in Figure P10-3A using a the **Solid** hatch on the layer **A-Anno-Ttlb-Text**.
4. Save the drawing to a template file as **Architectural D-Size.DWT**.

Figure P10-3A

Project 10-3b: Architectural B-Size Border—Continued from Chapter 9

1. Open the template file **Architectural B-Size.DWT**.
2. Hatch the logo outline similar to what is shown in Figure P10-3A using a two-color gradient hatch on the layer **A-Anno-Ttlb-Logo**.
3. Save the drawing to a template file as **Architectural B-Size.DWT**.

Project 10-4: Electrical Distribution Panel—Continued from Chapter 7

1. Open drawing **P7-4** from Chapter 7.
2. Add the hatching shown in Figure P10-4. Make sure the hatching is placed in back of the outlines.
3. Save your drawing as **P10-4**.

Figure P10-4

Project 10-5: Residential Architectural Plan—Continued from Chapter 9

1. Open drawing **P9-5** from Chapter 9.
2. Hatch the patio and driveway as shown in Figure P10-5. Use the **GRAVEL** hatch pattern. Experiment with the scale and rotation angle to achieve the desired stone pattern.
3. Create the solid fill areas in the walls and the north arrow.
4. Use appropriate layers for all objects.
5. Save your drawing as **P10-5**.

Figure P10-5

Project 10-6: Bearing—English Units—Continued from Chapter 9

1. Open drawing **P9-6** from Chapter 9.
2. Create the hatch pattern on the **HATCH** layer as shown in Figure P10-6.
3. Save the drawing as **P10-6**.

ANSI31 Hatch Pattern
Scale: 1

Figure P10-6

Project 10-7a: Hub—Metric

1. Start a new drawing using the acadiso.dwt template.
2. Create the following layers:

Name	Color	Linetype	Lineweight	Description
Object	7	Continuous	0.35 mm	Object lines
Hidden	1	Hidden	Default	Hidden lines
Center	2	Center	Default	Centerlines
Hatch and fills	4	Continuous	Default	Hatch patterns
Notes	3	Continuous	Default	Text and notes
Dims	2	Continuous	Default	Dimensions

3. Draw the Front view and Section view of the hub shown in Figure P10-7A.
4. Draw object lines as shown in Figure P10-7A on layer **Object**.
5. Draw hidden lines as shown in Figure P10-7A on layer **Hidden**.
6. Draw centerlines as shown in Figure P10-7A on layer **Center**.
7. Adjust the **LTSCALE** system so linetypes appear properly.
8. Hatch the section view as shown in Figure P10-7A on layer **Hatch**.
9. Do **not** include text or dimensions.
10. Save the drawing as **P10-7A**.

Figure P10-7A

Project 10-7b: Window Extrusion—Continued from Chapter 9

1. Open drawing **P9-7** from Chapter 9.
2. Add the hatching to the Window Extrusion as shown in Figure P10-7B on layer **Pattern**.
3. Save the drawing as **P10-7B**.

Figure P10-7B

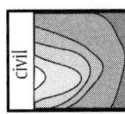

Project 10-8: Civil Site Plan—Continued from Chapter 9

1. Open drawing **P9-8** from Chapter 9.
2. Draw the site outline, elevation lines, and building site as shown in Figure P10-8. Place the corner of the site at 0,0 as shown. Draw the elevation lines approximately where shown. Do **not** include dimensions or text.
3. Save the drawing as **P10-8**.

Figure P10-8

Chapter Objectives

- Control the appearance of text using text styles and fonts
- Understand the difference between TrueType fonts and AutoCAD SHX fonts
- Create and edit multiline text
- Create and automate horizontal, diagonal, and tolerance type stacked text
- Create and edit single-line text
- Insert intelligent text fields
- Find and replace text in a drawing
- Check text spelling for a whole drawing

INTRODUCTION

They say a picture is worth a thousand words, and while the lines, arcs, and circles on a drawing can convey a great deal of design information, at the end of the day you will need to ***annotate*** your drawings in order to completely communicate your design.

annotate: To add text, notes, and dimensions to a drawing

Text on a drawing comes in many different shapes, sizes, and forms. It is used in a drawing's title block to tell the reader who created the drawing and when. Title block text might also provide information about who checked the drawing or at what revision of a design you are viewing—both very important pieces of information. Of course, there is also the text that is created directly on a drawing in the form of notes, labels, and callouts with specific design instructions, references to other drawings, part numbers, and specifications, to name but a few. Figure 11-1 shows a few examples of different types of drawing annotation.

Manually annotating a drawing on the drafting board, originally referred to as *lettering,* was a tedious and time-consuming task. In fact, some considered it an art form because of the skill and dexterity needed to annotate a drawing properly.

Those days are long gone. AutoCAD provides a number of tools that allow you to annotate your drawings, in a fashion that meets or exceeds industry drafting standards quickly, and with minimum effort. You can add multiple lines of text by simply defining a boundary area that the text should fill so that as you type, AutoCAD automatically formats the text to fit. It is also possible to add text, known as a *field,* which can automatically update itself with the current date, the name of drawing file, or the properties of an object in a drawing!

In this chapter, we look at the tools AutoCAD provides for annotating your drawing. We also examine the tools used to *edit* annotation features. Once again, AutoCAD makes it quick and easy to change information once it is created in a drawing so that updating text is as simple as double-clicking with your mouse.

Figure 11-1   Examples of drawing annotation

TIP

Text and other annotation features should be placed on a unique layer so that you can control their visibility. Text can be one of the most resource-intensive objects in a drawing. A drawing with a lot of text can become significantly bogged down. Being able to freeze text on its layer can significantly increase drawing performance.

CONTROLLING THE APPEARANCE OF TEXT

The appearance of text on a drawing is very important. Text should be created as legibly as possible so that it can be easily read and understood with minimum effort. Because of this, different standards have been established to control everything from the text font and height to how text should be located and oriented in a drawing.

FOR MORE DETAILS   See Appendix A for detailed information about drafting industry text standards.

Fonts

typeface: The style or design of a font

These days most people are familiar with text fonts. The font is what determines how text looks by defining its *typeface*.

Some of the more popular TrueType® fonts are shown in Figure 11-2.

TIP

A drawing named TrueType.DWG, located in the AutoCAD Sample folder, shows the character map for many of the TrueType fonts.

Arial, **Arial Black**, Arial Narrow
City Blueprint, Country Blueprint, Stylus BT
Courier New, Times New Roman
Swis721 BT, Swiss721 Lt BT
Impact, Comic Sans MS, **Vineta BT**
SansSerif, Trebuchet MS, Verdana
Wingdings ✌☜♋♌☞✋⌧■Ⓨ♦☺

Figure 11-2   Examples of TrueType fonts

TXT	–	AaBbCcDdEe123456790
MONOTXT	–	AaBbCcDdEe123456790
SIMPLEX	–	AaBbCcDdEe123456790
ROMANS	–	AaBbCcDdEe123456790
ROMANC	–	AaBbCcDdEe123456790
ROMAND	–	AaBbCcDdEe123456790
ROMANT	–	AaBbCcDdEe123456790
BOLD	–	**AaBbCcDdEe123456790**
COMPLEX	–	AaBbCcDdEe123456790

Figure 11-3   Examples of AutoCAD fonts

TrueType Fonts Versus AutoCAD Fonts.   The fonts shown in Figure 11-2 are known as TrueType fonts. TrueType fonts are the standard font type provided as part of Microsoft® Windows. TrueType is actually a specification developed by Apple Computer and later adopted by Microsoft that allows for scaleable text, meaning the same font can be displayed at any size and resolution. A TrueType font typically has a three-letter TTF filename extension.

In addition to TrueType fonts, AutoCAD comes with its own set of fonts referred to as *SHX fonts* because of their three-letter SHX filename extension. Some of the standard AutoCAD SHX fonts are shown in Figure 11-3.

As you can see from Figure 11-3, the AutoCAD fonts range from simple to complex. The most basic AutoCAD font is TXT.SHX. Text can be one of the most demanding factors on your computer system resources. Text with a complex font consumes more memory than text with a simple font. If you have a drawing with a lot of text, a complex double- or triple-line font takes much longer to regenerate than a simple font such as TXT.SHX.

Note:
The **TEXTFILL** system variable controls the filling of TrueType fonts while plotting and rendering. Setting **TEXTFILL=0** turns off the solid fill. Setting **TEXTFILL=1** turns the solid fill on.

TIP   A good balance of performance versus legibility is provided by both the ROMANS.SHX and SIMPLEX.SHX AutoCAD fonts.

Fonts are typically assigned to text styles because this provides the most control over the appearance of text in your drawing. It is possible to assign fonts directly to text objects using multiline text, but this approach is typically avoided because of the increased management needs. Text styles and multiline text are both discussed later in this chapter.

TIP   The **FONTALT** system variable specifies an alternate font to be used when a particular font file cannot be located on your system. By default, the **FONTALT** system variable is set to the AutoCAD SIMPLEX.SHX font.

Text Height

The height of text in a drawing is very important and, as mentioned earlier, is also determined by industry drafting standards. Text that is used for notes on a drawing is typically 0.100″ to 0.125″ (2 mm to 3 mm) tall while text for titles is typically 0.188″ to 0.25″ (5 mm to 6 mm) tall. These are the standard heights that text should be on the final plotted or printed drawing, but they are not always the heights used when text is added to a drawing. Remember from Chapter 1 that if the final printed drawing is not at a scale of 1:1, you must scale annotation features up or down so that they plot at the correct size. This is accomplished by multiplying the desired printed text height by the reciprocal of the plot or viewport scale. This multiplier is referred to as the *drawing scale factor*.

> **FOR MORE DETAILS** See Chapter 1 for more details about calculating the drawing scale factor manually.

Annotation Scale

Instead of calculating the scale factor manually as just described, it is possible to automate the process of scaling text so that it is created at the correct height for the final plotted drawing scale using the AutoCAD **Annotation Scale** feature located on the right side of the Status Bar.

When text with its **Annotative** property enabled is added to the drawing, it automatically scales up or down by the current **Annotation Scale** so that it is the correct height.

Taking it a step further, it is even possible to add additional different **Annotation Scales** to text automatically so that it can be viewed at different heights for different scale factors. Using this feature, each time the **Annotation Scale** is changed, all the text that has its **Annotative** property enabled is resized accordingly.

Note: Remember that even though text with multiple **Annotation Scales** can be viewed at multiple scales, it is in reality represented by only one text object. AutoCAD does not make multiple copies for each scale representation. In fact, the **Annotation Scale** feature was developed to eliminate the need to create new text for each scale and to have to rely on layers to turn different scales off and on.

> **FOR MORE DETAILS** See Chapter 1 for a detailed description of the **Annotation Scale** feature. See Chapter 14 for an example of applying the **Annotation Scale** features using paper space layouts and viewports.

The best way to take advantage of the **Annotation Scale** feature when you are working with text is to enable the **Annotative** feature in the current text style. Text styles are explained in detail in the next section.

Text Styles

The font, height, and other characteristics that affect the appearance of text are typically managed using text styles. All text in a drawing has a text style associated with it. When you add text to a drawing, it is created using the current text style settings. The current text style can be set by selecting it from the text style list on the **Annotation** panel on the **Home** ribbon or the **Text** panel on the **Annotate** ribbon shown in Figure 11-4, selecting it from the text style list in the multiline text editor explained later, or typed in if you are creating single-line text.

The default text style is named STANDARD, which is assigned the Arial TrueType font with a text height of 0.000″.

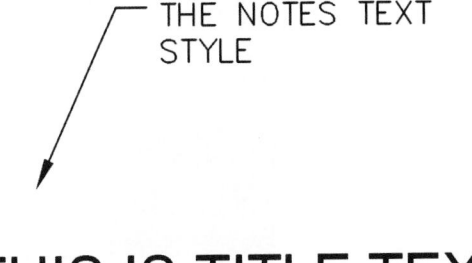

THIS IS A NOTE
CREATED USING
THE NOTES TEXT
STYLE

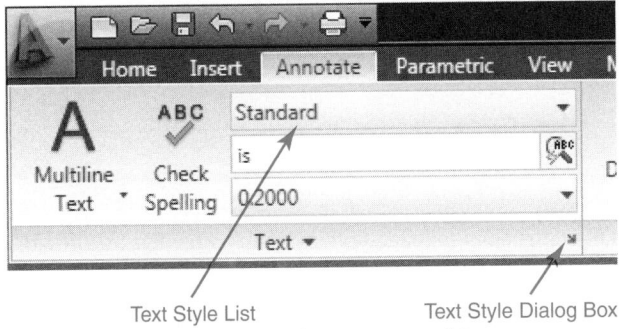

Text Style List   Text Style Dialog Box

Figure 11-4   **Text** panel on the **Annotate** ribbon

THIS IS TITLE TEXT CREATED USING THE TITLE TEXT STYLE

Figure 11-5   Examples of different text styles.

TIP   The **Annotate** ribbon provides quick and easy access to the most commonly used annotation tools. For this reason, you should select the **Annotate** tab to display the **Annotate** ribbon whenever you are adding text.

It is possible to modify the STANDARD text style or create one or more new text styles with user-defined names that can have different fonts, heights, or other properties.

Different text styles should be used to manage the different text types in a drawing. You might create a font named NOTES that is assigned the SIMPLEX.SHX font with a height set to 0.125″ that can be used for all note-type text in a drawing. You can then create another style named TITLES that is assigned the bold ARIAL True-Type font and a height of 0.25″ that can be used for all the title type text in a drawing. See Figure 11-5.

Using text styles to control the appearance of the different text types in a drawing provides a number of advantages. First, text styles make it easier to change the appearance of text if required. For instance, if the font specification changes for a certain type of text, you need to update only the corresponding text style. Otherwise, you must find every instance of text in a drawing that uses the old font and change it manually.

Using text styles to control the appearance of text also helps promote the use of drafting standards by providing the ability to have text look consistent for an entire project or organization.

Note:
Text height can either be controlled by the text style height setting, or it can be specified when the text is created. If the text height is set to 0.000″ in the text style, you must specify the text height when text is added to a drawing. If the text style height is set to any value greater than 0.000″, the text height is set automatically when text is added to a drawing.

Note:
Text style names can be up to 255 characters long and can consist of letters, numbers, and a few other special characters such as underscores, hyphens, and even spaces. The default style name created by AutoCAD is "Style" followed by an integer value (i.e., Style1, Style2, etc.).

TIP Use AutoCAD template files to your advantage by creating all your standard default text styles in a template file that can be used when you start a new drawing. You can also use DesignCenter to copy text styles from another drawing using drag-and-drop techniques.

FOR MORE DETAILS See Chapter 16 for more details about how to use DesignCenter.

The Text Style Dialog Box

The **Text Style** dialog box allows you to control and manage text styles in a drawing by allowing you to do the following:

- Set a text style current
- Add or delete a text style
- Rename a text style
- Assign or change the text style font
- Set the text height
- Apply different text effects that make text read upside down, backwards, or even vertically
- Change the text width so it is wider or narrower
- Slant text at a specified angle so it leans forward or backwards

The **Text Style** dialog box can be displayed by selecting the **Text Style** button on the **Text** panel shown in Figure 11-4, by selecting **Text Style...** from the **Format** menu, or by typing **STYLE** or **ST**.

The **Text Style** dialog box is shown in Figure 11-6. The following sections explain the different text style settings and features.

Text Style	
Ribbon & Panel:	Annotate| Text
Styles Toolbar:	
Menu:	Format| Text Style...
Command Line:	STYLE
Command Alias:	ST

Figure 11-6   The **Text Style** dialog box

Styles List.   **Styles:** is where you can select a text style to be current, rename a text style, or delete an existing text style. The text style list contains all the text styles in the drawing and displays the current text style. To change the current style, you can double-click on it, right-click and select **Set Current**, or select the **Set Current** button.

Type Style Name Here

Figure 11-7   The **New Text Style** dialog box.

To create a new text style, select the **New...** button.

The **New...** button displays the **New Text Style** dialog box shown in Figure 11-7.

The default style name is "Style" followed by a sequenced number (i.e., Style1, Style2, Style3, etc.). Typically you want to supply your own style name. One common approach is to name the style the same name as its associated font. For instance, if you are going to assign the SIMPLEX.SHX font, you would name the text style "Simplex." This way when you go to make a text style current, you can immediately tell what font will be used based on its name.

The **Delete** button on the **Text style** dialog box deletes the selected text style.

Note:
Only unreferenced text styles can be deleted. There can be no text in the drawing that uses the text style you wish to delete. In fact, the <Del> button is disabled if the selected text style is referenced anywhere in the drawing.

Font Area.   The **Font** area of the **Text Style** dialog box allows you to change the style's font name and style.

The **Font Name:** drop-down list contains a list of all the registered TrueType fonts *and* the AutoCAD SHX compiled shape fonts. The TrueType fonts are preceded with the "TT" icon, and the AutoCAD fonts are preceded with an icon that looks like a compass.

The **Font Style:** list box specifies font character formatting such as italic, bold, or regular for TrueType fonts. The **Font Style:** list is disabled when an Auto-CAD SHX type font is selected. When the **Use Big Font** check box is selected, this option changes to **Big Font Name** and is used to select a **Big Font** file name.

The **Use Big Font** check box is used to specify an Asian-language Big Font file. Big Font files provide an extended character set needed for many Asian languages with large alphabets. The **Use Big Font** check box is enabled only when an AutoCAD SHX font file is selected. TrueType fonts do not have this capability.

Note:
Changing a text style's font will automatically update all the text in the drawing that uses the selected text style with the new font. In fact, that is a good reason to use text styles to manage your fonts—you have centralized control over the text appearance.

TIP   It is possible to define several text styles that use the same font.

Size Area.   The **Size** area of the **Text Style** dialog box allows you to control the height of text based on the text style.

The **Height:** text box is where you enter the desired text height for all the text created using the selected text style. Remember earlier it was explained that if you use the default height of 0.00″, AutoCAD requires you to specify a text height each time you add text and the selected text style is current. Specifying a height greater than 0.00″ sets the text height for this style so that you do not need to specify a height every time you add text. Some TrueType fonts may be displayed at a smaller height than AutoCAD SHX fonts with the same height setting.

Selecting the **Annotative** check box enables the automated **Annotation Scale** feature discussed earlier for all text that is created using the current text style. When the **Annotative** check box is selected, the **Height:** text box is relabeled the **Paper Text Height** text box, and the **Match text orientation to layout** check box is enabled.

The **Paper Text Height** text box reflects what you want the final plotted text height to be. AutoCAD, in turn, will automatically scale the **Annotative** text up or down to match this height based on the current **Annotation Scale**.

Selecting the **Match text orientation to layout** check box automatically sets the orientation of the text in paper space viewports to match the orientation of the current layout.

> **Note:**
> Unlike changing the font, changing the height does not affect any existing text in the drawing that was created using the selected style. The new text height **will** be used by any new text that is created. Changing the height of existing text is discussed later in this chapter.

FOR MORE DETAILS   See Chapter 14 for more information about using the **Annotation Scale** feature with paper space layouts and viewports.

TIP   It is another common convention to name a text style to reflect the text height if it is set to anything other than 0.00″. For instance, a text style assigned the SIMPLEX.SHX font and a height set to 0.125″ might be named **Romans.125** or **Romans_125**. This way you know the font *and* the height when you set a text style current.

Effects Area.   The **Effects** area of the **Text Style** dialog box allows you to apply different font effects such as whether text is displayed upside down, backwards, or stacked vertically. You can also change the text width factor so that text can be made wider or narrower, as well as set at an oblique angle that will slant the text forward or backwards the specified angle—a technique that can be used to create italicized text.

The **Upside down** setting displays text upside down when it is selected. The **Backwards** setting displays text backwards. The **Vertical** setting displays text stacked vertically. See Figure 11-8. The **Vertical** setting is available only if the selected font supports dual orientation.

The **Width Factor:** setting controls horizontal text spacing. The default width is 1.0. Specifying a value greater than 1.0

> **Note:**
> The **Upside down** setting affects single-line text only. New and existing multiline text are not affected by the **Upside down** setting.

> **Note:**
> The **Backwards** setting affects single-line text only. New and existing multiline text are not affected by the **Backwards** setting.

BACKWARDS

ΠPSIDE DOWN

V
E
R
T
I
C
A
L

Figure 11-8   The **Backwards**, **Upside down**, and **Vertical** effects

WIDTH FACTOR = 0.5
WIDTH FACTOR = 1.0
WIDTH FACTOR = 2.0

Figure 11-9   Examples of **Width Factor** effects

OBLIQUE ANGLE = +30
OBLIQUE ANGLE = −30

Figure 11-10   Examples of **Oblique Angle** effects

expands the text so that it is wider. Specifying a value less than 1.0 condenses the text so it is narrower. See Figure 11-9.

The **Oblique Angle**: setting controls the oblique angle, or slant, of the text. The angle entered is measured from 90° vertical so that a positive angle slants text forward and a negative angle slants text backwards. It is possible to enter a value between −85° and 85°. See Figure 11-10.

Applying Changes to a Text Style.   The **Apply** button applies any changes made in the **Text Style** dialog box to any text in the drawing that uses the selected style.

The **Cancel** button will discard any changes and exit the **Text Style** dialog box. The **Cancel** button changes to a **Close** button whenever you click on the **Apply** button. Creating, renaming, or deleting a text style are all actions that cannot be canceled.

> **Note:**
> The **Vertical** setting affects only text styles that are assigned an SHX type font. TrueType fonts cannot be displayed vertically.

> **Note:**
> Some TrueType fonts using the effects described in this section might appear bold in your drawing. Don't be too concerned because their appearance has no effect on the plotted output.

Exercise 11-1: Creating and Modifying Text Styles

1. Start a new drawing using the acad.dwt drawing template.
2. Update the STANDARD text style so that its font is set to the SIMPLEX.SHX AutoCAD font.
3. Create a text style named **NOTES** with the following settings:
   a. Font = **Simplex.shx**
   b. Height = **0.125″**
4. Create a text style named **TITLES** with the following settings:
   a. Font = **Arial**
   b. Height = **0.25″**
5. Create a text style named **ARCHITECTURAL** with the following settings:
   a. Font = **CityBlueprint**
   b. Height = **0.125″**
6. Create a text style named **MECHANICAL** with the following settings:
   a. Font = **GDT.shx**
   b. Height = **0.100″**
7. Save the drawing as **EX11-1**.

CREATING MULTILINE TEXT

Multiline text is a complex text object that can consist of multiple lines of text that you enter in paragraph form using an in-place text editor that resembles a simple word processing program. The text is automatically formatted to fit a rectangular boundary area that you define using two corner points before the text editor is displayed. AutoCAD automatically determines the horizontal length of the line of text by inserting soft returns similar to a word processor. The vertical height of the multiline text object depends on the amount of text, not the vertical height of the bounding box. See Figure 11-11.

MULTILINE TEXT IS A COMPLEX
TEXT OBJECT THAT CAN CONSIST
OF MULTIPLE LINES OF TEXT
THAT YOU ENTER IN PARAGRAPH
FORM. THE TEXT IS
AUTOMATICALLY FORMATTED TO
FIT A RECTANGULAR BOUNDARY
AREA THAT YOU DEFINE USING
TWO POINTS BEFORE THE TEXT
EDITOR IS DISPLAYED. AUTOCAD
AUTOMATICALLY DETERMINES THE
HORIZONTAL LENGTH OF THE LINE
OF TEXT BY INSERTING SOFT
RETURNS SIMILAR TO A WORD
PROCESSOR.

Rectangular Text Boundary Area

Figure 11-11 Multiline text

The in-place text editor creates and edits the text in its current location and is transparent so you can see the drawing linework below to locate text accordingly. Some of the features and benefits of multiline text include:

- Setting tabs and indents
- Automated field insertion
- Importing external text files in ASCII or RTF format
- Enhanced symbol and special character insertion
- Bulleted and numbered list creation
- Creating stacked fractions and geometric tolerances
- Resizing the text boundary area using grips, and reformatting the text line length automatically
- The ability to switch selected text between uppercase and lowercase with the click of a mouse
- The ability to create multiple columns of text

The **MTEXT** command is used to create multiline text using the in-place text editor. Editing multiline text using the in-place editor is explained later in this chapter.

When you start the **MTEXT** command, AutoCAD displays the current text style and height at the command line as follows:

```
Current text style: "Standard" Text height: 0.2000
```

AutoCAD prompts you to *Specify first corner:* and the text "abc" is displayed on the cursor crosshairs as shown in Figure 11-12.

Because the size of the text is the *actual size* that the text will be created based on the current text height setting, it is affected by zooming in and out of your drawing. Select the first corner of the rectangular area that you want to use to create the text. AutoCAD prompts you to

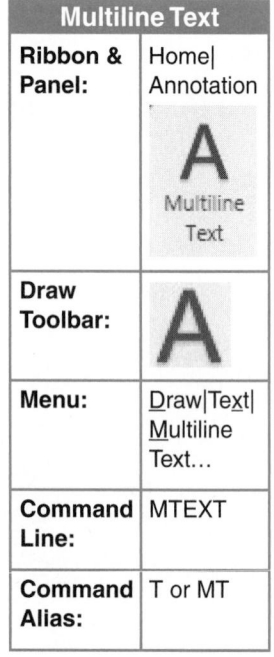

Multiline Text	
Ribbon & Panel:	Home|Annotation **A** Multiline Text
Draw Toolbar:	**A**
Menu:	Draw|Text|Multiline Text...
Command Line:	MTEXT
Command Alias:	T or MT

First Corner Point
Text Preview Is Actual Size

Figure 11-12 First corner of the multiline text boundary area

Specify first corner: 3.8869 5.2740

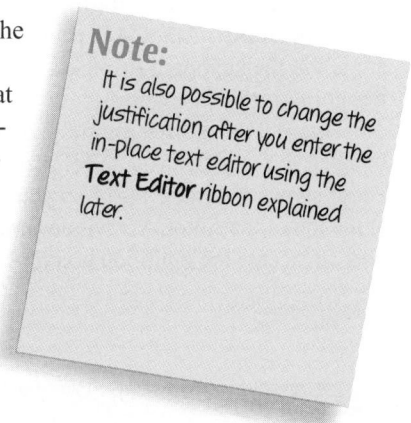

Figure 11-13   Second corner of the multiline text boundary area

Specify opposite corner or ↓ and displays a preview of the rectangular area as shown in Figure 11-13.

The arrow at the bottom of the rectangle indicates that the text flow is top to bottom. This is because the default justification for multiline text is the top left corner. It is possible to change the justification by selecting the **Justify** option when AutoCAD prompts you to *Specify opposite corner or* ↓ by typing **J<Enter ↵>** or by using your arrow keys if you are using **Dynamic Input**. The different multiline justification options are shown in Figure 11-14.

Notice how the arrows change to indicate how the justification affects the text flow.

> **Note:**
> It is also possible to change the justification after you enter the in-place text editor using the **Text Editor** ribbon explained later.

TL - Top Left

TC - Top Center

TR - Top Right

ML - Middle Left

MC - Middle Center

MR - Middle Right

BL - Bottom Left

BC - Bottom Center

BR - Bottom Right

Figure 11-14   Multiline text justification options

The other options that are available before you select the second text boundary corner point are as follows:

- Height
- Justify
- Line spacing
- Rotation
- Style
- Width
- Columns

Most options can also be set in the in-place text editor *after* selecting the second corner point, whereas the rotation angle must be indicated *before* selecting the second corner point.

The **Rotation** option allows you to specify the angle for the complete multiline text object so that the whole paragraph of text is rotated at the angle you specify. To change the multiline text rotation angle, type **R<Enter ↵>** or use the arrow keys if you're using **Dynamic Input**. AutoCAD prompts you to *Specify rotation angle <0>:*. You can enter an angle via the keyboard or pick a point in your drawing to define the angle using the first corner point as the base point.

Once all the desired multiline options are set, select the second point to define the initial text boundary area. After you select the second point, AutoCAD displays the in-place multiline text editor shown in Figure 11-15 so you can start entering text. At the same time, the current ribbon at the top of the AutoCAD window switches to the **Text Editor** ribbon shown in Figure 11-15 so you can access the multiline text tools and formatting options.

Figure 11-15   The in-place multiline text editor

The In-Place Multiline Text Editor

The in-place multiline text editor consists of the following components and features:

- In-place text editor window
- Ruler
- **Text Editor** ribbon
- Right-click shortcut menu

The in-place text editor window is where you enter the text. As mentioned, it works like most text editors and word processor software. As you type and the text reaches the end of the text editor window, AutoCAD automatically enters what is commonly referred to as a "soft" return to break the line. You can also enter your own "hard" returns if you wish by pressing the **<Enter ↵>**

key. All the other common text editor keyboard controls are available to help you navigate, select, copy, paste, delete, and edit text as you type:

Multiline Text Editor Keyboard Controls	
Key or Key Combination	**Description**
Home	Moves cursor to the beginning of the current line
End	Moves cursor to the end of the current line
\<Ctrl\> + \<Home\>	Moves cursor to the first column of the first line
\<Ctrl\> + \<End\>	Moves cursor to the end of the last line
Delete	Deletes character to the right of cursor
\<Ctrl\> + \<Del\>	Deletes complete word to the right of cursor
Page Up	Moves cursor to beginning of paragraph
Page Down	Moves cursor to end of paragraph
Arrow Keys	Moves cursor one position the direction of the arrow
\<Shift\> + Arrow Keys	Selects and highlights text under cursor as it moves
\<Bk Sp\>	Deletes character to the left of cursor
\<Ctrl\> + \<Bk Sp\>	Deletes word to the left of cursor
\<Ctrl\> + \<Shift\> + Space	Inserts a nonbreaking space
\<Ctrl\> + A	Selects all text
\<Ctrl\> + C	Copies selected text to the Windows clipboard
\<Ctrl\> + V	Pastes text from Windows clipboard at current cursor position
\<Ctrl\> + X	Cuts selected text so that the text is not copied to the Windows clipboard
\<Ctrl\> + Z	Undoes last operation
\<Ctrl\> + \<Shift\> + U	Changes selected text to all uppercase
\<Ctrl\> + \<Shift\> + L	Changes selected text to all lowercase

TIP   You can use the Windows Clipboard to copy and paste text between other Windows applications and AutoCAD.

When you are finished entering text, you have three ways to exit the multiline text editor and create the text in the drawing:

- Select the **Close Text Editor** button on the **Text Editor** ribbon.
- Click anywhere outside the text editor with your mouse.
- Hold down the **\<Ctrl\>** key and press **\<Enter ↵\>**.

To close the text editor without saving the text or any changes press the **\<Esc\>** key.

Exercise 11-2: Creating Multiline Text

1. Continue from Exercise 11-1.
2. Set the **NOTES** text style current.
3. Create the following paragraph of multiline text within an area that is 3″ wide and 3″ tall:

   ```
   The in-place text editor window is where you enter text. As men-
   tioned, it works similarly to most text editors and word processor
   software you might be familiar with. As you type and the text reaches
   the end of the text editor window, AutoCAD automatically enters what
   is commonly referred to as a "soft" return to break the line.
   ```

4. Save the drawing as **EX11-2**.

The Ruler.   The ruler indicates the width of the text using the current units setting. The double horizontal arrow at the right end of the toolbar can be used to adjust the width of the multiline text boundary box by clicking and dragging with your mouse.

     The arrow on the top left side of the ruler can be used to set the indent for the first line of a paragraph by clicking on it and dragging it to the desired position with your mouse as shown in Figure 11-16.

Figure 11-16   Setting the first line paragraph indent distance.

     The arrow on the bottom left side of the ruler can be used to set the indent for the whole paragraph by clicking on it and dragging it to the desired position with your mouse as shown in Figure 11-17.

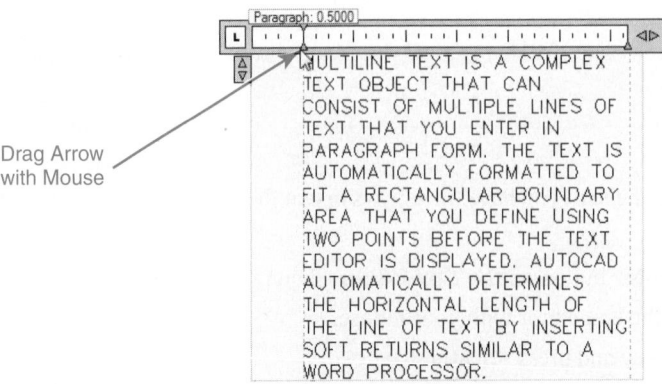

Figure 11-17   Setting the entire paragraph indent distance

Figure 11-18   Setting tab stops

You can create one or more tab stops by clicking with your mouse in the ruler where you want to locate the tab stop as shown in Figure 11-18.

The button on the far left sets the tab type. Clicking on it goes through the left, center, right, and decimal tab types.

Once a tab stop is created, you can move it by placing your cursor over the top of it and dragging it when the cursor changes to a double horizontal arrow. To remove a tab stop, simply click on it with your cursor and drag it off the toolbar.

> **Note:**
> You can turn the ruler off using the **Text Editor** ribbon explained in the next section. The ruler stays off the next time you use the multiline text editor.

Exercise 11-3: Using Tabs

1. Continue from Exercise 11-2.
2. Set the **NOTES** text style current.
3. Create the following table of multiline text within an area that is 4″ wide and 4″ tall with tab stops at every 1″:

   1   2   3   4

   5   6   7   8

   9   10   11   12

4. Save the drawing as **EX11-3**.

The Text Editor Ribbon

The **Text Editor** ribbon is used to control all aspects of the text's appearance ranging from the text style and font to the text height and justification. The various settings can be applied to new text or existing text that has already been selected (highlighted). The different **Text Editor** ribbon panels are explained in the following sections.

TIP

Remember that it is common to control most of the different format settings using text styles as explained earlier in this chapter because it provides central control over the text appearance, making text formatting easier to update. Applying different format options to text directly in the multiline text editor is considered a text style override. Using overrides is typically avoided if possible.

The Style Panel.   The **Style** list specifies the text style to use for new text or changes the text style of any selected text. Text styles and their usage were discussed in detail at the beginning of this chapter.

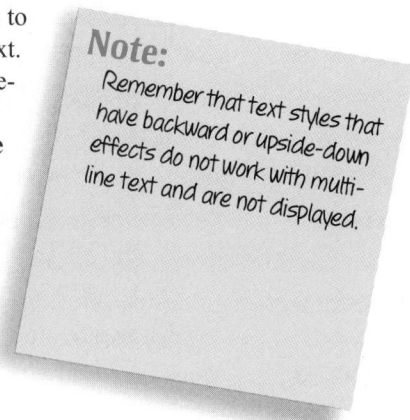

The **Annotative** button toggles the text **Annotative** property on and off for automatic text height scaling.

The **Text Height** list box sets the character height for new text or changes the height of selected text. A multi-line text object can contain characters of various heights. If the height you wish to use is not listed, you must click in the **Text Height** box and type it. It then becomes part of the list so you can select it from the list box the next time.

Note: Remember that text styles that have backward or upside-down effects do not work with multi-line text and are not displayed.

TIP   If the current text style height is set to **0.0**, you can change the default multiline text height displayed in the **Text Height** list box by setting the **TEXTSIZE** system variable. The default text height is **0.20**.

The Formatting Panel.   The **Bold** button turns bold formatting on and off for new or selected text. This option is available only for characters using TrueType fonts.

The **Italic** button turns italic formatting on and off for new or selected text. This option is available only for characters using TrueType fonts.

The **Underline** button turns underlining on and off for new or selected text.

The **Overline** button places a line over selected text.

The **Make Uppercase** button converts all selected text to uppercase.

The **Make Lowercase** button converts all selected text to lowercase.

The **Font** list specifies the font to use for new text or changes the font of any selected text. Both TrueType and the AutoCAD SHX fonts are listed. It is possible to mix different fonts within the same paragraph of multiline text.

The **Color** list specifies a color for new text or changes the color of selected text. You can also select one of the colors in the **Color** list or select the **Select Colors** option to display the **Select Color** dialog box.

The **Background Mask** button displays the **Background Mask** dialog box shown in Figure 11-19. This dialog box allows you to make the background of the finished multiline text boundary box opaque, as well as set its color. The **Use background mask** check box turns the background on and off. The **Border offset factor**: setting allows you to extend the background area beyond the original multiline text boundary area.

You can either apply a fill color to the background area via the color list in the **Fill Color** area at the bottom of the dialog box, or you can elect to use the drawing background color by selecting the **Use drawing background color** check box. Using the drawing background color allows you to block out linework underneath the multiline text boundary box so you can't see it.

Figure 11-19   The **Back-ground Mask** dialog box

The **Oblique Angle** box controls the oblique angle, or slant, of new or selected text. The angle entered is measured from 90° vertical so that a positive angle slants text forward and a negative angle slants text backward. It is possible to enter a value between −85° and 85°. You can either type a value in the box or select the up and down arrows on the right to increase or decrease the value by 1. See Figure 11-10 for examples of text that has been obliqued.

The **Tracking** box decreases or increases the space between characters for new or selected text. You can either type a value in the box or select the up and down arrows on the right to increase or decrease the value by 0.1.

The **Width Factor** box controls the text character width. The default width is 1.0. Specifying a value greater than 1.0 expands the text so that it is wider. Specifying a value less than 1.0 condenses the text. You can either type a value in the box or select the up and down arrows on the right to increase or decrease the value by 0.1. See Figure 11-9 for examples of **Width Factor** settings.

The Paragraph Panel.   The **Justification** button displays a menu with the same two-letter multiline text justification options shown earlier in Figure 11-14 (**Top Left TL**, **Middle Left ML**, etc.) when using the **Justify** option when you first start the **MTEXT** command. The **Justification** menu allows you to change the text justification within the multiline text editor.

The **Bullets and Numbering** button displays the menu shown in Figure 11-20 with the three different list formats (**Numbered, Lettered**, and **Bulleted**) along with various options:

Figure 11-20   The **Bullets and Lists** menu

- **Off**   Removes letters, numbers, and bullets from the selected text without changing the indentation
- **Numbered**   Creates a numbered list using numbers with periods for each list item
- **Lettered** cascade menu   Allows you to switch between uppercase and lowercase letters with periods for each list item. Double letters are used if the list has more items than the alphabet
- **Bulleted**   Creates a bulleted list using round filled circles for each list item
- **Start**   Starts a new numbering or lettering sequence
- **Continue**   Adds selected text to the list above and continues the numbering or lettering sequence
- **Allow Auto-list**   Toggles the **Auto-list** feature on and off. **Auto-list** creates a list when you enter a letter or number followed by a period "." or closing parenthesis ")", press the space bar or <**Tab**> key, and enter at least one character of text followed by <**Enter ↵**>
- **Use Tab Delimiter Only**   Will use only the <**Tab**> key for automatic list creation
- **Allow Bullets and Lists**   Disables the **Bullets and Numbering** feature.

The **Line Spacing** button displays a menu that allows you to set the text line spacing for the multiline text object. Line spacing for multiline text is the distance between the bottom of one line of text and the bottom of the next line of text where single spacing is 1.66 times the text height. You can set the spacing increment to a multiple of single-line spacing using the following predefined scale factors:

- **1.0x**   Single-line spacing
- **1.5x**   One-and-a-half-line spacing
- **2.0x**   Double-line spacing
- **2.5x**   Two-and-a-half-line spacing

Selecting **More...** from the **Line Spacing** menu displays the **Paragraph** dialog box so you can make additional adjustments. The **Paragraph** dialog box is explained in detail next.

Selecting the down arrow on the far right of the pane title bar displays the **Paragraph** dialog box shown in Figure 11-21 so that you can do the following:

- Add and remove tab stops
- Set left and right indents
- Set the horizontal paragraph justification

Figure 11-21   The
Paragraph dialog box

- Set the spacing between paragraphs
- Set the line spacing for the paragraph

The **Tab** area allows you to add and remove left, center, right, and decimal tab stops. To add a tab, enter the tab distance and select the **Add** button. To delete a tab, select it from the list and select the **Remove** button.

The **Left Indent** area allows you to set the first line and hanging indent distance.

The **Right Indent** area allows you to set the right side indent distance.

The **Paragraph Alignment** area allows you to control the horizontal paragraph justification, text flow, and spacing using one of the following methods:

> **Note:**
> Different tabs can also be selected from the **Tab** button on the left side of the ruler and then dragged into position.

- The **Left** option aligns text on the left-hand margin so text flows right.
- The **Center** option centers text on the centerline of the text boundary and flows both directions.
- The **Right** option aligns text on the right-hand margin so text flows left.
- The **Justified** option spreads text out to fill the text boundary width by putting space between words.
- The **Distributed** option spreads text out to fill the text boundary width by putting space between letters.

The **Paragraph Spacing** area controls the spacing between paragraphs. Selecting the **Paragraph Spacing** check box enables the **Before**: and **After**: text boxes so that it is possible to set different spacing before and after a paragraph.

The **Paragraph Line Spacing** area sets the spacing between individual lines in the current or selected paragraphs using the **Exactly, At least**, and **Multiple** options. **Multiple** is the default.

The **Paragraph Line Spacing** area controls the multiline line spacing. Line spacing for multiline text is the distance between the bottom of one line of text and the bottom of the next line. The default for single line spacing is 1.66 times the height of the text. The default spacing is **Multiple**, which is basically a multiplier that is applied to the preceding formula. The default setting is 1X, or one time. For double-line spacing, you would set **Multiple** to 2X and so on. The **Exactly** option maintains a consistent spacing using the absolute distance you specify. Using the **Exactly** option, it is possible to overlap rows. The **At least** line spacing option automatically increases line spacing to accommodate characters that are too large to fit.

Select **OK** in the **Paragraph** dialog box to exit and save your changes.

The five buttons to the right of the **Paragraph** button on the **Paragraph** panel control the horizontal justification and text spacing using the same **Paragraph Alignment** options provided in the **Paragraph** dialog box:

- The **Left** button aligns text on the left-hand margin so text flows right.
- The **Center** button centers text on the centerline of the text boundary and flows both directions.
- The **Right** button aligns text on the right-hand margin so text flows left.
- The **Justified** button spreads text out to fill the text boundary width by putting space between words.
- The **Distributed** button spreads text out to fill the text boundary width by putting space between letters.

Exercise 11-4: Formatting Multiline Text

1. Continue from Exercise 11-3.
2. Start the **MTEXT** command.
3. Define a text boundary area 3″ wide by 2″ tall.
4. Using the **Text Editor** ribbon, do the following:
   a. Set the style to **TITLES**.
   b. Set the text height to **0.125″**.
   c. Turn on the **Italic** option.
   d. Set the **Justification** to **Middle Center**.
5. Type the following paragraph:

   ```
   The in-place text editor window is where you enter text. As men-
   tioned, it works similarly to most text editors and word processor
   software you might be familiar with. As you type and the text reaches
   the end of the text editor window, AutoCAD automatically enters what
   is commonly referred to as a "soft" return to break the line.
   ```

6. Save the drawing as **EX11-4**.

The Insert Panel.   The **Columns** button displays the menu shown in Figure 11-22 that allows you to format multiline text into multiple columns. You can use either a static approach in which you specify the number of columns explicitly or a dynamic approach that creates new columns automatically as you type. Both methods allow you to specify the width and height of each column, as well as the gutter width. Special grips allow you to edit the column width and height quickly after the text is added to the drawing.

To use dynamic columns, select either **Auto height** or **Manual height** from the **Dynamic Columns** cascade menu. Both approaches use the current width of the multiline text boundary box that you defined for the initial column width. The difference is that the **Auto height** method

Figure 11-22   **Columns** menu

uses the current height of the boundary box as the column height so that when text gets to the bottom of the boundary area it automatically jumps to the next column and starts at the top. When you select **Manual height**, the text boundary box height collapses to a single row with a double arrow size control at the bottom that you must click and drag to set the column height.

TIP It is possible to ignore the column height and simply start entering text. The text will flow down in the same column using the current column width. You can then press **<Alt>** + **<Enter ↵>** to jump to another column, and it will be created using the same width and height as the first column.

To use static columns, you must select the number of desired columns (2–6) from the **Static Columns** cascade menu. The column width is determined by the number of columns and the gutter width that can be fit within the defined text boundary area.

If you need to specify more than six columns, select the **More...** menu item on the **Static Columns** cascade menu to display the **Column Settings** dialog box shown in Figure 11-23.

Figure 11-23   The **Columns Setting** dialog box

As you can see, the **Column Settings** dialog box controls all the other main column settings such as the number of columns, column width, height, and gutter width. This is also where you can turn existing columns off by selecting **No Columns** in the **Column Type** area at the top left. The easiest way to display the **Column Settings** dialog box is to select **Column Settings** from the main **Columns** menu shown in Figure 11-22.

The **Symbol** button displays a menu that allows you to insert a symbol or a nonbreaking space at the current cursor position. Some of the more commonly used symbols are listed on the menu with either their AutoCAD %% control code or Unicode string as shown in Figure 11-24.

Selecting the **Other...** menu item at the bottom of the menu displays the **Character Map** dialog box shown in Figure 11-25 so you can insert symbols that are not included on the menu. This dialog box contains the entire character set for every available font. To insert a symbol from the **Character Map** dialog box, you must first select a symbol and then click the **Select** button to place it in the **Characters to copy** box. To insert the symbol, you must select the

Note:
The **Character Map** dialog box is actually a separate program that shows up on the Windows taskbar when you display it. It must be closed and exited manually. If you do not close the dialog box, you might find yourself running multiple copies of the program if you repeatedly display it.

Figure 11-24   The **Symbols** menu

Figure 11-25   The **Character Map** dialog box

Copy button to copy the symbol to the Windows clipboard. You can then switch back to the multiline editor in AutoCAD and paste the selected symbol in the desired location.

The **Field** button allows you to insert a field using the **Field** dialog box. Fields and the **Field** dialog box are explained in detail later in this chapter.

Exercise 11-5: Creating Lists and Inserting Symbols

1. Continue from Exercise 11-4.
2. Set the **NOTES** text style current.
3. Create the following bulleted list of multiline text within an area that is 4″ wide and 4″ tall:
   - This is a degree symbol °
   - This is a plus/minus symbol ±
   - This is a diameter symbol Ø
   - This is a boundary line symbol ℞
   - This is a centerline symbol ℭ
   - This is a delta symbol Δ
   - This is a property line symbol ℞
4. Change the bulleted list to a lettered list.
5. Change the lettered list to a numbered list.
6. Save the drawing as **EX11-5**.

The Spell Check Panel.   The **Spell Check** button turns on and off the **Check Spelling As You Type** feature that allows you to check spelling as you enter text in the multiline text editor. Any word you enter is checked for spelling errors when it is completed so that any word that is misspelled is underlined in red. Spelling suggestions display when you right-click the underlined word.

The **Edit Dictionaries** button displays the **Dictionaries** dialog box explained later in "The Spell Checker" section so you can switch dictionaries to check spelling in other languages, add new words to a dictionary, and perform other dictionary management tasks.

Figure 11-26   The **Find and Replace** dialog box

The Tools Panel.   The **Find & Replace** tool displays the **Find and Replace** dialog box shown in Figure 11-26 so you can search for a specific string of text and replace it with a new string of text.

- The **Find what**: text box is where you enter the text you want to search for.
- The **Replace with**: text box is where you enter the replacement text for the text entered in the **Find what**: text box.
- Selecting the **Match case** check box allows you to search for text that matches the uppercase and/or lowercase of the text entered in the **Find what**: text box exactly.
- Selecting the **Find whole words only** check box allows you to search only for text as a complete word with a space before and after; otherwise, the search will also find text that is part of a word.
- The **Use wildcards** check box allows the use of wildcard characters in searches. For more information on wildcard searches, see the "Finding and Replacing Text" section later in this chapter.
- The **Match diacritics** check box allows you to match diacritical marks, or accents, in search results.
- The **Match half/full width forms (East Asian languages)** check box matches half- and full-width Asian characters in search results.

After all the search criteria are entered you can choose one of three options:

- Select the **Find Next** button to search for and highlight the next occurrence of the search text.
- Select the **Replace** button to replace the highlighted text in the multiline text editor to update the text with the text entered in the **Replace with**: text box.
- Select the **Replace All** button to search and replace all the text in the multiline text editor that matches the search criteria with the text entered in the **Replace with**: text box. A message box is displayed indicating how many occurrences were replaced so that you know if, and how many, text strings were replaced.

The **Import Text** button allows you to import an ASCII (American Standard Code for Information Interchange) text file or an RTF (Rich Text Format) text file into the multiline text editor. Selecting the **Import Text...** button displays the **Select File** dialog box shown in Figure 11-27 so you can navigate your computer or network and find the text file to import.

Once you locate the file, select it so it is highlighted and select the **Open** button to import the text. You can then edit the text if necessary using the standard methods explained in this chapter.

Figure 11-27   Importing a text file into the multiline text editor

TIP   You can store text that is used in multiple drawings in an external text file so that you don't have to type the text in every drawing. For instance, you might store general notes in a file named General Notes.txt. If you locate the file on a network, all team members can then import the same text file. This approach both provides consistency and increases production.

The **AutoCAPS** button turns the **AutoCAPS** feature on and off. **AutoCAPS** can be used to lock your keyboard so only uppercase letters can be entered similar to the **<Caps Lock>** key. This is a handy feature in the drafting field because most drawing notes are uppercase according to industry standards.

The Options Panel.   The **Ruler** tool toggles the ruler on and off. Once the ruler is turned off, it remains off the next time you display the in-place multiline text editor. See the preceding section "The Ruler" for detailed information about the ruler feature.

The **Undo** tool undoes actions in the multiline text editor, including changes to either text content or text formatting.

The **Redo** tool redoes actions in the multiline text editor, including changes to either text content or text formatting.

The **More** tool displays a menu with a few other multiline text options and features that are also located on the right-click menu explained in the next section.

The Right-Click Menu

The right-click shortcut menu shown in Figure 11-28 provides additional multiline text options and features, as well as access to some of the same features found on the **Text Editor** ribbon explained earlier.

Note:
The **AutoCAPS** feature overrides the **<Caps Lock>** key so that it cannot be used to toggle uppercase on and off. You must turn **AutoCAPS** off in order to type lowercase.

Select All	Ctrl+A
Cut	Ctrl+X
Copy	Ctrl+C
Paste	Ctrl+V
Paste Special	▶
Insert Field...	Ctrl+F
Symbol	▶
Import Text...	
Paragraph Alignment	▶
Paragraph...	
Bullets and Lists	▶
Columns	▶
Find and Replace...	Ctrl+R
Change Case	▶
AutoCAPS	
Character Set	▶
Combine Paragraphs	
Remove Formatting	▶
Background Mask...	
Editor Settings	▶
Learn about MTEXT	▶
Cancel	

Figure 11-28   The right-click shortcut menu

The right-click shortcut menu can be displayed by right-clicking with your mouse anywhere in the multiline text editor window. At the top of the menu are a few text editing specific commands:

- **Select All**   Selects all the text in the text editor
- **Cut**   Deletes text and places it on the Windows clipboard so you can paste it later
- **Copy**   Copies text to the Windows clipboard so you can paste it later
- **Paste**   Inserts text that is currently on the Windows clipboard
- **Paste Special**   Displays a cascade menu that allows you to perform the following special paste operations:
  - **Paste without Character Formatting**   Pastes and ignores any character-based formatting such as font, text height, etc. while maintaining any paragraph-based formatting such as justification, line spacing, etc.
  - **Paste without Paragraph Formatting**   Pastes and ignores any paragraph-based formatting such as justification, line spacing, etc. while maintaining any character-based formatting such as font, text height, etc.
  - **Paste without Any Formatting**   Ignores all original formatting and uses the current formatting

The **Insert Field** menu item allows you to insert a field using the **Field** dialog box. Fields and the **Field** dialog box are explained in detail later in this chapter.

The **Symbol** menu item displays a cascade menu that allows you to insert a symbol or a non-breaking space at the current cursor position. The **Symbol** cascade menu is the same as the **Symbols** menu displayed when you select the **Symbol** button on the **Insert** panel on the **Text Editor** ribbon. See the preceding section "The Insert Panel" for complete information about using the **Symbols** menu.

The **Import Text...** menu item allows you to import a text file using the **Select File** dialog box shown in Figure 11-27.

The **Paragraph Alignment** menu item displays a cascade menu with the same horizontal paragraph justification, text flow, and spacing options found in the **Paragraph Alignment** area in the **Paragraph** dialog box shown earlier in Figure 11-20 in the "The Paragraph Panel" section:

- The **Left** option aligns text on the left-hand margin so text flows right.
- The **Center** option centers text on the centerline of the text boundary and flows both directions.
- The **Right** option aligns text on the right-hand margin so text flows left.
- The **Justified** option spreads text out to fill the text boundary width by putting space between words.
- The **Distributed** option spreads text out to fill the text boundary width by putting space between letters.

The **Paragraph...** menu item displays the same **Paragraph** dialog box shown earlier in Figure 11-21 in the "The Paragraph Panel" section so that you can control tabs, indents, paragraph alignment, and other paragraph features and settings. Please see the "The Paragraph Panel" section for detailed information regarding the **Paragraph** dialog box.

The **Bullets and Lists** menu item displays the same **Bullets and Lists** cascade menu shown earlier in Figure 11-20 in the "The Paragraph Panel" section so that you can create lettered, numbered, or bulleted lists. Please see the "The Paragraph Panel" section for detailed information regarding the **Bullets and Lists** menu.

The **Columns** menu item displays the same **Columns** cascade menu shown earlier in Figure 11-22 in the "The Insert Panel" section so that you can create dynamic and static columns. Please see the "The Insert Panel" section for detailed information regarding the **Columns** menu.

The **Find and Replace...** menu item displays the same **Find and Replace** dialog box shown earlier in Figure 11-26 so you can search for a specific string of text and replace it with a new string of text. Please see the "The Tools Panel" section for detailed information regarding the **Find and Replace** dialog box.

The **Change Case** menu item displays the cascade menu shown in Figure 11-29. This menu can be used to change the selected text to all uppercase or all lowercase.

UPPERCASE	Ctrl+Shift+U
lowercase	Ctrl+Shift+L

Figure 11-29   Change Case cascade menu

The **AutoCAPS** menu item turns the **AutoCAPS** feature explained earlier on and off.

The **Character Set** menu item displays the cascade menu shown in Figure 11-30. The **Character Set** menu item can be used to change the *character set* used so that text in other languages appears properly.

The **Combine Paragraphs** menu item will combine multiple paragraphs of selected text together, removing any line feeds so that the selected text becomes one paragraph. The original text properties are retained.

The **Remove Formatting** menu item displays a cascade menu that provides different options for removing the formatting overrides for selected text so that those overrides revert back to the text's assigned text style:

- **Remove Character Formatting**   Removes any character-based formatting such as font, text height, etc. while maintaining any paragraph-based formatting such as justification, line spacing, etc.

- **Remove Paragraph Formatting**   Removes any paragraph-based formatting such as justification, line spacing, etc., while maintaining any character-based formatting such as font, text height, etc.

- **Remove All Formatting**   Removes all formatting

- The **Background Mask** menu item displays the **Background Mask** dialog box shown earlier in Figure 11-19 so you can set the background of one text boundary box opaque and set its color

> **Note:**
> The **Remove Formatting** menu item is displayed only when text is selected in the multiline text editor.

The **Editor Settings** menu item displays a cascade menu that allows you to control the following multiline text editor display features:

- **Always Display as WYSIWYG**
- **Show Toolbar**   Turns the **Text Formatting** toolbar on and off
- **Show Options**   Turns the bottom portion of the **Text Formatting** toolbar on and off
- **Show Ruler**   Turns the **Ruler** on and off
- **Opaque Background**   Allows you to make the background of the editor opaque. By default, the editor is transparent
- **Check Spelling**   Turns the **Check Spelling As You Type** feature on and off. This option is on by default
- **Check Spelling Settings...**   Displays the **Check Spelling Settings** dialog box so you can specify text options that will be checked for spelling errors within your drawing
- **Dictionaries...**   Displays the **Dictionaries** dialog box so you can control the dictionary that is checked against any found misspelled words
- **Text Highlight Color...**   Allows you to change the color used to highlight text

The **Learn about MTEXT** menu item displays a cascade menu that allows you to get help and information about using multiline text:

- **New Features Workshop**   Introduces you to what's new in AutoCAD using a series of slides and/or animations
- **Help**   Displays the multiline text help topic

character set: The set of numeric codes used by a computer system to represent the characters (letters, numbers, punctuation, etc.) of a particular country or place

Central Europe
Cyrillic
Hebrew
Arabic
Baltic
Greek
Turkish
Vietnamese
Japanese
Korean
CHINESE_GB2312
CHINESE_BIG5
✔ Western
Thai

Figure 11-30   Character Set cascade menu

Exercise 11-6: Using the Right-Click Menu

1. Continue from Exercise 11-5.
2. Using Windows Notepad, create a text file that contains the following text:

   This is text that is in an external file named Notes.txt that I am
   going to import into the multiline text editor and reformat.

> **TIP** The Notepad program can typically be started by selecting the Windows **Start** button and navigating to the **Accessories** folder. You can also start Notepad by typing **NOTEPAD** <**Enter.⏎**> in AutoCAD.

3. Save the file as **Notes.txt** in a location where you can find it and exit out of the Notepad program.
4. Switch back to AutoCAD and start the **MTEXT** command.
5. Define a text boundary area 2″ wide by 2″ tall.
6. Using the right-click menu, do the following:
   a. Import the **Notes.txt** text file.
   b. Set the background mask to red.
   c. Set the paragraph alignment to **Center**.
   d. Find all occurrences of the word "text" and replace it with "test."
   e. Make all the text uppercase.
7. Save the drawing as **EX11-6**.

Creating Stacked Text

As mentioned earlier, it is possible to format text representing a fraction or tolerance so that the left character is placed on top of the right character as a horizontal fraction, diagonal fraction, or tolerance based on the following special stack characters:

- ^ Caret converts to left-justified tolerance values.
- / Forward slash converts to a center-justified fraction with a horizontal bar.
- \ Backward slash converts to a center-justified fraction with a horizontal bar.
- # Pound sign converts to a fraction with a diagonal bar the height of the two text strings.

This can be done manually using the **Stack** menu item located on the right-click shortcut menu or, even better, it can be automated using the **AutoStack** feature in the multiline text editor so that the desired fraction type is created automatically as you type. The **AutoStack** feature and properties are explained in the following section.

AutoStack Properties Dialog Box.   The first time you type in a fraction or tolerance using the special characters listed in the previous section, AutoCAD displays the **AutoStack Properties** dialog box shown in Figure 11-31. This dialog box allows you to define specific text stacking properties that can be applied automatically as you type when a number is entered followed by any of the special stacking characters.

The **Enable AutoStacking** check box allows you to turn **AutoStacking** on and off. If checked, text is automatically stacked when a number is typed in followed by any of the special characters.

The **Remove leading blank:** check box allows you to remove automatically any space between the whole number and the fraction if it is checked.

You can control whether a forward slash converts to a horizontal or diagonal fraction via the **Specify how "x/y" should stack:** radio buttons. If the **Convert it to a diagonal fraction** button is selected, diagonal fractions are created. If the **Convert it to a horizontal fraction** button is selected, horizontal fractions are created.

Selecting the **Don't show this dialog again; always use these settings** check box makes the **AutoStack** settings permanent so the **AutoStack Properties** dialog box is not displayed the next time you type a number followed by one of the special characters. The **AutoStack** properties are automatically applied as you type.

> **TIP** If you select the **Don't show this dialog again; always use these settings** check box, the only way to display the **AutoStack Properties** dialog box again is select an existing fraction in the multiline text editor, right-click with your mouse, and select **Stack Properties** from the shortcut menu to display the **Stack Properties** dialog box. You can then select the **AutoStack...** button from the **Stack Properties** dialog box, explained in the next section.

Figure 11-31   The **AutoStack Properties** dialog box

Figure 11-32   The **Stack Properties** dialog box

Stack Properties Dialog Box.   The **Stack Properties** dialog box shown in Figure 11-32 allows you to edit the text content, stack type, alignment, and size of stacked text. To display the dialog box, you must first select existing stacked text, right-click with your mouse, and select **Stack Properties** from the shortcut menu. The following options are available:

- The **Upper** and **Lower** text boxes in the **Text** section allow you to change the upper and lower numbers of a stacked fraction.

- The **Appearance** section allows you to edit the style, position, or text size of a stacked fraction.

- The **Style** list allows you to switch between the horizontal fraction, diagonal fraction, and tolerance stacking styles.

- The **Position** list allows you to switch between the following text alignments:
    - **Top**   Aligns the top of the fraction with the top of the previous text
    - **Center**   Centers the fraction vertically at the center of the previous text
    - **Bottom**   Aligns the bottom of the fraction with the previous text

Note:
Both the **Top** text and the **Bottom** text use the same alignment specified.

- The **Text size** list controls the size of the stacked text as a percentage relative to the size of the whole number text height. Valid values are between 25% and 125%. The default text size is 70%.

- The **Defaults** button allows you to either restore the default stacked text properties or save the current stacked text properties as the new default.
- The **AutoStack...** button displays the **AutoStack Properties** dialog box so you can either modify or turn off **AutoStack** properties.

Exercise 11-7: Creating Stacked Text

1. Continue from Exercise 11-6.
2. Start the **MTEXT** command.
3. Define a text boundary area 3″ wide by 3″ tall.
4. Enter the following line of text in the multiline text editor and press **<Enter ↵>**:

   THIS IS A HORIZONTAL STACKED FRACTION 1/2

5. The **AutoStack Properties** dialog box shown in Figure 11-31 is displayed.
6. Enable Autostacking so that "x/y" changes to a horizontal fraction.
7. Select the **Don't show this dialog again** check box.
8. Select **OK** to exit the **AutoStack Properties** dialog box.
9. Enter the following line of text in the multiline text editor and press **<Enter ↵>**:

   THIS IS A DIAGONAL STACKED FRACTION 1#2

10. Enter the following line of text in the multiline text editor and press **<Enter ↵>**:

    THIS IS A TOLERANCE VALUE 001^002

11. Save the drawing as **EX11-7**.

CREATING SINGLE-LINE TEXT

In addition to multiline text, you can also create what is referred to as *single-line text* to create one or more lines of text. Single-line text is the original text type in AutoCAD that preceded the more complex and feature-rich multiline text explored in the last section. With single-line text, each line of text is an independent object that can be modified. Multiple lines of single-line text *can be* entered at the same time in paragraph form with consistent vertical spacing between each line— it's just that you must break each line at the end using the **<Enter ↵>** key. See Figure 11-33.

Each Line of Text Is a
Separate Object

Press <Enter ↵> to
End Line

MULTIPLE LINES OF SINGLE LINE TEXT
CAN BE ENTERED BY PRESSING THE
<ENTER> KEY AT THE END OF EACH
LINE.

Figure 11-33　Single-line text

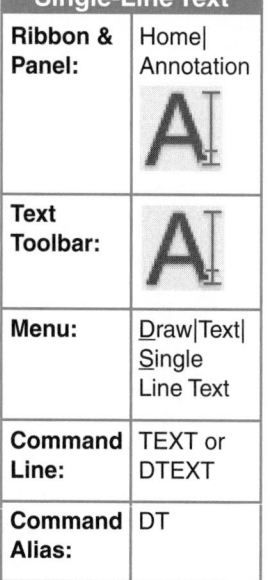

Single-Line Text	
Ribbon & Panel:	Home|Annotation
Text Toolbar:	
Menu:	Draw|Text|Single Line Text
Command Line:	TEXT or DTEXT
Command Alias:	DT

The **TEXT** command or the **DTEXT** command can be used to create single-line text.

When you start either command, AutoCAD displays the current text style and height at the command line as follows:

Current text style: "Standard" Text
height: 0.2000

The text styles used for single-line text are the same as those used for multiline text, explained earlier. You can change the styles via the **Style** option explained below, although using the **Text Style** list box on the **Text** panel on the **Annotate** ribbon shown in Figure 11-4 is much easier as you will see. The text height can also be changed after you select the starting point for the text.

Note:
Remember from the beginning of the chapter that if you set the current text style height to anything other than 0.00″ you will not be prompted for a text height when creating single-line text.

After starting either command, AutoCAD prompts you to *Specify start point of text or* ↓. Select a starting point for the text by either picking a point in your drawing or by entering a coordinate location via the keyboard.

After locating the text start point, AutoCAD prompts you to *Specify height <0.2000>:*. Enter the desired text height and press **<Enter ↵>**. The height entered becomes the default the next time you create single-line text.

After entering the height, AutoCAD prompts you to *Specify rotation angle of text <0>:*. Enter the desired text angle or press **<Enter ↵>** to use the default.

> **Note:**
> By default, single-line text is left justified. This means that text that you type will flow to the right of the text start point. You can change the default justification using the **Justification** option explained in one of the next sections.

TIP   You can also use your cursor to input the angle by selecting a point in response to the *Specify rotation angle of text <0>:* prompt. The text start point is used as the base point of the angle with the second point defining the angle. You can even utilize Object Snaps to align the text by snapping to points on existing objects.

After you enter the desired text angle, AutoCAD displays the no frills in-place single-line text editor, which is basically a dynamically sized box that grows longer as you type as shown in Figure 11-34.

Edit Box Grows Longer as You Type

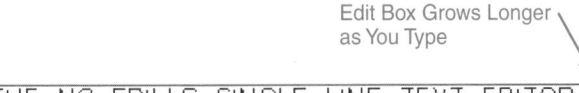

THE NO FRILLS SINGLE LINE TEXT EDITOR]

Figure 11-34   Entering single-line text

As mentioned, it is possible to create multiple lines of text using single-line text; however, you must input the line breaks manually by pressing **<Enter ↵>** at the end of the line. Pressing **<Enter ↵>** places the cursor on the next line in the in-place single-line text editor so you can continue typing as shown in Figure 11-35.

Cursor Location

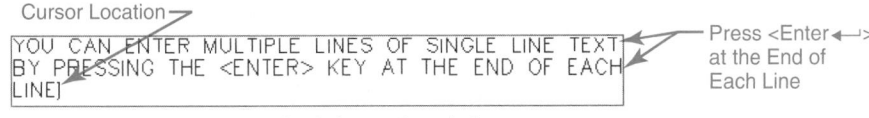

YOU CAN ENTER MULTIPLE LINES OF SINGLE LINE TEXT
BY PRESSING THE <ENTER> KEY AT THE END OF EACH
LINE]

Press <Enter↵> at the End of Each Line

Figure 11-35   Entering multiple lines of single-line text

You can continue to add lines of text until you press the **<Enter ↵>** key twice—meaning that you press **<Enter ↵>** without entering any text on the current line. You can also pick a point outside the edit box with your mouse to end the command. Remember that each line of text is still a separate object even though it was all entered at the same time as shown in Figure 11-36.

> **Note:**
> The line spacing used for single-line text is 1.5 times the text height from the bottom of one line of text to the bottom of the next line.

Each Line of Text
Is a Separate Object

Figure 11-36   Multiple lines of single-line text

TIP   If **TEXT** or **DTEXT** was the last command entered, when you create additional new single-line text you can simply press **<Enter ↵>** at the *Specify start point of text or ↓* prompt and skip the prompts for a text height and rotation angle. AutoCAD automatically displays the in-place single-line text editor directly below the last line of text created in the drawing using the same height, rotation angle, and justification so you can just start typing!

The Right-Click Menu

The single-line text editor also has the right-click menu shown in Figure 11-37, which provides additional functionality. The menu shares some of the same tools and features found on the right-click menu in the multiline text editor explained earlier:

- **Undo/Redo**   Allows you to undo/redo one or more actions in the text editor
- **Cut**   Deletes text and places it on the Windows clipboard so you can paste it later
- **Copy**   Copies text to the Windows clipboard so you can paste it later
- **Paste**   Inserts text that is currently on the Windows clipboard
- **Editor Settings**   Cascade menu with the same editor options found in multiline text editor
- **Insert Field...**   Allows you to insert a field using the **Field** dialog box. Fields and the **Field** dialog box are explained in detail later in this chapter.
- **Find and Replace...**   Displays the **Find and Replace** dialog box so you can search for and replace text
- **Select All**   Selects all the text in the single-line text editor

Undo	Ctrl+Z
Redo	Ctrl+Y
Cut	Ctrl+X
Copy	Ctrl+C
Paste	Ctrl+V
Editor Settings	▶
Insert Field...	Ctrl+F
Find and Replace...	Ctrl+R
Select All	Ctrl+A
Change Case	▶
Help	F1
Cancel	

Figure 11-37   Single-line text editor right-click menu

- **Change Case**   Cascade menu that allows you to change the case of text
  - **UPPERCASE**   Changes text to uppercase
  - **lowercase**   Changes text to lowercase

- **Help**   Displays the single-line text help topic
- **Cancel**   Exits the single-line text editor

Single-Line Text Justification

Single-line text has a justification property similar to multiline text that determines how the text is aligned relative to the insertion point, although unlike multiline text, single-line justification affects only one line of text, not the complete paragraph. The different justification options are shown in Figure 11-38.

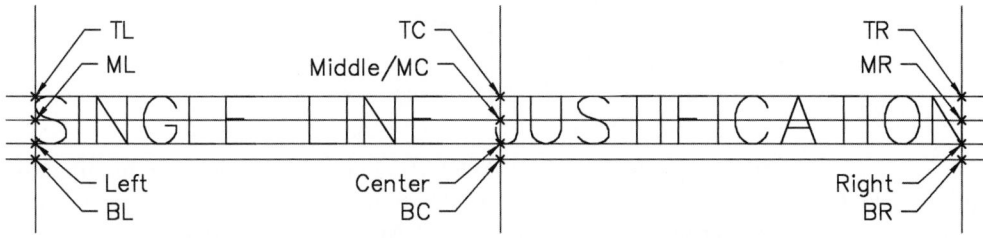

Figure 11-38   Single-line text **Justification** options

The single-line text **Justification** option can be used to specify any of the justifications shown in Figure 11-38. To change the text justification, start the **TEXT** or **DTEXT** command and either type **J<Enter ↵>** or select the **Justification** option using your arrow keys if you are using **Dynamic Input**. AutoCAD prompts you to *Enter an option:*. After you select a justification, you specify a start point, height, and rotation angle using the methods explained earlier. The in-place single-line text editor is then displayed, and you can begin typing.

The text flow as you type is determined by the **Justification** option. Specifying **Right** justification makes text flow from the right to the left, whereas the **Center** justification option makes text spill out in both directions from the start point (see Figure 11-39).

Except for the first two options, **Align** and **Fit**, most of the justification options are fairly self-explanatory. The **Align** and **Fit** justification options both allow you to locate text using two points to define the width and angle of the text. Both options force the text to fit between the two points specified—although with different methods. The **Align** option changes the height of the text (shorter or taller) to make the text fit, and the **Fit** option changes the text's width scale factor (narrower or wider) to make the text fit.

◄——— Text Flows This Way As You Type...

RIGHT JUSTIFIED TEXT FLOWS FROM RIGHT TO LEFT

Text Start Point ⟋

◄——— Text Flows Both Ways As You Type... ———►

CENTER JUSTIFIED TEXT FLOWS BOTH DIRECTIONS

Text Start Point ⟋

Figure 11-39   Using the **Right** and **Center** justification options

To use the **Align** option, start the **TEXT** or **DTEXT** command and select the **Justification** option using the methods explained above. AutoCAD prompts you to *Specify first endpoint of text baseline:*. Select the starting point for the text. AutoCAD then prompts you to *Specify second endpoint of text baseline:*. This point determines both the angle and final overall width of the text. Remember that the **Align** option changes the height of the text in order to make it fit between the two points. Because of this, the in-place single-line text editor box starts out tall and gets shorter as you type as shown in Figure 11-40.

Figure 11-40   Using the **Align** justification option

To use the **Fit** option, start the **TEXT** or **DTEXT** command and select the **Justification** option using the methods explained above. AutoCAD prompts you to *Specify first endpoint of text baseline:*. Select the starting point for the text. AutoCAD then prompts you to *Specify second endpoint of text baseline:*. This point determines both the angle and final overall width of the text. The **Fit** option changes the width scale factor of the text in order to make it fit between the two points. Because of this, AutoCAD prompts you to *Specify height <0.1000>:*. After you enter the desired height, the in-place single-line text editor box is displayed and you can begin typing. The text is either expanded or compressed to fit between the two points as you type but the height is maintained as shown in Figure 11-41.

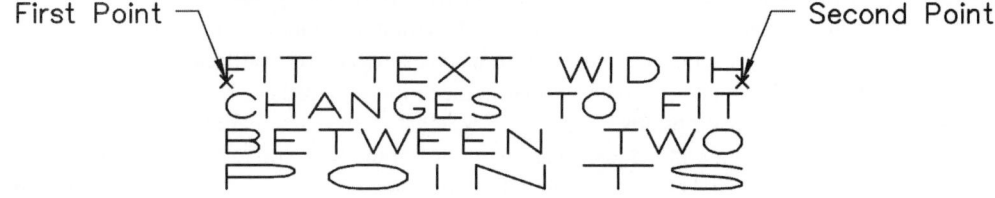

Figure 11-41   Using the **Fit** justification option

Exercise 11-8: Creating Single-Line Text

1. Open drawing **EX11-1**.
2. Create the single-line text shown in Figure 11-42 using the text style, height, and justification indicated.
3. Save the drawing as **EX11-8**.

Start Point (Typical)

STANDARD — 1/8" HIGH JUSTIFICATION=LEFT

NOTES — 1/8" HIGH JUSTIFICATION=RIGHT

TITLE - 1/4" TALL JUSTIFICATION=MIDDLE

ARCHITECTURAL - 1/8" HIGH JUSTIFICATION = ALIGN

MECHANICAL — 0.10" HIGH JUSTIFICATION = FIT

STANDARD - 1/8" HIGH JUSTIFICATION=LEFT OBLIQUE=30

STANDARD - 1/8" HIGH JUSTIFICATION=LEFT OBLIQUE=-30

Figure 11-42   Creating single-line text

Inserting Special Symbols in Single-Line Text

You can insert a number of the same special symbols using the single-line text editor that you can insert using the multiline text editor, but your options are somewhat limited. There is no access to the **Character Map** dialog box, and the symbols you can use must be typed in using either their corresponding AutoCAD "%%" control code or their "\U+" Unicode string. The available Auto-CAD control codes are as follows:

- %%C   Draws circle diameter dimensioning symbol (Ø)
- %%D   Draws degree symbol (°)
- %%P   Draws plus/minus tolerance symbol (±)
- %%O   Toggles overscoring on and off
- %%U   Toggles underscoring on and off
- %%%   Draws a single percent sign (%)

The control codes are immediately converted into their corresponding symbol as you type. For instance, entering **%%D** in the single-line text editor inserts the degree symbol shown in Figure 11-43.

TO CREATE A DEGREE SYMBOL ° — ENTER %%D

Figure 11-43   Using the %%D control code to insert a degree symbol

The underscore (%%U) and overscore (%%O) control codes are toggles that can be turned on and off as shown in Figure 11-44.

TO OVERSCORE A WORD — ENTER %%O
TO UNDERSCORE A WORD — ENTER %%U

Figure 11-44   Using the %%U and %%O control codes to underscore and overscore text

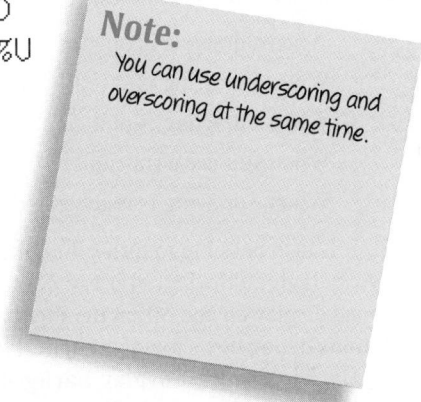

Note:
You can use underscoring and overscoring at the same time.

TIP You can also insert the Euro symbol. If your keyboard does not have a Euro symbol key, you hold down the **<Alt>** key and enter **0128** via the numeric keypad.

Exercise 11-9: Inserting Symbols in Single-Line Text

1. Open drawing **EX11-1**.
2. Set the **STANDARD** text style current.
3. Create the single-line text shown in Figure 11-45 at **0.125″** high, **0°** rotation angle, and justification set to **Left**.
4. Save the drawing as **EX11-9**.

THIS IS A DIAMETER SYMBOL ø
THIS IS A DEGREE SYMBOL °
THIS IS A PLUS/MINUS SYMBOL ±
THIS TEXT IS OVERSCORED AND UNDERSCORED
THIS IS A SINGLE PERCENT SIGN %

Figure 11-45   Inserting symbols in single-line text

Text Fields

A field is intelligent text you can insert in your drawing that dynamically updates according to the data it is based on and/or represents. A classic example is the **Date** field. You can create a **Date** field in a drawing that automatically updates to reflect the current date, and even time, using a variety of different formats:

- 2/5/2010
- Saturday, February 05, 2010
- 2010-02-05
- 5-Feb-10
- …

Fields can be created by themselves, so they stand alone, or they can be inserted in any kind of text, attribute, or attribute definition. A field uses the same text style as the text object in which it is inserted and is displayed with a light gray background that is not plotted.

FOR MORE DETAILS	See Chapter 16 for more details about blocks and block attributes.

When a field is updated, the latest data are displayed. Fields can be set to update automatically via one or all of the following events and actions:

- When a drawing is opened
- When a drawing is saved
- When a drawing is plotted
- When you use eTransmit
- When a drawing is regenerated

It is also possible to turn off all the automatic update features so you must manually update any fields in a drawing. You can control how fields are updated, and then turn the field background display on and off, in the **Fields** area at the bottom left of the **User Preferences** tab of the **Options** dialog box shown in Figure 11-46.

Unchecking the **Display background of fields** check box turns off the light gray background. Selecting the **Field Update Settings...** button displays the **Field Update Settings** dialog box shown in Figure 11-47.

This dialog box allows you to indicate what actions or events will automatically update fields. By default, they are all on. If you uncheck all the check boxes, you must update fields manually.

> **Note:**
> A field that currently has no value displays all hyphens (--). For instance, the **PlotDate** field is not set to anything until a drawing is plotted. An invalid field displays all pound signs (# # #).

Inserting Text Fields

There are several different ways to insert a field. To create a single stand-alone field, you use the **FIELD** command.

To insert a field into multiline text, you can either select **Insert Field...** from the multiline editor right-click menu (see Figure 11-28), or you can use the **Field** button on the **Text Editor** ribbon explained earlier (see Figure 11-15). To insert a field into single-line text, you must select **Insert Field...** from the single-line editor right-click menu explained earlier. Any of these methods displays the **Field** dialog box shown in Figure 11-48.

Insert Field	
Ribbon & Panel:	Insert| Data Field
Text Formatting Toolbar:	
Toolbar:	None
Menu:	Insert| Field...
Command Line:	FIELD
Command Alias:	None

Figure 11-46   **Fields** settings on the **User Preferences** tab of the **Options** dialog box

Figure 11-47   The **Field Update Settings** dialog box

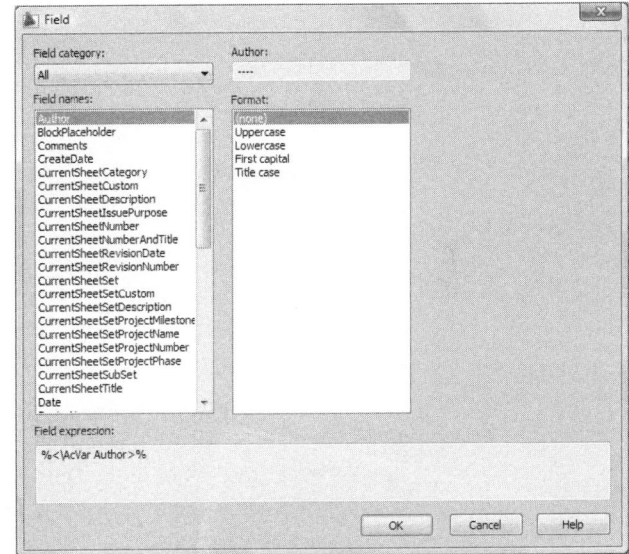

Figure 11-48   The **Field** dialog box

The **Field category**: list box lists the different types of fields available broken down into the following categories:

- **All**   All fields
- **Date & Time**   Date/time–related fields (created, saved, plotted)
- **Document**   Drawing file–related fields (file name, size, saved by)
- **Linked**   Hyperlink information
- **Objects**   Object information (formulas, block names, drawing object properties)
- **Other**   Miscellaneous information (diesel expressions, system variable values)
- **Plot**   Plot information (plot device, paper size, scale)
- **Sheetset**   Sheet set information

The **Field names**: list box changes based on the category selected. All the other options in the **Field** dialog box change based on the field category and field name that are selected. For instance, selecting the **Date & Time** field category displays a list of the following date-related field names:

- CreateDate
- Date
- PlotDate
- SaveDate

All the date fields allow you to specify a date format in the **Date format**: box and control how the date appears in the drawing. You can either enter your own format via the keyboard using the control codes shown in the **Hints** area on the right side of the **Field** dialog box or, even easier, select a predefined format from the **Examples**: list in the middle of the dialog box shown in Figure 11-49.

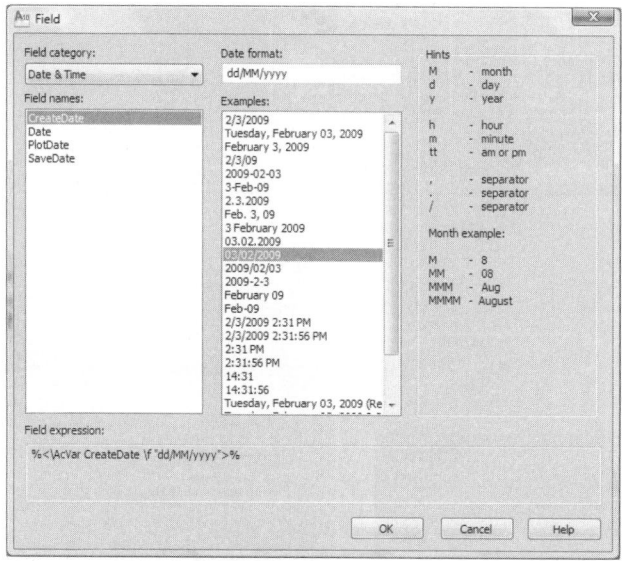

Figure 11-49   The **Field** dialog box with the **Date & Time** options

The **Field expression**: box displays the actual field expression that underlies the field and cannot be edited. It is possible to use the field expression as a guide so that you can construct your own expressions in the **Date format**: text box.

When you have selected the desired field name and all its formatting options, you can select **OK** to insert the field. Figure 11-50 shows a **Date** field inserted in a multiline text object.

Figure 11-50   A **Date** field inserted into a paragraph of multiline text

Editing Text Fields

Text fields are part of either a multiline or single-line text object. If you insert a stand-alone field as described earlier, it is created as multiline text. Because of this, you must use the same tools to edit a field as you do to edit multiline and single-line text. When a field is selected, the **Edit Field** option is available on the shortcut menu, or you can double-click the field to display the **Field** dialog box. Any changes are applied to all text in the field.

If you no longer want to update a field, you can preserve the value that is currently displayed by converting the field to text.

Exercise 11-10: Inserting Text Fields

1. Open drawing **EX11-1**.
2. Set the **NOTES** text style current.
3. Start the **TEXT** or **DTEXT** command to create single-line text.
4. Pick a start point for the text anywhere in your drawing.
5. Enter a rotation angle of **0°** when AutoCAD prompts you to *Specify rotation angle of text* **<0>:**.
6. Enter the following text followed by a space but *do not* press the **<Enter ↵>** key:

   ```
   Drawing plotted on:
   ```

7. Right-click with your mouse while still in the single-line text editor and select **Insert Field...** from the shortcut menu (see Figure 11-37) to display the **Field** dialog box (see Figure 11-48).
8. Select **Date & Time** from the **Field category:** list box to display the **Date & Time** field names.
9. Select **PlotDate** from the **Field names:** list box.
10. Select **OK** to insert the field.
11. Press **<Enter ↵>** twice to exit the **TEXT** command.
12. The text should read as follows:

    ```
    Drawing plotted on: - - - -
    ```

13. Plot your drawing to any plotting device or file.
14. Text is updated so that it looks similar to the following, only with today's date:

    ```
    Drawing plotted on: 2/9/2010
    ```

15. Save the drawing as **EX11-10**.

EDITING TEXT

Both multiline and single-line text can be modified using any of the modify commands introduced earlier in the book. You can move, copy, rotate, scale, and array text just like any other drawing object. Multiline text can even be broken down into individual single-line text objects using the **EXPLODE** command.

You can also use grips to modify text. Both single-line text and multiline text can be moved using the grip located at the text insertion point. Multiline text has grips at the four corner points of the text boundary that can be used to resize the boundary area using the **Stretch** option as shown in Figure 11-51.

Editing Text Content

The easiest way to edit the text content is to simply double-click on the text you want to edit. If you double-click on multiline text, the same in-place multiline text editor used to create the text is displayed with the selected text as shown in Figure 11-52. You can then update the text and any of its properties using the same methods and techniques introduced earlier.

Double-clicking on single-line text displays the in-place single line text editor shown in Figure 11-53.

You can also use the **DDEDIT** or **ED** command to edit text content. After starting the **DDEDIT** command, AutoCAD prompts you to *Select an annotation object or* ↓. Select the text to edit and press **<Enter ↵>**. AutoCAD displays either the in-place multiline or single-line text editor depending on the type of text selected. You can then update the text using the methods and techniques explained earlier.

Original Multiline
Text

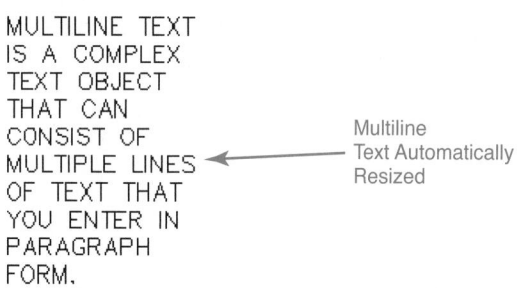

Select and Move
Grip with Mouse

New Corner Point
Location

Specify stretch point or   1.7561   < 204°

MULTILINE TEXT
IS A COMPLEX
TEXT OBJECT
THAT CAN
CONSIST OF
MULTIPLE LINES
OF TEXT THAT
YOU ENTER IN
PARAGRAPH
FORM.

Multiline
Text Automatically
Resized

Figure 11-51   Using grips to resize the multiline text boundary

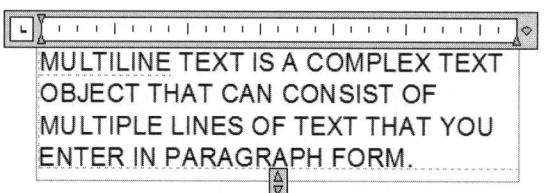

Figure 11-52   Editing text using the multiline text editor

SOME SINGLE LINE TEXT

Figure 11-53   Editing text using the
single-line text editor

Editing Text Using the Properties Palette

The **Properties** palette allows you to change all facets of a text object, including text content, text style, height, justification, and rotation, to name but a few. Plus, using the **Properties** palette, you can also change the text's general properties, such as layer, color, and so on. It's the Swiss army knife of text-editing tools. The properties of a multiline text object are shown in Figure 11-54.

Selecting the button to the right of the **Contents** property displays the appropriate text editor so you can update the text contents as explained earlier.

Edit Text	
Ribbon & Panel:	None
Text Toolbar:	
Menu:	Modify| Object Text|Edit
Command Line:	DDEDIT
Command Alias:	ED

TIP   You can update multiple text objects using the **Properties** palette. For instance, you can use the **Properties** palette to update the text height for all text in a drawing. In fact, you can even update the text height for both single-line and multiline text at the same time.

Figure 11-54 Properties of a multiline object

Exercise 11-11: Editing Text

1. Open drawing **EX11-2**.
2. Select the multiline text object so grips are displayed.
3. Select the bottom right corner grip and stretch the text boundary corner to the right (see Figure 11-51).
4. Press the **<Esc>** key to turn off grips.
5. Double-click on the multiline text object to display the in-place multiline text editor.
6. Resize the text width to **3″** using the arrows on the right-hand side of the ruler (see Figure 11-15).
7. Press **<Ctrl>+A** to select all the text in the editor.
8. Use the **Text Editor** ribbon toolbar to change the following:
   a. Set the style for all text to **ARCHITECTURAL**.
   b. Make all text uppercase.
   c. Deselect all text so nothing is highlighted by clicking anywhere in the text editor window with your cursor.
   d. Select the text "in-place editor" on the first line so it is highlighted.

e. Change the selected text to bold and italic.

f. Set the first line indent to **1″** and the paragraph indent to **0.5″** using the ruler.

9. Select **OK** or click outside the multiline text editor to exit and save your changes.

10. Save the drawing as **EX11-11A**.

11. Open drawing **EX11-8**.

12. Double-click on any of the single-line text objects to display the in-place single-line text editor.

13. Type the following over the highlighted text:

THIS IS SOME NEW TEXT!

14. Press **<Enter ⏎>** to exit the editor.

15. Hit **<Esc>** to exit the **DDEDIT** command.

16. Select all the text in the drawing and open the **Properties** palette (see Figure 11-54).

17. Change the **Height** property to **0.1″** to update the text height for all the selected text.

18. Change the **Justification** property to **Right** for all the selected text.

19. Press **<Esc>** to deselect all the text.

20. Save the drawing as **EX11-11B**.

Scaling Text

Scale Text	
Ribbon & Panel:	Annotate|Text 🅰 Scale
Text Toolbar:	🅰
Menu:	Modify| Object| Text|Scale
Command Line:	SCALE-TEXT
Command Alias:	NONE

The **SCALETEXT** command allows you to change the height of one or more text objects using the following methods using a base point that you specify:

• Specifying a new height

• Specifying a scale factor

• Matching the height of an existing text object

You can elect to use each text object's insertion point as the base point about which the text is scaled, or you can select one of the different justification options explained earlier in the chapter. AutoCAD uses the base point to scale each text object but it *doesn't change* the justification point for each object as shown in Figure 11-55.

Justification Point (Typical) →

STANDARD – 1/8″ HIGH JUSTIFICATION=LEFT

NOTES – 1/8″ HIGH JUSTIFICATION=RIGHT

TITLE - 1/4" TALL JUSTIFICATION=MIDDLE

ARCHITECTURAL - 1/8″ HIGH JUSTIFICATION = ALIGN.

MECHANICAL — 0.10″ HIGH JUSTIFICATION = FIT

STANDARD – 1/8″ HIGH JUSTIFICATION=LEFT OBLIQUE=30

STANDARD – 1/8′ HIGH JUSTIFICATION=LEFT OBLIQUE=30

Before Scaling x 0.5

Justification Points Remain in Original Location

STANDARD – 1/8′ HIGH JUSTIFICATION=LEFT

NOTES – 1/8″ HIGH JUSTIFICATION=RIGHT

TITLE - 1/4" TALL JUSTIFICATION=MIDDLE

ARCHITECTURAL - 1/8″ HIGH JUSTIFICATION = ALIGN

MECHANICAL — 0.10″ HIGH JUSTIFICATION = FIT

STANDARD – 1/8″ HIGH JUSTIFICATION=LEFT OBLIQUE=30

STANDARD – 1/8′ HIGH JUSTIFICATION=LEFT OBLIQUE=30

After Scaling x 0.5

Figure 11-55 Changing text height using the **SCALETEXT** command

When you start the **SCALETEXT** command, AutoCAD prompts you to *Select objects:*. Select the text you want to update using any of the selection methods and press **<Enter ⏎>**. AutoCAD prompts you to *Enter a base point option for scaling:*. You can press **<Enter ⏎>** to use the existing text insertion points as base points, or you can select one of the different **Justification** options. Remember that the justification point entered is used only as a temporary base point for each text object.

After you have selected a base point option, AutoCAD prompts you to *Specify new height or* ↓. You have three options: you can enter a new height, you can specify a scale factor to multiply each text height by, or you can match the height of an existing text object in the drawing. The default is to enter a new height.

Exercise 11-12: Scaling Text

1. Open drawing **EX11-8**.
2. Start the **SCALETEXT** command.
3. Type **ALL** and press **<Enter ↵>** twice when AutoCAD prompts you to *Select objects:* to select everything in the drawing.
4. AutoCAD prompts you to *Enter a base point option for scaling* ↓.
5. Type **E<Enter ↵>** or select the **Existing** option using your arrow keys.
6. AutoCAD prompts you to *Specify new height or* ↓.
7. Type **.1<Enter ↵>**.
8. All the text is resized to 0.1″ tall using its current insertion point.
9. Save the drawing as **EX11-12**.

Changing Text Justification

The **JUSTIFYTEXT** command allows you to change the justification property of one or more text objects without changing their location in the drawing. Typically, when you change the justification property of text using the **Properties** palette, the text is relocated about the new justification point as shown in Figure 11-56.

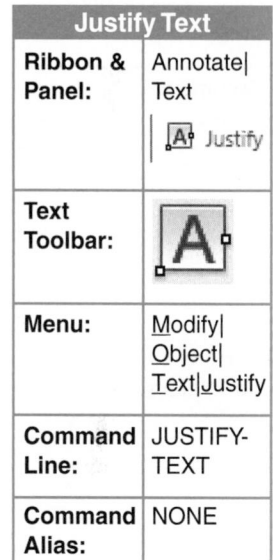

Justify Text	
Ribbon & Panel:	Annotate| Text [A] Justify
Text Toolbar:	A
Menu:	Modify| Object| Text|Justify
Command Line:	JUSTIFY- TEXT
Command Alias:	NONE

Figure 11-56   Changing text justification using the **Properties** palette

The **JUSTIFYTEXT** command provides a way around this problem. When you start the **JUSTIFYTEXT** command, AutoCAD prompts you to *Select objects:*. Select the text you want to update using any of the selection methods and press **<Enter ↵>**. AutoCAD prompts you to *Enter a justification option:*. You can select one of the different justification options either via the keyboard or by using your arrow keys if you are using **Dynamic Input**. The insertion points for all the selected text objects are changed to the justification point specified, but they remain in their original locations as shown in Figure 11-57.

Figure 11-57   Changing text justification using the **JUSTIFYTEXT** command

Exercise 11-13: Changing Text Justification

1. Open drawing **EX11-8**.
2. Start the **JUSTIFYTEXT** command.
3. Type **ALL** and press **<Enter ↵>** twice when AutoCAD prompts you to *Select objects:* to select everything in the drawing.
4. AutoCAD prompts you to *Enter a justification option* ↓.
5. Type **R<Enter ↵>** or select the **Right** justification option using your arrow keys.
6. All the text justification points are changed to **Right,** but the text remains in its original location.
7. Save the drawing as **EX11-13**.

Finding and Replacing Text

The **FIND** command allows you to find and replace text that you specify. AutoCAD searches through *all* the different text types in a drawing including:

- Single-line and multiline text
- Block attributes
- Dimensions
- Tables
- Hyperlinks

It is possible to limit what type of text to search for so you can refine your search via the **FIND** command's options explained later. When you start the **FIND** command, AutoCAD displays the **Find and Replace** dialog box shown in Figure 11-58.

Find Text	
Ribbon & Panel:	Annotate| Text
Text Toolbar:	
Toolbar:	None
Menu:	Edit| Find...
Command Line:	FIND
Command Alias:	None

Figure 11-58 The **Find and Replace** dialog box

The **Find what**: combo box is where you type in the text string for which you want to search. You can enter a text string or choose one of the recently used strings from the list. It is also possible to use wildcard characters to enhance your search possibilities.

You can enter text directly via the box to the left of the **Find Text** button on the **Text** panel on the **Annotate** ribbon. Selecting the **Find Text** button automatically starts the search for the first match and displays the **Find and Replace** dialog box.

The **Replace with**: combo box is where you type in the text string you want to replace for any found text. You can enter a text string or choose one of the recently used strings from the list.

The **Find where**: list box allows you to specify where to search. You can search the current space/layout, the entire drawing, or selected objects. If one or more objects are already selected, the **Current selection** option is the default value; otherwise the **Current space/layout** option is the default.

The **Select objects** button to the right of the **Search in**: list box closes the dialog box temporarily so that you can select objects in your drawing. Accepting the selection set by pressing **<Enter ↵>** returns to the dialog box.

The **More Options** button on the lower left expands the dialog box as shown in Figure 11-59 so you can view and modify the search options and text types to search.

The **Replace** button replaces the found text with the text that you enter in the **Replace with**: combo box.

The **Replace All** button finds *all* occurrences of the text entered in the **Find what**: combo box and replaces them with the text entered in the **Replace with**: combo box. AutoCAD reports the success or failure of the replacement attempt in a separate dialog box by indicating how many objects have been changed.

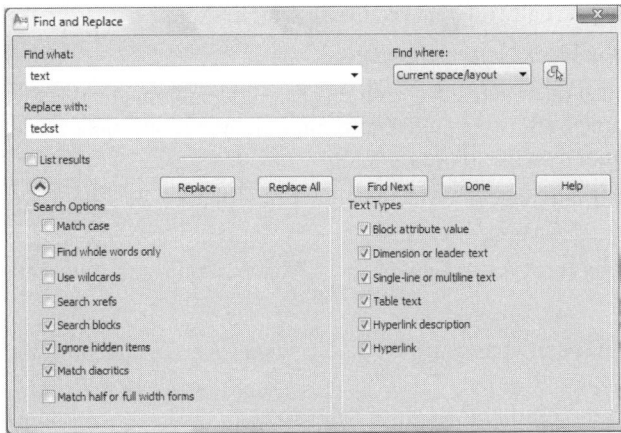

Figure 11-59   The **Find and Replace Options** dialog box

The **Find Next** button in the **Find and Replace** dialog box searches for the text that you enter in the **Find what**: combo box. Any text that is found is automatically zoomed into so you can see it in context. After finding the first occurrence of the text, the **Find** button becomes the **Find Next** button to allow you to search for the next text occurrence.

Selecting the **List results** check box displays a table with the text location (model or paper space), object type, and text string where the text was found showing it in context. Clicking on a column header in the table sorts the information based on the content in that column.

When **List results** are displayed the **Zoom** button on the right allows you to zoom to the highlighted object. Additional buttons allow you to quickly create a selection set that includes all text objects in the list or only the highlighted items.

Selecting the **More Options** arrow button expands the dialog box so you can specify different search options and text types to search.

The different **Search Options** include:

- **Match case**   Includes the case of the text in **Find what** as part of the search criteria
- **Find whole words only**   Finds only whole words that match the text in **Find what**. For example, if you select **Find whole words only** and search for "is," **Find and Replace** does not locate the text string "this"
- **Use wildcards**   Allows the use of the following wildcard characters in searches:

Find and Replace Wildcard Characters	
Wildcard Character	**Description**
*(Asterisk)	Matches any text string
@ (At)	Matches any letter *only*
# (Pound)	Matches any number *only*
? (Question mark)	Matches any single character (letters and numbers)
. (Period)	Matches any nonalphanumeric character
~ (Tilde)	Matches anything *but* the pattern
[ ] (Square brackets)	Matches any of the characters enclosed in the brackets
[~] (Tilde)	Matches any character not enclosed in the brackets
[-] (Hyphen and brackets)	Specifies a range for a single letter
' (Reverse quote)	Reads the next character literally

- **Search xrefs**   Include text in externally referenced files in search results
- **Search blocks**   Includes text in blocks in search results
- **Ignore hidden items**   Ignores hidden items in search results. Hidden items include text on layers that are frozen or turned off, text in block attributes created in invisible mode, and text in visibility states within dynamic blocks
- **Match diacritics** (Latin-based languages)   Matches diacritical marks, or accents, in search results
- **Match half or full width forms** (East Asian Languages)   Matches half- and full-width characters in search results

The **Text Types** area allows you to specify the type of text objects you want to include in the search. By default, all options are selected

The **Done** button closes and exits the **Find and Replace** dialog box.

TIP   The **FIND** command can also be found near the bottom of many of the right-click menus for easy access.

Exercise 11-14: Finding and Replacing Text

1. Open drawing **EX11-8**.
2. Type the word "text" in the **Find Text** box on the **Text** panel on the **Annotate** ribbon.
3. Select the **Find Text** button on the right to display the **Find and Replace** dialog box shown in Figure 11-58.
4. Type the word "teckst" in the **Replace with**: list box.
5. Select the **Replace** button to replace the current text.
6. Select the **Find Next** button to find the next occurrence.
7. Select the **Replace All** button to replace all the text in the drawing.
8. Note how many matches were found and how many objects were changed and select the **OK** button.
9. Select the **Close** button to exit the dialog box.
10. Save the drawing as **EX11-14**.

The Spell Checker

Check Spelling	
Ribbon & Panel:	Annotate| Text ABC ✓ Check Spelling
Text Toolbar:	ABC ✓
Menu:	Tools| Spelling...
Command Line:	SPELL
Command Alias:	SP

The **SPELL** command allows you to check and correct the spelling for the following text object types:

- Single-line and multiline text
- Dimensions
- Block attribute values
- External references

Entering the **SPELL** command displays the **Check Spelling** dialog box shown in Figure 11-60.

The **Where to check**: drop-down list allows you to limit where and what text AutoCAD checks for spelling errors. You have the following three options:

- Entire drawing
- Current space/layout
- Selected objects

By default, AutoCAD checks the entire drawing for spelling errors. If you select **Selected objects**, you must select some text objects in the drawing by selecting the **Select objects** button to the right of the **Where to check**: drop-down list. Otherwise, the **Start** button will be disabled.

Figure 11-60   The **Check Spelling** dialog box

Select the **Start** button to begin the spell-checking process. If no misspelled words are found, AutoCAD displays a message box indicating that the *Spelling Check is complete.* Otherwise, AutoCAD will automatically zoom to the first misspelled word in the drawing and highlight the offending text.

The **Not in dictionary**: area displays the highlighted word that is spelled incorrectly or was not found in the current dictionary. This is the text that will be updated if you select the **Change** or **Change All** button.

The **Suggestions**: box displays a list of suggested replacement words from the current dictionary. You can either select a replacement word from the list or type in a replacement word in the box.

The **Add to Dictionary** button adds the current word to the current custom dictionary. A different custom dictionary can be selected using the **Dictionaries...** button explained below.

The **Ignore** button skips the current word and begins searching for the next misspelled word.

The **Ignore All** button skips all the remaining occurrences of the misspelled word that match the current word.

The **Change** button replaces the current word with the word in the **Suggestions**: text box.

The **Change All** button replaces all occurrences of the misspelled word in the drawing based on the current **Where to check**: selection.

The **Dictionaries...** button displays the **Dictionaries** dialog box shown in Figure 11-61.

The **Dictionaries** dialog box allows you to switch dictionaries so you can check spelling in other languages. The default main dictionary is American English. To change to another language dictionary, select it from the **Current main dictionary**: list box at the top.

To add one or more words to the dictionary, enter it in the **Content**: text box and select the **Add** button. Any words you add in the **Check Spelling** dialog box or the **Dictionaries** dialog box are stored in the custom dictionary. By default, the custom dictionary is named sample.cus and is located in your AutoCAD Support folder.

You can manage custom dictionaries by selecting **Manage custom dictionaries...** from the **Current custom dictionary**: drop-down list to display the **Manage Custom Dictionaries** dialog box. The **Manage Custom Dictionaries** dialog box allows you to add dictionaries to check, create new dictionaries from scratch, and remove existing dictionaries.

The **Settings** button in the **Check Spelling** dilog box displays the **Check Spelling Settings** dialog box shown in Figure 11-62, which allows you to control various aspects of the spell-checking behavior.

At the top of the **Check Spelling Settings** dialog box in the **Include** area, you can choose whether to check dimension text, block attributes, and external references.

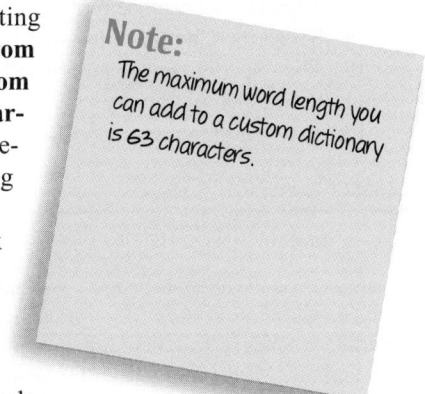

Note:
The maximum word length you can add to a custom dictionary is 63 characters.

Figure 11-61   The **Dictionaries** dialog box

Figure 11-62   The **Check Spelling Settings** dialog box

At the bottom of the dialog box in the **Options** area, you can choose to ignore certain types of words commonly found in technical drawings such as words with numbers and words containing punctuation.

 The **Undo** button allows you to undo changes if you change the wrong text.

Exercise 11-15: Using the Spell Checker

1. Open drawing **EX11-14**.
2. Start the **SPELL** command.
3. The **Check Spelling** dialog box is displayed.
4. Select the **Start** button.
5. AutoCAD zooms to the word "teckst" in your drawing while also displaying it in the **Not in dictionary**: text box.
6. **Suggestions**: is set to "text".
7. Select the **Change** button to update the current text.
8. The next occurrence of "teckst" is found.
9. Select the **Change All** button to update all occurrences of the misspelled word.
10. The "Spelling check complete" message box is displayed.
11. Select **OK**.
12. Save the drawing as **EX11-15**.

CHAPTER SUMMARY

This chapter showed you how to create and edit the different annotation features found in AutoCAD.

Remember that there are two different kinds of text: multiline and single-line. Each serves its own purpose. Many times you will want to rely on single-line text for short notes, titles, and labels in a drawing. Other times you may want the benefits of multiline text, which allows you to do things like easily insert special symbols from a menu, and create bulleted, numbered, and lettered lists.

Think about how you might incorporate text fields in your drawings. There are many fields that are well suited for title blocks. You could incorporate fields to automatically update the date, file name, and even your name!

FOR MORE DETAILS   See Chapter 16 for more information about extracting block attributes.

CHAPTER TEST QUESTIONS

Multiple Choice

1. A font determines how text looks by defining its:
   a. Boldness
   b. Typeface
   c. Language
   d. All of the above

2. AutoCAD fonts have what three-letter file extension?
   a. SHP
   b. FNT
   c. TTF
   d. SHX

3. The system variable that controls the font substituted for a font not found on your system is named:
   a. **ALTFONT**
   b. **FONTSUB**
   c. **SUBFONT**
   d. **FONTALT**

4. A common approach to naming text styles is to create the name by combining the:
   a. Font name and height
   b. Text type and height
   c. Font name and width
   d. Text height and oblique angle

5. The end of a line of multiline text is created using:
   a. A hard return
   b. A soft return
   c. **<Ctrl>+<Enter ↵>**
   d. a and b

6. The text height displayed in the in-place multiline editor is:
   a. The specified text height
   b. Real size
   c. Font size
   d. Text style height

7. To exit the in-place multiline text editor and save your text and any changes, you:
   a. Select **Close Text Editor** on the **Text Editor** ribbon
   b. Press **<Ctrl>+<Enter ↵>**
   c. Click outside the editor window with your mouse
   d. All of the above

8. The system variable that controls the default text height displayed in the multiline text editor **Text height**: list box is:
   a. **TEXTHEIGHT**
   b. **SIZETEXT**
   c. **TXTHEIGHT**
   d. **TEXTSIZE**

9. What file type can be imported into the multiline text editor?
   a. Rich Text Format file
   b. Microsoft Word document
   c. ASCII text file
   d. a and c

10. The name of the feature in the multiline text editor that locks your keyboard so only uppercase letters can be typed is:
    a. **CaseLock**
    b. **CapLocks**
    c. **AutoCAPS**
    d. **CapAuto**

11. The **AutoStack** feature automatically stacks numeric text when what character is placed between two numbers?
    a. /
    b. #
    c. ^
    d. All of the above

12. What single-line **Justification** option allows you to squeeze text between two points without changing the text height?
    a. **Align**
    b. **Fit**
    c. **Center**
    d. None of the above

13. The prefix used to insert special symbols into single-line text is:
    a. @
    b. %%
    c. \U++
    d. b and c

14. A text field that currently has no value assigned displays:
    a. ####
    b. Nothing
    c. - - - -
    d. Empty

15. To edit existing text, you can:
    a. Double-click on the text
    b. Use the **Properties** palette
    c. Use the **DDEDIT** command
    d. All of the above

16. To change the justification point of text without moving it in the drawing, use:
    a. The **JUSTIFYTEXT** command
    b. The **SCALETEXT** command
    c. The **Properties** palette
    d. a and c

Matching

a. Annotate

b. Typeface

c. **TEXTFILL**

d. **FONTALT**

e. Text style

f. Multiline text

g. **AutoCAPS**

h. Character set

i. **AutoStack**

j. Field

1. System variable that controls the filling of TrueType fonts while plotting and rendering

2. Locks your keyboard so only uppercase letters can be entered, similar to the **<Caps Lock>** key

3. The set of numeric codes used to represent the characters of a particular country or place

4. Controls the font, height, and other characteristics that affect the appearance of text

5. Creates different formats of stacked text as you type

6. To add text, notes, and dimensions to a drawing

7. Intelligent text that dynamically updates according to the data it is based on and/or represents

8. System variable that specifies an alternate font to be used when a particular font file cannot be located on your system

9. Complex text object that can consist of multiple lines of text that you enter in paragraph form

10. The style or design of a font

CHAPTER PROJECTS

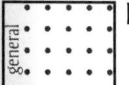

Project 11-1a: Calculator—Continued from Chapter 10

1. Open drawing **P10-1A** from Chapter 10.
2. Modify the **Standard** text style to use the **ROMANS.SHX** font file. Add the text shown in Figure P11-1A.
3. Save your drawing as **P11-1A**.

Figure P11-1A

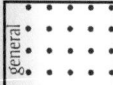

Project 11-1b: Classroom Plan—Continued from Chapter 8

1. Open drawing **P8-1** from Chapter 8.
2. Add the text shown in Figure P11-1B. Create a text style called **ARCH** using the **CountryBlueprint.SHX** font.
3. Save your drawing as **P11-1B**.

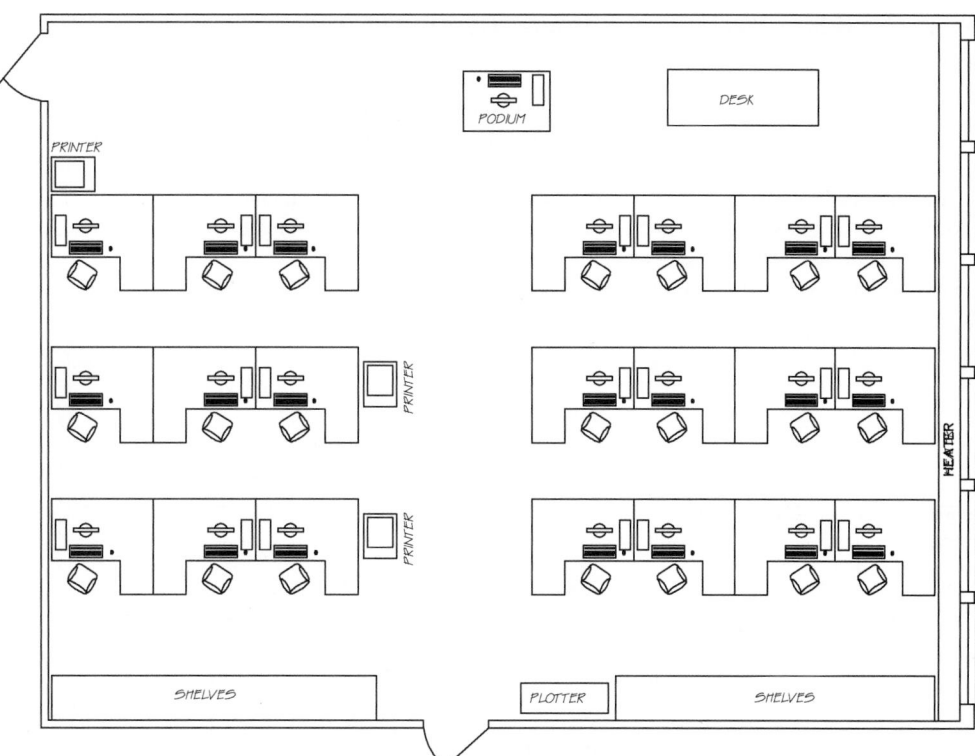

Figure P11-1B

Project 11-1c: Circuit Board—Continued from Chapter 10

1. Open drawing **P10-1B** from Chapter 10.
2. Modify the **Standard** text style to use the **ROMANS.SHX** font file. Add the text shown in Figure P11-1C.
3. Save your drawing as **P11-1C**.

Figure P11-1C

Project 11-2a: B-Size Mechanical Border—Continued from Chapter 6

1. Open the template file **Mechanical B-Size.DWT** from Chapter 6.
2. Modify the **Standard** text style to use the **ROMANS.SHX** font file.
3. Set the **Snap Mode** setting to **1/16"** and add the text shown in Figure P11-2A. Large text is **1/8"** tall, and smaller text is **1/16"**. Use multiline text for the tolerance note and single-line text for all other text. Use text fields for the drawing name, plot date, and user name.
4. Save the drawing to a template file as **Mechanical B-Size.DWT**.

Figure P11-2A

Project 11-2b: C-Size Mechanical Border—Continued from Chapter 7

1. Open the template file **Mechanical C-Size.DWT** from Chapter 7.
2. Modify the **Standard** text style to use the **ROMANS.SHX** font file.
3. Set the **Snap Mode** setting to **1/16"**. Add the zone division lines and text as shown in Figure P11-2B. All text is **1/4"** tall.

Figure P11-2B

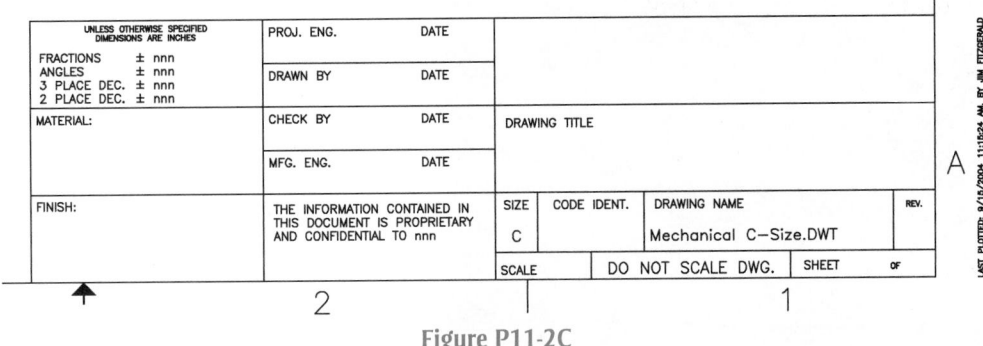

Figure P11-2C

4. Add the text shown in Figure P11-2C. Large text (the drawing name, "*C*," and "*DO NOT SCALE*") is **1/8″** tall. The plot stamp and "*UNLESS OTHERWISE SPECIFIED...*" text are **1/16″** tall. All other text is **3/32″**. Use multiline text for the tolerance note and single-line text for all other text. Use text fields for the drawing name, plot date, and user name.
5. Save the drawing to a template file as **Mechanical C-Size.DWT**.

Project 11-2c: A-Size Portrait Mechanical Border—Continued from Chapter 8

1. Open the template file **Mechanical A-Size-Portrait.DWT** from Chapter 8.
2. Modify the **Standard** text style to use the **ROMANS.SHX** font file.
3. Set the **Snap Mode** setting to **1/16″** and add the text shown in Figure P11-2D. Large text is **1/8″** tall, and smaller text is **1/16″**. Use text fields for the drawing name, plot date, and user name. *Hint:* Use aligned text for the drawing name field to ensure the file name fits in the allotted space.
4. Save the drawing to a template file as **Mechanical A-Size-Portrait.DWT**.

Figure P11-2D

Project 11-2d: Logo—Continued from Chapter 10

1. Open drawing **P10-2** from Chapter 10.
2. Create a new text style called **PEARSON** using the **Lucinda Sans.TTF** TrueType font. Assign a width factor of **1.10** to the text style.
3. Create a second text style called **PH** using the **Times New Roman.TTF** TrueType font.
4. Add the text shown in Figure P11-2E. All text is **0.375** high. Assign the color **255** as a hard-coded color to all text. *Hint:* Use the **DRAWORDER** command to send the solid fill areas to the back of the borders and text.
5. Save the drawing as **P11-2**.

Figure P11-2E

Project 11-3a: Architectural D-Size Border—Continued from Chapter 10

1. Open the template file **Architectural D-Size.DWT**.
2. Create a text style named **Border** assigned the text font **Simplex.shx**.
3. Create a text style named **Logo** assigned the text font **Century Gothic.ttf**.
4. Create a text style named **Arch** assigned the text font **CountryBlueprint.ttf**.
5. Create all text in the following steps at the approximate heights shown. Try to use standard heights when possible.
6. Create all the logo text as shown in Figure P11-3A using the text style **Logo** on the layer **A-Anno-Ttlb-Logo**.
7. Create the text on the bottom right that says, "Last plotted on MM/DD/YYYY" by inserting the date as a field using the **PlotDate** field so it updates each time the drawing is plotted.
8. Create all the remaining title border text as shown in Figure P11-3A using the text style **Border** on the layer **A-Anno-Ttlb-Text**.
9. Save the drawing to a template file as **Architectural D-Size.DWT**.

Figure P11-3A

Project 11-3b: Architectural B-Size Border—Continued from Chapter 10

1. Open the template file **Architectural B-Size.DWT**.
2. Create a text style named **Border** assigned the text font **Simplex.shx**.
3. Create a text style named **Logo** assigned the text font **Century Gothic.ttf**.
4. Create a text style named **Arch** assigned the text font **CountryBlueprint.ttf**.
5. Create all text in the following steps at the approximate heights shown. Try to use standard heights when possible.
6. Create all the logo text as shown in Figure P11-3B using the text style **Logo** on the layer **A-Anno-Ttlb-Logo**.
7. Create the text on the bottom left that says, "Last plotted on MM/DD/YYYY" by inserting the date as a field using the **PlotDate** field so it updates each time the drawing is plotted.
8. Create all the remaining title border text as shown in Figure P11-3B using the text style **Border** on the layer **A-Anno-Ttlb-Text**.
9. Save the drawing to a template file as **Architectural B-Size.DWT**.

Figure P11-3B

Project 11-3c: Architectural A-Size Border—Continued from Chapter 8

1. Open the template file **Architectural A-Size.DWT**.
2. Create a text style named **Border** assigned the text font **Simplex.shx**.
3. Create a text style named **Arch** assigned the text font **CountryBlueprint.ttf**.
4. Create all text in the following steps at the approximate heights shown. Try to use standard heights when possible.
5. Create the text on the bottom left that says, "Last plotted on MM/DD/YYYY" by inserting the date as a field using the **PlotDate** field so it updates each time the drawing is plotted.
6. Create all the remaining title border text as shown in Figure P11-3C using the text style **Border** on the layer **A-Anno-Ttlb-Text**.
7. Save the drawing to a template file as **Architectural A-Size.DWT**.

Figure P11-3C

Project 11-4a: Electrical Plan—Continued from Chapter 10, Problem 5

1. Open drawing **P10-5** from Chapter 10.
2. Create a text style called **E-Symbol** using the **ROMANS.SHX** font.
3. Add/modify the existing symbols and create the electrical symbols as shown in Figure P11-4A. Use **4″** text for all annotation within the symbols. Use **6″** text for the symbol description. Use the **E-Lite** or **E-Powr** layer to place the symbol annotation. Place all description annotation on the **E-Anno** layer.
4. Add/modify the symbols and wiring as shown in Figure P11-4B.
5. Save the drawing as **P11-4A**.

ELECTRICAL   NOTES:

⏁	110 CONVENIENCE OUTLET	⌇	SINGLE POLE SWITCH	○	CEILING MOUNTED LITE FIXTURE
⏁ GFI	110 C.O. GROUND FAULT 1NTERRUPTER	⌇³	THREE—WAY SWITCH	⊙	CAN CEILING LITE FIXTURE
⏁ WP	110 WATER PROOF	⊕⊕	LITE, HEATER, & FAN		WALL MOUNTED LITE
⏁ ⁴	MULTIPLE DUPLEX OUTLET	● S.D.	SMOKE DETECTOR	□	RECESSED LITE FIXTURE
⏁	220 OUTLET	Ⓟ	PHONE OUTLET	⊖	FLOOR OUTLET
CH	CHIME	Ⓣⱽ	CABLE T.V. OUTLET		48″ SURFACE MOUNTED FLOURESCANT LITE FIXTURE
		⊏⊅	DOOR BELL		

Figure P11-4A

Figure P11-4B

Project 11-4b: Electrical Distribution Panel—Continued from Chapter 10

1. Open drawing **P10-4** from Chapter 10.
2. Add the electrical annotation shown in Figure P11-4C. Place all annotation on the **E-Anno** layer.
3. Save your drawing as **P11-4B**.

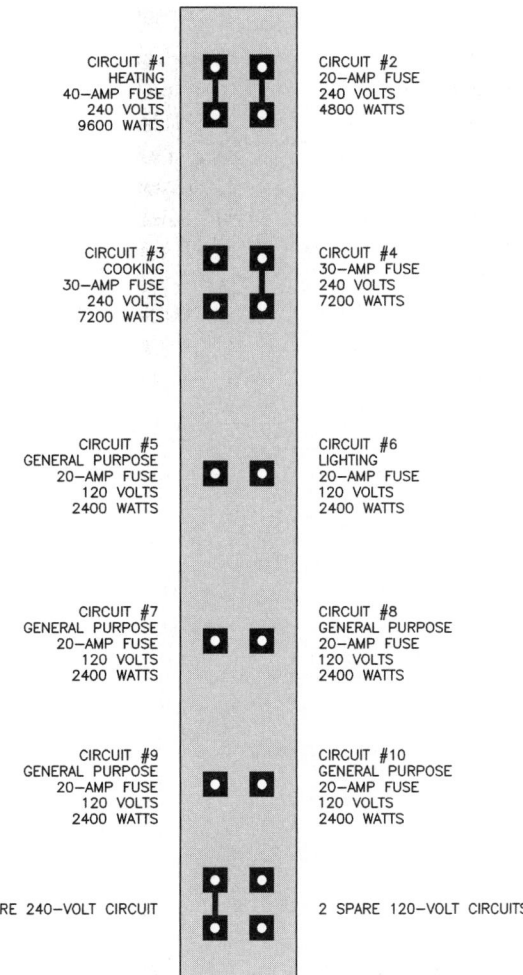

CIRCUIT #1
HEATING
40—AMP FUSE
240 VOLTS
9600 WATTS

CIRCUIT #2
20—AMP FUSE
240 VOLTS
4800 WATTS

CIRCUIT #3
COOKING
30—AMP FUSE
240 VOLTS
7200 WATTS

CIRCUIT #4
30—AMP FUSE
240 VOLTS
7200 WATTS

CIRCUIT #5
GENERAL PURPOSE
20—AMP FUSE
120 VOLTS
2400 WATTS

CIRCUIT #6
LIGHTING
20—AMP FUSE
120 VOLTS
2400 WATTS

CIRCUIT #7
GENERAL PURPOSE
20—AMP FUSE
120 VOLTS
2400 WATTS

CIRCUIT #8
GENERAL PURPOSE
20—AMP FUSE
120 VOLTS
2400 WATTS

CIRCUIT #9
GENERAL PURPOSE
20—AMP FUSE
120 VOLTS
2400 WATTS

CIRCUIT #10
GENERAL PURPOSE
20—AMP FUSE
120 VOLTS
2400 WATTS

SPARE 240—VOLT CIRCUIT

2 SPARE 120—VOLT CIRCUITS

Figure P11-4C

Project 11-5: Residential Architectural Plan—Continued from Chapter 11

1. Open drawing **P11-4A** from Chapter 11, Project 4. If you are not completing Project 4a, open drawing **P10-5** from Chapter 10.
2. Create the following layers:

Name	Color	Linetype	Description
A-Door-Iden	White	Continuous	Door tags
A-Glaz-Iden	White	Continuous	Window tags
A-Area-Iden	White	Continuous	Room numbers, room identification, and area calculations
A-Anno-Legn	White	Continuous	Door and window schedules
A-Anno-Note	White	Continuous	General notes
A-Anno-Dims	White	Continuous	Dimensioning

Note:
This project continues from Project 4a—Electrical Plan, presented earlier. If you are not completing Project 4a, continue from the Project 5 drawing in Chapter 10.

3. Create a text style called **A-SYMBOL** using the **ROMANS.SHX** font and set it current.
4. Create the door and window schedules and tags as shown in Figure P11-5A using lines and text. Use a text height of **6″** for the door and window tags and the small text in the schedule. Use a text height of **8″** for the column heads in the table and a text height of **12″** for the schedule titles.
5. Place the door and window tags and add the room labels as shown in Figure P11-5B. Place all objects on their appropriate layer.
6. Save the drawing as **P11-5**.

WINDOW SCHEDULE			
SYM.	SIZE	TYPE	QTY.
A	3'-0" X 3'-6"	S.H.	10
B	2'-0" X 3'-6"	S.H./FROSTED	1
C	2'-0" X 3'-0"	S.H.	4
D	3'-0" X 3'-0"	PCT.	2
E	5'-0" X 5"-0"	TEMP. PCT.	3
F	1'-0" X 3'-0"	S.H.	2
G	2'-0" X 6'-0"	GLASS SKY.	2

DOOR SCHEDULE			
SYM.	SIZE	TYPE	QTY.
1	3'-0" X 6'-8"	M.I./R.P.	1
2	2'-8" X 6'-8"	M.I./S.C.	2
3	2'-8" X 6'-8"	H.C.	8
4	2'-6" X 6'-8"	POCKET/H.C.	2
5	2'-6" X 6'-8"	H.C./BI-FOLD	2
6	6'-0" X 6'-8"	TEMP. SLIDER	2
7	8'-0" X 6'-8"	GARAGE	2

Figure P11-5A

Figure P11-5B

Project 11-6: Socket Head Cap Screws—English Units—Continued from Chapter 7

1. Open drawing **P7-6** from Chapter 7.
2. Modify the **Standard** text style to use the **ROMANS.SHX** font.
3. Create the table shown in Figure P11-6 using lines and text on the **NOTES** layer. Use a text height of **.125** for the table text and **.250** for the table title. Set the height of the top row to **.5** and the row height of all other rows to **.25**.
4. Save the drawing as **P11-6**.

Socket Head Cap Screw

Nominal Size (D)	Thread/In	A	B	C	L
4 (.112)	40	.183	3/32	.103	1.00
5 (.125)	40	.205	3/32	.113	1.00
6 (.138)	32	.226	7/64	.125	1.25
8 (.164)	32	.270	9/64	.150	1.25
10 (.190)	24	.312	5/32	.171	1.50
¼ (.250)	20	.375	3/16	.225	1.50

Figure P11-6

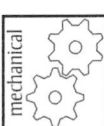

Project 11-7a: Gasket—Continued from Chapter 4

1. Open drawing **P4-7** from Chapter 4.
2. Create a text style named **Notes** assigned the text font **Simplex.shx** with a height of **5 mm**.
3. Create a text style named **Title** assigned the text font **Arial.ttf** with a height of **10 mm**.
4. Add the scale shown in Figure P11-7A using the text style **Notes** on layer **Text**.
5. Add the underlined title text shown in Figure P11-7A using the text style **Title** on layer **Text**.
6. Save the drawing as **P11-7A**.

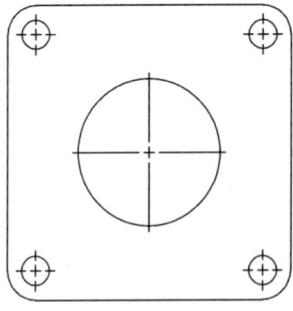

Project 11-7b: Widget—Continued from Chapter 5

1. Open drawing **P5-7** from Chapter 5.
2. Create a text style named **Notes** assigned the text font **Simplex.shx** with a height of **10 mm**.
3. Create a text style named **Title** assigned the text font **Arial.ttf** with a height of **20 mm**.
4. Add the scales shown in Figure P11-7B using the text style **Notes** on layer **Text**.
5. Add the underlined title text shown in Figure P11-7B using the text style **Title** on layer **Text**.
6. Save the drawing as **P11-7B**.

GASKET
SCALE: 1:2

Figure P11-7A

FRONT VIEW
SCALE: 1:4

RIGHT—SIDE VIEW
SCALE: 1:4

Figure P11-7B

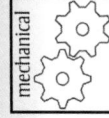

Project 11-7c: Hex Head Bolts and Nuts—Continued from Chapter 6

1. Open drawing **P6-7** from Chapter 6.
2. Create a text style named **Title** assigned the text font **Arial.ttf** with a height of **5 mm**.
3. Add the underlined title text shown in Figure P11-7C using the text style **Title** on layer **Text**.
4. Save the drawing as **P11-7C**.

M6x1   M8x1

Figure P11-7C   M10x1   M12x1.5

Project 11-7d: Motorcycle Head Gasket—Continued from Chapter 7

1. Open drawing **P7-7** from Chapter 7.
2. Create a text style named **Notes** assigned the text font **Simplex.shx** with a height of **5 mm**.
3. Create a text style named **Title** assigned the text font **Arial.ttf** with a height of **10 mm**.

4. Add the scale and general note shown in Figure P11-7D using the text style **Notes** on layer **Text**.
5. Add the underlined title text shown in Figure P11-7D using the text style **Title** on layer **Text**.
6. Save the drawing as **P11-7D**.

NOTE:
ALL FILLETS R12.7 UNLESS OTHERWISE NOTED

HEAD GASKET
SCALE: 1:2

Figure P11-7D

Project 11-7e: 68-Tooth Rear Sprocket—Continued from Chapter 8

1. Open drawing **P8-7** from Chapter 8.
2. Create a text style named **Notes** assigned the text font **Simplex.shx** with a height of **10 mm**.
3. Create a text style named **Title** assigned the text font **Arial.ttf** with a height of **20 mm**.
4. Add the scale shown in Figure P11-7E using the text style **Notes** on layer **Text**.
5. Add the underlined title text shown in Figure P11-7E using the text style **Title** on layer **Text**.
6. Save the drawing as **P11-7E**.

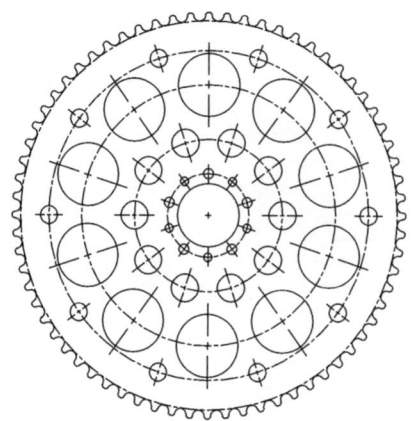

68 TOOTH REAR SPROCKET
SCALE: 4:1   Figure P11-7E

Project 11-7f: Window Extrusion—Continued from Chapter 9

1. Open drawing **P9-7** from Chapter 9.
2. Create a text style named **Notes** assigned the text font **Simplex.shx** with a height of **2.5 mm**.
3. Create a text style named **Title** assigned the text font **Arial.ttf** with a height of **5 mm**.
4. Add the scale shown in Figure P11-7F using the text style **Notes** on layer **Text**.
5. Add the underlined title text shown in Figure P11-7F using the text style **Title** on layer **Text**.
6. Save the drawing as **P11-7F**.

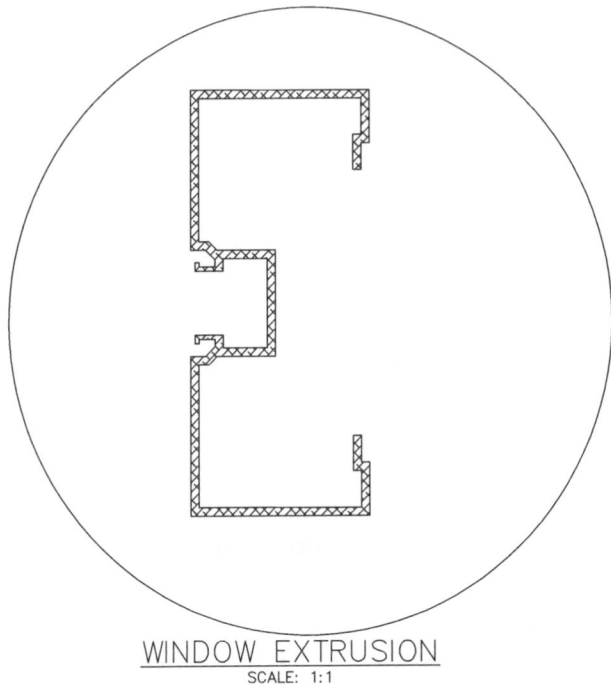

WINDOW EXTRUSION
SCALE: 1:1

Figure P11-7F

Project 11-7g: Hub—Continued from Chapter 10

1. Open drawing **P10-7A** from Chapter 10.
2. Create a text style named **Notes** assigned the text font **Simplex.shx** with a height of **5 mm**.
3. Create a text style named **Title** assigned the text font **Arial.ttf** with a height of **10 mm**.
4. Add the scale shown in Figure P11-7G using the text style **Notes** on layer **Text**.

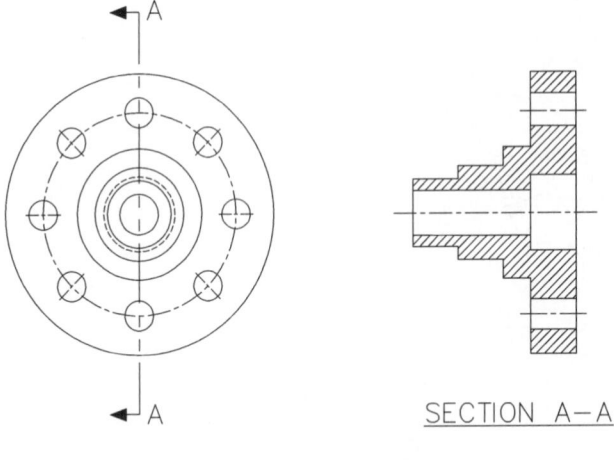

SECTION A—A

HUB
SCALE: 1:2

Figure P11-7G

5. Add the underlined title text shown in Figure P11-7G using the text style **Title** on layer **Text**.
6. Save the drawing as **P11-7G**.

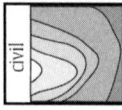

Project 11-8: Civil Site Plan—Continued from Chapter 10

1. Open drawing **P10-8** from Chapter 10.
2. Create a text style called **C-NOTE** using the **ROMANS.SHX** font and set it current.
3. Place the notes and spot elevations as shown in Figure P11-8. Use the appropriate layers for each object. *Hint:* Select **Symbol>Centerline** from the right-click menu within the **MTEXT** command to create the centerline symbol ().
4. Use the **HATCHEDIT** to modify the hatch patterns so the text is not obscured.
5. Save the drawing as **P11-8**.

Figure P11-8

Working with Tables

12

Chapter Objectives

- Create tables from scratch by entering the data manually
- Create tables by linking with a Microsoft® Excel spreadsheet
- Manage data links using the Data Link Manager
- Control the appearance of tables using table styles
- Modify tables using grips
- Insert formulas in a table

INTRODUCTION

A table is an AutoCAD annotation object type that consists of data in rows and columns similar to an accounting spreadsheet. Many of the common spreadsheet features you may be familiar with work exactly the same in AutoCAD tables. It is even possible to paste a Microsoft Excel spreadsheet so that it converts directly into a static AutoCAD table with the desired formatting and fonts. Even better, you can link a dynamic AutoCAD table directly to an external Excel spreadsheet so that it updates automatically if the spreadsheet changes. Figure 12-1 shows an example of a table being used for an Architectural door schedule.

You can create a table based on three different types of data:

- **Static data** Manually enter data into a table created from scratch or from pasting Excel data using the Windows clipboard

- **Externally linked data** Create a dynamic AutoCAD table by linking to an existing Excel spreadsheet

- **Object data** Create an AutoCAD table from object data in the drawing using the **Data Extraction** wizard, which allows you to extract different object properties, including blocks and block attributes

FOR MORE DETAILS See Chapter 16 for detailed information about using the **Data Extraction** wizard.

Using table styles, you can control all aspects of a table including the *cell* data format, the text and border properties, table direction, and other formatting options.

After the table has been created, the complete table, or individual rows and columns, can be resized using grips. Additional modifications can be made using the right-click shortcut menus or the **Table** ribbon explained later in the section on modifying tables.

cell: The box at the intersection of a table row and column that contains the table data or a formula. A cell is typically referenced using its column letter and row number separated with a colon. For example, the cell in column A and row 1 is referenced as A:1

WINDOW SCHEDULE

TAG	TYPE	MANUFACTURER	HEIGHT	WIDTH	COUNT
A	Fixed	ACME Glass Co.	4'-0"	4'-0"	20
B	Fixed	ACME Glass Co.	4'-0"	3'-6"	4
C	Fixed	ACME Glass Co.	3'-0"	2'-6"	4
D	Casement	Glassarama, Inc.	3'-0"	2'-0"	3
E	Sidelite	Season All Windows	4'-0"	1'-0"	1

Figure 12-1   Table used for an Architectural window schedule

CREATING TABLES FROM SCRATCH

The **TABLE** command creates a table object by inserting an empty table in the drawing at a specified point or defined window area using the table style, number of rows, columns, and sizes you specify.

When you start the **TABLE** command, AutoCAD displays the **Insert Table** dialog box shown in Figure 12-2.

Table	
Ribbon & Panel:	Home| Annotation
Draw Toolbar:	
Menu:	Draw| Table...
Command Line:	TABLE
Command Alias:	TB

Figure 12-2   The **Insert Table** dialog box

The **Table style** area at the top left side of the dialog box is used to control the appearance of the table.

The drop-down list allows you to select an existing table style and make it current. The default style is Standard. Selecting the button to the right displays the **Table Style** dialog box so that you can update the current style or add a new table style. Table styles are discussed later in this chapter.

Below the **Table style** area is the **Insert options** area where you select one of the three ways to insert a table. The default method is **Start from empty table**. If you select any of the other table **insert options**, most of the other options on the right will be disabled.

Note:
You can also set the current table style using the expanded **Annotation** panel on the **Home** ribbon.

The table **Preview** provides an example of what the current table style looks like.

The **Insertion behavior** section allows you to select how you want to locate the table. You can use an insertion point or specify a window boundary area.

The **Specify insertion point** option allows you to specify the location of the upper left corner of the table. You can either select a point with your mouse, or you can specify absolute coordinates via the keyboard.

The **Specify window** option allows you to locate and size the table by defining a rectangular window area either by using your mouse or by specifying absolute coordinates via the keyboard. The specified column width and the final number of rows depend on the size of the boundary area.

The table is sized using the number and size of the rows and columns specified in the **Column & row settings** area on the right side of the dialog box.

The **Columns:** box is used to specify the number of columns. You can enter a value directly, or you can increase and decrease the current values using the up and down arrows on the right.

The **Column width:** box is used to specify the width of the columns. You can enter a value directly, or you can increase and decrease the current values using the up and down arrows on the right.

The **Data rows:** box is used to specify the number of rows. You can enter a value directly, or you can increase and decrease the current values using the up and down arrows on the right. A table style with a title row and a header row has a minimum of three rows.

The **Row height:** box is used to specify the row height in lines. The height of a line is based on the current text height and the cell margin settings in the current table style. Table styles are explored later in this section. You can enter a value directly, or you can increase and decrease the current values using the up and down arrows on the right. The minimum row height is one line.

It is possible to create and apply different cell styles per row so that you can create different formatting for titles, headers, and data, if desired. The **Set cell styles** area allows you to assign the different styles independent of the current Table style.

The **First row cell style** list box controls the cell style for the first row in the table. The **Title** cell style is used by default.

The **Second row cell style** list box controls the cell style for the second row in the table. The **Header** cell style is used by default.

The **All other row cell styles** list box controls the cell style for all other rows in the table. The **Data** cell style is used by default.

Selecting **OK** closes the dialog box, and AutoCAD prompts you to *Specify insertion point:*. You can pick a point using your mouse, or you can enter an absolute coordinate using the keyboard. The table is inserted, and you are placed in **Edit** mode. The **Text Editor** ribbon explained in Chapter 11 is displayed, and your cursor is in the first data cell ready for data entry. Adding and modifying table data are explained in the following section.

Note:
If the table direction is set to **UP** in the current table style, the insertion point locates the lower left corner of the table.

Note:
When the **Specify window** option is used to locate the table and indicate its overall width, you can either specify the number of columns so that the column widths are set automatically, or you can specify the column width so that the number of columns is calculated automatically.

Note:
When the **Specify window** option is used to locate the table and indicate its overall height, you can either specify the number of rows so that the row height is set automatically, or you can specify the row height so that the number of rows is calculated automatically.

TIP   If you already have data in an Excel spreadsheet, you can copy and paste the Excel data as **AutoCAD Entities** using **Edit|Paste Special…** with the **Paste** option selected. Pasting Excel data as **AutoCAD Entities** automatically creates a new table with the static values already entered.

ENTERING TABLE DATA

When a table is inserted, you are placed in **Edit** mode so that the **Text Editor** ribbon is displayed and the first data cell is highlighted so that you can begin entering data. To move to an adjacent cell in the same row, you can use the left and right arrow keys or press the **<Tab>** key to go to the cell on the right. To move to an adjacent cell in the same column, you can use the up and down arrow keys or press **<Enter ↵>** to go to the cell directly below in the next row.

TIP   Table cells can contain text, fields, blocks, and even formulas. Inserting formulas is explored later in the section "Inserting Formulas."

You can use any of the text formatting features and options explained earlier in the "Creating Multiline Text" section in Chapter 11 to format the text in each cell. When you are editing text, the arrow keys move the text cursor and do not take you to another cell.

When you are finished adding data to the table, you can use the same methods used for multiline text to close out of **Edit** mode and accept any additions and changes:

Note:
The row height of a cell increases to accommodate multiple lines of text if the specified row height is exceeded.

- Select **Close Text Editor** in the **Close** panel of the **Text Editor** ribbon.

- Click anywhere outside the text editor with your mouse.

- Hold down the **<Ctrl>** key and press **<Enter ↵>**.

TIP   By default, the in-place text editor displays column letters and row numbers when a table cell is selected for editing. Use the **TABLEINDICATOR** system variable to turn this display on and off. To set a new background color, select a table and click **Table Indicator Color** on the shortcut menu. The text color, size, style, and line color are controlled by the settings for column heads in the current table style.

CREATING TABLES BY INSERTING A DATA LINK

The second way to insert a table is to link it to an existing Microsoft Excel spreadsheet using the **From a data link** method in the **Insert options** area of the **Insert Table** dialog box shown in Figure 12-2. Using data links, you can display tabular data from a spreadsheet as an AutoCAD table. This allows you to take advantage of AutoCAD fonts, colors, text styles, and all of the other

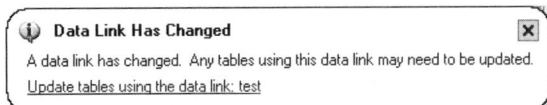

Figure 12-3   The **Data Link Notification** balloon

Data Link Manager	
Ribbon & Panel:	Insert Linking & Extraction
Toolbar:	
Menu:	Tools|Data Links|Data Link Manager…
Command	DATALINK
Command Alias:	DL

table formatting options while still maintaining a link to the original Excel data. If the Excel spreadsheet is updated, a notification balloon like the one shown in Figure 12-3 is displayed in the Status Tray on the right side of the Status Bar. It contains a link that lets you quickly update the table in the drawing so that it matches the Excel spreadsheet.

The Data Link Manager

When a new data link is created, you must give it a name, usually related to the type of data, and select the external file to which it links (XLS or CSV) using the **Data Link Manager** shown in Figure 12-4.

After entering a name and choosing a file, AutoCAD displays the **New Excel Data Link** dialog box shown in Figure 12-5. There you can choose which sheet in the file you want to link and whether you want to link to the entire sheet or just a specific range of cells.

Once the link has been established, select **OK** to close the **Data Link Manager** and return to the **Insert Table** dialog box. A preview of the linked table is shown at the bottom of the dialog box.

Selecting **OK** closes the dialog box, and AutoCAD prompts you to *Specify insertion point:.* You can pick a point using your mouse, or you can enter an absolute coordinate using

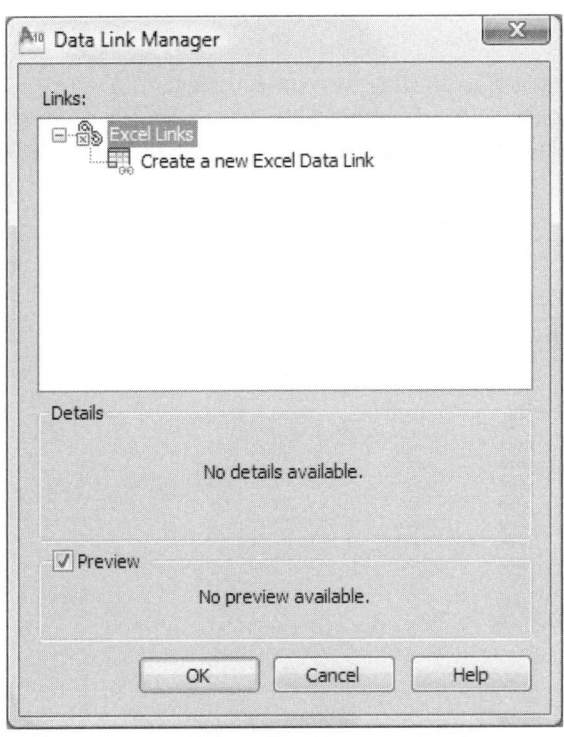

Figure 12-4   The **Data Link Manager** dialog box

Figure 12-5   The **New Excel Data Link** dialog box

the keyboard. The table is inserted without putting you in **Edit** mode because the data are already created. It is possible to modify the table after it is inserted using the methods explained in the next section. Be careful, though, because changes made in the table do not automatically update the linked Excel spreadsheet.

Note:
To guard against linked data getting out of sync, the range of linked cells is indicated by green corner brackets, and the linked cells are locked to prevent editing from within AutoCAD. If you select a linked cell, its status is indicated by the locked and linked icons as well as by information in a tooltip. It is possible to unlock a cell so that it can be updated via the **Locking** cascade menu on the right-click menu or the **Table** ribbon explained in the following section.

TIP   If you already have data in an Excel spreadsheet, you can copy and link the Excel data as **AutoCAD Entities** using **Edit|Paste Special...** with the **Paste** option selected. Pasting Excel data as **AutoCAD Entities** automatically creates a new table with the dynamic values already entered.

Table Style	
Ribbon & Panel:	Home| Annotation
Styles Toolbar:	
Menu:	Format| Table Style...
Command Line:	TABLESTYLE
Command Alias:	TS

MANAGING TABLE STYLES

Table styles are used to control the appearance of tables by allowing you to:

- Set the cell text style, height, data type, and alignment
- Control the cell border properties so you can set the border line thickness and color and turn border lines on and off
- Set the table text flow direction from top to bottom or bottom to top
- Set the horizontal and vertical cell margin distance

You can modify the default Standard table style, or you can create a new style. The **TABLESTYLE** command allows you to modify an existing table style or create a new one.

When you start the **TABLE** command, AutoCAD displays the **Table Style** dialog box shown in Figure 12-6.

Figure 12-6   The **Table Style** dialog box

To create a new table style, select the **New...** button and enter the new table style name in the **Create New Table Style** dialog box. You can select an existing table style as a starting point by selecting it from the **Start With**: list. Selecting the **Continue...** button displays the **New Table Style** dialog box shown in Figure 12-7.

Figure 12-7   The **New Table Style** dialog box

The options in the **Modify Table Style** dialog box displayed when you select the **Modify...** button on the **Table Style** dialog are exactly the same as the **New Table Style** dialog box.

You can select a table in your drawing to use as a starting point for the new table style in the **Starting table** area at the top left of the dialog box.

The **Table direction**: list box controls the direction of the text flow for the table.

- **Down**   Text reads from top to bottom (Default)
- **Up**   Text reads from bottom to top. The title row and column heads row are located at the bottom of the table

On the right side of the dialog box, there are three tabs that control the properties for the three default cell types in the **Cell styles** list box at the top:

- **Data**
- **Header**
- **Title**

You can set up and apply these different cell types to any row when you insert a table. You can also create your own cell styles via the **Manage Cell Styles** dialog box accessible by selecting the button to the right of the **Cell styles** list box.

The **General** tab controls general formatting and data type settings:

- The **Fill color**: list: box controls the background color of the cell. The **Select color...** list item displays the AutoCAD **Select Color** dialog box.

- The **Alignment**: list box controls justification and alignment for text in a cell. The same justification options are available as used for multiline text explained earlier in the chapter.

- The **Format**: setting controls the data type and display for the text in the cell. Selecting the **...** button to the right of the current **Format**: setting displays the **Table Cell Format** dialog box shown in Figure 12-8.

Figure 12-8 The **Table Cell Format** dialog box

- The **Cell Margins** area is used to control the spacing, or margin, between the cell border and the cell content. The default margin setting is 0.06″.
  - The **Horizontal:** text box sets the distance between the cell text and the left and right cell borders.
  - The **Vertical:** text box sets the distance between the cell text and the top and bottom cell borders.

The **Text** tab controls different text formatting settings:

- The **Text style:** list box lists all of the text styles in the drawing. The **…** button to the right displays the **Text Style** dialog box so you can create a new text style.
- The **Text height:** box sets the text height. The default text height for data and column head cells is 0.1800. The default text height for the table title is 0.25.
- The **Text color:** list box controls the text color. The **Select color…** list item displays the AutoCAD **Select Color** dialog box.

The **Borders** tab allows you to control the lineweight, linetype, and color of all four cell borders:

- The **Lineweight:** list box controls the lineweight for the borders you specify by selecting a border button below.
- The **Linetype:** list box controls the linetype for the borders you specify by selecting a border button below.
- The **Color:** list box controls the color for the borders you specify by selecting a border button below. The **Select color…** list item displays the AutoCAD **Select Color** dialog box.
- Checking the **Double line** check box will draw a double line border using the spacing specified below.

The buttons across the bottom determine to which border lines the properties above are applied.

- The **All Borders** button applies the border property settings to all four cell borders.
- The **Outside Border** button applies the border property settings to just the outside border of all cells.
- The **Inside Border** button applies the border property settings to the inside border of all cells. This option does not apply to title row cells.
- The **Bottom Border** button applies the border property settings to the bottom borders of all cells.
- The **Left Border** button applies the border property settings to the left borders of all cells.
- The **Top Border** button applies the border property settings to the top borders of all cells.

- The **Right Border** button applies the border property settings to the right borders of all cells.
- The **No Border** button hides borders for all cells.

Exercise 12-1: Creating a Table from Scratch

1. Start a new drawing using the acad.dwt drawing template.
2. Create a text style named **Notes** with the following settings:
   a. Font = **Simplex.shx** AutoCAD font
   b. Height = **0.125″**
3. Create a text style named **Titles** with the following settings:
   a. Font = **Arial** TrueType font
   b. Height = **0.25″**
4. Create a text style named **Architectural** with the following settings:
   a. Font = **CityBlueprint** TrueType font
   b. Height = **0.125″**
5. Create a new table style named **Schedule** with the following settings:
   a. Set the **Data rows** text style to **Notes**.
   b. Set the **Title row** text style to **Titles**.
   c. Set the **Header row** text style to **Architectural**.
   d. Set the text alignment to **Middle Center** for all rows.
   e. Set all border line lineweights to **0.50 mm** for all rows.
6. Create the window schedule shown in Figure 12-9 using the **TABLE** command with the **Schedule** table style you just created.
7. Save the drawing as **EX12-1**.

WINDOW SCHEDULE					
TAG	TYPE	MANUFACTURER	HEIGHT	WIDTH	COUNT
A	Fixed	ACME Glass Co.	4'-0"	4'-0"	20
B	Fixed	ACME Glass Co.	4'-0"	3'-6"	4
C	Fixed	ACME Glass Co.	3'-0"	2'-6"	4
D	Casement	Glassarama, Inc.	3'-0"	2'-0"	3
E	Sidelite	Season All Windows	4'-0"	1'-0"	1

Figure 12-9   Window schedule

MODIFYING TABLES

There are two levels of modifying and editing an existing table: table level and cell level. Both methods rely on using grips.

> **FOR MORE DETAILS**   See Chapter 7 for more details about using grips.

You select a table by clicking directly on a table line so that the table level grips are displayed as shown in Figure 12-10.

You can use the table grips to resize the table by stretching any corner except the insertion corner point. The insertion grip point moves the table. When you change the height or width of a table using grips, the rows and columns change proportionally.

You can change column widths by selecting a grip at the top of a column line and stretching it to another location. To also change the table width, press **<Ctrl>** while selecting the column grip.

Figure 12-10 Selecting a table for editing using grips

The light blue triangle grip at the bottom center of the table is the table-breaking grip. A table with a large amount of data can be broken into primary and secondary table fragments. You can use the table-breaking grips found at the bottom of a table to make a table span multiple columns in your drawing or to manipulate the different table parts that have already been created.

The Right-Click Menu

All the other table level editing options are provided via the right-click menu shown in Figure 12-11.

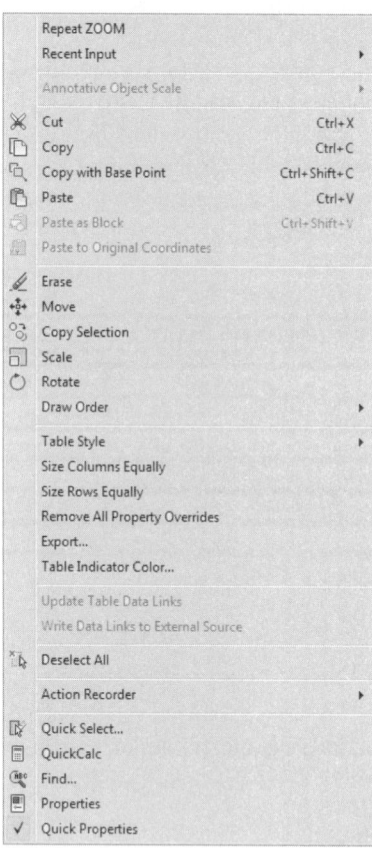

Figure 12-11 The **Table Editing** right-click menu

The **Table Style** menu item displays a cascade menu with the available table styles in the current drawing so you can change styles.

The **Size Columns Equally** menu item resizes all columns equally.

The **Size Rows Equally** menu item resizes all rows equally.

The **Remove All Property Overrides** menu item will reset the table back to its default format.

The **Export...** menu item allows you to export the table to a comma-delimited file via the **Export Data File** dialog box.

Note:
You can also use the **TABLEEXPORT** command to export a table to a comma-delimited file.

The **Table Indicator Color...** menu item allows you to change the color of the row/column indicators in the table editor using the standard AutoCAD **Select Color** dialog box.

The **Update Table Data Links** menu item updates the table with any changes in linked data if applicable.

The **Write Data Links to External Source** menu item writes any table data changes back to any linked source files.

MODIFYING TABLE CELLS

To modify a table cell, you must click inside the cell with your mouse so the four cell grips display at the midpoints of each cell border line as shown in Figure 12-12.

	A	B	C	D	E	F
1			WINDOW SCHEDULE			
2	TAG	TYPE	MANUFACTURER	HEIGHT	WIDTH	COUNT
3	A	Fixed	ACME Glass Co.	4'-0"	4'-0"	20
4	B	Fixed	ACME Glass Co.	4'-0"	3'-6"	4
5	C	Fixed	ACME Glass Co.	3'-0"	2'-6"	4
6	D	Casement	Glassarama, Inc.	3'-0"	2'-0"	3
7	E	Sidelite	Season All Windows	4'-0"	1'-0"	1

Figure 12-12   Selecting a table cell for editing using grips

You can select multiple cells by clicking and dragging your cursor to create a crossing window over multiple cells. You can also select a range of cells by selecting the first cell and holding down the **<Shift>** key to select the last cell and all the cells in between.

The four cell grips can be used to resize a row or column by selecting the appropriate grip and dragging it to a new location.

The blue diamond in the bottom right corner can be dragged to copy and increment data automatically.

The Table Ribbon

When you click inside a table cell, the **Table** ribbon shown in Figure 12-13 is displayed.

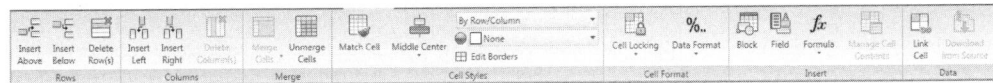

Figure 12-13   The **Table** ribbon

Using the **Table** ribbon, you can do the following:

- Edit rows and columns
- Merge and unmerge cells
- Alter the appearance of cell borders
- Edit data formatting and alignment
- Lock and unlock cells from editing
- Insert blocks, fields, and formulas
- Create and edit cell styles
- Link the table to external data

The Right-Click Menu

With a cell selected, you can also right-click and use the options on the shortcut menu shown in Figure 12-14.

The **Cell Style** cascade menu allows you to change the cell style.

The **Alignment** cascade menu allows you to change the cell's text justification using one of the standard multiline text justification options.

The **Borders...** menu item displays the **Cell Border Properties** dialog box shown in Figure 12-15 so you can change the lineweight, linetype, and/or color of one or more of the cell border lines.

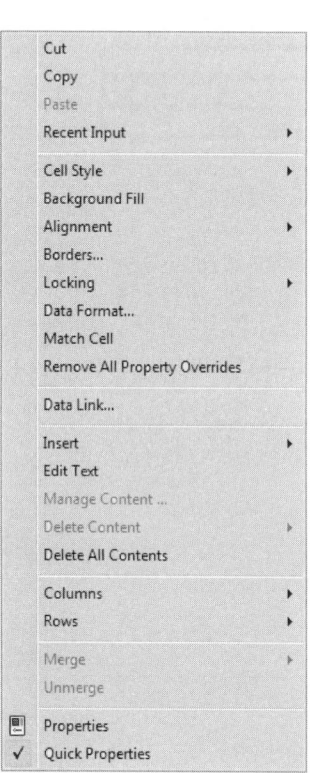

Figure 12-14   The **Cell Editing** right-click menu

Figure 12-15   The **Cell Border Properties** dialog box

The **Locking** cascade menu allows you to lock and unlock data cell content and/or data cell formatting. Tables created using data linking or data extraction are automatically locked to prevent inadvertent changes and preserve data integrity.

The **Data Format...** menu item displays the **Table Cell Format** dialog box so that you can change the data type and format for a cell.

The **Match Cell** menu item allows you to copy the selected cell properties to one or more additional cells.

The **Remove All Property Overrides** will remove all property overrides and revert back to the original table style.

The **Data Link...** menu item allows you to create or edit data links using the **Data Link Manager**.

The **Insert** cascade menu allows you to insert the following items into a cell:

- The **Block...** menu item displays the **Insert a Block in a Table Cell** dialog box so you can insert a block in a cell.

- The **Field...** menu item displays the **Field** dialog box so you can insert an automated text field. See the "Text Fields" section in Chapter 11 for complete information about inserting and using fields.

- The **Formula** cascade menu allows you to insert a formula that does calculations using values in other table cells. Inserting formulas is discussed in detail in the next section.

The **Edit Text** menu item displays the table editor and **Text Editor** ribbon so you can edit the cell text.

The **Delete All Contents** menu item deletes the cell contents.

The **Columns** cascade menu allows you to insert a new column to the left or right of the current cell, delete columns, or size multiple columns equally.

The **Rows** cascade menu allows you to insert a new row above or below the current cell, delete rows, or size multiple rows equally.

The **Merge** cascade menu item allows you to merge two or more cells into one block, row, or column.

The **Unmerge** menu item turns merged cells back into individual cells.

The **Properties** menu item displays the **Properties** palette with the cell properties displayed as shown in Figure 12-16 so you can make any formatting or content changes.

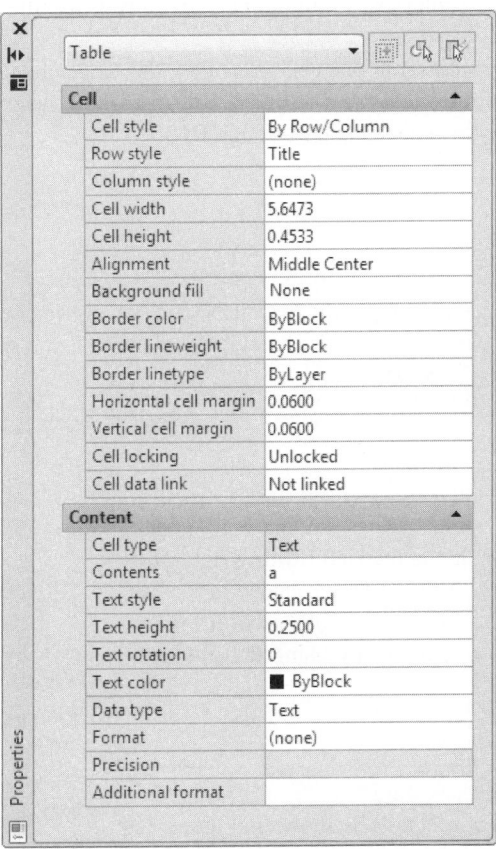

Figure 12-16   The **Properties** palette with a table cell selected

> **TIP**   The **Properties** palette provides you most of the editing features you might need, including access to many of the right-click shortcut menu items above.

INSERTING FORMULAS

Table cells can contain formulas similar to an accounting spreadsheet program. AutoCAD provides the following spreadsheet type functions:

- **=Sum(A1:A10)**   Sums the values in the first 10 rows in column A
- **=Average(A10:E10)**   Calculates the average of the values in the first five columns in row 10
- **=Count(A1:D100)**   Displays the total number of cells in columns A through D in rows 1 through 100
- **=A1+D1**   Adds the values in A1 and D1
- **=A1−D1**   Subtracts the value in D1 from the value in A1
- **=A1*D1**   Multiplies the values in A1 and D1
- **=A1/D1**   Divides the value in A1 by the value D1
- **=A1^2**   Squares the value in A1. The number after ^ is the exponent

All formulas must start with an equal sign (=). Formulas perform calculations using the values in other specified table cells by referencing their column letter and row number and/or constant values. The top left cell in a table is referenced using A1. A cell range is referenced using the first and last cells separated by a colon. For example, the range A1:D10 references the cells in rows one through 10 and columns A through D. Merged cells use the letter and number of the top left cell.

When you copy a formula from one cell to another, the range changes to reflect the new location. For example, if the formula in A11 sums A1 through A10, when you copy it to B11, the range changes so that the formula sums B1 through B10.

> **TIP**   You can create an absolute cell address that doesn't change when it is copied by preceding the row and column with a dollar sign ($). For example, if you specify A1, the column and row will always stay the same.

You can insert a formula via the **Cell Editing** right-click menu shown in Figure 12-14 that was introduced in the last section, select it from the cascade menu shown in Figure 12-17, or you can enter it in manually using the in-place text editor.

> **Note:**
> The Sum, Average, and Count formulas ignore empty cells and cells that do not contain a numeric value. The other mathematical formulas display pound signs (# # #) when a formula references empty or nonnumeric data.

Exercise 12-2: Modifying a Table

1. Continue from Exercise 12-1.
2. Modify the window schedule as shown in Figure 12-18.
3. Save the drawing as **EX12-2**.

```
Sum
Average
Count
Cell
Equation
```

Figure 12-17   The **Insert Formula** cascade menu

WINDOW SCHEDULE						
TAG	TYPE	MANUFACTURER	HEIGHT	WIDTH	SCREEN	COUNT
A	Fixed	ACME Glass Co.	4'-0"	4'-0"	No	20
B	Fixed	ACME Glass Co.	4'-0"	3'-6"	No	4
C	Fixed	ACME Glass Co.	3'-0"	2'-6"	No	4
D	Casement	Glassarama, Inc.	3'-0"	2'-0"	Yes	3
E	Sidelite	Season All Windows	4'-0"	1'-0"	No	1
F	Slider	Alumicore	7'-0"	8'-0"	Yes	1
G	Double Hung	Season All Windows	4'-0"	3'-0"	Yes	2
					TOTAL UNITS	33

Figure 12-18   Updated window schedule

CHAPTER SUMMARY

Tables can be used for many different purposes ranging from parts lists to door and window schedules. Using AutoCAD, your tables can come alive rather than remain static. You can insert intelligent fields and blocks directly into table cells. Live data can be linked from an Excel spreadsheet. It is even possible to mix and match data types so that some data are static and some are dynamically linked. In Chapter 16, we take it a step further by extracting and linking object data such as block attributes directly to a table. Stay tuned for more!

CHAPTER TEST QUESTIONS

Multiple Choice

1. Tables in AutoCAD are created using what type of data?
   a. Object
   b. Static
   c. Linked
   d. All of the above

2. The box at the intersection of a row and column is referred to as:
   a. Field
   b. Square
   c. Cell
   d. A:1

3. The best way to modify a table after it is inserted is by using:
   a. **Properties** palette
   b. **Table** ribbon
   c. Grips
   d. All of the above

4. A table's appearance and formatting is typically controlled using:
   a. Text styles
   b. Table styles
   c. Dimension styles
   d. All of the above

5. The current table style can be set using:
   a. **Annotation** panel
   b. **Insert Table** dialog box
   c. **Format** menu
   d. a and b

6. The default table insertion behavior is:
   a. Specifying a window boundary
   b. Picking a point
   c. Entering an absolute coordinate value
   d. b and c

7. To insert data from an Excel spreadsheet and convert it into an AutoCAD table, you can:
   a. Use the **PASTESPEC** command.
   b. Drag-and-drop an XLS file from Windows Explorer

   c. Select **Paste Special...** from the **Edit** pull-down menu
   d. a and c

8. Table cells can contain what type of data?
   a. Text
   b. Fields
   c. Blocks
   d. All of the above

9. The system variable that controls whether the in-place text editor displays column letters and row numbers is:
   a. **TABLECOLS**
   b. **TABLEROWS**
   c. **TABLEDISPLAY**
   d. **TABLEINDICATOR**

10. The **Data Link Manager** allows you to link to what file type?
    a. XLS
    b. CSV
    c. MDB
    d. a and b

11. The different options for starting a new table style include:
    a. Copying an existing table style
    b. Starting from scratch
    c. Picking an existing table in the drawing
    d. a and c

12. The best method to modify and update an existing table in a drawing is to:
    a. Use grips
    b. Rely on right-click menus
    c. Turn on the **Table** ribbon
    d. All of the above

13. All table formulas start with:
    a. Equal sign (=)
    b. Parentheses
    c. F
    d. None of the above

Matching

a. Table

b. Cell

c. Table styles

d. Cell style

e. **Paste Special**

f. **TABLEINDICATOR**

g. **Data Link Manager**

h. **TABLEEXPORT**

i. **Table** ribbon

1. Controls individual cell characteristics that affect the appearance of cell text and borders

2. System variable that controls the display of column letters and row numbers in the table editor

3. Ribbon used to modify tables

4. Command used to export a table to a comma-delimited file

5. Creates, edits, and manages data links

6. Command used to paste or link Excel data as an AutoCAD table

7. Controls the cell data format, the text and border properties, table direction, and other table formatting options

8. AutoCAD annotation object type that consists of data in rows and columns similar to an accounting spreadsheet

9. The box at the intersection of a table row and column that contains the table data or a formula

CHAPTER PROJECTS

Project 12-1: Parts List

1. Start a new drawing using the acad.dwt template.
2. Create a table style named **Parts List** with the following settings:
   a. Text font—**Simplex.shx**
   b. Title row text height—**0.25**
   c. Header row text height—**0.125**
   d. Data row text height—**0.125**
   e. Border lineweight = **0.60 mm**
3. Create the Parts List table shown in Figure P12-1 using the **TABLE** command.
4. Save the drawing as **P12-1**.

PARTS LIST			
ITEM	PART NUMBER	DESCRIPTION	QUANTITY
1	3VD-14602-01-00	EXHAUST PIPE COMP	1
2	92906-06600-00	WASHER	2
3	90101-06576-00	BOLT	2
4	3VD-14613-00-00	GASKET, EXHAUST PIPE	2
5	90179-08345-00	NUT, SPECIAL SHAPE	4
6	3VD-14710-03-00	MUFFLER ASSEMBLY	1
7	3VD-14755-00-00	GASKET, SILENCER	1
8	99999-01790-00	BOLT, FLANGE	1
9	90201-081H4-00	WASHER, PLATE	2
10	91316-08110-00	BOLT, HEXAGON	2

Figure P12-1

Project 12-2: Bill of Materials

1. Start a new drawing using the acad.dwt template.
2. Create a table style named **BOM** with the following settings:
   a. Text font—**Romans.shx**
   b. Title row text height—**0.25**
   c. Header row text height—**0.125**
   d. Data row text height—**0.125**
   e. Border lineweight = **0.60 mm**
3. Create the Bill of Materials table shown in Figure P12-2 using the **TABLE** command.
4. Save the drawing as **P12-2**.

BILL OF MATERIALS					
PART NUMBER	PART NAME	QUANTITY	DESCRIPTION	MATERIAL	PRICE
30431	TOP	1	6" X 9" SHEET METAL	STEEL	$3.00
34572	BODY	1	12" X 23 SHEET METAL	STEEL	$6.00
90321	HANDLES	2	C-TYPE	ALUMINUM	$12.00
36780	LATCHES	4	FRENCH MEDIUM	BRASS	$11.00
68857	FEET	4	ONE-INCH DIAMETER	RUBBER	$2.00
25410	SHELVES	5	5" X 11" SHEET METAL	STEEL	$6.00
20983	DIVIDERS	4	3" X 6" SHEET METAL	STEEL	$3.00
65382	HINGES	2	2" X 2"	BRASS	$2.00
76379	PADDING	5	5" X 11"	RUBBER	$6.00
98776	SCREWS	16	SHEET METAL SCREWS	STEEL	$2.00
TOTAL NUMBER OF ITEMS		44		TOTAL COST	$53.00

Figure P12-2

Project 12-3: Residential Architectural Plan—Continued from Chapter 11

1. Open drawing **P11-5** from Chapter 11.
2. Create a table style named **Schedule** with the following settings:
   a. Text font—**Romans.shx**
   b. Title row text height—**12**
   c. Header row text height—**8**
   d. Data row text height—**6**
   e. Border lineweight = **0.60 mm**
3. Re-create the door and window schedules created for drawing P11-5 using the **TABLE** command.
4. Save your drawing as **P12-3**.

Project 12-4: Socket Head Cap Screws—Continued from Chapter 11

1. Open drawing **P11-6** from Chapter 11.
2. Create a table style named **Screws** with the following settings:
   a. Text font—**Romans.shx**
   b. Title row text height—**0.25**
   c. Header row text height—**0.125**
   d. Data row text height—**0.125**
   e. Border lineweight = **0.60 mm**
3. Re-create the screw table created for drawing P11-6 using the **TABLE** command.
4. Save your drawing as **P12-4**.

13

Dimensioning Drawings

Chapter Objectives

- Create different types of dimension objects
- Create dimensions that match industry standards
- Control dimension associativity
- Create and manage dimension styles
- Create leader notes
- Update dimensions
- Match the settings of an existing dimension style

INTRODUCTION

Dimensioning drawings can be one of the more challenging aspects of using AutoCAD. Although creating dimension objects is fairly straightforward, controlling their look and behavior can be tricky. This is due to the many different types of dimension objects and the large number of variables that control how they look and behave. How you use dimensions and how they look and behave can also vary greatly depending on your industry (mechanical design, AEC, electronics, etc.). In this chapter, you'll examine how to place dimension objects as well as how to use dimension styles to control their look and behavior.

DIMENSION TOOLS

The most common dimension tools are located on the **Dimension** flyout menu on the **Annotation** panel on the **Home** ribbon for easy access (see Figure 13-1). These same tools and most of the other dimension tools are located on the **Dimensions** panel on the **Annotate** ribbon (see Figure 13-2).

TYPES OF DIMENSIONS

There are many types of dimension objects available in AutoCAD. Figure 13-3 shows some examples of the different types of dimension objects as well as some of the features found in a dimension object. The linear, radius, diameter, and angular dimensions are commonly used, but the type of dimensions you create will vary greatly based on your industry and discipline.

DIMENSION ASSOCIATIVITY

In Chapter 2, you saw briefly how associativity works with dimensioning. Dimension objects are linked to the geometry and update automatically when the geometry changes. AutoCAD has different levels of associativity depending on a number of factors. Sometimes AutoCAD will "flake out" and association will be lost. When this happens,

> **Note:**
> Dimensions can be placed in either model space or layout (paper) space in AutoCAD. The decision of where to place dimensions (model or paper space) can be a hotly debated topic in the AutoCAD world. Regardless of how dimensioning is handled, the important thing is to maintain consistency among drawings for any given project. Your company's CAD standards should provide clear guidelines for how dimensioning should be handled and where dimensions should be placed.

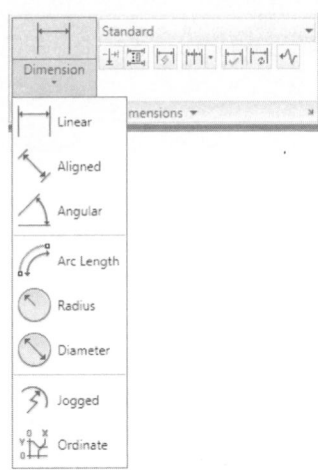

Figure 13-1   The **Annotation** panel on the **Home** ribbon

Figure 13-2   The **Dimensions** panel on the **Annotate** ribbon

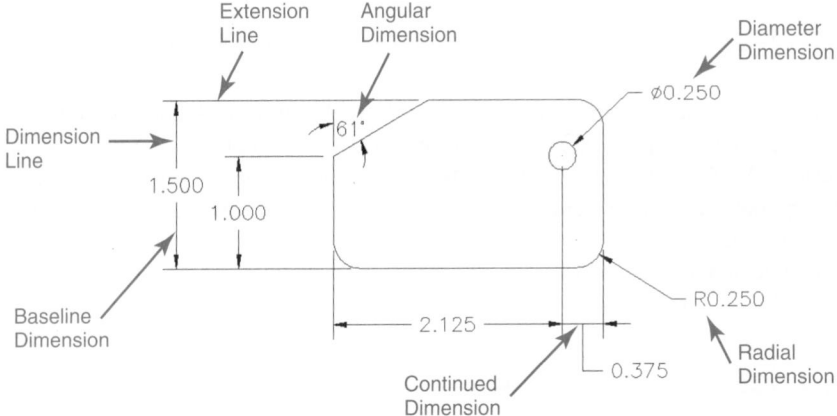

Figure 13-3   Types of dimension objects

it is sometimes possible to manually reassociate dimensions using the **REASSOCIATE** command. Controlling dimension associativity is discussed later in this chapter.

Definition Points

defpoint: Point created when placing dimensions that define the measurement value of the dimension

When you place dimension objects, you first choose the type of dimension you want to create, and then either pick points or select an object to define the placement of the dimension object. Using either method, AutoCAD automatically creates point objects that define the distance. These defining points are called *defpoints*. AutoCAD measures the distance between these defpoints and uses that distance as the default dimension text. For example, to dimension a line, you create a linear dimension. AutoCAD places defpoints at each end of the line and measures the distance between those defpoints. You then choose a location for the placement of the dimension text.

When you create dimensions, AutoCAD automatically creates a layer called **Defpoints**. All defpoints are placed on the **Defpoints** layer.

Note:
The **Defpoints** layer is unique in that it doesn't plot, regardless of its **Plot/Noplot** setting. Also, once created, the **Defpoints** layer cannot be deleted with either the **PURGE** command or the **Delete Layer** button in the **LAYER** command.

TIP If your drawing has a **Defpoints** layer, but no dimension objects, and you wish to get rid of the **Defpoints** layer, you can simply rename the layer. Once it is renamed, it will behave like any other layer and can be deleted or purged as needed.

CREATING HORIZONTAL AND VERTICAL DIMENSIONS

Vertical and horizontal dimensions are created with a single command, **DIMLINEAR**. The **DIMLINEAR** command measures the vertical or horizontal dimension between two definition points and allows you to pick the location of the dimension line.

Selecting Definition Points

There are two ways to create a linear dimension: pick points or select an object. Using the pick point method, you select any two points in your drawing and then select the location of the dimension text. Where you place the dimension text determines whether a vertical or horizontal dimension is created. If you place the dimension text above or below the points, AutoCAD will create a horizontal dimension. Selecting to the left or right of the selected points will create a vertical dimension (see Figure 13-4).

Linear	
Ribbon & Panel:	Home| Annotation
	⊢—⊣ Linear
Dimension Toolbar:	⊢—→
Menu:	Dimension| Linear
Command Line:	DIMLINEAR
Command Alias:	DIMLIN

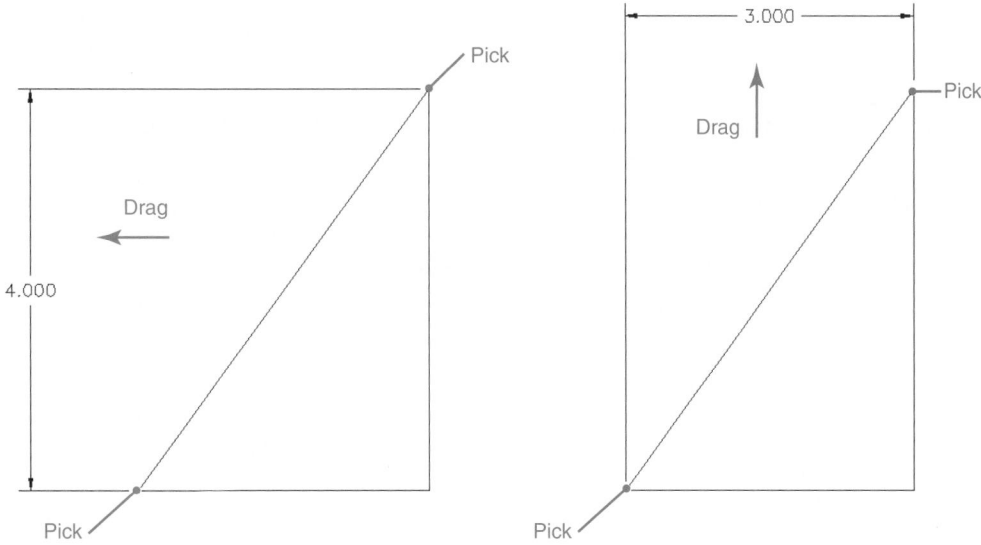

Figure 13-4 Placing a vertical or horizontal dimension

Selecting an Object

You can also create a linear dimension by selecting a line, arc, or circle. When you start the **DIMLINEAR** command, AutoCAD prompts you to *Specify first extension line origin or <select object>:*. Press **<Enter ↵>** to select a line, arc, or circle. When you select an object, AutoCAD will select the two points at the ends of the object as the definition points. Figure 13-5 shows the results of selecting different objects.

Note:
When selecting an object, you can select only line, arc, or circle objects. Ellipses, text points, or spline curves are not allowed. When you select a polyline object, AutoCAD will dimension the line or arc segment of the polyline at the point you selected.

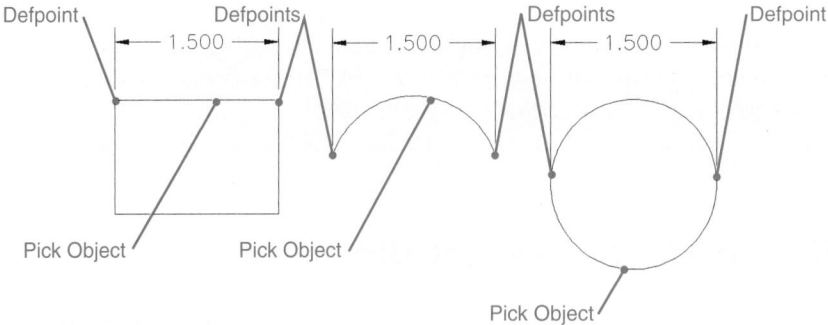

Figure 13-5   Linear dimensions on selected objects

The DIMLINEAR Options

After you select the definition points, AutoCAD provides a number of options for creating and placing the dimensions. These options are listed below.

Mtext	This option allows you to change the default dimension text using the Mtext text editor.
Text	The **Text** option allows you to modify the default dimension text at the command prompt. This is similar to the **Mtext** option, except you can place only a single line of text.
Angle	The **Angle** option allows you to specify the angle of the dimension text. The dimension text will be rotated to the specified angle.
Horizontal	By default, a horizontal or vertical dimension is placed depending on where you drag your cursor. This option allows you to override the cursor location and explicitly tell AutoCAD to place a horizontal dimension.
Vertical	This is like the **Horizontal** option, except you explicitly tell AutoCAD to place a vertical dimension.
Rotated	The **Rotated** option allows you to change the measurement angle of the dimension. For example, specifying an angle of 30 will cause AutoCAD to measure the distance between the two definition points along a 30° angled line (see Figure 13-6).

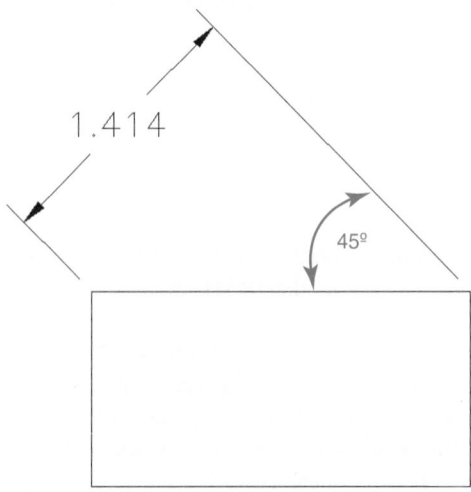

Figure 13-6   Rotated dimension
text

Exercise 13-1: Creating Linear Dimensions

1. Open the drawing **EX13-1** in the student data files. Make sure Object Snaps are turned on and set to detect **Endpoint** and **Center**.
2. Start the **DIMLINEAR** command. AutoCAD prompts you to *Specify first extension line origin or <select object>:.*
3. Pick the endpoint P1 shown in Figure 13-7. AutoCAD prompts you to *Specify second extension line origin:.*
4. Pick the endpoint P2 shown in Figure 13-7. AutoCAD prompts you to *Specify dimension line location or ↓* and starts dragging the dimension line.
5. Place the dimension line as shown in Figure 13-8. AutoCAD places the dimension and ends the **DIMLINEAR** command.

To access student data files, go to www.pearsondesigncentral.com.

Figure 13-7   Selecting the definition points   **Figure 13-8**   Linear dimensions

6. Restart the **DIMLINEAR** command. AutoCAD prompts you to *Specify first extension line origin or <select object>:.*
7. Press **<Enter ↓>**. AutoCAD prompts you to *Select object to dimension.*
8. Pick the line at P3 shown in Figure 13-7. AutoCAD places the defpoints at the ends of the line and prompts you to *Specify dimension line location or ↓.*
9. Place the dimension line as shown in Figure 13-8. AutoCAD places the dimension and ends the **DIMLINEAR** command.
10. Save your drawing as **EX13-1**. Your drawing should look like Figure 13-8.

Overriding Dimension Text.   The **DIMLINEAR** command has two text options: **Mtext** and **Text.** These options allow you to override the default text associated with the dimension. By default, AutoCAD places the numerical distance between the two definition points as the dimension text. By using the **Mtext** and **Text** options, you can modify or even override the measured distance. For example, you may want to include a note or other additional text along with the default dimension, or you may want to type in a specific dimension instead of using the measured dimension value.

The <> Brackets.   When you use the **Mtext** option, AutoCAD displays the multiline text editor with the default dimension text highlighted (see Figure 13-9). The default dimension text is the measured distance between the definition points. You can type any text before or after the default dimension text or you can delete it, but you cannot modify the value of the highlighted text. If you remove the default text, AutoCAD will ignore the measured distance and display only the text you specify.

If you delete the default dimension text, you can re-create it by typing <>. When AutoCAD sees the <> brackets, it will replace it with the measured distance between the definition points.

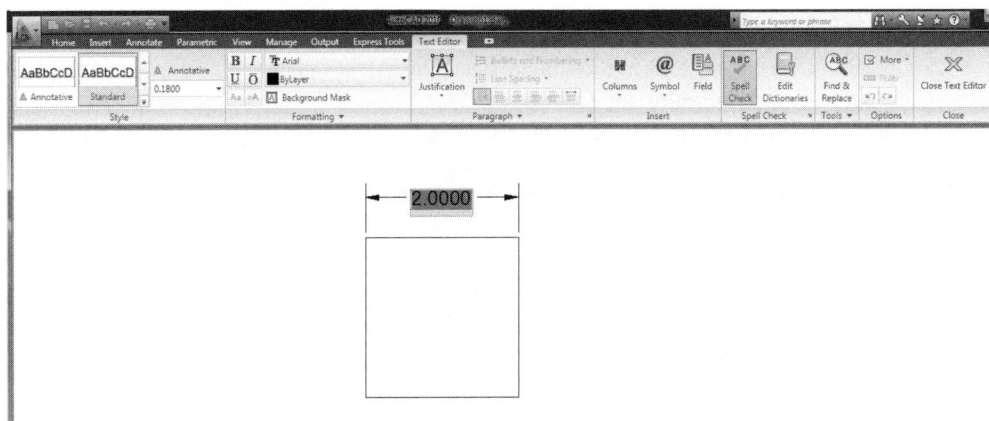

Figure 13-9   The default dimension text

You can use the < > brackets with the **Text** option as well. When using the **Text** option, Auto-CAD will display the measured dimension as a default and allow you to type a single line of text. You can type whatever text you want, using the < > brackets as a placeholder for the measured distance between the definition points.

TIP   You can also use the **DDEDIT** command to edit dimension text.

Exercise 13-2: Modifying Dimension Text

1. Continue from Exercise 13-1.
2. Start the **DIMLINEAR** command. AutoCAD prompts you to *Specify first extension line origin or <select object>:*.
3. Press **<Enter ↵>**. AutoCAD prompts you to *Select object to dimension.*
4. Pick the line at P1 shown in Figure 13-10. AutoCAD places the defpoints at the ends of the line and prompts you to *Specify dimension line location or ↓*.

Figure 13-10   Specifying an object to dimension

5. Choose the **Mtext** option. AutoCAD displays the multiline text editor with the default dimension text highlighted. Delete the default dimension text and type **1.00** in the mtext editor. Close the mtext editor. AutoCAD shows the dimension as 1.00.
6. Select the line you just dimensioned to activate its grips. Select the grip at one endpoint and drag it to a new location. Pick anywhere on the screen to place the end of the line. AutoCAD stretches the line and the dimension moves along with it, but the value of the dimension text does not update.

Figure 13-11   The modified dimension

7. Start the **DDEDIT** command and select the **1.00** dimension text. Delete the **1.00** text and type <>. AutoCAD replaces the <> brackets with the measured length of the line.
8. Select the line to activate its grips and return the endpoint to its original location. AutoCAD stretches the line, and the dimension moves with it. The dimension text updates to show the change.
9. Save your drawing as **EX13-2**. Your drawing should look like Figure 13-11.

CREATING ALIGNED DIMENSIONS

An aligned dimension is another type of linear dimension. However, while horizontal and vertical dimensions measure distances along either the *X*- or *Y*-axis, respectively, an aligned dimension measures the true distance between any two points. The dimension text is placed parallel to a line between the two points (see Figure 13-12). Aligned dimensions are created with the **DIMALIGNED** command.

When using the **DIMALIGNED** command, you can select the two definition points, or you can select a line, arc, or circle. Once you specify the definition points, the **Mtext, Text**, and **Angle** options are available. These options are identical to the **Mtext, Text**, and **Angle** options in the **DIMLINEAR** command.

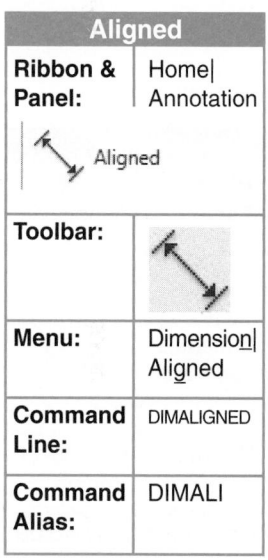

Aligned	
Ribbon & Panel:	Home| Annotation
	Aligned
Toolbar:	
Menu:	Dimension| Aligned
Command Line:	DIMALIGNED
Command Alias:	DIMALI

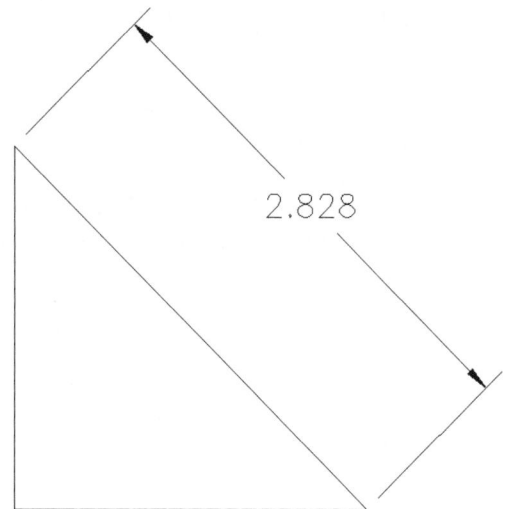

2.828

Figure 13-12   An aligned dimension

Exercise 13-3: Creating Aligned Dimensions

1. Continue from Exercise 13-2.
2. Start the **DIMALIGNED** command. AutoCAD prompts you to *Specify first extension line origin or <select object>:*.
3. Press **<Enter ↵>**. AutoCAD prompts you to *Select object to dimension*.

Figure 13-13   An aligned dimension

4. Pick the line at P1 shown in Figure 13-13. AutoCAD places the defpoints at the ends of the line and prompts you to *Specify dimension line location or ↓*.
5. Place the dimension line as shown in Figure 13-13.
6. Save your drawing as **EX13-3**. Your drawing should look like Figure 13-13.

TIP   You can also select the extension line origin points to define the angle of the aligned dimension. Typically. you would rely on Object Snaps to snap to endpoints or intersections.

Radius	
Ribbon & Panel:	Home|Annotation
	⊙ Radius
Dimension Toolbar:	⊘
Menu:	Dime<u>n</u>sion|<u>R</u>adius
Command Line:	DIMRADIUS
Command Alias:	DIMRAD

DIMENSIONING CIRCLES AND ARCS

When dimensioning circles and arcs, you will typically be calling out either radius or diameter dimensions or, in the case of arcs, the length of an arc segment. AutoCAD provides a dimensioning command for each of these types of dimensions.

Radius Dimension

Radius dimensions are placed with the **DIMRADIUS** command. When you select this command, AutoCAD will prompt you to select an arc or circle. You can select circles, arcs, and polyline arc segments. Once you select an arc or circle, AutoCAD measures the radius of the arc and prompts you for the location of the text. You can place the text inside or outside the arc. AutoCAD will place a leader line perpendicular to the arc through the specified point on the arc and put a center mark in the center of the circle or arc. When you place the text, AutoCAD will automatically place an **R** prefix before the measured radius (see Figure 13-14). Like the **DIMLINEAR** and **DIMALIGNED** commands, you have the **Mtext, Text**, and **Angle** options for modifying the dimension text.

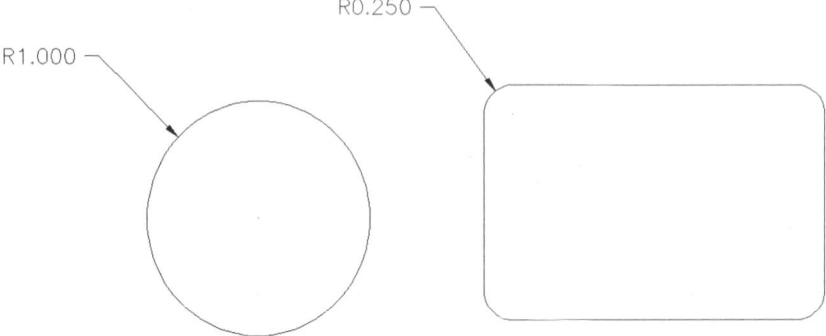

Figure 13-14   The radius prefix

Creating a Jogged Radius Dimension

With the **DIMRADIUS** command, the leader line will always point perpendicular to the circle or arc segment. The start point of the leader will always be in line with the center point of the arc (see Figure 13-15). A jogged radius dimension is similar to a regular radius dimension except the leader line has an offset jog built into it. This allows you to specify a different center point for the leader. This can be useful when dimensioning large radii in which the center point lies outside of your drawing area. Jogged radius dimensions are created with the **DIMJOGGED** command.

Jogged	
Ribbon & Panel:	Home| Annotation
Dimension Toolbar:	
Menu:	Dimension| Jogged
Command Line:	DIMJOGGED
Command Alias:	JOG

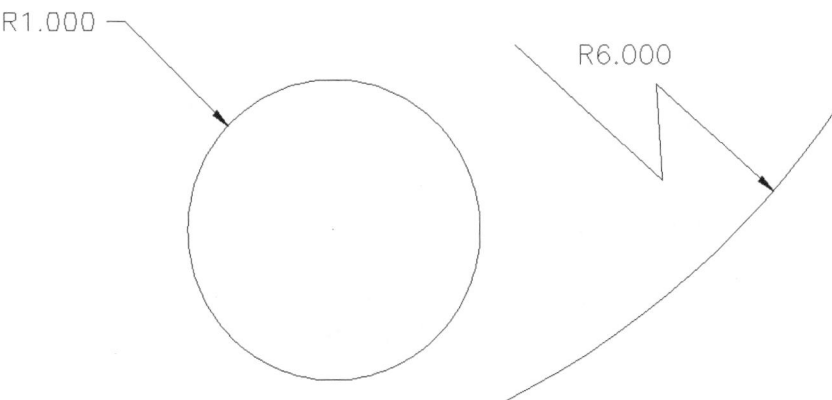

Figure 13-15   A radial and a jogged dimension

When you start the **DIMJOGGED** command, you are prompted to select a circle or arc. Once you select an object, AutoCAD prompts you to *Specify center location override:*. This is the location of the starting point (nonarrow end) of the leader line. The leader line is drawn from this point to a point on the circle or arc segment. You are then prompted for the location of the dimension text. Once you place the text, you can adjust the location of the jogged segment (see Figure 13-16).

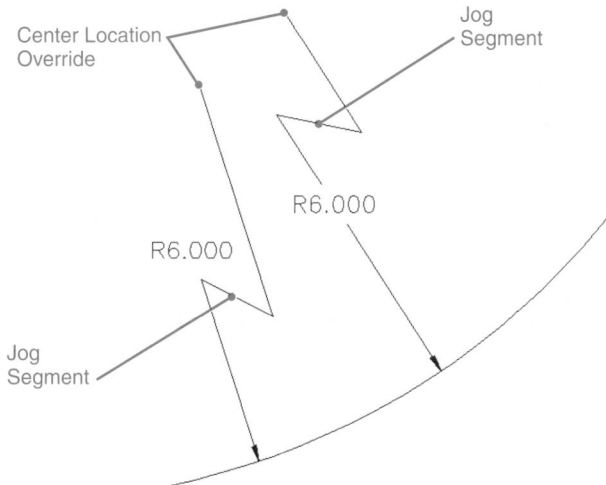

Figure 13-16   The jogged segment

Diameter Dimension

Diameter dimensions are placed with the **DIMDIAMETER** command. The **DIMDIAMETER** command behaves just like the **DIMRADIUS** command. The only difference is that text shown is the diameter of the arc or circle, and AutoCAD places the diameter symbol Ø in front of the text.

Diameter	
Ribbon & Panel:	Home| Annotation
	Diameter
Dimension Toolbar:	
Menu:	Dimension| Diameter
Command Line:	DIMDIAMETER
Command Alias:	DIMDIA

TIP   It is possible to dimension an arc beyond its endpoints. AutoCAD automatically creates an arc extension line.

Figure 13-17   Radial and diameter dimensions

Exercise 13-4: Creating Radius and Diameter Dimensions

1. Continue from Exercise 13-3.
2. Start the **DIMRADIUS** command. AutoCAD prompts you to *Select arc or circle:*.
3. Pick the arc at P1 shown in Figure 13-17. AutoCAD places the defpoints at the center of the arc and at the point you selected on the arc. You are then prompted to *Specify dimension line location or ↓*.
4. Choose the **Mtext** option and type **TYP** after the default dimension text. Close the mtext editor.
5. Place the dimension line as shown in Figure 13-17.
6. Start the **DIMDIAMETER** command. AutoCAD prompts you to *Select arc or circle:*.
7. Pick the circle at P2 shown in Figure 13-17. AutoCAD places the defpoints at the center of the arc and at the point you selected on the circle. You are then prompted to *Specify dimension line location or ↓*.
8. Place the dimension line as shown in Figure 13-17.
9. Save your drawing as **EX13-4**. Your drawing should look like Figure 13-17.

Dimensioning the Length of an Arc

Arc Length	
Ribbon & Panel:	Home| Annotation
	Arc Length
Dimension Toolbar:	
Menu:	Dime<u>n</u>sion| Arc Leng<u>t</u>h
Command Line:	DIMARC
Command Alias:	None

Similar to a linear dimension, AutoCAD can dimension the length of an arc using the **DIMARC** command. When using the **DIMARC** command, you select an arc segment, and AutoCAD measures the distance along the arc. By default, AutoCAD will dimension the entire length of the arc from endpoint to endpoint, but you can also opt to dimension a portion of the arc length. In addition to the **Mtext, Text**, and **Angle** options, the **Partial** option allows you to pick a start and endpoint along the arc segment and dimension only the portion of the arc between the two points.

When you place an arc length dimension, AutoCAD automatically places the arc symbol ⌒ in front of the dimension value (see Figure 13-18).

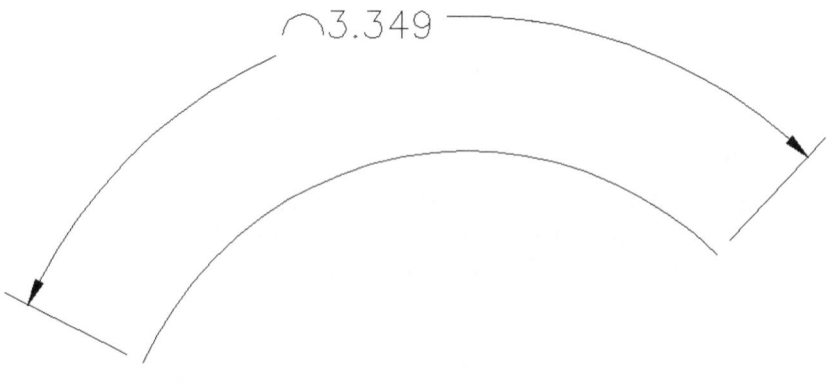

Figure 13-18   The ⌒ symbol

To access student data files, go to www.pearsondesigncentral.com.

Exercise 13-5: Creating an Arc Length Dimension

1. Open the drawing **EX13-5** in the student data files.
2. Start the **DIMARC** command. AutoCAD prompts you to *Select arc or polyline arc segment:*.

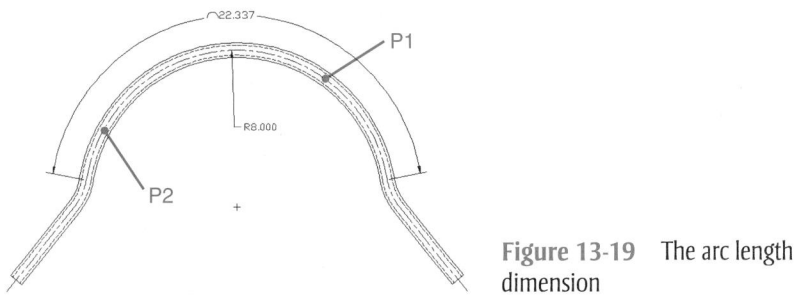

Figure 13-19 The arc length dimension

3. Pick the arc at P1 shown in Figure 13-19. AutoCAD places the defpoints at the center of the arc and at the point you selected on the arc. You are then prompted to *Specify dimension line location or ↓*.
4. Place the dimension line as shown in Figure 13-19.
5. Start the **DIMRADIUS** command. AutoCAD prompts you to *Select arc or circle:*.
6. Pick the arc at P2 shown in Figure 13-18. You are prompted to *Specify arc length dimension location or ↓*.
7. Place the dimension line as shown in Figure 13-19.
8. Save your drawing as **EX13-5**. Your drawing should look like Figure 13-19.

Creating Center Marks

When dimensioning arcs and circles, AutoCAD places marks at the center of the dimensions (see Figure 13-20). You may have a need to place center marks on arcs and circles that are not dimensioned. AutoCAD has a number of ways to create center marks. One option is to simply draw center marks using either the **LINE** or **PLINE** command. Another way is to use the **DIMCENTER** command.

The **DIMCENTER** command places orthogonal line segments at the center of a circle or arc segment. When you start the **DIMCENTER** command, AutoCAD prompts you to select a circle or an arc segment and then places center mark line segments.

Note:
When you use the DIMCEN-TER command, the resulting lines are not dimension objects but simply line segments.

Center Mark	
Ribbon & Panel:	Annotate| Dimensions
Dimension Toolbar:	
Menu:	Dimension| Center Mark
Command Line:	DIMCENTER
Command Alias:	None

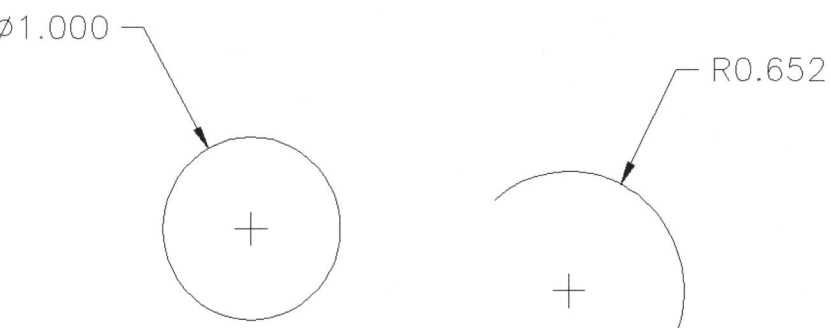

Figure 13-20 Center marks

FOR MORE DETAILS The **DIMCEN** system variable controls the size of center marks. Dimension variables are typically controlled through dimension styles, which are covered later in this chapter. For more information on the **DIMCEN** system variable, see Appendix D.

ANGULAR DIMENSIONS

With linear dimensions, AutoCAD needs to have two definition points in order to calculate the dimension value. With radius and diameter dimensions, AutoCAD can calculate the dimension value directly from the arcs and circles. When dimensioning angles, AutoCAD needs to know

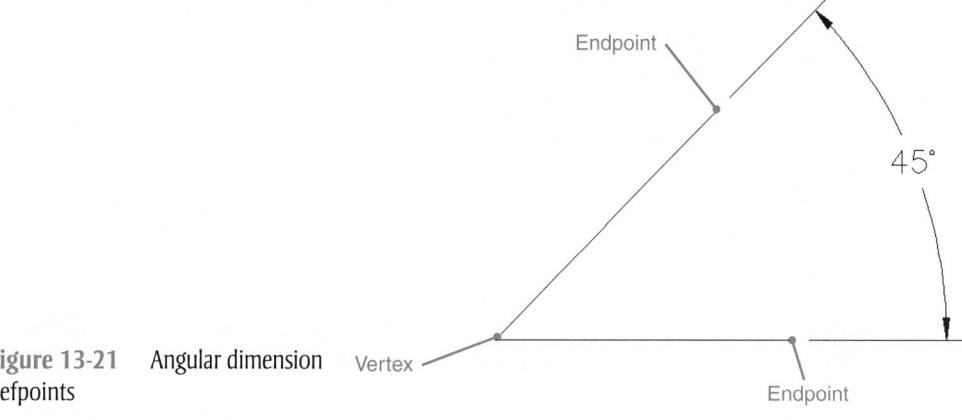

Angular	
Ribbon & Panel:	Home| Annotation
	<img> Angular
Dimension Toolbar:	<img>
Pull-down Menu:	Dime_n_sion| _A_ngular
Command Line:	DIMANGULAR
Command Alias:	DIMANG

Figure 13-21   Angular dimension defpoints

three points in order to define the angular dimension: a center vertex and two endpoints (see Figure 13-21). Angular dimensions are placed with the **DIMANGULAR** command. When using this command, you have three options for defining angular dimension: selecting an arc or circle, selecting two intersecting lines, or picking three points to define the vertex and the two endpoints.

Selecting Objects

When you start the **DIMANGULAR** command, AutoCAD prompts you to _Select arc, circle, line, or <specify vertex>_. If you select an arc, AutoCAD uses the center and ends of the arc to determine the angular dimensions.

If you select a circle, AutoCAD uses the selection point as one endpoint of the angle and the center of the circle as the vertex. AutoCAD then prompts you for a second endpoint and allows you to place the dimension text.

If you select a line segment, AutoCAD will ask you to select another line segment and will dimension the angle between endpoints of the first and second lines. AutoCAD will use the endpoints closest to the selection point of the line. Figure 13-22 shows the results of selecting two lines at various points.

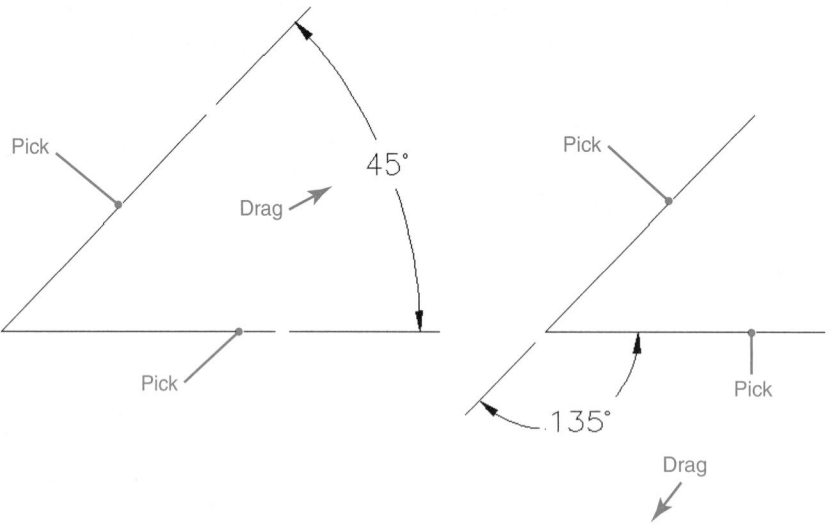

Figure 13-22   Specifying angular defpoints

Selecting Vertex and Angle Endpoints

To specify the vertex and angle endpoints, press **<Enter ↵>** when AutoCAD prompts you to _Select arc, circle, line, or <specify vertex>_. AutoCAD will prompt you for a vertex point and then prompt you for two endpoints.

The Quadrant Option

The **Quadrant** option allows you to place dimension text outside of the angle being measured. The only way to access the **Quadrant** option is from the right-click menu after selecting the angle to measure when AutoCAD prompts you: _Specify dimension arc line location or ↓_.

The **Quadrant** option prompts you to specify the quadrant that you want to dimension separate from specifying the dimension arc line location. If the dimension arc line is outside of the quadrant that is being measured, AutoCAD automatically creates an arc extension line using the current extension line settings.

Exercise 13-6: Creating an Angular Dimension

1. Continue from Exercise 13-5.
2. Start the **DIMANGULAR** command. AutoCAD prompts you to *Select arc, circle, line, or <specify vertex>*.
3. Pick the line at P1 shown in Figure 13-23. AutoCAD prompts you to *Select second line:*.
4. Pick the line at P2 shown in Figure 13-23. AutoCAD prompts you to *Specify dimension arc line location or ↓*.
5. Place the dimension line as shown in Figure 13-23. Notice that the angle that is dimensioned varies with your cursor location.
6. Save your drawing as **EX13-6**. Your drawing should look like Figure 13-23.

> **Note:**
> If you select two parallel lines, AutoCAD will show you the message *Lines are parallel* in the command window and end the command. If you select anything but a line segment for the second line, AutoCAD will display the message *Object selected is not a line* in the command window and prompt you to *Select second line.*

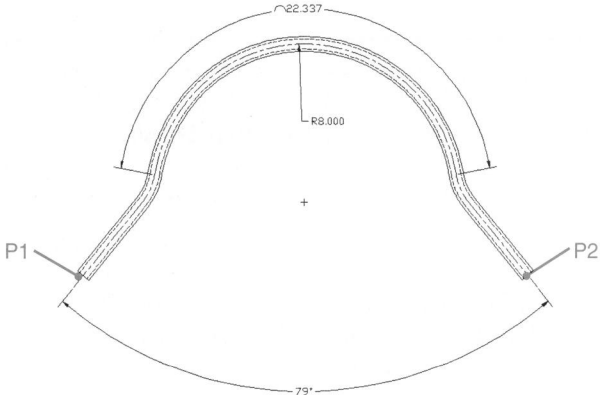

Figure 13-23   An angled dimension

CREATING DATUM AND CHAIN DIMENSIONS

Datum and chain dimensioning refers to linear dimensions that share common extension lines. A datum dimension is also known as a *baseline* dimension, in which multiple features are measured from a common feature. Chain dimensions are also known as *continued* dimensions, in which linear dimensions continue end-to-end. Figure 13-24 shows examples of baseline and continued dimensions.

Figure 13-24   Continued and baseline dimensions

Continue	
Ribbon & Panel:	Annotate| Dimensions
	Continue
Dimension Toolbar:	
Menu:	Dimension| Continue
Command Line:	DIMCONTINUE
Command Alias:	DIMCONT

Baseline	
Ribbon & Panel:	Annotate| Dimensions
	Baseline
Dimension Toolbar:	
Menu:	Dimension| Baseline
Command Line:	DIMBASELINE
Command Alias:	DIMBASE

Continued Dimension

A continued dimension is similar to a baseline dimension. It requires an existing linear or angular dimension, and it allows you to place multiple dimension lines in a single command. The only difference is that while baseline dimensions measure dimensions from a common extension line, continued dimensions measure from the last placed dimension line. The result is a chain of dimensions, each one measured from the last. Continued (or chain) dimensions are created with the **DIMCONTINUE** command.

When you start the **DIMCONTINUE** command, AutoCAD will place the dimension line at the second extension line of the last linear or angular dimension placed in the drawing. If you want to continue the dimension from dimension, you can press **<Enter ↵>** to select a different extension line. Like the **DIMBASELINE** command, the **DIMCONTINUE** command will repeat until you end the command. You also have the **Undo** and **Select** options to undo the last continued dimension or to select a different extension line to continue from.

Baseline Dimension

Baseline dimensions are measured from an extension line of an existing linear or angular dimension. When you place a baseline dimension, each dimension is measured from this extension line, and the dimension lines are spaced at a predefined distance. Baseline dimensions are created with the **DIMBASELINE** command.

> **FOR MORE DETAILS**
>
> The **DIMDLI** system variable controls the spacing of the baseline dimension lines. Dimension variables are typically controlled through dimension styles, which are covered later in this chapter. For more information on the **DIMDLI** system variable, see Appendix D.

The **DIMBASELINE** command requires an existing linear or angular dimension. By default, AutoCAD will use the first extension line of the last linear or angular dimension as the baseline. If you want to use a different extension line, you can press **<Enter ↵>** to select a different extension line. If AutoCAD cannot locate or determine where the last dimension line is, it will prompt you to select an extension line to use for the baseline.

Once you've specified the extension line to use as the baseline, AutoCAD prompts you to pick a definition point for the next extension line. The **DIMBASELINE** command will continue to place baseline dimensions until you end the command. While placing baseline dimensions, you can use the **Undo** option to undo a dimension line placement or press **<Enter ↵>** to select a different extension baseline.

Exercise 13-7: Creating Continued and Baseline Dimensions

To access student data files, go to www.pearsondesigncentral.com.

1. Open the drawing **EX13-7** in the student data files.
2. Start the **DIMLINEAR** command and place the horizontal dimension between P1 and P2 as shown in Figure 13-25.
3. Start the **DIMCONTINUE** command. AutoCAD starts dragging a dimension from the previous dimension. You are prompted to *Specify a second extension line origin or* ↓.
4. Place the dimensions P3 and P4 as shown in Figure 13-25. Press **<Esc>** to exit the **DIMCONTINUE** command.
5. Start the **DIMBASELINE** command. AutoCAD starts dragging a dimension from the previous dimension. You are prompted to *Specify a second extension line origin or* ↓.
6. Press **<Enter ↵>** to choose the **Select** option. AutoCAD prompts you to *Select base dimension:*.

Figure 13-25   Specifying dimension points

Figure 13-26   Continued and baseline dimensions

7. Choose the extension line at P1 shown in Figure 13-26. AutoCAD prompts you to *Specify a second extension line origin or ↓* .
8. Select the end of the line shown at point P2 shown in Figure 13-26. AutoCAD automatically spaces the dimension above the selected dimension.
9. Save your drawing as **EX13-7**. Your drawing should look like Figure 13-26.

DIMASSOC System Variable

There are actually three levels of associativity for a dimension object. The **DIMASSOC** system variable controls which level of dimension associativity AutoCAD uses.

The **DIMASSOC** system variable can be set to a value of **0, 1**, or **2**. When set to **2** (the default setting), dimension defpoints are associated with objects in the drawing. For example, if you dimension between the two endpoints of a line, AutoCAD will create defpoints at the endpoints of the line, and these defpoints will be associated with the line object. If the line moves, the dimension will move along with it. If an endpoint of the line is moved (stretched, trimmed, extended, etc.), the defpoint associated with that endpoint will move, and the dimension will update.

When **DIMASSOC** is set to **1**, AutoCAD still creates associative dimensions, but the defpoints are not associated with any particular geometry. To update a dimension, you must modify (move or stretch) the defpoints associated with the dimension explicitly. For example, if you dimension a line with **DIMASSOC** set to **1**, AutoCAD will create defpoints at the ends of the line. But if you move the line, the dimension will not follow it. You would have to select and move the dimension along with the line to keep them together. If you move the end of the line (by stretching, trimming, extending, etc.), you will need to move the defpoint located at the end of the line as well in order for the dimension to update.

When **DIMASSOC** is set to **0**, AutoCAD creates exploded dimensions with no associativity. No defpoints are created, and each part of the dimension is created as a separate object (lines and text).

TIP

While it's possible to create exploded dimensions, it's considered bad practice in most CAD work environments. Exploded dimensions are difficult to manage and update and can lead to sloppy and inaccurate drawings.

You can toggle the **DIMASSOC** variable with the **Associative Dimensioning** check box in the **User Preferences** tab of the **Options** dialog box (see Figure 13-27). When this box is checked, **DIMASSOC** is set to **2**. With the check removed, **DIMASSOC** is set to **1**.

Figure 13-27 The **Dimension Associativity** check box

Adjust Space	
Ribbon & Panel:	Annotate| Dimensions 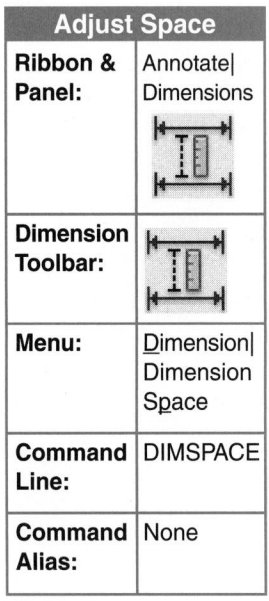
Dimension Toolbar:	
Menu:	Dimension| Dimension Space
Command Line:	DIMSPACE
Command Alias:	None

DIMENSION TOOLS

AutoCAD provides a few handy dimension tools that allow you to automate tasks that used to be much more time-consuming. There are tools to evenly space stacked dimensions and to break dimension lines and extension lines that cross other dimensions, as well as that have the ability to create jog lines in linear dimensions when a distance is too long to fit on the specified sheet size.

The Adjust Space Tool

The **Adjust Space** tool allows you to evenly space selected dimensions as shown in Figure 13-28. You can specify the spacing distance between dimension lines or let AutoCAD automatically determine a minimum spacing distance.

When you select the **Adjust Space** tool, AutoCAD prompts you to *Select the base dimension:* so that you can select the first dimension in the stack. After selecting a base dimension, AutoCAD then prompts you to *Select dimensions to space:*. Select the dimensions you want to space and either enter a distance or press **<Enter ↵>** to select the **Auto** option. The **Auto** option automatically spaces the dimensions based on the current dimension text height.

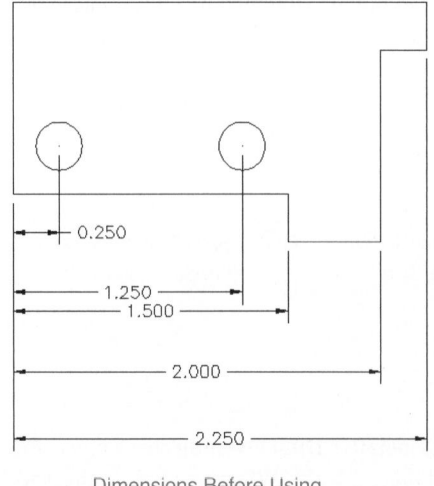

Dimensions Before Using Adjust Space Tool

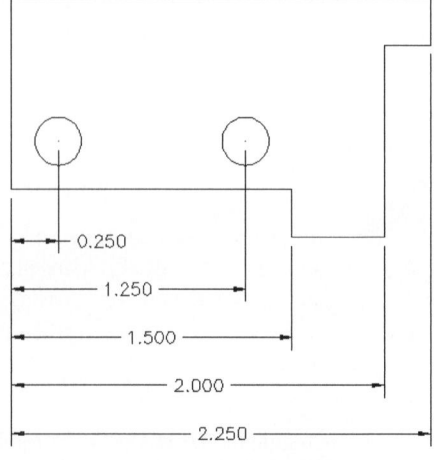

Dimensions After Using Adjust Space Tool

Figure 13-28 The **Adjust Space** tool

The Break Tool

The **Break** tool allows you to break dimension or extension lines where they intersect other dimensions or objects in your drawing as shown in Figure 13-29.

Dimensions Before Using
Break Tool

Dimensions After Using
Break Tool

Figure 13-29   The **Break** tool

Break	
Ribbon & Panel:	Annotate| Dimensions
Dimension Toolbar:	
Menu:	Dimension| Dimension Break
Command Line:	DIMBREAK
Command Alias:	None

When you select the **Break** tool, AutoCAD prompts you to *Select dimension to add/remove break or* ↓ so that you can select the dimension. After selecting the dimension, you have four options:

- Select intersecting objects to use as cutting edges for the break. AutoCAD prompts for objects until you press **<Enter ↵>**.

- Use the **Auto** option to automatically trim around all intersecting objects

- Use the **Manual** option so that you have to manually pick break points

- Use the **Remove** option to remove all the breaks from selected dimensions or leaders

Note:
When you break a dimension either by selecting objects or by using the **Auto** option, the breaks will automatically update when the intersection point moves. If the objects are moved so that they no longer intersect, the break will disappear; if they are moved back, the break will automatically return to the original location.

 TIP   You can break more than one dimension at a time by selecting the **Multiple** option after the **Break** tool.

The Jog Line Tool

The **Jog Line** tool allows you to add a jog, or breakline, to linear dimensions to represent measurements whose values are not the same length as the dimension line. Jogged dimension lines are typically used when a sheet is too small to display the true length of a dimension line as shown in Figure 13-30.

When you select the **Jog Line** tool, AutoCAD prompts you to *Select dimension to add jog or* ↓ so that you can select the dimension to add the jog. After selecting a dimension, AutoCAD then prompts you to *Specify jog location (or press Enter):*. You can either pick the location on the dimension line to locate the jog line or press **<Enter ↵>** to place the jog line automatically based on the direction of the dimension definition points. The jog line is created closest to the first dimension definition point.

Note:
The linear jog size can be specified on the **Symbols and Arrows** tab of the Dimension Style Manager dialog box explained later.

Jog Line	
Ribbon & Panel:	Annotate| Dimensions
Dimension Toolbar:	
Menu:	Dimension| Jogged Linear
Command Line:	DIMJOGLINE
Command Alias:	None

Figure 13-30   The **Jog Line** tool

TIP You can change the jog location using grips. You can turn off a jog line or edit its height using the **Properties** palette.

QUICK DIMENSIONING

When creating dimension objects, you may find that placing dimensions can be a somewhat tedious, repetitive process. Many times you may wish to simply place some dimensions on the drawing and then go back and adjust their placement and orientation to suit your drawing. AutoCAD helps automate the process of placing dimensions by allowing you to create multiple dimensions at once. The **QDIM** command (quick dimension) allows you to select multiple objects and then select a type of dimension to place. AutoCAD will then automatically detect definition points and place the specified dimensions based on those points.

Quick Dimension

When you start the **QDIM** command, AutoCAD will prompt you to *Select geometry to dimension:*. Once you have built your selection set of objects, press **<Enter ↵>**, and AutoCAD will provide a number of options. These options are described below.

Continuous.   The **Continuous** option places continuous dimensions from the outermost points of the selected geometry. When you select this option, AutoCAD will place the dimension objects and allow you to select a placement point for the dimensions. The dimensions will be either vertical or horizontal based on where you drag your cursor.

Staggered.   The **Staggered** option places a series of staggered or nested linear dimensions, starting from the innermost pair of definition points. From there, it will place a linear dimension on the next outer level of points and continue outward until the geometry is dimensioned. Figure 13-31 shows some examples of staggered dimensions placed with the **QDIM** command.

datumPoint.   The **datumPoint** option sets a base point for the **Baseline** and **Ordinate** dimension options. By default, when you use the **Baseline** option, it places the datum or base point of the dimensions on the definition point nearest to 0,0. The **datumPoint** option allows you to override this and place the datum point at any point in the drawing.

Baseline.   The **Baseline** option creates a series of baseline dimensions starting either at 0,0 or at the point specified with the **datumPoint** option. Figure 13-32 shows you some examples of baseline dimensions.

Quick Dimension	
Ribbon & Panel:	Annotate| Dimensions
	Jogged
Dimension Toolbar:	
Menu:	Dimension| Quick Dimension
Command Line:	QDIM
Command Alias:	None

Ordinate.   Ordinate dimensioning displays *X*- and *Y*-datum coordinates based on an origin, or datum point. The datum point is typically located at a key point on the geometry such as the corner of a part. The **Ordinate** option of the **QDIM** command creates a set of ordinate dimensions with the origin being either 0,0 or a point specified with the **datumPoint** option.

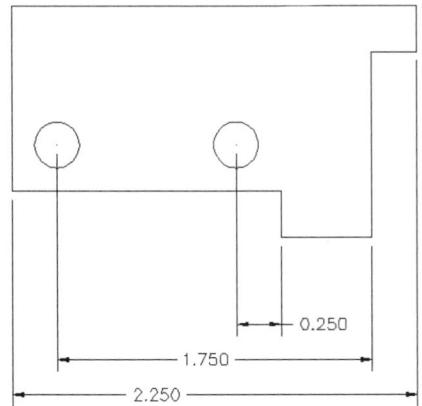

Figure 13-31   Staggered quick dimensions

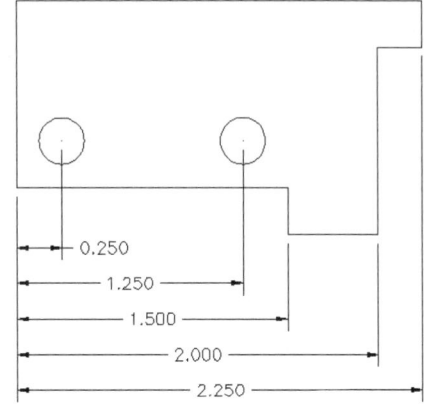

Figure 13-32   Baseline quick dimensions

TIP   Ordinate dimensions can also be created with the **DIMORDINATE** command. However, the **DIMORDINATE** command does not allow you to set a 0,0 datum point. To use the **DIMORDINATE** command, you must first establish a User Coordinate System (UCS) with its origin located at your desired datum point, which is beyond the scope of this book. Using the **QDIM** command with the **datumPoint** and **Ordinate** options is a much quicker way of creating ordinate dimensions.

Radius.   The **Radius** option will search through your selection of objects and find any circles or arcs. You are then prompted for a location for the leaders. The leaders are placed in the same relative position on each arc or circle. Figure 13-33 shows an example of using the **Radius** option.

Figure 13-33   Radius quick dimensions

Diameter.   The **Diameter** option works the same way as the **Radius** option. AutoCAD places diameter dimensions at the same relative points on each arc or circle.

Edit.   The **Edit** option allows you to edit the definition points within the selection set. When you choose this option, AutoCAD will show you all the definition points found in the selection set. You can add or delete definition points prior to placing your dimensions.

seTtings.   The **seTtings** option allows you to set the preference for determining definition points. By default, AutoCAD will look for endpoints of objects. You can set it to **Intersection** or **Endpoint**.

To access student data
files, go to
www.pearsondesigncentral.com.

Exercise 13-8: Creating Quick Dimensions

1. Open the drawing **EX13-8** in the student data files.
2. Start the **QDIM** command. AutoCAD prompts you to *Select geometry to dimension:*.
3. Type **ALL<Enter ↵>** to select all the geometry in the drawing. AutoCAD prompts you to *Specify dimension line position or ↓*.
4. Choose the **datumPoint** option and pick the endpoint P1 shown in Figure 13-34. AutoCAD prompts you to *Specify dimension line position or ↓*.

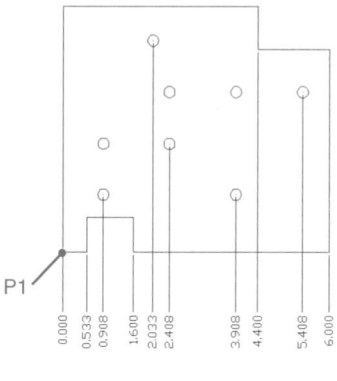

Figure 13-34 Selecting a datum point

5. Choose the **Ordinate** option. AutoCAD prompts you to *Specify dimension line position or ↓*.
6. Place the *X*-datum dimensions as shown in Figure 13-34. AutoCAD prompts you to *Specify dimension line position or ↓*.
7. Restart the **QDIM** command. AutoCAD defaults to the **Ordinate** option. Place the *Y*-datum dimensions shown in Figure 13-35.
8. Save your drawing as **EX13-8**. Your drawing should look like Figure 13-35.

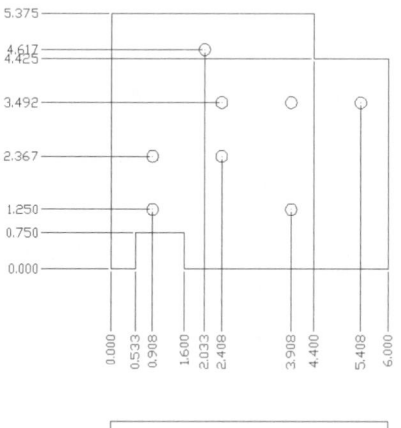

Figure 13-35 Ordinate quick dimensions

Dimension Style	
Ribbon & Panel:	Home|Annotation
Dimension Toolbar:	
Menu:	Dime<u>n</u>sion|Dimension Style…
Command Line:	DIMSTYLE
Command Alias:	DDIM

MANAGING DIMENSION STYLES

So far, we've looked at how to create and place dimension objects. Creating and placing dimension objects is only part of the process. In this section, you'll examine how to control the look of dimension objects through dimension styles.

A dimension style is a collection of dimension settings that is assigned a name and is applied as a group to dimension objects. Dimension styles control the look and behavior of dimension objects, such as the type of arrowhead used, the text style used in the dimensions, tolerance values and formatting, and the overall scale of the dimension.

Dimension styles work similarly to text styles or layers: you set a dimension style current and then any new objects are created using the settings contained within that style. Dimension styles are managed with the **DIMSTYLE** command.

When you start the **DIMSTYLE** command, AutoCAD displays the **Dimension Style Manager** dialog box (see Figure 13-36). From this dialog box, you can create dimension styles, modify dimension styles, compare dimension styles, and set a dimension style current. The **Styles** list shows dimension styles defined in your drawing. The **List** options allow you to control which dimension styles are shown in the **Styles** list. You can choose to show all dimension styles or only the ones currently used in the drawing. You can also choose to show or hide dimension styles contained in referenced drawings.

FOR MORE DETAILS	See Chapter 17 for more on referencing drawings.

Figure 13-36   The **Dimension Style Manager** dialog box

Figure 13-37   The **Create New Dimension Style** dialog box

The **Preview** area shows a preview image of the current dimension style and tells you which dimension style is current. The buttons along the right-hand side of the dialog box allow you to create, modify, override, and compare dimension styles.

Creating a Dimension Style

AutoCAD comes with two predefined dimension styles: **Annotative** and **Standard. Standard** is AutoCAD's default dimension style. Both can be modified, renamed, or even deleted if one is not the current style. The settings for the dimension styles are defined in the template file used to create the drawing. To create a new dimension style, choose the **New...** button. AutoCAD will display the **Create New Dimension Style** dialog box (see Figure 13-37).

When you create a new dimension style, AutoCAD will create a copy of an existing dimension style as the starting point. In the **Create New Dimension Style** dialog box, you specify the name for the new dimension style and tell AutoCAD which style to copy as the starting point. You can also create a dimension style that applies only to a certain type of dimension. For example, you might want all your dimension text to align with the dimension line, except for radial and diameter dimensions, where you might want the text to be horizontal. These styles are known as *child dimension styles* and appear as a substyle of the parent dimension style.

TIP   When you select a child dimension style in the **Dimension Style Manager** dialog box, the **Preview** area shows you only the dimension settings that are different from the parent style, and the **Description** area lists the differences between the parent and child dimension styles.

Exercise 13-9: Creating a New Dimension Style

1. Continue from Exercise 13-8.
2. Start the **DIMSTYLE** command. AutoCAD displays the **Dimension Style Manager** dialog box. Choose **New...** to display the **Create New Dimension Style** dialog box.
3. Type **Mech** in the **New Style Name** box and make sure the **Start With** box is set to **Standard** and the **Use for** box is set to **All Dimensions**. Choose **Continue** to create the new dimension style. AutoCAD displays **New Dimension Style** dialog box.
4. Choose **OK** to accept the dimension style settings. AutoCAD returns you to the **Dimension Style Manager** dialog box. The new dimension style is listed in the **Styles** list. Choose the **Close** button to end the **DIMSTYLE** command.
5. Start the **DIMLINEAR** command and place the dimension shown at P1 in Figure 13-38.
6. Save your drawing as **EX13-9**.

Figure 13-38   Creating a new
dimension style

Modifying an Existing Dimension Style

To modify a dimension style, select the style name from the **Dimension Style Manager** and choose the **Modify** button. This will display the **Modify Dimension Style** dialog box (see Figure 13-39). This dialog box is divided into seven different tabs that contain the settings for various aspects of your dimensions. These tabs are described in the following sections.

Lines Settings.   The **Lines** tab (see Figure 13-39) controls the dimension and extension lines within a dimension object. Figure 13-40 shows how these various settings map to dimension objects. The **Dimension lines** area allows you to set the **Color, Linetype**, and **Lineweight** of the dimension lines as well as the spacing between dimension lines when creating baseline dimensions. The **Extend beyond ticks** setting is available only when certain types of arrowheads are specified. For example, when an architectural tick is used, the **Extend beyond ticks** setting controls how far past the tick to extend the dimension line. You can suppress the dimension line on either side of the text. This comes in handy when dimensioning in tight areas where the dimension lines tend to obscure dimension text.

The **Extension lines** area has similar controls for extension lines. You can set the **Color, Linetype**, and **Lineweight** of the extension lines as well as control the length of the extension line and the gap between the extension line and the object you are dimensioning.

Checking the **Fixed length extension lines** check box will create extension lines that are all the same length specified in the **Length:** box regardless of their origin point locations. The fixed length is calculated using the distance from the second extension line origin point (second pick point) to the dimension line location point (third pick point) minus the distance specified in the **Offset from origin:** box.

Symbols and Arrows.   The **Symbols and Arrows** tab (see Figure 13-41) allows you to set the size and type of arrowheads used in dimensions. You can set different arrowheads for the first and second dimension lines as well as a separate arrowhead for leaders. The **Center marks** area allows you to set the size and type of center marks. This affects how center marks

Figure 13-39   The **Modify Dimension Style** dialog box

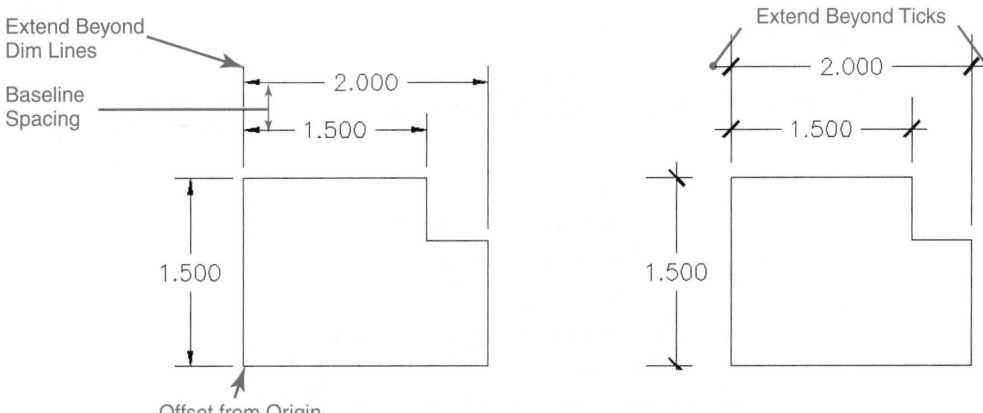

Figure 13-40   Dimension line settings

Figure 13-41   The **Symbols and Arrows** tab

are shown in radial and diameter dimensions and also controls how center mark lines are created with the **DIMCENTER** command. The **Arc length symbol** area controls where the arc length symbol is displayed with the **DIMARC** command, and the **Jog angle** setting controls the angle of the jogged segment in the **DIMJOG** command. Figure 13-42 shows examples of settings in the **Symbols and Arrows** tab.

The **Jog height factor** setting controls the height of the jog created by the **Jogged Line** tool explained earlier.

Note:
The **Leader:** arrowhead setting is used only by the old style QLEADER command. Use the **Multileader Style Manager** introduced to control the arrowhead for the default leader type.

Figure 13-42   Symbols and Arrows settings

Text Settings.   The **Text** tab (see Figure 13-43) controls how text is placed and how it looks. The **Text appearance** area allows you to set the text style used. The **...** button displays the **Style** dialog box to allow you to create and modify text styles. The **Text color** and **Fill** buttons control the color of the text and the color of the text background. You can also draw a box around the text by turning on the **Draw frame around text** option.

The **Text height** and **Fraction height scale** settings control text height. The **Fraction height scale** is a scale factor applied to numerator and denominator text in a fraction. For example, if the **Text height** is set to .125 and the **Fraction height scale** is set to .5, the size of the numerator and denominator would be .0625, making the overall height of the fraction .125. Figure 13-44 shows examples of the **Text appearance** settings.

The **Text placement** area controls how text is placed in regard to the dimension lines and extension lines. The **Offset from dim line** setting controls the gap between the dimension line and the dimension text. The **Vertical** setting allows you to place the text above, below, or centered on the dimension line. You can also choose **JIS**, which places the dimension text to conform to the Japanese Industrial Standard. Figure 13-45 shows the effects of the **Vertical** setting.

The **Horizontal** setting controls where the text is placed in reference to the extension lines. You can place the text near the first or second extension line, or have the text drawn over the first or second extension line. Figure 13-46 shows the effects of the **Horizontal** setting.

The **View Direction** setting controls whether text reads from left to right or from right to left.

Figure 13-43   The **Text** tab

Architectural Text Style

Text Height .25

Ø0.187

2.000

1.500

Fraction Height Scale .75

$1\frac{1}{2}$

Text Height .125

Ø0.250

Ø0.500

Frame Around Text

Figure 13-44   **Text appearance** settings

Centered

2.000

1.500

1.500

ø0.250

Above

2.000

1.500

1.500

ø0.250

JIS

2.000

1.500

1.500

ø0.250

Figure 13-45   **Vertical** text settings

Centered

2.000

1.500

Near First Extension

2.000

1.500

Over First Extension

2.000

1.500

Figure 13-46   **Horizontal** text settings

The **Text alignment** area controls whether text is always displayed horizontally or aligned with the dimension line. The **ISO standard** setting allows you to align text with one dimension line when text is inside the extension lines, but align it horizontally when it is outside the extension lines.

Fit and Scale Settings.   The **Fit** tab (see Figure 13-47) controls the behavior and scale of dimension objects. The **Fit** options control how dimensions behave when AutoCAD cannot place both the dimension lines and text between the extension lines. Figure 13-48 shows examples of each of these settings.

Figure 13-47   The **Fit** tab

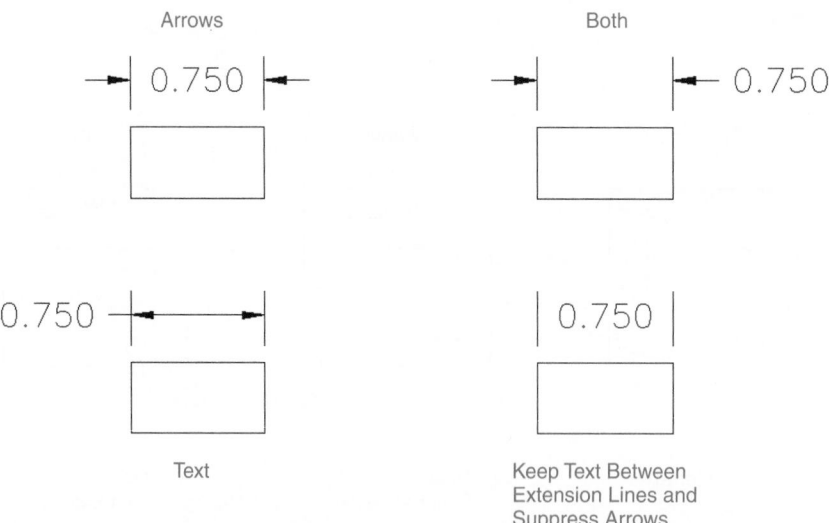

Figure 13-48   **Fit** settings

The **Text placement** area controls where text is placed when it is not in its default position. You can choose to have AutoCAD move the text beside the dimension line (outside the extension line), over the dimension line with a leader line running between the text and the dimension line, or over the dimension line without a leader. Figure 13-49 shows the effect of each of these options.

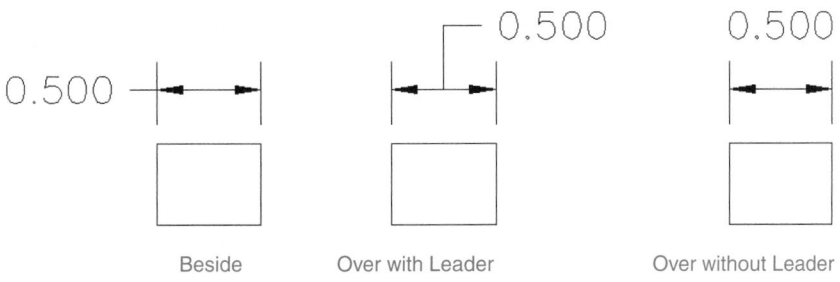

Figure 13-49 **Text placement** settings

Chapter 1 discussed annotation scale factors. For example, if you have a drawing plotted at a scale of 1/8″ = 1-0″, you need to scale all of your model space annotation by a factor of 96. This ensures that as the drawing is scaled down for plotting, the annotation appears at the correct size. The **Scale for dimension features** area controls the overall annotation scale of dimension objects.

The **Annotative** scale setting utilizes the AutoCAD **Annotation Scale** feature located on the right side of the Status Bar so that dimension features are scaled automatically when dimensions are added to your drawing. This setting will also add different scaled dimension features if you are using the **Annotation Scale** feature that automatically adds annotative scale objects.

Note:
It's important to note that the **Scale for dimension features** setting affects only the size of dimension objects, not the values of the dimensions themselves.

> **FOR MORE DETAILS** See Chapter 1 for a detailed description of the **Annotation Scale** feature.

The **Scale dimensions to layout** setting will automatically scale all your dimension features to match the scale of the layout viewport. This feature requires that you add dimensions through the paper space viewport so that AutoCAD knows what scale you are currently using.

The **Use overall scale of** setting is a manual scale factor that is applied to all dimension features. For example, if your text and arrowheads are set to a height of **.125** and the overall scale is set to **2**, AutoCAD will draw your text and arrowheads at a size of **.25**. Figure 13-50 shows an example of setting the overall dimension scale factor.

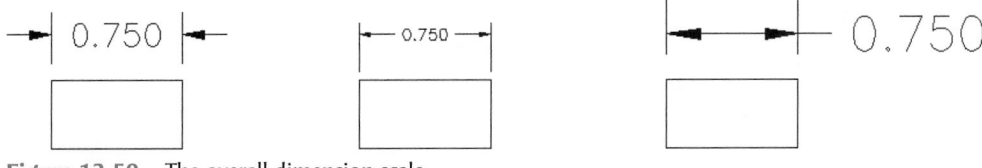

Figure 13-50   The overall dimension scale

> **FOR MORE DETAILS** See Chapter 14 for a detailed description of using paper space layouts and the different scale options for annotation features. Chapter 14 also includes directions on how to place and scale dimensions in paper space.

The **Fine tuning** area gives you some additional options for controlling the look of your dimension. When turned on, the **Place text manually** box adds an additional prompt when

Figure 13-51   Draw dim line between ext lines options

Normal

Draw Dim Line
Between Ext Lines

you are creating dimensions, which allows you to specify a location for the dimension text after you locate the dimension line.

The **Draw dim line between ext lines** option will force a dimension line to be placed between the extension lines, regardless of the location of the dimension text. Figure 13-51 shows some examples of turning on this option.

Primary Units Tab. The **Primary Units** tab (see Figure 13-52) controls the formatting of the dimension text. The **Linear dimensions** area allows you to control how units are displayed; the **Angular dimensions** area controls the display of angular dimensions. The options are listed next.

Unit Format. This option sets the units format for all dimension types except angular. This is typically set to match the units of your drawing. In addition to the standard AutoCAD unit settings, you can also choose the **Windows Desktop** units, which use the settings contained in the **Regional and Language Options** in the Windows **Control Panel** (see Figure 13-53).

In the **Angular dimensions** area, the **Units format** list allows you to control how angular dimensions are displayed. You can choose from **Decimal Degrees, Degrees Minutes Seconds, Gradians**, or **Radian** units.

> **Note:**
> Although it is common to set the dimension units of a dimension style the same as the display units used in the drawing, it is not required. As an example, you might have **Decimal** display units set in the drawing and **Architectural** units set in a dimension style. The separate unit settings also make it possible to create additional dimension styles with distinct dimension unit settings so that you can use different dimension standards in the same drawing.

Figure 13-52   The Primary Units tab

Figure 13-53   The Windows Regional and Language Options dialog box

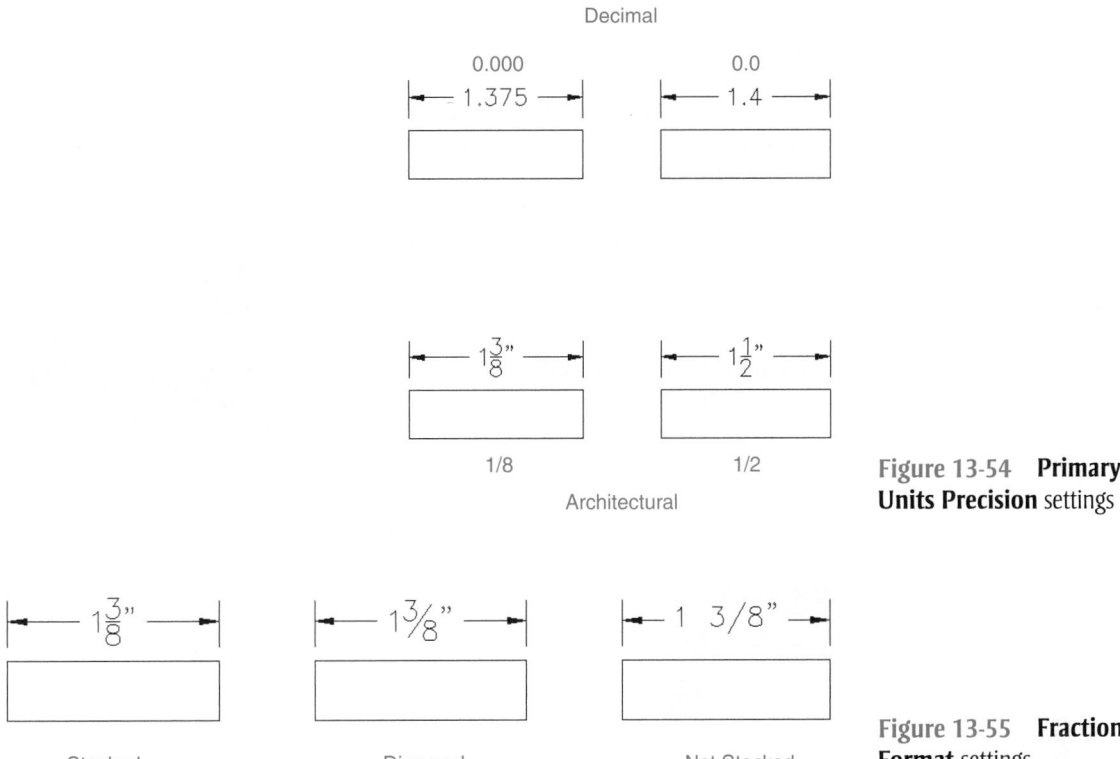

Figure 13-54 **Primary Units Precision** settings

Figure 13-55 **Fraction Format** settings

Precision.   This option controls the number of decimal places in the dimension text. This setting controls only how the dimension text is displayed; it does not change the drawing geometry or affect the actual measured value of the dimension. There are two settings: one for linear dimensions and one for angular dimensions. Figure 13-54 shows some examples of this setting.

Fraction Format.   This controls how fractions are displayed. This option is available only when the **Unit Format** is set to either **Architectural** or **Fractional**. This format is used in conjunction with the **Fractional height scale** in the **Text** tab. Figure 13-55 shows examples of these settings.

Decimal Separator.   When the **Unit format** is set to **Decimal**, this option sets the character used for the decimal separator.

Round Off.   This option sets the rounding rules for all dimension types except angular. If you enter a value of **0.25**, all distances are rounded to the nearest 0.25 unit. If you enter a value of **1.0**, all dimension distances are rounded to the nearest integer. The number of digits displayed after the decimal point depends on the **Precision** setting. Like the **Precision** setting, this setting affects only how dimensions are displayed; it does not change the geometry or the actual measured value of the dimension.

Prefix.   The **Prefix** option allows you to set a prefix in the dimension text. The specified text is placed in front of the default dimension text. You can enter any text you want or use control codes to display special symbols. For example, entering the control code **%%c** displays the diameter symbol.

Suffix.   The **Suffix** option works the same as the **Prefix** option except the specified text is placed after the default dimension text. For example, specifying the inch character (″) would place a ″ mark after each dimension.

Note:
When you enter a prefix, it replaces any default prefixes such as those used in diameter and radius dimensioning. If you specify tolerance values, the prefix is also added to the tolerance text as well as to the regular dimension text.

Measurement Scale. The **Measurement Scale** area allows you to define a scale factor for the default dimension text values. The **Scale factor** option sets a scale factor for linear dimension measurements. The value of any linear dimension is multiplied by this scale factor, and the resulting value is used as the default dimension text. For example, if you set a measurement scale factor of **2**, the dimension text for a 1-inch line is displayed as two inches. The value does not apply to angular dimensions and is not applied to rounding values or to plus or minus tolerance values.

When the **Apply to layout dimensions only** is turned on, AutoCAD will apply the measurement scale value only to dimensions created in layout (paper space) viewports.

> **Note:**
> Do not confuse the **Measurement Scale** with the **Use overall scale of:** setting located on the **Fit** tab discussed earlier. The **Measurement Scale** factor changes the numerical value of a dimension so that it no longer represents the actual length in the drawing. The **Use overall scale of:** setting, or dimension scale, affects only the appearance of dimension features like arrowheads and text size. The numerical dimension value always reflects its true length.

FOR MORE DETAILS	See Chapter 14 for more on dimensioning in layout (paper) space.

Zero Suppression. These options control the display of leading and trailing zeros in dimension text. For example, when set to decimal units, turning on the **Leading** option means that a dimension value of 0.5000 would be shown as .5000. With the **Trailing** option turned on, a dimension of 12.5000 would be displayed as 12.5. There are separate settings for both linear dimensions and angular dimensions.

The **0 feet** and **0 inches** options control the display of zeros in feet and inches dimensions. For example, when the **0 feet** option is turned on, 0'-8" would be displayed as 8". With **0 inches** turned on, 12'-0" would be displayed as 12'.

The **Sub-units factor** and **Sub-unit suffix** settings allow you to specify a sub-units factor and suffix so that when a dimension value is less than 1, you can switch to smaller units instead of displaying a leading zero.

Alternate Units Tab. The **Alternate Units** tab (see Figure 13-56) allows you to show dimensions in two different formats. A typical example of this is to show both inch and millimeter dimensions such as **2.00 [50.8mm]**. The **Alternate Units** tab contains settings that are similar to the **Primary**

Figure 13-56 The **Alternate Units** tab

Units tab. To enable alternate units, select the **Display alternate units** box. Once this is selected, the remaining options are enabled.

The **Unit format** and **Precision** options work the same as the **Primary Units** tab settings. When using fractional unit formats (**Architectural** and **Fractional**), you can choose between stacked or unstacked fractions.

Multiplier for Alternate Units and Round Distances To.   The **Multiplier for alt units:** setting specifies the conversion factor between the primary units and the alternate units. For example, to convert inches to millimeters, specify a multiplier of 25.4. The value has no effect on angular dimensions. The **Round distances to:** setting allows you to apply a rounding value to the alternate dimensions. This rounding value is independent of the primary units round-off value.

Prefix and Suffix and Zero Suppression.   The **Prefix:** and **Suffix:** values work the same as the primary units. To place an mm notation after the alternate dimensions, set the suffix to **mm**. The **Zero suppression** settings also work the same as the **Primary Units** tab settings.

Placement.   This controls where the alternate units are displayed. You can choose between **After Primary Value** and **Below Primary Value**.

The Tolerances Tab.   The **Tolerances** tab allows you to control the display and values of tolerances for both primary and alternate units. The **Zero suppression** and **Precision** settings work the same way as the primary and alternate units settings but control only the tolerance values. The **Upper** and **Lower** values control the upper and lower limits of the tolerance settings.

Method.   The **Method** setting controls how the tolerances are displayed. These settings are described below. Figure 13-57 shows an example of each setting.

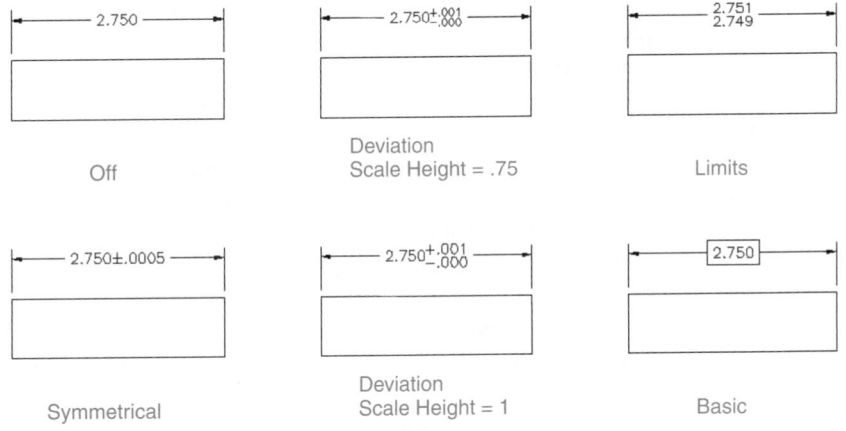

Figure 13-57   The tolerance **Method** settings

None	This setting turns off the tolerance display.
Symmetrical	This setting adds a plus/minus tolerance to the dimension measurement. A plus or minus sign appears before the tolerance. The **Symmetrical** setting uses the upper tolerance value. For example, when using the **Symmetrical** setting, if the upper tolerance value is set to **.001**, a **1″** dimension would be displayed as 1.0060.001.
Deviation	This is similar to symmetrical but allows you to display separate upper (+) and lower (−) tolerance values. The values appear stacked after the primary dimension.
Limits	The **Limits** setting replaces the primary dimension value with two stacked values. The upper value represents the sum of the primary dimension and the upper tolerance value. The lower value represents the primary dimension minus the lower tolerance value.
Basic	This setting creates a basic dimension, which displays a box around the full extents of the dimension.

Scaling for Height. The **Scaling for height** setting controls the relative size of the tolerance text. The value is a scale factor, which is multiplied by the primary unit text height. For example, if you set a **Scaling for height** value of **.5**, the tolerance text would be half the size of the primary units. This is primarily used with the **Deviation** and **Limits** methods.

Vertical Position. This option controls the vertical location of the primary dimension text in relation to the tolerance text. You can choose either **Top, Middle,** or **Bottom.** Figure 13-58 shows examples of the **Vertical position** setting.

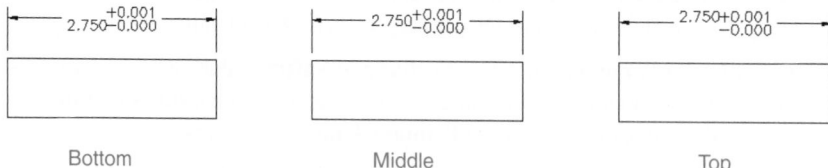

Bottom   Middle   Top

Figure 13-58 Vertical position settings

Exercise 13-10: Modifying an Existing Dimension Style

1. Continue from Exercise 13-9. Start the **DIMSTYLE** command to display the **Dimension Style Manager** dialog box.
2. Choose the **Mech** dimension style and choose the **Modify...** button. This will display the **Modify Dimension Style** dialog box.
3. In the **Symbols and Arrows** tab, set the **Arrow size** to **.125**.
4. In the **Text** tab, choose the **...** button next to the **Text style** list. This displays the **Text Style** dialog box. Choose **New** and create a text style named **DIM** using the romans.shx font. Choose **Apply** and then **Close** to close the **Text Style** dialog box. AutoCAD returns you to the **Text** tab of the **Modify Dimension Style** dialog box.
5. Choose the **Dim** text style you just created in the **Text style** list and set the **Text height** to **.125**.
6. Choose **OK** to save the dimension style changes and return to the **Dimension Style Manager** dialog box. Select the **Mech** dimension style and choose **Set Current** to set the dimension style current. Choose the **Close** button to end the **DIMSTYLE** command. Any dimensions that have this style are updated.
7. Select the dimensions created in Exercises 13-8 and 13-9 and change their dimension styles to **Mech** via the **Quick Properties** palette.
8. Save your drawing as **EX13-10**. Your drawing should resemble Figure 13-59.

Figure 13-59 The modified dimension style

Modifying Dimension Styles Versus Overriding Dimension Styles

When modifying dimensions, any changes made to the dimension style will affect all the dimensions that use that style. There may be times when you want to change the settings for a single dimension without making changes to the dimension style. In this case, a dimension override is what you need.

A dimension override allows you to make changes to dimension settings without applying them to the dimension style. Once you make a dimension override, any new dimensions will be placed with the settings of the dimension override until that override is changed or deleted. The dimension objects created with the override will retain the override setting until the dimension style is reapplied to the dimension.

Note:
A dimension override is similar to hard-coding object properties. For example, Chapter 6 showed how an object can have color, linetype, and lineweight settings that are different from the layer setting.

Overriding a Dimension Style.   To create a dimension override, choose the **Override** button from the **Dimension Style Manager** dialog box. When you choose this button, AutoCAD displays the **Override Current Style** dialog box (see Figure 13-60). This dialog box is the same as the **Modify Dimension Style** dialog box and allows you to make changes to the current dimension style settings. The difference is that the changes are not applied to the dimension style, but stored in a **<style overrides>** setting that appears as a child style of the parent dimension (see Figure 13-61).

Figure 13-60   The **Override Current Style** dialog box

Figure 13-61   A dimension style override

Once you create an override, the override settings are set current and are applied to all new dimensions.

Dimension Variables.   Another way to create a dimension override is to change the dimension variables directly. The dimension variables are system variables that control the dimension settings. When you make changes to the dimension style, its corresponding dimension variable is also set accordingly. A dimension style is basically a collection of these dimension variable settings. AutoCAD's dimension variables are listed in Appendix D. To change a dimension variable, just type the variable name and set the value. When you change a dimension variable, AutoCAD creates a dimension style override.

Note:
When you save a style override to a new dimension style, any dimensions created with the style overrides keep their original dimension style and the override settings. They are not changed to the new dimension style.

Saving an Override to a Style.   If you decide you want to keep the override setting, you can save the setting to the current dimension style, making the changes permanent. To make the dimension overrides permanent, right-click on the **<style over-rides>** in the **Dimension Style Manager** dialog box in the **DIMSTYLE** command and choose **Save to current style** in the menu. Doing this will apply the dimension override settings to all the dimensions that use the current style.

You can also save the dimension override settings to a new dimension style. To do this, right-click on the **<style overrides>** in the **Dimension Style Manager** dialog box in the **DIMSTYLE** command and choose **Rename**. You can then type in a name for the new dimension style. When you press **<Enter ↵>**, AutoCAD will save the dimension style overrides to a new dimension style and move that style to the top level in the style list.

Deleting an Override. There are two ways to delete a style override. One way is to set another dimension style current. AutoCAD will display an **Alert box** stating that the over-rides will be deleted (see Figure 13-62). Choose **Yes** to delete the current style override.

Another way to delete an override is to select the override name in the **Dimension Style Manager** dialog box and press the **<Delete>** key on your keyboard. You can also right-click on the override name and choose **Delete** from the menu. AutoCAD will ask if you're sure you want to delete the override. Choose **Yes** to delete the override.

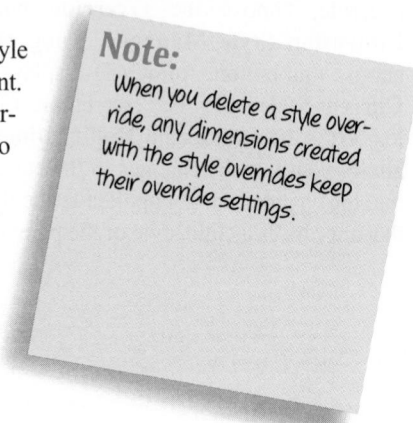

Note: When you delete a style over-ride, any dimensions created with the style overrides keep their override settings.

Figure 13-62 Delete overrides **Alert box**

Figure 13-63 The **Mech** dimension style override

Exercise 13-11: Overriding a Dimension Style

1. Continue from Exercise 13-10.
2. Start the **DIMSTYLE** command. AutoCAD displays the **Dimension Style Manager** dialog box. Select the **Mech** dimension style and choose the **Override...** button. AutoCAD displays the **Override Current Style** dialog box.
3. In the **Tolerances** tab, set the **Method** to **Deviation**. Set the **Upper Value** to **.005** and the **Lower Value** to **0**. Set the **Scaling for height** to **.5** and turn on the **Leading** zero suppression. Choose **OK** to finish creating the overrides. AutoCAD returns you to the **Dimension Style Manager** dialog box. You should see the override listed as a child style of the **Mech** dimension style (see Figure 13-63). Choose **Close** to end the **DIMSTYLE** command.
4. Start the **DIMDIAMETER** command and select the circle shown at P1 in Figure 13-64. Place the dimension as shown. The new dimension has the settings of the override while the existing dimensions remain unchanged.
5. Save your drawing as **EX13-11**. Your drawing should look like Figure 13-64.

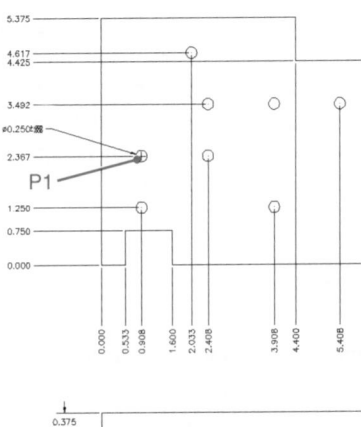

Figure 13-64   Overriding a dimension style

Comparing Dimension Styles

If you have a dimension style override or more than one dimension style, it is often helpful to know the differences between these styles. AutoCAD can compare two dimension styles and tell you which settings are different. When you select a dimension style in the **Dimension Style Manager** dialog box, AutoCAD will give you a description of the dimension style. If that style was based on an existing dimension style, AutoCAD will list the changes in the **Description** area (see Figure 13-65).

Description

Figure 13-65   The **Description** area of the **Dimension Style Manager** dialog box

Another way to compare dimensions is to choose the **Compare** button in the **Dimension Style Manager** dialog box. When you choose this button, AutoCAD will display the **Compare Dimension Styles** dialog box (see Figure 13-66).

Copy Button

Figure 13-66   The **Compare Dimension Styles** dialog box

To compare two dimension styles, select one dimension style in the **Compare** list and one style in the **With** list. AutoCAD will display the differences in the bottom portion of the dialog box. To see a listing of all the settings for a given dimension style, select the style in the **Compare** list and choose **<none>** in the **With** list. AutoCAD will list all the dimensions settings for that style. You can copy the list of results to the Windows clipboard by choosing the **Copy** button (see Figure 13-66). The list is copied as tab-separated text, which can then be pasted into another Windows application.

CREATING LEADERS

Leaders are used for a variety of items when annotating a drawing, such as manufacturing notes, detail bubbles, etc. In general, a leader consists of an end symbol (arrow head, dot, circle, etc.), a leader line (either curved or straight), and a callout (mtext, block, tolerance, etc.). Figure 13-67 shows some different examples of leaders. Leaders are created with the **MLEADER** command.

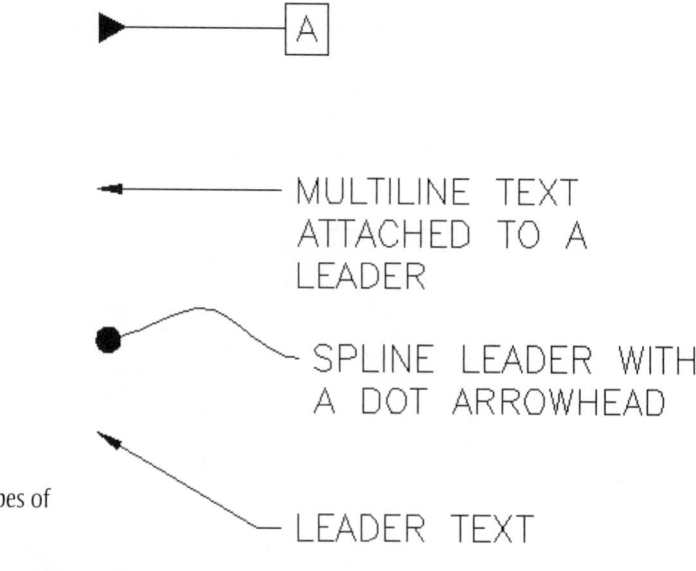

Multileader	
Ribbon & Panel:	Home| Annotation
Multileader	
Multileader Toolbar:	
Menu:	Dimension| Multileader
Command Line:	MLEADER
Command Alias:	MLA

Figure 13-67 Different types of leaders

The Multileader Tool

By default, when you start the **MLEADER** command, AutoCAD prompts you to *Specify leader arrowhead location or* ↓ so that you first select the arrowhead location. AutoCAD then prompts you to *Specify leader landing location or* ↓. Picking a point creates the landing, or tail of the leader, and puts you in the multiline text editor so you can begin adding text.

It is possible to create a leader by locating either the arrowhead, the landing, or text first. You can specify which option to use via the command options when you start the **MLEADER** command or via a right-click menu. The method you specify remains in effect for subsequent leaders.

You can change the multileader properties by selecting **Options** when you start the **MLEADER** command:

Note:
AutoCAD's **MLEADER** command replaces the **QLEADER** command, which created Auto-CAD quick leaders. It is still possible to create quick leaders by entering **QLEADER** or **LE** at the keyboard.

- **Leader type**   Allows you to switch between straight line segments and a spline
- **Leader landing**   Turns the leader landing (tail) on or off
- **Content type**   Allows you to specify whether to use text, a block, or nothing
- **Maxpoints**   The maximum number of pick points used to create a leader. Default value is two points

- **First angle**   Allows you to constrain the angle of the first line to a specific angle increment
- **Second angle**   Allows you to constrain the angle of the second line to a specific angle increment

You must use the **Exit** option to exit the **Options** settings and begin drawing leaders.

| **FOR MORE DETAILS** | See the next section in this chapter for more on creating geometric dimension and tolerance callouts. See Chapter 16 for more on creating and using blocks. |

After you create a leader, the easiest way to edit it is by using grips. Grips can be used to relocate the arrowhead location and resize a leader tail by selecting special arrow grips. Leaders are associative just like dimensions; that is, if you move the text, the leader line will follow.

Note: The **MLEADEREDIT** command can also be used to add and remove leader lines. The command alias is **MLE.**

The Leaders Panel.   The **Leaders** panel shown in Figure 13-68 provides quick access to all the commands and options discussed so far plus some additional useful multileader tools.

Using the **Leaders** panel, you can create new multileaders, add and remove leader lines, align multiple leaders, combine multiple block–type multileaders into a single multileader, and manage multileader styles.

The Add Leader Tool.   You might be wondering about the word *multi* in the multileader name. The **Add Leader** tool allows you to add one or more leaders and arrowheads to an existing multileader object so that it points to multiple features. All the additional leader lines remain associated with the original leader so that if the text moves, so do the leader lines.

When you select the **Add Leader** tool, AutoCAD prompts you to *Specify leader arrowhead location:* so that you can select as many arrowhead locations as needed. You must press **<Enter ↵>** to end command.

Add Leader	
Ribbon & Panel:	Home| Annotation
	Add Leader
Multileader Toolbar:	
Command Line:	None
Command Alias:	None

Figure 13-68   The **Leaders** panel

The Remove Leader Tool.   The **Remove Leader** tool allows you to remove one or more leaders from an existing multileader.

When you select the **Remove Leader** tool, AutoCAD prompts you to *Select a multileader:* so you can select the multileader to update. AutoCAD then prompts you to *Specify leaders to remove:* so that you can continue to remove leaders until you press **<Enter ↵>** to end the command.

Remove Leader	
Ribbon & Panel:	Home| Annotation
	Remove Leader
Multileader Toolbar:	
Command Line:	None
Command Alias:	None

TIP   It is also possible to add and remove multileaders by selecting the multileader and right-clicking to display the shortcut menu in Figure 13-69.

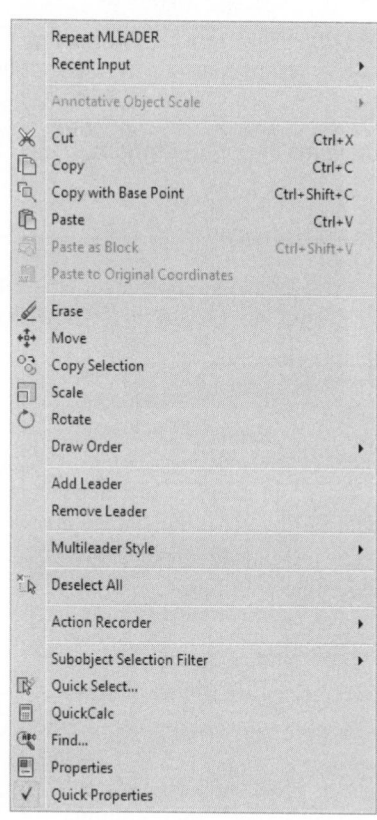

Figure 13-69   The **Multileader** right-click menu

Align	
Ribbon & Panel:	Home| Annotation [icon] Align
Multileader Toolbar:	[icon]
Menu:	None
Command Line:	MLEADERALIGN
Command Alias:	MLA

The Multileader Align Tool.   The **Multileader Align** tool allows you to quickly align a group of leaders along a line that you specify as shown in Figure 13-70.

Leaders Before Using Multileader Align Tool

Leaders After Using Multileader Align Tool

Figure 13-70   The **Multileader Align** tool

You can control the leader spacing by selecting **Options** when you start the **Multileader Align** tool:

- **Distribute**   Distributes leaders evenly (default)
- **Make leader segments Parallel**   Makes angle portion of leader lines parallel
- **Specify Spacing**   Allows you to specify the spacing distance
- Use current spacing

Collect	
Ribbon & Panel:	Home| Annotation [icon] Collect
Multileader Toolbar:	[icon]
Menu:	None
Command Line:	MLEADERCOLLECT
Command Alias:	MLC

The Multileader Collect Tool.   The **Multileader Collect** tool allows you to collect and combine multiple blocks so that they are attached to one landing line as shown in Figure 13-71.

Using the **Multileader Collect** tool, blocks can be collected horizontally, vertically, or within a user-defined area.

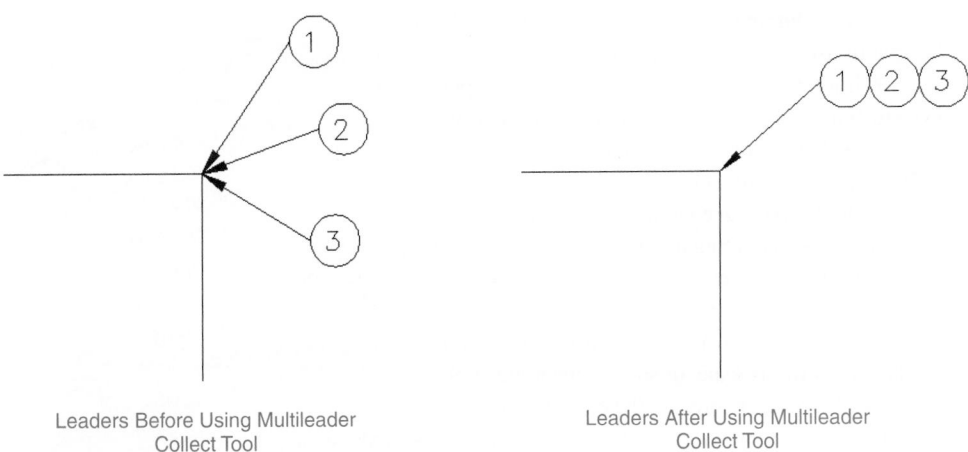

Leaders Before Using Multileader
Collect Tool

Leaders After Using Multileader
Collect Tool

Figure 13-71 The **Multileader Collect** tool

FOR MORE DETAILS	See Chapter 16 for more on creating and using blocks.

Multileader Style.   The **Multileader Style Manager** shown in Figure 13-72 allows you to control the multileader format and display options using a multileader style in a similar fashion to text styles, table styles, and dimension styles.

Selecting the **New...** or **Modify...** button displays the **Modify Multileader Style** dialog box shown in Figure 13-73.

Multileader Style	
Ribbon & Panel:	Home| Annotation
Multileader Toolbar:	
Menu:	None
Command Line:	MLEADERSTYLES
Command Alias:	MLS

Figure 13-72 The **Multileader Style Manager**

Figure 13-73 The **Modify Multileader Style** dialog box

The **Leader Format** tab allows you to specify the type of leader line to use (straight or spline), control general properties (color, linetype, and lineweight), as well as specify the arrowhead type and size. The **Leader break** setting determines the break size for the selected multileader when the **DIMBREAK** command is used.

The **Leader Structure** tab allows you to control constraints such as the maximum number of points and the first and second segment angles. You can also turn the landing (tail) on and off, as well as specify its length. The **Scale** area allows you to take advantage of **Annotative** scaling, use the layout viewport scale, or specify the scale explicitly so text and arrows are created the correct size.

Note:
AutoCAD provides a number of predefined annotation blocks that allow you to quickly create detail callouts, circles, boxes, and other standard items that include attribute information. See Chapter 16 for more information about blocks and attributes.

The **Content** tab allows you to indicate whether to use text, blocks, or nothing when creating leaders using the **Multileader type** drop-down list. If you are using text, the **Text options** and **Leader connection** areas are enabled so that you can control default text, text style, angle, color, and height. The **Leader connection** area allows you to control where the text is attached and specify the gap distance between the end of the landing and the beginning of the text.

If you specify a block as the **Multileader type**, the **Text options** and **Leader connection** areas change to **Block options** so that you can specify a block name, where the block will be attached, its color, and scale.

When possible, you should try to use multileader styles to control the appearance of multiline leaders in your drawings.

TIP   The **Properties** palette also provides access to all the multileader settings discussed in this section for easy updating after a multileader is created.

Exercise 13-12: Creating a Leader

1. Continue from Exercise 13-11.
2. Display the **Multileader Style Manager** dialog box. Select the **Modify** button and on the **Leader Format** tab of the **Modify Multileader Style** dialog box, set the **Arrowhead** to **Dot** and the **Size:** to **0.125**.
3. On the **Content** tab set the **Text height:** to **0.125** and the **Text style** to **Dim**.
4. Choose **OK** to save the change and close the **Multiline Style Manager** dialog box by selecting **Close**.
5. Start the **MLEADER** command. AutoCAD prompts you to *Specify leader arrowhead location or ↓*.
6. Pick the points P1 and P2 shown in Figure 13-74 and press **<Enter ↵>** to end the point placement. AutoCAD starts the multiline text editor.

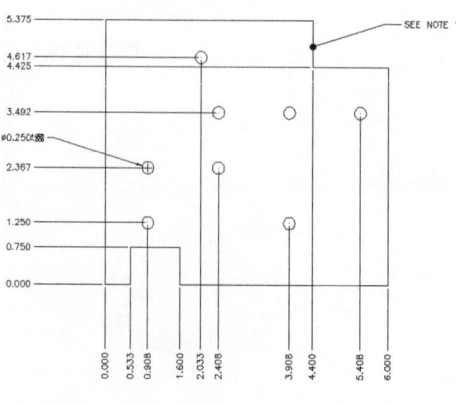

Figure 13-74   Creating a leader

7. Type **SEE NOTE 1** and select **Close Text Editor** or click anywhere outside the multiline text editor to end the **MLEADER** command.
8. Save your drawing as **EX13-12**. Your drawing should look like Figure 13-74.

CREATING GEOMETRIC DIMENSION AND TOLERANCE SYMBOLS (GD&T)

Geometric dimensioning and tolerancing (GD&T) is a method of specifying geometry requirements in mechanical engineering drawings. GD&T callouts use a series of symbols and numbers to convey specifications for mechanical parts and assemblies. Figure 13-75 shows an example of a GD&T callout (also called a *feature control frame*). GD&T is used primarily in mechanical design environments such as automotive, aerospace, electronic, and other manufacturing industries.

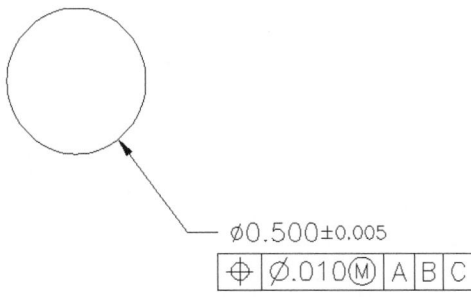

Figure 13-75 A feature control frame

GD&T symbols denote acceptable variations in form, profile, orientation, location, and runout of a feature. You add GD&T callout symbols in feature control frames. These frames contain all the tolerance information for a single dimension. In AutoCAD, GD&T control feature frames are created with either the **LEADER** or **TOLERANCE** command. The **LEADER** command creates GD&T callouts with a leader attached to them, whereas the **TOLERANCE** command creates callouts without leaders.

Tolerance	
Ribbon & Panel:	Annotate|Dimensions
Dimension Toolbar:	
Menu:	Dimension|Tolerance
Command Line:	TOLERANCE
Command Alias:	TOL

FOR MORE DETAILS	Geometric tolerancing is covered by ASME Y14.5M—1994, which supercedes ANSI Y14.5M—1982. See Appendix A for more on drafting standards.

When you create a GD&T callout, AutoCAD displays the **Geometric Tolerance** dialog box (see Figure 13-76). With this dialog box, you can construct GD&T callouts. To construct a callout, work from left to right to specify the symbols and tolerance values that apply to the feature you are dimensioning. When you select the **Sym** box, AutoCAD displays the **Symbol** dialog box (see Figure 13-77).

Figure 13-76 The **Geometric Tolerance** dialog box

Figure 13-77 The **Symbol** dialog box

GDT Font

The GDT font used in the **TOLERANCE** command, as well as other mechanical callout symbols, can be found in the GDT.SHX font file. The GDT.SHX font uses geometric symbols for the lower-case letters a–z, and the capital roman simplex letters for the uppercase letters A–Z. The symbols used in the GDT.SHX font are shown in Figure 13-78 along with their corresponding keystrokes.

GDT.SHX Characters	
a	∠
b	⊥
c	▱
d	⌒
e	○
f	//
g	⌀̸
h	⌖
i	≡
j	⊕
k	⌒
l	Ⓛ
m	Ⓜ
n	⌀
o	□
p	Ⓟ
q	¢
r	◎
s	Ⓢ
t	⌖⌖
u	—
v	⊔
w	▽
x	⊽
y	▷
z	▷
`	±

Figure 13-78   The GDT.SHX font characters

Inspect	
Ribbon & Panel:	Annotate| Dimensions
Dimension Toolbar:	
Menu:	Dimension| Inspection
Command Line:	DIMINSPECT
Command Alias:	None

INSPECTION DIMENSIONS

Inspection dimensions allow you to communicate how often manufactured parts should be checked to ensure that the tolerances of a part stay within the range specified in the dimension value. This is done using an inspection label, dimension value, and inspection rate as shown in Figure 13-79.

The dimension value is the value of the dimension before the inspection dimension is added. It can contain tolerances, text, and the measured value. The label and inspection rate fields are added using the **Inspection** tool explained below.

The **DIMINSPECT** command allows you to add or remove inspection dimensions and control their appearance including the shape, label, and inspection rate via the **Inspection Dimension** dialog box shown in Figure 13-79.

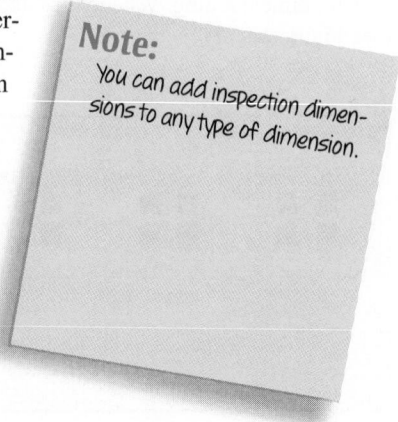

Note:
You can add inspection dimensions to any type of dimension.

Figure 13-79   The **Inspection Dimension** dialog box

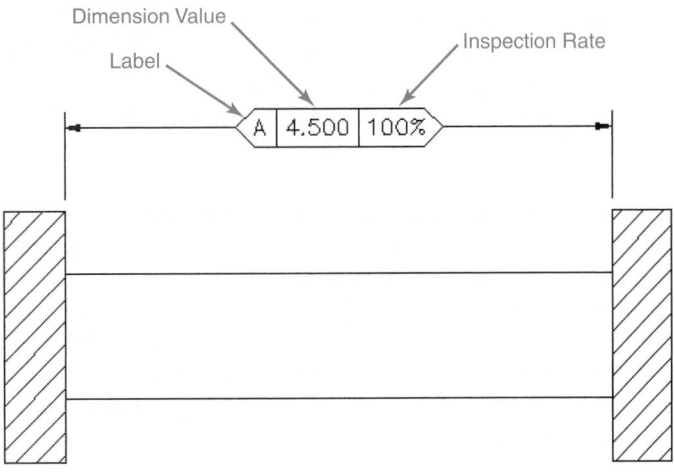

Figure 13-80   Inspection dimension

The **Shape** area allows you to control the type of inspection dimension shape used. You can switch between angular, round, and none.

The **Label** check box allows you to add a text label to the inspection dimensions. The label is located on the far left of the inspection dimension as shown in Figure 13-80.

The **Inspection Rate** check box allows you to indicate the frequency that the dimension should be inspected and is typically expressed as a percentage. The inspection rate is located on the far right of the inspection dimension as shown in Figure 13-80.

TIP   You can change the shape, label, and inspection rate of an inspection dimension after it is created using the **Properties** palette under the **Miscellaneous** category.

MODIFYING DIMENSIONS

When you use associative dimensions and make changes to your geometry, the dimensions will change right along with it. However, you may need to modify dimension objects for a number of other reasons: to relocate the dimension text, to flip the arrowheads to the other side of the dimension line, or to modify the dimension text. In this section, you'll look at some ways to make changes to dimension objects.

Dimensions are objects, just as lines, arcs, circles, and text are objects. As such, they can be moved, copied, rotated, and so on just like other objects. However, unlike other objects, dimensions contain multiple parts (text, dimension lines, extension lines, etc.), and each part can be modified. In the next sections, you'll take a look at some different methods of modifying dimensions.

Grip Editing Dimensions

Grip editing is one way to modify dimensions. When you select a dimension object, AutoCAD will display grip edit points at the definition points, the ends of the dimension lines, and the insertion point of the dimension text. By selecting and moving these grips, you can quickly and easily modify dimension objects.

Right-Click Shortcut Menu

AutoCAD's right-click context menu provides some unique editing abilities with dimensions. To activate the right-click menu, first select the dimension object(s) to activate its grips and then right-click anywhere on the drawing to display the menu. When dimensions are selected, the right-click menu will display the menu options shown in Figure 13-81. These are described in the following sections.

Note:
Take care when you use grip editing on dimension definition points. If you have associate dimensioning turned on (**DIMASSOC** set to **2**), modifying the definition points of a dimension will drop the association between the dimension and its object. When this happens, AutoCAD will display a message in the command line window stating: *Dimension extension disassociated.* This occurs only when modifying the definition points; modifying the dimension line or text grips has no effect on associativity.

Dim Text Position.   The **Dim Text position** item allows you to modify the placement of the dimension text. You can place the dimension text above the dimension line, centered on the dimension line, or you can move it back to its default position. When you select one of these options, AutoCAD moves the text immediately to the selected position.

You can also move the dimension text by dragging only the text, the text along with a leader, or both the text and dimension line. When you select one of these options, you are returned to the drawing and can place the dimension text by dragging your cursor and selecting a new position for the dimension text.

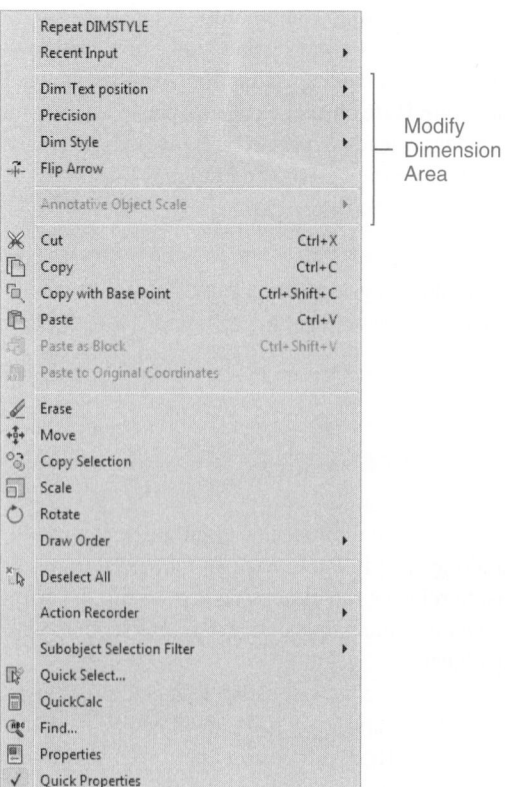

Figure 13-81   The **Dimension Editing** right-click menu

TIP The **Move text alone** menu item found on the **Dim Text position** cascade menu is the only way to break text free from a dimension so that you can move it alone without affecting the dimension line appearance and configuration.

Precision. This option allows you to modify the precision setting of the dimension text. The options for this menu change depending on the units set in the objects dimension style.

Dim Style. This option allows you to apply a different dimension style to the selected dimensions. When you choose this option, you can select from a list of currently defined dimension styles. If you've made changes to the dimension and want to save those changes to a new style, choose the **Save as New Style** option. AutoCAD will display the **Save as New Dimension Style** dialog box, where you can type a new dimension style name or choose an existing dimension style name to overwrite.

Flip Arrow. You can flip dimension arrowheads to the opposite side of the extension line by selecting the **Flip arrow** option. The arrowhead closest to the selection point will flip to the opposite side of the extension line. This option is available only when a single dimension object is selected.

Annotative Object Scale. This option is enabled only if you are using the **Annotation Scale** feature for dimensions. When enabled, this option displays a cascade menu with options to add or remove annotation scales so the same dimension can be used for multiple scale drawings. It is also possible to align multiple scale representations so they are in the same location using the **Synchronize Multiple-scale Positions** option.

> **FOR MORE DETAILS** See Chapter 1 for a detailed description of the **Annotation Scale** feature.

Exercise 13-13: Relocating Dimension Text

1. Open the drawing **EX13-13** in the student data files. This drawing has a number of overlapping dimensions.
2. Select the dimension shown at P1 in Figure 13-82. Right-click the dimension and choose **Dim Text position|Move with leader**. AutoCAD will start dragging the dimension text. Place the dimension text as shown in Figure 13-83.
3. Select the arrowhead shown at P2 in Figure 13-82. Right-click the arrowhead and choose **Flip Arrow**. The arrowhead flips to the other side of the extension line.
4. Save your drawing as **EX13-13**.

To access student data files, go to www.pearsondesigncentral.com.

Figure 13-82   Relocating dimension text

Figure 13-83   The modified dimensions

Modifying Dimension Text and Extension Lines

Sometimes it is necessary to modify dimension text and extension lines after a dimension has been created. The following sections provide an overview of some of the available tools and methods to replace, relocate, and modify dimension text, as well as change the angle of dimension extension lines in order to create oblique dimensions.

The DDEDIT Command.   The **DDEDIT** command works on dimension objects as well as regular **Text** and **Mtext** objects. Simply select the dimension object when you are prompted to *Select annotation object*: AutoCAD will display the dimension text in the multiline text editor. AutoCAD's default dimension text will appear highlighted. You can place additional text before or after the default text, or replace it altogether.

If you delete the default dimension text, you can restore it by typing <> brackets in the mtext editor. AutoCAD will replace the <> brackets with the measured distance between the definition points.

Oblique	
Ribbon & Panel:	Annotate| Dimensions
Dimension Toolbar:	
Menu:	Dime̱nsion| Obli̱que
Command Line:	DIMEDIT
Command Alias:	DIMED

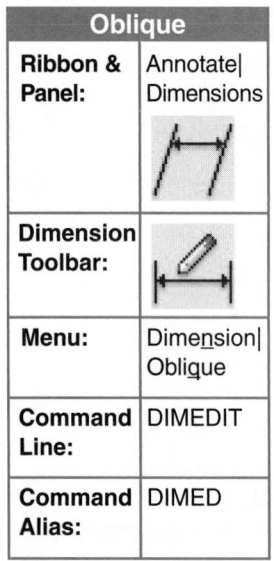

> **TIP** If alternate dimensions are turned off, you can show the alternate dimension text by placing the square brackets [] along with the default brackets text <>. This works only if the default dimension text is present.

The Oblique Tool.   The **Oblique** tool allows you to adjust the angle of the extension lines for linear dimensions using the **Oblique** option of the **DIMEDIT** command. The **Oblique** tool is useful when extension lines conflict with other features of the drawing or you need to dimension an isometric drawing.

When you start the **Oblique** tool, AutoCAD prompts you to *Select objects:* so you can select one or more dimensions and press **<Enter ↵>**. AutoCAD then prompts you to *Enter obliquing angle (press Enter for none):* so you can enter the desired oblique angle.

Align Text Tools.   The **Align Text** tools allow you to relocate or rotate dimension text using any of the **DIMTEDIT** command options described in the following table.

Align Text	
Ribbon & Panel:	Annotate| Dimensions
Dimension Toolbar:	A
Menu:	Dime̱nsion| Align Te̱xt
Command Line:	DIMTEDIT
Command Alias:	DIMTED

Home	This moves the dimension text back to its default position.
Angle	This changes the angle of the dimension text. Entering an angle of **0** degrees puts the text in its default orientation.
Left	This left-justifies the dimension text along the dimension line. This option works only with linear, radial, and diameter dimensions.
Center	This centers the dimension text on the dimension line.
Right	This right-justifies the dimension text along the dimension line. This option works only with linear, radial, and diameter dimensions.

Exercise 13-14: Editing Dimension Text and Extension Lines

1. Open the drawing **EX13-14** in the student data files.
2. Select the **Oblique** tool from the expanded **Dimensions** panel on the **Annotate** ribbon.
3. Select the dimensions shown at P1 and P2 in Figure 13-84 and press **<Enter ↵>**. Auto-CAD prompts you to *Enter obliquing angle (press ENTER for none):*.
4. Type **30** and press **<Enter ↵>**. AutoCAD adjusts the angle of the extension lines.
5. Select the **Oblique** tool again. Select the dimension shown at P3 in Figure 13-84 and press **<Enter ↵>**.

To access student data files, go to www.pearsondesigncentral.com.

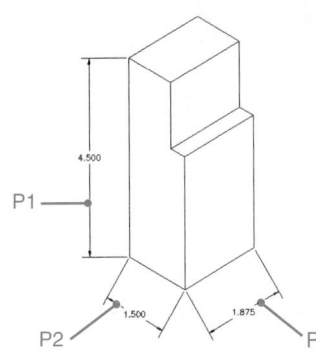

Figure 13-84   Selecting dimension text

6. Set the oblique angle to **150**. AutoCAD adjusts the extension line angle.
7. Select the **Text Angle** tool from the expanded **Dimensions** panel on the **Annotate** ribbon. AutoCAD prompts you to *Select dimension:*. Select the dimension text shown at P1 in Figure 13-84.
8. AutoCAD prompts you to *Specify angle for dimension text:*. Enter **−30** for the dimension text angle. AutoCAD rotates the dimension text.
9. Restart the **Text Angle** tool and select the dimension shown at P2 in Figure 13-84. Enter **30** for the dimension text angle. AutoCAD rotates the dimension text.
10. Restart the **Text Angle** tool and select the dimension shown at P3 in Figure 13-84. Enter **30** for the dimension text angle. AutoCAD rotates the dimension text.
11. Start the **DDEDIT** command and select the dimension text P1. AutoCAD displays the multiline text editor with the default dimension text shown. Highlight the dimension text and set the oblique angle to **30**. Choose **OK** to close the text editor.
12. Repeat step 11 with the text at points P2 and P3. Set the oblique angle to **30** and **−30**, respectively.
13. Save your drawing as **EX13-14**. Your drawing should resemble Figure 13-85.

Figure 13-85   The modified dimension text

Reassociate	
Ribbon & Panel:	Annotate| Dimensions
Toolbar:	None
Menu:	Dimension| Reassociate Dimensions
Command Line:	DIMREASSOCIATE
Command Alias:	None

Reassociating Dimensions

The association between a dimension object and other drawing objects can be somewhat precarious. There are times when, in the course of editing object geometry, the original drawing objects may be redefined or modified in such a way that the objects' association with a dimension object is lost. This may happen when polylines are exploded, when objects are trimmed or broken, or when multiple objects are joined. You may want to change the association to have the dimension be associated with another drawing object. AutoCAD provides a way to change dimension associativity with the **DIMREASSOCIATE** command.

When you start the **DIMREASSOCIATE** command, AutoCAD asks you to select a dimension object. When you select a dimension object, AutoCAD places an X at the first definition point and asks you to specify a new location for it. You can simply pick a new location for the definition point or skip to the next definition point by pressing **<Enter ↵>**. Depending on the type of dimension, AutoCAD will continue to prompt you for a new location for each definition point until the dimension is completely defined.

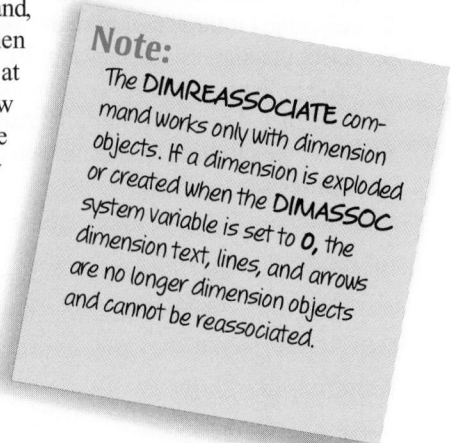

Note:
The **DIMREASSOCIATE** command works only with dimension objects. If a dimension is exploded or created when the **DIMASSOC** system variable is set to **0**, the dimension text, lines, and arrows are no longer dimension objects and cannot be reassociated.

If you want to reassociate the dimension with a new object, use the **Select object** option and select a new object to associate with your dimension. The type of object you select will depend on the type of dimension you select.

Exercise 13-15: Reassociating a Dimension

1. Continue from Exercise 13-14.
2. Select the dimension shown at P1 in Figure 13-86. The grips for the dimension appear.
3. Select the definition point grip shown at P1 and drag it off the object. AutoCAD displays the message *Dimension extension disassociated* in the command line window. The dimension is no longer associated with the geometry.
4. Start the **DIMREASSOCIATE** command. Select the dimension you just modified and press **<Enter ↵>**. AutoCAD places an X at the first defpoint and prompts you to *Specify first extension line origin or ↓*.
5. Choose the **Select object** option and select the line shown at P2 in Figure 13-86. AutoCAD reassociates the dimension with the selected line.
6. Save your drawing as **EX13-15**.

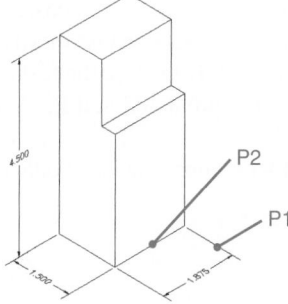

Figure 13-86   The reassociated dimension

Applying Dimension Styles

When working with multiple dimension styles, you may need to apply the settings on one style to an existing dimension. AutoCAD provides a number of ways to do this.

The Dimension Style Lists.   One of the simplest ways to control the dimension styles in a drawing is via the **Dimension Style** list on the expanded **Annotation** panel on the **Home** ribbon. See Figure 13-87.

Selecting a dimension style from the dimension style drop-down list when no objects are selected will set the dimension style current so that any new dimensions will be created using that style. If one or more dimensions are selected so that their grips are displayed, selecting a different dimension style from the list will change the object's associated dimension styles to the new dimension style.

You can also control dimension styles via the **Dimension Style** list on the **Dimensions** panel on the **Annotate** ribbon. See Figure 13-88.

Dimension Style List

Figure 13-87   Using the **Dimension Style** list on the **Annotation** panel

Dimension Style List

Figure 13-88   The **Dimension Style** list on the **Dimensions** panel

Properties Palette.   A dimension style is simply an object property that applies only to dimension objects. Like other object properties, the **Properties** palette allows you to change the style of any selected dimension objects (see Figure 13-89). In addition to changing the style, you can also change the value of any style settings within the selected dimensions. This effectively creates dimension overrides for these dimension objects.

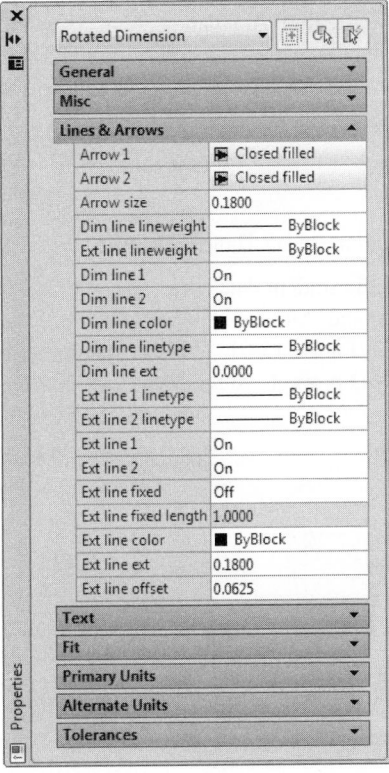

Figure 13-89   The **Properties** palette

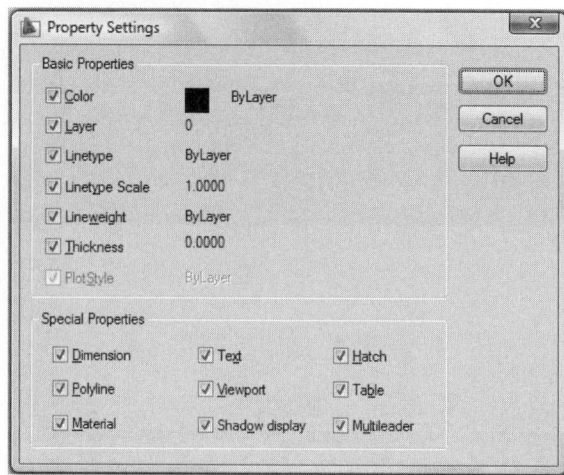

Figure 13-90   The **Property Settings** dialog box

Match Properties.   Because dimension styles are just a property of dimension objects, the **MATCHPROP** command can be used to match the dimension style properties of an existing dimension object. When you start the **MATCHPROP** command, you are prompted to select a source object and then destination object(s). The properties of the source object are applied to the destination objects.

When you use the **MATCHPROP** command, by default, all valid properties of the source object are applied to the destination objects, including layer, color, linetype, etc. To control which properties are applied, choose the **Settings** option of the **MATCHPROP** command. This will display the **Property Settings** dialog box (see Figure 13-90). This allows you to select which properties you want to apply to the destination objects. To apply only the dimension style properties, place a check in the **Dimension** box and remove the checks from all other boxes. Selecting only the **Dimension** option will filter the properties so that only the dimension style properties of the source object are applied to the destination objects.

It is possible to use the **MATCHPROP** command between drawings so you can select the source object in a drawing other than the destination object(s). This is a handy way to copy dimension style settings from one drawing to another without re-creating it from scratch or using DesignCenter.

Exercise 13-16: Using Match Properties to Update Dimension Styles

To access student data files, go to www.pearsondesigncentral.com.

1. Open the drawing **EX13-16** in the student data files.
2. Start the **MATCHPROP** command. AutoCAD prompts you to *Select source object:*.
3. Select the leader shown at P1 in Figure 13-91. This dimension has a dimension style override for the arrowhead. AutoCAD prompts you to *Select destination object(s) or* ↓ .

Figure 13-91   Matching dimension properties

4. Choose the **Settings** option. AutoCAD displays the **Property Settings** dialog box. In the **Special Properties** area, remove the check from all the settings except **Dimension**. Press **OK** to close the dialog box. AutoCAD prompts you to *Select destination object(s) or* ↓.

5. Select the leader shown at P2 in Figure 13-91. AutoCAD updates the leader to match the source object and prompts you to *Select destination object(s) or* ↓. Press **<Enter ↵>** to end the **MATCHPROP** command.

6. Save your drawing as **EX13-16**.

The Dimension Update Tool. If you've created dimension style overrides and want to apply those overrides to an existing dimension, AutoCAD provides a tool for applying dimension styles (including overrides) to existing dimension objects.

When you choose this tool, AutoCAD lists the current dimension style, along with any overrides, in the command window (see Figure 13-92) and prompts you to *Select objects:*. Once you select the dimension object, AutoCAD applies the current dimension style settings, including overrides, to the selected dimensions.

Note:
The Dimension Update tool is not technically a command. It is actually the **Apply** option of the **-DIMSTYLE** command, which is the command window version of the **DIMSTYLE** command. When you select this tool, AutoCAD starts the **-DIMSTYLE** command and automatically selects the **Apply** option.

Update	
Ribbon & Panel:	Annotate| Dimensions
Dimension Toolbar:	
Menu:	Dime<u>n</u>sion| <u>U</u>pdate
Command Line:	-DIMSTYLE/ Apply
Command Alias:	None

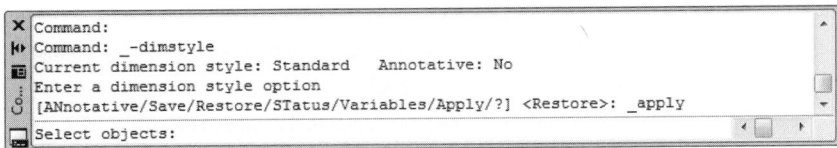

Figure 13-92   Updating dimensions

CHAPTER SUMMARY

Dimensioning can be one of the more difficult aspects of AutoCAD. Managing all the various settings can be daunting at times. However, AutoCAD provides a wide variety of tools to create, modify, and update dimension objects. The effective use of dimension styles and the ability to make changes to the dimension settings is key to being successful with AutoCAD.

CHAPTER TEST QUESTIONS

Multiple Choice

1. When using the **DIMLINEAR** command, which of the following is not a valid selection object?

   a. Line
   b. Arc
   c. Ellipse
   d. Circle

2. An arc length dimension:

   a. Is a linear dimension between the endpoints of an arc
   b. Measures the true distance along an arc segment
   c. Cannot be used on circles
   d. None of the above

3. To create a dimension with angled (oblique) extension lines you would:

   a. Use the **DIMOBLIQUE** command
   b. Use the **DIMEDIT** command and select the **Oblique** option
   c. Use grips to drag the extension lines to the desired angle
   d. None of the above; you cannot create angled extension lines.

4. A dimension style override:

   a. Allows you to make temporary changes to a dimension style
   b. Is applied to all dimensions with the current dimension style
   c. Cannot be saved to a dimension style
   d. None of the above

5. Setting the **DIMASSOC** system variable to **1**:

   a. Creates exploded dimensions

   b. Creates dimensions that are not associated with other drawing objects

   c. Creates dimensions that are associated with other drawing objects

   d. You cannot set **DIMASSOC** to **1**

6. In the **Fit** tab of the **Modify Dimension Style** dialog box, the **Use overall scale of** setting:

   a. Controls the overall size of all elements of a dimension object

   b. Controls the value of dimension text

   c. Does not apply to dimensions placed in model space

   d. All of the above

7. The **Angle** option of the **DIMLINEAR** command:

   a. Creates an angular dimension instead of linear dimension

   b. Creates extension lines at the specified angle

   c. Controls the angle of the dimension line

   d. Controls the angle of the dimension text

8. To flip a dimension arrowhead:

   a. Select the arrowhead and choose **Flip Arrow** from the right-click menu

   b. Delete the dimension and re-create it picking different defpoints

   c. Use the **MIRROR** command

   d. You cannot flip dimension arrowheads once they are placed

9. A baseline dimension:

   a. Creates dimensions that are aligned end to end

   b. Creates dimensions that are referenced from a common extension line

   c. Must be placed first before any other linear dimensions are created.

   d. None of the above

10. Diameter dimensions:

   a. Automatically have the Ø symbol placed in front of the dimension text

   b. Can be used with either arcs or circles

   c. Cannot be used on an ellipse

   d. All of the above

Matching

a. Linear dimension

b. Angular dimension

c. **Defpoints** layer

d. Associativity

e. Aligned dimension

f. Radius dimension

g. Dimension style override

h. Diameter dimension

i. Arc length dimension

j. **DIMASSOC**

1. Layer automatically created for definition points

2. A link between two drawing objects so that when one changes, the other updates

3. A linear dimension between two points along an angled line

4. A dimension of an angle

5. A dimension from the center to the edge of an arc or circle

6. The system variable that controls dimension associativity

7. A link between dimension definition points and other drawing geometry

8. A dimension between two opposite points on a circle or arc

9. A temporary change to dimension style settings

10. A dimension of the true length of an arc segment

CHAPTER PROJECTS

Project 13-1: Classroom Plan—Continued from Chapter 11

1. Open drawing **P11-1B** from Chapter 11.

2. Create a dimension style called **ARCH**. Use the settings shown in Figures P13-3A–E.

3. Add the dimensions shown in Figure P13-1.

4. Save your drawing as **P13-1**.

Figure P13-1

Project 13-2a: B-Size Mechanical Border—Continued from Chapter 11

1. Open the template file **Mechanical B-Size.DWT** from Chapter 11.
2. Create a dimension style called **Mech** based on the **Standard** dimension style. Use the settings shown in Figures P13-2A–E.
3. Save the drawing to a template called **Mechanical B-Size.DWT** with the following description:
   Mechanical Drawing Template:
   B-Size - 17.0 × 11.0
   Decimal Units - 0.000
   Decimal Angles - 0.0
   Dimension Style - Mech

Figure P13-2A

Project 13-2b: C-Size Mechanical Border—Continued from Chapter 11

1. Open the template file **Mechanical C-Size.DWT** from Chapter 11.
2. Create a dimension style called **Mech** based on the **Standard** dimension style. Use the settings shown in Figures P13-2A–E.
3. Save the drawing to a template called **Mechanical C-Size.DWT** with the following description:

   Mechanical Drawing Template:
   C-Size - 22.0 × 17.0
   Decimal Units - 0.000
   Decimal Angles - 0.0
   Dimension Style - Mech

Project 13-2c: A-Size Portrait Mechanical Border—Continued from Chapter 11

1. Open the template file **Mechanical A-Size-Portrait.DWT** from Chapter 11.
2. Create a dimension style called **Mech** based on the **Standard** dimension style. Use the settings shown in Figures P13-2A–E.

Figure P13-2B

Figure P13-2C

Figure P13-2D

Figure P13-2E

3. Save the drawing to a template called **Mechanical A-Size-Portrait.DWT** with the following description:
   Mechanical Drawing Template:
   A-Size Portrait - 8.50 × 11.0
   Decimal Units - 0.000
   Decimal Angles - 0.0
   Dimension Style - Mech

Project 13-3a: Architectural D-Size Border—Continued from Chapter 11

1. Open the template file **Architectural D-Size.DWT** from Chapter 11.
2. Create a dimension style named **ARCH** with the settings shown in Figures P13-3A–E.
3. Dimension the graphic scales as shown in Figure P13-3F using the dimension style Standard on the layer **A-Anno-Dims**.
4. Save the drawing to a template file as **Architectural D-Size.DWT**.

Project 13-3b: Architectural B-Size Border—Continued from Chapter 11

1. Open the template file **Architectural B-Size.DWT** from Chapter 11.
2. Create a dimension style named **ARCH** with the settings shown in Figures P13-3A–E.
3. Save the drawing to a template file as **Architectural B-Size.DWT**.

Project 13-3c: Architectural A-Size Border—Continued from Chapter 11

1. Open the template file **Architectural A-Size.DWT** from Chapter 11.
2. Create a dimension style named **ARCH** with the settings shown in Figures P13-3A–E.
3. Save the drawing to a template file as **Architectural A-Size.DWT**.

Figure P13-3A

Figure P13-3B

Figure P13-3C

Figure P13-3D

Figure P13-3E

Figure P13-3F

Project 13-4: Electrical Distribution Panel

1. Create a new drawing using the acad.dwt template.
2. Create a dimension style called **Mech** based on the **Standard** dimension style. Use the settings shown in Figures P13-2A–E. *Hint:* You can use DesignCenter to drag-and-drop the dimension style from the mechanical drawing templates.
3. Draw the electrical panel drawing shown in Figure P13-4. Include all dimensions and text.
4. Save your drawing as **P13-4**.

Figure P13-4

Project 13-5: Residential Architectural Plan—Continued from Chapter 11

1. Open the drawing **P11-5** from Chapter 11.
2. Create the following layer:

Name	Color	Linetype	Lineweight	Description
C-Anno-Dims	7	Continuous	Default	Dimensioning

3. Create a dimension style called **ARCH**. Use the settings shown in Figures P13-3A–E. *Hint:* You can use DesignCenter to drag-and-drop the dimension style from the architectural drawing templates.
4. Add the dimensions shown in Figure P13-5.
5. Save your drawing as **P13-5**.

Figure P13-5

Project 13-6: Optical Mount—English Units—Continued from Chapter 8

1. Open the drawing **P8-6** from Chapter 8.
2. Create a dimension style called **Mech** based on the **Standard** dimension style. Use the settings shown in Figures P13-2A–E. *Hint:* You can use DesignCenter to drag-and-drop the dimension style from the mechanical drawing templates.
3. Add the dimensioning shown in Figure P13-6. *Hint:* Use the **QDIM** command to create ordinate dimensioning.
4. Save the drawing as **P13-6**.

Figure P13-6

Project 13-7a: Gasket—Continued from Chapter 11

1. Open drawing **P11-7A** from Chapter 11.
2. Update the **Standard** text style so that it is assigned the text font **Simplex.shx** with a height of **0.0 mm**.
3. Update the **ISO-25** dimension style so that decimal separator is set to a period (**.**) instead of the default comma (**,**) and the dimension scale factor is set to **2**. *Hint:* You can set the dimension scale factor as an override by updating the **DIMSCALE** system variable.
4. Add the dimensions shown in Figure P13-7A using the **ISO-25** dimension style on layer **Dimensions**.
5. Save the drawing as **P13-7A**.

GASKET
SCALE: 1:2

Figure P13-7A

Project 13-7b: Widget—Continued from Chapter 11

1. Open drawing **P11-7B** from Chapter 11.
2. Update the **Standard** text style so that it is assigned the text font **Simplex.shx** with a height of **0.0 mm**.
3. Update the **ISO-25** dimension style so that decimal separator is set to a period (**.**) instead of the default comma (**,**) and the dimension scale factor is set to **4**. *Hint:* You can set the dimension scale factor as an override by updating the **DIMSCALE** system variable.
4. Add the dimensions shown in Figure P13-7B using the **ISO-25** dimension style on layer **Dimensions**.
5. Save the drawing as **P13-7B**.

FRONT VIEW
SCALE: 1:4

RIGHT—SIDE VIEW
SCALE: 1:4

Figure P13-7B

Project 13-7c: Hex Head Bolts and Nuts—Continued from Chapter 11

1. Open drawing **P11-7C** from Chapter 11.
2. Update the **Standard** text style so that it is assigned the text font **Simplex.shx** with a height of **0.0 mm**.
3. Update the **ISO-25** dimension style so that decimal separator is set to a period (**.**) instead of the default comma (**,**).
4. Add the dimensions shown in Figure P13-7C using the **ISO-25** dimension style on layer **Dimensions**.
5. Save the drawing as **P13-7C**.

Figure P13-7C

Project 13-7d: Motorcycle Head Gasket—Continued from Chapter 11

1. Open drawing **P11-7D** from Chapter 11.
2. Update the **Standard** text style so that it is assigned the text font Simplex.shx with a height of **0.0 mm**.
3. Update the **ISO-25** dimension style so that decimal separator is set to a period (**.**) instead of the default comma (**,**) and the dimension scale factor is set to **2**. *Hint:* You can set the dimension scale factor as an override by updating the **DIMSCALE** system variable.
4. Add the dimensions shown in Figure P13-7D using the **ISO-25** dimension style on layer **Dimensions**.
5. Save the drawing as **P13-7D**.

HEAD GASKET
SCALE: 1:2

Figure P13-7D

Project 13-7e: 68-Tooth Rear Sprocket—Continued from Chapter 11

1. Open drawing **P11-7E** from Chapter 11.
2. Update the **Standard** text style so that it is assigned the text font **Simplex.shx** with a height of **0.0 mm**.
3. Update the **ISO-25** dimension style so that decimal separator is set to a period (.) instead of the default comma (,) and the dimension scale factor is set to **4**. *Hint:* You can set the dimension scale factor as an override by updating the **DIMSCALE** system variable.
4. Add the dimensions shown in Figure P13-7E using the **ISO-25** dimension style on layer **Dimensions**.
5. Save the drawing as **P13-7E**.

68 TOOTH REAR SPROCKET

Figure P13-7E

Project 13-7f: Window Extrusion—Continued from Chapter 11

1. Open drawing **P11-7F** from Chapter 11.
2. Update the **Standard** text style so that it is assigned the text font **Simplex.shx** with a height of **0.0 mm**.
3. Update the **ISO-25** dimension style so that decimal separator is set to a period (**.**) instead of the default comma (**,**).
4. Add the dimensions and leader shown in Figure P13-7F using the **ISO-25** dimension style on layer **Dimensions**.
5. Save the drawing as **P13-7F**.

WINDOW EXTRUSION
SCALE: 1:1

Figure P13-7F

Project 13-7g: Hub—Continued from Chapter 11

1. Open drawing **P11-7G** from Chapter 11.
2. Update the **Standard** text style so that it is assigned the text font **Simplex.shx** with a height of **0.0 mm**.
3. Update the **ISO-25** dimension style so that decimal separator is set to a period (**.**) instead of the default comma (**,**) and the dimension scale factor is set to **2**. *Hint:* You can set the dimension scale factor as an override by updating the **DIMSCALE** system variable.
4. Add the dimensions shown in Figure P13-7G using the **ISO-25** dimension style on layer **Dimensions**.
5. Save the drawing as **P13-7G**.

HUB
SCALE: 1:2

Figure P13-7G

Project 13-8: Civil Site Plan—Continued from Chapter 11

1. Open the drawing **P11-8** from Chapter 11.
2. Create the following layer:

Name	Color	Linetype	Lineweight	Description
A-Anno-Dims	7	Continuous	Default	Dimensioning

3. Create a dimension style called **ARCH.** Use the settings shown in Figures P13-3A–E. *Hint:* You can use DesignCenter to drag-and-drop the dimension style from the architectural drawing templates.
4. Place the dimensions as shown in Figure P13-8.
5. Save the drawing as **P13-8**.

Figure P13-8

Managing Paper Space Layouts

14

Chapter Objectives

- Understand how and why paper space layouts are used
- Associate a printer/plotter with a layout
- Set the page size of a layout
- Create and import page setups
- Create layout viewports
- Set the viewport display scale
- Lock the viewport display
- Control layer visibility per viewport
- Modify viewports
- Create and manage layouts
- Use advanced paper space scaling features
- Create dimensions in paper space instead of model space

INTRODUCTION

In Chapter 1, we explained how AutoCAD has two distinct drawing environments: model space and paper space.

Remember that model space is the theoretically infinite 3D drawing environment where you locate most of the linework and annotation features that make up a drawing. To draw in model space, you select the **Model** tab at the bottom left of the drawing window as shown in Figure 14-1 to make it current.

> **Note:**
> When model space is the active drawing environment, the **UCS** icon in the lower left-hand corner of the drawing window defaults to the icon shown in Figure 14-2.

To reiterate, paper space is the 2D environment where you lay out the drawing information created in model space for plotting/printing on the desired size of paper and at a specified scale factor. In effect, a layout represents what the drawing will look like when it is printed.

TIP It is common to locate the title border information in a layout. Locating the border and title text in paper space allows them to be drawn at a scale of 1:1 because the plot scale in paper space is typically 1:1. Many of the default AutoCAD template files have the title border located in paper space.

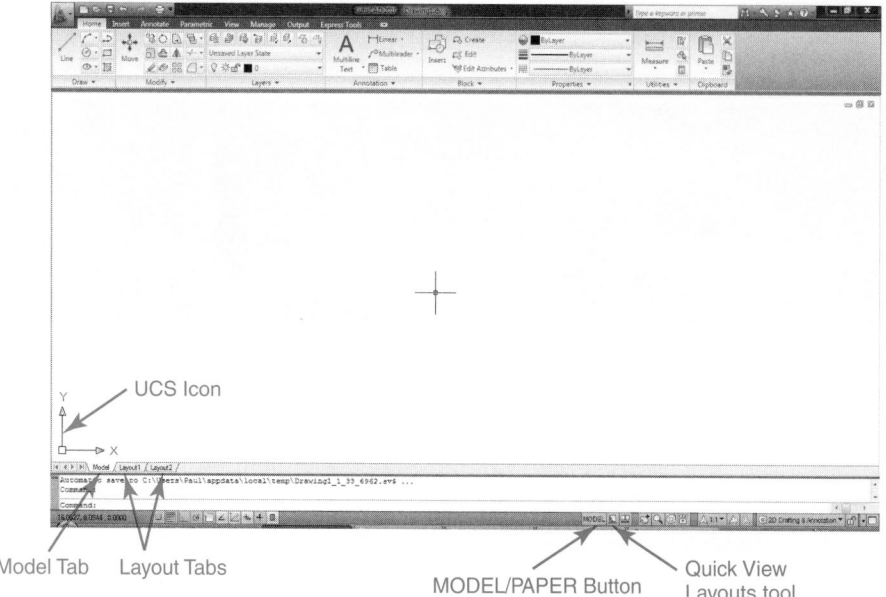

UCS Icon

Model Tab   Layout Tabs

MODEL/PAPER Button

Quick View
Layouts tool

Figure 14-1   Switching between model space and paper space layouts

Figure 14-2   The model
space **UCS** icon

It is possible to have multiple layouts in a drawing, each one a different paper size and scale. A new AutoCAD drawing that is based on the default template file (Acad.dwt) contains two generic layouts named **Layout1** and **Layout2**.

The quickest and easiest way to switch between layouts is to select the desired layout tab on the bottom left of the drawing window shown in Figure 14-1.

QUICK VIEW LAYOUTS

Another way to switch between model space and the paper space layouts is using the **Quick View Layouts** tool located on the right side of the Status Bar shown in Figure 14-1.

The **Quick View Layouts** tool displays a horizontal row of layout preview images at the bottom of the AutoCAD window so you can quickly switch between model space and all the layouts contained in a drawing. See Figure 14-3.

> **Note:**
> When paper space is the active drawing environment, the **UCS** icon in the lower left-hand corner of the drawing window defaults to the icon shown in Figure 14-4.

Plot   Publish

Model   Layout1   Layout2

Pin Quick View Layouts

New Layout

Close Quick View Layouts

Publish

Figure 14-3   The **Quick View Layouts** tool

Figure 14-4
The paper space
UCS icon

In addition, moving your cursor over a layout preview displays **Plot** and **Publish** buttons in the upper corners of the image so that you can print directly from the **Quick View Layouts** tool.

Note: Move the mouse past the edge of the row of images to display layouts that extend beyond the edge of screen.

TIP You can increase or decrease the layout preview image size by holding down the **<Ctrl>** key while rolling the mouse wheel in and out.

Using the accompanying control panel displayed below the preview images you can select the **Pin Quick View Layouts** button to keep the **Quick View Layouts** tool open so the previews are visible while you work. You can then select the **Close Quick View Layouts** button to turn off previews when you no longer want them displayed.

The **New Layout** button instantly creates a new generic layout in the drawing and displays its preview at the end of the current row of preview images. Creating and managing layouts is explained in detail later in this chapter.

The **Publish** button displays the **Publish** tool so you can quickly plot all the currently open drawings and layouts.

FOR MORE DETAILS See Chapter 15 for more detailed information about using the **Publish** tool for quickly plotting multiple drawings and layouts.

LAYOUT PAPER SIZE

The paper size used by an AutoCAD layout is controlled via its *page setup,* similar to setting the paper size of a document in a word processing program.

The difference is that, using AutoCAD, the available paper sizes are determined by the limits of the layout's associated plotting/printing hardware device. For instance, if you are printing on a printer whose maximum paper size capability is $8\frac{1}{2}'' \times 11''$ (A-size/letter), then an $8\frac{1}{2}'' \times 11''$ paper size is the maximum size you can specify for the layout. Applying this logic, a large format plotter that is capable of printing up to a $36'' \times 24''$ drawing (D-size) has many more paper size settings available than the average $8\frac{1}{2}'' \times 11''$ office printer. Associating a printer/plotter with a layout and selecting the desired paper size are both controlled using the **Page Setup Manager** explained later in this chapter.

LAYOUT VIEWPORT SCALE

The scale of a drawing is controlled via one or more *layout viewports* created in a layout.

In Chapter 1 we used the analogy that an AutoCAD paper space layout can be thought of as a 2D sheet of paper that hovers over your 3D model space drawing information. Views of the model space information are created by cutting one or more holes referred to as layout viewports in the paper so that you can see the drawing model below. You scale the model space information displayed in the viewport by zooming in and out at a specific scale factor. It is even possible to create multiple viewports and specify a different scale factor for each individual viewport, as shown in Figure 14-5, allowing you to easily create multiscaled drawings.

layout viewport: The user-defined window created in a paper space layout that allows you to view drawing information that resides in model space

Viewport Scale
1/8" = 1'-0"

Viewport
Scale
1/4" = 1'-0"

Figure 14-5 Paper space layout with multiple scaled viewports

TIP

AutoCAD provides a list of all of the standard viewport scales on the Status Bar so that you can quickly set a viewport scale without having to calculate the zoom scale factor each time. Both methods are described later in this chapter.

Being able to create plots with differently scaled viewports is one of the primary benefits of using paper space layouts. This is something you simply can't do in model space unless you scale the actual drawing information—which should be avoided at all costs. Remember that in Auto-CAD, the key is to draw everything exactly as it exists in the real world.

CONTROLLING LAYERS PER LAYOUT VIEWPORT

Another very useful capability of layout viewports is that you can freeze and thaw layers per viewport using the viewport layer freeze option introduced in Chapter 6. This allows you to create multiple viewports on one or more layouts that each displays different model space drawing information.

You can also control the layer color, linetype, lineweight, and plot style properties per viewport using viewport layer overrides. Viewport layer overrides allow you to change the layer color, linetype, lineweight, and plot style properties in each viewport while retaining the original layer properties in model space and in the other layout viewports. Viewport layer overrides are discussed in detail later in this chapter.

FOR MORE DETAILS   See Chapter 6 for more information about using layers to organize drawing information.

SETTING UP A LAYOUT

Once you are ready to lay out a drawing for plotting from paper space, select one of the default layouts (**Layout1** or **Layout2**).

Figure 14-6   Switching to a layout the first time

When you switch to a layout for the first time, a single layout viewport is displayed on the page with a dashed line indicating the ***printable area*** as shown in Figure 14-6.

The first thing you need to do when you are setting up a layout is to specify the desired printer/plotter output device. Once you specify an output device, *then* you can select a paper size. Remember that the two are intimately related because the available paper sizes are determined by the capabilities of the currently associated printer/plotter. The printer/plotter, paper size, and most of the other plot settings are controlled via the page setup associated with the layout.

To modify the settings for the page setup, you use the **Page Setup Manager** explained in the next section.

printable area: The actual physical area that can be printed for the currently specified plotting device and paper size

The Page Setup Manager

The **Page Setup Manager** allows you to do the following:

- Display details of the current page setup
- Set another page setup current
- Modify an existing page setup
- Create a new page setup
- Import a page setup from another drawing

The **Page Setup Manager** dialog box is shown in Figure 14-7.

Current page setup: displays the page setup that is applied to the current layout. By default it is set to **<None>**.

The **Page setups** box lists the page setups that can be modified or applied to the current layout.

By default, a page setup is automatically applied to each layout with the same name as the layout with an asterisk (*) added to the beginning and end of the layout name. For instance, the default page setups for the **Layout1** and **Layout2** layouts are ***Layout1*** and ***Layout2***, respectively.

Any new or imported page setups are automatically added to the **Page setups** list. You can make a page setup current by double-clicking on it in the list or by highlighting the page setup and selecting the **Set Current** button.

Page Setup Manager	
Ribbon & Panel:	Output|Plot
Layouts Toolbar:	
Menu:	File|Page Setup Manager...
Command Line:	PAGESETUP
Command Alias:	None

Figure 14-7   The **Page Setup Manager** dialog box

TIP   If you right-click in the **Page setups** list box, a shortcut menu is displayed that allows you to set current, delete, or rename a page setup.

The **Selected page setup details** area at the bottom of the dialog box displays the following information about the currently selected page setup:

Note:
It is not possible to set current, rename, or delete any of the default page setups that begin and end with an asterisk.

- **Device name**   Name of the plot device specified in the currently selected page setup
- **Plotter**   Type of plot device specified in the currently selected page setup
- **Plot size**   Plot size and orientation specified in the currently selected page setup
- **Where**   Physical location of the output device specified in the currently selected page setup
- **Description**   Description of the output device specified in the currently selected page setup

The **Display when creating a new layout** check box allows you to control whether the **Page Setup Manager** is displayed when a new layout tab is selected or a new layout is created.

TIP   You can also control whether the **Page Setup Manager** is displayed for new layouts via the **Show Page Setup Manager for new layouts** option on the **Display** tab of the **Options** dialog box.

Modifying a Page Setup.   You can modify the settings of a page setup at any time. In order to modify any default page setup, the layout the page setup is associated with must first be set current. Selecting the **Modify...** button in the **Page Setup Manager** displays the **Page Setup** dialog box shown in Figure 14-8.

Figure 14-8   The **Page Setup** dialog box

The **Page Setup** dialog box is almost exactly the same as the **Plot** dialog box shown in Figure 14-9. In fact, the two dialog boxes control the same settings. The only differences between the two are:

- Changes made in the **Page Setup** dialog box are saved with the layout. Changes made in the **Plot** dialog box are *not* saved, unless you select the **Apply to Layout** button.

- You can plot from the **Plot** dialog box. You *cannot* plot from the **Page Setup** dialog box.

- The **Plot** dialog box can be toggled to display more plot options using the **More Options** arrow button at the bottom right of the dialog box as shown in Figure 14-9, or it can be set to display a limited number of options.

In this chapter, the main concern is controlling the paper size of the layout so that you can properly set up a drawing for plotting (discussed in Chapter 15). For this reason, most of the other plot-related page setup settings are mentioned only briefly. The following sections explain primarily how to associate an output device so that you can select the desired layout paper size.

Selecting a Printer/Plotter Device.   The **Printer/plotter** area of the **Page Setup** dialog box allows you to specify a printer/plotter by selecting it from the **Name:** list box shown in Figure 14-10.

The **Name:** list box provides a list of the available printers/plotters you can associate with a layout. The list includes both *.PC3 files* and system printers that are prefixed with different icons—a plotter icon for a .PC3 file and a printer icon for a system printer.

The **Properties** button displays the **Plotter Configuration Editor** so you can view or modify the current plotter configuration.

.PC3 file: Plotter configuration file used to store and manage printer/plotter settings

---

FOR MORE DETAILS   See Chapter 15 for more on using the **Plotter Configuration Editor** to manage .PC3 files.

Figure 14-9   The **Plot** dialog box

Click Here
to Save Settings

Toggles More
Options On/Off

Select Desired Output
Device from List

Figure 14-10   Selecting a printer/plotter from the **Name**: list box

Other information provided about the currently selected printer/plotter includes the following:

- **Plotter**   Displays the current name
- **Where**   Displays the physical location or port
- **Description**   Displays a description if available

The **Preview** window displays the plot area relative to the paper size and the printable area.

<table>
<tr><td>FOR MORE
D E T A I L S</td><td>See Chapter 15 for more on using the **Add-A-Plotter** wizard.</td></tr>
</table>

Selecting a Paper Size.   The **Paper size** list box displays the standard paper sizes that are available for the associated printer/plotter. Every time a different printer/plotter is selected, the **Paper size** list is updated with the paper sizes supported by that device. If no plotter is selected so that the **Name**: list box is set to **None**, a list of all the standard paper sizes is provided.

If you are plotting a raster image, such as a BMP or TIFF file, the size of the plot is specified in pixels, not in inches or millimeters.

Note:
If the printer/plotter you wish to use is not listed, you can add it using the **Plotter Manager**'s **Add-A-Plotter** wizard.

TIP   If you are unsure what printer/plotter to specify, you can set the plotter to **None** so that it is still possible to select the desired paper size.

Other Page Setup Settings.   The following is a brief overview of a few of the other page setup settings.

The **Plot area** settings determine the area of the drawing to plot. The **What to plot**: list box provides five different options:

- **Display**   The current screen display
- **Extents**   The extents of the drawing
- **Layout**   The current layout
- **View**   A named view (must have at least one named view to be enabled)
- **Window**   User-specified window area

The **Plot area** is typically set to **Layout** for a paper space layout. The other **Plot area** settings are more commonly used when plotting in model space.

Note:
If the selected printer/plotter doesn't support the current paper size, the warning shown in Figure 14-11 is displayed. If you select **OK**, the paper size is changed to the default paper size for the new printer/plotter. If you select **Cancel**, the printer/plotter is changed to **None**, and the paper size is not changed.

Figure 14-11 Unsupported
paper size warning

The **Plot offset** area allows you to offset the plot area relative to the lower-left corner of the printable area or the edge of the paper.

FOR MORE DETAILS	See Chapter 15 for more detailed information about controlling the other plot settings and plotting your drawing.

The **Plot scale** area controls the ratio of the plotted units to the drawing units. Most of the standard drafting scales are listed in the **Scale**: list box. The default scale is 1:1 when plotting a layout. In fact, if the **Layout** option is selected as **What to plot**: in the **Plot area**, AutoCAD ignores the scale selected in the **Scale**: list box and prints the layout at 1:1.

Note:
You can change what the offset is relative to via the **Specify plot offset relative to** options on the **Plot and Publish** tab of the **Options** dialog box.

Creating a New Page Setup.   If you think that you might use the same page setup settings in another layout in the current drawing or even in a layout in another drawing, you can create a named page setup. Named page setups are saved in the drawing file so that they can be applied to other layouts or imported into other drawing files. Importing page setups is explained in the next section.

Using named page setups also allows you to plot the same layout more than one way. You can apply different named page setups to the same layout so that there are different output results each time. For example, you might create different named page setups to plot to printers/plotters that are in different locations.

To create a new named page setup, select the **New...** button in the **Page Setup Manager**. The **New Page Setup** dialog box shown in Figure 14-12 is displayed.

Enter the name for the new page setup in the **New page setup name**: text box. The default name is **Setup** followed by an integer representing a sequential number (i.e., **Setup1, Setup2**, etc.). You should enter a descriptive name indicating the page setup's purpose.

The **Start with**: list allows you to select a page setup to use as a starting point for the new page setup:

- **<None>**   No page setup is used as a starting point.
- **<Default output device>**   The default output device specified on the **Plot and Publish** tab of the **Options** dialog box is set as the printer in the new page setup.
- **<Previous plot>**   The new page setup uses the settings specified in the last plot.

When you select the **OK** button at the bottom of the **New Page Setup** dialog box, the **Page Setup** dialog box shown earlier in Figure 14-8 is displayed using the settings saved with the

Enter Descriptive
Name for Layout Here

Figure 14-12   The **New Page Setup** dialog box

selected starting point page setup. You can then modify any settings if necessary. When you exit the **Page Setup** box, the new named page setup is displayed in the list of page setups in the **Page Setup Manager** as shown in Figure 14-13.

New Page Setup

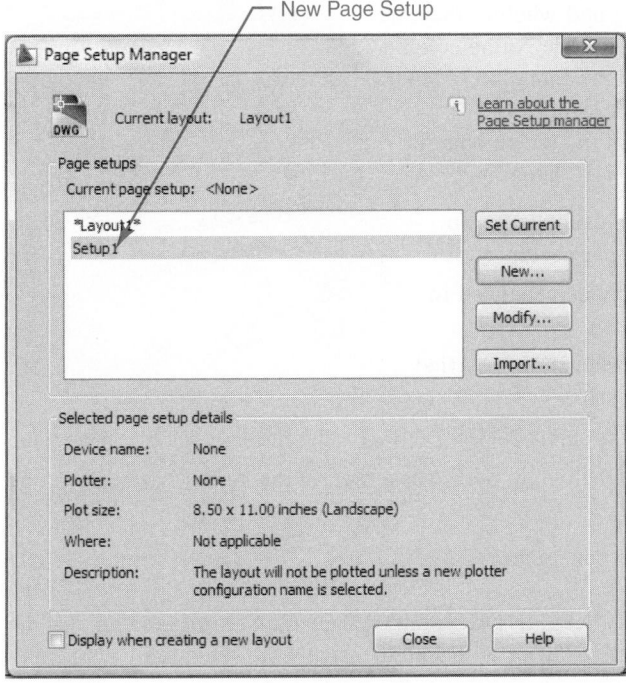

Figure 14-13   The **Page Setup Manager** with new page setup

Importing a Page Setup from Another Drawing.   A named page setup can be imported from another drawing file (DWG), drawing template file (DWT), or drawing exchange format file (DXF). To import a named page setup, select the **Import...** button in the **Page Setup Manager** shown in Figure 14-7. The **Select Page Setup from File** dialog box is displayed so that you can select the source file from which you want to import. After you locate the file and select the **Open** button, the **Import Page Setups** dialog box shown in Figure 14-14 is displayed so you can select one or more page setups.

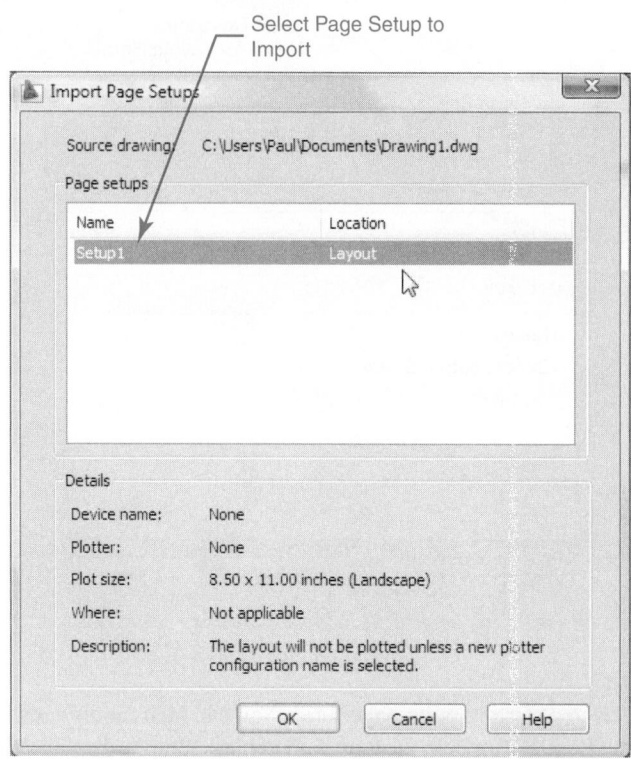

Select Page Setup to Import

Figure 14-14   The **Import Page Setups** dialog box

The **Page setups** list box lists the page setups that can be imported from the selected drawing and whether they are located in model space or paper space. The **Name** column lists the name of the page setup, and the **Location** column lists the page setup location (model or layout).

The **Details** area at the bottom of the dialog box displays information about the selected page setup.

> **Note:** If a page setup with the name selected already exists in the drawing, a warning is displayed asking you if you want to redefine it. Selecting **OK** overwrites the page setup with the new page setup settings.

- **Device name**   The name of the plot device specified in the currently selected page setup
- **Plotter**   The type of plot device specified in the currently selected page setup
- **Plot size**   The plot size and orientation specified in the currently selected page setup
- **Where**   Physical location of the output device specified in the currently selected page setup
- **Description**   Description of the output device specified in the currently selected page setup

Select **OK** to import the selected page setup.

Setting a Page Setup Current.   The **Set Current** button on the **Page Setup Manager** sets the selected page setup current for the active layout so that all the page setup settings are updated to match the selected page setup.

Exercise 14-1: Using the Page Setup Manager

To access student data files, go to www.pearsondesigncentral.com.

1. Open the building floor plan drawing named **EX14-1** in the student data files to display the building floor plan shown in Figure 14-15.
2. Select the **Layout1** tab so that paper space is active and **Layout1** is the current layout.
3. Use the **Page Setup Manager** to set the associated plotter to **None** and the paper size to **ARCH D (36.00 × 24.00 Inches)**.
4. Select the **Layout2** tab and switch to the **Layout2** layout.

Figure 14-15   Building floor plan

5. Use the **Page Setup Manager** to set the associated plotter to **None** and the paper size to **ANSI B (17.00 × 11.00 Inches)**.
6. Save the drawing as **EX14-1**.

Creating Layout Viewports

Layout viewports are the windows that you create in paper space that allow you to view the drawing information in model space at a specified scale (refer to Figure 14-5). Just like the windows in a building, layout viewports can be many different shapes and sizes. A layout viewport can be rectangular, polygonal, or even circular! You can create a single viewport that fits the paper size of the layout, or you can create multiple viewports. Each viewport is controlled independently so that different model space information can be displayed in each viewport, even at different scales if necessary.

> **Note:**
> Do not attempt to create one layout viewport completely within the borders of another layout viewport because unpredictable results can occur. It is possible, though, to overlap viewports.

A layout viewport is treated just like other basic AutoCAD drawing objects such as lines, circles, and arcs. Similar to drawing other AutoCAD objects, a new viewport assumes the current object properties such as layer, color, and linetype when it is created.

After a viewport is created, you can modify it using any of the standard modify commands (**ERASE, MOVE, COPY, SCALE**, etc.). You can even use grips to resize a viewport quickly using the **STRETCH** option.

TIP   Typically, you do not want viewports to be displayed on the final plotted drawing. Because of this, layout viewports should be created on a unique layer so that you can control their visibility. The best approach is to create layout viewports on a layer whose **Plot** property is set to **No plot** so that you can see the viewports in the AutoCAD drawing window, but they do not plot.

You can create one or more layout viewports using the **MVIEW, -VPORTS**, or **VPORTS** command. Creating layout viewports using each of these commands is explained in the following sections.

Creating a Single Rectangular Viewport.   The most common type of layout viewport is a single rectangular viewport. A single rectangular viewport is created by selecting two corner points. It is the default viewport option when you use either the **MVIEW** or **-VPORTS** command.

Single Viewport	
Ribbon & Panel:	None
Viewports Toolbar:	▣
Menu:	Views| Viewports|1 Viewport
Command Line:	MVIEW, VPORTS, -VPORTS
Command Alias:	MV

Do not forget to create a unique viewport layer set to **No plot** and make it current before you create a viewport using the **MVIEW** or **-VPORTS** command. Some typical layer names used include **Viewport** or **Vport**.

When you start either command, AutoCAD prompts you to *Specify corner of viewport or* ↓ as shown in Figure 14-16.

Figure 14-16   Locating the first corner point of a layout viewport

Select the first corner of the viewport or enter a coordinate value at the keyboard. AutoCAD then prompts you to *Specify opposite corner:* as shown in Figure 14-17 so you can specify the second point.

Figure 14-17   Locating the opposite corner point of a layout viewport

New Viewport with Display Zoomed to Extents

Figure 14-18   New layout viewport defaults to zoom extents

The viewport is immediately zoomed to the extents of the model space drawing information as shown in Figure 14-18.

At this point, the viewport is not set at any standard scale. You must manually set the viewport scale factor using the techniques explained later in this chapter.

TIP   You can create a rectangular viewport that is the exact size of the layout's printable area using the **Fit** option. **Fit** is the default option so that you can simply press the **<Enter ↵>** key when you run either the **MVIEW** or **-VPORTS** command before specifying the first viewport corner point.

Creating a Polygonal Viewport.   You can create an irregularly shaped viewport with three or more sides using the **Polygonal** option of the **MVIEW** or **-VPORTS** command. A polygonal viewport is created by selecting multiple points.

To create a polygonal viewport, start the **MVIEW** or **-VPORTS** command and either type **P<Enter ↵>** or select the **Polygonal** option using your arrow keys if you are using **Dynamic Input**. AutoCAD prompts you to *Specify start point:*. After selecting the first point, AutoCAD prompts you to *Specify next point or ↓* so you can start selecting points and define the viewport polygon as shown in Figure 14-19.

To finish the polygon viewport, you close it either by typing **C<Enter ↵>** or by selecting the **Close** option using your arrow keys. The **Close** option draws a viewport segment from the last current point to the start point and exits the command. Similar to a rectangular viewport, a polygonal viewport is immediately zoomed to the extents of the model space drawing information as shown in Figure 14-20.

Polygonal Viewport	
Ribbon & Panel:	View| Viewports
Viewports Toolbar:	
Menu:	Views| Viewports| Polygonal Viewport
Command Line:	MVIEW, VPORTS
Command Alias:	MV

TIP   You can also press **<Enter ↵>** to close a polygonal viewport after three or more viewport points have been defined.

Figure 14-19   Creating a polygonal viewport

Figure 14-20   Using the **Close** option to complete a polygonal viewport

The **Arc** option allows you to create arc segments when you are defining a polygonal viewport. You can pick a second point to define the arc, or you can select from a number of arc suboptions. The arc creation suboptions are the same as those used with the **PLINE** command.

> **FOR MORE DETAILS** See Chapter 9 for more detailed information about using the **PLINE** command **Arc** options.

The **Length** option creates a viewport segment a specified length at the same angle as the previous segment. If the previous viewport segment is an arc, the new segment is drawn tangent to that arc segment.

The **Undo** option will undo the most recent viewport segment.

Converting an Object into a Viewport.   You can convert any of the following objects into a layout viewport:

- Polyline
- Circle
- Ellipse
- Region
- Spline

> **Note:**
> In order to convert a polyline into a viewport, the polyline must be closed, and it must have more than three vertices.

To convert an object into a layout viewport, start the **MVIEW** or **-VPORTS** command and either type **O<Enter ↵>** or select the **Object** option using your arrow keys if you are using **Dynamic Input.** AutoCAD prompts you to *Select object to clip viewport:* so you can pick the object to convert. A circle is shown converted to a viewport in Figure 14-21.

Object	
Ribbon & Panel:	View| Viewports
Viewports Toolbar:	
Menu:	Views| Viewports| Object
Command Line:	MVIEW, VPORTS
Command Alias:	MV

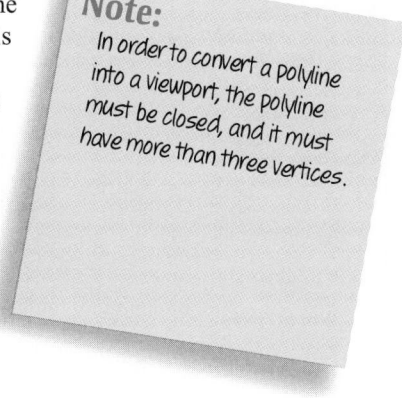

Circle Converted to Viewport

Figure 14-21   Converting a circle to a viewport

New Viewport	
Ribbon & Panel:	View| Viewports New
Viewports Toolbar:	
Menu:	Views| Viewports| New Viewports...
Command Line:	VPORTS
Command Alias:	None

Using the Viewports Dialog Box.   You can automatically create one or more rectangular viewports using the **Viewports** dialog box. The **VPORTS** command displays the **Viewports** dialog box shown in Figure 14-22.

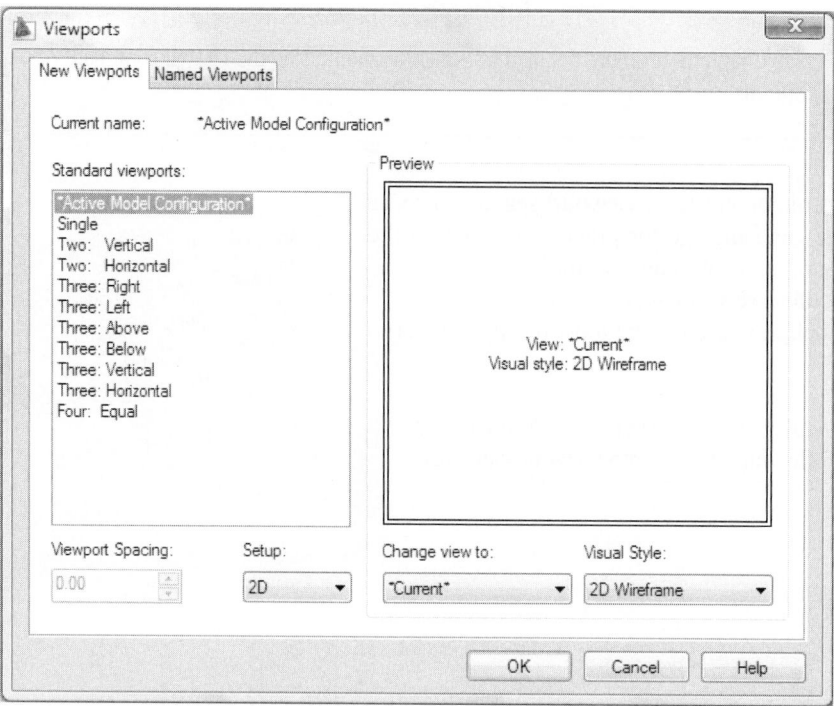

Figure 14-22 The **Viewports** dialog box

The **Standard viewports** box on the left displays a list of standard viewport configurations that you can select. The **Preview** window displays a preview of the selected viewport configuration.

The **Viewport Spacing** box allows you to specify the spacing you want to apply between the viewports for the selected configuration. The **Preview** window is updated to show the results of the spacing indicated.

The **Setup**: list box allows you to switch between a 2D and a 3D viewport setup. When you select 3D, standard orthogonal 3D views are applied to the selected viewport configuration. The **Change view to**: list box replaces the view in the selected viewport with the view you select from the list.

Select **OK** after you have specified the desired configuration and spacing to exit the **Viewports** dialog box. After the dialog box is closed, AutoCAD asks you to specify the rectangular area within which to fit the viewport configuration by prompting you to pick two corner points.

TIP   You can use the **Fit** option to make the viewport configuration fill the layout's printable area by pressing the **<Enter ↵>** key when AutoCAD prompts for the first corner point.

Exercise 14-2: Creating Layout Viewports

1. Continue from Exercise 14-1.
2. Select the **Layout1** tab so that paper space is active and **Layout1** is the current layout.
3. Create a new layer named **Viewport**, set its **Plot** property to **No plot**, and make it the current layer.
4. Create a rectangular viewport using the **MVIEW** or **-VPORTS** command that is the same size as the printable area. *Hint:* The **Fit** option creates a viewport the same size as the printable area.
5. Select the **Layout2** tab and switch to the **Layout2** layout.

6. Create a rectangular viewport using the **MVIEW** or **-VPORTS** command that is the same size as the printable area.
7. Save the drawing as **EX14-2**.

Making a Viewport Current

There are three ways to make a layout viewport current:

- Select the **PAPER** button on the Status Bar.

- Enter the **MSPACE** or **MS** command.

- Double-click with your mouse inside a viewport.

The first two methods work best when you are working with a single layout viewport. If you have more than one viewport, you must double-click with your mouse inside the viewport you want to make current. When a viewport is current, its borderline becomes bold, and your mouse pointer changes to the cursor crosshair mode as shown in Figure 14-23.

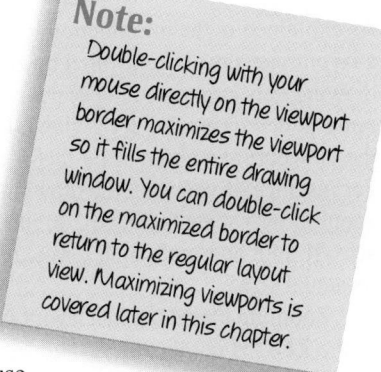

Note: Double-clicking with your mouse directly on the viewport border maximizes the viewport so it fills the entire drawing window. You can double-click on the maximized border to return to the regular layout view. Maximizing viewports is covered later in this chapter.

Cursor Crosshairs

Bold Outline Indicates Current Viewport

Figure 14-23   Making a layout viewport current

When a viewport is current, you can work on the model space drawing just like you are in model space—although it can be somewhat cumbersome working "through" the viewport. The ability to maximize viewports, which is discussed later in the chapter, makes this process much more user-friendly.

Switching Back to Paper Space.   There are three ways to switch back to paper space so that no viewports are current:

- Select the **MODEL** button on the Status Bar.

- Enter the **PSPACE** or **PS** command.

- Double-click with your mouse outside all viewports.

All information that is created when paper space is active and no viewports are current is added to paper space exclusively (**TILEMODE = 0**). In this mode, it is possible to add information (such as titles and drawing scales) directly above a viewport. This approach allows you to add information to your drawing that is displayed on the plotted drawing but does not need to be part of the model space design.

Setting the Viewport Scale

As explained in the introduction to the chapter, the scale of the drawing information displayed in a layout viewport is controlled by zooming in and out of the active viewport. If you zoom in, the drawing gets larger, and the scale is increased. If you zoom out, the drawing gets smaller, and the scale is decreased. To set a viewport to a standard drafting scale, you must zoom in or out in the viewport at a zoom scale factor equal to the scale you want the drawing information to plot. For instance, if you want the drawing information in a viewport to plot at a scale of 2:1, you must zoom in by a scale factor of 2 in the viewport so that everything appears twice as large as actual size. To plot at a scale of 1:2, you zoom out by a scale factor of 1/2 so that everything is half of its actual size.

Zooming in and out in a layout viewport to a specific scale factor is done using the **XP** option of the **ZOOM** command.

FOR MORE DETAILS	See Chapter 3 for more details about using the **ZOOM** command.

The **X** in the **XP** option represents a multiplication sign, and the **P** stands for paper space. The number preceding the **XP** is the value the view is scaled relative to the paper space scale, which is 1:1. For example, to create a viewport that is scaled at 2:1 you enter **2XP** in response to the **ZOOM** command. In order to create a view that is scaled 1:2, you would enter **1/2XP** or **.5XP**.

Using the **ZOOM** command with the **XP** option to set the viewport scale is fine when you are working with simple scales such as 2:1 or 1:2. Converting standard drafting scales such as $\frac{1}{4}'' = 1'\text{-}0''$ or $1\frac{1}{2}'' = 1'\text{-}0''$ to their equivalent scale factors takes a little more time and effort. Luckily, AutoCAD provides some easier ways to set a viewport's scale, which are explained in the following sections.

Setting the Viewport Scale on the Status Bar.   The easiest way to set the viewport scale is via the **Viewport Scale** button on the right side of the AutoCAD Status Bar. The arrow to the right of the **Viewport Scale** button displays a list of standard drafting scales that you can use to set the zoom scale factor of the current viewport as shown in Figure 14-24.

The **Viewport Scale** is displayed on the Status Bar only when a viewport is current. You can make a viewport current by double-clicking in the viewport with your mouse. Select the desired scale factor from the list, and the viewport is zoomed in or out by the pre-established scale factor.

TIP   After the viewport scale is set, zooming in and out using any **Zoom** tools should be avoided. Any incremental zoom is enough to change the zoom scale factor so that it is no longer correct. Panning the display is not a problem because the zoom factor remains the same. The easiest way to prevent inadvertent zooms is to lock the viewport by selecting the **Lock/Unlock Viewport** button to the left of the **Viewport Scale** button on the Status Bar when the viewport is current and toggling it so the **Lock** icon is closed.

Using the Properties Palette to Set the Viewport Scale.   You can also control the viewport scale factor via the **Properties** palette. Setting the viewport scale using the **Properties** palette requires that you are in paper space in order to select the viewport object. Selecting a viewport displays the properties shown in Figure 14-25 so that you can select a **Standard scale** from the list.

Figure 14-24   Setting the
Viewport Scale

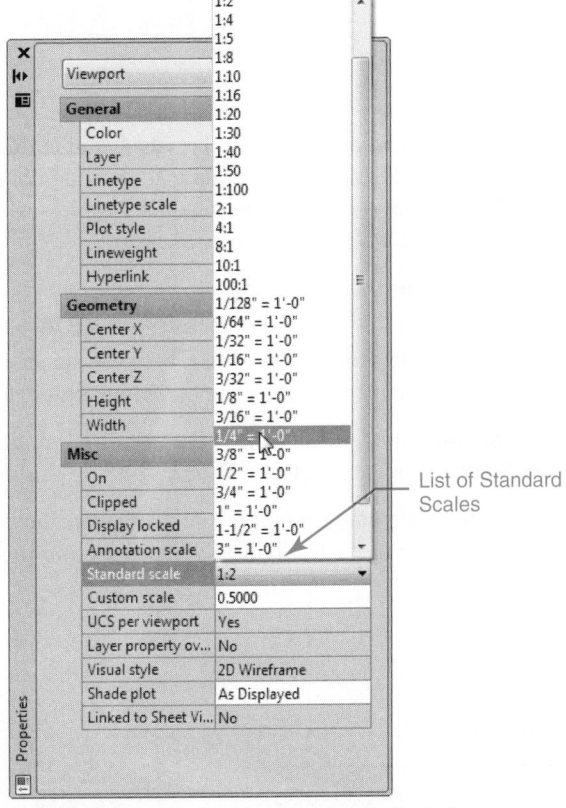

Figure 14-25   Setting the viewport scale via the
Properties palette

List of Standard
Scales

TIP   You can also set a custom scale using the **Properties** palette if the scale you need is not in the **Standard scale** list. To specify a custom scale, enter the desired scale factor in the **Custom scale** property text field.

Adding and Editing Scales in the Standard Scale List.   The **SCALELISTEDIT** command allows you to add new scales or edit existing scales that appear in the **Scale List** box. You can either type in the command, or you can select **Custom...** from the bottom of the scale list. The **Edit Scale List** dialog box shown in Figure 14-26 is displayed.

Figure 14-26   The **Edit Scale List** dialog box

The **Scale List** on the left displays the list of currently defined scales. Selecting a scale from the list displays the ratio of paper units to drawing units at the bottom of the **Scale List**.

The **Add** button allows you to add a custom scale to the list via the **Add Scale** dialog box shown in Figure 14-27. In this dialog box:

- The **Scale name** area is where you enter the descriptive or numeric name as you want it to appear in the list in the **Name appearing in scale list**: text box.
- The **Scale properties** area is where you set the ratio of paper units to drawing units by entering the numeric values in the **Paper units**: and **Drawing units**: text boxes.

The **Edit** button in the **Edit Scale List** dialog box allows you to edit an existing scale via the **Edit Scale** dialog box shown in Figure 14-28. In this dialog box:

- The **Scale name** area is where you update the descriptive or numeric name as you want it to appear in the list in the **Name appearing in scale list**: text box.

Figure 14-27   The **Add Scale** dialog box

Figure 14-28   The **Edit Scale** dialog box

- The **Scale properties** area is where you change the ratio of paper units to drawing units by entering new numeric values in the **Paper units:** and **Drawing units:** text boxes.

The **Move Up** button in the **Edit Scale List** dialog box moves the currently selected scale in the **Scale List** up one position so that it appears in that position in all scale list boxes. The **Move Down** button moves the currently selected scale in the **Scale List** down one position so that it appears in that position in all scale list boxes.

The **Delete** button permanently removes the currently selected scale from the **Scale List**. The **Reset** button deletes any custom scales that were added and restores the default list of standard AutoCAD scales.

Locking the Viewport Display

You can protect the viewport scale from being accidentally changed by locking the viewport display so it is impossible to zoom or pan inside the viewport when it is current. When a viewport is locked, any attempt to zoom or pan affects the entire paper space layout similarly to if you were working in paper space. The current viewport remains active; it is just temporarily disabled during the zoom or pan process. The easiest way to lock a viewport is to select the **Lock/Unlock Viewport** button on the Status Bar as shown in Figure 14-29. In addition, you can also use the following methods:

- Select viewport and right-click to display the shortcut menu and set the **Display locked** menu item to **Yes**.
- Set the **Display locked** property to **Yes** via the **Properties** palette.
- Use the **MVIEW** command's **Lock** option and select the viewport.

Figure 14-29   The **Lock/Unlock Viewport** button

To unlock a viewport, select the **Lock/Unlock Viewport** button or use any of the options listed above and set the **Locked** property to **Off** or **No**.

Exercise 14-3: Setting the Viewport Scale

1. Continue from Exercise 14-2.
2. Select the **Layout1** tab so that paper space is active and **Layout1** is the current layout.
3. Make the viewport created in Exercise 14-2 the active viewport and **Zoom Extents** so that the entire floor plan fills the viewport.
4. Set the viewport scale to **1/4″ = 1′-0″** by selecting it from the **Viewport Scale** list on the right side of the Status Bar.
5. Select the **Lock/Unlock Viewport** button to the left of the **Viewport Scale** list to lock the viewport.
6. Make paper space the active drawing environment by selecting the **MODEL** button on the Status Bar and toggling it to **PAPER**.
7. **Layout1** should now look similar to Figure 14-30.
8. Select the **Layout2** tab and switch to the **Layout2** layout.
9. Make the viewport created in Exercise 14-2 the active viewport and **Zoom Extents** so that the entire floor plan fills the viewport.

1/4" = 1'-0" Scale Viewport

Figure 14-30   Layout1 with **1/4″ = 1′-0″** scale viewport

1/8" = 1'-0" Scale Viewport

Figure 14-31   Layout2 with **1/8″ = 1′-0″** scale viewport

10. Set the viewport scale to **1/8″ = 1′-0″** by selecting it from the **Viewport Scale** list on the right side of the Status Bar.
11. Select the **Lock/Unlock Viewport** button to the left of the **Viewport Scale** list to lock the viewport.
12. **Layout2** should now look similar to Figure 14-31.
13. Make paper space the active drawing environment by selecting the **MODEL** button on the Status Bar and toggling it to **PAPER**.
14. Save the drawing as **EX14-3**.

Controlling Layers per Layout Viewport

As mentioned earlier, it is possible to control layers per layout viewport so that you can display different model space drawing information in each individual viewport while not affecting the information in model space. You can freeze and thaw layers in individual viewports, as well as control the color, linetype, and lineweight used. These individual viewport specific layer settings are referred to as *viewport layer overrides*.

The most popular viewport layer override is the ability to freeze a layer in an individual viewport. This allows you to leave all of the layers on (thawed) in model space but then freeze different layers in each viewport to create multiple views of the same model space information and create different drawings. For example, one layout could be used to display the electrical plan information, and another layout might display only the HVAC plan information. The possibilities are endless, especially when combined with the concept of external reference drawings.

FOR MORE DETAILS	See Chapter 17 for more information about using external reference drawings (xrefs).

There are two different ways to freeze layers per viewport: in the current viewport or in any new viewports. Freezing layers in the **New VP Freeze** column means that any information on the selected layers will not be displayed when you create any new layout viewports in the future.

Freezing layers in the current viewport is most common. Obviously, to freeze layers in the current viewport, you must first make the viewport current. After the viewport is current, start the **LAYER** command to display the **Layer Properties Manager**.

The viewport layer override columns are displayed at the right before the **Description** column as shown in Figure 14-32.

To freeze a layer in the current viewport, click on the sun icon in the **VP Freeze** column and change it to a snowflake icon, just like the regular **Freeze** option. The selected layer is frozen in the current viewport as shown in Figure 14-33.

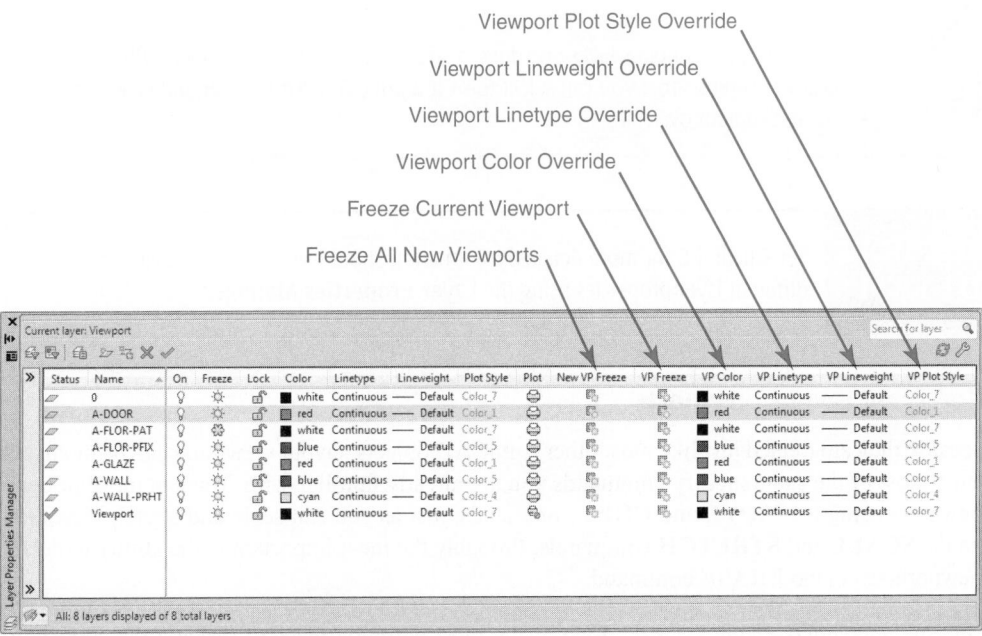

Figure 14-32   The **Layer Properties Manager** in paper space

Figure 14-33   Freezing layers per viewport

The same technique can be used to override the other layer settings (color, linetype, lineweight, and plot style). Simply make the viewport current and select the desired overrides.

You can remove viewport layer overrides using the right-click menu in the **Layer** list in the **Layer Properties Manager**. The **VPLAYEROVERRIDESMODE** system variable allows you to temporarily turn off all viewport layer overrides.

> **Note:**
> When any viewport layer override is applied, a different background color is used in the **Layer Properties Manager**.

TIP   When a viewport contains layer overrides, a **Viewport Overrides** property filter is automatically created so that you can select the **Viewport Overrides** filter and view only the layers that contain overrides.

FOR MORE DETAILS   See Chapter 6 for more detailed information about layers and controlling the different layer properties using the **Layer Properties Manager**.

Modifying Layout Viewports

Because they are treated just like most other AutoCAD objects, layout viewports can be modified using most of the same modify commands you are already familiar with. You can move or copy viewports using the **MOVE** and **COPY** commands, just as you can scale and stretch viewports via the **SCALE** and **STRETCH** commands. Probably the most important is the ability to delete viewports using the **ERASE** command.

Resizing Viewports Using Grips.   One of the most common ways to resize a viewport is to simply rely on grips. Using a viewport's grips and the **STRETCH** option allows you to modify a viewport quickly and make it the size needed as shown in Figure 14-34.

Selected
Viewport Grip

New Viewport
Corner Location

Specify stretch point or

Figure 14-34   Using grips to resize a viewport

FOR MORE DETAILS	See Chapter 7 for detailed information about using grips.

Clipping Viewports.   You can change the shape of a viewport using the **VPCLIP** command.

Using the **VPCLIP** command you can either select a different object to convert into a viewport, or you can redefine the viewport using a new polygon viewport.

When you start the **VPCLIP** command and a viewport is not already selected, AutoCAD prompts you to *Select viewport to clip:* so you can select a viewport. Once a viewport is selected, AutoCAD prompts you to *Select clipping object or ↓.* You can either select an object to convert into a viewport, or you can define a new polygon window by typing **P<Enter ↵>** or selecting the **Polygon** option using your arrow keys. The options for creating a polygon viewport are the same as explained earlier in the chapter. The new viewport that is created to replace the existing viewport is referred to as a *clipping boundary,* as shown in Figure 14-35.

The **Delete** option deletes the clipping boundary of a selected viewport. The **Delete** option is available only if the selected viewport has already been clipped once using the **VPCLIP** command.

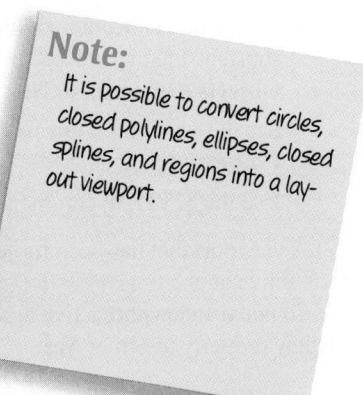

Note:
It is possible to convert circles, closed polylines, ellipses, closed splines, and regions into a layout viewport.

Viewport Clip	
Ribbon & Panel:	View| Viewports
Viewports Toolbar:	
Pull-down Menu:	None
Command Line:	VPCLIP
Command Alias:	None

TIP   You can determine whether a viewport has been clipped using the **VPCLIP** command by checking the viewport's **Clipped** property via the **Properties** palette. If it is set to **Yes**, the viewport has been clipped.

New Viewport
Clipping Boundary

Figure 14-35   Clipping a viewport using the **VPCLIP** command

Turning Viewport Display Off and On

You can turn the viewport display on and off temporarily so that the model space objects displayed in the viewport are no longer visible. This can be used to either speed up drawing regeneration time or control what drawing information is plotted. There are three ways to turn a viewport off:

Note:
The viewport boundary is still displayed if a viewport is turned off. Only the model space information is turned off.

- Select the viewport, right-click to display the shortcut menu, and set the **Display Viewport Objects** menu item to **No.**
- Set the viewport's **On** property to **No** via the **Properties** palette.
- Use the **MVIEW** command's **Off** option and select the viewport.

A viewport that has been turned off is considered inactive. You can only have up to 64 viewports active at one time.

To make a viewport active again, use any of the options listed above to toggle the viewport's **Display** property to **On** or **Yes**.

TIP   The maximum number of active viewports is controlled using the **MAXACTVP** system variable. The maximum value is 64.

Maximizing a Viewport

You can maximize a layout viewport so that it fills the entire drawing window area, which makes it easier to work on your model space design without switching entirely from paper space to model space. This feature was introduced to get around the complications of working "through" a layout viewport to get to the model space drawing information while you were still in paper space. There are four ways to maximize a layout viewport:

- Select the **Maximize Viewport** button on the right side of the Status Bar.
- Double-click on the viewport.
- Select the viewport, right-click to display the shortcut menu, and select the **Maximize Viewport** menu item.
- Type **VPMAX<Enter ↵>**.

Either method enlarges the viewport to fit the drawing window display area and changes the border to a thick red hashed line (see Figure 14-36).

Maximized Viewport Border

Figure 14-36   Drawing display with a layout viewport maximized

To pan and zoom when a viewport is maximized and not change the original viewport display when you switch back to the viewport, use the **Minimize Viewport** commands listed below. When a viewport is maximized, it is almost as if you were working in model space on the **Model** tab.

There are four ways to restore the maximized layout viewport back to its original size and display:

- Select the **Minimize Viewport** button on the right side of the Status Bar.
- Double-click on the maximized viewport.
- Select the viewport, right-click to display the shortcut menu, and select the **Minimize Viewport** menu item.
- Type **VPMIN<Enter ↵>**.

Exercise 14-4: Working with Multiple Annotation Scales

1. Continue from Exercise 14-3.
2. Create a text style named **Notes** with the following settings:
   a. Font = **Simplex.shx** AutoCAD font
   b. **Annotative** should be checked
   c. Paper Text Height = **0.125″**
3. Create the following layer:

Name	Color	Linetype	Lineweight	Description
A-Anno-Note	3	Continuous	Default	Drawing note text

4. Select the **PAPER** button on the Status Bar and toggle it to **MODEL** so that model space is active.
5. Set the **Notes** text style current on the **Annotation** panel.
6. Set the **A-Anno-Note** layer current in the **Layer** list box.
7. Set the **Viewport Scale** to **1/8″ = 1′-0″** by selecting it from the **Viewport Scale** list on the right side of the Status Bar.
8. Create the text shown in Figure 14-37 using the **Center** justification option.

Figure 14-37   1/8″ = 1′-0″ scale view with text

9. Select the **Automatically add scales to annotative objects when the annotation scale changes** icon on the far right of the **Viewport Scale** button on the Status Bar so it is on.
10. Set the **Viewport Scale** to **1/4″ = 1′-0″** by selecting it from the list on the right side of the Status Bar. All text in the drawing should scale down by 1/2.
11. Center the 1/4″ = 1′-0″ text in each room by using the upper left grip to move each piece of text individually of its 1/8″ = 1′-0″ scale representation as shown in Figure 14-38.

Figure 14-38   1/4″ = 1′-0″ scale view with text

12. Select the **Layout1** tab so that paper space is active and **Layout1** is the current layout. Only the 1/4″ = 1′-0″ text is visible.
13. Select the **Layout2** tab and switch to the **Layout2** layout. Only the 1/8″ = 1′-0″ text is visible.
14. Make paper space the active drawing environment by double-clicking outside the viewport.
15. Save the drawing as **EX14-4**.

Managing Layouts

The following sections describe how to manage layouts so that you can do the following:

- Create a new layout
- Rename a layout
- Move or copy a layout
- Delete a layout

One of the easiest ways to accomplish any of these tasks is to rely on the layout's right-click shortcut menu. Right-clicking with your mouse on any layout tab displays the shortcut menu shown in Figure 14-39.

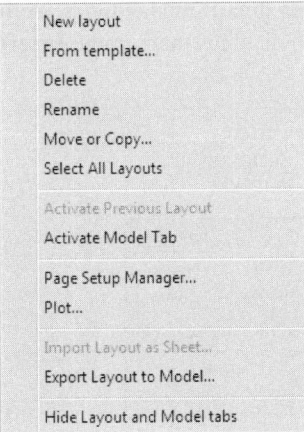

Figure 14-39   The **Layout** right-click shortcut menu

TIP   The **Select All Layouts** menu item on the **Layout** right-click menu provides a quick way to perform a task on all the layouts at one time.

The **LAYOUT** command also provides most of the same functionality, but as you might expect, it's not quite as user-friendly. Emphasis is placed on using the right-click menu where appropriate in the following sections.

Creating a New Layout

There are four ways to create a new layout:

- Add a new generic layout tab with the default settings so that the settings must be updated via the **Page Setup Manager**.
- Import a layout from an existing drawing file (DWG), drawing template file (DWT), or drawing exchange format file (DXF).
- Use the **Create Layout Wizard** that steps you through the layout setup.
- Copy an existing layout tab in the current drawing file and rename it.

New Layout	
Ribbon & Panel:	None
Layouts Toolbar:	
Menu:	Insert| Layout| New Layout
Command Line:	LAYOUT
Command Alias:	LO

Layout from Template	
Ribbon & Panel:	None
Layouts Toolbar:	
Menu:	Insert| Layout| Layout from Template
Command Line:	LAYOUT
Command Alias:	LO

The first three methods are described in the following sections. Copying a layout is covered a little later.

Adding a Generic Layout with Default Settings.   You can quickly add a generic layout with default page setup settings. You must then use the **Page Setup Manager** described earlier in this chapter to set up the layout as required.

You can add a generic layout by selecting **New layout** from the **Layout** cascade menu on the **Insert** menu, by right-clicking and selecting **New layout** from the shortcut menu, or by using the **New** option of the **LAYOUT** command.

AutoCAD prompts you to *Enter new Layout name <Layout3>:* if you add a new layout via the **Insert** menu or the **LAYOUT** command. The default layout name is "Layout" followed by an integer representing the layout number in the sequence.

When you select **New layout** from the right-click shortcut menu, a layout is added with the default name, and you must rename it. Renaming layouts is covered later in this chapter.

Importing a Layout from a Drawing Template.   To save time and effort, you can import a layout that is already set up with the correct paper size and plot settings from an existing drawing file (DWG), drawing template file (DWT), or drawing exchange format file (DXF).

You can import a layout by selecting **Layout from Template...** from the **Layout** cascade menu on the **Insert** menu, by right-clicking and selecting **From template...** from the shortcut menu, or by using the **Template** option of the **LAYOUT** command.

AutoCAD displays the **Select Template From File** standard file dialog box so you can select the file from which you want to import the layout. Selecting the **Open** button gets a list of the layouts in the selected file and displays them in the **Insert Layout(s)** dialog box shown in Figure 14-40.

Select Layout to Import

Insert Layout(s)

Layout name(s):   OK

Architectural Title Block   Cancel

Note:
If a layout with the same name already exists in the current drawing during the import process, the layout is still added, but it is renamed by prefixing the layout name with a default layout name and a dash (-).

Figure 14-40   The **Insert Layout(s)** dialog box

Create Layout Wizard	
Ribbon & Panel:	None
Layouts Toolbar:	None
Menu:	Insert| Layout| Create Layout Wizard
Command Line:	LAYOUTWIZARD
Command Alias:	None

Select one or more layouts you want to import in the **Layout name(s):** list box and select **OK**. The selected layout(s) are imported with all their settings and drawing information and added to the right end of the layout tabs at the bottom of the drawing window.

Creating a New Layout Using the Layout Wizard.   The **Create Layout Wizard** automates the process of creating, *and setting up,* a new layout by prompting you for information about the different layout settings in a series of preprogrammed steps.

You can start the **Create Layout Wizard** by selecting **Create Layout Wizard** from the **Layout** cascade menu on the **Insert** menu or by using the **LAYOUTWIZARD** command. The **Create Layout** dialog box is displayed with the **Begin** step displayed as shown in Figure 14-41.

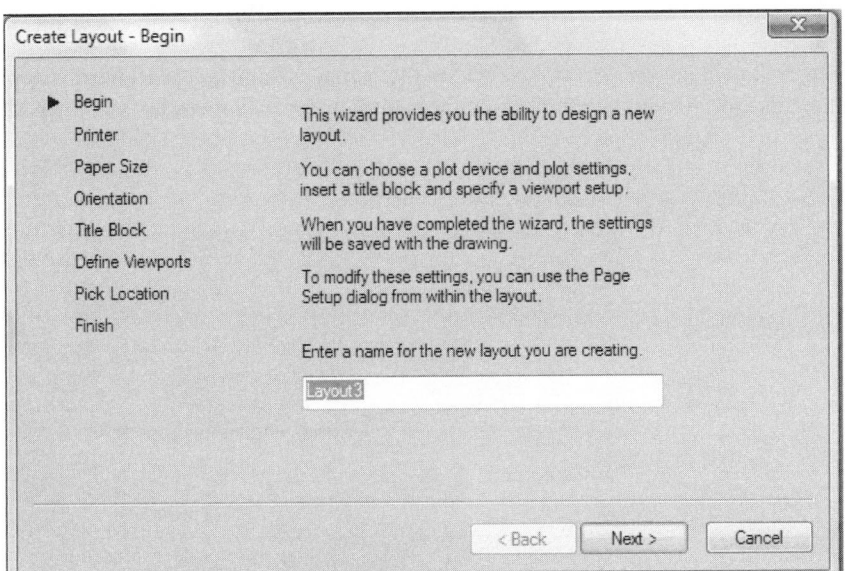

Figure 14-41   The **Create Layout—Begin** step

The steps that the wizard will take you through are listed on the left in sequence from top to bottom with the arrow to the left indicating the current step. Select the **Next** button to continue to the next step or the **Back** button to return to a previous step if you want to verify or change anything. The setup steps and options are as follows:

- **Begin**   Allows you to enter the desired name for the new layout
- **Printer**   Allows you to select a system printer/plotter output device
- **Paper Size**   Allows you to specify a paper size based on the printer selected in the previous step and switch drawing units between millimeters and inches
- **Orientation**   Allows you to switch between the portrait and landscape paper orientation modes
- **Title Block**   Allows you to insert a predefined title block in the layout as a block or an xref. The title block drawings listed are located in the default AutoCAD template folder

---

FOR MORE DETAILS   See Chapter 16 for more information about blocks. See Chapter 17 for more information about external references (xrefs).

- **Define Viewports**   Allows you to select a layout viewport configuration and set the viewport scale from a list of predefined standard scales
- **Pick Location**   Allows you to define the area to fill with the viewport configuration selected in the previous step by picking two corner points. If no location is selected, AutoCAD uses the layout's printable area
- **Finish**   Exits the **Layout Wizard** and creates the new layout with the selected settings

Note:
You can always change the information entered in the **Create Layout Wizard** later by selecting the layout and using the **Page Setup Manager** explained earlier in the chapter.

Renaming a Layout

The easiest way to rename a layout is to right-click on the layout tab and select **Rename** from the shortcut menu. You can then update the layout name directly on the layout tab as shown in Figure 14-42.

Figure 14-42   Renaming a layout

Enter New Layout Name Here

You can also rename a layout using the **Rename** option of the **LAYOUT** command. Using the **LAYOUT** command requires that you enter the layout to change in response to *Enter layout to rename <Layout1>:* where the current layout is the default name. AutoCAD then prompts you to *Enter new layout name:* so you can enter the new name.

TIP   You can double-click on a layout tab to automatically rename a layout.

Moving and Copying a Layout

The easiest way to move or copy a layout is to right-click on the layout tab and select **Move or Copy...** from the shortcut menu to display the **Move or Copy** dialog box shown in Figure 14-43.

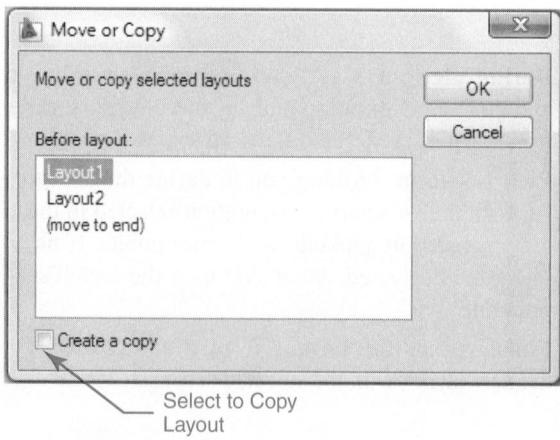

Figure 14-43   The **Move or Copy** dialog box

Select to Copy Layout

Select the layout from the list in the **Before layout**: list box that you want to locate the current layout *before*. When you select **OK**, the layout will be moved or copied so it appears as the layout tab directly preceding, or to the left of, the selected tab.

If you want to make a copy of a layout and move it at the same time, select the **Create a copy** check box on the bottom of the dialog box. AutoCAD creates a copy of the layout with the same name as the current layout with a numerical suffix representing the sequence appended in parentheses. For instance, **Layout1** becomes **Layout1(2)**.

It is possible to select a layout tab and drag it into another position with your mouse.

Deleting a Layout

The easiest way to delete a layout is to right-click on the layout tab and select **Delete** from the shortcut menu. AutoCAD displays a warning before deleting the layout so you can cancel the operation or select **OK** to continue.

You can also delete a layout using the **Delete** option of the **LAYOUT** command. Using the **LAYOUT** command requires that you enter the layout to delete in response to *Enter name of layout to delete <Layout1>:* where the current layout is the default name.

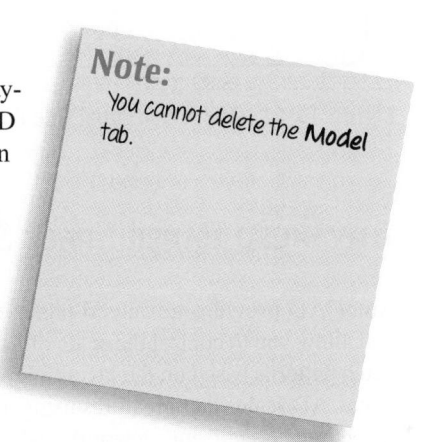

Note:
You cannot delete the **Model** tab.

Exercise 14-5: Managing Layouts

1. Continue from Exercise 14-4.
2. Right-click on a layout tab and select the **From template…** menu item on the Layout tab right-click menu in order to insert a new **Architectural D-Size** layout from an existing AutoCAD drawing template file.
3. Select the **Architectural D-Size.dwt** template file in the student data files in the **Select Template From File** dialog box and the **Open** button to display the **Insert Layout(s)** dialog box.
4. Select the **Architectural Title Block** layout and select the **OK** button.
5. Select the **Architectural Title Block** tab and switch to the **Architectural Title Block** layout.
6. Set the viewport scale to **1/4″ = 1′-0″** using the techniques learned in Exercise 14-3 and center the floor plan in the viewport so it looks similar to Figure 14-44.
7. Rename the **Architectural Title Block** layout to **ANSI D Title Block** by right-clicking with your mouse on the **Architectural Title Block** tab and selecting **Rename** from the shortcut menu.
8. Rename the **Layout2** layout to **ANSI B Title Block** by right-clicking with your mouse on the **Layout2** tab and selecting **Rename** from the shortcut menu.
9. Delete the **Layout1** layout by right-clicking with your mouse on the **Layout1** tab and selecting **Delete** from the shortcut menu.
10. Save the drawing as **EX14-5**.

To access student data files, go to www.pearsondesigncentral.com.

Center Floor Plan
in Viewport

Figure 14-44   The **Architectural Title Block** layout with **1/4″ = 1′-0″** viewport

ADVANCED PAPER SPACE SCALING FEATURES

AutoCAD provides advanced paper space scaling options that allow you to control the scale of linetype definitions and hatch patterns based on the layout viewport scale. Basically, AutoCAD scales these features using a multiplier that is the inverse of the current viewport scale. For instance, for a viewport with a scale set to 1/4″ = 1′-0″, the zoom factor scale is 1/48XP. To make linetype definitions and hatch patterns display correctly, they must be scaled up by 48, the inverse of 1/48.

Note:
In order to use any of these features, you must be in paper space working through a layout viewport in model space (**TILEMODE = 0**). It is possible to use the **Maximize Viewport** feature discussed earlier but do not zoom in or out because the viewport scale is affected.

Paper Space Linetype Scale

The **PSLTSCALE** system variable allows you to scale linetype definitions based on the viewport scale so that linetype definitions will display the same in multiple viewports that have different scale factors. Without paper space linetype scaling, the same linetype definition will appear at different scales in each viewport as shown in Figure 14-45.

Setting **PSLTSCALE** to **1** (on) tells AutoCAD to scale the linetype definitions of all the objects displayed in a viewport by the inverse of the viewport scale factor as shown in Figure 14-46.

Be aware that the global linetype scale controlled using the **LTSCALE** system variable is still in effect when paper space linetype scale is turned on and can have some unintended effects. Typically, the **LTSCALE** system variable is set to **1** when paper space linetype scale is being used (**PSLTSCALE = 1**).

FOR MORE DETAILS   See Chapter 6 for more information about linetype definitions and the **LTSCALE** system variable.

1/4" = 1'0" Scale
Viewport

1/8" = 1'0" Scale
Viewport

Different Linetype
Display Scales

Figure 14-45   Paper space linetype scaling not turned on

1/4" = 1'0" Scale
Viewport

1/8" = 1'0" Scale
Viewport

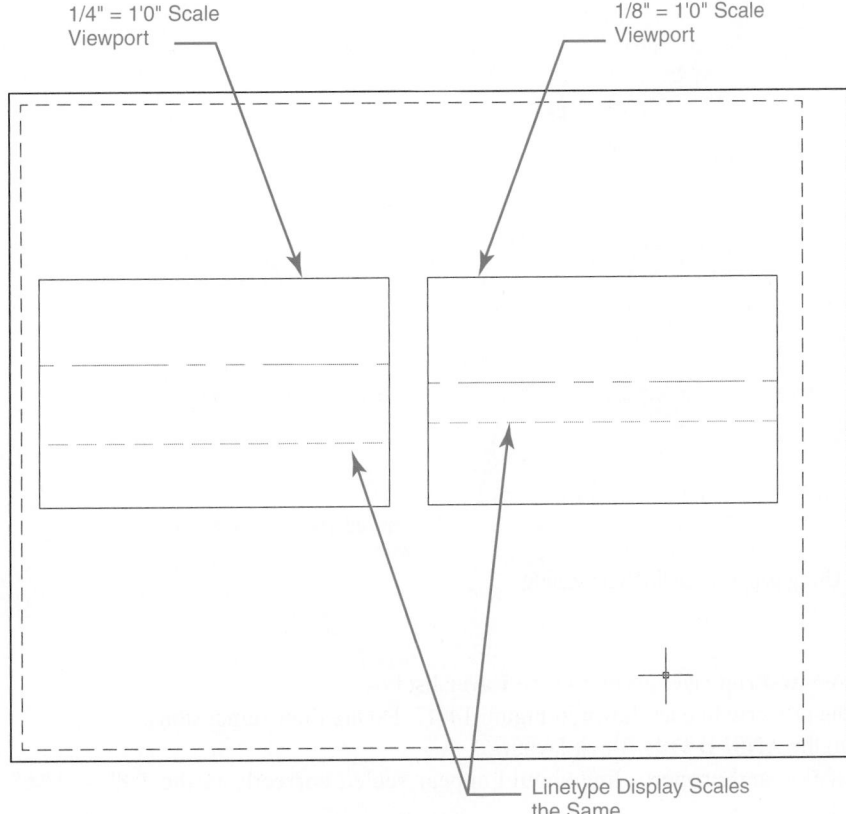

Linetype Display Scales
the Same

Figure 14-46   Paper space linetype scaling turned on

Exercise 14-6: Paper Space Linetype Scaling

1. Continue from Exercise 14-5.
2. Create the following layers:

Name	Color	Linetype	Lineweight	Description
A-Roof-Otln	1	Hidden	Default	Roof outline
A-Site-Prop	5	Phantom	Default	Property line

3. Set the **PSLTSCALE** system variable to **1** so paper space linetype scaling is turned on.
4. Set the **LTSCALE** system variable to **1** to so that global linetype scaling is turned off.
5. Switch to the **ANSI D Title Block** layout.
6. Maximize the viewport using the **Maximize Viewport** button on the right side of the Status Bar so you can work in model space.
7. Set the **A-Roof-Otln** layer current in the **Layer** list box.
8. Create the roof outline as shown in Figure 14-47. Do *not* draw dimensions.

Roof Outline   Property Line

6'-0" TYP.
2'-0" TYP.

2'-0" TYP.
6'-0" TYP.

Maximized 1/4" = 1' - 0" Scale Viewport

Figure 14-47   Using paper space linetype scaling

9. Set the **A-Site-Prop** layer current in the **Layer** list box.
10. Create the property line as shown in Figure 14-47. Do *not* draw dimensions.
11. Switch to the **ANSI B Title Block** layout.
12. The roof line and property line should appear scaled correctly in the 1/8″ = 1′-0″ viewport.
13. Save the drawing as **EX14-6**.

Paper Space Hatch Pattern Scale

You can create a boundary hatch that is automatically scaled relative to the layout viewport scale when using the **BHATCH** command so that you do not have to manually calculate the hatch scale factor. The hatch scale is set to the inverse of the current layout viewport scale.

To calculate the hatch scale automatically, select the **Relative to paper space** check box in the **Angle and scale** area of the **Hatch and Gradient** dialog box as shown in Figure 14-48.

Be aware that AutoCAD multiplies the viewport scale factor by the scale factor specified in the **Scale:** list box to come up with the final calculated scale factor. For this reason, the hatch scale factor specified in the **Scale:** list box is also typically set to **1** if you are going to use the **Relative to paper space** option.

Note: Hatch pattern scales must be updated manually using the **HATCHEDIT** command if the viewport scale is changed by zooming in or out.

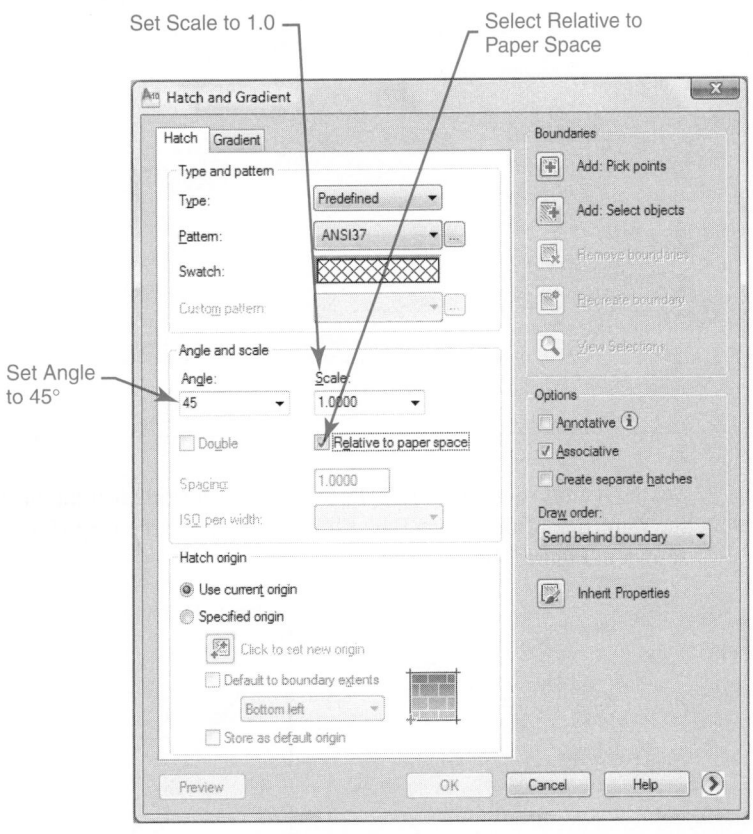

Set Scale to 1.0

Select Relative to Paper Space

Set Angle to 45°

Figure 14-48   Setting the hatch scale factor relative to paper space

The **Annotative** option allows you to take this concept a step further by using the **Annotation Scale** setting to control the hatch scale. This approach is superior when you have multiple scaled views because each scaled hatch pattern is displayed separately similar to the **Annotative** text styles discussed in Chapter 11.

FOR MORE DETAILS	See Chapter 10 for more information about the **BHATCH** and **HATCHEDIT** commands.

Exercise 14-7: Annotative Hatch Pattern Scaling

1. Continue from Exercise 14-6.
2. Select the **Model** tab so that model space is active.

3. Thaw the **A-Flor-Pat** layer in the **Layer** list box so the floor tile hatch outlines are displayed on the building floor plan and make it the current layer.
4. Set the **Annotation Scale** to **1/8″ = 1′-0″** by selecting it from the **Viewport Scale** list on the right side of the Status Bar.
5. Start the **BHATCH** command to display the **Hatch and Gradient** dialog box.
6. Set the **Pattern**: list box to the **AR-HBONE** hatch pattern, the **Scale**: list box to **2**, and select the **Annotative** check box.
7. Select the **Add**: **Pick points** button and pick three points on the building floor plan to add the hatch patterns to as shown in Figure 14-49.

Figure 14-49 Adding hatching to the 1/8″ = 1′-0″ scale view of a floor plan

8. Set the **Annotation Scale** to **1/4″ = 1′-0″** by selecting it from the **Viewport Scale** list on the right side of the Status Bar. All hatching in the drawing should scale down by 1/2 as shown in Figure 14-50.

Figure 14-50   1/4″ = 1′-0″ scale view with hatching

9. Switch to the **ANSI B Title Block** layout. Only the 1/8″ = 1′-0″ hatching is visible.
10. Switch to the **ANSI D Title Block** layout. Only the 1/4″ = 1′-0″ text is visible.
11. Save the drawing as **EX14-7**.

PAPER SPACE AND DIMENSIONING

There are three different ways that paper space can influence how, *and where,* you dimension a drawing. The different approaches are explained in the following sections.

Scaling Dimension Features Using the Viewport Scale

Rather than providing a dimension scale factor (**DIMSCALE**) to control the size of dimension features such as text height and arrow sizes, you can rely on the viewport scale to control dimension feature sizes automatically. The only requirement is that, just like the other paper space scaling features described earlier, you must dimension the drawing while in paper space working through the layout viewport—yet another good reason to utilize the **Maximize Viewport** feature.

To scale dimension features using the viewport scale, select the **Scale dimensions to layout** button on the **Fit** tab of the **Modify Dimension Style** dialog box shown in Figure 14-51.

Select Scale Dimensions to Layout Button

Figure 14-51   Setting dimension features to scale using the **Viewport Scale**

You can also set the system variable **DIMSCALE** to **0** to turn on the **Scale dimensions to layout** feature.

When the **Scale dimensions to layout** feature is on, or **DIMSCALE** is set to **0**, dimension features are automatically scaled by the inverse of the current viewport scale as shown in Figure 14-52.

1/4" = 1'-0" Scale Viewport
Current

Dimension Features Scaled
by 48

Figure 14-52 Scaling dimension features using the **Viewport Scale**

If the viewport scale changes by zooming in or zooming out, dimension features are *not* automatically rescaled even if the **Scale dimensions to layout** feature is currently on. You must update the dimensions by selecting **Update** from the **Dimensions** panel on the **Annotate** ribbon.

> **FOR MORE DETAILS**   See Chapter 13 for more details about scaling and updating dimension features.

Scaling Dimension Features Using the Annotation Scale

As mentioned in Chapter 13, the **Annotative Scale** setting utilizes the AutoCAD **Annotation Scale** feature located on the right side of the Status Bar so that dimension features are scaled automatically when dimensions are added to your drawing. Once again, this setting is superior when you have multiple scale viewports because it will also add different scaled dimension features if the **Automatically add scales to annotative objects when the annotation scale changes** button to the right of the **Annotation Scale** setting is on. The best part is that each scale representation is displayed separately depending on the current **Annotation Scale** so that you no longer need to create duplicate information on separate layers!

> **FOR MORE DETAILS**   See Chapter 1 for a detailed description of the **Annotation Scale** feature.

Exercise 14-8: Scaling Dimension Features Using the Annotation Scale

1. Continue from Exercise 14-7.
2. Create the following layers:

Name	Color	Linetype	Lineweight	Description
A-Anno-Dims-Ms	1	Continuous	Default	Dimensions located in model space
A-Anno-Dims-Ps	1	Continuous	Default	Dimensions located in paper space

3. Select the **Model** tab so that model space is active.
4. Set the **Annotation Scale** to **1/4″ = 1′-0″** by selecting it from the **Viewport Scale** list on the right side of the Status Bar.
5. Set the **A-Anno-Dims-Ms** layer current in the **Layer** list box.
6. Add the dimensions as shown in Figure 14-53.
7. Save the drawing as **EX14-8**.

New Dimensions

Figure 14-53 Scaling dimension features using the **Annotation Scale**

Dimensioning in Paper Space

Historically in AutoCAD, it has been the practice to locate all dimensions in model space with the drawing model information. Doing so made it possible to take advantage of dimension associativity so that when the drawing model changed, the dimensions updated automatically.

> **FOR MORE DETAILS**   See Chapter 13 for more details about the benefits of associated dimensioning.

It is now possible in AutoCAD to locate associated dimensions in paper space that update automatically when the drawing model changes—even though the drawing information is in model space and the dimensions are located in paper space. It is even possible to switch completely to model space, change the drawing model, and have the associated dimensions update in paper space so that the dimensions are correct when you switch to the layout.

One of the main advantages of locating dimensions in the paper space layout is that you do not have to worry about scaling dimension features such as text height and arrow sizes as you do when you locate dimensions in model space. This is particularly advantageous on drawings with multiple scaled viewports. This is because everything in paper space is drawn at the size it will plot because the final plotted scale is typically 1:1.

Except for the scaling part, dimensioning in paper space is almost the same as dimensioning in model space. All that is required is that you create dimensions in paper space when no viewport is current. You can either use Object Snaps to snap to dimension definition points on the objects in model space, or you can select the objects and dimension them automatically—even though you are still in paper space as shown in Figure 14-54.

Figure 14-54 Dimensioning in paper space

The one caveat to locating dimensions in paper space is that if the viewport display changes because you are panning or zooming inside the viewport, the paper space dimensions become temporarily detached from the model space drawing. Don't fret though; the **DIMREGEN** command can be used to "reattach" the paper space dimensions to their model space counterparts. Unfortunately, the **DIMREGEN** command is not found on any menu or toolbar, so you must type **DIMREGEN** **<Enter ↵>**. All paper space dimensions are automatically reassociated with the appropriate model space drawing information.

Note:
Dimension features for dimensions located in paper space are still affected by the current dimension scale (DIMSCALE) setting on the Fit tab of the **Dimension Style** dialog box. Typically, DIMSCALE is set to 1 when locating dimensions in paper space because there is no need to scale the dimension features.

Exercise 14-9: Placing Dimensions in Paper Space

1. Continue from Exercise 14-8.
2. Switch to the **ANSI B Title Block** layout.
3. Toggle the **PAPER** button on the right side of the Status Bar to **MODEL** so that model space is the current environment.
4. Freeze the **A-Anno-Dims-Ms** layer in the current viewport by changing the **Freeze or thaw in current viewport** column (third from left) to the snowflake in the **Layer** list box.
5. Toggle the **MODEL** button to **PAPER** so that paper space is the current environment.

Figure 14-55   Placing dimensions in paper space

6. Set the **A-Anno-Dims-Ps** layer current in the **Layer** list box.
7. Set the **DIMSCALE** system variable to **1** so that dimension features are not scaled and add the dimensions as shown in Figure 14-55 in paper space.
8. Save the drawing as **EX14-9**.

CHAPTER SUMMARY

In this chapter, we explained the different ways to set up and lay out a drawing using paper space techniques so that it is ready for output to the associated printer, plotter, or other output device.

As you found out in this chapter, using paper space to lay out a drawing is the industry standard for good reason. Using the techniques and methods you learned in this chapter will enable you to take advantage of benefits that include:

- Creating multiple layouts that are different sheet sizes
- Associating multiple printer/plotter devices to create different output results
- Setting up layouts with multiple scale views
- Controlling layer visibility individually per layout viewport

In addition to setting up a drawing for output, we also introduced some advanced paper space scaling techniques that allow you to rely on the scale of the current layout viewport to save time and increase productivity.

Finally, locating dimensions in the paper space layout instead of the traditional method of locating dimensions in model space was explored. While creating dimensions in paper space has some distinct advantages, it is still common to locate dimensions in model space. Both approaches have advantages and disadvantages. For this reason, no real consensus exists as to which approach should be used.

FOR MORE DETAILS   See Chapter 15 for detailed information about plotting to different output devices. See Chapter 13 for detailed information about dimensioning.

CHAPTER TEST QUESTIONS

Multiple Choice

1. Most of a drawing's linework and annotation features are drawn in:
   a. Paper space
   b. Model space
   c. Drawing space
   d. None of the above

2. The system variable that controls whether model space or paper space is active is named:
   a. **DRAWMODE**
   c. **TILEMODE**
   b. **SPACEMODE**
   d. **MODETILE**

3. The paper size of a layout is controlled via its:
   a. Drawing limits
   b. Associated plotting device
   c. b and d
   d. Page setup

4. The user-defined window created in a paper space layout that allows you to view and scale information in model space is referred to as a:
   a. Layout portal
   c. Layout window
   b. Layout viewport
   d. Layout aperture

5. The printable area of a layout is represented by:
   a. Shadow
   b. Edge of the layout
   c. Dashed line
   d. Drawing limits

6. The command used to create a layout viewport is:
   a. **MVIEW**
   c. **-VPORTS**
   b. **VPORTS**
   d. All of the above

7. The layout viewport creation option that creates a viewport the same size as a layout's printable area is:
   a. **Polygonal**
   c. **Fit**
   b. **Object**
   d. **Restore**

8. To make a layout viewport current:
   a. Double-click with the mouse inside the viewport
   b. Type **MS<Enter ↵>**
   c. Type **PS<Enter ↵>**
   d. a and b

9. Layout viewport scale is controlled by:
   a. **SCALE** command
   b. Zooming in and out of a viewport
   c. Panning the display in the viewport
   d. **VPSCALE** system variable

10. The scale of a layout viewport can be set using:
    a. The **Viewport Scale** list on the Status Bar
    b. The **ZOOM** command to specify a zoom scale factor
    c. The **Properties** palette
    d. All of the above

11. To prevent a viewport scale from changing accidentally, it is best to:
    a. Turn the viewport off
    b. Work only in model space
    c. Freeze the viewport layer
    d. Lock the viewport display

12. The command that allows you to change the shape of a viewport is:
    a. **SCALE**
    c. **MOVE**
    b. **VPORTCLIP**
    d. **VPCLIP**

13. The **LAYOUT** command allows you to:
    a. Rename a layout
    b. Delete a layout
    c. Create a new layout
    d. All of the above

14. The system variable used to control whether paper space linetype scaling is on or off is:
    a. **PSLTSCALE**
    b. **LTSCALE**
    c. **PAPERSCALE**
    d. All of the above

15. To make dimension features scale according to the viewport scale, you can set the **DIMSCALE** system variable to:
    a. **1**
    b. Inverse of the plot scale
    c. **0**
    d. None of the above

Matching

a. TILEMODE

b. Page setup

c. Layout viewport

d. Printable area

e. **Page Setup Manager**

f. .PC3 file

1. Displays details of the current page setup, creates new page setups, and modifies existing page setups

2. System variable that controls whether paper space linetype scaling is on or off

3. Command used to create one or more layout viewports

4. Plotter configuration file used to store and manage printer/plotter settings

5. Command used to create one or more layout viewports

6. System variable that controls whether you are working in model space or paper space

g. **MVIEW** command

h. **-VPORTS** command

i. **VCLIP** command

j. **PSLTSCALE**

7. User-defined window created in a paper space layout that allows you to view drawing information in model space

8. Controls the settings that affect the appearance of a plotted drawing

9. Actual physical area that can be printed for the currently specified plotting device and paper size

10. Command used to change the shape of a viewport

CHAPTER PROJECTS

Project 14-1: Classroom Plan—Continued from Chapter 13

1. Open drawing **P13-1** from Chapter 13.
2. Right-click on a layout tab and select **From template…** from the shortcut menu to import a layout.
3. Open the **Architectural D-Size.dwt** drawing template in the student data files and import the **Architectural Title Block** layout from the template.
4. Select the **Architectural Title Block** layout to set it current. There is a single viewport in this layout. Make the viewport current by double-clicking inside the viewport boundary.
5. **Zoom Extents** so the drawing fills the viewport and set the viewport scale to **1/2″ = 1′-0″**. Position the drawing within the viewport so it matches Figure P14-1.
6. Start the **DIMSTYLE** command and modify the **Arch** dimension style. On the **Fit** tab, set the **Scale for dimension features** to **Scale dimensions to layout**.
7. Switch back to paper space by double-clicking outside the viewport.
8. Delete the **Layout1** and **Layout2** layouts.
9. Save the drawing as **P14-1**.

To access student data files, go to www.pearsondesigncentral.com.

Figure P14-1

Project 14-2a: B-Size Mechanical Border—Continued from Chapter 13

1. Open template file **Mechanical B-Size.DWT** from Chapter 13.
2. Press the **<Ctrl>+A** keyboard combination to select everything in the drawing.
3. Press the **<Ctrl>+<Shift>+C** keyboard combination and specify **0,0** as the base point.

4. Press the **<Del>** key or use the **ERASE** command to delete all the selected objects.

5. Select the **Layout1** tab to switch to paper space.

6. Erase the existing default viewport.

7. Use the **Page Setup Manager** to set the associated plotter to **None** and the paper size to **ANSI B (17.00 × 11.00 Inches)**.

8. Press the **<Ctrl>+V** keyboard combination and enter **-.25,-.75** when AutoCAD prompts you to *Specify insertion point:* to paste the title border in paper space.

9. Create a polygonal viewport on layer **Viewport** at the inside border edges as shown in Figure P14-2A.

10. Rename the **Layout1** layout to **Mechanical B-Size** and delete the **Layout2** layout.

11. Right-click on the **Mechanical B-Size** layout and choose **Move or Copy...** Choose **(move to end)** and check the **Create a copy** box and choose **OK**. Rename the layout **Metric Mechanical B-Size**.

12. Use the **Page Setup Manager** and set the **Plot scale** to **1 inches = 25.4 units**.

13. Start the **SCALE** command and select all the geometry in the **Metric Mechanical B-Size** layout. Use a base point of **0,0** and a scale factor of **25.4**.

14. Save the drawing as a template file named **Mechanical B-Size.DWT**.

Figure P14-2A

Project 14-2b: C-Size Mechanical Border—Continued from Chapter 13

1. Open template file **Mechanical C-Size.DWT** from Chapter 13.

2. Press the **<Ctrl>+A** keyboard combination to select everything in the drawing.

3. Press the **<Ctrl>+<Shift>+C** keyboard combination and specify **0,0** as the base point.

4. Press the **<Del>** key or use the **ERASE** command to delete all the selected objects.

5. Select the **Layout1** tab to switch to paper space.

6. Erase the existing default viewport.

7. Use the **Page Setup Manager** to set the associated plotter to **None** and the paper size to **ANSI C (22.00 × 17.00 Inches)**.

8. Press the **<Ctrl>+V** keyboard combination and enter **-.25,-.75** when AutoCAD prompts you to *Specify insertion point:* to paste the title border in paper space.

9. Create a polygonal viewport on layer **Viewport** at the inside border edges as shown in Figure P14-2B.
10. Rename the **Layout1** layout to **Mechanical C-Size** and delete the **Layout2** layout.
11. Make sure that paper space is the current drawing environment by double-clicking outside the viewport.
12. Save the drawing as a template file named **Mechanical C-Size.DWT**.

Figure P14-2B

Project 14-2c: A-Size Portrait Mechanical Border—Continued from Chapter 13

1. Open template file **Mechanical A-Size-Portrait.DWT** from Chapter 13.
2. Press the **<Ctrl>+A** keyboard combination to select everything in the drawing.
3. Press the **<Ctrl>+<Shift>+C** keyboard combination and specify **0,0** as the base point.
4. Press the **<Del>** key or use the **ERASE** command to delete all the selected objects.
5. Select the **Layout1** tab to switch to paper space.
6. Erase the existing default viewport.
7. Use the **Page Setup Manager** to set the associated plotter to **None** and the paper size to **Letter (8.50 × 11.00 Inches)**.
8. Press the **<Ctrl>+V** keyboard combination and enter **-.25,-.25** when AutoCAD prompts you to *Specify insertion point:* to paste the title border in paper space.
9. Create a polygonal viewport on layer **Viewport** at the inside border edges as shown in Figure P14-2C.
10. Rename the **Layout1** layout to **Mechanical A-Size-Portrait** and delete the **Layout2** layout.
11. Make sure that paper space is the current drawing environment by double-clicking outside the viewport.
12. Save the drawing as a template file named **Mechanical A-Size-Portrait.DWT**.

Figure P14-2C

Project 14-3a: Architectural D-Size Border—Continued from Chapter 13

1. Open template file **Architectural D-Size.DWT** from Chapter 13.
2. Press the **<Ctrl>+A** keyboard combination to select everything in the drawing.
3. Press the **<Ctrl>+<Shift>+C** keyboard combination and select the bottom left corner of the border corner tick marks using the **Endpoint** Object Snap.
4. Press the **<Del>** key or use the **ERASE** command to delete all the selected objects.
5. Select the **Layout1** tab to switch to paper space.
6. Erase the existing default viewport.
7. Use the **Page Setup Manager** to set the associated plotter to **None** and the paper size to **ARCH D (36.00 × 24.00 Inches)**.
8. Press the **<Ctrl>+V** keyboard combination and enter **-.25,-.75** when AutoCAD prompts you to *Specify insertion point:* to paste the title border in paper space.
9. Create a rectangular viewport on layer **A-Anno-Vprt** at the inside border edges as shown in Figure P14-3A.
10. Rename the **Layout1** layout to **Architectural D-Size** and delete the **Layout2** layout.
11. Make sure that paper space is the current drawing environment by double-clicking outside the viewport.
12. Save the drawing to a template file as **Architectural D-Size.DWT**.

Project 14-3b: Architectural B-Size Border—Continued from Chapter 13

1. Open template file **Architectural B-Size.DWT** from Chapter 13.
2. Press the **<Ctrl>+A** keyboard combination to select everything in the drawing.
3. Press the **<Ctrl>+<Shift>+C** keyboard combination and select the bottom left corner of the border corner tick marks using the **Endpoint** Object Snap.

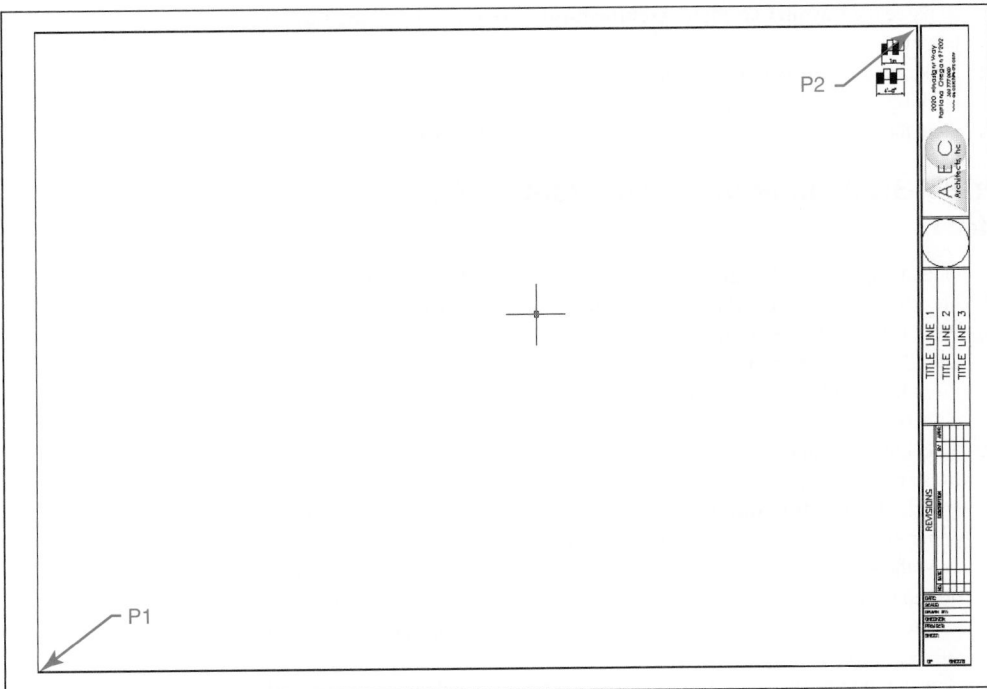

Figure P14-3A

4. Press the **<Del>** key or use the **ERASE** command to delete all the selected objects.
5. Select the **Layout1** tab to switch to paper space.
6. Erase the existing default viewport.
7. Use the **Page Setup Manager** to set the associated plotter to **None** and the paper size to **ANSI B (17.00 × 11.00 Inches)**.
8. Press the **<Ctrl>+V** keyboard combination and enter **-.25,-.75** when AutoCAD prompts you to *Specify insertion point:* to paste the title border in paper space.
9. Create a rectangular viewport on layer **A-Anno-Vprt** at the inside border edges as shown in Figure P14-3B.

Figure P14-3B

10. Rename the **Layout1** layout to **Architectural B-Size** and delete the **Layout2** layout.
11. Make sure that paper space is the current drawing environment by double-clicking outside the viewport.
12. Save the drawing to a template file as **Architectural B-Size.DWT**.

Project 14-3c: Architectural A-Size Border—Continued from Chapter 13

1. Open template file **Architectural A-Size.DWT** from Chapter 13.
2. Press the **<Ctrl>+A** keyboard combination to select everything in the drawing.
3. Press the **<Ctrl>+<Shift>+C** keyboard combination and select the bottom left corner of the border corner tick marks using the **Endpoint** Object Snap.
4. Press the **<Del>** key or use the **ERASE** command to delete all the selected objects.
5. Select the **Layout1** tab to switch to paper space.
6. Erase the existing default viewport.
7. Use the **Page Setup Manager** to set the associated plotter to **None** and the paper size to **ANSI A (8.50 × 11.00 Inches)**.
8. Press the **<Ctrl>+V** keyboard combination and enter **-.25,-.75** when AutoCAD prompts you to *Specify insertion point:* to paste the title border in paper space.
9. Create a rectangular viewport on layer **A-Anno-Vprt** at the inside border edges as shown in Figure P14-3C.
10. Rename the **Layout1** layout to **Architectural A-Size** and delete the **Layout2** layout.
11. Make sure that paper space is the current drawing environment by double-clicking outside the viewport.
12. Save the drawing to a template file as **Architectural A-Size.DWT**.

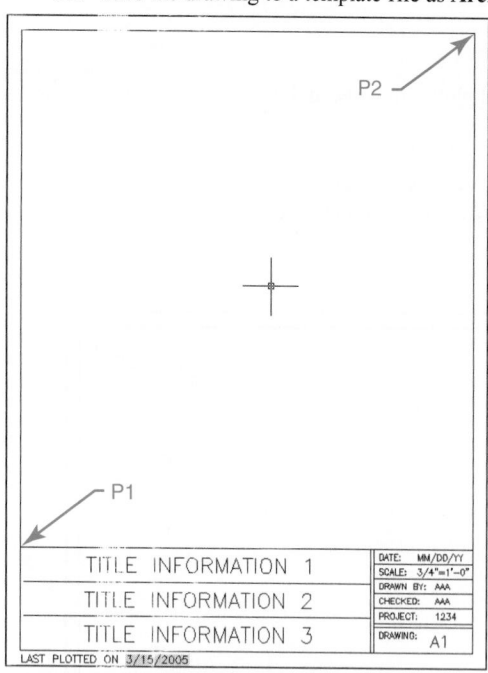

TITLE INFORMATION 1	DATE: MM/DD/YY
	SCALE: 3/4"=1'-0"
TITLE INFORMATION 2	DRAWN BY: AAA
	CHECKED: AAA
TITLE INFORMATION 3	PROJECT: 1234
	DRAWING: A1
LAST PLOTTED ON 3/15/2005	

Figure P14-3C

Project 14-4: Electrical Schematic—Continued from Chapter 13

1. Open drawing **P13-4** from Chapter 13.
2. Select **From template...** from the **Layout** right-click menu to import a layout.
3. Import the **Architectural D-Size** layout and border from the **Architectural D-Size.dwt** template file created in Project 14-3a.
4. Select the **Architectural D-Size** layout to make it current.
5. Set the viewport scale to **1:2** and center the view as shown in Figure P14-4.
6. Lock the viewport display so the view scale doesn't change.
7. Start the **DIMSTYLE** command and modify the **Arch** dimension style. On the **Fit** tab, set the **Scale for dimension features** to **Scale dimensions to layout**.

8. Delete the **Layout1** and **Layout2** layouts.
9. Save the drawing as **P14-4**.

Figure P14-4

Project 14-5: Residential Architectural Plan—Continued from Chapter 13

1. Open drawing **P13-5** from Chapter 13.
2. Select **From template…** from the **Layout** right-click menu to import a layout.
3. Import the **Architectural D-Size** layout and border from the **Architectural D-Size.dwt** template file created in Project 14-3a.
4. Select the **Architectural D-Size** layout to make it current.
5. Set the viewport scale to **1/4″ = 1′-0″** and center the view as shown in Figure P14-5.
6. Lock the viewport display so the view scale doesn't change.
7. Delete the **Layout1** and **Layout2** layouts.
8. Save the drawing as **P14-5**.

Figure P14-5

Project 14-6: Optical Mount—English Units—Continued from Chapter 13

1. Open drawing **P13-6** from Chapter 13.
2. Select **From template...** from the **Layout** right-click menu to import a layout.
3. Import the **Mechanical B-Size** layout and border from the **Mechanical B-Size.dwt** template file created in Project 14-2a.
4. Select the **Mechanical B-Size** layout to make it current.
5. Set the viewport scale to **2:1** and center the view as shown in Figure P14-6.
6. Lock the viewport display so the view scale doesn't change.
7. Delete the **Layout1** and **Layout2** layouts.
8. Save the drawing as **P14-6**.

Figure P14-6

Project 14-7a: Gasket—Continued from Chapter 13

1. Open drawing **P13-7A** from Chapter 13.
2. Select **From template...** from the **Layout** right-click menu to import a layout.
3. Insert the **Metric Mechanical B-Size** layout and border from the **Mechanical B-Size.dwt** template file created in Project P14-2a.
4. Select the **Metric Mechanical B-Size** layout to make it current.
5. Set the viewport scale to **1:2** and center the view as shown in Figure P14-7A.
6. Lock the viewport display so the view scale doesn't change.
7. Delete the **Layout1** and **Layout2** layouts.
8. Save the drawing as **P14-7A**.

Figure P14-7A

Project 14-7b: Widget—Continued from Chapter 13

1. Open drawing **P13-7B** from Chapter 13.
2. Select **From template…** from the **Layout** right-click menu to import a layout.
3. Insert the **Metric Mechanical B-Size** layout and border from the **Mechanical B-Size.dwt** template file created in Project 14-2a.
4. Select the **Metric Mechanical B-Size** layout to make it current.
5. Set the viewport scale to **1:4** and center the view as shown in Figure P14-7B.
6. Lock the viewport display so the view scale doesn't change.
7. Delete the **Layout1** and **Layout2** layouts.
8. Save the drawing as **P14-7B**.

Figure P14-7B

Project 14-7c: Hex Head Bolts and Nuts—Continued from Chapter 13

1. Open drawing **P13-7C** from Chapter 13.
2. Select **From template...** from the **Layout** right-click menu to import a layout.
3. Insert the **Metric Mechanical B-Size** layout and border from the **Mechanical B-Size.dwt** template file created in Project 14-2a.
4. Select the **Metric Mechanical B-Size** layout to make it current.
5. Set the viewport scale to **1:1** and center the view as shown in Figure P14-7C.
6. Relocate bolts and nuts as necessary to fit in viewport.
7. Lock the viewport display so the view scale doesn't change.
8. Delete the **Layout1** and **Layout2** layouts.
9. Save the drawing as **P14-7C**.

Figure P14-7C

Project 14-7d: Motorcycle Head Gasket—Continued from Chapter 13

1. Open drawing **P13-7D** from Chapter 13.
2. Select **From template...** from the **Layout** right-click menu to import a layout.
3. Insert the **Metric Mechanical B-Size** layout and border from the **Mechanical B-Size.dwt** template file created in Project 14-2a.
4. Select the **Metric Mechanical B-Size** layout to make it current.
5. Set the viewport scale to **1:2** and center the view as shown in Figure P14-7D.
6. Lock the viewport display so the view scale doesn't change.
7. Delete the **Layout1** and **Layout2** layouts.
8. Save the drawing as **P14-7D**.

Figure P14-7D

Project 14-7e: 68-Tooth Motorcycle Sprocket—Continued from Chapter 13

1. Open drawing **P13-7E** from Chapter 13.
2. Select **From template...** from the **Layout** right-click menu to import a layout.
3. Insert the **Metric Mechanical B-Size** layout and border from the **Mechanical B-Size.dwt** template file created in Project 14-2a.
4. Select the **Metric Mechanical B-Size** layout to make it current.
5. Set the viewport scale to **1:4** and center the view as shown in Figure P14-7E.
6. Lock the viewport display so the view scale doesn't change.
7. Delete the **Layout1** and **Layout2** layouts.
8. Save the drawing as **P14-7E**.

Figure P14-7E

Project 14-7f: Window Extrusion—Continued from Chapter 13

1. Open drawing **P13-7F** from Chapter 13.
2. Select **From template...** from the **Layout** right-click menu to import a layout.
3. Insert the **Metric Mechanical B-Size** layout and border from the **Mechanical B-Size.dwt** template file created in Project 14-2a.
4. Select the **Metric Mechanical B-Size** layout to make it current.
5. Set the viewport scale to **1:1** and center the view as shown in Figure P14-7F.
6. Lock the viewport display so the view scale doesn't change.
7. Delete the **Layout1** and **Layout2** layouts.
8. Save the drawing as **P14-7F**.

Figure P14-7F

Project 14-7g: Hub—Continued from Chapter 13

1. Open drawing **P13-7G** from Chapter 13.
2. Select **From template...** from the **Layout** right-click menu to import a layout.
3. Insert the **Metric Mechanical B-Size** layout and border from the **Mechanical B-Size.dwt** template file created in Project 14-2a.
4. Select the **Metric Mechanical B-Size** layout to make it current.
5. Set the viewport scale to **1:2** and center the view as shown in Figure P14-7G.
6. Lock the viewport display so the view scale doesn't change.
7. Delete the **Layout1** and **Layout2** layouts.
8. Save the drawing as **P14-7G**.

Project 14-8: Civil Site Plan—Continued from Chapter 13

1. Open drawing **P13-8** from Chapter 13.
2. Select **From template...** from the **Layout** right-click menu to import a layout.
3. Import the **Architectural D-Size** layout and border from the **Architectural D-Size.dwt** template file created in Project 14-2a.
4. Select the **Architectural D-Size** layout to make it current.

Figure P14-7G

5. Set the viewport scale to **1/8″ = 1′-0″** and center the view as shown in Figure P14-8.
6. Lock the viewport display so the view scale doesn't change.
7. Start the **DIMSTYLE** command and modify the **Arch** dimension style. On the **Fit** tab, set the **Scale for dimension features** to **Scale dimensions to layout**.
8. Delete the **Layout1** and **Layout2** layouts.
9. Save the drawing as **P14-8**.

Figure P14-8

Plotting and Publishing

Chapter Objectives

- Plot from both model space and layout space
- Control the final look of a plotted sheet
- Create, import, and manage page setups with the **PLOT** command
- Select, add, and configure various plotting devices
- Create electronic plot files including DWF and various raster file formats
- View and mark up DWF files in the Autodesk Design Review application

INTRODUCTION

In most cases, the purpose of creating AutoCAD drawings is to create a set of printed hard-copy drawings. In AutoCAD, this process is called *plotting*. In Chapter 14, we looked at how to create and manage paper space layouts, which (among other things) allow you to define the default settings for a plot. In this chapter, we examine various ways of outputting drawings, including how to plot from model space and how to plot to various file formats.

plotting: The process of printing a drawing in AutoCAD

PAGE SETUPS AND PLOTTING

In Chapter 14, we looked at how to create a page setup using the **PAGESETUP** command. Page setups are simply collections of plot settings that have a name assigned to them. When creating a page setup, you specify the default printer/plotter, the default paper size, and other default output options. Each drawing space (model space and each paper space layout) has a default page setup assigned to it that contains all the default plot settings for that drawing space.

Note:
In the early days of AutoCAD, drawings were typically output to pen plotters, which would create hard-copy prints by physically grabbing a pen and moving it around a piece of paper or Mylar. While these types of plotters are rarely used today, the terminology has remained. Today, the terms print and plot are synonymous in AutoCAD.

FOR MORE DETAILS See Chapter 14 for more on creating and managing page setups.

Plotting is done with the **PLOT** command. When you start the **PLOT** command, AutoCAD looks at the current page setup and displays those settings in the **Plot** dialog box (see Figure 15-1).

Figure 15-1   The **Plot**
dialog box

Plot	
Ribbon & Panel:	Output| Plot Plot
Standard Toolbar:	
Menu:	<u>F</u>ile|<u>P</u>lot...
Command Line:	PLOT/ PRINT
Command Alias:	CTRL+P

TIP The quickest way to start the **PLOT** command is by selecting the **Plot...** button on the **Quick Access** toolbar, which is always displayed on the top left of the AutoCAD window.

The **Plot** dialog box has the same settings as the **Page Setup** dialog box and allows you to make any final adjustments to your plot settings before outputting your drawing. The **Plot** dialog box also has additional controls, which allow you to create and modify page setups.

To create a plot using the default page setup values, you can simply start the **PLOT** command and choose **OK**. However, before you commit your drawing to paper, it's a good idea to check over your default settings and preview your plot.

Note:
Page setups can be created both for paper space layouts and for model space; however, page setups cannot be shared between paper space and model space. Page setups created for a paper space layout cannot be used in model space, and page setups created for model space cannot be used in a paper space layout.

Previewing Your Plot

Preview	
Ribbon & Panel:	Output|Plot Preview
Standard Toolbar:	
Menu:	<u>F</u>ile|<u>P</u>lot Pre<u>v</u>iew
Command Line:	PREVIEW
Command Alias:	None

The **Preview...** button in the **Plot** dialog box allows you to see a preview of the final output before you commit it to paper. When you choose the **Preview...** button, AutoCAD switches to plot preview mode (see Figure 15-2). In preview mode, the AutoCAD toolbars and pull-down menus are replaced with the **Preview** toolbar. These tools allow you to zoom and pan around the drawing to inspect it before you send it to the printer. If you are satisfied with the preview, you can choose the **Plot** button to send the drawing to the printer. Otherwise, you can choose **Cancel** to return to the **Plot** dialog box. The tools available in the **Preview** toolbar are also available in the right-click menu (see Figure 15-3).

The PREVIEW Command.   If you're confident in your plot settings, you can go directly to a plot preview with the **PREVIEW** command. The **PREVIEW** command bypasses the **PLOT** command and goes directly to plot preview mode. If you're satisfied with the plot preview, you can choose the **Plot** button and output your drawing. However, if you need to make changes, choosing **Cancel** will return you to your drawing. You then have to use the **PLOT** or **PAGESETUP** command to make changes to your default plot settings.

Figure 15-2   Plot preview mode

Figure 15-3   The preview mode right-click menu

Plotting from Model Space

The process of plotting is the same whether you plot from model space or paper space. However, there are some things to keep in mind when plotting from model space, particularly with regard to plot scale.

Specifying the Plot Area.   When plotting a layout space, you will typically plot the entire layout. Selecting the **Layout** option in the **What to plot:** list tells AutoCAD to plot the area defined in the paper space layout. When plotting from model space, the **Layout** option is not available, and you must choose a specific area to plot. The **What to plot:** drop-down list allows you to specify a number of different plot areas. The options are described below.

Display	Plots the objects currently displayed on the screen.
Extents	Plots all the objects currently visible in the drawing. Does not include objects on frozen layers but does include objects on layers that are turned off.
Limits	Plots objects located within the drawing limits.
View	Plots named views saved with the **VIEW** command. When selected, a list of named views is enabled, allowing you to select the view you wish to plot.
Window	Allows you to select a plot area by picking a window area. When selected, a **Window** button is enabled. Picking the **Window** button temporarily hides the dialog box and allows you to pick a window area to plot.

Setting the Plot Scale.   Because a paper space layout represents an actual piece of paper, the plot scale of a paper space layout is typically 1:1. The plot scale of your model is set within each viewport.

However, model space represents the actual full-size version of your design. When you plot from model space, you typically need to adjust the plot scale so that the full-size version of your design will fit on a piece of paper.

The **Plot scale** area of the **Plot** dialog box allows you to set the drawing scale. When selected, the **Fit to paper** check box will examine the specified plot area and scale it to fit the specified paper size. The calculated scale will appear grayed out in the **Scale** area.

To plot at a specific scale, remove the check from the **Fit to paper** box to enable the **Scale** area. Once enabled, you can specify a plot scale by selecting it from the **Scale** list or by selecting

Custom from the list and specifying a custom scale. Custom scales are entered as plotted (paper) units in either inches or millimeters (mm) and their equivalent drawing units. For example, to specify a scale of $1/4'' = 1' -0''$, you could either choose it from the **Scale** list or choose **Custom** and specify **.25 inch = 12 units**, or **1 inch = 48 units**.

> **TIP**   You can add to and modify the list of available plot scales with the **SCALELISTEDIT** command. See Chapter 14 for more information about the **SCALELISTEDIT** command.

Setting the Plot Offset.   The **Plot offset** area allows you to position your plot area on your paper. When set to **X: 0** and **Y: 0,** AutoCAD will place the specified plot area of your drawing at the lower left corner of the printable area of your paper. Recall from Chapter 14 that the printable area is the actual physical area that can be printed for a specified plotting device and paper size. This area varies with the printer and paper size you select.

By changing the X and Y offset values, you can reposition the drawing plot area on the paper. If your plot area goes outside the printable area, AutoCAD will warn you by showing a red line in the preview area of the **Plot** dialog box (see Figure 15-4).

Figure 15-4   The preview area of the **Plot** dialog box

The **Center the plot** check box will compare the printable area of your paper to the plot area of your drawing and calculate the appropriate X and Y offset values to center the plot area in the printable area of your paper.

Exercise 15-1: Plotting from Model Space

To access student data files, go to www.pearsondesigncentral.com.

1. Open the drawing **db_samp** located in the student data files.
2. Start the **PLOT** command to display the **Plot** dialog box.
3. Select the **DWF6 ePlot.pc3** printer and then select the **ARCH D (36.00 × 24.00 Inches)** paper size.
4. Select **Extents** from the **What to plot**: list.
5. Remove the check from the **Fit to paper** box and choose **3/32″ = 1′-0″** from the **Scale** list.
6. Choose **Center the plot** option in the **Plot offset** area and choose **Preview....**
7. AutoCAD will display the plot preview shown earlier in Figure 15-2. You can zoom and pan to examine the plot preview. When done, choose the **Close Preview Window** button to return to the **Plot** dialog box.
8. In the **What to plot**: list, choose **Window**. AutoCAD will close the dialog box and prompt you to *Specify first corner:*.
9. Draw a window around the upper right corner of the building as shown in Figure 15-5. After drawing the window, AutoCAD returns you to the **Plot** dialog box.
10. Choose **1/4″ = 1′-0″** from the **Scale** list and choose **Preview....** AutoCAD displays the plot preview as shown in Figure 15-6.
11. Choose the **Close Preview Window** button to exit the plot preview and choose **Cancel** to close the **Plot** dialog box. Do *not* save the drawing.

Figure 15-5   Selecting a plot window

Figure 15-6   The plot preview of the selected area

Plotting a Page Layout

Plotting a page layout is in many aspects simpler than plotting from model space. In setting up the page layout, you will typically define many or all of the plotting defaults. However, when you plot, you will still want to double-check your plot settings and do a plot preview before sending it to the printer. This also gives you the opportunity to temporarily override plot settings for any given plot.

Exercise 15-2: Plotting a Page Layout

1. Open the drawing **Welding Fixture-1** in the student data files.
2. Select the **Mounting Bar Casting Support** page layout tab.
3. Start the **PLOT** command to display the **Plot** dialog box and choose **Preview...** to display the plot preview. Notice that the viewports are displayed on the plot preview (see Figure 15-7). This is because the viewports are currently on a plotting layer.
4. Choose the **Close Preview Window** button to exit the plot preview and choose **Cancel** to close the **Plot** dialog box.
5. Select the two viewports and choose **Viewport** from the **Layer** drop-down list. This places the viewports on the nonplotting **Viewport** layer.
6. Restart the **PLOT** command. Notice that the plot preview area shows a red bar on the right-hand side of the page. This is because the **Plot offset X** value is set to **0.010**.

To access student data files, go to www.pearsondesigncentral.com.

Viewport
Borders

Figure 15-7   Viewport outlines in the plot preview

Figure 15-8   The corrected plot preview

7. Set the **X** value in the **Plot offset** to **0.00** and choose **Preview....** This displays the plot preview. The plot preview now looks correct, and the drawing is ready to plot (see Figure 15-8).

8. Choose the **Close Preview Window** button to exit the plot preview and choose **Cancel** to close the **Plot** dialog box. *Do not* save the drawing file.

Default Plot Settings and Page Setups

Keep in mind that each drawing environment (model space and each layout) has a set of default plot settings associated with it. A page setup is a collection of default plot settings that are assigned a name and saved in the drawing. Once a page setup is created, its settings can be applied to a given drawing space. Model space page setups can be applied to the model space environment, and layout page setups can be applied to layout (paper) spaces.

Selecting a Page Setup.   In the **Plot** dialog box, the **Page setup** area allows you to apply the settings stored in a page setup to the current plot. When you start the **PLOT** command, AutoCAD displays the name of the current page setup in the **Name** drop-down list. When you select the **Name**

drop-down list, you'll see a list of page setups stored in the drawing. Selecting one of these page setups will apply the settings stored in the page setup to the current plot.

In addition to page setups, there are three additional items in the **Name** list: **<None>**, **<Previous plot>**, and **Import...**. The **<None>** setting tells you that the current plot settings do not match any stored page setups. If you are using a page setup and make any changes to the setting in the **Plot** dialog box, the **Name** setting will change to **<None>**, noting that the current plot settings no longer match the settings stored in the page setup.

The **<Previous plot>** setting will reuse the settings from the last successful **PLOT** command.

Importing a Page Setup.   Selecting **Import...** from the **Name** list allows you to import a page setup from another drawing. When you select **Import...**, AutoCAD displays the **Select Page Setup From File** dialog box (see Figure 15-9), which allows you to select a drawing file. Once you select a drawing file, AutoCAD will display the **Import Page Setups** dialog box (see Figure 15-10), which displays all the saved page setups within a drawing. Select a page setup from the dialog box and choose **OK** to import the page setup into your current drawing. The imported page setup will now be listed in the **Name** drop-down list.

Figure 15-9   The **Select Page Setup From File** dialog box

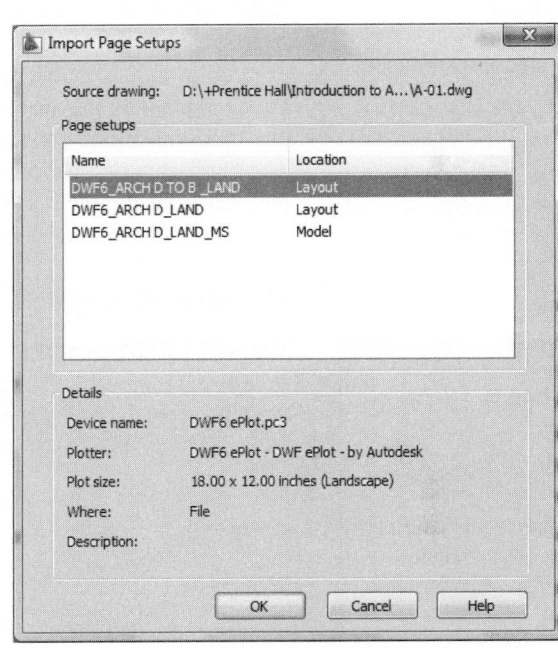

Figure 15-10   The **Import Page Setups** dialog box

Creating a Page Setup.   AutoCAD also allows you to save your current plot settings to a page setup. Once you have your plot settings to your liking, choose the **Add...** button in the **Page setup** area. AutoCAD will display the **Add Page Setup** dialog box (see Figure 15-11). Simply type a name and choose **OK** to save the current plot settings to the new page setup.

You can update an existing page setup by entering the existing page setup name into the **Add Page Setup** dialog box. AutoCAD will display a **Question** dialog box (see Figure 15-12) telling

Figure 15-11   The **Add Page Setup** dialog box

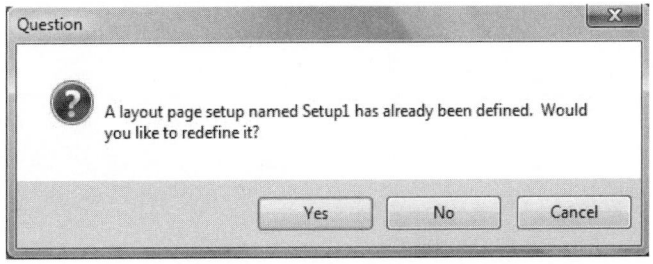

Figure 15-12   The **Add Page Setup Question** dialog box

you the page setup already exists and asking whether you'd like to redefine it. Choose **Yes** to update the existing page setup with the current plot settings.

Applying Plot Settings to the Current Layout.   As we mentioned earlier, each drawing space has a set of default plot settings. The **Apply to Layout** button allows you to take the settings displayed in the **Plot** dialog box and apply them to the current layout. These settings then become the default plot settings for that layout or model space.

PLOT STYLES AND LINEWEIGHTS

As noted earlier in the chapter, in the early days of AutoCAD, pen plotters were commonly used. These plotters typically had a pen carousel in which you loaded pens. You would load pens with different pen widths or different colors in each position in the carousel. You would also have a pen table that would tell AutoCAD which pen to use for each AutoCAD color. For example, use pen 4 for color 1, pen 2 for colors 2 and 3, etc. Modern printers no longer use physical pens, but AutoCAD still allows you to use pen tables to control the final look of your plot. Today, AutoCAD refers to these pen tables as *plot styles*.

A plot style is a table of settings that allows you to control all aspects of your plotted output. For example, you may have a plot table that converts AutoCAD colors to grayscale colors or a plot table that allows you to screen back certain colors.

There are two types of plot styles: ***named plot styles*** and ***color-dependent plot styles***. Named plot styles are stored in .STB files. Color-dependent plot styles are stored in .CTB files. A drawing can use either color-dependent plot styles or named plot styles, but not both.

Plot Style Manager

The **STYLESMANAGER** command will open the folder where the plot style table files are stored (see Figure 15-13). From this folder, double-clicking on a .CTB or an .STB file will start the **Plot Style Table Editor** application (see Figure 15-14). This is a stand-alone Windows program that runs outside of AutoCAD. This program allows you to create and modify AutoCAD

named plot style: Plot style that is organized by a user-defined name. Named plot styles are stored in .STB files

color-dependent plot style: Plot style that is organized by the AutoCAD Color Index (ACI) number. Color-dependent plot styles are stored in .CTB files

Plot Style Manager	
Ribbon & Panel:	None
Toolbar:	None
Menu:	File|Plot Style Manager...
Command Line:	STYLESMANAGER
Command Alias:	None

Figure 15-13   **Plot Styles** folder

Figure 15-14   The **Plot Style Table Editor**

Figure 15-15   The **Form View** tab of the **Plot Style Table Editor**

plot style tables. The **General** tab displays information about the plot style. The **Table View** and **Form View** tabs display the table settings in different formats. The **Form View** tab (see Figure 15-15) is useful for setting the properties of multiple colors at once. In this view, you can select multiple pens and apply settings to them in a single step.

Color-Dependent Plot Styles

Color-dependent plot styles map AutoCAD colors within your drawing to specific plotter settings. When you use color-dependent plot styles, all objects with the same color are plotted with the same plotter settings.

Named Plot Styles

Named plot styles allow you to assign plotter settings directly to AutoCAD objects or AutoCAD layers. Within each .STB file, plotter settings are assigned to plot style names (see Figure 15-16). These plot styles are then assigned to each drawing layer and therefore to each object in the drawing. When named plot styles are used in a drawing, the **Plot Style** column is enabled in the **Layer Properties Manager** palette (see Figure 15-17). This allows you to assign a named plot style to a layer.

When using named plot styles, AutoCAD creates a plot style called **Normal**. This is AutoCAD's default named plot style name and is included in each .STB file. This is similar to the **0** layer name and the **Continuous** linetype. It cannot be deleted and is always available.

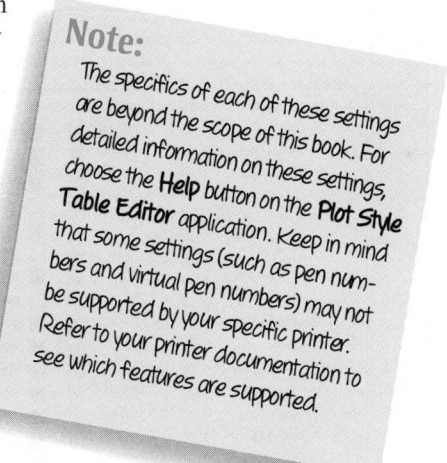

Note:
The specifics of each of these settings are beyond the scope of this book. For detailed information on these settings, choose the **Help** button on the **Plot Style Table Editor** application. Keep in mind that some settings (such as pen numbers and virtual pen numbers) may not be supported by your specific printer. Refer to your printer documentation to see which features are supported.

Note:
When you use named plot styles, the plot style name behaves like other object properties. By default, plot styles are assigned by layer, but you can hard-code a plot style for any specific object.

Figure 15-16   Named plot styles

Figure 15-17   The **Plot Style** column of the **Layer Properties Manager** palette

Using Plot Styles

As mentioned earlier, an AutoCAD drawing can use either color-dependent plot styles or named plot styles but not both. When you create a new drawing file, the drawing template typically determines whether AutoCAD uses color-dependent plot styles or named plot styles as well as the default plot style file (see Figure 15-18).

Figure 15-18   Drawing templates with various plot styles

Figure 15-19   The **Select Plot Style** dialog box

TIP   You can use the **CONVERTPSTYLES** command to convert a named plot style drawing to a color-dependent plot style drawing or vice versa.

Once a drawing has been created and the type of plot styles has been set, the **Plot style table** area of the **Plot** dialog box will show either .STB or .CTB files. From this list, you can tell AutoCAD which plot style table to use for your plot.

When working with named plot styles, it is possible to assign a plot style table that does not include plot styles that are used in your drawing. For example, say you create a drawing and assign the plot style named **40% Screen** that's defined in the **Autodesk-MONO.STB** file. If you then select the **ACAD.STB** plot style table, the **40% Screen** style is not defined in that .STB file. When this happens, AutoCAD will display the **Select Plot Style** dialog box (see Figure 15-19) and ask you to select a different plot style for that layer.

When you select a plot style table, the **Edit plot styles** button is enabled (see Figure 15-20), which starts the **Plot Style Table Editor** application (see Figure 15-14). This allows you to view and/or modify the selected plot style table.

> **Note:**
> When you plot from model space, selecting a plot style table will cause AutoCAD to ask whether you want this plot style table applied to all paper space layouts. If you answer **Yes**, AutoCAD will update the default plot settings for each layout to use the selected plot style table.

Plot Options

The **Plot options** area of the **Plot** dialog box allows you to specify options for plotting lineweights, plot styles, shaded plots, and the order in which objects are plotted.

Plot in Background.   This option specifies that the plot is processed in the background. Typically, when you plot, AutoCAD stops all other activity while the drawing is plotting and will show you a plotting progress bar (see Figure 15-21).

When the **Plot in background** option is turned on, AutoCAD will return you to the drawing environment and process the plot in the background. This allows you to work while the plot is being generated, but may also increase the time it takes to plot the drawing.

Figure 15-20   The **Edit plot styles** button

Figure 15-21   The **Plot Job Progress** bar

Plot Object Lineweights.   This option specifies whether lineweights assigned to objects and layers are plotted. When turned on, any lineweight information assigned in your drawing will be applied to the plot. When turned off, a lineweight of 0 will be applied to all objects in the plot, which results in all objects being plotted with a very thin lineweight.

Plot with Plot Styles.   This option specifies whether plot styles applied to objects and layers are plotted. This means that the plot style settings contained in the specified .CTB or .STB file will be applied to the plot. When you select this option, the **Plot Object Lineweights** option is automatically enabled.

Plot Paperspace Last.   This option allows you to control which space is plotted first. Generally, paper space geometry is usually plotted before model space geometry. Turning this option on will force AutoCAD to plot the model space geometry first.

Hide Paperspace Objects.   This option typically affects only 3D drawings and is available only when plotting from a paper space layout. When plotting a 3D object, you may want to have AutoCAD do a hidden line removal, which eliminates any lines appearing behind a 3D object. This option tells AutoCAD whether the hidden line removal process applies to objects in the paper space as well as objects in model space.

Plot Stamp On.   Turning this option on places a plot stamp on a specified corner of each drawing and/or logs it to a file.

Plot stamp settings are specified in the **Plot Stamp** dialog box (see Figure 15-22), which allows you to control the information that you want to appear in the plot stamp, such as drawing name, date and time, plot scale, and so on. To open the **Plot Stamp** dialog box, turn on the **Plot Stamp** option and then click the **Plot Stamp Settings** button.

Figure 15-22   The **Plot Stamp** dialog box

You can also open the **Plot Stamp** dialog box by clicking the **Plot Stamp Settings** button on the **Plot and Publish** tab of the **Options** dialog box.

Figure 15-23   The **Advanced Options** dialog box

From the **Plot Stamp** dialog box, you can select what information you want to display, and you can also create user-defined text to display a custom plot stamp.

Selecting the **Advanced** button displays the **Advanced Options** dialog box (see Figure 15-23), which allows you to control the placement and orientation of the plot stamp as well as the font and height of the plot stamp text.

PLOTTER SETUP

The **Printer/plotter** area of the **Plot** dialog box lists all the printers available when plotting a drawing. To select a printer, simply select it from the **Name** list. Once selected, AutoCAD will display information about the printer beneath the name, including the name of the printer driver, the printer port, and any description about the printer. The list of printers is divided into two types: Windows-configured printers and AutoCAD-configured printers.

Windows System Printers

The Windows printers are printers that are configured with the **Printers** applet in the Windows **Control Panel** (see Figure 15-24). These are printers that are available to all Windows applications. Any printer configured for Windows will be listed in the **Name** list.

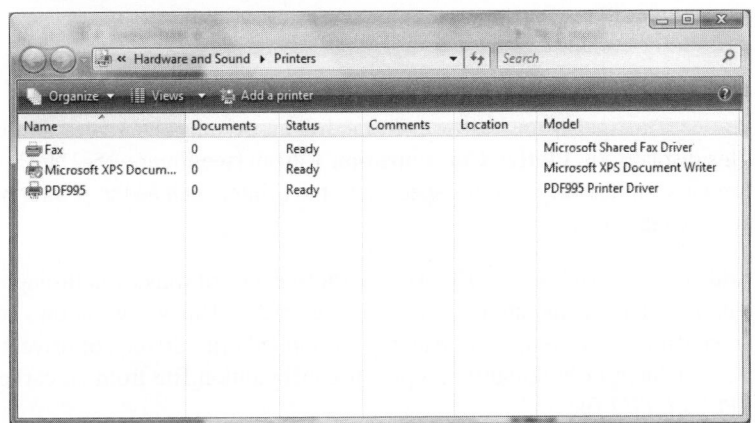

Figure 15-24   The **Printers** control window

AutoCAD Printers

AutoCAD printers are configured and controlled by AutoCAD directly. They bypass the Windows printing system and allow AutoCAD to print directly to the printer. AutoCAD-configured printers may also have features available that are not available in a Windows printer. There are also AutoCAD printer drivers that allow you to convert AutoCAD drawings to various raster and vector file formats, such as JPG, BMP, or HPGL.

Figure 15-25   The
Printer/plotter Name list

PC3 and PMP Files.   AutoCAD-configured printers are stored in plotter configuration files (.PC3 files). These files are also listed in the **Printer/plotter Name** list (see Figure 15-25).

In addition to .PC3 files, AutoCAD also uses plot model parameter (.PMP) files to store custom plotter calibration settings as well as user-defined custom paper sizes.

Plotter Manager	
Ribbon & Panel:	Output| Plot
Toolbar:	None
Menu:	File|Plotter Manager...
Command Line:	PLOTTERMANAGER
Command Alias:	None

Plotter Manager.   The **PLOTTERMANAGER** command displays the folder containing AutoCAD .PC3 files (see Figure 15-26). From this folder, you can create new plotter configurations and modify existing ones.

Figure 15-26   AutoCAD's
plotters folder

Plotter Configuration Editor.   To modify an existing .PC3 file, simply double-click the file. This displays the **Plotter Configuration Editor** (see Figure 15-27). From this dialog box, you can view and modify settings specific to the printer such as the printer port, custom page sizes, and printable areas.

Add-A-Plotter Wizard.   The **Add-A-Plotter** wizard walks you through the process of creating a new plotter configuration file (see Figure 15-28). This wizard allows you to create a new plotter configuration using either AutoCAD-supplied print drivers, or drivers supplied by the printer manufacturer, or by importing a plotter configuration file from an earlier version of AutoCAD (.PCP or .PC2 files).

Overriding a .PC3 File.   When you select a printer from the **Printer/plotter Name** list, the **Properties** button is enabled. When you select this button, AutoCAD displays the **Plotter Configuration Editor** (see Figure 15-27). This allows you to make changes to the plotter configuration within the **PLOT** command. When you make changes to the plotter configuration from within the **PLOT** command, AutoCAD will ask you whether you want to save the changes to the .PC3 file or make the changes only for the current plot (see Figure 15-29).

Figure 15-27   The **Plotter Configuration Editor**

Figure 15-28   The **Add-A-Plotter** wizard

Figure 15-29   The **Changes to a Printer Configuration File** dialog box

Exercise 15-3: Adding a New Plotter

1. Open the drawing **db_samp** located in the student data files.
2. Start the **PLOTTERMANAGER** command to display the **Plotters** folder.
3. Double-click the **Add-A-Plotter** wizard. AutoCAD displays the **Add Plotter** dialog box. Choose **Next** to begin the wizard.
4. Choose **My Computer** to tell AutoCAD that the printer will be controlled locally from your computer (see Figure 15-28). Choose **Next** to continue to the **Plotter Model** step.
5. Choose **Hewlett-Packard** in the **Manufacturers** list and **Draftpro (7570A)** from the **Models** list (see Figure 15-30). Choose **Next** to continue to the **Import Pcp or Pc2** step.
6. You are given the opportunity to import a .PCP or .PC2 file from an older version of AutoCAD. Choose **Next** to continue to the **Ports** step.
7. Because this plotter is not actually hooked up to your computer, select the **Plot to File** option (see Figure 15-31). This will redirect the printer output to a file. Choose **Next** to continue to the **Plotter Name** step.
8. Accept the default name of **DraftPro (7570A)**. Choose **Next** to continue to the **Finish** step.
9. At this point, you can modify the plotter defaults by choosing the **Edit Plotter Configuration...** button (see Figure 15-32). The **Calibrate Plotter...** button allows you to verify the accuracy of the plotter output by creating a sample plot, measuring the output, and inputting the measured results back into the plotter calibration. Choose **Finish** to complete the plotter configuration.

To access student data files, go to www.pearsondesigncentral.com.

Figure 15-30   Selecting a plotter

Figure 15-31   Specifying a port

Figure 15-32   The configured plotter

10. From AutoCAD, start the **PLOT** command. The **Draftpro (7570A).PC3** file is now listed in the **Printer/plotter Name** list.

11. Choose **Cancel** to close the **Plot** dialog box. *Do not* save the drawing.

Plotting to a File

As mentioned earlier, when you select a plotter in the **Plot** dialog box, AutoCAD will display information about the printer, including the port. The port describes where the plot output will be directed—for example, a USB port, an LPT port, or a network printer location. The output port for any particular printer is defined within the plotter configuration (.PC3) file for the printer.

Plot File—PLT.   The **Plot to file** box in the **Plot** dialog box allows you to redirect the output from the specified port to a plot file. Plot files can be used in various ways. Some office environments use plot management software that may require plot files. Some plot files can be used in other programs. The Hewlett-Packard Graphics Language (HPGL or HPGL/2) is a plot file format used in many Hewlett-Packard plotters. Some graphics programs support HPGL files instead of AutoCAD files. If you have a need to create a plot file, select the **Plot to file** option in the **Plot** dialog box. When you plot, AutoCAD will ask you for the name and location of the plot file. Plot files typically use a .PLT file extension.

Design Web Format File—DWF/DWFx.   The Design Web Format (DWF) is a file format developed by Autodesk that allows you to publish your drawing on the World Wide Web or an intranet network. DWF files can contain one or more drawing sheets (layouts) and also support real-time panning and zooming as well as control over the display of layers and named views. DWF files cannot be opened in AutoCAD.

> **Note:**
> The DWFx format allows you to view drawings using Microsoft's XPS Viewer, which is automatically installed with Windows Vista and Internet Explorer version 7 and higher.

DWF files can be reviewed, marked up, and plotted using the free Autodesk® Design Review software. DWF files can also be viewed and shared using Autodesk's free Web service named Freewheel at http://freewheel .autodesk.com.

To plot to a DWF file, select either the **DWF6 ePlot.pc3** or the **DWFx ePlot (XPS compatible).pc3** plot configuration in the **Printer/plotter Name** list. To change the DWF preferences, choose the **Properties** button in the **Plot** dialog box and choose the **Custom Properties** on the **Device and Document Settings** tab of the **Plotter Configuration Editor** dialog box (see Figure 15-33). The **DWF6 ePlot Properties** dialog box is shown in Figure 15-34.

Figure 15-33   The **Device and Document Settings** tab

Figure 15-34   The **DWF6 ePlot Properties** dialog box

In this dialog box, you can set the resolution of the raster and vector components of the DWF file, control which fonts are embedded in the DWF file, set the background color, and control whether layer control is included in the DWF file.

Adobe® Portable Document Format—PDF.   PDF files are the industry standard for sharing graphical information. Using PDF files, you can share drawings with almost anyone because the Adobe Reader® is already installed on most computers. If the Adobe Reader is not installed, it can be easily downloaded and installed for free from the Internet, most of the time, automatically.

To plot to a PDF file, select the **DWG to PDF.PC3** plot configuration in the **Printer/plotter Name** list. When you plot, the standard Windows file dialog box is displayed so that you can specify a file name and location to save the PDF file.

Raster Image File—BMP/CALS/JPEG/PNG/TIFF.   AutoCAD comes with a number of plot drivers that allow you to plot to various raster file formats. When you plot a drawing to a raster file, AutoCAD objects are converted to a series of pixels. When plotting to a raster image file, sheet size is measured in pixels instead of inches or millimeters. The resolution and color depth of the raster file determines the quality of the final output and also affects the size of the final file.

To configure AutoCAD to plot to a raster image file, run the **Add-A-Plotter** wizard, select **My Computer, Next**, and choose **Raster File Formats** in the **Manufacturers** list (see Figure 15-35). AutoCAD provides support for a number of raster file formats.

Figure 15-35   Plotting to a raster image file

Exercise 15-4: Plotting to a File

1. Continue from Exercise 15-3.
2. Start the **PLOT** command to display the **Plot** dialog box.
3. Select the **DWF6 ePlot.pc3** printer and then select the **ARCH D (36.00 × 24.00 Inches)** paper size.
4. Select **Extents** from the **What to plot**: list.
5. Remove the check from the **Fit to paper** box and choose **3/32″ = 1′-0″** from the **Scale** list.
6. Choose the **Center the plot** option in the **Plot offset** area (see Figure 15-36) and choose **Preview...**.
7. AutoCAD will display the plot preview. You can zoom and pan to examine the plot preview. When done, choose the **Plot** button to create the plot.
8. AutoCAD prompts you for the name and location of the plot file. Save the plot as **EX15-4.DWF** and choose **Save** to create the DWF file. AutoCAD plots the drawing and ends the **PLOT** command.

Figure 15-36   The **Plot** dialog box

PLOTTING A SET OF DRAWINGS

Although the **PLOT** command allows you to create a single plot, there are many times when you need to create a set of drawings. This might include multiple layouts within a single drawing or include layouts from other drawing files. You may even need to mix model space plots with paper space layout plots. AutoCAD's **PUBLISH** command allows you to create multiple plots and to save the settings so the plot set can be re-created.

Batch Plotting

When you start the **PUBLISH** command, AutoCAD displays the **Publish** dialog box (see Figure 15-37).

Batch Plot	
Ribbon & Panel:	Output|Plot Batch Plot
Standard Toolbar:	
Menu:	File|Plot...
Command Line:	PUBLISH
Command Alias:	None

Figure 15-37   The **Publish** dialog box

When the **PUBLISH** command starts, AutoCAD automatically imports all of the currently open drawings and shows them in the list. The drawings are listed by their file name and drawing tab name and also show the current page setup and the status of the last plot. You can change the page setup used for a plot sheet by selecting the page setup and selecting an available page setup from the drop-down list. You can also import page setups from other drawings to use in your plot sheet set.

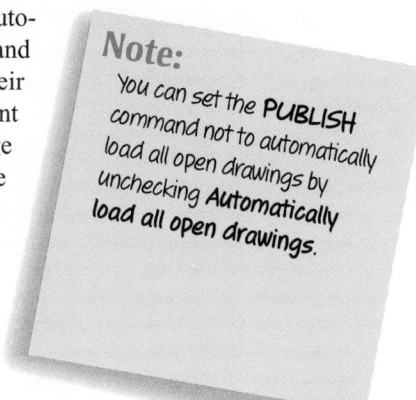

Note:
You can set the **PUBLISH** command not to automatically load all open drawings by unchecking **Automatically load all open drawings**.

TIP   It is possible to save a list of sheets to a .dsd (Drawing set Description) file so that you can plot the same list of sheets again in the future by selecting the **Save Sheet List** button. Select the **Load Sheet List** button to load a previously saved list. The **Sheet List:** drop-down list allows you to quickly select previous sheet lists.

Creating a Plot File Drawing Set.   The **Add** and **Remove** buttons allow you to make changes to the list of plot sheets. To remove a plot sheet from the list, simply select the plot sheet(s) and choose the **Remove** button.

To add plot sheets to the list, choose the **Add** button. AutoCAD displays the **Select Drawings** dialog box (see Figure 15-38), which allows you to select a drawing file. Once you select a drawing, AutoCAD will add a plot sheet for each drawing tab in the selected drawing. You can control whether AutoCAD imports model space and/or layout tabs using the **Include:** drop-down list.

The **Move Sheet Up** and **Move Sheet Down** buttons allow you to control the order of the plot sheets in the list. AutoCAD will plot the sheets in the order listed in the plot sheet list.

When you're ready to publish your plot sheet list, the **Preview** button allows you to see a plot preview of each plot sheet. The **PUBLISH** command preview mode works exactly like the single sheet plot preview but includes forward and back arrows (see Figure 15-39) that allow you to move through the plot sheet previews.

Figure 15-38   The **Select Drawings** dialog box

Previous Sheet   Next Sheet

Figure 15-39   The **Publish** preview controls

Creating an Electronic Drawing Set.   When you publish a set of plot sheets, you have the option of plotting to the printer defined in the layout or overriding that printer and creating an electronic drawing set in either a DWF, DWFx, or PDF format via the **Publish to:** drop-down list at the top of the **Publish** dialog box. When you select either option, AutoCAD will ignore the printer specified in the page setup and create the selected file type. DWF/DWFx files can be viewed and marked up using Autodesk Design Review introduced later in this chapter. PDF files can be viewed using the ubiquitous Adobe Reader, version 7 or later.

The **Publish Options...** button displays the **Publish Options** dialog box shown in Figure 15-40 and enables you to view and modify settings for the DWF/PDF output.

Because DWF/PDF files support multiple sheets, you have the option printing each sheet to a separate file or plotting all sheets to a single, multisheet file. You also have the option of including layer and block information and enabling password protection.

Figure 15-40   The **Publish Options** dialog box

Publish Output.   The **Include plot stamp** option allows you to turn plot stamping on and off. Selecting the **Plot Stamp Settings** button displays the **Plot Stamp** dialog box (see Figure 15-41), which allows you to change the plot stamp options.

Figure 15-41   The **Plot Stamp** dialog box

The **Publish in background** option allows you to process the list of drawings and layouts in the background so that you can continue to work in AutoCAD. A notification balloon is displayed in the AutoCAD Status Tray on the right side of the Status Bar when plotting is complete.

The **Open in viewer when done** option allows you to view DWF, DWFx, or PDF files in their respective viewer programs when plotting is complete.

To access student data files, go to www.pearsondesigncentral.com.

Exercise 15-5: Publishing an Electronic Drawing Set

1. Open the drawing **Welding Fixture-1** in the student data files. This drawing contains multiple paper space layouts for a welding fixture.
2. Start the **PUBLISH** command to display the **Publish** dialog box (see Figure 15-37).
3. Because we're interested in plotting only the paper space layouts, select the **Welding Fixture-1-Model** sheet from the list of sheet names. Choose the **Remove** button to remove this sheet from the list.
4. Select the **DWF** option from the **Publish to**: drop-down list to direct the results to a DWF file.
5. Choose the **Publish Options...** button to display the **Publish Options** dialog box (see Figure 15-40).
6. Verify that the DWF type is set to **Multi-sheet file**. Choose **Include** in the **Layer information** list and choose **OK** to close the dialog box.
7. Choose the **Preview** button to switch to preview mode. Examine the plot sheets to make sure they look correct. Choose the **Close Preview Window** button to end the preview.
8. Choose **Publish** to create the DWF file. AutoCAD will prompt you for the name of the DWF file. Specify **EX15-5.DWF** and choose **Select** to create the DWF file.
9. AutoCAD will publish the DWF file and ask you whether you'd like to save the plot sheet list. Choose **No** to return to the drawing. Do *not* save the drawing file.

WORKING WITH DWF FILES

Once you've created a DWF file, you have a couple of options for viewing and sharing them. Autodesk Design Review is installed when AutoCAD is installed and is also available as a free download from the Autodesk Website for those who do not have AutoCAD.

> **TIP** It is possible to view and share DWF files without Autodesk Design Review software by uploading your file to the Autodesk Freewheel Website located at http://freewheel.autodesk.com.

Autodesk Design Review

Autodesk Design Review allows you to view, measure, mark up, and print AutoCAD DWF files, making it possible to share your drawings with others who may not have AutoCAD while also maintaining your intellectual property because DWF files cannot be edited. The best part is that Autodesk Design Review is free and easily available at www.autodesk.com. The multisheet DWF file of the **Welding Fixture-1** drawing from the last exercise is shown open in **Autodesk Design Review** in Figure 15-42.

Most of the **Autodesk Design Review** tools are provided on the ribbon at the top of the screen, which has three tabs:

Note: For additional information about the Autodesk Design Review Program please refer to the Autodesk Design Review online help information or go to www.autodesk.com.

- **Home**   Controls views, workspaces, searching for text, getting help
- **Markup & Measure**   Clipboard, formatting, add callouts, draw tools, measure tools, stamps, and symbols
- **Tools**   Compare sheets, 3D tools, create new sheets by taking snapshot

Navigation tools are located on the toolbar at the upper right of the drawing window so you can pan, zoom, and navigate to the previous or next sheet using the **Previous Page** or **Next Page**

Figure 15-42 **Autodesk Design Review**

arrow buttons. The palette at the top left displays all of the open sheet information and has four tabs:

- **List View** List of sheets
- **Thumbnails** Previews of sheets
- **Markups** List of marked-up sheets
- **Model** Model view

Properties for the selected tab are displayed on the palette below. The tabs along the right side of the window display the following information about the drawing in a palette format that is set to auto-hide by default:

- **Sheet Properties** Lists the properties for the selected sheet
- **Object Properties** Lists the properties for the selected object
- **Views** Lists standard 2D and 3D views created in **Autodesk Design Review** and views created by AutoCAD
- **Cross Sections** Lists the cross sections created by you or the publisher of the 3D model
- **Layers** Lists all layers on the currently displayed sheet
- **Text Data** Lists all textual data
- **Grid Data** Lists all detail associated with a selection

> **Note:**
> Autodesk Design Review comes with AutoCAD so that you can install it from the Auto-CAD installation CD. It is typically installed by default.

Exercise 15-6: Viewing a DWF File

1. Continue from Exercise 15-5.
2. Start **Autodesk Design Review**.
3. Open the file **EX15-5.DWF** you created in the previous exercise.
4. Navigate around the DWF file and examine the multiple plot sheets.
5. Switch to the **Markup & Measure** tab and try the different tools.

Autodesk DWF Writer

The Autodesk DWF Writer is a Windows system printer driver that allows you to publish DWF files by simply selecting **Autodesk DWF Writer** from your standard **Printer Name** drop-down list in any Windows application. The DWF Writer allows you to create DWF files from any application that does not offer built-in DWF publishing. The DWF Writer is available as a free download from the Autodesk Website (www.autodesk.com).

CHAPTER SUMMARY

Whether you do quick check plots to check your work, create drawing sets to send to contractors, create full-color presentation drawings, or create electronic plots to share and collaborate with others over the Internet, plotting is an integral part of using AutoCAD.

AutoCAD provides a large number of options to precisely control the look and format of your output. This chapter gave you an overview of AutoCAD's plotting capabilities and some of the options available to controlling the output.

CHAPTER TEST QUESTIONS

Multiple Choice

1. A page setup is:
   a. A paper space layout
   b. A set of default plot settings
   c. A way to assign lineweights to AutoCAD objects
   d. A print driver

2. Which of the following model space plot scales will result in a drawing scaled to $1/2'' = 1'-0''$?
   a. $.5 = 1$
   b. $1 = 24$
   c. $24 = 1$
   d. $1 = .5$

3. Named plot style tables are stored in:
   a. .CTB files
   b. .PC3 files
   c. .DWF files
   d. .STB files

4. Plotter configurations are stored in:
   a. .CTB files
   b. .PC3 files
   c. .DWF files
   d. .STB files

5. To plot everything visible in the drawing, you would set the plot area to:
   a. Limits
   b. Extents
   c. Layout
   d. Display

6. A DWF file:
   a. Is a Design Web Format file
   b. Can be viewed only electronically; it cannot be printed
   c. Can be opened in AutoCAD
   d. Does not show layer information

7. Which of the following AutoCAD commands does not print drawings?
   a. **PREVIEW**
   b. **PLOT**
   c. **SAVEAS**
   d. **PUBLISH**

8. Color-dependent plot style tables are stored in:
   a. .CTB files
   b. .PC3 files
   c. .DWF files
   d. .STB files

9. Plot stamps:
   a. Can contain only specific preset information
   b. Always appear in the lower left corner of the plot
   c. Use only the TXT.SHX text font
   d. None of the above

10. Raster files:
    a. Contain only pixels, no actual AutoCAD objects
    b. Are not supported in AutoCAD
    c. Must not exceed 640×480 resolution
    d. None of the above

Matching

a. .PC3
b. DWF
c. Page setup
d. .STB
e. .CTB
f. **PLOT**
g. **PUBLISH**
h. **Plot Stamp**
i. PLT
j. BMP

1. Plotter configuration file
2. Text added to a drawing at plot time
3. Command used to print multiple plot sheets
4. Color-dependent style table file
5. Command used to print a single plot sheet
6. An electronic plot file format
7. A group of default plot settings
8. A type of raster file
9. Named plot style table file
10. An AutoCAD plot file

CHAPTER PROJECTS

Project 15-1: Classroom Plan—Continued from Chapter 14

1. Open drawing **P14-1** from Chapter 14.
2. Start the **PLOT** command so that the **Plot** dialog box is displayed.
3. Set the **Printer/plotter Name** to a large format plotter capable of printing on 36″ × 24″ paper (D-size). If you do not have access to a large format plotter, set the **Printer/plotter Name** to **DWF6 ePlot.pc3** to create a Drawing Web Format (DWF) file.
4. Make sure the **Paper size** is correct.
5. Make sure that the **Plot area** is set to **Layout**.
6. Make sure that the **Plot scale** is set to **1:1**.
7. Select the **More Options** arrow button at the bottom right of the dialog box to display the additional plotting options.
8. Turn off the **Plot with plot styles** option in the **Plot options** area and turn on the **Plot object lineweights** option.
9. Select the **Preview** button at the bottom left of the dialog box to preview the plot and make sure that everything is OK.
10. Select the **Apply to Layout** button at the bottom of the dialog box to save the changes with the layout.
11. Select **OK** to plot the drawing.
12. Save the drawing as **P15-1**.

Project 15-2a: B-Size Mechanical Border—Continued from Chapter 14

1. Open template file **Mechanical B-Size.DWT** from Chapter 14.
2. Start the **PLOT** command so that the **Plot** dialog box is displayed.
3. Set the **Printer/plotter Name** to a printer or plotter capable of printing on 11″ × 17″ paper (B-size). If you do not have access to a printer/plotter that can print 11″ × 17″, set the **Printer/plotter Name** to **DWF6 ePlot.pc3** to create a Drawing Web Format (DWF) file.
4. Make sure the **Paper size** is correct.
5. Make sure that the **Plot area** is set to **Layout**.
6. Make sure that the **Plot scale** is set to **1:1**.
7. Select the **More Options** arrow button at the bottom right of the dialog box to display the additional plotting options.
8. Turn off the **Plot with plot styles** option in the **Plot options** area and turn at the **Plot object lineweights** option.
9. Select the **Preview** button at the bottom left of the dialog box to preview the plot and make sure that everything is OK.
10. Select the **Apply to Layout** button at the bottom of the dialog box to save the changes with the layout.
11. Select **OK** to plot the drawing.
12. Save the drawing as **P15-2A**.

Project 15-2b: C-Size Mechanical Border—Continued from Chapter 14

1. Open template file **Mechanical C-Size.DWT** from Chapter 14.
2. Start the **PLOT** command so that the **Plot** dialog box is displayed.
3. Set the **Printer/plotter Name** to a printer or plotter capable of printing on 22″ × 17″ paper (C-size). If you do not have access to a printer/plotter that can print 22″ × 17″, set the **Printer/plotter Name** to **DWF6 ePlot.pc3** to create a Drawing Web Format (DWF) file.
4. Make sure the **Paper size** is correct.
5. Make sure that the **Plot area** is set to **Layout**.
6. Make sure that the **Plot scale** is set to **1:1**.

7. Select the **More Options** arrow button at the bottom right of the dialog box to display the additional plotting options.
8. Turn off the **Plot with plot styles** option in the **Plot options** area and turn on the **Plot object lineweights** option.
9. Select the **Preview** button at the bottom left of the dialog box to preview the plot and make sure that everything is OK.
10. Select the **Apply to Layout** button at the bottom of the dialog box to save the changes with the layout.
11. Select **OK** to plot the drawing.
12. Save the drawing as **P15-2B**.

Project 15-2c: A-Size Portrait Mechanical Border—Continued from Chapter 14

1. Open template file **Mechanical A-Size-Portrait.DWT** from Chapter 14.
2. Start the **PLOT** command so that the **Plot** dialog box is displayed.
3. Set the **Printer/plotter Name** to **Default Windows System Printer.pc3**. If you do not have access to a printer/plotter, set the **Printer/plotter Name** to **DWF6 ePlot.pc3** to create a Drawing Web Format (DWF) file.
4. Make sure the **Paper size** is correct.
5. Make sure that the **Plot area** is set to **Layout**.
6. Make sure that the **Plot scale** is set to **1:1**.
7. Select the **More Options** arrow button at the bottom right of the dialog box to display the additional plotting options.
8. Turn off the **Plot with plot styles** option in the **Plot options** area and turn on the **Plot object lineweights** option.
9. Select the **Preview** button at the bottom left of the dialog box to preview the plot and make sure that everything is OK.
10. Select the **Apply to Layout** button at the bottom of the dialog box to save the changes with the layout.
11. Select **OK** to plot the drawing.
12. Save the drawing as **P15-2C**.

Project 15-3a: Architectural D-Size Border—Continued from Chapter 14

1. Open template file **Architectural D-Size.DWT** from Chapter 14.
2. Start the **PLOT** command so that the **Plot** dialog box is displayed.
3. Set the **Printer/plotter Name** to a large format plotter capable of printing on 36″ × 24″ paper (D-size). If you do not have access to a large format plotter, set the **Printer/plotter Name** to **DWF6 ePlot.pc3** to create a Drawing Web Format (DWF) file.
4. Make sure the **Paper size** is correct.
5. Make sure that the **Plot area** is set to **Layout**.
6. Make sure that the **Plot scale** is set to **1:1**.
7. Select the **More Options** arrow button at the bottom right of the dialog box to display the additional plotting options.
8. Turn off the **Plot with plot styles** option in the **Plot options** area and turn on the **Plot object lineweights** option.
9. Select the **Preview** button at the bottom left of the dialog box to preview the plot and make sure that everything is OK.
10. Select the **Apply to Layout** button at the bottom of the dialog box to save the changes with the layout.
11. Select **OK** to plot the drawing.
12. Save the drawing as **P15-3A**.

Project 15-3b: Architectural B-Size Border—Continued from Chapter 14

1. Open template file **Architectural B-Size.DWT** from Chapter 14.
2. Start the **PLOT** command so that the **Plot** dialog box is displayed.

3. Set the **Printer/plotter Name** to a printer or plotter capable of printing on 11″ × 17″ paper (B-size). If you do not have access to a printer/plotter that can print 11″ × 17″, set the **Printer/plotter Name** to **DWF6 ePlot.pc3** to create a Drawing Web Format (DWF) file.
4. Make sure the **Paper size** is correct.
5. Make sure that the **Plot area** is set to **Layout**.
6. Make sure that the **Plot scale** is set to **1:1**.
7. Select the **More Options** arrow button at the bottom right of the dialog box to display the additional plotting options.
8. Turn off the **Plot with plot styles** option in the **Plot options** area and turn on the **Plot object lineweights** option.
9. Select the **Preview** button at the bottom left of the dialog box to preview the plot and make sure that everything is OK.
10. Select the **Apply to Layout** button at the bottom of the dialog box to save the changes with the layout.
11. Select **OK** to plot the drawing.
12. Save the drawing as **P15-3B**.

Project 15-3c: Architectural A-Size Border—Continued from Chapter 14

1. Open template file **Architectural A-Size.DWT** from Chapter 14.
2. Start the **PLOT** command so that the **Plot** dialog box is displayed.
3. Set the **Printer/plotter Name** to **Default Windows System Printer.pc3**. If you do not have access to a printer/plotter, set the **Printer/plotter Name** to **DWF6 ePlot.pc3** to create a Drawing Web Format (DWF) file.
4. Make sure the **Paper size** is correct.
5. Make sure that the **Plot area** is set to **Layout**.
6. Make sure that the **Plot scale** is set to **1:1**.
7. Select the **More Options** arrow button at the bottom right of the dialog box to display the additional plotting options.
8. Turn off the **Plot with plot styles** option in the **Plot options** area and turn on the **Plot object lineweights** option.
9. Select the **Preview** button at the bottom left of the dialog box to preview the plot and make sure that everything is OK.
10. Select the **Apply to Layout** button at the bottom of the dialog box to save the changes with the layout.
11. Select **OK** to plot the drawing.
12. Save the drawing as **P15-3C**.

Project 15-4: Electrical Schematic—Continued from Chapter 14

1. Open drawing **P14-4** from Chapter 14.
2. Start the **PLOT** command so that the **Plot** dialog box is displayed.
3. Set the **Printer/plotter Name** to a large format plotter capable of printing on 36″ × 24″ paper (D-size). If you do not have access to a large format plotter, set the **Printer/plotter Name** to **DWF6 ePlot.pc3** to create a Drawing Web Format (DWF) file.
4. Make sure the **Paper size** is correct.
5. Make sure that the **Plot area** is set to **Layout**.
6. Make sure that the **Plot scale** is set to **1:1**.
7. Select the **More Options** arrow button at the bottom right of the dialog box to display the additional plotting options.
8. Turn off the **Plot with plot styles** option in the **Plot options** area and turn on the **Plot object lineweights** option.
9. Select the **Preview** button at the bottom left of the dialog box to preview the plot and make sure that everything is OK.
10. Select the **Apply to Layout** button at the bottom of the dialog box to save the changes with the layout.
11. Select **OK** to plot the drawing.
12. Save the drawing as **P15-4**.

Project 15-5: Architectural Plan—Continued from Chapter 14

1. Open drawing **P14-5** from Chapter 14.
2. Start the **PLOT** command so that the **Plot** dialog box is displayed.
3. Set the **Printer/plotter Name** to a large format plotter capable of printing on 36″ × 24″ paper (D-size). If you do not have access to a large format plotter, set the **Printer/plotter Name** to **DWF6 ePlot.pc3** to create a Drawing Web Format (DWF) file.
4. Make sure the **Paper size** is correct.
5. Make sure that the **Plot area** is set to **Layout**.
6. Make sure that the **Plot scale** is set to **1:1**.
7. Select the **More Options** arrow button at the bottom right of the dialog box to display the additional plotting options.
8. Turn off the **Plot with plot styles** option in the **Plot options** area and turn on the **Plot object lineweights** option.
9. Select the **Preview** button at the bottom left of the dialog box to preview the plot and make sure that everything is OK.
10. Select the **Apply to Layout** button at the bottom of the dialog box to save the changes with the layout.
11. Select **OK** to plot the drawing.
12. Save the drawing as **P15-5**.

Project 15-6: Optical Mount—English Units—Continued from Chapter 14

1. Open drawing **P14-6** from Chapter 14.
2. Start the **PLOT** command so that the **Plot** dialog box is displayed.
3. Set the **Printer/plotter Name** to a large format plotter capable of printing on 36″ × 24″ paper (D-size). If you do not have access to a large format plotter, set the **Printer/plotter Name** to **DWF6 ePlot.pc3** to create a Drawing Web Format (DWF) file.
4. Make sure the **Paper size** is correct.
5. Make sure that the **Plot area** is set to **Layout**.
6. Make sure that the **Plot scale** is set to **1:1**.
7. Select the **More Options** arrow button at the bottom right of the dialog box to display the additional plotting options.
8. Turn off the **Plot with plot styles** option in the **Plot options** area and turn on the **Plot object lineweights** option.
9. Select the **Preview** button at the bottom left of the dialog box to preview the plot and make sure that everything is OK.
10. Select the **Apply to Layout** button at the bottom of the dialog box to save the changes with the layout.
11. Select **OK** to plot the drawing.
12. Save drawing as **P15-6**.

Project 15-7a: Gasket—Continued from Chapter 14

1. Open drawing **P14-7A** from Chapter 14.
2. Start the **PLOT** command so that the **Plot** dialog box is displayed.
3. Set the **Printer/plotter Name** to a printer or plotter capable of printing on 11″ × 17″ paper (B-size). If you do not have access to a printer/plotter that can print 11″ × 17″, set the **Printer/plotter Name** to **DWF6 ePlot.pc3** to create a Drawing Web Format (DWF) file.
4. Make sure the **Paper size** is correct.
5. Make sure that the **Plot area** is set to **Layout**.
6. Make sure that the **Plot scale** is set to **1:1**.
7. Select the **More Options** arrow button at the bottom right of the dialog box to display the additional plotting options.
8. Turn off the **Plot with plot styles** option in the **Plot options** area and turn on the **Plot object lineweights** option.
9. Select the **Preview** button at the bottom left of the dialog box to preview the plot and make sure that everything is OK.

10. Select the **Apply to Layout** button at the bottom of the dialog box to save the changes with the layout.
11. Select **OK** to plot the drawing.
12. Save the drawing as **P15-7A**.

Project 15-7b: Widget—Continued from Chapter 14

1. Open drawing **P14-7B** from Chapter 14.
2. Start the **PLOT** command so that the **Plot** dialog box is displayed.
3. Set the **Printer/plotter Name** to a printer or plotter capable of printing on 11″ × 17″ paper (B-size). If you do not have access to a printer/plotter that can print 11″ × 17″, set the **Printer/plotter Name** to **DWF6 ePlot.pc3** to create a Drawing Web Format (DWF) file.
4. Make sure the **Paper size** is correct.
5. Make sure that the **Plot area** is set to **Layout**.
6. Make sure that the **Plot scale** is set to **1:1**.
7. Select the **More Options** arrow button at the bottom right of the dialog box to display the additional plotting options.
8. Turn off the **Plot with plot styles** option in the **Plot options** area and turn on the **Plot object lineweights** option.
9. Select the **Preview** button at the bottom left of the dialog box to preview the plot and make sure that everything is OK.
10. Select the **Apply to Layout** button at the bottom of the dialog box to save the changes with the layout.
11. Select **OK** to plot the drawing.
12. Save the drawing as **P15-7B**.

Project 15-7c: Hex Head Bolts and Nuts—Continued from Chapter 14

1. Open drawing **P14-7C** from Chapter 14.
2. Start the **PLOT** command so that the **Plot** dialog box is displayed.
3. Set the **Printer/plotter Name** to a printer or plotter capable of printing on 11″ × 17″ paper (B-size). If you do not have access to a printer/plotter that can print 11″ × 17″, set the **Printer/plotter Name** to **DWF6 ePlot.pc3** to create a Drawing Web Format (DWF) file.
4. Make sure the **Paper size** is correct.
5. Make sure that the **Plot area** is set to **Layout**.
6. Make sure that the **Plot scale** is set to **1:1**.
7. Select the **More Options** arrow button at the bottom right of the dialog box to display the additional plotting options.
8. Turn off the **Plot with plot styles** option in the **Plot options** area and turn on the **Plot object lineweights** option.
9. Select the **Preview** button at the bottom left of the dialog box to preview the plot and make sure that everything is OK.
10. Select the **Apply to Layout** button at the bottom of the dialog box to save the changes with the layout.
11. Select **OK** to plot the drawing.
12. Save the drawing as **P15-7C**.

Project 15-7d: Motorcycle Head Gasket—Continued from Chapter 14

1. Open drawing **P14-7D** from Chapter 14.
2. Start the **PLOT** command so that the **Plot** dialog box is displayed.
3. Set the **Printer/plotter Name** to a printer or plotter capable of printing on 11″ × 17″ paper (B-size). If you do not have access to a printer/plotter that can print 11″ × 17″, set the **Printer/plotter Name** to **DWF6 ePlot.pc3** to create a Drawing Web Format (DWF) file.
4. Make sure the **Paper size** is correct.
5. Make sure that the **Plot area** is set to **Layout**.
6. Make sure that the **Plot scale** is set to **1:1**.

7. Select the **More Options** arrow button at the bottom right of the dialog box to display the additional plotting options.

8. Turn off the **Plot with plot styles** option in the **Plot options** area and turn on the **Plot object lineweights** option.

9. Select the **Preview** button at the bottom left of the dialog box to preview the plot and make sure that everything is OK.

10. Select the **Apply to Layout** button at the bottom of the dialog box to save the changes with the layout.

11. Select **OK** to plot the drawing.

12. Save the drawing as **P15-7D**.

Project 15-7e: 68-Tooth Motorcycle Sprocket—Continued from Chapter 14

1. Open drawing **P14-7E** from Chapter 14.

2. Start the **PLOT** command so that the **Plot** dialog box is displayed.

3. Set the **Printer/plotter Name** to a printer or plotter capable of printing on 11″ × 17″ paper (B-size). If you do not have access to a printer/plotter that can print 11″ × 17″, set the **Printer/plotter Name** to **DWF6 ePlot.pc3** to create a Drawing Web Format (DWF) file.

4. Make sure the **Paper size** is correct.

5. Make sure that the **Plot area** is set to **Layout**.

6. Make sure that the **Plot scale** is set to **1:1**.

7. Select the **More Options** arrow button at the bottom right of the dialog box to display the additional plotting options.

8. Turn off the **Plot with plot styles** option in the **Plot options** area and turn on the **Plot object lineweights** option.

9. Select the **Preview** button at the bottom left of the dialog box to preview the plot and make sure that everything is OK.

10. Select the **Apply to Layout** button at the bottom of the dialog box to save the changes with the layout.

11. Select **OK** to plot the drawing.

12. Save the drawing as **P15-7E**.

Project 15-7f: Window Extrusion—Continued from Chapter 14

1. Open drawing **P14-7F** from Chapter 14.

2. Start the **PLOT** command so that the **Plot** dialog box is displayed.

3. Set the **Printer/plotter Name** to a printer or plotter capable of printing on 11″ × 17″ paper (B-size). If you do not have access to a printer/plotter that can print 11″ × 17″, set the **Printer/plotter Name** to **DWF6 ePlot.pc3** to create a Drawing Web Format (DWF) file.

4. Make sure the **Paper size** is correct.

5. Make sure that the **Plot area** is set to **Layout**.

6. Make sure that the **Plot scale** is set to **1:1**.

7. Select the **More Options** arrow button at the bottom right of the dialog box to display the additional plotting options.

8. Turn off the **Plot with plot styles** option in the **Plot options** area and turn on the **Plot object lineweights** option.

9. Select the **Preview** button at the bottom left of the dialog box to preview the plot and make sure that everything is OK.

10. Select the **Apply to Layout** button at the bottom of the dialog box to save the changes with the layout.

11. Select **OK** to plot the drawing.

12. Save the drawing as **P15-7F**.

Project 15-7g: Hub—Continued from Chapter 14

1. Open drawing **P14-7G** from Chapter 14.

2. Start the **PLOT** command so that the **Plot** dialog box is displayed.

3. Set the **Printer/plotter Name** to a printer or plotter capable of printing on 11″ × 17″ paper (B-size). If you do not have access to a printer/plotter that can

print 11″ × 17″, set the **Printer/plotter Name** to **DWF6 ePlot.pc3** to create a Drawing Web Format (DWF) file.

4. Make sure the **Paper size** is correct.
5. Make sure that the **Plot area** is set to **Layout**.
6. Make sure that the **Plot scale** is set to **1:1**.
7. Select the **More Options** arrow button at the bottom right of the dialog box to display the additional plotting options.
8. Turn off the **Plot with plot styles** option in the **Plot options** area and turn on the **Plot object lineweights** option.
9. Select the **Preview** button at the bottom left of the dialog box to preview the plot and make sure that everything is OK.
10. Select the **Apply to Layout** button at the bottom of the dialog box to save the changes with the layout.
11. Select **OK** to plot the drawing.
12. Save the drawing as **P15-7G**.

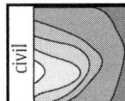

Project 15-8: Civil Site Plan—Continued from Chapter 14

1. Open drawing **P14-8** from Chapter 14.
2. Start the **PLOT** command so that the **Plot** dialog box is displayed.
3. Set the **Printer/plotter Name** to a large format plotter capable of printing on 36″ × 24″ paper (D-size). If you do not have access to a large format plotter, set the **Printer/plotter Name** to **DWF6 ePlot.pc3** to create a Drawing Web Format (DWF) file.
4. Make sure the **Paper size** is correct.
5. Make sure that the **Plot area** is set to **Layout**.
6. Make sure that the **Plot scale** is set to **1:1**.
7. Select the **More Options** arrow button at the bottom right of the dialog box to display the additional plotting options.
8. Turn off the **Plot with plot styles** option in the **Plot options** area and turn on the **Plot object lineweights** option.
9. Select the **Preview** button at the bottom left of the dialog box to preview the plot and make sure that everything is OK.
10. Select the **Apply to Layout** button at the bottom of the dialog box to save the changes with the layout.
11. Select **OK** to plot the drawing.
12. Save the drawing as **P15-8**.

Blocks and Block Attributes 16

Chapter Objectives

- Learn how to create and insert blocks
- Understand the difference between a block definition and a block reference
- Explore the different types of blocks
- Create unit blocks that can be inserted with different X and Y scale factors
- Manage block object properties such as layer, color, linetype, and lineweight
- Understand the significance of creating blocks on layer **0**
- Insert drawing files as blocks using Windows Explorer
- Create a drawing file (DWG) out of an internal block
- Create and update block attributes
- Extract block attributes to an AutoCAD table or external file
- Use DesignCenter to insert blocks
- Use and customize tool palettes
- Introduction to dynamic blocks

INTRODUCTION

Blocks, also referred to as *symbols,* are one of the most valuable features in AutoCAD. A block is a named collection of AutoCAD objects treated as a single complex object that can be inserted in a drawing one or more times. Blocks provide the following benefits and features:

- Provide the ability to reuse drawing information repeatedly in one or more drawings
- Increase drawing uniformity and consistency
- Promote and help maintain drafting standards
- Reduce drawing size
- Reduce amount of time and effort to update and revise drawings
- Add intelligence to drawings

Blocks can be made from practically any type of AutoCAD objects including lines, circles, text, dimensions, and even hatching. They may be as simple as a single line or as complex as a complete drawing. There are three basic types of blocks as shown in Figure 16-1:

- **Annotation** Detail bubbles, section marks, door/window tags
- **Schematic** Electrical symbols, plumbing symbols, weld symbols
- **Real-Size** Furniture, doors/windows, plumbing fixtures

Annotation blocks need to be scaled up or down when they are inserted to account for the drawing scale, just like text and dimensions. For instance, a detail bubble drawn with a 1/2″-diameter circle as shown in Figure 16-1 would have to be scaled up by 48 in a drawing with the scale of 1/4″ = 1′-0″ in order to plot at the correct size.

Schematic Block—
Scaled at 1:1

Annotation
Block—Must Be
Scaled by Drawing Scale

Real-Size Block—
Actual Size

Figure 16-1   Examples of block types

> **TIP** It is possible to make a block **Annotative** so it scales up or down automatically using the current **Annotation Scale**.

Schematic blocks are created at the size they will plot so that you can create schematic drawings at a scale of 1:1. For instance, the electrical symbol in Figure 16-1 is drawn with a 1/4″ diameter so that it can easily be located in a schematic drawing created on a 1/4″ or 1/8″ grid layout.

Real-size blocks are created at the actual size that the objects exist in the real world so that they can be used to accurately lay out a drawing. For instance, a 2′-0″ wide chair is drawn 24″ wide so that when it is located on a floor plan it represents the actual furniture.

It is even possible to attach dynamic intelligent text referred to as a ***block attribute*** that can be updated when a block is inserted or anytime later.

block attribute: A dynamic text-like object that can be included in a block definition to store alphanumeric data

Existing block attributes can be extracted directly to an AutoCAD table so that you can automatically create schedules, parts lists, bills of materials, and other tabular type information. In fact, block attributes can even be extracted to an external text file, spreadsheet, or database so that the attribute information can be shared with others, used to generate reports, and used to perform other tasks.

> **Note:** Like other complex objects, a block can be converted back into its original subobjects using the **EXPLODE** command. Using the **EXPLODE** command with blocks is examined later in this chapter.

As you can see, blocks are very useful. The following sections explain how to exploit the power of blocks and block attributes in your AutoCAD drawings.

CREATING BLOCKS

The named group of AutoCAD objects that make up a block is referred to as a ***block definition***.

Every time a block is inserted in a drawing it refers back to the centrally located block definition. In fact, when a block is inserted in a drawing, it is referred to as a ***block reference*** because it refers back to the block definition to determine its appearance and other properties.

block definition: A user-defined collection of drawing objects assigned a base point and a name that is stored centrally in a drawing

block reference: An instance of a block definition inserted in a drawing that references the central block definition drawing data

All that is stored with the block reference is the block's insertion point, scale (*X, Y,* and *Z*), and rotation angle. The rest of the information is derived from the block definition. This arrangement provides a couple of advantages. One advantage is that the drawing size is reduced because the block definition is centrally stored

> **Note:** It is possible to create blocks that are made up of other blocks. Creating a block within a block is a concept referred to as block nesting because one block is nested inside another block.

in *one* place, regardless of how many references of the block exist in a drawing. The other advantage is that if you update a block definition, all references to that block definition in a drawing are automatically updated, regardless of how many references there are.

Creating a new block definition is easy. You simply draw the objects you want the block to consist of using standard drawing techniques and then start the **BLOCK** command so you can select the objects and give them a descriptive name that you can reference later.

The BLOCK Command

The **BLOCK** command creates a block definition using the objects you select with the name specified via the **Block Definition** dialog box shown in Figure 16-2.

Create Block	
Ribbon & Panel:	Insert| Block Create
Draw Toolbar:	
Menu:	Draw| Block| Make...
Command Line:	BLOCK, BMAKE
Command Alias:	B

Figure 16-2   The **Block Definition** dialog box

The **Name:** list box is where you enter the desired block name. The name can be up to 255 characters long and can include letters, numbers, or blank spaces. Typically, you want to use a descriptive name that reflects the block's contents and/or usage.

Selecting an existing block name from the list will redefine all references to that block in the drawing if you make any changes. Redefining blocks is explained later in this chapter.

The **Base point** area allows you to specify an insertion point for the block. This point is used to locate the block in the drawing when it is inserted later. The default insertion point is 0,0,0. You can either enter the *X*, *Y*, and *Z* coordinate values directly in their respective text boxes or pick a point in your drawing by selecting the **Pick point** button. The **Pick point** button temporarily closes the **Block Definition** dialog box so that you can pick a point in the drawing as shown in Figure 16-3.

Note:
Do not use the block names AVE_RENDER, DIRECT, LIGHT, OVERHEAD, RM_SDB, or SH_SPOT. These names are reserved for special AutoCAD objects.

TIP Typically, you should rely on Object Snaps to snap to a key point on the objects that comprise the block. For instance, you might select the center point if you are creating a detail bubble block or the endpoint at a corner of a desk block.

Figure 16-3   Selecting a block insertion point

Figure 16-4   Selecting objects that will make up the block

The **Objects** area allows you to select the objects to include in the new block definition if there are none already selected in the drawing, as well as to indicate what to do with the selected objects after the block definition is created.

The **Select objects** button closes the **Block Definition** dialog box temporarily so you can select objects in the drawing as shown in Figure 16-4.

You can use any standard selection process. When you finish selecting objects, press **<Enter ↵>** to redisplay the **Block Definition** dialog box and continue defining the block. Pressing the **<Esc>** key when selecting objects will deselect the objects so that nothing is selected and redisplay the **Block Definition** dialog box.

The **QuickSelect** button closes the **Block Definition** dialog box temporarily and displays the **Quick Select** dialog box shown in Figure 16-5 so you can select objects by filtering one or more object properties.

Note:
If no objects are selected, the **No objects selected** warning shown in Figure 16-2 is displayed at the bottom of the **Objects** area. Otherwise, the number of objects that are currently selected is displayed.

Figure 16-5   The **Quick Select** dialog box

The other three options in the **Objects** area directly below the **Select objects** button determine what happens to the selected objects after the block is created:

- **Retain**   Retains the original selected objects in the drawing without doing anything
- **Convert to block (default)**   Converts the selected objects to a block reference "in-place"
- **Delete**   Deletes all the selected objects after the block is created so that they no longer exist

TIP   If you use the **Delete** option by accident, you can use the **OOPS** command to undelete the block subobjects. Type **OOPS <Enter ↵>** immediately after the block is created in order to return the original block subobjects to your drawing.

The **Settings** area at the bottom is where you specify different settings for the block.

The **Block unit**: list box lists the different possible insertion units for the block. If you insert a block that is created with different block drawing units than the insertion scale units currently set for the drawing, the block is automatically scaled up or down according to the scale factor equivalent of the ratio between the different unit systems.

Note:
The insertion scale units are set via the **Drawing Units** dialog box, which can be displayed by selecting **Units** from the **Drawing Utilities** menu on the big "A" Application Menu or using the **UNITS** command.

The **Hyperlink...** button displays the **Insert Hyperlink** dialog box so that you can associate a hyperlink with the block definition. Hyperlinks can be attached to almost any AutoCAD object so that it is possible to link objects to Websites and even other documents.

The **Behavior** area at the top right is where you control what happens after a block is inserted.

The **Annotative** check box indicates if the block can be scaled up and down automatically using the current **Annotation Scale**.

The **Scale uniformly** check box indicates whether or not the block reference can be nonuniformly scaled when it is inserted so that the X, Y, and Z scales are not all equal.

The **Allow exploding** check box indicates whether or not the block reference can be exploded when it is inserted or afterwards.

The **Description**: text box allows you to input a text description for the block that appears in the **DesignCenter** block drawing content management tool discussed later in this chapter.

Note:
The block definition is created in the current drawing only. To use the block in any other drawing, you must first export it to a separate drawing file using the **WBLOCK** command explained later in this chapter.

The **Open in block editor** check box opens the current block definition in the **Block Editor** after you select **OK**. The **Block Editor** is described briefly later in this chapter.

After you have entered a name for the block, selected one or more objects, and specified the desired settings described above, select **OK** to close the dialog box and create the block.

Block Object Properties

When you insert a block, the block reference assumes the current object properties (layer, color, linetype, lineweight) just like other AutoCAD objects. Be aware that the current properties are assigned to the overall complex block reference *only*. The object properties of the subobjects that make up the block are determined by how the objects were originally created before they were made into a block.

There are three different techniques for controlling the properties of a block's subobjects that result in the following effects when the block is inserted:

- Create subobjects on layer **0** with the color, linetype, and lineweight set to **ByLayer**
- Create subobjects on any layer other than **0**
- Create subobjects using the **ByBlock** property set for color, linetype, or lineweight

Creating Blocks on Layer 0. Creating block subobjects on layer **0** with object properties set to **ByLayer** is the most popular approach to creating blocks because it provides the most flexibility. Blocks with subobjects created on layer **0** have the special ability to assume the current object properties when they are inserted. This allows you to create one block that can be used in multiple scenarios based on the layer that is current when the block is inserted.

Hard-Coding a Block's Object Properties. Creating block subobjects on any layer other than **0** locks the subobjects on the layer on which they were created so that the subobjects always maintain their original properties regardless of what layer or other properties are current when the block is inserted. This approach provides the least amount of flexibility because the block's subobjects are always located on the layer on which they were created regardless of the current layer and object properties in the drawing when the block is inserted. However, this hard-coded approach can have its uses, especially if standards dictate that a particular layer should be maintained for the life of a drawing.

Using the ByBlock Object Property. The **ByBlock** property allows you to create block subobjects that will assume the current color, linetype, or lineweight property when the block is inserted. Normally, a block and its subobjects ignore the color, linetype, and lineweight properties when the block is inserted. If you create a block subobject with any of these properties set to **ByBlock**, the subobject will assume the current setting for the property during the insertion process. For instance, setting a line's color property to **ByBlock** and including it in a block definition forces the line to assume the current color when the block is inserted. If the current color setting is **red**, then the line subobject is **red**. The same logic applies to the linetype and lineweight properties.

Exercise 16-1: Creating Blocks

1. Start a new drawing using the acad.dwt drawing template.
2. Create the following layers:

Name	Color	Linetype	Lineweight	Description
WINTAG-B	1	Continuous	Default	Layer used for all WINTAG-B block subobjects
A-Glaze-Iden	3	Continuous	Default	Window tag layer

3. Create the "A" window tag shown in Figure 16-6 on layer **0**.
4. Create the "B" window tag shown in Figure 16-6 on layer **WINTAG-B**.
5. Create the "C" window tag shown in Figure 16-6 on layer **0** with the color, linetype, and lineweight properties all set to **ByBlock**.
6. Start the **BLOCK** command to display the **Block Definition** dialog box.
7. Enter the name **WINTAG-A** in the **Name:** list box.
8. Select the **Pick point** button in the **Base point** area.
9. Select the center point of the "A" window tag circle using the **Center** Object Snap.
10. Select the **Select objects** button in the **Objects** area.
11. Select the "A" window tag circle and text and press **<Enter ↵>** to return to the **Block Definition** dialog box.
12. Make sure that the **Convert to block** button is selected.
13. Select the **Annotative** check box in the **Behavior** area.
14. Select **OK** to create the block.

Wintag-A   Wintag-B   Wintag-C

Figure 16-6   Window tag blocks

15. Repeat steps 6 through 13 to create blocks named **WINTAG-B** and **WINTAG-C** for the "B" window tag and the "C" window tag, respectively.
16. Save the drawing as **EX16-1**.

INSERTING BLOCKS

As mentioned earlier, when you insert a block, it creates a block reference. Remember that the information about the objects that make up the block and what the block looks like is determined by the block definition explained in the previous section. All that you need to specify when inserting a block is the following:

- Block name
- Insertion point
- *X, Y,* and *Z* scale
- Rotation angle

In fact, besides the standard object properties such as layer, color, and linetype discussed later, this constitutes the majority of the information that is stored with the block reference. This is evident when you list a block reference using the AutoCAD **LIST** command:

```
BLOCK REFERENCE Layer: "0"
Space: Model space
Handle = a4
Block Name: "WINTAG-A"
at point, X=   0.0000  Y=   0.0000  Z=   0.0000
X scale factor: 1.0000
Y scale factor: 1.0000
rotation angle: 0
Z scale factor: 1.0000
InsUnits: Inches
Unit conversion: 1.0000
Scale uniformly: No
Allow exploding: Yes
```

Remember that a block reference assumes the object properties that are current when the block is inserted just like any other AutoCAD object. However, how the object properties affect the appearance of the block reference is dependent on how the block was created as explained earlier in the section, "Creating Blocks."

The INSERT Command

The **INSERT** command allows you to insert a block reference by specifying the block name, insertion point, scale, and rotation angle via the **Insert** dialog box shown in Figure 16-7.

The **Name:** list box lists the names of all the blocks defined in a drawing that can be inserted.

The **Browse...** button displays the standard **Select Drawing File** dialog box so you can select a block or drawing file to insert.

The **Path:** label specifies the path to the block if you select an external drawing file using the **Browse...** button above.

The **Locate using Geographic Data** check box will insert the block using geographic data as the reference. This option is enabled only if both the block and the current drawing have geographic data.

The **Preview** window displays a preview of the specified block to insert. A lightning bolt icon in the lower-right corner of the preview indicates that the block is dynamic.

The **Insertion point** area allows you to specify the insertion point for the block. You can either pick a point in the drawing after you select **OK** (default), or you can specify the coordinate position

Insert Block	
Ribbon & Panel:	Insert|Block
	Insert
Draw Toolbar:	
Menu:	Insert|Block...
Command Line:	INSERT
Command Alias:	I

Figure 16-7   The **Insert** dialog box

in the **X:, Y:,** and **Z:** text boxes. The **Specify On-screen** check box toggles between the two methods.

The **Scale** area allows you to specify the *X, Y,* and *Z* scale factors for the inserted block. You can either enter the scale factors in the **X:, Y:,** and **Z:** text boxes (default), or you can enter the scale factors after you select **OK**. The **Specify On-screen** check box toggles between the two methods.

The **Uniform Scale** check box forces a single scale value for the *X-, Y-,* and *Z*-axes. When the **Uniform Scale** check box is selected, the *Y* and *Z* scales default to the value specified for *X*.

The **Rotation** area allows you to specify the rotation angle for the inserted block in the current UCS. You can either enter the rotation angle in the **Angle:** text box (default), or you can enter the rotation angle after you select **OK**. The **Specify On-screen** check box toggles between the two methods.

> **Note:**
> It is possible to insert an external drawing file (DWG) file from anywhere on your computer or network. Inserting external drawing files is explained in detail later in this chapter.

The **Block Unit** area displays information about the block units. The **Unit:** label indicates the insert units for the block. The **Factor:** displays the unit scale factor, which is calculated based on the insert units of the block and the drawing units. Neither of these settings can be changed in the **Insert** dialog box.

The **Explode** check box explodes the block immediately after it is inserted. It is possible to specify a uniform scale factor only when the **Explode** check box is selected.

After all the desired settings have been specified, select **OK** to insert the block as shown in Figure 16-8.

Figure 16-8 shows a block being inserted using the default settings, which prompt you to *Specify insertion point or ↓* on-screen during the insertion process.

If the **Specify On-screen** check box is selected for the **Scale** settings, AutoCAD prompts you to *Enter X scale factor, specify opposite corner, or ↓* so that you can either enter the desired scale for the *X* axis at the keyboard or pick a corner point in your drawing that dynamically defines both the *X* and *Y* scales. The default scale factor is always **1**.

If you enter an *X* scale and press **<Enter ↲>**, AutoCAD then prompts you to *Enter Y scale factor <use X scale factor>: ↓*. You can either press **<Enter ↲>** so that the *X* and *Y* scales are equal, or you can enter a different scale factor to create a nonuniformly scaled block. Nonuniformly scaled blocks are discussed in the next section.

If the **Specify On-screen** check box is selected for the **Rotation** settings, AutoCAD prompts you to *Specify rotation angle <0>:* so that you can either enter the desired rotation angle at the

Figure 16-8   Inserting a block

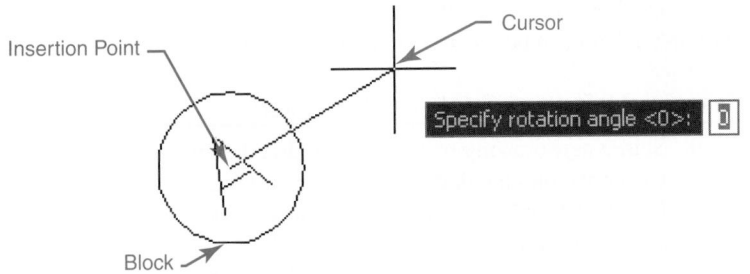

Insertion Point

Figure 16-9 Inserting a block and specifying the rotation angle on-screen

keyboard or pick a point in your drawing that dynamically defines the angle using the insertion point as the angle base point as shown in Figure 16-9.

Exercise 16-2: Inserting Blocks

1. Continue from Exercise 16-1.
2. Set the current layer to **A-Glaze-Iden** via the **Layers** drop-down list.
3. Set the current color to **Blue** via the **Properties** panel on the **Home** ribbon.
4. Use the **INSERT** command to insert the **WINTAG-A**, **WINTAG-B**, and **WINTAG-C** blocks anywhere in the drawing so that you can see all three block references in the drawing window.
5. Compare how the object properties are different for each block reference.
6. Turn on the **Automatically add scales to annotative objects when the annotation scale changes** button on the right side of the Status Bar.
7. Change the **Annotation Scale** to **12**.
8. Insert one of the WINTAG blocks.
9. Change the **Annotation Scale** to **2:1**.
10. Insert another WINTAG block.
11. Save the drawing as **EX16-2**.

Nonuniformly Scaled Unit Blocks

If the **Scale uniformly** check box was not selected when the block was created, you can specify different *X, Y,* and *Z* scale factors when a block is inserted so that the block can be scaled along a single axis. In fact, this is a technique that is used to create what are known as ***unit blocks***.

Unit blocks can be scaled along one axis so that one block definition can serve multiple purposes. A classic example is a structural lumber section, which is typically represented by a nominally sized rectangle with a cross through it. See Figure 16-10. Creating the lumber section as a

unit block: A block or symbol drawn within a 1 × 1 unit square that is inserted in the drawing with different *X* and *Y* scales to achieve different final sizes

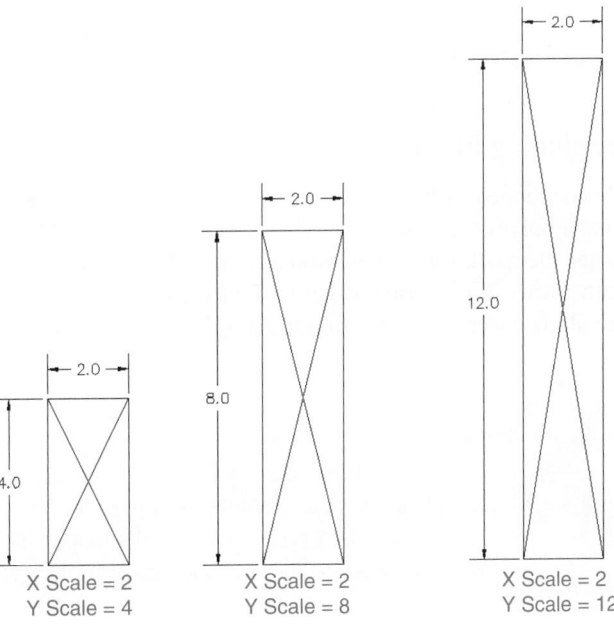

Figure 16-10 Structural lumber section inserted as a unit block with nonuniform scales

unit block allows you to specify different *X* and *Y* scales when the block is inserted so that different lumber sizes can be created as shown in Figure 16-10.

Exercise 16-3: Nonuniformly Scaled Unit Blocks

1. Start a new drawing using the acad.dwt drawing template.
2. Create the unit block drawing shown in Figure 16-11.
3. Use the **BLOCK** command to create a block named **STUD** that consists of the line work created in step 2 with a base point at the lower left-hand corner.
4. Start the **INSERT** command to display the **Insert** dialog box.
5. Select **STUD** from the **Name:** list box.
6. Make sure the **Specify On-screen** check box is unselected in the **Scale:** area.
7. Set the **X:** scale to **2.0**.
8. Set the **Y:** scale to **4.0**.
9. Select **OK** to insert the 2 × 4 stud anywhere in your drawing.
10. Start the **INSERT** command to display the **Insert** dialog box.
11. Select **STUD** from the **Name:** list box if not selected.
12. Set the **X:** scale to **2.0**.
13. Set the **Y:** scale to **8.0**.
14. Select **OK** to insert the 2 × 8 stud anywhere in your drawing.
15. Start the **INSERT** command to display the **Insert** dialog box.
16. Select **STUD** from the **Name:** list box if not selected.
17. Set the **X:** scale to **2.0**.
18. Set the **Y:** scale to **12.0**.
19. Select **OK** to insert the 2 × 12 stud anywhere in your drawing.
20. Your drawing should look like Figure 16-10.
21. Save the drawing as **EX16-3**.

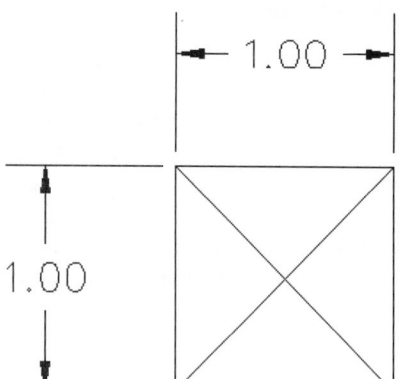

Figure 16-11   1 × 1 unit block

Exploding Blocks

As mentioned earlier in the Introduction, a block reference is considered a complex object just like a polyline, boundary hatch, or dimension. If the **Allow exploding** check box was selected when the block was created, you can explode a block back into its original individual subobjects either after it is inserted using the **EXPLODE** command or when it is inserted by selecting the **Explode** check box in the **Insert** dialog box shown in Figure 16-7.

TIP   Typically, you do not want to explode blocks because you lose all the advantages of using them in the first place. Not only can you no longer automatically update an exploded block using the techniques explained later in this chapter, but you also increase the size of the drawing because each subobject is added as a new object and is no longer simply a reference.

Inserting a Drawing File as a Block

It is possible, and actually quite common, to insert an entire drawing file (DWG) as a block. When you insert a drawing file, a block definition with the same name as the file is automatically created using all the information in the drawing file.

There are a couple of ways to insert a drawing file as a block. To insert a drawing file via the **Insert** dialog box explained earlier, select the **Browse** button shown in Figure 16-7 to display the **Select Drawing File** dialog box shown in Figure 16-12.

Note:
When you insert a drawing file as a block, only model space information is included. Objects located in paper space are ignored.

Select File to Insert

Figure 16-12   Selecting a drawing file to insert as a block

Find the file you want to insert and select the **Open** button. A block definition with the same name as the drawing file is added to the **Name** list box, and it becomes the current block to insert as shown in Figure 16-13.

Once a drawing has been selected and it has been made a block definition, the exact same settings can be specified. You can select **OK** to insert the block.

Note:
When you insert a drawing file, all the nongraphical named information defined in the drawing such as layers, linetypes, text styles, dimension styles, etc., comes along for the ride so that any named information defined in the original drawing becomes part of the current drawing.

TIP   By default, the insertion base point for a drawing file inserted as a block is the coordinate location 0,0,0 in the original drawing file. You can change the insertion base point by opening the drawing file and using the **BASE** command to set it to another location. Don't forget to save the drawing.

Drawing File Added as Block

Figure 16-13 New block definition added to list

Cursor · · · · · Block

Figure 16-14 Inserting drawing files as blocks

Exercise 16-4: Inserting a Drawing File as a Block

1. Start a new drawing using the acad.dwt drawing template.
2. Start the **INSERT** command to display the **Insert** dialog box.
3. Select the **Browse...** button to display the **Select Drawing File** dialog box and locate the **EX16-4.DWG** drawing file in the student data files.
4. Select the **EX16-4.DWG** file and select the **Open** button to return to the **Insert** dialog box.
5. Select **OK** to insert the block anywhere in the drawing as shown in Figure 16-14.
6. Save the drawing as **EX16-4**.

To access student data files, go to
www.pearsondesigncentral.com.

Using Windows Explorer to Insert a Drawing File

You can use Windows® Explorer to drag-and-drop a drawing file directly into the current drawing. You can start Windows Explorer a number of ways including double-clicking on the **My Computer** icon on the Windows desktop, by right-clicking on the Windows **Start** button and selecting **Explore** from the menu, or even by typing the **EXPLORE** command in AutoCAD.

In order to use drag-and-drop techniques, you must be able to have both AutoCAD and Explorer visible on your computer at the same time, as shown in Figure 16-15.

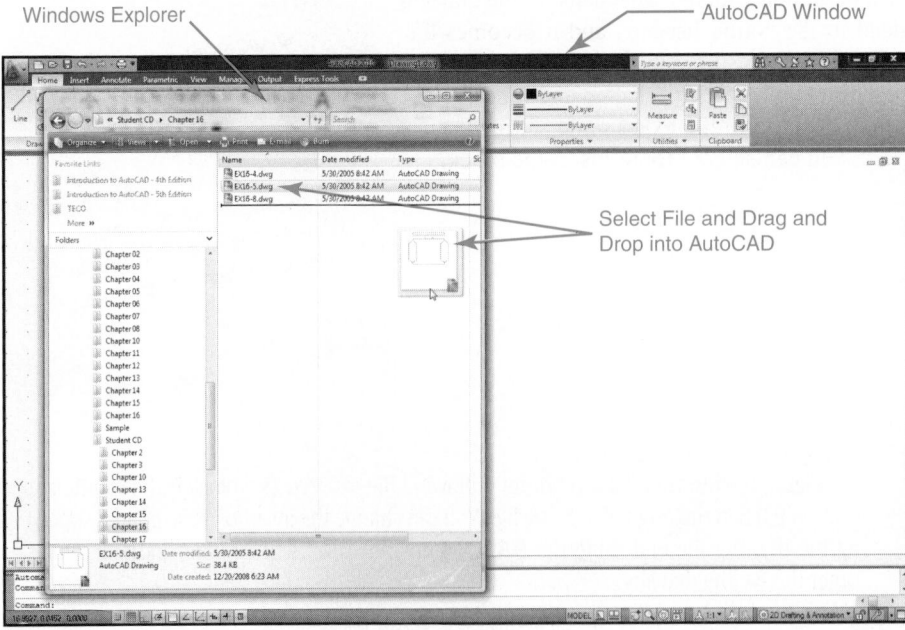

Windows Explorer   AutoCAD Window

Select File and Drag and Drop into AutoCAD

Figure 16-15 Using Windows Explorer to insert files

If you select a file with the *left* mouse button and drag-and-drop it into your drawing, the same insertion point, scale factor, and rotation angle command prompts are displayed as if the **Specify On-screen** check boxes were selected in the **Insert** dialog box described earlier.

If you select a file with the *right* mouse button and drag-and-drop it into your drawing, the shortcut menu shown in Figure 16-16 is displayed.

Using the shortcut menu, you can elect to do one of the following:

> **Note:**
> It is possible to drag-and-drop only one drawing file at a time.

Figure 16-16   Right-click drag-and-drop shortcut menu

- **Insert Here**   Inserts the file as a block the same as above
- **Open**   Opens the drawing file in a new window
- **Create Xref**   Attaches the drawing as an xref
- **Create Hyperlink Here**   Creates a hyperlink to the drawing on the object you select
- **Cancel**   Cancels drag-and-drop operation

> **FOR MORE DETAILS**   See Chapter 17 for more details about using xrefs (external references).

Exercise 16-5: Using Windows Explorer to Insert a Drawing File

1. Start a new drawing using the acad.dwt drawing template.
2. Start Windows Explorer using one of the techniques explained above.
3. Set up your computer display so that the AutoCAD drawing window and Windows Explorer window are both visible, similar to the display shown in Figure 16-15.
4. In Windows Explorer, locate the **EX16-5.DWG** drawing file in the student data files.
5. Select the **EX16-5.DWG** drawing file with your *left* mouse button and drag-and-drop it into the current drawing.
6. Select the **EX16-5.DWG** drawing file with your *right* mouse button and drag-and-drop it into the current drawing.
7. Select **Insert Here** from the shortcut menu.
8. Select an insertion point in the drawing and press **<Enter ↵>** three times to accept the defaults for the *X* scale (1), *Y* scale (1), and rotation angle (0).
9. Save the drawing as **EX16-5**.

To access student data files, go to www.pearsondesigncentral.com.

EXPORTING BLOCKS

As mentioned earlier in the "Creating Blocks" section, by default, a block definition is stored *only* in the drawing it is created. In order to use the block in another drawing, you must first export it to a drawing file (DWG). You can then insert it using the techniques explained above.

The WBLOCK Command

The **WBLOCK** command, short for "write block," writes a block definition to an external drawing file (DWG) with the file name and location you specify using any of the following methods:

- Write an existing block definition that is already defined internally in a drawing
- Create a new block definition *and* write the block to an external drawing file
- Create a new block definition using *all* the information in the drawing and write the block to an external drawing file

Starting the **WBLOCK** command displays the **Write Block** dialog box shown in Figure 16-17. The **Source** area is the main area of the dialog box used to specify how to create the block.

Write Block	
Ribbon & Panel:	None
Toolbar:	None
Menu:	None
Command Line:	WBLOCK
Command Alias:	W

Figure 16-17   The **Write Block** dialog box

The **Block** option allows you to select a block that has already been defined in the drawing from the list on the right. This option and the list are disabled if there are no blocks defined in the drawing. The **Entire drawing** option creates a block out of the entire drawing and writes it out to a file.

> Using **WBLOCK** to create a block out of the entire drawing and write it to a file is an old trick used to quickly purge a drawing of all its unreferenced drawing information such as layers, linetypes, text styles, dimension styles, other blocks, and so on, so that the file size is reduced.

The **Objects** option allows you to create a new block on the fly and write it out to an external file using the exact same techniques as the **BLOCK** command explained earlier in the chapter. See the earlier section, "Creating Blocks," for complete, detailed information about creating a block from scratch.

The **Base point** area allows you to specify a base point for the block. The default value is 0,0,0.

The **Select objects** button closes the **Write Block** dialog box temporarily so you can select objects in the drawing as shown earlier in Figure 16-4. The **QuickSelect** button closes the **Write Block** dialog box temporarily and displays the **Quick Select** dialog box shown earlier in Figure 16-5 so you can select objects by filtering on one or more object properties.

The other three options in the **Objects** area directly below the **Select objects** button determine what happens to the selected objects after the block is created:

- **Retain (default)**   Retains the original selected objects in the drawing without doing anything

- **Convert to block**   Converts the selected objects to a block reference "in-place"

- **Delete from drawing**   Deletes all the selected objects after the block is created so that they no longer exist

The **Destination** area is where you specify the file name and location and the units of measurement to be used when the block is inserted.

The **File name and path**: text box allows you to enter the file name and path where the block will be saved.

Selecting the **[...]** button displays the standard **Browse for Drawing File** dialog box so you can select a file or specify another drive and folder location. The selected file and location are displayed in the **File name and path**: text box above when you exit the dialog box by selecting the **Save** button.

The **Insert units**: list box lists the different possible insertion units for the block. If you insert a block that is created with different block drawing units from the insertion scale units currently set for the drawing, the block is automatically scaled up or down according to the scale factor equivalent of the ratio between the different unit systems.

Exercise 16-6: Using the WBLOCK Command to Export a Block

1. Continue from Exercise 16-1.
2. Start the **WBLOCK** command to display the **Write Block** dialog box.
3. Select the **Block** option in the **Source** area at the top of the dialog box.
4. Select the **WINTAG-A** block from the **Block** list box.
5. Set the **File name and path**: setting in the **Destination** area to a folder location of your choice using the **WINTAG-A.DWG** file name and select **OK** to export the block.
6. Draw a "D" window tag similar to the others with the same circle diameter and text height somewhere in the drawing.
7. Start the **WBLOCK** command to display the **Write Block** dialog box again.
8. Select the **Objects** option in the **Source** area at the top of the dialog box.
9. Select the **Pick point** button in the **Base point** area.
10. Select the center point of the "D" window tag circle you just created using the **Center** Object Snap.
11. Select the **Select objects** button in the **Objects** area.
12. Select the "D" window tag circle and text and press **<Enter ⏎>** to return to the **Write Block** dialog box.
13. Set the **File name and path**: setting in the **Destination** area to a folder location of your choice with the file name **WINTAG-D.DWG** and select **OK** to export the block.
14. Save the drawing as **EX16-6**.

BLOCK ATTRIBUTES

As explained in the Introduction, an attribute is a text-like object included in a block definition that is used to store alphanumeric information. It can be either updated dynamically when a block is inserted or updated manually after the block is inserted later by selecting the block. Updated attribute data can then be used to automatically create tables or exported to external files using the **Data Extraction** wizard explained later in this chapter.

The key to an attribute is its tag, which is used to store and retrieve the attribute data. A tag is an attribute's unique identifier, similar to a field in a database or a row/column in a spreadsheet. The tag allows you to specify which attributes to extract when you use the **Data Extraction** wizard. Tags are always all uppercase and cannot include any spaces or special characters. They are typically given a descriptive name indicating the type of data they are storing. For example, the attribute tags for a window tag block that contains information about the window type, width, height, and manufacturer might be defined as shown in Figure 16-18.

Figure 16-18 shows what the window tag block looks like prior to being defined. Attributes that are defined to be invisible are not turned off until the block is defined and inserted as a block reference in the drawing as shown later in Figure 16-21.

Note:
Attributes can be set to be invisible so that you can attach nongraphical information to a block that can be updated and extracted even though you can't see it in the drawing and it doesn't plot. This and other special attribute properties are discussed later in the section "Creating Attributes."

Figure 16-18 Window tag block with attribute tags—before block definition

The other key parts of an attribute definition are its prompt and default value. The prompt is what you see when you insert the block so you know what type of information to enter. The default value is what the attribute is automatically set to if no information is entered. The attribute tag, prompt, and default value for the window tag block's manufacturer attribute are shown in Figure 16-19.

Figure 16-19 Manufacturer attribute tag, prompt, and default value

After the block is defined and you insert it, you are automatically prompted to enter the attribute values either individually at the command prompt or en masse via the **Edit Attributes** dialog box shown in Figure 16-20.

Figure 16-20 The **Attributes** dialog box

After the attribute values have been entered either via the **Edit Attributes** dialog box or at the command prompt, a block reference is created as shown in Figure 16-21.

Notice that the attributes that were defined as invisible are now no longer displayed, although it is possible to turn them on if necessary.

It is possible to update the attributes after the block is inserted using a number of different approaches, all of which are explained later in the section "Updating and Editing Attributes." First, though, we need to create a block with some attributes.

> **Note:**
> Attribute display is controlled via the **Attributes** panel on the **Insert** ribbon. The **Display All** setting turns all invisible attributes on and the **Hide All** setting turns off all attributes. The **Retain Display** setting displays attributes as they were originally defined. You can also use the **ATTDISP** command to control the same settings.

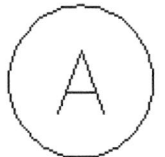

Figure 16-21 The inserted block reference with attributes

CREATING ATTRIBUTES

When working with attributes, you follow the same steps you would for creating a standard block. First you draw any line work and/or text that will make up the block, and then you can define the attributes. Attributes share many of the same properties as text, including the ability to assign text styles and fonts. When you add an attribute, you must also specify a justification and insertion point, similar to the manner in which you add single-line text.

Just like other AutoCAD objects, attributes also assume the current object properties such as layer, color, and linetype. Some organizations create attributes on their own individual layer so you can further control their visibility and appearance.

FOR MORE DETAILS	See Chapter 11 for more details about the different text properties and effects. See Chapter 6 for more details about managing object properties.

Attribute Definition

The **ATTDEF** command creates an attribute definition via the **Attribute Definition** dialog box shown in Figure 16-22.

The **Mode** area is where you control the visibility and other attribute options that are set when you insert the block. The **Mode** options are as follows:

- **Invisible** Specifies that attribute values are not displayed or printed when you insert the block
- **Constant** Makes attribute a constant value so that it cannot be updated either when it is inserted or anytime later
- **Verify** Has you verify that the attribute value is correct when you insert the block by prompting you for the attribute information twice
- **Preset** Sets the attribute to its default value and does not prompt you for the attribute information, although it is still possible to update the attribute after it is inserted using the techniques explained in the following section
- **Lock Position** Locks the position of the attribute definition in the block so that it cannot be moved after the block is inserted using grips

Define Attributes	
Ribbon & Panel:	Insert| Attributes Define Attributes
Toolbar:	None
Menu:	Draw| Block| Define Attributes…
Command Line:	ATTDEF
Command Alias:	ATT

Figure 16-22   The
Attribute Definition
dialog box

- **Multiple lines**   Allows you to create multiple line attributes by selecting the [**…**] button next to the **Default** value to display a stripped-down version of the multiline text editor introduced in Chapter 11 and add multiple lines of text

The **Attribute** area is where you define the attribute tag, prompt, and default value:

Note:
The **Verify** and **Preset** attribute modes work only when you enter attributes at the command prompt. They have no effect whenever the **Edit Attributes** dialog box is used to update attribute information.

- **Tag**   The unique alphanumeric key used to identify the attribute. Enter a descriptive name using any combination of characters except spaces. Lowercase letters are automatically changed to uppercase. Attribute tags can contain up to 256 characters
- **Prompt**   The prompt that is displayed either in the **Edit Attributes** dialog box or at the command prompt when you insert the block. If the prompt field is left blank, the attribute tag is used as a prompt. The **Prompt** option is disabled if you are defining an attribute with the **Constant** mode selected
- **Default**   Specifies the default attribute value used

The **Insert Field** button displays the **Field** dialog box so you can insert a field into the attribute default value.

> **FOR MORE DETAILS**   See Chapter 11 for more details about using about text fields.

The **Insertion Point** area specifies the location for the attribute in the drawing. You can enter coordinate values via the keyboard, or if you select the **Specify On-screen** check box, you can pick a point in your drawing after you select **OK** and the dialog box closes.

The **Text Settings** area sets the justification, text style, height, and rotation of the attribute text:

- **Justification**   Allows you to set the attribute justification from a list of standard single-line text justification options

- **Text style**   Allows you to assign a text style from a list of text styles defined in the current drawing
- **Annotative**   Allows you to make the attribute **Annotative** so that it scales up and down automaticaly based on the current **Annotation Scale**
- **Text height**   Allows you to specify the height of the attribute text. You can enter a height value via the keyboard, or select the **Text height** button to define the height by picking points with your mouse. The **Text height** option is disabled if a text style with a height greater than 0.0 is selected or if the justification is set to **Align**
- **Rotation**   Allows you to specify the rotation angle of the attribute text. You can enter a value via that keyboard or select the **Rotation** button to define the rotation angle by picking points with your mouse. The **Rotation** option is disabled if the justification is set to **Align** or **Fit**

FOR MORE DETAILS   See Chapter 11 for more details about the different text options

---

The **Align below previous attribute definition** check box allows you to automatically locate an attribute tag directly below the previously defined attribute using all of the same text options. If selected, both the **Insertion Point** and **Text Settings** areas of the dialog box are disabled. This option is disabled if you have not previously created an attribute definition.

Selecting **OK** closes the dialog box, and AutoCAD prompts you to *Specify start point:* so you can locate the attribute in the drawing. If the **Align below previous attribute definition** check box is selected, the attribute is automatically located directly below the last attribute that was defined.

TIP   Although you can change the prompt order of the attributes after a block is defined, it is best to select the attributes individually in the order you want to be prompted. If you select all the attributes using any of the window selection methods, the ordering of the attributes can be random.

Exercise 16-7: Creating a Block with Attributes

1. Start a new drawing using the acad.dwt drawing template.
2. Create the window tag drawing shown in Figure 16-23 on layer **0** at **0,0,0** with the following attributes and settings:

Tag	Prompt	Default	Mode
TAG	Enter window tag:	A	Visible
TYPE	Enter window type:	Fixed	Invisible
WIDTH	Enter window width:	4'-0"	Invisible/Verify
HEIGHT	Enter window height:	4'-0"	Invisible/Verify
MANUFACTURER	Enter window manufacturer:	ACME Glass Co.	Invisible/Preset

3. Save the drawing as **EX16-7**.

Figure 16-23 Window tag block
definition with attributes

Updating and Editing Attributes

By default, when you insert a block with attributes, you automatically get prompted to update the attribute values individually at the command prompt in the order in which the attributes were created. The alternate **Edit Attributes** dialog box can be displayed during the insertion process by setting the **ATTDIA** system variable to **1** (on). Setting **ATTDIA** to **0** (off) turns the **Edit Attributes** dialog box off.

> **TIP** It is possible to turn attribute prompts off temporarily when you are inserting a block by setting the **ATTREQ** system variable to **0** (off). When **ATTREQ = 0**, an attributed block is inserted as though there are no attributes attached. The attributes can still be updated after the block is inserted using the techniques explained below. Set **ATTREQ** to **1** (on) to turn attribute prompts back on.

The easiest way to update attributes after they are inserted is to simply double-click on the attributed block. Double-clicking on a block with attributes displays the **Enhanced Attribute Editor** dialog box discussed in the next section so that you can update attribute values, as well as change attribute text options and attribute object properties.

The **Block Attribute Manager** discussed a little later in this section allows you to edit block attribute definitions on a global scale so that you can change the attribute modes, the attribute prompt order, and even remove attributes, so that *all* existing and future block references in the drawing are updated.

Note: Changes made to attribute properties using the **Enhanced Attribute Editor** affect only the individually selected block reference.

> **TIP** It is possible to use grips to modify attributes so that you can perform basic editing tasks such as moving, rotating, and scaling attributes. Any changes affect the whole block if the **Lock position** check box was selected when the block was created.

FOR MORE DETAILS   See Chapter 7 for more details about using grips.

Editing Attributes Individually

The **EATTEDIT** command allows you to update attributes via the **Enhanced Attribute Editor** dialog box so that you can do the following:

- Update attribute values
- Control attribute text options (text style, height, etc.)
- Manage attribute object properties (layer, color, linetype, etc.)

After starting the **EATTEDIT** command, AutoCAD prompts you to *Select a block:*. Select the block to update and press **<Enter ↵>** to display the **Enhanced Attribute Editor** dialog box shown in Figure 16-24.

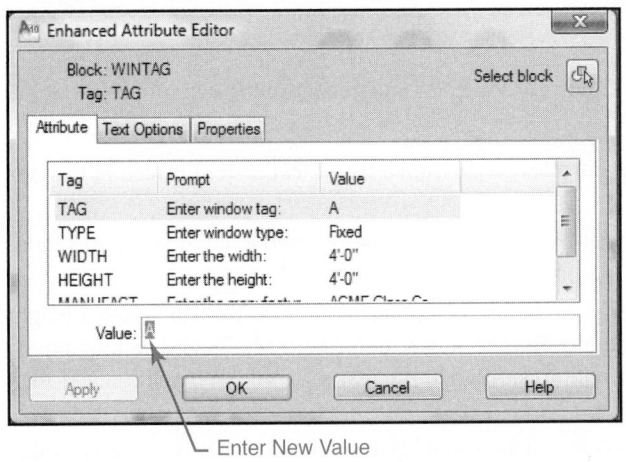

Figure 16-24   The **Enhanced Attribute Editor** dialog box— **Attribute** tab

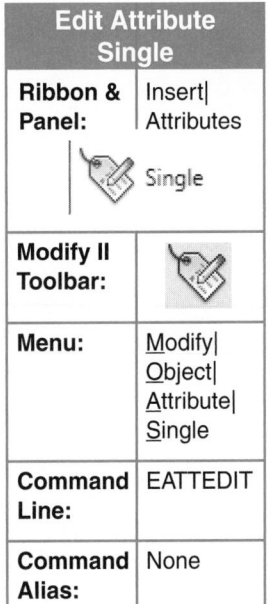

Edit Attribute Single	
Ribbon & Panel:	Insert| Attributes
	Single
Modify II Toolbar:	
Menu:	Modify| Object| Attribute| Single
Command Line:	EATTEDIT
Command Alias:	None

The name of the selected block along with the current attribute tag is displayed at the top left of the dialog box. The **Select block** button on the right temporarily closes the dialog box so you can select another block to update.

The **Attribute** tab is the default tab shown in Figure 16-24 that allows you to update attribute values. All the block's attribute tags and their corresponding prompts and values are displayed in a tabulated list that you can navigate by selecting an attribute with your mouse or by pressing **<Enter ↵>** while the **Value:** text box below is selected. Pressing **<Enter ↵>** while the **Value:** text box is current cycles through all the block attributes in the list.

The **Value:** text box displays the current value assigned to the attribute highlighted in the list box above. Enter a new value and press **<Enter ↵>** to update the attribute and proceed to the next attribute in the list.

Note:
If you modify a block and then select another block before saving the changes, you are prompted to save the changes first. To save changes and update the selected block, select the **Apply** button at the bottom of the dialog box.

TIP You can insert a field in a value by right-clicking and selecting **Insert Field...** on the shortcut menu to display the **Field** dialog box.

If a multiline attribute is selected, the **[...]** button is displayed to the right of the **Value:** text box so you can select it to display the stripped-down multiline text editor and edit multiline attribute values.

Figure 16-25   The **Enhanced Attribute Editor** dialog box—**Text Options** tab

The **Text Options** tab shown in Figure 16-25 allows you to control the text properties of the currently selected attribute:

- **Text Style**   Allows you to assign a text style from a list of text styles defined in the current drawing
- **Justification**   Allows you to set the attribute justification from a list of standard single-line text justification options
- **Height**   Allows you to specify the height of the attribute text. You can enter a height value via the keyboard or select the **Height** button to define the height by picking points with your mouse. The **Height** option is disabled if a text style with a height greater than 0.0 is selected or if the justification is set to **Align**
- **Rotation**   Allows you to specify the rotation angle of the attribute text. You can enter a value via the keyboard or select the **Rotation** button to define the rotation angle by picking points with your mouse. The **Rotation** option is disabled if the justification is set to **Align** or **Fit**
- **Backwards**   Specifies whether or not the attribute text is displayed backwards
- **Upside down**   Specifies whether or not the attribute text is displayed upside down
- **Width Factor**   Sets the character spacing for the attribute text. Entering a value less than 1.0 condenses the text. Entering a value greater than 1.0 expands it
- **Oblique Angle**   Specifies the angle that the attribute text is slanted
- **Annotative**   Specifies if annotation scaling is on or off

FOR MORE DETAILS   See Chapter 11 for more details about the different text properties and effects.

The **Properties** tab shown in Figure 16-26 allows you to control the general object properties of the currently selected attribute:

- **Layer**   Specifies the attribute layer
- **Linetype**   Specifies the attribute linetype
- **Color**   Specifies the attribute color
- **Lineweight**   Specifies the attribute lineweight
- **Plot style**   Specifies the attribute plot style

When you are done making changes or updates, you can either select **OK** to exit the dialog box and update the block, or you can select **Apply** to update the block and keep the **Enhanced Attribute Editor** open so you can make more changes.

Note: If the current drawing uses color-dependent plot styles, the **Plot style** list is disabled.

Figure 16-26   The **Enhanced Attribute Editor** dialog box— **Properties** tab

Editing Attributes Globally

The **-ATTEDIT** command allows you to quickly update attribute values globally throughout an entire drawing at the same time.

The **-ATTEDIT** command is rather archaic. In fact, the **-ATTEDIT** command is actually just the old command line version of the **ATTEDIT** dialog box driven command. It may be an old, clunky command, but it is the only way to update more than one attribute at a time in a drawing so that you don't have to select and update each block individually.

After starting the **-ATTEDIT** command, AutoCAD prompts: *Edit attributes one at a time?* ↙. Enter **N** or **No** **<Enter ↙>** to update attributes globally. AutoCAD then prompts: *Edit only attributes visible on screen?* ↙ Typically, you should enter **No** **<Enter ↙>** to ensure all attributes in the drawing are updated accordingly and not just those shown in the drawing window.

AutoCAD then prompts you for the block name, attribute tag, and attribute value to be found. The default asterisk (*) value represents a wildcard, meaning that all blocks that match that category will be processed. If you know the block name, attribute tag, or attribute value for the block you want to update, you can enter the information to limit the number of blocks that are processed. Pressing **<Enter ↙>** in response to all these prompts forces AutoCAD to process all the attributed blocks in the drawing.

AutoCAD then requests the original value of the attribute text value to change by prompting *Enter string to change:* so you can enter the current attribute value. You are then prompted for a new attribute value *Enter new string:* so you can enter a new value. Immediately after you press **<Enter ↙>**, AutoCAD searches the drawing for all the attributes with a value of the text to change and updates the attribute with the new value as shown in Figure 16-27.

Edit Attributes Multiple	
Ribbon & Panel:	Insert| Attributes Multiple
Toolbar:	None
Menu:	Modify| Object| Attribute| Global
Command Line:	-ATTEDIT
Command Alias:	-ATE

Figure 16-27   Updating attributes globally in a drawing

<table>
<tr><td colspan="2">Block Attribute Manager</td></tr>
<tr><td>Ribbon & Panel:</td><td>Insert| Attributes</td></tr>
<tr><td colspan="2">Manage</td></tr>
<tr><td>Modify II Toolbar:</td><td></td></tr>
<tr><td>Menu:</td><td>Modify| Object| Attribute| Block Attribute Manager</td></tr>
<tr><td>Command Line:</td><td>BATTMAN</td></tr>
<tr><td>Command Alias:</td><td>None</td></tr>
</table>

Managing Attributes

The **BATTMAN** command allows you to update one or more block attribute definitions via the **Block Attribute Manager** dialog box so that you can do the following:

- Edit attribute definitions so that you can change the tag, prompt, default, and even the modes (invisible, constant, verify, preset)
- Control attribute definition text options (text style, height, etc.)
- Manage attribute definition object properties (layer, color, linetype, etc.)
- Change the attribute prompt order
- Remove attribute definitions

Changes made with the **Block Attribute Manager** update the block definition so that all future block insertions reflect the changes. It is also possible to synchronize the changes with blocks that have already been inserted.

Starting the **BATTMAN** command displays the **Block Attribute Manager** dialog box shown in Figure 16-28.

The **Select block** button allows you to choose a block definition to edit by selecting a corresponding block reference in the current drawing. Selecting the **Select block** button temporarily closes the **Block Attribute Manager** dialog box and prompts you to *Select a block:*. Select the block to update, and the dialog box is redisplayed.

The **Block:** list box allows you to select the block from the list of blocks currently defined in the drawing.

The tag, prompt, default, and mode properties of all the attributes defined for the selected block are displayed in the list box in the middle of the dialog box. The number of block references found in the drawing and whether or not they are located in the current layout are displayed directly below the list box.

The **Settings...** button at the bottom of the dialog box allows you to control what information is displayed in the attribute list box. Selecting the **Settings...** button displays the **Block Attribute Settings** dialog box shown in Figure 16-29.

Note:
If you modify a block and then select another block before saving the changes, you are prompted to save the changes first. To save changes and update the selected block, select the **Apply** button at the bottom of the dialog box.

Figure 16-28   The **Block Attribute Manager** dialog box

Figure 16-29   The **Block Attribute Settings** dialog box

The following options are available:

- The **Display in list** area is where you select which properties you want to display in the attribute list. Selected properties are displayed as an additional column in the list. The **Tag** property is always displayed.

- The **Select All** button selects all of the properties in the **Display in list** area above.

- The **Clear All** button clears all of the properties in the **Display in list** area above.

- The **Emphasize duplicate tags** check box turns duplicate tag emphasis on and off. When the **Emphasize duplicate tags** check box is selected, duplicate tag names are changed to red in the attribute list in the **Block Attribute Manager** dialog box so they can be easily identified.

- The **Apply changes to existing references** check box indicates whether or not to update all the existing block references in the drawing when any changes are made. When the **Apply changes to existing references** check box is selected, all existing and new block references are updated with the new attribute definitions. If it is not selected, only new block references have the new attribute definitions.

- The **OK** button accepts any setting changes, closes the **Block Attribute Settings** dialog box, and returns you to the **Block Attribute Manager** so you can continue to make any changes.

In the **Block Attribute Manager** dialog box, there are several more options:

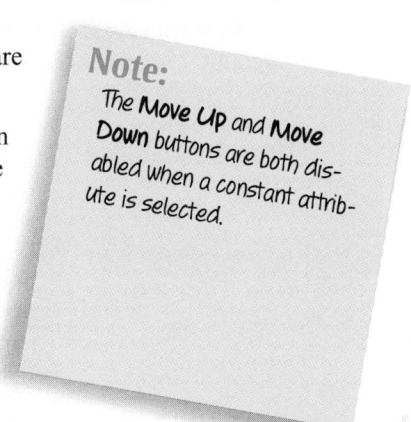

Note:
The **Move Up** and **Move Down** buttons are both disabled when a constant attribute is selected.

- The **Sync** button updates all block references in the drawing with the currently defined attribute properties. Attribute values are not affected by any changes.

- The **Move Up** button moves the selected attribute tag up in the prompt order.

- The **Move Down** button moves the selected attribute tag down in the prompt order.

- The **Edit...** button displays the **Edit Attribute** dialog box shown in Figure 16-30.

Using the **Edit Attribute** dialog box, you can modify the attribute definition properties. The name of the selected block is displayed at the top left of the dialog box. The **Attribute** tab is the default tab shown in Figure 16-30 that allows you to update attribute; definitions; you can control:

- The **Mode** area is where you update the visibility and other attribute options that are set when you insert the block. There are five different options:
    - **Invisible**   Specifies that attribute values are not displayed or printed when you insert the block

Figure 16-30   The **Edit Attribute** dialog box

- **Constant**   Makes attribute a constant value so that it cannot be updated either when it is inserted or anytime later. This option is disabled when using the **Block Attribute Manager**. The **Constant** option can be used only when an attribute is first defined
- **Verify**   Has you verify that the attribute value is correct when you insert the block by prompting you for the attribute information twice
- **Preset**   Sets the attribute to its default value and does not prompt you for the attribute information although it is possible to still update the attribute after it is inserted using the techniques explained in the following section
- **Multiple lines**   Allows you to use multiline attributes

- The **Data** area is where you update the attribute tag, prompt, and default value:
  - **Tag**   The unique alphanumeric key used to identify the attribute. Enter a descriptive name using any combination of characters except spaces. Lowercase letters are automatically changed to uppercase. Attribute tags can be up to 256 characters long
  - **Prompt**   The prompt that is displayed either in the **Edit Attribute** dialog box or at the command prompt when you insert the block. If the prompt field is left blank, the attribute tag is used as a prompt. The **Prompt** option is disabled if you are defining an attribute with the **Constant** mode selected
  - **Default**   Specifies the default attribute value used

Figure 16-31   The **Edit Attribute** dialog box—**Text Options** tab

The **Text Options** tab shown in Figure 16-31 allows you to control the text properties of the currently selected attribute definition:

- **Text Style**   Allows you to assign a text style from a list of text styles defined in the current drawing
- **Justification**   Allows you to set the attribute justification from a list of standard single-line text justification options
- **Height**   Allows you to specify the height of the attribute text. The **Height** option is disabled if a text style with a height greater than 0.0 is selected or if the justification is set to **Align**
- **Rotation**   Allows you to specify the rotation angle of the attribute text. The **Rotation** option is disabled if the justification is set to **Align** or **Fit**
- **Backwards**   Specifies whether or not the attribute text is displayed backwards
- **Upside down**   Specifies whether or not the attribute text is displayed upside down
- **Width Factor**   Sets the character spacing for the attribute text. Entering a value less than 1.0 condenses the text. Entering a value greater than 1.0 expands it
- **Oblique Angle**   Specifies the angle that the attribute text is slanted
- **Annotative**   Specifies whether the attribute scales up and down using the current **Annotation Scale**

FOR MORE DETAILS   See Chapter 11 for more details about the different text properties and effects.

Figure 16-32   The **Edit Attribute** dialog box—**Properties** tab

The **Properties** tab shown in Figure 16-32 allows you to control the general object properties of the currently selected attribute definition:

- **Layer**   Specifies the attribute layer
- **Linetype**   Specifies the attribute linetype
- **Color**   Specifies the attribute color
- **Lineweight**   Specifies the attribute lineweight
- **Plot style**   Specifies the attribute plot style

The **Auto preview changes** check box allows you to immediately display any updates or changes made in the **Edit Attribute** dialog box. If the **Auto preview changes** check box is selected, any changes are immediately displayed.

The **OK** button accepts any setting changes, closes the **Edit Attribute** dialog box, and returns you to the **Block Attribute Manager** so you can continue to make any changes.

The **Remove** button removes the selected attribute from the block definition. The **Remove** button is disabled when a block has only one attribute.

The **Apply** button applies the changes you made to all block references in the drawing but does not close the **Block Attribute Manager**.

Select **OK** to accept any updates and close the **Block Attribute Manager** dialog box.

Note:
The **Auto preview changes** check box is disabled if the **Apply changes to existing references** check box is not selected in the **Settings** dialog box described earlier.

Exercise 16-8: Updating and Editing Attributes

1. Open the building floor plan drawing named **EX16-8** in the student data files.
2. Set layer **A-Glaze-Iden** current.
3. Start the **INSERT** command.
4. Select the **Uniform Scale** check box and set the **X Scale** to **48**.
5. Insert the **EX16-7.DWG** file created in Exercise 16-7 as a block using the **Browse...** button.

To access student data files, go to www.pearsondesigncentral.com.

6. Locate the window tags as shown in Figure 16-33 and update them with the following attribute values:

Attribute	Window Type				
TAG	A	B	C	D	E
TYPE	Fixed	Fixed	Fixed	Casement	Sidelite
WIDTH	4'-0"	3'-6"	2'-6"	2'-0"	1'-0"
HEIGHT	4'-0"	4'-0"	3'-0"	3'-0"	4'-0"
MANUFACTURER	ACME Glass Co.	ACME Glass Co.	ACME Glass Co.	Glassarama, Inc.	Season All Windows

7. Change the window manufacturer from **Glassarama, Inc.** to **SpectorLite** for all "D" type window tags in the drawing using either the **EATTEDIT** or the **ATTEDIT** command.
8. Change the attribute text color to **blue** for the **TAG** attribute for all blocks in the building plan drawing using the **BATTMAN** command.
9. Save the drawing as **EX16-8**.

Insert Ex16-7.DWG Window Tag Block (Typical)

Figure 16-33   Building floor plan with window tags

EXTRACTING ATTRIBUTES

It is possible to extract property information from objects in drawings, including blocks and their attributes, to a formatted table in the current drawing or to an external file so that you can quickly create schedules, parts lists, bills of materials, and other tabular-type information based on the current drawing, or even multiple drawings.

TIP   The extracted data can even be merged and linked with information in a Microsoft Excel® spreadsheet so that is possible to include additional external information.

To make the extraction process as easy as possible, AutoCAD provides the **Data Extraction** wizard, which guides you through a series of preprogrammed steps so that you can provide the following information.

- Data source for information to extract
  - Current drawing
  - Multiple drawings or sheet set
  - Selected objects
- The block names and attribute tags to extract
- Whether to output the attribute information to an AutoCAD table or to output the information to one of the following external file types:
  - Comma-delimited text file (CSV)
  - Microsoft Excel® spreadsheet (XLS)
  - Microsoft Access® database (MDB)
  - Generic text file (TXT)

The **Data Extraction** wizard saves all the settings you specify in each step to an external file (DXE) so that you can use it the next time you use the **Data Extraction** wizard.

Extracting Attribute Data

The **DATAEXTRACTION** command starts the **Data Extraction** wizard to guide you through the steps to extract attribute information.

Starting the **DATAEXTRACTION** command displays the **Data Extraction** wizard on the **Begin** page as shown in Figure 16-34.

Extract Data	
Ribbon & Panel:	Insert| Linking & Extraction
	Extract Data
Modify II Toolbar:	
Menu:	Tools|Data Extraction...
Command Line:	DATAEXTRACTION
Command Alias:	DX

Figure 16-34   The **Data Extraction** wizard—**Begin** page

The **Begin** page allows you to select whether you want to specify new extraction settings from scratch or use settings previously saved in an attribute extraction file (DXE or BLK).

If you select the **Use previous extraction as a template** option, you must select the **[...]** button on the right to select a file using the standard file selection dialog box.

The **Edit an existing data extraction** option allows you to modify an existing data extraction (DXE) file. You must select the **[...]** button on the right to select a file using the standard file selection dialog box.

Select the **Next >** button on the bottom to proceed to the **Define Data Source** page shown in Figure 16-35 or the **Cancel** button to close the wizard.

Note:
If you are creating a new data extraction, you must create a data extraction template file (DXE) before proceeding to the **Define Data Source** page.

The **Define Data Source** page allows you to select one of the following data sources from which to extract the attribute information:

- **Drawings/Sheet Set**   Enables the **Add Folder...** and **Add Drawings...** buttons so you can add a folder or more drawings (DWG) or sheet sets (DST) using the standard file selection dialog box. The current drawing is included by default.
- **Select objects in the current drawing**   Enables the **Select objects** button so you can select one or more blocks in the current drawing.

The **Drawing files and folders** list box lists all the drawing files or sheets in the selected sheet set from which attributes will be extracted.

The **Settings...** button displays the **Data Extraction— Additional Settings** dialog box shown in Figure 16-36.

Note: You can delete one or more files from the list by selecting the file(s) and selecting the **Remove** button on the right.

The **Additional Settings** dialog box allows you specify whether or not to include nested blocks and xrefs, as well as specify which types of blocks should be included in the overall block count.

The **Extraction settings** area allows you to control which blocks are included in the attribute extraction process and whether or not to include xrefs in the block count.

- **Extract objects from blocks**   Includes blocks nested within other blocks
- **Extract objects from xrefs**   Includes blocks located in any attached xrefs
- **Include xrefs in block counts**   Includes attached xrefs as blocks in block counts.

FOR MORE DETAILS   See Chapter 17 for more details about xrefs.

The **Extract from** area provides options for which objects to include in the extraction process.

- **Objects in model space**   Extracts from only block references in model space and ignores any blocks located in paper space layouts
- **All objects in drawing**   Extracts from all block references in the entire drawing (model space and paper space)

The **OK** button accepts any setting changes, closes the **Additional Settings** dialog box, and returns you to the **Data Extraction** wizard so you can continue to the next step.

Select the **Next >** button on the bottom to proceed to the **Select Objects** page shown in Figure 16-37, the **Cancel** button to close the wizard, or the **< Back** button to return to the previous page.

Figure 16-37   The **Data Extraction** wizard—**Select Objects** page

The **Select Objects** page allows you to select the objects and drawing information to be extracted. Just about any AutoCAD object information can be extracted including blocks and non-blocks.

 TIP   It is possible to resize columns with your mouse and reverse the sort order by clicking on the column header. You can also select or unselect all objects via a right-click shortcut menu.

The **Objects** list displays each object by its name in the **Object** column. Blocks are listed by block name, and non-blocks are listed by their object name.

The **Display Name** column allows you to enter an optional alternative name for an object as it will appear in the extracted information. To change a display name, right-click in the **Display Name** column and select **Edit Display Name** from the shortcut menu.

The **Type** column indicates whether the object is a block or non-block.

The **Preview** image displays a preview image of the checked block in the **Objects** list.

You can limit the types of objects displayed in the **Objects** list in the **Display options** area at the bottom.

The **Display all object types** option displays a list of all object types (blocks and non-blocks) in the **Objects** list. It is on by default.

Turning off the **Display all object types** option allows you to toggle between the **Display blocks only** option and the **Display non-blocks only** option so you can further filter the **Objects** list.

The **Display blocks with attributes only** option displays only those blocks that have attributes in the **Objects** list.

The **Display objects currently in-use only** will limit the **Objects** list to objects that exist in the selected drawings.

Select the **Next >** button at the bottom to proceed to the **Select Properties** page shown in Figure 16-38, the **Cancel** button to close the wizard, or the **< Back** button to return to the previous page.

Figure 16-38   The **Data Extraction** wizard—**Select Properties** page

The **Select Properties** page allows you to control the object, block, and drawing properties to extract.

Each row in the **Properties** list displays a property name, display name, and category.

> It is possible to resize columns with your mouse and reverse the sort order by clicking on the column header. You can also select or unselect all properties via a right-click shortcut menu.

The **Property** column displays the properties of all the objects selected on the **Select Objects** page in the previous step. These are the same object properties displayed in the **Properties** palette in AutoCAD.

The **Display Name** column allows you to enter an optional alternative name for a property as it will appear in the extracted information. To change a display name, right-click in the **Display Name** column and select **Edit Display Name** from the shortcut menu.

The **Category** column displays a category for each property. For example, **General** designates ordinary object properties, such as color or layer. **Attribute** designates user-defined attributes. These are the same object categories displayed in the **Properties** palette in AutoCAD.

The **Category filter** check box list allows you to filter the list of properties shown in the **Properties** list based on the category listed in the **Category** column. Only checked categories are displayed.

Select the **Next >** button on the bottom to proceed to the **Refine Data** page shown in Figure 16-39, the **Cancel** button to close the wizard, or the **< Back** button to return to the previous page.

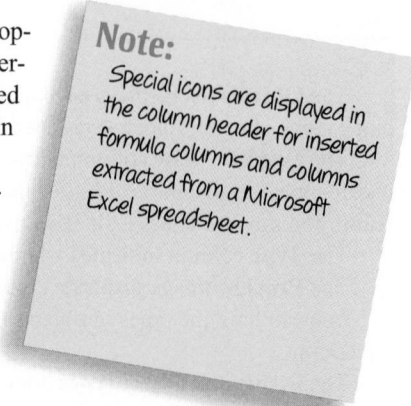

Note:
Special icons are displayed in the column header for inserted formula columns and columns extracted from a Microsoft Excel spreadsheet.

Figure 16-39   The **Data Extraction** wizard—**Refine Data** page

The **Refine Data** page allows you to modify the structure of the data extraction table. You can reorder and sort columns, filter results, add formula columns and footer rows, and even create a link to data in a Microsoft Excel spreadsheet.

The grid in the middle of the dialog box displays properties that were selected in the **Select Properties** page in the previous step in a tabular format. The **Count** and **Name** columns display by default and can be turned off as explained below.

The **Combine identical rows** check box groups identical records by row in the table and updates the **Count** column with the sum total.

The **Show count column** check box toggles the **Count** column on and off in the table display.

The **Show name column** check box toggles the **Name** column on and off in the table display.

The **Link External Data...** button displays the **Link External Data** dialog box, where you can create a link between the extracted drawing data and data in an Excel spreadsheet.

The **Sort Columns Options...** button displays the **Sort Columns** dialog box, where you can sort data across multiple columns.

The **Full Preview...** button displays a full preview of the final output, including linked external data. The preview is for viewing only.

Right-clicking in a column displays the shortcut menu shown in Figure 16-40 that gives you the following options:

Option	Description
Sort Descending	Sorts column data in a descending order
Sort Ascending	Sorts column data in an ascending order
Sort Column Options	Displays the **Sort Columns** dialog box so you can sort data across multiple columns
Rename Column	Allows in-place editing of the selected column name
Hide Column	Hides the selected column
Show Hidden Columns	Displays the hidden column. The cascade menu allows you to **Display All Hidden Columns**
Set Column Data Format	Displays the **Set Cell Format** dialog box so you can set a data type for cells in the selected column

Insert Formula Column	Displays the **Insert Formula Column** dialog box so you can insert a formula into the table to the right of the selected column
Edit Formula Column	Displays the **Edit Formula Column** dialog box. Available only when a formula column is selected.
Remove Formula Column	Removes the selected formula column. Available only when a formula column is selected.
Combine Record Mode	Displays numeric data in the selected column as separate values or collapses identical property rows into one row and displays the sum of all the numeric data in the selected column. This option is available when the **Combine Identical Rows** is checked and the selected column contains numerical data
Show Count Column	Displays a **Count** column that lists the quantity of each property
Show Name Column	Displays a **Name** column that displays the name of each property
Insert Totals Footer	Displays a cascade menu with options for **Sum, Max, Min,** and **Average** formulas. Creates a footer row for the selected column that is placed below all data rows and displays values based on the selected arithmetic function. Available only for columns that have a numeric data type
Sum	Displays a sum of all the values in the selected column in a footer row
Max	Displays the maximum value in the selected column in a footer row
Min	Displays the minimum value in the selected column in a footer row
Average	Displays the average value in the selected column in a footer row
Remove Totals Footer	Removes the **Totals** footer. Available only when a footer row exists
Filter Options	Displays the **Filter Column** dialog box so you can specify filter conditions for the selected column
Reset Filter	Restores the default filter for the selected column
Reset All Filters	Restores default filters for all columns that have filters
Copy to Clipboard	Copies selected data cells to the clipboard

Select the **Next >** button at the bottom to proceed to the **Choose Output** page shown in Figure 16-41, the **Cancel** button to close the wizard, or the **< Back** button to return to the previous page.

The **Choose Output** page allows you to select the type of output to which the data are extracted.

Figure 16-40   The **Data Extraction** wizard—**Refine Data** shortcut menu

Figure 16-41   The **Data Extraction** wizard—**Choose Output** page

The **Insert data extraction table into drawing** check box allows you to extract the attribute information to an AutoCAD table.

The **Output data to external file** check box allows you to export the attribute information to the file type and location you specify. Selecting the **[…]** button displays the standard **Save As** file dialog box so you can select the file type via the **File of type:** list box at the bottom of the dialog box and the folder location to save the file. By default, the file name is the same name as the current drawing file. The three-character file extension is determined by the file type selected. The four file output options are as follows:

- XLS   Microsoft Excel spreadsheet
- MDB   Microsoft Access database
- CSV   Comma-separated file format
- TXT   Tab-separated file format

Select the **Next >** button at the bottom to proceed to either the **Table Style** page shown in Figure 16-42 or the **Finish** page shown in Figure 16-43, the **Cancel** button to close the wizard, or the **< Back** button to return to the previous page.

The **Table Style** page allows you to control the appearance of the table before it is inserted in the drawing.

The **Table style** area at the top allows you to control the table style used for the extracted data. The **Select the table style to use for the inserted table** list box allows you to sel-ect an existing table style. You can also select the **Table Style** button to the right to display the **Table Style** dialog box to modify an existing table style or create a new one.

The **Formatting and structure** area allows you to fine-tune the final table structure and format.

The **Use table in table style for label rows** option creates the data extraction table with a set of top rows that contain label cells and a bottom set of label rows that contain header and footer cells. Extracted data are inserted between the top and bottom label rows.

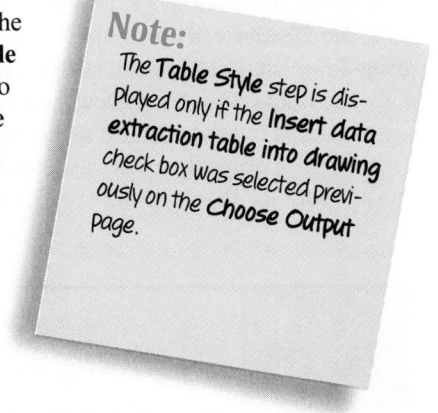

Note:
The Table Style step is displayed only if the Insert data extraction table into drawing check box was selected previously on the Choose Output page.

Figure 16-42 The **Data Extraction** wizard—**Table Style** page

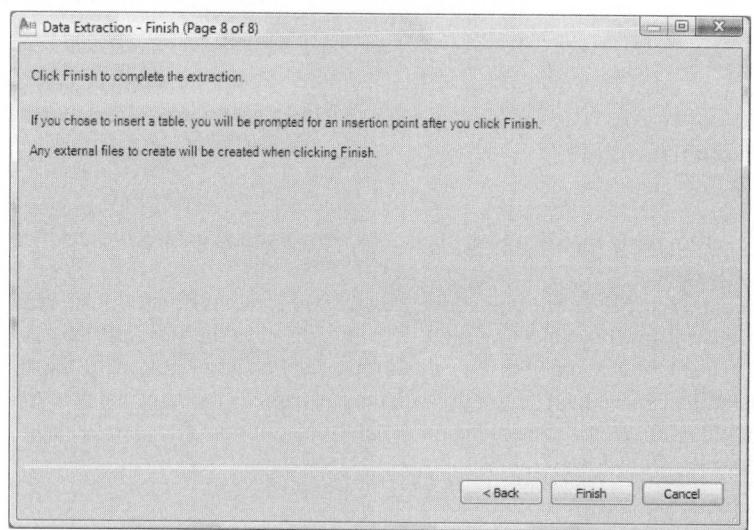

Figure 16-43 The **Data Extraction** wizard—**Finish** page

The **Manually setup table** option allows you to manually enter a title and select a specific title, header, and data cell style.

The **Enter a title for your table** text box allows you to enter a title for the table. This row is not overwritten when the table is updated. If the selected table style does not include a title row, this option is not available. The default table style, **Standard**, includes a title row.

The **Title cell style** list allows you to select a separate style for the title cell. Select the drop-down list to select a title cell style defined in the selected table style.

The **Header cell style** allows you to select a separate style for the header row. Select the drop-down list to select a cell style defined in the selected table style.

The **Data cell style** list allows you to select a separate style for data cells. Select the drop-down list to select a cell style defined in the selected table style.

The **Use property names as additional column headers** check box includes column headers and uses the **Display Name** property as the header row.

| FOR MORE DETAILS | See Chapter 12 for more details about controlling table format using table styles. |

Select the **Next >** button at the bottom to proceed to the **Finish** page shown in Figure 16-43, the **Cancel** button to close the wizard, or the **< Back** button to return to the previous page.

The **Finish** page allows you to complete the process of extracting object property data that was specified in the wizard and creates the output type that was specified on the **Choose Output** page.

If you select the **Insert data extraction table into drawing** check box on the **Choose Output** page, when you select the **Finish** button, a table will be attached to your mouse cursor. AutoCAD then prompts you to *Specify insertion point:* so you can locate the table as shown in Figure 16-44.

If the **Output data to external file** option was selected, the extracted data are saved to the specified file type.

Note:
If data linking and column matching to an Excel spreadsheet was defined in the **Link External Data** dialog box, the selected data in the spreadsheet are also extracted.

Figure 16-44 Table created using the **Data Extraction** wizard

Updating Data Extraction Table Data Manually

Data extraction table data are locked by default to prevent the data from being updated and possibly getting out of sync with the source data (attributes). When you click on a table cell, a **Lock** icon is displayed along with the data extraction information as shown in Figure 16-45.

Figure 16-45   Locked cell in a data extraction table

You can unlock a cell by selecting **Locking** from the right-click menu and checking the **Unlocked** cascade menu item. Table data that are overwritten manually will be updated when the table data are updated using the automated update data links options explained in the following section.

Updating Data Extraction Table Data Automatically

You can update data extraction table data automatically when the extracted source data (attributes) change.

AutoCAD locates a **Data Link** icon in the Status Tray on the far right of the Status Bar anytime a data extraction table is located in your drawing. You can right-click on the icon and select **Update All Data Links...** from the shortcut menu shown in Figure 16-46, and AutoCAD will read all the attributes in the drawing and update the table data with any changes.

You can select to be notified when extracted data have changed. When information in the data source has changed that affects the extracted data in a table, the **Data Extraction—Outdated Table** dialog box is displayed so that you can update the table data automatically (see Figure 16-47).

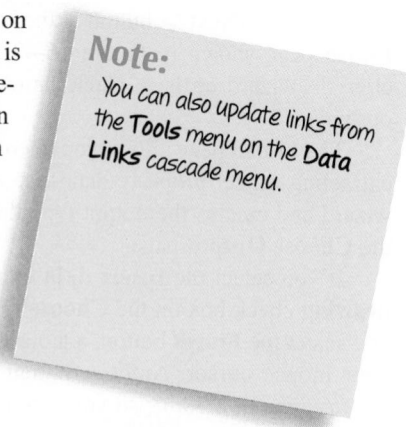

Note:
You can also update links from the **Tools** menu on the **Data Links** cascade menu.

Figure 16-47   The **Data Extraction—Outdated Table** dialog box

Figure 16-46   Updating data links via the **Data Link** shortcut menu

Notification is controlled by the current **DXEVAL** system variable setting. By default, **DXEVAL** is set to check if the extracted data is not current only when the **PLOT** or **PUBLISH** command is used. It can also be set to occur with the **OPEN, SAVE,** and **ETRANSMIT** commands. The **DXEVAL** system is stored as an integer using the sum of the following values:

- **0**   No notification
- **1**   Open
- **2**   Save
- **4**   Plot
- **8**   Publish
- **16**   eTransmit/Archive
- **32**   Save with Automatic Update
- **64**   Plot with Automatic Update
- **128**   Publish with Automatic Update
- **256**   eTransmit/Archive with Automatic Update

The default value of **DXEVAL** is **12**.

Exercise 16-9: Extracting Attributes

1. Continue from Exercise 16-8.
2. Use the **Data Extraction** wizard and extract all of the **CH16_EX7** block attributes to create the window schedule shown in Figure 16-44 using the AutoCAD table option.
   Hint: Use your mouse to reorder and sort the columns as needed in the **Refine Data** page shown in Figure 16-39. Table must be scaled by a drawing scale factor of **48** after the table is inserted if it is inserted in model space.
3. Save the drawing as **EX16-9**.

REDEFINING BLOCKS

One of the greatest benefits of using blocks in your drawings is that it makes it possible to quickly redefine a block so that all existing and future block references are automatically updated in the drawing to match the new block definition. You may have hundreds, or even thousands, of references of a block in a drawing, and they will all be updated. Think how much time it would take to update each one manually, and it's easy to appreciate why it is such a great feature.

Updating Blocks Created in the Current Drawing

To redefine a block in the current drawing, you simply follow the steps outlined earlier in the chapter to create the updated block information. You then use the **BLOCK** command to save the drawing information with the same block name as the existing block name to update by selecting it from the **Name:** list box at the top of the **Block Definition** dialog box, as shown in Figure 16-48.

When you select **OK** to update the block information, AutoCAD displays a message like the one shown in Figure 16-49. This informs you that the block definition already exists and asks you whether you want to update it.

Figure 16-48   Redefining an existing block

Figure 16-49   Updating a block definition

Selecting the **Redefine block** button replaces the existing block definition with the new one, and all the existing block references in the drawing are immediately updated to reflect the new definition. All future block insertions will also refer to the new block definition.

The easiest way to update a block is to insert the original block and explode it so that you can update its subobjects and then redefine it using the **BLOCK** command as explained above.

TIP

Be sure that when you insert the original block that you specify a base point that you can remember, a uniform scale of 1.0, and a rotation angle of 0.0. If the base point, scale, or rotation angle is different from the original when you redefine the block, all block references will be updated to reflect the change, causing unpredictable results.

Updating Blocks Inserted from an External Drawing File

Block definitions created by inserting an external drawing file are not automatically updated when the original drawing file is modified. The easiest way to update a block definition created by inserting a drawing file is to simply reinsert the updated drawing file using the **INSERT** command explained earlier to display the **Insert** dialog box shown in Figure 16-7 and select the **Browse...** button to select the updated drawing file using the standard **Select Drawing File** dialog box.

When you select **OK** to exit the **Insert** dialog box and insert the updated block, AutoCAD displays a message like the one shown in Figure 16-49. This informs you that the block definition already exists and asks whether you want to update it. Rather than insert another block reference by picking a point in the drawing you can press the **<Esc>** key to cancel the insertion process. All the existing block references are still updated, but you don't end up with a new unwanted block reference in your drawing.

Editing Blocks In-Place

Edit Reference	
Ribbon & Panel:	Insert|Reference Edit Reference
Toolbar:	None
Menu:	Tools| Xref and In-place Block Editing| Edit Reference In-Place
Command Line:	REFEDIT
Command Alias:	None

The **REFEDIT** command, which was originally created to edit xrefs, can be used to quickly redefine a block "in-place" without having to explode the block and re-create it using the **BLOCK** command as explained above.

FOR MORE DETAILS	See Chapter 17 for more details about xrefs and using the **REFEDIT** command.

After starting the **REFEDIT** command, AutoCAD prompts you to *Select reference:*. Select the block to redefine and press **<Enter ↵>** to display the **Reference Edit** dialog box shown in Figure 16-50.

Figure 16-50   The **Reference Edit** dialog box

This dialog box provides the following options:

- The **Identify Reference** tab is used to identify and select the block definition you want to edit.
  - The block name is listed on the left in the **Reference name:** box along with any blocks that might be nested within the block. If multiple blocks are displayed, you must select the block you want to modify from the list. Only one block can be edited in place at a time.
  - The **Preview** window displays a preview image of the currently selected block.
  - The **Automatically select all nested objects** option controls whether nested blocks are included automatically in the block editing session.
  - The **Prompt to select nested objects** option controls whether nested blocks must be selected individually in the block editing session.
- The **Settings** tab is used to control various block editing settings.
  - The **Create unique layer, style, and block names** check box allows you to control how xref layers and other named objects are managed.
  - The **Display attribute definitions for editing** check box allows you to control whether all the attribute definitions in a block reference are displayed during the block editing session.

> **Note:**
> When **Display attribute definitions for editing** is selected, attribute values are turned off, and all the block attribute definitions are displayed so that they can be edited. The updated attribute definitions affect only future block insertions—the attributes in existing block references are unchanged. Attributes defined as **Constant** cannot be updated.

Additionally, the **Lock objects not in working set** check box allows you to lock all objects not in the ***working set*** so that you don't inadvertently modify other objects in the drawing while in a block editing session. Locked objects behave similarly to objects on a locked layer—they can be viewed, but they cannot be selected.

Selecting **OK** puts you in the block editing mode where all the objects that are not part of the working set are locked *and* faded back so that the objects to edit in the working set stand out as shown in Figure 16-51.

working set: The group of objects selected for in-place editing using the **REFEDIT** command

Block to Update   Drawing Faded and Locked   Edit Reference Panel

Figure 16-51 Drawing display in block editing mode

When you are in block editing mode, the **Edit Reference** panel shown in Figure 16-52 is turned on to allow you to manage the working set and save or discard any changes made to the block definition.

Figure 16-52   The **Edit Reference** panel

In block editing mode, you can edit the block definition using any of the standard AutoCAD drawing and editing commands. You can add information, erase information, and change object properties—almost anything you would normally do in the AutoCAD drawing editor.

When you are done updating the block definition, select the **Save Changes** button on the left side of the **Edit Reference** panel shown in Figure 16-52 to save the changes and exit block editing mode. You can discard any changes and exit block editing mode by selecting the **Discard Changes** button shown in Figure 16-52.

Redefining Blocks with Attributes

It is possible to redefine block attributes using any of the standard techniques explained so far, but there are a few idiosyncrasies to be aware of. For the most part, only future block references will reflect the changes made to the attribute definition properties and modes—existing block references do not get updated.

Note:
When an attribute definition is updated, the current attribute value remains the same; only the attribute properties are updated.

Adding new attribute definitions is even more problematic—adding a new attribute to a block affects only future block insertions. Not even the **BATTMAN** command described earlier allows you to add new attributes. Fortunately, AutoCAD provides the **ATTREDEF** command to solve the issues surrounding updating blocks with attributes.

The ATTREDEF Command.   The **ATTREDEF** command redefines the specified block and its attribute definitions by prompting you to select the objects that will make up the block, similar to when you created the block originally. Because of this, the easiest process is to explode the block to make any changes and/or add any new attribute definitions.

Because the **ATTREDEF** command is not on any menu or ribbon, you must type it at the command prompt. After starting the **ATTREDEF** command, AutoCAD prompts you to *Enter name of the block you wish to redefine:*. You must enter the block name at the keyboard. AutoCAD then prompts you to *Select objects:* so you can select the objects and attributes that make up the block. After you have selected all the block objects, press the **<Enter ⏎>** key, and AutoCAD prompts you to *Specify insertion base point of new Block:* so you can select the insertion point. You should select an insertion point in the exact location as the original base point, or any existing block references in the drawing will move.

Exercise 16-10: Redefining Blocks

1. Continue from Exercise 16-9.
2. Start the **REFEDIT** command and select any one of the **CH16_EX7** window tag blocks.
3. Select **OK** in the **Reference Edit** dialog box to enter block editing mode.
4. Change the window tag circle to a hexagon as shown in Figure 16-53 by erasing the circle and using the **POLYGON** command to create the hexagon.

Figure 16-53   Redefined window tag blocks

5. Select the **Save Changes** button on the **Edit Reference** panel to save your changes. All window tags in the drawing should immediately change to hexagons.
6. Save the drawing as **EX16-10**.

USING DESIGNCENTER TO MANAGE BLOCKS

AutoCAD's **DesignCenter** is a multipurpose tool that provides easy access to blocks, hatch patterns, layers, linetypes, text styles, dimension styles, and other named object information contained in other drawings on your computer, on a network location, or even on the Internet.

DesignCenter allows you to "open" another drawing so that you can view the drawing's named objects, referred to as *drawing content,* in list or icon form. You can then copy any of the drawing content from the source drawing to your current drawing by simply dragging-and-dropping it with your mouse. You can even select multiple objects, making it possible to copy a group of named objects as one. For instance, using this approach, you could copy all the layer definitions from one drawing to another, saving a lot of time. In addition to layers, **DesignCenter** provides access to the following drawing content:

- Blocks
- Dimension styles
- Layers
- Linetypes
- Table styles
- Text styles
- Xrefs

For the purpose of this chapter, we are going to concentrate on using **DesignCenter** to manage and insert blocks.

TIP   Using **DesignCenter**, you can create a standard drawing, or drawings, that contains all of your organization's standard layers, linetypes, text styles, and so on. Then locate it centrally on a network drive, giving your coworkers access to it so all they have to do is drag-and-drop to set up their drawings.

<table>
<tr><td colspan="2">DesignCenter</td></tr>
<tr><td>Ribbon
& Panel:</td><td>Insert|
Content</td></tr>
<tr><td colspan="2" align="center">Design Center</td></tr>
<tr><td>Standard
Toolbar:</td><td></td></tr>
<tr><td>Menu:</td><td>Tools|
Design
Center</td></tr>
<tr><td>Command
Line:</td><td>ADCENTER</td></tr>
<tr><td>Command
Alias:</td><td>ADC</td></tr>
</table>

The DesignCenter Window

The **ADCENTER** command displays the **DesignCenter** window so that you can locate and insert drawing content from other drawings located on your computer, a network, or the Internet.

Starting the **ADCENTER** command displays the **DesignCenter** window shown in Figure 16-54.

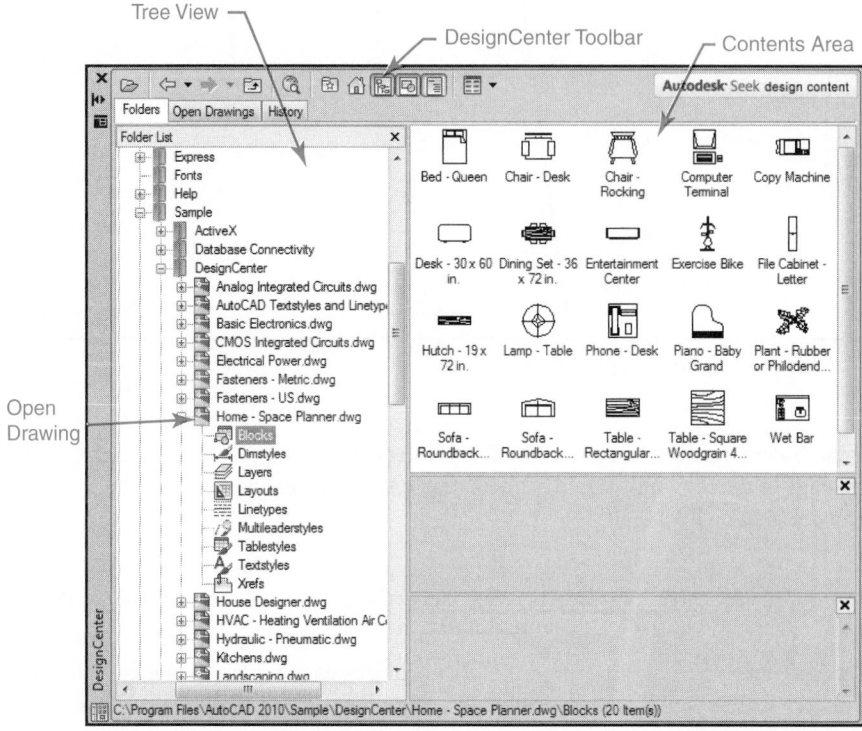

Figure 16-54 The **DesignCenter** window

The **DesignCenter** window consists of three parts:

- **Tree view** (left pane)   Navigation tools used to locate drawing files and Web-based content
- **Contents area** (right pane)   Displays the contents of a drawing or Web content once it is located
- **Toolbar** (top)   Additional navigation and display tools

The following sections explain each of these parts as well as other **DesignCenter** features.

> **Note:**
> If the Tree view is not displayed, select the **Tree View Toggle** toolbar button at the top of the **DesignCenter** window shown in Figure 16-54.

Tree View.   The Tree view on the left allows you to locate a drawing file using the following methods so that you can display the drawing's contents in the Contents area on the right:

- **Folders** tab   Explorer-like interface that allows you to navigate the hierarchy of files and folders on your computer or attached network drives (see Figure 16-54)
- **Open Drawings** tab   List of all currently open drawings
- **History** tab   History of the last drawings accessed

You can remove a file from the **History** tab by selecting the file, right-clicking, and selecting **Delete** from the shortcut menu.

Contents Area. The Contents area on the right side of the window displays the contents of the drawing, or named object collection currently selected in the Tree view on the left. When a block is selected it is possible to display a preview and a description as shown in Figure 16-55.

Figure 16-55 The Contents area

The Preview window and Description window can be toggled on and off by selecting the **Preview** and **Description** buttons on the **DesignCenter** toolbar shown in Figure 16-57. It is also possible to switch how the information is viewed in the Contents pane via the **Views** flyout menu on the right side of the **DesignCenter** toolbar shown in Figure 16-57 to one of the following standard Explorer-type formats:

- Large icons
- Small icons
- List
- Details

You can navigate in the Contents area by double-clicking an icon with your mouse to display its contents. You can then select the **Up** arrow on the **DesignCenter** toolbar shown in Figure 16-57 to go back up one level in the hierarchy.

Right-clicking on a block icon displays the shortcut menu shown in Figure 16-56 so that you can do the following:

- **Insert Block...** Displays the **Insert** dialog box
- **Insert and Redefine** Inserts the selected block and redefines all block definitions in the drawing
- **Redefine only** Redefines a block in the drawing but does not insert a copy
- **Block Editor** Displays the dynamic block editor
- **Copy** Copies the block to the Windows clipboard
- **Create Tool Palette** Creates a custom tool palette

DesignCenter Toolbar. The **DesignCenter** toolbar shown in Figure 16-57 provides the following navigation tools and display options:

- **Load** Displays the standard file selection dialog box so you can locate a file and load its information in the Contents area
- **Back** Returns to the most recent location in the history list

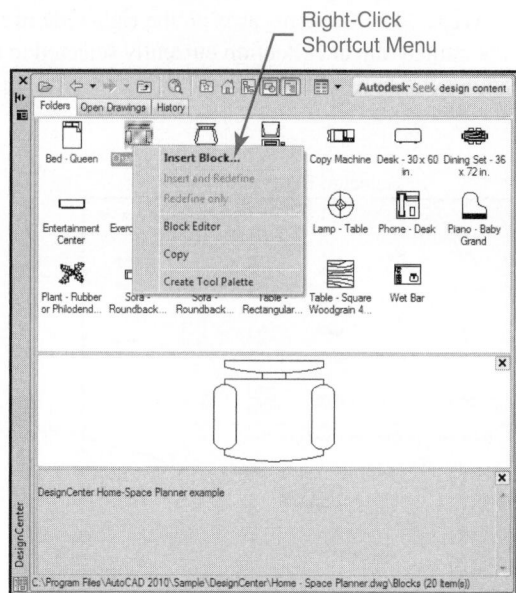

Figure 16-56 The **Contents area shortcut** menu

Figure 16-57 The **DesignCenter** toolbar

- **Forward**   Moves forward to a recent location in the history list
- **Up**   Displays the contents of the next level up in the hierarchy
- **Search**   Displays the **Search** dialog box so you can enter search criteria to locate drawings, blocks, and other named objects within drawings
- **Favorites**   Displays the contents of the **Favorites** folder in the Contents area. You can add items to the **Favorites** folder by right-clicking and selecting **Add to Favorites** from the shortcut menu
- **Home**   Returns **DesignCenter** to the home folder. You can change the home folder by navigating to the desired folder in the Tree view, right-clicking, and selecting **Set as Home** from the shortcut menu.
- **Tree View Toggle**   Displays and hides the tree view. When the Tree view is hidden, you can still navigate in the Contents area using the techniques described earlier.
- **Preview**   Toggles the Preview window on and off in the Contents area
- **Description**   Toggles the Description window on and off in the Contents area
- **Views**   Allows you to switch between different display formats in the Contents area

Figure 16-58 The **DesignCenter Properties** shortcut menu

DesignCenter Properties.   Just like other AutoCAD windows and palettes, the **DesignCenter** window can be moved, resized, and docked using your mouse. You can also control these and other features by selecting the **Properties** button on the window title bar to display the shortcut menu shown in Figure 16-58.

Using the shortcut menu, you can prevent the **DesignCenter** window from being docked. You can also toggle on and off the **Auto-hide** feature that collapses the window, so that only the title bar is visible when the mouse pointer is not directly over the window.

TIP The **<Ctrl>+2** keyboard combination can be used to quickly toggle **DesignCenter** on and off.

Inserting Blocks. Once you locate a block using one of the methods described above and it is visible in the Contents area, there are three ways you can insert the block into the current drawing using **DesignCenter**:

- Drag-and-drop the block into the current drawing using your mouse.
- Double-click on the block in the Contents area to display the **Insert** dialog box.
- Right-click on the block in the Contents area to display the shortcut menu shown earlier in Figure 16-56.

Note:
The following exercise requires that you install the sample **DesignCenter** drawing files that come with AutoCAD 2010. By default, the sample drawings are located in the **C:\Program Files\AutoCAD 2010\ Sample\DesignCenter** folder.

Each method has its merits. Dragging-and-dropping a block is obviously the fastest method, while double-clicking on a block provides the most control because you can specify different block settings in the **Insert** dialog box. Finally, right-clicking provides the only option to redefine a block. Practice using each method so that you are prepared for any situation.

Autodesk Seek. **Autodesk Seek** is an online utility that allows you to search product information and drawings from the Web and download them directly into your AutoCAD drawing. It can be accessed either from the right side of the **DesignCenter** toolbar shown in Figure 16-57 or by entering your search criteria directly on the **Content** panel on the **Insert** ribbon in the **Seek design content** search box.

Either method will launch your Internet browser and take you to the http://seek .autodesk.com Website so you can find the product you are searching for. Once you locate a drawing, you can drag-and-drop the content into the current AutoCAD drawing.

It is also possible to share your blocks and other content with other **Autodesk Seek** users by selecting the **Share with Autodesk Seek** tool on the **Autodesk Seek** panel on the **Output** ribbon. Selecting the **Share with Autodesk Seek** tool asks you what content you want to share and then takes you through an online submittal process where the selected content is then uploaded to the **Autodesk Seek** Website.

Exercise 16-11: Using DesignCenter

1. Continue from Exercise 16-10.
2. Set layer **A-Furn** current.
3. Start **DesignCenter** and navigate to the **Home-Space Planner.dwg** file located in the **DesignCenter** folder as shown in Figure 16-54.
4. Select the **Blocks** icon so you can see the blocks defined in the drawing in the Contents area on the right as shown in Figure 16-55.
5. Select the **Tree View Toggle** button on the **DesignCenter** toolbar shown in Figure 16-57 to turn off the Tree view.
6. Insert blocks using the techniques explained above and furnish the floor plan in a manner similar to Figure 16-59.
7. Save the drawing as **EX16-11**.

Furniture
Blocks
(Typical)

Block
Contents of
Home Space Planner.dwg
in Design Center

Figure 16-59 Building
floor plan with office
furniture and equipment
blocks inserted using
DesignCenter

TOOL PALETTES AND DYNAMIC BLOCKS

Tool Palettes	
Ribbon & Panel:	View| Palettes
Standard Toolbar:	
Menu:	Tools| Palettes| Tool Palettes
Command Line:	TOOL PALETTES
Command Alias:	TP

Tool palettes are highly customizable palette-type windows that allow you to group and organize blocks, hatch patterns, and even commands, using graphical icons on easily accessible palettes organized in a series of named tabs.

Dynamic blocks are multipurpose blocks that can be changed after they are inserted using special grips that allow you to display multiple block views, sizes, block behavior, and more. Using dynamic blocks, one block definition can be used for a myriad of different scenarios and situations. Dynamic blocks are covered in detail later in this section. The AutoCAD **Dynamic Blocks Tool** palettes are shown in Figure 16-60.

Tool palette tools can be either dragged and dropped directly into your drawing to perform the associated action or selected like a toolbar button by left-clicking on the tool's icon with your mouse. Figure 16-61 shows the **Door-Imperial** block being inserted in the drawing by dragging-and-dropping it from the sample **Architectural** palette.

> **Note:**
> All dynamic blocks have a lightning bolt in the lower right corner of their **Tool palette** icon as shown in Figure 16-60 to indicate that they can be dynamically updated after they are inserted. Inserting and updating dynamic blocks is explained later in this section.

Controlling Tool Palettes

Because they utilize the palette-type window, **Tool** palettes can be hidden when you are not using them via the **Auto-hide** palette feature, as well as made transparent so that you can see through them to your drawing below using the **Transparency** palette feature. These and other features can be controlled via the **Properties** shortcut menu that can be displayed by clicking on the **Properties** button at the top of the palette title bar. See Figure 16-60.

TIP The **Auto-hide** feature can also be quickly turned on and off via the **Auto-hide** button located directly above the **Properties** button. See Figure 16-60.

FOR MORE DETAILS See Chapter 1 for more information about controlling different palette properties such as **Auto-hide** and **Transparency**.

Figure 16-60   AutoCAD **Dynamic Blocks Tool** palettes

Figure 16-61   Inserting the **Door-Imperial** block from the sample **Architectural** palette

More options are available by right-clicking anywhere on the title bar to display the shortcut menu shown in Figure 16-62.

In addition to the **Auto-hide** and **Transparency** palette features, the **Tool** palette title bar right-click menu allows you to do the following:

- Turn **Tool** palette docking off so that if you drag a palette to the far left or right side of your screen, the palette will remain in a floating state and not attach itself to the AutoCAD window.

- **Anchor Tool** palettes on the left or right side of the AutoCAD window. Anchored palettes are palettes that are docked but hidden using the **Auto-hide** feature so that only the title bar is visible. Placing your mouse over the palette title bar displays the entire palette, but it remains anchored.

- Create new empty **Tool** palettes and rename existing **Tool** palettes.

- Turn **Tool** palette groups off and on. Related **Tool** palettes can be grouped together in categories so you can control what palettes are displayed by category.

- Customize **Tool** palette groups. The **Customize Palettes...** menu item displays the **Customize** dialog box shown in Figure 16-63 so you can do the following:
  - Add/remove/move palettes by dragging palettes with your mouse. A palette can be added to a group by dragging it from the **Palettes:** list box on the left to the desired palette group on the right.
  - Add/remove palette groups by right-clicking on a group in the **Palette Groups:** list box on the right and using the shortcut menu.
  - Export and import **Tool** palettes using the XTP file format so that palettes can be shared with other users by right-clicking on a palette in the **Palettes:** list box on the left and selecting **Export...** or **Import...** from the shortcut menu to display the Windows file dialog box.

- Add custom commands. The **Customize Commands...** menu item displays the **Customize User Interface** dialog box with a list of all the AutoCAD commands. To add a command to a **Tool** palette, you simply drag it from the **Command List:** and drop it onto the **Tool** palette of your choice.

Figure 16-62   **Tool** palette title bar
right-click menu

Figure 16-63   The **Customize** dialog box

But wait, there's more. There are a total of four different **Tool** palette right-click shortcut menus depending on where you right-click with your mouse. If you right-click on a **Tool** palette anywhere between toolbar icons on an empty space on the palette background, the shortcut menu in Figure 16-64 is displayed.

In addition to most of the commands and features already discussed, this menu also allows you to control different display options. The **View Options...** menu item displays the **View Options** dialog box so that you can switch between icon and list view, as well as control the size of the images used for the icons. The **Sort By** cascade menu allows you to automatically sort tool icons by name or type.

Right-clicking on the named tab on a **Tool** palette displays yet another shortcut menu. This menu allows you to move a palette up and down in the palette order, rename a palette, or create a new palette.

Finally, right-clicking directly over a **Tool** palette icon displays a shortcut menu that allows you to cut, copy, delete, rename, and control the selected tool's properties.

Figure 16-64   **Tool** palette background right-click menu

Figure 16-65   The **Tool Properties** dialog box for a block

Tool Properties

The **Properties...** menu item located on the bottom of a tool's right-click shortcut menu displays the **Tool Properties** dialog box shown in Figure 16-65 so you can edit the tool's name and description, as well as control tool-specific properties like block locations, hatch pattern names, and command macros depending on the tool type selected. The properties for a block are shown in Figure 16-65.

Each tool also has general properties such as layer, color, and linetype that can be controlled via the **Tool Properties** dialog box. See Figure 16-65. These properties are applied to any object type that is created when the corresponding **Tool palette** icon is selected. For instance, setting a block's **Layer** property to any layer setting other than "—use current" will insert the block on the layer specified.

TIP   It is possible to rearrange the order of the tools on a **Tool** palette by left-clicking a tool icon and dragging it to another location.

Exercise 16-12: Using Tool Palettes

1. Continue from Exercise 16-11.
2. Turn on **Tool** palettes via the **Palettes** panel on the **View** ribbon.
3. Right-click anywhere on the **Tool** palettes title bar and select **Annotation and Design** from the shortcut menu to turn on only the **Annotation and Design Tool** palettes shown in Figure 16-60.
4. Size and position the palettes on the screen using your mouse.
5. Turn the **Auto-hide** feature on by selecting the **Auto-hide** button at the top of the palette title bar directly above the **Properties** button.
6. Move your mouse off the palette so that the palette closes and only the palette title bar is visible.

7. Right-click anywhere on the **Tool** palettes title bar again and select **Anchor Right >** to anchor the **Tool** palette on the right side of the screen.
8. Put your cursor over the anchored **Tool** palette to display it and select the **Architectural** palette tab to make it active.
9. Select the **Door-Imperial** block at the top of the **Architectural** palette by clicking on it with your left mouse button. AutoCAD should prompt you to *Specify insertion point or* ↓.
10. Pick a point to locate the block anywhere on the floor plan.
11. Select the **Fluorescent (Recessed)-Imperial** block, hold your mouse button down, and drag-and-drop the light fixture block anywhere in the drawing.
12. Right-click on the **Door-Imperial** block on the **Architectural** palette and select **Properties...** from the shortcut menu to display the **Tool Properties** dialog box.
13. Change the **Layer** property under the **General** category from "—use current" to "A-DOOR" and select **OK** to close the dialog box.
14. Insert another **Door-Imperial** block. It should now always insert on the **A-DOOR** layer regardless of what layer is current.
15. Save the drawing as **EX16-12**.

Adding Tools to Tool Palettes

One of the coolest things about **Tool** palettes is that you can add information to a palette by simply selecting an object in your drawing and dragging it onto the **Tool** palette where you want it to be located. If the object is a block, it is added to the palette as a block. If the object is a hatch pattern, the hatch pattern is added to the palette. If the object selected is not a block or hatch pattern, the command used to create the object is added to the palette. For instance, dragging a piece of multiline text from a drawing onto a **Tool** palette will add the **MTEXT** command using the default multiline text icon as shown in Figure 16-66.

Figure 16-66   Adding tools by dragging-and-dropping them from the drawing

There are a couple of different ways to add blocks to a palette besides dragging them from the drawing.

Using the **DesignCenter** palette described earlier, it is possible to automatically create a new palette that contains all the blocks in a drawing by right-clicking on a drawing on the **DesignCenter Folders** tab and selecting the **Create Tool Palette** menu item from the shortcut menu. A new palette with the same name as the drawing is added to the current palette group with blocks and tool icons generated for each block.

DesignCenter can also create a new palette that consists of all the drawing files located in a folder. If you right-click on a folder that contains drawing (DWG) files and select **Create Tool Palette of Blocks** from the shortcut menu, AutoCAD will create a new tool palette with the same name as the folder with blocks and icons for each drawing file in the folder.

TIP Drawing (DWG) files can also be added to a **Tool** palette by dragging-and-dropping them from Windows Explorer onto the desired palette. It is even possible to add multiple drawings at the same time using the **<Ctrl>** and **<Shift>** keys to select multiple files.

Exercise 16-13: Adding Tools to Tool Palettes

1. Continue from Exercise 16-12.
2. Right-click anywhere on the **Tool** palettes title bar and select **New Palette** from the shortcut menu to create a new palette. Name the new palette **My Tools**.
3. Select any toilet block on the floor plan in the drawing so it is highlighted and add it to the **My Tools** palette by dragging-and-dropping it onto the palette from the drawing. *Be careful not to select a grip when dragging it.*
4. Select any wall line so it is highlighted and add it to the **My Tools** palette by dragging and dropping it onto the palette from the drawing. You should now have a **Line** tool with a fly-out of assorted drawing commands.
5. Select the **Line** tool and create a line.
6. Right-click on the **My Tools** tab and select **Move Up** from the shortcut menu to move the **My Tools** palette up in the palette order.
7. Repeat step 6 until the **My Tools** palette is the top-level palette.
8. Select the **Line** tool and, while holding your left mouse button down, drag the tool to the top of the palette and release the mouse button to move the tool to the top of the palette.
9. Save the drawing as **EX16-13**.

Introduction to Dynamic Blocks

As mentioned earlier, dynamic blocks are multipurpose blocks that allow you to use a single block to represent many different variations, sizes, and typical actions that would normally require a block library consisting of numerous different block definitions. Using dynamic blocks, you typically insert a generic version of the block and then use the special grips shown in the following table to update it dynamically:

Dynamic Block Grips		
Grip		**Description**
▽	**List Arrow**	Selecting grip displays a list of block options such as size, configuration, number, or views to choose from.
▷	**Stretch Arrow**	Dragging grip allows you to stretch, scale, and array a block to predefined sizes and configurations.
■	**Locater Box**	Dragging grip allows you to stretch or move a block or block subcomponent.
◁	**Flip Arrow**	Selecting grip flips a block in the direction of the arrow.
⬠	**Alignment**	Dragging grip aligns a block with existing objects in the drawing.
●	**Rotate**	Selecting grip allows you to rotate a block to predefined angles using your cursor.

For example, using dynamic block technology, one single block of an architectural-type door for a floor plan can be updated so that you can:

- Switch between different standard door opening angles
- Resize the door using standard door opening and frame widths
- Flip the door horizontally or vertically about the center of the door opening
- Automatically align the door along a wall

FOR MORE DETAILS   See Chapter 7 for more information about using grips to modify objects.

Many of a block's dynamic options and features can be set *prior* to inserting the block using the **Properties** palette instead of using grips after the block is inserted. If you turn on the **Properties** palette and select a dynamic block on a **Tool** palette, the dynamic block options that can be updated prior to insertion are listed under the **Custom** category.

Using the **List Arrow** grip, the door opening angle can be set to 30°, 45°, 60°, 90°, or even appear closed as shown in Figure 16-67.

Figure 16-67   Using the dynamic **List Arrow** grip to change the door opening angle

Using the **Stretch Arrow** grip, you can resize the door to any predefined opening size (24″, 28″, 30″, 32″, 36″, or 40″) as shown in Figure 16-68.

Using the **Flip Arrow** grip, you can mirror the door about the center of the opening either horizontally or vertically as shown in Figure 16-69.

With the **Alignment** grip, you can drag the door near a wall, and it will automatically align itself along the same angle as the wall as shown in Figure 16-70.

Figure 16-68   Using the dynamic **Stretch Arrow** grip to change the door opening size

Figure 16-69   Using the dynamic **Flip Arrow** grip to mirror the door

TIP   The dynamic block alignment feature also works as the dynamic block is inserted so that you can instantly align doors, windows, and other blocks with existing objects in your drawing.

Unfortunately, covering all the dynamic block update options and features is beyond the scope of this textbook, as is the complex process involved in creating a dynamic block. Because of their complex nature, AutoCAD includes a special **Block Editor** environment for creating and updating dynamic blocks that has its own set of "authoring" palettes where you define parameters and actions. You might have started it accidentally at some point and wondered what it was because it changes the color of the AutoCAD background as shown in Figure 16-71.

Figure 16-70   Using the **Alignment** grip to align the door with the wall

Figure 16-71   The AutoCAD dynamic block editor

If this happens, the best thing to do at this point is to select the **Close Block Editor** button on the toolbar at the top of the screen to exit the editor and get back to your drawing.

Fortunately, AutoCAD has many sample dynamic blocks available on the sample **Tool** palettes that come with AutoCAD (shown earlier in Figure 16-60) that you can play with and use in your drawings.

Exercise 16-14: Using Dynamic Blocks

1. Continue from Exercise 16-13.
2. Select one of the **Door-Imperial** blocks inserted in Exercise 16-12 so that dynamic grips are displayed.

3. Select the **Alignment** grip and align the door with the vertical wall by dragging it with your mouse close to the wall until the block rotates 90° and is aligned with the wall as shown in Figure 16-70. Select a point to locate the door on the wall.
4. Select the **List Arrow** grip to display all the door opening angle options and select **Open 45°** so that the door angle is updated as shown in Figure 16-67.
5. Select the vertical **Stretch Arrow** grip and stretch the door so that the door opening is 36″ wide as shown in Figure 16-68.
6. Select the horizontal **Stretch Arrow** grip and stretch the door so the door frame width is 4″ wide, the same as the wall thickness.
7. Select the vertical **Flip Arrow** grip and mirror the door horizontally as shown in Figure 16-69.
8. Save the drawing as **EX16-14**.

CHAPTER SUMMARY

In this chapter, we learned how to create, insert, and manage blocks. Blocks have been around for a long time and are one of the primary features of most CAD software because you can draw something once and use it many times. This simple capability provides three basic but overwhelmingly important benefits:

- *Increased productivity*   Draw it once and use it over and over again.
- *Increased precision*   If you take the time to draw a block right the first time, it is always correct for each subsequent insertion.
- *Increased standards compliance*   Draw a block that you are sure meets the standards of your organization and then distribute it so that it is used throughout a project.

Many blocks already exist that can be downloaded on the Internet from various manufacturers, suppliers, trade organizations, and others. The **Autodesk Seek design content** feature provides access to much of this content. It is even possible to download complete symbol libraries of blocks.

Take the time to consider when to make a block. If you are going to use something in a drawing more than three times, it might be a good candidate for a block. Think about creating a block library and what it might look like. You can create several separate block drawing files and organize them in folders so they can be inserted using Windows Explorer, or you might put all the blocks in a single drawing file and access them using **DesignCenter**. Each approach has its pros and cons.

The ability to add nongraphical alphanumeric intelligence to your drawings in the form of block attributes is another huge productivity enhancer. Now you can create a single block definition and assign different alphanumeric information each time it is inserted—visible or invisible! Using invisible attributes, you can attach important alphanumeric information to blocks that will not plot but can be extracted to an AutoCAD table, text file, spreadsheet, or even database. What you do with this information is up to your own imagination.

TIP   Be careful when downloading any information from the Internet. You will want to examine any blocks you download and check them for accuracy and standards compliance. As with anything on the Internet, there is some bad information to be found—you must take the time to separate the wheat from the chaff.

CHAPTER TEST QUESTIONS

Multiple Choice

1. An AutoCAD block is best described as a:
   a. Hatch pattern
   b. Named collection of AutoCAD objects treated as a single complex object
   c. Title border
   d. Group of layers

2. The advantage of using blocks in a drawing is:
   a. Reduced drawing size
   b. Increased accuracy
   c. Ease of updating drawings
   d. All of the above

3. When inserting an annotation-type block, it is necessary to:
   a. Put it on a text layer
   b. Scale the block by the drawing scale
   c. Set the text style
   d. All of the above

4. A block attribute is:
   a. An object property such as layer, color, linetype, or lineweight
   b. A scale
   c. A rotation
   d. Dynamic text used to store alphanumeric data

5. The only information stored with a block reference is the:

   a. Insertion point
   b. Scale factor
   c. Rotation angle
   d. All of the above

6. Defining a block within another block is referred to as:

   a. Block assembly
   b. Impossible
   c. Block reference
   d. Block nesting

7. Block subobjects created on layer **0** with all their object properties set to **ByLayer** assume what current object property when the block is inserted?

   a. Color
   b. Lineweight
   c. Layer
   d. All of the above

8. Unit blocks allow you to:

   a. Maintain consistent grid and snap settings
   b. Scale a block differently in the *X* and *Y* scale for different results
   c. Transfer blocks from one unit system to another
   d. All of the above

9. Dragging-and-dropping a drawing from Windows Explorer into a drawing using the right mouse button allows you to:

   a. Open a drawing
   b. Insert a drawing as a block
   c. Attach an xref
   d. All of the above

10. By default, when you create a block using the **WBLOCK** command, it does what with the original objects selected to make the block?

    a. Converts them to a block in-place
    b. Deletes the original objects
    c. Retains them in the drawing
    d. None of the above

11. The command that allows you to turn invisible attributes on so they are displayed in the drawing is:

    a. **ATTREQ**
    b. **ATTDIA**
    c. **ATTDISP**
    d. **-ATTEDIT**

12. The command that allows you to update the value of an attribute is:

    a. **-ATTEDIT**
    b. **BATTMAN**
    c. **EATTEDIT**
    d. a and c

13. The easiest way to update a changed block definition after it has been inserted is:

    a. Explode all block references and redraw each of them in-place
    b. Explode the block and redefine it using the **BLOCK** command
    c. Use the **REFEDIT** command
    d. Freeze the layer the block is on and draw over it

14. To insert a block from **DesignCenter**, you can:

    a. Drag-and-drop the block using your mouse
    b. Double-click on the block
    c. Right-click on the block and use a shortcut menu command
    d. All of the above

Matching

a. Block attribute

b. Block definition

c. Block reference

d. **BLOCK** command

e. **ByBlock** property

f. **INSERT** command

g. Unit block

h. **WBLOCK** command

i. **ATTDIA** system variable

j. **REFEDIT** command

1. Block drawn within a 1 × 1 unit square that is inserted in the drawing with different *X* and *Y* scales

2. Writes a block definition to an external drawing file (DWG)

3. Dynamic text-like object that can be included in a block definition to store alphanumeric data

4. User-defined collection of drawing objects stored centrally in a drawing

5. Controls whether the **Edit Attributes** dialog box is displayed during the insertion process

6. Creates a block definition using the objects you select with the name specified

7. Property that will assume the current color, linetype, or lineweight property when a block is inserted

8. Redefines a block "in-place" without having to explode the block

9. Inserts a block reference by specifying the block name, insertion point, scale, and rotation angle

10. Instance of a block definition inserted in a drawing that references the central block definition drawing data

CHAPTER PROJECTS

Project 16-1: Classroom Plan—Continued from Chapter 14

1. Open drawing **P14-1** from Chapter 14.
2. Create separate blocks for each of the items shown in Figure P16-1 using the insertion points shown.

3. Create blocks for the left- and right-hand workstations as shown in Figure P16-1 using the insertion points shown. Use the blocks created in the previous step as components of the workstation blocks.
4. Replace the original workstations with the new workstation blocks.
5. Save your drawing as **P16-1**.

Figure P16-1

Project 16-2a: B-Size Mechanical Border—Continued from Chapter 15

1. Open template file **Mechanical B-Size.DWT** from Chapter 15.
2. Create the title block attribute definitions shown in Figure P16-2A. Place the attributes on the **Title** layer. Use the definitions shown in the following table:

Tag	Prompt	Default	Justification	Height
TITLE	Drawing Title	Title	Center	0.2
DESCRIPTION	Description	Description	Center	0.125
PARTNO	Part Number	xxx	Left	0.125
SCALE	Drawing Scale	1:1	Left	0.09375
DWN	Drawn By	AAA	Left	0.09375
SHEET	Sheet Number	1 of 1	Left	0.09375
REV	Revision Number	0	Center	0.125
PROJ_ENG	Project Engineer	AAA	Left	0.09375
PE_DATE	Date	mm/dd/yy	Left	0.09375
DWN_BY	Drawn By	AAA	Left	0.09375

DWN_DATE	Date	mm/dd/yy	Left	0.09375
CHK_BY	Checked By	AAA	Left	0.09375
CHK_DATE	Date	mm/dd/yy	Left	0.09375
MFG_ENG	Manufacturing Engineer	AAA	Left	0.09375
ME_DATE	Date	mm/dd/yy	Left	0.09375

3. Use the **WBLOCK** command to create a block/drawing named **Title Attributes Mechanical B-Size.DWG** by selecting the attributes defined above and shown in Figure P16-2B using the following settings:
   a. Set the **Base point** to **0,0,0**.
   b. Set the **Objects** option to the **Delete from drawing** setting so the attributes are deleted.
   c. Set **Insert units** to **Unitless**.

4. Create the revision block geometry and attribute definitions shown in Figure P16-2A. Place the geometry and attributes on the **Title** layer. Use the definitions shown in the following table:

Tag	Prompt	Default	Justification	Height
ZONE	ZONE	A1	Left	0.09375
REV	Revision Number	1	Left	0.09375
DESCRIPTION	Description	xxx	Left	0.09375
REV_DATE	Revision Date	MM/DD/YY	Left	0.09375
APRVD_BY	Approval By	AAA	Left	0.09375

5. Use the **WBLOCK** command to create a block/drawing named **Revision Block - Mechanical.dwg** by selecting the revision block attributes defined above and shown in Figure P16-2A using the following settings:
   a. Set the **Base point** by snapping to the lower left corner of the revision block.
   b. Set the **Objects** option to the **Delete from drawing** setting so the attributes are deleted.
   c. Set **Insert units** to **Unitless**.

Insertion Point

| ZONE | REV | DESCRIPTION | | REV_DATE | APRVD_BY |

Revision Block - Mechanical

Figure P16-2A

Title Attributes Mechanical B-size

Figure P16-2B

6. Use the **WBLOCK** command to create a block/drawing named **Mechanical B-Size.DWG** by selecting all the remaining title border line work and static text that never changes using the following settings:
   a. Set the **Base point** to **0,0,0**.
   b. Set the **Objects** option to the **Delete from drawing** setting so the attributes are deleted.
   c. Set **Insert units** to **Unitless**.
7. Close the drawing template. *Do not save changes to the drawing template.*

Project 16-2b: C-Size Mechanical Border—Continued from Chapter 15

1. Open template file **Mechanical C-Size.DWT** from Chapter 15.
2. Create the title block attribute definitions shown in Figure P16-2C. Place the attributes on the **Title** layer. Use the definitions shown in the following table:

Tag	Prompt	Default	Justification	Height
TITLE	Drawing Title	Title	Center	0.2
DESCRIPTION	Description	Description	Center	0.125
PARTNO	Part Number	xxx	Left	0.125
SCALE	Drawing Scale	1:1	Left	0.09375
SHEET	Sheet Number	n	Left	0.09375
TOT_SHT	Total Number of Sheets	n	Left	0.09375
REV	Revision Number	0	Center	0.125
PROJ_ENG	Project Engineer	AAA	Left	0.09375
PE_DATE	Date	mm/dd/yy	Left	0.09375
DWN_BY	Drawn By	AAA	Left	0.09375
DWN_DATE	Date	mm/dd/yy	Left	0.09375
CHK_BY	Checked By	AAA	Left	0.09375
CHK_DATE	Date	mm/dd/yy	Left	0.09375
MFG_ENG	Manufacturing Engineer	AAA	Left	0.09375
ME_DATE	Date	mm/dd/yy	Left	0.09375

3. Use the **WBLOCK** command to create a block/drawing named **Title Attributes Mechanical C-Size.DWG** by selecting the attributes defined above and shown in Figure P16-2C using the following settings:
   a. Set the **Base point** to **0,0,0**.
   b. Set the **Objects** option to the **Delete from drawing** setting so the attributes are deleted.
   c. Set **Insert units** to **Unitless**.
4. Use the **WBLOCK** command to create a block/drawing named **Mechanical C-Size.DWG** by selecting all the remaining title border line work and static text that never changes using the following settings:
   a. Set the **Base point** to **0,0,0**.
   b. Set the **Objects** option to the **Delete from drawing** setting so the attributes are deleted.
   c. Set **Insert units** to **Unitless**.
5. Close the drawing template. *Do not save changes to the drawing template.*

Figure P16-2C

Project 16-2c: A-Size Portrait Mechanical Border—Continued from Chapter 15

1. Open template file **Mechanical A-Size-Portrait.DWT** from Chapter 15.
2. Create the title block attribute definitions shown in Figure P16-2D. Place the attributes on the **Title** layer. Use the definitions shown in the following table:

Tag	Prompt	Default	Justification	Height
TITLE	Drawing Title	Title	Center	0.2
DESC	Description	Description	Center	0.125
PARTNO	Part Number	xxx	Left	0.125
SCALE	Drawing Scale	1:1	Left	0.09375
DWN	Drawn By	AAA	Left	0.09375
SHEET	Sheet Number	1 of 1	Left	0.09375
REV	Revision Number	0	Center	0.125
PROJ_ENG	Project Engineer	AAA	Left	0.09375
PE_Date	Date	mm/dd/yy	Left	0.09375
Dwn_By	Drawn By	AAA	Left	0.09375
Dwn_Date	Date	mm/dd/yy	Left	0.09375
CHK_BY	Checked By	AAA	Left	0.09375
Chk_Date	Date	mm/dd/yy	Left	0.09375
MFG_ENG	Manufacturing Engineer	AAA	Left	0.09375
ME_Date	Date	mm/dd/yy	Left	0.09375

Figure P16-2D

3. Use the **WBLOCK** command to create a block/drawing named **Title Attributes Mechanical A-Size-Portrait.DWG** by selecting the attributes defined above and shown in Figure P16-2D using the following settings:
   a. Set the **Base point** to **0,0,0**.
   b. Set the **Objects** option to the **Delete from drawing** setting so the attributes are deleted.
   c. Set **Insert units** to **Unitless**.
4. Use the **WBLOCK** command to create a block/drawing named **Mechanical A-Size-Portrait.DWG** by selecting all the remaining title border line work and static text that never changes using the following settings.
   a. Set the **Base point** to **0,0,0**.
   b. Set the **Objects** option to the **Delete from drawing** setting so the attributes are deleted.
   c. Set **Insert units** to **Unitless**.
5. Close the drawing template. *Do not save changes to the drawing template.*

Project 16-3a: Architectural D-Size Border—Continued from Chapter 15

1. Open template file **Architectural D-Size.DWT** from Chapter 15.
2. Create a layer named **A-ANNO-TTLB-ATTS** with default properties. Set its color to **red** and make it the current layer.
3. Replace all the updateable title block text with the attribute definitions shown in Figure P16-3A and defined in the following table:

Tag	Prompt	Default
DATE	Enter the date:	MM/DD/YY
SCALE	Enter the scale:	1/4″ = 1′-0:
DRNBY	Enter drawn by initials:	AAA
CHKBY	Enter checked by initials:	AAA
PROJECT	Enter project number:	1234
SHTNO	Enter the sheet number:	1
TOTAL	Enter the total number of sheets:	100
TITLE1	Enter the first title line:	TITLE
TITLE2	Enter the second title line:	INTRODUCTION TO AUTOCAD
TITLE3	Enter the third title line:	PRENTICE HALL

4. Use the **WBLOCK** command to create a block/drawing named **Title Attributes Architectural D-Size.DWG** by selecting the attributes defined above and shown in Figure P16-3A using the following settings:
   a. Set the **Base point** to **0,0,0**.
   b. Set the **Objects** option to the **Delete from drawing** setting so the attributes are deleted.
   c. Set **Insert units** to **Unitless**.
5. Replace all the updateable revision text with the attribute definitions shown in Figure P16-3A and defined in the following table:

Tag	Prompt	Default
REVNO	Enter the revision number:	1
REVDATE	Enter the revision date:	MM/DD/YY
REVDESC	Enter the revision description:	REVISED
REVBY	Enter revision by initials:	AAA
APPBY	Enter revision approved by initials:	AAA

6. Use the **WBLOCK** command to create a block/drawing named **Revision Block - Architectural.DWG** by selecting the revision block attributes defined above and shown in Figure P16-3A using the following settings:
   a. Set the **Base point** by snapping to the left endpoint of the line directly above the **REVNO** attribute definition as shown in Figure P16-3A.
   b. Set the **Objects** option to the **Delete from drawing** setting so the attributes are deleted.
   c. Set **Insert units** to **Unitless**.

Figure P16-3A

7. Use the **WBLOCK** command to create a block/drawing named **Architectural D-Size.DWG** by selecting all the remaining title border line work and static text that never changes as shown in Figure P16-3A using the following settings.
    a. Set the **Base point** to **0,0,0**.
    b. Set the **Objects** option to the **Delete from drawing** setting so the objects are deleted.
    c. Set **Insert units** to **Unitless**.
    Note: Do not include the graphic scale in the upper right-hand corner as part of title block definition!

Project 16-3b: Architectural B-Size Border—Continued from Chapter 15

1. Open template file **Architectural B-Size.DWT** from Chapter 15.
2. Create a layer named **A-ANNO-TTLB-ATTS** with default properties. Set its color to **red** and make it the current layer.
3. Replace all the updateable title block text with the attribute definitions shown in Figure P16-3B and defined in the following table:

Tag	Prompt	Default
DATE	Enter the date:	MM/DD/YY
SCALE	Enter the scale:	1/8″ = 1′-0:
DRNBY	Enter drawn by initials:	AAA
CHKBY	Enter checked by initials:	AAA
PROJECT	Enter project number:	1234
DWGNO	Enter the drawing number:	1
TITLE1	Enter the first title line:	TITLE
TITLE2	Enter the second title line:	INTRODUCTION TO AUTOCAD
TITLE3	Enter the third title line:	PRENTICE HALL

Figure P16-3B

4. Use the **WBLOCK** command to create a block/drawing named **Title Attributes Architectural B-Size.DWG** by selecting the attributes defined above and shown in Figure P16-3B using the following settings:
   a. Set the **Base point** to **0,0,0**.
   b. Set the **Objects** option to the **Delete from drawing** setting so the attributes are deleted.
   c. Set **Insert units** to **Unitless**.

5. Use the **WBLOCK** command to create a block/drawing named **Architectural B-Size.DWG** by selecting all the remaining title border line work and static text that never changes as shown in Figure P16-3B using the following settings:
   a. Set the **Base point** to **0,0,0**.
   b. Set the **Objects** option to the **Delete from drawing** setting so the attributes are deleted.
   c. Set **Insert units** to **Unitless**.

Project 16-3c: Architectural A-Size Border—Continued from Chapter 15

1. Open template file **Architectural A-Size.DWT** from Chapter 15.
2. Create a layer named **A-ANNO-TTLB-ATTS** with default properties. Set its color to **red** and make it the current layer.
3. Replace all the updateable title block text with the attribute definitions shown in Figure P16-3C and defined in the following table:

Tag	Prompt	Default
DATE	Enter the date:	MM/DD/YY
SCALE	Enter the scale:	1/4″ = 1′-0:
DRNBY	Enter drawn by initials:	AAA
CHKBY	Enter checked by initials:	AAA
PROJECT	Enter project number:	1234
SHTNO	Enter the sheet number:	1
TITLE1	Enter the first title line:	TITLE
TITLE2	Enter the second title line:	INTRODUCTION TO AUTOCAD
TITLE3	Enter the third title line:	PRENTICE HALL

4. Use the **WBLOCK** command to create a block/drawing named **Title Attributes Architectural A-Size.DWG** by selecting the attributes defined above and shown in Figure P16-3C using the following settings:
   a. Set the **Base point** to **0,0,0**.
   b. Set the **Objects** option to the **Delete from drawing** setting so the attributes are deleted.
   c. Set **Insert units** to **Unitless**.

5. Use the **WBLOCK** command to create a block/drawing named **Architectural A-Size.DWG** by selecting all the remaining title border line work and static text that never changes as shown in Figure P16-3C using the following settings:
   a. Set the **Base point** to **0,0,0**.
   b. Set the **Objects** option to the **Delete from drawing** setting so the attributes are deleted.
   c. Set **Insert units** to **Unitless**.

Figure P16-3C

Project 16-4: Electrical Schematic—Continued from Chapter 14

1. Open drawing **P14-5** from Chapter 14.
2. Create blocks for each of the electrical symbols shown in Figure P16-4. Choose appropriate names and insertion points for each block. Use the **E-Lite** or **E-Powr** layers to place the symbol annotation. Place all description annotation on the **E-Anno** layer.
3. Replace the symbols in the drawing with the new blocks you just created.
4. Freeze all layers *except* the electrical layers (layers starting with E-).
5. Use the **WBLOCK** command to create a drawing called **Electrical Plan.dwg** by selecting all the geometry on the electrical layers using the following settings:
   a. Set the **Base point** to **0,0,0**.
   b. Set the **Objects** option to the **Delete from drawing** setting so geometry is deleted.
   c. Set **Insert units** to **inches**.
6. Use the **PURGE** command to remove the **E-** layers and all electrical blocks from the drawing.
7. Save the drawing as **P16-4**.

ELECTRICAL SYMBOLS:

Figure P16-4

Project 16-5: Architectural Plan—Continued from Project 16-4

1. Open drawing **P16-4**.
2. Freeze the **L-Walk, L-Walk-Pat, A-Area,** and **A-Area-Iden** layers.
3. Create blocks for each of the symbols shown in Figure P16-5A. Choose appropriate insertion points for each block. For the door and window callouts, create attributes with the definitions shown in the following table. Choose appropriate default values for the door and window attributes. Place all geometry on appropriate layers.

Tag	Prompt	Invisible	Justification	Height
SYM	Callout Symbol	N	Middle	4
SIZE	Size	Y	Middle	4
TYPE	Type	Y	Middle	4

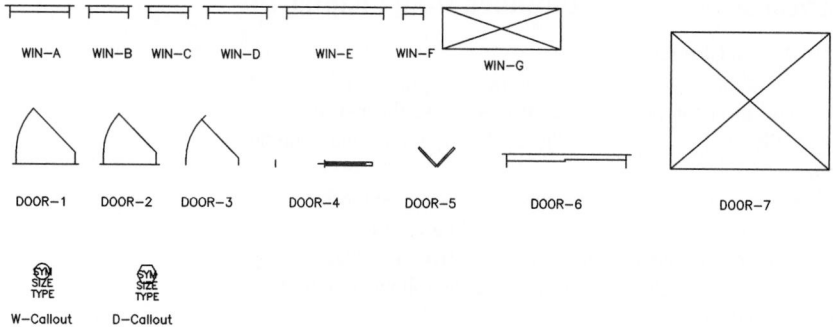

Figure P16-5A

4. Replace the symbols in the drawing with the new blocks. Delete the door and window schedules from the model space environment. Place the new blocks on the appropriate layer.
5. Switch to **Architectural D-Size** layout. Select the **Extract Data** tool on the **Linking & Extraction** panel on the **Insert** ribbon to start the **Data Extraction** wizard. Create a window schedule by extracting the **W-Callout** block attributes to a table. Arrange the columns in the order shown and sort the table by the **SYM** field. Create/modify table styles as needed to match the table shown in Figure P16-5B.
6. Create another table for the door schedule shown in Figure P16-5B by extracting the **D-Callout** block attributes to a table.
7. Save the drawing as **Architectural Plan.dwg**.

Figure P16-5B

Project 16-6: Socket Head Cap Screws—English Units—Continued from Chapter 11

1. Open drawing **P11-6** from Chapter 11.
2. Create blocks from the metric fasteners created for Chapter 11 using the following settings:
   a. Name the block as indicated in Figure P16-6. Do not include the text in the block definition.
   b. Specify the base point shown with "X" in Figure P16-6.
   c. Select the **Convert to block** option so the block is converted in place.
   d. Select the **Allow exploding** option.

10-24-T   10-24-500   25-20-T   25-20-750

Figure P16-6

3. Save the drawing as **Socket Head Cap Screws** but leave the drawing open.
4. Start a new drawing using the acad.dwt template.
5. Start **DesignCenter** and select the **Open Drawings** tab.
6. Select the plus symbol (+) next to the **Socket Head Cap Screws.dwg** drawing to expand the tree.
7. Select the **Blocks** icon so that the fastener blocks you created in step 2 are displayed in the Contents area on the right.
8. Practice dragging-and-dropping fastener symbols into your drawing using both the left and right mouse buttons.
9. Double-click on a block to display the **Insert** dialog box.

Project 16-7: Metric Fastener Symbol Library—Continued from Chapter 6

1. Open drawing **P6-7** from Chapter 6.
2. Create blocks from the metric fasteners created for Chapter 6 using the following settings:
   a. Name the block as indicated in Figure P16-7. Do not include the text in the block definition.
   b. Specify the base point shown with "X" in Figure P16-7.

   c. Select the **Convert to block** option so the block is converted in place.
   d. Select the **Allow exploding** option.
3. Save the drawing as **Fastener Symbols** but leave the drawing open.
4. Start a new drawing using the acad.dwt template.
5. Start **DesignCenter** and select the **Open Drawings** tab.
6. Select the plus symbol (+) next to the **Fastener Symbols.dwg** drawing to expand the tree.
7. Select the **Blocks** icon so that the fastener blocks you created in step 2 are displayed in the Contents area on the right.
8. Practice dragging-and-dropping fastener symbols into your drawing using both the left and right mouse buttons.
9. Double-click on a block to display the **Insert** dialog box.

Figure P16-7

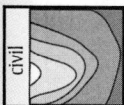

Project 16-8: Civil Site Plan—Continued from Chapter 14

1. Open drawing **P14-8** from Chapter 14.
2. Create blocks for the landscaping objects and North arrow as shown in Figure P16-8.
3. Replace the landscaping symbols with the blocks.
4. Save the drawing as **P16-8**.

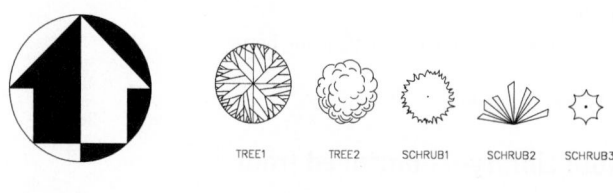

Figure P16-8

Working with External References 17

INTRODUCTION

Rapidly produced, high-quality drawings are the objective of any drafter or designer. When changes are made to a design, drawings must be updated to reflect the changes. Opening and editing each drawing affected by a change can be a time-consuming process. AutoCAD can help with this process by allowing changes in one drawing to be automatically reflected in other files. This is done through the use of externally referenced drawings, called *xrefs*.

When you create an xref, you are placing a reference to another drawing into your drawing. When changes are made to the referenced drawing, your drawing is updated to reflect the changes.

For example, consider the design of a building where multiple people are working on various aspects of the building at once. People working on the HVAC, piping, and electrical systems need to see where the walls, doors, and windows are located. In this situation, the HVAC, piping, and electrical designers could place an xref of the floor plan into their drawings. That way, when changes are made to the floor plan, the xref will update to show those changes, and they can adjust their design as needed.

AutoCAD also allows you to create similar references to raster images. Raster images can enhance your drawing by providing additional visual information to your drawing. Civil or architectural drawings can use an image as a background to locate placement points or structural positions. Satellite or aerial views can be used to trace or locate utilities or roadways. Raster images can also be used to enhance the appearance of your company name or logo. Images are similar to xrefs in that AutoCAD creates a reference to the raster image file. If and when the raster image updates, the changes are automatically reflected in your drawing.

In many design environments, design data can come from many different sources and in different formats. Often, vector drawing data may be provided in a format that you only wish to view, but not modify. To accommodate this, AutoCAD provides a way to display and view this type of CAD information, called *underlays*. An underlay is similar to both xref drawings and raster images.

xref: A drawing that is referenced by another drawing. The drawing references are updated when the source drawing is modified.

underlay: A CAD file that is not directly modifiable by AutoCAD but is still displayed within a drawing and updated when the source data is changed.

AutoCAD allows you to display DWF (Design Web Format), DGN (MicroStation Design), and PDF (Adobe Portable Document Format) files as underlays. The DWF file format is a compressed vector-based drawing file format developed by Autodesk that allows you to share your drawings with other individuals who do not have AutoCAD and/or who should not have access to sensitive, proprietary design information.

DWF files cannot be modified; they can only be viewed and marked up. Autodesk provides free downloadable software on its Website, called Design Review, that allows you to view, mark up, and print DWF files. Another advantage of DWF files is that DWF file sizes are significantly smaller than the original drawing files (DWG) so that they take up less room and can be transferred faster electronically via email or the Internet.

DGN files are vector-based drawing files created by MicroStation, a CAD package similar to AutoCAD. AutoCAD currently supports DGN files created by version 8 (V8) of MicroStation. DGN files cannot be modified by AutoCAD directly; however, AutoCAD can convert DGN files to the DWG file format. AutoCAD can also export drawing data to the DGN file format. See Chapter 18 for more on importing and exporting drawing data.

PDF files, which are also a vector-based format, are the industry standard for sharing electronic information because they can be easily viewed and printed using the free Adobe Reader software (version 7 or later) that is installed on most computers. Using PDF files, you can share drawings with practically anyone. You can download the Adobe Reader software at www.Adobe .com if you do not have it installed. While it is not possible to convert a PDF file into the AutoCAD DWG format, you can create PDF files from your AutoCAD drawings. See Chapter 15 for more information about plotting and the procedure for creating PDF files.

In this chapter, we'll examine xrefs, images, and underlays, the different ways they can be embedded in a drawing, how they are updated, and how to manage and keep track of their relationships.

THE REFERENCE PANEL

Located on the **Insert** ribbon, the **Reference** panel shown in Figure 17-1 provides most of the tools needed to work with the different types of reference files described above. The **Attach** tool allows you create a reference to any of the different file types using one standard file selection dialog box. The **Clip** tool helps you reduce visual clutter and increase drawing performance by allowing you to "clip," or cut out, portions of a reference file that do not need to be viewed in your drawing. The **Adjust** tool allows you to adjust the fade, contrast, and monochrome settings of referenced images and underlays. Other tools allow you to control reference layer settings, whether a frame or border is displayed around the edges of a reference, and turn on/off the ability

Note:

By default, xrefs appear lighter than nonreferenced drawing information so that you can distinguish between information that is part of your drawing and can be modified and information that is part of a reference file and cannot be modified unless you open the xref or use one of the xref editing tools explained later. The xref fade level can be adjusted using the **Xref fading** slider control that can be displayed by clicking on the down arrow on the bottom of the **Reference** panel to display the expanded panel. It is set to 70 percent by default.

Figure 17-1   The **Reference** panel

to snap to reference features using AutoCAD's Object Snap feature. All these tools and more are covered in detail in the following sections.

EXTERNAL REFERENCES PALETTE

Xrefs, raster images, and underlay files are all managed using the **External References** palette shown in Figure 17-1. The **External References** palette can be displayed by selecting the angled down arrow on the right side of the **Reference** panel shown in Figure 17-2.

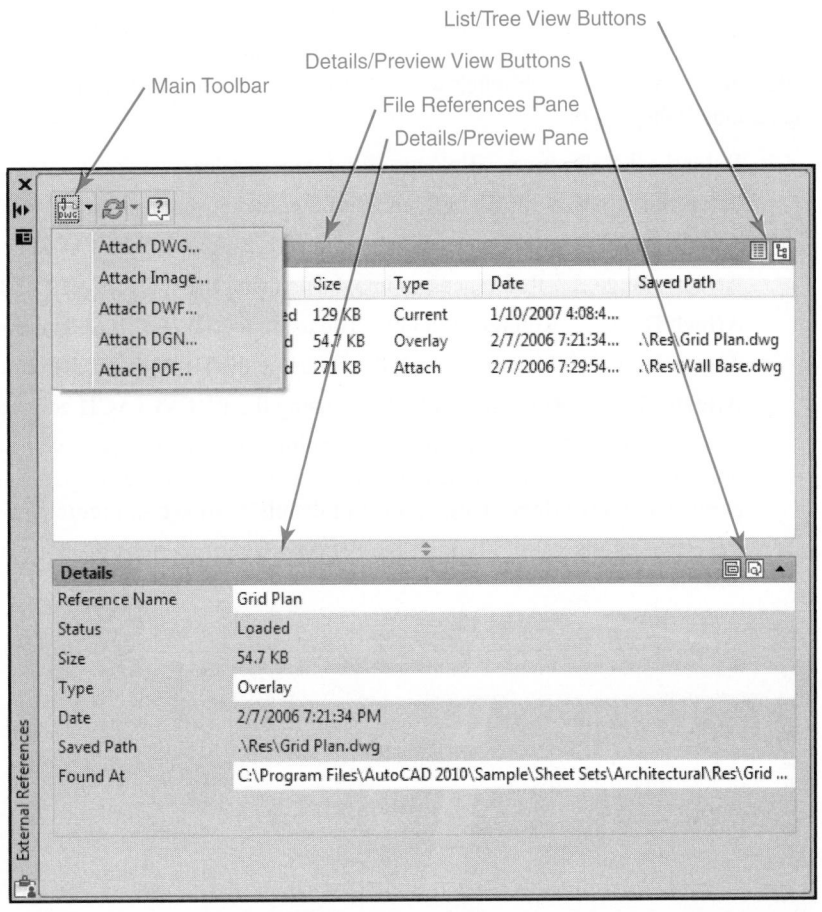

External References	
Ribbon & Panel:	Insert|Reference
Reference Toolbar:	
Menu:	Insert|External References...
Command Line:	XREF
Command Alias:	XR

Figure 17-2   The **External References** palette

The toolbar on the top of the **External References** palette allows you to create new file references and refresh the status of existing file references. The button on the left of the toolbar displays a drop-down menu with the following reference attachment options:

- **Attach DWG...**   References another drawing file (DWG) using the **XATTACH** command
- **Attach Image...**   References a raster image file (BMP, JPG, GIF, etc.) using the **IMAGEATTACH** command
- **Attach DWF...**   References a Drawing Web Format file (DWF) using the **DWFATTACH** command
- **Attach DGN...**   References a DGN file using the **DGNATTACH** command
- **Attach PDF...**   References a PDF file using the **PDFATTACH** command

Whichever of these attachment options is selected becomes the default button displayed on the toolbar.

The **Refresh** button in the middle updates the status of reference files so that they are current, and the question mark (?) button displays the AutoCAD Help topic for External References.

The **File References** pane lists the current drawing, referred to as the *master drawing,* and any referenced drawings, raster images, or underlays along with their current status, size, type, and the date/time they were last updated. Files can be displayed in the default **List View** mode (F3) or in **Tree View** mode (F4) using the buttons on the top right of the **File References** pane or their corresponding function key. The **Tree View** mode makes it possible to view any nested references and how they are related.

> In the **List View** mode, you can select two or more files using the standard Windows **<Shift>** and **<Ctrl>** key methods.

Right-click shortcut menus provide most of the options for working with the files in the **File References** pane. If you right-click when no files are selected, a shortcut menu with the following options is displayed:

- **Reload All References**   Reloads all referenced files
- **Select All**   Selects all file references except the current drawing
- **Attach DWG...**   References another drawing using the **XATTACH** command
- **Attach Image...**   References an image file using the **IMAGEATTACH** command
- **Attach DWF...**   References a DWF file using the **DWFATTACH** command
- **Attach DGN...**   References a DGN file using the **DGNATTACH** command
- **Attach PDF...**   References a PDF file using the **PDFATTACH** command
- **Tooltip Style**   Allows you to set the tooltip style shown when you hover your mouse pointer over a reference name to display either the file name of the reference, a graphical preview in one of three sizes, or a list of details as shown in Figure 17-3
- **Preview/Details Pane**   Toggles the **Preview/Details** pane at the bottom of the palette on and off

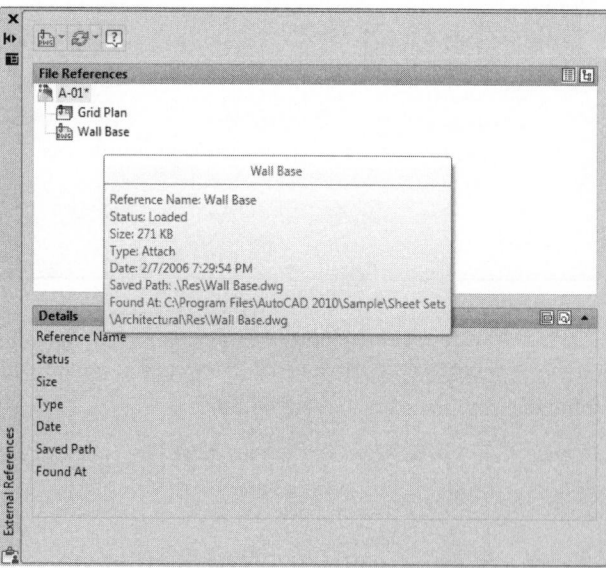

Figure 17-3   Tooltip Style set to Details mode

Right-clicking when one or more files are selected displays a shortcut menu with some or all of the following options, depending on the file type(s) selected:

- **Open**   Opens the selected file reference using the associated application
- **Attach...**   Displays the attach dialog box corresponding to the selected reference type
- **Unload**   Unloads the selected file reference
- **Reload**   Reloads the selected file reference
- **Detach**   Detaches the selected file reference

- **Bind...**   Displays the **Bind Xrefs** dialog box so that you can make an xref part of the current drawing (available only for referenced DWG files)

The **Details/Preview** pane on the bottom can either display properties for the selected file references or a thumbnail preview if available. Use the buttons on the top right of the **Details/Preview** pane to switch between the two different modes. The default **Details** pane displays the following properties for all reference files types:

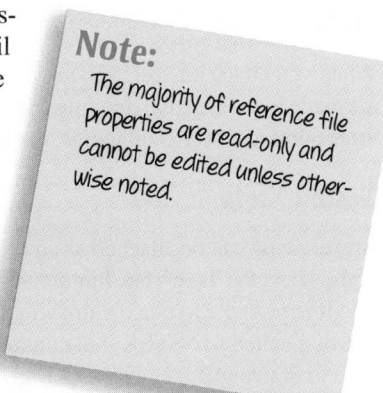

Note:
The majority of reference file properties are read-only and cannot be edited unless otherwise noted.

- **Reference Name**   File reference name in drawing. Displays *Varies* if multiple file references are selected (Editable)

- **Status**   Displays whether file reference is loaded, unloaded, or not found (Read-only)

- **Size**   Displays the file size of selected file reference (Read-only)

- **Type**   Indicates if a DWG file reference is an attachment or overlay, the image file type or underlay (Editable for DWG files/Read-only for images, DWF, DGN, and PDF files). You can use this property to quickly switch referenced drawings between the Attach and Overlay attachment type after an xref has been attached without having to detach and reattach it again.

- **Date**   Displays last date the file reference was modified (Read-only)

- **Saved Path**   Displays the saved path of the selected file reference. This path can be different from where the file was found because of the different options available for locating reference files (Read-only).

- **Found At**   Displays full path of the selected file reference. This path is where the referenced file is actually found and might not be the same as the **Saved Path** property above. Selecting the [...] button to the right displays the **Select new path** dialog box where you can select a different file or file location. Valid path changes are stored to the **Saved Path** property above (Editable).

TIP   It is possible to specify a different reference file using the [...] button on the right. When you do this, AutoCAD simply references the specified file instead of the file specified in the **Reference Name**. This allows you to quickly swap one reference file for another.

If you select a referenced raster image file, additional image-specific properties are displayed such as the image size and resolution. All the additional image properties are read-only and cannot be edited.

The specifics of using the **External References** palette to reference and manage file types are detailed in the following sections beginning with the first, and arguably the most popular of the reference file types, external drawing (DWG) references. These are commonly referred to in the industry as *xrefs*.

BLOCKS VERSUS XREFS

Xrefs are similar to blocks but with a few notable exceptions.

Blocks

When you insert a block, you are creating a reference to a block definition that exists entirely inside the drawing file. When you insert an external drawing file with the **INSERT** command,

AutoCAD converts the external drawing file into an internal block definition. Changes to the original drawing file are not reflected in the drawings containing the inserted blocks.

Xrefs

When you attach an xref, you are directly referencing an external drawing file. Whenever changes are made to the external drawing file, all the references to that drawing are updated as well. Because xrefs point to external drawings, the location of the drawing file (the file path) is important.

Nested Xrefs

Any drawing can be attached as an xref to another xref, a concept known as nesting. To view nested xrefs, select the **Tree View** button on the **File References** pane on the **External References** palette.

It is possible to place a drawing that contains an xref as an xref. For example, say you have a drawing called MASTER that contains a reference to drawing A, and drawing A contains a reference to drawing B (see Figure 17-4). In this example, drawing B is referred to as a ***nested xref***.

Xref nesting can lead to some interesting or unexpected results. In the example above, when you reference drawing A, drawing B comes along as a nested xref. However, drawing B could also contain an xref (drawing C), and drawing C might also contain an xref, and the nesting could go on and on. You can also create circular xrefs where drawings reference one another. For example, drawing A could reference drawing B, and drawing B could reference drawing A.

If AutoCAD detects circular xrefs, it will display a warning that circular references are detected (see Figure 17-5) and ask if you want to continue. If you choose Yes, AutoCAD will break the circular reference and proceed with loading the xref.

> **nested xref:** An xref within an xref. This occurs when the drawing you are referencing contains a reference to another drawing.

Figure 17-4   Nested xrefs

Figure 17-5   Circular xrefs warning

DWG Reference	
Ribbon & Panel:	Insert| Reference
	Attach
Reference Toolbar:	
Menu:	Insert| DWG Reference...
Command Line:	XATTACH
Command Alias:	XA

ATTACHING AN XREF

When you attach an xref, you create a link to an external drawing file in your drawing. You can attach an xref by either selecting **Attach DWG...** from the drop-down or right-click menu in the **External References** palette or via the **Attach** tool on the **Reference** panel. Once you've selected a drawing, and select **OPEN**, AutoCAD displays the **External Reference** dialog box (shown in Figure 17-6).

Attach Versus Overlay

When you attach an xref, you can tell AutoCAD how you want that xref to behave when referenced in other

Note: When AutoCAD references a drawing, only model space objects are included. Objects in paper space are ignored.

Figure 17-6   The **Attach External Reference** dialog box

drawings. The **Attach** option tells AutoCAD to load this drawing and any nested xrefs. The **Overlay** option tells AutoCAD to ignore any nested xrefs and load only the top-level drawing.

The **Attach** and **Overlay** options control only how nested xrefs behave when the drawing is referenced in another drawing.

Setting the Path Type

When AutoCAD loads an xref, it must locate the drawing on your computer or network. The file path is the location of the drawing file on your system. It includes the drive letter or server name along with the list of folders and subfolders where the drawing file is located.

When you create an xref, you can tell AutoCAD how you want to store the path to the drawing file. You have the option of saving the **Full path, Relative path,** or **No path**:

- **Full path**   If the **Path type** is set to **Full path**, AutoCAD stores the entire path, including the local hard drive name or the network location and the entire list of folders and subfolders where the drawing is located. For example, *C:\Design\Projects\8013\arch* describes the full path to a drawing file. In this example, the xref is located on the local *C:* drive, in the *Design\Projects\8013\arch* folder.

- **Relative path**   Using the **Relative path** option, AutoCAD automatically updates the xref path to assume the current path of the master, or host, drawing so that drive letters and network server names are not a factor as long as the subfolder structure stays the same. AutoCAD replaces the period (.) in the relative path with the path to the master drawing file. For example, if the relative path is set to *.\Xrefs*, the referenced drawings can be located at *C:\Design\Projects\8013\Xrefs* on one computer or at the network location *N:\Consultants\AEC Architects\Projects\8013\Xrefs* on another computer. The only requirement is that the master drawing is located in the *8013* folder on both computers so that the subfolder structure is the same.

- **No path**   Using **No path**, AutoCAD will store only the xref drawing name and no path information. When AutoCAD opens the drawing, it will look for the xref in the current drawing folder. If it doesn't find the xref there, it will then search the folders defined in the AutoCAD **Support File Search Path**. The **Support File Search Path** is defined in the **Files** tab on the **Options** dialog box. If it still doesn't find the xref, it will display a note in the **Command Line** window that the xref cannot be found.

If your drawing files remain at a single location and are never moved or sent to another site, the drawing file paths will remain the same every time you load a drawing file. However, if you send your drawings to other sites (to a contractor, client, manufacturer, etc.), you need to consider how your drawings will be loaded at these remote sites. Using the **Relative path** or **No path** options may make it easier for others to locate the xref drawings.

Insertion Point, Scale, and Rotation

Once you set the reference **Type** and the **Path** type, the rest of the attachment process is identical to inserting a block. The **Insertion point**, **Scale**, and **Rotation** options work exactly like those in the **INSERT** command. You can specify these values in the dialog box or by selecting them in the drawing.

MANAGE XREFS ICON

When xrefs are attached to a drawing, the **Manage Xrefs** icon is displayed in the system tray in the lower-right corner (see Figure 17-7). Clicking on the icon displays the **External References** palette, providing a quick way to check xrefs and their status in the current drawing. If an attached xref changes, a notification balloon is also displayed in the system tray, indicating that the xref needs to be reloaded with a link to reload it (see Figure 17-12).

Manage Xrefs Icon

Figure 17-7   The **Manage Xrefs** icon

Exercise 17-1: Attaching an Xref

To access student data files, go to www.pearsondesigncentral.com.

1. Start a new drawing using the **Architectural D-size.DWT** drawing template located in the student data files.
2. Switch to the **Model** tab.
3. Create a layer named **References** and assign a **Continuous** linetype and color **7**. Set this layer **Current**.
4. Select the **Insert** tab to display the **Reference** panel and select the **External References** button to display the **External References** palette.
5. Select **Attach DWG...** from the **External References** palette toolbar. Select the **Grid Plan.dwg** located in AutoCAD's **\Sample\Sheet Sets\Architectural\Res** folder.
6. Set the **Reference Type** to **Attach**. Set the **Insertion point** to **0,0**, the **Scale** to **1**, and the **Rotation** to **0**. Choose **OK** to place the xref in your drawing. Do a **Zoom Extents** to see the entire xref.
7. Select **Attach DWG...** from the **External References** palette toolbar again. Select the **Wall Base.dwg** located in the **\Sample\Sheet Sets\Architectural\Res** folder.
8. Set the **Reference Type** to **Attach**. Set the **Insertion point** to **0,0**, the **Scale** to **1**, and the **Rotation** to **0**. Choose **OK** to place the xref in your drawing. Do another **Zoom Extents** to see the entire xref.
9. Save the drawing as **EX17-1**. Your drawing should resemble Figure 17-8.

LAYERS AND XREFS

When you attach an xref to a drawing, all the drawing's layers come with it. However, AutoCAD distinguishes between layers in the current drawing and layers in an xref by appending the file name along with the pipe (|) character to the layer name. For example, if you reference a drawing called **Grid**, which contains a layer called **S-Grid**, AutoCAD will display the layer name as **Grid|S-Grid** in the **Layer Manager** palette.

If your drawing contains multiple references to the same drawing file, AutoCAD will assign a number to each reference and append it along with the file name. For example, if you have two references to the drawing **Grid** in your drawing, AutoCAD will display the layers **Grid|1_S-Grid** and **Grid|2_S-Grid** in the **Layer Manager** palette. The **Layer Manager** palette also gives you filters for displaying the layers for any given xref.

Figure 17-8   The attached xrefs

Changing Xref Layers

The initial state of the xref layers will be the state in which the source drawing was saved. A layer that was frozen in a drawing will initially appear frozen when that drawing is referenced. You can make changes to xref layers, but there are some limitations on what you can do. You cannot set an xref layer as the current layer, and you cannot rename xref layers. However, you can change the color, linetype, lineweight, and visibility of xref layers. This allows you to change how xref layers are displayed and plotted within your drawing.

When you make changes to xref layers settings, AutoCAD will retain any changes to the layer settings the next time the drawing is loaded.

TIP

You can control the retention of xref layer settings with the **VISRETAIN** system variable. Setting **VISRETAIN** to **1** tells AutoCAD to retain any changes made to xref layers. Setting **VISRETAIN** to **0** tells AutoCAD to ignore changes made to xref layers and use the setting stored in the reference drawing each time the reference is loaded. This variable can also be set with the **Retain changes to Xref layers** box in the **Open and Save** tab of the **OPTIONS** command.

Exercise 17-2: Xref Layers

1. Continue from Exercise 17-1.
2. Start the **LAYER** command. AutoCAD displays the **Layer Manager** palette.

Figure 17-9   The modified xref layers

3. Expand the **Xref** tree in the filters on the left side of the palette. You'll see the loaded xrefs listed in the tree. Choose the **Wall Base** xref to show only the layers in that xref.
4. Freeze all the layers that start with **Wall Base|1_**. Thaw all the **Wall Base|2_** layers. Freeze all the **Wall Base|2_Arch_Reflected_Ceiling_Plan_** layers. This isolates the second-floor layers for this building. Choose **OK** to close the **Layer Manager** palette.
5. Save the drawing as **EX17-2**. Your drawing should resemble Figure 17-9.

MANAGING XREFS

The **External References** palette discussed earlier is the main xref management tool (see Figure 17-10).

The default **List** view shows each reference along with its status (loaded or unloaded), file size, attachment type (attach or overlay), file date, and the full path to where the reference is located. The list can be sorted by any column type by selecting the column header at the top of the list as shown in Figure 17-10.

The **Tree** view shows the hierarchy of the loaded xrefs. This allows you to see nested xrefs and their relationship with other xrefs in the drawing as shown in Figure 17-11.

Click on Any Column Header to Sort Info

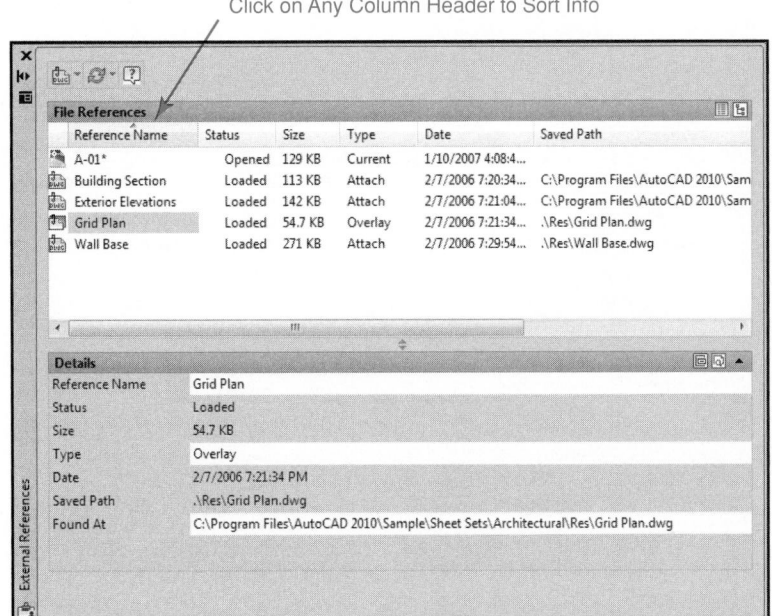

Figure 17-10   **External References** palette – **List** view

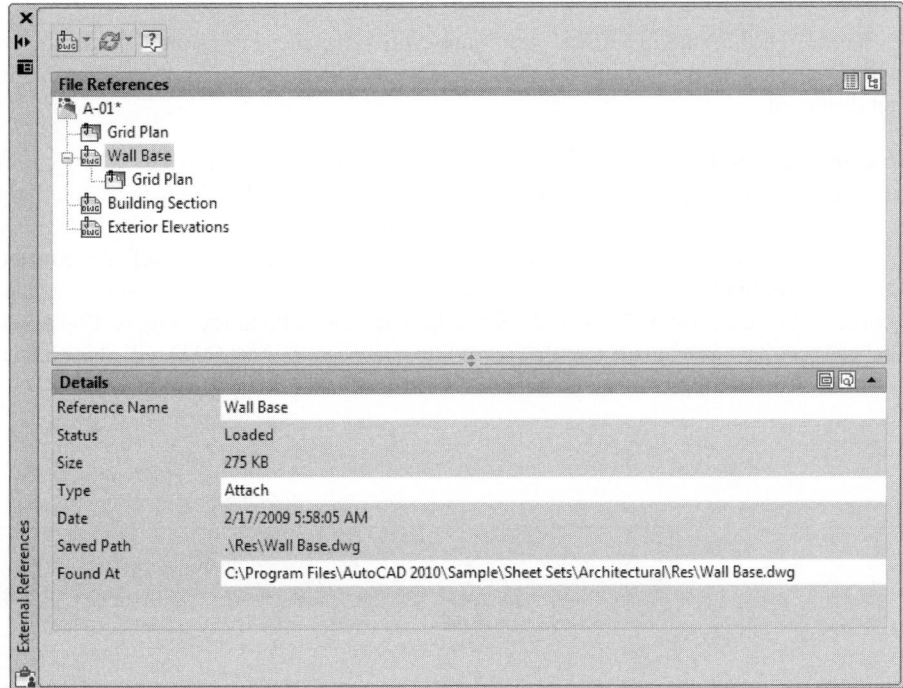

Figure 17-11   **External References** palette – **Tree** view

The Right-Click Menu

As mentioned earlier, most of the xref options and settings are provided via a shortcut menu that is displayed when you right-click on an xref in the **File References** pane as shown in Figure 17-12.

Open.   The **Open** menu item will open the selected referenced drawing(s) in a new drawing window. When you select **Open**, AutoCAD changes the status of the drawing(s) to **Opened** in the **External References** palette. This is the same as choosing **Open** from the **File** pull-down menu and opening the referenced file directly. The advantage of using **Open** from the **File References** palette is that AutoCAD will locate the drawing and open it automatically. It also allows you to open multiple drawings at the same time.

Attach....   The **Attach...** menu item will display the corresponding attach-type dialog box for the currently selected file type so you can attach another reference file of the same type. This option is unavailable when more than one file is selected.

Right-Click Shortcut Menu

Figure 17-12   **External References** palette – right-click menu

Unload.   The **Unload** menu item will remove the selected xref(s) from the drawing screen but will retain the reference within the drawing. The xref layers are still retained but the drawing is not displayed.

Reload.   The **Reload** menu item reloads xref(s) in the current drawing. When you reload an xref, AutoCAD reopens the drawing from the location specified in the path. Reloading is necessary when changes are made to an xref while the current drawing is open. The **Reload** menu item also allows you to reload any unloaded xrefs. Once you reload an xref, the **Status** column changes to **Reloaded**. If you have an xref loaded into your drawing and changes are made to the source of the xref, AutoCAD will display a notification balloon (see Figure 17-13) telling you that changes have been made and that reloading is necessary. AutoCAD will also change the status in the **File References** pane to note that reloading is necessary (see Figure 17-14).

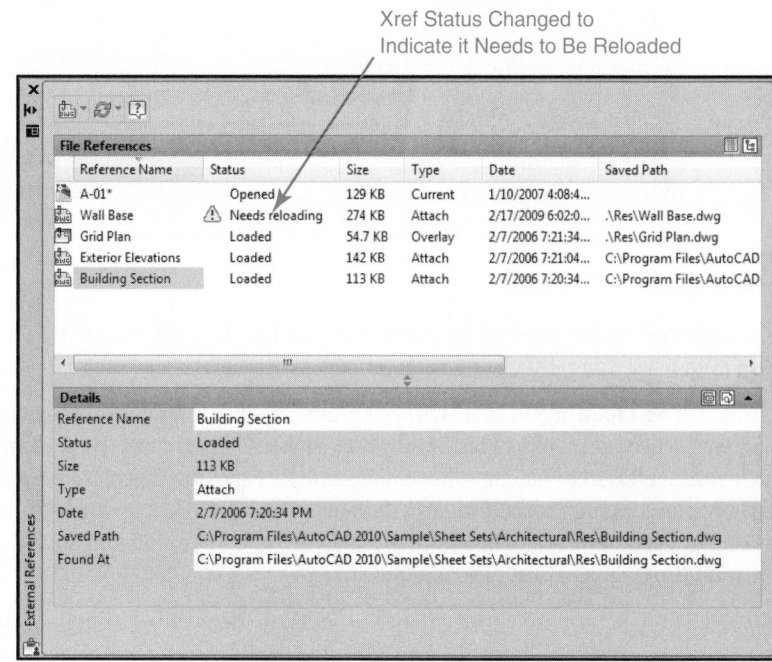

Xref Status Changed to
Indicate it Needs to Be Reloaded

Figure 17-13   The xref notification balloon

Figure 17-14   The xref status

Detach.   The **Detach** menu item will remove attached xref(s). This completely removes the xref and any nested xrefs from your drawing. All xref layer information is also removed from your drawing.

Bind.   The **Bind...** menu item converts an externally referenced drawing to an AutoCAD block in the master drawing. When you bind an xref, the xref becomes a permanent part of the current drawing, and any link to the referenced file is broken. The file is removed from the **File References** palette and changes made to the original referenced drawing will not be updated. When you bind an xref, you have some options for how to deal with layer names. When you choose the **Bind** button, AutoCAD displays the **Bind Xrefs** dialog box (see Figure 17-15), which allows you to control how the xrefs are bound.

Figure 17-15   The **Bind Xrefs** dialog box

The Bind Option.   The **Bind** option binds the selected xref to the current drawing. Xref layers are converted from the format *xref|layer* to the format *xref%n%layer*, where the number *n* is assigned automatically. This allows xref-dependent layers to retain their unique identity.

For example, if you have an xref named **FLOOR1** containing a layer named **WALL**, this layer would appear as **FLOOR1|WALL** while the drawing is an xref. Once you bind the xref using the **Bind** option, the layer name is converted to **FLOOR1$0$WALL**. If the layer **FLOOR1$0$WALL** already existed, the layer **FLOOR1|WALL** would be converted to **FLOOR1$1$WALL**.

Note:
Other named objects (i.e., dimension styles, block definitions, text styles, etc.) are renamed in a similar fashion. For example, if the FLOOR1 drawing contained a block named DOOR, the block definition would be renamed FLOOR1$0$DOOR.

TIP   The **BINDTYPE** system variable allows you to change how object definitions are renamed when bound. When **BINDTYPE** is set to **0** (the default), object definitions are renamed using the numbering convention. For example, **FLOOR1|WALL** is converted to **FLOOR1$0$WALL**.

When **BINDTYPE** is set to **1**, object definitions are not renamed, and the xref name is ignored. For example, **FLOOR1|WALL** is converted to **WALL**.

The Insert Option.   The **Insert** option binds the xref to the current drawing in a way similar to detaching and inserting the reference drawing. Rather than renaming xref layers, the layers are stripped of their xref name and no numbering occurs. If a layer already exists, the layers are simply merged into a single layer, and the layer retains the properties of the existing layer.

For example, if you have an xref named **FLOOR1** containing a layer named **WALL**, after binding it with the **Insert** option, the xref-dependent layer **FLOOR1|WALL** becomes layer **WALL**.

Exercise 17-3: Managing Xrefs

1. Continue from Exercise 17-2.
2. Display the **External References** palette if it is not already displayed.
3. Select the **Grid Plan** reference. In the **Type** property, select **Attach** and change the attachment type to **Overlay**. Repeat this for the **Wall Base** reference.
4. Select the **Wall Base** reference, right-click, and select **Unload...** from the shortcut menu. The **Status** column changes to **Unload**.
5. The **Wall Base** reference drawing is unloaded and disappears from your drawing.

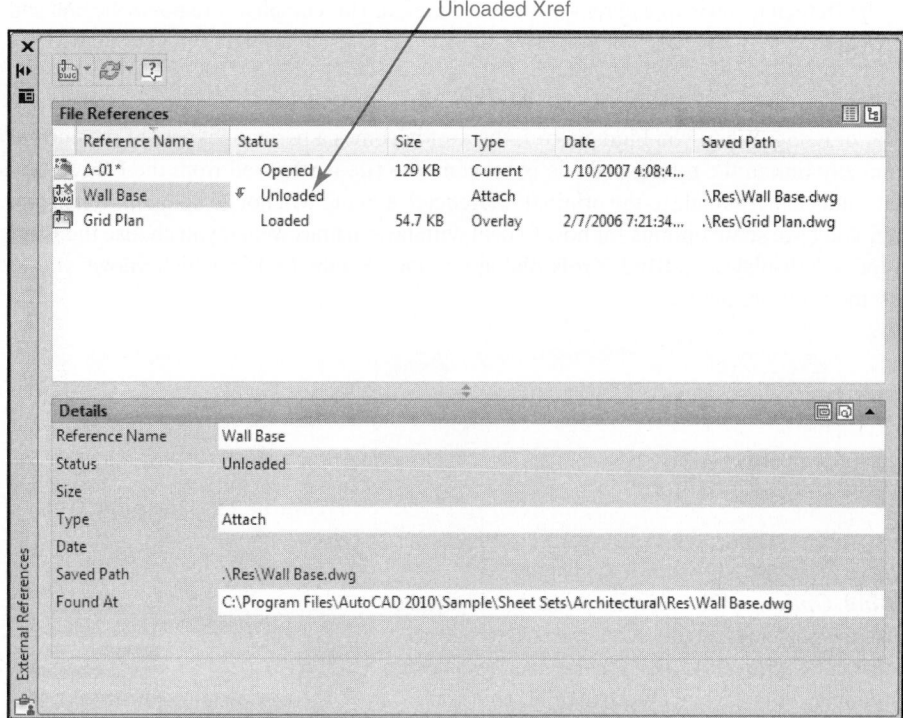

Figure 17-16   The unloaded xref

6. The **Wall Base** drawing is shown as unloaded but is still referenced in the drawing (see Figure 17-16). Select the **Wall Base** drawing and choose **Reload...** from the right-click shortcut menu. The status changes to **Reload**.
7. AutoCAD reloads the reference drawing, and it is displayed in its original location.
8. Save your drawing as **EX17-3**.

EDITING XREFS

The easiest way to modify an xref is to select it in the drawing so that the **External Reference** context ribbon shown in Figure 17-17 is displayed, allowing you to easily access the most useful xref modification tools and controls.

The **Edit Reference** context ribbon provides tools to perform the following tasks:

- Edit the xref in-place so that you do not have to open the xref drawing file in a separate window.
- Open the attached xref in a new AutoCAD drawing window so that you can make any changes and updates as you would normally in AutoCAD and then save the drawing.
- Cut out, or clip, an xref so that only the portion of the xref you need to see is loaded and displayed.

The following sections explore these xref editing tools in detail.

Edit Reference In-Place

edit reference in-place:
Using the **REFEDIT** command to make changes to an externally referenced drawing

It is possible to edit an xref directly within the host drawing. In Chapter 16, you looked at how to use the **REFEDIT** command to modify block definitions. The **REFEDIT** command also allows you to modify an xref from within your current drawing. This is known as *edit reference in-place*.

Edit Reference In-Place	
Ribbon & Panel:	External Reference| Edit
	Edit Reference In-Place
Refedit Toolbar:	
Menu:	Xref and Block In-Place Editing| Edit Reference In-Place
Command Line:	REFEDIT
Command Alias:	None

FOR MORE DETAILS   See Chapter 16 for more on using the **REFEDIT** command.

Selecting the **Edit Reference In-Place** tool on the **External Reference** ribbon displays the **Reference Edit** dialog box and displays the selected reference drawing along with any blocks or nested xrefs contained in the reference drawing. Selecting the **OK** button will put you in edit mode so that the reference drawing is no longer one complex block-type object and you can modify the individual drawing objects using the regular AutoCAD modify commands.

Note:
You need to have the proper access privileges to the disk where the reference is stored in order to use the **REFEDIT** command on an xref. If you are referencing a read-only drawing from a CD or network drive, you will not be able to make changes to the xref.

After you have completed modifying the drawing and you save it, all the host or parent drawings that reference the modified drawing will show the most recent changes when they are opened the next time. If you or someone else has a host or parent drawing that is currently open, a notification balloon should appear in the system tray on the bottom right of the AutoCAD window informing you that the xref has been changed with a link to reload it. Clicking on the link will reload the xref and display the most recent changes.

TIP   To prevent others from using the REFEDIT command to edit your drawing, remove the check from the **Allow other users to Refedit current drawing** option in the **Open and Save** tab on the **Options** dialog box.

Opening Xrefs

Of course, one of the easiest ways to make changes to an xref is to simply open the referenced drawing file with the **OPEN** command. When you make changes to the referenced drawing and save them, AutoCAD will notify you that changes have been made to the referenced drawing and allow you to update the xref by reloading it.

The **Open** option on the right-click menu in the **External References** palette allows you to open referenced drawings directly, by passing the **Select File** dialog box. As we discussed in the previous section, selecting one or more xrefs in the **External References** palette and choosing **Open** from the right-click menu will cause AutoCAD to open each xref in a separate drawing window.

The **Open Reference** tool on the **External Reference** ribbon also allows you to open referenced drawings directly. Selecting the **Open Reference** tool simply opens the selected xref. Like the **REFEDIT** command, saving the xref will ensure all host drawings that reference the modified file are updated as well.

Open Reference	
Ribbon & Panel:	External Reference| Edit
	Open Reference
Toolbar:	None
Menu:	Tools|Xref and Block In-place Editing| Open Reference
Command Line:	XOPEN
Command Alias:	None

Exercise 17-4: Editing Xrefs

1. Continue from Exercise 17-3.
2. Display the **External Reference** palette if it is not already displayed.
3. Select the **Grid Plan** reference and choose **Open...** from the right-click shortcut menu. The status changes to **Open**.
4. AutoCAD opens the **Grid Plan.dwg** file in a new window (see Figure 17-18).
5. Close the **Grid Plan** drawing. *Do not save any changes*.

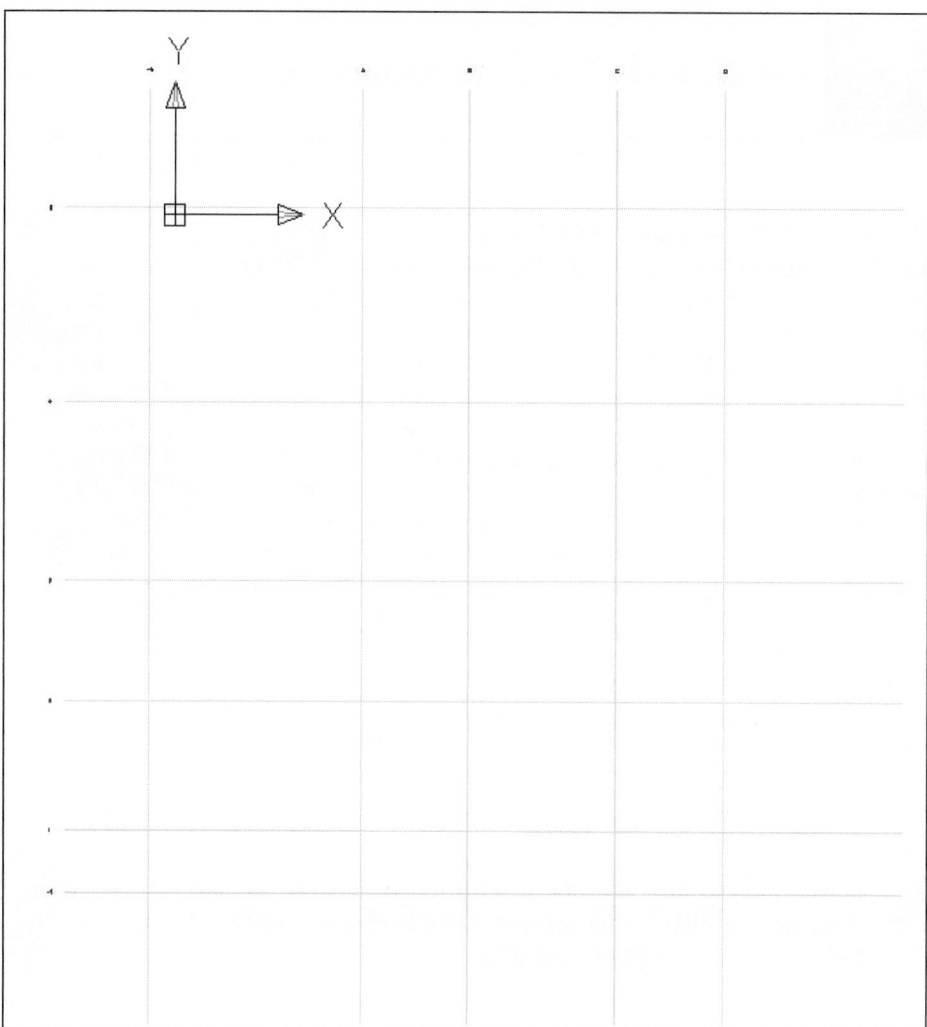

Figure 17-17   The External Reference context ribbon

Clip Xref	
Ribbon & Panel:	External Reference| Clipping
	Create Clipping Boundary
Reference Toolbar:	
Menu:	Modify| Clip|Xref
Command Line:	XCLIP
Command Alias:	XC

Figure 17-18   The opened xref

Clipping an Xref

There may be times when you only want to view a portion of an xref. The **XCLIP** command allows you to "clip out" part of the displayed xref. The drawing or xref is not altered, but the xref is clipped to limit the display to only a portion of the xref. Clipping xrefs also speeds up the performance of a drawing. Information that is outside the clipping boundary is not processed by AutoCAD.

When you start the **XCLIP** command, AutoCAD asks you to select an xref and then presents a number of options. These are described below:

On / Off	Turns clipping on and off for a given xref. Turning clipping Off will cause AutoCAD to ignore any clipping boundaries assigned the xref.
Clip Depth	This option is used in 3D xrefs. The Clip Depth allows you to set the viewing depth of 3D models.
Delete	Deletes any xclip boundaries associated with an xref.
Generate Polyline	Draws a polyline around the edge of an xclip area. When you choose this option, AutoCAD will create a polyline along the outline of a clipped xref. Once the polyline is created, it has no association with the xref. It is simply a polyline object in the drawing.
New Boundary	Defines a new clipping area. If the xref has an existing clipping boundary, AutoCAD will ask you if you want to delete the old boundary. You then have three methods for defining a new clipping area.
Select Polyline	Uses an existing polyline to define a new clipping area. The existing polyline remains after the new clipping area is defined.
Polygonal	Allows you to draw a polygon to define the clip area. The polygon does not remain after the clipping area is defined.
Rectangular	Allows you to draw a box or rectangle to define the clipping area. The rectangle does not remain after the clipping area is defined.
Invert Clip	Inverts the clipping boundary. Clipped objects are shown, and shown object are hidden

Xref clipping is similar to cropping an image in other Windows applications. When you clip an xref, you are simply selecting an area of the xref to display.

It is possible to edit the boundary of a clipped xref using grips to resize the area, as well as, invert the clipping area. Before editing a clipping boundary it must first be visible, so you can select it. The easiest way to control the visibility of xref clipping boundaries is via the **Reference** panel on the **Insert** ribbon. Reference clipping boundaries are referred to as *frames*. By default, frames are hidden and do not display. You can turn them on so they are visible in the drawing by clicking on the **Hide frames** option on the **Reference** panel and selecting either the **Display and plot frames** or **Display but don't plot frames** option from the flyout menu.

Note:
You can also change the visibility of an xref clipping boundary by changing the **XCLIPFRAME** system variable. Setting the **XCLIPFRAME** variable to **1** makes xref clipping boundaries visible. Setting it to **0** hides xref clipping frames.

Exercise 17-5: Clipping Xrefs

1. Continue from Exercise 17-4.
2. Start the **XCLIP** command and select both the **Grid Base** and **Wall Base** drawings and press **<Enter ↵>**.
3. Select the **New boundary** option and then choose **Rectangular** to create a rectangular clipping boundary.

4. Pick the endpoints at **P1** and **P2** as shown in Figure 17-19. AutoCAD clips the xrefs around the rectangular area.
5. Save your drawing as **EX17-5**.

Figure 17-19   Xref clipping area

BINDING PARTS OF AN XREF

Bind	
Ribbon & Panel:	None
Reference Toolbar:	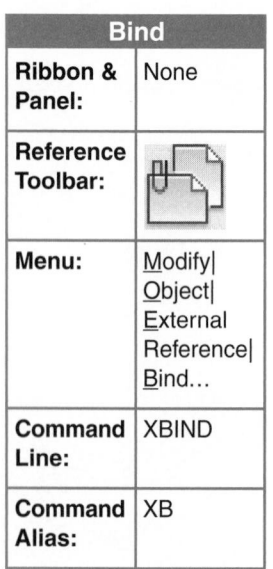
Menu:	Modify| Object| External Reference| Bind...
Command Line:	XBIND
Command Alias:	XB

Using the **Bind** option within the **External References** palette allows you to bind an entire reference file to your current drawing. This results in the entire drawing being converted to a block and inserted into your drawing. The **XBIND** command allows you to selectively bind individual named objects (layers, blocks, text styles, etc.) to your current drawing.

When you start the **XBIND** command, AutoCAD displays the **Xbind** dialog box (see Figure 17-20). The **Xrefs** area displays all the xrefs in the drawing. Clicking on an xref name will display a list of all the named objects within the xref. To bind an individual object, select the object

Figure 17-20   The **Xbind** dialog box

and choose the **Add->** button to add it to the **Definitions to Bind** list. You can add and remove objects from the list. When you are satisfied with the list of object definitions, choose **OK** to bind those object definitions to your current drawing.

DEMAND LOADING XREFS

Demand loading is designed to help make AutoCAD run faster and more efficiently. If you have a number of xrefs loaded, or your referenced drawings are large and complex, you may notice slower system performance. To help with this, AutoCAD uses a method called *demand loading*.

Demand loading works by loading only the parts of an xref that AutoCAD is actually showing. Layers that are turned off or frozen or any geometry hidden by a clipping boundary are not loaded into your drawing until they are needed. When a layer state or a clipping boundary changes, AutoCAD loads the geometry from the referenced drawing. AutoCAD gives you some options for controlling demand loading. These options are found in the **Open and Save** tab on the **Options** dialog box (see Figure 17-21). Demand loading can be set to **Disabled, Enabled** or **Enabled with Copy**. These options are described below:

demand loading: Loading only the visible part of a referenced drawing

Disabled	Turns off demand loading. Each referenced drawing is completely loaded when AutoCAD loads your drawing.
Enabled	Turns demand loading on, making AutoCAD run faster and regenerate views quicker. However, the referenced drawings will be locked, preventing others from modifying the referenced drawing while your drawing is open.
Enabled with Copy	This is AutoCAD's default setting. AutoCAD will make a temporary copy of any referenced drawings and load this copy into your drawing. This enables demand loading while still allowing other users to modify the referenced drawings.

Figure 17-21   Options for demand load xrefs

The **Enabled with Copy** option provides the benefits of demand loading while still allowing others to work on the referenced drawings. If you use the **REFEDIT** command while the **Enabled with Copy** option is set, AutoCAD will save the changes back to the original referenced file, not the temporary copy.

Raster Image Reference	
Ribbon & Panel:	Insert| Reference Attach
Reference Toolbar:	
Menu:	Insert| Raster Image Reference...
Command Line:	IMAGEATTACH
Command Alias:	IAT

WORKING WITH RASTER IMAGES

Raster images can enhance your drawings in a number of ways. They can provide colorful backgrounds with a company logo or background images for accurately tracing shapes. Architectural and civil drawings can benefit greatly by attaching satellite or aerial images to show site locations or conditions.

These views can then serve as backgrounds to help the reader visualize locations or to help the designer to locate utility points for xrefs or inserts. An image can also help provide vital information about your drawing or the function of your part.

An image can be just about any of the popular raster image formats including .BMP, .GIF, .PNG, .TIF, and others. Much like xrefs, the images are simply linked to your drawing so they can be quickly changed, updated, or removed.

Raster images are treated and behave much the same way as xrefs but have additional controls to control image quality and transparency as well as brightness, contrast, and background fading.

Attaching Raster Images

You can attach a raster image by either selecting **Attach Image...** from the drop-down or right-click menu in the **External References** palette (see Figure 17-22) or via the **Attach** tool on the **Reference** panel. Once you select an image and choose **Open**, AutoCAD displays the **Attach Image** dialog box (see Figure 17-23), which allows you to set the type of path along with the **Insertion point, Scale**, and **Rotation** angle. All these functions work the same as the **XREF** command.

The **Show Details** button will display information about the resolution and size of the raster image (see Figure 17-24). This will tell you how AutoCAD will convert raster image resolution to physical size. For example, a raster image that has a resolution of 72 pixels per inch, and is 144 pixels by 108 pixels, will be converted to 2″ × 1.5″ in AutoCAD. The **Show Details** button displays information about the image resolution, AutoCAD units, and the image size in both pixels and AutoCAD units.

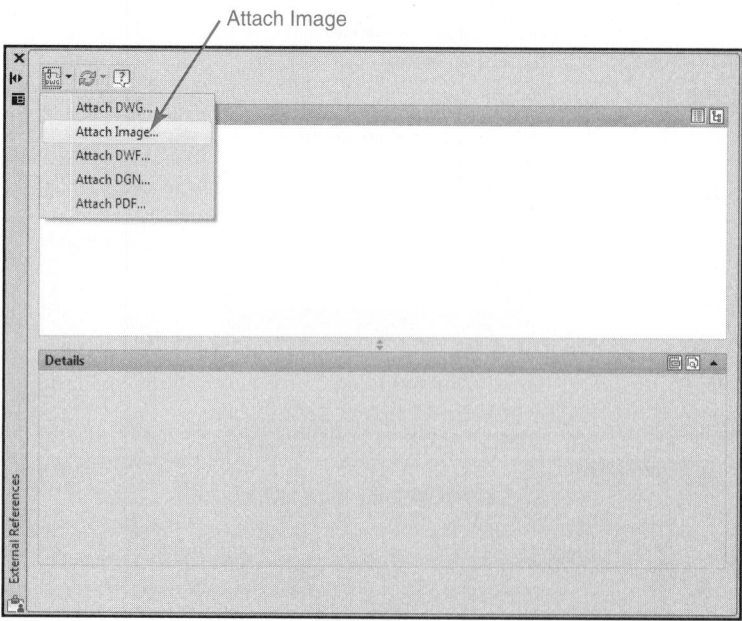

Figure 17-22 The **External References** palette

Figure 17-23   The **Attach Image** dialog box

Figure 17-24   Raster image details

Exercise 17-6: Attaching Raster Images

1. Continue from Exercise 17-5.
2. Switch to the **Architectural Title Block** layout. Use grips to move and resize the viewport as shown in Figure 17-25. Set the viewport scale to ⅛″ = 1′-0″.
3. Display the **External Reference** palette if it is not already displayed.
4. Choose **Attach Image…** and select the image **EX17-6.jpg** in the student data files. Check the **Specify on-screen** option for the **Insertion point** and set the **Scale** at **2**. Choose **OK** and place the image as shown in Figure 17-25.
5. Save the drawing as **EX17-6**.

To access student data files, go to www.pearsondesigncentral.com.

Figure 17-25   The attached image

Managing Images

Once you have loaded images into your drawing, AutoCAD will list the images, their status, file type, file date, and the saved path to the image file. **Detach, Reload**, and **Unload** work identically to their xref counterparts. You can also update the **Saved Path** property via the **Found at** property on the **Preview/Details** pane in the **External Reference** palette.

Controlling Image Settings

Placing and displaying images can be a somewhat subjective process. The quality, size, and format of raster images can vary widely. AutoCAD provides some tools for controlling and managing raster images.

The easiest way to control an image's settings and appearance is to select it in the drawing so that the **Image** context ribbon shown in Figure 17-26 is displayed, allowing you easy access to the most useful image settings.

Figure 17-26   The **Image** context ribbon

Controlling Image Frames. Before you can select an image in a drawing you must first turn on the image borders or frames. The easiest way to do that is via the **Reference** panel on the **Insert** ribbon. Click on the **Hide frames** option and select either the **Display and plot frames** or **Display but don't plot frames** option from the layout menu. The **IMAGEFRAME** system variable also controls the display of the image outline. If an image is clipped, it controls the display of the clipping boundary. There are three settings for the **IMAGEFRAME** variable: **0, 1**, or **2**. These are described below:

> **Note:**
> When image frames are not displayed, you will not be able to select images from within AutoCAD.

0	Image frames are not displayed or plotted.
1	Image frames are both displayed and plotted.
2	Image frames are displayed but not plotted.

Image Adjust	
Ribbon & Panel:	Image| Adjust
Reference Toolbar:	
Menu:	Modify| Object| Image| Adjust...
Command Line:	IMAGEADJUST
Command Alias:	IAD

Adjusting Image Brightness, Contrast, and Fade Settings.   The **Brightness** adjustment changes the brightness of an image. This can range from completely black to completely white.

The **Contrast** adjustment allows you to control the relative difference between dark and light areas of the image.

The **Fade** adjustment allows you to blend the image into the background. Moving the **Fade** control towards the right will adjust the overall color of the image to match the background color. If AutoCAD's background is set to black, increasing the Fade setting causes

> **Note:**
> Many of the image settings discussed in the section can also be controlled via the **Image** cascade menu located on the right-click menu displayed when an image is selected, as well as in the **Properties** palette.

the image to fade to black. If the background color is set to white, increasing the Fade setting causes the image to fade to white.

Image Clipping.   Like xrefs, you can apply clipping boundaries to images. The **Create Clipping Boundary** tool allows you to define and control clipping boundaries associated with images. The options are identical to the **XCLIP** command discussed earlier.

Image clipping boundaries can be modified directly using grips. When you select a clipped image, AutoCAD displays grips at the corners of the clipping boundary. If the clippingl boundary is rectangular, moving a grip changes the length and width of the clipping boundary. If the boundary is polygonal, moving a grip will change the shape of clipping boundary.

Transparency.   Some image file formats (such as GIF or PNG) support transparent pixels. When using images with transparency, you can turn the transparency on and off by selecting the **Transparency** button on the options panel. If your image file format supports transparency, setting it to **On** will allow objects behind the image to be seen through the transparent pixels in the image.

Exercise 17-7: Controlling Image Settings

1. Continue from Exercise 17-6.
2. Select the raster image so the **Image** context ribbon is displayed.
3. Select the **Create Clipping Boundary** tool on the **Clipping** panel. Select the **Rectangular** option and clip the image as shown in Figure 17-27. Position the image as necessary to match Figure 17-27.
4. Adjust the **Brightness** and **Contrast** settings to your liking using the settings on the **Adjust** panel.
5. Save your drawing as **EX17-7**.

Figure 17-27   The clipped image

Clip Image	
Ribbon & Panel:	Image|Clipping
	Create Clipping Boundary
Reference Toolbar:	
Menu:	Modify|Clip|Image
Command Line:	IMAGECLIP
Command Alias:	ICL

Image Transparency	
Ribbon & Panel:	Image|Options
	Transparency
Reference Toolbar:	
Menu:	Modify|Object|Image|Transparency
Command Line:	TRANSPARENCY
Command Alias:	IAD

WORKING WITH DWF UNDERLAYS

Remember from the beginning of the chapter that the DWF file format is a compressed vector-based drawing file format that allows you to share your drawings with other individuals who should not have access to sensitive, proprietary design information.

It is possible to reference DWF files in a similar fashion as xref drawings and raster images using the **DWF Underlay** feature by specifying a file path, insertion point, scale, and rotation angle.

You can modify the appearance of a DWF underlay after it is attached so that it is possible to change the DWF underlay from color-based to monochrome, adjust its fade and contrast, as well as automatically adjust the DWF colors to match the drawing background. It is also possible to define a clipping boundary to limit the visible area of the DWF underlay in a fashion similar to xrefs and images.

Attaching DWF Underlays

You can attach a DWF underlay either by selecting **Attach DWF...** from the drop-down or right-click menus in the **External References** palette or by selecting the **Attach** tool on the **Reference** panel on the **Insert** ribbon.

Either method displays the **Select Reference File** dialog box so you can select a DWF file to attach to your drawing. After you select a file and choose **Open**, AutoCAD displays the **Attach DWF Underlay** dialog box shown in Figure 17-28 where you set the type of path along with the **Insertion point, Scale**, and **Rotation** angle. These options are the same as those for the **XREF** command.

Figure 17-28   The **Attach DWF Underlay** dialog box

If the DWF file consists of multiple sheets, you must select the sheet to attach from the **Select a sheet from the DWF file:** list box on the left.

Managing DWF Underlays

Once you attach one or more DWF underlays in your drawing, AutoCAD will list the DWF file names, their status, file type, file date, and the saved path to the DWF file in the **External References** palette as shown in Figure 17-29.

Similar to xrefs, most of the DWF underlay options and settings are provided via a right-click shortcut menu similar to the xref shortcut menu shown earlier in Figure 17-12. The DWF underlay options work the same as the xref file options, with a few subtle differences.

Selecting **Open...** from the shortcut menu will open the DWF file using the downloadable Autodesk Design Review software mentioned earlier so that you can view, *but not edit*, the DWF file.

The **Attach...** menu item displays the **Select DWF File** dialog box so that you can attach another DWF File; the other DWF underlay options, **Unload, Reload**, and **Detach**, work the same as their xref counterparts.

Controlling DWF Underlay Settings

The easiest way to control a DWF underlay's settings is to select it in the drawing so that the **DWF Underlay** context ribbon shown in Figure 17-30 is displayed, allowing you to easily access the most useful DWF underlay settings and options.

DWF Underlay

Ribbon & Panel:	Insert| Reference Attach
Insert Toolbar:	DWF
Menu:	Insert| DWF Underlay...
Command Line:	DWFATTACH
Command Alias:	None

Figure 17-29   The External References palette with a DWF Underlay attached

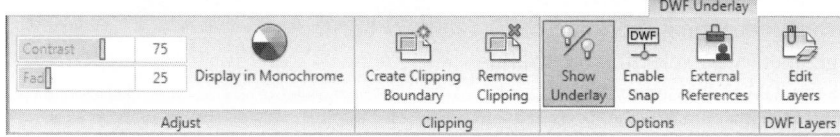

Figure 17-30   The DWF Underlay context ribbon

Controlling DWF Underlay Frames.   You can control whether a border outline is displayed around the edges of a DWF underlay via the **Hide frames** flyout menu on the **Reference** panel on the **Insert** ribbon. Unlike raster images, DWF frames do not need to be on in order to select a DWF Underlay. To turn frames on, select either **Display and plot frames** or **Display but don't plot frames** options from the flyout menu.

The **DWFFRAME** system variable also controls the display of the DWF underlay outline. If a DWF underlay is clipped, it controls the display of the clipping boundary. There are three settings for the **DWFFRAME** variable: **0, 1**, and **2**. These are described below.

0	DWF underlay frames are not displayed and are not plotted.
1	DWF underlay frames are both displayed and plotted.
2	DWF underlay frames are displayed but not plotted (default).

Adjusting Fade Effect, Contrast, and Color Settings.   The options and settings on the **Adjust** panel allow you to set the fade effect, contrast, and whether a DWF underlay is displayed in color or monochrome.

You have the following options:

- **Fade**   Controls the fade effect of the underlay. Valid settings, are from 0 to 80. The higher the setting, the lighter the linework in the underlay. The lower the setting, the darker the linework. (Default = 25)

- **Contrast**   Controls the contrast of the underlay. Values settings are from 0 to 100. The greater the setting, the higher the contrast between dark and light colors, and vice versa. (Default = 75)

DWF Adjust	
Ribbon & Panel:	DWF Underlay| Adjust
Toolbar:	None
Menu:	None
Command Line:	DWFADJUST
Command Alias:	None

- **Monochrome**   Toggles the DWF underlay between color display and monochrome display (black and white). (Default = On)

DWF Underlay Clipping.   Similar to both xrefs and images, you can apply clipping boundaries to DWF underlays. The **Create Clipping Boundary** tool allows you to define and control clipping boundaries associated with DWF files. The options are identical to the **XCLIP** and **IMAGECLIP** commands.

Adjusting Colors for the Current Background.   The **Adjust Colors for Background** option controls whether the DWF underlay colors are visible against the current drawing background color. The option is only accessible via the **Properties** palette under the **Underlay Adjust** category.

The default setting of **Yes** forces AutoCAD to analyze the background colors of the DWF underlay and the drawing environment to determine if they are both light or both dark. If necessary, the colors of the DWF underlay are adjusted so the underlay is visible.

If the **Adjust Colors for Background** option is changed to **No**, the original colors of the underlay are always used regardless of the current background color. If you use this setting, the DWF underlay might not always be visible.

Note:
The **DWFOSNAP** system variable allows you to control whether object snapping to objects that are part of a DWF file is enabled. Setting **DWFOSNAP = 1** (default) allows you to snap to DWF underlay objects. Setting **DWFOSNAP = 0** turns DWF underlay object snaps off.

Turning Object Snaps On and Off.   You can control whether object snapping is enabled for the DWF underlay geometry by selecting the **Enable Snap** button on the **DWF Underlay** context ribbon and toggling on or off.

DWF Layer Control

When a DWF file is created, the user has the option of including layer information within the DWF file. This allows people viewing the DWF file to turn layers on and off. People viewing the DWF file cannot control the name, color, linetype, etc., of DWF layers, only the layer visibility.

When you attach a DWF underlay, if the DWF file contains layer information, AutoCAD allows you this same ability. The **DWFLAYERS** command allows you to turn on and off the layers within a DWF file. The **DWFLAYERS** command is also available by selecting a DWF underlay and choosing **DWF Layers...** from the right-click menu or the **DWF Underlay** context ribbon.

Note:
You can control layers in other attached xrefs by selecting them in the **Reference Name:** list box at the top.

When you start the **DWFLAYERS** command, AutoCAD will prompt you to select the DWF underlay. If the DWF underlay contains layer information, AutoCAD will display the layer names in the **Underlay Layers** dialog box (Figure 17-31). In this dialog box, you can turn DWF layers on and off by clicking the light bulb icon next to each layer. You can select multiple layers by pressing the **<Ctrl>** or **<Shift>** key while clicking layer names. You can also turn layers on and off by right-clicking highlighted layers and choosing **Layer(s) On** or **Layer(s) Off** from the right-click menu.

WORKING WITH DGN UNDERLAYS

Similar to the DWF Underlay, AutoCAD supports the referencing of MicroStation V8 DGN design files. Like a DWF underlay, a DGN underlay is a view-only version of the design data contained in the DGN file. DGN underlays are attached in the same way DWF files are, with some minor

DWF Clip	
Ribbon & Panel:	DWF Underlay| Clipping Attach
Toolbar:	None
Menu:	None
Command Line:	DWFCLIP
Command Alias:	None

DWF Layers	
Ribbon & Panel:	DWF Underlay| DWF Layers Edit Layers
Reference Toolbar:	None
Menu:	None
Command Line:	DWFLAYERS
Command Alias:	None

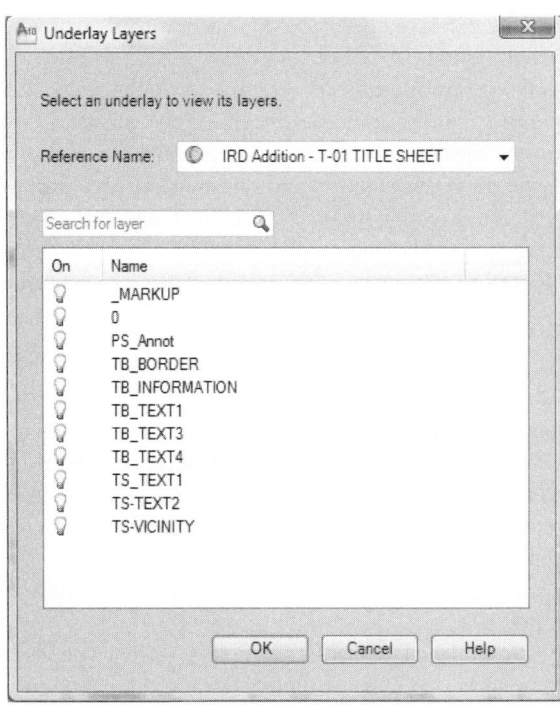

Figure 17-31   The **Underlay Layers** dialog box

differences. You can also control the DGN underlay settings via a context ribbon that is displayed when you select a DGN file in a drawing.

Attaching DGN Underlays

You can attach a DGN underlay either by selecting **Attach DGN...** from the drop-down or right-click menus in the **External References** palette or by selecting the **Attach** tool on the **Reference** panel on the **Insert** ribbon.

Either method displays the **Select Reference File** dialog box so you can select a DGN file. After you select a file and choose **Open**, AutoCAD displays the **Attach DGN Underlay** dialog box shown in Figure 17-32 where you set the type of **Path Type** along with the **Insertion point, Scale**, and **Rotation** angle.

Unlike AutoCAD, which has only one model design space, DGN files can contain multiple design models. Select the desired design model from the **Select a Design Model from the DGN**

DGN Underlay	
Ribbon & Panel:	Insert| Reference Attach
Insert Toolbar:	DGN
Menu:	Insert| DGN Underlay...
Command Line:	DGNATTACH
Command Alias:	None

Figure 17-32   **Attach DGN Underlay** dialog box

File list. Only a single design model can be displayed per underlay. Sheet models within a DGN file (similar to DWF sheets) are not listed.

The **Conversion Units** area of the dialog box allows you to control how units are converted in the DGN file. DGN files use *working units* (imperial or metric) called *master units* and *sub-units*. Some number of sub-units is equal to one master unit. Select the unit you wish to use in your AutoCAD drawing. For example, if master units are set to feet and sub-units are set to inches, then 12 sub-units would equal 1 master unit (feet). Selecting master units in the **Conversion Units** area would convert DGN master units (feet) to AutoCAD's unit of measurement.

The **Insertion Point, Scale**, and **Rotation** settings are the same as those for xrefs and DWF underlays.

Managing DGN Underlays

Once you attach one more DGN underlay in your drawing, AutoCAD will list all of them along with all the other xrefs, images, and DWF underlays in the **External Reference** palette.

Like DWF underlays, the different DGN underlay options and settings are provided via a right-click shortcut menu. The DGN underlay options work exactly the same as their DWF underlay counterparts with some slight differences.

The **Open...** option from the shortcut menu is not selectable. This is because AutoCAD does not include a DGN file viewer with AutoCAD.

The **Attach...** menu item displays the **Select DGN File** dialog box so that you can attach another DGN file; all the other DGN underlay options—**Unload, Reload**, and **Detach**—work exactly the same as their xref counterparts and DWF underlay.

Controlling DGN Underlay Settings.   The easiest way to control a DGN underlay's settings is to select it in the drawing so that the **DWF Underlay** context ribbon shown in Figure 17-33 is displayed, allowing you to easily access the most useful DGN underlay settings and options.

DGN Adjust	
Ribbon & Panel:	DGN Underlay| Adjust
Toolbar:	None
Menu:	None
Command Line:	DGNADJUST
Command Alias:	None

DGN Clip	
Ribbon & Panel:	DGN Underlay| Clipping
	Attach
Toolbar:	None
Menu:	None
Command Line:	DGNCLIP
Command Alias:	None

Figure 17-33   The **DGN Underlay** context ribbon

DGN Underlays share all the same settings and options as DWF Underlays so that you can do the following:

- Adjust the contrast, fade, and monochrome settings
- Clip portions of a DGN underlay so it is not displayed
- Enable/disable object snapping to the DGN underlay geometry
- Turn on/off DGN underlay layers if they are included

Refer to the Controlling DWF Underlay Settings section earlier for detailed descriptions of all the DGN underlay options and options.

WORKING WITH PDF UNDERLAYS

AutoCAD also supports the referencing of PDF (Adobe Portable Document Format) files, the de facto standard for sharing electronic information. PDF underlays are attached using basically the same methods as DGN files. You can also control the PDF underlay settings after it is attached by selecting it in your drawing to display a context ribbon with the same settings and options as a DGN underlay.

Attaching PDF Underlays

You can attach a PDF underlay by either selecting **Attach PDF...** from the drop-down or right-click menus in the **External References** palette or by selecting the **Attach** tool on the **Reference** panel on the **Insert** ribbon.

Either method displays the **Select Reference File** dialog box so you can select a PDF file. After you select a file and choose **Open**, AutoCAD displays the **Attach PDF Underlay** dialog box shown in Figure 17-34 where you set the **Path Type** along with the **Insertion point, Scale**, and **Rotation** angle.

PDF Underlay	
Ribbon & Panel:	Insert| Reference
Insert Toolbar:	
Menu:	Insert| PDF Underlay
Command Line:	PDFATTACH
Command Alias:	None

Figure 17-34   **Attach PDF Underlay** dialog box

PDF files with more than one page are attached one *page* at a time (as opposed to one *sheet* at a time for DWF files or one *model* at a time for DGN files). If the PDF file has more than one page, you must select the desired page from the **Select one or more pages from the PDF File** list.

The **Insertion Point, Scale** and **Rotation** settings work the same as the other types of underlays.

Note:
Hypertext links in PDF files are converted to straight text and digital signatures are not supported.

Managing PDF Underlays

Once you attach one or more PDF underlays in your drawing, AutoCAD will list them along with all the other xrefs, images, and underlays in the **External Reference** palette.

Like the other underlays, the different PDF underlay options and settings are provided via a right-click shortcut menu.

Controlling PDF Underlay Settings.   The easiest way to control a PDF underlay's settings is to select it in the drawing so that the **PDF Underlay** context ribbon shown in Figure 17-35 is displayed, allowing you to easily access the most useful PDF underlay settings and options.

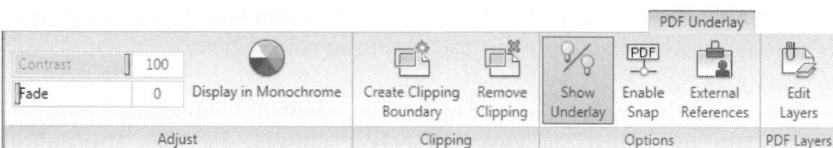

Figure 17-35   The **PDF Underlay** context ribbon

PDF Adjust	
Ribbon & Panel:	PDF Underlay| Adjust
Toolbar:	None
Pull-down Menu:	PDFADJUST
Command Line:	None
Command Alias:	None

PDF underlays share all the same settings and options as DGN underlays so that you can do the following:

- Adjust the contrast, fade, and monochrome settings
- Clip portions of a PDF underlay so it is not displayed
- Enable/disable object snapping to the PDF underlay geometry
- Turn on/off PDF underlay layers if they are included

Refer to the Controlling DGN Underlay Settings section earlier for detailed descriptions of all the PDF underlay options.

PDF Clip	
Ribbon & Panel:	PDF Underlay| Clipping
	Create Clipping Boundary
Toolbar:	None
Pull-down Menu:	None
Command Line:	PDFCLIP
Command Alias:	None

TRANSMITTING DRAWINGS WITH REFERENCES

When creating drawings that use referenced drawings or images, it's important to consider what happens to those drawings when they are given to others (clients, contractors, vendors, etc.). When you provide drawings to others, any referenced files must be supplied as well. This can be a difficult task when there are multiple references stored in different locations. The problem is compounded if nested xrefs are used.

Fortunately, AutoCAD provides the **ETRANSMIT** command to help manage these external files. The **ETRANSMIT** command helps solve the problem of sending incomplete files by compiling all external files into a separate folder or ZIP file. You can also create an email and automatically attach the files to the email.

Using eTRANSMIT

eTransmit	
Application Menu:	Send
Toolbar:	None
Menu:	File| eTransmit...
Command Line:	ETRANSMIT
Command Alias:	None

Before using the **ETRANSMIT** command, you need to save any changes to your drawing. If you start the command before you save any changes, AutoCAD will ask you to save the changes before continuing (see Figure 17-36).

Figure 17-36   The Save Changes notification

Selecting Files.   When you start the **ETRANSMIT** command, AutoCAD displays the **Create Transmittal** dialog box (see Figure 17-37). The **Files Tree** tab shows you a hierarchical tree view of your drawing and any files that are associated with it. From this view, you can see the relationships of the files and also which files are attached to which.

The **Files Table** tab (see Figure 17-38) shows you a flattened list of all files associated with your drawing. This view does not show file relationships but may be easier to work with because all the files are displayed in a single list.

With either view, you can select the files you wish to include in your transmittal by checking or unchecking the box next to the file.

The **Add File...** button allows you to specify additional files you wish to include in your transmittal, such as design specifications, product data sheets, or cover letters.

The Transmittal Report.   When you create your transmittal, AutoCAD will create a transmittal report to include with the transmittal. The **View Report** button displays the **View Transmittal**

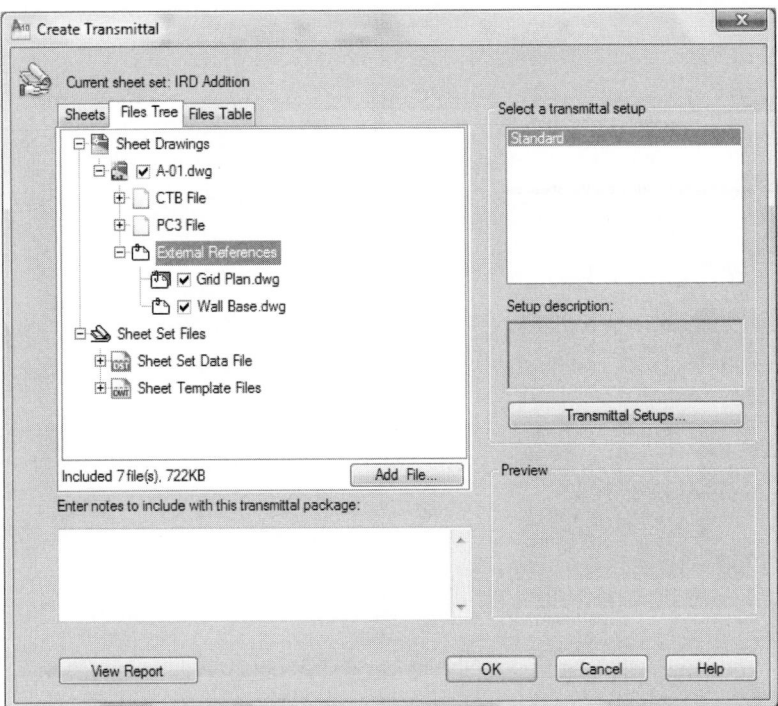

Figure 17-37   The **Create Transmittal** dialog box

Figure 17-38   The **Files Table** tab

Report dialog box, which shows you a copy of the information that will be included in this report. The **Save As...** button allows you to save this report to a text file. The **Close** button closes the **View Transmittal Report** dialog box.

You can add additional information to this report by typing it into the text area above the **View Report** button. Any text typed here will be added to the transmittal report (see Figure 17-39).

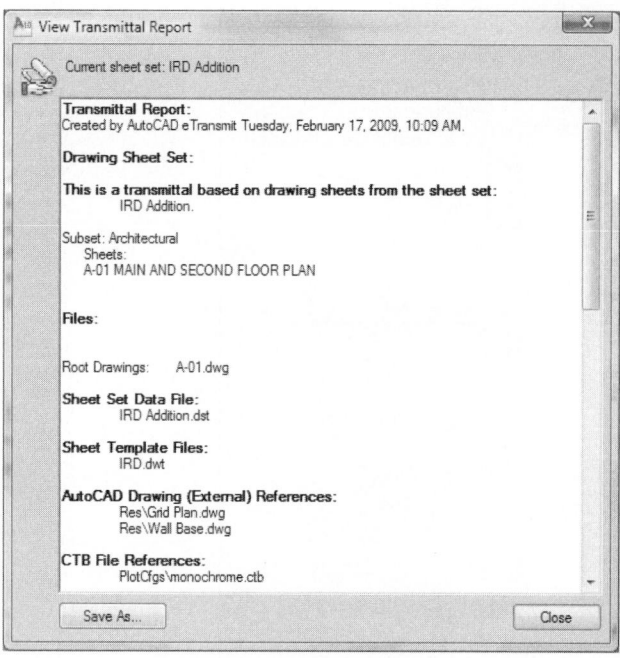

Figure 17-39   The sample transmittal report

Configuring the Transmittal

A transmittal setup contains all the settings for the transmittal, including which files to include, how the files are organized, and how xrefs are included with the drawing. Multiple transmittal setups can be created and saved. This allows you to create different setups for different clients or needs. When you choose the **Transmittal Setups...** button, AutoCAD displays the **Transmittal Setups** dialog box (see Figure 17-40). This allows you to modify, rename, or delete an existing setup or create a new transmittal setup. Transmittal setups are similar to page setups or dimension styles in that they simply assign a name to a collection of settings.

Figure 17-40   The **Transmittal Setups** dialog box

To create a new setup, choose the **New...** button in the **Transmittal Setups** dialog box. This displays the **New Transmittal Setup** dialog box (see Figure 17-41) where you can assign a name to your new transmittal setup. Each new transmittal setup is created from an existing setup. The **Based on:** list allows you to choose which setup to use as a basis for your new setup.

Once you create a new setup or choose the **Modify...** button, AutoCAD will display the **Modify Transmittal Setup** dialog box (see Figure 17-42). This dialog box allows you to modify the setting for the transmittal.

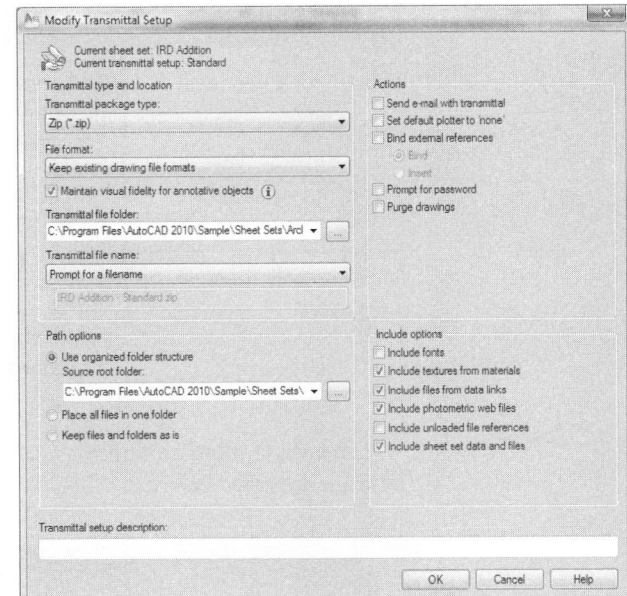

Figure 17-42   The **Modify Transmittal Setup** dialog box

Figure 17-41   The **New Transmittal Setup** dialog box

Transmittal Settings.   The **Transmittal package type**: allows you to select how the files will be stored. The options are described below:

Folder (Set of Files)	Packages the files in a single file folder. The **Transmittal file folder**: setting specifies the location of the folder. You may want to create a new folder to store the transmittal files.
Self-extracting Executable (.exe)	Packages the files in a self-extracting file. This is similar to a zip file but does not require a separate zip program to open the files. The user can simply double-click on the files to open, decompress, and extract them.
Zip (*.zip)	Packages the files in compressed zip file. All files are compressed into a single file, which makes them easy to send electronically. Windows XP systems have built-in support for zip files. Earlier versions of Windows way require a zip program such as Winzip.

The **File format**: option lets you convert AutoCAD 2010 drawings back to the AutoCAD 2007 and 2007 LT, AutoCAD 2004 and 2004 LT, or AutoCAD 2000 and 2000 LT release formats. All drawing files and xrefs are converted back to the selected file format prior to packaging them.

The **Transmittal file folder**: is the location for the transmitted files. The drop-down list will display the nine previous locations that have been used, or you can choose the **Browse** button to specify a new location.

The **Transmittal file name**: determines the ZIP or EXE file name and tells AutoCAD which method is used for naming. By default, AutoCAD combines the drawing file name with the transmittal setup name. For example, a drawing called **Plan.dwg** using the **Standard** transmittal setup with the **Zip** package option would have a transmittal file name called **Plan - Standard.zip**. You can change the default file name by typing a new name in the space below the **Transmittal file name**:. This option is disabled if the **Folder** package type is used. These options are described below:

Prompt for a file name	This method will prompt you for a file name each time you create a transmittal. The file will be stored in the folder set in the **Transmittal file folder**: setting.
Overwrite if necessary	This option will automatically name the file. If that file already exists, AutoCAD will automatically overwrite the existing file.
Increment file name if necessary	This option will automatically name the file. If the file already exists, AutoCAD will create a new file name by adding a number to the end of the file name. For example, a Zip file called **Plan - Standard.zip** would be incremented to **Plan - Standard 1.zip**.

The **Path Options** area allows you to choose how the files are organized within the package. These are described below:

Use organized folder structure	This method duplicates the folder structure for the files being transmitted. The root folder is the top-level folder for the transmittal. For files that lie within the root folder path, a folder is created for each file's parent folder. Files that are outside the root folder path are placed in the root folder. Other folders are created as needed for fonts and plot configurations.
Place all files in one folder	This option places all files in a single folder defined in the **Transmittal file folder**: option. No subfolders are created.
Keep files and folders as is	This option replicates the existing folder structure of all the files included in the transmittal. This option works well when you have xrefs or images stored with full paths because it retains the complete folder structure for all files.

The **Send e-mail with transmittal** option will cause AutoCAD to start a new email message with the transmittal files included as attachments.

The **Set default plotter to 'none'** option changes the default plotter for all model and paper space layouts to **None**. This prevents AutoCAD from trying to communicate with plotters that may not be configured on another user's system.

The **Bind external references** option causes AutoCAD to bind all xrefs in the transmittal drawing file. This means that no xref files are included with the transmittal and that all xrefs are automatically bound before packaging. This does not affect the source drawing file, only the transmittal copy. The advantage of using this option is that the person receiving the transmittal will not have to deal with xref paths or missing files. The disadvantage is that for large or complex drawings, binding xrefs may cause the file size to increase significantly.

The **Prompt for password** option is available only when packaging the transmittal as a ZIP or EXE file. When this option is selected, AutoCAD will password-protect the ZIP or EXE file. When using this option to create the transmittal package, AutoCAD will display the **Transmittal-Set Password** dialog box (see Figure 17-43) that will prompt you for a password and ask you to confirm that password. The recipient of the transmittal package will need to type in the password to gain access to the files.

The **Purge Drawings** option will do a complete purge of all the drawings in the transmittal package.

The **Include options** area allows you to specify whether to include associated fonts, textures from materials, external files referenced by a data link, and photometric web files that are associated with web lights.

Figure 17-44   Transmittal settings

Figure 17-43   The **Set Password** dialog box

Exercise 17-8: Transmitting Xrefs

1. Continue from Exercise 17-7.
2. Start the **ETRANSMIT** command. If you have any unsaved changes, AutoCAD will ask if you want to save them. Choose **OK** to save any changes.
3. Look at the **Files Tree** and **Files Table** tabs to see which files are going to be included in the transmittal.
4. Choose the **Transmittal setups...** button and choose **New** to create a new transmittal setup. Name the transmittal setup **Chapter 17** and choose **Continue** to continue setting up the transmittal.
5. Set the **Transmittal package type**: to **Zip** and **Keep existing drawing file formats**. Select a location from the **Transmittal file folder**: and choose **Prompt for a filename**.
6. Choose **Place all files in one folder** and **Include fonts**. Turn all other options off. Choose **OK** to save the transmittal setup and **Close** to return to the **Create Transmittal** dialog box. Your settings should be set to match Figure 17-44.
7. Choose **OK** to create the transmittal. Save the transmittal as **EX17-8**.

CHAPTER SUMMARY

Using xrefs and images allows you to share and update information across multiple drawings with relative ease. This can greatly facilitate the sharing of information in a group environment. Planning and CAD standards are key to successfully using these features, especially in multiuser environments. One of the challenging aspects of using referenced files is tracking and managing all the files related to a particular drawing. The **ETRANSMIT** command provides an easy way to track and assemble all files associated with a drawing into a single location.

CHAPTER TEST QUESTIONS

Multiple Choice

1. One advantage of using xrefs in a team environment is:
   a. The ability to share drawings with team members
   b. The ability to attach drawings to other drawings
   c. The ability to bind drawings to other drawings
   d. All of the above

2. Which of the following statements best defines an xref?
   a. A drawing that is independent of all other drawings
   b. A drawing attached to the current or host drawing with a link back to the original drawing
   c. A drawing that can bind only to the current drawing
   d. All of the above

3. Which of the following are commonly used options when attaching an xref?

    a. Attach and Bind
    b. Block and Insert
    c. Cut and Paste
    d. None of the above

4. The insertion point of an xref from the **External Reference** dialog box can be which of the following options?

    a. Fix-and-place at origin
    b. Drag-and-drop
    c. Cut-and-paste
    d. Specify on-screen or X, Y, and Z coordinate specification

5. Which of the following are options of the **Attach** option?

    a. Scale
    b. Rotation
    c. Block unit
    d. All of the above

6. Why would "Reload" be needed when using xrefs?

    a. To lock changes out of the current drawing
    b. To check updates to a current attached drawing
    c. To bind changes to a current drawing
    d. All of the above

7. Binding an attached xref drawing will:

    a. Isolate the drawing from any more updates
    b. Make the attached drawing more editable
    c. Bind it somewhat permanently to the current drawing
    d. All of the above

8. Which of the following is true when using the **Open** option in the **External References** palette?

    a. Opens a new drawing to attach to the current drawing
    b. Opens the xref drawing in a new drawing window
    c. Opens only current layers in an xref
    d. All of the above

9. Which bind-type option will bind named xref objects such as layers, linetypes, and textstyles, and not rename them with the xref name and a "0" prefix?

    a. Bind option
    b. Insert option
    c. Setting **BINDTYPE** system variable to **0**
    d. None of the above

10. The **XOPEN** command is used for:

    a. Opening a deleted drawing
    b. Opening a new drawing
    c. Directly opening an attached xref
    d. All of the above

11. The **XBIND** command is used for:

    a. Adding or removing individual dependent definitions from the xrefed drawing to the host drawing.
    b. Managing xref layer settings.

    c. Adding or removing layers definitions to the current host drawing.
    d. All of the above

12. Options on the **REFEDIT** panel include:

    a. Edit in place
    b. Add to working set
    c. Remove from working set
    d. All of the above

13. The purpose of clipping an xref would be to:

    a. Clip out unused layers
    b. Clip out part of the displayed xref
    c. Trim portions of the host drawing
    d. All of the above

14. An eTransmit report contains the following information:

    a. Date and drawing name
    b. File paths and xref file paths
    c. Any excluded files
    d. All of the above

15. eTransmit files can be which of the following?

    a. .exe (self-extracting executable files)
    b. .ZIP (zip files)
    c. Folder (set of files)
    d. All of the above

16. Why would "demand loading" be applied to xrefs?

    a. To automatically load your drawing when AutoCAD is opened
    b. To speed up AutoCAD and make it run more efficiently
    c. To block others from using your xrefs
    d. All of the above

17. Why would raster images be applied to a drawing?

    a. To provide a company logo background image
    b. To provide location points for satellite topographical drawings
    c. To trace shapes or profiles
    d. All of the above

18. Which of the following is an option when applying a raster image?

    a. Scale
    b. Rotation
    c. Insertion point
    d. All of the above

19. Reloading an image would be for what benefit?

    a. To block further changes to the drawing
    b. To restrict uploading of the image
    c. To update any changes that may have been done to the image
    d. All of the above

20. What "details" can be adjusted or included in an image?

    a. Brightness
    b. Resolution
    c. The image frame
    d. All of the above

Matching

a. **External Reference**

b. **ETRANSMIT**

1. Displays the **Select Image File** dialog box

2. Bypasses the **External Reference** palette and directly attaches an xref

c. **IMAGEATTACH**

3. A reference to a drawing file that retains a link back to the original drawing file

d. **XCLIP**

4. Opens an attached xref directly in your current drawing

e. **REFEDIT**

5. Packages drawing and dependent files for file transfer

f. **XATTACH**

6. Binds individual named object definitions from an xref drawing

g. **XBIND**

7. Toggles an image between draft and high-quality mode

h. **IMAGEADJUST**

8. Opens a referenced drawing in a new drawing window

i. **XOPEN**

9. Sets contrast, brightness, and fade on an attached image

j. **IMAGEQUALITY**

10. Crops an external reference to a defined boundary

CHAPTER PROJECTS

Project 17-1: Classroom Plan—Continued from Chapter 16

1. Open drawing **P16-1**.
2. Switch to the **Architectural Title Block** layout. Attach the drawing **Architectural D-Size.dwg** created in Chapter 16 as an overlay xref. Place the xref at the coordinates **-.75,-.5**.
3. Insert the drawing **Title Attributes D-Size.dwg** as a block. Use an insertion point of **-.5,.25**. Fill in appropriate values for the attributes. Your drawing should resemble Figure P17-1.
4. Save your drawing as **P17-1**.

Figure P17-1

Project 17-2A: Logo—Continued from Chapter 11

1. Open drawing **P11-2D**. Move the geometry so the lower left corner of the logo is located at 0,0.
2. Scale the logo so the height is **.375** as shown in Figure P17-2A.
3. Save the drawing as **PH-Logo**.

0.375

0,0

Figure P17-2A

Project 17-2B: B-Size Mechanical Border—Continued from Chapter 16

1. Open the template file **Mechanical B-Size.DWT**.
2. Set the **Mechanical B-Size** layout current and attach the drawing **PH-Logo** as an overlay reference. Place the drawing as shown in Figure P17-2B.
3. Switch to the **Metric Mechanical B-Size** layout and attach the drawing **PH-Logo** as an overlay reference. Set a uniform scale of **25.4** and place the logo as shown in Figure P17-2B.
4. Save the drawing as **Mechanical B-Size.DWT**.
5. Open the **Mechanical B-Size.DWG**.
6. Attach the drawing **PH-Logo** as an overlay reference. Place the drawing as shown in Figure P17-2B.
7. Save the drawing as **Mechanical B-Size.DWG**.

Figure P17-2B

Project 17-2C: C-Size Mechanical Border—Continued from Chapter 16

1. Open the template file **Mechanical C-Size.DWT**.
2. Set the **Mechanical C-Size** layout current and attach the drawing **PH-Logo** as an overlay reference. Place the drawing as shown in Figure P17-2C. Scale as necessary.
3. Save the drawing as **Mechanical C-Size.DWT**.
4. Open the **Mechanical C-Size.DWG**.
5. Attach the drawing **PH-Logo** as an overlay reference. Place the drawing as shown in Figure P17-2C.
6. Save the drawing as **Mechanical C-Size.DWG**.

Figure P17-2C

Project 17-2D: A-Size Portrait Mechanical Border—Continued from Chapter 16

1. Open the template file **Mechanical A-Size-Portrait.DWT**.
2. Set the **Mechanical A-Size-Portrait** layout current and attach the drawing **PH-Logo** as an overlay reference. Place the drawing as shown in Figure P17-2D.
3. Save the drawing as **Mechanical A-Size-Portrait.DWT**.
4. Open the **Mechanical A-Size-Portrait.DWG**.
5. Attach the drawing **PH-Logo** as an overlay reference. Place the drawing as shown in Figure 17-2D.
6. Save the drawing as **Mechanical A-Size-Portrait.DWG**.

Project 17-3A: Architectural D-Size Border—Continued from Chapter 16

1. Start a new drawing using the **acad.dwt** template.
2. Create the architect's professional seal shown in Figure P17-3 as follows:
   a. All information should be drawn on layer **0**.
   b. Use the **DONUT** command to create a donut at 0,0 with an inside diameter of **1.70″** and an outside diameter of **1.75″**.
   c. Use the **CIRCLE** command to create the inside circle with a diameter of **1.25″**.
   d. Use the **TEXT** command to create all text as single-line text. Outside curved text is **0.125″** high. Inside text is **0.093″**.
   e. Save the drawing as **Seal.DWG**.

SIZE	PART NO.	DWG NAME
A		Mechanical A–Size–Portrait.DWT
SCALE:	DWN BY:	SHEET:

REV

Figure P17-2D

3. Open the template file **Architectural D-Size.DWT**.
4. Attach the architect's professional seal drawing created above (**Seal.DWG**) as an external reference at the center of the title border circle as shown in Figure P17-3 so that it is rotated **90°**.
5. Save the drawing to a template file as **Architectural D-Size.DWT**.
6. Open the D-size title border drawing file **Architectural D-Size.DWG**.
7. Attach the architect's professional seal drawing created above (**Seal.DWG**) as an external reference at the center of the title border circle as shown in Figure P17-3 so that it is rotated **90°**.
8. Save the **Architectural D-Size.DWG** drawing file.

Location on
Title Border —
Rotated 90°

Seal.DWG

Figure P17-3

Project 17-3B: Architectural B-Size Border—Continued from Chapter 16

1. Open the template file **Architectural B-Size.DWT**.
2. Attach the architect's professional seal drawing created above **(Seal.DWG)** as an external reference at the center of the title border circle similar to that shown in Figure P17-3. Xref does *not* need to be rotated in this drawing.
3. Save the drawing to a template file as **Architectural B-Size.DWT**.
4. Open the B-size title border drawing file **Architectural B-Size.DWG**.
5. Attach the architect's professional seal drawing created above **(Seal.DWG)** as an external reference at the center of the title border circle similar to as shown in Figure P17-3. Xref does *not* need to be rotated in this drawing.
6. Save the **Architectural B-Size.DWG** drawing file.

Project 17-4: Electrical Schematic—Continued from Chapter 16

1. Open drawing **Electrical Plan.dwg**.
2. In model space, attach the drawing **Architectural Plan.dwg** as an overlay xref. Place the reference at **0,0** at a scale of **1** and a rotation angle of **0**.
3. Set the color of the layers associated with the **Architectural Plan** xref to **9**.
4. Switch to the **Architectural D-Size** layout. Erase the existing title block geometry, leaving only the viewport.
5. Attach the drawing **Architectural D-Size.DWG** as an overlay xref. Place the reference at **0,0** at a scale of **1** and a rotation angle of **0**.
6. Insert the drawing **Title Attributes D-Size.dwg** as a block. Place the block at **0,0** at a scale of **1** and a rotation angle of **0**. Enter appropriate values for the title block attributes. Your drawing should look like Figure P17-4.
7. Save the drawing as **Electrical Plan.dwg**.

Figure P17-4

Project 17-5: Architectural Plan—Continued from Chapter 16

1. Open drawing **Architectural Plan.dwg**.
2. Switch to the **Architectural D-Size** layout. Erase the existing title block geometry, leaving only the viewport.
3. Attach the drawing **Architectural D-Size.DWG** as an overlay xref. Place the reference at **0,0** at a scale of **1** and a rotation angle of **0**.
4. Insert the drawing **Title Attributes D-Size.dwg** as a block. Place the block at **0,0** at a scale of **1** and a rotation angle of **0**. Enter appropriate values for the title block attributes. Your drawing should look like Figure P17-5.
5. Save the drawing as **Architectural Plan.dwg**.

Figure P17-5

Project 17-6: Optical Mount—English Units—Continued from Chapter 14

1. Open drawing **P14-6**.
2. Switch to the **Mechanical B-Size** layout. Erase the existing title block geometry, leaving only the viewport.
3. Attach the drawing **Mechanical B-Size.DWG** as an overlay xref. Place the reference at **0,0** at a scale of **1** and a rotation angle of **0**.
4. Insert the drawing **Title Attributes Mechanical B-Size.dwg** as a block. Place the block at **0,0** at a scale of **1** and a rotation angle of **0**. Enter appropriate values for the title block attributes. Your drawing should look like Figure P17-6.
5. Save the drawing as **P17-6.dwg**.

Project 17-7A: Gasket—Continued from Chapter 14

1. Open drawing **P14-7A**.
2. Select the **Metric Mechanical B-Size** layout to make it current.
3. Erase all the title border information except the polygonal viewport.

Figure P17-6

4. Attach the **Mechanical B-Size.DWG** title block drawing from Problem P16-2A as an external reference file at **0,0,0** in paper space. The title block should scale automatically using the insert units. If it does not scale, you must set the *X, Y,* and *Z* scale factors to **25.4**.

5. Insert the **Title Attributes Mechanical B-Size.dwg** block at **0,0,0** and update the attributes accordingly.

6. Save the drawing as **P17-7A**.

Project 17-7B: Widget—Continued from Chapter 14

1. Open drawing **P14-7B**.
2. Select the **Metric Mechanical B-Size** layout to make it current.
3. Erase all the title border information except the polygonal viewport.
4. Attach the **Mechanical B-Size.DWG** title block drawing from Problem P16-2A as an external reference file at 0,0,0 in paper space. The title block should scale automatically using the insert units. If it does not scale, you must set the *X, Y,* and *Z* scale factors to **25.4**.
5. Insert the **Title Attributes Mechanical B-Size.dwg** block at **0,0,0** and update the attributes accordingly.
6. Save the drawing as **P17-7B**.

Project 17-7C: Hex Head Bolts and Nuts—Continued from Chapter 14

1. Open drawing **P14-7C**.
2. Select the **Metric Mechanical B-Size** layout to make it current.
3. Erase all the title border information except the polygonal viewport.
4. Attach the **Mechanical B-Size.DWG** title block drawing from Problem P16-2A as an external reference file at **0,0,0** in paper space. The title block should scale automatically using the insert units. If it does not scale, you must set the *X, Y,* and *Z* scale factors to **25.4**.
5. Insert the **Title Attributes Mechanical B-Size.dwg** block at **0,0,0** and update the attributes accordingly.
6. Save the drawing as **P17-7C**.

Project 17-7D: Motorcycle Head Gasket—Continued from Chapter 14

1. Open drawing **P14-7D**.
2. Select the **Metric Mechanical B-Size** layout to make it current.
3. Erase all the title border information except the polygonal viewport.
4. Attach the **Mechanical B-Size.DWG** title block drawing from Problem P16-2A as an external reference file at **0,0,0** in paper space. The title block should scale automatically using the insert units. If it does not scale, you must set the *X, Y,* and *Z* scale factors to **25.4**.
5. Insert the **Title Attributes Mechanical B-Size.dwg** block at **0,0,0** and update the attributes accordingly.
6. Save the drawing as **P17-7D**.

Project 17-7E: 68-Tooth Motorcycle Sprocket—Continued from Chapter 14

1. Open drawing **P14-7E**.
2. Select the **Metric Mechanical B-Size** layout to make it current.
3. Erase all the title border information except the polygonal viewport.
4. Attach the **Mechanical B-Size.DWG** title block drawing from Problem P16-2A as an external reference file at **0,0,0** in paper space. The title block should scale automatically using the insert units. If it does not scale, you must set the *X, Y,* and *Z* scale factors to **25.4**.
5. Insert the **Title Attributes Mechanical B-Size.dwg** block at **0,0,0** and update the attributes accordingly.
6. Save the drawing as **P17-7E**.

Project 17-7F: Window Extrusion—Continued from Chapter 14

1. Open drawing **P14-7F**.
2. Select the **Metric Mechanical B-Size** layout to make it current.
3. Erase all the title border information except the polygonal viewport.
4. Attach the **Mechanical B-Size.DWG** title block drawing from Problem P16-2A as an external reference file at **0,0,0** in paper space. The title block should scale automatically using the insert units. If it does not scale, you must set the X, Y, and Z scale factors to **25.4**.
5. Insert the **Title Attributes Mechanical B-Size.dwg** block at **0,0,0** and update the attributes accordingly.
6. Save the drawing as **P17-7F**.

Project 17-7G: Hub—Continued from Chapter 14

1. Open drawing **P14-7G**.
2. Select the **Metric Mechanical B-Size** layout to make it current.
3. Erase all the title border information except the polygonal viewport.
4. Attach the **Mechanical B-Size.DWG** title block drawing from Problem P16-2A as an external reference file at **0,0,0** in paper space. The title block should scale automatically using the insert units. If it does not scale, you must set the X, Y, and Z scale factors to **25.4**.
5. Insert the **Title Attributes Mechanical B-Size.dwg** block at **0,0,0** and update the attributes accordingly.
6. Save the drawing as **P17-7G**.

Project 17-8: Civil Site Plan—Continued from Chapter 16

1. Open drawing **EX16-11**.
2. In model space, attach the drawing **Architectural Plan.dwg** as an overlay xref. Align the reference to the building outline at a scale of **1** and a rotation angle of **E (0)**.
3. Set the color of the layers associated with the **Architectural Plan** xref to **9**.
4. Switch to the **Architectural D-Size** layout. Erase the existing title block geometry, leaving only the viewport.
5. Attach the drawing **Architectural D-Size.DWG** as an overlay xref. Place the reference at **0,0** at a scale of **1** and a rotation angle of **0**.
6. Insert the drawing **Title Attributes D-Size.dwg** as a block. Place the block at **0,0** at a scale of **1** and a rotation angle of **0**. Enter appropriate values for the title block attributes. Your drawing should look like Figure P17-8.
7. Save the drawing as **Civil Plan.dwg**.

Figure P17-8

File Management and Object Linking and Embedding

18

Chapter Objectives

- Understand the backup and AutoSave settings
- Fix a corrupt drawing
- Purge a drawing
- Import and export different drawing file types
- Copy and paste information between different software applications
- Use Object Linking and Embedding objects in AutoCAD drawings
- Automate repetitive tasks using the Action Recorder
- Use the Measure tools

INTRODUCTION

Successful AutoCAD file management requires thorough attention to drawing file creation, maintenance, saving, and naming conventions. File management also includes addressing corrupt drawing files, importing and exporting various CAD drawing formats as well as combining and sharing data using the Windows clipboard feature or Object Linking and Embedding (OLE). In this chapter, we will examine the AutoCAD Drawing Utilities and additional file management procedures to use when different source applications are needed to increase productivity.

DRAWING FILE BACKUP AND RECOVERY

Anyone who has used a computer has undoubtedly experienced computer problems. Operating systems that lock up, programs that stop responding, viruses, power outages, and equipment failures are a routine part of working with computers. How do you protect your drawings which represent many hours of valuable work? For starters, safe computing practices such as regular backups, up-to-date anti-virus and anti-spyware software scans, and routine computer maintenance can greatly reduce the risk of data loss. AutoCAD offers some additional ways of backing up your design data as well as some tools to help monitor file integrity and recover lost design data.

File Safety Precautions

The **File Safety Precautions** area of the **Open and Save** tab on the **Options** dialog box allows you to control some of these backup and file recovery options (see Figure 18-1).

Backup Files.   By default, when you save a drawing in AutoCAD, the file is saved with a DWG file extension. The previously saved version of that drawing is renamed with a BAK file extension. For example, you have a drawing called A-06.DWG. When you open that drawing, make changes to it, and then save your drawing, the previously saved file is renamed A-06.BAK, and the new changes are saved to A-06.DWG. If a BAK file already exists, it is overwritten with the new BAK file.

Figure 18-1 The **Open and Save** tab on the **Options** dialog box

If you are unable to open your current drawing, or if you need to recover changes made to your drawing, you can simply rename the BAK file extension to DWG and open the backup file in AutoCAD. You may want to change the file name as well to avoid confusion. For example, you have two files: A-06.BAK and A-06.DWG. You wish to open the BAK file to recover some objects you deleted. To avoid confusing the two files, you can rename the BAK file to A-06-Backup.DWG and then open the backup file in AutoCAD.

By default, AutoCAD has backup files enabled. To disable the backup file creation, remove the check from the **Create backup copy with each save** box in the **Open and Save** tab on the **Options** dialog box (see Figure 18-1).

Autosave Files. Backup files (BAK) are created only when you save your drawing. For this reason, it's considered good practice to save your drawing often. However, there are times when AutoCAD quits before you have the opportunity to save. To help recover from these instances, AutoCAD can automatically save your drawing file at regular intervals. This is known as an *autosave*. By default, AutoCAD does this every 10 minutes.

autosave: The practice of AutoCAD automatically saving your drawing at regular intervals. The default save interval is 10 minutes.

Files created with the **Autosave** feature are considered temporary files. When AutoCAD performs an autosave, it assigns a name consisting of the file name combined with a random number and the file extension .SV$. These files are placed in the **Windows Temp** folder and are created as a failsafe to recover drawing information in the event of a program failure or power failure. If your drawing is closed normally, these temporary save files are deleted. If the drawing does not close normally, the temporary files are retained and can be renamed and opened in AutoCAD.

When you start a command, AutoCAD looks at the time since the last autosave was done. If the time is greater than the autosave interval, AutoCAD will do an autosave before it starts your command. AutoCAD displays a message when it is performing an automatic save while you are working. Following is an example:

```
Automatic save to C:\DOCUME~1\JIMFIT~1\LOCALS~1\Temp\
Drawing1_1_1_0372.sv$ ...
```

If you do not see a message from AutoCAD, you should check that the **Autosave** feature is enabled and that a reasonable save interval is set. You can set this in the **Automatic save** box in the **Open and Save** tab on the **Options** dialog box (see Figure 18-1). The **Automatic Save File Location** setting in the **Files** tab on the **Options** dialog box allows you to change the location where the files are saved.

Temporary Files.   In addition to the autosave files, AutoCAD also creates temporary files in the **Windows Temp** folder. These temporary files are used by AutoCAD and Windows to manage data while your drawing file is open. These keep track of Undo and Redo information as well as store changes to your drawing in between saves. These files are given a random name with a .AC$ file extension.

Like the autosave files (.sv$) when a drawing is closed normally, these temporary files are deleted. However, if a drawing is not closed properly, these temporary files are retained. They can also be renamed as .DWG and opened in AutoCAD. Since these files are randomly named, finding the exact file you are looking for can be hit-and-miss. Also, there is no guarantee that the information you're seeking will be contained in these files, but it does give you some additional places to look if you lose valuable design information.

The **File extension for temporary files** box in the **Open and Save** tab on the **Options** dialog box (see Figure 18-1) allows you to change the file extension of these temporary files. Also, the **Temporary Drawing File Location** setting in the **Files** tab on the **Options** dialog box allows you to change the location where these temporary files are stored (see Figure 18-2).

Figure 18-2 The **Files** tab on the **Options** dialog box

Corrupt Drawing Objects.   Drawing corruption can occur when a drawing object is not defined properly within the drawing file. This can happen when importing drawing information from other CAD applications, if you are using custom software applications inside AutoCAD, or if AutoCAD closes without saving your drawing.

Corrupt objects can cause a variety of problems from AutoCAD locking up to a drawing failing to load properly. When you consider that drawings can be used as xrefs and that nested references may be used, a single corrupt object can wreck havoc on a design project.

If you suspect that corrupt objects may be causing a problem, AutoCAD allows you to turn on a cyclic redundancy check (CRC) to monitor all new objects created during the drawing session. This option will check all new objects to ensure they are well defined before AutoCAD adds them to the drawing. This is set by checking the **Full-time CRC validation** box in the **Open and Save** tab on the **Options** dialog box (see Figure 18-1). This checking can slow down the drawing process slightly, so this option should be turned on only as needed to help track down the source of corrupt drawing objects.

Drawing Recovery Manager	
Application Menu	Drawing Utilities
Toolbar:	None
Menu:	<u>F</u>ile | Drawing Utilities | Drawing Recovery Manager…
Command Line:	DRAWINGRECOVERY
Command Alias:	None

Recovering Lost or Corrupt Drawings

If your AutoCAD session locks up or closes before you can save your drawing, AutoCAD provides some tools for recovering lost drawing information and fixing corrupt drawings.

The Drawing Recovery Manager. If your AutoCAD session ends prematurely, the next time you start Auto-CAD, it will display a message about Drawing Recovery (see Figure 18-3), and the **Drawing Recovery Manager** (see Figure 18-4) will start automatically. You can also start the **Drawing Recovery Manager** with the **DRAWINGRECOVERY** command.

> **Note:**
> Although these tools can recover many damaged or corrupt drawings, they are not guaranteed to recover all lost information. Remember to save often and back up critical drawing files on a regular basis.

Figure 18-3   The **Drawing Recovery** message

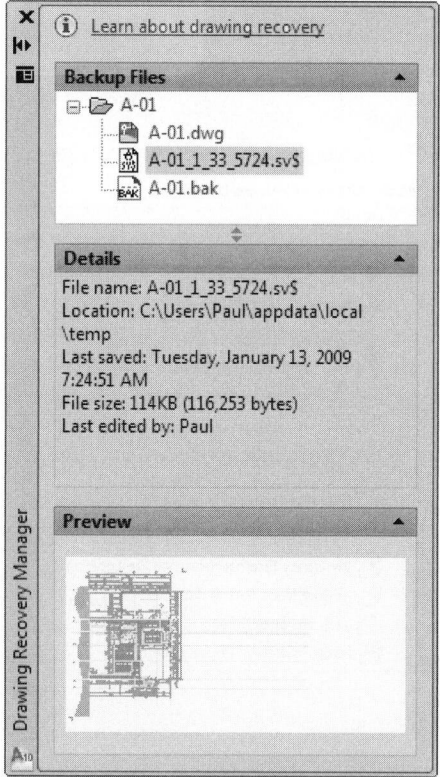

Figure 18-4   The **Drawing Recovery Manager** palette

The **Drawing Recovery Manager** provides an easy way to examine backup and autosave files. When the **Drawing Recovery Manager** starts, it searches for backup (BAK) and autosave (SV$) files along with their associated DWG files and displays them in the **Drawing Recover Manager** palette (see Figure 18-4).

The **Backup** area displays all the backup, autosave, and drawing files associated with a given drawing. Selecting one of the listed files will display information about the file in the **Details** area and a preview of the file in the **Preview** area.

> **Note:**
> The Drawing Recovery Manager will start automatically every time you start AutoCAD until you remove the drawings from the Backup Files area.

You can open the selected file by double-clicking it or choosing **Open** from the right-click menu. This allows you to examine in detail the various backup files. When you find the one you want to keep, save it using the file name of your choosing. You can then remove the drawing from the **Drawing Recovery Manager** by selecting the drawing file name folder in the **Backup Files** area and choosing **Remove** from the right-click menu (see Figure 18-5).

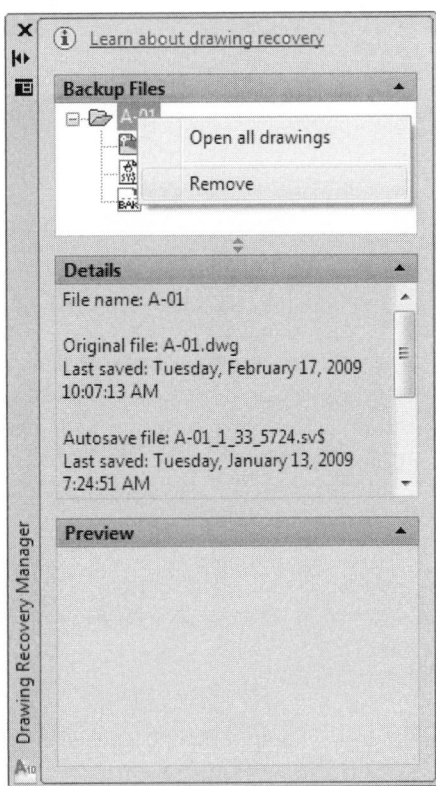

Figure 18-5   Removing drawings from the **Drawing Recovery Manager**

Fixing Corrupt Drawings.   If you find yourself with a corrupt drawing file, AutoCAD provides two commands to examine and repair these files: **AUDIT** and **RECOVER**.

The **AUDIT** and **RECOVER** commands will both scan a drawing for any corruption and will allow you to attempt to correct any problems they find. The **RECOVER** command allows you to select any drawing file to scan. The **AUDIT** command only scans the currently open drawing file. In addition, the **AUDIT** command gives you the option of just scanning the file without attempting to correct the problems.

The **AUDIT** and **RECOVER** commands only operate on a single drawing file. If the drawing has any xrefs, the xrefs will not be scanned for problems. If you wish to scan a drawing and all of its associated xrefs, you should use the **RECOVERALL** command. The **RECOVERALL** command scans the drawing and any xrefs attached to the drawing. The **RECOVERALL** command also displays a report at the end of the command showing the results for each drawing it scans (see Figure 18-6).

Cleaning Up Drawing Files

As you have seen, AutoCAD drawings consist of both graphical and nongraphical elements. Layer settings, block definitions, linetypes, text styles, plot styles, table styles, dimension styles, and other nongraphical elements can be stored in a drawing, even if they may not be

Audit	
Application Menu	Drawing Utilities ?
Toolbar:	None
Menu:	File | Drawing Utilities | Audit
Command Line:	AUDIT
Command Alias:	None

Recover	
Appli-cation Menu	Drawing Utilities Recover
Toolbar:	None
Pull-down Menu:	File | Drawing Utilities | Recover…
Command Line:	RECOVER
Command Alias:	None

Recover with Xrefs	
Appli-cation Menu	Drawing Utilities Recover with Xrefs
Toolbar:	None
Menu:	File | Drawing Utilities | Recover drawing and xrefs…
Command Line:	RECOVERALL
Command Alias:	None

Purge	
Appli-cation Menu	Drawing Utilities
Toolbar:	None
Menu:	File | Drawing Utilities | Purge
Command Line:	PURGE
Command Alias:	None

Figure 18-6   The RECOVERALL error report

used within the drawing. It is possible to have empty layers, unused linetypes, dimension styles, etc.

Although these elements can reside in the drawing without being used, they do add to the size of the drawing file and can add complexity to a drawing. For example, a CAD layering standard may have hundreds of potential layers, but only a handful of them are used in any given drawing. Similarly, you may have a block library that consists of many symbols, but you may only use a few in any single drawing. There is no need to have all of these extra settings and block definitions stored with every drawing.

To help manage these various definitions and style settings, AutoCAD provides the **PURGE** command to view unused styles and definitions and remove them from the drawing.

The PURGE Command.   When you start the **PURGE** command, AutoCAD displays the **Purge** dialog box (see Figure 18-7). This dialog box has a list of the various items that can be purged from a drawing. By default, AutoCAD shows you all the items that can be purged. A plus (+) symbol next to any item denotes a category that contains items that can be purged. Clicking on the + symbol expands the tree to show you the specific items. To purge an item, simply select the object from the list and choose the **Purge** button. You can select multiple items using either **<Ctrl>** or **<Shift>** while selecting items. To purge all unused objects from a drawing, choose the **Purge All** button. Placing a check in the **Confirm each item to be purged** check box will cause AutoCAD to prompt you before it purges each object.

You can also choose to display items that cannot be purged by selecting the **View items you cannot purge** button. Keep in mind that only unused objects can be purged from the drawing. When the **View items you cannot purge** button is selected, you will not be able to purge any objects. In addition, the following default AutoCAD objects cannot be purged from a drawing.

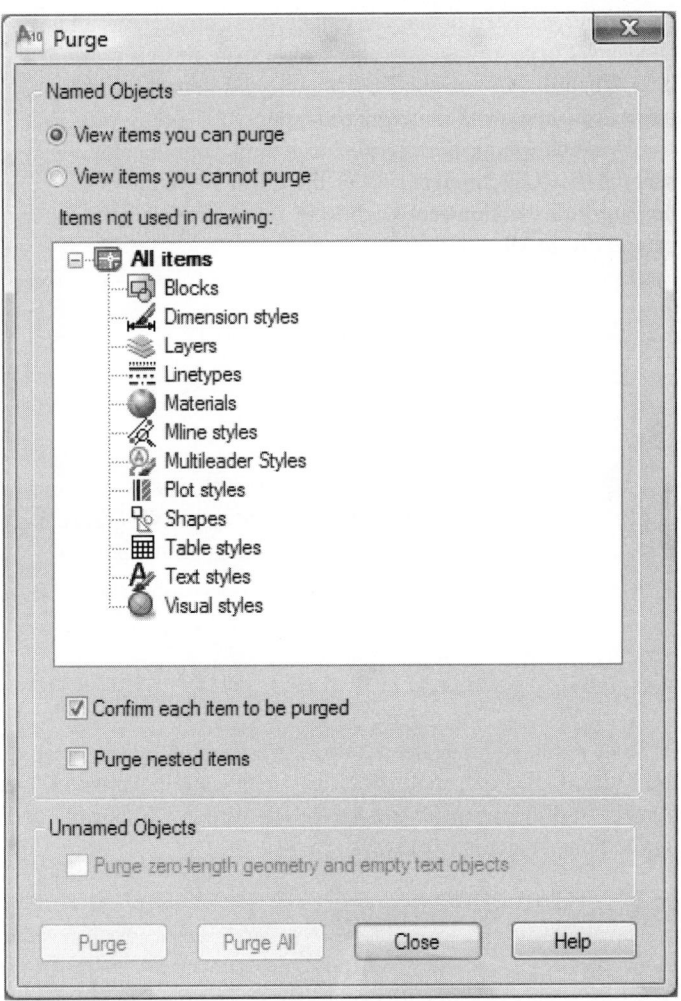

Figure 18-7   The **Purge** dialog box

Default Objects	Name
Layers	0, Defpoints
Linetypes	ByLayer, Continous, ByBlock
Multileader Style	Standard
Multiline Style	Standard
Dimension Style	Standard
Plot Style	Normal
Table Style	Standard
Text Style	Standard

Purging Nested Items.   Some objects may be nested, meaning that unused objects are dependent on other unused objects. For example, you may have a block definition that contains an unused layer definition. In order for the layer definition to be purged, the block definition containing the layer definition must first be purged.

To purge nested items, you can keep selecting items and choosing **Purge**, or you can check the **Purge nested items** box. When this box is checked, all selected items and any items nested below them will also be purged.

To quickly purge all unused objects from your drawing, start the **PURGE** command, check the **Purge nested items** box, turn off the **Confirm each item to be purged**, and choose **Purge All**.

Note:
It is possible to purge zero-length geometry and text objects that consist only of spaces by selecting the checkbox in the **Unamed Objects** area at the bottom of the **Purge** dialog box.

TIP   Sometimes you may have a layer that appears to be unused but cannot be purged. Layers that are frozen within a layout viewport (**VP Freeze** in the **Layer** dialog box) cannot be purged until they are thawed within that viewport.

WORKING WITH DIFFERENT CAD FILE FORMATS

At some point, you may need to work with a drawing file created in another drafting program or use AutoCAD data in another software application. AutoCAD has the ability to read and write a number of different raster and vector file formats. Importing and exporting various file formats can be done in a variety of ways.

Exporting to DWF/PDF Files

In Chapter 15, we saw how it is possible to create DWF/DWFx (Drawing Web Format) and PDF (Adobe Portable Document Format) files using the **PLOT** command. It is also possible to export a file directly to the DWF/DWFx and PDF formats using the tools and settings on the **Export to DWF/PDF** panel on the **Output** ribbon shown in Figure 18-8.

Figure 18-8   The **Export to DWF/PDF** panel

FOR MORE DETAILS   See Chapter 15 for more information about the DWF/DFWx and PDF file formats.

The **Export** list box at the top of the panel allows you to specify what information to export. In a paper space layout you can export the current layout or all layouts at one time. In model space, you can export what is currently displayed, the drawing extents, or pick a window area.

The **Page Setup** list box allows you to control what page setup settings to apply. By default, the current page setup is used. The **Override** option displays the **Page Setup Override** dialog box so you can change the paper size, the plot style table (pen assignments), plot scale, and other plot settings.

The **Export to DWF/PDF Options** button displays the **Export to DWF/PDF Options** dialog box shown in Figure 18-9 so you can control the output settings, such as whether to create a multisheet file or to include layer information.

The **Preview** button allows you to preview the file before exporting it so you can check it to make sure everything looks correct.

Figure 18-9   The **Export to DWF/PDF Options** dialog box

Once all the desired settings and options have been selected and you are ready to export your file, select one of the three export types from the flyout menu on the left (DWFx, DWF, PDF) to display its corresponding "Save As" dialog box so you can specify a file name and location. All three output formats share a dialog box similar to the **Save As PDF** dialog box shown in Figure 18-10.

Figure 18-10   The **Save As PDF** dialog box

Select the **Save** button once the file name and location has been specified to export the file. The **Plot and Publish Job Complete** notification balloon is displayed in the AutoCAD system tray in the lower right-hand corner of the AutoCAD window when AutoCAD is done exporting the file, indicating the success or failure of the export process.

Importing and Exporting Other File Types

The **IMPORT** and **EXPORT** commands are the most common ways of reading and writing other file formats. AutoCAD also provides a number of commands that work with specific file formats.

The following table describes the various file formats that AutoCAD supports and the commands that are available to read or write.

Note:
This section will cover some of the basics of importing and exporting various file formats. However, the specifics of working with each individual file type are beyond the scope of this book. If you have a specific file format you need to read or write, please consult the AutoCAD 2010 Help feature and search for your specific file format.

File Format	Description	Import Commands	Export Commands
DXF	Drawing Exchange File. A text file used by Autodesk to exchange CAD information. The most common way of exchanging AutoCAD drawing information between various CAD packages.	**OPEN, DXFIN**	**SAVEAS, DXFOUT**
DGN	MicroStation Design file. A 2D/3D vector file format created by MicroStation. Currently, only the V8 version of this file format is supported.	**IMPORT DGNIMPORT**	**EXPORT DGNEXPORT**
DXB	Drawing Exchange Binary file. A binary version of the DXF file. This file is typically used to flatten 3D models to 2D drawings. 3D models are plotted to a flat 2D DXB file.	**DXBIN**	**PLOT**
ACIS/SAT	Standard Acis Text. A 3D solid file format. Only **REGION** or **3DSOLID** objects are supported in this file format.	**IMPORT, ACISIN**	**EXPORT, ACISOUT**
STL	Stereolithography file. A 3D solid file format typically used in rapid prototyping applications. Only **REGION** or **3DSOLID** objects are supported in this file format.	Not Supported	**STLOUT**
3DS	3D Studio file. Typically a 3D file format used primarily with rendering and animation applications.	Not Supported	**3DSOUT**
DXX	Attribute extract DXF file. An abbreviated type of DXF file created by the **ATTEXT** command in AutoCAD. Only block and attribute information is included in a DXX file.	Not Supported	**EXPORT, ATTEXT**
EPS	Encapsulated Postscript file. Used in a variety of desktop publishing applications and maintains a high resolution print capability.	Not Supported	**EXPORT, PSOUT**

| WMF | Windows Metafile. A combination of raster and vector formats used in Microsoft Windows and Office applications. | IMPORT, WMFIN | EXPORT, WMFOUT |
| BMP, JPG, PNG, TIF | Various raster file formats. | IMAGE | BMPOUT, JPGOUT, PNGOUT, TIFOUT |

The EXPORT Command. The **EXPORT** command allows you to export AutoCAD drawing information to various file formats. When you start the **EXPORT** command, AutoCAD will display the **Export Data** dialog box (see Figure 18-11) where you can specify the output file type as well as the file name.

Once you specify the file name and file type, AutoCAD will prompt you to select the objects you want to export. Once you select the objects to export, press **<Enter ↵>** to export the objects to the specified file.

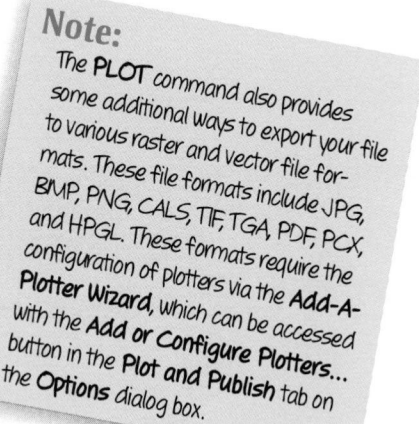

Note:
The **PLOT** command also provides some additional ways to export your file to various raster and vector file formats. These file formats include JPG, BMP, PNG, CALS, TIF, TGA, PDF, PCX, and HPGL. These formats require the configuration of plotters via the **Add-A-Plotter Wizard**, which can be accessed with the **Add or Configure Plotters...** button in the **Plot and Publish** tab on the **Options** dialog box.

Export	
Appli-cation Menu	Send
Toolbar:	None
Menu:	File | Export…
Command Line:	EXPORT
Command Alias:	EXP

Figure 18-11   The **Export Data** dialog box

Import	
Ribbon & Panel:	Insert| Import
Insert Toolbar:	
Menu:	File| Import...
Command Line:	IMPORT
Command Alias:	IMP

The IMPORT Command. The **IMPORT** command allows you to convert various file formats to AutoCAD objects. When you start the **IMPORT** command, AutoCAD will display the **Import File** dialog box (Figure 18-12) and allow you to specify the file type as well as the file name.

After you specify the file name and file type, AutoCAD imports the data and places it in the drawing. The imported objects are typically converted to a block and placed as a single object, which can then be exploded.

Note: Take care when exporting objects from paper space layouts. Because you are prompted to select objects, only selected objects in the current drawing space will be exported. Exporting objects from both model space and paper space is not allowed.

Figure 18-12   The **Import File** dialog box

Working with DXF Files

DXF stands for *Drawing Exchange File* and is the primary method that AutoCAD uses for importing and exporting data between CAD applications. A DXF file can be either binary or ASCII text (most commonly used) and is widely used and supported by most CAD applications. DXF Files can be created in AutoCAD with the **SAVEAS** or **DXFOUT** commands. The **DXFOUT** command is actually a command alias for the **SAVEAS** command.

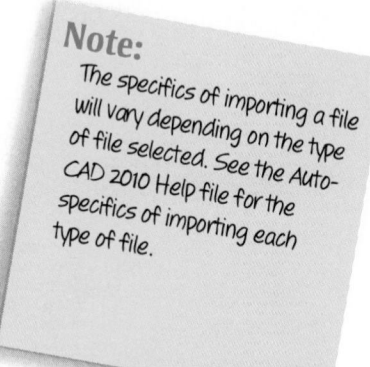

Note: The specifics of importing a file will vary depending on the type of file selected. See the AutoCAD 2010 Help file for the specifics of importing each type of file.

Creating a DXF File.   Although the **EXPORT** command only allows you to export selected objects within a drawing, a DXF file represents the entire drawing (paper space, model space, layers, blocks, etc.). Like the DWG file format, the DXF file format has changed over the various releases of AutoCAD. AutoCAD can currently create DXF files in the following formats: AutoCAD 2010, AutoCAD 2007, AutoCAD 2004, AutoCAD 2000, and AutoCAD R12.

When you start the **SAVEAS** command, AutoCAD displays the **Save Drawing As** dialog box (Figure 18-13). Specify the file name, location, and type of file you wish to create and choose **Save**.

> **Note:**
> The DXF file format is defined in the AutoCAD Customization Guide section of the AutoCAD 2010 Help.

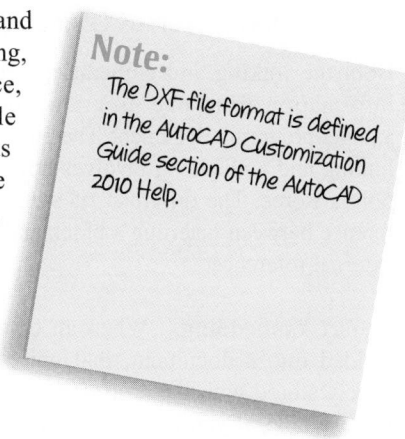

> **Note:**
> Keep in mind that some object types are not supported in earlier versions of AutoCAD and will be translated to their earlier object types. For example, ellipses and spline curves are converted to polylines in the R12 file format.

Figure 18-13   The **Save Drawing As** dialog box

OBJECT LINKING AND EMBEDDING

Another way to share information between AutoCAD and other applications is to use Object Linking and Embedding (OLE). OLE allows you to share information between two Windows applications. To use OLE, you need both the source and the destination applications that support OLE. The source application is the program used to create the document. The destination application is the program that is going to receive the source document. For example, if you were to embed an AutoCAD drawing in a Word document, AutoCAD is the source, and Word is the destination.

Object Linking Versus Object Embedding

Both the linking and embedding processes insert information from one program's document into another program's document. The difference between linking and embedding involves how the information is stored. The difference is similar to the difference between inserting a block and creating an external reference.

Note:
Although the Windows OLE feature can use AutoCAD as either a source or a destination application, this chapter focuses primarily on placing OLE objects in AutoCAD drawings. Keep in mind that the behavior of data from other applications will vary from program to program. To link or embed AutoCAD drawings in other applications, refer to the documentation for that application for specifics on using OLE within that program.

Object Embedding.   When an object is embedded into a document, that object is completely stored with the destination application. For example, if you created a Word document and then embedded it into an AutoCAD drawing, you would not need to save the Word file to a separate file. That Word document would exist entirely within the AutoCAD drawing. When the AutoCAD drawing is saved, the embedded Word document is saved along with it. This is similar to the relationship between an AutoCAD drawing and a block definition. Block definitions are defined and stored entirely within the AutoCAD drawing. The block does not need to exist as a separate drawing file.

Object Linking.   When an object is linked, Windows simply creates a link between the source file and the destination file. Any changes made to the source document will be reflected in the destination document. If the source document is deleted, the link will be broken, and the OLE object will not be updated. This is similar to the relationship between an AutoCAD drawing and an xref. The drawing file does not store the entire xref, only a link to the referenced file. When the referenced file is updated, the AutoCAD drawing containing the xref is also updated.

Insert OLE Object	
Ribbon & Panel:	Insert|Data
	OLE Object
Insert Toolbar:	
Menu:	Insert|OLE Object...
Command Line:	INSERTOBJ
Command Alias:	None

Inserting OLE Objects

There are a number of ways to create and insert OLE objects within an AutoCAD drawing. The method you use will depend primarily on whether you want to link or embed the OLE object and how you want the OLE object to be displayed within the drawing.

The INSERTOBJ Command.   The **INSERTOBJ** command allows you to create a linked or embedded object. When the command starts, AutoCAD displays the **Insert Object** dialog box (Figure 18-14).

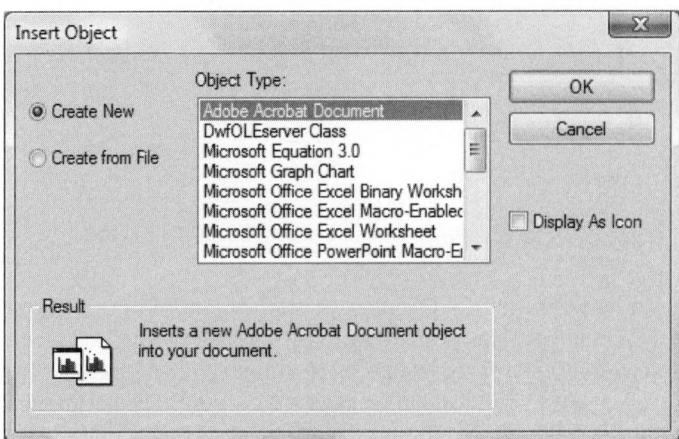

Figure 18-14   The **Insert Object** dialog box

From this dialog box, you can choose whether you want to create a new OLE source document or use an existing file as the source document. Select the **Create New** button to create a new embedded document. Selecting this will only allow you to embed a new file. Once you select the type of file you wish to embed, Windows will launch that application with a new document for you to modify. Once you are done modifying the embedded object, select **File|Update Drawing** in the source application, and the embedded object will appear in your drawing. Because the object is now embedded in the AutoCAD drawing, you can close the source application.

> **Note:**
> The list of **Object Types** in the **Insert Object** dialog box will vary depending on the software you have installed on your computer. Also, the exact method of updating the AutoCAD drawing may vary depending on the source application.

If you want to use insert an existing document as on OLE object, select the **Create from File** button and then choose **Browse...** to select the source document. Once you select the source file, you can choose whether you want to link to the source file by putting a check in the **Link** box. Not checking the **Link** box will embed the source file in your drawing.

Placing a check in the **Display As Icon** box will display the OLE object as an icon within the drawing. This only affects how the OLE object is displayed in AutoCAD and does not affect the contents of the OLE object.

Using the Windows Clipboard.   The Windows Clipboard feature can also be used to link and embed data from other applications. The Windows Clipboard provides a way to store data temporarily from most Windows programs. In most Windows applications, you can select data and choose **Copy** from the **Edit** pull-down menu or press **<Ctrl>+C** within that application. Once information is copied to the Windows Clipboard, it can be pasted into other locations within the same program or into other Windows applications.

The Windows Clipboard can be used to store information from within a file or to copy entire files or multiple files and folders.

When data is stored in the Windows Clipboard, it can be placed into an AutoCAD drawing using either the **PASTECLIP** or **PASTESPEC** commands.

The **PASTECLIP** command will place the contents of the Clipboard as an embedded OLE object. When you start the **PASTECLIP** command, AutoCAD will prompt you for an insertion point. Depending on the type of data in the Clipboard, AutoCAD may display the **OLE Text Size** dialog box (see Figure 18-15). This dialog box allows you to control how Windows fonts are displayed within AutoCAD and allows you to convert the Windows text point size to AutoCAD text height.

Paste	
Ribbon & Panel:	Home|Clipboard Paste
Standard Toolbar:	
Menu:	Edit|Paste
Command Line:	PASTECLIP
Command Alias:	Ctrl+V

Paste Special	
Ribbon & Panel:	Home|Clipboard Paste Special
Toolbar:	None
Menu:	Edit|Paste Special...
Command Line:	PASTESPEC
Command Alias:	None

Figure 18-15   The **OLE Text Size** dialog box

The **PASTESPEC** command gives you a little more control over how the Clipboard data is stored in AutoCAD. When you start the **PASTESPEC** command, AutoCAD displays the **Paste Special** dialog box (see Figure 18-16).

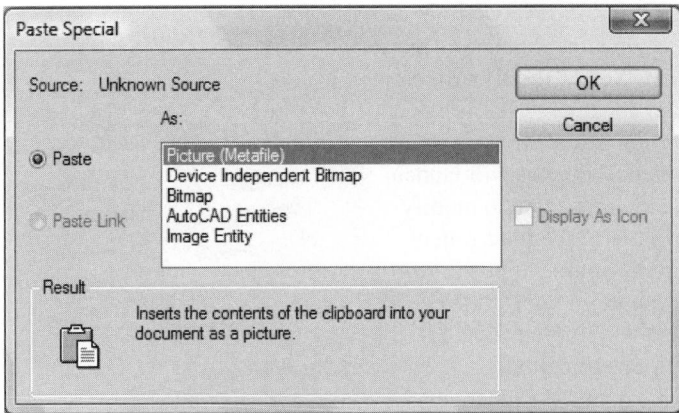

Figure 18-16   The **Paste Special** dialog box

The **PASTESPEC** command allows you to place an OLE object as either a linked or embedded object. It also gives you the ability to convert the Clipboard contents to AutoCAD entities. The types of entities created depend on the type of data in the Clipboard. AutoCAD will automatically convert the Clipboard data to the most appropriate AutoCAD object. For example, Excel spreadsheet data is converted to an AutoCAD table, Word data is converted to AutoCAD text, raster image data is converted to AutoCAD image overlays, etc.

Drag-and-Drop. Another feature of Windows is the ability to drag-and-drop data between Windows applications. Drag-and-drop involves selecting data in the source application and, while holding your left mouse button down, dragging the data onto your AutoCAD drawing. This can take a little practice and preplanning because both applications must be visible and accessible.

Drag-and-drop works the same as **PASTECLIP**; the only difference is that drag-and-drop bypasses the Windows Clipboard.

Editing OLE Objects

The nature of OLE objects is that they are edited in their source application. Double-clicking an OLE object will launch the source application with the OLE data. You can make changes to the source data and then either close the source application or, in most applications, choose **Close and Return to Drawing** from the **File** menu in the source application.

Managing Linked Objects. Linked objects, because they rely on the coordination of multiple files, require a little more attention than embedded objects. The location of the linked file is critical to updating and maintaining the information in the OLE object. The way in which you want the information updated and the ability to terminate a link are also part of maintaining an OLE linked object. The **OLELINKS** command allows you to manage linked OLE objects from within AutoCAD.

The **OLELINKS** command only works if you have linked OLE objects in your AutoCAD drawing. When you start the **OLELINKS** command, AutoCAD displays the **Links** dialog box (see Figure 18-17). The **Update Now** button will refresh the OLE object from the source file. The **Open Source** button will open the source file and allow you to make changes. The **Change Source** button allows you to specify a different source file for the OLE object. When you change the source file, the new source file must be the same type of file as the original source file. The **Break Link** button will terminate the link between AutoCAD and the source file and turn the linked object into an embedded object.

At the bottom of the **Links** dialog box are two buttons which allow you to control how the OLE objects are updated. Choosing **Automatic** causes AutoCAD to update the OLE object whenever the source file changes. Choosing **Manual** tells AutoCAD not to update the OLE object until you choose the **Update Now** button.

OLE Links	
Ribbon & Panel:	None
Toolbar:	None
Menu:	Edit|OLE Links
Command Line:	OLELINKS
Command Alias:	None

Figure 18-17   The **Links** dialog box

Plot Quality.   OLE objects are treated as raster objects when a raster plotter is used. Because large, high-resolution, color-rich rasters can be expensive to plot, you can set the **OLEQUALITY** system variable to control how each OLE object is plotted. There are four possible settings: 0 (Monochrome), 1 (Low Quality), 2 (High Quality), and 3 (Automatically Select). The default setting, Automatically Select, assigns a plot-quality level based on the type of object. The higher the plot-quality setting, the more time and memory are used to plot. The **OLEQUALITY** variable can be applied separately to each OLE object in the drawing.

Controlling the Visibility of OLE Objects.   While working on a drawing, you may want to suppress the display or plotting of OLE objects. The **OLEHIDE** system variable allows you to control the visibility and plotting of OLE objects in model space, paper space, or both. The default setting is **0** which displays and plots all OLE objects in both model and paper space. Setting **OLEHIDE** to **1** displays and plots OLE objects in paper space only. Setting **OLEHIDE** to **2** displays and plots OLE objects in model space only. Setting **OLEHIDE** to **3** suppresses the display and plotting of all OLE objects in both model and paper space. The **OLEHIDE** variable applies globally to all OLE objects in a drawing.

OLEFRAME System Variable.   When OLE objects are placed in AutoCAD, they behave like other AutoCAD objects in that they have default properties, such as layer color and linetype, associated with them. Like raster image overlays, these properties apply to the frame surrounding the OLE objects. The **OLEFRAME** system variable controls the display and plotting of the OLE object frame. Setting **OLEFRAME** to **0** turns off the OLE frame, and it will not be displayed or plotted. Setting **OLEFRAME** to **1** displays the OLE frame both on screen and in plots. Setting **OLEFRAME** to **2** displays the OLE frame in the display but suppresses it in plots. The **OLEFRAME** variable applies globally to all OLE objects in a drawing.

OLE Properties.   As stated earlier, OLE objects behave similarly to other objects in a drawing. They can be moved, copied, resized, etc. The **Properties** palette (see Figure 18-18) displays information specific to OLE objects, such as the location and the height and width scale of the OLE object. You can also control the plot quality of the OLE object.

Action Recorder

The **Action Recorder** tool allows you to automate repetitive tasks by recording the AutoCAD commands, inputs, and options you enter as an **Action Macro** that you, or anyone else, can replay later. If you find yourself doing the same series of steps over and over again, the **Action Recorder** can help by recording them so that the next time you need to do the same thing, all you have to do is press the **Play** button. The **Play** button and all the other **Action Recorder** tools and features are located on the **Action Recorder** panel on the **Tools** ribbon shown in Figure 18-19.

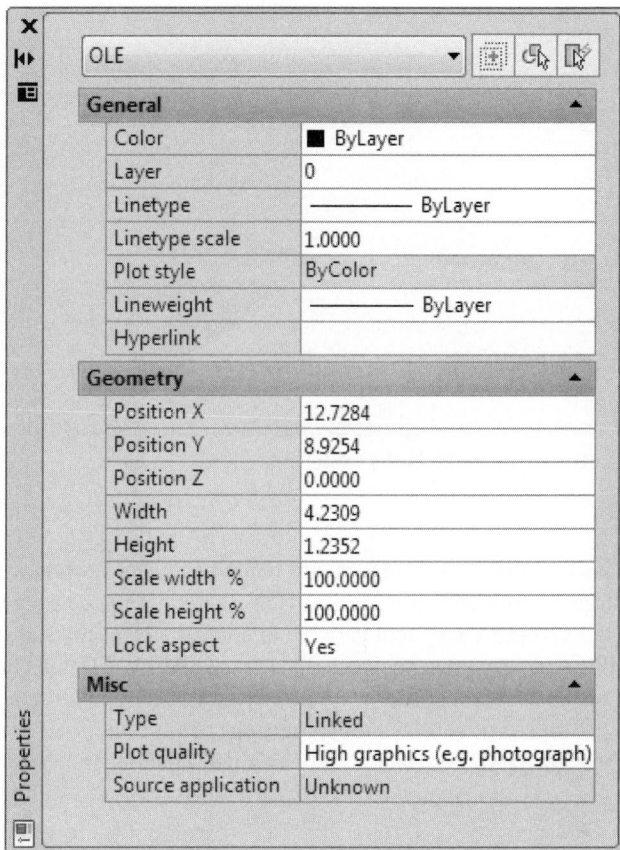

Figure 18-18   The **Properties** palette

Figure 18-19   The **Action Recorder** panel

To use the **Action Recorder** you simply press the **Record** button and step through the series of commands that you would normally go through to complete a task and push the **Stop** button when you are done. The **Action Recorder** can record actions entered via the command line, ribbon panels, menus, the **Layer Properties Manager**, the **Properties** palette, tool palettes and even toolbars. While recording an **Action Macro**, a red recording circle icon is displayed near the crosshairs to indicate that the **Action Recorder** is running and any commands and input are being recorded.

Note:
There are certain actions that cannot be recorded—specifically, file operation commands such as **OPEN** and **CLOSE**, as well as any type of grip editing. While it is possible to display a dialog box, it is not possible to track and record your actions once it is displayed. Additionally, the **Quick Properties** Palette is not recognized and certain tool palette commands cannot be recorded.

TIP   Many commands have an alternate command line only version that can be accessed by prefixing the command with a hyphen (–) that allows you to work around the **Action Recorder's** inability to record dialog box actions. For instance, while the **HATCH** command displays the **Hatch & Gradient** dialog box, which cannot be recorded, the -**HATCH** commands allows you to place hatches by entering all the command options via the keyboard so that the **Action Recorder** can record them.

When you press the **Stop** button the **Action Macro** dialog box shown in Figure 18-20 is displayed so you can enter a command name for the macro.

Figure 18-20   The **Action Macro** dialog box

All the actions entered are saved to an **Action Macro** file with an **.ACTM** file extension. The default macro and file name provided is **ActMacro001**, where the 3-digit suffix is incremented each time. It is suggested that you enter a more descriptive name that better indicates the nature of the macro.

The best thing about **Action Macros** is that after you are done recording a macro you can go back and customize it by adding your own text messages and pauses for user input by right-clicking on an action in the **Action Tree** window and using the shortcut menu shown in Figure 18-21.

> **Note:**
> There are a few limitations when naming an **Action Macro**. An **Action Macro** cannot have the same name as an AutoCAD command. For instance, you cannot create a macro named **LINE**. It is also not possible to use spaces or special characters. It is suggested you substitute a dash (-) or an underscore (_) when a space is required.

Figure 18-21 Adding messages and pauses for user input

The **Preferences** button on the **Action Recorder** panel displays the **Action Recorder Preferences** dialog box shown in Figure 18-22, which allows you to control whether the **Action Recorder** panel expands when recording or playing back an action macro, and if you are prompted to provide a command name for the **Action Macro** when you press the **Stop** button and recording is stopped.

TIP

By default, **Action Macro** files are stored in the folder specified in the **Actions Recording File Location** setting under **Action Recorder Settings** on the **Files** tab in the **Options** dialog box. The **Additional Actions Reading File Locations** setting allows you share **Action Macro** files in a network location so multiple people on different computers can access and run them.

Figure 18-22   **Action Recorder Preferences** dialog box

Measure Tools

The **Measure** tools located on the **Utilities** panel on the **Home** ribbon shown in Figure 18-23 allow you to measure the distance, radius, angle, area, or volume of a selected object or sequence of points.

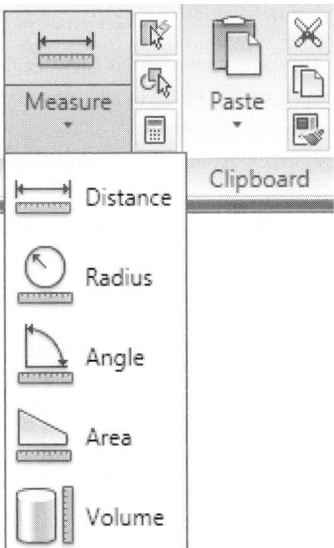

Figure 18-23   The **Measure** tools on the **Utilities** panel

The **Distance** tool allows you to measure the distance between two points. After you select two points, AutoCAD displays the distance, delta x, delta y, and angle directly on your screen and at the AutoCAD command line. The **Multiple** option allows you to continue picking points and display a cumulative distance.

The **Radius** tool allows you to measure the radius of a selected arc or circle.

The **Angle** tool allows you to measure the angle of a selected arc, circle, or line. The default **Specify vertex** option allows you pick three points starting with the vertex.

The **Area** tool allows you to select objects or pick points and display the included area. The **Add** and **Subtract** options allow you calculate cumulative areas.

The **Volume** tool allows you to calculate an area using techniques similar to the **Area** tool and then specify a height to determine the volume. It is also possible to display the volume of selected solids or regions.

Chapter Summary

This chapter explored additional file management techniques that include recovering and fixing corrupt files and changing settings in AutoCAD to create backup files. Remember that AutoCAD drawings can be shared with other CAD programs and viewed in other software applications. In turn, other CAD and Windows-based files can be translated into AutoCAD. Sharing data from one software application to another is cost efficient, productive, and becoming commonplace in the design industry. AutoCAD has internal tools to assist with these file translations. As with most Windows software, AutoCAD provides all the Object Linking and Embedding tools such as **Copy, Cut,** and **Paste**, as well as a Clipboard that makes sharing information even easier. Last, AutoCAD provides ways to enhance OLE objects with system variables that control display, plotting, and editing options.

Chapter Test Questions

Multiple Choice

1. The **PURGE** command can remove unused:

   a. Layers
   b. Linetypes
   c. Blocks
   d. All of the above

2. The **EXPORT** command supports the following file type:

   a. WMF, JPG, EPS, DXX, BMP, DWG, 3DS
   b. WMF, SAT, EPS, DXX, BMP, 3DS, DWG
   c. JPG, PNG, DXX, BMP, DXX, EPS, SAT
   d. None of the above

3. The command that saves and exports an AutoCAD object into a drawing file is:

   a. **WBLOCK**
   b. **WMFOUT**
   c. **JPGOUT**
   d. **DWGOUT**

4. The Backup File extension is:

   a. AC$
   b. BAC
   c. SV$
   d. BAK

5. A DXF file can be created by:

   a. Pasting a DWG file into Word
   b. Using the **SAVE** or **SAVEAS** command
   c. Using the **XREF** command
   d. None of the above

6. A source application file:

   a. Is where an object is linked
   b. Can never be changed or edited
   c. Is the same as a destination file
   d. None of the above

7. Dragging-and-dropping objects is the same as:

   a. Embedding and linking
   b. Copying and pasting
   c. Cutting and pasting
   d. All of the above

8. An AutoCAD file with linked objects:

   a. Can be automatically updated if there are changes to the source file
   b. Tends to be smaller in file size than files with embedded objects
   c. Must be updated if either the source or destination file is moved to another drive or directory
   d. All of the above

9. An embedded object can be changed or edited in an AutoCAD file:

   a. By right-clicking on the object and selecting **Edit**
   b. By double-clicking on the object to bring up the source application
   c. By deleting the object, recreating an updated version in the source file, and bringing it back into AutoCAD through the Clipboard
   d. Is not allowed

10. The **OLEHIDE** system variable will display and plot OLE objects in model space if the value is:

    a. Set to **0**
    b. Set to **1**
    c. Set to **2**
    d. Set to either **0** or **2**

Matching

a. BAK
b. **PASTECLIP**
c. **AUDIT**
d. Drawing Recovery Manager
e. **Options** dialog box
f. **OLELINKS**
g. **PURGE**
h. DXX
i. **IMPORT**
j. **EXPORT**

1. Eliminates unused lines, blocks, and layers
2. Pastes copied objects
3. Controls settings of AutoCAD software
4. AutoCAD backup file
5. Attribute extract DXF file
6. Changes other file types into an AutoCAD drawing file
7. Modifies existing OLE links
8. Changes AutoCAD drawing file types into a specific file format
9. Checks and fixes errors in a drawing file
10. Attempts to restore or retrieve open and backup drawing files

Introduction to 3D in the AutoCAD Program

19

Chapter
Objectives

- Know the advantages of 3D modeling and recognize the different ways to represent a 3D model.
- Become familiarized with the location of the commands related to the 3D environment and the different methods available to access them.
- Understand the 3D viewing system and manage the procedures to change, save, and restore the viewing point.
- Understand the 3D coordinate system (WCS and UCS) and its relationship to the viewing system.
- Use the predefined orthogonal UCS and user-created UCS.
- Learn the different systems to express the 3D coordinates of a point.
- Use the **3DORBIT** command and other navigation tools related to it.
- Learn to use the mouse wheel efficiently to navigate the 3D space.
- Understand and use the predefined visual styles.
- Learn advanced drafting aids to find points in the 3D space.

INTRODUCTION

2D DRAWING VS. 3D MODEL

Drawings have long been regarded as the universal technical language. They are used to represent any object's shape, dimensions, and specifications on a piece of paper.

With the development of the computer in the 1980s, programmers began to focus on Computer Aided Design (CAD), which led to the development of pioneering software to perform important drawing tasks. This marked the beginning of a new era for designers and drafters, allowing them to greatly increase their accuracy and productivity with less work strain.

As the speed and power of computers increased, the concept of three-dimensional (3D) modeling started to develop as well. This new capability gave designers the most efficient tool they had ever had, substituting for costly prototypes in many cases.

Most two-dimensional (2D) drawings simply show an object's projections, and in many cases they tend to confuse personnel in charge of interpreting them. 3D models, however, give an exact understanding of what the real object looks like. With some experience, you will look at 2D work the same way you looked at hand drafting when you first started to work with AutoCAD.

WAYS OF REPRESENTING A 3D MODEL

Regardless of specific conventions used in particular disciplines, the main purpose of generating electronic drawings is to represent objects as accurately as possible. Using the AutoCAD software, you can represent objects electronically in either two or three dimensions.

The two-dimensional ways of representing objects are:

- 2D drawings
- Isometric drawings using the Isometric snap style

The three-dimensional ways of representing 3D objects are:

- Wireframe models
- Surface models
- Solid models

In all the three-dimensional ways of representing objects, the entities or elements that are used are actually placed throughout the 3D space. Creating 3D models with AutoCAD is not limited to a particular method or set of tools. You can use as many tools and objects as you wish in conjunction with representing a 3D object.

A 3D object is represented as a *wireframe* model simply by placing lines, polylines, arcs, splines, and 3D polylines in the 3D space where the edges of the object are located. For example, to represent a box by modeling its wires you will need 12 *lines* or *polylines* to represent its 12 edges. A cylinder would be represented less clearly because it has no physical vertical edge, but rather a single continuous surface (Figure 19-1).

Representing a box with a hole, therefore, would require the same 12 straight lines and the two circles (Figure 19-2).

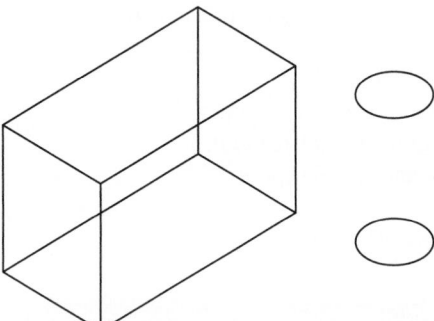

Figure 19-1   Wireframe representation of a box and a cylinder

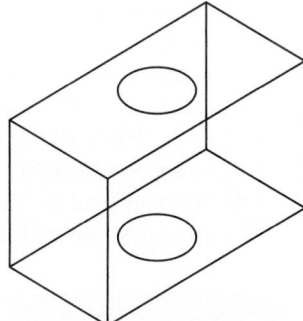

Figure 19-2   Wireframe representation of a box with a cylindrical hole

A wireframe or skeleton model is the simplest way to represent objects three-dimensionally; however, it is more difficult to achieve. A wireframe model does not allow you to perform an operation in which the supposedly occulted lines of the represented 3D object are actually hidden. Thus, this procedure is rarely used as a final representation of 3D objects. In most cases, a wireframe model is merely used to find points in the 3D space, or to create objects that will be used in the creation of other 3D entities.

A *surface model* is the representation of a 3D object's skin. Any type of surface entity can hide objects located behind it when tools related to this operation are invoked. Representing the box as a surface model requires placing six planar surfaces. The cylinder would be composed of three surfaces: two planar surfaces for the top and bottom, and a nonplanar surface to represent the cylindrical face (Figure 19-3).

Regions are the most suitable entity to represent planar surfaces. Nonplanar surfaces are commonly represented by faceted surfaces or true surfaces; however, faceted surfaces or meshes offer very few tools for further modifications. Figure 19-4 shows a box with a hole. The top and bottom planar surfaces of the box are represented by two regions, whereas the cylindrical surface of the hole is represented by a polygon mesh. This is one of many approaches that can be used to represent this particular object as a surface model.

Using a solid model is the easiest way of representing a 3D object three-dimensionally, and the most realistic one. Unlike wireframe and surface models, a single 3D solid can be used to

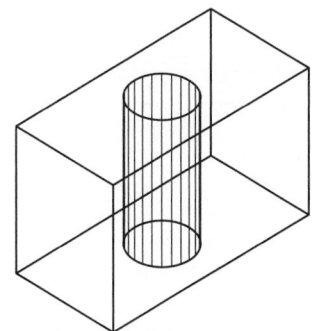

Figure 19-3   Surface representation of a box and a cylinder

Figure 19-4   Surface representation of a box with a cylindrical hole

represent the entire 3D model of an object. 3D solids can also hide objects located behind them and hide occulted edges.

The process of creating the box with a hole is as simple as subtracting a solid cylinder from a solid box. Figure 19-5 shows the 3D solid model of the box in a wireframe mode on the left, and with the hidden lines removed on the right.

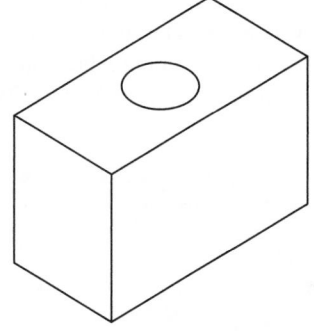

Figure 19-5   Box with a cylindrical hole represented with a 3D solid

Valuable mathematical information such as volume, center of gravity, moments of inertia, and other data can be obtained from 3D solid entities. A 3D solid can be edited using many 3D operations.

Preparing clear, concise, and accurate conceptual 3D models based on engineering information received electronically or by other means is part of the activity of designers and drafters. In order to properly visualize, conceive, and provide solutions to design problems and prepare appropriate engineering documentation, 3D users must be able to properly identify the different techniques used to represent 3D models. A complete understanding of these methods will assure a better comprehension and analysis of any information received. It will also ensure that data is properly generated according to the process and the use for which it is intended.

CUSTOMIZATION FOR 3D

ACCESS TO 3D COMMANDS AND OTHER SETTINGS

Using Workspaces

Due to the number of toolbars, menus, and dockable windows available in the AutoCAD program, it is necessary to switch back and forth between different screen arrangements. The ***Workspaces*** customization tools allow you to save these arrangements and quickly switch

workspaces: Specific arrangements of user interface elements, including their contents, properties, display status, and locations.

Figure 19-6   Workspaces can be selected from the toolbars' drop-down lists, or from the menu that shows on the status bar when clicking the Workspace switching button

between them. This prevents the screen from filling up with toolbars and windows that are not necessary for a particular task.

The AutoCAD program comes with three predefined workspaces: **3D Modeling, AutoCAD Classic**, and **2D Drafting & Annotation**. To switch between these workspaces, you can use the drop-down lists located in the **Workspaces** toolbars, the **Tools** drop-down menu **(Tools/Workspaces)**, or the Workspace switching button located at the right end of the status bar (Figure 19-6).

You can create a new workspace or modify an existing one. The easiest way to create a new workspace is by selecting **Save Current As. . .** from the drop-down list in the **Workspaces** toolbars after arranging the toolbars and dockable windows. You can overwrite a workspace by simply reselecting it in the **Save Workspace** dialog box (Figure 19-7).

Figure 19-7   The **Save Workspace** dialog box

The Command Line Window

Just as in 2D work, the *command line* can be used to access 3D command tools and settings. Due to the occasionally large amount of information that you must read at one time, three text lines should be opened above the bottom line in the command line window when working in a 3D environment (Figure 19-8). This can be achieved by moving the mouse pointer slowly toward the command line window's top border. When the pointer changes its appearance, pick, drag, and drop the window. If needed, the command line window can be undocked or closed, and its transparency can be changed. To do such operations, you will have to pick it from the left ribbon and drag it to the drawing area, then you can right-click on its ribbon to display the controls. You can open or close the command line window by clicking on Tools > Command Line.

TIP   Reading the command line window frequently can make the difference between learning to use the AutoCAD program faster, or slower.

Figure 19-8   The command line window

The Ribbon and Tool Palettes

The ***Ribbon*** is a special palette that contains the commands and controls most frequently used to create, view, and render 3D models. The commands and controls contained in the Ribbon palette are organized by ***Ribbon Panels***, which at the same time are organized into ***Ribbon Tabs***. Each one of the Ribbon Panels that is prebuilt in AutoCAD contains tools that are organized by category to help you find a particular tool more easily. In the Ribbon palette (Figure 19-9), practically everything can be customized: the Ribbon Tabs that will be available, the Ribbon Panels that will be displayed within each Ribbon Tab, and the tools that will be available in each Ribbon Panel. Furthermore, you can define a different Ribbon palette for each saved Workspace. The Ribbon palette can be closed or opened by invoking the **RIBBONCLOSE** or the **RIBBON** commands, respectively. The Ribbon Tabs in particular allow you to quickly display a complete set of categorized tools by themselves. This is extremely helpful in the 3D work, where the screen gets crowded occasionally with so many toolbars that you can hardly find a place to draw.

Ribbon: A totally customizable palette where you can organize the tools and controls most frequently used to create, view, and render 3D models.

Ribbon Tab: The most general grouping element in the *Ribbon palette*; each *Ribbon Tab* can contain several *Ribbon Panels*.

Ribbon Panel: The panels contained in each *Ribbon Tab*; each *Ribbon Panel* can contain different commands and controls.

> **FOR MORE DETAILS**   The customization of Workspaces and Ribbon palettes is made in the Customize User Interface, and it will be discussed further in this chapter.

In any particular Ribbon palette displayed, you can choose to hide or to show any of the Ribbon Tabs available; this is done by unchecking or checking the Tab from the list displayed in the shortcut menu. Right-clicking the top ribbon on the Ribbon palette or inside an empty area

Figure 19-9   The **Home** tab (above) and the **View** tab (below) showing the different panels contained in each one according to the predefined **3D Modeling** Workspace

Figure 19-10   Different shortcut menus on the Ribbon to access the list of **Tabs** available on the current Workspace and the list of Panels available on the current Tab. The shortcut on the right shows the **Undock** operation.

will show this shortcut menu (Figure 19-10); in the same way, you can hide or show Panels individually from the currently selected Tab. In a different shortcut menu, displayed by right-clicking the side ribbon on the Ribbon palette, you can specify whether the Ribbon palette will **Allow Docking**, so it can be anchored to the top right or left of the drawing area; to do so, you must grab it from its side ribbon, or the top one when it is docked at one of the sides. Other settings such as **Auto-hide** or **Transparency** can be controlled as well. You should turn the **Allow Docking** property off if you intend to use the **Auto-hide** feature. This will allow you to move the Ribbon palette to one of the ends of the drawing area without docking it.

Many of the panels of the Ribbon palette expand to show additional tools. Take a look at the **Navigation** panel located in the **View** tab in Figure 19-11 as an example.

To expand a control panel you can click on the small triangle located at the bottom (when it is docked at the top) or the side of the panel. You can choose to keep the panel expanded by clicking on the pushpin located at the bottom corner.

Figure 19-11   The **3D Modeling** panel on the Ribbon shown in an expanded mode

Flyout buttons for tools that do not fit in a particular row, as well as frequently used drop-down lists (i.e., the predefined view), can also be accessed from the Ribbon palette (Figure 19-12).

The **Tool Palettes** window, on the other hand, allows you to organize commands, materials, visual styles, blocks, hatches, and many other customizable tools. Right-clicking the title ribbon of this window shows its shortcut menu (Figure 19-13).

The ***Tool Palettes*** window is basically a group of palettes organized as a stack of pages. Clicking on a tab will bring a specific palette up; just like the tabs on any dialog box, it allows you to see the tools contained in it. You can create and customize palettes, as well as groups of palettes.

Tool Palettes: Customizable AutoCAD window that allows the user to organize tools and many other settings by palettes. You can add a tool by dragging objects into a palette.

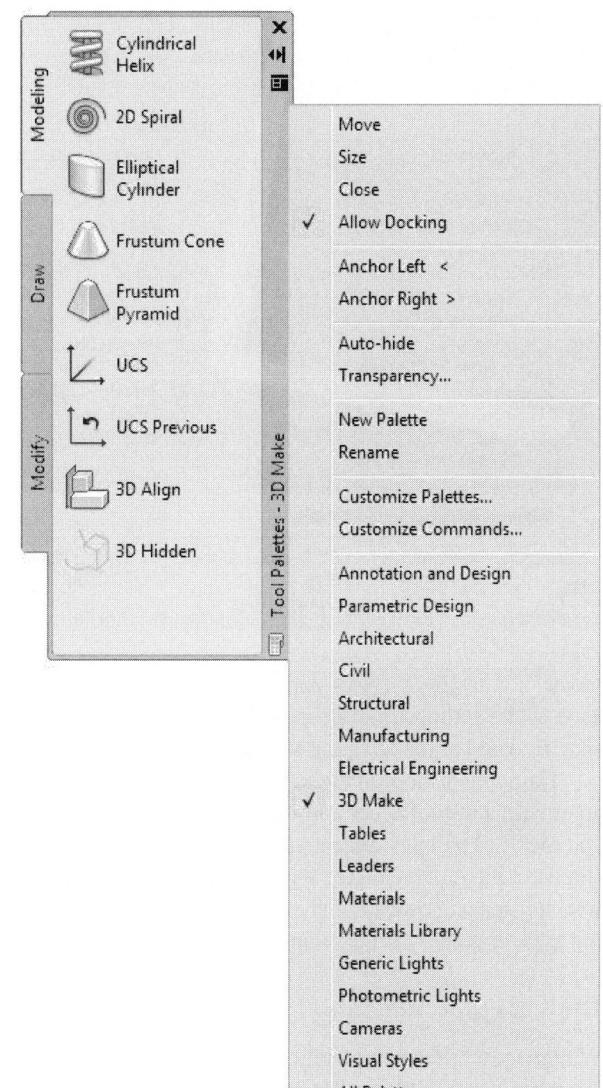

Figure 19-12   The predefined view drop-down lists on the **View** panel

Figure 19-13   The **Tool Palettes** window and its main shortcut menu

When customizing the palettes, you can add your most-used tools inside them. You add each tool by dropping it inside the palette. You can add commands as well as objects such as blocks, hatches, dimensions, polylines, raster images, materials, visual styles, and so on. Commands must be dragged from the **Command List**: section of the **Customize User Interface** window and dropped into the palette.

FOR MORE DETAILS   See the Customize User Interface (CUI) in this chapter for details about accessing the **Customize User Interface** window.

The groups of palettes are customized in the **Customize** window, which can be accessed by clicking on **Customize Palettes. . .** from the shortcut menu (Figure 19-14). In the **Customize** window you can drag and drop palettes from the list of **Palettes** into specific **Palette Groups**.

The control panels on the Ribbon palette can be linked to one of the existing **Palette Groups**. To do so you must right-click on the specific panel and select a **Tool Palette Group** in the shortcut

Figure 19-14   The **Customize** window

menu (Figure 19-15). Now you can slide down a Ribbon panel that contains your most frequently used tools, settings, and drop-down lists while selecting the palette group that you previously specified and associated to it in one single action.

Using the panels on the Ribbon palette, along with the palette group associated with them, is an effective way of accessing the AutoCAD tools and settings used in 3D modeling. The Ribbon and the Tool palettes can be placed one below the other to make effective use of the workspace (Figure 19-16). If you have a widescreen display, this particular arrangement could benefit your working space; however, there is a tendency to dock the Ribbon panel on the top side of the drawing area, especially if you plan not to display any toolbar at all.

Toolbars and Menus

With the use of the completely customizable Ribbon palette, there is not much need to display the Toolbars; some of the predefined Workspaces do not even show any Toolbar by default. However, you can choose to display them if you prefer to. The displaying of any Toolbar is easy if there is

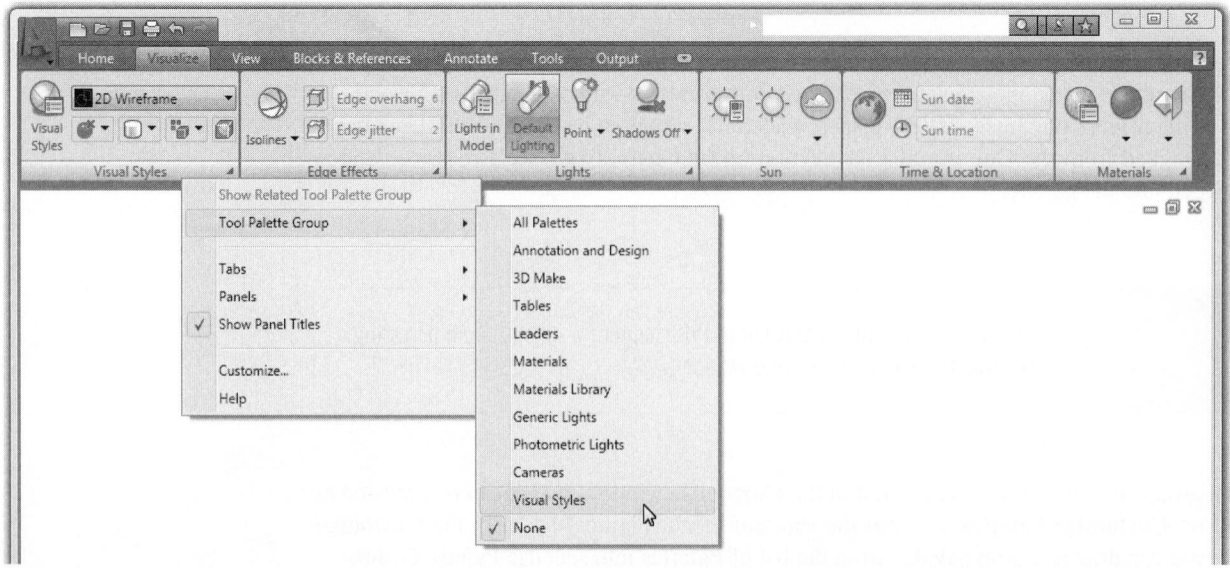

Figure 19-15   Linking a Ribbon panel to a palette group. The **Show Related Tool Palette Group** becomes available after the **Tool Palette Group** is defined.

Figure 19-16   Using the Ribbon and the Tool Palettes jointly

any other toolbar already shown; just right-click on the toolbar to display a complete list of toolbars and check one by one those you need. Then you can drag the Toolbars to your preferred location. Such arrangement is only temporary because it is not saved with any Workspace in particular, which means that recalling the current Workspace will hide them.

If you want to show a Toolbar in a Workspace that has no Toolbars displayed, then you need to redefine the customization of this particular Workspace. Choosing to display Toolbars in this way will become part of the definition of the Workspace; therefore, they will be shown every time the Workspace is recalled.

FOR MORE DETAILS	You will learn more about customizing Workspaces and Ribbon palettes later in this chapter.

Many of the tools that are used to generate 2D work are also used to generate 3D work, and there are other toolbars that contain commands and settings specifically related to 3D work. These toolbars are shown in Figure 19-17 for your reference. When docking the **View, UCS II, Viewports**, and **3D Navigation** toolbars, make sure they are placed horizontally; otherwise, the drop-down list won't show up. Toolbars now are not so useful as they used to be because the **Ribbon** and the **Tool Palettes** provide much easier access.

The standard drop-down menus can be shown by setting the **MENUBAR** command to **1**. The menus, like the toolbars, are not the most practical way to acces the commands; however, you may choose to use those as well.

Modeling

Solids Editing

View

3D Navigation

Orbit

UCS

UCS II

Visual Styles

Inquiry

Render

Lights

Mapping

Viewports

Figure 19-17 Toolbars containing commands and settings specifically related to 3D work

Shortcut Menus Customization

When working in 3D, it is very important to speed up access to the command options and suboptions. Shortcut menus can save a good amount of time if they are used correctly.

By default, the AutoCAD shortcut menus are enabled. But if you ever need to change this setting, you can do so through the **Options** dialog box. Clicking on the **Right-click Customization. . .** button located under the **User Preferences** tab (Figure 19-18) will open the **Right-Click Customization** dialog box. You must enable **Shortcut Menu** for each mode (Figure 19-19).

To invoke the **OPTIONS** command, you can use one of the methods shown in the grid located at the margin of the page.

After enabling shortcut menus, which is the default setting, right-clicking in the drawing area will bring up a general shortcut menu if no command is in progress. This is where the **Options** dialog box can also be accessed, along with the **Edit** tools (Figure 19-20).

When a command is in progress, you can make a shortcut menu pop up by right-clicking in the drawing. A list of the command's options will be included in the shortcut menu, providing you with easier access than typing. As an example, look at the following prompts that are displayed in the command line window when the **CIRCLE** command is invoked. These same options are displayed in the shortcut menu shown in Figure 19-21, allowing easier access with the mouse pointer.

Options	
Pull-down Menu	Tools/ Options. . .
Command Line	options
Alias	op

Command: _circle Specify center point for circle or [3P/2P/Ttr (tan tan radius)]:

Figure 19-18   Location of the **Right-click Customization. . .** button

Figure 19-19   The **Right-Click Customization** dialog box

Figure 19-20   The standard shortcut menu when no command is in progress

Figure 19-21 The **CIR-CLE** command shortcut menu

The Customize User Interface (CUI)

The **Workspace** is the most general element in terms of customization. In the **Customize User Interface** window (Figure 19-22), you can create, customize, set as default, and delete workspaces. For each selected workspace, you can then customize which toolbars, menus, and other palettes in general will show up; you can also customize which Tabs will be available for the Ribbon palette corresponding to the selected Workspace, as well as the Panels that will be available for each Tab.

To add or remove Ribbon Tabs, you must enter the customize mode; this is achieved by selecting **Customize Workspace** from the shortcut menu, displayed after right-clicking on the selected Workspace (Figure 19-22); you can also click on the **Customize Workspace** button on the **Workspace Contents** pane. Once in the customization mode, you can add Tabs to the Workspace's Ribbon by checking them in the **Customization in ALL CUI files** pane (Figure 19-23). You can exit the customization mode by clicking on the **Done** button in the **Workspace Contents** pane. To add or remove panels to a particular tab, you can drag them from the **Ribbon Panels** list into the desired tab from the **Ribbon Tabs** list. This operation must be performed while not in the customization mode (Figure 19-24). You can also set other default properties of a selected workspace (e.g., showing or not showing the Model/Layout tabs). The **Customize User Interface** window can be opened by clicking the **User Interface** button on the **Manage** panel of the Ribbon, or by invoking the **CUI** command. It is also possible to create new workspaces, toolbars, Ribbon Tabs, Ribbon Panels, and many other elements by using the options on the shortcut menus.

Figure 19-22 The **Customize User Interface** window

Figure 19-23   The **Home-2D** Tab is added to the list of Ribbon Tabs by checking its box on the left while in customization mode

Figure 19-24   The **Draw-2D** panel is added to the list of panels included in the **Output-3D** Tab when not in the customization mode

In the **Customize User Interface**, you can use drag and drop actions to remove commands and tools from toolbars, menus, Ribbon Panels, and so on. In the **Customization in All CUI Files** pane, you can also customize which elements will show up inside the default shortcut menus and also for specific objects selected (Figure 19-25). Another important task you can perform while in the customize mode is the selection of the commands that will show on the **Quick Access Toolbar**, located at the top left corner on the AutoCAD display.

TIP

The **Customize User Interface** window shows the **Command List** pane only when accessed through the shortcut menu that appears by right-clicking on any of the toolbar's icons.

Figure 19-25   Customizing a shortcut menu in the CUI window

Exercise 19-1: Creating a Custom Workspace

In this exercise you will create a new workspace containing the toolbars, windows, and settings that you will use in other exercises, tutorials, and projects.

1. Start a **NEW** drawing by selecting **File/New** in the drop-down menu or using any method. In the **Select template** dialog box (Figure 19-26), select **acad** from the list of template files and click on the **Open** button.

2. Open the **Customize User Interface** window through the enhanced drop-down menus by clicking on the AutoCAD logo and then selecting Tools /Workspaces/Customize... In the **Customization in All CUI Files** pane, open the list of Workspaces and select the **3D Modeling** workspace. Right-click on it and select **Duplicate** from the shortcut menu. When the copy is created, rename it as **My 3D Workspace** also from its shortcut menu.

3. In the **Customization in All CUI Files** pane, right-click on **Ribbon Tabs** and select **New Tab**. Rename the new Tab *Modeling 1*.

Note:
Throughout the book, you will start any new drawing by using either the **Acad.dwt** or the **Acadiso.dwt** template. That way, you can start any drawing from the familiar 2D environment. The difference between these two templates is that **acad** uses imperial units (feet, inches) and **acadiso** uses metric units.

Figure 19-26   The **Select template** window

Repeat the same operation to add a new tab named *Modeling 2*.

4. Now you will add some panels to the Tabs you just created. Click the plus icon next to **Ribbon Panels** to show the complete list of panels. Holding the control key down, drag one by one the panels listed under *Modeling 1,* and drop them into the **Modeling 1** Tab. If needed, re-order the panels so they are shown in the same order as below. Repeat the same procedure for *Modeling 2*.

Note:
The Panels in a Ribbon Tab can be reordered in the **Workspace Content** pane. To reorder them, you must first click the plus sign to show the list of Panels, then pick and drag the Panel to the new position.

Modeling 1:	*Modeling 2:*
Draw—3D	Layers 3D
Modify—3D	Render
3D Modeling	Light
Solid Editing	Materials
View	Properties—3D
UCS—3D	Visual Styles
3D Palettes	Edge Effects

5. Click on **My 3D Modeling** workspace to display the content on the right pane. Drag the **Modeling 1** tab and drop it into the Ribbon Tabs on the right pane (**Workspace Content**). Do the same with the **Modeling 2** tab.

6. On the right pane, click the plus sign to show the list of Tabs and delete all the Tabs except the ones you just created: *Modeling 1* and *Modeling 2*. You can delete Tabs by right-clicking on it and selecting **Remove from Workspace**, or by pressing the Delete key.

7. On the right pane, click the plus sign next to **Palettes** to display the list of palettes; select **Tool Palettes** and change its **Show** property to **No**.

8. Select **My 3D Modeling** workspace and click the **Customize Workspace** button; make sure the Menus checkbox located in the **Customization in All CUI Files** pane is checked, as well as all of the menus available. If you would like, check some of the toolbars that you would like to display. When you are finished, click on the **Done** button to exit the customize mode.

9. On the **Properties** pane, make sure **Model/Layout tabs** is set to on.

10. Right-click on **My 3D Workspace** and select **Set Current** from the shortcut menu.

11. Click **OK** to close the **Customize User Interface** window and save the settings. Your AutoCAD screen should lock similar to the one shown in Figure 19-27.

Note:

My 3D Modeling workspace is not set to be your default workspace; it is just for practicing. If you leave the AutoCAD program and open it again, the default workspace will show up again. You are encouraged, however, to keep adding tools, palettes, and other elements as you move forward with the book. This way you can create, little by little, a workspace you are familiar with, one that contains the tools and settings more related to your particular work.

TIP Selecting **My 3D Workspace** will bring up all the toolbars and windows arranged as they were when you saved the workspace. You should use this workspace for every exercise, tutorial, or project in this book.

Figure 19-27   A custom work environment

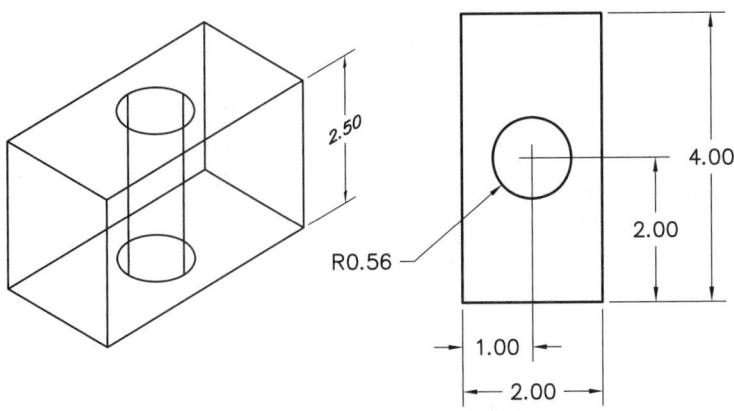

Figure 19-28   Dimensions for the simple 3D solid model

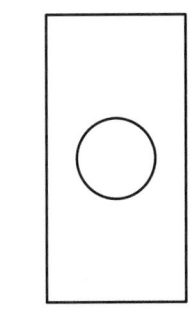

Figure 19-29   Drawing the profile

MODELING A SIMPLE SOLID: A QUICK TUTORIAL

In this first tutorial, you will create the simple 3D solid model that was discussed in the "Ways of Representing a 3D Model" section. The dimensions are shown in Figure 19-28. (Any new command used in this tutorial will be explained later in this book.)

1. Start a **NEW** drawing, using the **acad** template.
2. **SAVE** the drawing **AS** *SimpleSolid*.
3. Select the workspace named **My 3D Workspace** to set it as current.
4. Draw the objects shown in Figure 19-29, using the **RECTANGLE** and the **CIRCLE** commands. Enter 1,0.5 when prompted to specify the first corner point.

TIP   As a general rule, you should not place dimensions when creating 3D models. Rather, you can use the **DIST** command to find distances between points in your 3D objects.

5. Change the viewing point to look at the model from **SE Isometric** view (Figure 19-30). Use one of the methods shown in the grid in the margin.
6. **EXTRUDE** the two profiles to create the box and the cylinder, as shown in Figure 19-31. Use one of the methods shown in the grid to invoke the **EXTRUDE** command, and respond to the prompts as follows:

```
Select objects to extrude: Select the rectangle and the circle in
any order.
Select objects to extrude: ↲ (To end the selection)
Specify height of extrusion or [Direction/Path/Taper angle]: 2.5 ↲
```

SE ISOMETRIC	
View Toolbar	
Ribbon View Panel	Drop-down list
Pull-down Menu	View/3D Views/SE Isometric

EXTRUDE	
Modeling Toolbar	
Ribbon Modeling panel	
Pull-down Menu	Draw/ Modeling/ Extrude
Command Line	extrude
Alias	ext

Figure 19-30   The profile viewed from the **SE Isometric** viewing point

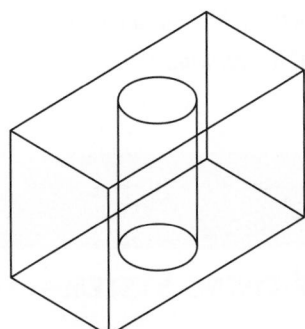

Figure 19-31   The extruded profile

SUBTRACT	
Solids Editing Toolbar	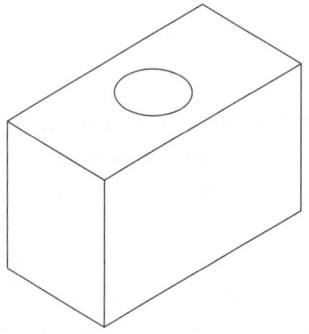
Ribbon Solid Editing	
Pull-down Menu	Modify/ Solids Editing/ Subtract
Command Line	subtract
Alias	su

7. **SUBTRACT** the cylinder volume from that of the box. Use one of the methods shown in the grid to invoke the command, and respond to the prompts as follows:

```
Select solids and regions to subtract from..
Select objects: Select the box.
Select objects: ↵ (To end the selection)
Select solids and regions to subtract..
Select objects: Select the cylinder.
Select objects: ↵ (To end the selection)
```

FOR MORE DETAILS   **SUBTRACT** is one of the Boolean commands. It is performed on regions and 3D solids, and will be discussed in Chapters 22 and 23.

HIDE	
Render Toolbar	
Pull-down Menu	View/Hide
Command Line	hide
Alias	hi

8. Invoke the **HIDE** command. Use one of the methods shown in the grid. The 3D solid should now look as shown in Figure 19-32.

Note:
An alternative solution to this model is to convert the Rectangle and the Circle into two Regions, and then subtract one Region from the other to create a composite Region that would simply have to be extruded. You will learn more about this choice in later chapters.

Figure 19-32   The 3D solid model with the occulted lines hidden

TIP   The **ZOOM Realtime** and **PAN** commands cannot be used immediately after the **HIDE** command has been invoked, unless the display is regenerated.

REGEN	
Pull-down Menu	View/ Regen
Command Line	regen
Alias	re

9. Invoke the **REGEN** command to revoke the effects of the **HIDE** command. Use one of the methods shown in the grid to access the command.
10. **SAVE** the drawing.

WORKING IN THE 3D ENVIRONMENT

THE 3D VIEWING SYSTEM

The 3D space is always present within the model space in the AutoCAD program. The 3D viewing system allows you to control the viewing point from where you look at objects in the 3D space. It is based on three infinite imaginary planes (typically called *TOP, RIGHT,* and *FRONT*), each of which is perpendicular to the others (Figure 19-33). The TOP plane is the plane where all the objects are normally placed when working in 2D.

The planes divide the entire 3D space into eight spaces because of their relative location. An object can be located anywhere inside these eight spaces or between them. Let's focus our attention on one of these eight spaces and locate an object inside it (Figure 19-34).

The location from where you look at an object determines the face(s) of the object that you see. This location is known as the *viewing point*.

A person looking at an object from a viewing point that is perpendicular to the TOP plane will see the **Top** view of the object, which is the same as the projection of the object onto the TOP plane. The same will happen if a person looks from a direction perpendicular to the FRONT and the RIGHT imaginary planes (Figure 19-35).

Note:
The viewing system is not limited to looking at the objects perpendicularly to the imaginary planes. You can actually look at the object from any point in the 3D space, just as you can when holding an object in your hand.

viewing point: The point in the 3D space that establishes the viewing direction of the user.

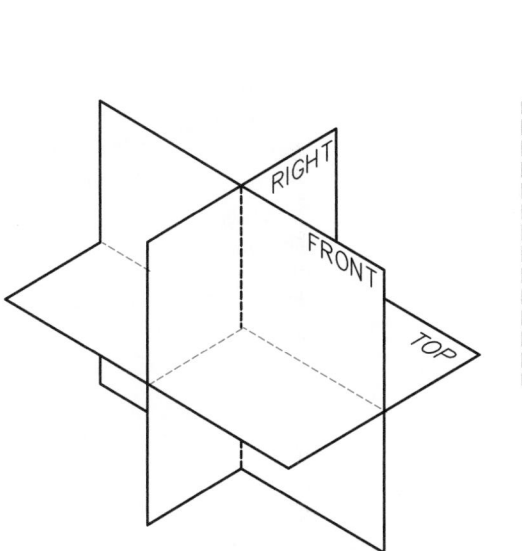

Figure 19-33   The TOP, RIGHT, and FRONT imaginary planes

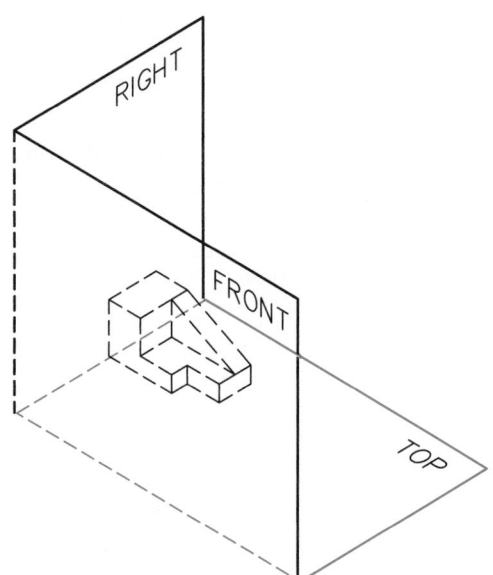

Figure 19-34   An object inside the positive octant

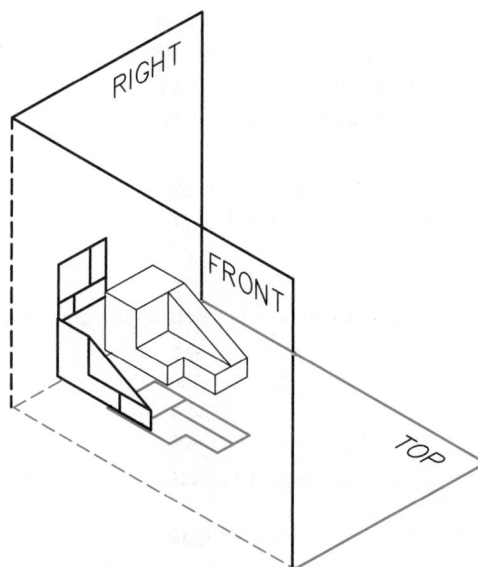

Figure 19-35   The object is seen from the TOP, FRONT, and RIGHT imaginary planes as it projects onto the planes

Orthographic Views

The projection of an object onto an imaginary plane is known as an ***orthographic view***. AutoCAD stores the six possible orthographic views, allowing you to quickly switch between them. Three of the orthographic views are **Top, Right**, and **Front**, just like the three imaginary planes. The other three orthographic views are **Bottom, Left**, and **Back**, the opposite sides of the three imaginary planes.

Selecting one of the orthographic views makes AutoCAD rotate the entire viewing system to align the selected plane parallel to your display.

TIP   Most 3D operations are better performed from a viewing point that is different from the orthogonal views.

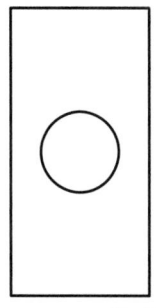

Figure 19-36   The Top view of the Simple Solid model

Exercise 19-2: Selecting Orthographic Views

1. **OPEN** *SimpleSolid*.
2. Change the viewing point to the **Top** view. Access this tool through the View toolbar or through the drop-down menus by selecting View/3D Views/. . .
3. **ZOOM** out as needed! Your drawing should look like Figure 19-36.
4. Select the **Front** view (Figure 19-37).
5. Select the **Right** view (Figure 19-38).

Note:
Our model is symmetrical, so you will view the same edges whether you select **Front** or **Back** (which is its opposite view). The same would happen by selecting **Left** and **Right**, or **Top** and **Bottom**.

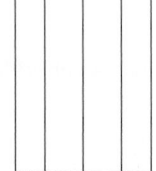

Figure 19-37   The Front view of the Simple Solid model

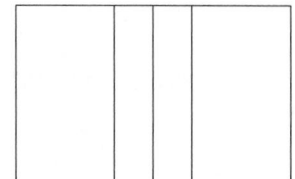

Figure 19-38   The Right view of the Simple Solid model

6. Practice selecting the rest of the orthographic views.
7. Select the **SE Isometric** viewing point.
8. **SAVE** the drawing.

Isometric Viewing Points

Other predefined viewing points in AutoCAD are the four Isometric viewing points:

- **SW Isometric**
- **SE Isometric**
- **NE Isometric**
- **NW Isometric**

An Isometric viewing point is the computer version of the ***isometric view*** used in manual drafting. An isometric view was a quick way of creating 3D views of objects in the days of manual drafting. It was based on the thesis that the projection of the three axes onto the drawing paper would have the same angle (120°) between them.

Isometric views remain the standard 3D view in drawing documents. The AutoCAD program still allows you to use this technique of 2D drafting by enabling the **Isometric** snap type in the **Drafting Settings** dialog box; however, creating actual 3D models is easier, faster, and more accurate.

Figure 19-39 shows the four different Isometric viewing directions from which objects can be seen. Because the current viewing point is **SE Isometric**, its arrow is viewed as a circle, which is the projection of the arrow onto the viewing plane or display. From the **SE Isometric** viewing point you can see the TOP, FRONT, and RIGHT faces of the model.

isometric view: A 3D drawing view in which the three principal dimensions of the objects are aligned with three axes 120° apart as they project onto the viewing plane.

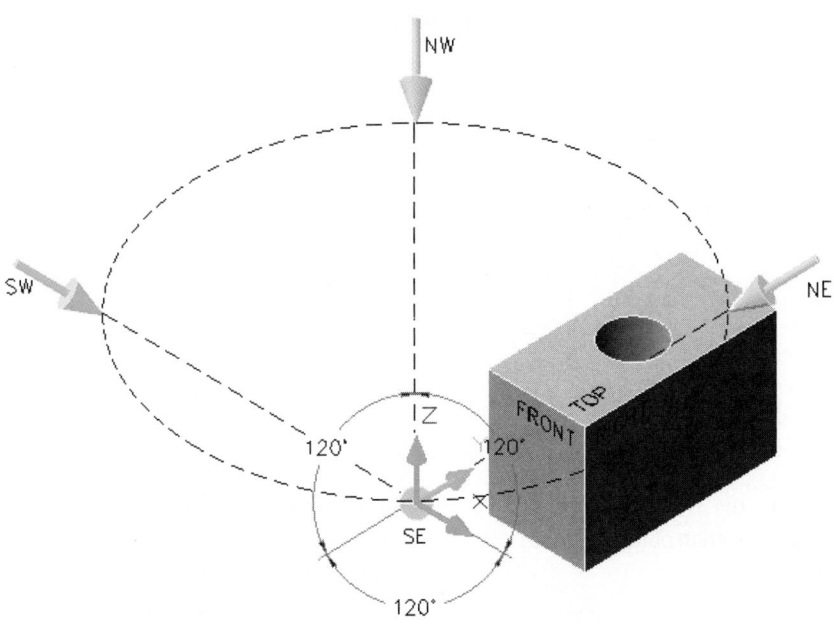

Figure 19-39   The four predefined Isometric viewing directions

Exercise 19-3: Selecting the Isometric Views

1. **OPEN** *SimpleSolid*.
2. Select each of the four Isometric viewing points. Access these tools through the **View** toolbar, or through the drop-down menus by selecting **View/ 3D Views/...**
3. Invoke the **HIDE** command after changing the viewing point.
4. Select the **SE Isometric** viewing point.
5. **SAVE** the drawing.

Note:
The Isometric viewpoints are extremely practical to use when working in 3D.

TIP   The **REGEN** command need not be invoked if you select a different viewing point; this operation also regenerates the display.

THE 3D COORDINATE SYSTEM

Mathematically, the 3D space is represented by three imaginary planes: *XY*, *YZ*, and *ZX*. Similar to the three viewing planes, the *XY*, *YZ*, and *ZX* planes are perpendicular to each other. The intersecting lines between these planes are the three axes *X*, *Y*, and *Z* (Figure 19-40). AutoCAD shows you the axes of its coordinate system through the UCS icon.

The *X*-axis is the intersecting line between the *XY* and *ZX* planes, whereas the *Y*-axis is the intersecting line between the *XY* and *YZ* planes. Analogously, the *XY* plane goes through the *X*- and *Y*-axes. The point where the three axes meet is called the *origin*.

From the **Top** view, which is the default view of a new drawing, the *Z*-axis is not shown in the UCS icon. The reason is that from this viewing point, you can look at the *Z*-axis only perpendicular to it (Figure 19-41). The hatched area is the default area of the *XY* plane where you typically perform 2D work every time you start a new drawing from scratch.

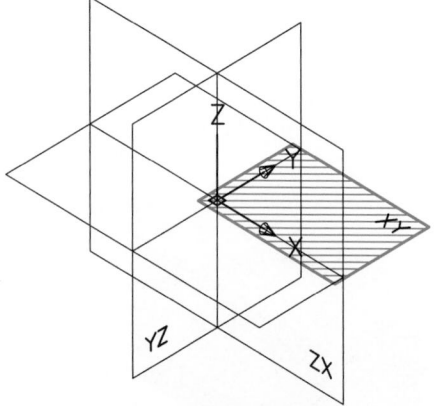

Figure 19-40 The *XYZ* coordinate system with the positive portion of the *XY* plane highlighted

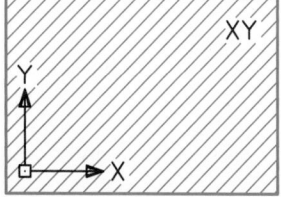

Figure 19-41 The positive portion of the *XY* plane as seen when starting a new drawing from scratch, where 2D work is typically done

Changing the viewing point allows you to look at the same imaginary *XY* plane so that the *Z*-axis is not perpendicular to the display, as it is by default. By simply doing so, you can be said to be working in a 3D environment (Figure 19-42).

Figure 19-42 Looking at the positive portion of the *XY* plane from different viewing points in which the *Z*-axis is not perpendicular to the display

The WCS and the UCS

By default, the *XY*, *YZ*, and *ZX* planes of the coordinate system are located exactly where the three imaginary viewing planes (TOP, RIGHT, and FRONT) are, respectively (Figure 19-43). The coordinate system that has this characteristic is known as the ***World Coordinate System (WCS)***. The WCS icon is always shown with a little square in its origin.

World Coordinate System (WCS): The AutoCAD program's reference coordinate system. It serves as a reference for any user coordinate system.

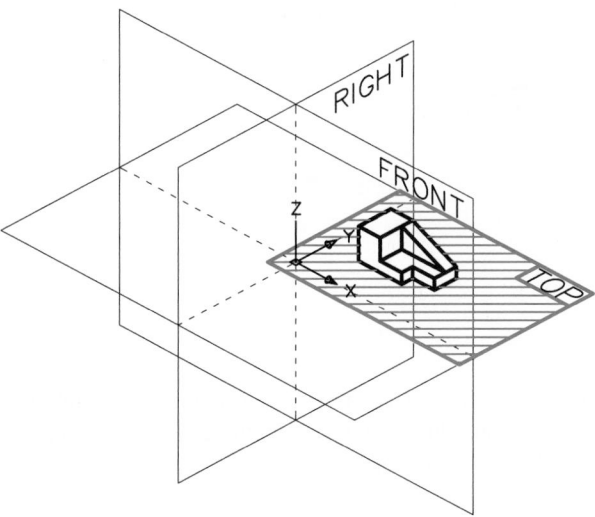

Figure 19-43   The *XY* plane of the World Coordinate System (WCS) is coincident with the imaginary Top plane

As you will learn later, the user can modify the coordinate system. A coordinate system that has been modified to reflect any arrangement of the viewing planes that is different from the WCS is known as the ***User Coordinate System (UCS)***. Figure 19-44 shows the **Front** UCS. Notice that the square in the UCS icon has disappeared.

User Coordinate System (UCS): The WCS after it has been reoriented using one of many possible methods.

Orthographic UCS

AutoCAD has six predefined ***orthographic UCSs*** (**Top, Right, Front, Bottom, Left**, and **Back**). Selecting any orthographic UCS rotates the entire coordinate system so that its *XY* plane aligns with the corresponding orthographic view. The origin for any orthographic UCS is the same.

orthographic UCS: A reorientation of the WCS in which the *XY* plane aligns parallel to the corresponding imaginary orthographic viewing planes.

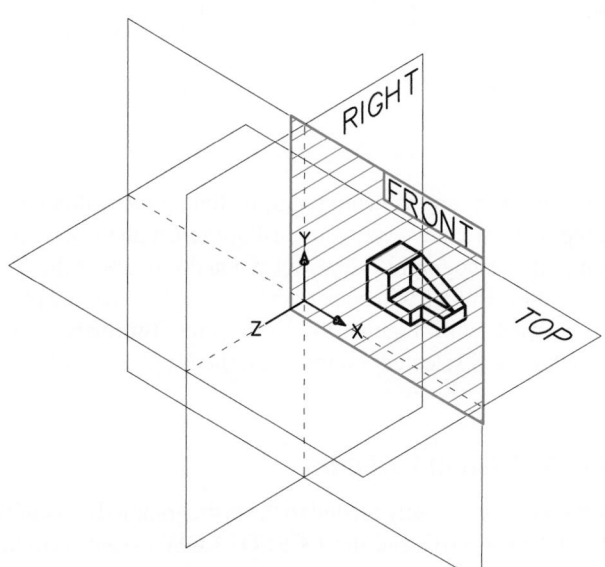

Figure 19-44   The *XY* plane of the Front UCS is coincident with the imaginary Front plane

Exercise 19-4: Using the Orthographic UCS

1. **OPEN** *SimpleSolid*.
2. Select each of the orthographic UCSs. Use the drop-down list located in the **UCS II** toolbar (Figure 19-45).

Figure 19-45 The UCS drop-down list located in the **UCS II** toolbar

3. Select the **SE Isometric** viewing point.
4. Select the **World** UCS.
5. **SAVE** the drawing.

Figure 19-46 shows all the orthographic UCSs viewed from the same viewing point. The **Bottom, Back**, and **Right** orthographic UCS icons show the *Z*-axis in hidden lines. This means that the positive portion of the *Z*-axis is behind the imaginary *XY* plane.

Figure 19-46 All the orthographic UCSs viewed from the same viewing point

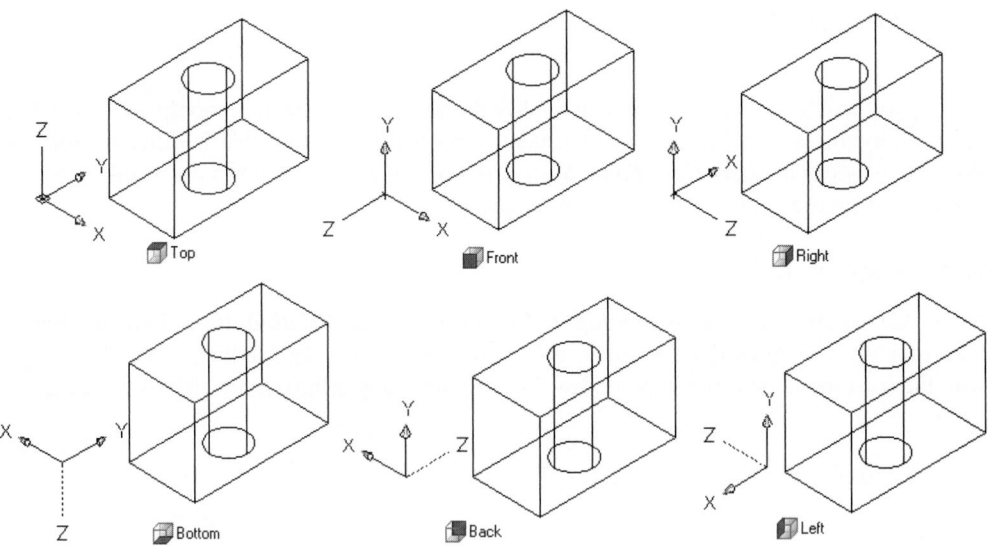

An orthographic UCS can be activated from any viewing point, including the orthographic views. When using one of the orthographic views, however, you must not select an orthographic UCS other than the one corresponding to the orthographic view. But if you do so, either the *X*- or the *Y*-axis will not be seen and, therefore, the *XY* plane will be perpendicular to the viewing plane. Such a situation is almost impossible to work with. Figure 19-47 shows the **Top** orthographic view on the left, with the **Top** orthographic UCS selected; on the right, the *Y*-axis disappears after the **Right** UCS is selected.

The UCSORTHO and UCSFOLLOW System Variables

The orthographic views of the viewing system are closely related to the orthographic UCSs of the coordinate system. The settings of the **UCSORTHO** and the **UCSFOLLOW** system variables determine the way each affects the other.

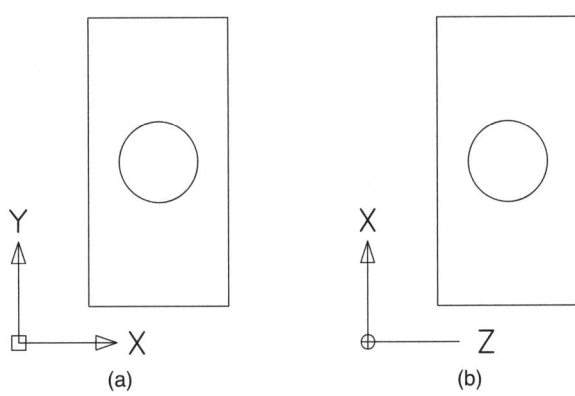

Figure 19-47 (a) The Top view and the Top UCS (b) The Y-axis disappears after you select the Right UCS

The **UCSORTHO** system variable determines whether or not selecting an orthographic view automatically sets its corresponding orthographic UCS. When this variable is turned on (**1**), which is the default value, selecting the **Front** view, for example, will automatically set the **Front** UCS.

The **UCSFOLLOW** system variable, on the other hand, determines whether or not selecting an orthographic UCS automatically displays its corresponding orthographic view. When it is turned on (**1**), selecting the **Front** UCS, for example, will automatically display the **Front** view. This system variable is turned off (**0**) by default. It is more convenient to work with the **UCSFOLLOW** system variable turned off. The **PLAN** command can be invoked to align the view with any current UCS.

The PLAN Command

The **PLAN** command can change the viewing point so that the view is aligned with the *XY* plane of the current UCS.

Modifying the UCS

Many tools are available in the AutoCAD program to make specific modifications to the current UCS. You can use these tools to align the UCS at your convenience throughout the 3D space. Occasionally, you must perform two or more of these operations in order to achieve the desired result.

Note:
As specified by the right-hand rule, the relationship or arrangement among the *X*-, *Y*- and *Z*-axes is unchangeable.

PLAN	
Pull-down Menu	3D Views/ Plan View/ Current UCS
Command Line	plan

FOR MORE DETAILS See the information regarding the use of the right-hand rule later in this chapter.

UCS ORIGIN	
UCS Toolbar	
Ribbon UCS panel	
Pull-down Menu	Tools/ New UCS/ Origin
Command Line	ucs ↵ o

The following is a list of the operations that can be made to the UCS in order to modify it. These are all options of the **UCS** command.

1. Relocate the **Origin** of the UCS.

   With the **Origin UCS** command, you can move the UCS origin to a different location. Its orientation will remain the same.

   ```
   Specify new origin point <0,0,0>:
   ```

2. Specify a **Z Axis Vector**.

The first point defines the UCS origin. The second point defines the positive direction of the *Z*-axis (Figure 19-48).

```
Specify new origin point or [Object] <0,0,0>:
Specify point on positive portion of Z-axis <-1.2598,
-4.7789,5.1736>:
```

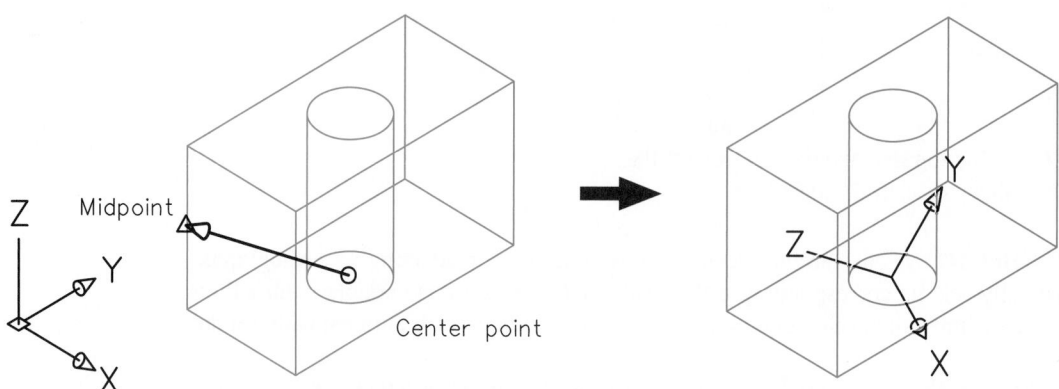

Figure 19-48   Modifying the UCS by specifying a *Z*-Axis Vector

UCS Z-AXIS	
UCS Toolbar	
Ribbon UCS panel	
Pull-down Menu	Tools/ New UCS/ Z Axis Vector
Command Line	ucs ↵ za

The **Object** option of this method aligns the *XY* plane normal to an open curve, locating the origin at the endpoint closest to the point where the selection was made. The *Z*-axis will be aligned in the opposite direction of the curve (Figure 19-49). This type of alignment is very useful when specifying the path for the **EXTRUSION** or the **SWEEP** commands.

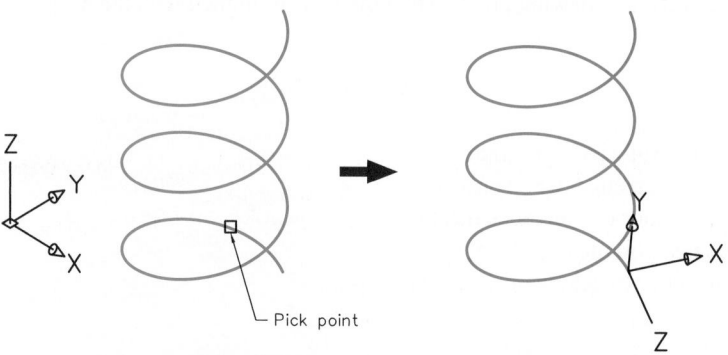

Figure 19-49   Modifying the UCS by using an object to specify a *Z*-Axis Vector

UCS 3 POINTS	
UCS Toolbar	
Ribbon Coordinates panel	
Pull-down Menu	Tools/ New UCS/ 3 Point
Command Line	ucs ↵ 3

FOR MORE DETAILS   See Chapter 23 to learn more about the EXTRUSION and SWEEP commands.

3. Specify three points (**3 Point**).

The first point defines the UCS origin. The second point defines the positive direction of the *X*-axis. The third point defines the location and orientation of the UCS (Figure 19-50).

4. Rotate about the **X-**, **Y-**, or **Z-**axis.

This option simply rotates the UCS about the axis specified. The positive rotational direction can be determined by the right-hand rule.

```
Specify rotation angle about X axis <90>:
```

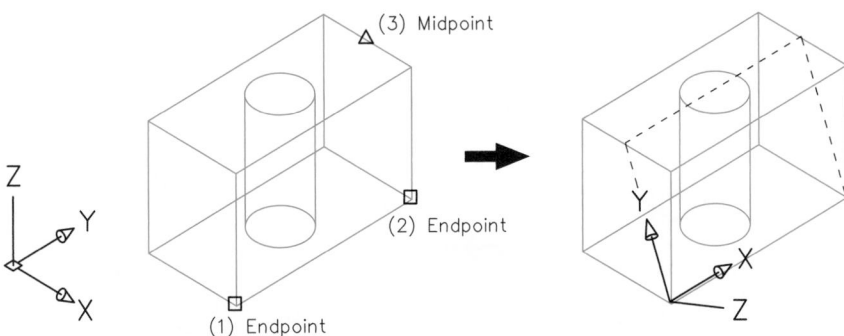

Figure 19-50   Modifying the UCS by specifying three points (**3 Point**)

5. Align the UCS with the **View**.

The UCS is aligned with the current viewing plane or display. This modification is very useful when you have saved views, or when placing text aligned with the current viewing plane.

FOR MORE DETAILS	See the information regarding the use of the right-hand rule later in this chapter.

TIP   If you make a mistake when entering a positive or negative angle value, just **UNDO** the operation and enter its opposite value.

6. Align the UCS with an **Object**.

The resulting UCS depends on the object selected. For instance, if a circle is selected, the origin will relocate on its center, the *XY* plane will align with the plane in which the circle lies, and the *X*-axis will go through the point where you picked the circle.

Selecting an arc will relocate the UCS origin in its centerpoint as well. The *X*-axis, however, will pass through one of the endpoints of the arc.

```
Select object to align UCS:
```

7. Align the UCS with a 3D solid's **Face**.

This method can be used only with a planar face of a 3D solid. To select a 3D solid's face you can either click within the boundary of the face or on one of its edges. If you click within the boundary of the face, the origin will relocate on the corner of the face closest to the point where it is selected, and the *X*-axis will align with the closest edge (Figure 19-51).

Because an edge is always shared by two adjacent faces, when selecting an edge you will most likely have to refine your selection. You can do this by using the **Next** option. You can also flip the UCS around the *X*- and *Y*-axes, if necessary.

```
Enter an option [Next/Xflip/Yflip] <accept>:
```

FOR MORE DETAILS	See Chapter 24 to learn more about face selection techniques on 3D solids.

UCS X-ROTATE	
UCS Toolbar	
Ribbon Coordinates panel	
Pull-down Menu	Tools/ New UCS/ X
Command Line	ucs ↵ 3

UCS Y-ROTATE	
UCS Toolbar	
Ribbon Coordinates panel	
Pull-down Menu	Tools/ New UCS/ Y
Command Line	ucs ↵ y

UCS Z-ROTATE	
UCS Toolbar	
Ribbon Coordinates panel	
Pull-down Menu	Tools/ New UCS/ Z
Command Line	ucs ↵ z

UCS VIEW	
UCS Toolbar	
Ribbon Coordinates panel	
Pull-down Menu	Tools/New UCS/View
Command Line	ucs ↵ v

UCS OBJECT	
UCS Toolbar	
Ribbon Coordinates panel	
Pull-down Menu	Tools/ New UCS/ Object
Command Line	ucs ↵ ob

Figure 19-51   Modifying the UCS by aligning it with a 3D solid's face

UCS FACE	
UCS Toolbar	
Ribbon Coordinates panel	
Pull-down Menu	Tools/New UCS/Face
Command Line	ucs ↵ fa

8. Go back to a **Previous** UCS.

   This option allows you to go back to a UCS that you previously defined in the drawing, regardless of whether it has been saved or not. You can go back up to the last ten UCSs used.

9. Restore the **World** UCS.

   The **UCS** shortcut menu, shown in Figure 19-52, provides easy access to the different options used to modify the UCS. You can display this menu by right-clicking in the drawing area while the **UCS** command is in progress.

Exercise 19-5: Modifying the UCS by Specifying 3 Points

1. **OPEN** *SimpleSolid* from the location where you saved it.

2. Invoke the **3 Point** option of the **UCS** command. Respond to the prompts as follows:

   Specify new origin point <0,0,0>: *Snap to the top center point of the cylinder [Figure 19-53(a)].*

   Specify point on positive portion of X-axis <Current X,Y,Z>: *Snap to the top-right edge's midpoint.*

   Specify point on positive-Y portion of the UCS XY plane <Current X,Y,Z>: *Snap to the endpoint shown in Figure 19-53(b).*

> **Note**
>
> The X-axis is defined by the first two points. The third point defines the XY plane and the rest of the UCS. The Y-axis is then defined as contained in that plane. The third point is on the same side of the X-axis as the Y-axis. A point along the previously defined X-axis is not a valid entry.

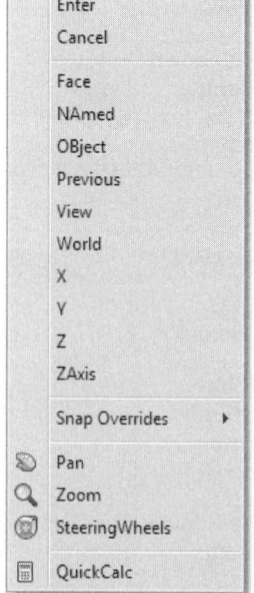

Figure 19-52   The **UCS** shortcut menu

(a)

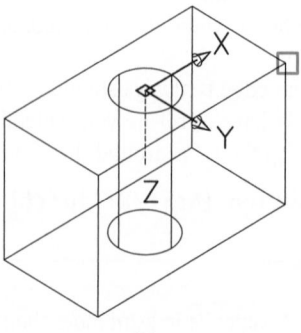

(b)

Figure 19-53   Snap to the geometry as shown

3. Select the **SE Isometric** viewing point.
4. Select the **World** UCS.
5. **SAVE** the drawing.

Saving a UCS

After the UCS has been modified, you can save it in order to access it later. By using a saved UCS, you can even modify the location of the planes for the viewing system (Top, Front, Right, etc.) by changing the UCS that these planes are relative to. You will learn more about the procedure to save a UCS in the following exercise.

Exercise 19-6: Working with the UCS Manager

1. **OPEN** *SimpleSolid*.
2. Rotate the **UCS** 30° around the *X*-axis.

   Specify rotation angle about X axis <90>: 30 ⏎

3. Open the **UCS** dialog box to save the UCS you just created.
4. In the **UCS** dialog box (Figure 19-54), click in the **Named UCSs** tab, right-click on the **Unnamed** UCS, and select **Rename** from the list. Type in the new name **MyUCS**. Click on the white area and then click the **OK** button. The new name will appear in the drop-down dialog box on the **UCS II** toolbar (Figure 19-55).
5. Select the **SE Isometric** viewing point.
6. Select the **World** UCS.
7. **SAVE** the drawing.

UCS PREVIOUS	
UCS Toolbar	
Ribbon Coordinates panel	
Command Line	ucs ⏎ p

UCS WORLD	
UCS Toolbar	
Ribbon Coordinates panel	
Command Line	ucs ⏎
Drop-down List	UCS II Toolbar

UCS VIEW	
UCS II Toolbar	
Ribbon Coordinates panel	
Pull-down Menu	Tools/ Named UCS ...
Command Line	ucsman

Figure 19-54   Saving a UCS in the **UCS** dialog box by giving it a name

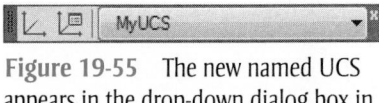

Figure 19-55   The new named UCS appears in the drop-down dialog box in the **UCS II** toolbar

Deleting a UCS

To delete a previously saved UCS, open the **UCS** dialog box. In the **Named UCSs** tab, right-click on the saved UCS and click **Delete** (Figure 19-56).

Figure 19-56 Deleting a saved UCS in the **UCS** dialog box

CONCLUDING REMARKS ON THE 2D AND 3D ENVIRONMENTS

As mentioned earlier, the 3D space is always present in AutoCAD. The **2D environment**, however, is the one in which the geometry is placed on a single plane parallel to the current viewing plane, such as the default working condition that is used to generate 2D drawings. This type of work is normally performed on the *XY* plane of the WCS, using the **Top** orthographic view.

An operation that either uses or generates geometry that is not contained in the *XY* plane of the current UCS is considered to be performed in a **3D environment**. This environment requires you to view the model from different viewing points and use different techniques, regardless of how simple the 3D model is.

THE UCS ICON

In the **UCS Icon** dialog box (Figure 19-57), you can change the default appearance of the UCS icon by choosing **2D** under the **UCS icon style** setting. You can also change the UCS icon size and modify other settings. The **UCS Icon** dialog box can be accessed by selecting **Properties** from the **View** drop-down menu (Figure 19-58).

Figure 19-57 The **UCS Icon** dialog box

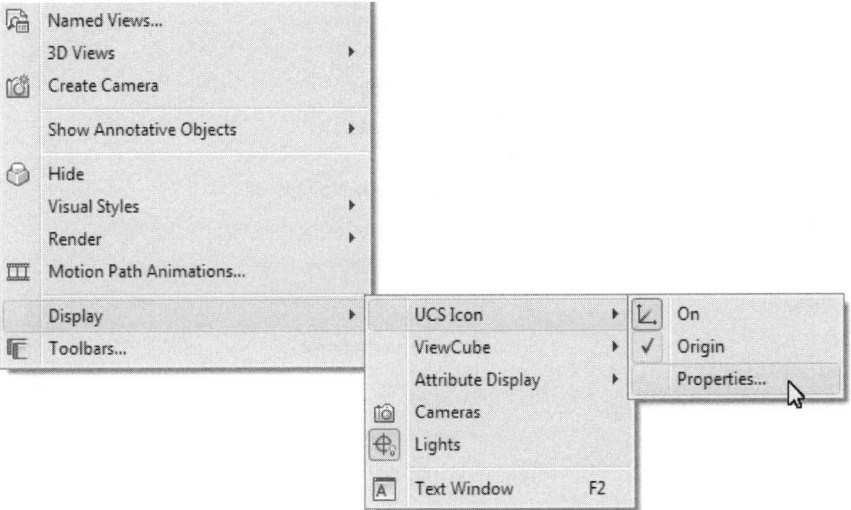

Figure 19-58   Accessing the **UCS Icon** dialog box from the **View** drop-down menu

In the same drop-down menu, you can turn the UCS icon either on or off. You can also choose whether the UCS icon will display at the origin or in the lower-left corner on the drawing area.

THE 3D CROSSHAIRS CURSOR

When working in a 3D environment, you can choose one of the two following looks for the crosshairs cursor:

- The traditional look, showing only two hairs aligned with the X- and Y-axes [Figure 19-59(a)].
- The 3D look, which shows all three axes aligned with the current UCS. The longer portions of the hairs show the positive direction of each axis [Figure 19-59(b)].

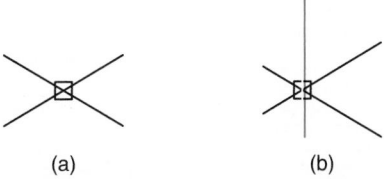

(a)   (b)

Figure 19-59   (a) The traditional appearance of the UCS icon (b) Its 3D appearance

You can control this setting in the **3D Modeling** tab of the **Options** dialog box (Figure 19-60) by selecting **Show Z axis in crosshairs** under **3D Crosshairs**. The 3D look will not show if you switch to a 2D environment (i.e., select an orthogonal view, align the UCS to the viewing plane, or align the viewing plane with the XY plane of the current UCS). You can also control where the 3D crosshairs will show the labels for the X-, Y-, and Z-axes, or any other customized labels.

You can display the crosshairs either in different colors (red, green, and blue) or in a single color. You can change this setting in the **Drawing Window Colors** dialog box (Figure 19-61). This window is accessed by clicking the **Colors . . .** button on the **Display** tab of the **Options** dialog box.

In the **Drawing Window Colors** dialog box, you select **3D parallel projection** from the **Context**: window, which is the preferred working context for 3D modeling. Then you select **Crosshairs** from the **Interface element**: window and, finally, check the **Tint for X, Y, Z** checkbox. You cannot change the color of the three hairs; you can, however, change the tint of the three colors used from lighter to darker by selecting a different **Color**.

Figure 19-60   Controlling the UCS icon's appearance in the **3D Modeling** tab of the **Options** dialog box

Figure 19-61   Changing the UCS icon's colors in the **Drawing Window Colors** dialog box

USING THE DYNAMIC UCS

When the **Dynamic UCS** is on, you can easily create objects on the faces of 3D solids, regardless of the UCS currently in use. This feature temporarily auto-aligns the UCS with one of the faces of the 3D solid as you place the crosshairs close to it in a situation in which the progress of a command requires you to specify a point. The faces will highlight and the crosshairs change their orientation as you hover over the different faces. Clicking or snapping to geometry while a face is highlighted concludes the definition of the UCS with which the object will be aligned.

The **Dynamic UCS** feature is controlled by the **DUCS** button on the status bar. You can also change its setting by pressing the **<F6>** key or by invoking the **UCSDETECT** system variable. This feature should be turned on only at the precise moment of placing objects on a face of a 3D solid to avoid affecting other 3D operations.

Exercise 19-7: Using the Dynamic UCS

1. **OPEN** *SimpleSolid*.
2. **SAVE** the drawing **AS** *Exercise 19-7*.
3. Turn **DUCS** mode on.
4. Invoke the **BOX** command by typing it in the command line, and respond to the prompts as follows:

   Specify first corner or [Center]: *Move the crosshairs over the right face of the 3D solid. Once the face is highlighted, snap to the top rightmost endpoint.*

   Specify other corner or [Cube/Length]: *Snap to the midpoint of the bottom edge.*

   Specify height or [2Point] <1.0000>: *1 ↵*

5. The 3D model should look like Figure 19-62. Invoke the **CIRCLE** command, and respond to the prompts as follow:

   Specify center point for circle or [3P/2P/Ttr (tan tan radius)]: *m2p ↵*

   First point of mid: *Snap to the midpoint of any of the four edges of the front face.*

   Second point of mid: *Snap to the midpoint of its opposite parallel edge.*

   Specify radius of circle or [Diameter]: *.5 ↵*

6. Invoke the **HIDE** command. The 3D model should look like Figure 19-63.
7. **SAVE** the drawing.

> **Note:**
> m2p is the alias for the Middle Between two points object snap.

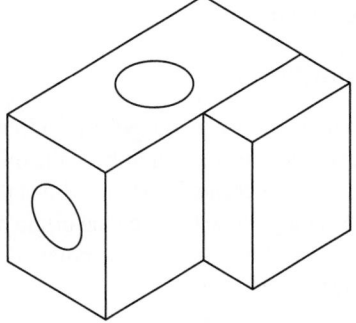

Figure 19-62 The 3D model after adding a box using the **Dynamic UCS**

Figure 19-63 The 3D model after invoking the **HIDE** command

ENTERING POINT COORDINATES IN 3D

Rectangular Coordinates

In a 2D coordinate system, the rectangular coordinates of a point are expressed as *X,Y,* where *X* is the distance from the origin 0,0 to the point parallel to the *X*-axis, and *Y* is the distance from the origin 0,0 to the point parallel to the *Y*-axis. Figure 19-64 shows the point 1.25, 0.75 located on the *XY* plane.

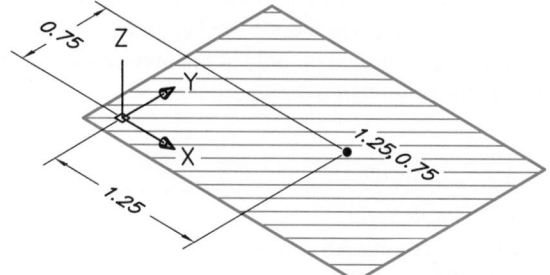

Figure 19-64   The 2D rectangular coordinates of the point 1.25, 0.75

Working in 2D does not require a specified *Z* value. All objects are placed on the *XY* plane, where the *Z* value for any given point is 0. This operation simulates drawing on a piece of paper.

In a 3D coordinate system, the rectangular coordinates of a point are expressed as *X,Y, Z.* Here *Z* is the distance from the origin 0,0,0 to the point parallel to the *Z*-axis. Figure 19-65 shows the point 1.25,0.75,1.00.

Note:
Any point in the AutoCAD display has 3D coordinates. The *Z* coordinate is simply assumed to be 0 when its value is not specified.

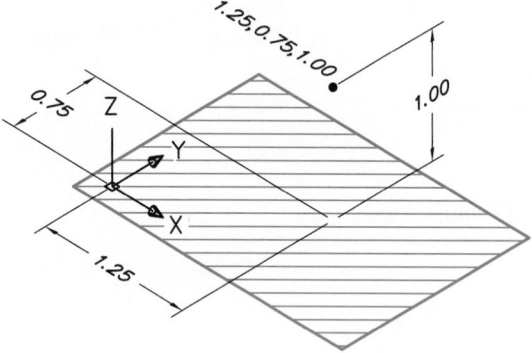

Figure 19-65   The 3D rectangular coordinates of the point 1.25,0.75,1.00

Polar Coordinates

In a 2D coordinate system, the polar coordinates of a point are expressed as $r < \theta$, where *r* is the distance of a straight line measured from the origin 0,0 to the point (or the radius of an imaginary circle whose center is located at 0,0) and θ is the angle, measured counterclockwise, between the *X*-axis and the straight line between the origin and the point. Figure 19-66 shows the point 1.46<31.

In a 3D coordinate system, the polar coordinates of a point can be expressed in one of the following ways:

- Cylindrical coordinates
- Spherical coordinates

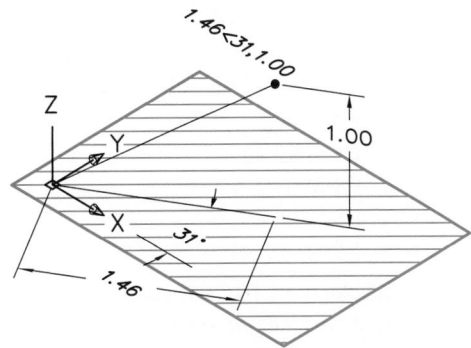

Figure 19-66   The 2D polar coordinates of the point 1.46<31

Figure 19-67   The cylindrical coordinates of the point 1.46<31,1.00

The polar cylindrical coordinates of a point are expressed as $r < \theta$, Z. This expression is just an extension of the 2D polar coordinates. $r < \theta$ are the 2D polar coordinates of the projection of the point onto the XY plane. Z is the distance from the XY plane to the point. Figure 19-67 shows the cylindrical coordinates of the point 1.46<31,1.00.

The polar spherical coordinates of a point are expressed as $r < \theta < \varphi$. These are not as close to the 2D polar coordinates because r now is the 3D distance of an imaginary line that extends from the origin 0,0,0 to the point itself, θ is still the angle between the X-axis and a line between the origin and the point projected onto the XY plane, and φ is the angle between the imaginary line representing the 3D distance and the XY plane. Figure 19-68 shows the spherical coordinates of the point 1.77<31<34 (the same point as 1.46<31,1.00, but expressed in a different manner).

Unless necessary, entering 3D points in either rectangular or polar coordinates is impractical, and may result in extensive work. In many 3D operations, AutoCAD generates geometry whose points can be specified later in any command. Figure 19-69 shows a 3D solid box after it has been sliced and moved away. This operation generates new geometry, which you can snap to when specifying a point, such as the midpoint shown.

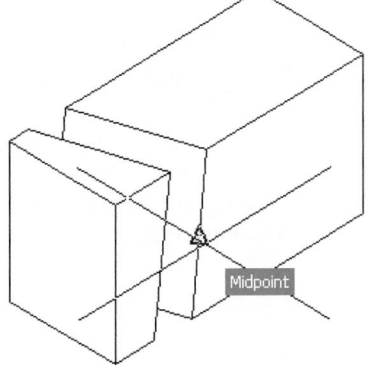

Figure 19-68   The spherical coordinates of the point 1.77<31<34

Figure 19-69   New geometry generated after slicing a 3D solid box

Exercise 19-8: Specifying Points in Cylindrical Coordinates

1. Start a **NEW** drawing using the **acad** template.
2. **SAVE** the drawing **AS *Exercise 19-8***.
3. Select the **Isometric SE** viewing point.
4. Using the **PAN** command, displace the drawing area so that the UCS icon appears more or less centered on the screen.

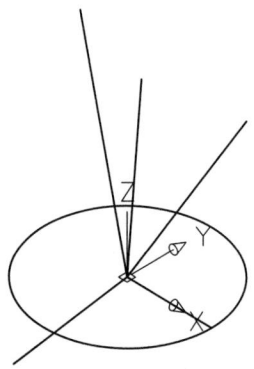

Figure 19-70 The 3D model after drawing the circle

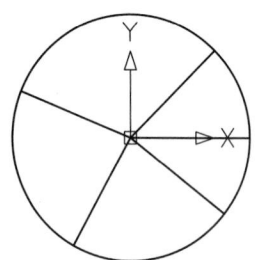

Figure 19-71 The 3D model as seen from the Top view

5. Invoke the **LINE** command five times to draw five lines. Each line will start on the point 0,0,0 and will end on each of the following points:
   - 1.5<158,3
   - 1.5<45,2.32
   - 1.5<0,0
   - 1.5<–38, 4
   - 1.5<214.2,–1

6. Invoke the **CIRCLE** command and draw a circle with the center on 0,0,0 and a radius of **1.5** (Figure 19-70).
7. Select the **Top** orthographic view. The drawing should look like Figure 19-71.
8. **SAVE** the drawing.

Note:
All the endpoints of the lines were specified using the same r value. Therefore all the points are located on the surface of an imaginary cylinder, which projects on the Top plane as a circle of equal radius.

Exercise 19-9: Specifying Points in Spherical Coordinates

1. Start a **NEW** drawing using the **acad** template.
2. **SAVE** the drawing **AS** *Exercise 19-9*.
3. Select the **Isometric SE** viewing point.
4. Using the **PAN** command, displace the drawing area so that the UCS icon appears more or less centered on the screen.
5. Invoke the **LINE** command five times to draw five lines. Each line will start on the point 0,0,0 and will end on each of the following points:
   - 1.5<158<31
   - 1.5<45<–91.5
   - 1.5<0<0
   - 1.5<–38<47
   - 1.5<214.2<–31

Note:
As you can see, all the lines stick out the same distance from the sphere (0.1 unit). In spherical coordinates, the r value determines the imaginary sphere in which the point is located in the 3D space.

6. Invoke the **SPHERE** command by typing it in the command line. When prompted, specify **0,0,0** for the center and **1.4** for the radius.
7. Change the color of the 3D solid sphere to yellow.
8. Set the **FACETRES** system variable value to **6**.
9. Select the **Realistic** visual style from the drop-down menus, located at **View/Visual Styles**.
10. Invoke the **3DORBIT** command by typing its name in the command line window. In the drawing area, hold the click button of the mouse and drag it to interactively change the viewing point (Figure 19-72).
11. **SAVE** the drawing.

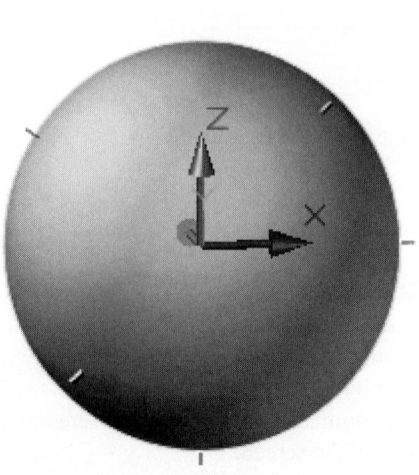

Figure 19-72 The 3D model after rotating the viewing point

THE RIGHT-HAND RULE

When working in a 3D environment you can use your right hand as a mnemonic tool to easily orient yourself in the 3D space. Two different uses of the ***right-hand rule*** can be given:

right-hand rule: A method used to remember the unchangeable relationship between the three axes of the coordinate system and the positive rotation about them.

    1. Determining the positive direction of the *X-, Y-,* and *Z*-axes.

    The relationship between the positive directions of the three axes is unchangeable. By knowing the positive direction of any two axes you can determine the positive direction of the third one.

    Close all your right-hand fingers, open the thumb and index finger until they make a square, then open the middle finger halfway. The thumb represents the *X*-axis, the index finger represents the *Y*-axis, and the middle finger the *Z*-axis (Figure 19-73). Rotating your hand so that any two fingers align with the positive direction of their corresponding axes determines the positive direction of the third one.

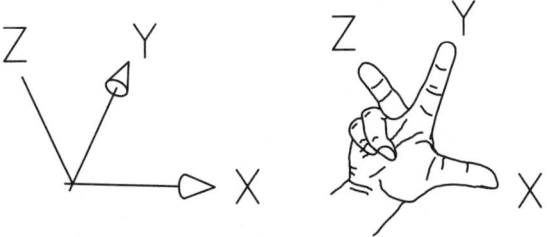

Figure 19-73   Using the right-hand rule to determine the relationship among the three axes

    This rule was very useful in AutoCAD 2000 or earlier versions for determining the positive direction of the *Z*-axis because no 3D UCS icon was available. You can still use it as an aid to visualize the 3D coordinate system.

    2. Determining the positive rotation about an axis.

    Curling the fingers of your right hand while pointing the thumb in the positive direction of any axis shows you the positive direction of rotation about the axis (Figure 19-74).

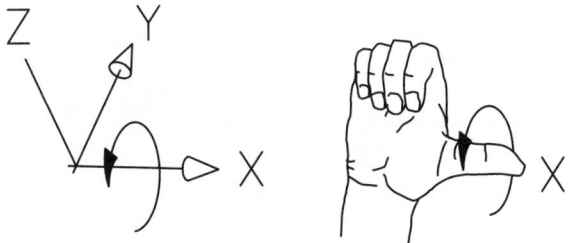

Figure 19-74   Using the right-hand rule to determine the positive rotation about any axis

TIP
You should use the right-hand rule to find the positive direction within any tool where rotation is involved.

THE 3D ORBIT TOOL

Besides the six orthographic views and the four Isometric viewing points, you can use the ***3D Orbit*** viewing tool to dynamically change the viewing point. The **3DORBIT** command launches this viewing tool. After it is invoked, all you need to do is to click and drag the cursor in the drawing area to interactively rotate the entire viewing system. This operation does not affect the UCS; it

3D Orbit: The most useful viewing tool for quickly selecting any viewing point.

just follows whatever rotation is made to the viewing system. The UCS icon changes to shaded 3D look while the 3D Orbit is active because the AutoCAD program automatically changes to the **3D Wireframe** visual style in case the **2D Wireframe** visual style is being used.

> **FOR MORE DETAILS**   To learn more about the different visual styles, see the "Using the Predefined Visual Styles" section in this chapter.

3D Orbit must be used when an Isometric viewing point does not provide a clear picture due to the location of the object's edges in the 3D space. Figure 19-75(a) is a clear example of such a situation. Slightly changing the viewing point [Figure 19-75(b)] shows the edges of the same 3D model more clearly.

Figure 19-75   Slightly changing the viewing point shows the edges of the 3D model more clearly

  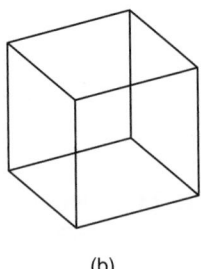

(a)   (b)

3DORBIT	
3D Navigation Toolbar	
Ribbon Navigate panel	
Pull-down Menu	View/ Orbit/ Cons- trained Orbit
Command Line	3dorbit

The **3D Orbit** viewing tool can be used in two different modes. Each mode is activated by a different command:

- **Constrained Orbit**, invoked with the **3DORBIT** command
- **Free Orbit**, invoked with the **3DFORBIT** command

The **Constrained Orbit** mode constrains orbiting so that the Z-axis maintains its verticality at all times, as well as any edges parallel to it. The Arcball is not shown while this command is active. The **Free Orbit** mode, on the other hand, allows orbiting in any direction, and it shows the Arcball.

You can invoke the **3DFORBIT** command by pressing the **<Shift>** key and the wheel button of the mouse simultaneously. The **3DORBIT** command can be invoked by pressing the **<Shift>** + **<Ctrl>** keys and the wheel button of the mouse simultaneously, too. While using these methods all you have to do is drag the mouse while the wheel button and the specific key(s) are pressed.

> **Note:**
> Regardless of which command you invoke, you can switch between these two modes within the same operation by using the **3D Orbit** shortcut menu. You will see more details about this in the next topic.

3DFORBIT	
3D Navigation Toolbar	
Ribbon Navigate panel	
Pull-down Menu	View/ 3D Orbit
Command Line	3dforbit

TIP   Both the **3DORBIT** and **3DFORBIT** commands can be used transparently while other commands are in progress.

When invoking the **3DFORBIT** command, you will see the Arcball, which is represented as a big circle with four smaller ones on its quadrants (Figure 19-76). The UCS icon changes its appearance, and the cursor changes to an orbit-like type.

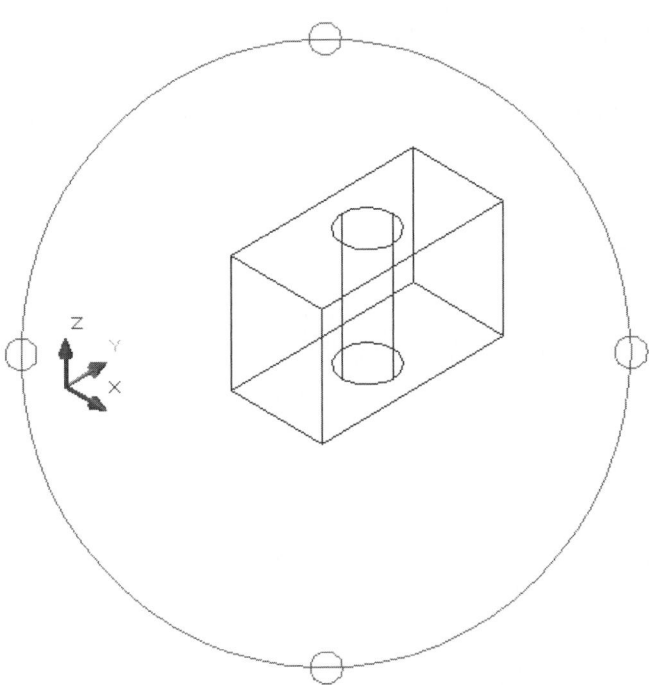

Figure 19-76   The Arcball after invoking the **3DFORBIT** command

The pointer changes its appearance as you move it from one location to another. Clicking and dragging the mouse in each particular location causes a different effect (Table 19-1). If the command is invoked by pressing the **<Shift> + <Ctrl>** keys along with the wheel button, such effects will not be available.

Table 19-1   Appearances of the Mouse Pointer in Different Zones of the Arcball

Pointer	Location where it shows up	Effect
	Inside the Arcball	Spins your model around an imaginary axis that is perpendicular to the direction you are moving your pointer to
	Outside the Arcball	Spins your model around an imaginary axis that is perpendicular to the display
	Inside the left or right small circles	Spins your model around an imaginary vertical axis
	Inside the top or bottom small circles	Spins your model around an imaginary horizontal axis

Exercise 19-10: The 3D Orbit

1. **OPEN** *SimpleSolid*.
2. Select the **SW Isometric** view and invoke the **ZOOM Realtime** command to zoom into your drawing.
3. Invoke the **3DORBIT** command and spin the object around to inspect all its faces.
4. Select the **SE Isometric** viewing point.
5. Select the **World** UCS.
6. **SAVE** the drawing.

Note:
When using the **3D Orbit** tool, remember that the object does not move with respect to the coordinate system. It is actually the entire coordinate system that has been rotated because it is seen from a different point.

The 3D Orbit Shortcut Menu: Other 3D Navigation Tools

Right-clicking in the drawing area while the **3D Orbit** tool is activated displays the **3D Orbit** shortcut menu (Figure 19-77). Through this shortcut menu you can perform the following operations:

- Select different visual styles
- Select preset and named views
- Use other visual aids: compass, grid, and UCS icon

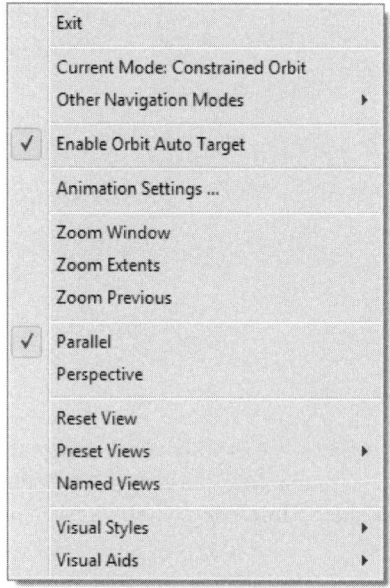

Figure 19-77 The **3D Orbit** shortcut menu

- Switch between parallel and perspective views
- Enable Orbit Auto Target
- Use other navigation modes

FOR MORE DETAILS   The **Visual Styles** and **Named Views** options are explained later in this chapter.

Other Visual Aids.   Deactivating the **UCS Icon** turns this element off, even after exiting the 3D Orbit tool. Activating the **Grid** displays this element, which is the same as pressing the **<F7>** key outside the **3D Orbit** tool. Activating the **Compass** enhances the **3D Orbit** appearance by showing a scale around the axes and their rotations.

perspective view: View in which the 3D objects represented give the impression not only of height, width, and depth, but also of relative distance from the viewing point to the viewing target.

Parallel and Perspective Views.   You can switch between these two viewing modes by selecting them from the shortcut menu while in the **3DORBIT** command. You can also change this setting outside the **3DORBIT** command through the **PERSPECTIVE** system variable. The parallel view and *perspective view* are compared in Figure 19-78.

Figure 19-78 Comparison between the parallel and perspective views

Parallel View

Perspective View

Orbit Auto Target.   This feature keeps the target point on the objects you are viewing rather than on the center of the viewport. It is turned on by default. Besides this feature, you can also use the **3DORBITCTR** command, which allows you to specify the exact center of the orbiting operation.

Other Navigation Modes.   Inside the **Other Navigation Modes** submenu (Figure 19-79) you will find tools associated with the viewing system:

- **Continuous Orbit** causes the 3D model to spin continuously in a direction specified by briefly clicking and dragging the left mouse button in the drawing area.

- **Swivel** simulates the effect of swiveling the camera.

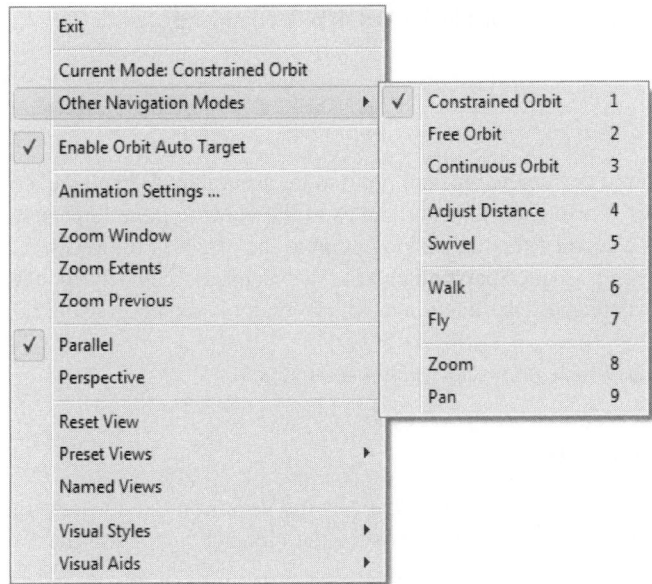

Figure 19-79   The **Other Navigation Modes** submenu

- **Walk** allows you to move the viewing point as if you were walking through the 3D model at a fixed height above the *XY* plane. This operation is available only in a perspective view.

- **Fly** allows you to move the viewing point to simulate flying through the 3D model without being restricted to a fixed height above the *XY* plane. This operation is available only in a perspective view.

- **Zoom** and **Pan** allow you to use the **3DZOOM** and **3DPAN** commands inside the **3D Orbit** tool.

FOR MORE DETAILS   See Chapter 27 for more details about the **Walk** and **Fly** operations, using the **3DWALK** and **3DFLY** commands.

Visualizing objects three-dimensionally requires special imaginative and abstract skills. The 3D viewing system of the AutoCAD program, along with the **3D Orbit** tool, allow users to observe 3D models from virtually anywhere, regardless of whether 3D abstract visualization is present or not.

Therefore, achieving a complete understanding of the 3D viewing system is a key factor for success in 3D modeling. Recognizing the different operations of the 3D viewing system and becoming proficient in their use will automatically improve the user's 3D visualization, which is an asset for the workplace.

The 3DZOOM and 3DPAN Commands

Using the **ZOOM** and **PAN** commands provides effects similar to those of the **3DZOOM** and **3DPAN** commands. The two last commands, however, are much better tools for a 3D environment.

The regular **ZOOM** and **PAN** commands sometimes require invoking the **REGEN** command intermediately to be able to proceed. With the **3DZOOM** and **3DPAN** commands, however, this is not necessary.

The **3DZOOM** and **3DPAN** commands can be invoked in the following ways:

- From the icons located in the **3DORBIT** toolbar
- Entering **3dzoom** or **3dpan** in the command line
- Activating the standard **ZOOM** and **PAN** commands while any visual style is active (except the default **2D Wireframe** visual style)
- Through the **3DORBIT** command's shortcut menu
- By manipulating the mouse wheel while inside the **3DORBIT** command

THE VPOINT COMMAND

The **VPOINT** command allows you to define the viewing point more accurately. When invoked through the command line, it allows you to enter the coordinates of the viewing point anywhere in the 3D space. This point defines a vector from the viewing point to the origin of the WCS.

The viewing plane on your screen is aligned perpendicular to the vector defined between the viewing point and the origin. This establishes the direction in which you look at objects in the 3D space.

The **Rotate** option specifies a new viewing vector using two angles:

```
Enter angle in XY plane from X axis <315>:
Enter angle from XY plane <35>:
```

The first angle is the angle between the projection of the viewing vector on the *XY* plane of the WCS and its *X*-axis. The second angle is measured between the viewing vector and the *XY* plane of the **World** UCS.

For example, the two angles corresponding to the **SE Isometric** viewing point are **315°** and **35°**; and the angles corresponding to the **Right** view are **0°** and **0°**.

Pressing **<Enter ↵>** displays a compass and axis tripod, allowing you also to define a viewing direction.

Exercise 19-11: Using the VPOINT Command

1. **OPEN** *SimpleSolid*.
2. **SAVE** the drawing **AS** *Exercise 19-11*.
3. Invoke the **VPOINT** command by typing its name in the command line. When prompted to specify a viewing point, enter **1,0.5,2.5**.
4. **ZOOM** out. The display reflects the new viewing direction (Figure 19-80).
5. Draw a line from the point **0,0,0** to the point **1,0.5,2.5**.

Note:
The line cannot be seen before the **SE Isometric** viewing point is selected because it is located in the same direction as the viewing vector.

Figure 19-80 The viewing point modified with the **VPOINT** command

6. Select the **SE Isometric** viewing point to see the location of the line.
7. **SAVE** the drawing.

THE **CAMERA** COMMAND

The **CAMERA** command allows you to specify and save different viewing directions by specifying the camera location, or viewing point, and the target location. The **VPOINT** command, on the other hand, allows you to specify only the viewing point because the viewing target is always the origin of the WCS.

The **CAMERA** command creates a special object or entity called a *camera*. The **CAMERADISPLAY** system variable controls whether or not the cameras are shown. Its value, however, is automatically set to **1** (on) whenever a camera is created. Selecting a camera object will display a pyramid representing its viewing field (Figure 19-81). It will also display the **Camera Preview** window, containing a perspective preview of the 3D model as seen by the selected camera (Figure 19-82). You can use the grips of the viewing field to manipulate the camera lens length as well as the camera and target locations.

camera: An object that encapsulates the geometric definitions of a particular view.

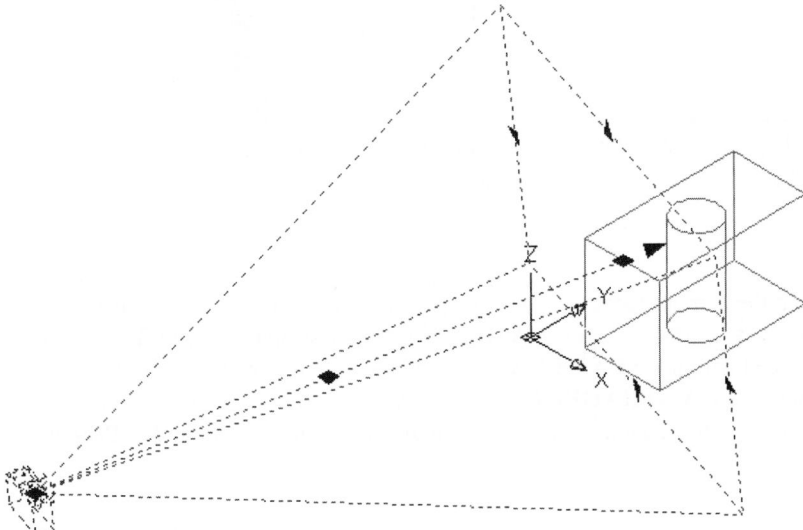

Figure 19-81   A camera object selected

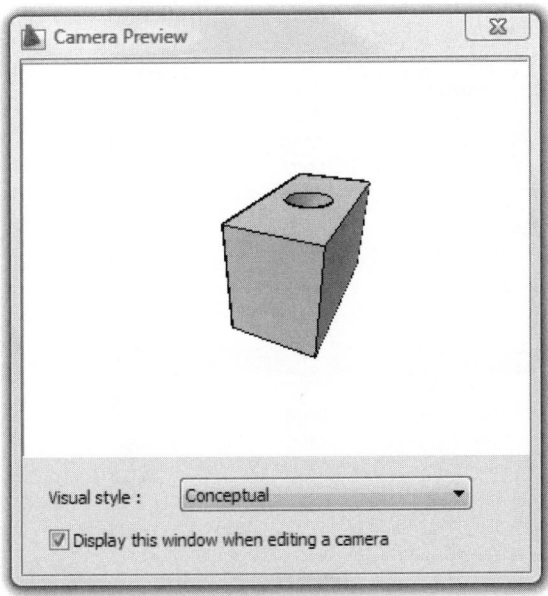

Figure 19-82   The **Camera Preview** window

Each camera creates a new model view, which allows you to quickly change between previously defined viewing points. Model views are displayed in the drop-down list of the **View** toolbar (Figure 19-83). Selecting a model view changes the display to a perspective view according to the camera geometric definitions (Figure 19-84).

Figure 19-83   The drop-down list of the **View** panel on the Ribbon

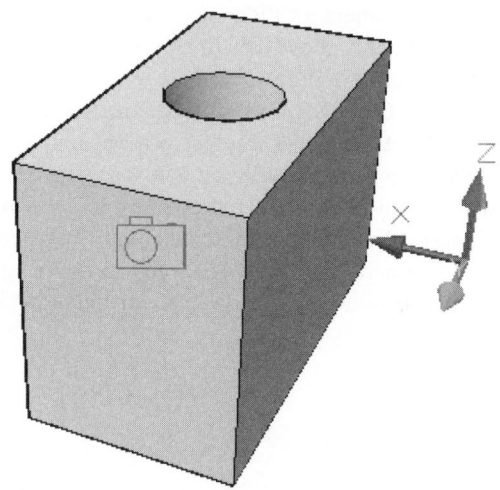

Figure 19-84   A perspective view displayed according to the camera definitions

When specifying the camera location, you can specify only the X and Y coordinates of the point. The Z coordinate is controlled by the **CAMERAHEIGHT** system variable. The Z coordinate can also be changed within the **CAMERA** command by selecting the **Height** option, which automatically updates the **CAMERAHEIGHT** system variable. This and other properties or definitions of the camera object, such as its name, can also be changed through the **Properties** window (Figure 19-85).

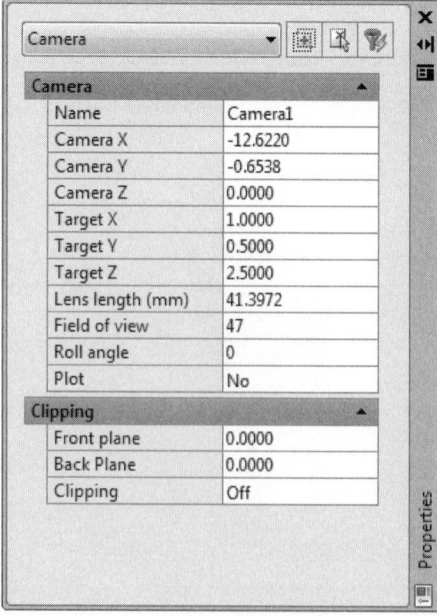

Figure 19-85   The camera properties shown in the **Properties** palette

Exercise 19-12: Working with the Camera

CAMERA	
View Toolbar	
Ribbon Camera panel	
Pull-down Menu	View/ Create Camera
Command Line	camera
Alias	cam

1. **OPEN** *SimpleSolid*.
2. **ZOOM** out as needed and **SAVE** the drawing **AS** *Exercise 19-12*.
3. Invoke the **CAMERA** command using one of the methods shown in the grid, and respond to the prompts as follows:

   `Specify camera location:` *-9,-6* ↵

   `Specify target location:` *1,0.5,2.5* ↵

   `Enter an option`

   `[?/Name/LOcation/Height/Target/LEns/Clipping/View/eXit]:` ↵*(To exit the command)*

4. Invoke the **CAMERA** command again to create a second camera. Specify the camera and target locations as **–7,3** and **1,4.5,2.5**.
5. The 3D model should look like Figure 19-86. Select the second camera you created. Right-click in the drawing area and select **Properties** from the shortcut menu.

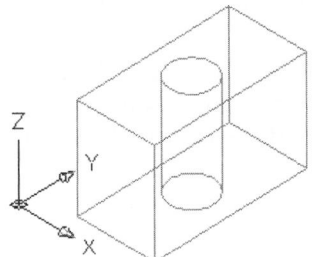

Figure 19-86   The 3D model with the two cameras shown

6. In the **Properties** window, change the **Name** to **High Camera**, and change the camera *Z* value to **6**. Close the **Properties** window and press the **<Esc>** key to close the **Camera Preview** window and hide the camera viewing field pyramid.
7. Click on the drop-down list of views located on the **View** panel of the Ribbon (Figure 19-87). Select **High Camera** from the list.

Figure 19-87   The views drop-down list located on the **View** panel of the Ribbon

8. Invoke the **ZOOM Realtime** command and zoom out to obtain a smaller view of the 3D model.
9. Invoke the **CAMERADISPLAY** system variable to hide the cameras. The 3D model should look like Figure 19-88.
10. **SAVE** the drawing.

Figure 19-88   The 3D model as seen by the camera

SAVING AND USING MODEL VIEWS

model view: A combination of geometric specifications that define a view plus additional elements such as UCS, layer snapshot, and visual style.

AutoCAD uses *model views* to store viewing points and other parameters associated with them. You can create or save a model view either by using the **CAMERA** command or through the **View Manager** dialog box (Figure 19-89).

Figure 19-89   The **View Manager** dialog box

In the **View Manager** dialog box you can see the coordinates of any camera and target points. Through this dialog box you can also specify certain details for any saved model view such as linking a previously saved UCS or visual styles to it. You can also rename a model view and specify whether the view will show in parallel or perspective mode.

The procedure to save a model view through the **View Manager** dialog box is explained in the next exercise.

Exercise 19-13: Using the View Manager

1. **OPEN** *Exercise 19-12*.
2. **SAVE** the drawing **AS** *Exercise 19-13*.
3. Select the **SE Isometric** viewing point.
4. Invoke the **Rotate** option of the **VPOINT** command. Specify **300** and **15** when prompted for the first and second angles.
5. Change the **PERSPECTIVE** system variable to **0.** Invoke this setting by entering its name in the command line.
6. **ZOOM** the view out to make the 3D model smaller. The 3D model should look like Figure 19-90.

VIEW	
View Toolbar	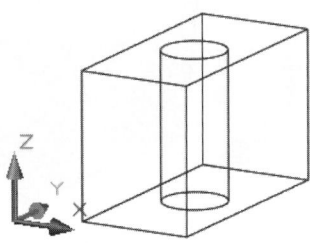
Pull-down Menu	View/ Named Views . . .
Command Line	view
Alias	v

Figure 19-90 The 3D model shows the new viewing point after zooming out

7. Invoke the **VIEW** command by using one of the methods from the grid. In the **View Manager** dialog box, click on the **New . . .** button to open the **New View** dialog box (Figure 19-91). In this dialog box, type **My3Dview** in the **View Name:** field and click **OK** to return to the **View Manager**.

Figure 19-91 The **New View** dialog box

8. The new model view is added to the list. Under the **General** category of properties, select the **Conceptual** visual style. Under the **View** category, set **Perspective** as **On**. Click **OK** to close the **View Manager** dialog box.
9. Select **My3Dview** from the drop-down list on the **View** toolbar. The 3D model should look like Figure 19-92.
10. **SAVE** the drawing.

Figure 19-92 The 3D model after selecting **My3Dview** from the drop-down list on the **View** toolbar

USING THE MOUSE WHEEL IN THE AUTOCAD PROGRAM

In AutoCAD the mouse wheel can be used to perform the following four **3D Navigation** operations:

- **ZOOM Realtime**
- **PAN**
- **ZOOM Extents**
- **Transparent 3D Orbit**

ZOOM Realtime enables you to zoom in or zoom out by rotating the mouse wheel forward and backward. This feature allows you to keep a specific area of the display stationary by simply positioning the pointer there. With the standard **ZOOM Realtime** command, you cannot control this because this command always zooms from the center of the screen.

One complete turn of the wheel is divided into small steps. Each step tells the AutoCAD program to zoom in or out by a certain factor. The **ZOOMFACTOR** system variable allows you to set a value ranging from 3 to 100.

PAN allows you to perform a panning operation in the drawing area. Just click and drag the mouse wheel in the drawing area. You must set the **MBUTTONPAN** system variable to **1** (the default value) in order to use the wheel button for this purpose. Otherwise, AutoCAD displays the **Object Snap** shortcut menu.

ZOOM Extents works just like the **Extents** option of the **ZOOM** command. It zooms in or out automatically to the factor where all the existing objects in the model fit in the screen. This operation is performed simply by double-clicking the mouse wheel.

The **3D Swivel** navigation mode is activated by pressing the **<Ctrl>** key and the wheel button together while the dragging the mouse.

Transparent 3D Orbit activates the constrained mode of the **3D Orbit** tool. It is activated by pressing the **<Shift>** key and the wheel button at the same time, and then dragging in the drawing area. Releasing either key or the wheel button will cancel the function.

You can use the **3DORBIT** command transparently inside other commands. But using this feature is more convenient because you save the time needed to invoke and exit the command.

In most cases, all these operations can be performed without any problems. Sometimes, however, the AutoCAD program might not respond properly to one or more of these operations. The cause is probably an incompatibility between the mouse settings and the AutoCAD software. To solve these issues, you can first try changing some mouse settings regarding the wheel. Second, you can download your mouse's driver from the manufacturer's website and install it in your computer. If none of the above work, you can purchase a different wheel mouse.

TIP   Using the mouse wheel increases productivity, especially when working in a 3D environment. Its main advantage is that it can be used at any stage of a command without having to invoke other commands.

THE STEERINGWHEELS

The **SteeringWheel**, or wheel to simplify, is a relatively new navigation device that provides quick and easy access to the different navigation tools. The steering wheel is divided into different sections, known as wedges; each *Wedge* activates a different navigation tool when you click on the wedge, or when you click on the wedge and hold the pointing down device while dragging it. Most navigation tools, however, need to be activated by clicking on their corresponding wedge and holding the pointing down device while dragging it.

Wheels can be shown in seven different modes; the mode is controlled by the **NAVSWHEELMODE** system variable, which can be set from 0 to 6. Figure 19-93 shows the different types of wheels, and the corresponding mode for the **NAVSWHEELMODE** system variable. Each of the wheel modes contains a particular set of navigation tools. Besides using the **NAVSWHEELMODE** system variable, you can also switch between the different modes through the shortcut menu that is displayed by right-clicking the drawing area while the wheel is in use (Figure 19-94), or by clicking the arrow located in the lower right corner of the wheel.

One important aspect common to any of the SteeringWheels is that they travel along with your cursor wherever it goes throughout the

Wedge: When talking about SteeringWheels, refers to the different areas that these tools are divided into; each Wedge activates a different navigation tool.

Notes:
1. The arrow used to bring up the SteeringWheels shortcut menu is available only in the Big Steering-Wheels.
2. When the **2D Navigation Wheel** mode is active, you cannot switch to any other mode through the shortcut menu; it can be changed only through the **NAVSWHEELMODE** system variable.

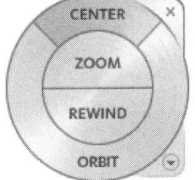

0   Big View Object wheel

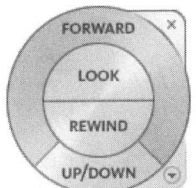

1   Big Tour Building wheel

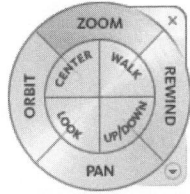

2   Big Full Navigation wheel

3   2D Navigation wheel

4   Mini View Object wheel

5   Mini Tour Building wheel

6   Mini Full Navigation wheel

Figure 19-93   The different types of SteeringWheels, the value of the **NAVSWHEELMODE** system variable associated with each one, and a brief description

Figure 19-94   The **SteeringWheels** shortcut menu

entire drawing area. This can save you a great amount of time because it shortens by much the distance that the pointing device has to be moved to reach the navigation tool. Different properties on the SteeringWheels, such as the transparency and the size, among others, can be adjusted in the **SteeringWheels Setting** dialog box (Figure 19-95). You can access this dialog box through the shortcut menu as well.

Figure 19-95   The **Steering Wheels Settings** dialog box

SteeringWheels: Navigation tool that provides quick and easy access to the different navigation tools. Each tool is activated though its corresponding Wedge.

Most of the navigation tools contained in the ***SteeringWheels*** work just as discussed in previous topics. For example, the Center wedge works similar to the **3DORBITCTR** command, allowing you to define the orbiting center. A tool that is unique to this group is **Rewind**. This tool allows you to go back and forth through the most recent views you have used. The view stages you can go through can even be previewed in a thumbnail picture, that is, if the **CAPTURETHUMBNAILS** system variable is set to **1** or **2**, which you can also control in the **SteeringWheels Settings** dialog box.

THE VIEWCUBE

The *ViewCube,* or simply the cube (Figure 19-96), is another new navigation device that provides quick and easy access to displaying the different predefined viewing points, including the standard and isometric views. The **ViewCube** is displayed whenever you switch to a visual style other than the **2D Wireframe** visual style. The **NAVVCUBE** command serves two purposes in the displaying of the **ViewCube:**

1. To turn the **ViewCube** on and off while you are in an appropriate visual style.
2. To determine whether the **ViewCube** will show up the next time you leave the **2D Wireframe** visual style to go to another one. Figure 19-97 shows the options of this command in its shortcut menu.

ViewCube: 3D navigation tool that appears when a Visual style other than the **2D Wireframe** is selected. This tool allows you to switch quickly between the different predefined viewing points, including the standard and isometric views.

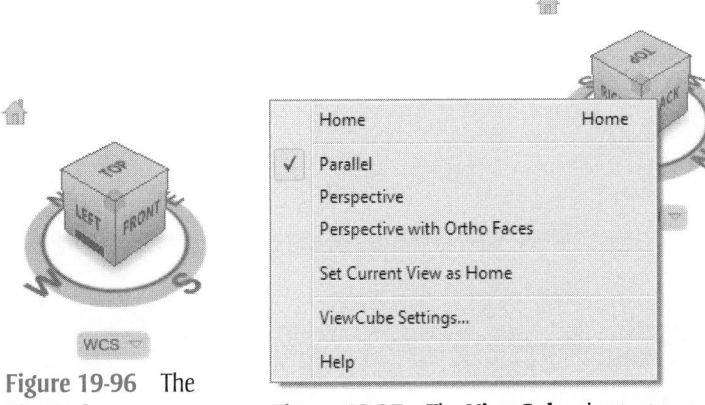

Figure 19-96 The **ViewCube**

Figure 19-97 The **ViewCube** shortcut menu

> **FOR MORE DETAILS**   See "Using the Predefined Visual Styles" to learn about visual styles.

By hovering the mouse pointer over each element, you can highlight the different elements of the **ViewCube**. Clicking on a highlighted geometrical element, which could be a face, an edge, or a vertex, you can change the viewing point accordingly. The four top vertices of the box, for instance, will bring the four predefined Isometric viewing points. You can also spin around the 3D model by spinning the compass below the cube. Right-clicking on the cube will bring up its shortcut menu, where you can change between parallel and perspective views and access the **ViewCube** settings. The orientation of the views can be made with respect to the WCS or to any UCS stored or currently in use.

VIEWPORTS IN MODEL SPACE

In general, two types of *viewports* are available in AutoCAD:

- Model space viewports
- Paper space viewports, also called *floating viewports*

When you start a new drawing from scratch, the entire model space consists of a single viewport. Working with multiple viewports splits the model space into smaller drawing areas or viewports

viewports: Areas into which the model space is divided.

Figure 19-98   The drawing areas split into smaller areas or viewports

(Figure 19-98). In each viewport you can select the viewing point and the UCS independently. The viewports cannot overlap each other, and only one can be active at a time. To make a viewport active you just click inside it.

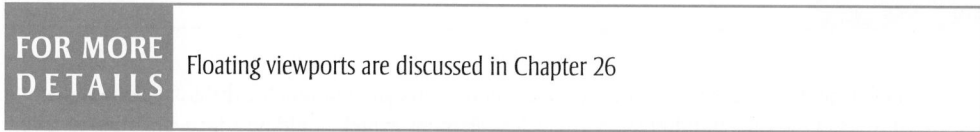

FOR MORE DETAILS   Floating viewports are discussed in Chapter 26

Using more than one viewport enables you to look at the 3D model from different viewing points at the same time. You can invoke a command while a viewport is active and then switch to another viewport within the command. Because you can **ZOOM** in each viewport independently, you can make a detailed modification through a specific viewport while seeing the changes in another one, without having to **ZOOM** back and forth.

Splitting the display into multiple viewports also reduces the work area, so you might want to use multiple viewports only when they are really needed. A 3D model can always be created in a single viewport.

With the **UCSVP** system variable you can specify whether or not the UCS on a specific viewport is free to update its UCS, so it reflects the same UCS as that of the current viewport. The UCS is free or unlocked when the value of the **UCSVP** variable is **0**; and when its value is **1** (the default value), the UCS is locked, remaining unchanged.

Different configurations are preestablished by the AutoCAD software, but you are not limited to them. If you have divided the default single viewport into four equal viewports, you can keep dividing each of these four viewports into any other configuration.

The **VPORTS** command is used to perform operations on viewport configurations. It can be invoked in two different ways through the command line:

1. **VPORTS:** Opens up the **Viewports** dialog box.
2. **−VPORTS:** Prompts you to enter one of the following options in the command line.

```
Enter an option [Save/Restore/Delete/Join/SIngle/?/2/3/4] <3>:
```

You can join two viewports into one as long as the two viewports together form a rectangle. For example, in Figure 19-100, you could join only the two viewports at the bottom of the screen. The UCS and the viewing point of the resulting viewport will be the same as those of the first viewport selected. You can also save, retrieve, and delete your own viewport configurations. When you save a configuration, the UCS and the **UCSVP** system variable information contained in each viewport are saved together with it.

Exercise 19-14: Creating Viewports in Model Space

1. **OPEN** *SimpleSolid*.
2. **SAVE** the drawing **AS** *Exercise 19-14*.
3. Make sure the **SW Isometric** view and the **World** UCS are selected.
4. Set the **UCSFOLLOW** system variable to **0**. Set the **UCSORTHO** and **UCSVP** system variables to **1**.
5. Split the display into three viewports with the biggest one on top. To do this, open the **Viewports** dialog box. In the **New Viewports** tab, click on the **Three: Above** Standard viewport configuration.
6. Select **3D** from the **Setup** drop-down list (Figure 19-99). Click on the **OK** button to close the **Viewports** dialog box.

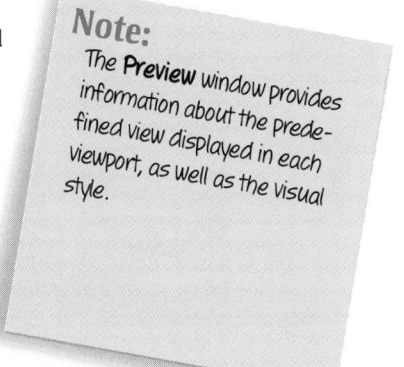

Note:
The **Preview** window provides information about the predefined view displayed in each viewport, as well as the visual style.

VIEWPORTS	
Viewports Toolbar	
Pull-down Menu	View/ Viewports/ New Viewports . . .
Command Line	viewports
Alias	vports

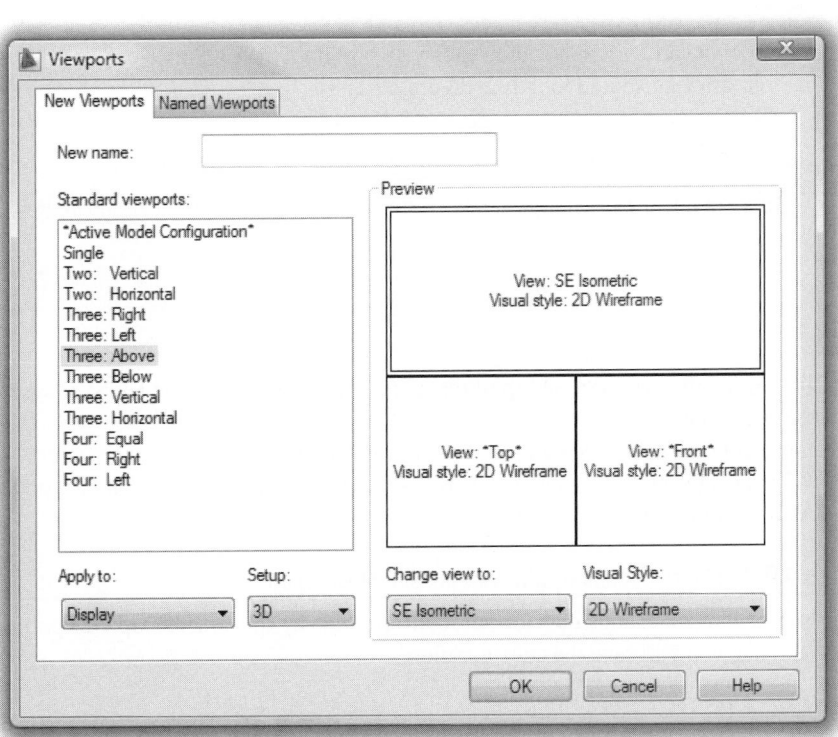

Figure 19-99   The **Viewports** dialog box with a 3D setup configuration

Figure 19-100   After zooming out in each individual viewport

7. In the drawing area, **ZOOM** out in each viewport until the UCS icon can be seen at its origin. Your drawing should look like Figure 19-100.

TIP   To zoom out in a viewport, you must first make it current by clicking inside its area.

8. Click inside the viewport on top to make it current and change the **UCSVP** system variable value to **0**.
9. Click inside the bottom-left and the bottom-right viewports, in that order. Observe how the UCS in the top viewport is automatically updated when you make the other viewport current.
10. **SAVE** the drawing.

Exercise 19-15: More Operations with Viewports in Model Space

In this exercise, you will change the viewport configuration by splitting the top viewport into four equal areas. Then you will save the configuration.

1. **OPEN** *Exercise 19-14*.
2. **SAVE** the drawing **AS** *Exercise 19-15*.
3. Make the top viewport current, and open the **Viewports** dialog box.

4. In the **New Viewports** tab, click on the **Two: Vertical** standard viewport configuration. In the **Apply to**: drop-down dialog box, choose **Current Viewport**. Click the **OK** button.

5. Repeat the same process to subdivide the new top-right and top-left viewports into **Two: Vertical** viewports each. By doing so, you will end up splitting the initial top viewport into four viewports.

6. Select the **SW Isometric, SE Isometric, NE Isometric**, and **NW Isometric** viewing points from left to right on each viewport. Your display should look like Figure 19-101.

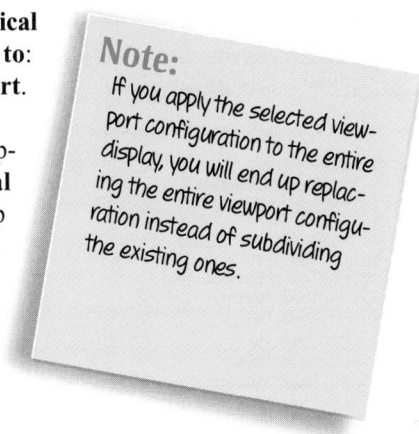

Note: If you apply the selected viewport configuration to the entire display, you will end up replacing the entire viewport configuration instead of subdividing the existing ones.

Figure 19-101   In three steps, the top viewport is divided into four viewports

7. Save the viewport configuration you just created. To do so, open the **Viewports** dialog box again. In the **New Viewports** tab, type **Six-Two below** in the **New Name**: field (Figure 19-102). Click the **OK** button.

8. Change the viewport configuration to **Three: Vertical**. Open the **Viewports** dialog box again. In the **New Viewports** tab of the **Viewports** dialog box, select the **Three: Vertical** Standard viewport configuration. This time, leave the **Apply to**: drop-down dialog box as its default **Display** so you can change the entire display. Then, click the **OK** button.

Figure 19-102   Saving the **Six-Two below** viewport configuration

9. Open the **Viewports** dialog box again to retrieve your saved configuration. In the **Named Viewports** tab, click on the **Six-Two below** viewport to make it current. Click the **OK** button.

10. Invoke the **–VPORTS** command by typing its entire name in the command line. Respond to the prompts as follows.

Enter an option [Save/Restore/Delete/Join/SIngle/?/2/3/4] <3>: *j* ↵

Select dominant viewport <current viewport>: *Click inside one of the viewports you want to join.*

Select viewport to join: *Click inside the other viewport you want to join.*

11. **SAVE** the drawing.

USING THE PREDEFINED VISUAL STYLES

visual style: A collection of settings or modifiers that control the display of edges and faces of 3D objects.

predefined visual styles: Predefined collections of settings, saved as visual styles, that control the display of edges and faces of 3D objects.

3D models are always displayed in a particular *visual style*. The default visual style is **2D Wireframe**. By selecting a different visual style you can create different shaded displays of the 3D objects in each viewport.

AutoCAD supplies five *predefined visual styles*. These styles combine the most useful display styles for 3D models:

- **2D Wireframe**
- **3D Hidden**
- **3D Wireframe**
- **Conceptual**
- **Realistic**

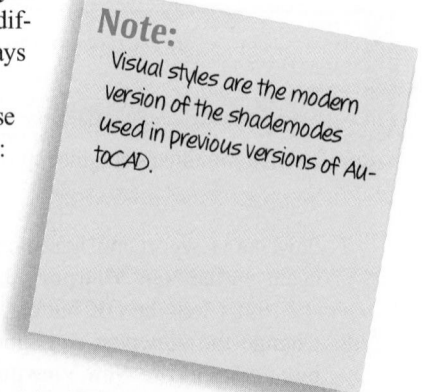

Note:
Visual styles are the modern version of the shademodes used in previous versions of AutoCAD.

The **2D Wireframe** visual style shows all the edges of the 3D model and displays the standard UCS icon (Figure 19-103). The **DISPSILH** system variable controls whether or not the silhouette lines are shown.

Figure 19-103   The **2D Wireframe** visual style

The **3D Wireframe** visual style shows all the edges of the 3D model and displays the 3D UCS icon (Figure 19-104). The **DISPSILH** system variable controls whether or not the silhouette lines are shown.

Figure 19-104   The **3D Wireframe** visual style

The **3D Hidden** visual style removes the obscured edges and objects from the view (Figure 19-105).

Figure 19-105   The **3D Hidden** visual style

The **Conceptual** visual style provides a shaded display of the 3D model, using the color of the object in a warm-cool face style (Figure 19-106).

Figure 19-106   The **Conceptual** visual style

The **Realistic** visual style provides a shaded display of the 3D model using the color and texture of the material applied to the object, or the color of the objects in its defect. Faces are shown in a real style (Figure 19-107).

Figure 19-107   The **Realistic** visual style

VISUALSTYLES	
Visual Styles Toolbar	
Ribbon Visual Styles panel	
Pull-down Menu	View/ Visual Styles/ Visual Styles Manager. . .
Command Line	visual-styles

You can quickly apply a predefined visual style in the following ways:

- Clicking the visual style icon directly on the **Visual Styles** toolbar
- Through the **Visual Styles** panel in the Ribbon (Figure 19-108)
- Using the **Visual Styles Manager** palette (Figure 19-109)

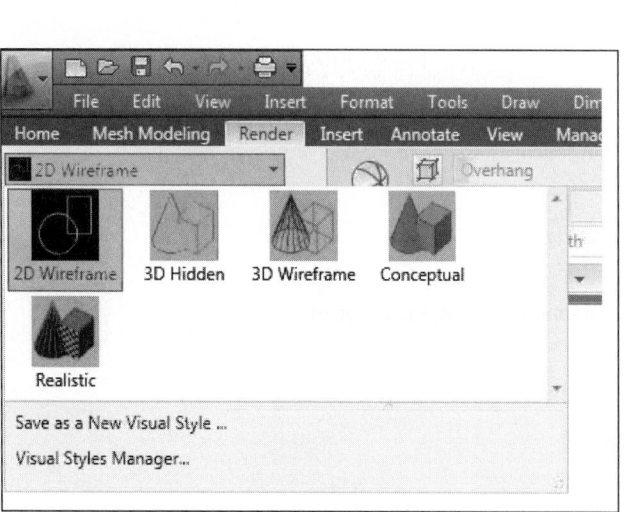

Figure 19-108   The predefined visual styles can be selected from the **Visual Styles** panel in the Ribbon

Figure 19-109   Selecting the predefined visual styles from the **Visual Styles Manager** palette

You can display the **Visual Styles Manager** palette by invoking the **VISUALSTYLES** command or by selecting it from the **Tools** drop-down menu under **Palettes**. To apply a visual style from the **Visual Styles Manager** palette specifically, you can perform one of the following operations:

- Drag and drop one of the sample images into the drawing area or a specific viewport.
- Double-click the sample image to apply the visual style on the current viewport.
- Click the **Apply Selected Visual Style to Current Viewport** button.

You can modify a visual style in two different ways:

- Using the controls on the **Visual Style** panel in the Ribbon
- Using the categorized settings in the **Visual Styles Manager** palette

Changes made using the controls located in the **Visual Style** panel of the Ribbon (Figure 19-110) are not saved to the visual style.

On the other hand, changes made to the settings in the **Visual Styles Manager** palette are permanently stored in the visual styles for the current drawing.

You can always **Reset to default** any of the AutoCAD program's predefined visual styles by right-clicking on its sample image. These visual styles cannot be deleted.

By simply changing some of the visual style modifiers, you can obtain a pictorial result similar to Figure 19-111.

Figure 19-110   The display of the objects can be temporarily modified through the **Edge Effects** panel of the Ribbon

Figure 19-111   You can obtain pictorial illustrations by modifying the predefined **Visual Style**

HIDE	
Render Toolbar	
Pull-down Menu	View/Hide
Command Line	hide
Alias	hi

> **FOR MORE DETAILS**   To learn specific details about creating and modifying visual styles, see Chapter 27.

THE HIDE COMMAND

The **HIDE** command is the traditional tool used to quickly inspect the 3D model when using the **2D Wireframe** visual style. This command hides the *obscured lines* by default; however, you can customize or fine-tune this effect in the **Visual Styles Manager** window. The **HIDE** command can be invoked by using one of the methods shown in the grid. To access the hidden line settings, the **2D Wireframe** sample image must be selected (Figure 19-112).

obscured lines: Edges or other objects that cannot be seen from the current viewing point because of their position relative to other objects.

TIP   Invoking the **HIDE** command while a visual style other than the **2D Wireframe** is current will simply apply the **3D Hidden** visual style.

Under **2D Hide – Obscured Lines**, you can change the default settings for the **Linetype** and **Color** of the obscured lines. When the linetype is off, the obscured lines are completely removed. Figure 19-113(a) shows all of the objects' edges. Figure 19-113(b) shows the obscured lines removed, and Figure 19-113(c) shows the obscured lines in a different linetype and color.

Figure 19-112   The **2D Wireframe** visual style settings

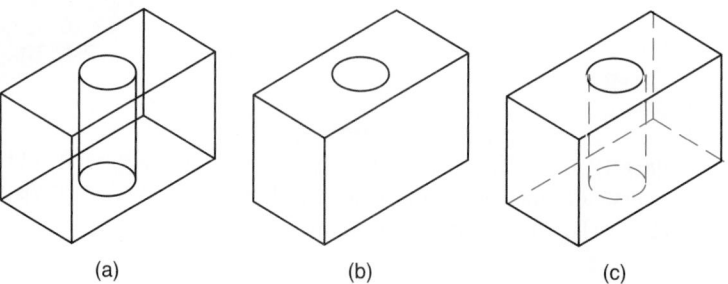

Figure 19-113   (a) Before invoking the **HIDE** command (b) After invoking the **HIDE** command with linetype off (c) With the Dashed linetype

Under **2D Hide – Intersection Edges**, you can change the settings for the **Linetype** and **Color** of the intersecting curves between 3D objects. Figure 19-114 compares the effects after the **HIDE** operation with and without enabling this setting. The color of the intersecting lines can also be changed.

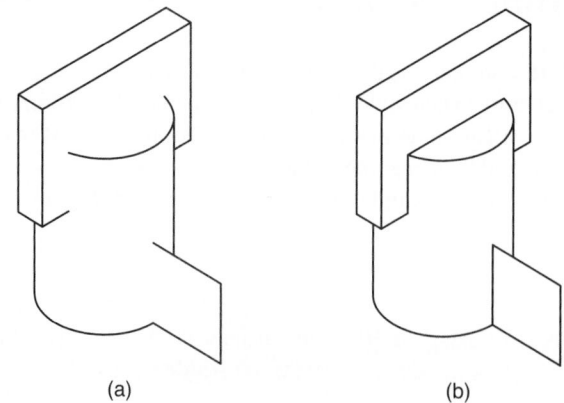

Figure 19-114   After invoking the **HIDE** command; with **Intersection Edges** disabled (a) and enabled (b)

Other settings that can be controlled in the **Visual Styles Manager** palette for the **2D Wireframe** visual style are:

- **Contour lines:** Controls the number of isolines displayed per curved face. This setting is also controlled by the **ISOLINES** system variable.

- **Draw true silhouettes:** Controls the display of silhouettes. This setting is also controlled by the **DISPSILH** system variable.

- **Halo gap %:** Controls the gap displayed where an object is hidden by another object.
- **Arc/circle smoothing:** This value controls the appearance of curves. Increasing its value will cause arc, circles, ellipses, and splines to look smoother. It is also controlled by the **VIEWRES** command.
- **Spline segments:** Sets the number of line segments to be generated for each spline-fit polyline generated by the **Spline** option of the **PEDIT** command. This value is also set by the **SPLINESEGS** system variable.
- **Solid smoothness:** Controls the smoothness of 3D solids by increasing or reducing the number of facets on curved faces. This setting is also controlled by the **FACETRES** system variable.

After invoking the **HIDE** command, you can revoke its effect by invoking the **REGEN** command. This operation is necessary prior to performing **ZOOM Realtime** or **PAN** operations.

USING POINT FILTERS AND TRACKING METHODS

When working in a 3D environment, finding points throughout the 3D space is essential. Because there are sometimes no physical objects to snap to, you will place objects temporarily in order to find these points. Or you can use methods such as point filters and tracking tools.

Point Filters

When you enter a point by either clicking or typing it, you enter all three coordinates (X, Y, and Z) at the same time. Using *point filters,* on the other hand, allows you to subdivide the process of entering the coordinates of a point into two or three steps. For example, you can specify the Y coordinate, and then the X and Z coordinates as the AutoCAD program prompts you to do so.

Point filters can be accessed whenever you are prompted to specify a point (Figure 19-115). There are two ways of specifying point filters:

- Shortcut menu: **<Shift>** + Right-click or **<Ctrl>** + Right-click (Figure 19-115)
- Keyboard entry: [.X .Y .Z .XY .YZ .ZX] ↵

point filters: A method of entering a point by which the *X, Y,* and *Z* coordinates are given in separate stages using any combination.

Figure 19-115   The **Point Filters** shortcut menu

SPHERE	
Solids Toolbar	
Ribbon Modeling panel	
Pull-down Menu	Draw/ Solids/ Sphere
Command Line	sphere

Exercise 19-16: Using Point Filters to Place Geometry

In this exercise, you will create a sphere in the center of the model by using point filters.

1. **OPEN** *SimpleSolid*.
2. **SAVE** the drawing **AS** *Exercise 19-16*.
3. Make sure the **DUCS** (Dynamic UCS) mode in the status bar is turned off.
4. Set the **ISOLINES** system variable to **4**.
5. Invoke the **SPHERE** command by using one of the methods in the grid. Respond to the prompts as follows:

   Specify center of sphere <0,0,0>: *.xy* ↵

   Of: *Click on the center 1 of the top circle [Figure 19-116(a)].*

   Of (need Z): *Click on the midpoint 2 of the edge.*

   Specify radius of sphere or [Diameter]: *0.5* ↵

6. The model should look like Figure 19-116(b). **SAVE** the drawing.

> **Note:**
> You could also have drawn a line temporarily from the bottom circle to the top circle of the cylindrical hole. When prompted for the center of the sphere, you then could have just clicked on the line's midpoint and then erased the line (if you did not plan to use it anymore).

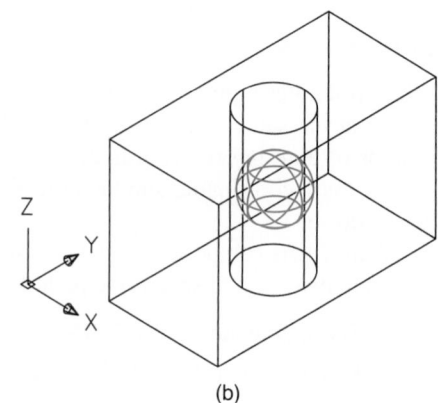

(a)   (b)

Figure 19-116 (a) Using point filters to specify the *XY* coordinates of the point and then the *Z* coordinate. (b) The resulting sphere

AutoTrack

AutoTrack: A powerful drafting tool that allows you to find points or to align objects along specified directions named *traces,* instead of snapping directly to the objects.

AutoTrack is a useful drafting aid to specify points in both 2D and 3D work. Using this tool, you can achieve the same results as those obtained by using the point filters, only in a more efficient way (especially when working with orthogonal views).

To turn **AutoTrack** mode on, you can press **<F11>** or click on the **OTRACK** button in the status bar.

Exercise 19-17: Using the Tracking Tools

In this exercise, you will create the same sphere in the same place as in the previous exercise. This time you will use a different method to find its center point.

1. **OPEN** *SimpleSolid*.
2. **SAVE** the drawing **AS** *Exercise 19-17*.
3. Turn **AutoTrack** mode on.
4. Open the **Drafting Settings** dialog box (Figure 19-117) and make sure that **Center** is one of the **Object Snap modes** checked.

TIP   You must enable a particular object snap before using it for tracking.

Figure 19-117   The **Center** object snap enabled in the **Drafting Settings** dialog box

5. Click on the **Polar Tracking** tab. Make sure that the **Track orthogonally only** choice is selected (Figure 19-118).
6. Turn **DUCS** (Dynamic UCS) off on the status bar.
7. Set the **ISOLINES** system variable to **2**.
8. Invoke the **SPHERE** command. When prompted for the *center point,* place the crosshairs cursor at the *center point* of the bottom circular edge for about a second to place a mark. Then move your pointer up.
9. While the vector is still showing, type **1.25** and press **<Enter ↵>**.

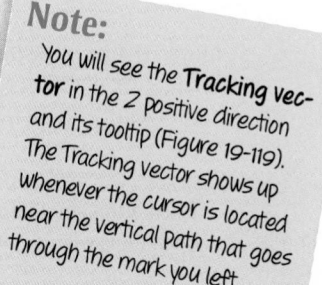

Note:
You will see the **Tracking vector** in the Z positive direction and its tooltip (Figure 19-119). The Tracking vector shows up whenever the cursor is located near the vertical path that goes through the mark you left.

Figure 19-118   Selecting the **Track orthogonally only** option allows tracking in four directions only

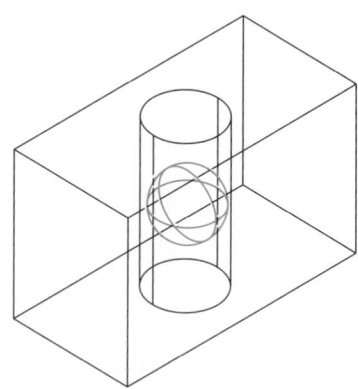

Figure 19-119   The tracking vector in the *Z* positive direction and its tooltip

Figure 19-120   After placing the sphere

TIP — Placing the crosshairs back on a mark for about a second will eliminate the mark. Zoom operations will eliminate the mark as well.

10. Finish the command by specifying the sphere radius as **0.5**. The sphere should be placed as in Figure 19-120.
11. **SAVE** the drawing.

In the **Polar Tracking** tab of the **Drafting Settings** dialog box (Figure 19-118), you can select the **Track orthogonally only** option. This will allow you to restrain the tracking along the axes, including the *Z*-axis. You can also choose to **Track using all polar angle settings**. In this option, the tracking is made according to the established polar angle settings. You can use any angle increment plus any other additional angles and along the *Z*-axis. Tracking along *Z* is not possible if one of the angle increments is coincident with the direction of the *Z*-axis in the current view. For example, you cannot track along *Z* in the **SE Isometric** viewing point if the angle increments are set to **45°**.

You can change **AutoTrack Settings** in the **Drafting** tab of the **Options** dialog box (Figure 19-121). Clicking the **Drafting Tooltip Settings. . .** button will allow you to modify the **Tooltip Appearance** as well, as long as **Override OS settings for all drafting tooltips** is selected in the **Tooltip Appearance** dialog box (Figure 19-122).

The tracking of a point occurs in a plane that is parallel to the *XY* plane of the current UCS. The plane goes through the point you are tracking and along the *Z*-axis.

Leaving tracking marks on two points will enable you to find the intersection of two tracking vectors. You should use this method only if the two points and the intersection point are located on a common plane parallel to any of the major planes of the current UCS (*XY*, *YZ*, or *ZX*).

Figure 19-121   The **Drafting Tooltip Settings ...** button in the **Drafting** tab of the **Options** dialog box opens the **Tooltip Appearance** dialog box

Figure 19-122   The **Tooltip Appearance** dialog box

Exercise 19-18: Copying Objects Using Tracking Techniques

In this exercise you will create a copy of the sphere using the tracking tool. You will locate the center of the new sphere in the middle of the left face of the box.

1. **OPEN** *Exercise 19-17*.
2. **SAVE** the drawing **AS** *Exercise 19-18*.

3. Turn **ORTHO** mode off, and select the **Front** UCS.

4. Invoke the **COPY** command, and respond to the prompts as follows:

Select objects: *Select the sphere.*

Select objects: ↵ *(To end the selection)*

Specify base point or [Displacement] <Displacement>: *Snap to the center point of the sphere.*

Specify second point or <use first point as displacement>: *Leave a mark in the midpoint of the two edges shown in* Figure 19-123 *and move the pointer near the center of the front face. Slightly move the pointer until you see the two tracking vectors. Click to specify the point.*

Specify second point or [Exit/Undo] <Exit>: ↵ *(To end the command)*

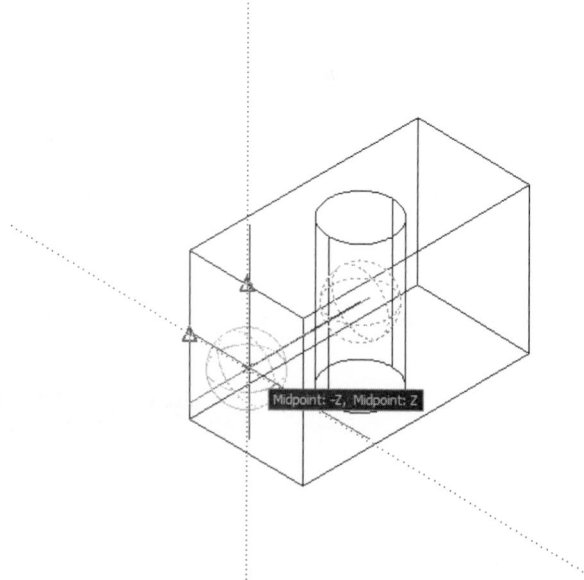

Figure 19-123 The tracking vectors for the two midpoints show up when near the intersection

5. A second sphere should be placed in the middle of the left face. **SAVE** the drawing.

6. Select the **Right** view and **ZOOM** out to make the 3D model view smaller.

7. Turn **ORTHO** mode on.

8. Invoke the **COPY** command again and, when prompted, select the sphere. Respond to the remaining prompts as follows:

Specify base point or [Displacement] <Displacement>: *Snap to the center point of the sphere.*

Specify second point or

<use first point as displacement>: *Leave a mark in the lower-right endpoint of the 3D solid (Figure 19-124). Then move the pointer up to find the intersection between the vertical tracking vector and the Ortho alignment of the center point.*

Specify second point or [Exit/Undo] <Exit>: ↵ *(To end the command)*

9. Select the **SE Isometric** viewpoint. The 3D model should look like Figure 19-125.

10. **Save** the drawing.

> **Note:**
> The copied sphere maintains the Z coordinate of the original object. This occurs even though the point used for tracking does not have the same Z coordinate as the first point.

Figure 19-124   Leaving a mark in the lower-right endpoint allows you to use a vector that tracks this point

Figure 19-125   The original sphere and two other spheres copied using different tracking techniques

Polar Tracking

Activating the **POLAR** mode automatically deactivates the **ORTHO** mode, and vice versa. This tool allows you to use an angle increment and the additional angles specified in the **Drafting Settings** dialog box (Figure 19-126). This tool also allows you to find the polar coordinates of the points.

Figure 19-126   **POLAR** tracking mode uses an angle increment and the additional angles, as specified in the **Drafting Settings** dialog box

When using the **POLAR** mode, you can specify points by first finding the direction predefined in the angle settings. You just move the mouse around until you see a path, like the one in Figure 19-127, that indicates the specific preset angle you want. Then you release the mouse and enter the distance from the tracking point to finish specifying the polar coordinate.

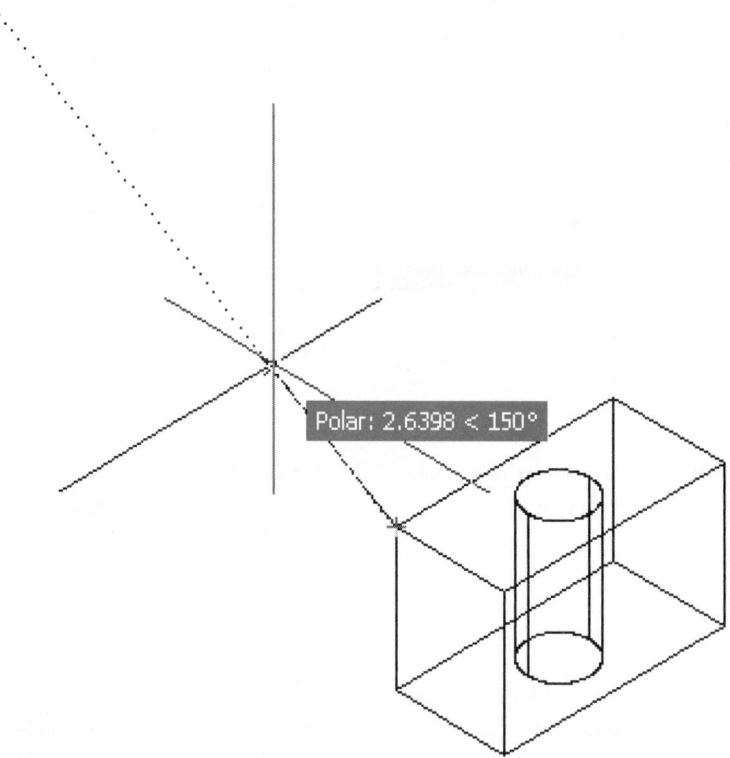

Figure 19-127 A polar coordinate on a plane parallel to the current *XY* plane in the direction of 150°

TIP You can use **POLAR** tracking and **AutoTrack** jointly to find points by the intersection of the tracking paths generated by both tools.

Direct Distance Entry

direct distance entry: A practical method of specifying the coordinates of the next point by entering a distance while the cursor indicates a specific known direction.

Direct distance entry can be used with either the **ORTHO** or **POLAR** mode. In this method you release the mouse while the pointer indicates a known direction. You then enter the distance directly in the command line.

Now you can also use the direct distance entry method in the direction of the *Z*-axis.

DYNAMIC INPUT

Dynamic input consists of a group of elements that allow you to interface with the AutoCAD software near the cursor. It is not intended to completely replace the command line window. The three dynamic input features are **Pointer Input, Dimension Input**, and **Dynamic Prompts**. These features can be turned on and off individually according to your needs, level of usage, and preferences (Figure 19-128). You can also turn the entire **Dynamic Input** mode on and off by clicking the **DYN** button in the status bar, or by pressing the **<F12>** key.

Pointer Input allows you to see the current coordinates of the cursor and enter them in the tooltip boxes. You move to the next box by typing one of the coordinate separators (, or <), or by pressing the **<Tab>** key (Figure 19-129).

Figure 19-128   The **Pointer Input, Dimension Input**, and **Dynamic Prompts** features can be turned on and off in the **Dynamic Input** tab of the **Drafting Settings** dialog box

Figure 19-129   The **Pointer Input** feature of **Dynamic Input**

The **Dimension Input** element is activated by specifying the first point on most of the commands that require the specification of more than one point or distances (i.e., **LINE, CIRCLE, CYLINDER, BOX**, and **CONE**). Instead of coordinates, the tooltip boxes display current distances and angle, depending on the particular command invoked. Pressing the **<Tab>** key allows you to move from one tooltip box to the next (Figure 19-130).

The **Dynamic Prompts** element allows you to read the command prompts in a tooltip near the cursor. In case other options are available in a command, they can be selected from the dynamic prompt list after pressing the **<Down Arrow>** key, similarly to the shortcut menu (Figure 19-131).

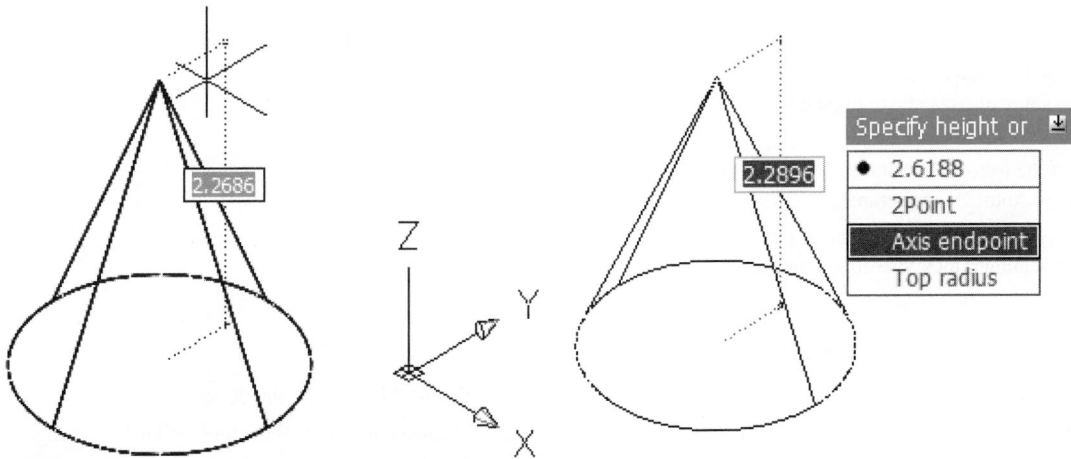

Figure 19-130   The **Dimension Input** feature of **Dynamic Input**

Figure 19-131   The **Dynamic Prompt** feature of **Dynamic Input**

CHAPTER SUMMARY

After going though this chapter, you should have clarified your idea about what working in 3D space means. You should also have become familiar with some of the main tools involved. Many important topics have been discussed here, although isolated in some cases. These will be very useful in your future 3D work, so you can consult this particular chapter as a reference from time to time.

The key point of the entire chapter is that you must understand how important is the relationship between the way you look at the 3D space, and the location of the current working plane. That is,

you must clearly grasp the relationship between the 3D viewing system and the 3D coordinate system. The mathematics of the coordinate system, along with the introduction to the third coordinate (Z), will allow you, understand more clearly what the computer 3D space is.

Many 3D modeling aids and tools, such as the visual styles, the 3D Orbit, and the tracking tools in 3D, among others, have been presented in this chapter. These are some of the tools that will be essential for your future success.

CHAPTER TEST QUESTIONS

Multiple Choice

1. The AutoCAD program's 3D space:
   a. Is always present
   b. Needs to be activated
   c. Interferes with 2D work
   d. Requires additional software

2. Which of the following can be linked to specific Tool palette groups?
   a. **Design Center**
   b. **Properties**
   c. **Ribbon Panels**
   d. **Visual Styles Manager**

3. The number of viewing points you can use in the AutoCAD program:
   a. Is ten (six Orthographic and four Isometric)
   b. Depends on whether you are working in 3D or 2D
   c. Is infinite
   d. Depends on the current UCS

4. The UCS can be modified by:
   a. Selecting an object
   b. Specifying a Z-axis vector
   c. Rotating it around the Y-axis
   d. All of the above

5. The **3D Orbit** tool is used mainly to:
   a. Rotate objects in the 3D space
   b. Change the viewing point
   c. Place some objects closer to others
   d. Relocate the UCS

6. Which of the following methods cannot be used to create a new UCS in the AutoCAD program?
   a. Specify two points to align the Z-axis
   b. Rotate counterclockwise about the Y-axis

   c. Align with a selected face
   d. Locate the XY plane normal to a selected line

7. Turning on (**1**) the **UCSORTHO** system variable causes:
   a. A change in the viewing point when an orthographic UCS is selected
   b. A change in the UCS when an orthographic view is selected
   c. A viewport to update its UCS to agree with the current one
   d. None of the above

8. Which of the following is not one of the AutoCAD program's predefined visual styles?
   a. **3D Hidden**
   b. **Gouraud Shaded**
   c. **Conceptual**
   d. **Realistic**

9. Which of the following actions does not change the viewing point?
   a. Using the **3D Orbit** tool
   b. Selecting a new Isometric viewing point
   c. Invoking the **PLAN** command
   d. Zooming into the drawing area

10. Which of the following is a method used to find points in the 3D space?
    a. Point filters
    b. **AutoTrack**
    c. Direct entry method
    d. All of the above

Matching

a. **NW Isometric** view

b. **3D Orbit**

c. Top imaginary plane

d. Cylindrical coordinates

e. UCS

f. Conceptual

1. Shows the object's silhouettes

2. Changes the viewpoint when the UCS is changed

3. Provides easy access to many command options

4. AutoCAD's default viewing point

5. A predefined viewing point

6. A tool to change the viewing point freely

g. **DISPSILH**

h. Shortcut menu

i. **REGEN**

j. **UCSFOLLOW**

7. A method of entering the 3D coordinates of a point

8. Revokes the effect of the **HIDE** command

9. Gives the object an artistic shaded appearance

10. The World Coordinate System, modified by the user

CHAPTER TUTORIALS

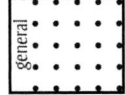

Tutorial 19-1: UCS Manipulation

In this tutorial you will practice the different procedures used to manipulate the UCS. Mastering this aspect of 3D work is a key factor for successful future learning. Figure 19-132 shows how the final 3D model will look after we add the different texts throughout the 3D space.

1. **OPEN** the finished *SimpleSolid* drawing you created earlier in this chapter.
2. **SAVE** it **AS** *Tutorial 19-1*.

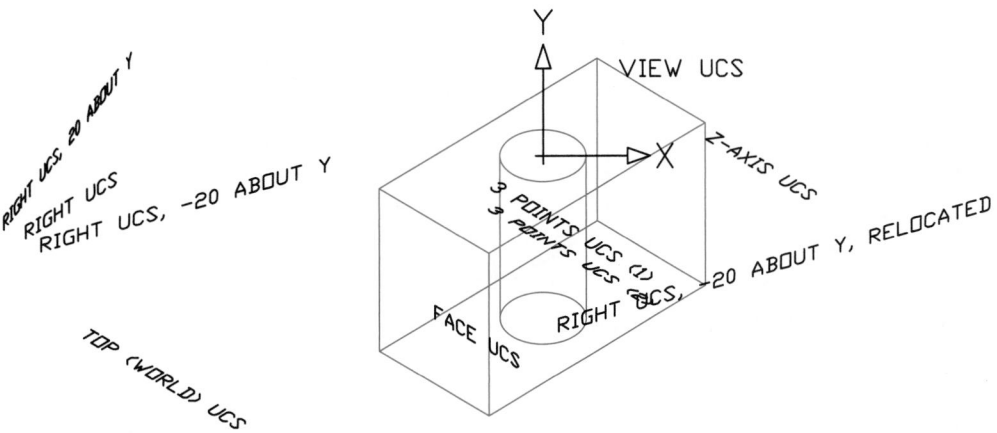

Figure 19-132   Preview of the final model after adding the texts throughout the 3D space

3. Make sure the **UCSORTHO** system variable is set to **1**.
4. Select the **Top** view.
5. **MOVE** the 3D solid **3″** orthogonally to the right (along the positive *X*-axis).
6. **MOVE** the 3D solid **3″** orthogonally up (along the positive *Y*-axis) (Figure 19-133).

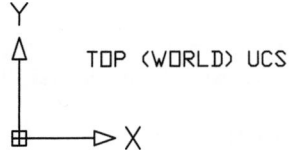

Figure 19-133   A Top view of the moved 3D solid

Figure 19-134   Text placed in the WCS

7. Invoke the **TEXT** command through the command line, and respond to the prompts as follows:

   `Specify start point of text or [Justify/Style]: 1,1 ↵`

   `Specify height <0.2000>: ↵ (To accept the height value)`

   `Specify rotation angle of text <0>: ↵(To accept the height value)`

8. When the simplified text editor opens, type **TOP (WORLD)** UCS and press **<Enter>** twice to exit the **TEXT** command (Figure 19-134).

9. Invoke the **COPYBASE** command through the drop-down menu: **Edit/Copy with Base Point**. When prompted for the base point, enter 0,0,0. Select the text when prompted to select the objects, and press **<Enter ↵>** to exit the command.

10. Select the **SE Isometric** viewing point (Figure 19-135).

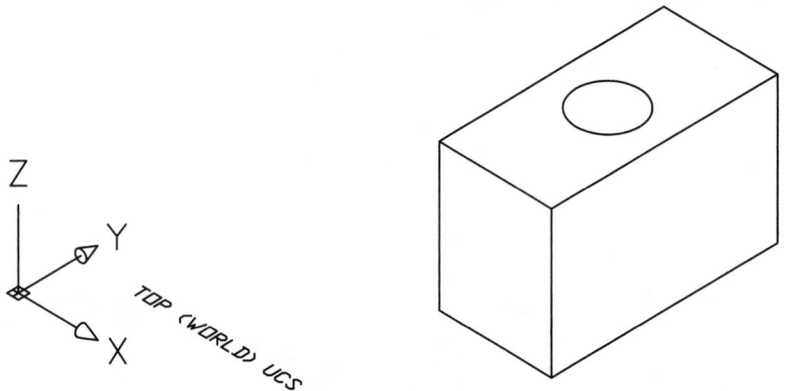

Figure 19-135   The **SE Isometric** view of the 3D model

11. Select the **Right** UCS.

12. Invoke the **PASTECLIP** command through the drop-down menu: **Edit/Paste**. When prompted for the insertion point, enter **0,0,0.**

13. Double-click the text to open the simplified text editor (**DDEDIT**) and edit it to read **RIGHT UCS** (Figure 19-136). Press **<Enter ↵>** twice to exit the **DDEDIT** command.

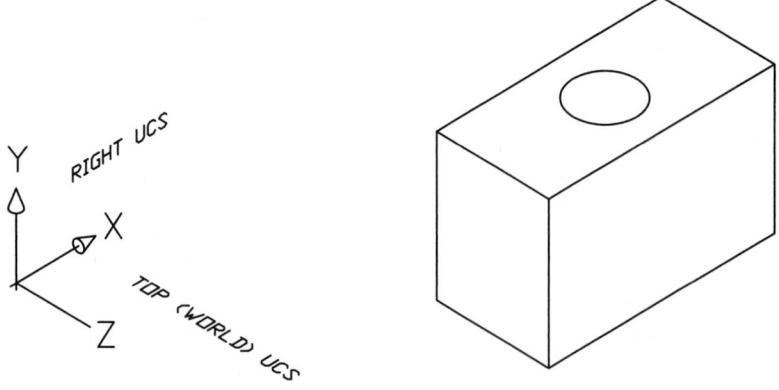

Figure 19-136   New text placed in the Right UCS

14. Rotate the UCS **20°** about the *Y*-axis, using the icon on the UCS toolbar.

15. Double-click the text and edit it to read **RIGHT UCS, 20 ABOUT Y** (Figure 19-137).

16. Select the **Right** UCS again.

17. Rotate the UCS **−20°** about the *Y*-axis.

18. Invoke the **PASTECLIP** command, and enter **0,0,0** for the insertion point.
19. Double-click the text and edit it to read **RIGHT UCS, -20 ABOUT Y** (Figure 19-138).

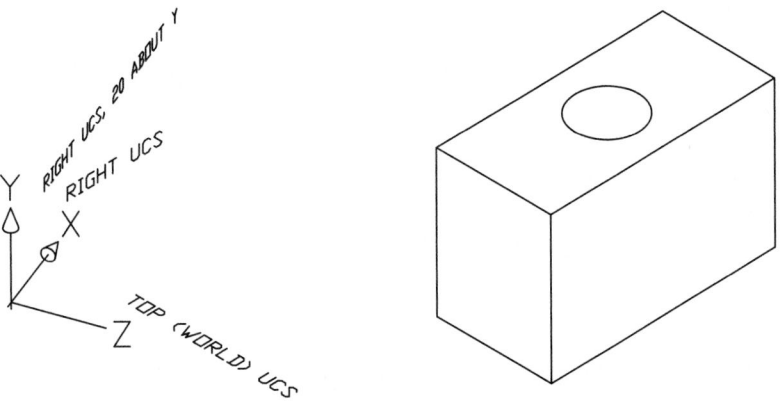

Figure 19-137   New text placed in a user-defined UCS, 20° about the Y-axis with respect to the previous UCS

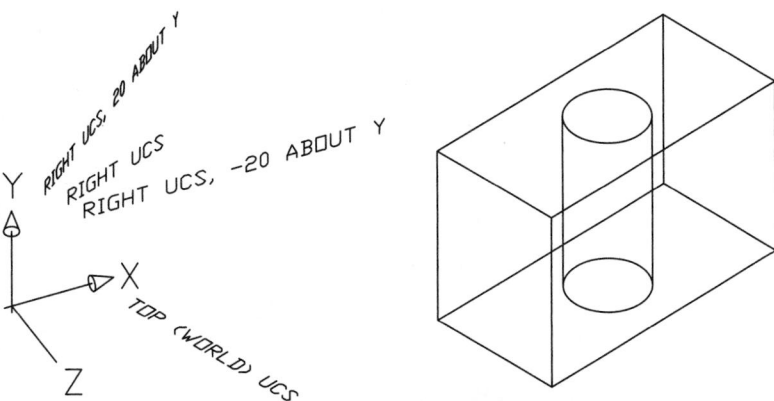

Figure 19-138   New text placed in a user-defined UCS, –20° about the Y-axis with respect to the previous UCS

20. Relocate the origin of the UCS, using the icon on the **UCS** toolbar. When prompted to specify the new origin point, snap on the endpoint of the 3D solid indicated in Figure 19-139.

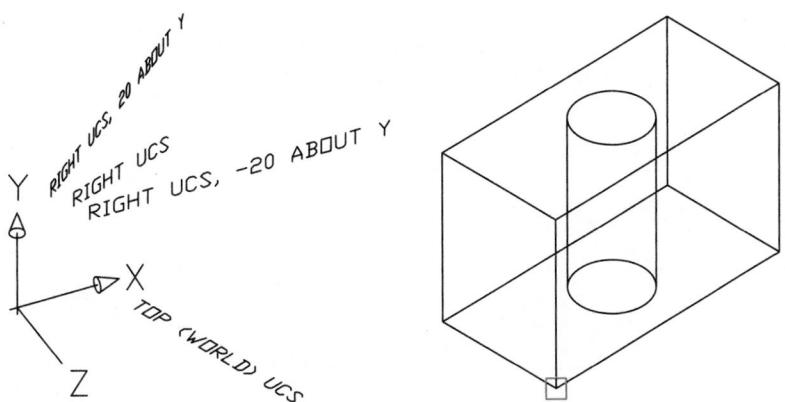

Figure 19-139   Specifying a point to relocate the origin of the UCS

21. Invoke the **PASTECLIP** command, and enter **0,0,0** for the insertion point.
22. Double-click the text and edit it to read **RIGHT UCS, −20 ABOUT Y, RELOCATED** (Figure 19-140).

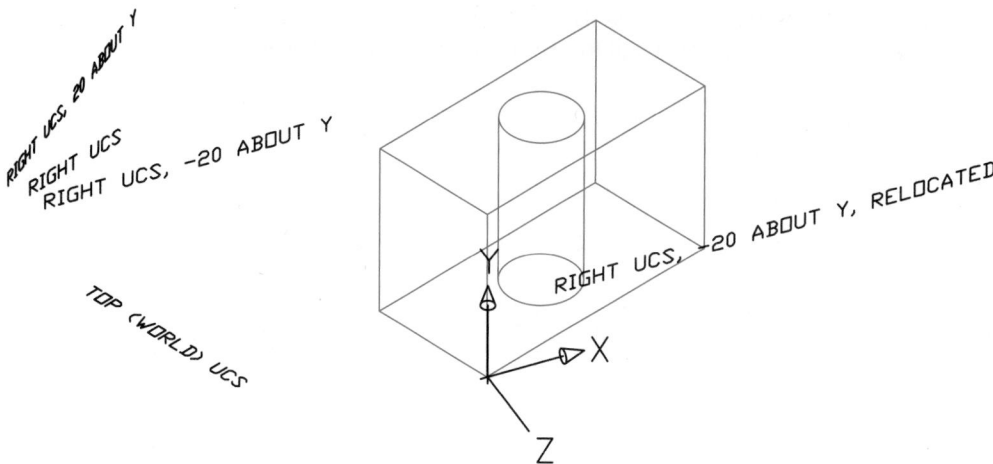

Figure 19-140   New text placed in a user-defined UCS, in a different location with respect to the previous UCS

23. Define the next orientation of the UCS by specifying three points. Use the icon on the **UCS** toolbar. To specify the three points, snap to the 3D solid's points in the order indicated in Figure 19-141.

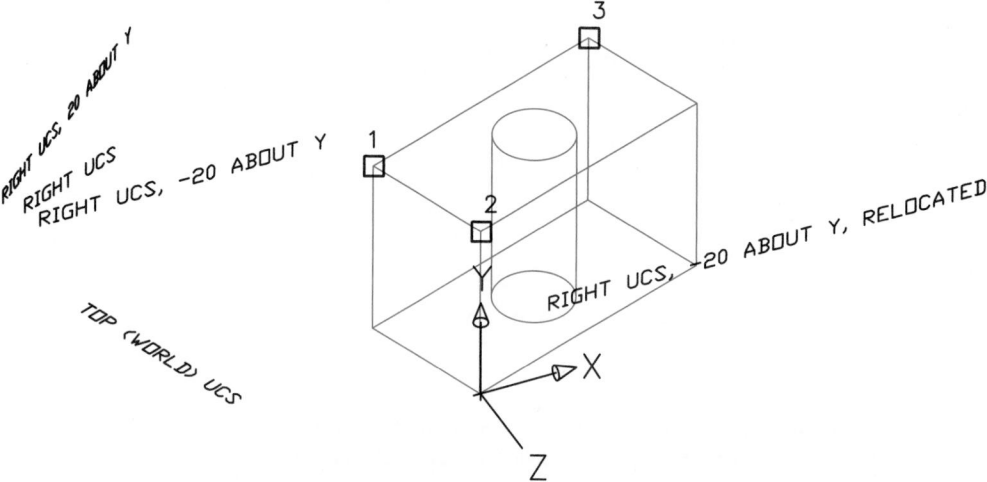

Figure 19-141   The three points used to specify the new user-defined UCS

24. Invoke the **PASTECLIP** command, and enter **0,0,0** for the insertion point.
25. Double-click the text and edit it to read **3 POINTS UCS (1)** (Figure 19-142).

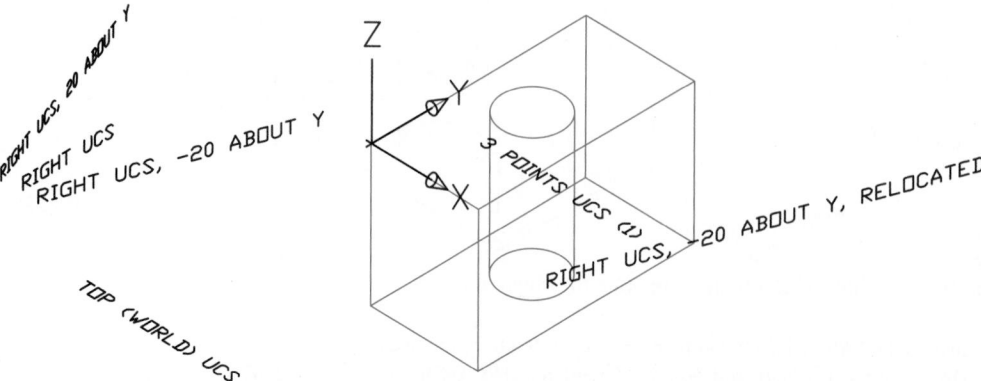

Figure 19-142   New text placed in the new user-defined UCS

26. Define the orientation of the UCS by specifying three points again. Use the icon on the **UCS** toolbar. Snap to the 3D solid's points in the order indicated in Figure 19-143.

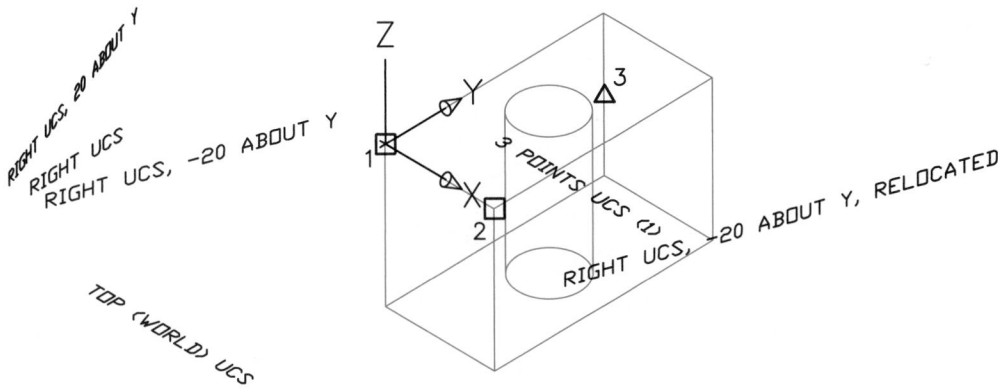

Figure 19-143   The three points used to specify the new user-defined UCS

27. Invoke the **PASTECLIP** command, and enter **0,0,0** for the insertion point.
28. Double-click the text and edit it to read **3 POINTS UCS (2)** (Figure 19-144).

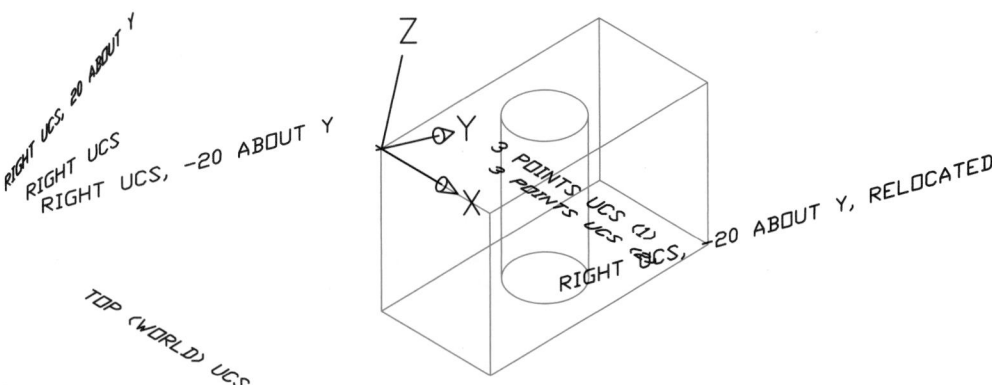

Figure 19-144   New text placed in the new user-defined UCS

29. Define the orientation of the UCS by selecting the face of a 3D solid. Use the corresponding icon on the **UCS** toolbar. When prompted to select the face of the 3D solid object, click as close as possible to the area indicated in Figure 19-145. Press **<Enter ↵>** to accept the selected face.

Note:
Selecting the face of the 3D solid in a particular area, when defining the UCS, is interpreted by the AutoCAD program in the following way:
• The closest corner locates the origin.
• The closest edge locates the X-axis.

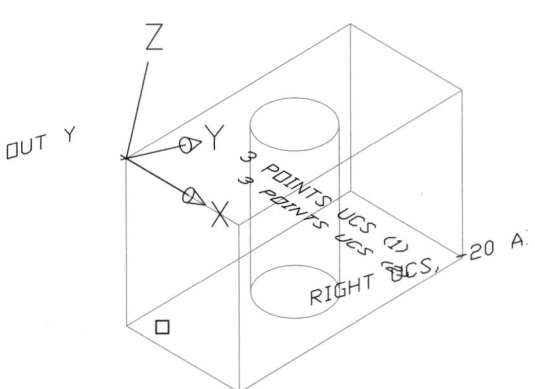

Figure 19-145   The selected face of the 3D solid used to define the new UCS

30. Invoke the **PASTECLIP** command, and enter 0,0,0 for the insertion point.
31. Double-click the text and edit it to read **FACE UCS** (Figure 19-146).

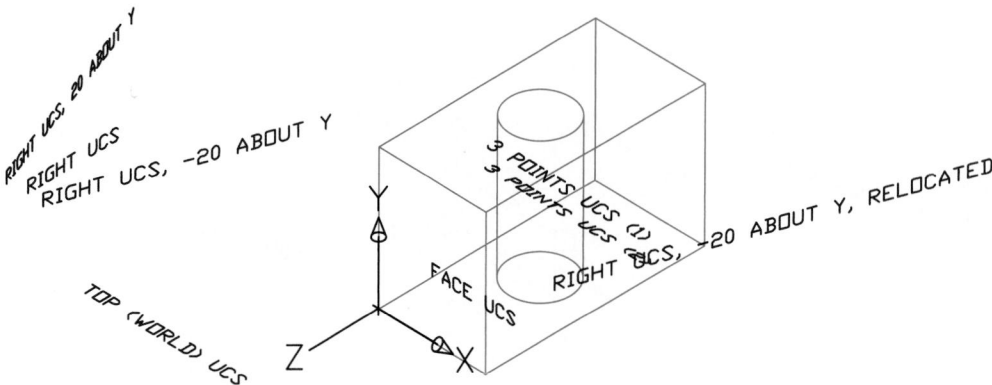

Figure 19-146   New text placed in the new user-defined UCS

32. Define the orientation of the UCS by specifying a **Z axis Vector**, using the corresponding icon on the **UCS** toolbar. To specify the new origin point and a point on the positive portion of the Z-axis, snap to the 3D solid's points in the order indicated in Figure 19-147.

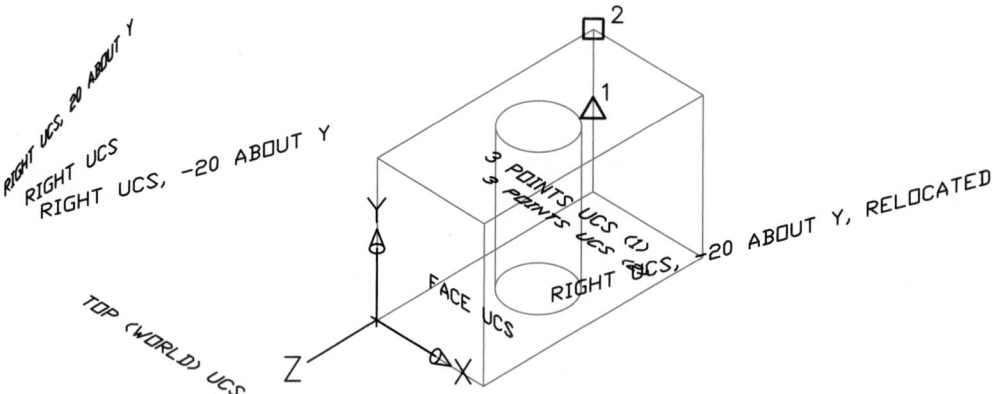

Figure 19-147   Points used to define a new UCS using the **Z Axis Vector** option

33. Invoke the **PASTECLIP** command, and enter **0,0,0** for the insertion point.
34. Double-click the text and edit it to read **Z-AXIS UCS** (Figure 19-148).
35. Relocate the origin of the UCS. When prompted to specify the new origin point, snap to the center point on the top circular edge of the 3D solid.
36. Relocate the UCS again to align it with the current view. Use the corresponding icon on the **UCS** toolbar.

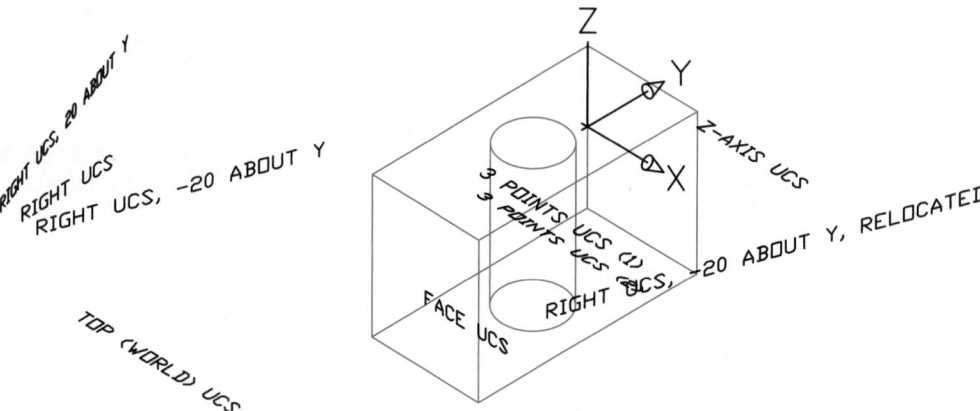

Figure 19-148   New text placed in the new user-defined UCS

37. Invoke the **PASTECLIP** command, and enter **0,0,0** for the insertion point.
38. Double-click the text and edit it to read **VIEW UCS** (Figure 19-149).

> **Note:**
> When the UCS is aligned with the current viewing plane, the Z-axis letter disappears, indicating that this axis is perpendicular to the display at this moment.

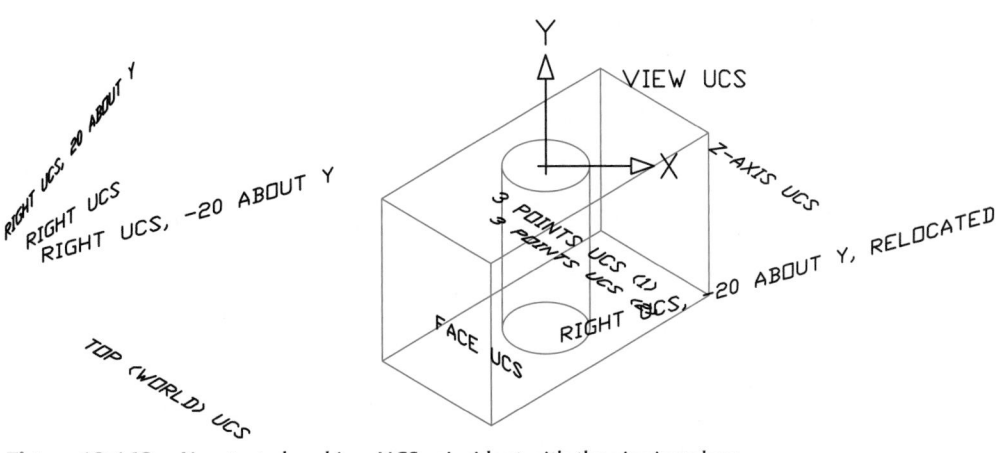

Figure 19-149   New text placed in a UCS coincident with the viewing plane

> **Note:**
> AutoCAD stores and allows you to go back to the last ten UCSs you defined.

39. Relocate the UCS by selecting the **Previous** one. Use the corresponding icon on the **UCS** toolbar.
40. Repeat the **Previous** operation until the UCS no longer changes.
41. Relocate the UCS by selecting an **Object**. Use the corresponding icon on the **UCS** toolbar. When prompted to select the object, select any of the text objects you edited.
42. Repeat the **Object** operation for each of the text objects.
43. Invoke the **3DORBIT** command to explore in greater depth the alignments of the text objects and the planes that they define in the 3D space.
44. **SAVE** the drawing.

> **Note:**
> The AutoCAD program stores the information of the UCS when each object is created, allowing you to go back to its particular UCS. The origin of the UCS relocates on the insertion point of the text. What is more difficult to achieve is not precisely relocating the origin of the UCS, but aligning the UCS in the 3D space.

Quick-Start Tutorials: 3D 20

Chapter Objectives

- Create two real 3D modeling projects, starting them from scratch.
- Know the difference between representing 3D models with 3D solid objects and with surface-type objects.
- Become familiar with the commands and tools most frequently used to generate 3D models.
- Employ commands typically used for 2D design in a 3D environment.
- Strengthen the argument that working in 3D is not an isolated task, but rather the usage of advanced tools along with those commonly used in 2D.
- Observe the effects and capabilities of the tools used in modifications to the viewing point and other visual effects.

INTRODUCTION

These introductory tutorials will provide you with the opportunity to get a better idea about what 3D modeling is. Hands-on practice will help you better comprehend the further detailed explanation of these concepts.

Before you start the projects, make sure all the toolbars and dockable windows used in 3D modeling are available. You can do so by simply recalling the workspace you created in the previous chapter.

MODELING THE SOFA TABLE

In this part of the project you will create 3D solid objects to represent the 3D model. As you will see, the same commands you use to generate 2D drawings are also used in a 3D environment.

Many assembling details, such as the connections between the pieces of the sofa table, have been omitted for simplicity. If designing furniture is one of your areas of interest, then you may want to try adding some more details on your own.

1. Start a **NEW** drawing, using the **acad** template.
2. **SAVE** the drawing AS *SofaTable*.

TIP During the rest of the project, you will not be directed to **SAVE** the drawing. But it is important that you do so every few steps or when taking a break to prevent losing the work you have done. 3D operations typically demand more from a computer than 2D operations. This may cause your system to stop responding depending on its level of use and properties.

3. Open the **Visual Styles Manager** palette and click on the **2D Wireframe** sample image.

4. Under **2D Hide – Obscured Lines**, set the **Linetype** to **Dashed** and the **Color** to **Green** or any other color you like. Close the **Visual Styles Manager** palette.

5. Select the **SE Isometric** viewing point.

6. Invoke the **BOX** command using one of the methods in the grid. Respond to the prompts as follows:

   Specify first corner or [Center]: *Click anywhere in the drawing area.*

   Specify other corner or [Cube/Length]: *Move the mouse to open a rectangle and click anywhere in the drawing area.*

   Specify height or [2Point]: *Move the mouse up and click anywhere in the drawing area.*

7. Select the **3D Solid** box and right-click in the drawing area. Select **Properties** from the shortcut menu.

8. In the **Properties** palette, under **Geometry**, change the values of the following elements as shown:

   * Position X=12
   * Position Y=12
   * Length=24
   * Width=24
   * Height=1

9. **ZOOM** to extents and invoke the **HIDE** command. The 3D model should look now like Figure 20-2.

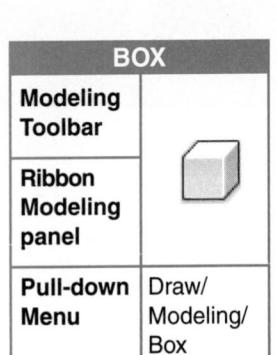

BOX	
Modeling Toolbar	
Ribbon Modeling panel	
Pull-down Menu	Draw/ Modeling/ Box
Command Line	box

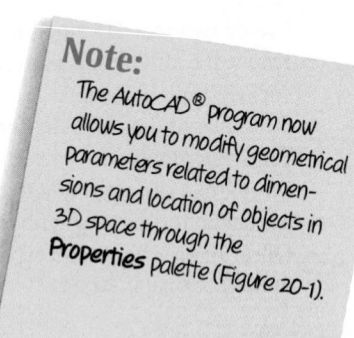

Note: The 3D solid box is interactively created as you specify the points.

Note: The AutoCAD® program now allows you to modify geometrical parameters related to dimensions and location of objects in 3D space through the **Properties** palette (Figure 20-1).

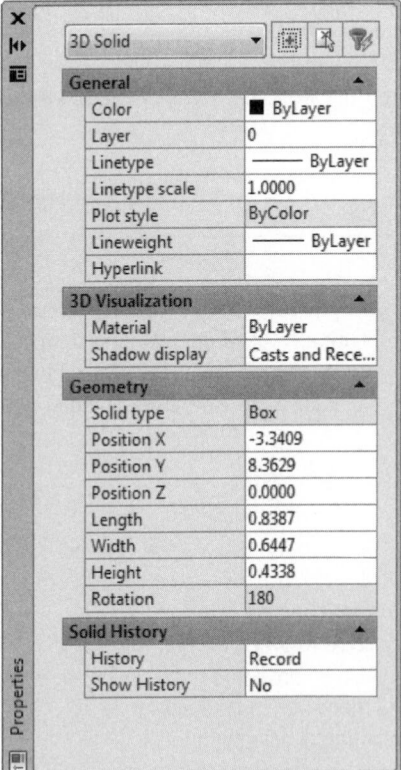

Figure 20-1   Using the **Properties** palette to modify the 3D solid box

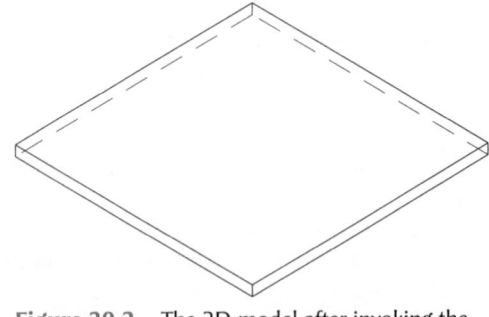

Figure 20-2   The 3D model after invoking the **HIDE** command

10. Using the **RECTANGLE** command, draw a square as shown in Figure 20-3. When prompted for the first corner, snap to the top endpoint of the tabletop and enter **@8,8** for the second corner.

11. **MOVE** the square away from the tabletop corner, as shown in Figure 20-4.

Figure 20-3   An 8 × 8 square is placed on the top face   **Figure 20-4**   The square is moved to the proper place

12. Select the **Top** view.

13. Using the **MIRROR** command, obtain the other three squares shown in Figure 20-5.

14. Select the **SE Isometric** viewing point. Invoke the **EXTRUDE** command and respond to the prompts as follows:

    Select objects to extrude: *Select the four squares.*

    Select objects to extrude: ↵ *(To end the selection process)*

    Specify height of extrusion or [Direction/Path/Taper angle]: *-6* ↵
    (The minus sign causes the extrusion to be made downward.)

15. The 3D model should look like Figure 20-6. Invoke the **SUBTRACT** command, and respond to the prompts as follows:

    Select solids and regions to subtract from ..

    Select objects: *Select the tabletop.*

    Select objects: ↵ *(To end the selection)*

    Select solids and regions to subtract ..

    Select objects: *Select the four new solid blocks.*

    Select objects: ↵ *(To end the selection)*

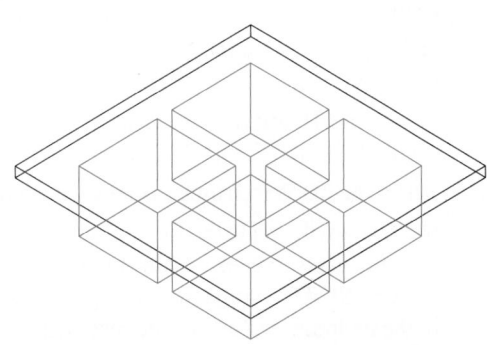

Figure 20-5   The other three squares are created   **Figure 20-6**   The four squares are extruded downward

16. Select the **Realistic** visual style. The 3D model now should look like Figure 20-7.

17. Select the **2D Wireframe** visual style.

18. Make sure either the **Top** or the **World** UCS is shown as current. Otherwise, select one of them.

19. With the **RECTANGLE** command, draw the square highlighted in Figure 20-8, using the endpoints for the square hole on the board. Using a different color will help you visualize the new object.

Figure 20-7 The four holes are created by subtracting the four 3D solids from the board

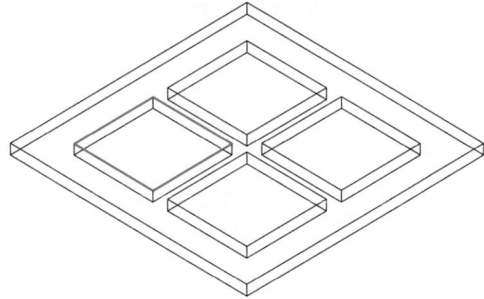

Figure 20-8 A new square using the geometry originated

20. **OFFSET** the square **3/8″** outward. **ERASE** the original rectangle (Figure 20-9).

21. **EXTRUDE** the new rectangle **–1/4″** (down).

22. **COPY** the new 3D solid from any endpoint on the square hole where it is located to the same point in the rest of the holes (Figure 20-10).

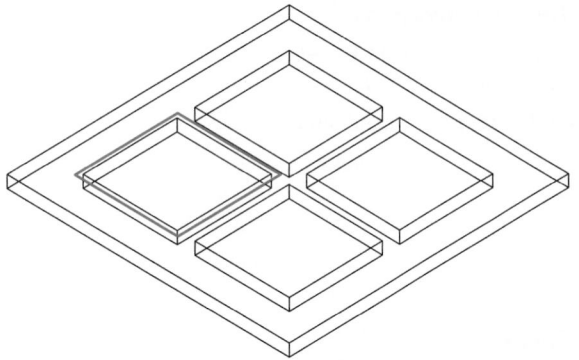

Figure 20-9 The offset square

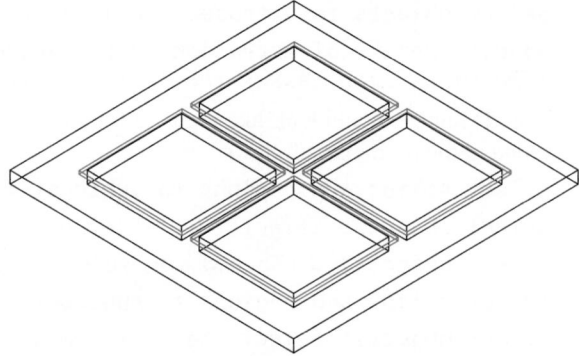

Figure 20-10 The four thin 3D solids are placed in the right locations

PLANESURF	
Modeling Toolbar	
Ribbon Modeling panel	
Pull-down Menu	Draw/ Modeling/ Planesurf
Command Line	planesurf

23. **SUBTRACT** the four new 3D solids from the tabletop to create a recessed surface where the glass pieces will sit.

24. Select the **Realistic** visual style. The 3D model should look like Figure 20-11.

25. Select the **2D Wireframe** visual style again.

26. Next, you will create the four 3D solids representing the glass pieces of the table. Invoke the **PLANESURF** command. When prompted, snap to the endpoints of one of the recessed holes on the board (Figure 20-12).

Note:
If you used 3D solids with different colors for the **SUBTRACT** operation, the resulting 3D faces of the solid will show both colors. By changing the color property of the resulting 3D solid, you can give it a uniform color.

Figure 20-11   The four recesses are created by subtracting the four thin 3D solids

Figure 20-12   A surface is created with the **PLANESURF** command

27. Invoke the **THICKEN** command. When prompted, select the surface and specify **–1/4″** for the thickness. The 3D model should look like Figure 20-13.

28. **COPY** the first 3D solid representing the piece of glass from any point on the square hole to the same point in the rest of the holes.

29. Open the **Layer Properties Manager** dialog box and create a new layer. Name it **Glass** and change its color to **cyan (4)** (Figure 20-14).

30. Select the four glass pieces and change their layer to **Glass**.

Note:
The **THICKEN** command transforms surfaces into 3D solids, by uniformly thickening them.

THICKEN	
Ribbon Solid Editing panel	
Pull-down Menu	Modify/ 3D Operation/ Thicken
Command Line	thicken

Figure 20-13   The surface is turned into a 3D solid using the **THICKEN** command

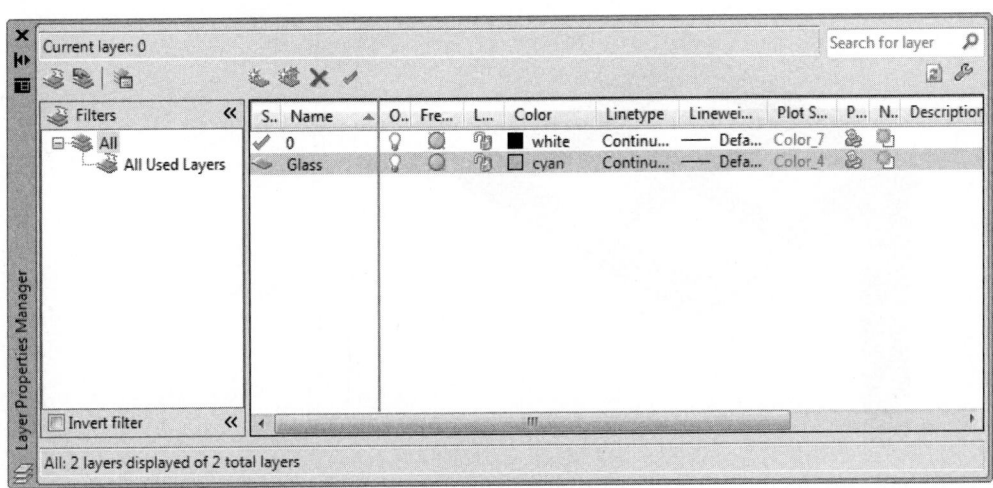

Figure 20-14   The **Layer Properties Manager** dialog box

31. Invoke the **HIDE** command. The 3D model should look now like Figure 20-15.

32. Turn the **Glass** layer OFF to hide all 3D solids representing the pieces of glass.

33. Invoke the **REGEN** command.

34. Next, you will create the table legs. Using the **RECTANGLE** command, draw a 2½ × 2½ rectangle anywhere in the drawing area. **MOVE** the rectangle to the endpoint of the rectangular hole, as shown in Figure 20-16.

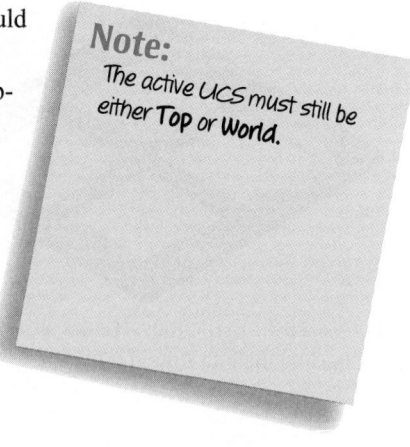

Note: The active UCS must still be either **Top** or **World**.

Figure 20-15   After invoking the **HIDE** command

Figure 20-16   A 3 × 3 square in the bottom face

35. **EXTRUDE** the rectangle **–22″** (down).

36. Select the **Realistic** visual style. The 3D model should look like Figure 20-17.

37. Select the **2D Wireframe** visual style.

38. Using the **3DORBIT** command, slightly change the viewing point to have a clearer picture. **ZOOM** into the bottom part of the leg.

39. Draw the polyline shown in Figure 20-18.

Figure 20-17   The extruded leg displayed in the **Realistic** visual style

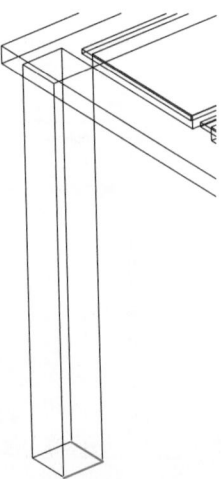

Figure 20-18   The polyline is created at the bottom of the leg

40. Select the **Front** UCS.

41. **MOVE** the polyline up **7″** (Figure 20-19).

42. Invoke the **IMPRINT** tool, and respond to the prompts as follows:

    Select a 3D solid: *Select the table leg 3D solid.*

    Select an object to imprint: *Select the polyline.*

    Delete the source object [Yes/No] <N>: *y ↵*

    Select an object to imprint: *↵ (To end the selection and end the command)*

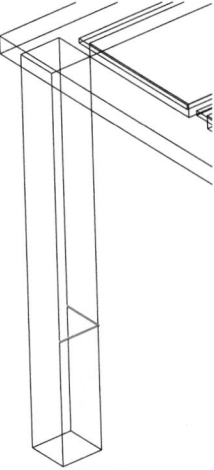

> **Note:**
> When you extrude a single profile, the extrusion height is interactively displayed as you move the crosshair cursor. This allows you to simply specify a distance or another point for the extrusion height.

Figure 20-19 The polyline is moved up

43. Invoke the **Taper faces** tool of the **SOLIDEDIT** Command. Use Figure 20-20 as a reference and respond to the prompts as follows:

    Select faces or [Undo/Remove]: *Pick edge 1.*

    Select faces or [Undo/Remove/ALL]: *↵ (To end the selection)*

    Specify the base point: *Snap to endpoint 2.*

    Specify another point along the axis of tapering: *Snap to endpoint 3.*

    Specify the taper angle: *7 ↵*

    Enter a face editing option

    [Extrude/Move/Rotate/Offset/Taper/Delete/Copy/coLor/Undo/eXit] <eXit>: *Press the <Esc> key to exit the SOLIDEDIT command.*

44. After the operation, the lower end of the leg should look like Figure 20-21. Invoke the **MIRROR3D** command to obtain the second leg. Respond to the prompts as follows:

    Select objects: *Select the table leg 3D solid.*

    Select objects: *↵ (To end the selection)*

IMPRINT	
Solid Editing Toolbar	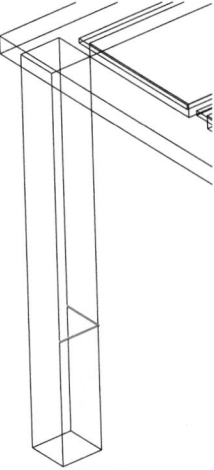
Ribbon Solid Editing panel	
Pull-down Menu	Modify/ Solid Editing/ Imprint
Command Line	imprint

TAPER FACES	
Solid Editing Toolbar	
Ribbon Solid Editing panel	
Pull-down Menu	Modify/ Solid Editing/Taper Faces
Command Line	solidedit ↵ f ↵ t

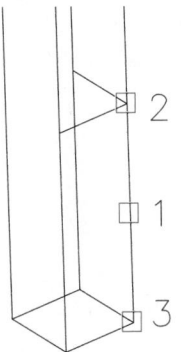

Figure 20-20 Points are specified for the **Taper faces** operation

Figure 20-21 The split faces after tapering

Specify first point of mirror plane (3 points) or [Object/Last/Zaxis/View/XY/YZ/ZX/3points] <3points>: *Specify any of the midpoints indicated* in Figure 20-22.

Specify second point on mirror plane: *Specify another midpoint indicated.*

Specify third point on mirror plane: *Specify a third midpoint indicated.*

Delete source objects? [Yes/No] <N>: *↵ (To keep the source object)*

45. The 3D model should look like Figure 20-23. Invoke the **MIRROR3D** command again and repeat the process of the previous step to obtain the two remaining legs. This time, the three midpoints must be specified perpendicularly to the ones specified previously.

Figure 20-22   Points specified in the **MIRROR3D** command

Figure 20-23   The second leg is mirrored

MIRROR3D	
Ribbon Modify panel	
Pull-down Menu	Modify/ 3D Opera- tion/3D Mirror
Command Line	3dmirror

46. Select the **Realistic** visual style. The 3D model should look like Figure 20-24.
47. Select the **Right** UCS. Then, using the **3D ORBIT** command, change the viewing point so that you can see the bottom face of the table top (Figure 20-25).

Figure 20-24   After obtaining the four legs

Figure 20-25   After changing the viewing point

48. Select the **2D Wireframe** visual style.
49. Draw a **1 × 3** rectangle anywhere in the drawing area.
50. Select the **3D Hidden** visual style and **MOVE** the rectangle to the endpoint of the leg, as shown in Figure 20-26.
51. Invoke the **EXTRUDE** command, and respond to the prompts as follows:

    Select objects: *Select the table rectangle.*

    Select objects: ↵ *(To end the selection)*

    Specify height of extrusion or [Direction/Path/Taper angle]: *Snap to the endpoint indicated* in Figure 20-27.

52. Turn off the **Linetype** generation of the **Obscured Lines**.

Figure 20-26   The **1 × 3** rectangle in the correct place

Figure 20-27   Point to indicate the height of extrusion

FOR MORE DETAILS   Refer to steps 3 and 4 for more details about changing this setting.

53. Select the **2D Wireframe** visual style and invoke the **HIDE** command. The first reinforcement 3D solid should look like Figure 20-28.

54. Select the **Top** view.

55. Draw a diagonal polyline, snapping to endpoints, as shown in Figure 20-29.

Figure 20-28   After invoking the **HIDE** command

Figure 20-29   A diagonal polyline to locate the center point of the table

56. Invoke the **ARRAY** command. In the **Array** dialog box (Figure 20-30), select **Polar Array**. Click the **Select objects** button to select the reinforcement 3D solid. Click the **Center point**: button and snap to the midpoint of the polyline you just drew. Click the **OK** button to close the dialog box.

57. **ERASE** the diagonal polyline.

58. Select the **SE Isometric** viewing point.

59. Select the **Realistic** visual style. The model should look like Figure 20-31.

60. Select the **2D Wireframe** visual style.

61. Select the **Bottom** view.

62. Invoke the **HIDE** command.

Figure 20-30   The **Array** dialog box

Figure 20-31   The resulting reinforcements after the **ARRAY** operation

63. Invoke the **PLINE** command. With **ORTHO** activated, draw the polyline highlighted in Figure 20-32. You should snap only to endpoints. Try using a different color to distinguish the object better.

64. Select the **SE Isometric** viewing point.

65. Select the **Front** UCS.

66. If necessary, **MOVE** the polyline to where the straight section of the legs begins. Use end-points to snap to (Figure 20-33).

67. **EXTRUDE** the polyline **1″** up.

Figure 20-32   A profile created from the Top view

Figure 20-33   The profile is moved to its final location

68. Turn on the **Glass** layer.

69. Select the **Conceptual** visual style.

70. In the **Visual Style** panel of the Ribbon, click on the **Edge jitter** button and move the slide bar to the third position from left to right (Figure 20-34).

71. Invoke the **3DORBIT** command to inspect the 3D model of the sofa table. It should look like Figure 20-35.

72. **SAVE** the drawing.

Figure 20-34   The **Edge Jitter** control on the **Edge Effects** panels of the Ribbon

Figure 20-35   The 3D model shown in a modified **Conceptual** visual style

The 3D models created with the AutoCAD program have many uses. As demonstrated in this tutorial, this versatile program can create 3D models of objects for interior design and space planning projects. The 3D representation of objects can provide different levels of complexity. Unlike 3D models prepared for manufacturing processes according to a company's specifications and standards, the construction of 3D models used for other purposes, such as interior design and space planning, can be simplified. Recognizing the procedures and techniques that enable the development of different levels of complexity of 3D models and systems is an important skill for the workplace. Organizations recognize this skill as efficiency and productiveness.

MODELING THE LAMP

In this tutorial, you will use surfaces, faceted surfaces, and regions jointly to create a 3D model of a lamp. As in the previous tutorial, many details have been avoided. As a general rule, you can create different levels of detail according to the purpose of the 3D model.

1. Start a **NEW** drawing, using the **acad** template.

2. **SAVE** the drawing **AS** *TableLamp*.

3. Set the **VIEWRES** system variable to **3000**. When prompted about fast zooms, respond **Yes** by pressing **<Enter>**.

4. Set the **DISPSILH** system variable to **1**.

5. By default, the **Top** view and the **WCS** should be current. Do not change these settings yet.

6. You will start by creating the lamp base. To do so, first draw the profile shown in Figure 20-36. The next few steps will assist you in creating the polyline that will be used as the profile.

TIP   When using the **Tan tan radius** option of the **CIRCLE** command, try to select the circles in a location close to where the tangent point will be, so you prevent AutoCAD from finding a second solution.

Figure 20-36   The lamp base profile

7. Start the curve or wire by drawing the objects shown in Figure 20-37. Draw all the objects without worrying about positioning or dimensioning them. You will use **Geometric Constraining** in the next step to do so.

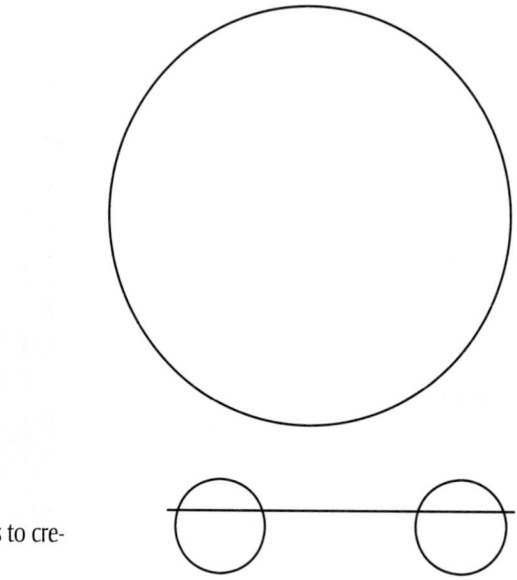

Figure 20-37 Instructions to create the profile

8. Select the **Equal:** constraint from the **Geometric** panel in the Ribbon, located in the **Parametric** tab. When prompted, select the two small circles.

 TIP When applying constraints, it is important to do it in a particular order so that the object that gets modified is the one you intend to modify.

9. Apply all the dimensions shown in Figure 20-38 using the **DIMCONSTRAINT** command; click on the **Linear** and **Diameter** button on the **Dimensional** panel to activate the command.

Figure 20-38 The diameter of one of the small circles is modified with the **Equal** parametric constraint

TIP   You can easily change the size of objects by changing the parametric dimensions when the dimension is placed or through the **Properties** palette. See Figure 20-39.

Figure 20-39   Parametric dimensions can be modified in the **Properties** palette

10. Apply the **Concentric** geometric constraint between the big circle and one of the small circles. Repeat the process between the big circle and the other small circle. The constrained geometry should look like the illustration in Figure 20-40.

Figure 20-40   The two small circles are made tangent to the big circle by applying the **Tangent** parametric constraint

11. **TRIM** the existing objects as necessary. Add the other highlighted objects as shown in Figure 20-41.

12. Perform the final **TRIM** operations without appling any constraints. Add an extra line as shown in Figure 20-42. Align its endpoints horizontally with the endpoints of the first and last objects.

Figure 20-41   Instructions to create the profile, continued

Figure 20-42   Placing the lamp base axis

13. Invoke the **PEDIT** command in order to join all the continuously drawn objects into a single polyline. Respond to the prompts as follows:

PEDIT	
Modify II Toolbar	
Ribbon Modify panel	
Pull-down Menu	Modify/ Object/ Polyline
Command Line	pedit
Alias	pe

Select polyline or [Multiple]: *Select any of the objects.*

Object selected is not a polyline

Do you want to turn it into one? <Y> ↵ *(To turn the selected object into a polyline)*

Enter an option [Close/Join/Width/Edit vertex/Fit/Spline/Decurve/Ltype gen/Undo]: *j* ↵

Select objects: *Using a selection window, select all the objects.*

Select objects: ↵ *(To end the selection)*

Enter an option [Close/Join/Width/Edit vertex/Fit/Spline/Decurve/Ltype gen/Undo]: ↵ *(To exit the command)*

Note:
Two or more wire-type objects can be joined as a single polyline object. As a requirement, all objects must lie in the same plane and the endpoints of two continuous objects must be located in the same place.

TIP You can check whether all the objects were joined by simply hovering the cursor above the polyline, or by selecting it.

14. Select the two objects by picking them directly. With the objects selected, invoke the **CUTCLIP** command to move them to the clipboard.

15. Select the **Front** view.

16. Invoke the **PASTECLIP** command. When prompted to specify the insertion point, click anywhere in the drawing area.

17. Select the **SE Isometric** viewing point and zoom as needed.

18. Select the **Top** UCS, and draw the two circles shown in Figure 20-43. Snap to the endpoints of the objects to specify the center and radius of both circles.

19. Invoke the **REGION** command. When prompted, select the two circles. This operation will turn the circles into regions.

20. Invoke the **REVOLVE** command. Respond to the command prompts as follows:

    Select object to revolve: *Select the polyline.*

    Select object to revolve: ↵ *(To end the selection)*

    Specify axis start point or define axis by [Object/X/Y/Z] <Object>: *o* ↵

    Select an object: *Select the line.*

    Specify angle of revolution or [STart angle] <360>: ↵ *(To accept the default angle)*

21. **ERASE** the line.

22. Set the **FACETRES** system variable to **8** to enhance the visual effects.

23. Invoke the **HIDE** command. The 3D model should look like Figure 20-44.

24. Invoke the **REGEN** command.

25. With the **Top** UCS still active, invoke the **CYLINDER** command. When prompted, specify the center point of the base in the center point of the top circular region. Specify **0.5** for the radius and **3** for the height (Figure 20-45).

26. Now you will create the 3D model of the lightbulb as a polygon mesh. Select the **Front** UCS and draw the three objects shown in Figure 20-46.

27. Invoke the **PEDIT** and join the arc with the small line as a single polyline.

28. Set the **SURFTAB1** and **SURFTAB2** system variables to **15**. To access these settings, enter their names in the command line.

29. Invoke the **REVSURF** command and create a revolved faceted surface. Respond to the prompts as follows:

    Select object to revolve: *Select the polyline.*

    Select object that defines the axis of revolution: *Select the line.*

    Specify start angle <0>: ↵ *(To accept the default)*

    Specify included angle (+=ccw, -=cw) <360>: ↵ *(To accept the default)*

Note:
The **Front** UCS should activate itself at the moment you select the Front view.

Note:
The objects inserted from the clipboard were simply moved from the **Top** plane to the **Front** plane, where the *XY* plane or the current UCS now lies. Cutting and pasting objects from one plane to another is equivalent to rotating the objects in the 3D space.

Note:
The open profile is revolved, becoming a true surface.

Figure 20-43   The top and bottom circles are drawn in place

REGION	
Draw Toolbar	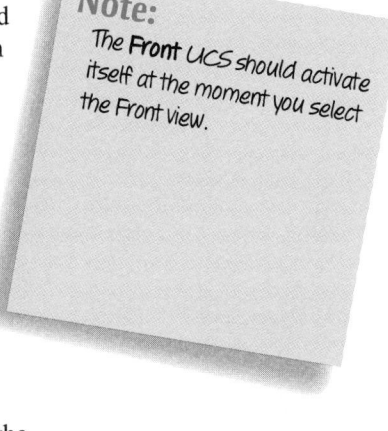
Ribbon Draw panel	
Pull-down Menu	Draw/ Region
Command Line	region

REVOLVE	
Modeling Toolbar	
Ribbon 3D Model- ing panel	
Pull-down Menu	Draw/ Modeling/ Revolve
Command Line	revolve
Alias	rev

Figure 20-44 The lamp base surface is generated with the **REVOLVE** command

Figure 20-45 A 3D solid cylinder is placed on top of the lamp base

Figure 20-46 Draw the three objects shown

Figure 20-47 After invoking the **HIDE** command

30. **ERASE** the polyline and the line. The result, after invoking the **HIDE** command, is shown in Figure 20-47.

31. Select the **Front** view and draw the two highlighted objects in an empty spot, as shown in Figure 20-48.

32. Select the **SE Isometric** viewing point.

33. **MOVE** the objects so that the lower endpoint of the line is placed at the bottom center point of the cylinder (Figure 20-49).

CYLINDER	
Modeling Toolbar	
Ribbon 3D Modeling panel	
Pull-down Menu	Draw/ Modeling/ Cylinder
Command Line	cylinder
Alias	cyl

REVSURF	
Ribbon 3D Modeling panel	
Pull-down Menu	Draw/ Modeling/ Meshes/ Revolved Mesh
Command Line	revsurf

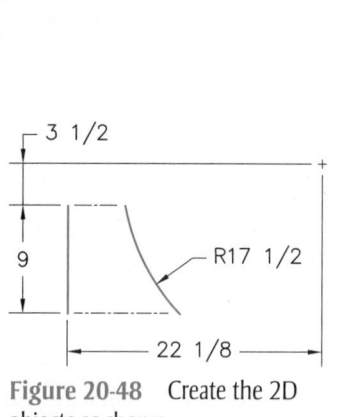

Figure 20-48 Create the 2D objects as shown

Figure 20-49 The 2D objects after they are moved to the proper location

34. Select the **World** UCS.

35. Select the arc and invoke the **ARRAY** command. In the **Array** dialog box (Figure 20-50), select **Polar Array**, click the **Center point**: button, and snap to the top endpoint of the line. In the **Total number of items**: field, specify **8**. After clicking on the **OK** button, the array should look like Figure 20-51.

36. Invoke the **3DORBIT** command to slightly change the viewing point.

37. Draw two lines between any two arcs as shown in Figure 20-52.

Figure 20-50   The **Array** dialog box

Figure 20-51   The arrayed copies of the arc

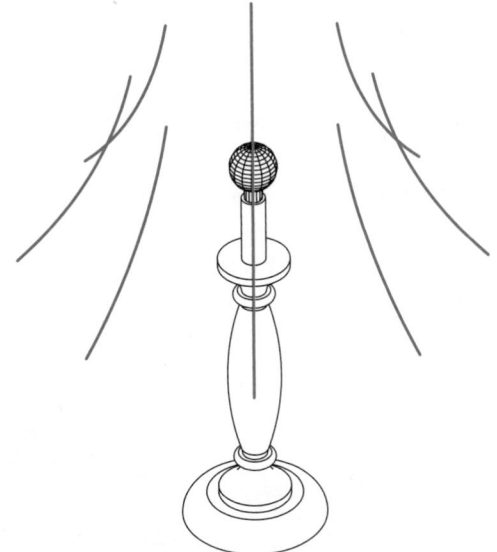

Figure 20-52   Draw the two lines shown

38. Change the values of the **SURFTAB1** and **SURFTAB2** system variables to **8**.

39. Invoke the **EDGESURF** command and, when prompted, select the two lines and the two arcs connecting them in any order.

40. Change the **Color** property of the polygon mesh you just created to any color you like.

41. Invoke the **DRAWORDER** command by entering its name in the command line and respond to the prompts as follows:

Select objects: *Select the polygon mesh.*

Select objects: ↵ *(To end the selection)*

Enter object ordering option [Above objects/Under objects/Front/Back] <Back>: ↵ *(To accept the default, which is sending it to the back)*

EDGESURF	
Ribbon 3D Modeling panel	
Pull-down Menu	Draw/ Modeling/ Meshes/ Edge Mesh
Command Line	edgesurf

TIP   Alternating the order in which overlapping objects are displayed facilitates the selection of the objects on top.

Figure 20-53 After erasing the lines and arcs

Figure 20-54 Modifying the edge display in the **Edge Effects** panel of the Ribbon

42. **ERASE** all the lines and arcs, except the vertical line in the middle of the lamp (Figure 20-53).

43. With the **World** or **Top** UCS still active, select the polygon mesh and invoke the **ARRAY** command. Use the same parameters as in the previous **ARRAY** operation. Use the endpoint of the vertical line in the middle to specify the **Center point:**.

44. **ERASE** the vertical line.

45. Change the **Color** property of the lamp base to color 42, the cylinder to color 251, and the lightbulb to yellow.

46. Select the **Realistic** visual style.

47. Invoke the **3DORBIT** command to inspect the 3D model from underneath.

48. Select **No edges** from the **Edges** flyout buttons located in the **Edge Effects** panel of the **Ribbon** (Figure 20-54).

49. Select **Desaturate Mode** from the **Face color mode** flyout buttons located in the same panel of the Ribbon (Figure 20-55).

50. The 3D model should look like Figure 20-56. **SAVE** the drawing.

Figure 20-55 Modifying the face display in the **Visual Style** panel of the Ribbon

Figure 20-56 A modified **Realistic** visual style to display the 3D model

CHAPTER SUMMARY

You have just walked though two different projects. In the first project, you were able to use operations related to the creation of 3D solid objects. In the second project, you mixed other types of objects used to generate 3D models. This project also allowed you to become familiar with parametric 2D modeling using geometric and dimensional constraints.

You should now have a better idea of what 3D modeling is about. Throughout the remaining chapters, you will find the answers to the many questions you might have gathered from these projects.

Wireframe Modeling

Chapter Objectives

- Learn to create and modify simple objects throughout the 3D space.
- Explore the behavior of common objects in the 3D environment.
- Learn the differences between modifying objects in 2D and 3D environments.
- Know other commands specifically used to modify objects in a 3D environment.
- Explore in depth polylines, 3D polylines, splines, and helixes.
- Learn to create 3D models represented as wireframes.
- Know the uses of 3D wireframes.
- Learn about editing with grips and using the grip tools.
- Use the wireframe modeling method in preparatory work to create more complex 3D models using other objects.

INTRODUCTION

ABOUT WIREFRAMES

If as its name implies, a wireframe represents a 3D model by placing its edges, or *wires,* in the 3D space using the most common AutoCAD® objects (lines, arcs, circles, ellipses, polylines, 3D polylines, splines, and helixes). To create a wireframe, you simply invoke the same commands used in 2D work to create and modify the objects. The difference between this type of work and 2D drafting is that the objects are placed in the 3D space, which requires you to modify the UCS and use other techniques to properly place the objects.

Wireframe representation is the simplest type because there are no surfaces where the light rays can hit. Thus, no shading or hiding effect can be obtained from this type of 3D model. In most cases, however, constructing a wireframe object is not a simple task. Imagine how laborious it would be to find the intersecting curve between a cone and an inclined cylinder throughout the 3D space using only wires. With other types of objects, however, such as 3D solids, this curve can be obtained by simply making the cone and cylinder intersect each other.

In practice, there are very few applications in which representing a 3D model as a simple wireframe is the final goal. (A pipeline diagram is an example, where substituting the traditional isometric drawing for a 3D wire can lead to better results.) But despite the difficulty involved in using wires, placing wires is usually a necessary task prior to using the commands and tools needed to create meshes, surfaces, and 3D solid objects.

TYPES OF OBJECTS USED TO REPRESENT WIRES OR EDGES

Any wire or edge of an object that is being modeled can be classified into one of the following categories:

- Straight edges
- Planar curve
- *Nonplanar curve*

nonplanar curve: A curve placed throughout the 3D space that is not completely contained in a plane.

AutoCAD wireframe objects or curves can also be classified into two different groups according to their behavior:

- Curves that belong to a particular plane and can be placed only on a plane parallel to the *XY* plane of the current UCS:
  - Circle
  - Ellipse
  - Arc
  - Polyline
- Curves that do not belong to a particular plane and can be placed anywhere in the 3D space, regardless of the current UCS:
  - Line
  - 3D polyline
  - Spline

Straight edges are represented using lines and polylines. Wires that have the characteristics of planar curves can be represented by almost any type of objects. Wires that are nonplanar curves, however, can be represented only by splines, 3D polylines transformed into splines, and helixes.

When creating objects that belong to a particular plane, the first point defines the location of the imaginary plane parallel to the current *XY* plane to which the object belongs. In the case of polylines, including those created with the **RECTANGLE** and **POLYGON** commands, any subsequent point specified that is not contained in such a plane is perpendicularly projected onto it.

When you create a circle in the default mode, for example, the plane is defined when you specify the circle's center. If you specify the circle's radius by specifying a second point, Auto-CAD considers the radius to be the 3D distance from the center to the second point.

Despite certain peculiarities, you will use all these objects to create 3D models exactly the same way you use them to create 2D drawings.

MODIFYING OBJECTS IN 3D

USING STANDARD COMMANDS IN THE 3D ENVIRONMENT

The following commands used to modify the objects in a 2D environment have special particularities or considerations when used in a 3D environment.

OFFSET: Works only for planar objects. The parallel offset copies are created on the same *XY* plane that the objects belong to.

TRIM/EXTEND: If the cutting edge and the object to be trimmed are contained in the same plane, the command works as a 2D operation. If the cutting edge and the object to be trimmed are not contained in the same plane, you can control its result by changing the **Projection** option after selecting the cutting edge(s).

```
Current settings: Projection=UCS, Edge=None
Select cutting edges...
Select objects: Select the objects.
```

```
Select objects: ↵ (To end the selection)
Select object to trim or shift-select to extend or
[Fence/Crossing/Project/Edge/eRase/Undo]: p ↵
Enter a projection option [None/Ucs/View] <Ucs>: Enter an option. ↵
```

Ucs: When using this option, the objects are trimmed as if both the object and the cutting edge were projected onto the current *XY* plane. You can also visualize this operation as if the cutting edge were a surface perpendicular to the *XY* plane extending to infinity in both directions (Figure 21-1).

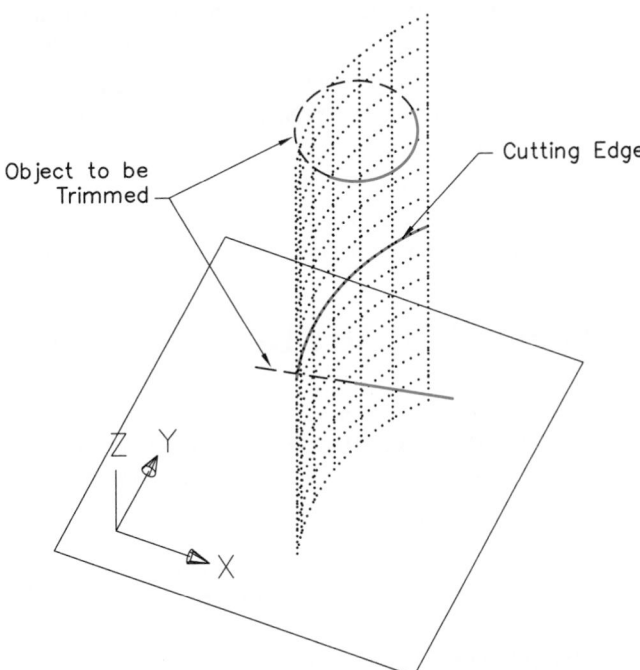

Object to be Trimmed

Cutting Edge

Figure 21-1   When the Projection option of the **TRIM/EXTEND** command is used, the objects interrelate as if placed on the same plane

None: With this option, you cannot trim any objects unless they really meet in the space. Because no projecting method is used, the current UCS does not affect the result.

View: Will project both the object and the cutting edge onto the viewing plane instead of the current *XY* plane.

Additionally, the **Edge** option can be changed to establish whether or not the cutting edge or the imaginary cutting surface resulting from its projection actually needs to intersect the object to be trimmed.

```
Select object to trim or shift-select to extend or [Fence/
Crossing/Project/Edge/eRase/Undo]: e ↵
Enter an implied edge extension mode [Extend/No extend] <No
extend>: Enter a choice. ↵
```

By choosing the **Extend** option, the cutting edge or the imaginary cutting surface will behave as if it were infinite.

MIRROR: Any object can be mirrored in the 3D space. When specifying the two points of the mirror line, however, AutoCAD accepts only points that belong to the *XY* plane of the current UCS. Specifying a point that is not contained in the *XY* plane causes the AutoCAD program to snap not to the point itself, but to its projection on the *XY* plane. It is always more comfortable to use this command in an orthogonal view, in which both the point and its projection appear to be the same.

SCALE: Its behavior is completely 3D. It will scale objects proportionally in all directions regardless of the current UCS.

STRETCH: For objects that can be drawn freely in the 3D space, you can stretch points freely as well. For objects that can be placed only on a plane parallel to the *XY* plane, the vertices can only be stretched, so they continue to pertain to the same plane.

FILLET and CHAMFER: Work only for objects that pertain to the same plane, regardless of the current UCS. By setting the radius value to **0**, in case of the **FILLET** command, you can make the two lines meet without generating an arc.

ROTATE: The 2D rotation of an object is produced around a point. This command, in a 3D environment, requires you to specify a point as well, but to better understand the rotation, you can think of that point as if it were an axis parallel to the *Z*-axis, so you do not necessarily have to specify a point on the current *XY* plane. The result of the rotation depends on the UCS you are currently using. The objects, however, can belong to any plane.

ARRAY: The arrayed copies of objects are generated relative to the *XY* plane of the UCS. You can, however, select objects that are placed in any plane.

COPY and MOVE: Any object can be freely moved or copied from any point to any other point, regardless of the current UCS.

Most of the standard commands used to modify objects work in a 2D way. Consequently, their results depend on the location of the working plane (the *XY* plane of the UCS).

COMMANDS SPECIALLY DESIGNED TO MODIFY OBJECTS IN 3D—

Another group of commands is used to modify objects in a 3D environment: **3DROTATE**, **ROTATE3D**, **3DMOVE**, **MIRROR3D**, **3DARRAY**, **3DALIGN**, and **ALIGN**. In general, these operations can be compared with 2D operations based on the following two rules:

- 2D rotations are made around a point, whereas 3D rotations are made around an axis.
- To create a 2D mirrored copy, you define a mirror line, whereas to create a 3D mirrored copy, you must define a mirror plane.

The 3DROTATE Command

imaginary axis of rotation: An imaginary vector defined by specifying two points, or a direction vector and a point, about which the objects are rotated.

rotate grip tool: Editing tool that enables you to choose among three directions of rotation that are aligned with the axes of the current UCS.

This command allows you to rotate the selected object about an ***imaginary axis of rotation*** that is parallel to one of the three axes of the current UCS (*X, Y,* and *Z*). The axis to which the imaginary axis of rotation is parallel is defined by picking one of the axis handles of the ***rotate grip tool***. The display switches to the **3D Wireframe** visual style while this command is in progress if the current visual style is **2D Wireframe** (Figure 21-2).

3DROTATE	
Modeling Toolbar	
Ribbon Modify panel	
Pull-down Menu	Modify/ 3D Operation/3D Rotate
Command Line	3drotate

Figure 21-2   The **3DROTATE** command in action

The command prompts are as follows:

Select objects: Specify opposite corner: *Select the objects.*

Select objects: ↵ *(To end the selection)*

Specify base point: *Specify a base point to locate the rotate grip tool.*

Pick a rotation axis: *Specify which of the three axes the objects will be rotated around. You do so by clicking on the axis handle of the rotate grip tool.*

Specify angle start point: *Enter the angle of rotation and end the command, or specify the angle start point.*

Specify angle endpoint: *Specify the angle endpoint (this prompt appears only if you specify the angle start point).*

TIP You can interactively view the rotation by specifying the angle start and end points by clicking in the drawing area. This is useful when you intend to approximate the alignment of an object.

The ROTATE3D Command

The **ROTATE3D** command allows you to rotate selected objects about an imaginary axis of rotation that can be defined anywhere in the 3D space by using different options, some of which depend on the UCS currently in use. Figure 21-3 shows the shortcut menu containing these options. The **ROTATE3D** command can be invoked only through the command line.

2points: Is the default option; by specifying a first point, you are prompted to specify the second one. The two points can be specified anywhere independently of the current UCS. The right-hand rule can be used to determine the positive direction of rotation, by knowing that the vector goes from the first point to the second one (Figure 21-4).

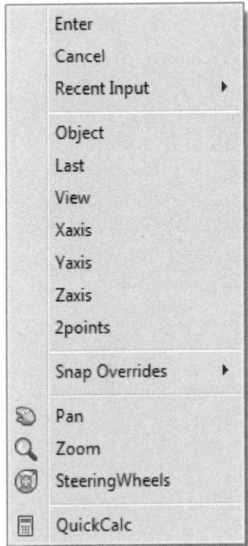

Figure 21-3 The **ROTATE3D** command's shortcut menu

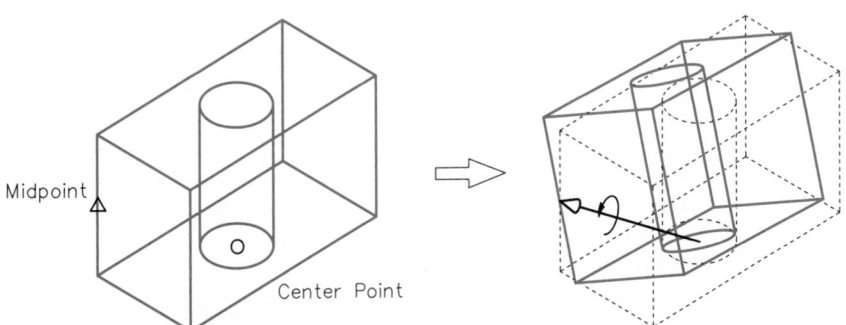

Figure 21-4 The imaginary axis of rotation defined with the **2points** option of the **ROTATE3D** command

Object: Allows you to select an object to define the imaginary axis of rotation; however, only lines, circles, arcs, and 2D polyline segments are valid selections. Lines and straight 2D polyline segments are used directly as the imaginary axis of rotation. Circles and arcs, on the other hand, define the imaginary axis of rotation perpendicular to the object's plane and through its center point.

View: The imaginary axis of rotation is defined normal to the viewing plane (monitor display) and through a point that you specify (Figure 21-5).

Xaxis/Yaxis/Zaxis: These options work similar to the **3DROTATE** command in that they define the imaginary axis of rotation parallel to one of the three major axes of the current UCS (*X, Y,* and *Z*), and a point that you specify. In Figure 21-6, the objects are rotated about the endpoint specified using the **Xaxis** option.

Last: In this option, the AutoCAD program uses the imaginary axis of rotation you defined in the previous operation.

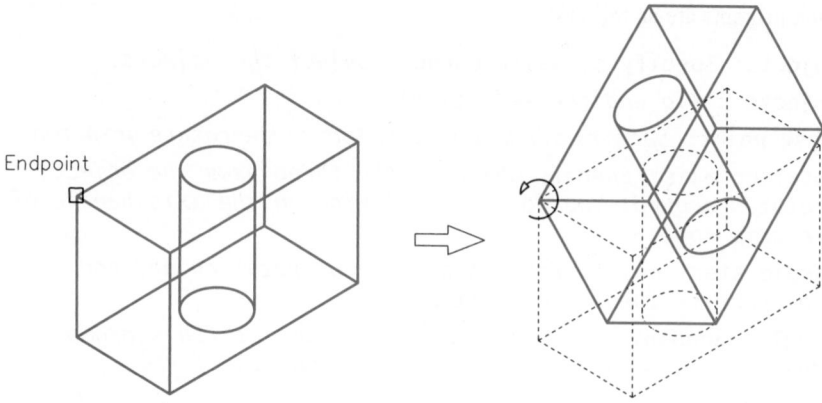

Figure 21-5   The imaginary axis of rotation defined with the **View** option of the **ROTATE3D** command

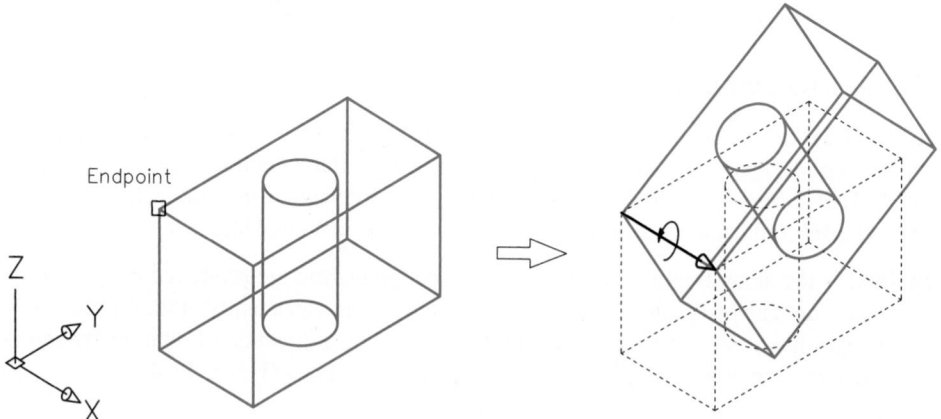

Figure 21-6   The imaginary axis of rotation of the **ROTATE3D** command defined parallel to the *X*-axis

Exercise 21-1: Using the **ROTATE3D** Command

To access student data files, go to www.pearsondesigncentral.com.

1. **OPEN** the drawing named *Exercise 21-00-A* in the student data files.
2. **SAVE** the drawing **AS** *Exercise 21-1*.
3. Invoke the **ROTATE3D** command by typing its name in the command line. Respond to the prompts as follows:

   Select objects: *Using a selection window, select all the objects.*

   Select objects: ↵ *(To end the selection)*

   Specify first point on axis or define axis by

   [Object/Last/View/Xaxis/Yaxis/Zaxis/ 2points]: *y* ↵

   Specify a point on the Y axis <0,0,0>: *-1,20,-1* ↵

   Specify rotation angle or [Reference]: *30* ↵

4. Your drawing should look like Figure 21-7. Invoke the **ROTATE3D** command again and respond to the prompts as follows:

   Select objects: *p* ↵ *(To use the previous selection)*

   Select objects: ↵ *(To end the selection)*

Note:
Because the imaginary axis is defined as an infinite axis parallel to the Y-axis, the Y coordinate of the point is not significant. Only the X and Z coordinates of the point define the imaginary axis.

Figure 21-7   The 3D model rotated 30° about an imaginary axis parallel to the *Y*-axis

```
Specify first point on axis or define axis by
[Object/Last/View/Xaxis/Yaxis/Zaxis/2points]: 1 ↵
Specify rotation angle or [Reference]: -30 ↵
```

5. This will take the model back to its original position. **SAVE** the drawing.

The 3DMOVE Command

This command allows you to move selected objects throughout the 3D space. By using the elements of the ***move grip tool***, you can change the movement behavior as follows:

Figure 21-8   The move grip tool

- Freely, when no element of the move grip tool is selected.
- Constrained along the direction of one of the axes of the current UCS. This direction is specified by clicking one of the three handles of the move grip tool (Figure 21-8).
- Constrained to a plane that is parallel to one of the three planes of the current UCS. You specify this behavior by clicking one of the squares on the move grip tool, which automatically selects two handles.

move grip tool: Editing tool that allows you to choose among six movements along one of the three axes or parallel to one of the three planes.

As with **3DROTATE**, the display switches to the **3D Wireframe** visual style while this command is in progress if the current visual style is **2D Wireframe**. Figure 21-9 shows the **3DMOVE** command in action.

3DMOVE	
Modeling Toolbar	
Ribbon Modify control panel	
Pull-down Menu	Modify/ 3D Opera- tion/3D Move
Command Line	3dmove

Figure 21-9   The **3DMOVE** command in action

3DARRAY	
Ribbon Modify panel	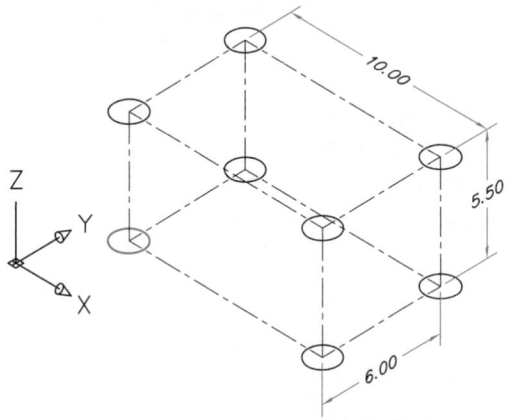
Pull-down Menu	Modify/ 3D Opera-tion/3D Array
Command Line	3darray

The 3DARRAY Command

The **3DARRAY** command is a 3D version of the standard **ARRAY** command. With this command you can create both rectangular and polar 3D arrays.

With the rectangular 3D array you are allowed to create multiple objects arranged not only in rows and columns but also in levels. In the event you enter **1** as the number of levels, the array will behave just like a standard 2D array.

The result of a rectangular 3D array depends on the current UCS. The rows are created in the Y-axis direction, the columns in the X-axis direction, and the levels in the Z-axis direction. For example, a $2 \times 2 \times 2$ array of the highlighted circle with the dimensions rows, columns, levels = 6,10,5.5 will be as shown in Figure 21-10.

Figure 21-10   A 3D array of the highlighted circle

With the polar 3D array, you can create multiple objects that are uniformly distributed around an imaginary axis of rotation. Unlike the rectangular 3D array, the results do not depend on the current UCS, but on the two points you specify to establish the axis of rotation.

Exercise 21-2: A 3D Rectangular Array Operation

To access student data files, go to www.pearsondesigncentral.com.

1. **OPEN** the drawing named ***Exercise 21-00-A*** in the student data files.
2. **SAVE** the drawing **AS** ***Exercise 21-2***.
3. Invoke the **3DARRAY** command and respond to the prompts as follows:

   Select objects: *Select the two circles representing the hole on the 3D model.*

   Select objects: ↵ *(To end the selection)*

   Enter the type of array [Rectangular/Polar] <R>: ↵ *(To accept the default)*

   Enter the number of rows (---) <1>: *2* ↵

   Enter the number of columns (|||) <1>: *2* ↵

   Enter the number of levels (...) <1>: *2* ↵

   Specify the distance between rows (---): *6* ↵

   Specify the distance between columns (|||): *10* ↵

   Specify the distance between levels (...): *5.5* ↵

4. Invoke the **3DORBIT** command to inspect the 3D model.
5. The drawing should look like Figure 21-11.
6. **SAVE** the drawing.

Figure 21-11   The 3D model
after the **3DARRAY** operation

Exercise 21-3: A 3D Polar Array Operation

1. **OPEN** the drawing named *Exercise 21-00-A* in the student data files.
2. **SAVE** the drawing **AS** *Exercise 21-3*.
3. Select the **Front** UCS.
4. Draw a line from the center point of the top circle to the center point of the bottom circle (Figure 21-12).
5. With ORTHO activated, **MOVE** the line **3″** along the negative *X*-axis direction.
6. **ROTATE** the line **15°** using the lower endpoint as the rotation base point (Figure 21-13).

To access student data files, go to www.pearsondesigncentral.com.

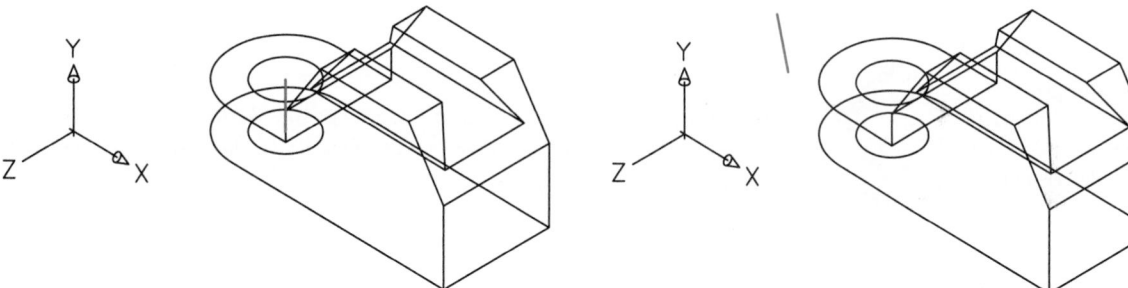

Figure 21-12   A line is drawn between the center points   Figure 21-13   After the line is moved and rotated

7. Invoke the **3DARRAY** command and respond to the prompts as follows:

    Select objects: *all ↵ (To select all the objects)*

    Select objects: *↵ (To end the selection)*

    Enter the type of array [Rectangular/Polar] <R>: *p ↵*

    Enter the number of items in the array: *4 ↵*

    Specify the angle to fill (+=ccw, -=cw) <360>: *↵ (To accept the default)*

    Rotate arrayed objects? [Yes/No] <Y>: *↵ (To accept the default)*

    Specify center point of array: *Select one of the endpoints of the line you drew.*

    Specify second point on axis of rotation: *Select the other endpoint of the line.*

8. The drawing should look like Figure 21-14.
9. Invoke the **3DORBIT** command to inspect the operation you just performed.
10. **SAVE** the drawing.

Figure 21-14   The resulting 3D array about the line

MIRROR3D	
Ribbon Modify panel	
Pull-down Menu	Modify/ 3D Opera- tion/3D Mirror
Command Line	mirror3d

imaginary mirror plane:
Imaginary plane about which the selected object is copied to the opposite side as a mirror image.

Figure 21-15   The **MIRROR3D** command shortcut menu

The MIRROR3D Command

This command is the 3D version of the standard **MIRROR** command. It allows you to create mirror copies of objects in 3D by specifying an *imaginary mirror plane*. With the standard **MIRROR** command, you simply define an imaginary mirror line.

After selecting the object, you can choose one of the options to define the imaginary mirror plane. At this stage, right-clicking in the drawing area will display the shortcut menu (Figure 21-15). Or, if **DYN** (Dynamic Input) is on, you can also see the options by using the **<Down Arrow>** key.

> **TIP** Regardless of whether a plane is to be used in the **MIRROR3D** command or any other, knowing how to define planes in the 3D space is a key aspect of 3D modeling in general.

3points: This is the default option. If you enter a point instead of specifying another option, you are automatically asked for two more points. The mirror plane is defined by specifying any three noncollinear points. The UCS currently in use does not affect the result.

Object: If you select this option, AutoCAD will ask you to select an object in order to use the plane it defines as the imaginary mirror plane. Only circles, arcs, and polylines can be selected. Selecting any other type of object will cause AutoCAD to prompt the following message:

```
Improper type of object picked.
```

Zaxis: With this option you define a plane by specifying two points (Figure 21-16). The first point (1) defines a point on the imaginary mirror plane. The second point (2) defines the direction of a vector to which the imaginary plane is normal.

View: In this option the imaginary mirror plane is defined parallel to the viewing plane (your monitor display). Because the orientation of the plane is already known with this option, all you are required to do is to specify the point that defines its location.

XY/YZ/ZX: By selecting one of the planes of the current UCS, you define the imaginary mirror plane parallel to it. As with the **View** option, the plane requires an additional point

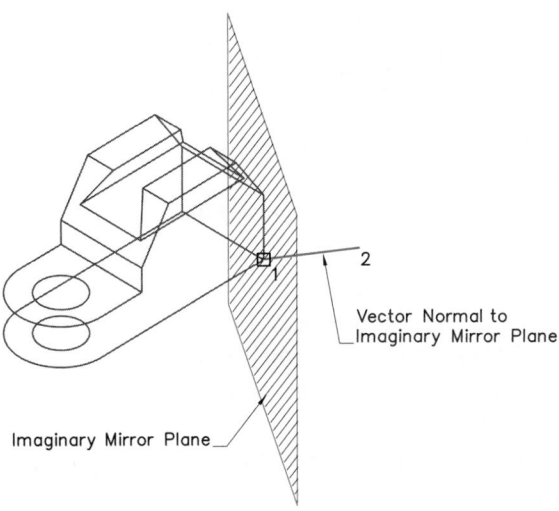

Figure 21-16   The imaginary mirror plane defined with the **Zaxis** option of the **MIRROR3D** command

to fully define its location. These three options and the **3points** option are the most frequently used in practice.

Last: Reuses the last imaginary mirror plane you defined.

Exercise 21-4: A 3D Mirror Operation by Specifying Three Points

1. **OPEN** the drawing named *Exercise 21-00-A* in the student data files.
2. **SAVE** the drawing **AS** *Exercise 21-4*.
3. Invoke the **MIRROR3D** command and respond to the prompts as follows:

To access student data files, go to www.pearsondesigncentral.com.

   Select objects: *all ↵ (To select all the objects)*

   Select objects: *↵ (To end the selection)*

   Specify first point of mirror plane (3 points) or [Object/Last/Zaxis/View/XY/YZ/ZX/3points] <3points>: *Specify any point on the wires of the face highlighted in Figure 21-17.*

   Specify second point on mirror plane: *Specify a second point on the same face.*

   Specify third point on mirror plane: *Specify a third point on the same face.*

   Delete source objects? [Yes/No] <N>: *↵ (To accept the default)*

4. The 3D model should look like Figure 21-18. Invoke the **3DORBIT** command and inspect the mirror image you just created.
5. **SAVE** the drawing.

Figure 21-17   Reference face to specify the three points for the **MIRROR3D** operation

Figure 21-18   The 3D model after the **MIRROR3D** operation

Exercise 21-5: A 3D Mirror Operation by Using an Object

You will create a mirrored copy of the model using the bottom circle that represents the hole in the model.

Figure 21-19   The 3D model is turned over using a **MIRROR3D** operation

1. **OPEN** the drawing named *Exercise 21-00-A* in the student data files.
2. **SAVE** the drawing **AS** *Exercise 21-5*.
3. Invoke the **MIRROR3D** command and respond to the prompts as follows:

   Select objects: *all* ↵ *(To select all the objects)*

   Select objects: ↵ *(To end the selection)*

   Specify first point of mirror plane (3 points) or [Object/Last/Zaxis/View/XY/YZ/ZX/3points] <3points>: *o* ↵

   Select a circle, arc, or 2D-polyline segment: *Select the bottom circle.*

   Delete source objects? [Yes/No] <N>: *y* ↵ *(To flip the model without creating a copy)*

4. The 3D model should look like Figure 21-19. Explore the model with the **3DORBIT** command.
5. **SAVE** the drawing.

Exercise 21-6: A 3D Mirror Operation Using a *Z*-Axis Vector

You will mirror the objects of the 3D model by specifying a vector perpendicular to the mirroring plane.

1. **OPEN** the drawing named *Exercise 21-00-A* in the student data files.
2. **SAVE** the drawing **AS** *Exercise 21-6*.
3. Select the **SW Isometric** viewing point.
4. Invoke the **MIRROR3D** command and respond to the prompts as follows:

   Select objects: *all* ↵ *(To select all the objects)*

   Select objects: ↵ *(To end the selection)*

   Specify first point of mirror plane (3 points) or [Object/Last/Zaxis/View/XY/YZ/ZX/3points] <3points>: *z* ↵

   Specify point on mirror plane: *Specify the endpoint shown in Figure 21-20.*

   Specify point on Z-axis (normal) of mirror plane: *@2,-1,0* ↵

   Delete source objects? [Yes/No] <N>: ↵ *(To accept the default)*

5. Select a **Top** view. Your drawing should look like Figure 21-21.
6. **SAVE** the drawing.

Figure 21-20   Point to specify the imaginary mirror plane for the **Zaxis** option of the **MIRROR3D** command

Figure 21-21   The 3D model after the **MIRROR3D** operation

Exercise 21-7: A 3D Mirror Operation Using the View Option

In this exercise you will create a mirror image of the model by specifying a mirroring plane that is parallel to the viewing plane.

Note: Because the mirroring plane is specified parallel to the viewing plane, you will not be able to see the mirrored copy until you change the viewing point.

To access student data files, go to www.pearsondesigncentral.com.

1. **OPEN** the drawing named *Exercise 21-00-A* in the student data files.
2. **SAVE** the drawing **AS** *Exercise 21-7*.
3. Select the **Top** view.
4. Invoke the **MIRROR3D** command and respond to the prompts as follows:

   Select objects: *Use a selection window to select all the objects.*

   Select objects: ↵ *(To end the selection)*

   Specify first point of mirror plane (3 points) or [Object/Last/Zaxis/View/XY/YZ/ZX/3points]<3points>: *v* ↵

   Specify point on view plane: *0,0,6* ↵

   Delete source objects? [Yes/No] <N>: ↵ *(To accept the default)*
5. Select the **SE Isometric** view. Your drawing should look like Figure 21-22.
6. **SAVE** the drawing.

Note: Once the alignment of a plane is known, all that is needed to fully define it is a point through which the plane goes.

Figure 21-22   The 3D model after the **MIRROR3D** operation using the **View** option

Exercise 21-8: A **3DMIRROR** Operation Using One of the Planes of the Current UCS

You will now create a mirror image of the same model by specifying the mirroring plane oriented parallel to the *ZX* plane.

1. **OPEN** the drawing named *Exercise 21-00-A* in the student data files.
2. **SAVE** the drawing **AS** *Exercise 21-8*.

To access student data files, go to www.pearsondesigncentral.com.

3. Invoke the **MIRROR3D** command and respond to the prompts as follows:

Select objects: *Use a selection window to select all the wires.*

Select objects: ↵ *(To end the selection)*

Specify first point of mirror plane (3 points) or [Object/Last/Zaxis/View/XY/YZ/ZX/3points] <3points>: *Right-click in the drawing area to open the shortcut menu and click on* **ZX.**

Specify point on ZX plane <0,0,0>: *15,-1,15* ↵

Delete source objects? [Yes/No] <N>: ↵ *(To accept the default)*

4. Your drawing should look like Figure 21-23.
5. **SAVE** the drawing.

Figure 21-23   The 3D model after the **MIRROR3D** operation using one of the current UCS planes

3DALIGN	
Modeling Toolbar	
Ribbon Modify panel	
Pull-down Menu	Modify/ 3D Operation/3D Align
Command Line	3dalign
Command Alias	al

The 3DALIGN Command

This is probably the most complex and useful command in this group. In general, this command allows you to align objects by matching a source-oriented plane to the destination-oriented plane, regardless of the combinations of displacements and rotations involved. Both oriented planes can be visualized as imaginary coordinate systems.

Specifying all three points enables you to fully define the two imaginary coordinate systems. However, you can also specify one or two points for either of the imaginary coordinate systems, which gives you a total of nine different combinations. Throughout the process, the imaginary coordinate system is defined regardless of the number of points specified. The current UCS provides the missing alignment information in case fewer than three points are specified.

The example in Figure 21-24 shows two 3D solids before and after one of them is aligned with the other 3D solid, using fully defined imaginary coordinate systems.

After selecting the object(s), you start by defining the source imaginary coordinate system. The first point simply locates its origin. Choosing to specify only this point would define the imaginary coordinate system as shown in Figure 21-25. If you specified only one point to define the destination imaginary coordinate system, it would simply become a **MOVE** operation.

The second point defines the X'-axis of the imaginary coordinate system (Figure 21-26). Using two points will enable you to align the object so that its edge is flush with the destination imaginary coordinate system.

Note: Because the mirroring plane is parallel with the ZX plane, only the Y coordinate of the point is read.

Note: The imaginary coordinate system will not show up in the program. It is just an illustrative element to show you the object's current location and orientation. Because the coordinate system is not real, its axes are named X', Y', and Z' for the source imaginary coordinate system and X'', Y'', and Z'' for the destination imaginary coordinate system.

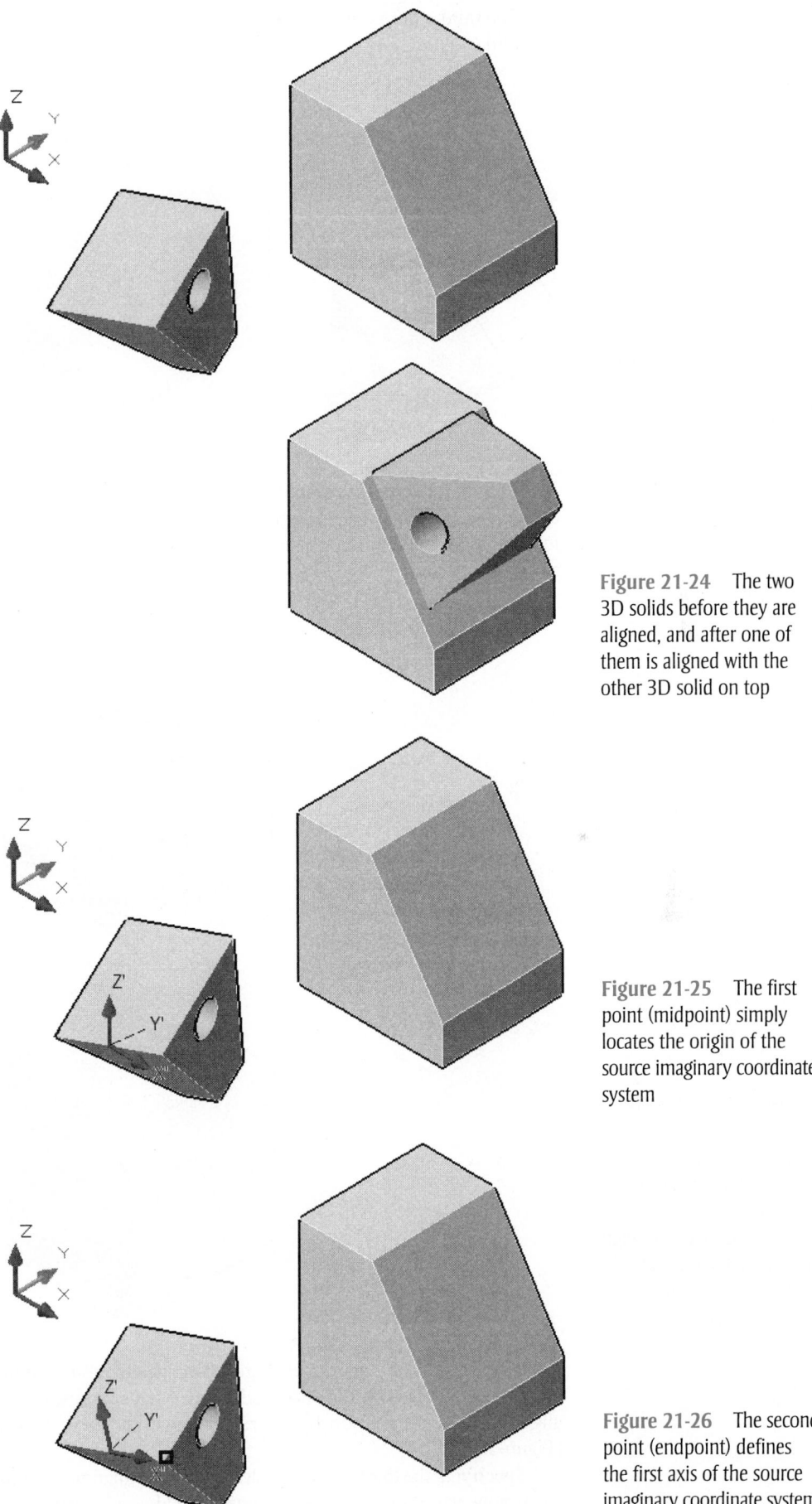

Figure 21-24   The two 3D solids before they are aligned, and after one of them is aligned with the other 3D solid on top

Figure 21-25   The first point (midpoint) simply locates the origin of the source imaginary coordinate system

Figure 21-26   The second point (endpoint) defines the first axis of the source imaginary coordinate system

The third point finally aligns the $X'Y'$ plane to the face that we want to mate with the other 3D solid (Figure 21-27).

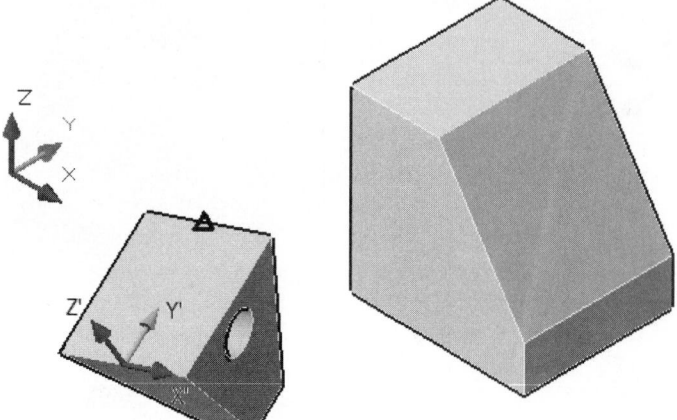

Figure 21-27 The third point (midpoint) fully aligns the source imaginary coordinate system

As with the source imaginary coordinate system, the first point of the destination imaginary coordinate system locates its origin (Figure 21-28). Using only this point will align the source object so that its imaginary coordinate system matches the destination imaginary coordinate system as defined so far.

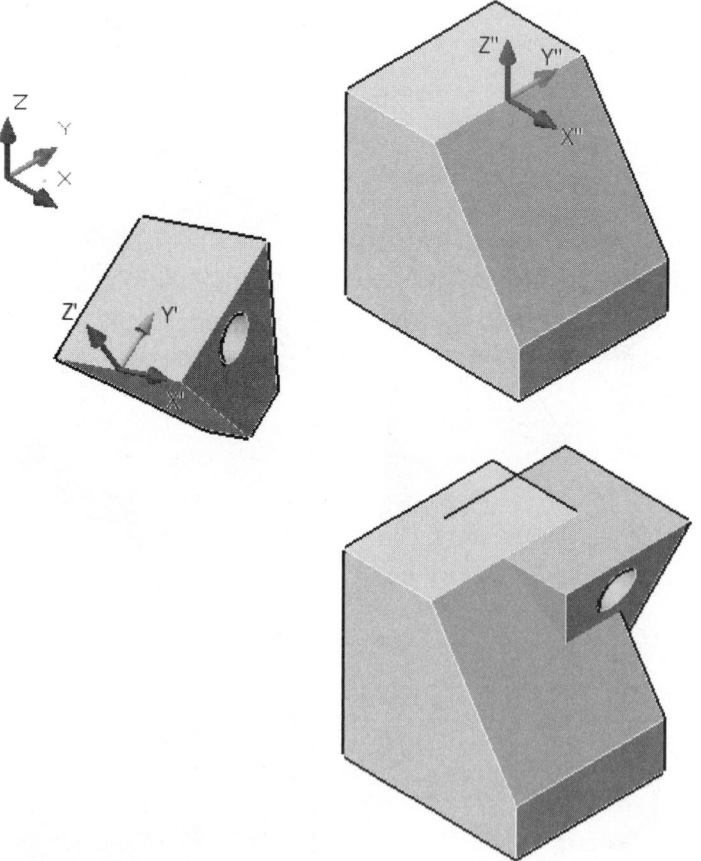

Figure 21-28 The first point (midpoint) of the destination imaginary coordinate system simply defines its origin. Ending the command at this stage will align the selected object so that both imaginary coordinate systems match

The second point continues aligning the destination imaginary coordinate system so that the X''-axis aligns with the specified point. Choosing not to specify the third point will also align the objects based on the current orientation of the two imaginary coordinate systems (Figure 21-29).

Specifying the third point fully defines the destination imaginary coordinate system. The object is now placed in the face we planned for (Figure 21-30).

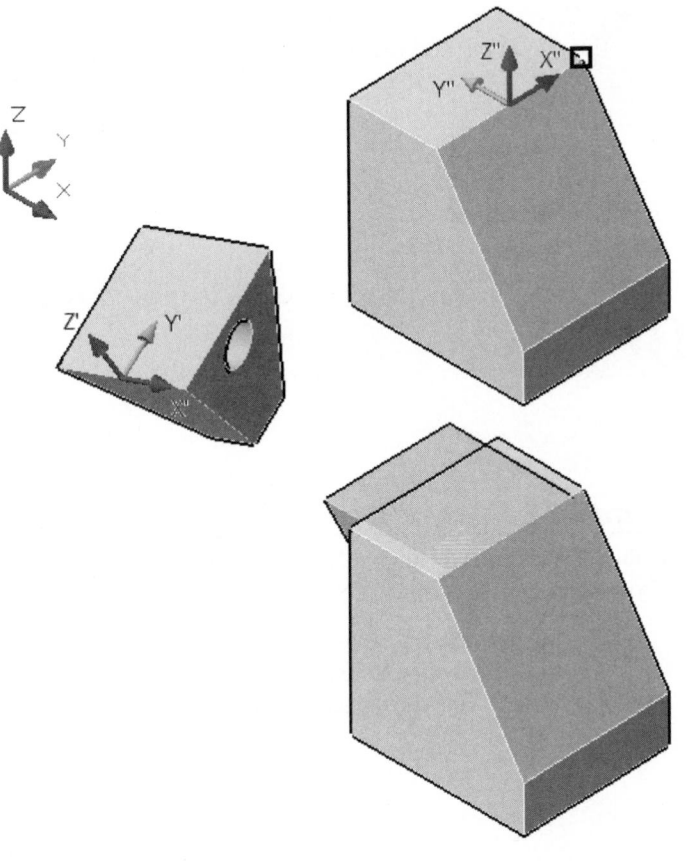

Figure 21-29   The second point (endpoint) of the destination imaginary coordinate system defines its first axis. Alignment is achieved if the command ends at this stage

Figure 21-30   The third point (midpoint) of the destination imaginary coordinate system fully defines it. By matching the two imaginary coordinate systems, the selected object is aligned exactly as expected

With the **3DALIGN** command, you can create a rotated copy of selected objects by using the **COPY** option.

TIP

You should turn **DUCS** (Dynamic UCS) mode off when using the **3DALIGN** command.

TIP

Exercise 21-9: Using the **3DALIGN** Command as a 2D Operation

In this exercise you will align a 2D shape contained in the current UCS with another object that is also contained in the current UCS. This is how this command is normally used when working in 2D.

To access student data files, go to www.pearsondesigncentral.com.

1. **OPEN** the drawing named *Exercise 21-00-A* in the student data files.
2. **SAVE** the drawing **AS** *Exercise 21-9*.
3. Draw the shape shown near the 3D model in Figure 21-31.

Figure 21-31   Draw the high-lighted objects

4. Invoke the **3DALIGN** command and respond to the prompts as follows:
   Select objects: *Select the entire shape you just drew.*
   Select objects: ↵ *(To end the selection)*
   Specify source plane and orientation ...
   Specify base point or [Copy]: *Snap to endpoint 1 (Figure 21-32).*
   Specify second point or [Continue] <C>: *Snap to endpoint 2.*
   Specify third point or [Continue] <C>: ↵ *(To continue with the other stage of the command)*
   Specify destination plane and orientation ...
   Specify first destination point: *Snap to endpoint 3.*
   Specify second destination point or [eXit] <X>: *Snap to endpoint 4.*
   Specify third destination point or [eXit] <X>: ↵ *(To exit the command)*
5. Your drawing should look like Figure 21-33. **SAVE** the drawing.

Figure 21-32 Follow this order to specify the points for the **3DALIGN** operation

Figure 21-33 The objects are aligned using two points to define both the source and the destination imaginary coordinate systems

Exercise 21-10: Using the **3DALIGN** Command to Align a Cylinder in a Hole

1. **OPEN** the drawing named ***Exercise 21-00-A*** in the student data files.
2. **SAVE** the drawing **AS** ***Exercise 21-10***.
3. Select the **Right** UCS.
4. Use the **CYLINDER** command to create a 3D solid cylinder near the model. When prompted, specify **0.7** as the radius and **3** for the height.
5. Invoke the **3DALIGN** command and respond to the prompts as follows:

To access student data files, go to www.pearsondesigncentral.com.

Select objects: *Select the cylinder.*

Select objects: ↵ *(To end the selection)*

Specify source plane and orientation...

Specify base point or [Copy]: *Snap to center point 1 (Figure 21-34).*

Specify second point or [Continue] <C>: *Snap to center point 2.*

Specify third point or [Continue] <C>: ↵ *(To continue with the other stage of the command)*

Specify destination plane and orientation...

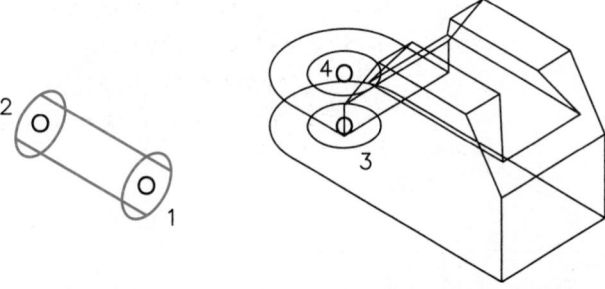

Figure 21-34 Follow this order to specify the points for the **3DALIGN** operation

Specify first destination point: *Snap to center point 3.*

Specify second destination point or [eXit] <X>: *Snap to center point 4.*

Specify third destination point or [eXit] <X>: ↵ *(To exit the command)*

6. Select the **Realistic** visual style. Your drawing should look like Figure 21-35.
7. **SAVE** the drawing.

Figure 21-35 The cylinder is aligned, using two points to define both the source and the destination imaginary coordinate systems

Exercise 21-11: The **3DALIGN** Command Using All Points to Specify the Source and Destination Imaginary Coordinate Systems

1. **OPEN** the drawing named *Exercise 21-00-A* in the student data files.
2. **SAVE** the drawing **AS** *Exercise 21-11*.
3. Re-create the 2D shape you drew in *Exercise 21-9*.
4. Invoke the **3DALIGN** command and respond to the prompts as follows:

   Select objects: *Select the shape's objects.*
   Select objects: ↵ *(To end the selection)*
   Specify source plane and orientation...
   Specify base point or [Copy]: *Snap to endpoint 1* (Figure 21-36).
   Specify second point or [Continue] <C>: *Snap to endpoint 2.*
   Specify third point or [Continue] <C>: *Snap to endpoint 3.*
   Specify destination plane and orientation...
   Specify first destination point: *Snap to endpoint 4.*
   Specify second destination point or [eXit] <X>: *Snap to endpoint 5.*
   Specify third destination point or [eXit] <X>: *Snap to midpoint 6.*

5. Your drawing should look like Figure 21-37. **SAVE** the drawing.

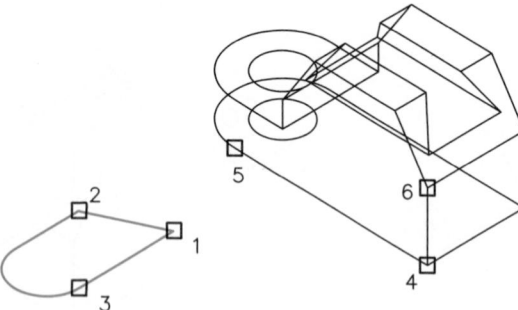

Figure 21-36 Follow this order to specify the points for the **3DALIGN** operation

Figure 21-37 The objects are aligned using fully defined source and destination imaginary coordinate systems

Exercise 21-12: Using the **3DALIGN** Command to Align a Cylinder in a Hole in a Specified Position

1. **OPEN** the drawing named *Exercise 21-00-B* in the student data files.
2. **SAVE** the drawing **AS** *Exercise 21-12*.
3. Select the **Right** UCS.

4. Invoke the **3DALIGN** command and respond to the prompts as follows:

Select objects: *Select the shape's objects.*

Select objects: ↵ *(To end the selection)*

Specify source plane and orientation...

Specify base point or [Copy]: *Snap to center point 1* (Figure 21-38).

Specify second point or [Continue] <C>: *Snap to center point 2.*

Specify third point or [Continue] <C>: *Snap to midpoint 3.*

Specify destination plane and orientation...

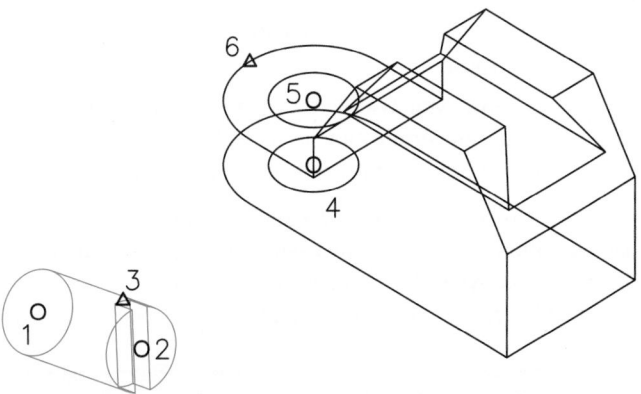

Figure 21-38   Follow this order to specify the points for the **3DALIGN** operation

Specify first destination point: *Snap to center point 4.*

Specify second destination point or [eXit] <X>: *Snap to center point 5.*

Specify third destination point or [eXit] <X>: *Snap to midpoint 6.*

5. Select the **Realistic** visual style. Your 3D model should look like Figure 21-39.
6. **SAVE** the drawing.

Figure 21-39   The cylinder and its slot are aligned using fully defined source and destination imaginary coordinate systems

ALIGN	
Pull-down Menu	Modify/3D Operation/ Align
Command Line	align
Command Alias	al

The ALIGN Command

The **ALIGN** command is very similar to the **3DALIGN** command. The only difference is the order in which it collects the source and destination points.

The **3DALIGN** command collects the source points first and then the destination points. By doing so, the command tries to define a 2D source imaginary coordinate system, or aligned plane, and match it with a 2D destination imaginary coordinate system, which is also an aligned plane.

The **ALIGN** command, on the other hand, performs the alignment by defining each pair of source-destination points one by one.

As with the **3DALIGN** command, the AutoCAD software determines all the necessary operations (move, rotate, and scale) needed to align the source points with the destination points. The command temporarily draws traces from each source point to its corresponding destination while it is still in process to help you preview the results.

Because you must enter complete pairs, the number of combinations you can obtain is smaller than you get with the **3DALIGN** command. Depending on the number of pairs entered, the **ALIGN** command can perform different operations in both the 2D and 3D environments. Pressing **<Enter ↵>** after you enter a complete pair of points will end the command, resulting in one of the following operations:

1 pair results in a **MOVE** operation. In practice, the **ALIGN** command is seldom used for this purpose.

2 pairs allows you to align the objects in two straight lines, where the first pair of points establishes the origin and the second pair the alignment. This operation is very useful when you are aligning objects by an imaginary axis (e.g., a bolt in a hole).

When you press **<Enter ↵>** after entering the second pair, the command will prompt for the scaling option. This is the only event in which the **Scale** operation can be performed.

Using the **ALIGN** command with two pairs of points is useful only in a 2D environment. This enables you to move, rotate, and scale objects at the same time.

> Both the **ALIGN** and the **3DALIGN** commands guarantee that objects can be repositioned throughout 3D space regardless of their relative location. Such reliability and versatility make these commands key operations in the development of 3D models for mechanical assemblies. A complete understanding of 3D modeling operations performed with these two commands constitutes a valuable skill for individuals involved in the creation of complex mechanical assemblies.

CREATING AND MODIFYING 3D CURVES

NONPLANAR CURVES

3D Polylines

3DPOLYLINE	
Ribbon Draw panel	(icon)
Pull-down Menu	Draw/3D Polyline
Command Line	3dpoly

A **3D polyline** is a single continuous object made of straight segments whose points can be located anywhere in the 3D space. This object is created with the **3DPOLY** command.

A polyline can be made of line and arc segments, whereas a 3D polyline can contain only line segments. The use of the 3D polyline is so limited that it cannot even be filleted. You can draw a 3D polyline on a plane; however, its characteristics will still be different from those of a regular polyline.

3D polyline: A curve made of straight segments that are placed in 3D space that does not belong to a plane.

Splines

spline: A nonplanar continuous curve that goes through a set of points specified anywhere in the 3D space.

A **spline** is a smooth curve that goes through a set of points located anywhere in the 3D space, turning and twisting so that it is *continuously curved* at any point. This object is created with the **SPLINE** command.

In Figure 21-40, the two-segment polyline is continuous in all its points. If you were to modify it by performing a **FILLET** operation, you would add a new arc segment and it would become a three-segment polyline. Then besides being continuous, it would also be *continuously tangent* at any point; however, there would still be an abrupt transition at the points where the lines and the arc segments met.

A spline, on the other hand, is a more complex object that is not only continuous and continuously tangent, but also *continuously curved* at any point. The AutoCAD program uses a larger number of segments, which are not physically seen, to achieve this effect.

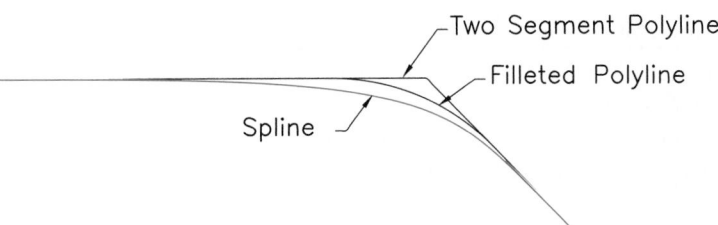

Figure 21-40   The spline is not only continuously tangent at any point but also continuously curved

SPLINE	
Draw Toolbar	
Ribbon Draw panel	
Pull-down Menu	Draw/ Spline
Command Line	spline
Command Alias	spl

There are many types of splines: Bezier curves, B-splines, uniform nonrational B-splines, nonuniform nonrational B-splines, Beta splines, V-splines, and so on. The AutoCAD program uses a particular type of spline known as a nonuniform rational B-spline (NURBS) curve. "Nonuniform" refers to the difference in segment lengths into which these curves are divided and "rational" to the fact that its control points can be given different weight values individually to change the curve path. "B-spline" stands for "Basis spline."

NURBS curves are the industry standard for the representation of complex geometry. They are very useful when creating irregular-shaped or free-form curves, for example, geographic contour curves, automobile design lines, and boat hull design lines.

The **SPLINE** command prompt is structured as follows:

Specify first point or [Object]: *Here you have two choices:*

- If you specify a first point, you will be prompted for the next one.
- When selecting **Object** as the initial option, the only type of object you can select to convert to a spline is a spline-fit polyline. This will be covered in the next topic.

Specify next point: *At least a second point has to be selected in order to enter the spline options.*

Specify next point or [Close/Fit tolerance] <start tangent>: *Here you have four choices:*

- Specify another point.
- Select the **Close** option to create a closed spline. You will be asked for a point tangent to the spline at the closing point.
- Change the **Fit tolerance**. By changing this option you allow AutoCAD to calculate a spline curve of a smaller degree of complexity. The curve will then go through different points than the ones you specified, but never farther than the fit tolerance value specified. A fit tolerance of 0, which is the default value, will make the spline go through each point exactly. These settings apply for all the points except the start and end ones.
- Hit the **<Enter>** key to let the AutoCAD program know that this is the last point. You will be then asked for the tangencies. An open spline has two tangencies; a closed spline has only one.

Specify start tangent: *Here you have two choices:*

- Press the **<Enter>** key to accept the default natural tangency of the start point.
- Specify a point to establish a different tangency.

Specify end tangent: *The same as with the start point*

TIP   In practice, when you specify the last point of the spline, and you do not want to specify any tangent, just remember to press **<Enter ↵>** three times consecutively.

Exercise 21-13: Creating Splines Using 3D Geometry

To access student data
files, go to
www.pearsondesigncentral.com.

1. **OPEN** the drawing named *Exercise 21-00-A* in the student data files.
2. **SAVE** the drawing **AS** *Exercise 21-13*.
3. Invoke the **SPLINE** command and respond to the prompts as follows:

   Specify first point or [Object]: *Snap to the endpoint 1* (Figure 21-41).

   Specify next point: *Snap to the endpoint 2.*

   Specify next point or [Close/Fit tolerance] <start tangent>: *Snap to the endpoint 3. (Repeat until endpoint 6.)*

   Specify next point or [Close/Fit tolerance] <start tangent>: ↵

   Specify start tangent: ↵

   Specify end tangent: ↵

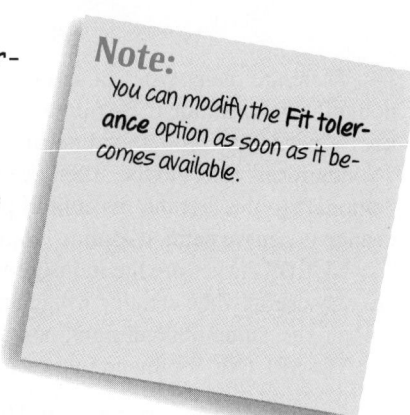

Note:
You can modify the **Fit tolerance** option as soon as it becomes available.

4. The drawing should look like Figure 21-42. Create another two splines. Specify the same points as the one before, but this time specify a **Fit tolerance** of **1.25** for the first one and **2.50** for the second one.

   Specify next point or [Close/Fit tolerance] <start tangent>: *f* ↵

   Specify fit tolerance <0.0000>: *1.25* ↵ *(2.50* ↵ *for the second spline)*

Figure 21-41   Create a spline through the specified points

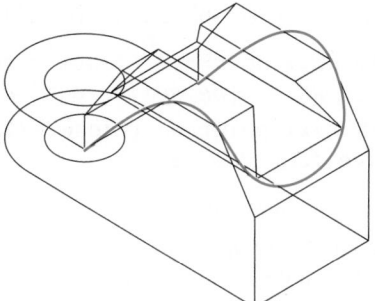

Figure 21-42   Resulting spline curve throughout the 3D space

5. Select the **3DWireframe** visual style.
6. Invoke the **3DORBIT** command to inspect the splines you just created (Figure 21-43).
7. **SAVE** the drawing.

Figure 21-43   A second spline curve through the same points using a different **Fit tolerance** value

Helixes

A *helix* is a continuous open spiral curve that smoothly grows horizontally, vertically, or in both directions. The **HELIX** command creates this type of object, allowing you to specify the six elements that define its geometric characteristics (Figure 21-44).

helix: 2D or 3D spiral curve that coils around an axis, gradually growing horizontally, vertically, or in both directions. 2D spiral curves grow only horizontally.

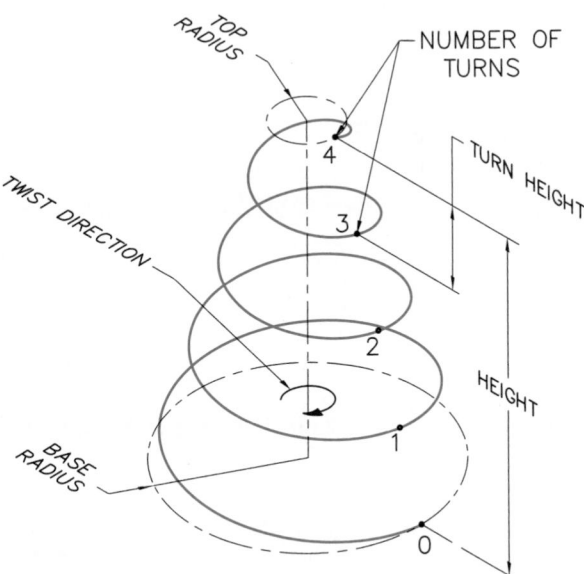

Figure 21-44   The six geometric elements that define a helix's shape

HELIX	
Modeling Toolbar	
Ribbon Draw panel	
Pull-down Menu	Draw/ Helix
Command Line	helix

According to the values of the parameters specified, you can create one of the three types of helixes (Figure 21-45):

- 2D spiral
- Cylindrical 3D spiral
- Conical 3D spiral

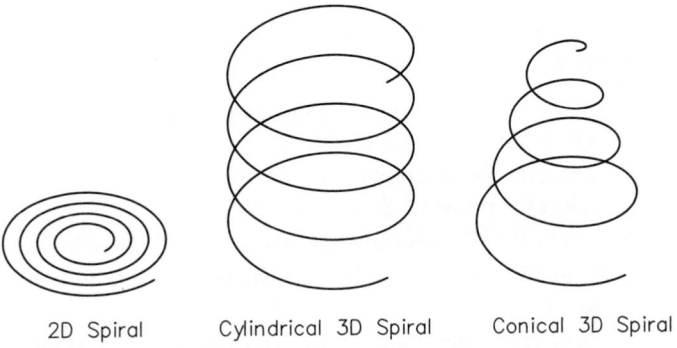

2D Spiral   Cylindrical 3D Spiral   Conical 3D Spiral

Figure 21-45   From left to right: 2D spiral, cylindrical 3D spiral, and conical 3D spiral

2D Spiral: Simply known as a *spiral,* this is a helix that grows only horizontally. This curve is obtained as the result of specifying the height as **0**, and the base and top radius as different values.

Cylindrical 3D Spiral: Also known as a *cylindrical helix,* this curve is a helix that grows only vertically. It is obtained as the result of specifying the base and top radius as the same value, and the height as a value different from **0**.

Conical 3D Spiral: Also known as a *conical helix,* this is a helix that grows in both directions, vertically and horizontally. This curve is obtained as the result of specifying the base and top radius as different values, and the height as a value different from **0**.

The six geometric elements of the helix can be modified in the **Properties** palette after it is created (Figure 21-46). The **Turn Height**, **Height**, and **Turns** parameters are related to each other by the expression:

Height = Turn Height × Turns

In the **Properties** palette, you can constrain one of the three values so that it is not affected when modifying the two others. For example, constraining the **Turn Height** will cause the number of **Turns** to change if the **Height** value is changed (Figure 21-47).

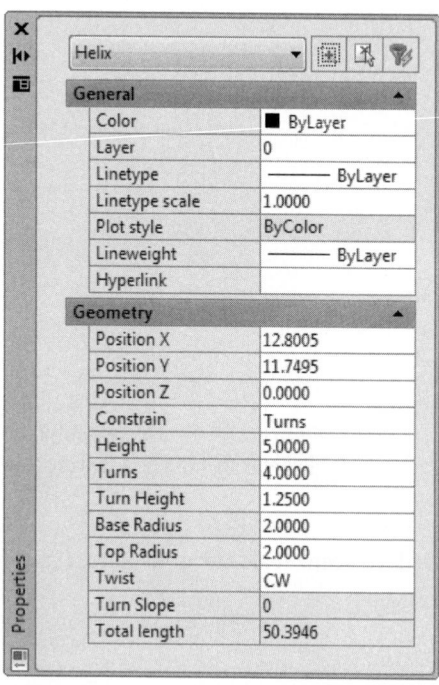

Figure 21-46   A helix's geometry can be modified through the **Properties** palette

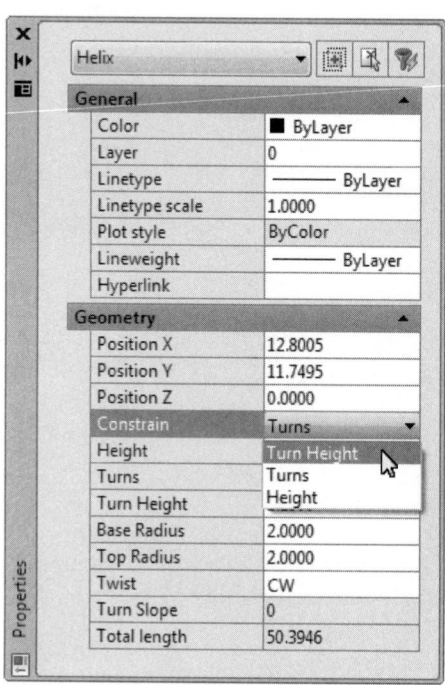

Figure 21-47   Changing the constrained parameter through the **Properties** palette

---

Exercise 21-14: Creating a Spiral and a Helix with the **HELIX** Command

1. Start a **NEW** drawing using the **acad** template.
2. **SAVE** it **AS** *Exercise 21-14*.
3. Select the **SE Isometric** viewing point.
4. Select the **Front** UCS.
5. Invoke the **HELIX** command and respond to the prompts as follows:

   Specify center point of base: *Click anywhere in the drawing area.*

   Specify base radius or [Diameter] <1.0000>: *2* ↵

   Specify top radius or [Diameter] <2.0000>: *6* ↵

   Specify helix height or [Axis endpoint/Turns/turn Height/tWist] 0.2727: *t* ↵ *(To specify the number of turns)*

   Enter number of turns <3.0000>: *5* ↵

   Specify helix height or [Axis endpoint/Turns/turn Height/tWist] <1.000>: *0* ↵

6. **ZOOM** as needed. The spiral should look like Figure 21-48.
7. Invoke the **HELIX** command again and respond to the prompts as follows:

   Specify center point of base: *Click anywhere in the drawing area.*

   Specify base radius or [Diameter] <2.0000>: *3.5* ↵

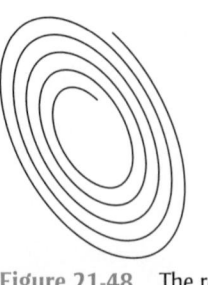

Figure 21-48   The resulting 2D spiral

Specify top radius or [Diameter] <3.5000>: ↵ *(To accept the same value as the base radius)*

Specify helix height or [Axis endpoint/Turns/turn Height/tWist] <0.2727>: *15* ↵

8. **ZOOM** as needed. The two spirals should look like Figure 21-49.
9. **SAVE** the drawing.

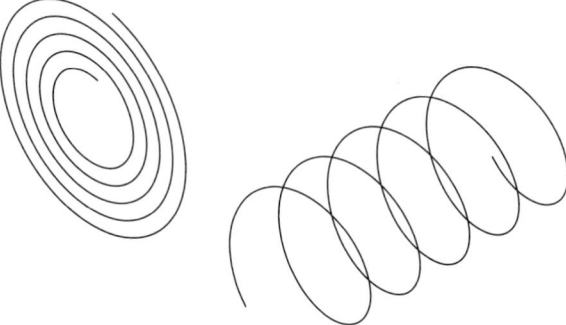

Figure 21-49   The resulting 3D cylindrical spiral next to the 2D spiral

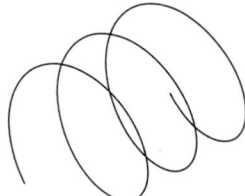

Figure 21-50   The 3D cylindrical spiral with three turns

Exercise 21-15: Modifying Helixes Through the **Properties** Palette

1. Open *Exercise 21-14*.
2. **SAVE** it **AS** *Exercise 21-15*.
3. Select the **Cylindrical Helix**, and right-click to select **Properties** from the shortcut menu.
4. In the **Properties** palette, constrain the **Turn Height** and change the value of the **Height** to **9**.
5. The number of **Turns** changes to **3.** Press the **<Esc>** key. The modified helix should look like Figure 21-50.
6. Select the **Cylindrical Helix** again. In the **Properties** palette, change the value of the top radius to **1.5**.
7. The cylindrical helix transforms into a conical helix. Press the **<Esc>** key. The modified helix should look like Figure 21-51.
8. Close the **Properties** palette.
9. **SAVE** the drawing.

Figure 21-51   You make the 3D spiral conical by changing its top radius value

Helixes are very complex objects. They are used by engineers, architects, and designers to prepare clear, concise, and accurate 3D models whose geometry is described by this type of curve. Identification of this type of geometry and its subsequent use, based on a complete understanding of its principles, will allow users to develop accurate 3D models of known elements such as threads, spiral stairs, and cams. Helixes can also be applied to perform research tasks and to find enhanced solutions to conceptual design problems in the development of new products and systems.

Job Skills

EDITING POLYLINES: THE PEDIT COMMAND

With the **PEDIT** command you can edit both polylines and 3D polylines. There are different options available for these two types of objects. Figure 21-52 shows the shortcut menus for these two objects once the command is in progress. The shortcut menu of options available for polylines is the one on the left. To invoke the **PEDIT** command, you can use one of the methods shown in the grid.

For a polyline, the following options are the ones you will use more frequently when working in the 3D environment:

- **Close** adds a new segment from the starting point of the first segment to the last point on the end segment.

PEDIT	
Modify II Toolbar	
Ribbon Modify panel	
Pull-down Menu	Modify/ Object/ Polyline
Command Line	pedit
Command Alias	pe

Figure 21-52   The **PEDIT** command's shortcut
menu shows the options available for a polyline
(to the left) and a 3D polyline (to the right)

- **Join** adds lines, arcs, or opened polylines to the selected line, arc, or polyline. In the event that the object is not a polyline, but a line or an arc, the AutoCAD program will ask you if you want to convert it into one.

- **Fit** converts the polyline to a continuously tangent curve called a *fit polyline,* which is made of arc segments only. For every segment, AutoCAD creates two new arc segments.

- **Spline** converts the polyline into a ***spline-fit polyline***. The endpoints of the original polyline segments become the control points of the spline-fit polyline.

- **Decurve** converts polylines, fit polylines, and spline-fit polylines to the simplest polyline made of straight segments only, eliminating all extra segments.

When converting polylines to fit polylines or spline-fit polylines, the arc segments are considered to be straight. This is why you obtain the same result from a polyline regardless of whether the **Decurve** operation was previously performed or not (Figure 21-53).

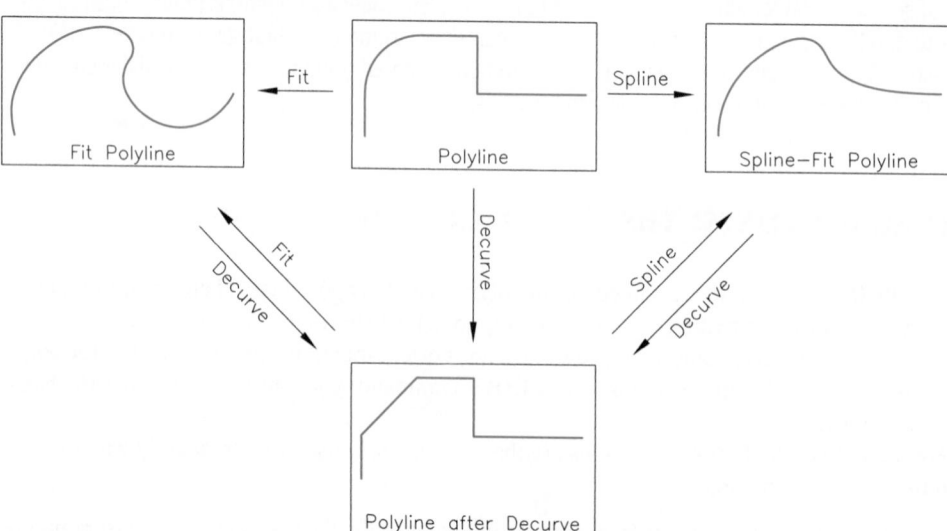

Figure 21-53   Polyline transformations

The **PEDIT** command has fewer options when used with 3D polylines. These are the most useful options:

- **Close** performs the same function as with polylines.
- **Spline curve** converts the 3D polyline to a 3D curve that is continuously curved at any point, called a *spline-fit polyline*. As with polylines, the endpoints of the polyline segments become the control points of the resulting spline-fit polyline.
- **Decurve** converts spline-fit polylines to their original 3D polylines.

Spline-Fit Polylines

The **Spline** and **Spline curve** options of the **PEDIT** command smooth polylines and 3D polylines by subdividing them into many straight segments that approximate a spline curve. This type of object is known as a spline-fit polyline.

If a spline-fit polyline is exploded, all the segments are separated. Two system variables control how polylines and 3D polylines are transformed into spline-fit polylines: **SPLINESEGS** and **SPLINETYPE**.

The **SPLINESEGS** variable controls the number of segments that polylines and 3D polylines will be divided into. The default value of this variable is **8**, but it can be set from **–32768** to **32767**. For polylines only, negative values tell AutoCAD to change the straight segments into arc segments, which are much better spline approximations.

You can change the **SPLINESEGS** value by typing the string entirely in the command line. You can also change it by changing the **Segments in a polyline curve** value on the **Display** tab of the **Options** dialog box (Figure 21-54).

Figure 21-54 The **SPLINESEGS** system variable can be specified as **Segments in a polyline curve** value on the **Display** tab of the **Options** dialog box

The **SPLINETYPE** variable controls the type of curve (cubic or quadratic) into which the **Spline-fit Polylines** operation will transform the original polyline. To change the value of the **SPLINETYPE** variable, enter its name in the command line.

There are two values for this system variable:

- **6** for cubic spline-fit polylines (default value)
- **5** for quadratic spline-fit polylines

The quadratic spline curves are less complex mathematically because they are third-order equations, whereas the cubic splines are fourth-order equations. Figure 21-55 shows the highlighted cubic splines, together with the highlighted quadratic splines in hidden line and the original polylines.

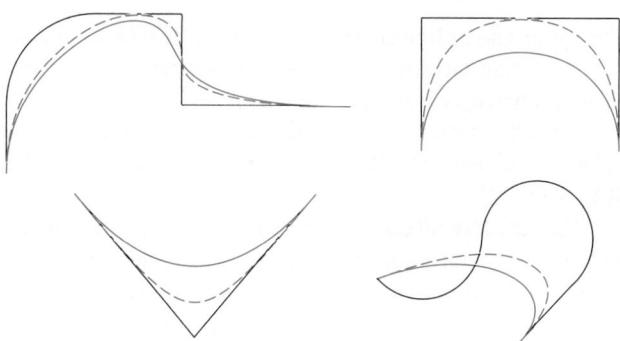

Figure 21-55   Cubic and quadratic spline-fit polyline transformations

EDITING SPLINES: THE SPLINEDIT COMMAND

SPLINEDIT	
Modify II Toolbar	
Ribbon Modify panel	
Pull-down Menu	Modify/ Object/ Spline
Command Line	splinedit

The **SPLINEDIT** command offers many editing operations that can be performed to modify splines. No operations are available, however, for splines without Fit data and spline-fit polylines. Figure 21-56 shows the **SPLINEDIT** command shortcut menu and submenus.

Figure 21-56   The **SPLINEDIT** command's shortcut menu and submenus

When you enter the **Fit data** submenu, you can **Add**, **Delete**, or **Move** the fit points. AutoCAD places an additional point in between the two highlighted points (the one you select and the one after it). The **Object Snap** needs to be turned off so you can select the desired fit point.

Other operations you can perform while in the **Fit data** submenu are: **Purge** the **Fit data** information and, together with it, its fit points; change the **Tangents** of the start and end points;

change the fit **toLerance**; and **Close** or **Open** splines, depending on the current status, without losing the **Fit data**. These operations are similar to the operations found in the **SPLINE** command menu. The fit points can be moved easily by selecting the grips, without entering the **SPLINEDIT** command.

By entering the **Refine** submenu you basically have three operations available: **Add control point**; **Elevate** the **order** of the spline to a maximum of 26; and change the **Weight** of the control points individually. This last option pulls the spline closer to the control points; the higher the **Weight** value, the closer the spline will be to the control points. All these operations will eliminate the **Fit data** at once.

In the main menu you have three other options: the **Close/Open** operation, which leads to a slightly different result; **Move** the **vertex** (control points); and **rEverse** the spline direction to switch the start and end points. The first two operations eliminate the **Fit data**.

The AutoCAD program allows you to either create a spline from scratch or transform a spline-fit polyline. In general, there are three methods you can use to obtain splines:

1. Invoking the **SPLINE** command and specifying a set of points.
2. Invoking the **SPLINE** command and selecting the **Object** option to select a spline-fit polyline, which is the only type of object that can be converted. The conversion is irreversible.
3. Invoking the **SPLINEDIT** command and selecting a spline-fit polyline.

The difference between creating a spline using the first method and using the other two methods is the **Fit data**. The information contained in a spline's **Fit data** is the fit points, the tangents of the start and end points, and the fit tolerance.

The fit points are the set of points you specified when you created the spline. All splines have control points, regardless of whether or not they have fit points.

The control points are not specified by you, but are the endpoints of the control polygon that controls the spline. The control polygon can be displayed, or not, on a spline with **Fit data** depending on the value of the **SPLFRAME** system variable.

The **SPLFRAME** system variable controls the visibility of the control polygon for splines and spline-fit polylines. When the value of this variable is **0** (default), the control polygon is not visible; when the value is **1**, it will be visible. As with many other display-related commands, a **REGEN** operation is needed after changing the value so you can see the result. The **SPLFRAME** system variable is invoked by entering its name in the command line.

Exercise 21-16: Transforming the Splines

1. Open a **NEW** drawing using the **acad** template.
2. **SAVE** it **AS** *Exercise 21-16*.
3. Invoke the **SPLINE** command. When prompted, specify five points following more or less the order shown in Figure 21-57. After completing the spline, it should look close to the one shown in Figure 21-58.

TIP   Remember to press **<Enter ⏎>** three times to accept the default tangent directions.

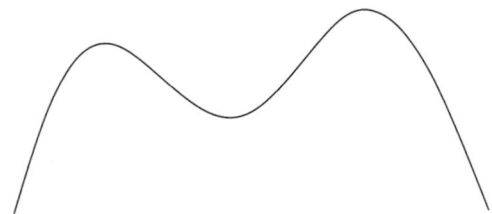

Figure 21-57   Ordered arbitrary points through which the spline will go

Figure 21-58   After completing the spline

Figure 21-59   The spline is copied

4. With **ORTHO** activated, **COPY** the spline to the right (Figure 21-59).
5. Invoke the **SPLINEDIT** command and respond to the prompts as follows:

   Select spline: *Select the spline on the left.*

   Enter an option [Fit data/Close/Move vertex/Refine/rEverse/Undo]: *f ↵*

   Enter a fit data option [Add/Close/Delete/Move/Purge/Tangents/toLerance/eXit] <eXit>: *p ↵*

   Enter an option [Close/Move vertex/Refine/rEverse/Undo/eXit] <eXit>: *x ↵*

> **Note:**
> After the **Fit data** of the left spline have been purged, its grips appear at the control points when the left spline is selected instead of appearing at the fit points, the default location.

6. Without having any command in progress, select the two splines in order to reveal their grips (Figure 21-60).
7. Press the **<Esc>** key to unselect the objects.

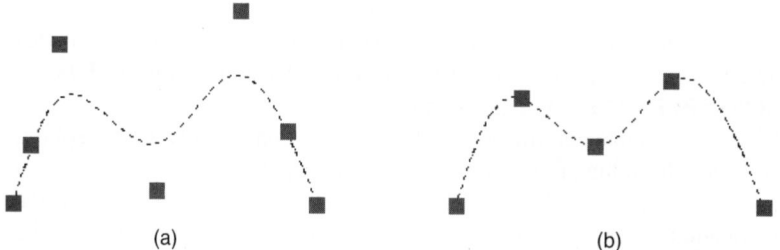

(a)   (b)

Figure 21-60   Splines selected, without (a) and with (b) **Fit data** information

8. Invoke the **SPLFRAME** command to turn on the display of the control polygon.

   Enter new value for SPLFRAME <0>: *1 ↵*

9. Invoke the **REGEN** command. The drawing should now look like Figure 21-61.
10. Select the two splines again to reveal their grips (Figure 21-62).

> **Note:**
> Now the right spline shows both the fit points and the control points.

Figure 21-61   Splines displayed after the **SPLFRAME** system variable is turned on

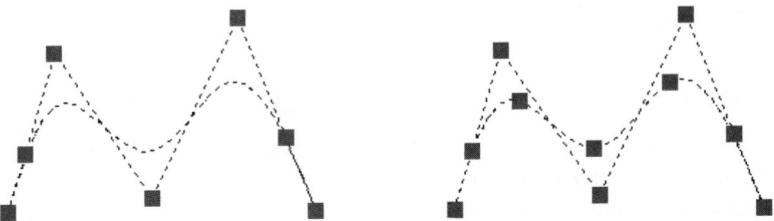

Figure 21-62   Selecting the splines reveals that the one on the left has lost its
Fit data

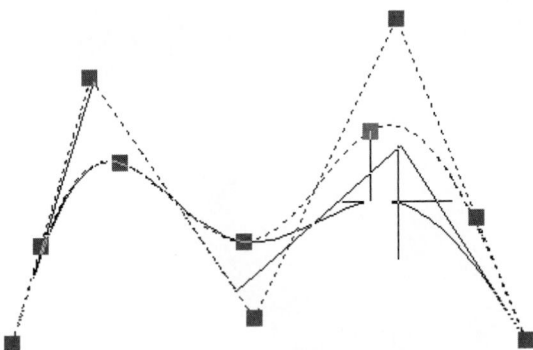

Figure 21-63   Moving a fit points grip

11. Select the fit points grip shown in the right spline and stretch it downward, as shown in Figure 21-63.
12. Select the control points grip and move it upward, as shown in Figure 21-65.
13. **SAVE** the drawing.

The splines created can lose the **Fit data** after any of these editing operations.

- **Purge**
- **Refine**
- **Move** a control point or control vertex
- **Add** control points

Note:
The spline is readjusted, without losing the fit points (Figure 21-64).

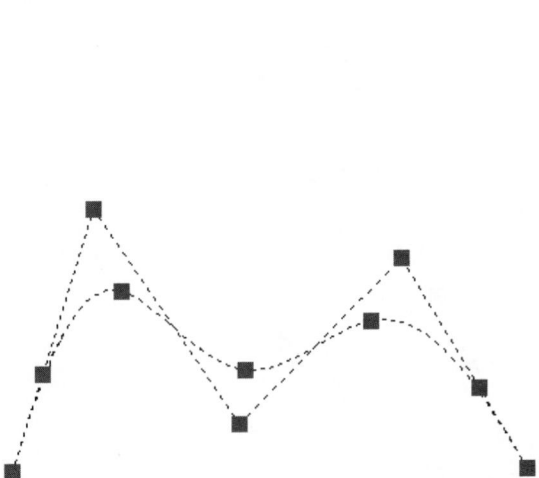

Figure 21-64   The spline maintains its fit points

Figure 21-65   Moving a control point grip

- **Open** or **Close** with the option of the main menu
- **Elevate** the **order**
- Change the **Weight** of a control point.

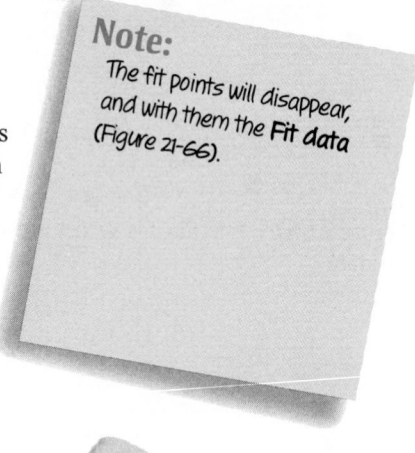

Note: The fit points will disappear, and with them the **Fit data** (Figure 21-66).

In practice, splines are not exactly the type of objects most used to create 3D models. Using more common geometry, such as straight segments and arcs, can lead to excellent results in most cases without necessarily creating a much simpler 3D model.

Most of the time, splines are not intentionally created but are obtained as the result of extracting them from existing geometry (e.g., the edge formed by the intersection of two faces [Figure 21-67]).

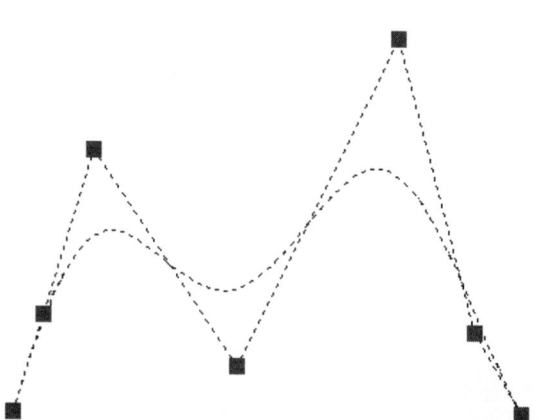

Figure 21-66   The spline does not maintain its **Fit data**

Figure 21-67   A spline edge formed by the intersection of two faces

USING GRIPS TO EDIT WIRES

When selecting a wire without any command in progress, the object not only changes its appearance, indicating that it has been selected, but also shows its grips. This operation is known as "revealing the object's grips." Figure 21-68 shows a group of different wire objects on top, and the same objects after their grips have been revealed at the bottom.

Figure 21-68   Objects before and after revealing their grips

The grips must be turned on so they show up when selecting an object. You turn the grips on in the **Selection** tab of the **Options** dialog box by checking the **Enable grips** option (Figure 21-69). You can also change the size and color of the grips.

Figure 21-69   The grips can be turned on in the **Selection** tab of the **Options** dialog box by checking the **Enable grips**

The grips are located at strategic places on the object. For example, a line will reveal a grip at each endpoint, and another one at the midpoint; a circle will reveal a grip on each quadrant, and another one in its center point. A polyline shows grips at each endpoint of the line segments, and at the endpoints and midpoints of the arc segments.

An originally blue grip changes its color to green when it is hovered, and to red when it is selected. Selecting any grip activates the grip editing routine, allowing you to perform one of the five following operations: **STRETCH**, **MOVE**, **ROTATE**, **SCALE**, and **MIRROR**.

To move on to the next operation, you must press the **<Space>** key.

```
** STRETCH **
Specify stretch point or [Base point/Copy/Undo/eXit]:
** MOVE **
Specify move point or [Base point/Copy/Undo/eXit]:
** ROTATE **
Specify rotation angle or [Base point/Copy/Undo/Reference/eXit]:
** SCALE **
Specify scale factor or [Base point/Copy/Undo/Reference/eXit]:
** MIRROR **
Specify second point or [Base point/Copy/Undo/eXit]:
```

The **STRETCH** command is the default and the most frequently used operation of this group. Stretching a selected grip modifies the geometry of the object so that the selected grip is placed in another location. You can select multiple grips by holding down the **<Shift>** key before selecting them. You can also create copies of the selected objects by selecting the **Copy** option within any operation.

Besides the standard grips, arcs and helixes also reveal special triangular grips, which allow you to perform other operations in a specific direction. For example, you can lengthen an arc by grabbing one of its triangular grips at the endpoints. Pulling one of the triangular grips along the axis of a helix modifies its **Height** value and the value of another parameter, depending on which one is constrained.

Grips and Their Relation to the UCS

The behavior of the grips is affected by the current UCS. Figure 21-70(a) shows the grips revealed when the current UCS is parallel to the object's UCS. Figure 21-70(b) shows the same objects selected when the current UCS is not parallel to the object's UCS.

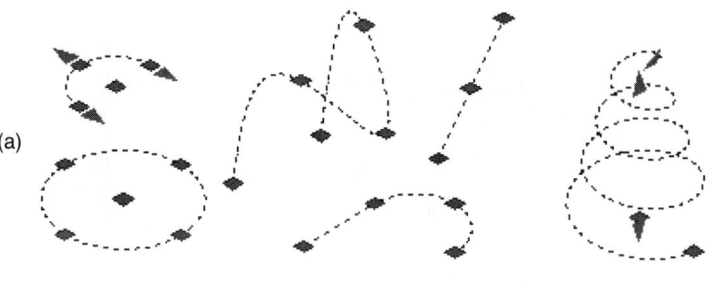

(a)

(b)

Figure 21-70   The grips of a planar object can be pulled only within its UCS, whereas the grips of a non-planar object can be pulled in any direction

The grips of a planar object are always aligned with the *XY* plane of the UCS that it belongs to. When stretching the grips of planar objects, the UCS temporarily changes to the object's UCS, allowing you to edit the object only in its plane.

The grips of nonplanar objects, on the other hand, can be stretched in any direction, and the UCS maintains its current orientation. The grips of nonplanar objects are aligned with the *XY* plane of the current UCS.

The Move Grip Tool

When the current visual style is not **2D Wireframe**, the move grip tool, in addition to the object's grips, also appears when selecting the objects. You can choose to use the standard grips selection by selecting a grip directly. However, placing the mouse for more than a second over a particular grip without selecting it will relocate the move grip tool to this grip, which changes its color to yellow (Figure 21-71).

To relocate a grip using the move grip tool, you must click one of the grip's elements instead of clicking on the grip itself (Figure 21-72).

FOR MORE DETAILS   See the **3DMOVE** command section for more information regarding the use of the move grip tool.

Figure 21-71   The move grip tool

Figure 21-72   Clicking the *Y*-axis of the move grip tool constrains the movement of the selected grip along the *Y*-axis

CHAPTER SUMMARY

Rather than showing you an isolated way of representing 3D models, this chapter has focused on how objects commonly used in 2D work behave in a 3D environment, and demonstrated the way they relate to the UCS. It has also given you key aspects to consider when using the standard 2D commands to modify objects in a 3D environment, allowing you to compare them with other commands that focus particularly on 3D modifications. You also learned about creating and editing complex objects with special uses in 3D, such as splines, polylines, 3D polylines, and helixes.

Understanding the behavior of wire objects or curves in 3D space is essential for success in 3D modeling. Always remember that regardless of which final objects you use to represent a 3D model, wire objects will always be involved.

CHAPTER TEST QUESTIONS

Multiple Choice

1. Which of the following objects can be drawn in the 3D space, without necessarily being parallel to the *XY* plane of the current UCS?

    a. Circle
    b. Line
    c. Arc
    d. Polyline

2. Which of the following can you perform using the move grip tool?

    a. Move the objects constrained to one of the three planes of the current UCS
    b. Move objects along one of the three axes of the current UCS
    c. Move an object to any point in the 3D space
    d. All of the above

3. Which of the following commands allow you to rotate objects around any specified imaginary axis, regardless of the current UCS?

    a. **ROTATE**
    b. **3DMIRROR**

    c. **3DROTATE**
    d. None of the above

4. Which of the following is not one of the options that define the imaginary mirror plane in the **3DMIRROR** command?

    a. **Xaxis**
    b. **XY**
    c. **Zaxis**
    d. **3points**

5. Which of the following characteristics best describes a spline curve?

    a. Continuous
    b. Continuously tangent
    c. Continuously curved
    d. Continuously tangent and curved

6. Which of the following objects can be edited by using the **PEDIT** command?

    a. Circle
    b. Polyline

c. Spline

d. None of the above

7. From a 3D viewing point, a circle appears to be an ellipse. Under what conditions can a circle appear completely round?

a. When it is parallel to the *XY* plane

b. When it is created using the **Ttr** (tan tan radius) option

c. When it is located on a plane parallel to the viewing plane

d. All of the above

8. When using the **MIRROR** command from a 3D viewing point, which of the following may cause you not to see the object snap when the command is certainly recognizing a snap point?

a. The current *XY* plane is not parallel to the viewing plane.

b. The projection of the point onto the current *XY* plane is out of the display.

c. None of the above

d. All of the above

9. Which of the following is not one of the options you could use to define the axis of rotation with the **ROTATE3D** command?

a. **Xaxis**

b. **XY**

c. **Zaxis**

d. **2points**

10. Which of the following is not one of the elements that define the geometric characteristics of helixes?

a. **Turn Height**

b. **Bottom Radius**

c. **Start Angle**

d. **Turns**

Matching

a. **SPLINESEGS**

b. **ROTATE3D**

c. **SPLINETYPE**

d. Spline-fit polyline

e. 3D polyline

f. Source point

g. Polyline

h. Helix

i. Spline

j. **ALIGN**

1. 2D or 3D spiral curve that coils around an axis

2. Planar object made of straight and arc segments

3. Sets the number of segments for the spline fit process

4. Point requested by the **ALIGN** command

5. A smooth 3D curve tangent and continuous at any point

6. Versatile command useful for 3D operations

7. Polylines and 3D polylines smoothed by adding segments

8. Command that allows you to rotate objects about any axis

9. Sets the type of curve for the spline fit process

10. 3D object made of straight segments only

CHAPTER TUTORIALS

Tutorial 21-1: The Bracket Wireframe

This tutorial will show you how to develop the 3D model that you have used in some of the exercises. It will also help you practice using common commands in a 3D environment. Bear in mind that when working in 3D, the most important aspect is controlling the UCS. Figure 21-73 shows the dimensions of the object, the edges of which you will represent three-dimensionally using wire objects.

1. Start a **NEW** drawing using the **acad** template.
2. **SAVE** it **AS** *Tutorial 21-1*.
3. Draw the shape shown in Figure 21-74.

TIP   You can start by creating two concentric circles and the three straight lines, and then trim the bigger circle.

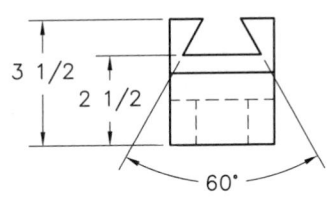

Figure 21-73   The dimensions of the object

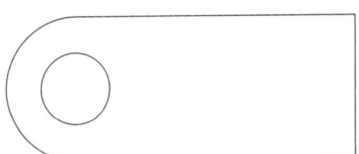

Figure 21-74   Drawing the first objects

4. Select the **SW Isometric** viewing point, using any of the methods you studied before.
5. Select the **Front** orthographic UCS from the **UCS II** toolbar drop-down window.
6. **COPY** all the objects 1¼″ up along the *Y*-axis (Figure 21-75).
7. Select the **Top** orthographic UCS. **MOVE** the short vertical line 4½″ to the left and **TRIM** the rest of the two horizontal lines.
8. Select the **Left** orthographic UCS. Draw the two **3/4″**-long vertical polylines shown in Figure 21-76.

> **Note:**
> You can use the **direct distance entry** method by establishing any point in the drawing area as the base point and, with **ORTHO** activated, moving the crosshairs so the path aligns with the positive *Y*-axis. While the path keeps the alignment, release the mouse, type the desired distance (**1.25**), and press the **<Enter ↵>** key.

Figure 21-75   The objects are copied up

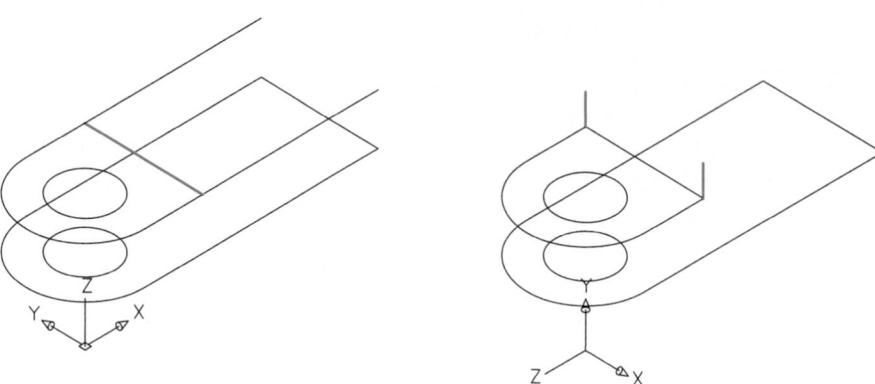

Figure 21-76   After placing the two vertical lines

9. With **Ortho** mode on, draw a polyline from point 1 to point 2 [Figure 21-77(a)]. When you are close to the second endpoint, you will notice that the snap symbol is projected automatically onto a plane parallel to the *XY* plane where the first point was specified [Figure 21-77(b)].

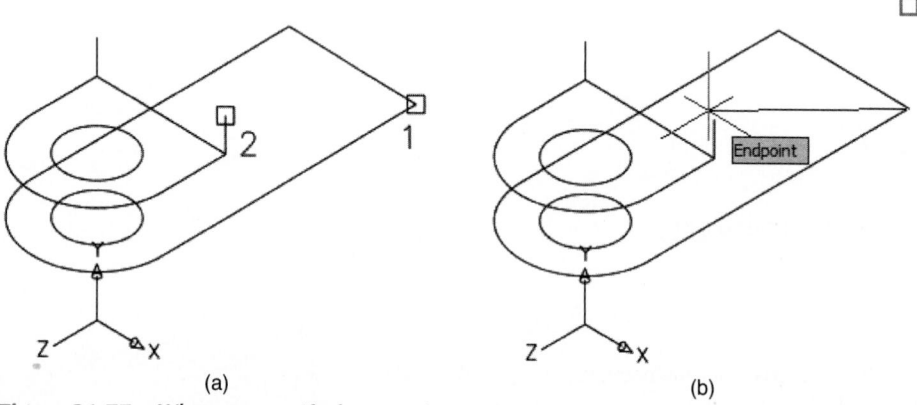

(a)   (b)

Figure 21-77   When you specify the second point for the polyline, the snap symbol is projected onto a plane parallel to the *XY* plane of the first point

10. **COPY** the polyline from endpoint to endpoint as shown in Figure 21-78.
11. Select the **Front** orthographic UCS.

Figure 21-78   The polyline is copied

12. Draw a line from the endpoint of one of the short vertical lines to the point **@1.00,1.50** (Figure 21-79).
13. Draw a horizontal line from the endpoint of one of the short vertical lines to the endpoint of the longer vertical line.
14. **MIRROR** the inclined line using the geometry of the horizontal line (Figure 21-80).

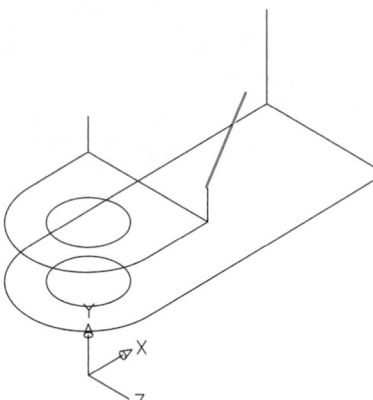

Figure 21-79   After placing the inclined line

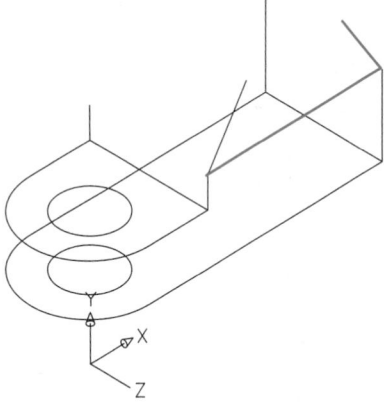

Figure 21-80   The inclined line is mirrored

TIP

When asked for the first point of the mirror line, place the cursor close to the midpoint of the horizontal line. AutoCAD projects the midpoint onto the *XY* plane. With **Ortho** mode on, specify the second point anywhere above or below the first one.

15. **ERASE** the horizontal line.
16. **COPY** the two inclined lines, from any endpoint on the front face of the model to the same point on the back face.
17. Select the **Top** orthographic UCS.
18. Relocate its origin to the top endpoint of any inclined line.
19. Using the **RECTANGLE** command, draw a rectangle by selecting any two top diagonal endpoints. The model should now look like Figure 21-81(a).
20. Draw the two lines that represent the edges between the vertical faces and the inclined faces [Figure 21-81(b)].

Note:
These lines could have been mirrored as well, if the **Top** UCS had been selected previously.

(a)

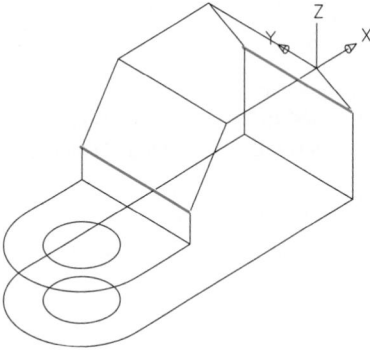

(b)

Figure 21-81   Placing the top rectangle, and then the two highlighted lines

21. Select the **Front** orthographic UCS.
22. **EXPLODE** the rectangle.
23. **COPY** the top edge of the back face **1.00″** down (Figure 21-83).
24. **EXTEND** the new line to the two inclined edges of the same face (Figure 21-84).

Note:
Your model is almost finished. All you need to do is add the geometry that represents the slot on the top. Our purpose now is to find points 1 and 2, which are the vertices of the edge of the intersection of one of the slot faces with the inclined face (Figure 21-82). The rest is simple; it can be done using the **MIRROR** command.

Figure 21-82   The next task is to find points 1 and 2

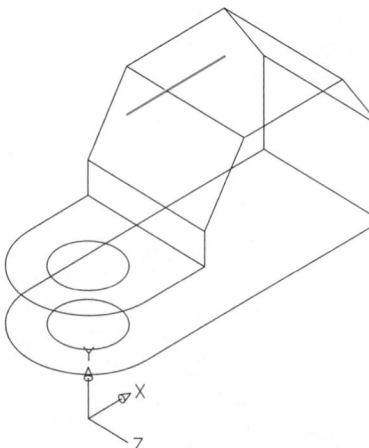

Figure 21-83   The top line is copied

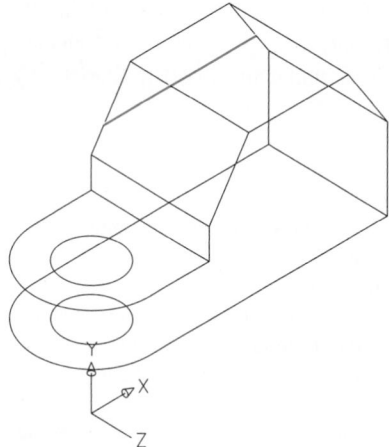

Figure 21-84   The new line is extended

25. Select the **Top** orthographic UCS.
26. **MOVE** the new line **3/8″** (0.375″) along the *Y*-axis inside the model (Figure 21-85). By doing this you have found point 1.

Note:
Remember that both entries (fractional or decimal) are accepted the same way by the AutoCAD program. Because the distance from the back or front face to point 2 is not known, finding point 2 is probably the most difficult part. You do know, however, that the inside walls of the slot are symmetrically inclined 60°.

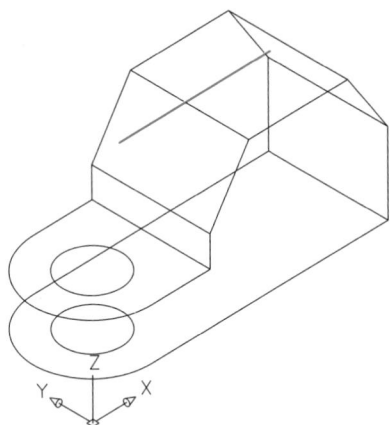

Figure 21-85 The extended line is moved in to find point 2

27. Select the **Left** orthographic UCS.
28. Draw a **2.50″** vertical line from point 1 [Figure 21-86(a)].
29. **ROTATE** the line **−30°** using point 1 as the base point [Figure 21-86(b)].
30. **TRIM** line **2**, using the top-left wire 1 as the cutting edge [Figure 21-87(a)]. The result is shown in Figure 21-87(b).
31. Select the **Top** UCS.
32. Draw a line from the endpoint of the trimmed line perpendicular to the top-right edge [Figure 21-88(a)].
33. **TRIM** the new line using the top-left edge [Figure 21-88(b)].

Note:
The line is trimmed by projecting the cutting edge toward the XY plane of the current UCS.

(a)

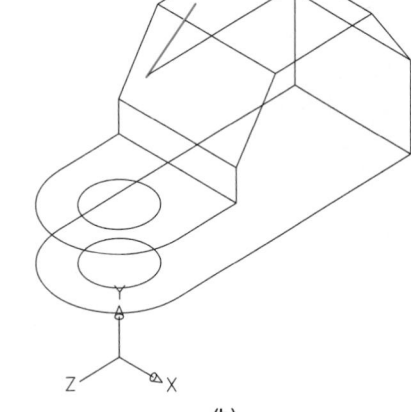

(b)

Figure 21-86 A new vertical line is created and then rotated

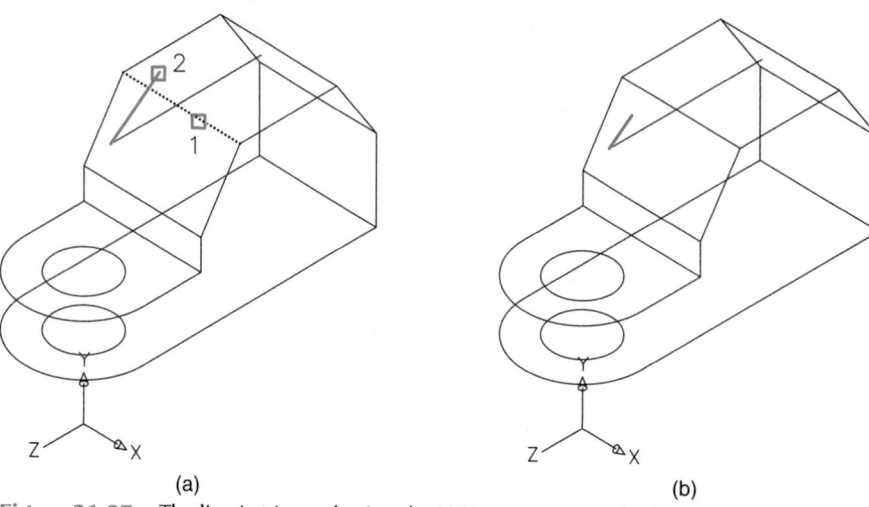

(a)   (b)

Figure 21-87   The line is trimmed using the UCS projection method

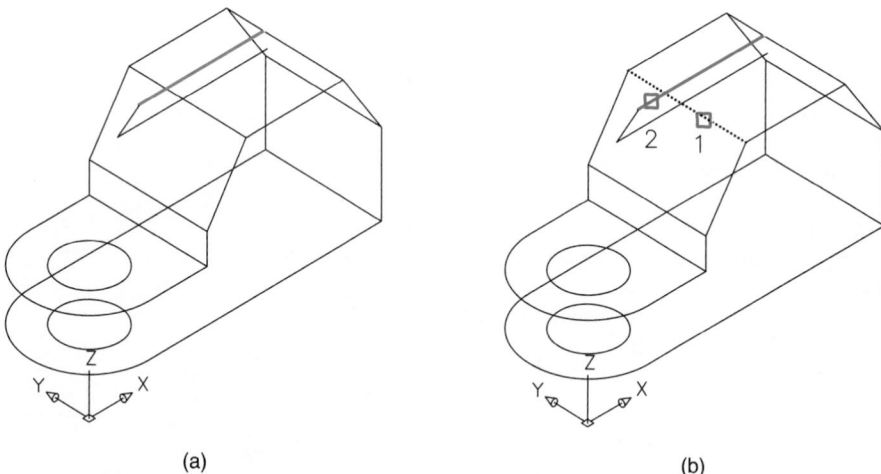

(a)   (b)

Figure 21-88   A new horizontal line is created and then trimmed

34. You have already found the two points needed (1 and 2). **ERASE** the small line 1 (Figure 21-89).

35. **MIRROR** the top and bottom edges of the slot face. Select the midpoint of any edge aligned with the *Y*-axis as the first point of the mirror line (Figure 21-90).

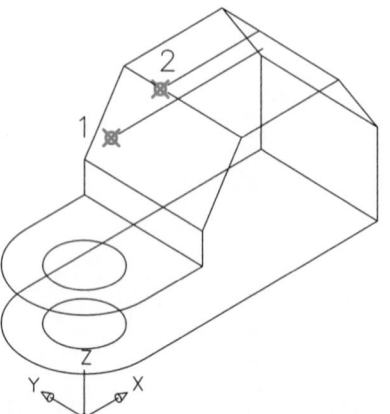

Figure 21-89   Points 1 and 2 are found

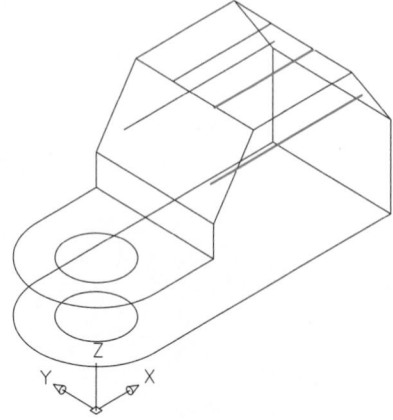

Figure 21-90   The two lines are mirrored

36. **TRIM** the top edges as shown in Figure 21-91. Select the two highlighted lines as cutting edges.
37. Invoke the **3DPOLY** command and draw the two highlighted 3D polylines as shown in Figure 21-92. Zoom in and out as needed.
38. Invoke the **3DORBIT** command to inspect the 3D model.
39. **SAVE** the drawing.

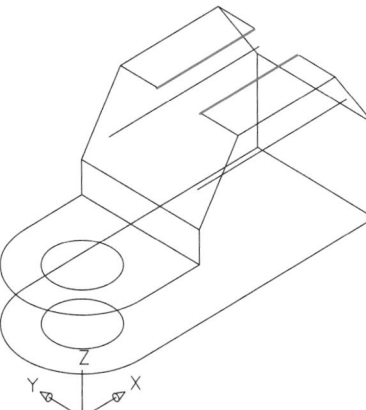

Figure 21-91   The two horizontal lines are trimmed

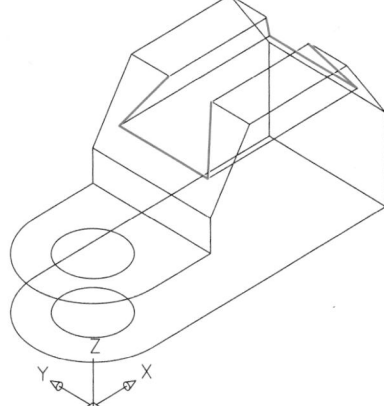

Figure 21-92   The two 3D polylines complete the 3D model

As you probably have noticed, building a wireframe model is certainly a laborious task. The main reason is that you have to place each of the wires one by one. Besides, the use of 3D models represented by wire objects is very limited; visual aids, such as the **HIDE** operation or applying the different visual styles, do not have any effect on them.

Tutorial 21-2: The Boat Hull

A hull is the main part of a boat. Typically made of fiberglass, its geometry is very complex because its shape is determined by hydrodynamic concepts. Designers prefer to represent 3D models of hulls using surface objects, which requires placing a wire skeleton first.

First, you will create several cross sections of the boat hull. Then, you will place the sections at the proper location aided by a main curve, which represents the side view of the boat. Finally, you will use the resulting locations of the points throughout the 3D space to generate the final curves defining the edges of the surface object.

1. Start a **NEW** drawing using the **acad** template.
2. **SAVE** the drawing **AS** *Tutorial 21-2*.
3. Select the **Front** view. The UCS should automatically change to **Front** as well, if the **UCSORTHO** system variable is set to **1**. Draw the 2D curve as shown in Figure 21-93. Locate the leftmost point on the UCS's origin **(0,0,0)**.
4. Invoke the **PEDIT** command and use the **Join** option to turn all the objects into a single polyline.

Figure 21-93   The main curve of the hull

5. Draw a **48″**-long vertical line anywhere. **MOVE** the line so its midpoint is located at the left endpoint of the curve.
6. Invoke the **ARRAY** command to create an arrayed set of copies of the line, as shown in Figure 21-94. Specify the array parameters as shown in Figure 21-95.

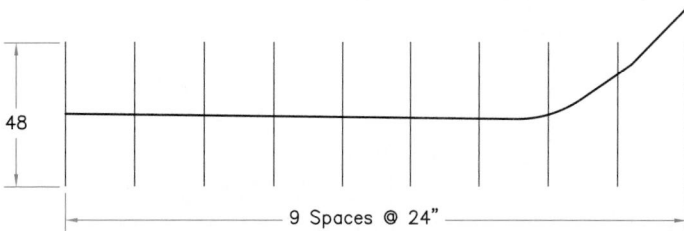

Figure 21-94   An arrayed copy of the line

Figure 21-95   The **Array** dialog box

7. Select the **Right** view.
8. Draw the 2D curve shown in Figure 21-96.
9. Select the **Isometric SE** viewpoint and **MOVE** all the objects belonging to the curve you just drew, placing its lower corner at the first intersection (or endpoint) (Figure 21-97). Any UCS may be used for this operation.

Note:
Do not be concerned about placing the objects in a specific place; they will be moved later. This curve does not need to be turned into a polyline.

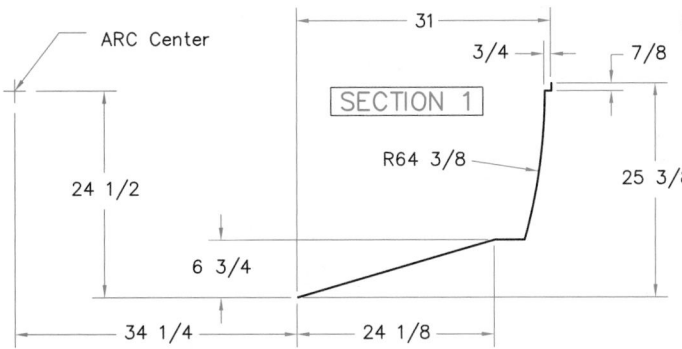

Figure 21-96   The first half section of the hull

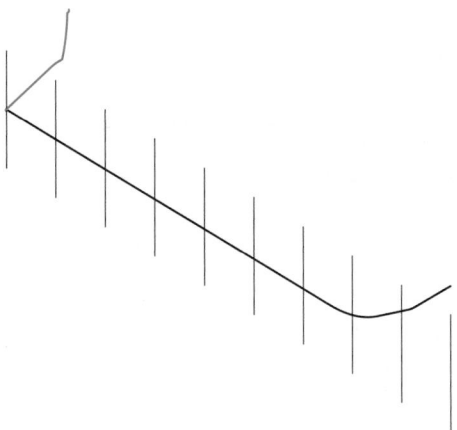

Figure 21-97   The first half section in place

10. Select the **Right** view again and draw the rest of the section's 2D curves, as shown in Figure 21-98. You can place them anywhere, but try to place them in order so that you don't get confused later. If possible, give them names such as *Section 2*, *Section 3,* and so on.
11. Select the **Isometric SE** viewpoint, or use the **3DORBIT** command to achieve an appropriate view.
12. **MOVE** each section one by one to its corresponding location. The results should look like Figure 21-99. Make sure you snap to the intersection when specifying the second point of displacement in each move operation.
13. **ERASE** all the vertical lines that were used to locate the hull's sections (Figure 21-100).

SECTION 2

7/8   3/4
18 3/4
7 3/8
24 1/2   3 5/8
31 1/4

SECTION 3

3 3/8   1
19 1/4
3/4
8 1/8
24 7/8   3 1/2
31 7/8

SECTION 4

4 1/8   1
19 3/4
3/4
8 3/4
25   3 3/8
32 1/4

SECTION 5

4 1/2   1 1/8
20
3/4
9 5/8
24 7/8   3 1/8
32

SECTION 6

4 1/2   1 5/8
19 3/4
3/4
10 3/4
23 7/8   2 7/8
30 7/8

SECTION 7

4 1/2   2 5/8
18 7/8
3/4
12 1/2
2 1/8
20 7/8
28 5/8

SECTION 8

4 5/8   4 1/8
16 7/8
3/4
13 1/2
1 1/8
14
24 7/8

SECTION 9

4 3/4   6 7/8
14 3/8
7/8
2 3/4   1/4
3 1/4
15 3/8

Figure 21-98   The rest of the sections

Figure 21-99   The sections are placed in their corresponding locations

Figure 21-100   The arrayed lines are erased

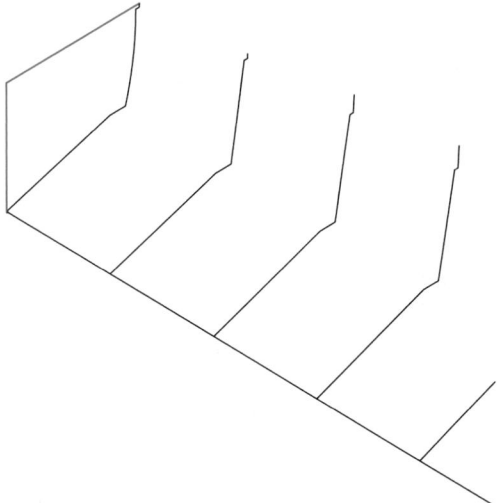

Figure 21-101   Two lines are placed at the first section

14. Select the **Right** UCS and draw the two lines shown in Figure 21-101.
15. Invoke the **SPLINE** command and create the first two splines going through the two sets of points that are closer to the main curve on each section, as shown in Figure 21-102.

> **Note:**
> In step 14, one of the lines is parallel to the X-axis and the other one is parallel to the Y-axis. In this case, Autotrack can be helpful.

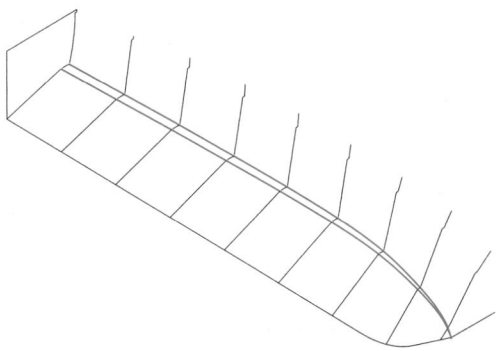

Figure 21-102   Two splines are created through a common set of points in the sections

> **Note:**
> An additional vertical line needs to be placed at the nose. It will locate the point where the next set of splines will meet.

TIP   When specifying the last point of the splines, you will need to press the **<Enter ↵>** key three times to accept the default tangency conditions.

16. Select the **Front** UCS and create the line shown in Figure 21-103. Do not be concerned about its length.

TIP   A line of sufficient length can be created on the rightmost endpoint, then moved toward the left 5 3/8″ and trimmed.

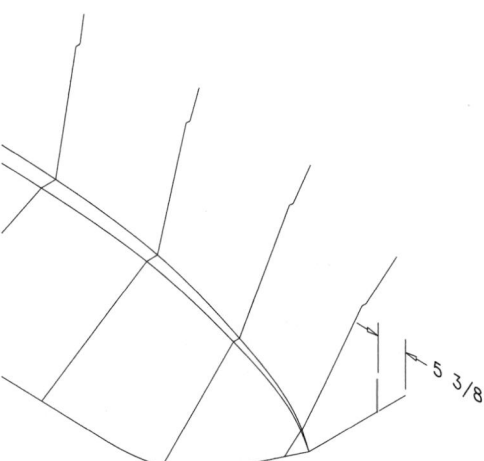

Figure 21-103   A new short line is created

17. Invoke the **SPLINE** command and place the last three splines through the remaining set of points.
18. **ERASE** the line you drew in the previous step (Figure 21-104).

Figure 21-104   Three more splines are created through a common set of points in the sections

19. **ERASE** all the intermediate sections (Figure 21-105).
20. Select the **Isometric SE** viewpoint. Double-click the mouse wheel to **ZOOM** to extents.
21. **SAVE** the drawing.

This project will continue at the end of Chapter 22, where you will add the polygon meshes.

Figure 21-105   The hull sections are erased and the desired wireframe is obtained

CHAPTER PROJECTS

Project 21-1: Objects: Part 1

Using the same objects that you use to generate 2D work, develop the wireframe 3D model of the object shown in Figure 21-106. Do not place any dimensions or use any linetypes other than **Continuous**. Their only purpose in the figure is to clarify your task.

Figure 21-106 Dimensions for objects: Part 1

Project 21-2: Objects: Part 2

Using the same objects that you use to generate 2D work, develop the wireframe 3D model of the object shown in Figure 21-107. Do not place any dimensions or use any linetypes other than **Continuous**. Their only purpose in the figure is to clarify your task.

Figure 21-107 Dimensions for objects: Part 2

Creating and Modifying Meshes 22

Chapter Objectives

- Explore the advantages and disadvantages of using meshes or faceted surfaces to represent 3D models.
- Study other objects that can be used along with faceted surfaces to represent 3D models.
- Learn to create 3D primitives with faceted surfaces.
- Know the system variable that controls the smoothness of meshes and polygon meshes.
- Learn how to create complex meshes.
- Learn the different procedures for modifying meshes and polygon meshes.
- Combine meshes with other objects to create the final 3D model.
- Know specific uses of grips with faceted meshes.
- Learn how to transform polygon meshes into smoother faceted surfaces.
- Learn how to modify the meshes using their subobjects.
- Learn and practice the uses of 2D solids and 3D faces.
- Change the system variable settings to control the quality of shaded faceted surfaces.
- Explore and create other objects used in surface modeling.
- Learn the details about Boolean operations with regions.
- Create 3D models of real objects using faceted surfaces.
- Learn how to convert meshes into solids, and vice versa.

INTRODUCTION

CLASSIFICATION OF SURFACES IN 3D MODELS

When 3D models are represented with faceted surfaces, only the outer skin is placed throughout the 3D space. In most cases, several faceted surfaces or meshes are placed next to each other to represent the delimited object's surfaces or faces. The surfaces of any object can be classified into three general types (Figure 22-1):

- Planar surfaces
- Surfaces with a single curvature (i.e., cylindrical and conical surfaces)
- Surfaces with curvature in both directions (i.e., a spherical surface)

Unlike wires, faceted surfaces or meshes, along with other entities that are used to represent the surfaces of objects, can hide objects located behind them. They can also be used to obtain shaded and rendered images.

TYPES OF OBJECTS USED TO REPRESENT FACETED SURFACES

Several types of objects or entities can be used to represent individual surfaces of a 3D model depending on the type of surface that is being modeled, as well as its geometric complexity. In some cases, a single object or entity can represent more than one surface.

Planar Surface

Surface with
Single Curvature

Surface with
Curvature in Both
Directions

Figure 22-1   Examples of an object's surfaces and how they are represented using faceted surfaces and similar entities

Planar surfaces can be represented with the following objects:

- Thickened objects (lines, circles, arcs, etc.)
- Regions
- 2D solids
- 3D faces
- Polygon meshes
- Meshes

Surfaces with a single curvature are represented with the following objects:

- Thickened objects (lines, circles, arcs, etc.)
- Polygon meshes

Surfaces with curvature in both directions can be represented only with polygon meshes.

Polygon Meshes and Meshes

polygon mesh: Surface object composed of individual three- or four-sided polygons joined together.

A ***polygon mesh*** is a surface object composed of individual three- or four-sided polygons joined together (Figure 22-2). The set of polygons is organized by an $N \times M$ set of vertices or matrices. A polygon mesh can be either *open* or *closed* in either of the two directions M or N (Figure 22-3). When a mesh is closed in a certain direction, the first or last row or column of vertices is shared.

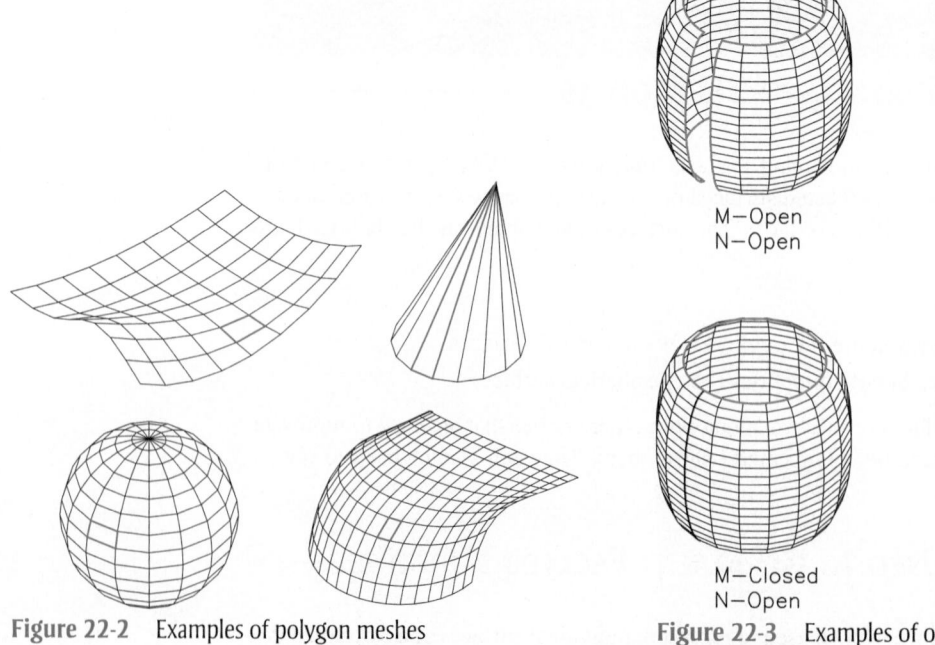

M−Open
N−Open

M−Open
N−Closed

M−Closed
N−Open

M−Closed
N−Closed

Figure 22-2   Examples of polygon meshes

Figure 22-3   Examples of open and closed polygon meshes in the M and N directions

Polygon meshes are very old types of objects. Meshes, however, are a more recent addition to the family of 3D objects. **Meshes** are surface-type objects that can be edited and converted to a solid. Meshes have much more editing capabilities and can be converted to solids. A good way to see the difference in editing capabilities between polygon meshes and meshes is by comparing their properties; see Figure 22-4.

meshes: Surface-type objects that can be edited and converted to a solid.

Figure 22-4   Different properties are available for polygon meshes and meshes

Polygon meshes and meshes are the primary objects used to create 3D models with faceted surfaces because they can represent any type of surface, and can be edited to generate more complex surfaces. Sometimes, however, it is much easier to use another type of object to achieve the same result.

Polyface meshes are another type of object used to represent faceted surfaces. Like polygon meshes and meshes, polyface meshes are made of smaller faces joined together. This type of object is typically created by applications rather than by the user. For example, 3D primitives such as boxes, wedges, and pyramids are created as polyface meshes by AutoCAD (Figure 22-5).

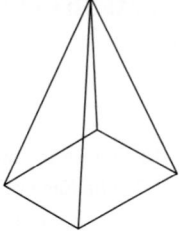

Figure 22-5   Examples of polyface meshes created by specific applications

The polygon mesh is an old type of object used to represent the surfaces of 3D models. With the AutoCAD software, besides polygon meshes, meshes, and polyface meshes, you can also create true surfaces for such purposes. Generally, true surfaces are more easily edited than are faceted surfaces. Unlike faceted surfaces, true surfaces can interact with 3D solids. Meshes are the most versatile type within the faceted surface type objects, but they are never as versatile as true surfaces.

> **FOR MORE DETAILS**
> See Chapters 23 and 24 to learn more about true surfaces.

Using faceted surfaces to represent 3D models, however, still has three remarkable advantages over using surfaces and 3D solids:

1. They can be transformed and smoothed into more complex surface shapes.
2. They are highly flexible. Their grips can be stretched in any direction in order to create free-form shapes.
3. Meshes in particular can be edited using subobjects and can be converted to 3D solids.

DECIDING WHEN TO USE FACETED SURFACES

The thickness of a real object is never 0. For certain objects, however, the thickness is not relevant to the design process. For those objects it is necessary to model only the outer or inner surfaces.

A molded fiberglass part such as a boat hull is an example in which the surfaces of an object are the only geometrically relevant aspect for the concept design. The design of an automobile body can also be considered conceptually as involving only surfaces.

Using meshes and other related objects can also be considered when the only purpose of the 3D model is to create a rendered image. An example is a drawing of the exterior walls of a building.

You can combine meshes, surfaces, and 3D solids in your 3D model. For instance, when creating 3D models for interior design, the inside face of walls can be represented with surfaces, whereas furniture and other objects can be created as 3D solids.

If the purpose of a model is totally artistic, a faceted surface may be the best choice because of its flexibility. For topographical and landscape representations of terrains, polygon meshes are also a good choice.

CREATING 3D PRIMITIVES AS FACETED SURFACES

THE 3D COMMAND

The **3D** command is used to create polygon meshes, meshes, and polyface meshes that look like 3D primitives such as boxes, cones, and spheres. Each of these is created by specifying one of the options of the **3D** command. This command can be invoked only through the command line window. Figure 22-6 shows the command's shortcut menu with the available options.

Objects such as cones, dishes, domes, spheres, and tori can either be created as polygon meshes or meshes. The value of the **MESHTYPE** system variable determines the result. When its value is <1>, it creates meshes.

The Box Option

The **Box** option creates a polyface mesh with the shape of a box. You need to specify the five geometric elements shown in Figure 22-7. The base of the box will be constructed parallel to the current UCS. The **MESHTYPE** system variable does not affect the resulting object.

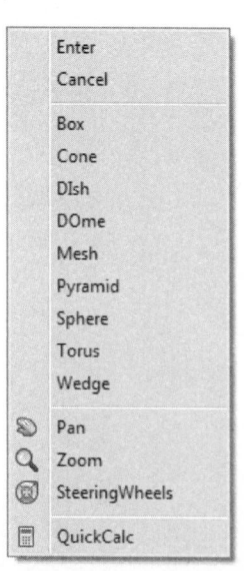

Figure 22-6 The **3D** command's shortcut menu

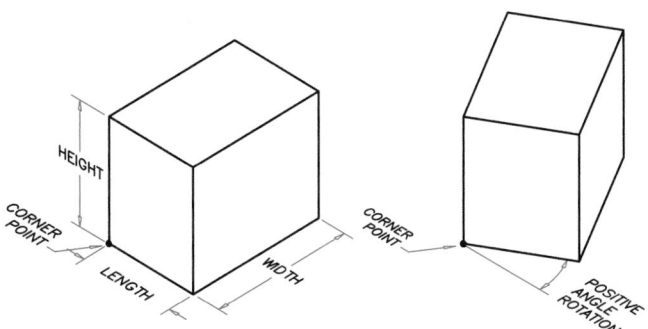

Figure 22-7   Geometric elements specified when creating a box-shaped polyface mesh using the **Box** option of the **3D** command

Exercise 22-1: Creating a Box Surface with the **3D** Command

1. Start a **NEW** drawing using the **acad** template.
2. **SAVE** the drawing **AS** *Exercise 22-1*.
3. Select the **SE Isometric** viewing point.
4. Invoke the **Box** option of the **3D** command to create the box shown in Figure 22-8. Respond to the prompts as follows:

   Specify corner point of box: *Click anywhere in the drawing area.*

   Specify length of box: *2* ↵

   Specify width of box or [Cube]: *3* ↵

   Specify height of box: *2.5* ↵

   Specify rotation angle of box about the Z axis or [Reference]: ↵ *(To accept the default value 0)*

> **Note:**
> The default value of the rotation angle is not always 0. It is updated depending on the last value you specified.

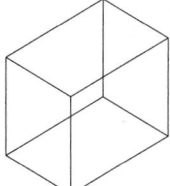

Figure 22-8   The resulting box

> **TIP**
> After entering the width dimension, you can use the **Cube** option to create a cube surface.

5. Invoke the **Box** option of the **3D** command again and respond to the prompts as follows:

   Specify corner point of box: *Specify endpoint 1 as shown in Figure 22-9.*

   Specify length of box: *4* ↵

   Specify width of box or [Cube]: *c* ↵

   Specify rotation angle of box about the Z axis or [Reference]: *Snap to midpoint 2.*

6. Invoke the **HIDE** command. The 3D model should look like Figure 22-10.
7. **SAVE** the drawing.

> **Note:**
> The object snaps are temporarily turned off when any of the objects of the **3D** command is invoked. To snap to a point, you can click on the specific object snap icon directly.

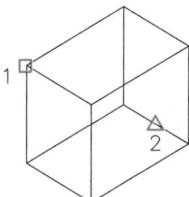

Figure 22-9   Points to be specified with the operation

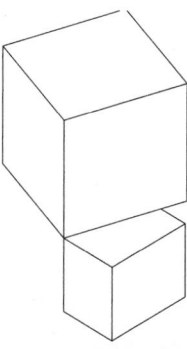

Figure 22-10   The resulting second box

The Wedge Option

The **Wedge** option creates a polyface mesh in the shape of a wedge (Figure 22-11). This command proceeds exactly like the **Box** option of the **3D** command. Again, the base of the wedge will be constructed parallel to the current UCS. The **MESHTYPE** system variable does not affect the result.

Figure 22-11   Geometric elements specified when creating a wedge-shaped polyface mesh using the **Wedge** option of the **3D** command

<u>Exercise 22-2:</u> Creating a Wedge Surface with the **3D** Command

1. Start a **NEW** drawing using the **acad** template.
2. **SAVE** the drawing **AS** *Exercise 22-2*.
3. Select the **SE Isometric** viewing point.
4. Invoke the **Wedge** option of the **3D** command.
5. Create two wedges, specifying the exact same values and snap points as in *Exercise 22-1*. After you invoke the **HIDE** command, the 3D model should look like Figure 22-12.
6. **SAVE** the drawing.

Note:
Because a wedge object cannot be a cube, this option will not be available for this type of object. You will need to specify the width and height using the same value as for the length.

The Pyramid Option

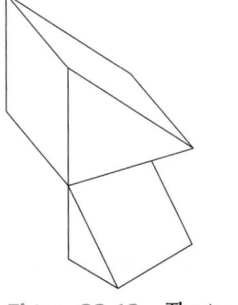

Figure 22-12   The two resulting wedges

The **Pyramid** option creates a polyface mesh in the shape of a pyramid or a tetrahedron, depending on whether the base has four or three vertices. Basically, you can combine these two types of bases with three different types of roof to achieve the desired final shape of the polygon mesh. Figure 22-13 shows the order in which the points will need to be specified according to the options you use. The **MESHTYPE** system variable does not affect the resulting object.

In this type of object, neither the base nor the roof has to lie in the current UCS in which the object is created. Therefore, you do not need to change the UCS before invoking the **3D** command.

When creating pyramids, you must pay special attention to the relative location of the points to avoid an undesired twisting of the object.

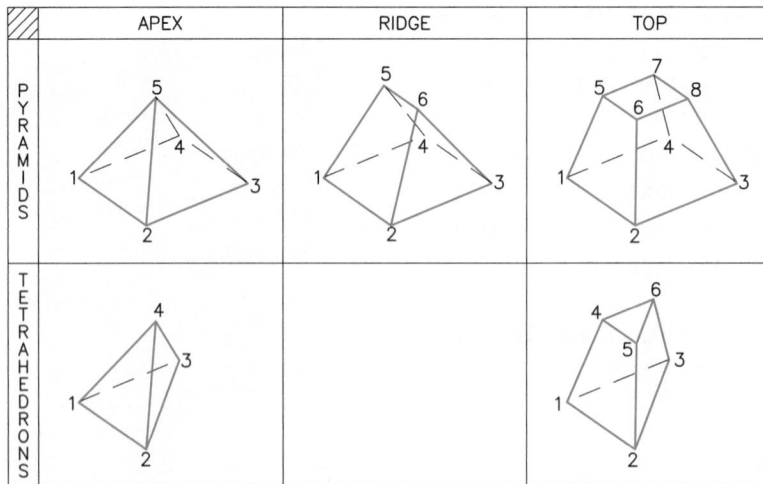

Figure 22-13   Different types of pyramids and tetrahedrons that can be created using the **Pyramid** option of the **3D** command, and the order in which the points must be specified

Exercise 22-3: Creating an Apex Pyramid Using the 3D Command

1. Start a **NEW** drawing using the **acad** template.
2. **SAVE** the drawing **AS** *Exercise 22-3*.
3. Select the **SE Isometric** viewing point.
4. Invoke the **Pyramid** option of the **3D** command. Respond to the prompts as follows:

    Specify first corner point for base of pyramid: *0,0* ⏎

    Specify second corner point for base of pyramid: *3,0* ⏎

    Specify third corner point for base of pyramid: *3,4* ⏎

    Specify fourth corner point for base of pyramid or [Tetrahedron]: *0,4* ⏎

    Specify apex point of pyramid or [Ridge/Top]: *1.5,3,4* ⏎

5. Invoke the **HIDE** command. The 3D model should look like Figure 22-14.
6. Practice creating other types of pyramids and tetrahedrons.
7. **SAVE** the drawing.

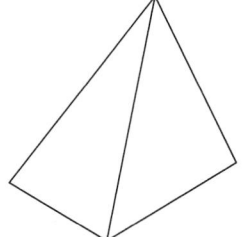

Figure 22-14   The resulting pyramid

The Cone Option

The **Cone** option creates M-open, N-closed polygon meshes in the shape of a cone or a cylinder. The command prompts you to specify points and distances to define the geometric figure. In the event the radius for the top and bottom is specified as the same, the surface obtained will be a cylinder. The base of the cone is placed on a plane parallel to the UCS; its axis is parallel to the current Z-axis (Figure 22-15). When the **MESHTYPE** system variable is set to 1, a mesh-type object is obtained instead of a polygon mesh.

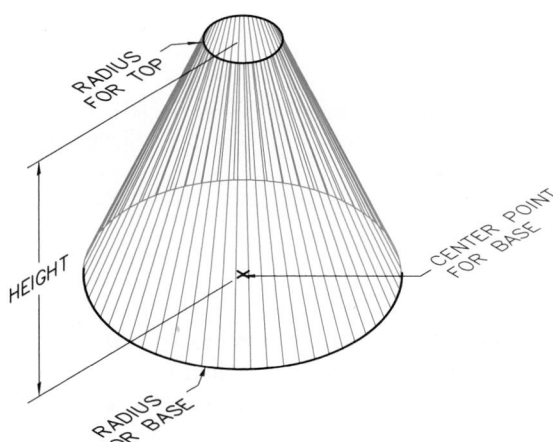

Figure 22-15   Geometric elements specified when creating a cone-shaped polygon mesh using the **Cone** option of the **3D** command

Exercise 22-4: Creating Cones with the **3D** Command

1. Start a **NEW** drawing using the **acad** template.
2. **SAVE** the drawing **AS** *Exercise 22-4*.
3. Select the **SE Isometric** viewing point.
4. Invoke the **Cone** option of the **3D** command. Respond to the prompts as follows:

    Specify center point for base of cone: *Click anywhere in the drawing area.*

    Specify radius for base of cone or [Diameter]: *3* ⏎

    Specify radius for top of cone or [Diameter] <0>: *1* ⏎

    Specify height of cone: *5* ⏎

    Enter number of segments for surface of cone <16>: *25* ⏎

5. Invoke the **Cone** option of the **3D** command again. Respond to the prompts as follows:

Specify center point for base of cone: *Click in the drawing area, next to the other cone.*

Specify radius for base of cone or [Diameter]: *3* ↵

Specify radius for top of cone or [Diameter] <0>: *(To accept the default 0)*

Specify height of cone: *5* ↵

Enter number of segments for surface of cone <16>: *4* ↵

Note:
The number of segments can be set between **2** and **32767**. The larger the value, the smoother and more accurate the cone will be. Too many segments, however, can affect the computer's performance.

6. Invoke the **HIDE** command. The two objects should look like Figure 22-16.
7. **SAVE** the drawing.

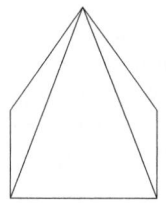

Figure 22-16   Two resulting objects created with the **Cone** option of the **3D** command

TIP   By simply specifying a small number of segments, you can create a polygon mesh shaped like a pyramid. Using the **Cone** option, you can also create a cylinder by specifying the same value for the top and base radii.

The Sphere, Dome, and Dish Options

The **Sphere, Dome,** and **Dish** options create M-closed, N-open polygon meshes in the shape of a sphere and the top and bottom halves of a sphere, respectively. For these options you must specify the center point and the radius, as well as the longitudinal and latitudinal number of segments. The imaginary line joining the two poles, or a pole with the center point, will be parallel to the Z-axis of the current UCS (Figure 22-17). When the **MESHTYPE** system variable is set to 1, a mesh-type object is created.

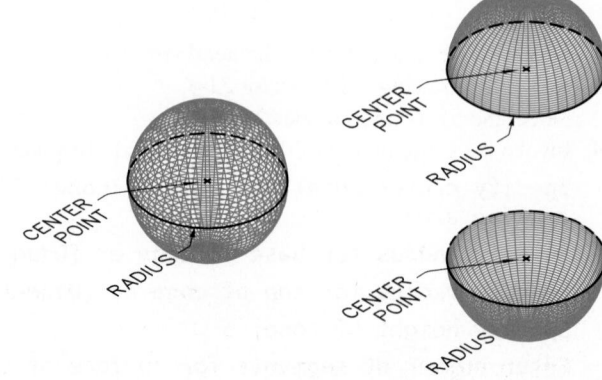

Figure 22-17   Geometric elements specified when using the **Sphere, Dome**, and **Dish** options of the **3D** command to create polygon meshes

Exercise 22-5: Creating a Dish with the **3D** Command

1. Start a **NEW** drawing using the **acad** template.
2. **SAVE** the drawing **AS** *Exercise 22-5*.
3. Select the **SE Isometric** viewing point.
4. Invoke the **Dish** option of the **3D** command. Respond to the prompts as follows:

   Specify center point of dish: *Click anywhere in the drawing area.*

   Specify radius of dish or [Diameter]: *3* ↵

   Enter number of longitudinal segments for surface of dish, <16>: *30* ↵

   Enter number of latitudinal segments for surface of dish <8>: *15* ↵

5. Invoke the **HIDE** command. The dish should look like Figure 22-18.
6. Practice creating a sphere and a dome.
7. **SAVE** the drawing.

Note:
As with the **Cone** option, the number of segments for a dish can be set between **2** and **32767**.

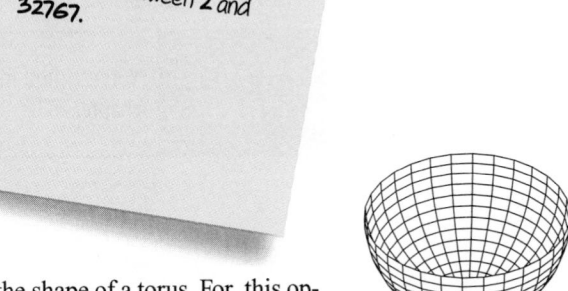

Figure 22-18   The resulting dish

The Torus Option

The **Torus** option creates an M-closed, N-closed polygon mesh in the shape of a torus. For this option you must specify the center point and radius of the torus, the tube radius, and the longitudinal and latitudinal number of segments. The midplane of the torus is located parallel to the current UCS (Figure 22-19). When the **MESHTYPE** system variable is set to 1, a mesh-type object is created.

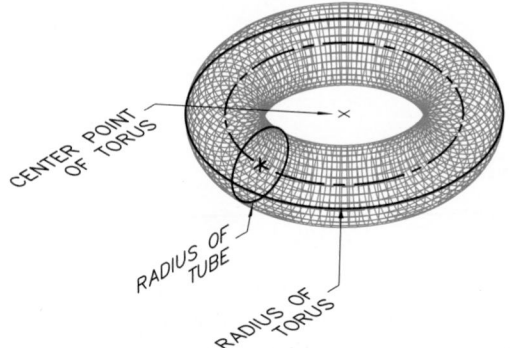

Figure 22-19   Geometric elements specified when creating a torus-shaped polygon mesh using the **Torus** option of the **3D** command

Exercise 22-6: Creating a Torus with the **3D** Command

1. Start a **NEW** drawing using the **acad** template.
2. **SAVE** the drawing **AS** *Exercise 22-6*.
3. Select the **SE Isometric** viewing point.
4. Invoke the **Torus** option of the **3D** command. Respond to the prompts as follows:

   Specify center point of torus: *Click anywhere in the drawing area.*

   Specify radius of torus or [Diameter]: *3* ↵

   Specify radius of tube or [Diameter]: *.75* ↵

   Enter number of segments around tube circumference <16>: *60* ↵

   Enter number of segments around torus circumference <16>: *20* ↵

5. Invoke the **HIDE** command. The torus should look like Figure 22-20.
6. **SAVE** the drawing.

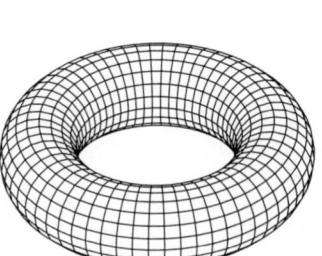

Figure 22-20   The resulting torus

The Mesh Option

The **Mesh** option creates an M-open, N-open polygon mesh by specifying its four corner points. The points must be entered in the form of a loop to avoid creating self-intersecting surfaces. If the four points are specified on the same plane, the result will be a planar polygon mesh. If one of the points does not belong to a common plane, the result will be a nonplanar polygon mesh (Figure 22-21). The **MESHTYPE** system variable does not affect the resulting object created.

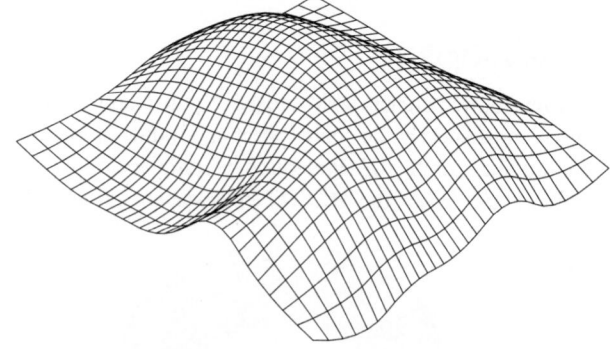

Figure 22-21 Depending on the points specified, the resulting mesh can be either planar or nonplanar

In practice, it is more useful to create a planar polygon mesh with this option. Its grips can then be edited to produce other shapes. Figure 22-22 shows a planar polygon mesh after stretching some of its grips and smoothing it.

FOR MORE DETAILS	You can find more information about deforming meshes with grips later in this chapter.

Figure 22-22 A mesh created with this command can be deformed by pulling its grips

CREATING 3D PRIMITIVES AS MESHES WITH THE MESH COMMAND

The **MESH** command allows you to create 3D primitives, similar to those created with the **3D** command. The **MESH** command is much newer than the **3D** command, so it works in an easier and more interactive fashion. With the **MESH** command, you can create only meshes, regardless of the value of the **MESHTYPE** system variable.

According to the command's option you choose, you can create boxes, cones, cylinders, pyramids, spheres, wedges, and tori. The options can be acessesed from the shortest menu or they can be easily invoked from the **Primitives** panel on the **Mesh Modeling** tab on the Ribbon (Figure 22-23).

Figure 22-23 The new AutoCAD primitive meshes

You can change the smoothness of the objects created with the command by accesing the **settings** option; the smoothness can be specified as 0, 1, 2, 3, or 4. As the smoothness value increases, the object becomes smoother and the edges become move round. You can also change the value of the object's smoothness through the **Properties** palette. Figure 22-24 shows 3D primitive objects with a 4 level of smoothness and the **Properties** palette where you can easily access this setting.

Figure 22-24   The smoothness of the edges of the new mesh primitives can be changed through the **Properties** palette

The **Tessellation** option within the settings opens the **Mesh Primitive Options** dialog box, where you can change the tessellation divisions for each of the 3D primitives independently (Figure 22-25). In the preview area, you can pan, zoom, and rotate the image. With the **MESH** command, you can create different mesh objects that look like 3D primitive shapes by combining the smoothness value and the number of tessellation divisions.

Figure 22-25   The **Tessellation Divisions** properties can be specified in different ways

THE 3DMESH COMMAND

Regardless of the **MESHTYPE** system variable, the **3DMESH** command creates an M-open, N-open polygon mesh by specifying first the number of vertices in terms of the M and N values, and then the location of every individual vertex. You can create a planar polygon mesh by specifying all the points on the same plane, or you can create a mesh in any 3D shape by specifying the locations of the vertices throughout the 3D space.

When using the **3DMESH** command, pay special attention to the order in which the points are entered to avoid creating self-intersecting meshes. You should try to enter the points in such a way that they form a zigzag relative to a particular plane; so that for each M number of vertices, you will enter an N number of vertices. Figure 22-26 shows the approximate order in which you would enter the location of the vertices for a **5 × 4** mesh (Figure 22-27).

Note:
You will have to enter the number of points given by the result of the multiplication M × N. Specifying a large number of vertex locations is a laborious task. Therefore, most of the time programmers have this command activated inside other applications rather than by the user directly. With the **Mesh** option of the **3D** command, you can easily create an M × N mesh and then change the location of each specific vertex individually.

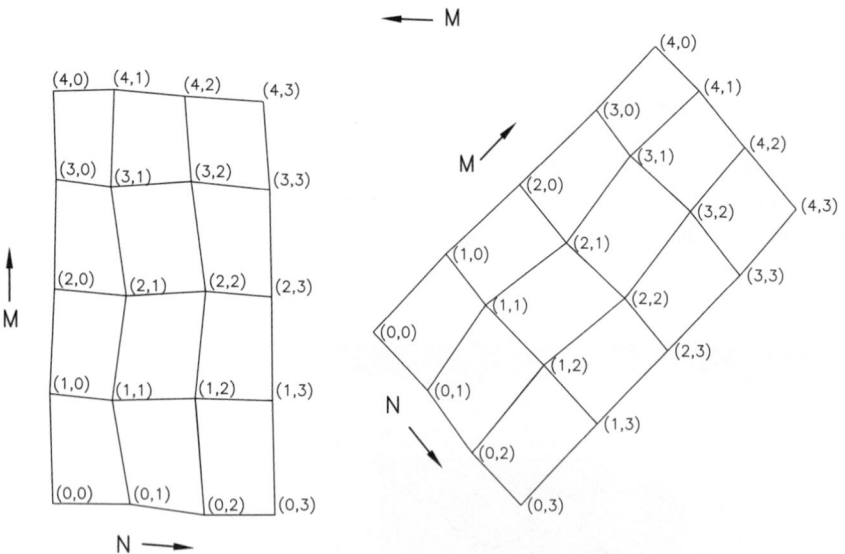

Figure 22-26   The zigzag order in which the points of the mesh must be entered

	N₁	N₂	N₃	N₄
M₁	(0,0)	(0,1)	(0,2)	(0,3)
M₂	(1,0)	(1,1)	(1,2)	(1,3)
M₃	(2,0)	(2,1)	(2,2)	(2,3)
M₄	(3,0)	(0,1)	(3,2)	(3,3)
M₅	(4,0)	(4,1)	(4,2)	(4,3)

Figure 22-27   Examples of meshes and the order in which to enter the points

CREATING COMPLEX POLYGON MESHES

COMMANDS USED TO CREATE COMPLEX POLYGON MESHES

The following group of commands is used to create complex polygon meshes:

- **REVSURF** (Revolved Surfaces)
- **TABSURF** (Tabulated Surfaces)

- **RULESURF** (Ruled Surfaces)
- **EDGESURF** (Edge Surfaces)

These commands are similar in that they all require other wire objects to be selected. Also, the current UCS does not affect the result for any of these commands. When the **MESHTYPE** system variable is set to 1, these commands create mesh-type objects instead of polygon meshes.

Unlike the **3D** command, the commands in this group cannot control the density of the polygon meshes internally. The density of the polygon meshes created by these commands has to be set prior to invoking the command.

The SURFTAB1 and SURFTAB2 System Variables

The **SURFTAB1** and **SURFTAB2** system variables control the number of vertices that the polygon meshes created with the **REVSURF, TABSURF, RULESURF,** and **EDGESURF** commands will have. The **SURFTAB1** variable affects the number of vertices in the N direction of meshes that are created with the **RULESURF** and **TABSURF** commands, and the number of vertices in the M direction of meshes created with the **REVSURF** and **EDGESURF** commands. The **SURFTAB2** variable, on the other hand, affects the number of vertices in the N direction of meshes created with the **REVSURF** and **EDGESURF** commands (Table 22-1).

Table 22-1   Resulting number of M and N tabulations according to the specific command

		RULESURF	TABSURF	REVSURF	EDGESURF
OPEN	M	2	2	SURFTAB1 + 1	SURFTAB1 + 1
OPEN	N	SURFTAB1 + 1	SURFTAB1 + 1	SURFTAB2 + 1	SURFTAB2 + 1
CLOSED	M			SURFTAB1	
CLOSED	N	SURFTAB1	SURFTAB1	SURFTAB2	

The values of the **SURFTAB1** and **SURFTAB2** variables can be set to any integer number between **2** and **32766**. The default value of both variables is **6**. Higher values generate denser, smoother polygon meshes, but they also affect computer performance.

When creating polygon meshes using polylines and 3D polylines that have not been transformed into fitted polylines or into spline-fit polylines using the **REVSURF** and **TABSURF** commands, the M and N values can be determined as shown in Table 22-2. This consideration is based on the fact that polyline straight segments and arc segments are treated differently. Arc segments are tabulated individually, whereas straight segments always have a tabulation of 1.

Table 22-2   The resulting number of M and N tabulations when using polylines and 3D polylines with the REVSURF and TABSURF commands

		TABSURF	REVSURF
OPEN	M	2	SURFTAB1 + 1
OPEN	N	SURFTAB1 × No. Arc Segments + No. Straight Segments + 1	SURFTAB2 × No. Arc Segments + No. Straight Segments + 1
CLOSED	M		SURFTAB1
CLOSED	N	SURFTAB1 × No. Arc Segments + No. Straight Segments	SURFTAB2 × No. Arc Segments + No. Straight Segments

The REVSURF Command

The **REVSURF** command creates a polygon mesh or mesh that looks like a revolved faceted surface by rotating a planar or nonplanar curve around a selected axis (Figure 22-28).

Revolved
Planar Curve

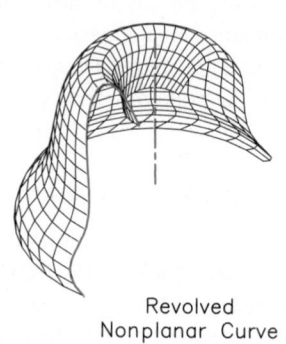

Revolved
Nonplanar Curve

Figure 22-28   Both planar and nonplanar curves can be used to generate polygon meshes and meshes by rotating them about a selected axis with the **REVSURF** command

The axis of revolution is defined by selecting a line, an open polyline, or an open 3D polyline. In the event that a polyline or a 3D polyline is selected, the axis will be considered to be a straight line that goes from the start point of the first segment to the endpoint of the last segment.

The curve defines the type and N size of the mesh. If the curve is closed, the mesh will be N-closed. The mesh will be M-closed only if the angle of revolution is specified as an entire turn (**360°**).

Exercise 22-7: Using the **REVSURF** Command

1. Start a **NEW** drawing using the **acad** template.
2. **SAVE** the drawing **AS** *Exercise 22-7*.
3. Select the **Front** viewing point.
4. Draw the two polylines shown in Figure 22-29.
5. Select the **SE Isometric** viewing point and **ZOOM** in as needed.
6. Set the **SURFTAB1** variable to **4** and the **SURFTAB2** variable to **20**.
7. Invoke the **REVSURF** command, using any of the methods shown in the grid. Respond to the prompts as follows:

Select object to revolve: *Select polyline 1* (Figure 22-30).

Select object that defines the axis of revolution: *Select polyline 2.*

Specify start angle <0>: ↵ *(To accept the default value)*

Specify included angle (+=ccw, -=cw) <360>: ↵ *(To accept the default value)*

Note:
Make sure the UCS has updated to **Front** as well. If not, select it manually.

REVSURF	
Ribbon Primitives panel	
Pull-down Menu	Draw/ Modeling/ Meshes/ Revolved Surface
Command Line	revsurf

Figure 22-29   Profile and axis to be created

Figure 22-30   Selection procedure

TIP You can use different colors to differentiate a surface from a curve.

8. Invoke the **3DORBIT** command to inspect your model.
9. Invoke the **HIDE** command. The 3D model should look like Figure 22-31.
10. **SAVE** the drawing.

Exercise 22-8: Using the **REVSURF** Command with Different **SURFTAB** Values

1. **OPEN** the drawing *Exercise 22-7*.
2. **SAVE** the drawing **AS** *Exercise 22-8*.
3. Select the **SW Isometric** viewing point.
4. **ERASE** the polygon mesh you just created, leaving only the two *polylines*.
5. Change the **SURFTAB1** variable to **20** and invoke the **REVSURF** command again. Respond to the prompts as follows:

   Select object to revolve: *Select the same polyline as in the previous exercise.*

   Select object that defines the axis of revolution: *Select the same polyline as in the previous exercise.*

   Specify start angle <0>: ↵ *(To accept the default)*

   Specify included angle (+=ccw, -=cw)<360>: *–180* ↵

6. **HIDE** the objects. The 3D model should look like Figure 22-32.
7. **SAVE** the drawing.

Figure 22-31   The resulting faceted surface model

Figure 22-32   The resulting faceted surface model

The TABSURF Command

The **TABSURF** command creates a polygon mesh or mesh that looks like an extruded faceted surface. With this command, you can extrude a planar or nonplanar curve along the direction of a selected vector (Figure 22-33).

Planar Curve   Nonplanar Curve

Figure 22-33   Both planar and nonplanar curves can be used to generate polygon meshes by extruding them along a selected vector with the **TABSURF** command

Lines, open polylines, and open 3D polylines are the only types of objects that can be selected to define the vector. As with the **REVSURF** command, if a polyline or a 3D polyline is selected, the vector will be considered to be a straight line that goes from the start point of the first segment to the endpoint of the last segment. The extrusion can be made toward one side or the other, depending on which of the two halves of the vector you click on when selecting it.

The curve defines whether the polygon mesh is open or closed in the N direction. You cannot create an M-closed mesh with this command. For this reason, the M size of meshes created with this command is always **2**.

Exercise 22-9: Using the **TABSURF** Command

TABSURF	
Ribbon Primitives panel	
Pull-down Menu	Draw/ Modeling/ Meshes/ Tabulated Surface
Command Line	tabsurf

1. **OPEN** *Exercise 22-8*.
2. **SAVE** the drawing **AS** *Exercise 22-9*.
3. Select the **Top** UCS.
4. **ERASE** the vertical polyline that served as the axis of revolution in the previous exercise.
5. Draw a 3″-long polyline from the endpoint shown in Figure 22-34 and parallel to the *Y*-axis.
6. Change the color of the polygon mesh.
7. Invoke the **DRAWORDER** command and select the polygon mesh to send it to the back. This allows the polyline to stand out, so it can be easily selected.
8. Invoke the **TABSURF** command, using any of the methods shown in the grid. Respond to the prompts as follows:

   `Select object for path curve:` *Select polyline 1 (Figure 22-35).*

   `Select object for direction vector:` *Select polyline 2.*

> **TIP** When selecting line 2, make sure to do it on its right half. Picking the opposite portion will change the direction in which the polygon mesh is created.

9. **HIDE** the objects. The 3D model should look like Figure 22-36.
10. **SAVE** the drawing.

Figure 22-34 The 3D model after adding a polyline

Figure 22-35 Selection order

Figure 22-36 The resulting tabulated faceted surface

The RULESURF Command

The **RULESURF** command creates polygon meshes and meshes that look like ruled faceted surfaces by specifying two curves, or a curve and a point. A cone is an example of a ruled faceted surface obtained by selecting a circle and a point.

Depending on the situation of the curves, you can create polygon meshes that have two, three, or four edges (Figure 22-37).

You can place planar and nonplanar curves anywhere in the 3D space to define the ruled faceted surface. It is important to pick the curve at the same half portion to avoid producing self-intersecting meshes (Figure 22-38).

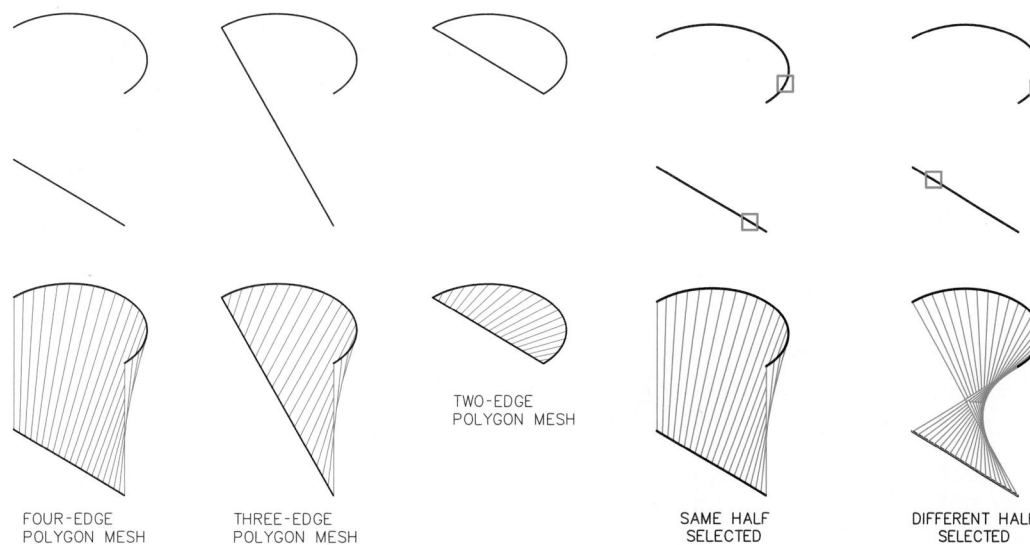

Figure 22-37   You can use the **RULESURF** command to create different polygon meshes according to the relative location of the curves

Figure 22-38   The two curves must be selected at the same half to avoid self-intersecting polygon meshes

Both the selected edges must be either open or closed. The AutoCAD program cannot create a polygon mesh between a closed and an open curve. Two closed curves will generate an N-closed mesh. The 3D model of the hood shown in Figure 22-39 can be represented by four ruled faceted surfaces.

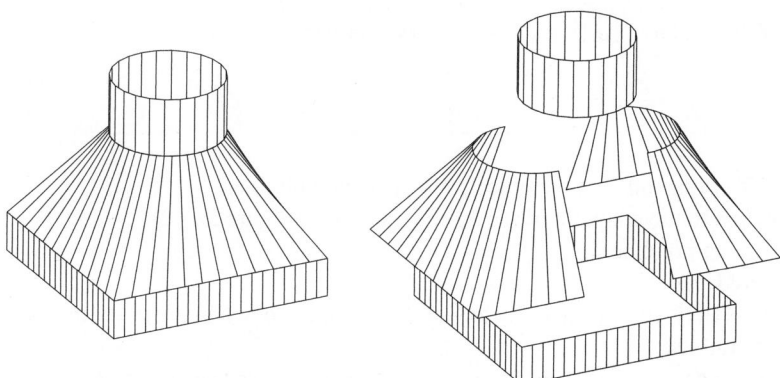

Figure 22-39   The hood shown is an example of the use of ruled faceted surfaces

Exercise 22-10: Using the **RULESURF** Command

1. **OPEN** *Exercise 22-9*.
2. **SAVE** the drawing **AS** *Exercise 22-10*.
3. Select the **Top** view.
4. Invoke the **MIRROR** command. Respond to the prompts as follows:

   Select objects: Specify opposite corner: *Using a selection window, select the polyline located between the two polygon meshes.*

   Select objects: ↵ *(To end the selection)*

   Specify first point of mirror line: *Snap to endpoint 1 (Figure 22-40).*

   Specify second point of mirror line: *With Ortho mode activated, specify a second point 2, vertically above endpoint 1.*

   Erase source objects? [Yes/No] <N>: ↵ *(To accept the default value and keep the selected polyline)*

5. Select the **SE Isometric** viewing point.

Figure 22-40   Selection order   **Figure 22-41**   Dimensions to draw the profile

6. Select the **Front** UCS.
7. Draw the object shown in Figure 22-41 anywhere in an empty space. It will be created on the *XY* plane of the UCS automatically.

RULESURF	
Ribbon Primitives panel	
Pull-down Menu	Draw/ Modeling/ Meshes/ Ruled Surface
Command Line	rulesurf

TIP   You can start by creating a circle, and then add other objects.

8. Using the **PEDIT** command, join the objects into a single polyline.
9. **MOVE** the polyline to the endpoint of the **30**-long polyline (Figure 22-42).
10. **ERASE** the 30″-long polyline.
11. Set the **SURFTAB1** variable to **40**.
12. Invoke the **RULESURF** command, using any of the methods shown in the grid. Respond to the prompts as follows:

Select first defining curve: *Select polyline 1 (Figure 22-43).*
Select second defining curve: *Select polyline 2.*

Figure 22-42   The profile after it has been moved   **Figure 22-43**   Selection order

TIP

Be careful to select both polylines in the same half. Otherwise, the result will be a twisted polygon mesh.

13. Invoke the **HIDE** command. The 3D model with the polygon mesh added should look like Figure 22-44.
14. **SAVE** the drawing.

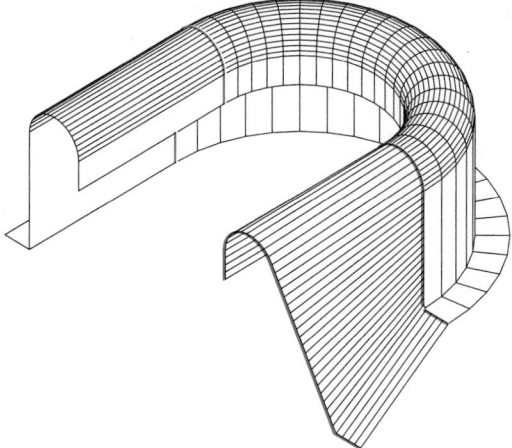

Figure 22-44   The resulting ruled faceted surface

The EDGESURF Command

The **EDGESURF** command creates a polygon mesh or a mesh that looks like a Coons patch faceted surface by specifying four edges. A *Coons patch* is a bicubic surface resulting from interpolating two curves, one controlling the curvature in the M direction and the other one controlling the curvature in the N direction. Examples of this type of surface are shown in Figure 22-45.

The four edges required can be selected in any order, but all must be open and placed end to end, forming a closed path. The side and back of a boat hull are examples of a faceted surface created with the **EDGESURF** command (Figure 22-46).

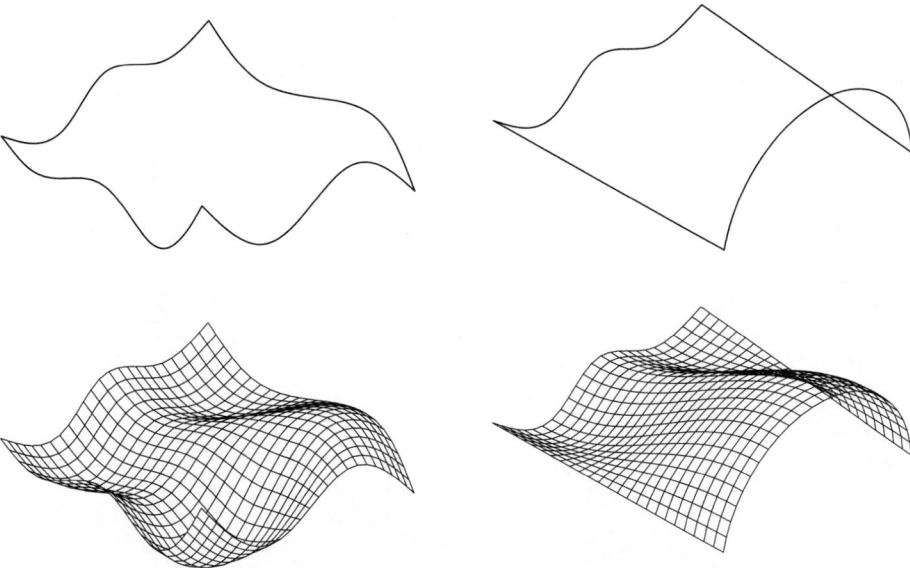

Figure 22-45   Wireframe models and their corresponding Coons patch faceted surfaces

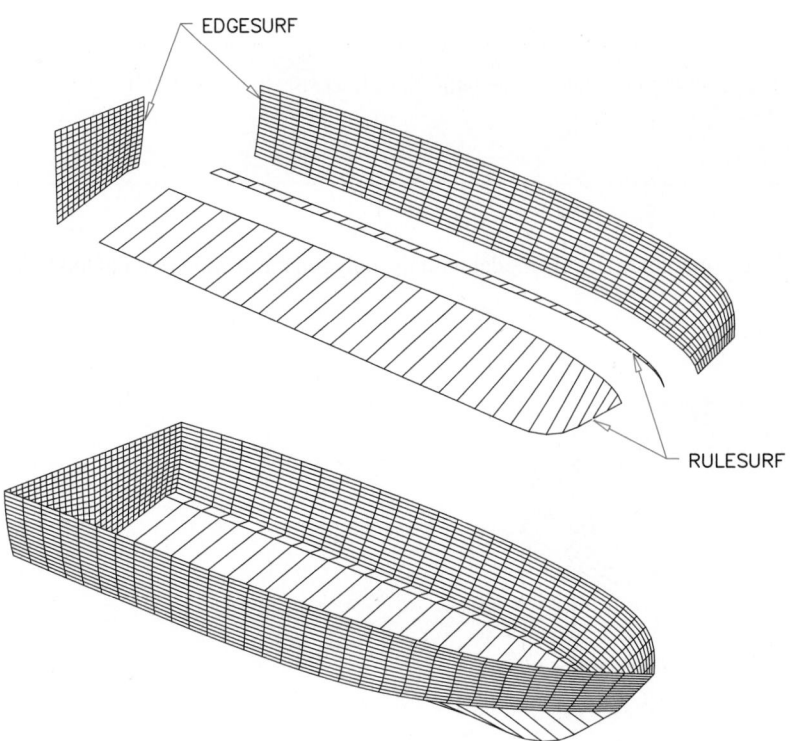

EDGESURF

RULESURF

Figure 22-46   Some of the surfaces of a boat hull can be created using the **EDGESURF** command

Exercise 22-11: Using the **EDGESURF** Command

1. **OPEN** *Exercise 22-10*.
2. **SAVE** the drawing **AS** *Exercise 22-11*.
3. Select the **SE Isometric** viewing point.
4. Your 3D model should still contain three polylines. **MOVE** the leftmost polyline to the other end of the tabulated faceted surface, snapping to any of the endpoints (Figure 22-47).
5. Select the **Top** UCS.
6. **MOVE** the three polygon meshes **4″** toward the positive direction of the *Y*-axis. This will separate the polylines so you can select them more easily.
7. **ERASE** the rightmost polyline.
8. Using the **2Points** option of the **CIRCLE** command and snapping to endpoints only, draw the three highlighted circles. Then with the **LINE** command, draw the two highlighted lines shown in Figure 22-48.

Figure 22-47   Polylines to be moved

Figure 22-48   Other objects to be added

Figure 22-49 After trimming the objects

9. Using the two lines as the cutting edges, **TRIM** the portions of the circles as shown in Figure 22-49. Make sure the projection option of the **TRIM** command is set to UCS after you select the objects.
10. **ERASE** the two lines and select the **Front** UCS.
11. Using the polylines as the cutting edges, **TRIM** each of its end straight segments. The result is shown in Figure 22-50.

Figure 22-50 After performing the final trims

12. Invoke the **EDGESURF** command using any of the methods shown in the grid. When prompted, select in any order the four edges that form a closed contour.
13. Select the **Top** UCS and **MOVE** the polygon mesh just created **4″** toward the positive direction of the *Y*-axis (Figure 22-51).
14. **ERASE** all the curves, leaving only the two arcs at the bottom.
15. Draw two small lines between the endpoints of the arcs, as shown in Figure 22-52.
16. Set the **SURFTAB2** variable to **4**.
17. Invoke the **EDGESURF** command again. When prompted, first select any of the arcs to make this the M direction of the mesh; then select the other three objects in any order.
18. **MOVE** the new polygon mesh 4″ toward the positive direction of the *Y*-axis.
19. **ERASE** the remaining arcs and lines.
20. Explore your 3D model using the **3DORBIT** command.
21. Invoke the **HIDE** command. The **3D** model should look like Figure 22-53.
22. **SAVE** the drawing.

EDGESURF	
Ribbon Primitives panel	
Pull-down Menu	Draw/ Modeling/ Meshes/ Edge Surface
Command Line	edgesurf

Figure 22-51   The resulting polygon mesh after it is moved to the 3D model

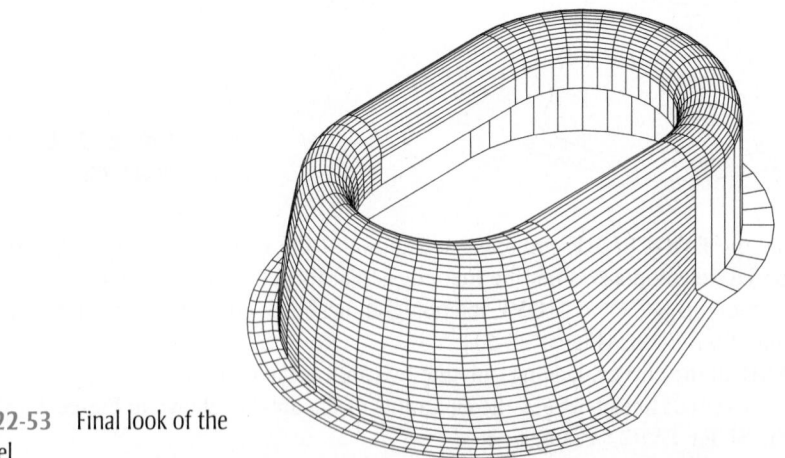

Figure 22-52   Preparing the last four edges

Figure 22-53   Final look of the 3D model

The different operations used to create faceted surfaces, in particular the **EDGESURF** command, are important tools in the development of complex shapes. The flexibility of polygon meshes and their possible transformations can be helpful in achieving complex designs. Understanding these tools is beneficial for the design process because they can assist users in the development of complex 3D models to support engineering documentation.

EDITING POLYGON MESHES

METHODS USED TO EDIT POLYGON MESHES AND MESHES

Polygon meshs and polyface meshes can be easily transformed by stretching their grips. It is precisely their flexibility that makes these particular objects useful for creating artistic and other free-form shapes. The following operations can be used to deform the vertices of a polygon mesh:

- Pulling the grips
- Using the **STRETCH** command
- Editing the polygon mesh with the **PEDIT** command
- Modifying the properties of the polygon mesh in the **Properties** palette

Deforming by Pulling the Grips and the Subobjects

Pulling the selected grips of a polygon mesh will deform its original shape. The jar spout model shown in Figure 22-54 is a typical example. The procedure is simple. The grips first must be revealed by selecting the polygon mesh. Then specific grips must be selected and pulled a certain distance toward the desired direction. You can use the move grip tool to move the grips only in the direction of one of the three axes or within one of the three planes. You can select more than one grip by holding the <**Shift**> key down.

FOR MORE DETAILS	See Chapter 21 for more information about using the move grip tool.

 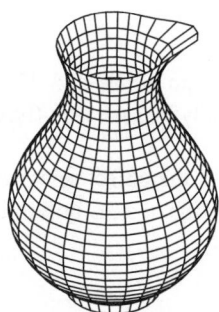

Figure 22-54   A jar spout is a typical example of how a shape can be produced by deforming the polygon mesh grips

If a grip is moved to the location of another grip, both grips will share the same location. You can move as many grips to the same location as you want. For example, by deforming the grips of a polyface mesh created with the **Box** option of the **3D** command, you can create another object such as a wedge (Figure 22-55).

 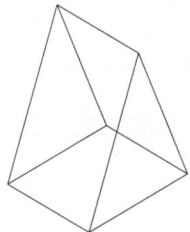

Figure 22-55   A ridge pyramid obtained by moving two grips of a box

Unlike polygon meshes, meshes have only one grip located in the center. However, meshes are even easier to deform than polygon meshes. To modify meshes you select **Subobjects** instead of grips; the subobjects are selected by holding the **<Ctrl>** key down while you make the selection. You can select faces, vertices, and edges when making your selection (Figure 22-56). The selection can be made more easily if you use the subobject selection filters located on the **Subobject** panel of the Ribbon (Figure 22-57).

Figure 22-56   Individual **Faces** in the mesh can be selected for additional operations

Figure 22-57   Using **Subobjects** selection filters makes the selection process easier

Editing with the STRETCH Command

The **STRETCH** command also can be used to pull the vertices of polygon meshes and meshes. All vertices enclosed with the crossing window are automatically selected for the operation.

Editing with the PEDIT Command

The **PEDIT** command is used to edit not only polylines and 3D polylines, but also polygon meshes. On the other hand, true meshes and polyface meshes (boxes, wedges, and pyramids), cannot be edited with the **PEDIT** command.

When the **PEDIT** command is invoked, and the object selected is a polygon mesh, the options available are different from those for a polyline or a 3D polyline. Figure 22-58 compares the shortcut menus for these three types of objects.

Figure 22-58   Comparison among the different **PEDIT** command shortcut menus displayed, depending on the type of object selected

The **Edit Vertex** option is used to move a specific vertex to a new location. You first specify the vertex by the submenu options (**Left, Right, Up, Down**), and then specify the **Move** option within this submenu. You will have to repeat the operation for the next vertex, or select the **eXit** option to return to the main menu.

`[Next/Previous/Left/Right/Up/Down/Move/REgen/eXit]<N>:`

It is easier to move a vertex by using the grips than with the **PEDIT** command. But if two vertices are in the same location, their common grip will move both vertices at the same time (Figure 22-59). The **PEDIT** command, on the other hand, allows you to select one specific vertex whether or not it shares the same location with another vertex.

The **Smooth surface** option smoothes the polygon mesh by fitting it into another type of surface generated by higher-degree mathematical equations.

Polygon meshes can be smoothed into three different types of surfaces (Figure 22-60). The value of the **SURFTYPE** system variable determines the type of surface that the original polygon mesh will be transformed to when smoothed.

- **5** will smooth the polygon mesh to a quadratic B-spline surface.
- **6** will smooth the polygon mesh to a cubic B-spline surface.
- **8** will smooth the polygon mesh to a Bezier surface.

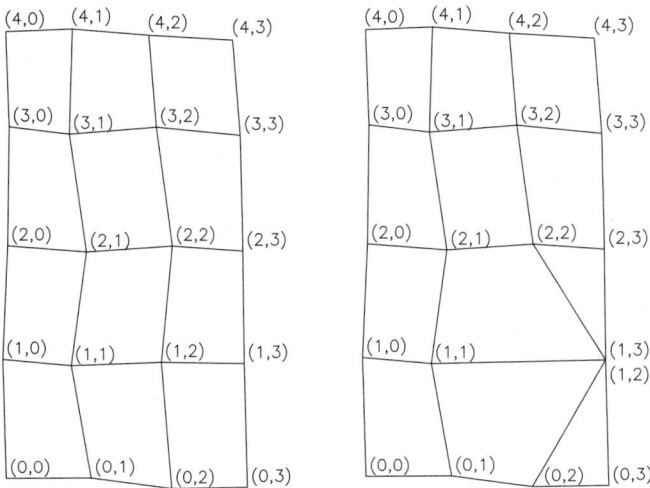

Figure 22-59   Two vertices located in the same place

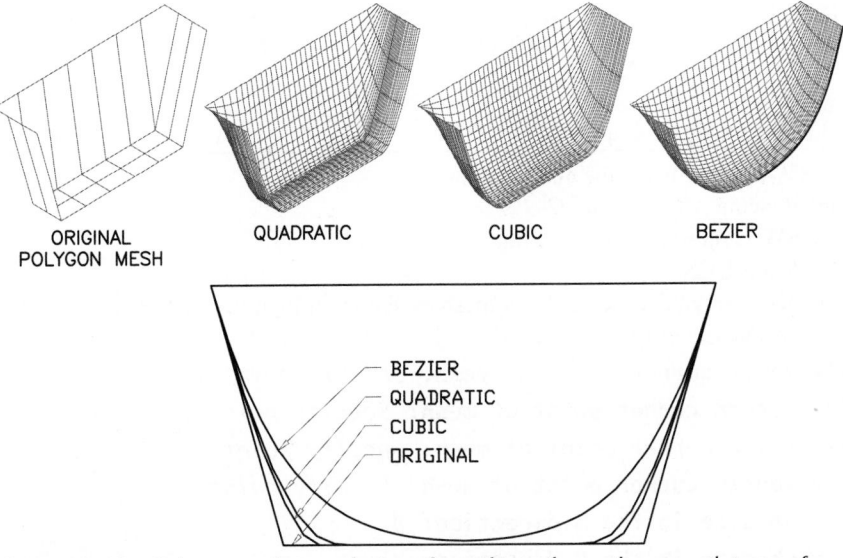

Figure 22-60   Polygon meshes can be transformed into three other smooth types of surfaces

The SURFU and SURFV System Variables

The **SURFU** and **SURFV** system variables control the density of the smoothed polygon mesh in the M and N directions, respectively. This is similar to the effect that the **SURFTAB1** and **SURFTAB2** system variables have on the number of vertices of the polygon meshes generated with the **REVSURF, TABSURF, RULESURF,** and **EDGESURF** commands.

The **SURFU** and **SURFV** variables can be set from **2** to **200, 6** being the default value. After you have established what type of surface the polygon mesh will be fitted into, and the density that it will have, you can proceed with the **Smooth surface** option.

The new smoothed faceted surface will have a different number of vertices placed in new locations, depending on the **SURFU** and **SURFV** values. The new M size will be **SURFU** + 1, and the new N size will be **SURFV** + 1.

The **Desmooth** option restores the smoothed mesh to the original polygon mesh. When a polygon mesh is in its smoothed state, its grips cannot be deformed, so this option will reset the polygon mesh back into its deformable stage.

The **Mclose** and **Nclose** options close or open a polygon mesh in the M or N direction by adding or removing the last set of polygons in the specified direction. The options change to **Mopen** and **Nopen** when the selected polygon mesh is closed in both directions (Figure 22-61).

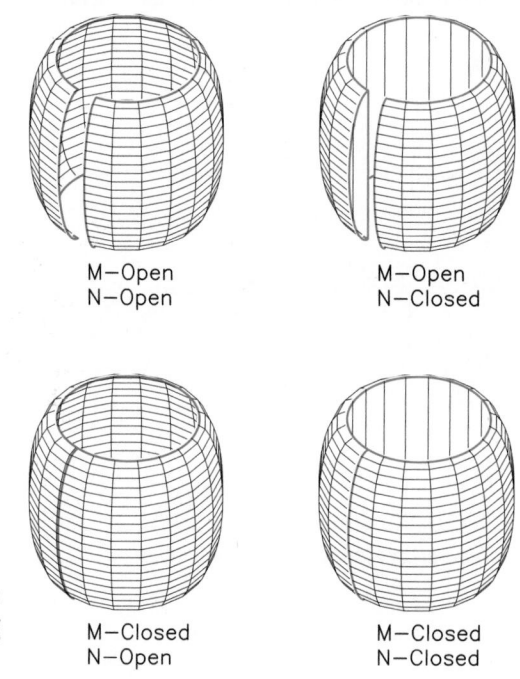

M—Open
N—Open

M—Open
N—Closed

Figure 22-61   Polygon meshes can be transformed by closing or opening them in the N and M directions

M—Closed
N—Open

M—Closed
N—Closed

Exercise 22-12: Deforming the Grips of a Polygon Mesh

1. Start a **NEW** drawing using the **acad** template.
2. **SAVE** the drawing **AS** *Exercise 22–12*.
3. Select the **SW Isometric** viewing point.
4. Select the **Front** UCS.
5. Using the **3D** command, create a 4 × 8 mesh as shown in Figure 22-62. Respond to the command prompts as follows:

   Specify first corner point of mesh: *Specify point 1.*

   Specify second corner point of mesh: *Specify point 2.*

   Specify third corner point of mesh: *Specify point 3.*

   Specify fourth corner point of mesh: *Specify point 4.*

   Enter mesh size in the M direction: *4 ↵*

   Enter mesh size in the N direction: *8 ↵*

6. Select the **Right** UCS.

7. Select the polygon mesh to reveal its grips. Stretch all the highlighted grips in Figure 22-63 **6″** orthogonally in the positive direction of the *X*-axis. If needed, you can stretch the grips in several stages. When you are finished, the mesh should look like Figure 22-64.

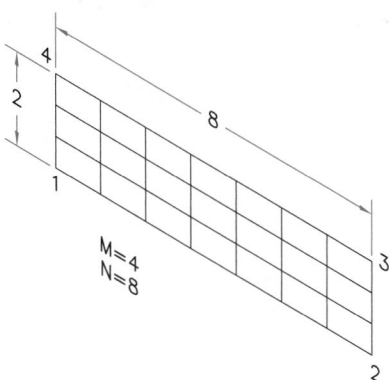

Figure 22-62 Mesh created with the **3D** command

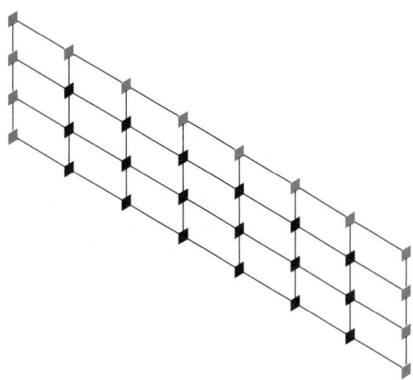

Figure 22-63 Grips to be selected

8. Select the polygon mesh to reveal its grips again. Stretch the two grips in the top rightmost edge **1″** up, orthogonally. The polygon mesh should look like Figure 22-65.
9. Set both system variables, **SURFU** and **SURFV**, to **30**.
10. Invoke the **PEDIT** command and respond to the prompts as follows:

    Select polyline or [Multiple]:
    Select the mesh.

    Enter an option [Edit vertex/ Smooth surface/Desmooth/Mclose/ Nclose/Undo]: *s ↵*

    Enter an option [Edit vertex/Smooth surface/Desmooth/Mclose/Nclose/Undo]:
    ↵ (To exit the command)

Note:
Because the default value of the **SURFTYPE** system variable is **6**, the polygon mesh smooths to fit a cubic surface.

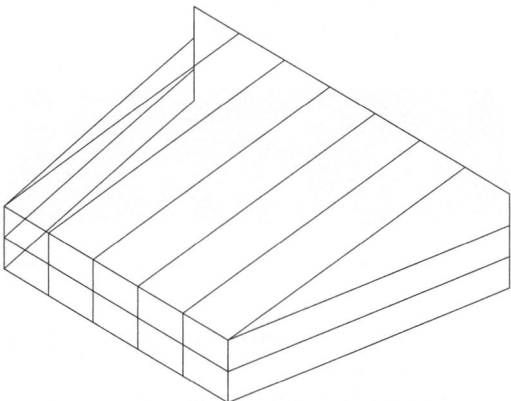

Figure 22-64 After the grips have been moved

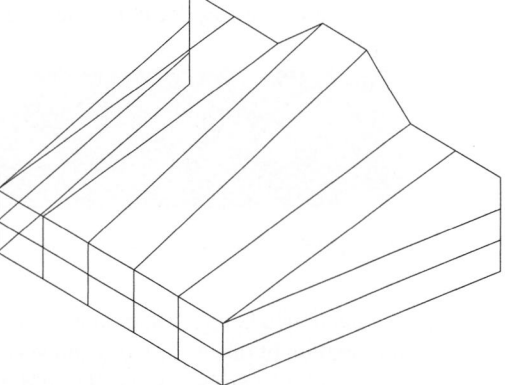

Figure 22-65 After the top grips have been moved

11. Invoke the **HIDE** command. The smoothed polygon mesh should look like Figure 22-66.
12. Select the **Realistic** visual style and use the **3DORBIT** command to check the other side of the 3D model.
13. Practice changing the **SURFTYPE** system variable to **5** and then **8** to smooth the polygon mesh into the quadratic and the Bezier types, respectively.
14. **SAVE** the drawing.

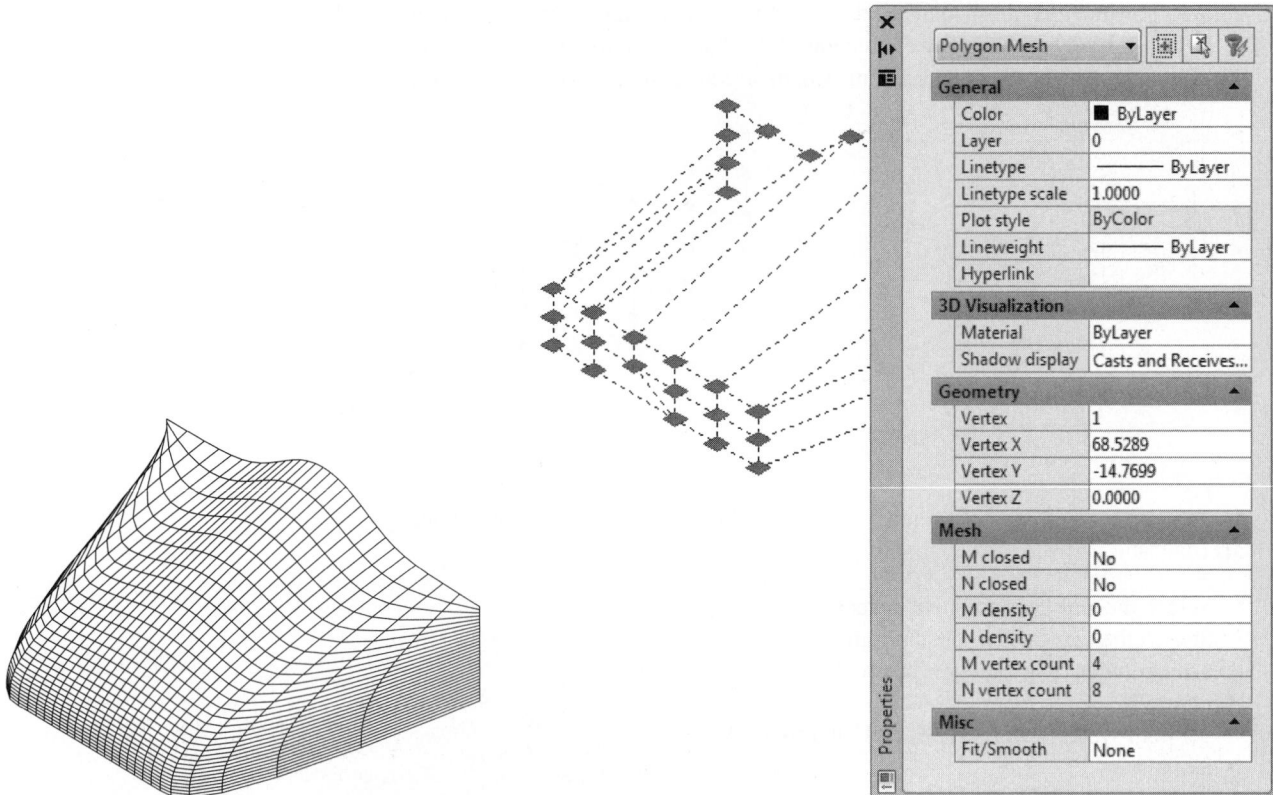

Figure 22-66   Polygon mesh smoothed into a cubic surface

Figure 22-67   The **Properties** palette can be used to see and modify a polygon mesh's properties

Editing Polygon Meshes Through the Properties Palette

The **Properties** palette is a very useful tool for editing operations with almost every object. When the selection is a polygon mesh, this palette allows you to access the same editing tools as with the **PEDIT** command. Selecting the vertices is easy when using the **Properties** palette, especially when more than one vertex shares the same place (Figure 22-67).

You can smooth meshes by fitting them to any type of surface through the **Properties** window, without having to change the **SURFTYPE** system variable beforehand.

ADDITIONAL OBJECTS USED ALONG WITH POLYGON MESHES AND MESHES

SOLIDS

As mentioned before, other simpler objects can be used along with polygon meshes to simplify the creation of planar surfaces and surfaces that curve in one direction.

A solid (also known as a 2D solid) is a planar object with four vertices, whose shape depends on the location of the vertices. Usually, a solid has a tetragonal shape, but it can also be triangular if two of its four edges are located in the same place. This type of object is created with the **SOLID** command. It allows you to specify either three or four points. Pressing the **<Enter↵>** key after specifying the third point will create a triangular solid. After you have drawn the first solid, the command will continue by asking for the points of the following solid.

A solid is always created in a plane parallel to the current *XY* plane of the current UCS. Its vertices can be moved individually to any other location within the *XY* plane of its UCS either by pulling its grips, or through the **Properties** palette (Figure 22-68).

Figure 22-68   The **Properties** palette allows you to move the vertices of a 2D solid

SOLID	
Ribbon 3D Model-ing panel	
Pull-down Menu	Draw/ Modeling/ Meshes/ 2D Solid
Command Line	solid
Command Alias	so

Solids are better to use when working in a 2D environment because they can be turned into filled objects only when the viewing direction is perpendicular to the *XY* plane of the current UCS. Both the **FILL** and **FILLMODE** system variables control this setting.

Exercise 22-13: Creating and Modifying 2D Solid Objects

1. Start a **NEW** drawing.
2. **SAVE** the drawing **AS** *Exercise 22-13*.
3. Set the **FILL** system variable to **0**.
4. Invoke the **SOLID** command. Draw, as closely as possible, the shape shown in Figure 22-69. Respond to the prompts as follows:

   Specify first point: *Specify point 1.*

   Specify second point: *Specify point 2.*

   Specify third point: *Specify point 3.*

   Specify fourth point or <exit>: *Specify point 4.*

   Specify third point: *Specify point 5.*

   Specify fourth point or <exit>: *Specify point 6.*

   Specify third point: *Specify point 7.*

   Specify fourth point or <exit>: *Specify point 8.*

   Specify third point: ↵

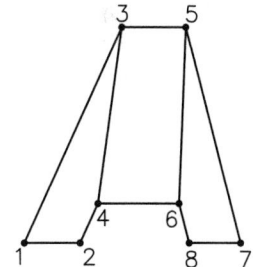

Figure 22-69   Shape to be drawn and the order in which the points should be specified

TIP

The AutoCAD® program uses the last two points entered on the first solid as the first two points for the next solid. That's why you are asked for only the third and fourth points. It is difficult to enter so many points at the same time without making mistakes, and the only advantage of doing so is to save time. If you prefer, you can stop the command right after the fourth point and start over. This way, you will simply create an individual solid in each operation, obtaining the same result.

5. Change the **FILL** system variable to **1**.
6. Invoke the **REGEN** command. The drawing should look like Figure 22-70.
7. Select the three 2D solids and practice stretching their grips while they are filled.
8. Select the **SE Isometric** viewing point. The fill should not show up from this viewing point.
9. Select the **Realistic** visual style to see the effects of shading this type of object.
10. Select the **2D Wireframe** visual style again.
11. Select the **Top** view again to see the fill.
12. **SAVE** the drawing.

Figure 22-70   The result-ing 2D solid with the **FILL** mode on

3D FACES

A 3D face is an object with four vertices that is similar to a 2D solid. A 3D face, however, does not necessarily need to be planar; its four vertices can be located anywhere in the space. This type of object is created with the **3DFACE** command.

When two of the four vertices of a 3D face share the same location, the result will be a triangular 3D face. When all four vertices are located at different points, the resulting object will have either a tetragonal planar shape (if all the vertices belong to a common plane) or two adjoined triangular planar faces (Figure 22-71). AutoCAD divides the 3D face into two triangles, with the sole purpose of reflecting the light when using a shaded visual style or creating a rendered image.

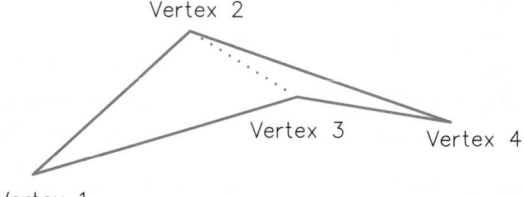

Figure 22-71   A nonplanar 3D face is shown by the AutoCAD program as two adjoined triangular planar faces

3D faces are also obtained by exploding polygon meshes. Depending on the shape of the mesh, some of the 3D faces can be planar and some nonplanar. But all of them can be used to represent a portion of any surface by stretching their vertices, just as if they were created with the **3DFACE** command.

Exercise 22-14: Using 3D Faces

1. Start a **NEW** drawing using the **acad** template.
2. **SAVE** the drawing **AS *Exercise 22-14***.
3. Set the **Drawing Units** to **Architectural,** by going to **Format/Units**...
4. Without placing any dimensions, draw the perimeter and the two centerlines shown in Figure 22-72.

You must use a zoom factor big enough to fit the perimeter into the display. To do so, you can simply create a line 80′ long or so without worrying about seeing it in its entirety. Then you can invoke the **ZOOM Extents** command. The line can be erased afterward.

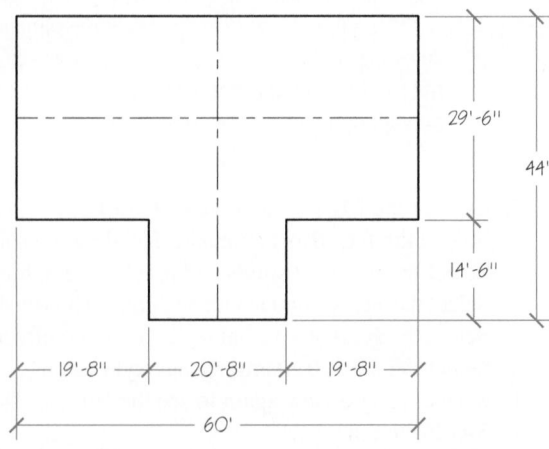

Figure 22-72   Contour shape to be drawn

5. Select the **SE Isometric** viewing point and the **2D Wireframe** visual style.
6. Select the **Front** UCS.
7. Place vertical lines as shown in Figure 22-73. Their endpoints will be used to create the roof using 3D faces. Two different linetypes show the two heights needed.
8. **ERASE** the two centerlines.

Figure 22-73   After the vertical lines are placed

9. Invoke the **3DFACE** command. Use one of the methods shown in the grid. Respond to the prompts as follows:

Specify first point or [Invisible]: *Specify endpoint 1 (Figure 22-74).*

Specify second point or [Invisible]: *Specify endpoint 2.*

Specify third point or [Invisible] <exit>: *Specify endpoint 3.*

Specify fourth point or [Invisible] <create three-sided face>: *Specify endpoint 4.*

Specify third point or [Invisible] <exit>: ↵ *(To end the command)*

Note:
After you specify the first point, you enter the rest of the points in a continuous order, either clockwise or counterclockwise, instead of in zigzag as with the **SOLID** command. Right after the third point is entered, you can specify the fourth one, or you can press the **<Enter>** key to create a triangular 3D face.

3DFACE	
Ribbon 3D Modeling panel	
Pull-down Menu	Draw/ Modeling/ Meshes/ 3D Face
Command Line	3dface

10. Invoke the **3DFACE** command again. Within the same operation, create two new 3D faces, one next to the other. Respond to the prompts as follows:

Specify first point or [Invisible]: *Specify endpoint 1 (Figure 22-75).*

Specify second point or [Invisible]: *Specify endpoint 2.*

Specify third point or [Invisible] <exit>: *Specify endpoint 3.*

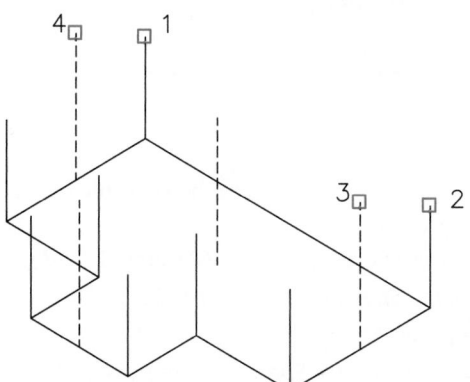

Figure 22-74   Order to specify the points for the **3DFACE** operation

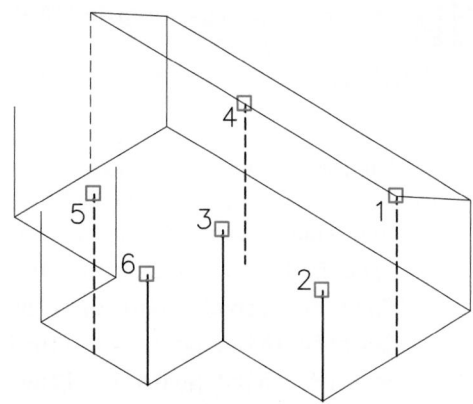

Figure 22-75   Order to specify the points for the **3DFACE** operation

Specify fourth point or [Invisible] <create three-sided face>: *Specify endpoint 4.*

Specify third point or [Invisible]<exit>: *Specify endpoint 5.*

Specify fourth point or [Invisible] <create three-sided face>: *Specify endpoint 6.*

Specify third point or [Invisible] <exit>: ↵ *(To end the command)*

11. Select the **SW Isometric** viewing point.
12. Invoke the **HIDE** command.
13. Create the two 3D faces on the other side. Repeat the procedure you performed in step 10, using Figure 22-76 as a reference on how to specify the points.

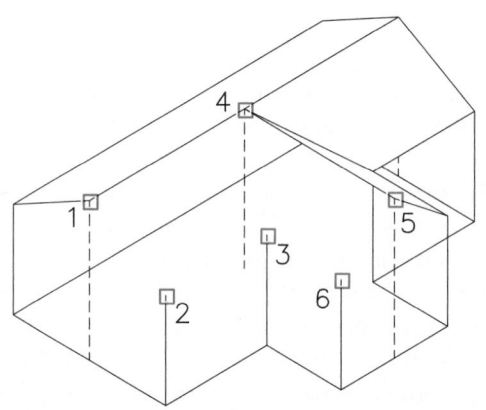

> **Note:**
> You can create as many 3D faces within the same command as you want, as long as you carefully study the order in which the points should be entered. If you prefer, you can also stop the command and create the faces one by one. Regardless of which way you do it, the result will always be individual 3D faces.

Figure 22-76 Order to specify the points for the **3DFACE** operation

TIP   Remember that to **ZOOM** or **PAN** after the **HIDE** command has been invoked, you must first invoke the **REGEN** command.

TIP   Because the last 3D faces created are symmetrical to the previous ones, you could also have obtained them with the **MIRROR** or the **MIRROR3D** command.

14. **ERASE** all the vertical lines.
15. Add two 3D faces to create the left side of the house. This time, use the **Invisible** option so that the common edge for both faces is not shown.

Specify first point or [Invisible]: *Specify endpoint 1* (Figure 22-77).

Specify second point or [Invisible]: *Specify endpoint 2.*

Specify third point or [Invisible] <exit>: *i* ↵

Specify third point or [Invisible] <exit>: *Specify endpoint 3.*

Specify fourth point or [Invisible] <create three-sided face>: *Specify midpoint 4.*

Specify third point or [Invisible] <exit>: *Specify endpoint 5.*

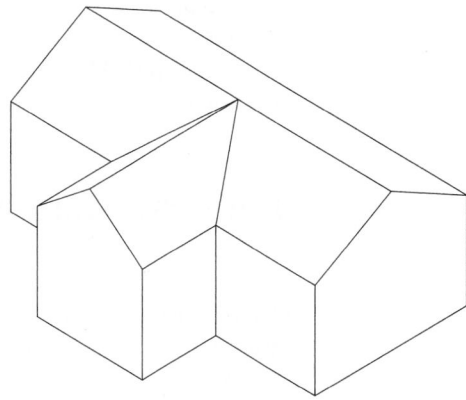

Figure 22-77   Order to specify the points for the **3DFACE** operation

Figure 22-78   3D model completed using 3D faces

```
Specify fourth point or [Invisible]
<create three-sided face>: Specify
endpoint 6.
```

```
Specify third point or [Invisible]
<exit>: ↵ (To end the command)
```

16. Create the rest of the walls to complete the 3D model. When you are finished, the model should look like Figure 22-78 from the **SE Isometric** viewing point.

17. Select the **Realistic** visual style and invoke the **3DORBIT** command to inspect the 3D model.

18. **SAVE** the drawing.

Note:
You must activate the **Invisible** option right before entering the first of the two points whose edge you intend to hide. Invisible edges are not shown while the **2D Wireframe** visual style is current.

EDGE	
Ribbon 3D Modeling panel	
Pull-down Menu	Draw/ Modeling/ Meshes/ Edge
Command Line	edge

By using several 3D faces next to one another, and hiding some of the edges by using the **Invisible** option, you can create many different surface models. Sometimes, however, it is difficult to make the correct edge invisible. To solve this problem, you can use one of two different methods:

1. Use the **Properties** palette (Figure 22-79) to change the visibility of each individual edge.

2. Use the **EDGE** command. It can be invoked by using any of the methods shown in the grid.

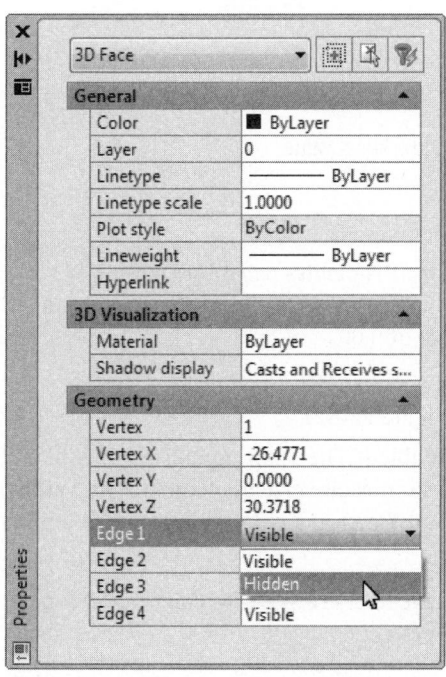

Figure 22-79   Using the **Properties** palette to hide edges

With the **EDGE** command, you can select as many edges as you need on multiple 3D faces. You then press the **<Enter.↵>** key to finish the selection and exit the command, toggling the display of selected edges.

The **Display All** option of the **EDGE** command can be used to temporarily show the hidden edges of all the 3D faces in the drawing.

THICKENED OBJECTS

This is the simplest type of 3D object. Simply changing the **Thickness** property of certain objects extrudes them perpendicularly to the *XY* plane of the object's UCS. An object can be thickened by a positive value, or by a negative value (to reverse the direction of the operation).

Objects whose thickness value can be changed are arcs, circles, lines, polylines, donuts, single-line texts, and 2D solids (Figure 22-80). Some of the objects whose thickness value cannot be changed include regions, ellipses, multiline texts, 3D polylines, splines, 3D faces, and polygon meshes.

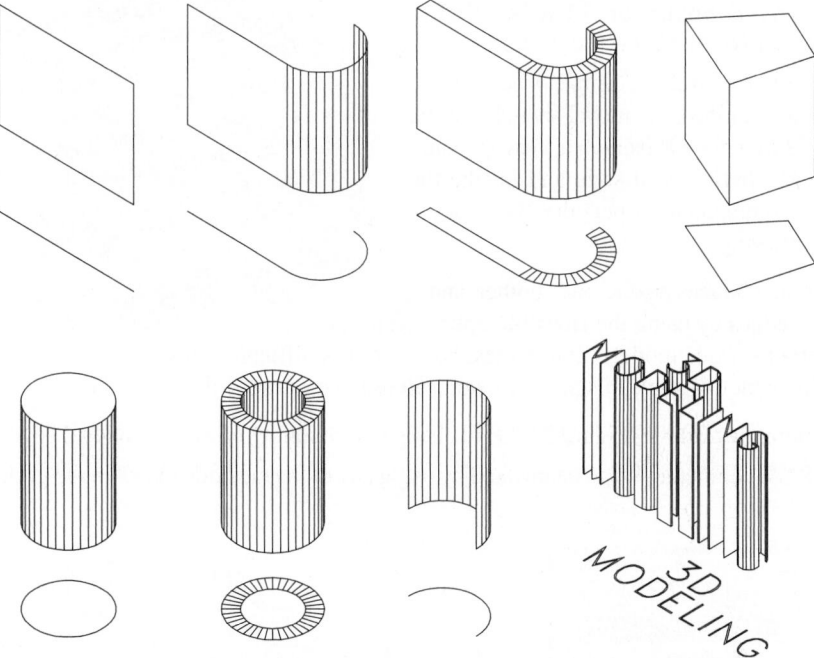

Figure 22-80   Different objects shown with and without a thickness value

The **Thickness** property can be easily changed in the **Properties** palette (Figure 22-81).

The following is a description of some of the characteristics that are added to the objects if the thickness property is different from the default value of 0.00.

Arcs and circles: When these objects are thickened, the number of points that you can snap to, as well as the number of grips, is doubled (Figure 22-82).

Lines and polylines: The number of grips is doubled. The snap points, besides being doubled, have an additional midpoint to snap to in each vertical element. The **Width** property in polylines does not give this type of object any extra grips or snap points (Figure 22-83).

When the default **2D Wireframe** visual style is active, the **VIEWRES** system variable controls the number of segments of thickened arcs and circles.

Figure 22-81 The **Thickness** property in the **Properties** palette

Snap Points   Grips

Figure 22-82 Points to snap to and grips are doubled for arcs and circles with a thickness value

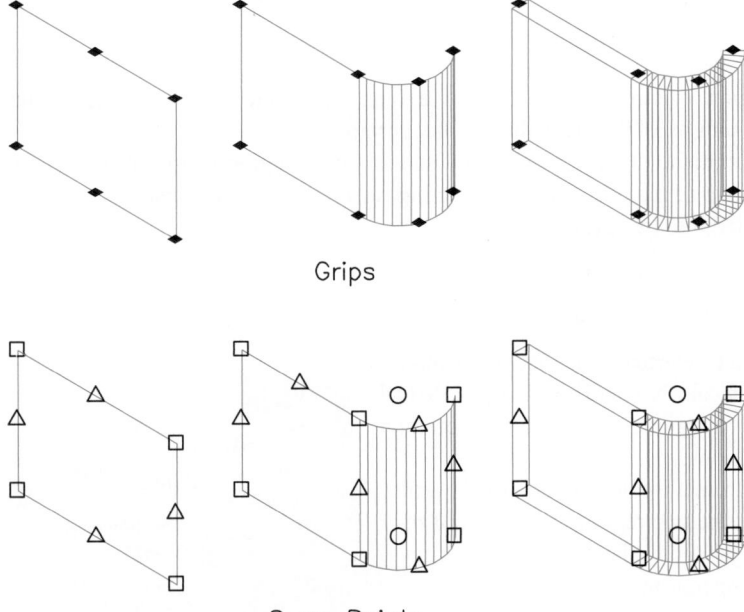

Grips

Snap Points

Figure 22-83 Points to snap to and grips on thickened lines and polylines

REGIONS

A *region* is a bounded 2D area that can more easily be used to represent any planar surface than can polygon meshes, 2D solids, and 3D faces. Regions can be obtained from a group of planar curves, using either the **REGION** or the **BOUNDARY** commands; or by performing 3D operations, such as sectioning a 3D solid with the **SECTION** command; or by copying planar faces with the **SOLIDEDIT** command.

FOR MORE DETAILS   See Chapter 23 for more information about the **SECTION** command.
See Chapter 24 for more information about the **SOLIDEDIT** command.

REGION	
Draw Toolbar	
Ribbon Draw panel	
Pull-down Menu	Draw/ Region
Command Line	region

Boolean operations: Union, subtract, and intersect operations that are performed on regions and 3D solids.

UNION	
Solids Editing Toolbar	
Ribbon Solid Editing panel	
Pull-down Menu	Modify/ Solids Editing/ Union
Command Line	union
Command Alias	uni

The **REGION** command is really simple to use. It simply prompts you to select the objects that will be turned into regions. Creating the objects is the part you must pay the most attention to because all the objects that will be turned into a region must meet the following conditions:

- They must all be either planar curves or straight lines.
- They must all be placed in the same plane.
- They must all be placed in contact with each other (their endpoints must meet).
- They must form a closed loop.
- No object can intersect another one.

Even though regions are infinitely thin objects, they accept the same *Boolean operations* that are used to modify 3D solids. Their mass property information, such as area, moment of inertia, and centroid, can be obtained with the **MASSPROP** command.

Another advantage of regions is that splines can also be used to create this type of object, allowing you to create more complex shapes.

Boolean Operations with Regions: UNION, SUBTRACT, and INTERSECT

You can combine regions that coexist in the same plane by using one of the following Boolean operation commands:

- **UNION**
- **SUBTRACT**
- **INTERSECT**

UNION creates a region by joining any number of regions that belong to the same plane. The resulting area will be the sum of all the areas that are not common.

The **SUBTRACT** command creates a region by subtracting a region or group of regions from another region or group of regions. When subtracting regions, you must consider the selection of regions to be divided into two groups:

- First group: Region(s) to subtract from
- Second group: Region(s) to subtract

If more than one region is selected in the first group, this part of the operation will automatically be considered to be a **UNION**.

INTERSECT creates a region from the unique common area among a group of regions.

The region resulting from a Boolean operation depends on the relative location of the two regions or groups of regions selected. Figure 22-84 shows the three possible situations for each particular operation:

Note:
In Figure 22-84, the region shown in hidden lines in the **SUBTRACT** operation is the one to be subtracted.

- The two regions have no area in common.
- One of the regions is completely contained inside the other region.
- One of the regions is partially contained inside the other region.

Regions are no longer rigid objects that can be edited only by performing Boolean operations. When you use the **MOVE, ROTATE,** or **SCALE** command, rather than selecting the entire region, you can now hold the **<Ctrl>** key down and select edges instead. Performing such operations on the edges of the region will readjust its geometry and location, as well as modify adjacent edges accordingly. The grips of the region, however, cannot be used to stretch the region.

	BEFORE THE OPERATION	RESULT	COMMENTS
U N I O N			THE TWO REGIONS BECOME A SINGLE ONE EVEN THOUGH THEY DO NOT SHARE ANY AREA.
			THE SMALL REGION DOES NOT PROVIDE ANY NEW AREA TO THE BIGGER ONE.
			THE NEW REGION IS THE SUM OF ANY AREAS THAT ARE NOT SHARED.
S U B T R A C T			THE REGION TO BE SUBTRACTED IS LOST BECAUSE NO AREA IS SHARED.
			THIS RESULTS IN A SINGLE REGION WITH A HOLE.
			ONLY THE SHARED AREA IS SUBTRACTED.
I N T E R S E C T			BECAUSE NO AREA IS SHARED, THE RESULT IS A NULL REGION.
			THE SHARED AREA IS EXACTLY THE SMALL REGION.
			AREA THAT IS NOT SHARED IS ELIMINATED.

Figure 22-84   The three possible situations and results for each Boolean operation with regions

SUBTRACT	
Solids Editing Toolbar	
Ribbon Solid Editing panel	
Pull-down Menu	Modify/ Solids Editing/ Subtract
Command Line	subtract
Alias	su

INTERSECT	
Solids Editing Toolbar	
Ribbon Solid Editing panel	
Pull-down Menu	Modify/ Solids Editing/ Intersect
Command Line	intersect
Command Alias	in

REGION	
Draw Toolbar	
Ribbon Solid Editing panel	
Pull-down Menu	Draw/ Region
Command Line	region

Exercise 22-15: Combining Different Types of Objects to Generate Surface Models

In this exercise you will create a simple 3D model in which you will combine regions and thickened objects to represent the surfaces.

1. Start a **NEW** drawing using the **acad** template.
2. **SAVE** the drawing **AS** *Exercise 22-15*.
3. Using only lines and arcs, draw the objects shown in Figure 22-85 anywhere in the drawing area. Instead of circles place two mirrored arcs. That way, you will create the effect of a cylindrical hole when changing their thickness.
4. With **Ortho** mode activated, **COPY** all the objects **5″** orthogonally to the right.
5. Invoke the **REGION** command, using one of the methods shown in the grid. When prompted, select the group of objects on the left. In the command line window, the AutoCAD program should advise you about the creation of three regions:

   3 loops extracted.

   3 Regions created.

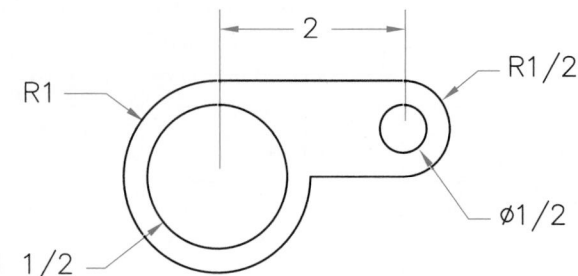

Figure 22-85 Dimensions for the objects to be drawn

6. Select the **SE Isometric** viewing point.
7. **ZOOM** in as needed.
8. Assign a **Color** to the two circular regions that is different from the color used for the bigger region.
9. Select the **Conceptual** visual style.
10. Invoke the **SUBTRACT** command. You will subtract the two circular regions from the main region. Respond to the prompts as follows:

    Select solids and regions to subtract from...

    Select objects: *Select the main region by picking on its border, not inside the shaded area.*

    Select objects: ⏎ *(To end the selection)*

    Select solids and regions to subtract...

    Select objects: *Select the two circular regions using selection windows.*

    Select objects: ⏎ *(To end the selection)*

11. Make sure no command is in progress and select the group of objects on the right. Right-click in the drawing area and select **Properties** from the shortcut menu. In the **Properties** palette, change the **Thickness** value of the selected objects to **2**.
12. Select the **2D Wireframe** visual style.
13. Invoke the **HIDE** command. The model should look like Figure 22-86.
14. **MOVE** the region from the center point of the bigger hole to the corresponding center point on the top of the thickened objects.
15. **COPY** the region from any endpoint on the thickened objects to the endpoint located vertically below it.
16. Invoke the **HIDE** command again. The 3D model should look now like Figure 22-87.
17. **SAVE** the drawing.

Note:
When copying the region, you might have some difficulty selecting it because it shares all its edges with the thickened objects. One way to make the selection easier is to use the **DRAWORDER** command. This command places selected objects under the other objects, changing the order in which they will be picked.

Figure 22-86 After hiding the occulted lines of the thickened objects

Figure 22-87 The 3D model after placing the regions

EXPLODING FACETED SURFACES

The **EXPLODE** command can be useful when working with faceted surfaces. When a polygon mesh or a polyface mesh is exploded, all the adjacent faces of the mesh are separated into 3D faces, which you studied previously.

On the other hand, solids and 3D faces cannot be exploded any further. If you need to explode a 3D face or a solid, the procedure requires converting it into regions first, which then can be exploded into lines. Just keep in mind that regions are planar objects, so only planar 3D faces can be converted to regions.

CHAPTER SUMMARY

Throughout this chapter you have learned the different operations used to develop 3D models that are represented by faceted surfaces and other similar objects. You have also been introduced to the considerations involved in determining whether surface modeling is the appropriate method to use. By following the tutorials, you should realize how important it is to develop the necessary curves throughout the 3D space prior to creating faceted surfaces.

You have studied in depth the different operations used to generate polygon meshes. These are the most important and complex objects used in this type of representation of 3D objects.

Other types of objects such as regions, 3D faces, solids, and thickened 2D objects have also been discussed in this chapter. Because of their characteristics, they are also suitable for use with polygon meshes in achieving the main purpose: covering all the surfaces of the 3D model with objects that can be shaded and that can hide other objects.

You have also learned that by performing Boolean operations with regions, you can easily obtain complex planar surfaces.

CHAPTER TEST QUESTIONS

Multiple Choice

1. Which of the following objects can represent any type of faceted surface?

   a. Region
   b. 3D face
   c. Polygon mesh
   d. 2D solid

2. Which primitive 3D model can be created with the 3D command?

   a. Cylinder
   b. Torus
   c. Sphere
   d. All of the above

3. Which of the following methods cannot be used to edit polygon meshes?

   a. The **STRETCH** command
   b. Pulling the grips
   c. The **PEDIT** command
   d. The **TRIM** command

4. Which of the following commands requires selecting four curves, one next to the other, forming a closed path?

   a. **REVSURF**
   b. **TABSURF**
   c. **EDGESURF**
   d. **RULESURF**

5. Which of the following can be used to perform Boolean operations?

   a. Polygon meshes
   b. 3D faces
   c. Regions
   d. Thickened objects

6. If you had to represent a flat piece of sheet metal with a slotted hole on it, which single object would you use to achieve your purpose?

   a. 3D face
   b. Region
   c. 2D solid
   d. Polygon mesh

7. For which of the following can the thickness value *not* be changed?

   a. 2D solids
   b. Regions
   c. Arcs
   d. Single-line texts

8. Which of the following is not a Boolean operation command?

   a. **INTERSECT**
   b. **UNION**
   c. **COMBINE**
   d. **SUBTRACT**

9. When converting objects into regions, the objects should meet which of the following conditions?

   a. All should be planar curves.
   b. All must coexist in the same plane.
   c. They must form a closed loop.
   d. All of the above

10. If you perform a **SUBTRACT** operation between two concentric circles of different diameters and select the bigger circle as the object to subtract, the result of the operation will be:

    a. The bigger circle
    b. The bigger circle, with a hole
    c. No object
    d. None of the above

Matching

a. **REVSURF**

b. **TABSURF**

c. **UNION**

d. **SURFTAB1**

e. **SURFTYPE**

f. **EDGESURF**

g. **INTERSECT**

h. **RULESURF**

i. 2D Solid

j. **SURFU**

1. Creates faceted surfaces that look like Coons patches

2. Controls the density of smoothed meshes

3. Creates surfaces between two curves

4. Returns the sum of all unshared areas of the regions selected

5. Planar surface having four vertices

6. Sets the type of surface to smooth the mesh

7. Creates faceted surfaces that look like extrusions

8. Creates faceted surfaces of revolution

9. Returns the unique area of selected regions

10. Controls the number of vertices for the M direction

CHAPTER TUTORIALS

Tutorial 22-1: The Boat Hull

Continuing with **Tutorial 21-2** from Chapter 21, you will give the boat hull its final touch. The task will consist of creating the polygon meshes needed to fill the entire surface of the object.

1. **OPEN** *Tutorial 21-2* created in Chapter 21.
2. **SAVE** it **AS** *Tutorial 22-1*.
3. Open the **Layer Manager** dialog box and create a new layer. Name it **Surfaces**, change its color to one you prefer, and turn it off. Close the **Layer Manager** dialog box by clicking on the **OK** button.
4. Set both system variables **SURFTAB1** and **SURFTAB2** to **15**.
5. You need to prepare the wireframes so they are suitable for the requirements of the commands used to create polygon meshes. **ZOOM** in to the back of the boat hull and select the **Right** UCS.
6. **COPY** the top line from its rightmost endpoint, as shown in Figure 22-88.
7. **TRIM** the portion of the copied line that extends beyond the boat's centerline. **TRIM** also the top portion of the vertical line (Figure 22-89).

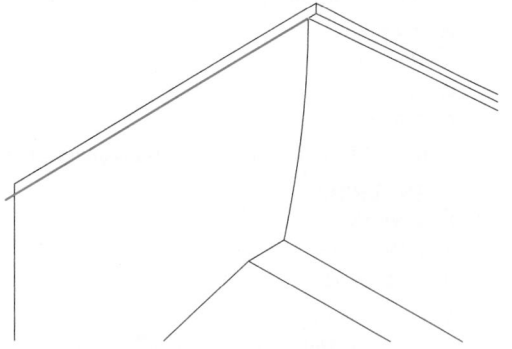

Figure 22-88   After copying the top line

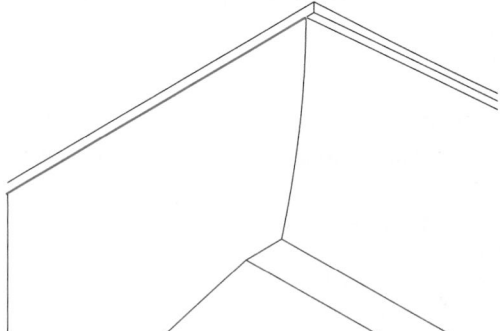

Figure 22-89   After trimming the lines

8. With the **Right** UCS still current, turn the second group of highlighted objects in Figure 22-90 into a single polyline, using the **Join** option of the **PEDIT** command.

> **FOR MORE DETAILS**   To find information about using the **PEDIT** command, refer to Chapter 21.

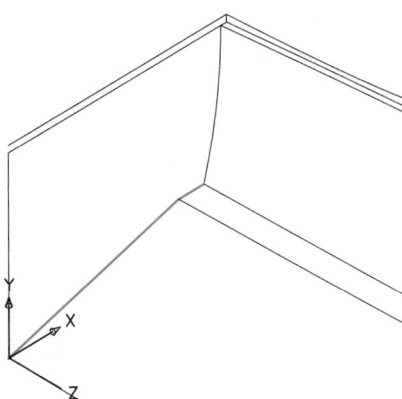

Figure 22-90   The highlighted objects must be joined into a single polyline

9. Select the **Front** UCS, and **ZOOM** into the front part of the boat hull.
10. **BREAK** the polyline along the hull into three portions. The polyline shown highlighted in Figure 22-91 should be independent from the other two segments.

Figure 22-91   The 2D polyline along the hull must be split into three portions so the highlighted segment is independent

11. Invoke the **EDGESURF** command. When prompted, select the four objects that define the outline of the polygon mesh shown highlighted in Figure 22-92.

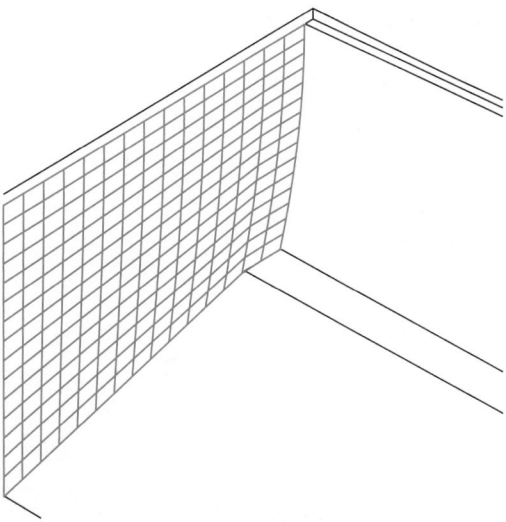

Figure 22-92   Polygon mesh generated with the **EDGESURF** command

12. Select the polygon mesh and change its layer to **Surfaces**. You can perform this operation either in the **Properties** palette or in the drop-down list on the **Layers** panel of the Ribbon (Figure 22-93). Because the new layer is turned off, the mesh will turn off as well. The message shown in Figure 22-94 will warn you.

Figure 22-93   Your choices for changing the layer of the polygon mesh

Figure 22-94   Warning from the AutoCAD program

13. Set the **SURFTAB1** system variable to **30**.
14. Invoke the **EDGESURF** command again. Select the four objects that define the outline of the highlighted polygon mesh (Figure 22-95).
15. Select the new polygon mesh and change its layer to **Surfaces** to hide the object shown.
16. Invoke the **RULESURF** command. When prompted, select the two highlighted curves in Figure 22-96.

Figure 22-95   New polygon mesh generated with the **EDGESURF** command

Figure 22-96   Curves to be selected for the **RULESURF** operation

17. Invoke the **RULESURF** command again and select the two curves highlighted in Figure 22-97.

18. Select the two polygon meshes and assign them the **Surfaces** layer.

19. Create the two remaining polygon meshes (Figure 22-98).

Figure 22-97   Curves to be selected for the new **RULESURF** operation

Figure 22-98   Creating two more polygon meshes

20. Set the **SURFTAB1** system variables to **15**.

21. **ZOOM** into the back of the boat. Invoke the **TABSURF** command. Respond to the prompts as follow:

Select object for path curve: *Select the horizontal line* (Figure 22-99).

Select object for direction vector: *Select the small vertical line.*

Figure 22-99   Polygon meshes created with the **TABSURF** command

22. Change the layer of the three polygon meshes to **Surfaces**.
23. You no longer need the wireframe objects. Make sure no polygon mesh is displayed and **ERASE** all the remaining objects in the screen.
24. Turn the **Surfaces** layer on.
25. Select the **Top** view and **MIRROR** all the polygon meshes to create a symmetrical copy (Figure 22-100).

Figure 22-100   After mirroring the polygon meshes

26. Select the **Realistic** visual style.
27. In the **Visual Style** panel of the Ribbon, change the **Edge** setting to show **No edges** (Figure 22-101).

Figure 22-101   The **Edge Effects** panel of the Ribbon

28. Invoke the **3DORBIT** command to inspect the faceted surface 3D model. It should look much like Figure 22-102.
29. **SAVE** the drawing.

Figure 22-102   A shaded view of the final 3D model represented by faceted surfaces

CHAPTER PROJECTS

Project 22-1: Industrial Hood

Using faceted surface objects, create the 3D surface model shown in Figure 22-103. The dimensions for this model can be found in Figure 22-104.

Hints for the Project

The four curved surfaces that represent the transition of the hood can be produced by creating a ruled surface between a quarter of the top circle and any other temporary

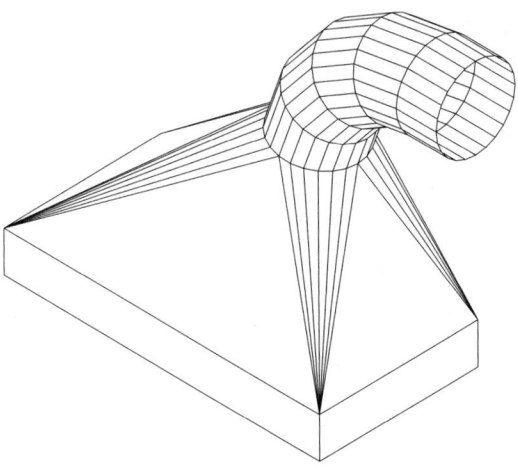

Figure 22-103   A 3D view of the project's model

Figure 22-104   Dimensions for the project

object such as a line. Subsequently, the grips along the temporary line can be stretched in order to be gathered at the same point, and the line can be erased. Figure 22-105 shows the steps just described. The same polygon mesh can also be created in an easier way between the same arc and a point.

Figure 22-105   Hints about how to create specific geometry

Project 22-2: Industrial Hood: The Flat Pattern

When only 2D capability exists, sheet metal work can get very complicated for designers and engineers, especially if the piece to be developed is an uncommon one. If carefully handled, the AutoCAD software can assist you with the task of generating an accurate flat pattern.

Open the drawing containing the 3D model you created in Project 22-1 and develop a 2D drawing that represents the flat pattern or development of the hood. When you finish, the drawing should look like Figure 22-106.

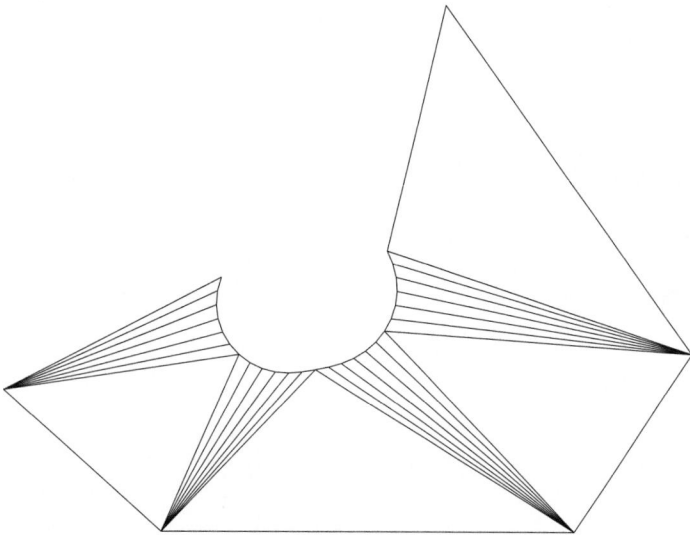

Figure 22-106   The resulting flat pattern

Hints for the Project

As you learned previously, when a polygon mesh is exploded, it disintegrates into individual 3D faces. Such objects can be moved and rotated throughout the 3D space one by one until all are placed in a common plane.

One sequence of operations that can be used is as follows:

1. Modify the UCS by three given points so that its *XY* plane is coincident with the 3D face object.
2. **CUT** the 3D face to remove it from its location.
3. Change the UCS to a common one that you will use over and over to **PASTE** all the 3D faces.
4. **PASTE** the 3D face.
5. Use the **ALIGN, MIRROR,** or **ROTATE** commands as necessary.
6. Repeat the process for the next 3D face. Its edge should be aligned with the corresponding edge of the 3D face that was previously placed.

Creating 3D Solids and Surfaces

23

Chapter Objectives

- Control the system variables to improve the visualization of 3D solids and surfaces.
- Understand the differences between surfaces and faceted surfaces.
- Learn the use of commands to create 3D primitives with 3D solids.
- Learn the use of commands to create complex surfaces and 3D solids.
- Learn other commands and operations to create surfaces and 3D solids.
- Use Boolean operations to create composite 3D solids.
- Learn an efficient way to convert 2D drawings into 3D models.
- Learn the practical usage of the **INTERFERE** command.
- Learn the operations to slice 3D solids and extract regions from their cross sections.
- Learn the specifics of using the **FILLET** and **CHAMFER** commands on 3D solids.
- Learn and practice how to generate 3D assemblies with the AutoCAD® program.

INTRODUCTION

ABOUT 3D SOLIDS

Without any doubt, the use of 3D solids is the easiest and most realistic way to generate a 3D model. Instead of simply representing the object's skeleton, or its outer skin, 3D solids represent the 3D model of real objects as a whole volumetric shape. 3D solids, along with the new true surfaces and their interaction possibilities, offer a complete set of tools to create excellent 3D models, which allow designers to develop better designs and innovations in less time.

The AutoCAD software's 3D solids can also be used to obtain important mathematical information such as volume, area, and moment of inertia. Data obtained from 3D solids can be exported into specific file formats and used by other applications to generate CNC (computer numeric control) programs, for FEA (finite element analysis), to produce rapid prototypes, and so on.

SURFACES VS. FACETED SURFACES

Faceted surfaces or meshes are only approximations of surfaces because they are made of smaller planar faces placed one next to the other. Faceted surfaces can be created through several operations, allowing you to obtain many different shapes. They can be shaded by the incidence of light, have materials applied, and be used to hide objects located behind them. Editing or post operations with faceted surfaces, however, are limited to simply deforming the vertices and smoothing the mesh.

Surfaces, on the other hand, are created with the same commands used to create 3D solids, and they are as smooth as the faces of 3D solids. Besides their capabilities of being shaded, having materials applied, and hiding objects, surfaces can be used in other post operations, such as slicing 3D solids, or be transformed into 3D solids by thickening them.

When 3D solids are exploded, regions and surfaces are obtained from the operation. Regions are created from the planar faces, and surfaces from the nonplanar faces of the 3D solids.

Depending on their type, surfaces can be edited by using their grips. Unlike 3D solids, however, surfaces cannot be used to generate 2D drawing views.

CONTROLLING THE DISPLAYING OF SURFACES AND 3D SOLIDS——

When creating a 3D model, it is important to know how to improve the display of the objects in order to ensure a clearer visualization. Depending on the visual style selected, specific system variables or settings concerning the visual style can drastically affect the way that 3D solids are displayed, particularly the nonplanar faces.

The **2D Wireframe** is the visual style you will most likely use to develop 3D model objects. For this reason, we will focus on this particular visual style. Other visual styles are used at the development stage of the 3D modeling process simply to temporarily visualize the result of the operations performed.

When the **2D Wireframe** is the current visual style, the **DISPSILH** system variable controls two important visual effects on surfaces and 3D solids:

1. Display of the *silhouettes* before hiding occulted lines with the **HIDE** command
2. Displaying of the edges of *facets* after hiding occulted lines with the **HIDE** command

The default value of the **DISPSILH** variable is **0** (off) and can be turned on by setting it to **1**. This setting affects only the current drawing. Figure 23-1 shows how the **DISPSILH** variable affects the display of a 3D solid's nonplanar faces and nonplanar surfaces before and after the **HIDE** command is invoked.

The **ISOLINES** system variable controls the number of contour lines that the AutoCAD program uses to represent nonplanar faces of 3D solids. Its default value is **4**. Faces with double curvature, such as spherical faces, generate contour lines in both directions.

silhouette: Outline that defines the limit or profile of the curved faces of an object in the 3D space, causing it to look more real. Silhouettes are not physical edges.

facets: Edges or subdivisions of a 3D solid's nonplanar faces and nonplanar surfaces, produced by internal calculations of the AutoCAD program.

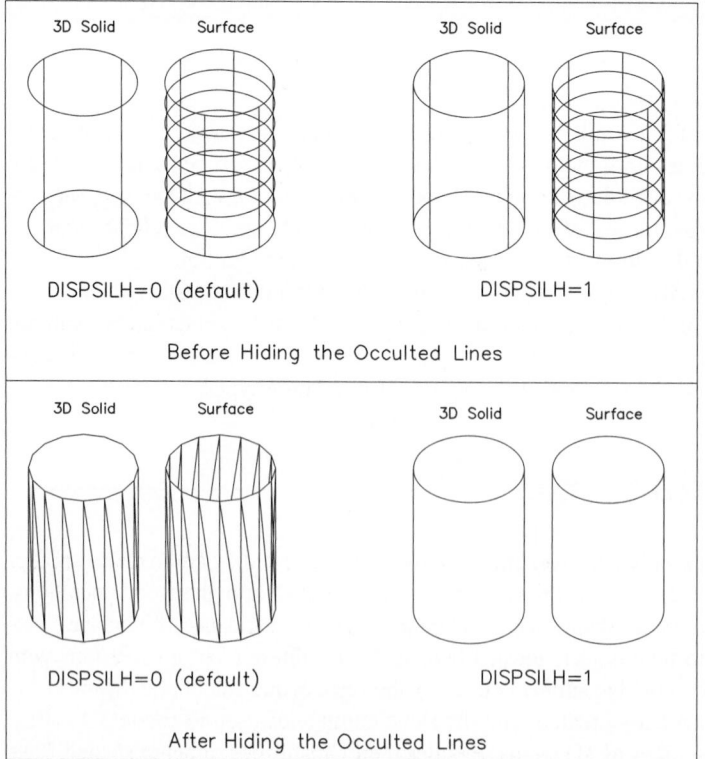

Figure 23-1   Effect of the **DISPSILH** system variable in the display of the 3D solids and surfaces

Figure 23-2 shows the effects of changing the **ISOLINES** variable on the display of 3D solids when the **DISPSILH** variable is **0**.

As you can see, setting both the **DISPSILH** and the **ISOLINES** system variables as **0** does not provide a clear display of 3D solids. Using **DISPSILH=1** and **ISOLINES=0** provides a good visualization of 3D solids when the occulted lines are not hidden (Figure 23-3).

ISOLINES=4   ISOLINES=0   ISOLINES=24
(default)

Figure 23-2   Effect of the **ISOLINES** system variable in the display of the 3D solids

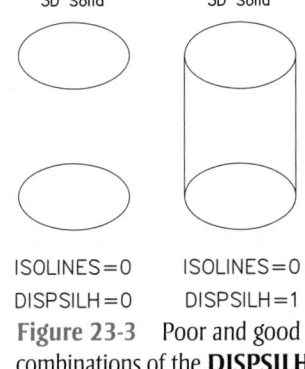

ISOLINES=0   ISOLINES=0
DISPSILH=0   DISPSILH=1

Figure 23-3   Poor and good combinations of the **DISPSILH** and **ISOLINES** system variables on 3D solids

For surfaces, the number of lines displayed in each direction is controlled by the **SURFU** and **SURFV** system variables, respectively. These variables also control the M and N density of smoothed meshes. Figure 23-4 shows how changing these two variables affects the display of surfaces when the **DISPSILH** system variable is **0**.

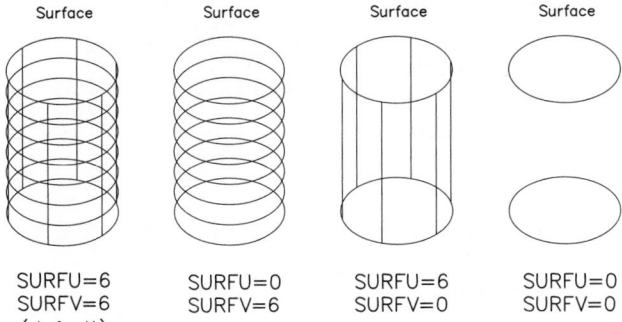

SURFU=6   SURFU=0   SURFU=6   SURFU=0
SURFV=6   SURFV=6   SURFV=0   SURFV=0
(default)

Figure 23-4   Effect of the **SURFU** and **SURFV** system variables on the display of the surfaces

As you can see, setting the **DISPSILH** system variable to **0** when the **SURFU** and **SURFV** values are both **0** does not provide a clear display of surfaces.

Using **DISPSILH=1** when the **SURFU** and **SURFV** values are both **0** provides a clear visualization of surfaces when the occulted lines are not hidden (Figure 23-5).

The **FACETRES** system variable improves the visualization of surfaces and 3D solids by increasing the number of facets used to represent nonplanar faces of 3D solids. Increasing its value will make the faces look smoother after hiding the occulted lines. Its default value is **0.50**, and it can be set between **0.01** and **10.00**. Figure 23-6 shows the comparison between high and low **FACETRES** values when the **DISPSILH** system variable is set to **1**.

Note:
As discussed in Chapter 1, most of the system variables that control the display of 3D objects can be changed either through the **Visual Styles Manager** palette or by entering them in the command line.

Figure 23-5 Effect of the **DISPSILH** system variables on surfaces when the **SURFU** and **SURFV** system variables are set to **0**

Figure 23-6 The **FACETRES** system variable smooths surfaces and 3D solids by increasing the number of facets

CREATING 3D SOLID PRIMITIVES

COMMANDS USED TO CREATE 3D SOLID PRIMITIVES

Typically, the creation of a 3D model represented by 3D solids starts with the creation of several simple 3D solids, such as 3D solid primitives. Then these simple 3D solids are combined, edited, and modified by using other operations until the final shape is achieved. The **BOX, WEDGE, CONE, SPHERE, CYLINDER, TORUS**, and **PYRAMID** commands are used to create 3D solid primitives. Figure 23-7(b) shows the location of these commands in the **Modeling** panel of the Ribbon. To display the list you must click on the down arrow [Figure 23-7(a)]; the last command you invoked from the list is displayed by default. Two different tooltips are displayed according to the delay time that you keep the mouse pointer over a particular command [Figures 23-7(b) and (c)]. Longer times will display a more detailed tooltip.

Note:
The type of 3D solid is shown in the **Properties** palette under **Geometry**, when the 3D solid is selected.

With the newly redesigned 3D solid primitives commands, you can create objects more easily while seeing their development process interactively as you move the cursor when specifying the points. Each command in this group generates its own type of 3D solid, which can be edited by using its unique grips or through the **Properties** palette.

FOR MORE DETAILS	To learn about editing 3D solid primitives, see Chapter 24.

BOX	
Modeling Toolbar	
Ribbon Modeling panel	
Pull-down Menu	Draw/ Modeling/ Box
Command Line	box

The BOX Command

The **BOX** command creates a box-shaped 3D solid, with the base located parallel to the current *XY* plane.

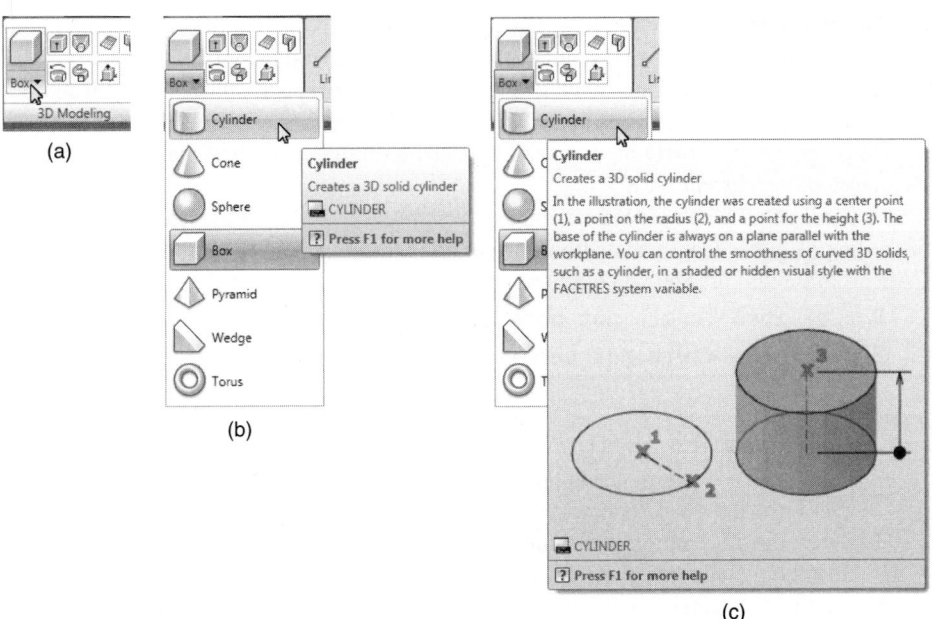

Figure 23-7 The commands used to create 3D solid primitives

You can combine the command's options to create boxes by using different procedures. The following, also shown in Figure 23-8, are most typically used to create a solid box:

- Specify a corner point, another corner in the same plane, and the height.
- Specify two corner points.
- Specify a corner point and a distance (length) using the **Cube** option.
- Specify the center point and one of the corner points.
- Specify a corner and three distances (length, width, and height).
- Specify the center and three distances (length, width, and height).

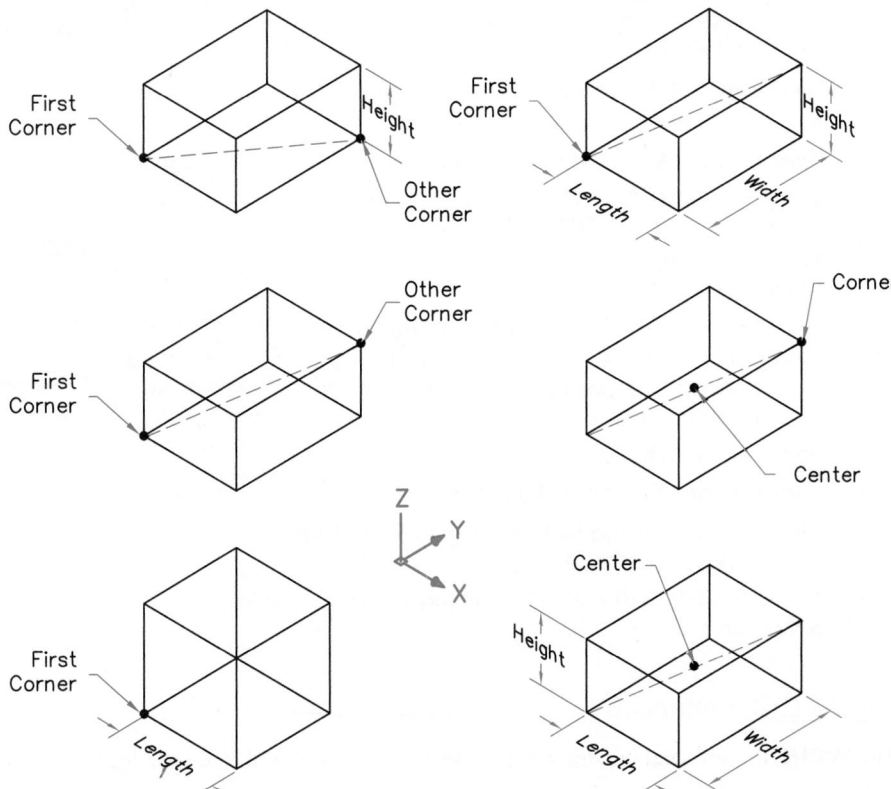

Figure 23-8 Different procedures used to create a box-shaped 3D solid

For procedures in which you specify a second corner point, AutoCAD uses the relative distances *X, Y,* and *Z* from the first point as the length, width, and height, respectively.

With any of the procedures in which you are required to specify the length, you automatically specify the alignment of the box as well, regardless of whether you enter a distance or specify a second point. The **ORTHO** mode must be turned on in order to align the faces of the box with the planes of the current UCS.

Regardless of which procedure you use, you must always enter the length, width, and height of the box. If either length or width information is missing from the points specified, the AutoCAD program will prompt you with one of the following messages:

> **Box of zero length not permitted.**
>
> **Box of zero width not permitted.**

Exercise 23-1: Creating 3D Solid Primitives with the **BOX** Command

1. Start a **NEW** drawing using the acad3D.dwt template.
2. **SAVE** the drawing **AS** *Exercise 23-1*.
3. Select the **SE Isometric** viewing point.
4. Select the **Conceptual** visual style.
5. Turn on the **GRID** by pressing the **<F7>** key, in case it is not turned on.
6. Turn off the **SNAP** mode by pressing the **<F9>** key.
7. Invoke the **BOX** command and respond to the prompts as follows:

   Specify first corner or [Center]: *Move the mouse pointer to the coordinates 1.0000, 1.0000, 0.0000 and click to specify this point.(Zoom in as needed.)*

   Specify other corner or [Cube/Length]: *Move the mouse pointer to the coordinates 2.0000, 3.0000, 0.0000 and click to specify this point.*

   Specify height or [2Point]: *Move the mouse pointer up and enter 1.5 as the height value.*

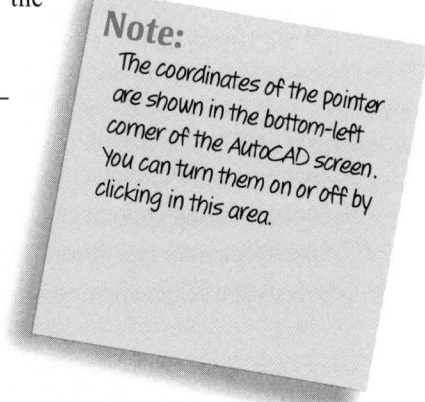

> **Note:**
> The coordinates of the pointer are shown in the bottom-left corner of the AutoCAD screen. You can turn them on or off by clicking in this area.

8. Invoke the **BOX** command again. Respond to the prompts as follows:

   Specify first corner or [Center]: *c* ↵

   Specify center: *Click on the coordinates 2.5000, 2.0000, 0.0000.*

   Specify other corner or [Cube/Length]: *L* ↵

   Specify length: *With ORTHO mode on, place the pointer so as to align the trace with the positive direction of the X-axis, and enter 1.*

   Specify width: *2* ↵

   Specify height or [2Point]: *1.5* ↵

> **Note:**
> When using the **Length** option, you use the **Length** value to specify this distance as well as the rotation in the *XY*-axis. In this exercise you also could have specified @1 <0. Specifying an angle different from 0 will not align the length side parallel to the *X*-axis.

9. The 3D model should look like Figure 23-9. Turn off the **GRID** and the **SNAP** modes.
10. Invoke the **3DORBIT** command to inspect the 3D model.
11. **SAVE** the drawing.

The WEDGE Command

The **WEDGE** command creates a wedge-shaped 3D solid with the base located parallel to the current *XY* plane.

WEDGE	
Modeling Toolbar	
Ribbon Modeling panel	
Pull-down Menu	Draw/ Modeling/ Wedge
Command Line	wedge

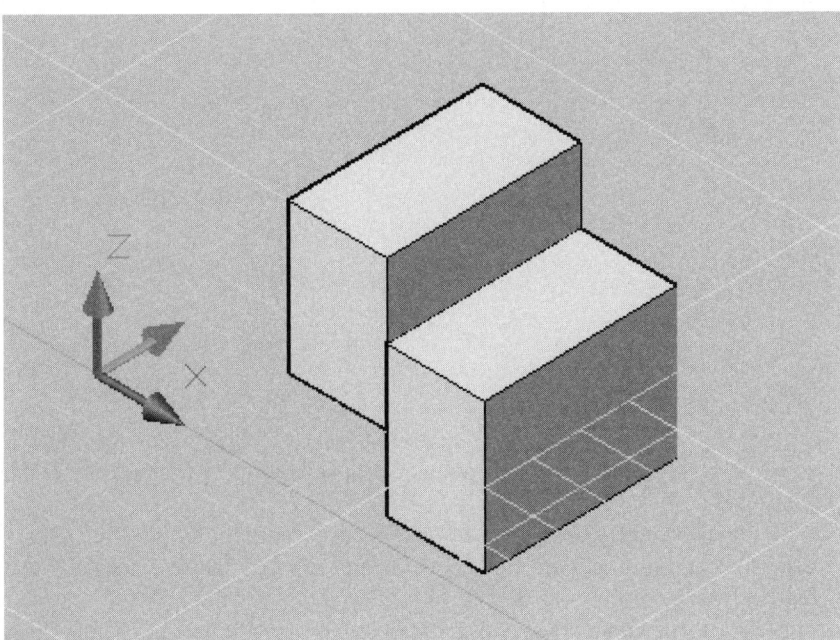

Figure 23-9   The two boxes created

The same procedures used to create a box can be used to create a wedge. You can easily visualize a wedge by thinking of a box diagonally sliced by a plane that is perpendicular to the *ZX* plane (Figure 23-10).

The CONE Command

The **CONE** command creates a cone-shaped 3D solid with a circular or elliptical base (Figure 23-11). Similar to the construction of the circle, the circular base of the cone can be specified by the **2 points,** **3 points**, or **Tangent, tangent, radius** options. Elliptical bases are specified by entering three

CONE	
Modeling Toolbar	
Ribbon Modeling panel	
Pull-down Menu	Draw/ Modeling/ Cone
Command Line	cone

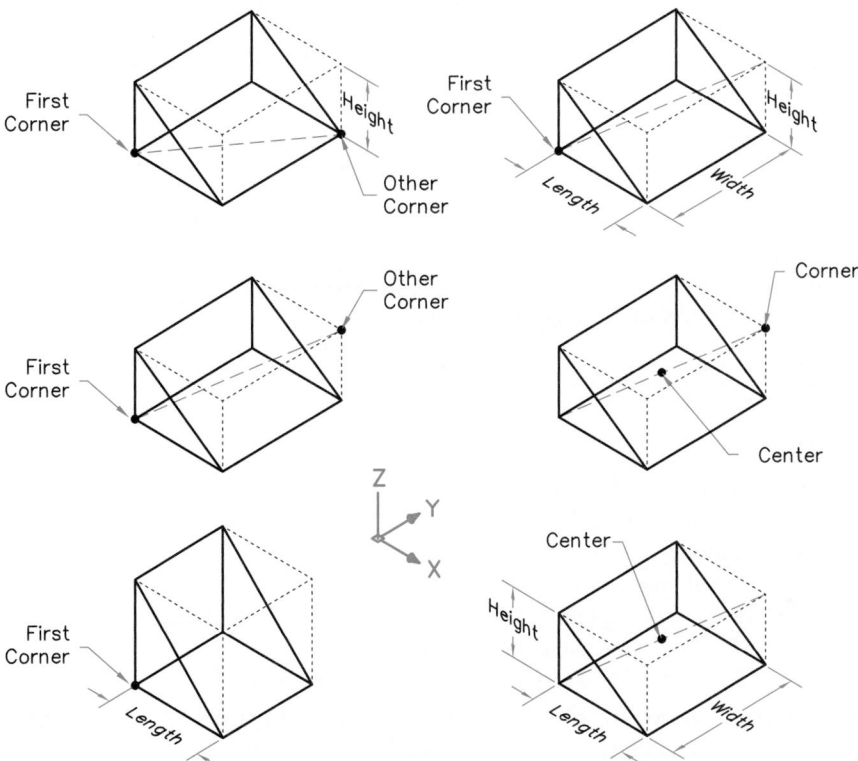

Figure 23-10   Different procedures used to create a wedge-shaped 3D solid

Figure 23-11 The parameters to specify both types of 3D solid cone (with a circular or elliptical base)

endpoints of the axis, or by entering the center point, the distance to the first axis, and the endpoint of the second axis.

If the height of the cone is specified, its base is located parallel to the current *XY* plane. Specifying a point with the **Axis endpoint** option, on the other hand, will align the base normal to the axis of the cone (Figure 23-12).

You can also create a cone that does not end in an apex point by specifying a value in the **Top radius** option (Figure 23-13). In cones with an elliptical base, the top radius value is the distance from the center to the major axis.

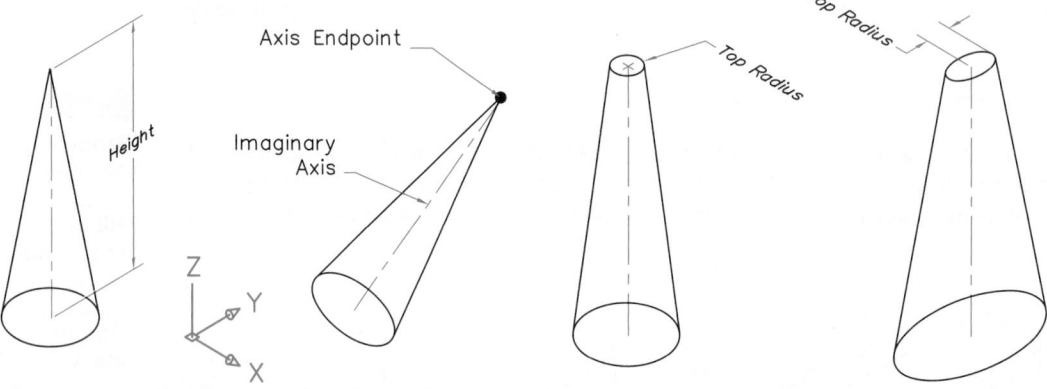

Figure 23-12 Specifying an axis endpoint aligns the imaginary axis of the cone differently

Figure 23-13 If you specify a top radius value, the cone does not end in an apex point

TIP By specifying the radius and the top radius as the same value, you can create a 3D solid in the shape of a cylinder, even though it would still be a cone.

Exercise 23-2: Creating 3D Solid Primitives with the **CONE** Command

1. Start a **NEW** drawing using the acad3D.dwf template.
2. **SAVE** the drawing **AS** *Exercise 23-2.*
3. Select the **SE Isometric** viewing point.
4. Select the **Conceptual** visual style.
5. Turn on the **GRID** by pressing the **<F7>** key, in case it is not turned on
6. Turn off the **SNAP** mode by pressing the **<F9>** key.
7. Invoke the **CONE** command and respond to the prompts as follows:

    Specify center point of base or [3P/2P/Ttr/Elliptical]: *Click on the coordinates 2.0000, 2.0000, 0.0000. (Zoom in as needed.)*

    Specify base radius or [Diameter]: *1 ↵*

    Specify height or [2Point/Axis endpoint/Top radius]: *3 ↵*

8. Invoke the **CONE** command again. Respond to the prompts as follows:

Specify center point of base or [3P/2P/Ttr/Elliptical]: *Click on the coordinates 4.0000, 4.0000, 0.0000. (Zoom in as needed.)*

Specify base radius or [Diameter]: 1 ↵

Specify height or [2Point/Axis endpoint/Top radius]: *t* ↵

Specify top radius: *0.5* ↵

Specify height or [2Point/Axis endpoint]: *a* ↵

Specify axis endpoint: *Click on the coordinates 4.0000, 2.0000, 0.0000.*

9. The 3D model should look like Figure 23-14. Turn off the **GRID** and the **SNAP** modes.
10. Invoke the **3DORBIT** command to inspect the 3D model.
11. **SAVE** the drawing.

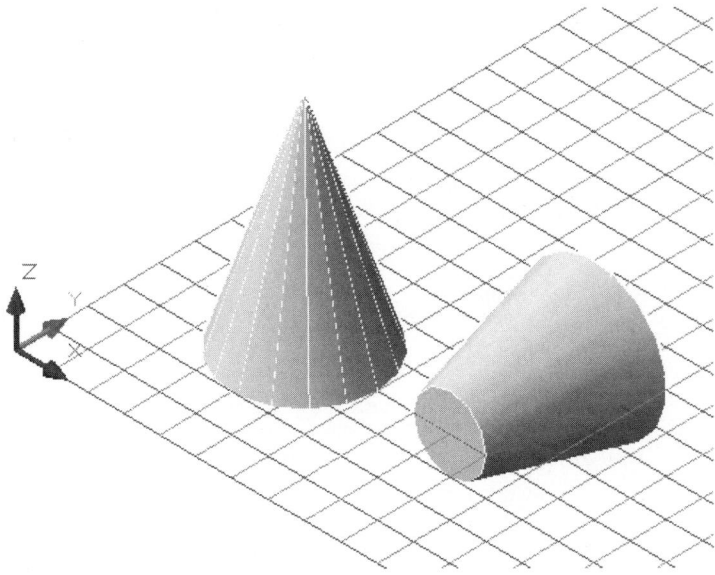

Figure 23-14   The two cylinders created

The SPHERE Command

The **SPHERE** command creates a sphere-shaped 3D solid with its midplane located parallel to the current *XY* plane. The default procedure for creating the sphere is by specifying its center and its radius or diameter (Figure 23-15). A 3D solid sphere can also be created by using the **3 points, 2 points**, and **Tangent, tangent, radius** options:

Specify center point or [3P/2P/Ttr]:

Using the other options allows you to have further control over the location and dimension of the sphere:

- **2P Option:**   Locates the center of the sphere on the midpoint between the two points specified. Its diameter is the distance between the two points [Figure 23-16(a)].

SPHERE	
Modeling Toolbar	
Ribbon Modeling panel	
Pull-down Menu	Draw/ Modeling/ Sphere
Command Line	sphere

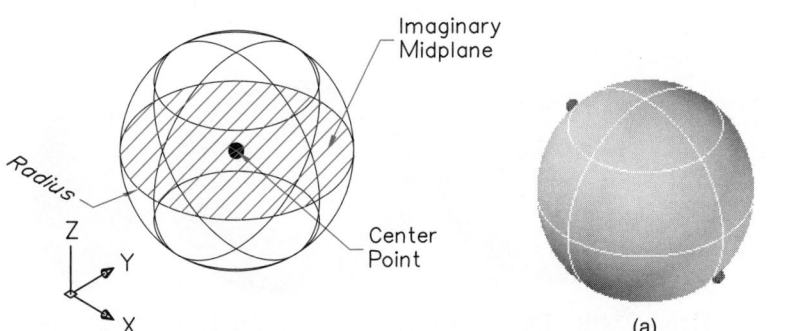

Figure 23-15   Parameters defined in the default procedure for creating the sphere

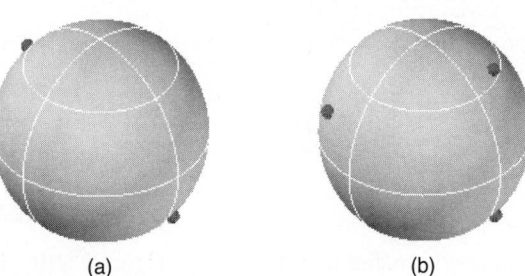

Figure 23-16   **2P** (a) and **3P** (b) options for creating the sphere

- **3P Option:**   Calculates the center point and the radius of the sphere, so that all three points are located exactly on its surface [Figure (23-16(b)].
- **Ttr Option:**   Creates a sphere that is tangent to two lines, arcs, circles, or similar edges of any other object.

The CYLINDER Command

CYLINDER	
Modeling Toolbar	
Ribbon Modeling panel	
Pull-down Menu	Draw/ Modeling/ Cylinder
Command Line	cylinder
Command Alias	cyl

The **CYLINDER** command creates a cylinder-shaped 3D solid with a circular or elliptical base. This command works similarly to the **CONE** command. Because the top and bottom faces of a cylinder are identical, however, there is not an option to specify the top radius (Figure 23-17).

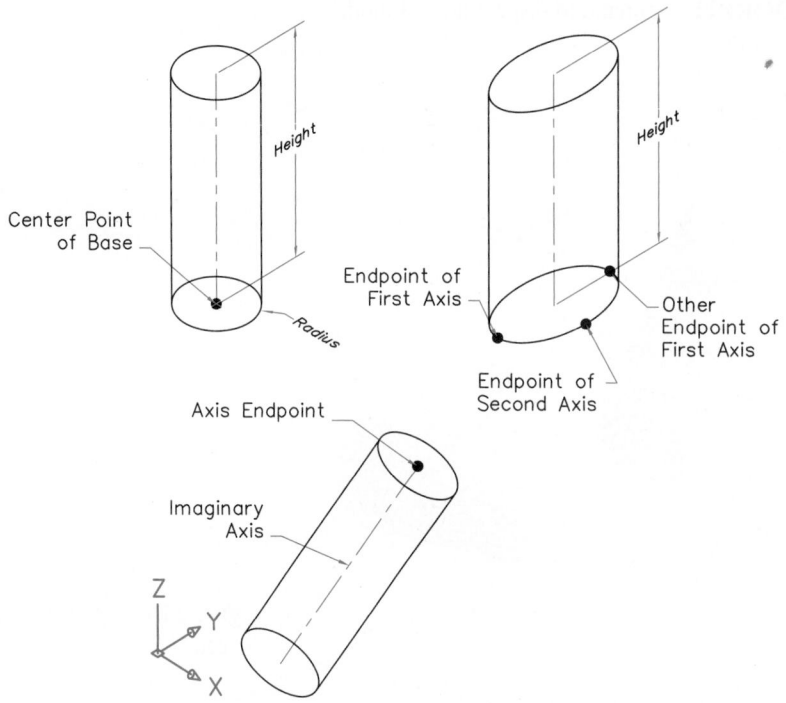

Figure 23-17   The parameters used to specify both types of 3D solid cylinder (with a circular or elliptical base); specifying an axis endpoint aligns the axis of the cylinder differently

The TORUS Command

TORUS	
Modeling Toolbar	
Ribbon Modeling panel	
Pull-down Menu	Draw/ Modeling/ Torus
Command Line	torus

The **TORUS** command creates a torus-shaped 3D solid, defined by the torus radius and a tube radius (Figure 23-18). Depending on the values specified, three different toroidal shapes can be obtained with this command (Figure 23-19).

- **Donut** The torus and tube radii are both positive. The torus radius is greater than the tube radius.

Figure 23-18   The parameters specified to create a torus-shaped 3D solid

Figure 23-19   Different 3D objects obtained according to the sign and relation of the values specified

- **Tangerine** The torus and tube radii are both positive. The torus radius is smaller than the tube radius.

- **Football** The torus radius is negative and the tube radius is positive. The tube radius must be positive and greater than the absolute value of the torus radius.

The imaginary circle defining the torus radius or centerline can be defined by its center point and a radius, or by the **3 points, 2 points**, and **Tangent, tangent, radius** options, similar to the construction of a circle. By using the **3 points** option, you can specify three points anywhere in the 3D space, which enables you to create a torus whose midplane is not parallel to the current *XY* plane.

The PYRAMID Command

The **PYRAMID** command creates a pyramid-shaped 3D solid. The polygonal base can have between 2 and 32 sides. If the polygonal base of the pyramid is created by specifying a center point, then, similar to the **POLYGON** command, it can be created circumscribed or inscribed on a circle. You can also determine the geometry of the base by specifying the first and second points of the leading edge. The default settings of the base are four sides circumscribed on a circle (Figure 23-20).

The rest of the geometry is determined very similarly to the **CONE** command. By specifying the height of the pyramid, you can locate its base parallel to the current *XY* plane. Specifying a point with the **Axis endpoint** option will align the base normal to the axis of the cone (Figure 23-21).

PYRAMID	
Modeling Toolbar	
Ribbon Modeling panel	
Pull-down Menu	Draw/ Modeling/ Pyramid
Command Line	pyramid

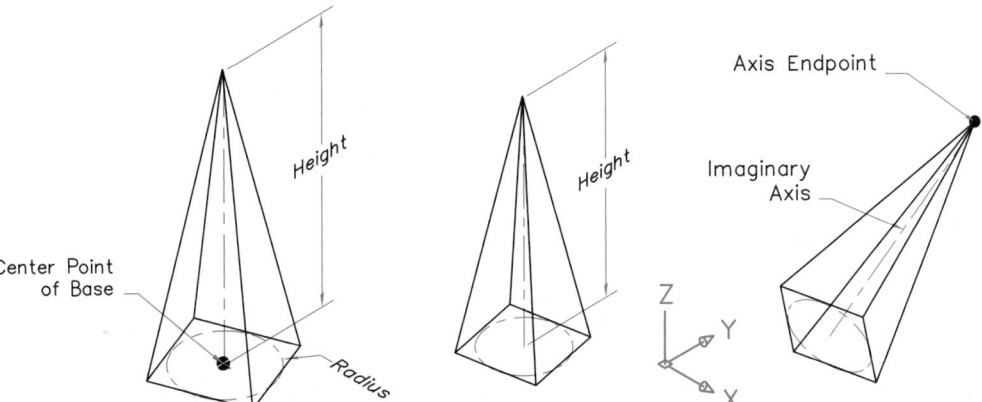

Figure 23-20   The parameters specified to create a pyramid-shaped 3D solid

Figure 23-21   Specifying an axis endpoint aligns the axis of the pyramid differently

As with the cone, you can create a pyramid that does not end in an apex point by specifying a value in the **Top radius** option (Figure 23-22).

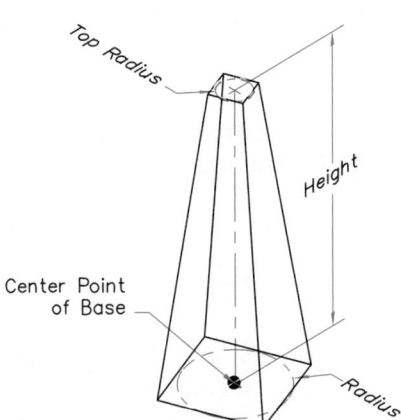

Figure 23-22   If you specify a top radius value, the pyramid does not end in an apex point

CREATING COMPLEX 3D SOLIDS AND SURFACES

DIFFERENT APPROACHES TO CREATING 3D SOLID OBJECTS

The commands that are used to create 3D solid primitives enable you to create the most common 3D objects. As you will learn later, you can combine 3D solid primitives through Boolean operations to create more complex 3D models. More complex commands (**EXTRUDE, REVOLVE, SWEEP**, and **LOFT**), however, can also be used to obtain the same 3D solids with less effort. Figure 23-23 shows two alternative ways of developing the same 3D solid model.

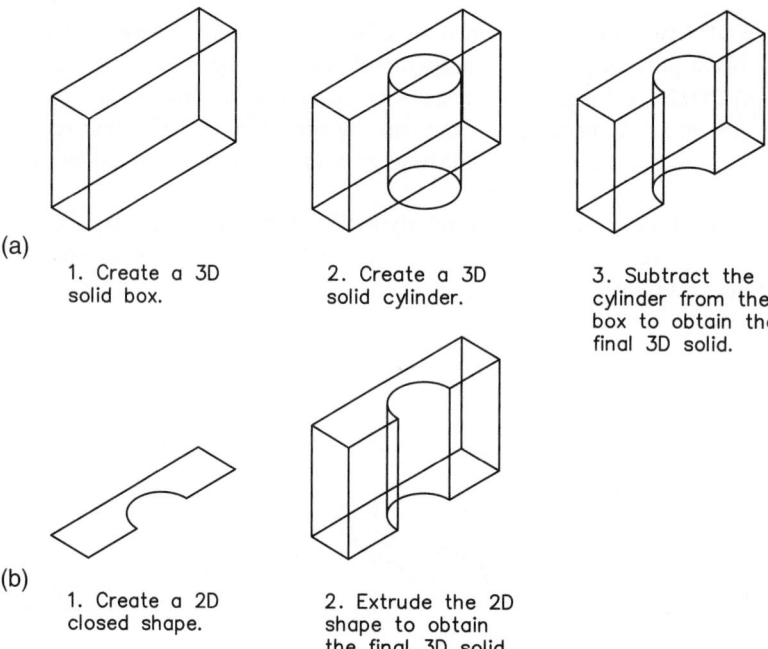

(a)

1. Create a 3D solid box.

2. Create a 3D solid cylinder.

3. Subtract the cylinder from the box to obtain the final 3D solid.

(b)

1. Create a 2D closed shape.

2. Extrude the 2D shape to obtain the final 3D solid.

Figure 23-23   Two approaches to creating a 3D solid model: (a) using and combining primitives and (b) using the **EXTRUDE** command

The **EXTRUDE, REVOLVE, SWEEP**, and **LOFT** commands also allow you to create 3D solids and surfaces of very complex shapes. All these commands require you to select certain types of objects depending on the operation performed. As a general rule, 3D solids are created from closed objects such as circles, regions, and closed polylines, whereas surfaces are created from open objects such as arcs, lines, and open polylines.

Each of these commands generates its own type of 3D solid and surface. Each particular type of 3D object contains properties unique to it. You can then use these properties to perform further editing.

FOR MORE DETAILS	To learn about editing different types of 3D solids and surfaces, see Chapter 24.

By default, the selected objects are deleted after the 3D solid or surface is created through the different operations. This setting is controlled by the **DELOBJ** system variable. You can change its value to **1** to keep the selected objects.

THE EXTRUDE COMMAND

The name **EXTRUDE** comes from a manufacturing process called *extrusion,* in which heat-softened metal or plastic is pushed under high pressure through a mold opening, producing bars with constant cross sections. Figure 23-24 shows a 3D solid model of an aluminum bar extrusion created with the **EXTRUDE** command.

Figure 23-24   Extruded aluminum bars can be created using the **EXTRUDE** command

Figure 23-25   Different ways of creating extrusions

The **EXTRUDE** command creates 3D solids and surfaces of the **Extrusion** type by protruding planar objects. Depending on the options you use, the extrusion can be performed in one of the following ways (Figure 23-25):

- Perpendicular to its plane (default)
- In a specified direction
- Following a path

By specifying the height of extrusion, the object is automatically extruded perpendicular to the plane where it exists. You can change this course by selecting either the **Direction** or the **Path** option.

Defining a **Direction** by specifying the start and end points creates the same 3D solid or surface shape as does selecting a line between these two points using the **Path** option. The types of 3D solids and surfaces created with the **Path** option, however, are not the same as those created with the **Direction** option. The **Path** option creates 3D solids and surfaces of the **Sweep** type, whereas using the **Direction** option or simply extruding the object perpendicular to its plane both create 3D solids and surfaces of the **Extrusion** type. These different types of 3D solids and surfaces offer different editing capabilities.

FOR MORE DETAILS   See Chapter 24 to find more information about procedures to edit the different types of 3D solids and surfaces.

You can also specify a **Taper angle** for any of the operations to create both 3D solids and surfaces (Figure 23-26).

The following AutoCAD objects or entities can be extruded into either 3D solids or surfaces:

- Lines
- Arcs
- Circles
- Regions
- Ellipses and elliptical arcs
- Non-self-intersecting polylines
- Non-self-intersecting, planar 3D polylines

Taper
Angle

PERPENDICULAR
TO ITS PLANE

IN A SPECIFIED
DIRECTION

FOLLOWING A PATH

Figure 23-26 A taper angle can also be specified for both 3D solids and surfaces

- Planar splines
- Planar 3D faces
- Non-self-intersecting 2D solids
- Planar surfaces
- Planar faces on 3D solids (see below)

You can create extruded 3D solids from planar faces of other 3D solids by holding down the **<Ctrl>** key while selecting objects. The 3D solids created from the selected faces will be independent of the original 3D solids whose faces were selected. You can select different faces on the same 3D solid or on different 3D solids. You can also select faces along with any other object.

Almost any object can be used as a path as well, as long as it is not placed in the same plane as the extruded object. The following list contains the objects allowed in the selection:

- Lines
- Arcs
- Circles
- Ellipses and elliptical arcs
- Non-self-intersecting polylines
- Non-self-intersecting 3D polylines
- Splines
- Edges of 3D solids and surfaces (see below)
- Helixes

You can create extruded 3D solids and surfaces using the edges of other 3D solids and surfaces by holding down the **<Ctrl>** key while selecting the object that defines the path.

Polylines are very useful for defining the path of extrusions. Two applications in which extruding objects by using this path can be helpful are the pipe and duct lines shown in Figure 23-27. If two continuous segments of the polyline path are not tangent, the resulting 3D solid will look as if it were mitered by the midplane between the two segments (Figure 23-28).

Extruding a circle along a helix path allows you to create springs (Figure 23-29).

Figure 23-27 Pipe and duct lines are easily created by extruding the profile through a path

Figure 23-28 Mitered transitions can be obtained by using a path with two continuous straight segments

Figure 23-29 Extruding along a helix path allows you to create springs

EXTRUDE	
Modeling Toolbar	
Ribbon Modeling panel	
Pull-down Menu	Draw/ Modeling/ Extrude
Command Line	extrude
Command Alias	ext

[TIP pencil icon] It is a good practice to place the object to be extruded on the starting point of the path in a plane perpendicular to the path curve. This helps to avoid unpredicted results. You can find the plane that is perpendicular to a curve by using the **Object** option of the **Z axis** method of modifying the UCS.

Exercise 23-3: Using the **EXTRUDE** Command

1. **OPEN** the drawing *Exercise 23-3* in the student data files.
2. **SAVE** the drawing **AS** *Exercise 23-3 solved* on your computer.
3. Select the **SE Isometric** viewing point.
4. Invoke the **EXTRUDE** command. Respond to the prompts as follows:

   Select objects to extrude: *Select the region.*

   Select objects to extrude: ↵ *(To end the selection)*

   Specify height of extrusion or [Direction/Path/Taper angle]: *t* ↵

   Specify angle of taper for extrusion: *−30* ↵

   Specify height of extrusion or [Direction/Path/Taper angle]: *−1.5* ↵

Note:
The extrusion is performed 1.5 units toward the negative direction of the Z-axis. Due to the negative taper angle, the cross section of the 3D solid gets bigger toward the extrusion end (Figure 23-30, with the hidden lines removed).

To access student data files, go to www.pearsondesigncentral.com.

Figure 23-30 After extruding the profile as specified

5. Invoke the **EXTRUDE** command again and respond to the prompts as follows:

Select objects to extrude: *Hold down the* **<Ctrl>** *and* **<Alt>** *keys, and click on the front face once it is highlighted.*

Select objects to extrude: *Holding down the* **<Ctrl>** *key, click inside the front face.*

Specify height of extrusion or [Direction/Path/Taper angle]: *p ↵*

Select extrusion path or [Taper angle]: *Select the open polyline.*

TIP   Now you can select the objects before invoking the **EXTRUDE** command. This enables you to avoid the selection process.

6. Invoke the **HIDE** command. The objects should look like Figure 23-31.
7. Invoke the **REGEN** command.
8. With **ORTHO** mode on, **COPY** the first extruded 3D solid and the polyline **12″** along the positive direction of the *X*-axis (Figure 23-32).

Figure 23-31   The resulting 3D model with occulted lines removed

Figure 23-32   After copying the objects

9. **EXTRUDE** the front face of the copied 3D solid. Use a **Taper angle** of **5°**, and a **Direction** specified between the two endpoints of the open polyline's first segment. The result should look like Figure 23-33 with the hidden lines removed.
10. With **ORTHO** mode on, **MOVE** the two open polylines **12″** along the negative direction of the *Z*-axis (Figure 23-34).
11. Select the leftmost polyline and invoke the **EXTRUDE** command to create an extruded surface. Enter **−8** when prompted to specify the height of extrusion.
12. **EXPLODE** the remaining polyline.
13. Select the longest of the separated segments and invoke the **EXTRUDE** command again. Respond to the prompts as follows:

Specify height of extrusion or [Direction/Path/Taper angle] <3.3500>: *p ↵*

Select extrusion path or [Taper angle]: *Holding down the* **<Ctrl>** *key, select the edge highlighted in* Figure 23-35.

Note:
Now you can select the objects before invoking the **EXTRUDE** command. This facilitates the selection process.

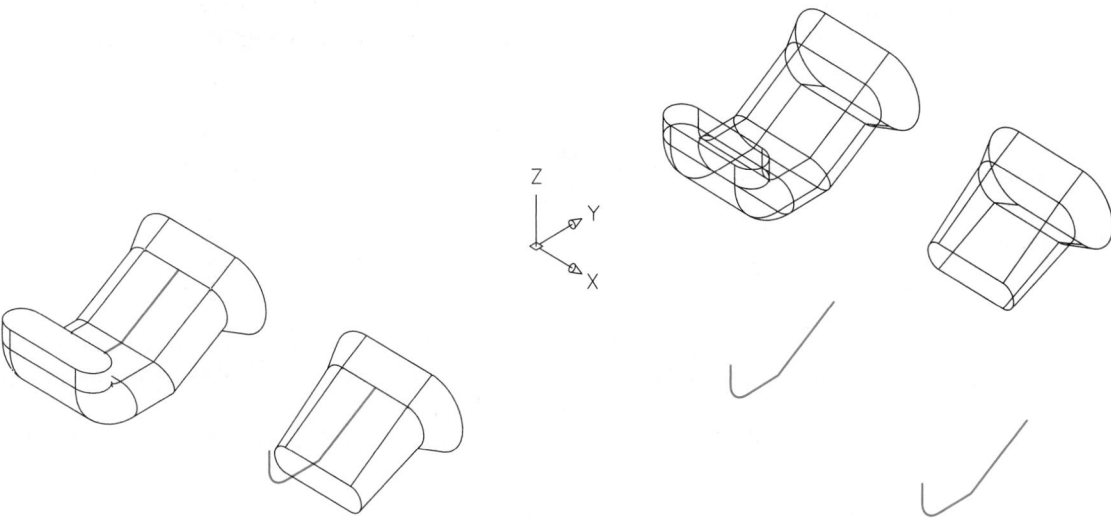

Figure 23-33   After extruding the profile using a taper angle

Figure 23-34   The polylines are moved

Figure 23-35   The highlighted edge is selected as the extrusion path

Figure 23-36   The resulting 3D objects

14. After invoking the **HIDE** command, the 3D objects should look like Figure 23-36.
15. **SAVE** the drawing.

Extruding Implied Faces: The PRESSPULL Command

EXTRUDE is the command most widely used in 3D modeling. You can also create 3D solids by extruding a bounded area perpendicular to its plane without even invoking the **EXTRUDE** command. This operation is known as **Extrude Implied Faces**.

The **Extrude Implied Faces** detection process is initiated automatically by holding down the **<Ctrl>** and **<Alt>** keys together, or by invoking the **PRESSPULL** command. Then you just click inside the bounded planar area or contour detected to extrude it in one of two directions by either entering a value or clicking on another point. For example, the rectangle and the line shown in Figure 23-37, which are placed on a common plane, contain two bounded planar areas that are recognized by this operation. Clicking on one of the detected implied faces and specifying a height creates the 3D solid.

Besides bounded planar areas, delimited by crossing coplanar objects, implied faces can also be detected from any single closed planar object, such as a closed polyline or a region. Moreover,

PRESSPULL	
Modeling Toolbar	
Ribbon Modeling	
Command Line	presspull

Figure 23-37 (a) Selecting one of the implied faces (b) The extruded implied faces

(a)   (b)

the faces of existing 3D solids can also become part of the implied face boundary along with other coplanar curves. Figure 23-38 shows the creation of a 3D solid by extruding an implied face between the bottom face of the 3D solid and a circle.

The **IMPLIEDFACE** system variable controls whether or not the implied faces are detected.

Figure 23-38 The faces of 3D solids are included in the implied face boundary selection

Exercise 23-4: Extruding Implied Faces

1. Start a **NEW** drawing using **Imperial** units.
2. **SAVE** the drawing **AS** *Exercise 23-4*.
3. Set the **DISPSILH** system variable to **1**.
4. Set the **ISOLINES** system variable to **0**.
5. Select the **SE Isometric** viewing point.
6. Invoke the **CYLINDER** command and create a cylinder anywhere in the drawing area. Specify **11/16″** for the radius, and **2½″** for the height.
7. **ZOOM** in as needed and create a **4 × 1** rectangle using the **RECTANGLE** command. Then **MOVE** the rectangle so the midpoint of its long side is located on the center point of the bottom face of the cylinder (Figure 23-39).
8. Press and hold down the **<Ctrl>** and **<Alt>** keys to initiate the **Extrude Implied Faces** process. Once recognized, click inside the area that is bounded by the rectangle and the circular edge of the cylinder.
9. Release the **<Ctrl>** and **<Alt>** keys. Move the pointer upward and type **4** in the command line. Press **<Enter↵>** to finish the operation.
10. After invoking the **HIDE** command, the two 3D solids should look like Figure 23-40.
11. **SAVE** the drawing.

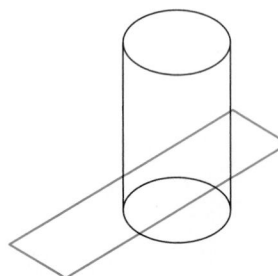

Figure 23-39 The rectangle is moved toward the cylinder

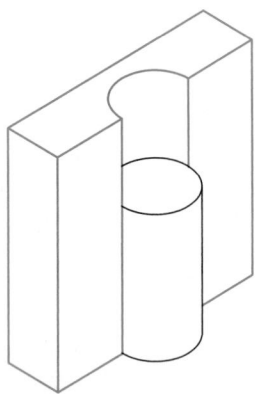

Figure 23-40 A new 3D solid created by extruding an implied face

imaginary axis of revolution: The vector, defined by specifying any two points, about which the objects are revolved. Its direction is defined from the first point to the second point.

THE REVOLVE COMMAND

The **REVOLVE** command creates revolved 3D solids and surfaces by turning closed and open objects in a circular direction around an *imaginary axis of revolution* at a specified angle. Objects machined in a lathe, such as the pulley shown in Figure 23-41, are good examples of 3D objects that can be easily created using this command.

Basically, the same type of objects that can be extruded can be revolved as well, including planar faces on 3D solids. As with the **EXTRUDE** command, holding down the **<Ctrl>** key while selecting objects allows you to select faces from one or more 3D solids, which you can combine with any other valid selection. The new revolved 3D solids and surfaces created by selecting the faces of 3D solids will be independent of the original 3D solid from which the faces were selected.

Figure 23-41   A pulley can easily
be created as a revolved 3D solid

The imaginary axis of revolution can be defined anywhere in the 3D space, as long as it is not perpendicular to the plane of the object to be revolved. Depending on the option selected, you can define the imaginary axis of revolution using one of the following methods:

- Two points
- The *X*-axis of the current UCS
- The *Y*-axis of the current UCS
- The *Z*-axis of the current UCS
- Using an existing object (lines, open polylines, and straight edges on 3D solids)

When using the **Object** option, you can select a straight edge of other 3D solids or surfaces by holding down the **<Ctrl>** key. If you select a polyline with more than one segment, the axis of revolution will be considered to be a vector between the start and end points of the polyline.

Exercise 23-5: Using the **REVOLVE** Command

1. **OPEN** the drawing *Exercise 23-5* in the student data files. It contains the objects shown in Figure 23-42.

To access student data files, go to www.pearsondesigncentral.com.

2. **SAVE** the drawing **AS** *Exercise 23-5 solved*.
3. Invoke the **REVOLVE** command, and respond to the prompts as follows:

   Select objects to revolve: *Select the region on the right.*

   Select objects to revolve: ↵ *(To end the selection)*

   Specify axis start point or define axis by [Object/X/Y/Z] <Object>: *Specify the leftmost endpoint of the line next to it.*

   Specify axis endpoint: *Specify the other endpoint of the line.*

   Specify angle of revolution or [STart angle] <360>: *225* ↵

4. Invoke the **HIDE** command. The 3D solid should look like Figure 23-43.

Figure 23-42   Objects contained in the student data files

Figure 23-43   The revolved 3D solid with the obscured lines removed

REVOLVE	
Modeling Toolbar	
Ribbon Modeling panel	
Pull-down Menu	Draw/ Modeling/ Revolve
Command Line	revolve
Command Alias	rev

FOR MORE DETAILS In a rotation, the positive angle direction is determined by the right-hand rule. See Chapter 19 for more information on this topic.

5. Invoke the **REGEN** command.
6. Invoke the **REVOLVE** command, and respond to the prompts as follows:

    Select objects to revolve: *Select the region on the left.*

    Select objects to revolve: ↵ *(To end the selection)*

    Specify start point for axis of revolution or

    Specify axis start point or define axis by [Object/X/Y/Z] <Object>: *o* ↵

    Select an object: *Select the line by picking it on the top half portion.*

    Specify angle of revolution or [STart angle] <360>: *180* ↵

7. **ERASE** the line you used to define the axis of revolution.
8. Invoke the **HIDE** command. The new revolved 3D solid should look like Figure 23-44.
9. Invoke the **REGEN** command and select the **Right** UCS.
10. Draw the two lines shown in Figure 23-45. Using AutoTrack might be helpful for this operation.
11. Invoke the **REVOLVE** command, and respond to the prompts as follows:

Note: When using an object to specify the axis of revolution, the portion of the object at which it is picked determines the positive angle for the **REVOLVE** operation.

Figure 23-44 Another revolved 3D Solid

Figure 23-45 Dimensions of lines to be created

Select objects to revolve: *Holding down the <Ctrl> key, click on the face shown highlighted in* Figure 23-46.

Select objects to revolve: ↵ *(To end the selection)*

Specify start point for axis of revolution or

Specify axis start point or define axis by [Object/X/Y/Z] Object: *o* ↵

Select an object: *Select the line by picking it on the left half portion.*

Specify angle of revolution or [STart angle] <360>: *60* ↵

12. **ERASE** the line you used to define the axis of revolution.
13. Create a third revolved 3D solid by revolving the other planar face 60° as well. Define the axis of revolution by selecting the line on its lower half portion.
14. **ERASE** the line and invoke the **UNION** command. When prompted, select the three 3D solids.
15. Select the **Conceptual** visual style.

Figure 23-46   Face to be selected for the **REVOLVE** operation

Figure 23-47   A shaded view of the resulting 3D model

16. In the **Edge Effects** panel of the Ribbon, make sure the **Obscured edges** button is turned off. The 3D model should look like Figure 23-47.
17. Invoke the **3DORBIT** command to inspect the geometry of the 3D model.
18. **SAVE** the drawing.

THE SWEEP COMMAND

The **SWEEP** command creates 3D solids of the **Sweep** type and surfaces by sweeping closed planar and open planar objects along a sweep path. Figure 23-48 shows a rectangular polyline and a line that have both been swept along a helical path. The operation aligns itself with the cross section normal to the path at any point.

The different options you can use to fine-tune the sweep operation once the objects are selected are shown in the **SWEEP** shortcut menu (Figure 23-49).

sweep: Operation in which open or closed planar objects are passed through a curve, creating 3D solids and surfaces.

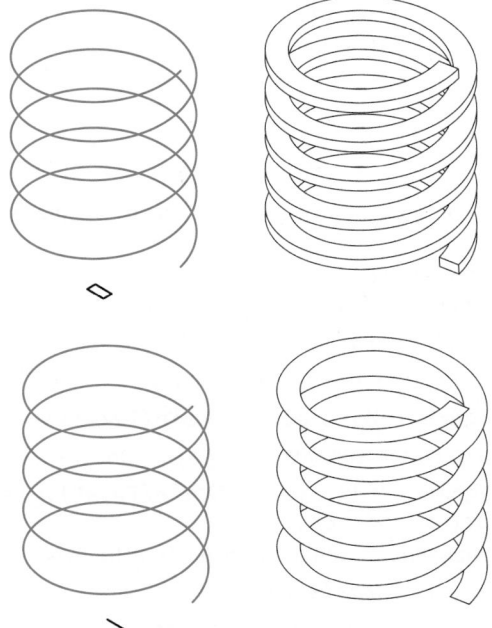

Figure 23-48   Objects swept along a helical path

Figure 23-49   The **SWEEP** command shortcut menu

The **Alignment** option determines whether the planar objects are aligned normal to the sweep path before the sweep operation or swept with their current alignment.

By default, the location of the selected objects with respect to the swept path is in the middle of all the objects selected. This setting can be changed through the **Base point** option, or by manually locating the objects at the desired location (Figure 23-50).

Figure 23-50 The **Base point** option controls the relative location of the cross section with respect to the path's start point

Default Base Point

Controlled Base Point

The **Scale** option allows you to create 3D solids and surfaces for which the cross section increases or decreases uniformly as they are swept along the path, depending on the scale factor you specify (Figure 23-51).

The **Twist** option rotates the cross section uniformly as the object is swept along the path, depending on the angle value you specify (Figure 23-52).

Figure 23-51   Using the **Scale** option creates swept 3D objects with cross sections that increase or decrease uniformly

Figure 23-52   The **Twist** option rotates the cross section uniformly

Exercise 23-6: Using the **SWEEP** Command

To access student data files, go to www.pearsondesigncentral.com.

1. **OPEN** the drawing *Exercise 23-6* in the student data files. It contains the objects shown in Figure 23-53.
2. **SAVE** the drawing **AS** *Exercise 23-6 solved.*
3. Invoke the **SWEEP** command, and respond to the prompts as follows:

   Select objects to sweep: *Select the small polyline.*

   Select objects to sweep: ↵ *(To end the selection)*

   Select sweep path or [Alignment/Base point/Scale/Twist]: *b* ↵

   Specify base point: *Snap to the rightmost endpoint on the polyline.*

   Select sweep path or [Alignment/Base point/Scale/Twist]: *Select the helix close to its bottom portion.*

4. Invoke the **SWEEP** command again, and respond to the prompts as follows:

   Select objects to sweep: *Select the small line.*

   Select objects to sweep: ↵ *(To end the selection)*

   Select sweep path or [Alignment/Base point/Scale/Twist]: *s* ↵

   Enter scale factor or [Reference] <1.0000>: *3* ↵

   Select sweep path or [Alignment/Base point/Scale/Twist]: *Select the spline on the topmost portion of the current view.*

5. Invoke the **HIDE** command. The 3D model should look like Figure 23-54.
6. Select the **Realistic** visual style and invoke the **3DORBIT** command to inspect the 3D model.
7. **SAVE** the drawing.

SWEEP	
Modeling Toolbar	
Ribbon Modeling panel	
Pull-down Menu	Draw/ Modeling/ Sweep
Command Line	sweep

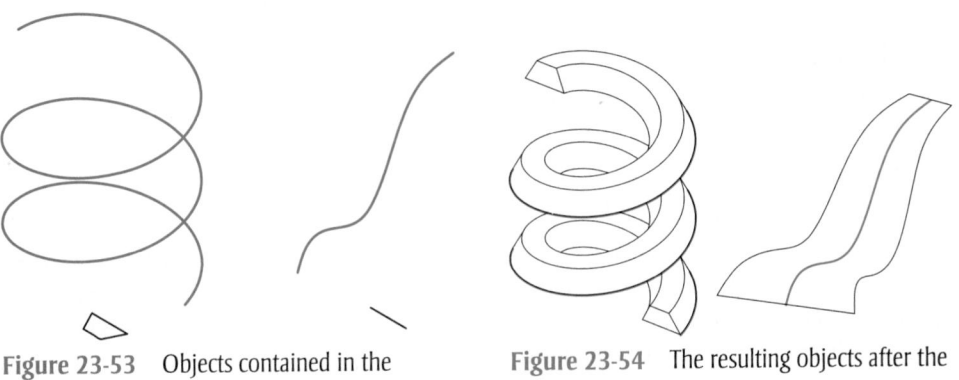

Figure 23-53   Objects contained in the drawing file

Figure 23-54   The resulting objects after the **SWEEP** operation

THE **LOFT** COMMAND

The **LOFT** command creates 3D solids or surfaces of the *loft* type by lofting a set of two or more cross sections. This operation can alternatively be assisted by a path or a set of guides. Unlike other commands, **LOFT** generates three different types of 3D solids and surfaces depending on which option you use:

- Loft with cross sections only
- Loft with path
- Loft with guide curves

Each of these types of 3D solids or surfaces contains properties that are unique to them, which you can then use to perform further editing. You can see the type of 3D solid or surface in the **Geometry** section of the **Properties** palette.

LOFT	
Modeling Toolbar	
Ribbon Modeling panel	
Pull-down Menu	Draw/ Modeling/ Loft
Command Line	loft

> **FOR MORE DETAILS**   To learn about editing different types of 3D solids and surfaces, see Chapter 24.

Each type of 3D solid or surface is created by using one of the options available. Figure 23-55 shows the **LOFT** command shortcut menu with the three options available.

The **Cross sections only** option is the default. It simply requires you to select a set of two noncoplanar curves. Sets of closed curves generate a 3D solid, whereas sets of open curves generate a surface (Figure 23-56). Closed and open curves cannot be combined in the same set of cross sections. Nonplanar curves can be used as cross sections, as long as they are not the first and last ones.

The following objects can be used as cross sections:

- Lines
- Arcs

loft: Operation in which a set of open or closed objects are connected through a blended smooth transition, creating 3D solids and surfaces.

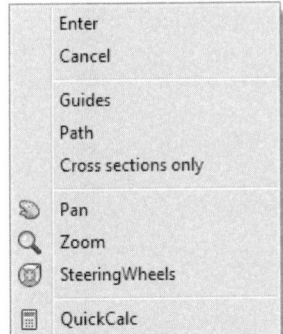

Figure 23-55   The **LOFT** command shortcut menu

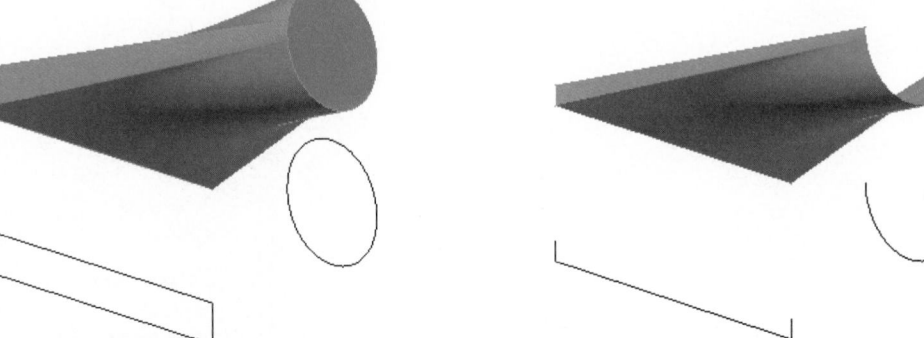

Figure 23-56   A simple **LOFT** operation using the **Cross sections only** option simply requires selecting two open or closed noncoplanar curves

- Circles
- Ellipses and elliptical arcs
- Non-self-intersecting polylines
- Non-self-intersecting 3D polylines
- Splines
- Points (only the start and end cross sections)

In the world of design, loft operations are known as *free-form generation tools.* They connect the cross section through a blended smooth transition, from which many different shapes can be obtained, depending on the options used (Figure 23-57). Many shampoo and liquid soap bottles, among other items, are designed using this operation.

Figure 23-57   Examples of shapes that can be achieved with the **LOFT** operation

Using the **Cross sections only** option opens the **Loft Settings** dialog box (Figure 23-58). Here you can choose from four different methods to control the behavior of the lofted 3D object at the cross sections:

- **Ruled**
- **Smooth Fit**

Figure 23-58   The **Loft Settings** dialog box

- **Normal to the Start, End, Start and End**, or **All cross sections**
- Using **Draft angles** for start and end cross sections

The difference between **Ruled** and **Smooth Fit** methods of creating a lofted 3D object is noticeable only when lofting more than two cross sections (Figure 23-59).

Creating a loft 3D object **Normal to**: specific cross sections forces the lofted geometry to protrude perpendicular to the specified cross sections (Figure 23-60).

Ruled Loft   Smooth Fit Loft

Figure 23-59   Lofted 3D solids using the **Ruled** and **Smooth Fit** methods

Ruled or Smooth Fit   Normal to All Cross Sections   Normal to Start Cross Section Only

Figure 23-60   Lofted 3D solids using the **Normal to**: specific cross sections option

The **Draft angles** setting allows you to control the angle between the lofted geometry and the start or end cross sections. Angles over 90° tilt the surfaces of the lofted geometry inward, whereas angles from 90° to 0° tilt the surfaces of the lofted geometry outward. Specifying both **Draft angles** as 0° enables you to create 3D solids without sharp edges (Figure 23-61). The **magnitude** value controls the relative distance that the lofted geometry is drafted from the specified cross section.

You can loft between cross sections that have different numbers of segments. Using cross sections with an equal number of edges whenever possible, however, will allow you to obtain smoother lofted 3D solids and surfaces. For example, a 3D solid lofted between a circle and an ellipse provides a smoother result than the one created between a circle and a rectangle because both the circle and ellipse cross sections contain a single segment (Figure 23-62). A loft operation between a rectangle and a triangle, on the other hand, might give you odd results (Figure 23-63). To prevent odd results, you can add another segment to the cross sections by creating a simple chamfer or fillet in one of the vertices.

Using the **Path** option or **Guides** option allows you to use a different approach to create lofted 3D objects. The settings or geometric conditions you specify when using the **Cross sections only**

Figure 23-61   Lofted 3D solids using **Draft angles**

Specifying a 110° Angle
at the Start Cross Section

Specifying a 110° Angle
at the Start Cross Section and
0° at the End Cross Section

Figure 23-62   Using cross sections with an equal number of segments is beneficial for the smoothness of the resulting 3D solid

Figure 23-63   A lofted 3D solid between a rectangle and a triangle

option do not apply with the **Path** option or **Guides** option. The **Path** option requires you to specify a single curve, which takes control over the centerline of the lofted 3D object between the cross sections. Using **Guides**, on the other hand, gives you the freedom of controlling specific areas on the surface of the lofted 3D object. Areas that are not guided will behave as a smooth-fit loft (Figure 23-64).

The **Path** curve must intersect the planes of all cross sections. The best results are obtained when it starts and ends on the center of the cross sections or close to it. Cross sections take priority over the path when using more than two cross sections; the path then tries to pull the loft centerline toward it in places having no cross sections. **Guides** must intersect the curve of each cross section, making the surface of the lofted 3D object follow them at their specific locations. When the cross section curves are made of several segments, guides are best used by placing their endpoints at the vertices of the curve of the cross section (Figure 23-65). In general, open continuously tangent and continuously curved wire objects such as lines, arcs, polylines, elliptical arcs, splines and spline-fit polylines, and 3D polylines behave very well when used as paths or guides. Helixes can be used only as paths.

Loft Normal to All   Loft Using a Path   Smooth-Fit Loft   Loft Using Two
Cross Sections   Guides

Figure 23-64   Lofted 3D solids using the **Path** option or **Guides** option compared with the **Cross sections only** construction

Figure 23-65   The **Path** must intersect all cross section planes, whereas **Guides** are required to intersect each cross section

Exercise 23-7: Using the **LOFT** Command

1. **OPEN** the drawing *Exercise 23-7* in the student data files. It contains the six curves shown in Figure 23-66.
2. **SAVE** the drawing **AS *Exercise 23-7 solved.***
3. Set the **DELOBJ** system variable to **0**.
4. Invoke the **LOFT** command and respond to the prompts as follows.

To access student data files, go to www.pearsondesigncentral.com.

    Select cross sections in lofting order: *Select the four closed curves in order from left to right.*

    Select cross sections in lofting order: ↵ *(To end the selection)*

    Enter an option [Guides/Path/Cross sections only] <Cross sections only>: *g* ↵

    Select guide curves: *Select the two open curves in any order.*

    Select guide curves: ↵ *(To end the selection)*

5. With **ORTHO** mode on, **MOVE** the lofted 3D solid **5″** along the positive direction of the *Y*-axis.
6. **ERASE** the two objects that you previously selected as guides.
7. Set the **DELOBJ** system variable to **1**.
8. Invoke the **LOFT** command and respond to the prompts as follows.

> **Select cross sections in lofting order:** *Select the four closed curves in the same order.*
>
> **Select cross sections in lofting order:** ↵ *(To end the selection)*
>
> **Enter an option [Guides/Path/Cross sections only] <Cross sections only>:** *(To open the Loft Settings dialog box)*

9. In the **Loft Settings** dialog box, select **Normal to:** and select **All cross sections** from its drop-down list. Click **OK** to close the dialog box.
10. Select the **Realistic** visual style.
11. Invoke the **3DORBIT** command to inspect the difference between a guided loft and a loft that is normal to all cross sections. The two lofted 3D solids should look like Figure 23-67.
12. **SAVE** the drawing.

Figure 23-66   Object contained in the drawing file

Figure 23-67   Two different results: a guided loft, and a loft that is normal to all cross sections

As a 3D CAD designer, you will analyze different procedures to ensure the creation of products that meet specific customer needs while achieving the desired aesthetics. The different types of loft operations are widely used to develop many of the modern free-form design shapes represented by 3D solids and surfaces. A complete understanding and demonstrated knowledge of these design tools and their concepts gives users a skill that is an extraordinary asset for many organizations.

POLYSOLID	
Modeling Toolbar	
Ribbon Modeling panel	
Pull-down Menu	Draw/ Modeling/ Polysolid
Command Line	polysolid

OTHER COMMANDS USED TO CREATE 3D SOLIDS AND SURFACES

The POLYSOLID Command

The **POLYSOLID** command creates a 3D solid of the **Sweep** type with a rectangular cross section that is swept along a segmented path defined by specifying a set of points. Each path segment can be straight or in the form of an arc. The base of the 3D solid is placed parallel to the current *XY* plane. The default height and width of the rectangular cross section are **4.00** and **0.25** units, respectively (Figure 23-68).

The different options you can use and the settings you can change in the **POLYSOLID** command are shown in its shortcut menu (Figure 23-69).

Figure 23-68   A 3D solid of the **Sweep** type created with the **POLYSOLID** command using the default **Height** and **Width** values

Figure 23-69   The **POLYSOLID** command shortcut menu

The **Height** and **Width** options allow you to change the dimensions of the rectangular cross section of the 3D solid. (You can do so only before specifying the first point.) The **Justify** option controls how the width of the rectangular cross section is justified or located with respect to specified points (Figure 23-70).

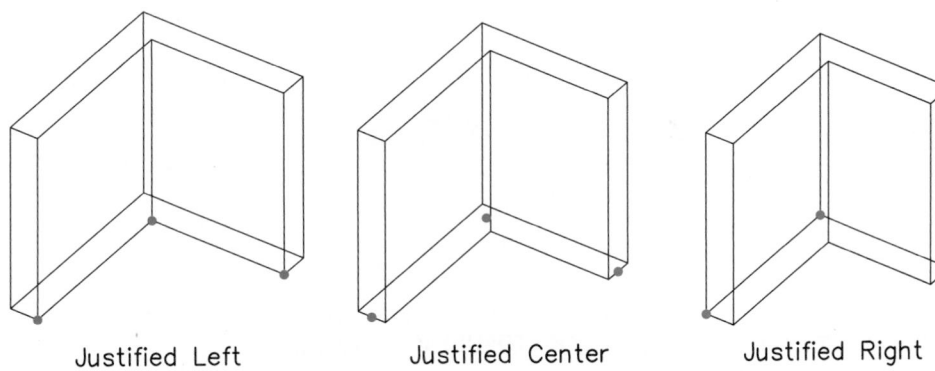

Justified Left   Justified Center   Justified Right

Figure 23-70   Different **Justify** options can be used

By using the **Object** option, you can convert lines, arcs, polylines, and circles into 3D solids. You can convert only one object at a time. The object must lie on the current UCS, so that the cross section of the 3D solid created is the one previously specified.

The CONVTOSOLID Command

The **CONVTOSOLID** command converts specific objects into 3D solids. Only the following objects can be converted by this operation (Figure 23-71):

- Thickened polylines with uniform width
- Thickened closed polylines with **0** width
- Thickened circles

Multiple objects can be selected with this operation, either before or after invoking the command. The **DELOBJ** system variable controls whether the selected objects are kept or deleted. Thickened polylines with uniform width must lie on the current UCS in order to be properly converted to 3D solids.

CONVTOSOLID	
Ribbon Solid Editing panel	
Pull-down Menu	Modify/ 3D Operation/Con vtosolid
Command Line	convto- solid

Figure 23-71 Objects (above) converted to 3D solids (below) with the **CONVTOSOLID** command

CONVTOSURFACE	
Ribbon Solid Editing panel	
Pull-down Menu	Modify/ 3D Operation/ Convto-surface
Command Line	convto-surface

The CONVTOSURFACE Command

The **CONVTOSURFACE** command converts surface-type objects into surfaces. Depending on the type of object selected, the conversion can generate planar surfaces or single-curvature surfaces.

In general, the objects selected must define a delimited surface. Planar objects such as circles, ellipses, closed polylines, regions, 2D solids, and planar 3D faces are converted to planar surfaces (Figure 23-72). The type of surface created with these objects is *planar*.

Thickened objects, which are used to represent surfaces with a single curvature such as lines, arcs, circles, and polylines, are converted into single-curvature surfaces (Figure 23-73). The type of surface created with these objects is *extrusion*.

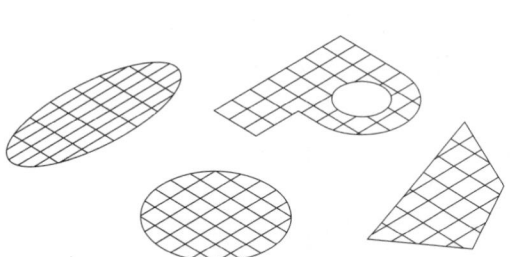

Figure 23-72 Closed planar objects can be converted to surfaces using the **CONVTOSURFACE** command

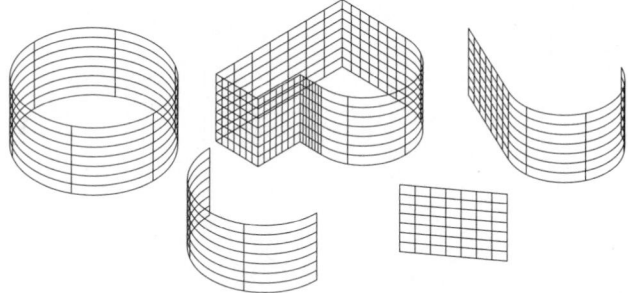

Figure 23-73 Thickened objects can be converted to surfaces using the **CONVTOSURFACE** command

As with the **CONVTOSOLID** command, more than one object can be selected with this operation, either before or after invoking the command. The **DELOBJ** system variable controls whether the selected objects are kept or deleted.

PLANESURF	
Modeling Toolbar	
Ribbon Modeling panel	
Pull-down Menu	Draw/ Modeling/ Planesurf
Command Line	planesurf

The PLANESURF Command

The **PLANESURF** command creates planar surfaces. By default, a rectangular planar surface is created by specifying two of its corner points. Alternatively, you can use the **Object** options and select planar objects such as circles, ellipses, closed polylines, regions, 2D solids, and planar 3D faces and convert them into planar surfaces. The thickness of the objects is ignored with this operation.

Surfaces created with the **PLANESURF** command by specifying two corner points are projected onto the current *XY* plane.

The THICKEN Command

The **THICKEN** command creates 3D solids by thickening surfaces, both planar and nonplanar. You can control the side to which the surfaces are thickened by specifying a positive or a negative value (Figure 23-74).

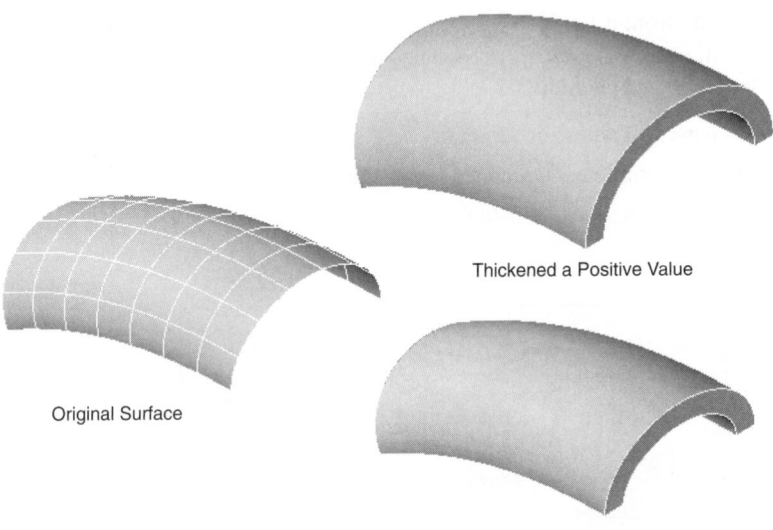

Original Surface

Thickened a Positive Value

Thickened a Negative Value

Figure 23-74   Using the **THICKEN** command, you can turn surfaces into 3D solids; the value sign determines which side the surface thickens to

THICKEN	
Ribbon Solid Editing panel	
Pull-down Menu	Modify/ 3D Operation/ Thicken
Command Line	thicken

OTHER OPERATIONS WITH 3D SOLIDS

OBTAINING COMPOSITE 3D SOLIDS WITH THE UNION, SUBTRACT, AND INTERSECT BOOLEAN OPERATIONS

Boolean operations can be performed only with regions or 3D solids. In the previous chapter, you learned details about using Boolean operations with regions. Here you will learn how to use Boolean operations with 3D solids.

One of the most important tasks in the development of a 3D model represented with 3D solids is to combine several elemental 3D solids into a single one, commonly known as a *composite 3D solid*.

3D solids can be combined by using the same Boolean operations as the ones used to combine regions:

- **UNION**
- **SUBTRACT**
- **INTERSECT**

While regions must be located in a common plane, 3D solids can be located anywhere in the 3D space. Although they are used similarly to regions and 3D solids, Boolean operations cannot be performed between 3D solids and regions.

UNION creates a 3D solid by joining any number of 3D solids. The resulting volume will be the sum of all the volumes that are not common.

SUBTRACT creates a 3D solid by subtracting a 3D solid or a group of 3D solids from another 3D solid or group of 3D solids. When subtracting 3D solids, you must consider the selection of two groups of 3D solids:

- First Group: 3D solids to subtract from
- Second Group: 3D solids to subtract

When more than one 3D solid is selected from the first group, the operation between them is automatically considered to be a **UNION** operation.

The **INTERSECT** operation creates a 3D solid from the unique common volume among a group of 3D solids.

composite 3D solids: 3D solids obtained by combining 3D solids using one of the three Boolean operations: **UNION**, **SUBTRACT**, or **INTERSECT**.

The 3D solid that results from a Boolean operation depends on the relative location of the two 3D solids or groups of 3D solids interacting with each other. Figure 23-75 shows the three possible situations for each particular operation:

- The two 3D solids have no volume in common.
- One of the 3D solids is completely contained inside the other 3D solid.*
- One of the 3D solids is partially contained inside the other 3D solid.*

	BEFORE THE OPERATION	RESULT	COMMENTS
UNION			EVEN WHEN THE TWO SOLIDS SHARE NO VOLUME, THEY ARE JOINED AS A SINGLE SOLID THAT IS MADE OF TWO PIECES.
			THE RESULTING SOLID IS THE SAME AS THE BIGGER ONE. THE SMALL SOLID IS CONTAINED INSIDE THE BIGGER SOLID, NOT PROVIDING ANY NEW VOLUME TO IT.
			RESULTS IN A NEW SOLID. EACH SOLID PROVIDES A CERTAIN NEW VOLUME.
SUBTRACT			BECAUSE NO VOLUME IS SHARED, THE SOLID TO BE SUBTRACTED SIMPLY DISAPPEARS WITHOUT AFFECTING THE MAIN SOLID.
			A HOLE IS MADE THROUGH THE MAIN SOLID.
			THE SHARED VOLUME IS SUBTRACTED FROM THE MAIN SOLID.
INTERSECT			BECAUSE NO VOLUME IS SHARED, THE RESULT IS A NULL SOLID.
			THE SHARED VOLUME IS THAT OF THE SMALL SOLID. ITS ENTIRE VOLUME IS PRECISELY THE VOLUME SHARED.
			THE RESULTING SOLID IS THE UNIQUE COMMON VOLUME SHARED BY THE TWO SOLIDS.

Figure 23-75 The three possible situations and results for each Boolean operation with 3D solids

* For the **SUBTRACT** command, the 3D solid shown in hidden lines is the one to be subtracted.

Exercise 23-8: Using Boolean Operations

In this exercise you will develop the same 3D model that you created in Tutorial 21-1: The Bracket Wireframe. This time you will make it a 3D solid model. The object's views and dimensions are shown in Figure 23-76. You will use these dimensions throughout the exercise to create the shapes, as well as the values for the height of the extrusion.

Figure 23-76   Dimensions to create the 3D solid model

Figure 23-77 shows two different approaches to starting the 3D model. The one on the right requires an extra step compared to the one on the left. The resulting shape, however, is closer to the final 3D model.

1. Start a **NEW** drawing.
2. **SAVE** the drawing **AS *Exercise 23-8***.
3. Set the **DISPSILH** system variable to **1** and the **ISOLINES** system variable to **0**.
4. Select the **SW Isometric** viewing point.

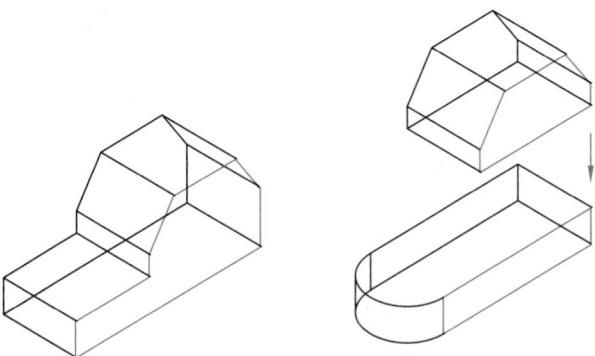

Figure 23-77   Two different approaches to starting the 3D model

5. Draw the profile shown in Figure 23-78.
6. Convert the profile to a closed polyline or a region.
7. **EXTRUDE** the profile. Refer to the drawing at the beginning of the exercise to find the value of the extrusion height (Figure 23-79).
8. Select the **Front** UCS and draw the profile highlighted in Figure 23-80 anywhere in the 3D space.
9. **EXTRUDE** the profile as required.

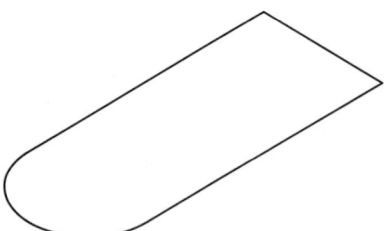

Figure 23-78   The first profile

Figure 23-79   The profile extruded

Figure 23-80   A second profile extruded

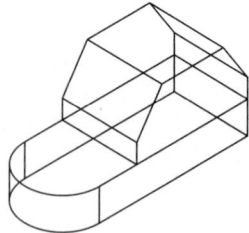

Figure 23-81   The two extruded 3D solids in their corresponding places

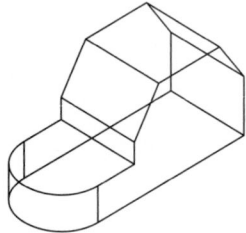

Figure 23-82   A single 3D solid is obtained after the **UNION** operation

Figure 23-83   A cylinder 3D solid

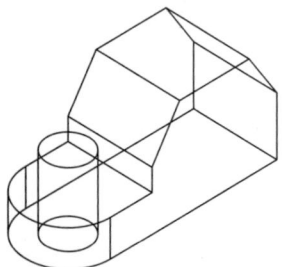

Figure 23-84   A cylinder 3D solid moved concentric with the cylindrical face

10. Snapping to the endpoints, **MOVE** the last 3D solid to the first 3D solid so it is located as shown in Figure 23-81.
11. Invoke the **UNION** command. When prompted, select both 3D solids and press **<Enter>** to end the command. The 3D model should look now like Figure 23-82.
12. Select the **Top** UCS.
13. Create a 3D solid in the shape of a cylinder (Figure 23-83). Its diameter should be the same as that of the hole. Make it **2 1/2″** high. For this operation you can either use the **CYLINDER** command or **EXTRUDE** a circle.
14. **MOVE** the cylinder from its bottom center point to the center point of the arc at the bottom of the main body (Figure 23-84).
15. Select the **Left** UCS.
16. Using the dimensions from the 2D drawing at the beginning of the exercise, create the profile highlighted in Figure 23-85 and **EXTRUDE** it **5″**.
17. **MOVE** the new 3D solid from the midpoint of its top-right edge to the midpoint of the top-right edge of the main 3D solid (Figure 23-86).
18. Make sure the **UCSORTHO** system variable is set to **1**. Select the **Front** view.
19. With **ORTHO** mode on, **MOVE** the last 3D solid **1″** to the right (Figure 23-88).
20. Invoke the **SUBTRACT** command and respond to the prompts as follows:

`Select solids and regions to subtract from...`
`Select objects:` *Select the main solid.*
`Select objects:` ↵ *(To end the selection)*

> **Note:**
> So far, you have created the main body of the model. The rest of the work will simply be to create and subtract the 3D solids that will give the 3D model its final shape.

> **Note:**
> The last 3D solid does not go all the way through the main 3D solid (Figure 23-87).

Figure 23-85   Create the 3D solid shown

Figure 23-86   The new 3D solid moved toward the main 3D solid

Figure 23-87   The front view

Figure 23-88   The new 3D solid is moved toward the right

Figure 23-89   The resulting 3D solid after the **SUBTRACT** operation

```
Select solids and regions to subtract...
Select objects: Select the cylinder solid.
Select objects: Select the small solid on top.
Select objects: (To end the selection)
```

21. Select the **SW Isometric** viewing point.
22. Invoke the **HIDE** command. The 3D solid should look like Figure 23-89.
23. **SAVE** the drawing.

Using the 3D Solids History to Modify Composite 3D Solids

AutoCAD allows you to modify a composite 3D solid. You can do this by modifying the original 3D solids that were used to create the composite 3D solid.

You can display the original 3D solids of a composite 3D solid, if their *history* is set to **Record**, by holding down the **<Ctrl>** key. Hovering the pickbox pointer over them allows you to select them.

The **History** and **Show History** settings of the composite 3D solids can be controlled individually on each 3D solid through the **Properties** palette under **Solid History** (Figure 23-90). They can also be globally controlled using the **SOLIDHIST** and **SHOWHIST** system variables.

history: Original 3D solids involved in the Boolean operations of a composite 3D solid.

Figure 23-90   The **History** and **Show History** settings can be controlled in the **Properties** palette

The **SOLIDHIST** system variable determines whether the history for a new 3D solid is set to **Record** (**1**) or is not (**0**). The history of a composite 3D solid, however, is determined by the history of its original 3D solids rather than by the **SOLIDHIST** system variable. Only composite 3D solids combined through the Boolean operations with at least one of the original 3D solid's history set to **Record** can show the history of their original 3D solids.

TIP It is more convenient to leave the **SOLIDHIST** system variable set at **Record** in order to retain the history of any new 3D solid created, which is the variable's default value. You can always change this property individually, prior to performing the Boolean operation.

The **SHOWHIST** system variable controls whether or not the original 3D solids or the history is shown in a drawing. It uses the following settings:

- **0** sets the **Show History** property to **No** for all solids. You cannot use the **Properties** palette to show the original 3D solids of individual composite 3D solids.

- **1** allows you to control the **Show History** property individually through the **Properties** palette.

- **2** displays the history of all solids. You cannot use the **Properties** palette to control the display of the original 3D solids of individual composite 3D solids. You need a **REGEN** operation to show the history.

TIP It is more convenient to leave the **SHOWHIST** system variable to **1**, its default value. This enables you to control the **Show History** property individually through the **Properties** palette.

Showing the history of a composite 3D solid might be confusing if you continue performing Boolean operations with it. You can choose when to stop recording the history of a composite 3D solid by changing its status to **None** in the **Properties** palette. You can also erase the history of any 3D solid by using the **BREP** command, which turns objects into a basic representation only.

The history of a composite 3D solid is automatically erased by performing post-operations such as **SLICE** or by performing editing operations with the **SOLIDEDIT** command.

FOR MORE DETAILS	See Chapter 24 for more details about performing editing operations with the **SOLIDEDIT** command.

Exercise 23-9: Modifying a Composite 3D Solid by Modifying Its Original 3D Solids

To access student data files, go to www.pearsondesigncentral.com.

1. **OPEN** the drawing *Exercise 23-9* in the student data files.
2. **SAVE** the drawing **AS** *Exercise 23-9 solved*.
3. Set both the **SOLIDHIST** and **SHOWHIST** system variables to **1**, if they are not already set. Access these settings by entering the name of each in the command line.
4. Invoke the **SUBTRACT** command, and subtract the cylinder from the box.
5. Select the **Realistic** visual style.
6. Select the composite 3D solid. Right-click in the drawing area and select **Properties** from the shortcut menu.
7. In the **Properties** palette, under **Solid History**, change the value of **Show History** to **Yes** (Figure 23-91).
8. Press the **<Esc>** key to unselect the composite 3D solid. The 3D model should look like Figure 23-92.

Note:
Subtracted 3D solids are transparent in the display.

Figure 23-91   Changing the value of the **Show History** setting to **Yes**

Figure 23-92   The composite 3D solid showing its history

9. Holding down the **<Ctrl>** key, select the original cylinder 3D solid that was used to create the hole (Figure 21-93).
10. Invoke the **MOVE** command. When prompted for the base point, click anywhere in the drawing area and start moving the pointer to see the hole move interactively.
11. Enter **@1.5,2,0** as the second point.
12. Select the composite 3D solid again and change the value of **Show History** to **No**. Change the **History** setting to **None**.
13. Press the **<Esc>** key to unselect the composite 3D solid. The 3D model should look like Figure 23-94.
14. **SAVE** the drawing.

Figure 23-93   3D solid history object selected independently of the composite solid

Figure 23-94   3D solid history object is relocated to modify the composite solid

Converting 2D Drawings into 3D Models

The 3D model you developed in Exercise 23-8 could have been solved in another way: by using the **INTERSECT** command rather than joining and subtracting 3D solids. This method provides an easy and more efficient way to proceed, especially when the drawing views already exist as a CAD file. This is one of the procedures that can be used to generate 3D models more efficiently from the input of a 2D drawing. As you will see, no special tools are required to achieve these results.

Exercise 23-10: Converting 2D Drawings into 3D Models

In this exercise you will develop the model you created in Exercise 23-9 one more time. This time, however, you will use the existing drawing's views.

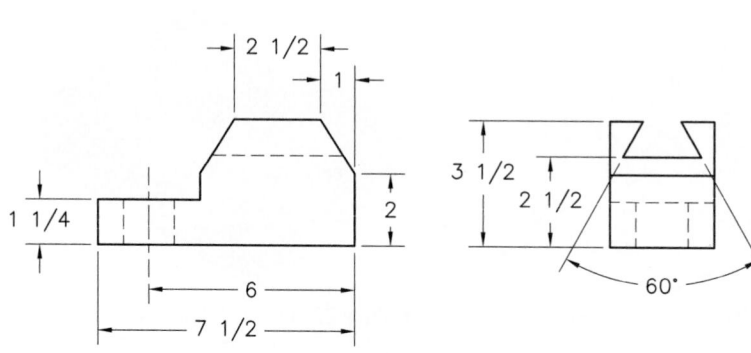

Figure 23-95 Objects contained in the drawing file

Suppose you need to convert the 2D drawing shown in Figure 23-95 into a 3D model. Your first task is to clean up the drawing views, leaving only the objects that define the outer profiles and islands. These objects will be used to create the regions that will be extended and finally intersected.

To access student data files, go to www.pearsondesigncentral.com.

1. **OPEN** the drawing *Exercise 23-10* in the student data files, and **SAVE** it on your computer as *Exercise 23-10 Solved*.
2. **ERASE** any unnecessary objects to clean up the drawing views. The drawing should look like Figure 23-96 after it is cleaned up.
3. Invoke the **REGION** command. Using a selection window, select all the objects to convert them into regions. The command prompt should advise you of the four regions created.

   4 loops extracted.

   4 Regions created.

4. Zoom into the objects representing the top view and **SUBTRACT** the circular regions from the outer one to create a single region with a hole.
5. Select the **SW Isometric** viewing point.

> **Note:**
> The top view region will remain in the same position. The other two views will be rotated and moved to the plane they belong to in 3D space.

Figure 23-96 After erasing all unnecessary objects

6. Select the **Left** UCS.
7. **ROTATE** both the region representing the front view and the region representing the side view **−90°**. When prompted for the base point, specify any endpoint along the bottom line of the front view region. The drawing should look like Figure 23-97.
8. **MOVE** the region representing the front view from its lower-right endpoint to the corresponding endpoint on the region representing the top view (Figure 23-98).
9. Select the **Top** UCS. **ROTATE** the region representing the side view 90°. Use any point on the region as a base point (Figure 23-99).

Note:
The three regions now have to be extruded a distance that goes farther than the model space with a 0° taper angle.

Figure 23-97   The regions corresponding to the front and the side views are rotated

Figure 23-98   The region corresponding to the front view is moved

Figure 23-99   The region corresponding to the front view is rotated

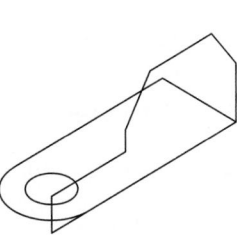

10. **MOVE** the region representing the side view from its lower-right endpoint to the corresponding endpoint on the other two regions (Figure 23-100).
11. With the **Top** UCS still current, **EXTRUDE** the top region **4** units.
12. **EXTRUDE** the region representing the front view **−3.5** units.
13. **EXTRUDE** the region representing the side view **−8** units (Figure 23-101).
14. Invoke the **INTERSECT** command and, when prompted, select the three 3D solids. Then press **<Enter↵>** to finish the operation.
15. Invoke the **HIDE** command. The 3D model should look like Figure 23-102.
16. **SAVE** the drawing.

Note:
The unique portion of the 3D space that is shared by the three 3D solids is exactly the 3D model.

Figure 23-100   The region corresponding to the front view is moved

Figure 23-101   All regions are extruded so that the volumes meet in the 3D space

Figure 23-102   The resulting 3D solid after the **INTERSECT** operation

THE **INTERFERE** COMMAND

The **INTERFERE** command has a certain similitude to the **INTERSECT** command. The **INTERFERE** command can, however, check for interference or shared volume between 3D solids without deleting the original 3D solids. The command can also create new 3D solids whose shape is the same as the interfering volume.

Depending on how you respond to the command prompts, the command can perform two different tasks:

> **Note:**
> The **Nested selection** option enables you to select individual 3D solid objects that are nested in blocks and external references.

- Check interference and create new 3D solids from each interfering pair in a set of 3D solids
- Check interference and create interfering 3D solids between two sets of 3D solids

The command prompts you to select two sets of 3D solids. You can choose not to select a second set of 3D solids by pressing **<Enter↵>** when prompted to do so. Pressing **<Enter↵>** will initiate the interference checking process between the objects selected in the first and only group. The visual style and the color of the objects will change automatically according to those specified in the **Interference Settings** dialog box (Figure 23-103), which you can open by selecting the **Settings** option while selecting the first set of objects:

```
Select first set of objects or [Nested selection/Settings]:
```

Figure 23-103   The **Interference Settings** dialog box

The **Interference Checking** dialog box is also displayed as soon as the selection process is finished. Figure 23-104 shows a set of three interfering 3D solids. Their corresponding **Interference Checking** dialog box is also displayed. Each 3D solid shares its volume with the other two, so in this particular case, three interference pairs are found.

Figure 23-104   A set of three interfering 3D solids with the corresponding **Interference Checking** dialog box displayed

During the interference testing process, you can **Zoom, Pan**, and **Orbit** around the objects only by using the viewing tool buttons in the **Interference Checking** dialog box. When you are finished using a particular viewing tool, pressing the **<Esc>** key will take you back to the dialog box.

The **Next** and **Previous** buttons will cycle through each interfering pair, highlighting and zooming into it (Figure 23-105).

Figure 23-105   Clicking the **Next** and **Previous** buttons cycles through each interfering pair

You can create new 3D solids from each interfering pair in a set of 3D solids by clearing the **Delete interference objects created on Close** checkbox. Figure 23-106 shows the three new separated individual 3D solids that can be obtained with this operation after you close the **Interference Checking** dialog box.

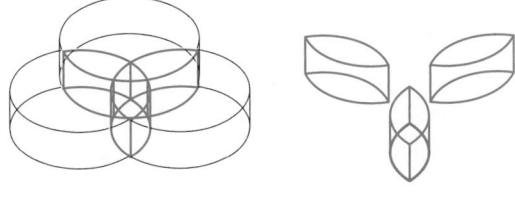

Figure 23-106   New 3D solids can be created from each interfering pair

Figure 23-107   Checking for interference between two sets of 3D solids

When you enter the two sets of 3D solids, the **INTERFERE** command checks for interference only between 3D solids of two different sets. Interference between 3D solids of the same group is ignored. Figure 23-107 shows two sets of 3D solids. The first set consists of 3D solids **A** and **B**. The second set is composed only of the 3D solid **C**. When these two independent sets of 3D solids interfere with each other, only two interferences are found and two 3D solids are generated.

As with the **Interference Checking** dialog box for objects within the same group, you can create new 3D solids from each interfering pair found between the two sets of objects by clearing the **Delete interference objects created on Close** checkbox.

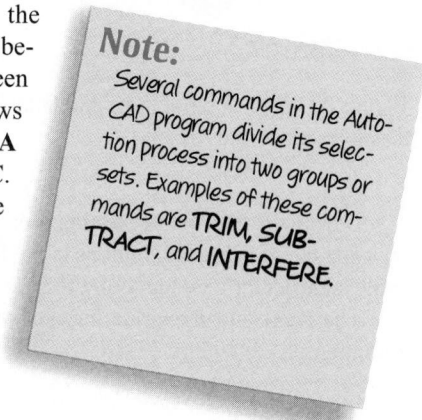

Note:
Several commands in the AutoCAD program divide its selection process into two groups or sets. Examples of these commands are *TRIM, SUBTRACT,* and *INTERFERE.*

Exercise 23-11: Using the **INTERFERE** Command

In this exercise you will use the **INTERFERE** command to detect parts that do not fit properly in an assembly design.

To access student data files, go to www.pearsondesigncentral.com.

1. **OPEN** the drawing *Exercise 23-11* in the student data files. It contains the assembly of several 3D solids: five hardware pieces and two other parts (Figure 23-108).
2. **SAVE** the drawing **AS** *Exercise 23-11 solved*.
3. Invoke the **INTERFERE** command using one of the methods shown in the grid. Respond to the prompts as follows:

   `Select first set of objects or [Nested selection/Settings]:` *Using a selection window, select all the 3D solids.*

INTERFERE	
Ribbon Solid Editing Panel	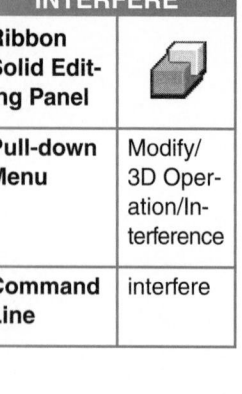
Pull-down Menu	Modify/ 3D Operation/Interference
Command Line	interfere

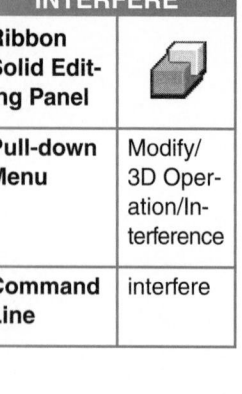

Figure 23-108   Objects contained in the drawing file

```
Select first set of objects or [Nested selection/Settings]: ↵
(To end the selection of the first set)
```

```
Select second set of objects or [Nested selection/checK first
set] <checK>: ↵ (Here a second set is not considered. The com-
mand checks for interference within the first set only.)
```

4. Five **Interfering pairs found**: is shown in the **Interference Checking** dialog box (Figure 23-109). Click on the **Next** and **Previous** buttons to navigate through each of the interfering pairs.

Figure 23-109   The interference checking scenario within a group of objects

5. Click on the **Close** button to close the **Interference Checking** dialog box.
6. Now let's find out how many of the hardware pieces interfere with the other two parts. Invoke the **INTERFERE** command again, and respond to the prompts as follows:

```
Select first set of objects or [Nested selection/Settings]:
Select the five bolts.
```

```
Select first set of objects or [Nested selection/Settings]: ↵ (To
end the selection of the first set)
```

```
Select second set of objects or
[Nested selection/checK first set]
<checK>: Select the other two 3D
solids.
```

```
Select second set of objects or
[Nested selection/checK first set]
<checK>: ↵ (To end the selection of
the second set)
```

7. Four **Interfering pairs found**: is shown in the **Interference Checking** dialog box after comparing the two main objects with any hardware (Figure 23-110). Click on the **Next** and **Previous** buttons to navigate through each of the interfering pairs. Then close the dialog box.

8. **SAVE** the drawing.

Note:
The **INTERFERE** command is a useful tool for detecting parts that may not fit properly, causing a mechanism to function incorrectly. In large assemblies you can use the **Highlight pair** setting to detect which pair of 3D solids is causing the interference. This allows you to correct design errors before production.

Figure 23-110   The interference checking scenario between two groups of objects

Determining possible failures is one of the most important tasks in the design of tools, engines, machines, and other mechanical devices. Therefore, the professional team in charge must make sure that components fit properly within mechanisms and assemblies in their different positions. The **INTERFERE** operation can incorporate an advanced method to perform this task accurately using 3D models. A complete knowledge and practical understanding of the **INTERFERE** operation and its applications gives 3D users a powerful tool. This skill can help many companies and organizations further enhance and understand design processes.

SLICING 3D SOLIDS WITH THE SLICE COMMAND

Many other tools are used jointly with Boolean operations to enable you to obtain a 3D solid's final shape in less time. The **SLICE** command is one of the most useful of these tools.

imaginary slicing plane:
Imaginary plane with which 3D solid objects are cut.

With the **SLICE** command, a 3D solid or group of 3D solids can be cut by an ***imaginary slicing plane*** or by a surface. Figure 23-111 shows the different options in the command's shortcut menu. Besides the **Surface** option, all other options are dedicated to defining the imaginary slicing plane.

You can slice a 3D solid according to the shape of the surface, creating faces on the 3D solid that have the same shape as the surface used to slice it (Figure 23-112). The surface must completely cross the 3D solid for the operation to proceed.

Using an imaginary slicing plane will create a flat cut through the 3D solids. The imaginary slicing plane can be defined by using one of the following options:

Perpendicular to the current *XY* plane: This is the default option. It activates itself when you specify the start point after completing the selection process. This option defines the imaginary slicing plane perpendicular to the current *XY* plane by specifying the start and second points (Figure 23-113). When you specify the second point, only the *X* and *Y* coordinates are read, and the Object Snap is projected onto the *XY* plane. This method is very useful when slicing 3D solids in an orthogonal view.

3points: With this option, the imaginary slicing plane is defined by specifying three different noncollinear points (Figure 23-114). This method substitutes for the default method if you press the **<Enter↵>** key before specifying any point.

Figure 23-111   The **SLICE** command shortcut menu

Figure 23-112   3D solids can be sliced by a surface

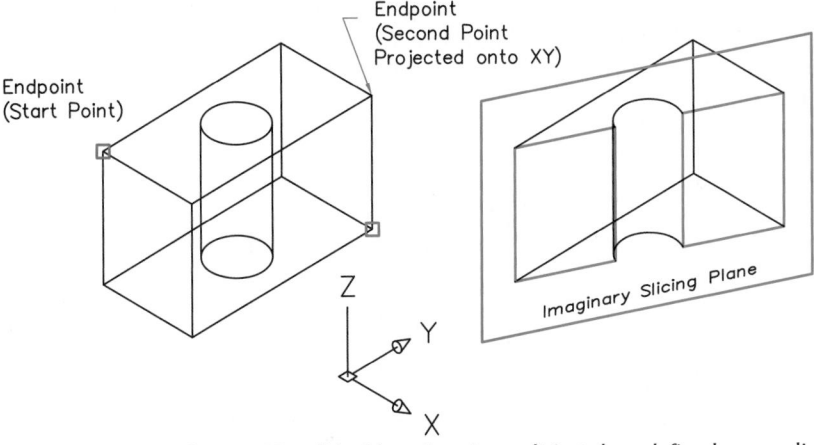

Figure 23-113   Slicing a 3D solid with an imaginary slicing plane defined perpendicular to the current XY plane

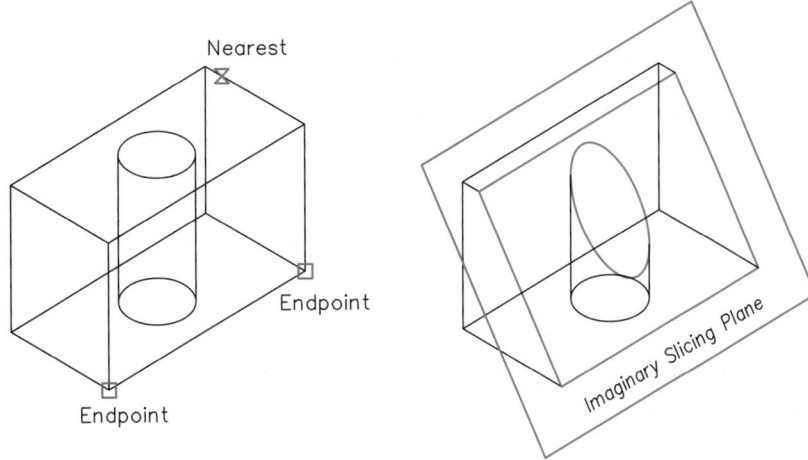

Figure 23-114   Slicing a 3D solid with an imaginary slicing plane defined by three points

XY, YZ,* and *ZX: When you specify one of these options, the imaginary slicing plane aligns parallel to the specified plane of the current UCS. An additional point is also required to specify where the plane will go through. Figure 23-115 shows a 3D solid that has been sliced parallel to the *YZ* plane and is going through the midpoint of the top-left edge.

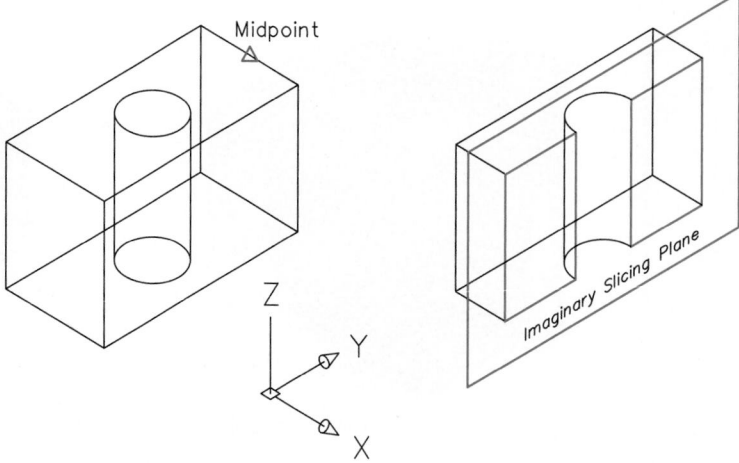

Figure 23-115   Slicing a 3D solid with an imaginary slicing plane defined parallel to one of the planes of the current UCS

Planar object: This option aligns the imaginary slicing plane with the plane to which a specific object belongs. Figure 23-116 shows an imaginary slicing plane aligned with the selected polyline. This option works for objects that are considered 2D objects and that belong to the *XY* plane of a specific UCS. Valid objects are circles, ellipses, arcs, planar splines, and polylines.

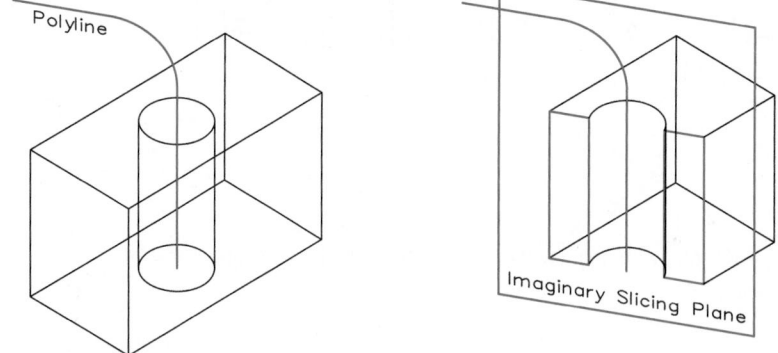

Figure 23-116   Slicing a 3D solid with an imaginary slicing plane defined by a planar curve (object)

View: This method defines the imaginary slicing plane parallel to the viewing plane, which is your monitor screen. An additional point is also required to specify where the plane will go through (Figure 23-117).

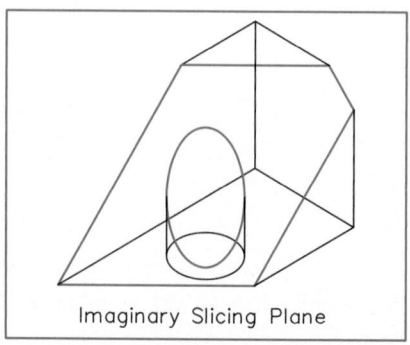

Figure 23-117   Slicing a 3D solid with an imaginary slicing plane defined parallel to the viewing plane

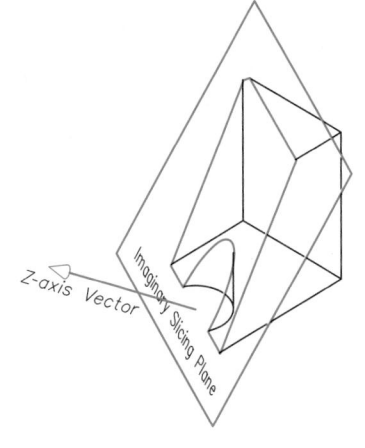

Figure 23-118   Slicing a
3D solid with an imaginary
slicing plane defined perpendicular to a Z-axis vector

Z-axis: With this option the imaginary slicing plane is aligned perpendicular to a vector between the two points specified and going through the first point specified (Figure 23-118).

After selecting the solids, and specifying an imaginary slicing plane or a surface, you must specify which portion to keep. You can keep only one of the two portions by specifying a point on the desired side, or you can keep both sides by pressing **<Enter>**.

Exercise 23-12: Using the **SLICE** Command

1. **OPEN** either *Exercise 23-8* or *Exercise 23-10 solved.*
2. **SAVE** the drawing **AS** *Exercise 23-12.*
3. Invoke the **SLICE** command to split the 3D solid. Respond to the prompts as follows:

   `Select objects to slice:` *Select the 3D solid.*

   `Select objects to slice:` ↵ *(To end the selection)*

   `Specify start point of slicing plane or [planar Object/Surface/Zaxis/View/XY/ YZ/ZX/3points] <3points>:` ↵ *(To use the 3 points option)*

   `Specify first point on plane:` *Snap to any of the three endpoints indicated in* Figure 23-119.

   `Specify second point on plane:` *Snap to any other indicated endpoint.*

   `Specify third point on plane:` *Snap to the third endpoint.*

   `Specify a point on desired side or [keep Both sides] <Both>:` ↵ *(To keep both sides)*

Note: At this last stage of the command, you can choose either to keep both portions, or to keep only one of them by specifying a point. Pressing **<Enter↵>** will automatically keep both sides.

SLICE	
Ribbon Solid Editing Panel	
Pull-down Menu	Modify/ 3D Operation/ Slice
Command Line	slice

Figure 23-119   Points used to specify the imaginary slicing plane

Figure 23-120   The sliced 3D solid after it is split

Figure 23-121   Another **SLICE** operation (after choosing to keep only one side)

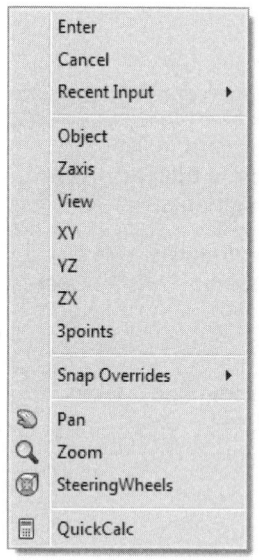

Figure 23-122   The **SECTION** command shortcut menu

4. Select the **Top** UCS.
5. With the **ORTHO** mode activated, **MOVE** the upper 3D solid **5″** along the positive direction of the *Y* axis.
6. Invoke the **HIDE** command. The split 3D solid should look like Figure 23-120.
7. Invoke the **SLICE** command again and respond to the prompts as follows:

    Select objects to slice: *Select the two 3D solids.*

    Select objects to slice: ↵ *(To end the selection)*

    Specify start point of slicing plane or [planar Object/Surface/Zaxis/View/XY/YZ/ZX/3points] <3points>: *yz* ↵

    Specify a point on the YZ-plane <0,0,0>: *Snap to any of the center points on the cylindrical holes.*

    Specify a point on desired side or [keep Both sides] <Both>: *Snap to any point on the right portion of the solids to leave only the portions shown in* Figure 23-121.

8. **SAVE** the drawing.

EXTRACTING REGIONS FROM 3D SOLIDS WITH THE SECTION COMMAND

Sometimes it is necessary to extract precise geometry from existing 3D solids in order to use them in other 3D operations or simply to inspect internal details. The **SECTION** command can assist you with this task. It can be invoked only through the command line.

With the **SECTION** command you define an imaginary plane, just as you do with the **SLICE** command. Other than defining it as perpendicular to the current *XY* plane, all other methods apply.

The results obtained with these two commands, however, are different. The **SLICE** command divides 3D solids into two portions, whereas the **SECTION** command extracts only regions from them. The regions obtained are exactly the cross section that results after the 3D solid is intersected by the *imaginary sectioning plane*.

imaginary sectioning plane: Imaginary plane that defines a section through 3D solids as it crosses these objects.

The methods used with the **SECTION** command to specify the imaginary sectioning plane are the same as those used to specify the imaginary slicing plane with the **SLICE** command. See the command's options shortcut menu in Figure 23-122.

The operation extracts a region even if the imaginary sectioning plane is specified flush with a planar face on a 3D solid (Figure 23-123).

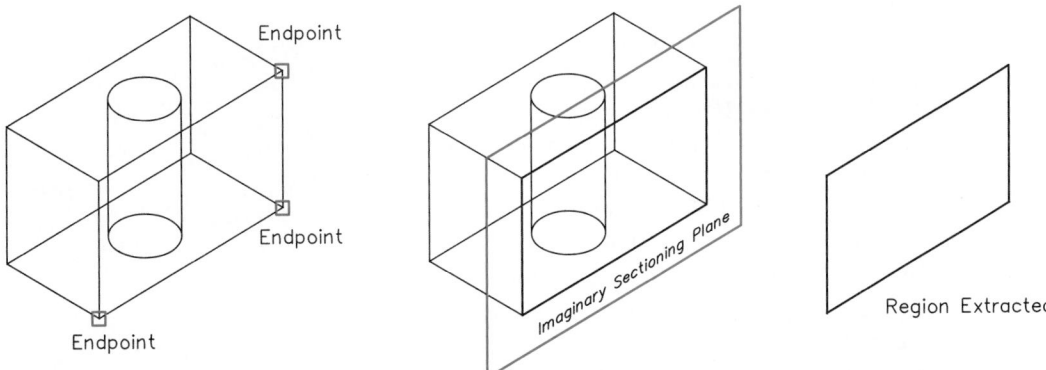

Figure 23-123   Specifying the imaginary sectioning plane flush with a planar face also extracts a region

Exercise 23-13: Using the **SECTION** Command

1. **OPEN** either *Exercise 23-8* or *Exercise 23-10 solved*.
2. **SAVE** the drawing **AS** *Exercise 23-13*.
3. Invoke the **SECTION** command by typing its name in the command line. Respond to the prompts as follows:

   Select objects: *Select the 3D solid.*

   Select objects: ↵ *(To end the selection)*

   Specify first point on Section plane by [Object/Zaxis/View/XY/YZ/ZX/ 3points] <3points>: *Snap to any of the three endpoints indicated in Figure 23-124.*

   Specify second point on plane: *Snap to any other indicated endpoint.*

   Specify third point on plane: *Snap to the third endpoint.*

4. Select the **Top** UCS.
5. With the **ORTHO** mode activated, **MOVE** the extracted region **6″** along the positive direction of the *Y*-axis. The 3D model should look like Figure 23-125.

Note:
Depending on the shape of the 3D solid and the place where the imaginary sectioning plane goes through, you will obtain simple and composite regions. In the example above, you created a composite region made of an external profile with an elliptical hole. You can modify the regions obtained, as you will do in this exercise.

Figure 23-124   Points used to specify the imaginary sectioning plane

Figure 23-125   The extracted region after it is moved away

6. Select the **Top** UCS.
7. **EXPLODE** the region extracted.
8. **ERASE** the elliptical hole.
9. Invoke the **REGION** command and select the remaining objects. A new region without a hole is created, as shown in Figure 23-126.
10. Invoke the **SECTION** command again and respond to the prompts as follows:

    Select objects: *Select the solid.*

    Select objects: ↵ *(To end the selection)*

    Specify first point on Section plane by [Object/Zaxis/View/XY/YZ/ZX/3points] <3points>: *xy* ↵

    Specify a point on the XY-plane <0,0,0>: *Snap to the midpoint shown in* Figure 23-127.

11. **MOVE** the extracted region **6″** along the negative direction of the *Y*-axis. The 3D model should look like Figure 23-128.
12. **EXPLODE** the new composite region to separate it into two individual regions.
13. **SAVE** the drawing.

> **Note:**
> In this case, the region extracted is made of two regions combined. By exploding regions with this characteristic, you can separate the composite regions into individual ones.

Figure 23-126 The extracted region can be used to generate other objects, such as the new region without the hole

Figure 23-127 Point used to specify the imaginary sectioning plane parallel to the XY plane

Figure 23-128 The extracted region after it is moved away

CREATING FILLETS AND CHAMFERS ON 3D SOLIDS

Most of the commands that belong to the **Modify** group of commands such as **COPY, MOVE, ROTATE**, and **ERASE**, to mention some, do not deviate from their ordinary process, regardless of the type of objects selected.

FILLET and CHAMFER commands, however, are a special case. Even though they also belong to the **Modify** group of commands, they work differently when the object selected is a 3D solid. If you select an edge of a 3D solid after invoking one of these two commands, the command deviates from its normal procedure.

The FILLET Command

In its standard 2D mode, the **FILLET** command prompts you to specify the two objects to be filleted (Figure 23-129). Picking on the edge of a 3D solid, on the other hand, provides enough information for the command to proceed. The command substitutes each selected edge with another face that is tangent to the two faces sharing that edge (Figure 23-130).

The **Chain** option of this command is available only after an edge of a 3D solid is selected. It enables you to select a group of edges that are continuously tangent, rather than selecting them one by one (Figure 23-131). You can switch back to the selection of individual edges at any time if needed.

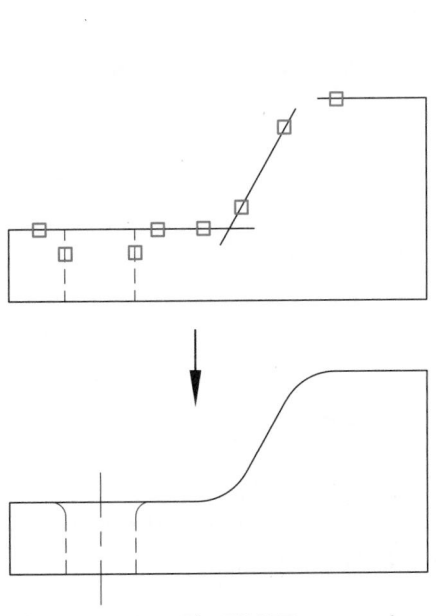

Figure 23-129   The **FILLET** command as used in a 2D operation

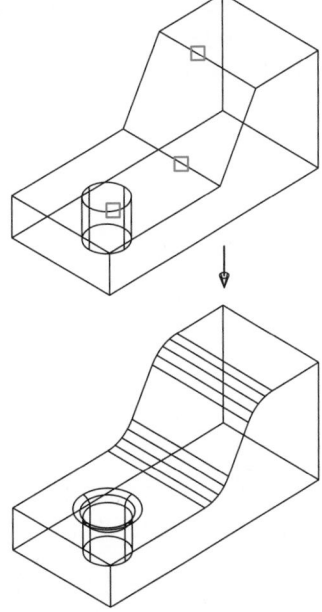

Figure 23-130   The **FILLET** command is used in a 3D operation by selecting the edge to be filleted

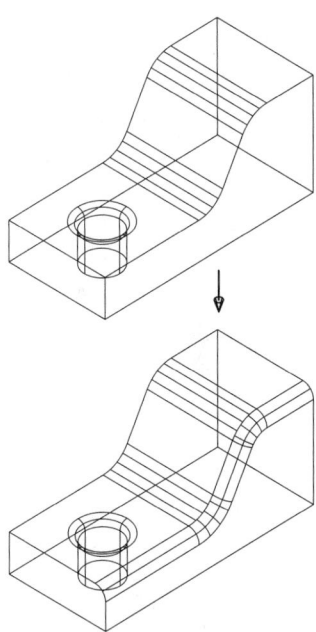

Figure 23-131   The **Chain** option of the **FILLET** command allows the selection of a group of continuously tangent edges

When creating fillets on three or more edges that converge on a common vertex, AutoCAD creates an additional blended face (Figure 23-132). This feature is possible only if performed within the same operation.

Another important aspect of the **FILLET** command is that you can change the **Radius** value within the same operation, prior to selecting any particular edge. In this case, a more complex blended face is created (Figure 23-133).

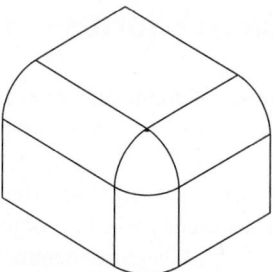

Figure 23-132 Fillets created on three converging edges

Figure 23-133 Fillets created on three converging edges using different **Radius** values

Exercise 23-14: Using the **FILLET** Command on 3D Solids

1. **OPEN** either *Exercise 23-8* or *Exercise 23-10 solved*.
2. **SAVE** the drawing **AS** *Exercise 23-14*.
3. Invoke the **FILLET** command and respond to the prompts as follows:

   Select first object or [Undo/Polyline/Radius/Trim/Multiple]: *Select the straight edge shown in* Figure 23-134.

   Enter fillet radius: *0.25* ↵

   Select an edge or [Chain/Radius]: *r* ↵

   Enter fillet radius <0.2500>: *0.125* ↵

   Select an edge or [Chain/Radius]: *Select the circular edge.*

   Select an edge or [Chain/Radius]: ↵ *(To end the selection)*

4. Invoke the **HIDE** command. The 3D model should look like Figure 23-135.

Figure 23-134   Edges to select

Figure 23-135   The 3D solid after the **FILLET** operation

5. Invoke the **REGEN** command.
6. Invoke the **FILLET** command again and respond to the prompts as follows:

   Current settings: Mode = TRIM, Radius = 0.1250

   Select first object or [Undo/Polyline/Radius/Trim/Multiple]: *Select either of the two straight edges shown in* Figure 23–136.

   Enter fillet radius <0.1250>: *0.25* ↵

   Select an edge or [Chain/Radius]: *c* ↵

   Select an edge chain or [Edge/Radius]: *Select the other straight edge.*

   Select an edge chain or [Edge/Radius]: ↵ *(To end the selection)*

7. Select the **Realistic** visual style. The 3D model should look like Figure 23-137.
8. **SAVE** the drawing.

Figure 23-136 Places to pick the chain of edges

Figure 23-137 A shaded view of the resulting 3D solid

The CHAMFER Command

In 2D usage, the **CHAMFER** command creates an inclined line between two lines or polyline objects coexisting on a common plane. Such a line is typically used to represent a beveled edge. When used on 3D solids, the command creates an actual beveled edge, substituting the selected sharp edge with a chamfered face between the two adjacent faces, depending on the geometry (Figure 23-138).

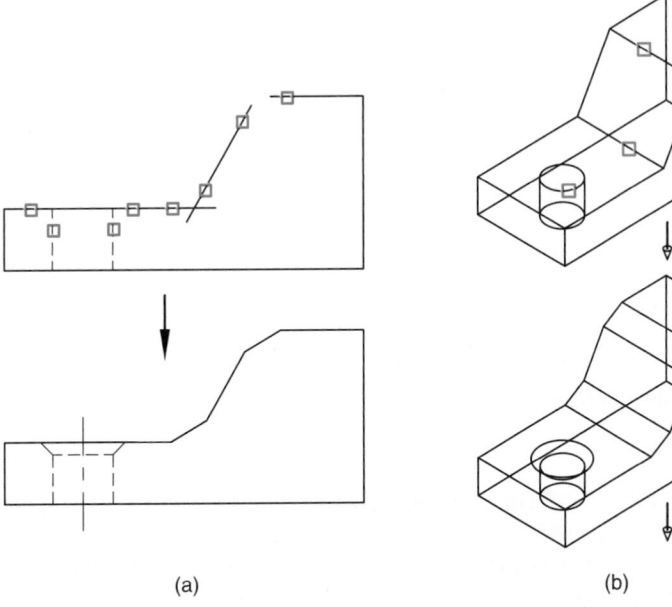

(a)

(b)

Figure 23-138
Comparison of the **CHAMFER** command as a 2D (a) and a 3D (b) operation

The selection process of this command differs quite a bit from that of the **FILLET** command. In each operation, you can select only edges that belong to a common face, which must be specified first. The AutoCAD program requires a face to be selected because the face establishes the base surface chamfer distance. In other words, the first chamfer distance is measured on this face from the edge to the inside of the 3D solid. The two options available are:

- Picking edges individually
- Selecting the entire loop

The last option will include all the edges of the specified face. Selecting the entire loop of a face will fail to chamfer if the edges pertaining to the loop are not all either interior or exterior edges. The loop of none of the three faces highlighted in Figure 23-139 can be selected because they include both types of edges.

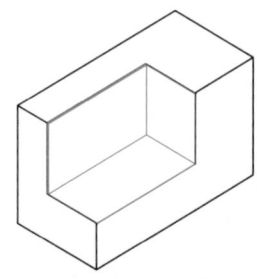

Figure 23-139 The loop cannot be selected for any of the three faces highlighted

Exercise 23-15: Chamfering the Edges of 3D Solids

1. **OPEN** either *Exercise 23-8* or *Exercise 23-10 solved*.
2. **SAVE** the drawing **AS** *Exercise 23-15*.
3. Invoke the **CHAMFER** command and respond to the prompts as follows:

   Select first line or [Undo/Polyline/Distance/Angle/Trim/mEthod/Multiple]: *Select the straight edge shown in* Figure 23-140.

   Base surface selection...

   Enter surface selection option [Next/OK (current)] <OK>: *n ↵ (To select the face highlighted in* Figure 23-141)

   Enter surface selection option [Next/OK (current)] <OK>: ↵ *(To accept the selection, once the correct face is selected)*

   Specify base surface chamfer distance <0.5000>: *0.25 ↵*

   Specify other surface chamfer distance <0.5000>: *0.25 ↵*

   Select an edge or [Loop]: *Select the straight and the circular edges shown in* Figure 23-142.

   Select an edge or [Loop]: ↵ *(To end the command and create the chamfers)*

> **Note:**
> By selecting a solid's edge, the command digresses to base surface selection. In this mode, you can specify one of the two faces adjacent to the selected edge.

Figure 23-140 Edge selected to specify the base surface

Figure 23-141 Face to be selected

Figure 23-142 Edges to be selected from the face specified

4. Invoke the **HIDE** command. The 3D solid should look like Figure 23-143.
5. Invoke the **REGEN** command.
6. Invoke the **CHAMFER** command again and respond to the prompts as follows:

   Select first line or [Undo/Polyline/Distance/Angle/Trim/mEthod/Multiple]: *Select the edge shown in* Figure 23-144.

   Base surface selection...

   Enter surface selection option [Next/OK (current)] <OK>: *Select the bottom face, choosing* **Next** *if necessary. Press ↵ when you are finished.*

   Specify base surface chamfer distance <0.1250>: *0.5 ↵*

   Specify other surface chamfer distance <0.1250>: *0.5 ↵*

   Select an edge or [Loop]: *1 ↵*

   Select an edge or [Loop]: *Select the same edge again, or any other edge on the selected face.*

   Select an edge or [Loop]: ↵ *(To end the command and create the chamfer)*

7. Invoke the **3DORBIT** command to inspect the chamfer around the loop. The 3D solid should look like Figure 23-145 after you invoke the **HIDE** command.
8. **SAVE** the drawing.

Figure 23-143   The 3D solid after the **CHAMFER** operation

Figure 23-144   Edge to be selected

Figure 23-145   The 3D solid after the **CHAMFER** operation using the **Loop** option

CREATING 3D ASSEMBLY MODELS

There are no special tools or commands in AutoCAD specifically related to assembly models. Parametric CAD programs, such as Autodesk® Inventor™, include tools specifically designed to be used with assemblies and allow you to establish and modify the relationships between different 3D objects. This type of program even uses a different type of file to perform assembly tasks.

With AutoCAD, assemblies can be created using the same file that you normally use to create 2D drawings and 3D models. This reduces the job to simply gathering all the 3D objects together inside the same drawing file and placing them in the right locations. You could also create all the 3D objects in the same drawing file if the resulting file size is not too large for your computer. Once all the necessary objects are together, all you need to do is to put them in the correct locations and make sure they are properly aligned.

Well-known commands such as **MOVE, COPY, ROTATE, MIRROR**, and so on, are the ones mainly used for assembly tasks. The **ALIGN** command, which is not so popular in 2D work, is the most useful one here. Additionally, you can take advantage of specialized commands such as **3DARRAY, MIRROR3D**, and **ROTATE3D** in 3D operations.

A single 3D solid object can better represent a complete object. Therefore, this type of object is more convenient to use in assemblies than any other type of 3D object.

FOR MORE DETAILS	See Chapter 21 for specific information about the usage of the **Modify** group of commands in a 3D environment, as well as the specialized commands used in 3D operations.

Exercise 23-16: An Assembly of 3D Solids

1. **OPEN** the drawing *Exercise 23-16* in the student data files. It contains a group of 3D solids disarranged throughout the 3D space. These objects will be used to create the assembly shown in Figure 23-146.
2. **SAVE** the drawing **AS** *Exercise 23-16 solved*.
3. **OPEN** either *Exercise 23-8* or *Exercise 23-10 solved*.
4. In the drawing that contains the bracket 3D solid, select the **SW Isometric** viewing point and the **Top** UCS.
5. Invoke the **COPYCLIP** (copy to clipboard) command and select the bracket.

Note:
The bracket 3D solid is missing from the group of objects. You will bring it into the assembly from another drawing.

To access student data files, go to www.pearsondesigncentral.com.

6. **CLOSE** the drawing that contains the bracket. Select **No** when prompted to **SAVE** the changes.
7. Go back into *Exercise 23-16 solved* and make sure the **SW Isometric** viewing point and the **World** UCS are current.
8. Invoke the **PASTECLIP** (paste from the clipboard) command and specify an insertion point by clicking anywhere in the 3D space (Figure 23-147).

Figure 23-146   The completed assembly

Figure 23-147   After pasting the bracket near the other components

9. Invoke the **ROTATE** command. When prompted, snap to any point on the bracket, and enter **90** as the rotation angle.
10. Select the Bracket and invoke the **ROTATE3D** command. Use the option that defines the axis aligned with the *Y*-axis. When prompted, snap to any point on the bracket and enter **−90** as the rotation angle (Figure 23-148).
11. Use the **Face** option of the **UCS** command to align the *XY* plane with one of the faces on the base. When prompted, select the highlighted face, picking it around the area shown in Figure 23-149. Press **<Enter↵>** to accept the face. The new UCS should align its *XY* plane as shown.

Note:
Cutting an object when a specific UCS is active and then pasting it into a new UCS is a good technique for aligning objects in the 3D space.

FOR MORE DETAILS   See Chapter 19 for further information about the different options used to modify the UCS.

12. Invoke the **CUTCLIP** (cut to clipboard) command and select the base.
13. Select the **Right** UCS.
14. **PASTE** the base back into the drawing area, anywhere in the 3D space.

Figure 23-148   After rotating the bracket   **Figure 23-149**   The UCS is aligned with the selected face

15. **MOVE** the base closer to the other 3D solids. The 3D assembly model should look like Figure 23-150.
16. **MOVE** the socket bolt close to one of the holes on the base.
17. Make sure the **DUCS** mode is turned off and invoke the **3DALIGN** command. When prompted, select the socket bolt. Figure 23-151 shows the order in which you must select the four center points to locate the socket bolt properly: 1 and 2 are the two source points, while 3 and 4 are the destination points. The result should look like Figure 23-152.

TIP   On certain occasions having the **DUCS** (Dynamic UCS) mode on might interfere with the specification of the points. It is a good idea to turn this setting off for this particular operation.

Figure 23-150   The base is moved closer to the other objects

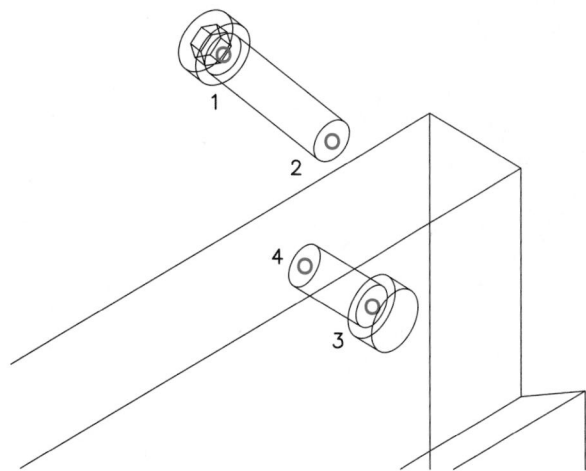

Figure 23-151   The order in which the points to align the bolt with its hole must be specified

Figure 23-152   After the bolt is aligned

18. Select the **Right** view.
19. **MIRROR** the socket bolt, as you would normally do in a 2D operation, to place mirrored copies of the socket bolt in each of the three remaining holes (Figure 23-153).
20. Select the **SW Isometric** viewing point.
21. **ZOOM** into the bracket and create a hole through it, as specified in Figure 23-154.
22. **MOVE** the leftmost end of the Allen wrench close to the set screw.
23. Invoke the **3DALIGN** command. When prompted, **ZOOM** in as needed and select the Allen wrench. Follow Figure 23-155 for the order in which you should snap to the six endpoints: 1, 2, and 3 are the three source points, while 4, 5, and 6 are the three destination points.

Note:
Remember to press **<Enter⏎>** after specifying all the points that define the source plane, as well as after specifying all the points that define the destination plane.

TIP   One of the approaches used to create a circular hole in a 3D solid is to place a circle in the correct location, **EXTRUDE** it long enough so it goes through the 3D solid, and **SUBTRACT** it from the 3D solid.

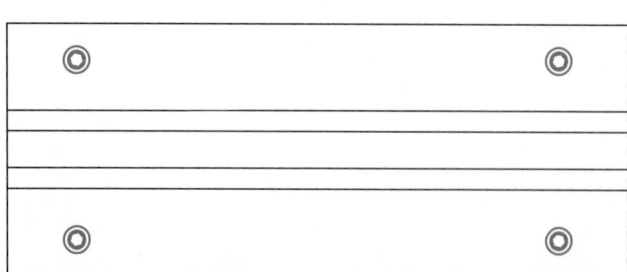

Figure 23-153   The three other bolts are obtained with **MIRROR** operations

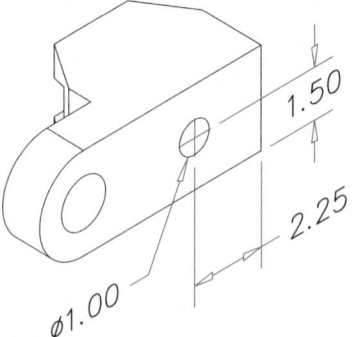

Figure 23-154   Dimensions for the hole

24. **MOVE** the socket screw and the Allen wrench together so the socket screw is close to the hole you opened on the bracket (Figure 23-156).
25. Invoke the **3DALIGN** command to align both the socket bolt and the Allen wrench with the hole of the bracket, as shown in Figure 23-157. Select the two center points on the socket bolt as the source points, and the two center points on the bracket hole as the destination points.

Figure 23-155 Order to specify the points for the **3DALIGN** operation

Figure 23-156 Objects moved closer to the base

Figure 23-157 After aligning the objects with the hole on the bracket

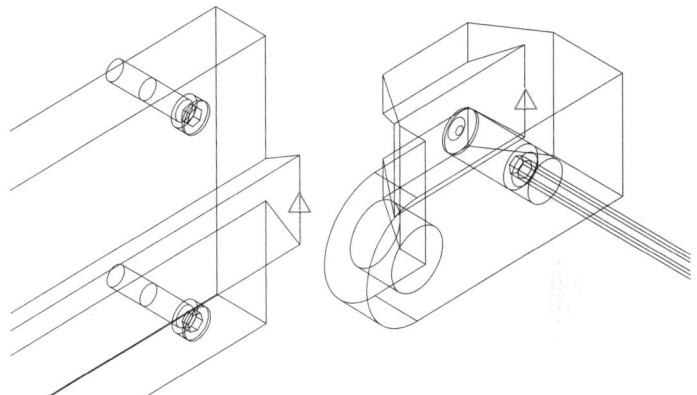

Figure 23-158 Points to be specified in the **MOVE** operation

26. **MOVE** the bracket together with the socket screw and the Allen wrench from the midpoint on the edge of the bracket to the midpoint on the edge of the base, as shown in Figure 23-158.
27. Once again, **MOVE** the previous 3D solids orthogonally along the base guide to locate them close to the middle of the base. The 3D assembly model should look like Figure 23-159.
28. **SAVE** the drawing.
29. On your own, try rotating the Allen wrench along with the set screw so that the bent end of the Allen wrench is aligned exactly downward.

Figure 23-159 The final arrangement, after the objects are moved orthogonally toward the middle of the base

CHAPTER SUMMARY

After reading this chapter, you should have learned the commands needed to create 3D solid primitives, as well as many other powerful tools related to the creation of 3D solids and surfaces such as **EXTRUDE, REVOLVE, SWEEP**, and **LOFT**. In addition, the Boolean operations with 3D solids, along with the many other operations you learned, will assist you in the development of very sophisticated 3D models. You have also learned how the **FILLET** and **CHAMFER** commands have a very specific use in these types of objects.

The many exercises contained in this chapter have given you the practice required to start using the tools contained in this chapter. They also have introduced you to the different approaches and uses for which 3D solids and surfaces are considered to be appropriate.

You have learned the techniques used to develop 3D assembly models in a practical way, as well as the methods needed to find possible failures caused by improper fitting of components, using the **INTERFERENCE** command.

CHAPTER TEST QUESTIONS

Multiple Choice

1. Which system variable controls the display of silhouettes on curved faces?

    a. **FACETRES**
    b. **DISPSILH**
    c. **ISOLINES**
    d. None of the above

2. Which of the following is not a method used to develop an extruded object?

    a. Following a path
    b. Perpendicular to its plane
    c. Between two cross sections
    d. In a specified direction

3. Which of the following objects will create a surface if an **EXTRUDE** operation is performed with it?

    a. A circle
    b. An open non-self-intersecting polyline
    c. A region
    d. A closed non-self-intersecting polyline

4. Which of the following options cannot be used to define the axis of rotation of the **REVOLVE** command?

    a. Two points
    b. The X-axis of the current UCS
    c. The XY plane of the current UCS
    d. The Z-axis of the current UCS

5. Which of the following can be controlled on the swept objects in a **SWEEP** operation?

    a. Location of the base point
    b. Scaling
    c. Twisting
    d. All of the above

6. Which of the following enables you to control the behavior of very specific areas on the surfaces of lofted 3D objects?

    a. Using a path
    b. Using draft angles

    c. Using guides
    d. None of the above

7. Two concentric cylinders of different diameters that have their bases in the same plane and have the same height are combined using an **INTERSECT** operation. What will the resulting object be?

    a. A pipe
    b. The smaller cylinder
    c. The bigger cylinder
    d. No object

8. Many of the commands used to create 3D objects require that a plane be defined in the 3D space. Which of the following is an appropriate way to define such a plane?

    a. Specify three noncollinear points
    b. Specify the parallelism with respect to another plane and a point
    c. Specify a point and the direction of a vector perpendicular to it
    d. All of the above

9. Suppose that when using the **SLICE** command, you define the imaginary slicing plane as parallel to the ZX plane. Which of the following points cannot be used to specify the portion of the 3D solid to keep?

    a. A point on the ZX plane
    b. A point on the slicing plane
    c. A point on the YZ plane
    d. None of the above can be used

10. Which of the following commands changes its procedure and its prompts when the selected object is a 3D solid?

    a. **MOVE**
    b. **SCALE**
    c. **ROTATE**
    d. **FILLET**

Matching

a. **SECTION**

b. **DELOBJ**

c. **ISOLINES**

d. **SLICE**

e. **LOFT**

f. **DISPSILH**

g. **FACETRES**

h. **INTERSECT**

i. **SWEEP**

j. **INTERFERE**

1. Operation in which objects are passed through a curve

2. Command used to cut the 3D solid into two pieces

3. Operation that connects cross sections in a smooth transition

4. One of the Boolean operation commands

5. Command used to extract regions from a 3D solid

6. Controls the deletion of objects selected after the operation

7. Controls the number of contour lines

8. Command used to check interference between 3D solids

9. Turns an object's silhouettes on or off

10. Controls the number of facets per curved face

Chapter Tutorials

Tutorial 23-1: A Plastic Part Design

A common characteristic of plastic parts is that all the surfaces along the ejection direction need to be tapered. That way, the part can easily be ejected from the mold cavity without being damaged.

In this tutorial, you will develop a plastic staple that is used to secure electrical wires to walls.

1. Open a **NEW** drawing, through the **File** drop-down menu using **Imperial** units.
2. **SAVE** the drawing **AS** *Tutorial 23-1*.
3. Draw the 2D profile shown in Figure 23-160. Turn the profile into either a region or a polyline.
4. Set the **DISPSILH** system variable to **1** and the **ISOLINES** system variable to **0**.
5. Set the **FACETRES** system variable to **6**.
6. Select the **SE Isometric** viewpoint.
7. **EXTRUDE** the profile **−0.375″** (down) using a **Taper angle** of **2** (Figure 23-161).
8. While in the WCS, draw two circles on top of the face. Draw the circles concentric with the arc edges and specify **0.094″** as the diameter (Figure 23-162).

> **Note:**
> To turn a closed group of objects into a region, you must use the **REGION** command. This command is the first choice in this type of work and does not require a specific UCS. In certain cases, however, you might find it easier or even necessary to use the **PEDIT** command instead to create a polyline.

Figure 23-160   Profile dimensions

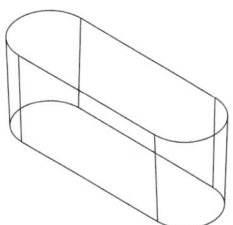

Figure 23-161   After a tapered **EXTRUSION** operation

Figure 23-162   Two concentric circles on the top face

9. **EXTRUDE** the circles **−0.375″** (down) using a **Taper angle** of **2**. This operation will create two thin cones.
10. **SUBTRACT** the two thin cones from the main 3D solid (Figure 23-163).
11. Draw another two circles (**0.188″** diameter) concentric with the two arcs on the top face.

Figure 23-163   Holes created by subtracting the cones

12. **EXTRUDE** the circles **−0.032″** (down) using a **Taper angle** of **2**.
13. **SUBTRACT** the two new 3D solids from the main one. The 3D model of the plastic part now should look like Figure 23-164 after you invoke the **HIDE** command.
14. Invoke the **REGEN** command.
15. Select the **Front** UCS.
16. Draw the 2D profile shown in Figure 23-165. Use the **Ttr (Tan tan radius)** option of the **CIRCLE** command to generate the arc.
17. Convert the profile into a region.
18. **EXTRUDE** the profile **1″** in any direction.
19. Draw a **LINE** at the bottom face from midpoint to midpoint (Figure 23-166).

> **Note:**
> The objects' endpoints must touch each other perfectly for the **REGION** command to proceed.

Figure 23-164   Recess created by subtracting the two new cones

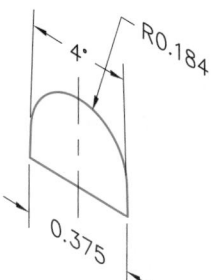

Figure 23-165   2D profile to be drawn

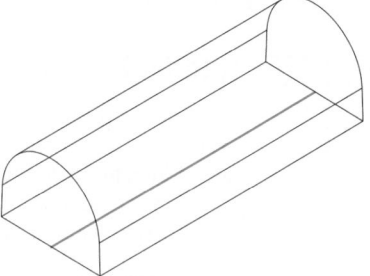

Figure 23-166   Extruded profile

20. **MOVE** the new 3D solid from the midpoint of the line to the midpoint of the straight edge at the bottom of the main 3D solid, as shown in Figure 23-167.

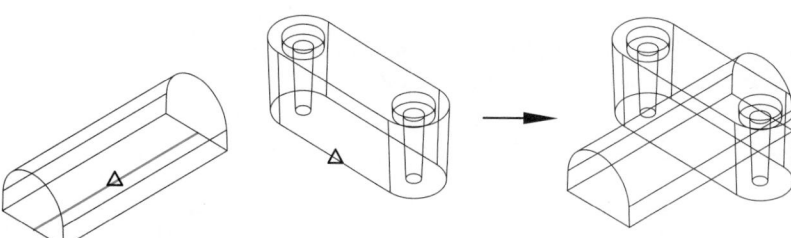

Figure 23-167   3D solid moved to the correct location

21. **ERASE** the line after the operation.
22. **SUBTRACT** the 3D solid that you just moved from the main 3D solid.
23. The 3D model should look like Figure 23-168 after you invoke the **HIDE** command.
24. **SAVE** your drawing.

Tutorial 23-2: The Spiral Stair

In this tutorial, you will add a 5′-diameter spiral stair to the interior of a building. Its partial model (Figure 23-169) has already been created for you.

You will start the project by installing the stair pole. Then you will add the treads, the posts, and the handrail. You will also need to modify the top slab and add the railing on the second floor.

Figure 23-168   Final 3D solid model

Figure 23-169 Partial model of a building contained in the drawing file

During this project you will not be asked to use the **3DORBIT** or the **HIDE** command. You should constantly use these commands, however, to obtain a clearer view.

1. **OPEN** *Tutorial 23-2* in the student data files, and **SAVE** it **AS** *Tutorial 23-2 solved* on your computer.
2. Draw the two circles (**4″** diameter and **2′-8″** radius), as shown in Figure 23-170.

Figure 23-170 Dimensions and location of the circles

3. **EXTRUDE** the two circles **126″** upward.
4. **SUBTRACT** the bigger cylinder from the top slab (Figure 23-171).

Figure 23-171   Hole opened in the slab by subtracting the cylinder and the stair pole

5. To create the tread, select the **Top** view. Then draw the profile and the circle shown in Figure 23-172 to the right of the 3D model.

Figure 23-172   Dimensions for the profile

6. Select the **SE Isometric** viewing point and **ZOOM** into the objects you just drew.
7. Using the **REGION** command, convert the objects into two regions. Afterward **EXTRUDE** both regions **1″**.
8. **SUBTRACT** the cylinder from the outer 3D solid to create a hole. The resulting 3D solid should look like Figure 23-173 with the **Realistic** visual style selected.
9. To finish the tread, you will place a piece of pipe on the bottom face. Select the **2D Wireframe** visual style. Draw the two circles in the bottom face of the tread, as shown in Figure 23-174.
10. Invoke the **REGION** command and turn the two circles into two regions. **SUBTRACT** the small circular region from the bigger one.

Figure 23-173   A shaded view of the finished tread

Figure 23-174   Dimensions for the profile

11. **EXTRUDE** the resulting regions −6″ downward. The tread with the pipe should look like Figure 23-175 with the **Realistic** visual style selected.

Figure 23-175   A shaded view of the tread and the piece of pipe

12. **MOVE** the two 3D solids (the tread with the tube) from the upper center point of the hole to the top center point of the pole.
13. **MOVE** the tread with the tube **7″** orthogonally along the negative direction of the Z-axis.
14. **COPY** the two 3D solids (the tread with the tube) **7″** down. The 3D model should look like Figure 23-176.

Figure 23-176   The first tread in place is copied down

15. Invoke the **ROTATE3D** command to rotate the copied tread. When prompted for the first point on the axis, specify the topmost center point on the pole. Specify another center point below it as the second point on the axis. Enter **28** for the rotation angle (Figure 23-177).

Figure 23-177   After rotating the copied tread

16. Repeat the last two steps until the tube of the last tread reaches the floor surface.

17. At this point, it is convenient to hide the walls and the top slab. To do so, create two new layers, named **Wall** and **Slab**. Specify different colors for them if you wish. Then assign each layer to the corresponding objects, and **Freeze** the two layers. The 3D model should look like Figure 23-178.

Note:
Next, you will draw the stair handrail. To create this 3D object you will perform a **SWEEP** operation along a helical path.

Figure 23-178   All the treads and pipes are created and located in the correct place

18. **COPY** one of the tubes on top of the last step also.
19. Make sure the **World** UCS is current, invoke the **HELIX** command, and respond to the prompts as follows:

    Specify center point of base: *Snap to the center point of the bottom circular edge of the pole.*

    Specify base radius or [Diameter]: *29* ↵

    Specify top radius or [Diameter]: *29* ↵

    Specify helix height or [Axis endpoint/Turns/turn Height/tWist]: *h* ↵

    Specify distance between turns: *90* ↵

    Specify helix height or [Axis endpoint/Turns/turn Height/tWist]: *t* ↵

    Enter number of turns: *2* ↵

20. Invoke the **HIDE** command. The resulting helix should look like Figure 23-179.
21. Invoke the **REGEN** command and create a cylinder with a diameter of **3″** and a height of **50″**. Place the center point of its base on the endpoint of the helix (Figure 23-180).

> **Note:**
> The **Turn Height** is the key element needed to create the helix correctly. This value is obtained by analyzing a common point between two contiguous treads. From one point to another, the helix path must rotate 28° while rising 7″. This means that a complete turn (360°) will rise $360 \times 7/28 = 90″$ height. Two complete turns will create a helix long enough to reach the last tread. The handrail will be cut to fit in place later.

Figure 23-179   The resulting helix

Figure 23-180   A cylinder is created

22. Draw a circle **1½″** in diameter next to the base of the cylinder.
23. Invoke the **SWEEP** command and sweep the circle along the helix.
24. **ERASE** the helix. The 3D model should look like Figure 23-181.
25. Select the **SE Isometric** viewing point.
26. With **ORTHO** mode on, **COPY** the 3″ cylinder **6″** orthogonally in the negative direction of the Z-axis.
27. **SUBTRACT** the copied cylinder from the swept handrail (Figure 23-182).

28. **ROTATE** the swept handrail and the **3″**-diameter cylinder (post) **66°** around any center point along the central pole.
29. **MOVE** the swept handrail **47″** orthogonally toward the positive direction of the Z-axis (Figure 23-183).

Figure 23-181 The swept handrail

Figure 23-182 Trimming the handrail with a **SUBTRACT** operation

Figure 23-183 The handrail is moved up

30. Draw three **1″**-diameter circles on the top face of the topmost tread, as shown in Figure 23-184.
31. **EXTRUDE** the three circles up **60″** to create three round posts.
32. Duplicate the swept handrail by creating a **COPY** in place. You can do so by snapping to the same point when specifying the base point and second point.
33. **SUBTRACT** one of the spiral railings from the three round posts.
34. Invoke the **Separate** option of the **SOLIDEDIT** command to separate the now-combined 3D solid into six independent 3D solid objects. When prompted, simply select the combined posts. Press **<Esc>** to end the operation.

Note:
If you subtract from more than one 3D solid when performing a **SUBTRACT** operation, these 3D solids are automatically combined as if you were first performing a **UNION** operation with them.

Figure 23-184 Dimensions to locate the circles in the top tread

SEPARATE	
Solid Editing Toolbar	
Ribbon Solid Editing panel	
Pull-down Menu	Modify/ Solid Editing/ Separate
Command Line	solidedit ← b ← p

<table>
<tr><td>FOR MORE
DETAILS</td><td>See Chapter 24 for more information about the SEPARATE operation.</td></tr>
</table>

35. **ERASE** the three remaining portions of the posts above the railing. The 3D model should look like Figure 23-185.
36. Select the **Top** UCS if it is not set current.
37. **COPY** the three posts **7″** orthogonally down in the direction of the Z-axis.
38. Invoke the **ROTATE** command. Rotate the three new posts, copied **−28°** around any center point of the center post or pole of the stair. Use the **3D Orbit** tool as needed. The 3D model should look like Figure 23-186.

Figure 23-185   Trimming the three posts with a **SUBTRACT** operation

Figure 23-186   The three posts copied to the next tread

39. Repeat the previous two steps until you have placed three posts on all of the treads. Use the **3DORBIT** command as needed. When you are finished, the 3D model should look like Figure 23-187.

TIP   Selecting the **Realistic** visual style before placing the three posts on the treads will give you a better understanding of the operation.

40. Thaw the **Wall** and **Slab** layers.
41. Now, you will create the top board. Select the **Top** view. In an empty spot, draw the objects shown in Figure 23-188.
42. When you are finished, convert the objects into two regions (the outer profile and the circular region).
43. **SUBTRACT** the circular region from the outer profile to create a hole in it.
44. Select the **SW Isometric** viewing point and **EXTRUDE** the resulting region **1″**.
45. **MOVE** the top board to the stair so it sits on top of the last cylinder you placed (Figure 23-189).

Figure 23-187 After placing the three posts on all the treads

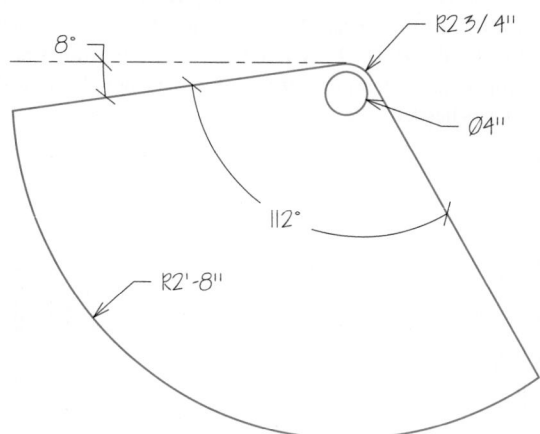

Figure 23-188 The top board profile

Figure 23-189 The top board moved to its location

46. Draw the four **3″**-diameter circles, as shown in Figure 23-190. The centerlines shown going through two of the circles should be parallel to the edges of the top board.

Figure 23-190 Dimensions to locate the three circles highlighted

47. **EXTRUDE** the four circles up **42″** to create the four posts.
48. Create an in-place **COPY** of the **3″** post that connects to the handrail in order to duplicate it.
49. **SUBTRACT** one of the duplicate posts from the swept handrail.
50. Invoke the **SEPARATE** command to make the two portions of the handrail independent.
51. **ERASE** the remaining portion of the handrail (Figure 23-191).

Figure 23-191   Trimming the handrail with a **SUBTRACT** operation

52. Use the **CYLINDER** command to create a **1½″**-diameter cylinder. Locate the center point of the base in one of the center points on the circular top edge of the posts. Use the **Axis endpoint** option and select the center point on the circular top edge of the other post (Figure 23-192).
53. Draw the arc shown in Figure 23-193 using the **Center, Start, End** method. Center it on the stair between the center points of the top circular edges of the posts.
54. Draw a **1½″**-diameter circle close to the arc.
55. **SWEEP** the circle along the arc.

Figure 23-192   Adding a straight cylindrical handrail

Figure 23-193   Arc created in place

56. **MOVE** the last cylinder created and the swept 3D solid **1″** down orthogonally, along the negative direction of the *Z*-axis (Figure 23-194).
57. **MOVE** the arc **42″** down orthogonally.
58. Invoke the **DDPTYPE** command and select the point style shown in Figure 23-195. Click **OK** to close the **Point Style** window.

Figure 23-194   The handrail swept along the arc

Figure 23-195   The **Point Style** window

59. Draw a polyline between the center points of the bottom edges of the posts located in the middle of the stair and the post receiving the two handrails.
60. Invoke the **DIVIDE** command. Select the polyline when prompted and divide it into **7** segments. Points are placed to indicate the divisions. Repeat the operation and divide the arc into **17** segments. The results of these operations are shown in Figure 23-196.

Note:
To create the remaining posts that connect to the handrails, follow the next steps.

Figure 23-196   Points placed by the **DIVIDE** command

Note:
You can set the **Object Snap** to snap only to nodes (points) in the **Drafting Settings** dialog box to make this operation easier.

61. Create a cylinder **1″** in diameter and **41″** in length, placing the base's center point on any of the point entities.
62. **COPY** the cylinder from the center point of its base to each of the other points.
63. Create a duplicate of the handrail with the **COPY** command.
64. **SUBTRACT** the copy of the handrail from all the **1″**-diameter posts on the second floor.

Figure 23-197   The finished top of the stairs

65. **ERASE** the arc, the polyline, and all the points. The top of the stairs should look like Figure 23-197.
66. Set the **PERSPECTIVE** system variable to **1** to select a perspective view.
67. Change the color of the elements of the stairs as you wish.
68. Invoke the **3DORBIT** to select a different viewing point.
69. Select the **Realistic** visual style. The 3D model should look like Figure 23-198.
70. **SAVE** the drawing.

Figure 23-198   A shaded perspective view of the spiral staircase

Tutorial 23-3: Design of a Valve in Metric Units

In this tutorial, you will develop the main part of a valve shown in Figure 23-199. This type of component is typically manufactured out of a hexagonal bar using lathe, mill, and drill operations. Pay special attention to the procedure by which the 3D

Figure 23-199   This valve will be developed in metric units

Figure 23-200   The **Create New Drawing** dialog box

solid model is developed. It has been prepared in a way that can be compared to the actual manufacturing process of the part.

This tutorial has also been prepared in metric units. This will give you practice in using the International Standards Organization (ISO) system of measurement.

1. Start a **NEW** drawing, using the **acadiso** template (Figure 23-200).
2. Change the **DISPSILH** system variable to **1**. Change the **ISOLINES** system variable to **0**. Change the value of the **FACETRES** system variable to **5**.
3. **SAVE** the drawing and specify *Tutorial 23-3* as the file name.
4. To start the 3D model, draw a **25**-mm-diameter circle and a six-sided **POLYGON** circumscribed in it (Figure 23-201).
5. Select the **SW Isometric** viewing point.
6. **EXTRUDE** the polyline up **60** mm (Figure 23-202).
7. Select the **Front** view. The **Front** UCS should be activated automatically.
8. Draw the profile shown in Figure 23-203 next to the 3D solid.

> **Note:**
> When invoking the **NEW** command from the drop-down menu, you can select **Metric** as the default setting in the **Create New Drawing** dialog box (Figure 23-200). The units can also be changed by using the **Drawing Units** dialog box in any existing drawing.

> **Note:**
> The profile in step 8 represents the material that would have to be removed in a lathe to start shaping the part (Figure 23-204).

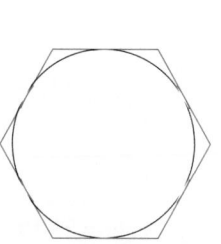

Figure 23-201   A circle with a circumscribed polygon

Figure 23-202   The extruded polygon

Figure 23-203   Dimensions for the profile

Figure 23-204   The profile shape is the section of the volume that will be removed from the 3D solid

9. Draw the highlighted reference line, as shown in Figure 23-205. This line represents the main axis of the object.
10. Select the **SW Isometric** viewing point.
11. Convert the objects into a region.
12. **MOVE** the region and the reference line from the bottom endpoint of the reference line to the center point of the reference circle (Figure 23-206).
13. **REVOLVE** the region, using the top and bottom endpoints of the reference line to specify the start and end points of the axis of revolution. Accept **360** as the angle of revolution (Figure 23-207).

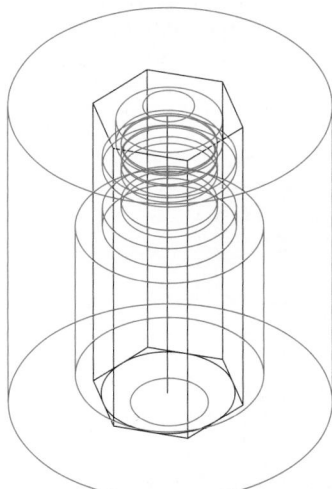

Figure 23-205   Dimensions for the reference line

Figure 23-206   The region and the reference line are moved to the extruded bar

Figure 23-207   The profile is revolved, generating a revolved 3D solid

14. **SUBTRACT** the revolved 3D solid from the extruded hexagonal bar.
15. **ERASE** both the reference line and the reference circle.
16. Invoke the **HIDE** command to check the new shape of the 3D solid. The result should look like Figure 23-208.

Figure 23-208   The 3D solid model is shaped by subtracting the revolved 3D solid

Figure 23-209   Dimensions for the profile

17. Select the **Front** view and draw the profile shown in Figure 23-209. This second profile will be used to create the 3D solid that will remove the material in the center of the object.
18. Select the **SW Isometric** viewing point.
19. Convert the profile into a region.
20. **MOVE** the region from its rightmost bottom endpoint to the center point of the bottom face (Figure 23-210).
21. **REVOLVE** the region **360°**, using any two center points on the 3D solid hexagonal bar to specify the start and end points of the axis of revolution.
22. **SUBTRACT** the new 3D solid from the hexagonal bar. The volume is removed from the part (Figure 23-211).

Figure 23-210   The region is moved to the 3D solid

Figure 23-211   The region is revolved and subtracted from the 3D solid, shaping the inside cavity

23. Select the **Front** view.
24. Draw the profile shown in Figure 23-212.
25. Select the **SW Isometric** viewing point.
26. Convert the profile into a region and then **EXTRUDE** the region **40** mm.
27. Draw a reference line diagonally on the top face, as shown in Figure 23-213, with the hidden lines removed.
28. **MOVE** the extruded 3D solid from the midpoint of the reference line to the center point of the bottom of the 3D solid.

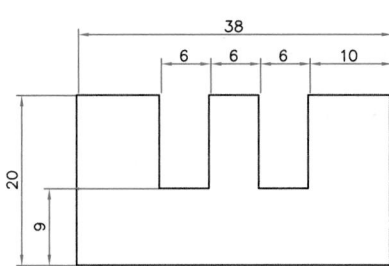

Figure 23-212   Dimensions for the profile

Figure 23-213   The extruded profile

29. **ERASE** the reference line.
30. With **ORTHO** mode on, **MOVE** the extruded 3D solid again **11** mm upward.
31. **SUBTRACT** the 3D solid from the hexagonal bar. The 3D solid model should now look like Figure 23-214.
32. Make sure the **Front** UCS is the current one and draw a **6**-mm-diameter circle with its center located on the topmost center point of the 3D solid. Figure 23-215 shows the result with the occulted lines removed.
33. **EXTRUDE** the circle **−20** mm.

Note:
This operation can be considered to be the milling operation of the manufacturing process.

Figure 23-214   The new extruded 3D solid is subtracted from the 3D solid model

Figure 23-215   Dimensions and location of the circle

Figure 23-216   The two cylinders next to each other

34. **COPY** the cylinder from the center point of its front face to the center point of its back face (Figure 23-216).
35. **COPY** the two cylinders in the same place in order to duplicate them.

TIP   You **COPY** a 3D solid over to duplicate it by simply specifying both the base point and the second point as the same.

36. Select the **Top** UCS.
37. **ROTATE** one of the duplicate cylinders **90°**. The result should look like Figure 23-217.
38. Select the **Left** UCS.
39. Use the **CYLINDER** command to create a **3**-mm-diameter cylinder. Select the midpoint of the bottom leftmost edge when prompted for the center point of the base of the cylinder and enter **–30** for the height (Figure 23-218).
40. **MOVE** the last cylinder up **4** mm orthogonally, then move it **6** mm along the positive direction of the *X*-axis (Figure 23-219).
41. **MOVE** the (**4**) cylinders on top **15.5** mm down orthogonally.
42. **SUBTRACT** the (**5**) cylinders from the 3D solid model.
43. Invoke the **HIDE** command. The 3D model should look like Figure 23-220.

Figure 23-217   The four cylinders intersecting the 3D solid model

Figure 23-218   A new cylinder based on the bottom midpoint

Figure 23-219   After moving the new cylinder

Figure 23-220   All cylinders are subtracted to generate the holes

44. To create the threads effect, you will simply create a set of triangular rings and subtract them from the 3D solid. Select the **Front** view and draw the profile shown in Figure 23-221.
45. Convert the profile into a region.
46. **MOVE** the region from the topmost left endpoint to the topmost right quadrant point on the 3D solid. The result should look like Figure 23-222.
47. Select the **SW Isometric** viewing point.
48. **REVOLVE** the region **360°**. Snap to the two topmost center points of the 3D solid to specify the axis of revolution.

Figure 23-221   Dimensions for the thread profile

Figure 23-222   Thread profile moved to the 3D solid model

49. **SUBTRACT** the threads from the 3D solid model.
50. **ZOOM** out to see the entire 3D model.
51. Select the **Realistic** visual style. The 3D model should look like Figure 23-223.
52. **SAVE** the drawing.

Figure 23-223   Shaded view of the final 3D model

CHAPTER PROJECTS

Project 23-1: Modeling a 3D Solid Part

Create the 3D solid model shown in Figure 23-224. Place the **6 × 4** face on the *XY* plane of the **World** UCS.

Hints for the Project

Create a 3D solid box, and then **SUBTRACT** two cylinders to open the holes. Finally, create a surface and slice the 3D solid with it to obtain the top shape.

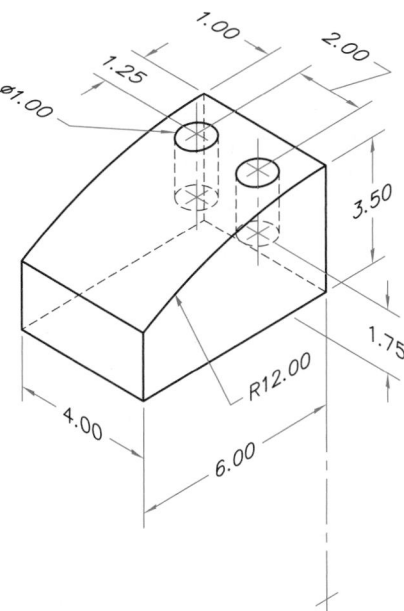

Figure 23-224   Dimensions for the solid part

Project 23-2: Designing a Turning Bracket

Start a **NEW** drawing in metric units and create the 3D solid model shown in Figure 23-225, as it is viewed from the **SW Isometric** viewing point on the left. Obtain the dimensions in millimeters from the 2D drawing in Figure 23-226. Save the drawing as *Project 23-2*.

Figure 23-225   Shaded views of the final 3D model

Figure 23-226   Dimensions for the turning bracket

Hints for the Project

Do not perform any filleting operation until all other faces of the 3D solid have been generated.

The order in which the fillets are created is important to achieve smooth, round edges. When creating corner fillets, first create the fillets that eliminate the sharp turns for other chain fillets, as shown in the example in Figure 23-227.

Figure 23-227   Hints for the **FILLET** operation

Project 23-3: 3D Solid Objects

Create the 3D solid models of the objects you previously created in Project 21-1 and Project 21-3.

Hints for the Project

You can use some of the wireframe objects to create the 3D solids.

Project 23-4: Creating a Bolt 3D Model with Real Thread

OPEN the drawing *Project 23-4* in the student data files. It contains the objects shown in Figure 23-228. You will use these objects to create the 3D model of the bolt with real thread shown in Figure 23-229.

To access student data files, go to www.pearsondesigncentral.com.

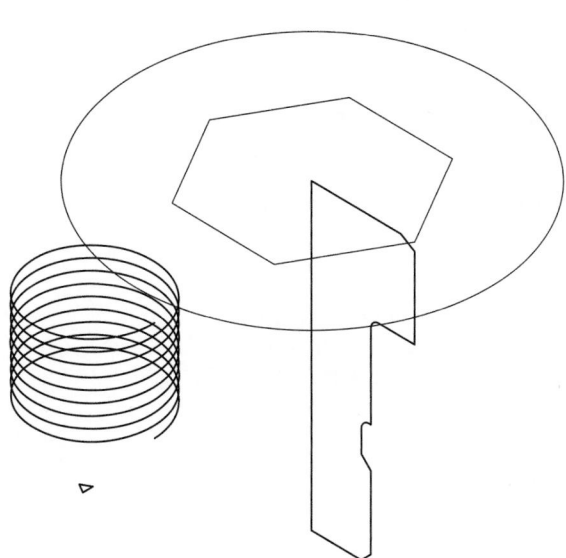

Figure 23-228   Objects contained in the drawing file

Figure 23-229   A shaded view of the final 3D model shows the bolt with a real thread

Hints for the Project

To create the thread, you can use the **Base point** option of the **SWEEP** command, and snap to the midpoint of the edge that is parallel to the *Y*-axis (Figure 23-230).

The hexagonal head can be created by subtracting a 3D solid having a hole of the same shape.

Figure 23-230
Hints for the **SWEEP** operation

Project 23-5: Creating the 3D Model of a Faucet

Using the knowledge you have acquired from this chapter, create the 3D model of the faucet shown in Figure 23-231. The dimensions of the object are shown in Figure 23-232.

Hints for the Project

The shape of the objects can be easily created with a **LOFT** operation following a centerline path. You can use some of the cross sections given as well as other sections to control the geometry of the 3D solid.

Figure 23-231 A shaded view of the faucet 3D model

Figure 23-232 Dimensions for the cross sections and the path

Project 23-6: Finding Interferences Between Components of the Spiral Staircase

Some of the components of the spiral staircase developed in Tutorial 23-2 interfere with each other. Find and eliminate these interferences.

Hints for the Project

You can use the **INTERFERE** command first to find any existing interferences. After you have found the interferences, you can eliminate them by giving the objects the correct shape. You can create duplicate in-place copies of the objects with which the components interfere and then **SUBTRACT** them.

Editing 3D Solids and Surfaces

24

Chapter Objectives

- Become familiar with the **SOLIDEDIT** command and its family of tools.
- Understand and control the process of selecting faces within a **SOLIDEDIT** operation.
- Modify a 3D solid's geometry by editing its edges.
- Modify a 3D solid's geometry by editing its faces.
- Modify a 3D solid's geometry by editing its body.
- Emphasize the use of the **Shell** operation.
- Extract geometry from the 3D solids for use in further operations.
- Understand the different types of 3D solids and surfaces.
- Use grips to edit 3D solids and surfaces.
- Modify composite 3D solids by modifying the history of their original 3D solids.

INTRODUCTION

ABOUT EDITING 3D SOLIDS

The activities of design and prototyping have much to do with constant modifications until the final product is defined. The more tools you have to make these changes, the less likely it is that you will have to restart your 3D model from scratch. The 3D solids editing tools or options contained in the **SOLIDEDIT** command are very helpful in this regard.

The 3D solids editing tools, however, can be used not only to make changes on 3D solid objects but also to achieve specific shapes in the design process. As you will learn in this chapter, without these important and handy tools, you could not create many shapes of 3D models, at least in a simple manner.

Because of the way in which they proceed, many of the 3D solids editing tools are similar to the **Modify** group tools used in 2D.

Using the **SOLIDEDIT** command is not the only way to edit 3D solids. Depending on the type of 3D solid, the value of its geometric characteristics can also be modified through the **Properties** palette. In addition, many other editing capabilities that employ grips, including the manipulation of subobjects, mean that 3D solids have become flexible objects. Modifications made to a composite 3D solid, studied in the previous chapter, by using the original 3D solids recorded in its history can also be considered part of the editing capabilities of this type of object. The new surfaces have similar editing capabilities.

THE SOLIDEDIT COMMAND

OVERVIEW OF THE SOLIDEDIT COMMAND

SOLIDEDIT is a general command that contains a wide range of tools that can be used to perform certain modifications on 3D solid objects. It erases the history of the 3D solid, as mentioned in the previous chapter.

Each tool of the **SOLIDEDIT** command is organized according to its category in one of three groups of options: **Face, Edge,** or **Body**. Figure 24-1 shows the shortcut menu with the options of the **SOLIDEDIT** command, and the shortcut menus with the options of each group.

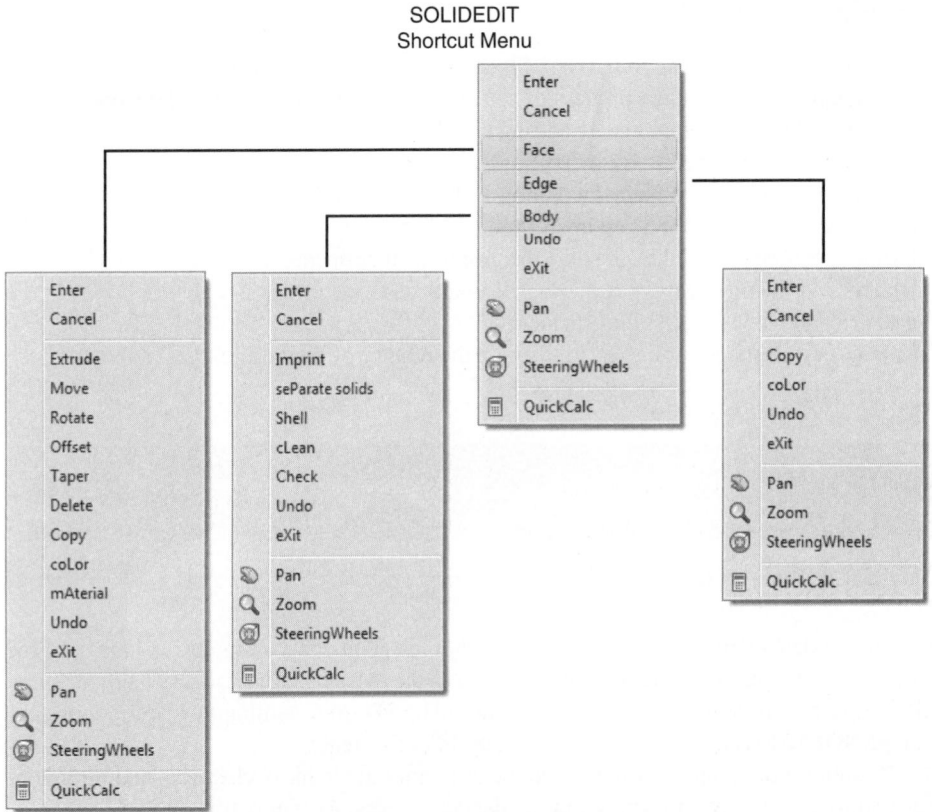

Figure 24-1   The **SOLIDEDIT** command and its subcategory shortcut menus

Accessing a particular **SOLIDEDIT** tool requires first invoking the command, then selecting the group and the particular option within this group. Accessing each individual tool from the **Solid Editing** panel of the Ribbon, however, is as simple as invoking any other command (Figure 24-2).

FACE EDITING TOOLS

The tools within this group are used to perform operations on the faces of 3D solids. Editing a face in most cases modifies the shape of the 3D solid as well. Because face editing tools use specific faces of a 3D solid, you can select faces only from a particular 3D solid in each operation.

Figure 24-2   Location of the **SOLIDEDIT** tools in the toolbar and the pull-down menus

Selecting the Faces

As with all other tools or commands that modify objects, the face editing tools involve a selection process. The selection process of this group of tools prompts you to select specific faces of 3D solids instead of entire objects, as with most other commands.

Selecting faces differs quite a bit from the standard method of selecting objects. Regardless of which face editing tool has been invoked, the following methods will enable you to select faces properly when you are prompted:

1. **Picking an Edge:**   An edge of a 3D solid is the border of any two adjacent faces. Because AutoCAD cannot distinguish between one face and another, picking an edge will automatically include the selection of both adjacent faces [Figure 24-3(a)]. If you want to remove one of these two faces, you can pick any edge of the face you want to remove while holding down the **<Shift>** key [Figure 24-3(b)].

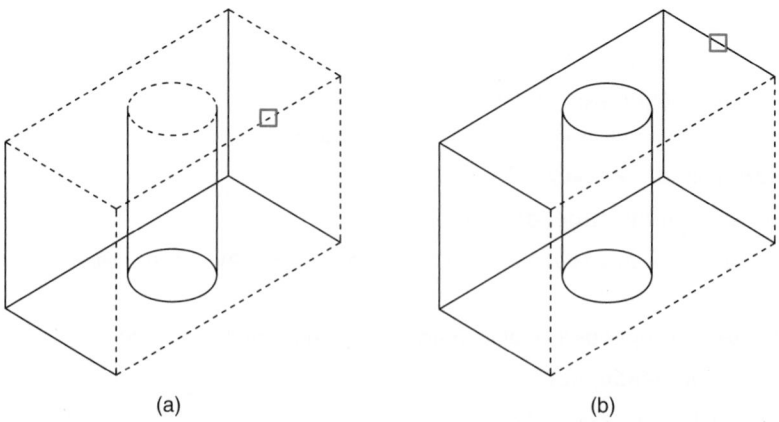

(a)   (b)

Figure 24-3   (a) Picking an edge selects both adjacent faces (b) Faces are deselected when you hold down the **<Shift>** key

2. **Picking a Face:**   Picking inside the face contour is the easiest way to select a face. To understand the face selection process, you must realize that regardless of what face of a 3D solid you are looking at, there is always at least one other face behind it.

Clicking inside the face contour selects the face closer to you. A second click in the same place will select the face behind it, a third click will select the face behind the second, and so on (Figure 24-4).

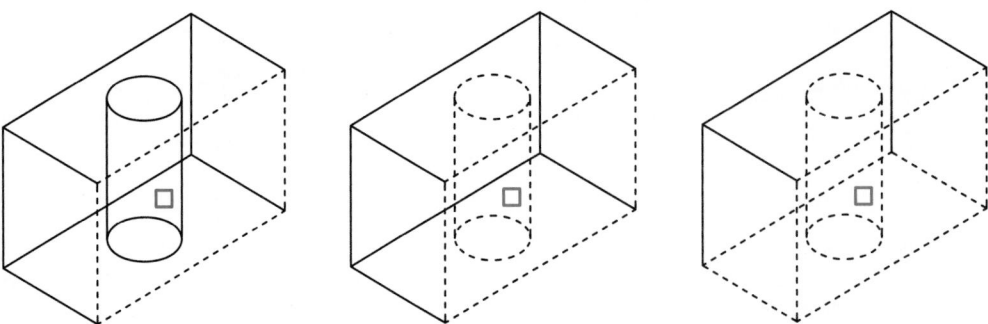

Figure 24-4   Picking on the same spot continuously selects the faces behind it

To remove faces from the selection, you must hold down the **<Shift>** key and click one of the edges of the face you want to remove. If you click any place other than an edge, including outside the 3D solid, while holding the **<Shift>** key down, you will remove the faces in the opposite order of their previous selection (Figure 24-5).

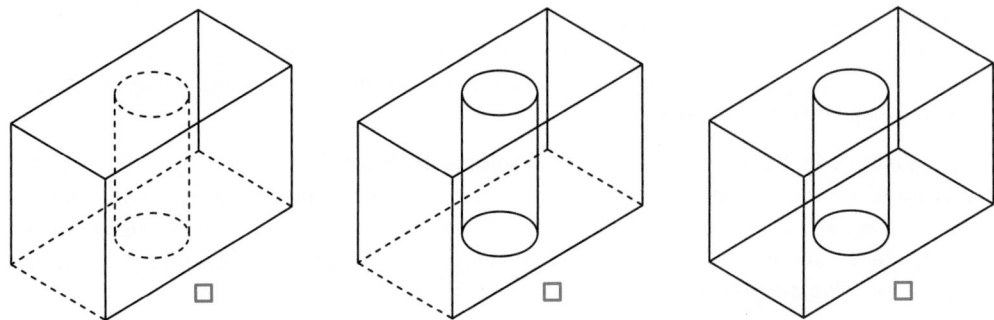

Figure 24-5   Holding down the **<Shift>** key while clicking on the same spot continuously deselects the faces in the same order

3. **Using the Command's Options:**   After you make your first selection, you can ease the selection process by using the options available at the command prompt:

Select faces or [Undo/Remove/ALL]:

all ↵ will select every face of the solid.

r ↵ will save you from having to hold the <Shift> key when removing a face.

After selecting **Remove**, the options available in the command prompt change to:

Remove faces or [Undo/Add/ALL]:

This allows you to switch back to the **Add** mode.

4. **Picking a Silhouette or an Isoline:**   You can use one of these methods when the **DISPSILH** system variable is on, or when the **ISOLINES** system variable is set at a value other than **0**. Isolines and silhouettes are not real entities; they are there only to represent curved faces. Picking an isoline or a silhouette will select only the curved face related to it. This is the most effective way of selecting curved faces, especially the interior ones (Figure 24-6).

5. **Using Selection Tools:**   Additionally, you can select faces by entering the aliases **C**, **F**, and **CP** followed by **<Enter↵>**. This will activate one of the following selection tools,

Crossing/Fence/CPolygon, in the same order. These are the only standard selection methods that can be used. Any other selection method, such as **Window, Previous, or Last**, will not work.

Combining different selection methods is also possible at any time. The **PICKADD** system variable, which determines whether the **<Shift>** key is used to **Remove** or to **Add** objects, is ignored in the selection of faces.

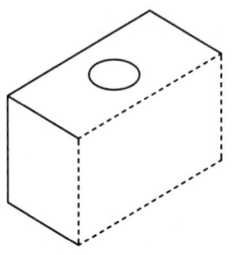

1. Create a region on the highlighted face, with the SECTION command going through that face.

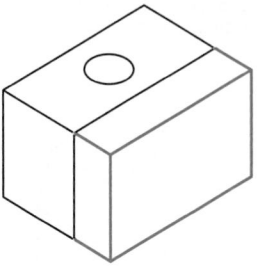

2. EXTRUDE the region created.

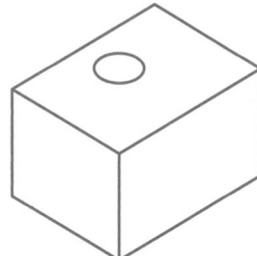

3. Perform a UNION Boolean operation to join the two 3D solids.

Figure 24-6   Picking an isoline or a silhouette selects only the curved face to which it belongs

Figure 24-7   Increasing one of the distances can take three steps using operations studied up to this point

Extrude Faces

Figure 24-7 shows the steps you would perform to increase the size of a 3D solid in a particular direction, using the tools you have learned so far.

TIP   To avoid any possible confusion, be aware that the **Extrude Faces** icon is exactly like the **EXTRUDE** command icon.

EXTRUDE FACES	
Solid Editing Toolbar	
Ribbon Solid Editing panel	
Pull-down Menu	Modify/ Solids Editing/ Extrude faces
Command Line	solidedit ↵ f ↵ e

The **Extrude faces** tool, on the other hand, reduces this work to one single step by extruding the face directly. You can use this tool to protrude planar faces just as you would extrude a shape. As with the **EXTRUDE** command, you can perform the following three extrusion operations in one of two directions, outside or inside the 3D solid (Figure 24-8):

- Perpendicular to the planar face
- Perpendicular to the planar face with a taper angle
- Following a path

Move Faces

Just like the **MOVE** command is used in 2D, the **Move faces** tool can be used when working with 3D solids to move selected faces from one point to another without changing the orientation and topology of the selected faces. Faces surrounding the moved face(s), however, can be modified with the operation to accommodate the new location of the moved face(s).

Depending on the situation in which the tool is used, different results can be obtained. This tool makes it easy to move a hole or any other internal face(s) from one point to another, and even remove it from the 3D solid. In Figure 24-9, the face representing the hole in the original 3D solid

MOVE FACES	
Solid Editing Toolbar	
Ribbon Solid Editing panel	
Pull-down Menu	Modify/ Solids Editing/ Move faces
Command Line	solidedit ↵ f ↵ m

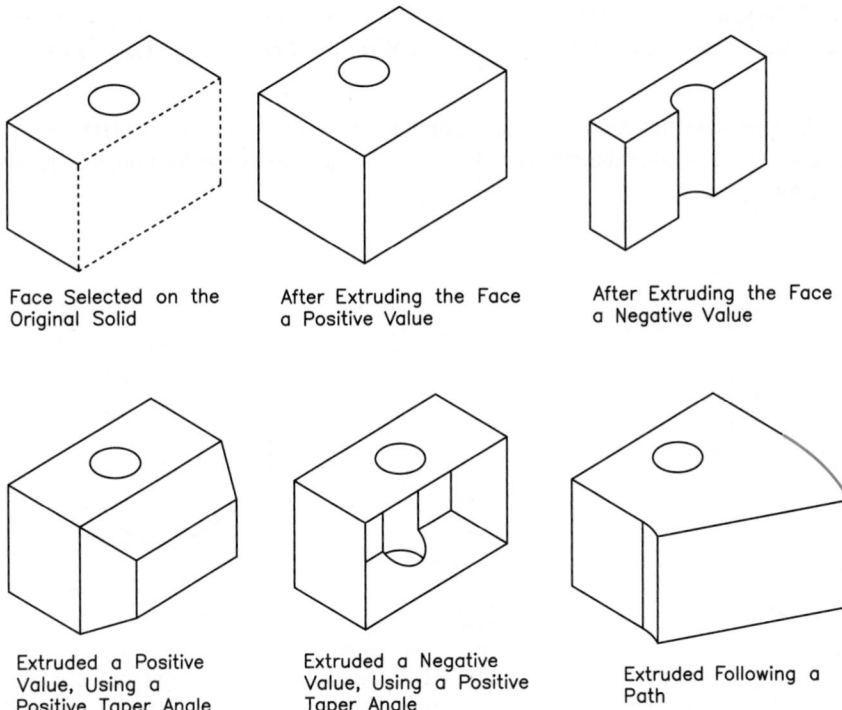

Face Selected on the
Original Solid

After Extruding the Face
a Positive Value

After Extruding the Face
a Negative Value

Extruded a Positive
Value, Using a
Positive Taper Angle

Extruded a Negative
Value, Using a Positive
Taper Angle

Extruded Following a
Path

Figure 24-8 Possible
modifications performed
with the **Extrude faces** tool

has been moved from one point to another in three different operations. In the first operation, the face was moved from point 1 to point 2; in the second operation, it was moved from point 1 to point 3; and in the third operation, from point 1 to point 4. In the last operation, the face is simply lost because it is moved to a point outside the 3D solid's body.

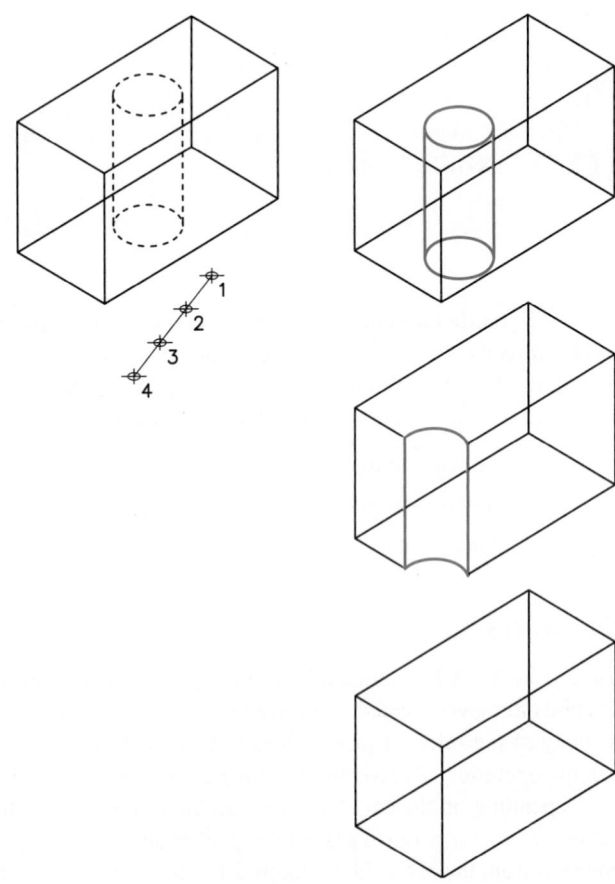

Figure 24-9 Moving a cylindrical
hole using the **Move faces** tool can
lead to different results

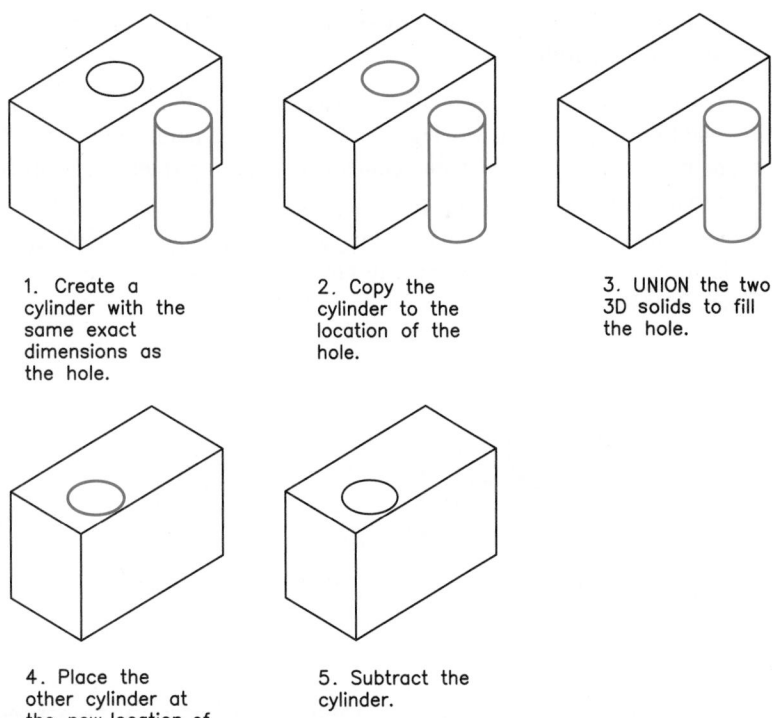

1. Create a cylinder with the same exact dimensions as the hole.

2. Copy the cylinder to the location of the hole.

3. UNION the two 3D solids to fill the hole.

4. Place the other cylinder at the new location of the hole.

5. Subtract the cylinder.

Figure 24-10   Without using the **Move faces** tool, moving a hole to a different location would result in a long list of steps

Without the use of the **Move faces** tool, the operation we previously described would result in a long list of steps (Figure 24-10).

Moved faces are automatically extended or trimmed in their new locations by the adjacent faces. This maintains the integrity of the 3D solid. In Figure 24-11, the two blind holes were moved parallel to the *X*-axis from point 1 to point 2. Their cylindrical faces then were trimmed due to the geometry condition of the top face.

An outer face that is moved also is extended or trimmed according to the adjacent faces that were not moved. For example, moving the selected face in Figure 24-12 from point 1 to point 2 will also modify all faces connected with it.

Figure 24-11   The faces are modified as they are moved to a different location

Figure 24-12   A visual approach to understanding the **Move faces** operation

To better understand the **Move faces** and **Extrude faces** tools, let's look at some of their differences and similarities:

1. Extruding the left face a positive distance (from point 1 to point 2) protrudes the face of the solid [Figure 24-13(a)]. Moving the same face from point 2 to point 1 also modifies all faces around it in order to preserve their geometric relationship [Figure 24-13(b)].

2. The **Extrude faces** and **Move faces** operations will achieve the same result when they are performed inside the 3D solid, as long as the taper angle of the **Extrude faces** operation is 0. This occurs regardless of whether or not the operation interferes with another face inside it [Figure 24-14(a)].

(a)

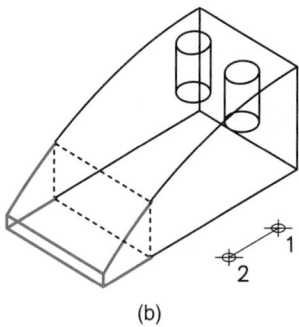

(b)

Figure 24-13   Difference between extruding (a) and moving (b) a single face the same distance

(a)

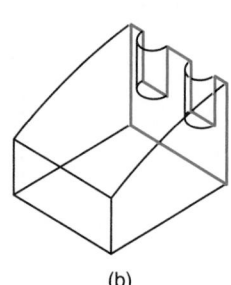

(b)

Figure 24-14   A face can be extruded or moved even if it encounters other faces in its new location

3. Extruding the left and front faces at the same time by a positive value protrudes each face individually. Moving these same two faces from point 1 to point 2 deforms the solid differently, so that the geometric relationship is maintained. In this case, the face parallel to the X-axis would move a distance of ΔY, while the face parallel to the Y-axis would move a distance of ΔX (Figure 24-15).

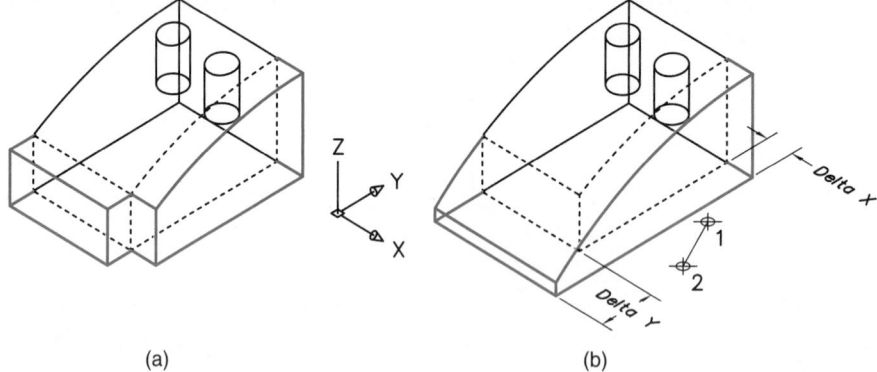

(a)   (b)

Figure 24-15   (a) More than one face is extruded with the same value (b) When multiple faces are moved from one point to another, the faces are displaced according to the coordinate deltas

OFFSET FACES	
Solid Editing Toolbar	⬚
Ribbon Solid Editing panel	
Pull-down Menu	Modify/ Solids Editing/ Offset faces
Command Line	solidedit ↵ f ↵ o

Offset Faces

Like the **OFFSET** command in 2D work, the **Offset faces** tool modifies the solid by relocating the selected face(s) a certain distance parallel to the previous original location. A positive offset distance value will offset the face(s) outside the solid, increasing its size; a negative distance will reduce the size of the solid, offsetting the face(s) inward (Figure 24-16).

The **Offset faces** tool is very useful when performing tasks such as increasing or decreasing the size of an internal face, like the slotted hole on Figure 24-17. If, however, you were to perform

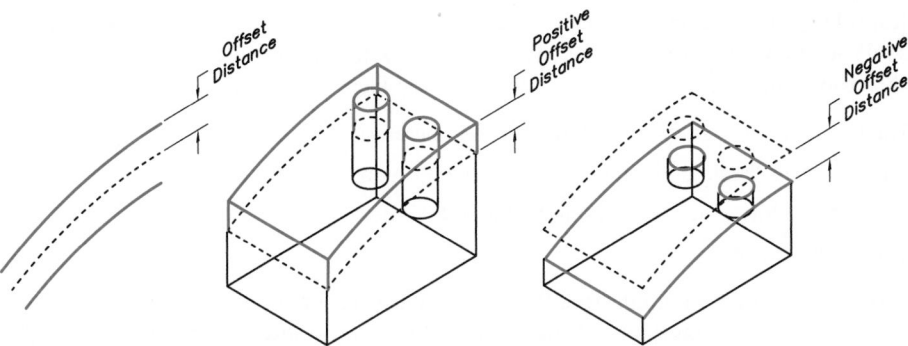

Figure 24-16   The faces can be offset outward and inward using the **Offset faces** tool

| Original 3D Solid with Faces selected | Positive Offset Distance | Negative Offset Distance |

Figure 24-17   The **Offset faces** tool is useful when changing the size of a hole

this task using Boolean operations, it would take many more steps, especially if you were to reduce the size of the slotted hole.

As with the **Move faces** tool, if more than one face is selected, the offset faces blend to maintain the topology of the adjacent faces. The difference in the results obtained using these two tools arises basically from the way in which the displacement distance is considered.

The **Move faces** tool uses distances independently, which depend on the orientation of the face and the delta component of an axis normal to it [Figure 24-18(a)]. The **Offset faces** tool, on the other hand, uses the same specified distance to displace all selected faces [Figure 24-18(b)].

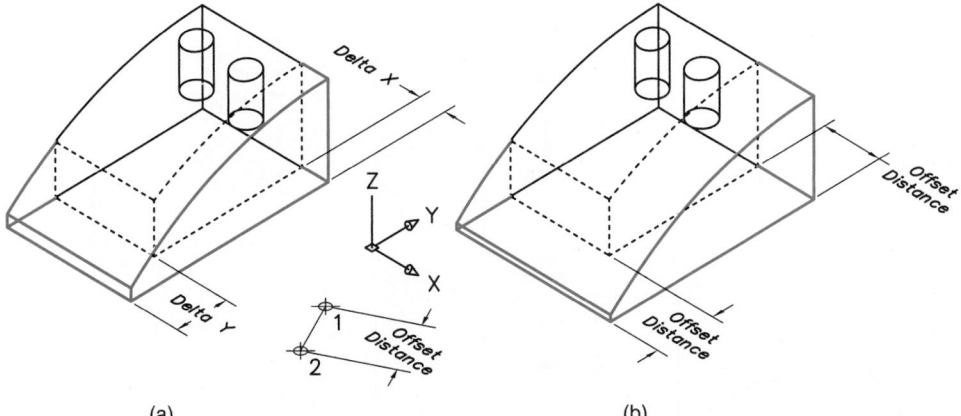

| (a) | (b) |

Figure 24-18   Unlike the **Move faces** operation (a), **Offset faces** displaces the faces an equal distance (b)

Delete Faces

You can use this tool to delete one or more faces on a solid, filling in the gap or empty volume between the removed face and its adjacent faces.

DELETE FACES	
Solid Editing Toolbar	
Ribbon Solid Editing panel	
Pull-down Menu	Modify/ Solids Editing/ Delete faces
Command Line	solidedit ↵ f ↵ d

Holes, fillets, and chamfers have faces that usually can be removed easily by this operation. Figure 24-19(a) shows the original 3D solid before the **Delete faces** operations. The same 3D solid is then shown in Figure 24-19(b) after the following faces have been deleted:

- The two faces created with the **CHAMFER** operation at the bottom
- The two faces created with the **FILLET** operation on top
- The two cylindrical faces representing the blind holes
- The leftmost face

The AutoCAD® program might find that certain face(s) cannot be filled due to geometric conditions. In these cases the tool will not proceed, and the following message will be displayed:

```
Modeling Operation Error:
Gap cannot be filled.
```

Rotate Faces

With this tool, you can rotate selected faces a specified angle around an imaginary axis of rotation, keeping the relationship with the adjacent faces.

The following are the options of the **Rotate faces** tool:

2points: Even though the **2points** option does not appear in its shortcut menu (Figure 24-20), it is available as the default. This option is the method most commonly used to rotate faces. Specifying a point will automatically activate this option. You will then be prompted to specify a second point. These two points define the imaginary axis of rotation through which the faces are to rotate.

ROTATE FACES	
Solid Editing Toolbar	
Ribbon Solid Editing panel	
Pull-down Menu	Modify/ Solids Editing/ Rotate faces
Command Line	solidedit ↵ f ↵ r

FOR MORE DETAILS	The positive rotation can be determined by pointing the thumb of your right hand from the first to the second point and curling the rest of the fingers, as the right-hand rule indicates. See Chapter 19 for further information.

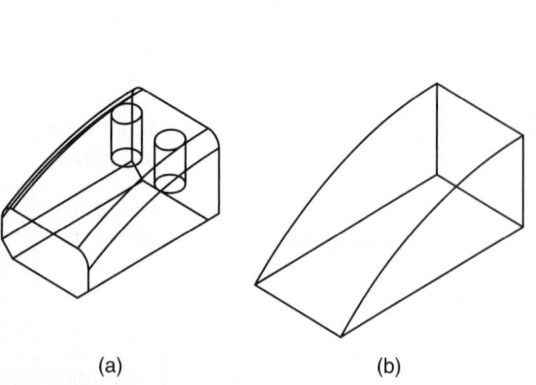

(a)   (b)

Figure 24-19   Holes, fillets, and chamfers can be removed easily by deleting their faces

ROTATE3D
Command

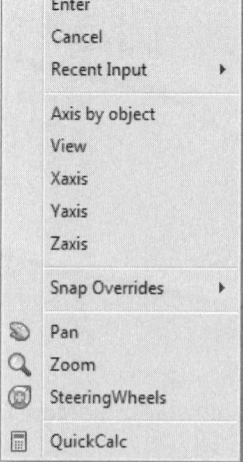

Rotate Faces
Operation

Figure 24-20   The **ROTATE3D** command operation and the **Rotate faces** shortcut menus

Axis by Object: This option differs from the **Object** option of the **ROTATE3D** command. Depending on the type of object, the AutoCAD program has three interpretations:

1. A line is used directly as the imaginary axis of rotation.

2. For circles, ellipses, and arcs, the imaginary axis of rotation is considered to be perpendicular to the plane that contains the object and goes through its center.

3. The start and end points of polylines, 3D polylines, and splines are extracted and used by AutoCAD to establish the axis of rotation.

View: This method aligns the axis of rotation perpendicular to the viewing plane, that is, perpendicular to the monitor screen. You will be prompted to specify a point to locate the axis.

Xaxis/Yaxis/Zaxis: These three options instruct the AutoCAD program to align the axis of rotation parallel to an axis of the current UCS, as specified. You will then be asked for a point to locate where it will go through.

In Figure 24-21 the cylindrical hole was rotated 90° around an imaginary axis that goes through the center of the other cylindrical hole. The face is redefined in its new location.

Similarly, if the top curved face is rotated 30° around an imaginary axis that goes from the midpoint of the left bottom edge to the midpoint of the right bottom edge (Figure 24-22), the solid modifies all adjacent faces to maintain the 3D solid's integrity.

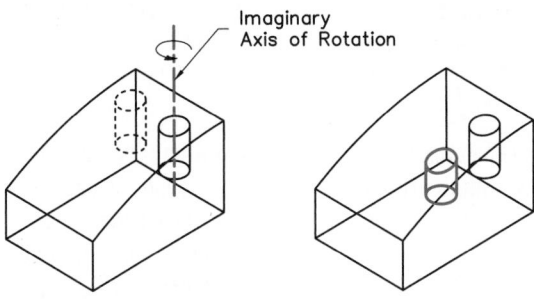

Figure 24-21   The selected face is rotated about the indicated imaginary axis

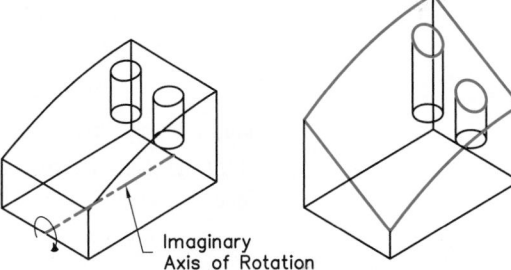

Figure 24-22   The top face is rotated about the indicated imaginary axis

As with the **Move faces** operation, a **Rotate faces** operation will proceed even if the selected face(s) moves outside the 3D solid's body. If, because of the rotation, the face falls completely outside the 3D solid, it will be deleted (Figure 24-23).

Figure 24-23   A face can be rotated farther than the limits of the 3D solid

Taper Faces

With this tool, the faces are tapered at a certain angle. Tapering planar faces will cause them to incline. Tapering cylindrical faces will turn them into conical faces. Faces that are not planar or cylindrical cannot be tapered.

As you have learned, the **EXTRUDE** command enables you to create 3D solids in which all faces parallel to the extrusion direction are tapered at the same angle. The end of the extrusion at which the original shape was located keeps its dimensions, while the dimensions of the other end are affected by the taper angle.

TAPER FACES	
Solid Editing Toolbar	
Ribbon Solid Editing panel	
Pull-down Menu	Modify/ Solids Editing/ Taper faces
Command Line	solidedit ↵ f ↵ t

With the **Taper faces** tool, you can taper planar and cylindrical faces of a 3D solid individually. You establish two necessary aspects of the face tapering operation by specifying two points:

tapering midplane: The cross section in the 3D solid that does not change its original dimensions when the **Taper faces** operation is performed.

1. The point through which the *tapering midplane* will go. AutoCAD refers to this point as the *base point.*

2. A second point that determines the direction of the tapering vector, which aligns the tapering midplane perpendicular to it. AutoCAD refers to this vector as the *axis of tapering.*

Figure 24-24 shows the modified 3D solid that results from tapering three of its faces, locating the base point on the midpoint of a vertical edge, and placing the second point on the top vertex of the same edge. This aligns the tapering midplane parallel to the bottom and top faces.

Try to keep the tapering midplane perpendicular to the extrusion direction. That way, you can avoid dealing with complicated combinations of angular displacements.

Internal faces such as holes are easy to taper as well. For cylindrical or conical faces, the tapering vector should be aligned with the centerline (Figure 24-25).

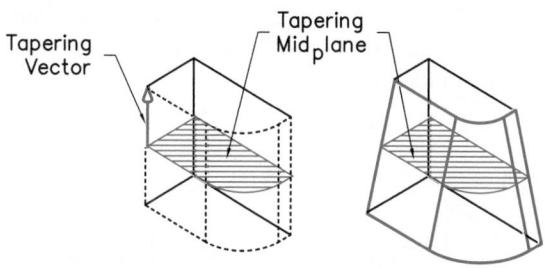

Figure 24-24 The tapering midplane defines the section of the 3D solids that remains unchanged with the **Taper faces** operation

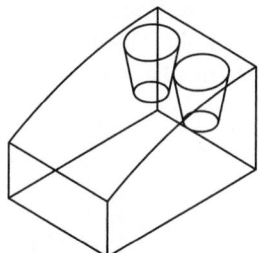

Figure 24-25 When tapering a cylindrical or conical face, the tapering vector should be aligned with its centerline

COPY FACES	
Solid Editing Toolbar	
Ribbon Solid Editing panel	
Pull-down Menu	Modify/ Solids Editing/ Copy faces
Command Line	solidedit ⏎ f ⏎ c

Copy Faces

This tool allows you to extract faces from a 3D solid to any location. Planar faces are extracted from a 3D solid as regions; nonplanar faces are extracted as surfaces.

Regions are typically copied for use in another 3D operation. For instance, let's assume that the bottom face of the 3D solid in Figure 24-26(a) needs to be modified so that it has the same exact curvature as the top face in Figure 24-26(d). This operation can be performed quickly by creating a copy of the front face down, for example, from point 1 to point 2 [Figure 24-26(b)] and then extruding the extracted region as shown in Figure 24-26(c) to create a new 3D solid. A third and final step would be to **SUBTRACT** the new 3D solid from the original one.

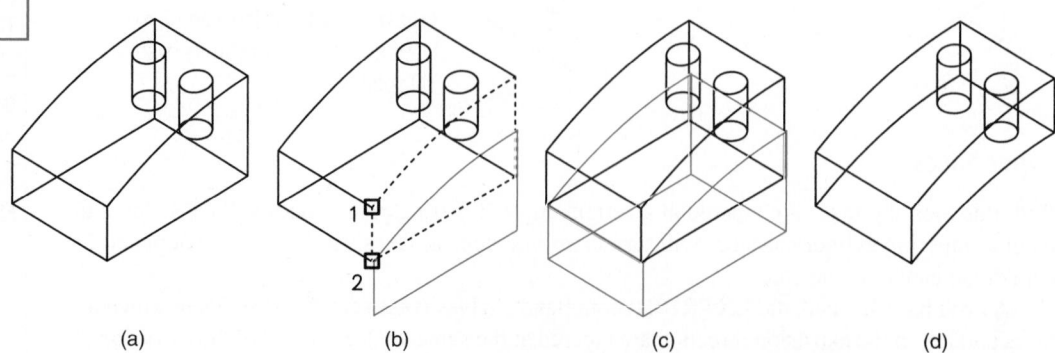

(a)   (b)   (c)   (d)

Figure 24-26 The new faces obtained with the **Copy faces** tool can be used to generate further modifications in the 3D solid

Color Faces

The **Color faces** tool enables you to change the color of individual faces on a 3D solid. Usually, the purpose of such a task is either to achieve a certain artistic look or to improve clarity when modeling.

There are two more aspects you need to know about the colors of solids:

1. Changing the **Color** property of a solid will turn all of its faces to this color.

2. The color of new faces generated by a slice or a Boolean operation will be affected by both the current color and the object's color.

Exercise 24-1: Using the Face Editing Tools

1. **OPEN** either the finished drawing *Project 23-1*, or *Exercise 24-1* in the student data files, in case you did not finish the project.

2. **SAVE** the drawing **AS** *Exercise 24-1 solved.*

3. Select the **SE Isometric** viewing point and the **Top** UCS.

4. Use the **Extrude faces** tool to protrude the front face of the 3D solid shown in Figure 24-27(a). After the operation, the results should look like Figure 24-27(b). Invoke the **Extrude faces** option of the **SOLIDEDIT** command and respond to the prompts as follows:

   `Select faces or [Undo/Remove/ALL]:` *Select the face as shown in* Figure 24-27(a).

   `Select faces or [Undo/Remove/ALL]:` ↵ *(To end the selection)*

   `Specify height of extrusion or [Path]:` *1* ↵

   `Specify angle of taper for extrusion:` *0* ↵

   `Enter a face editing option`

   `[Extrude/Move/Rotate/Offset/Taper/Delete/Copy/coLor/mAterial/Undo/eXit] <eXit>:` *<Esc> (To exit the command)*

To access student data files, go to www.pearsondesigncentral.com.

> **Note:**
> This 3D solid should have been created in one of the projects of the previous chapter. If you don't have this model, take a few minutes to re-create it.

COLOR FACES	
Solid Editing Toolbar	
Ribbon Solid Editing panel	
Pull-down Menu	Modify/ Solids Editing/ Color faces
Command Line	solidedit ↵ f ↵ L

(a)

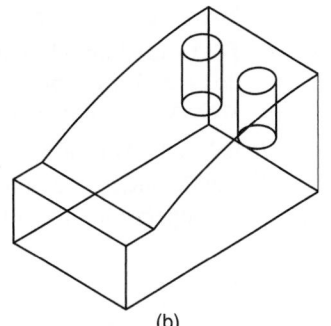

(b)

Figure 24-27   Face to select (a) and the modified 3D solid (b) after the **Extrude faces** operation

5. Invoke the **Move faces** option of the **SOLIDEDIT** command to relocate the two holes. After the operation, the 3D solid should look like Figure 24-28(a). Respond to the prompts as follows:

   `Select faces or [Undo/Remove/ALL]:` *Select the two cylindrical faces of the holes.*

   `Select faces or [Undo/Remove/ALL]:` ↵ *(To end the selection)*

   `Specify a base point or displacement:` *Specify endpoint 1 [Figure 24-28(b)].*

> **Note:**
> The face protrudes a positive distance, perpendicular to its plane.

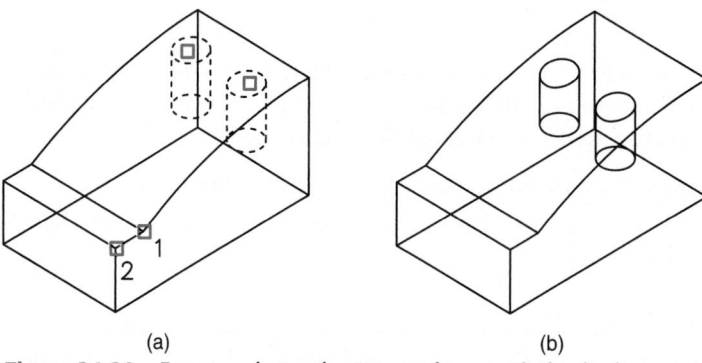

Figure 24-28   Faces to select and points used to specify the displacement
(a) The modified 3D solid after the **Move faces** operation (b)

Specify a second point of displacement:
Specify endpoint 2.

Enter a face editing option

[Extrude/Move/Rotate/Offset/Taper/
Delete/Copy/coLor/mAterial/Undo/eXit]
<eXit>: <Esc> *(To exit the command)*

6. Modify the size of one of the holes. After the operation, the 3D solid should look like Figure 24-29(b). Invoke the **Offset faces** option of the **SOLIDEDIT** command and respond to the prompts as follows:

Select faces or [Undo/Remove/ALL]:
Select the cylindrical face shown in
Figure 24-29.

Select faces or [Undo/Remove/ALL]: ⏎
(To end the selection)

Specify the offset distance: −1/4 ⏎

Enter a face editing option

[Extrude/Move/Rotate/Offset/Taper/
Delete/Copy/coLor/mAterial/Undo/eXit]
<eXit>: <Esc> *(To exit the command)*

7. Select the **Top** UCS.
8. Rotate one of the holes of the 3D solid. After the operation, the results should look like

> **Note:**
> The two holes moved the distance measured between the two points. The cylindrical faces adjust to the new geometric conditions.

> **Note:**
> The selected face enlarges by offsetting the specified distance, adapting its shape to the new geometric conditions.

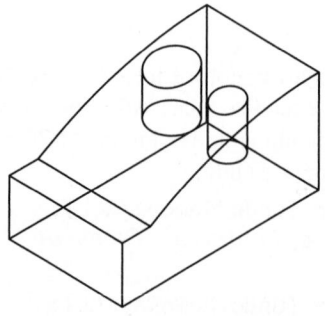

Figure 24-29   Face to select (a) and the modified 3D solid (b) after the
Offset faces operation

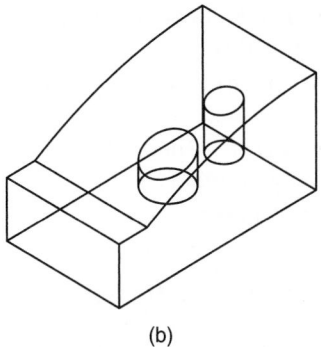

(a)   (b)

Figure 24-30   (a) Face to select and point used to specify the axis of rotation
(b) The modified 3D solid after the **Rotate faces** operation

Figure 24-30(b). Invoke the **Rotate faces** option of the
SOLIDEDIT command and respond to the prompts
as follows:

Select faces or [Undo/Remove/ALL]:
*Select the cylindrical face of the
larger hole [Figure 24-30(a)].*

Select faces or [Undo/Remove/ALL]: ↵
(To end the selection)

**Specify an axis point or [Axis by
object/View/Xaxis/Yaxis/Zaxis]
<2points>:** *z* ↵

**Specify the origin of the rotation
<0,0,0>:** *Specify center point 1.*

**Specify a rotation angle or [Ref-
erence]:** *90* ↵

**Enter a face editing option
[Extrude/Move/Rotate/Offset/Taper/Delete/Copy/coLor/mAterial/Undo
/eXit] <eXit>:** *<Esc> (To exit the command)*

> **Note:**
> The selected face rotates around an imaginary axis parallel to the Z-axis and going through endpoint 1. The face changes to adapt its shape to the new geometrical conditions.

 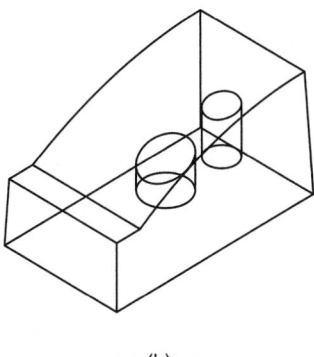

(a)   (b)

Figure 24-31   Faces to select and points used to specify the axis of tapering
(a) The modified 3D solid after the **Taper faces** operation (b)

9. Use the **Taper faces** option of the **SOLIDEDIT** command to modify the faces of the 3D
   solid so it looks like Figure 24-31(b). Respond to the prompts as follows:

   Select faces or [Undo/Remove/ALL]: *Select the two faces shown in
   Figure 24-31(a).*

Select faces or [Undo/Remove/ALL]: ⏎
(To end the selection)

Specify the base point: *Specify end-point 1.*

Specify another point along the axis of tapering: *Specify endpoint 2.*

Specify the taper angle: *5* ⏎

Enter a face editing option

[Extrude/Move/Rotate/Offset/Taper/ Delete/Copy/coLor/mAterial/Undo/ eXit] <eXit>: *<Esc> (To exit the command)*

Note:
The selected faces tilt at a positive angle relative to their base, which was determined by point 1.

10. Select the **Front** UCS.
11. Using the **Taper faces** option of the **SOLIDEDIT** command, taper the cylindrical face of one of the holes, turning it into a conical face. After the operation, the 3D solid should look like Figure 24-32(b). Respond to the prompts as follows:

    Select faces or [Undo/Remove/ALL]: *Select the cylindrical face of the hole as shown in* Figure 24-32(a).

    Select faces or [Undo/Remove/ALL]: ⏎ *(To end the selection)*

    Specify the base point: *Specify center point 1.*

    Specify another point along the axis of tapering: *With the ORTHO mode activated, move the cursor up to specify any point aligned vertically with point 1.*

    Specify the taper angle: *5* ⏎

    Enter a face editing option

    [Extrude/Move/Rotate/Offset/Taper/Delete/Copy/coLor/mAterial/Undo/ eXit] <eXit>: *<Esc> (To exit the command)*

12. Select the different orthographic views and invoke the **3DORBIT** command to inspect the modifications on the 3D solid.
13. **SAVE** the drawing.

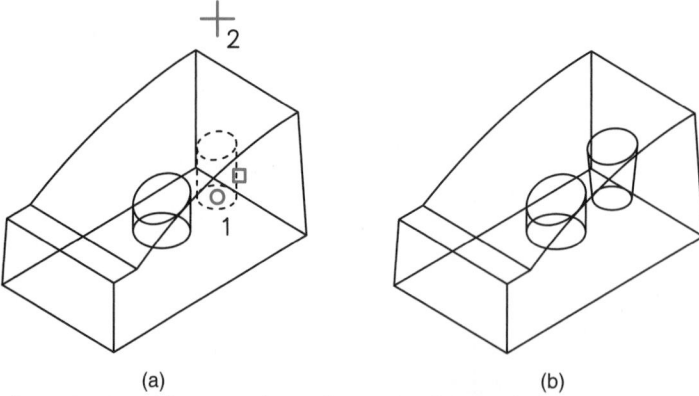

(a)   (b)

Figure 24-32   (a) Face to select and points used to specify the axis of tapering (b) The modified 3D solid after the **Taper faces** operation

EDGE EDITING TOOLS

The edge editing group has fewer tools to modify 3D solids. In fact, no geometric modification is performed on a 3D solid by using this group of tools. Edge editing is limited to extracting the edges or changing their color. As with the face editing tools, only one 3D solid can be used at a time.

Copy Edges

This tool allows you to extract one or more edges of a solid. The objects generated with this tool are lines, arcs, circles, ellipses, and splines.

This tool can save you a good amount of time whether the new extracted edge is used as an extrusion path, or for any other use. An alternative way of extracting edges is to copy the face with the **Copy faces** tool, and then explode the extracted face.

The **Copy edges** tool is also very helpful for other operations. An example is when you need to subtract material from a 3D solid that is swept along one of its edges.

Figure 24-33 shows the process where first the edge is copied over in the same place. (This step can be achieved by specifying the base point and the second point of displacement as the same point.) Next, a cross section is swept along the extracted path. Then the left face of the new 3D solid is extended using the **Offset faces** tool, just to make sure it goes completely through the main 3D solid. Finally, the new 3D solid is subtracted from the main one.

COPY EDGES	
Solid Editing Toolbar	
Ribbon Solid Editing panel	
Pull-down Menu	Modify/ Solids Editing/ Copy edges
Command Line	solidedit ↵ e ↵ c

Figure 24-33 The new edges obtained with the **Copy edges** tool can be used to generate further modifications in the 3D solid

Color Edges

This tool changes the color of the specified edges. Its purpose is mainly to improve clarity when modeling. The color of an edge might change automatically after certain operations are performed, depending on the color currently in use, or the color of the solids interrelating in Boolean operations. In addition, changing the **Color** property of an entire solid will also affect the color of a specific edge.

COLOR EDGES	
Solid Editing Toolbar	
Ribbon Solid Editing panel	
Pull-down Menu	Modify/ Solids Editing/ Color edges
Command Line	solidedit ↵ e ↵ L

BODY EDITING TOOLS

In general, this group contains tools that enable you to perform operations that modify the entire 3D solid. By using these operations you can perform such important modifications to 3D solids as creating a shell or splitting its faces.

Imprint

This tool adds temporary edges to the faces of a 3D solid. It does so by finding the intersections of the solid's faces with another object that passes through the solid or is placed inside it.

Objects that can be imprinted are:

- Wireframe-type objects: arcs, circles, lines, polylines, 3D polylines, ellipses, and splines
- Surface-type objects: regions and surfaces
- 3D solids

IMPRINT	
Solid Editing Toolbar	
Ribbon Solid Editing panel	
Pull-down Menu	Modify/ Solids Editing/ Imprint
Command Line	solidedit ↵ b ↵ i

Figure 24-34   Wireframe objects coincident with the face of the 3D solid are imprinted as edges

For a wireframe-type object to be imprinted, it must be placed on a specific face of the 3D solid (Figure 24-34).

If a wireframe-type object intersects a face of the 3D solid face [Figure 24-35(a)], it will simply be imprinted as a point [Figure 24-35(b)].

Surface-type objects can either be placed on a solid's face or intersect it. After the operation, the intersecting edges of regions and surfaces are imprinted on the 3D solid's faces (Figure 24-36).

(a)

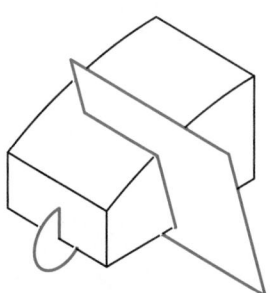

(b)

Figure 24-35   Wireframe objects intersecting the face (a) of the 3D solid are imprinted as points (b)

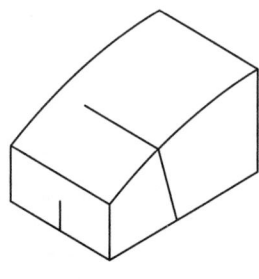

Figure 24-36   Surface-type objects intersecting the face of the 3D solid are imprinted as edges on the 3D solid's faces

A 3D solid object imprints an edge on a 3D solid for each intersection found between the faces of the objects (Figure 24-37).

Depending on the type of object imprinted, there are three types of impressions: points, nonsplitting edges, and splitting edges (Figure 24-38).

Split faces can be selected individually for purposes of performing some face editing operations. Edges imprinted on a 3D solid are automatically eliminated by performing most of the editing operations.

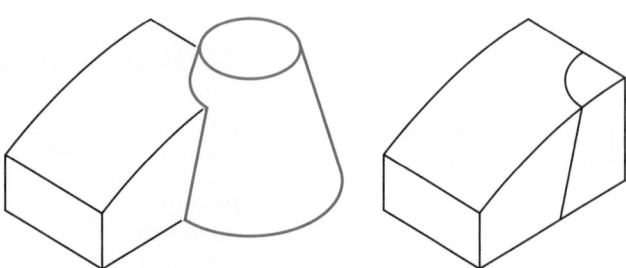

Figure 24-37   3D solids can also imprint their intersecting edges on the faces of other 3D solids

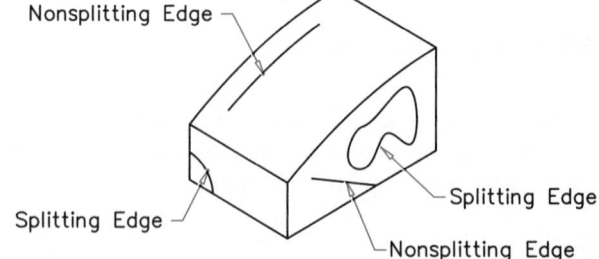

Figure 24-38   Imprinted edges can either split a face or not

---

Exercise 24-2: Splitting Faces with the **Imprint** Tool to Perform Further Face Editing Operations

To access student data files, go to www.pearsondesigncentral.com.

1. **OPEN** either the finished drawing *Project 23-1* or *Exercise 24-1* in the student data files, in case you did not finish *Project 23-1*.
2. **SAVE** the drawing **AS** *Exercise 24-2*.

3. Select the **SE Isometric** viewing point.
4. Select the **Right** UCS.
5. Use the **Copy edges** option of the **SOLIDEDIT** command to copy the selected edge, as indicated in Figure 24-39.
6. Use the **RECTANGLE** command to draw the rectangle in the face of the 3D solid, also as shown in Figure 24-39.

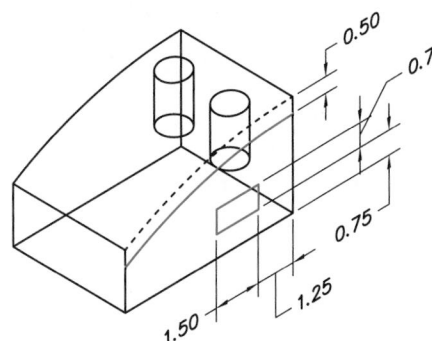

Figure 24-39   Edge to be copied and objects to be drawn on the 3D solid's face

7. Invoke the **Imprint** tool to imprint the arc and the polyline on the 3D solid's face. Respond to the prompts as follows:

   Select a 3D solid: *Select the original solid.*

   Select an object to imprint: *Select the arc.*

   Delete the source object [Yes/No] <N>: *y ↵*

   Select an object to imprint: *Select the rectangle.*

   Delete the source object [Yes/No] <N>: *y ↵*

   Select an object to imprint: <Esc> *(To exit the command)*

Note:
The objects to imprint need to be selected one by one. This enables you to control which particular object should be deleted or kept.

8. Select the **Extrude faces** option of the **SOLIDEDIT** command. When prompted, select the top portion of the face split by the arc and specify **—1**. The face is depressed 1″ after the operation (Figure 24-40).
9. Select the **Taper faces** option of the **SOLIDEDIT** command and click on the split face delimited by the imprinted rectangle (Figure 24-41). Specify midpoint **1** as the base point, and midpoint **2** as the other point along the axis of tapering. Enter **—20** for the taper angle. After the operation, the 3D solid should look like Figure 24-42.
10. With the **Rotate faces** option of the **SOLIDEDIT** command, select the face shown in Figure 24-43. Select endpoints 1 and 2 for the axis of rotation. Enter **45** as the rotation angle. After the operation, the 3D solid should look like Figure 24-44.
11. With the **Right** UCS still current, invoke the **Move faces** option of the **SOLIDEDIT** command and select the four faces of the wedge (Figure 24-45). Move the selected faces orthogonally **0.76″** downward. After the operation, the 3D solid should look like Figure 24-46.
12. **SAVE** the drawing.

Figure 24-40   After extruding the split face

Clean

In reality, imprinted edges do not make much sense geometrically. The **Clean** tool deletes all redundant edges and edges that have been imprinted but not used. This leaves only those that have become actual edges after a face editing operation.

CLEAN	
Solid Editing Toolbar	
Ribbon Solid Editing panel	
Pull-down Menu	Modify/ Solids Editing/ Clean
Command Line	solidedit ↵ b ↵ L

Figure 24-41 Order to specify the axis of tapering in the **Taper faces** operation

Figure 24-42 Resulting modification on the 3D solid

Figure 24-43 Order to specify the axis of rotation in the **Rotate faces** operation

Figure 24-44 Resulting modification on the 3D solid

Figure 24-45 Faces to be selected

Figure 24-46 Resulting modification on the 3D solid after completing the **Move faces** operation

Separate

On certain occasions, you would prefer that separate 3D solids be integrated. But there are many other cases in which they need to be separated. The **Separate** tool separates 3D solids that are made up of more than one isolated piece.

Typically, a 3D solid is made up of a single piece. Some 3D solids, however, are made up of several independent pieces. Two common operations that may result in a 3D solid made up of more than one piece are:

- A **UNION** Boolean operation of two or more 3D solids that do not share any common volume.

- A **SLICE** operation through an imaginary plane that causes the remaining portion of the 3D solid to be made up of more than one piece (Figure 24-47).

SEPARATE	
Solid Editing Toolbar	
Ribbon Solid Editing panel	
Pull-down Menu	Modify/ Solids Editing/ Separate
Command Line	solidedit ↵ b ↵ p

Figure 24-47   3D solid can be made up of more than one piece after a **SLICE** operation

Shell

This is probably the most complex tool of the body editing group. It transforms a 3D solid into a shell-type 3D solid by removing its inside volume, leaving only a solid skin layer of a thickness specified by you. The barrel in Figure 24-48 has been modeled by shelling the solid on its left.

SHELL	
Solid Editing Toolbar	
Ribbon Solid Editing panel	
Pull-down Menu	Modify/ Solids Editing/ Shell
Command Line	solidedit ↵ b ↵ s

Original 3D Solid   Original 3D Solid Section   3D Solid after Shell Operation   Section of 3D Solid after Shell Operation

Figure 24-48   The barrel has been created using a **Shell** operation

Shelling will occur inside the solid's faces if the specified thickness is a positive value. If the thickness is specified as a negative value, then the shelling will occur outside the solid; in this case, the original faces of the solid will become the inside of the shell (Figure 24-49).

Despite the fact that the **Shell** tool belongs to the body editing group, it involves a face selection process. When the tool is first invoked, all of the 3D solid's faces are selected automatically. Thereafter, each face can be individually removed or added to the selection.

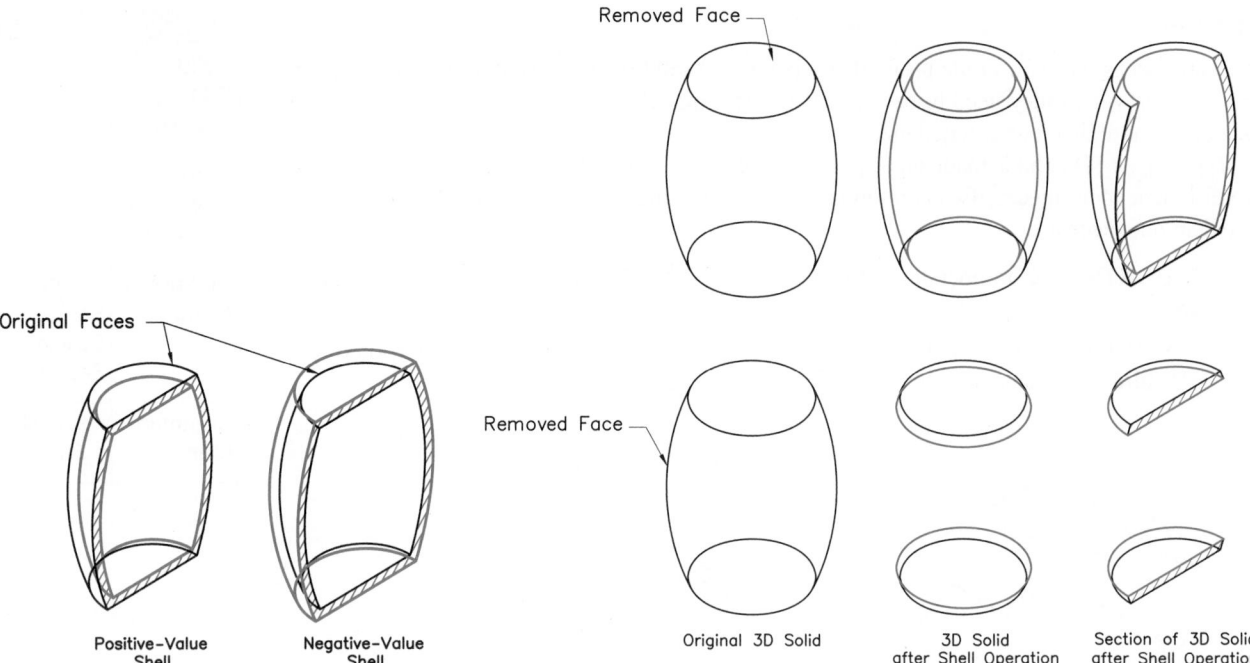

Figure 24-49 According to the sign of the value specified, the shell can occur inside or outside the 3D solid

Figure 24-50 Two **Shell** operations in which different original faces are unselected

After the selection process is completed, the unselected faces will disappear, creating an opening on the solid (Figure 24-50). Controlling the selection process is the key to success with the **Shell** tool.

Exercise 24-3: Using the **Shell** Tool

In this exercise you will perform a **Shell** operation on the 3D solid you have been using for the exercises in this chapter. Pay special attention during the selection process to remove only the bottom face.

1. **OPEN** the finished drawing *Exercise 24-2*.
2. **SAVE** the drawing **AS** *Exercise 24-3*.
3. Select the **SW Isometric** viewing point.
4. Invoke the **Shell** option of the **SOLIDEDIT** command and respond to the prompts as follows:

    Select a 3D solid: *Select the solid by picking any of its edges.*

    Remove faces or [Undo/Add/ALL]: *Select the edge shown in* Figure 24-51.

    Remove faces or [Undo/Add/ALL]: *a* ↵

    Select faces or [Undo/Remove/ALL]: *Select the right face by clicking on it as shown in* Figure 24-52.

    Select faces or [Undo/Remove/ALL]: ↵ *(To end the face selection process)*

    Enter the shell offset distance: *.125* ↵

    Enter a body editing option [Imprint/seParate solids/Shell/ cLean/Check/Undo/eXit] <eXit>: *<Esc> (To exit the command)*

> **Note:**
> By default, all the faces are selected with this tool when you select the 3D solid. From that time on, it is not necessary to hold down the **<Shift>** key to unselect a face because the operation will actually prompt you to select faces for removal.

> **Note:**
> Two faces were removed automatically by selecting the edge. The front face should not have been removed, so you will add it back to the selection.

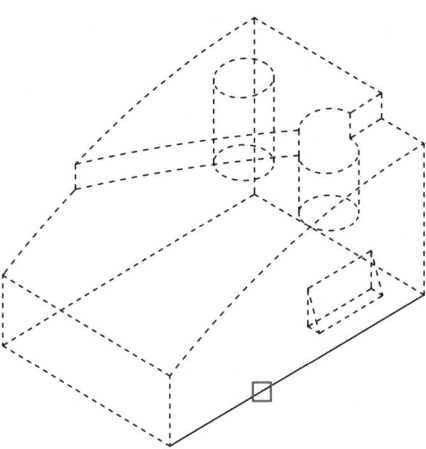

Figure 24-51   Picking the edge shown will remove two faces

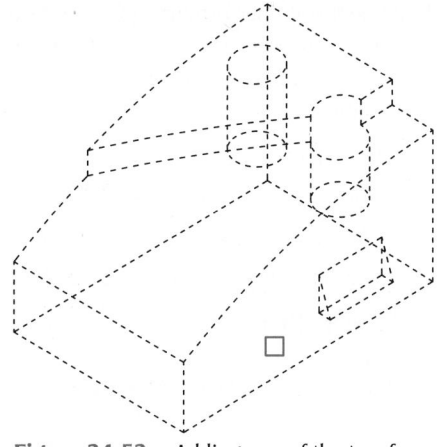

Figure 24-52   Adding one of the two faces removed

5. Select the **Realistic** visual style and invoke the **3DFORBIT** command to inspect the 3D solid with the volume removed. The results should look like Figure 24-53 from two different viewing points.
6. **SAVE** the drawing.

Note:
Even though it appears as if all the faces were selected, they were not. The bottom face was removed and never added back to the selection.

Plastic parts are typically developed as shell-type objects. They consist of thin walls that interconnect, forming the most dissimilar shapes and contours. The **Shell** operation is an excellent application for the design of plastic parts because it allows you to empty the volume of 3D solids, creating shell-type objects with constant wall thickness. Proficiency in the use of this particular tool can be seen as a potential benefit for organizations involved with this widespread manufacturing process.

Figure 24-53   Different shaded views of the final 3D model

CHECK	
Solid Editing Toolbar	
Ribbon Solid Editing panel	
Pull-down Menu	Modify/ Solids Editing/ Check
Command Line	solidedit ↵ b ↵ c

Check

The AutoCAD software uses a technology named ***ShapeManager*** to generate 3D solids. A complex 3D solid can become an invalid ShapeManager solid after a certain operation. If this happens, you

ShapeManager: Modeler or engine used by AutoCAD to change the form and appearance of 3D solids.

will not be able to perform any more edit operations on it. A way to confirm if a 3D solid has become an invalid ShapeManager solid is by invoking the **Check** tool.

Even though face editing operations are not permitted on invalid ShapeManager solids, many operations can still be performed:

- Boolean operations
- Body and edge editing operations
- **SLICE** and **SECTION** commands
- Any standard operation (**ERASE, MOVE, COPY**, etc.)

The **SOLIDCHECK** system variable is related to the **Check** tool. When activated (**1**), which is its default status, it automatically determines whether or not the operation created a valid ShapeManager solid. **SOLIDCHECK** should not be turned off.

OTHER EDITING OPERATIONS WITH 3D SOLIDS

EXTRACTING THE EDGES OF 3D OBJECTS WITH THE XEDGES COMMAND

XEDGES	
Ribbon Solid Editing panel	
Pull-down Menu	Modify/ 3D Operation/ Extract Edges
Command Line	xedges

The **XEDGES** command can be used to extract edges not only from 3D solids but from surfaces and regions as well. If you select the entire object, this command will extract every one of its edges. You can specify which edges to extract by holding down the **<Ctrl>** key and picking the edges directly, or by using any selection tool such as windows and crossing windows.

EDITING ORIGINAL TYPES OF 3D SOLIDS AND SURFACES THROUGH THE PROPERTIES PALETTE

AutoCAD gives a unique, distinctive name to original 3D solids and surfaces according to the operation from which they originated. This name is shown as the **type** of 3D solid or surface, for example:

- Cylinder 3D solid type
- Extrusion 3D solid type
- Sweep-type surface
- Loft with cross section only surface type

You can find out the type of 3D solid or surface of an object through the AutoCAD text window by invoking the **LIST** command. You can also obtain such information from the **Geometry** section in the **Properties** palette (Figure 24-54).

The **Geometry** section of the **Properties** palette contains specific geometric properties about original 3D solids and surfaces. Some of these properties can be modified directly in the **Properties** palette, allowing you to edit the 3D object without invoking any command. Each section of the **Properties** palette can be folded or unfolded by clicking on its double arrow.

In all, there are 13 types of 3D solids and six types of surfaces. Each of the seven types of 3D solid primitives is generated with its own command. The **EXTRUDE, REVOLVE, SWEEP**, and **LOFT** commands generate their own type of 3D solid or surface as well. As you learned in the previous chapter, the **LOFT** command in particular generates three different types of 3D objects, depending on the method used. The **EXTRUDE** command generates a swept 3D object when using the **Path** option.

3D solids that have lost their history due to a postediting operation, as well as those turned into basic representations using the **BREP** command, are not listed as any particular type of 3D solid. Their geometric properties cannot be changed through the **Properties** palette.

Figure 24-54   The **Properties** palette provides information about the type of 3D solid or surface selected

Exercise 24-4: Editing Original 3D Solids Through the **Properties** Palette

1. Start a **NEW** drawing in **Imperial** units.
2. **SAVE** the drawing **AS** *Exercise 24-4*.
3. Select the **SE Isometric** viewpoint.
4. Select the **Realistic** Visual Style.
5. Turn on the **Grid** (**<F7>**).
6. Set the **FACETRES** system variable to **6**.
7. Select the **Green** color in the **Properties** toolbar.
8. Invoke the **CONE** command and create a **Cone** type of 3D Solid. Specify the center point, radius, and height by clicking anywhere in the drawing area while visualizing the object being developed.
9. Select the 3D Solid and open the **Properties** palette. Under **Geometry**, change the following properties (Figure 24-55):
   - **Base radius:** 2.5
   - **Top radius:** 1
   - **Height:** 3
10. **EXPLODE** the cone.
11. **ERASE** the conical surface.
12. **EXPLODE** the top and bottom regions.
13. Invoke the **LOFT** command and create a **Loft with cross sections only** 3D solid. Select the two circles as the cross sections. Finally, accept the **Smooth Fit** surface control in the **Loft Settings** dialog box and click **OK** to close it.
14. Select the 3D solid and open the **Properties** palette if you have previously closed it. Under **Geometry**, change the **Surface Normals** to **Use draft angles**.

Figure 24-55 Modifying a cone-shaped 3D solid through the **Properties** palette

15. Set both the **Start draft angle** and **End draft angle** to **60**. The 3D model should look like Figure 24-56.
16. **SAVE** the drawing.

Figure 24-56 Modifying a **Loft with cross sections only** type of 3D solid through the **Properties** palette

Editing Composite 3D Solids Through the Properties Palette

Composites are not displayed under any particular type of 3D solid. Their geometric properties cannot be changed through the **Properties** palette either. However, the geometric properties of original 3D solids that are involved in the Boolean operation of a composite 3D solid whose **History** is set to **Record** can be changed in the **Properties** palette (Figure 24-57).

The original 3D solids of a composite 3D solid are selected by holding down the **<Ctrl>** key before making the selection. Only original 3D solids defined as a particular type display their geometric properties. Other composite 3D solids and basic representation 3D solids that were used to obtain the composite 3D solid will not display any geometric properties.

Figure 24-57   The properties of the original 3D solids that make up a composite 3D solid can be changed in the **Properties** palette

Using the Grips to Edit 3D Solids and Surfaces

Grips allow you to easily edit original 3D solids and surfaces. The number and location of grips depend on the type of 3D object selected, regardless of its shape. Figure 24-58 shows four identical shapes of different types of 3D solids. The grips show differently from one solid to another. Figure 24-59 shows a similar situation for three types of surfaces.

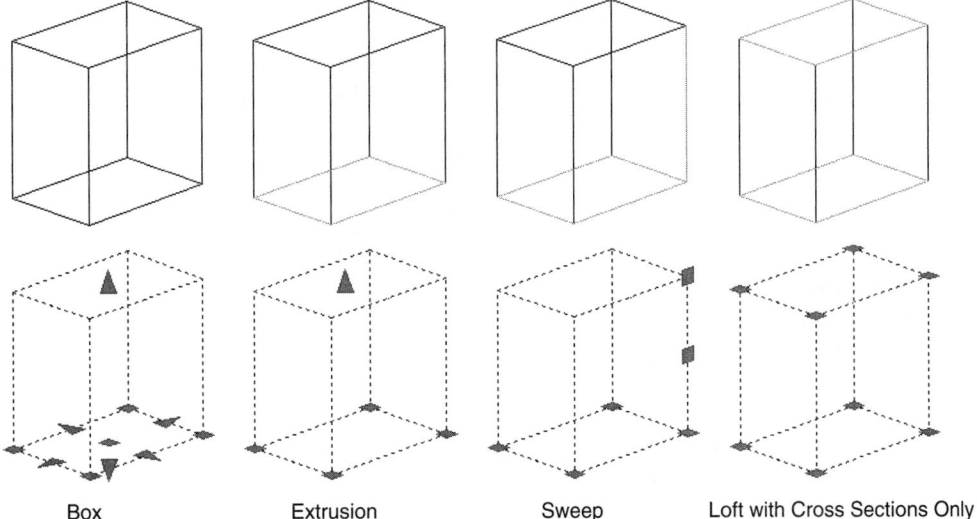

| Box | Extrusion | Sweep | Loft with Cross Sections Only |

Figure 24-58   Different grips are shown for different types of 3D solids

Triangular or directional grips control the length of the 3D solid in a specific direction. These grips are used by all the primitive types and the extrusion type of 3D solids. For example, selecting the directional grips located in the bottom of a box will modify the 3D solid in this specific direction (Figure 24-60).

The standard square grips located in vertices can be used to deform a 3D solid or surface depending on its type and the source object used to obtain it. For example, selecting any standard grip located on the vertex of a box-type 3D solid box can deform two of its dimensions (Figure 24-61).

The grips located on the vertices of an extrusion-type 3D solid can be used to deform the 3D solid only if the profile used was a closed polyline (Figure 24-62). If the 3D solid was created from a region or a surface, however, you will not be able to deform it using the standard grips.

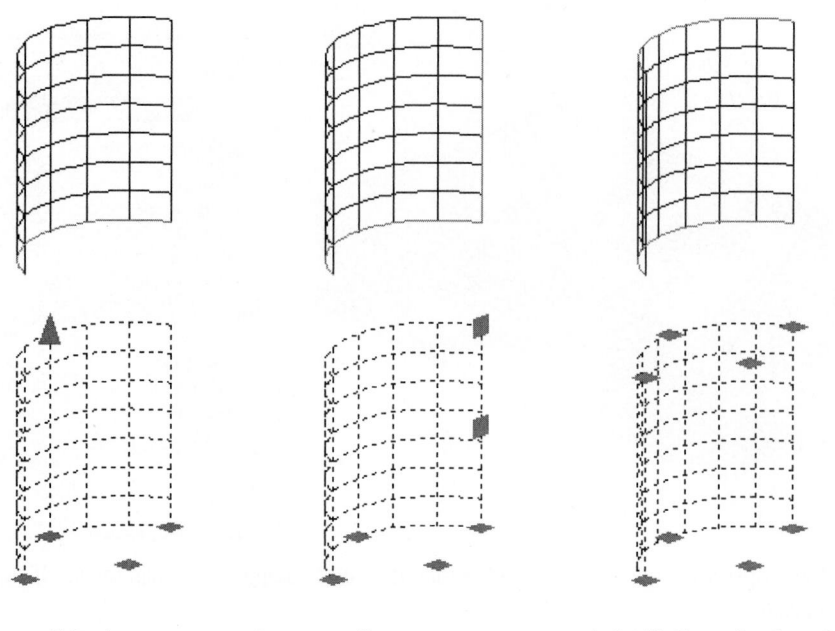

| Extrusion | Sweep | Loft with Cross Sections Only |

Figure 24-59   Different grips are shown for different types of surfaces

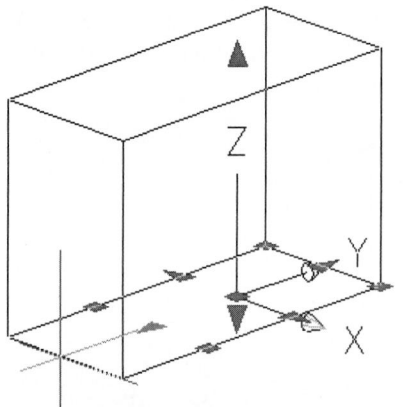

Figure 24-60   When triangular or directional grips are pulled, the 3D solid changes its size in the direction in which it is pulled

Figure 24-61   When a standard grip of a box-type 3D solid is pulled, it is deformed in two directions

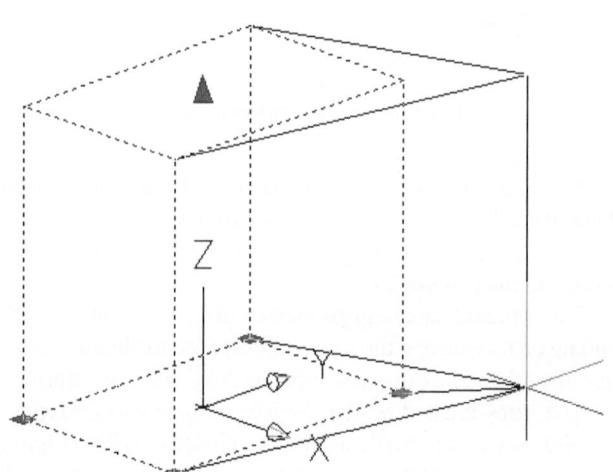

Figure 24-62   When a standard grip of an extruded-type 3D solid is pulled, the object is deformed differently from the box

Selecting the grips of swept-type 3D solids and surfaces enables you to modify both the profile and the sweep path control grips. Modifying the sweep path control grips also affects the plane in which the profile was placed in order to maintain its perpendicularity (Figure 24-63).

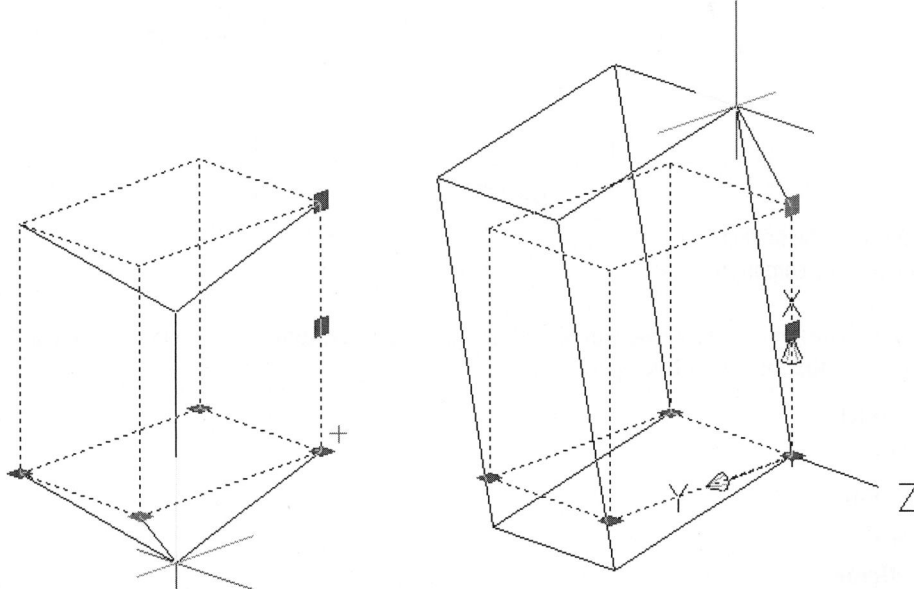

Figure 24-63   Different modifications can be made by pulling the grips of swept-type 3D solids

Loft with cross sections only and **Loft with path**–type 3D objects can be deformed by selecting the control grips of any of the cross sections' profiles, as well as the path (Figure 24-64). **Loft with guide curves**–type 3D objects cannot be deformed using standard grips.

Composite 3D solids, as well as other 3D solids that have lost their history due to a postediting operation or through the **BREP** command, will show only the base control grip when they are selected (Figure 24-65).

You can, however, select and modify the grips of the original 3D solids of a composite 3D solid by holding down the **<Ctrl>** key before making the selection (Figure 24-66).

Note:
Deforming a 3D object by selecting the standard grips will not cause the type of 3D object's condition to be lost. A swept-type surface, for example, will still be a swept-type surface after being edited using its grips.

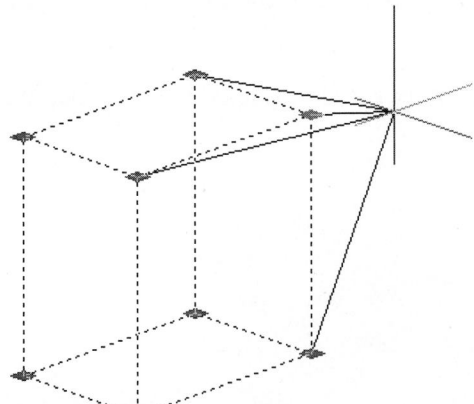

Figure 24-64   The cross sections of lofted 3D solids can be deformed by pulling the grips

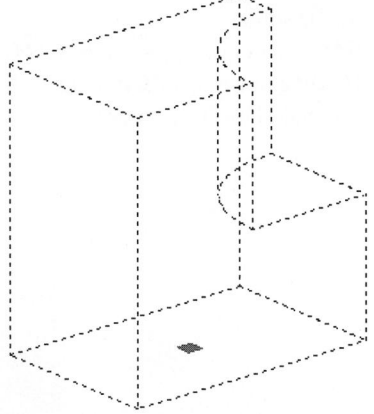

Figure 24-65   Only the positional grip shows up in a basic representation 3D solid

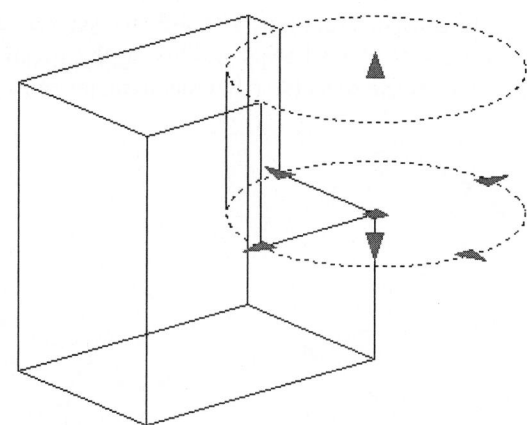

Figure 24-66 The original 3D solids of a selected composite

As with wire-type objects, you can cycle through the grip editing routine. This allows you to perform one of the following five operations:

- **Stretch**
- **Move**
- **Rotate**
- **Scale**
- **Mirror**

To move on to the next operation, you must press the **<Space>** key.

```
** STRETCH **
Specify stretch point or [Base point/Copy/Undo/eXit]:
** MOVE **
Specify move point or [Base point/Copy/Undo/eXit]:
** ROTATE **
Specify rotation angle or [Base point/Copy/Undo/Reference/eXit]:
** SCALE **
Specify scale factor or [Base point/Copy/Undo/Reference/eXit]:
** MIRROR **
Specify second point or [Base point/Copy/Undo/eXit]:
```

For the primitives type of 3D solids, these operations are available only when selecting the base control grip.

Exercise 24-5: Editing the Original 3D Solid of a Composite 3D Solid by Using the Grips

To access student data files, go to www.pearsondesigncentral.com.

1. **OPEN** the drawing *Exercise 24-5* in the student data files. It contains a simple composite 3D solid.
2. **SAVE** the drawing as *Exercise 24-5 solved*.
3. Holding down the **<Ctrl>** key, click on one of the arc edges (Figure 24-67) to select the original 3D solid cylinder.

Figure 24-67 The original cylinder of a composite 3D solid is selected

4. Select the arrow grip shown in Figure 24-68. With the **ORTHO** mode on, move the pointer toward the arrow direction and enter **0.5** in the command line to increase the radius of the cylinder by 0.5″.

5. Press the **<Esc>** key to clear the grips.

6. **SAVE** the drawing.

Figure 24-68   The original cylinder is modified by pulling one of its grips; as a result, the composite 3D solid is modified

EDITING 3D SOLIDS BY MODIFYING THE SUBOBJECTS

Subobjects are elements of an inferior order that are part of a 3D solid. Original 3D solids combined into a composite 3D solid can be considered to be subobjects as well. The term *subobjects,* however, more often refers to the elements forming part of any type of 3D solid, including basic representation solids. Faces, edges, and vertices are all subobjects of 3D solids.

You can select subobjects by holding down the **<Ctrl>** key, which is the same procedure used to select original 3D solids of a composite 3D solid. Figure 24-69 shows the three types of subobject selected, each on a different 3D solid. As with the meshes, the subobject filters can be used to ease the selection process.

subobject: Any face, edge, or vertex of a 3D solid. The original 3D solids of a composite 3D solid can be considered as subobjects as well.

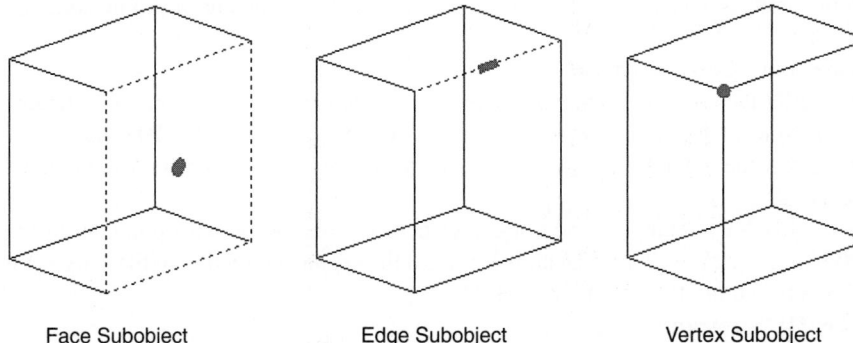

Face Subobject   Edge Subobject   Vertex Subobject

Figure 24-69   The three types of subobjects and their typical grips

You can simultaneously select multiple subobjects from different 3D solids, using any selection method such as windows and crossing windows (Figure 24-70).

After selecting the subobject, you can either select its grip to relocate it, or invoke the standard **MOVE, ROTATE,** and **SCALE** commands to deform the 3D object. For example, scaling down the selected face in Figure 24-71(a), based on the endpoint shown, will deform a box into the 3D solid shown in Figure 24-71(b).

As another example, moving down the selected edge in Figure 24-72(a) will deform the box into the 3D solid shown in Figure 24-72(b).

Selecting a 3D solid's subobjects creates an infinite number of editing possibilities. You can combine faces, edges, and vertices in the same operation.

Note:
Deforming a 3D object by using the subobjects will cause the information on the type of 3D object to be lost, turning the object into a basic representation 3D solid.

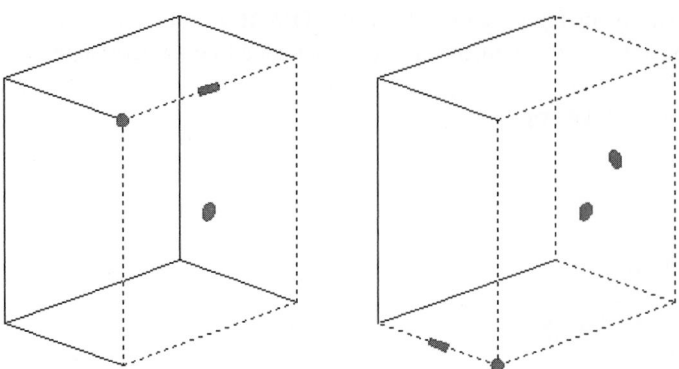

Figure 24-70   Several subobjects selected

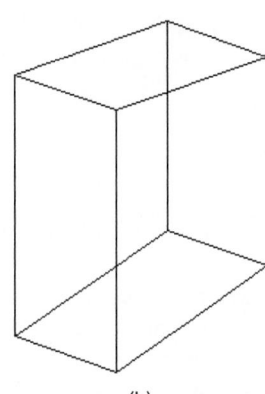

(a)   (b)   (a)   (b)

Figure 24-71   (a) A selected face subobject (b) After it is scaled down with its base on the selected endpoint

Figure 24-72   (a) A selected edge subobject (b) After it is moved down

---

Exercise 24-6: Editing the Original 3D Solid of a Composite 3D Solid by Using the Grips

To access student data files, go to www.pearsondesigncentral.com.

1. **OPEN** the drawing *Exercise 24-5* in the student data files. It contains a simple composite 3D solid.
2. **SAVE** the drawing as *Exercise 24-6.*
3. Invoke the **BREP** command by entering its name in the command line, or change the **History** property to **None** in the **Properties** palette. This will erase the history of the 3D solid.
4. Holding down the **<Ctrl>** key, click on the cylindrical face to select this subobject (Figure 24-73).
5. Invoke the **MOVE** command, and click anywhere to specify the base point. With the **ORTHO** mode activated, move the pointer toward the negative direction of the *Y*-axis and enter **0.5** in the command line (Figure 24-74).
6. Select the **2D Wireframe** visual style.
7. Practice deforming the 3D solid by selecting vertex and edge subobjects.
8. **SAVE** the drawing.

Figure 24-73   A selected face subobject

Figure 24-74   3D solid modified by moving the face subobject

CHAPTER SUMMARY

Just like 2D drawings, 3D models frequently need to be changed. Regardless of the nature of the revision, the changes need to be made somehow.

Throughout this chapter you have learned the use of tools that modify the geometry of 3D solids. The knowledge acquired here should allow you to perform many of these changes. It is not always easy, however, to make major modifications on 3D solids. Sometimes starting from scratch is the best solution.

Besides the editing operations performed with the **SOLIDEDIT** command, as well as the use of grips and subobjects with 3D solids,

you have also learned particular tools, such as the **Shell** tool, that are used to obtain specific geometric shapes. The **Shell** operation is a key operation in the design of objects with thin walls, such as plastic parts. Other tools will allow you to extract geometry that can be used in other operations (e.g., **Copy Faces**, **Copy Edges**, and the **XEDGES** command).

You have also learned how to split the faces of 3D solids with the **Imprint** tool. After you become familiar with this new tool as well as the others presented in this chapter, you should be able to create a greater number of different 3D solid shapes in less time.

CHAPTER TEST QUESTIONS

Multiple Choice

1. Which of the following is not one of the categorized groups of tools contained in the **SOLIDEDIT** command?
   a. Vertex
   b. Edge
   c. Face
   d. Body

2. When selecting faces within the **SOLIDEDIT** command, which of the following actions will be accepted by AutoCAD?
   a. Picking a face
   b. Picking an edge
   c. Picking a silhouette
   d. All of the above

3. If you had to change the location of a hole through a board-shaped 3D solid, which of the following operations could you not use?
   a. Subobject editing
   b. Grip editing
   c. **Taper faces**
   d. **Move faces**

4. If you had to modify the length of a slot through a board-shaped 3D solid, which of the following operations could you use?
   a. **Copy faces**
   b. **Offset faces**
   c. **Move faces**
   d. **Rotate faces**

5. A cylindrical face of a 3D solid having a radius of 1.25 is edited using the **Offset faces** tool. If the offset distance specified is **–0.25**, what will the final radius of the edited face be?
   a. 1.50
   b. 1.25
   c. 1.00
   d. None of the above

6. With the **Rotate faces** operation, which of the following options is not available to define the imaginary axis of rotation?
   a. Selecting an object
   b. Selecting an edge
   c. Specifying two points
   d. The viewing plane

7. Which of the following operations could not be used to transform a 3D solid cone into a cylinder?
   a. Changing the geometry in the **Properties** palette
   b. **Rotate faces**
   c. Grip editing
   d. **Taper faces**

8. Which of the following objects could not be imprinted on the face of a 3D solid?
   a. Polyline
   b. 3D solid
   c. Spline
   d. Polygon mesh

9. The tools of the **SOLIDEDIT** command will not allow you to change the color of which of the following elements of 3D solids?
   a. The edges
   b. The faces
   c. The entire body
   d. All of the above

10. Which of the following is not a valid type of 3D object?
    a. Swept 3D solid
    b. **Loft with cross sections only** surface
    c. Cone surface
    d. 3D solid cylinder

Matching

a. **Shell**

b. **Separate**

c. **XEDGES**

d. **Move faces**

e. **Imprint**

1. Faces, edges, and vertices of 3D solids

2. Causes the faces of 3D solids to incline

3. Moves the faces of a 3D solid

4. Extracts the 3D solid faces as surfaces and regions

5. Relocates the faces parallel to their original location

f. **Extrude faces**

g. **Copy faces**

h. **Offset faces**

i. **Subobjects**

j. **Taper faces**

6. Makes the isolated pieces of 3D solids independent

7. Removes the inside volume of a 3D solid

8. Extracts edges from a 3D solid

9. Protrudes planar faces of a 3D solid

10. Adds temporary edges to a 3D solid's faces

CHAPTER TUTORIALS

Tutorial 24-1: The Enclosure of a Light Fixture

1. Start the project by opening a **NEW** drawing using **Imperial** units.
2. **SAVE** the drawing **AS** *Tutorial 24-1*.
3. Set the **DISPSILH** system variable to **1**.
4. Set the **ISOLINES** system variable to **0**.
5. Set the **FACETRES** system variable to **6**.
6. Select the **SE Isometric** viewing point.
7. Select the **Right** UCS.
8. Draw a **4″**-diameter circle anywhere.
9. **EXTRUDE** the circle **–6″**. Specify 5° as the angle of taper by using the corresponding option.
10. Select the **Top** view.
11. Using the **RECTANGLE** command, draw the polyline highlighted in Figure 24-75. Place it as indicated.
12. **MIRROR** the rectangle symmetrically to the other side of the cone.

> **TIP** From an orthographic view you can use the quadrants or the center points to mirror objects around the axis of cones and cylinders.

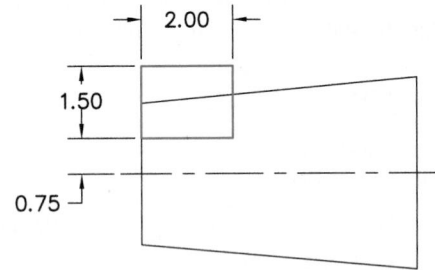

Figure 24-75   Dimensions for the rectangle

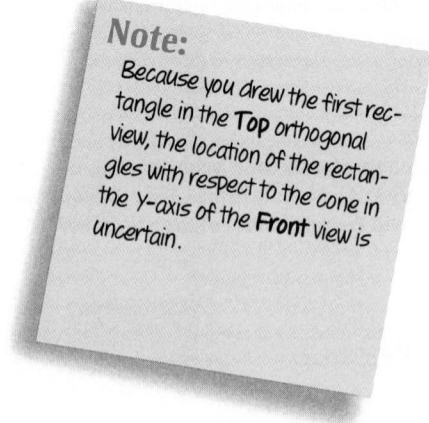

Note: Because you drew the first rectangle in the **Top** orthogonal view, the location of the rectangles with respect to the cone in the Y-axis of the **Front** view is uncertain.

13. Select the **Front** view.
14. **MOVE** the two rectangles down orthogonally so that all their points are below the cone (Figure 24-76).
15. **EXTRUDE** the two rectangles a positive height value, large enough to go over the top of the cone (Figure 24-77).

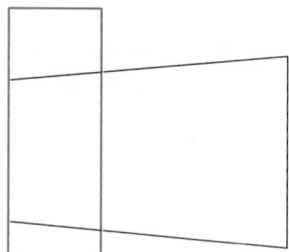

Figure 24-76   After the rectangles are moved

Figure 24-77   After the rectangles are extruded

TIP   A good approach here to specifying a distance without knowing the specific value is to click on any two points in the drawing area.

16. **SUBTRACT** the two new 3D solids from the cone.
17. Select the **SW Isometric** viewing point.
18. Invoke the **Rotate faces** option of the **SOLIDEDIT** command. Select the face highlighted in Figure 24-78. Specify the points for the axis of rotation by snapping to the endpoints indicated. Enter **30** for the rotation angle.
19. Repeat the same operation to rotate the corresponding face on the other side **30°**.
20. Select the **Top** view. The 3D model should look like Figure 24-79.
21. Select the **SW Isometric** viewing point.
22. After selecting the proper UCS, draw the three **1″**-diameter circles on the faces of the 3D solid, as shown highlighted in Figure 24-80.

Figure 24-78   Face to select and points specified to define the axis of rotation

Figure 24-79   A top view of the 3D model

Figure 24-80   Circles to be imprinted

TIP   Selecting the **Top** view will reveal whether the three circles are correctly placed on top of the planar faces.

23. Invoke the **Imprint** body editing tool, and imprint all three circles on the faces of the 3D solid. Select **Yes** when prompted to delete the source objects.
24. Invoke the **Extrude faces** tool, and select the three circular faces split by the **Imprint** operation. Protrude the three faces **0.375″** and accept **0** as the angle of taper (Figure 24-81).

TIP   To select faces located in the back, you can either use the **3D Orbit** tool within the command and pick the face directly, or you can select two faces by picking a common edge and then remove the one that is not needed.

25. Select the **SW Isometric** viewing point.
26. **SLICE** the 3D solid in half, keeping only the bottom half (Figure 24-82).
27. With the **Copy faces** tool of the **SOLIDEDIT** command, copy the face highlighted in Figure 24-83 over in the same place.
28. Invoke the **Delete faces** tool to delete the half cylinder in the back (Figure 24-84).

Figure 24-81   After extruding the split faces

Figure 24-82   The 3D solid sliced in half

Figure 24-83   The face copied in place

Figure 24-84   After deleting the half cylinder in the back

TIP   Remember, to copy a face over, specify the base point and the second point in the same place.

TIP   To delete the half cylinder, only two faces of the 3D solid should be selected for the operation: the face you just copied over and the cylindrical face.

29. Invoke the **Taper faces** tool of the **SOLIDEDIT** command. Incline the three highlighted faces, and specify the axis of tapering by snapping to the two endpoints shown in Figure 24-85. Specify **10** when prompted for the taper angle.

Because the three vertical faces are located one next to the other, they can be selected by picking the two shared edges.

30. After you invoke the **HIDE** command, the 3D solid should look like Figure 24-86.

Figure 24-85   Faces selected and points specified to define the axis of tapering

Figure 24-86   Resulting shape after the **Taper faces** operation

31. Select the **Front** view.
32. **EXTRUDE** the region extracted previously **–0.5,** with **0** as the angle of taper (Figure 24-87).

Figure 24-87   The region extruded toward the 3D solid

33. Join the two 3D solids with the **UNION** command.
34. Select the **SW Isometric** viewing point.
35. **FILLET** the four individual highlighted edges (Figure 24-88). Specify **0.125** as the **Radius** value.
36. **FILLET** the chain of highlighted edges (Figure 24-89) using the previous **Radius** value.

Figure 24-88   Edges to be selected for the **FILLET** operation

Figure 24-89   Chain of edges to be selected for a second **FILLET** operation

37. Invoke the **Offset faces** editing tool and select the two faces highlighted in Figure 24-90. Specify an offset distance of **–0.25** to shorten the length of the two half cylinders by 0.25″.

38. Invoke the **Shell** tool of the **SOLIDEDIT** command. When prompted, select the 3D solid, picking it on any of its edges. Pick the four highlighted edges in Figure 24-91 to remove the corresponding faces from the selection. Finally, press **<Enter↵>** to end the selection, and enter **0.09** as the shell offset distance.

Figure 24-90   Faces to select for the **Offset faces** operation

Figure 24-91   Edges where the 3D solid can be picked for the **Shell** operation; they will be picked to remove faces as well

39. Select the **Realistic** visual style.
40. Invoke the **3DORBIT** command to inspect the 3D solid (Figure 24-92).

Figure 24-92   A shaded view of the resulting **Shell** operation

41. Invoke the **MIRROR3D** command. When prompted, select the 3D solid and specify any three points on the top face.
42. Invoke the **UNION** command to join the two 3D solids. The 3D model should look like Figure 24-93.
43. **SAVE** your drawing.

Figure 24-93   The 3D model after joining the two mirrored halves

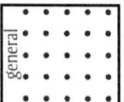

Tutorial 24-2: Revising Plastic Part Design

You have received a fax from one of your customers that informs you of several required changes on a product that you are designing. The customer has used a printout of the 3D view to write some comments for you (Figure 24-94).

1— ELIMINATE RECESS ON HOLES

2— CHANGE GENERAL TAPER TO 3°

3— ELIMINATE AT LEAST 30% OF MATERIAL, WITHOUT LOSING CONTACT AREA WITH WIRE

Figure 24-94   Revision request received from a customer via fax

1. **OPEN** the finished *Tutorial 23-1*.
2. **SAVE** the drawing **AS** *Tutorial 24-2*.
3. Select the **SE Isometric** viewing point.
4. Let's start with comment 1. Invoke the **Delete faces** tool and, when prompted, select the four faces that are related to the two recessed holes. Select the surfaces by picking the two edges highlighted in Figure 24-95. Finish the operation by pressing **<Enter.↵>** and then **<Esc>**.

Note:
To take care of the taper angle, you need to divide the process into three parts. This is because the two vertical flat faces of the middle tunnel through which the wire will run need to be tapered as well. These faces, however, do not start at the same height as the other vertical faces. The interior conical faces also need to be tapered, in the opposite direction.

Figure 24-95   Edges to be selected

5. Invoke the **Taper faces** option of the **SOLIDEDIT** command. When prompted, select the four outer vertical faces by picking the two edges highlighted in Figure 24-96. Specify the axis of tapering by snapping to the two center points in the order shown. Enter **1** for the taper angle.

Note: If you taper the vertical faces inside the tunnel, the plane of tapering will not move with the operation, regardless of where you locate it. This will cause the tangency between the planar face and the cylindrical face to be lost (Figure 24-97).

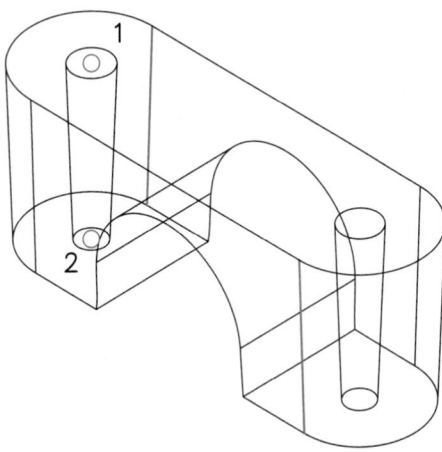

Figure 24-96   Edges to pick when selecting the faces and points to specify the axis of tapering

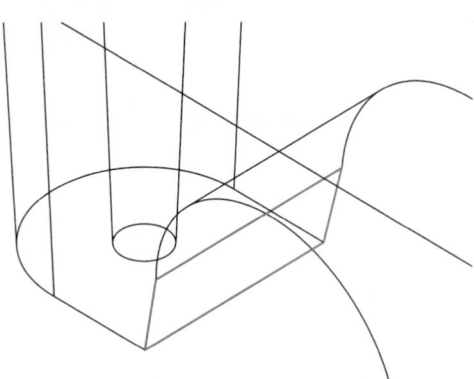

Figure 24-97   Tapering the highlighted face will lose the tangency with the cylindrical face

6. Invoke the **Rotate faces** option of the **SOLIDEDIT** command. When prompted, select the face inside the tunnel highlighted in Figure 24-98. Specify the axis of rotation by snapping to the two center points of the cylindrical face of the tunnel in the order shown. Enter **1** for the rotation angle.
7. Repeat the previous step for the other vertical face in the tunnel. Consider using the right-hand rule to determine which point to snap to first for a positive rotation angle.
8. Select the **Front** view.
9. Create an angular dimension to check whether the **Rotate faces** operation was successful or not. It should read **6°** (Figure 24-99).
10. **DELETE** the angular dimension.
11. Select the **SE Isometric** viewing point.
12. Invoke the **Taper faces** tool and, when prompted, select the two conical faces by picking a silhouette line on each face. Specify the axis of tapering by snapping to the bottom and top center points on either of these two faces. Select first the one at the bottom. Enter **1** for the taper angle.
13. Invoke the **MASSPROP** command. When prompted, select the 3D D solid and press **<Enter↵>**.
14. Select the **Front** UCS.
15. Invoke the **Move faces** option of the **SOLIDEDIT** command. When prompted, select the two conical faces highlighted on Figure 24-100. Move them orthogonally **0.0469″** along the negative direction of the *X*-axis.

Note: Before trying to provide a solution for comment 3, we must find out the current volume of the 3D solid so we can compare it with the new volume after certain modifications.

Note: After invoking the **MASSPROP** command, you can read that the actual volume of the 3D solid is **0.0706** cubic inch.

TIP When performing face editing operations with small values, you can determine whether the operation is performed correctly by looking at the display when pressing **<Enter.⏎>**.

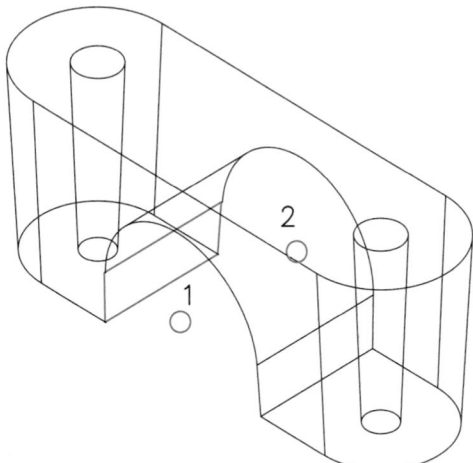

Figure 24-98   Face to select and points used to specify the axis of rotation

Figure 24-99   Checking the result of the operation

MASSPROP	
Inquiry Toolbar	
Ribbon Inquiry Editing panel	
Pull-down Menu	Tools/ Inquiry/ Region/ Mass Properties
Command Line	massprop

Figure 24-100   Faces to select for the **Move faces** operation

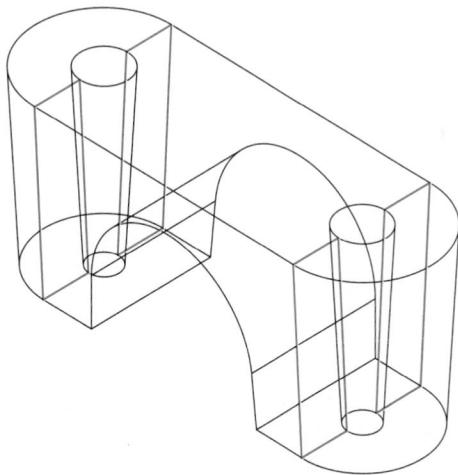

Figure 24-101   After splitting the 3D solid into three pieces

16. Repeat another **MOVE** operation, selecting the conical faces on the other side of the 3D solid. Move the faces **0.0469″** along the positive direction of the *XY*-axis.

17. Using the **SLICE** command, cut the 3D solid into three pieces by defining the imaginary slicing planes parallel to the *YZ* plane and going through one of the center points of each conical hole (Figure 24-101).

18. Invoke the **Offset faces** option of the **SOLIDEDIT** command. Offset each of the end conical faces **−0.0469″**.

19. With the **UNION** operation, join the three 3D solids again. The 3D model should look like Figure 24-102.

20. Invoke the **Taper faces** option of the **SOLIDEDIT** command. When prompted, select the four faces highlighted in Figure 24-103. Specify the axis of tapering by snapping to the two center points in the order shown. Enter **3** as the angle of taper.

Figure 24-102 After offsetting the extreme faces and performing the **UNION** operation

Figure 24-103 Faces to select and points used to specify the axis of tapering

Figure 24-104 The final 3D solid model after it is modified

Note:
Checking the mass properties of the 3D solid reveals that its new volume is **0.0630** cubic inch. Your goal, however, is to take it below **0.0494** cubic inch.

21. Check the volume of the 3D solid again. This time, its value is **0.0460** cubic inch, which achieves your goal. The final 3D solid should look like Figure 24-104 after you hide the lines.
22. **SAVE** your drawing.

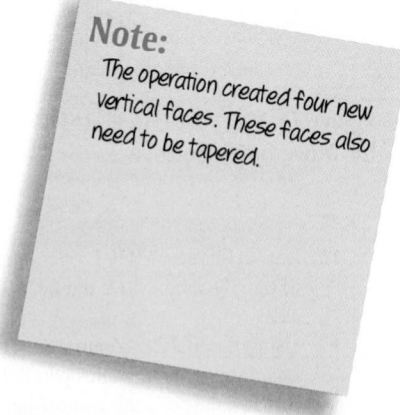

Note:
The operation created four new vertical faces. These faces also need to be tapered.

Most design time is usually dedicated to performing necessary adjustments, corrections, and other changes. This task can certainly be complicated in 3D models. The proper use of procedures and techniques, however, as exemplified in this tutorial can become an important asset. Understanding and applying these tools in the design process shows your ability to efficiently interact with customers in achieving specific objectives.

CHAPTER PROJECTS

Project 24-1: Solid Model of the Community Recreational Hall

In this project you will develop a community recreational hall using 3D solids and surface objects. Use as many of the solids editing tools as possible.

When you are finished, the building will look like Figure 24-105. The dimensions for this project are shown in Figure 24-106.

Figure 24-105   The completed 3D model of the community recreational hall

Figure 24-106   Dimensions for the community recreational hall

Hints for the Project

Because the purpose of this project is to use the solids editing tools, you will not use the Boolean operations. To create the openings in the walls, you can imprint 2D objects and then extrude the split faces. To create the roof as a single piece, you can create a block, and then split and taper all the vertical faces one by one.

Project 24-2: Finishing the Light Fixture

In this project you will finish the 3D model of the light fixture. The main part or enclosure was created in *Tutorial 24-1*.

This project will become an assembly after you put the other three components in their proper place. When you are finished, rotate the light fixture enclosure **20°** downward. The finished project will look like Figure 24-107.

It is recommended that you create the rest of the components in a separate file. This will allow your computer to process less information, and therefore work faster.

Hints for the Project

The dimensions for the rest of the components are shown in Figure 24-108. The revolved component can be produced easily by using the **Shell** body editing tool.

Figure 24-107   The completed 3D model of the light fixture

Figure 24-108   Dimensions for the components of the light fixture

Chapter Objectives

- Strengthen the knowledge you have acquired throughout previous chapters.
- Learn advanced approaches to quickly achieve complex 3D models.
- Walk through a real design process using 3D solid modeling.
- Put together the most-used tasks in a single project.
- Practice the manipulation of the UCS and the viewing system.
- Learn how to take advantage of the most commonly used solids editing tools.
- Evaluate different practical approaches that can be performed with 3D solids.
- Practice the different operations applied in the development of 3D assembly models.

INTRODUCTION

In this chapter you will go through the design process of a real product: a bench vise. In this detailed tutorial project, which starts from scratch, you will practice many of the tools learned in the previous chapters.

You will be able to achieve the final result by following the steps. You should not discard the possibility, however, of trying different approaches you could use at any step. There are always multiple possible solutions for almost every task in 3D modeling.

You can activate any visual style at any time. You can also invoke the **HIDE** or the **3DORBIT** command at any time. Using these tools will give you a clearer understanding of the operation you have just performed. Just remember to go back to the original viewing point and UCS so that the results reflect the assumed settings for the next step. Not having the correct settings for the viewing point and the UCS might end in an unexpected outcome.

Unless your 3D model has many parts, you don't need to use different layers for the modeling stage of a 3D project. Using different colors for different objects, however, is very helpful, especially for distinguishing which edge belongs to each object. Like any other object, 3D solids are created with the current color. Boolean operations affect the color of individual faces as well, depending on the color of the interacting objects.

MODELING THE MAIN BODY

You start the development of a 3D solid by creating one or more original 3D solids. These are then combined by performing several Boolean operations. Then other post-operations are performed to achieve the main geometry. Fillets, chamfers, and holes are performed at the end of the modeling process.

It is not necessary to place any dimensions, centerlines, or any other annotation. Their only purpose is to help you follow the instructions.

1. Start a **NEW** drawing using **Imperial** units. Select the **acad** template to do so.
2. **SAVE** it **AS** *Main Body*.
3. Set or check the value of the following system variables as specified:
   - **DISPSILH** to **1**.
   - **ISOLINES** to **0**.
   - **FACETRES** to **9**.
   - **VIEWRES** to **4000**.
   - **UCSORTHO** to **1**.
   - **UCSFOLLOW** to **0**.
4. Select the **Front** view.
5. Draw the objects shown in Figure 25-1 anywhere in the 3D space.
6. Invoke the **REGION** command and create a region from the objects.

TIP Remember, the objects must touch each other at their endpoints to form a closed profile. Otherwise, they will not become a region.

7. Select the **Right** view.
8. Draw the objects shown in Figure 25-2.

Figure 25-1   Profile dimensions

Figure 25-2   Profile dimensions

Figure 25-3   Shaded view of the composite region

9. Invoke the **REGION** command and, when prompted, select all the objects.
10. **SUBTRACT** the three circular regions from the main region.
11. Select the **Conceptual** visual style. If the operation was successfully performed, the shaded view should look like Figure 25-3.
12. Select the **2D Wireframe** visual style and the **SE Isometric** viewing point.

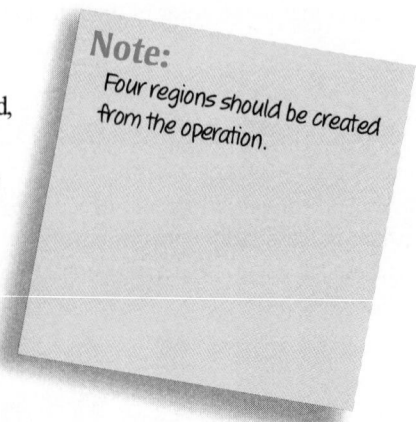

Note:
Four regions should be created from the operation.

13. **MOVE** one of the regions from one of its endpoints to the endpoint of the other region created (Figure 25-4).

14. With the **Right** UCS still current, **EXTRUDE** the profile on your left **–3.00** units and the one on your right **–1.50** units. Specify **0** as the angle of taper for both extrusions.

15. Invoke the **INTERSECT** command and select both 3D solids (Figure 25-5). The results with the occulted lines removed are shown on the right side of the figure.

Note:
This 3D solid object will be called Jaw.

Figure 25-4   One of the regions is moved to the other region

Figure 25-5   The 3D solid resulting from the **INTERSECT** operation

16. Select the **Right** UCS.
17. Create the region shown in Figure 25-6.
18. Select the **Front** UCS and create the region shown in Figure 25-7.
19. Select the **Front** UCS. Turn **ORTHO** mode off and **MOVE** the last region created from its top-left corner to the top-right corner of the other region. After the operation, your model should look like Figure 25-8.
20. Select the **Top** UCS and then create the region shown in Figure 25-10.

Note:
Due to the fillet radius in that particular corner, there is not a physical point to snap to. You can find the snap point by using the **AutoTrack** tools. In that case, you leave a blip mark on both endpoints, and then look for the intersection of the two orthogonal tracking traces (Figure 25-9). If you wish, you can move the region using a procedure other than the AutoTrack tools. Just make sure the region is placed in the proper location.

Figure 25-6   Profile dimensions

Figure 25-7   Profile dimensions

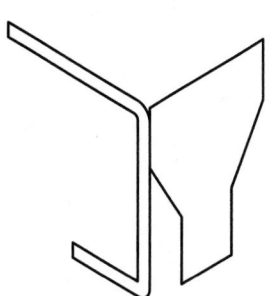

Figure 25-8   After the object is moved

> **FOR MORE DETAILS**   You can find more information about the **AutoTrack** tools in Chapter 19.

Figure 25-9   The destination point must be selected by using tracking techniques

Figure 25-10   Profile dimensions

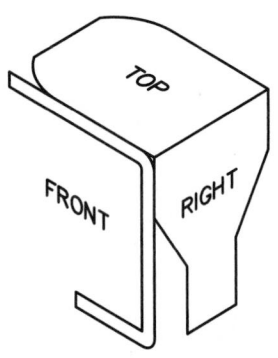

Figure 25-11   The last region is moved

21. **MOVE** the last region so that the three regions meet at the endpoint (Figure 25-11).

22. Make sure the **Top** UCS is still current and **EXTRUDE** the three regions individually. Specify the height of extrusion for each region as follows:

   - Region parallel to the front plane: **−1.75**
   - Region parallel to the right plane: **−2.5**
   - Region parallel to the top plane: **−2.5**

23. **INTERSECT** these three 3D solids. The results should look like Figure 25-12.

24. Next, you will combine the *Jaw* and the *Clamp.* Draw the line, shown highlighted in Figure 25-13, between the two endpoints of the *Jaw.*

> **Note:**
> We will refer to this 3D solid as a *Clamp.*

Figure 25-12   The 3D solid resulting from the **INTERSECT** operation

Figure 25-13   The highlighted line will be used as a reference

25. **MOVE** the *Clamp* from the midpoint of the tangent edge to the midpoint of the line you just created on the *Jaw*, as shown in Figure 25-14, with the hidden lines removed on the right.

26. **ERASE** the line you drew on the previous step.

27. **Top** should still be the current UCS. **MOVE** the *Jaw* **0.81** unit along the positive *X*-axis direction (Figure 25-15).

Note:
It is a good practice to intersect 3D solids throughout a design process. Such an operation avoids many other unnecessary steps, which saves time. If you are transforming a 2D drawing into a 3D model, it is also a good approach because you can get the profiles out of the drawing views.

Figure 25-14   After moving the *Clamp* and erasing the line

Figure 25-15   The *Clamp* moved again to its final location

28. Select the **Front** orthographic view (Figure 25-16).

29. **COPY** over the *Clamp* to create a duplicate of this object in the same place. Respond to the prompts as follows:

Select objects: *Select the Clamp portion.*

Select objects: ↵ *(To end the selection)*

Specify base point or [Displacement] <Displacement>: *0,0,0* ↵

Specify second point or <use first point as displacement>: *0,0,0* ↵

Specify second point or [Exit/Undo] <Exit>: ↵
(To exit the command)

Note:
Your next goal is to eliminate the portion of the *Jaw* that is interfering with the *Clamp*. The next few steps describe one of the possible approaches that can be used.

TIP   Avoid snapping to points in an orthogonal view. You cannot tell for sure whether you are snapping to the closest point or to the ones behind it.

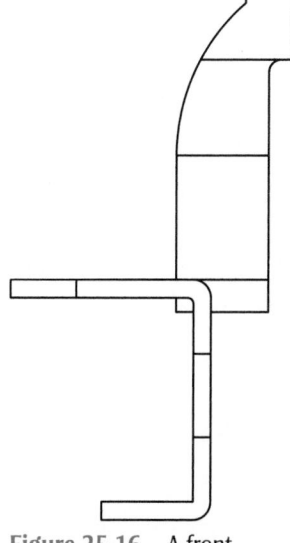

Figure 25-16   A front view of the 3D model

30. **SUBTRACT** one of the two *Clamps* from the *Jaw*.

TIP   Select the *Clamp* by picking it directly instead of using a window or a crossing window. Using either of these two selection tools will cause both clamps to be selected, when only one should be selected.

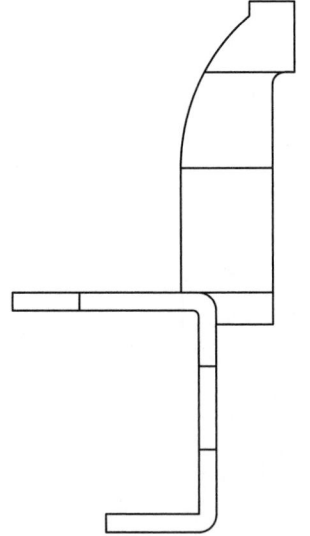

31. Use the **SEPARATE** command to disintegrate the 3D solid into two individual ones.

32. **ERASE** the smaller 3D solid located in the inside corner of the *Clamp*. After this, the 3D model should look like Figure 25-17.

33. With the **UNION** command, combine the *Clamp* and the *Jaw*. We will call this new 3D solid *Main Body*.

34. Select the **Right** view and create the region shown in Figure 25-18.

35. Select the **SE Isometric** viewing point.

Note:
After subtracting the *Clamp*, the *Jaw* portion is split into two joined 3D solids.

Figure 25-17   After eliminating the portion inside the *Clamp*

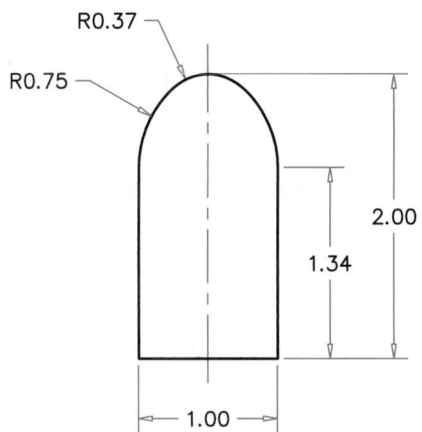

Figure 25-18   Profile dimensions

36. Invoke the **SECTION** command by entering its name in the command line and create a region on the *Main Body* parallel to the current *YZ* plane and going through the rightmost quadrant point of the upper circular edge highlighted in Figure 25-19.

37. Select the **Front** view.

38. Create the region shown in Figure 25-20.

39. Select the **SE Isometric** viewing point.

40. **MOVE** the region extracted with the **SECTION** command to the highlighted region shown in Figure 25-21, so that the two indicated endpoints meet.

Note:
You will use this region to extract some information when creating the next profile.

(a)   (b)

Figure 25-19   The extracted region (a); with the occulted edges removed (b)

Figure 25-20   Profile dimensions

41. Obtain the region shown in Figure 25-22 by subtracting the two regions with the **SUBTRACT** command.

42. **MOVE** one of the regions from its endpoint to the other region (Figure 25-23).

43. Select the **Top** UCS.

44. With **ORTHO** mode activated, **MOVE** the region on the right **0.5″** along the positive *X*-axis (Figure 25-24).

45. **EXTRUDE** the region on the right **−3.00** units, and the one on the left **−1.00** unit. Specify **0** as the angle of taper for both extrusions.

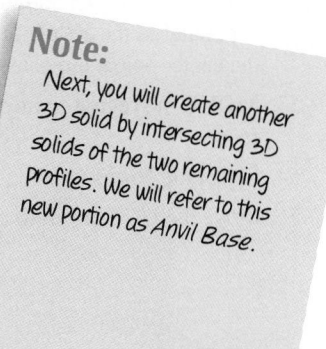

Note:
Next, you will create another 3D solid by intersecting 3D solids of the two remaining profiles. We will refer to this new portion as *Anvil Base*.

Figure 25-21   Point to be specified in the **MOVE** operation

Figure 25-22   The resulting composite region after the **SUBTRACT** operation

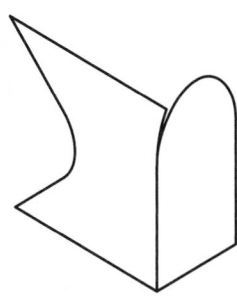

Figure 25-23   The region is moved to the other region

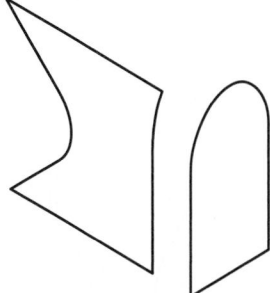

Figure 25-24   The region is moved away

46. With the **INTERSECT** command, create the new 3D solid shown in Figure 25-25. The 3D solid is shown with the hidden lines removed on the right side of the figure.

47. Invoke the **3DORBIT** command and rotate the viewing point to see the left side of the 3D models.

Figure 25-25   The 3D solid resulting from the **INTERSECT** operation

48. **MOVE** the *Anvil Base* to the *Main Body.* Snap to the endpoints to find the proper location (Figure 25-26).

49. With the **UNION** command, join the *Anvil Base* and the *Main Body.*

50. Select the **SE Isometric** viewing point.

51. Make sure the **Top** UCS is current.

52. Use the **SECTION** command to create a region that is parallel to the *YZ* plane and goes through any of the center points indicated in Figure 25-27.

53. **MOVE** the region to any empty place in the 3D space.

54. Select the **Right** view.

55. Move the UCS origin to any point on the extracted region.

Note:
In the following steps you will create the Anvil 3D solid and incorporate it into the Main Body with a smooth transition. In order to do that, you will extract a section and use its geometry to create the new profile tangent to it.

Figure 25-26   The *Anvil Base* is moved to the *Main Body*

Figure 25-27   The resulting region

FOR MORE DETAILS   To find further information concerning UCS modifications, see Chapter 19.

56. **EXPLODE** the extracted region two times to separate the object into lines and arcs.

57. Create the profile shown in Figure 25-28 using the objects obtained by exploding the region.

Note:
Because the region we are working with is composed of two individual areas, we will perform two **EXPLODE** operations. The first **EXPLODE** operation will separate the two regions. The second one will decompose the single region into 2D objects.

Figure 25-28   Profile dimensions

TIP You can obtain the arc by creating a circle tangent to the reference arc and tangent to another vertical reference line separated 0.76/2 from the symmetry line.

58. Select the **SE Isometric** viewing point.

59. Convert the new objects into a region.

60. **MOVE** the region from the midpoint of the extracted section to the midpoint of the *Main Body* (Figure 25-29).

61. **ERASE** the remaining objects from the exploded region.

Note:
This **MOVE** operation is the first of two steps needed to locate the profile in the proper place.

Figure 25-29   Points to perform the **MOVE** operation

TIP Keeping the model free of unnecessary objects is an important factor in avoiding errors and confusion.

62. Select the **Front** orthographic view.

63. With **ORTHO** mode activated, draw a **2.36″** polyline horizontally from the endpoint, as shown in Figure 25-30.

64. With **ORTHO** and **OTRACK** modes activated, **MOVE** the region from its top endpoint to align it vertically with the polyline's endpoint (Figure 25-31).

65. **ERASE** the polyline.

66. **EXTRUDE** the region **1.5** units (Figure 25-32).

> **Note:**
> Using the tracking tool to move the region guarantees that the region will move only in the X-axis direction, regardless of whether the two points specified have different Z coordinates.

Figure 25-30   After the polyline is placed

Figure 25-31   The region is moved to align it with the polyline

Figure 25-32   After extruding the region

67. With the **UNION** command, integrate the *Anvil* solid with the *Main Body*.

68. Select the **Isometric SW** viewing point (Figure 25-33).

69. Extract a new region using the **3 points** option of the **SECTION** command. Specify any three noncollinear points on the face highlighted on Figure 25-34.

70. **MOVE** the region away from the *Main Body* so you can work comfortably.

> **Note:**
> Next, you will cut off the volume inside the Anvil Base to clean up the path through which the bolt and the cylindrical guides will go. We will refer to this new 3D solid as Cavity.

Figure 25-33   The 3D solid resulting from the **UNION** operation

Figure 25-34   Face to specify the three points of the **SECTION** command

71. Select the **Left** view.

72. Move the UCS origin to any point on the extracted region.

73. Use the extracted region as a reference to draw the objects shown in Figure 25-35.

74. Convert the objects into a region.

75. Select the **Isometric SW** viewing point.

76. **EXTRUDE** the region **2.5** units to create the *Cavity*.

77. **MOVE** the *Cavity* from the midpoint of the region to the same point on the *Main Body* (Figure 25-36).

78. **ERASE** the region that you used as a reference.

79. Select the **Front** view.

80. **MOVE** the *Cavity* orthogonally to the right so that the right planar face aligns vertically with the inside flat face of the *Clamp*.

Note: Extracting regions and working on top of them clarifies the job and reduces the chance of making mistakes.

Figure 25-35   New profile created using the extracted region

Figure 25-36   Points to specify in the **MOVE** operation

TIP   You can use the **AutoTrack** tool to find the second point of displacement to make sure that the object moves only in the direction of the X-axis Figure 25-37).

Endpoint: 1.1962 < 90°

Figure 25-37   The *Cavity* moved using tracking methods

81. **SUBTRACT** the *Cavity* from the *Main Body*.

82. Select the **3D Hidden** visual style and inspect the 3D model with the **3DORBIT** command (Figure 25-38).

83. Select the **SE Isometric** viewing point.

84. Select the **Right** UCS.

85. Use the **Copy edges** option of the **SOLIDEDIT** command to copy the circular edge of the hole with the defect at the same place. Specify the base point and the second point of displacement as the same point.

Note:
By carefully inspecting the 3D model, you can see that the lower hole is not completely cylindrical. If a region were extracted along the center of the 3D solid, it would reveal such a defect (Figure 25-39).

Figure 25-38 The 3D solid resulting from the **SUBTRACT** operation

Figure 25-39 Inspecting the 3D model

TIP   The selection of the copied edge can easily be made using a selection window.

86. **EXTRUDE** the new circle **–1.5** units (Figure 25-40).

87. **SUBTRACT** the cylinder from the *Main Body* to correct the defect of the hole.

88. Select the **Top** UCS.

89. Invoke the **CYLINDER** command. Specify the midpoint of the highlighted edge for the center of the cylinder. Snap to the endpoint of the same edge to specify the radius. Specify **–0.66** for the height (Figure 25-41).

90. With the **UNION** command, join the cylinder with the *Main Body*.

91. Create a second cylinder with a radius of **0.21″** and a height of **1″**. Place its center concentric with the bottom circular edge of the previous cylinder.

92. **SUBTRACT** the second cylinder from the *Main Body* (Figure 25-42).

Note:
A rib is needed to give more stiffness to the *Clamp* portion. You will create the rib by sweeping a profile along a path.

Figure 25-40   The circle extruded

Figure 25-41   A cylinder created in place

Figure 25-42   A hole created by subtracting a second cylinder

93. Select the **Front** view.

94. Draw the curve shown in Figure 25-43 as a single polyline.

TIP   If necessary, use the **PEDIT** command to join the segments. Remember that all the objects to be joined need to lie in the same plane and such plane must be parallel to the current UCS. Start by drawing a circle concentric with the right angle edge, and create the rest of the geometry using the circle as a reference.

Figure 25-43   Curve dimensions

Figure 25-44   Profile dimensions

Figure 25-45   The profile is moved to the curve

95. Draw the region shown in Figure 25-44. This will be the cross section of the rib.

96. Select the **SE Isometric** viewing point.

97. **MOVE** the region from its bottom midpoint to the endpoint of the polyline (Figure 25-45).

98. **SWEEP** the region along the polyline.

99. **ERASE** the polyline used as the sweep path (Figure 25-46).

100. Select the **Top** view (Figure 25-47).

101. **MOVE** the rib orthogonally along the *Y*-axis to center it with the *Main Body*. You can do this either by

Note:
Because you created the extrusion path in an orthogonal view without knowing its *Z*-axis location, the swept rib will not be centered with the Main Body. Your next step will be to relocate and modify the rib before joining it with the Main Body.

Figure 25-46   After sweeping the profile

Figure 25-47   A **Top** view

Figure 25-48   A gap is revealed in a **Front** view

tracking points or by using the point filters. Use the point filters this time. To do so, respond to the prompts as follows:

Select objects: *Select the rib.*

Select objects: ⏎ *(To end the selection)*

Specify base point or displacement: *Specify any midpoint located at the center of the rib.*

Specify second point of displacement or <use first point as displacement>: *.y* ⏎

Of: *Specify any midpoint located at the center of the Main Body.*

(need XZ): *With ORTHO mode activated, move the pointer over the Main Body. Click anywhere in the drawing area while the cursor trace is aligned with the Y-axis.*

> **Note:**
> As shown in Figure 25-48, there is a gap between the rib and the Main Body. This happened because of the 4° angle of the polyline used as the path. This gap will have to be filled before joining the 3D solids.

102. Select the **Front** view.

103. With the **CHECK** command, determine whether the rib is a valid ShapeManager solid. After you finish the selection, the AutoCAD® program responds with the following message:

This object is a valid ShapeManager solid.

Enter a body editing option
[Imprint/sePerate solids/Shell/ cLean/Check/Undo/eXit] <eXit>: *Press <Esc> to exit the command.*

> **Note:**
> The prompted message indicates that face editing operations can be performed on the rib.

104. Select the **SW Isometric** viewing point.

105. With ORTHO mode activated, **MOVE** the rib orthogonally down **2″**. This will make it easier to specify the points in the next operation.

106. Invoke the **Rotate faces** option of the **SOLIDEDIT** command and respond to the prompts as follows:

Select faces or [Undo/Remove]: *Select the face highlighted in Figure 25-49.*

Select faces or [Undo/Remove/ALL]: ⏎ *(To end the selection)*

Specify an axis point or [Axis by object/View/Xaxis/Yaxis/Zaxis] <2points>: *Specify the center point of the leftmost arc edge.*

Specify the second point on the rotation axis: *Specify the other center point.*

Specify a rotation angle or [Reference]: *4 ↵*

Enter a face editing option [Extrude/Move/Rotate/Offset/Taper/ Delete/Copy/coLor/mAterial/Undo/eXit] <eXit>: *Press <Esc> to exit the command.*

107. Select the **Front** view.

108. **MOVE** the rib orthogonally back up the same **2″** (Figure 25-50).

109. Invoke the **Move faces** option of the **SOLIDEDIT** command and respond to the prompts as follows:

Select faces or [Undo/Remove]: *Select the face by clicking on the edge shown in Figure 25-51.*

> **Note:**
> There is another gap to be filled before joining the rib to the *Main Body*. You will extend the left portion of the rib so that it reaches the cylinder without getting into the hole.

Figure 25-49   Face to be selected and points to be specified

Figure 25-50   The corrected rib

Figure 25-51   Face to be selected

Select faces or [Undo/Remove/ALL]: ↵ *(To end the selection)*

Specify a base point or displacement: *Click anywhere in an empty space on the drawing area.*

Specify a second point of displacement: *0.5 ↵ (While ORTHO is activated and the pointer shows a direction to your left, that is, using the direct distance entry method)*

> **Note:**
> You will add two small pieces to the *Main Body*. We will call these pieces *Tube Teeth*. To make it simple, you will start by cutting a section through the model.

110. Invoke the **UNION** command to join the rib and the *Main Solid* (Figure 25-52).

111. Select the **SW Isometric** viewing point.

112. Invoke the **SECTION** command. Specify **XY** as the method to obtain the sectioning plane. Specify any center or midpoint that goes through the middle of the model.

113. With **ORTHO** activated, **MOVE** the new extracted region **2″** along the positive *X*-axis (Figure 25-53).

114. Select the **Front** view.

115. Change the UCS origin to any point in the extracted region.

Figure 25-52   The 3D solid resulting from the **UNION** operation

Figure 25-53   The extracted region is moved away

116. **ZOOM** in to the top part of the extracted region and, using the extracted region as a reference, create the region shown in Figure 25-54.

117. With **ORTHO** activated, **MOVE** the new region **2″** back along the negative *X*-axis.

118. **ERASE** the extracted region.

119. **EXTRUDE** the region **0.13** unit.

120. Select the **SE Isometric** viewing point.

121. Invoke the **Taper faces** option of the **SOLIDEDIT** command and respond to the prompts as follows:

Select faces or [Undo/Remove]: *Select only the highlighted face shown in* Figure 25-55.

Select faces or [Undo/Remove/ALL]: ↵ *(To end the selection)*

Specify the base point: *Specify endpoint 1.*

Specify another point along the axis of tapering: *Specify perpendicular point 2.*

Specify the taper angle: *-15* ↵

Figure 25-54   Profile based on the region and its dimensions

Figure 25-55   Face to be selected and points to be specified in the **Taper faces** operations

```
Enter a face editing option:
[Extrude/Move/Rotate/Offset/Taper/Delete/Copy/coLor/mAterial/Undo/
eXit] <eXit>: Press <Esc> to exit the command.
```

122. Select the **NE Isometric** view.

123. Invoke the **Taper faces** option of the **SOLIDEDIT** command again. Repeat exactly the same process to taper the face located at the other side of the *Tube Tooth*.

124. Select the **Top** viewing point.

125. With **ORTHO** mode activated, **MOVE** the *Tube Tooth* **0.38″** along the negative *Y*-axis.

126. **MIRROR** the *Tube Tooth* by using two midpoints or any other point aligned with the center of the model to define the mirror line (Figure 25-56).

127. Join the two *Tube Teeth* to the *Main Body* with the **UNION** command.

128. Select the **SW Isometric** view.

129. Invoke the **FILLET** command and respond to the prompts as follows:

> *Note:*
> The model is almost complete. Now you will add some fillets and chamfers as the final touches.

```
Select first object or [Polyline/
Radius/Trim]: Select one of the two
edges highlighted in Figure 25-57.
Enter fillet radius <0.5000>: 0.13 ↵
Select an edge or [Chain/Radius]: Select the second highlighted
edge.
Select an edge or [Chain/Radius]: ↵ (To end the selection)
```

Figure 25-56   The mirrored copy of the *Tube Tooth*

Figure 25-57   Edges to be filleted

130. Change the viewing point with the **3D Orbit** tool to see inside the *Cavity*.

131. **FILLET** the group of continuous edges highlighted in Figure 25-58. Use the **Chain** option and respond to the prompts as follows:

```
Select first object or [Polyline/Radius/Trim]: Select any edge of
the group.
Enter fillet radius <0.1300>: ↵ 0.03 ↵
Select an edge or [Chain/Radius]: c ↵
Select an edge chain or [Edge/Radius]: Select another edge of the
group.
Select an edge chain or [Edge/Radius]: ↵ (To end the selection)
```

Figure 25-58   Chain of edges to be filleted

132. Select the **SE Isometric** viewing point.

133. **FILLET** the two chains of edges highlighted in Figure 25-59, using a radius of **0.03″**.

134. **FILLET** the edges highlighted in Figure 25-60, using the same fillet radius of **0.03″**. The AutoCAD program will recognize all the edges that are continuous by using the **Chain** option, making the selection easier.

Figure 25-59   Chain of edges to be filleted

Figure 25-60   Chain of edges to be filleted

135. Using a radius value of **0.31″**, **FILLET** the four edges highlighted in Figure 25-61.

136. Invoke the **CHAMFER** command and respond to the prompts as follows:

> **Select first line or [Polyline/ Distance/Angle/Trim/Method]:** *Select any edge belonging to the face highlighted in* Figure 25-62.
>
> **Base surface selection...**
>
> **Enter surface selection option [Next/OK (current)] <OK>:** *n ↵ (In case the selected face is not the highlighted one)*
>
> **Enter surface selection option [Next/OK (current)] <OK>:** ↵ *(To end the selection)*

Note:

Next, you will create chamfers on the circular edges of all the holes, using the value of **0.02** for the two chamfer distances. Remember, unlike with the **FILLET** command, the edges selected in the **CHAMFER** command must belong to a common previously defined face.

Figure 25-61   Other edges to be filleted

Figure 25-62   Face to be selected for the **CHAMFER** operation

Specify base surface chamfer distance: *0.02* ⏎

Specify other surface chamfer distance: *0.02* ⏎

Select an edge or [Loop]: *Select the three circular edges highlighted in* Figure 25-63.

Select an edge or [Loop]: ⏎ *(To end the selection)*

137. Select the **SW Isometric** viewing point.

138. Create the other chamfers highlighted in Figure 25-64. Use the same chamfer distances as with the previous one.

139. Select the **SE Isometric** viewing point.

140. Select the **Top** UCS.

141. Draw the polyline shown in Figure 25-65 between the two center points of the highlighted arc edges.

Figure 25-63   Edges to be chamfered

Note: Now you will create the two countersunk holes to finish the 3D model.

Figure 25-64   Other edges to be chamfered

Figure 25-65   Polyline placed

142. Based on the polyline, create the region shown in Figure 25-66.

143. **REVOLVE** the region. Use two endpoints of the polyline to define the axis of revolution (Figure 25-67).

Figure 25-66   Profile dimensions

Figure 25-67   The revolved 3D solid

144. Invoke the **MIRROR3D** command. After you select the countersunk hole, specify any three of the many points that can define an imaginary plane going through the center of the 3D solid (Figure 25-68).

145. **SUBTRACT** the two countersunk holes from the *Main Body*.

146. After you invoke the **HIDE** command, the completed 3D model of the *Main Body* should look like Figure 25-69.

147. **SAVE** the drawing.

Figure 25-68   A mirrored copy of the re-volved 3D solid

Figure 25-69   The finished 3D model of the *Main Body*

MODELING THE MOVING JAW

The second 3D model you will create will be named *Moving Jaw*. Because much of this model is exactly like the *Main Body,* you will simply modify a copy of this file. Using this approach will save you a good amount of design time.

1. **OPEN** the *Main Body* drawing.

2. **SAVE** it **AS Moving Body**.

3. Select the **SW Isometric** viewing point.

4. Select the **Top** UCS.

5. Use the **SECTION** command to create the two regions shown in Figure 25-70. Their geom-etry will be used as a reference.

   • The first region will be parallel to the *ZX* plane, going through any point located at the center of the 3D solid.

   • The second one will be parallel to the *YZ* plane. Locate any point through which the highlighted region could go.

6. **MOVE** both regions anywhere outside the 3D solid.

7. Select the **Front** UCS.

8. Create the region shown in Figure 25-71, using the points or objects of the extracted re-gions as reference. Dimensions are given only for the geometry that is not yet defined.

TIP   To use the region's objects, **EXPLODE** the region as many times as needed. You can also leave the region intact and use only its points to place new objects. A circle can be drawn coradial with the arc to find the tangent point with the line.

Figure 25-70   Two sections extracted, shown with the hidden lines removed at right

Figure 25-71   Profile created based on one of the extracted regions

9. **ERASE** the old region (or the remaining objects, if it was exploded) to keep the drawing clean.

10. Select the **Left** view.

11. Follow the same procedure to create the region shown in Figure 25-72, using the other region extracted.

12. **ERASE** any remaining objects around the region, as well as the three circles inside it.

13. Select the **SW Isometric** viewing point.

14. **MOVE** one of the regions to the other region, as shown in Figure 25-73.

Note: Because all the objects you need are already contained in the second region, you will not need any new dimensions. This time you might prefer to **EXPLODE** the region and use its objects. Basically, all you have to do is **DELETE** one of the arcs at the bottom and **EXTEND** the other arc to the line.

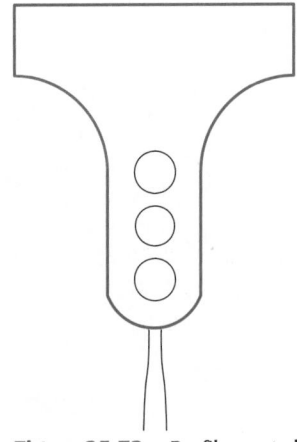

Figure 25-72   Profile created using the other extracted regions

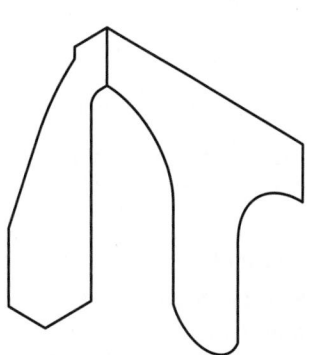

Figure 25-73   Regions placed together

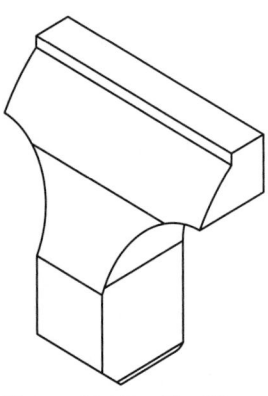

Figure 25-74 The 3D solid resulting from the **IN-TERSECT** operation

15. Make sure the **Left** UCS is current.

16. **EXTRUDE** the region that is on your right **2″**, and the one on your left **3″**.

17. **INTERSECT** the two 3D solids (Figure 25-74).

18. With the **SECTION** command, extract the same region on the *Main Body* you extracted before (Figure 25-75). Because the **Left** UCS is current, you can perform the operation parallel to the *XY* plane.

19. **MOVE** the region extracted to the *Moving Jaw.* Snap to the endpoints indicated in Figure 25-76 to place it correctly.

20. Select the **SE Isometric** viewing point.

21. Select the **Right** UCS.

22. Draw three circles concentric with the region's circular holes. Use the dimensions shown in Figure 25-77.

Note:
Now, you will create the three holes in the *Moving Jaw* piece. The most accurate way to make the holes concentric with the ones on the *Main Body* is by using the existing reference geometry.

Figure 25-75 An extracted region

Figure 25-76 The region moved to the *Moving Jaw* using the point shown

Figure 25-77 Circles created based on the reference region

23. **ERASE** the extracted region you used as a reference.

24. **EXTRUDE** the three circles, using the following heights:

   - **–2″** for the middle circle
   - **–0.75″** for the top and bottom circle

25. **SUBTRACT** the resulting three cylinders from the *Moving Jaw.* Your drawing should look like Figure 25-78.

26. Select the **Front** UCS.

27. Use the **SECTION** command to create a region on the *Main Body,* parallel to the *XY* plane and going through the center of the 3D solid (Figure 25-79).

28. **MOVE** the region out of the 3D solid.

29. Move the UCS origin to any point on the extracted region.

Note:
Next, you will extract the Tube Teeth from the *Main Body,* which is the only portion you need to add to the *Moving Jaw.* After this, you will no longer need the *Main Body* 3D solid.

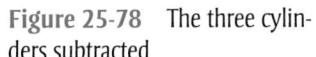

Figure 25-78 The three cylinders subtracted

Figure 25-79 Another region extracted from the *Main Body*

30. Create the region shown in Figure 25-80. **EXPLODE** the extracted region to use its objects, if needed.

31. Select the **NW Isometric** viewing point.

32. **MOVE** the created region from the endpoint of the region to the endpoint of the *Main Body,* as shown in Figure 25-81.

33. **ERASE** the extracted region or its remaining objects.

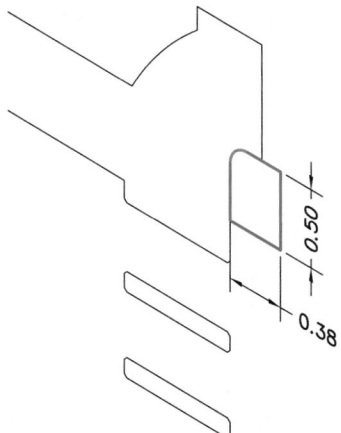

Figure 25-80 Profile to be created

Figure 25-81 Region moved to the *Main Body*

TIP You can change the viewing point by using the **3DORBIT** command, if needed, to make the selection of the objects easier.

34. Select the **SE Isometric** viewing point.

35. Select the **Front** UCS.

36. **EXTRUDE** the region 3″ (Figure 25-82).

37. Invoke the **Copy edges** option of the **SOLIDEDIT** command. When prompted, select the edge shown in Figure 25-83. Specify any point for both the base and the second point to copy the edge in the same place.

38. **INTERSECT** the *Main Body* and the extruded 3D solid. The resulting 3D solid and the extracted edge are shown in Figure 25-84.

Note:
Before you intersect these two 3D solids, you must leave a reference point. This is because the *Main Body* will disappear after the operation.

Figure 25-82 After extruding the region

Figure 25-83 Edge to be copied

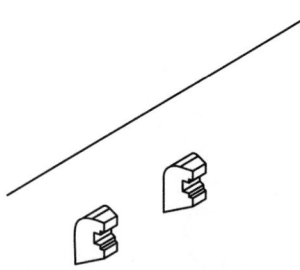

Figure 25-84 The 3D solid resulting from the **INTERSECT** operation

39. **MOVE** the resulting 3D solid from the endpoint of the reference edge to the corresponding endpoint of the *Moving Jaw* piece (Figure 25-85).

40. After you have placed the solid in the right position, perform a **UNION** operation to join the two 3D solids.

41. **ERASE** the reference line.

42. Invoke the **3DORBIT** command to get a viewpoint similar to the one shown in Figure 25-86. **FILLET** the highlighted edges, using a **Radius** value of **0.5"**.

43. **FILLET** the chain of edges shown in Figure 25-87, using a **Radius** value of **0.13"**.

TIP   Sometimes the complexity of the geometry makes the chain of edges appear to be continuously tangent when it is not. In this case, you can select the next chain of edges manually.

TIP   Selecting a cylindrical face for the **CHAMFER** operation allows you to select both of its circular edges.

Figure 25-85 Points to be specified in the **MOVE** operation

Figure 25-86 Edges to be filleted

Figure 25-87 Chain of edges to be filleted

44. **CHAMFER** the six circular edges of the holes. Use **0.02** for both chamfer distances. The result is shown in Figure 25-88.

45. **SAVE** your drawing.

Figure 25-88 Edges are chamfered

A key element in the design of components with complex shapes is efficiency. As you have learned so far in this tutorial, you must not discard any geometry contained in other 3D models before starting from scratch. The use of this technique and other similar ones demonstrates a complete understanding of the procedures used to generate competent 3D models, while showing a commitment to efficiency and productiveness.

MODELING THE MISCELLANEOUS COMPONENTS

In this part of the project, you will create the remaining 3D solids needed for the bench vise assembly. These 3D solids can all be created in the same drawing file. You will also modify the *Main Body* and the *Moving Jaw* to allow installation of the *Aluminum Blocks*.

1. Start a **NEW** drawing using the **acad** template.

2. **SAVE** it **AS** *Miscellaneous*.

3. Set or check the values of the following system variables as specified:
   - **DISPSILH** to **1**.
   - **ISOLINES** to **0**.
   - **FACETRES** to **9**.
   - **VIEWRES** to **2000**.
   - **UCSORTHO** to **1**.
   - **UCSFOLLOW** to **0**.

4. Next, you will create the *Main Bolt* and the *Fastening Bolt* 3D solids. Without changing the viewing point or the UCS, create the two regions shown in Figure 25-89.

Note: Real threads can be created because true helix curves are now supported by the AutoCAD program. Creating long threaded surfaces, however, can consume a large amount of memory and slow down the computer. Threaded surfaces can be perfectly represented by subtracting a set of individual concentric rings from the 3D solid, or by revolving a profile with a similar shape.

TIP A region will not be created unless the objects you select form a perfectly closed contour.

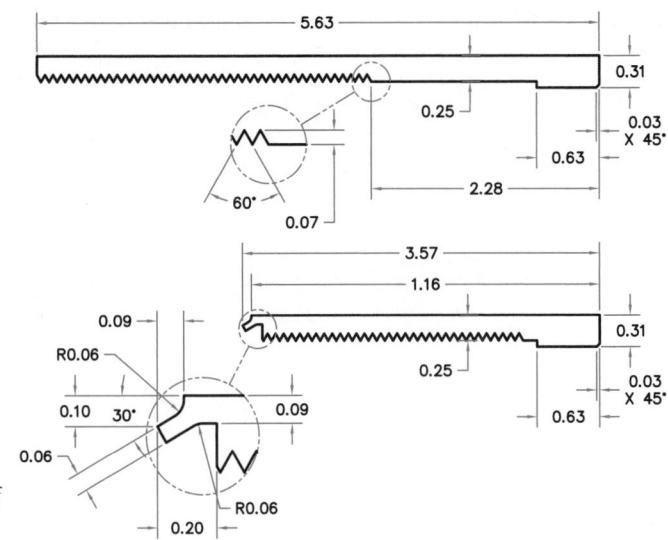

Figure 25-89   Dimensions of the profiles

5. **REVOLVE** each region around its highlighted edge, specifying any two points on it. Accept **360** as the angle of revolution for both operations (Figure 25-90).

Figure 25-90   Profiles will be revolved about the high-lighted axis

6. Draw the three circles shown in Figure 25-91. When prompted to specify the center point of the circles, snap to the center points of the circular edges as indicated.

7. With **ORTHO** mode activated, **MOVE** the circles to the left according to the distances shown in Figure 25-92.

8. Select the **SE Isometric** viewing point.

9. Select the **Right** UCS.

10. **MOVE** the circles orthogonally down **1″**.

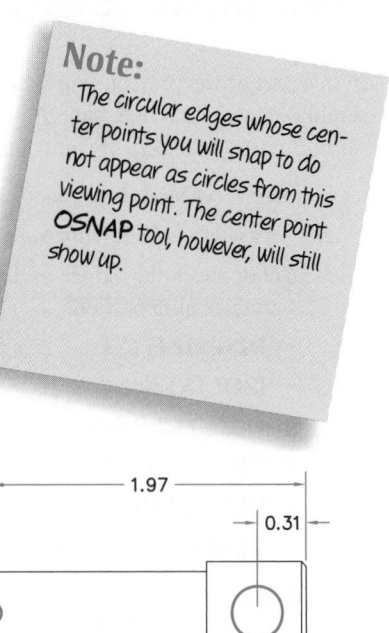

Note:
The circular edges whose center points you will snap to do not appear as circles from this viewing point. The center point OSNAP tool, however, will still show up.

Figure 25-91   Circles to be drawn

Figure 25-92   Dimensions to place the circles

11. **EXTRUDE** the circles **2″** (Figure 25-93).

12. Perform two **SUBTRACT** operations to create the holes in the *Main Bolt* and the *Fastening Bolt* individually (Figure 25-94).

Figure 25-93   Extruded circles

Figure 25-94   The holes resulting from the **SUBTRACT** operation

13. With the **CYLINDER** command, create the cylinder shown in Figure 25-95.

14. **CHAMFER** both circular edges of the 3D solid cylinder. Specify both chamfer distances as **0.03″** (Figure 25-96). We will refer to the 3D solid you have just completed as *Guide*.

15. In an empty place, create a 3D solid sphere with a radius of **0.19**.

16. With **ORTHO** mode activated, **COPY** the sphere **3.25″** along the *X*-axis (Figure 25-97).

Figure 25-95   Cylinder dimensions

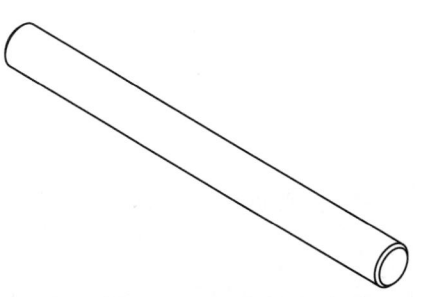

Figure 25-96   The chamfered cylinder

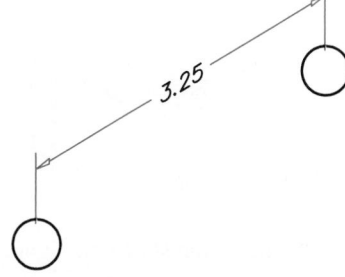

Figure 25-97   Two spheres created

17. Invoke the **CYLINDER** command and respond to the prompts as follows:

```
Specify center point of base or [3P/2P/Ttr/Elliptical]: Snap to
the sphere's center point.
Specify base radius or [Diameter]: 0.13 ↵
```

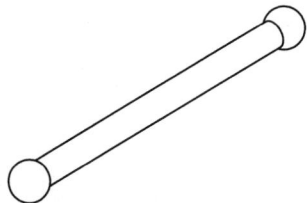

Figure 25-98 The 3D solid resulting from the **UNION** operation

```
Specify height or [2Point/Axis end-
point]: a ↵
Specify axis endpoint: Snap to the
center point of other sphere.
```

18. Perform a **UNION** operation to join the cylinder and the two spheres. You have now completed the *Handle* (Figure 25-98).

19. Select the **Right** view.

20. Create the two regions and the two lines (center-lines) shown in Figure 25-99, anywhere in the 3D space.

Note:
The objects you created were placed anywhere in the 3D space, without using any reference from other geometry. The objects appear farther apart than you thought when you change the viewing point.

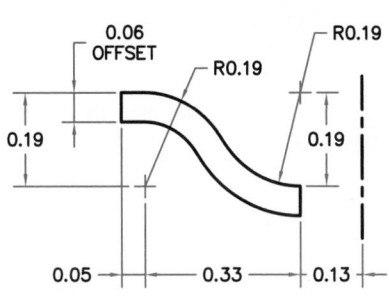

Figure 25-99 Dimensions of the profiles

21. **REVOLVE** each region individually **360°**. Use the endpoints of the centerlines to specify the axes of rotation.

22. **ERASE** the two centerlines. You nave just completed the *Pressing Plate* and the *Pin*.

23. **MOVE** the *Pressing Plate* and the *Pin* from their center points to the center point of the left spherical face of the *Handle*. Then move them orthogonally **2″** to the right (Figure 25-100).

TIP — Place the objects in a known location relative to other objects. This helps to keep them close together in the infinite 3D space, regardless of the current viewing point.

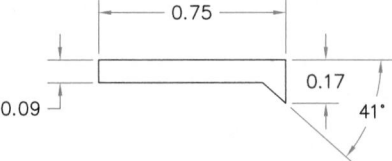

Figure 25-100 After the **MOVE** operation   **Figure 25-101** Profile dimensions

24. Create the region shown in Figure 25-101.

25. **REVOLVE** the region **360°** around any two points on the longer line. This 3D solid will be named *Screw*.

26. **MOVE** the new *Screw* from any point on it to the center point of the spherical face of the *Handle*. Then **MOVE** it orthogonally **1″** down (Figure 25-102).

27. Select the **SE Isometric** viewing point.

28. Select the **Top** UCS.

Figure 25-102   After the **MOVE** operation   **Figure 25-103**   The box dimensions

29. Create a box with the dimensions shown in Figure 25-103.

30. **ROTATE** the *Screw* **–90°**. Specify any point on it as the base point. From the current viewing point, the *Screw* should look like Figure 25-104.

31. **COPY** the *Screw* from its rightmost center point to the midpoint of the vertical edge, as shown in Figure 25-105 with the hidden lines removed.

32. With **ORTHO** mode activated, **MOVE** the copy of the *Screw* **0.50″** along the positive *Y*-axis.

Figure 25-104   After rotating the *Screw*

33. Use the **MIRROR3D** command to create another mirrored copy, as shown in Figure 25-106. Use three of the four midpoints of the box's longer edges to specify the points on the mirror plane.

Figure 25-105   A copy of the *Screw* placed on the edge of the box

Figure 25-106   The two screws after the **MIRROR** operation

34. **SUBTRACT** the two *Screws* from the box to create the countersunk holes (Figure 25-107). This 3D solid will be called *Aluminum Block*.

35. Select the **Right** UCS.

36. **ZOOM** into the *Screw* and draw a vertical line between the two quadrant points of the circular face.

37. **OFFSET** the line **0.015″** to both sides.

38. **DELETE** the original line.

39. Invoke the **Imprint** body option of the **SOLIDEDIT** command and imprint the two lines in the face of the *Screw* (Figure 25-108). Respond **Yes**, when prompted, to delete the source objects.

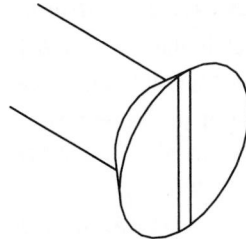

Figure 25-107   Holes created by subtracting the *Screws*

Figure 25-108   The two lines imprinted

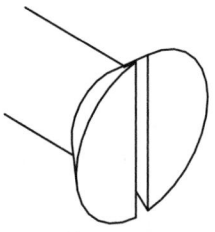

Figure 25-109 After extruding the split face inward

40. Invoke the **Extrude faces** option of the **SOLIDEDIT** command. Select only the split face, which represents the *Screw* slot, at the center. Specify **−0.03** as the height of the extrusion, and **0** as the angle of taper. The *Screw* with the slot should look like Figure 25-109.

41. Select the **Top** UCS.

42. **MOVE** the 3D solids around so they appear to be closer from this particular viewing point (Figure 25-110). The objects do not need to have the same arrangement in your drawing.

43. **SAVE** the drawing.

Figure 25-110 All of the miscellaneous components

Creating the Bench Vise Assembly

Now that you have created all the 3D solids, you are ready to assemble them. The approach is very simple. First, you will gather all the 3D solids in the same file. Then you will place each one in the right location in the 3D space so that the relationships among all the parts make the assembly functional.

For this task, it is important that you select a different color for each 3D solid to make the operations easier. You can choose any colors you want.

1. **OPEN** the file *Main Body*.

2. **SAVE** the file **AS** *Bench-Vise*.

3. Select the **SE Isometric** viewing point.

4. Select the **Top** UCS.

5. **OPEN** the file *Miscellaneous*.

6. Select the **Top** UCS.

7. Invoke the **COPYCLIP** (copy to clipboard) command. When prompted, select all the 3D solids contained in the file and press **<Enter↵>** to end the selection.

8. **CLOSE** the file *Miscellaneous*.

9. Back in the file *Bench-Vise*, invoke the **PASTECLIP** (paste from clipboard) command. When prompted, click anywhere close to the *Main Body*.

10. Repeat the same procedure to insert the *Moving Jaw* 3D solid into the **Bench-Vise** drawing file. Remember to change the UCS to **Top** before copying the 3D solid to the clipboard.

11. Turn the **OTRACK** mode off.

12. Invoke the **ALIGN** command and, when prompted, select the *Moving Jaw*. You will specify each of the three pairs of points one by one. For example, the first source point will be

Figure 25-111   All of the bench vise components

endpoint 1, and the first destination point will be its corresponding endpoint, shown by the arrow (Figure 25-112).

13. With **ORTHO** mode activated, **MOVE** the *Moving Jaw* **1″** along the positive *X*-axis to open up the two jaws (Figure 25-113).

14. **ROTATE** the *Fastening Bolt* **90°**. Select any point on it as the base point.

15. With **ORTHO** mode off, **MOVE** the *Pressing Plate* closer to the *Fastening Bolt*.

Figure 25-112   The order in which to specify the points for the **ALIGN** operation

Figure 25-113   The *Moving Jaw* moved away

16. Invoke the **3DALIGN** command to align the *Fastening Bolt* with the *Pressing Plate*. You will specify only two source center points, and then press **<Enter↵>** to specify the two corresponding destination center points (Figure 25-114). Center point 2 can be any center point in the threaded portion.

17. **MOVE** the *Fastening Bolt* and the *Pressing Plate* together from any center point on the threaded area to another center point on the vertical hole of the *Main Body* (Figure 25-115). The through hole on the *Fastening Bolt* should end up being aligned parallel to the *Y*-axis. Otherwise, invoke the **ROTATE** command and rotate the *Fastening Bolt* **90°** around any of its center points.

18. **MOVE** the *Pin* closer to the *Main Bolt*.

19. Using the **SECTION** command, extract a region through the *Main Bolt* parallel to the *XY* plane going through the middle of the 3D solid.

20. On the *Pin,* draw a reference line from the center point of the top face to the bottommost center point.

21. **MOVE** the *Pin* from the midpoint of the reference line to the center point of the circular edge of the region (Figure 25-116). **ZOOM** in as needed.

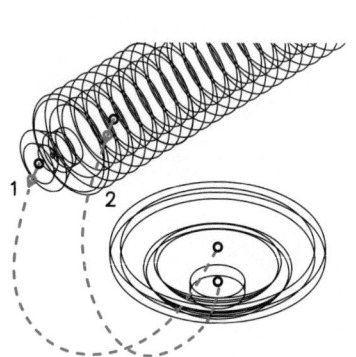

Figure 25-114   The order in which the points must be specified for the **3DALIGN** operation

Figure 25-115   After moving the *Fastening Bolt* and the *Pressing Plate*

Figure 25-116   Points to specify in the **MOVE** operation

22. **ERASE** both the extracted region and the line.

23. **MOVE** the *Main Bolt* along with the *Pin* from the center point of the *Main Bolt* to the center point of the *Main Body's* middle horizontal hole. Both center points are shown in Figure 25-117.

TIP   To avoid selecting the center point at the end of the chamfer instead of the one on the planar face, select the center point **OSNAP** tool directly, and click the proper circular edge.

24. **MOVE** the *Guide* from its rightmost center point to the end of one of the two holes on the *Moving Jaw*.

25. **COPY** the *Guide* to the other hole as well. The assembly should look like Figure 25-118.

26. Make sure the **Top** UCS is current.

27. With the **SECTION** command, extract a region from the *Fastening Bolt,* parallel to the *ZX* plane and going through any of the center points along the 3D solid.

28. **MOVE** the *Handle* from the center point of the leftmost circular edge to the center point of the region's hole.

Figure 25-117   Points to specify in the **MOVE** operation

Figure 25-118   The *Guide* copied to the other location

29. With **ORTHO** mode activated, **MOVE** the *Handle* **1.5″** orthogonally along the negative *Y*-axis (Figure 25-119).

30. **ERASE** the extracted region.

31. **COPY** the *Handle* close to the *Main Bolt* hole.

32. Invoke the **ROTATE3D** command to rotate the copied *Handle* **90°**. Define the axis of rotation parallel to the *X*-axis and going through any point on it.

33. On the *Main Bolt,* extract a region with the **SECTION** command, parallel to the *XY* plane, going through any of the center points along the 3D solid.

34. **MOVE** the new *Handle* from the center point of the top circular edge to the center point of the hole on the region.

35. **ERASE** the extracted region.

36. Select the **Front** UCS.

37. With **ORTHO** mode activated, **MOVE** the new *Handle* **0.3″** along the negative *Y*-axis (Figure 25-120).

Note:
Because the hole on the Fastening Bolt did not have any circular edges, you had to create additional geometry to snap to it.

Figure 25-119   The handle placed in its location

Figure 25-120   The second handle placed in its location

38. Invoke the **3DORBIT** command to obtain a view close to the one shown in Figure 25-121 (with the hidden lines removed).

39. Use the **RECTANGLE** command to draw a **0.25 × 0.50** rectangle anywhere in the 3D space.

40. **EXTRUDE** the rectangle **4″**.

41. **MOVE** the new 3D solid to the endpoint of the *Main Body*. Then **COPY** the 3D solid to the endpoint of the *Moving Jaw*. The result is shown in Figure 25-122.

42. With two independent **SUBTRACT** operations, subtract one of the 3D solids from the *Main Body* and the other one from the *Moving Jaw* (Figure 25-123).

Figure 25-121   The assembly with the hidden lines removed

Figure 25-122   The 3D solids shaped as boxes after being moved and copied

Figure 25-123   After subtracting the 3D solids

43. **MOVE** the *Aluminum Block* to the *Main Body*. Snap to the corresponding endpoints to place the *Aluminum Block* as shown in Figure 25-124.

44. Draw the highlighted reference line between the two endpoints as shown in Figure 25-125.

45. Use the **YZ** option of the **MIRROR3D** command to create a mirrored copy of the *Aluminum Block* on the *Moving Jaw*. Specify the midpoint of the line when prompted to specify the point on the *YZ* plane.

46. **ERASE** the reference line.

47. Invoke the **Copy edges** editing tool to copy the four circular edges highlighted in Figure 25-126, each in its own place.

Figure 25-124   The *Aluminum Block* moved to the *Main Body*

Figure 25-125   A reference line is placed

Figure 25-126   Edges are copied in place in both *Aluminum Blocks*

TIP   You can copy an object in its own place by specifying the base and the destination points as the same point. The editing tool operations work on only one 3D solid at a time.

48. **EXTRUDE** the two extracted circles on the *Main Body* **−0.19″** and the two extracted circles on the *Moving Jaw,* **0.19″**.

49. **SUBTRACT** the two cylinders from the *Main Body*. In a separate operation, **SUBTRACT** the two cylinders from the *Moving Jaw*.

50. Select the **World** UCS.

51. Invoke the **BLOCK** command to open the **Block Definition** dialog box. Type **Screw** under the **Name** field. Click on the **Select objects** button and select the *Screw*. Click on the **Pick point** button and snap to the center point of the circular edge between the cylindrical body and the head of the screw. Make sure **Convert to block** is selected, and click **OK** to close the dialog box.

> **Note:**
> Blocks are not exactly meant to be used with 3D objects. Using blocks, however, allows you to modify several objects at the same time. The next steps of this tutorial will demonstrate this fact.

Figure 25-127   The *Screw* block is placed in the hole

52. Select the *Screw* block, and then select its insertion point grid to move it to the first countersunk hole on the *Main Body*. Snap to the center point of the corresponding edge on the hole (Figure 25-127).

53. **COPY** the *Screw* block a few inches away from the *Main Body*.

54. **ROTATE** the new *Screw* block **180°**, using any point on it as the base point (Figure 25-128).

55. Select the copied *Screw* block, then select its insertion point grid to move it to the corresponding center point on the first countersunk hole of the *Moving Jaw*.

56. **COPY** both *Screw* blocks into the other holes of the *Aluminum Blocks* (Figure 25-129).

57. Select the **Front** view (Figure 25-130).

58. Use the **3D Orbit** tool to change the viewpoint to a viewpoint close to the one you had before.

59. Select the **World** UCS.

60. Double-click on any of the *Screw* blocks. Click **OK** in the **Edit Block Definition** dialog box. The screen changes to the **Block Editor** mode.

> **Note:**
> As you can see, the screws we are using are too long for our product. Because they all have the same block definition, editing one of them will change the others. Using blocks is a very helpful way of organizing the job in case you ever need to change large numbers of the same part in the 3D assembly.

61. Invoke the **Move faces** editing tool and respond to the prompts as follows:

Select faces or [Undo/Remove]: *Click on the circular edge at the left (seen as a line from this viewing point).*

Select faces or [Undo/Remove/ALL]: ↵ *(To end the selection)*

Specify a base point or displacement: *Click anywhere in the drawing area.*

Figure 25-128   The new *Screw* after it is rotated

Figure 25-129   The four screws are placed

Figure 25-130   Inspecting the 3D model from the front view

Specify a second point of displacement:
With **ORTHO** *mode activated, move the pointer toward the right and enter* *0.31* ↵

Enter a face editing option [Extrude/ Move/Rotate/Offset/Taper/Delete/Copy/ coLor/mAterial/Undo/eXit] <eXit>:
Press **<Esc>** *to exit the command.*

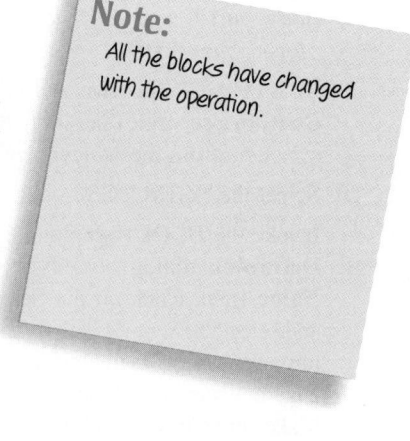

Note:
All the blocks have changed with the operation.

62. Press **<Esc>** to exit the command. Click on **Close Block Editor** on the **Block** toolbar, and select **Yes** to save the changes to the *Screw.*

63. Invoke the **HIDE** command. The 3D assembly model should look like Figure 25-131.

64. **SAVE** your drawing.

Figure 25-131   The final bench vise assembly

CHAPTER SUMMARY

The extensive tutorials in this chapter have given you the opportunity to use most of the operations learned in previous chapters. You have also learned some of the practical approaches that can be employed in a real design process to reduce the development time of 3D solid models and assemblies.

By comparing the 3D models developed in this tutorial with the 3D models developed in Chapter 20, you can measure your improvement in 3D modeling in general. You should also now be able to understand more clearly the specific operations performed in this chapter as well.

Generating Drawings and DWF Files

26

Chapter Objectives

- Learn to obtain accurate 2D and 3D sections using section objects.
- Use the **FLATSHOT** command to obtain quick projections of the drawing views.
- Learn to place dimensions throughout the 3D space.
- Generate exploded 3D views.
- Understand and manage the AutoCAD® program's paper space, and know the differences between paper space and model space.
- Generate and manipulate viewports, and be able to set view scales the correct way.
- Learn and practice the tools used to generate drawing views automatically from 3D models.
- Know the engineering information that can be obtained from 3D models.
- Learn to create DWF files of both 3D models and 2D drawings.

INTRODUCTION

DIFFERENT USES OF THE 3D MODELS

After you have finished the 3D model, you can use it to perform several other tasks, such as generating 2D drawings, obtaining rapid prototypes, rendering, publishing, and obtaining physical properties. Obtaining 2D drawings is probably the most important and common task. This chapter will take you through different techniques and processes that will allow you to generate quick and very precise drawings from 3D models.

The AutoCAD program allows you to create projected drawing views in both model space and paper space. In model space you can perform such tasks by using the following commands:

- **SECTIONPLANE**
- **FLATSHOT**

More automated ways of performing such tasks can be performed in paper space. Two different processes involving specific commands can be used:

- Simple views generation (**SOLPROF**)
- Automatic views generation (**SOLVIEW** and **SOLDRAW**)

Regardless of whether the orthogonal views are created in model space or paper space, the final preparation of the document should always be completed in the layouts, or paper space.

A REVIEW OF PAPER SPACE

DEFINITION OF PAPER SPACE

As you know, the model space mode is an infinite 3D space where you create both 2D and 3D models. The objects are represented in model space with real dimensions as they would appear in real life.

The paper space mode is the infinite 2D plane where you prepare the technical documents of the objects contained in model space. The drawing views are scaled according to the relative proportions between the objects and the sheet of paper used. You can look at the paper space only from the Top view.

WORKING WITH LAYOUTS

You can switch to paper space mode by simply clicking on the tabs named **Layout1** and **Layout2** located at the lower left corner of the drawing area; you can then go back to model space by clicking the **Model** tab next to them. See Figure 26-1(a). Clicking the **MODEL** button on the status

Figure 26-1   Accessing the paper space and model space modes through (a) the tabs and the status bar, and (b) the status bar. (c) Using the **Quick View Layouts**

bar will switch to the paper space as well; to completely switch back to the model space, you will have to click on the **Model** tab. The displaying of such tabs is controlled by the **Display Layout and Model tabs** in the **Options** dialog box (Figure 26-2).

Figure 26-2   The **Display** tab of the **Options** dialog box allows you to select and unselect the **Display Layout** and **Model** tabs

When the **Display Layout and Model tabs** option is not selected, you can use the buttons that appear one next to the other in the status bar to switch between model space and paper space [Figure 26-1(b)]. It is probably more convenient not to display the tabs because it gives you some more space for the drawing area. Whichever the case, you also click on the **Quick View Layouts** button to display a thumbnail image of each layout as well and the model space. You can click on the images to access the particular tab [Figure 26-1(c)]. Layout images are displayed differently, depending on whether you have accessed the layout or not.

If the **Show Page Setup Manager for new layouts** is enabled in the **Options** dialog box, the **Page Setup Manager** dialog box will open automatically the first time you enter any layout. After you close it, you can see the paper space elements (Figure 26-3). You can place any object throughout the infinite plane (the gray area); however, only the objects located inside the printable area of the sheet will be plotted. Notice the different look of the UCS icon in the paper space mode.

Right-clicking a Layout tab exposes a shortcut menu containing a group of tools [Figure 26-4(a)]. In this shortcut menu, you can **Rename** or **Delete** a layout. You can also **Move or Copy** the layout, or create a **New layout** from scratch. You can bring a layout from a specific drawing by using the **From template...** option as well. A similar shortcut menu shows up by right-clicking the **Quick View Layout** button on the status bar [see Figure 26-4(b)].

To properly prepare a layout or page for printing and publishing, you must specify the settings that control the following aspects:

- Page setup
- Viewports
- Objects placed directly on the paper, such as the title block

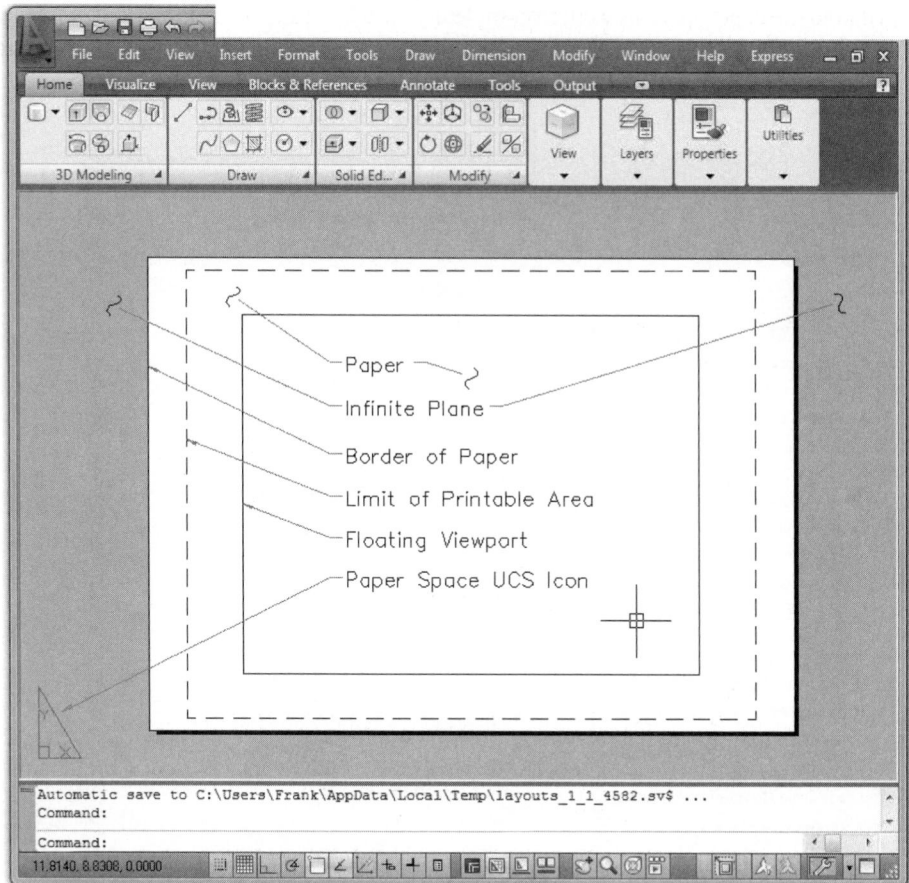

Figure 26-3   The paper space elements

(a)   (b)

Figure 26-4   Shortcut menu exposed by (a) right-clicking on a Layout tab or by (b) right-clicking on the **Quick View Layouts** button on the status bar

THE PAGE SETUP MANAGER

You open the **Page Setup Manager** dialog box (Figure 26-5) by invoking the **PAGESETUP** command. It can be accessed through the **Layouts** shortcut menu, the **File** pull-down menu, or the **Layouts** toolbar (Figure 26-6).

Figure 26-5 The **Page Setup Manager** dialog box

Figure 26-6 The **Layouts** toolbar

The **Page Setup Manager** gives you a report on the page setup details of the current layout. In essence, you can modify the page setup of the layouts directly by clicking the **Modify...** button, or you can apply a named page setup previously created such as the one named *My Page Setup* shown in Figure 26-7. You apply a named page setup by clicking the **Set Current** button. Doing so will override the current settings of the layout page setup.

Figure 26-7 Using a named page setup in the **Page Setup Manager** dialog box

In either case, the **Page Setup** dialog box is opened. It is similar to the **Plot** dialog box. The main difference is that clicking **OK** will not send the drawing to the plotter, but will apply and store any settings for future plots in this particular layout (Figure 26-8).

Figure 26-8   The **Page Setup** dialog box

FLOATING VIEWPORTS

floating viewport: A viewport entity created in paper space, through which you can display any view of the objects contained in the model space.

The paper space mode can be conceived of as an infinite plane covering the entire model space. Through this infinite plane you can see the object existing in the model space by turning an area transparent. This is made possible by placing a paper space viewport, also known as a *floating viewport*.

The model space viewports studied in Chapter 1 are not entities, but partitions of the drawing area. Paper space viewports, on the other hand, are specific AutoCAD entities that allow you to see the model space from any viewpoint and with any zoom factor. Floating viewports can be modified by different settings and operations, including some in the **Properties** palette.

The **VPORTS** command opens the **Viewports** dialog box, where you can create a specific arrangement of viewports in a specified area. In the **Viewports** dialog box, you can automatically generate a set of viewports that show the different views of the 3D model by selecting the **3D** option **Setup** (Figure 26-9).

Other operations to create and modify viewports are contained in the **Viewports** panel on the **Ribbon**. Additionally, other operations regarding the viewports can be accessed from the shortcut menu that displays by right-clicking on a selected viewport (Figure 26-10).

The **Viewports** toolbar should be used every time you work in a **Layout** tab. From left to right, the tools allow you to perform the following operations:

- Display the **Viewports** dialog box, where you can create a specific arrangement of viewports in a specified area
- Create a single rectangular viewport
- Create a polygonal viewport made of straight and arc segments, similar to creating a polyline
- Convert closed objects such as circles, ellipses, polylines, and regions into viewports
- Clip an existing viewport with a polygonal shape, or delete a viewport's clipping
- Use the viewport scale drop-down list to set a specific view scale on the active viewport.

Figure 26-9   The **Viewports** dialog box

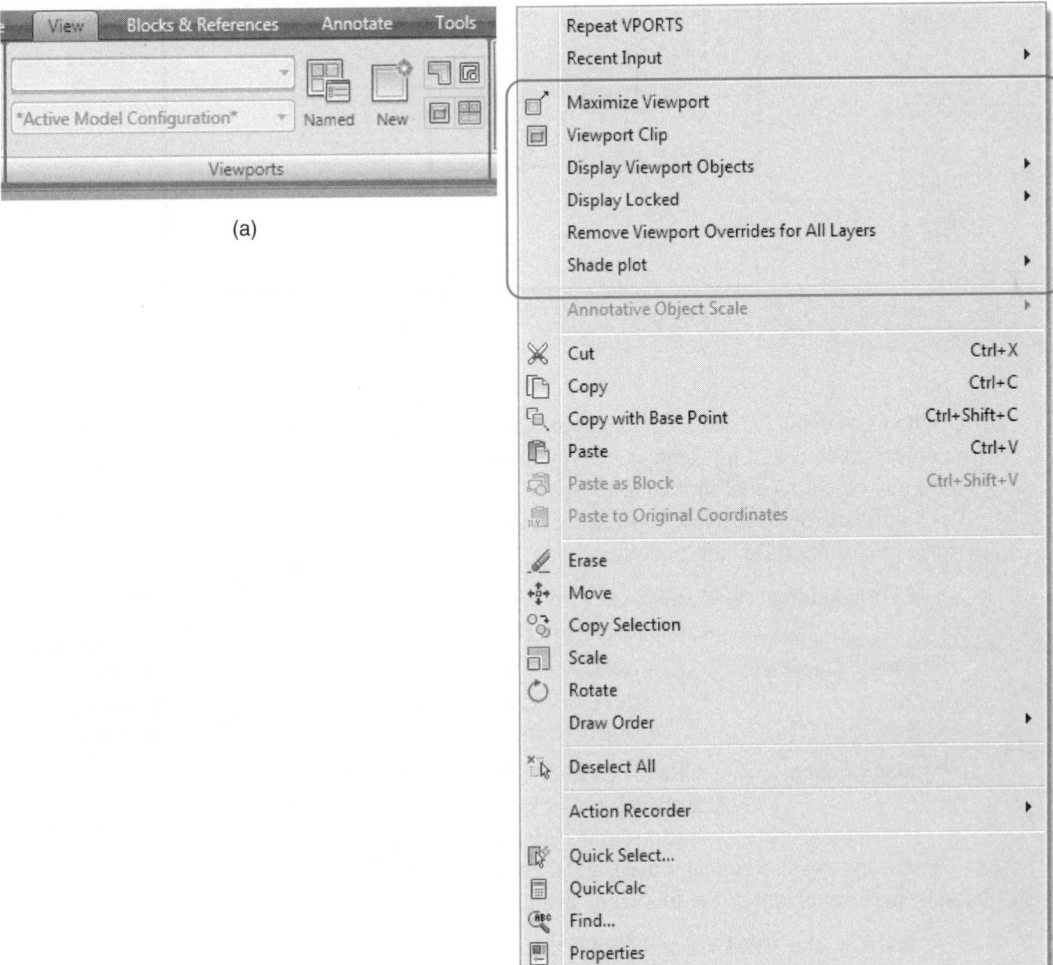

(a)

(b)

Figure 26-10   (a) The **Viewports** panel of the Ribbon (b) A special shortcut menu is displayed by right-clicking while a viewport is selected

The viewport's shortcut menu also allows you to specify settings for the selected viewports. You can **Lock** the view scale or set a specific type of **Shade** in each viewport, among other operations.

You can place floating viewports anywhere in the paper space. A viewport can overlap another viewport, or it can be located completely inside it. In any case, only the part of a viewport located inside the printable area of the paper will be plotted.

A floating viewport can also be modified using commands such as **ERASE, SCALE, MOVE**, and **COPY**. The most important property of a viewport, however, is that it enables you to activate or deactivate the model space seen through it.

When a viewport is activated (Figure 26-11), the contour of the viewport changes to a thicker line. Any object existing in model space can be selected and modified; even new objects can be placed in the model space though this window. **ZOOM** and **PAN** operations through an activated viewport make it possible to obtain the drawing views with specific scales.

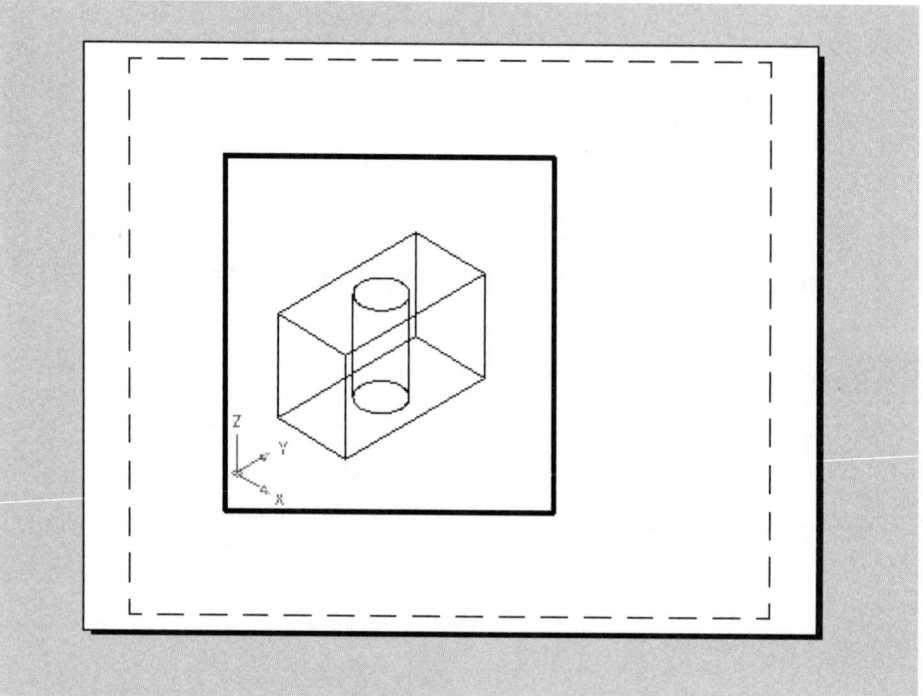

Figure 26-11   An activated viewport

When a viewport is deactivated (Figure 26-12), you can work only in the 2D infinite plane. Any object created will not appear when you switch to model space. You also cannot select or modify any object located in the model space.

To activate or deactivate a floating viewport, you can perform one of the following operations:

- Command line: . . . . . mspace ⏎ (to activate)
                    pspace ⏎ (to deactivate)
- Mouse double-click: . . . . . Inside a viewport (to activate) Outside a viewport (to deactivate)
- Status button[*]: . . . . . Click **PAPER** button (to activate) Click **MODEL** button (to deactivate)

Viewports can also be maximized, and then minimized back, by performing one of the following operations:

- Invoking the **VPMAX** and **VPMIN** commands
- Double-clicking on the viewport contour

Note:
Only one viewport can be activated at a time. To activate another viewport, you can just click inside it, or you can press the <Ctrl> and <R> keys to cycle through the viewports.

[*]Only when the **Layout** and **Model** tabs are enabled.

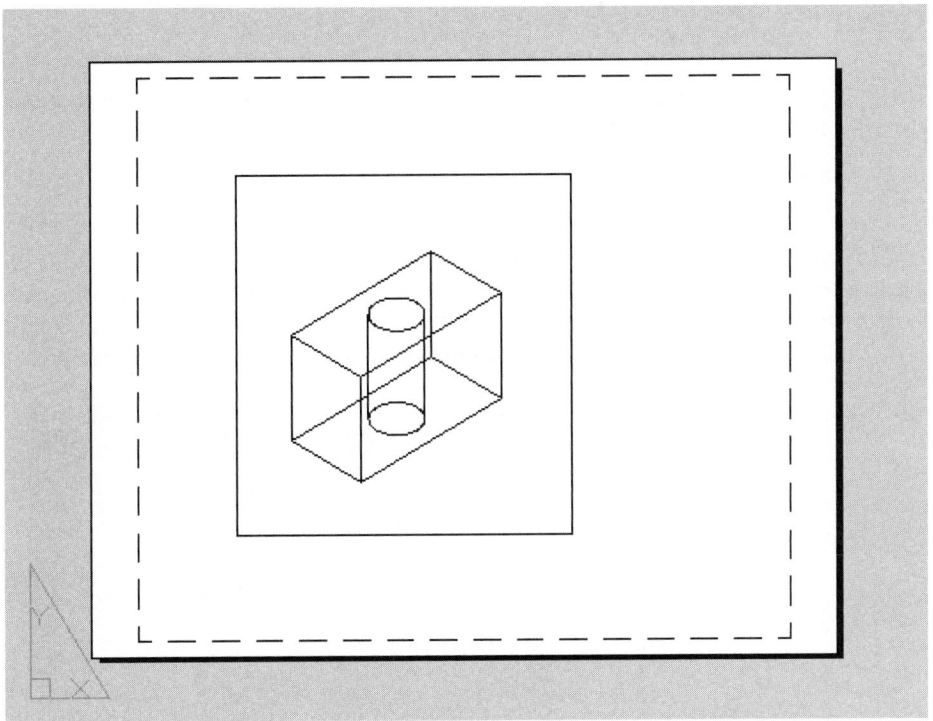

Figure 26-12   A deactivated viewport

- Using the **Maximize Viewport** button in the status bar
- Selecting **Maximize Viewport** on the shortcut menu, after selecting the viewport

USING LAYERS IN PAPER SPACE

In paper space, layers have two important additional properties that are not available in model space:

- Frozen/thawed in the currently active viewport
- Frozen/thawed in a new viewport

The first property enables you to show only a specific group of layers through each particular viewport. The second function, when turned on, helps you set the group of layers that will not automatically be shown on a new viewport. As you will see later, these properties are self-activated in the operations that generate the drawing views and, like any other property of layers, can be changed at any time. Other properties of the layers, such as **Color, Linetype**, and **Lineweight**, can be controlled in each viewport individually while the viewport is activated, or for the paper space in general with no viewport activated. Take a look at the **Current VP Freeze** and **New VP Freeze** columns in the **Layer Properties Manager** dialog box in Figure 26-13.

S..	Na..	O..	Fre..	L..	Color	Li..	Linewei...	Plot S...	Plot	New VP Freeze	VP Freeze	VP Color	VP Linetype	VP Lineweight	VP Plot Style	Des
✓	0				■ w...	Co...	— Defa...	Color_7				■ white	Continuous	— Default	Color_7	
	3D...				■ w...	Co...	— Defa...	Color_7				■ white	Continuous	— Default	Color_7	
	AS...				■ w...	Co...	— Defa...	Color_7				■ white	Continuous	— Default	Color_7	
	Def...				■ w...	Co...	— Defa...	Color_7				■ white	Continuous	— Default	Color_7	
	PH...				■ w...	HI...	— Defa...	Color_7				■ white	HIDDEN	— Default	Color_7	
	PH...				■ w...	HI...	— Defa...	Color_7				■ white	HIDDEN	— Default	Color_7	
	PH...				■ w...	HI...	— Defa...	Color_7				■ white	HIDDEN	— Default	Color_7	
	PV-...				■ red	Co...	— Defa...	Color_1				■ red	Continuous	— Default	Color_1	
	PV-...				■ red	Co...	— Defa...	Color_1				■ red	Continuous	— Default	Color_1	
	PV-...				■ red	Co...	— Defa...	Color_1				■ red	Continuous	— Default	Color_1	
	Vie...				■ w...	Co...	— Defa...	Color_7				■ white	Continuous	— Default	Color_7	

Current layer: 0

Filters ≪ · All · All Used Layers

☐ Invert filter ≪

All: 11 layers displayed of 11 total layers

Search for layer

Layer Properties Manager

Figure 26-13   The **Layer Properties Manager** dialog box

USING THE PLOT STYLE TABLE EDITOR

The plot styles are individual files that AutoCAD uses to store information about printing preferences. There are two different types of plot styles files:

- Color-dependent plot style files (*.ctb*)
- Named plot style files (*.stb*)

The type of file used to manage the plot style is established the moment you create a new drawing. It depends on the option selected in the **Default plot style behavior for new drawings** section in the **Plot Style Table Settings** dialog box (Figure 26-14). This dialog box is accessed by clicking the **Plot Style Table Settings...** button in the **Plot and Publish** tab of the **Options** dialog box (Figure 26-15).

Figure 26-14   The **Plot Style Table Settings** dialog box

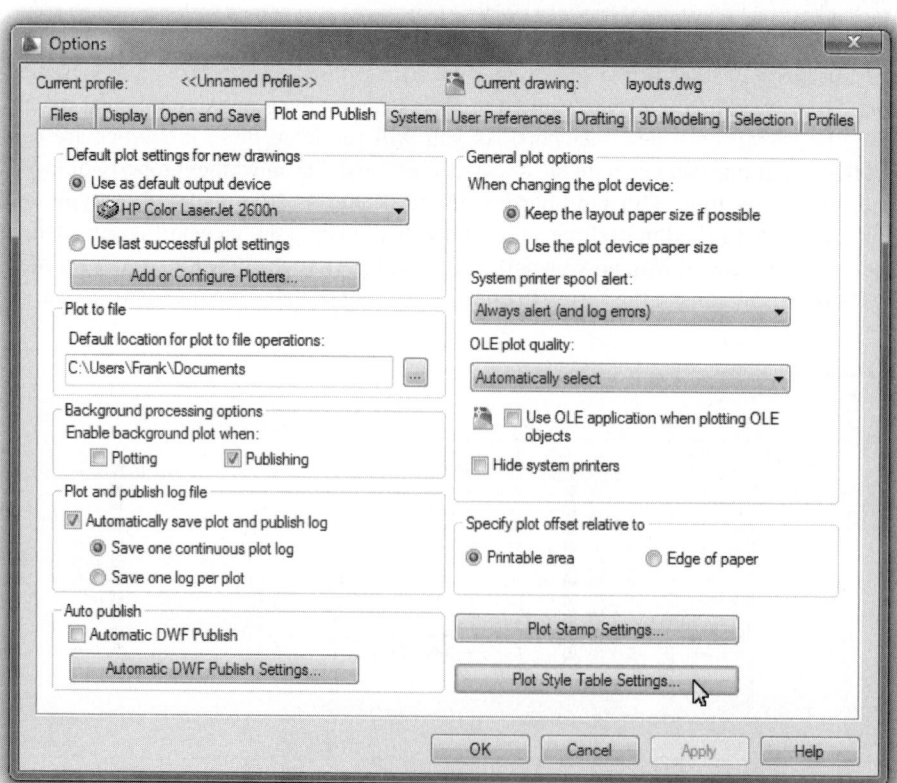

Figure 26-15   The **Plot and Publish** tab of the **Options** dialog box contains the **Plot Style Table Settings...** button

Color-dependent plot styles are the default when the AutoCAD software is first installed. Many users find these styles more convenient to use and to visualize because it is easy know how an object will be plotted by looking at its color. Other users prefer using named plot styles. These plot styles can be assigned to the objects independently of their color, either by changing this property on the object directly or through the object's layer. Regardless of which method you use, the final purpose is the same. We will use color-dependent plot styles for the exercises in the book.

A new *.ctb* file can be created by selecting **New...** from the drop-down list of *.ctb* files located in the **Plot** dialog box (Figure 26-16). This will take you through a short process, where you can select **Start from scratch** in the **Begin** screen, and then easily continue with the rest of the process.

Figure 26-16   The drop-down list of *.ctb* files located in the **Plot** dialog box

After you create the *.ctb* files, you can edit them or edit files that already exist. The **Edit...** button, located to the right of the drop-down list (Figure 26-17), opens the **Plot Style Table Editor** for the specific file in use (Figure 26-18).

In the **Plot Style Table Editor**, you can change the properties of the colors so that they are plotted with specific characteristics. Of all these properties, three are sufficiently important to consider:

- **Color:** You can set a specific color to be plotted in any other color. Usually, you will assign each color to be plotted in black or in its own color.

- **Screening:** The value of this property can be decreased from 100% to 1% to obtain faded or grayed tones. It is very helpful when plotting heavy hatches or when trying to save some ink in a plot for review.

- **Lineweight:** This is really the most important property because it controls the line thickness for each particular color.

Figure 26-17   The **Edit...** button located to the right of the drop-down list in the **Plot** dialog box

Figure 26-18   The **Plot Style Table Editor** dialog box

Specific line thickness values are used for the different drafting standards (ANSI, ISO, etc.), but most companies and draftpersons use their own thickness values to accommodate their unique needs, commonly within the following values:

Visible lines	0.3 to 0.6 mm (0.012 to 0.024″)
Hidden lines	0.15 to 0.3 mm (0.006 to 0.012″)
Dimensions, centerlines, break lines, and hatches	0.05 to 0.15 mm (0.002 to 0.006″)
Texts and annotations	0.2 to 0.4 mm (0.008 to 0.016″)
Titles and section lines	0.5 to 1.4 mm (0.197 to 0.055″)

GENERATING DRAWING VIEWS IN MODEL SPACE

CREATING 2D AND 3D SECTIONS USING SECTION OBJECTS

section object: An AutoCAD entity that allows you to temporarily slice 3D objects and create 2D and 3D sections from them.

A *section object* is an AutoCAD entity created with the **SECTIONPLANE** command. You can use section objects to perform multiple tasks. Their main use is to create live sectioning of 3D solids, surfaces, and regions, allowing you to see the interior geometry of the 3D solids (Figure 26-19). Additionally, you can generate 2D and 3D sections from the sliced objects.

Figure 26-19   A section object with live sectioning enabled

As with any other entity, you can modify section objects using operations such as **MOVE, ROTATE, COPY, ERASE**, and **MIRROR** (Figure 26-20). You can also assign a section object a layer and turn the layer off without canceling the sectioning effect (Figure 26-21).

When you invoke the **SECTIONPLANE** command, you can use one of four methods to create the section object. Two of the methods are implicit in the same first prompt. The other two can be optionally selected:

```
Select face or any point to locate
section line or [Draw section/Ortho-
graphic]:
```

1. **Selecting a Planar Face:** This method places a section object on the planar face of the 3D solid. The face is selected by clicking on it.

Note:
Turning off a layer that has been previously assigned to a section object simply hides the section object. The objects continue to be sectioned by the section object. Freezing the layer, on the other hand, not only hides the section object, but also cancels its slicing effect.

Figure 26-20   A section object can be moved, rotated, and more

Figure 26-21 The layer assigned to a section object can be turned off without affecting its sectioning effect

2. **Specifying Two Points:** If the first click does not find a planar face, it is considered to be the first point of the section line, and then a second, or through, point is required to create the section object. The slicing plane is created perpendicular to the current *XY* plane.

3. **Draw Section:** This option allows you to specify a set of points that define the segments of a jogged section object. Each segment of the section object defines a plane perpendicular to the current *XY* plane.

4. **Orthographic:** This method places a section object on the selected orthographic plane in the middle of the 3D object.

After you create a section object, you can change its appearance by selecting another type of slicing object. You can do so by clicking on the big down arrow that is revealed after the section object is selected [Figure 26-22(a)].

- **Section Plane:** The section object behaves as a plane that extends infinitely in all directions [Figure 26-22(a)].

Section Object's Base Plane

Section Boundary

(b)

✓ Section Plane
Section Boundary
Section Volume

Section Plane
(a)

Section Volume

(c)

Figure 26-22 A section object can be manifested in three different ways

- **Section Boundary:** The section object behaves as a boundary delimited in length and width by its corners, extending infinitely high in both directions [Figure 26-22(b)].
- **Section Volume:** The section object behaves as a box, enclosing a volume delimited in length, width, and height by its vertices [Figure 26-22(c)].

You can manipulate the available grips of a selected section object depending on its type. Figure 26-23 shows the uses of the different grips.

Right-clicking in the drawing area while a section object is selected displays a special section in the shortcut menu that contains other settings and tools (Figure 26-24).

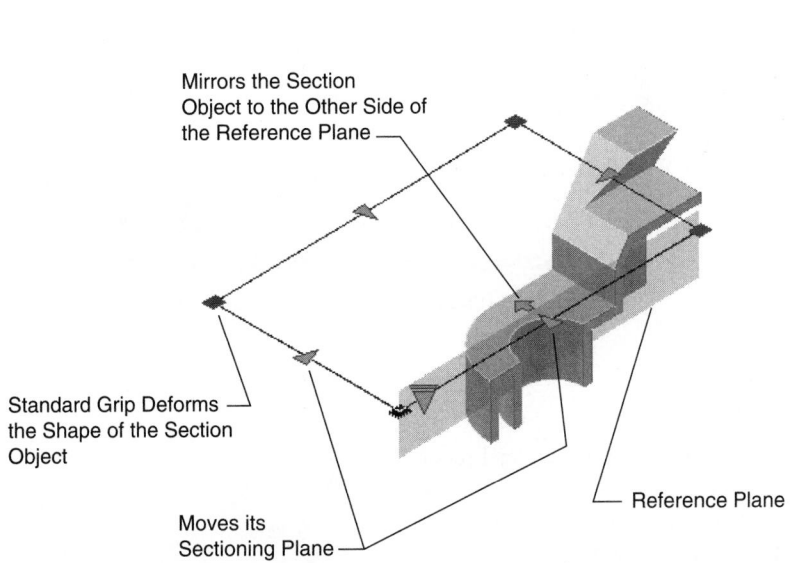

Mirrors the Section Object to the Other Side of the Reference Plane

Standard Grip Deforms the Shape of the Section Object

Moves its Sectioning Plane

Reference Plane

Figure 26-23   Uses of the different grips of the section object

Figure 26-24   A special section in the shortcut menu is displayed by right-clicking the drawing area while a section object is selected

In this section of the shortcut menu, you can perform the following tasks:

- Activate or deactivate the live sectioning
- Show or hide the sliced portion of the 3D objects in a different color
- Modify the section object by adding a step or jog
- Open the **Generate Section/Elevation** dialog box to generate 2D or 3D sections (Figure 26-25).
- Open the **Section Settings** dialog box to modify settings affecting **Live Section**, as well as the creation of 2D and 3D sections with the section object (Figure 26-26).

Figure 26-25   The **Generate Section/Elevation** dialog box

Figure 26-26   The **Section Settings** dialog box

The **Properties** palette also contains a special section where you can control other properties of the section object. These properties include the section object's **Name, Color**, and **Plane Transparency** (Figure 26-27).

Live sectioning can be activated or deactivated, allowing you to inspect inside the 3D objects whenever needed. 2D section and 3D section operations are used to extract geometry from the 3D objects whether or not live sectioning is enabled.

The geometry is extracted as block entities through the **Generate Section/Elevation** dialog box. You can choose to select specific objects under **Source Geometry**. You can also choose to replace existing block definitions or to save blocks as separate drawing files under **Destination**. Clicking the **Create** button closes the **Generate Section/Elevation** dialog box and takes you through a series of prompts. Here you can specify different scale factors along the three axes, as well as the rotation of the block generated.

Note:
Section objects created by specifying two points or using the **Draw section** option are initially placed with **Activate live sectioning** disabled. This setting can be modified by invoking the **LIVESECTION** command, through the section objects shortcut menu, or through the **Properties** palette.

Figure 26-27   Section objects can be modified through the **Properties** palette

Figure 26-28   A section view generated when a section object goes through the object

2D section blocks are placed in the current *XY* plane. If the section object cuts the 3D object, a section view is generated (Figure 26-28).

On the other hand, if the section object does not cut the 3D object and is located in front of it, a projected view is generated (Figure 26-29). You cannot, however, create projected views with different linetypes for hidden and visible edges in the same 2D section block. As you will learn later, other operations enable you to create projected views in a more effective way.

Figure 26-29   A projected view generated when a section object does not go through the object

One of the most important uses of section objects is creating jogged 2D sections. This procedure is the only one that allows you to obtain this type of drawing view (Figure 26-30).

3D section blocks maintain the orientation of the sectioned objects (Figure 26-31). When a 3D section block is exploded, it ungroups into a sliced copy of the 3D object, a hatch, and its boundary objects (Figure 26-32).

By adding jogs to the section object, you can create 3D section blocks slicing the 3D objects virtually anywhere (Figure 26-33).

Figure 26-30   A section object containing jogs can be used to generate jogged section views

Figure 26-31   A 3D section block obtained with a section object

Figure 26-32   A 3D section block is composed of a 3D solid, a hatch, and its boundary objects

Figure 26-33   A 3D section block obtained with a jogged section object

Exercise 26-1: Using Section Objects

1. **OPEN** *Exercise 26-1* in the student data files.
2. **SAVE** it **AS** *Exercise 26-1 solved*.
3. Invoke the **SECTIONPLANE** command and respond to the prompts as follows:

   `Select face or any point to locate section line or [Draw section/Orthographic]:` *Click to the left and over the 3D solid (Figure 26-34).*

   `Specify through point:` *With ORTHO mode activated, click to the right of the 3D solid so that the section object crosses it.*

Note: The two points specified by clicking in the drawing area to create the section object are placed on the current *XY* plane.

To access student data files, go to www.pearsondesigncentral.com.

SECTIONPLANE	
Ribbon: Solid Editing panel	
Pull-down Menu	Draw/ Modeling/ Section Object
Command Line	section-plane

Point to Locate Section Line

Z

Y

X

Ortho: 10.8863 < 0°

Through Point

Figure 26-34   Points to be specified in the **SECTIONPLANE** command

4. Select the **Realistic** visual style.
5. Select the section object by clicking its plane and open the **Properties** palette.
6. In the **Properties** palette (Figure 26-35), change the **Plane Color** property to **Red**.
7. While the section object is still selected, right-click in the drawing area and select **Activate live sectioning** to turn this feature on.
8. Press **<Esc>** to unselect the section object. The sectioned 3D object should look more or less like Figure 26-36.
9. Select the section object again and right-click in the drawing area. Select **Generate 2D/3D section...** from the shortcut menu.
10. In the **Generate Section/Elevation** dialog box, select **2D Section/Elevation** and click on the **Section Settings...** button.
11. In the **Section Settings** window, make sure **2D section/elevation block creation settings** is selected and scroll down to **the Cut-away Geometry** settings. Set both **Show** and **Hidden Line** to **No** (Figure 26-37).

Note: Because the points of the section object were not specified in an exact location, your section object might end up located in a different place.

Figure 26-35 The **Properties** palette

Figure 26-36 After activating live sectioning

12. Scroll to the **Background Lines** settings and set **Hidden Lines** to **No**.
13. Scroll to the **Intersection Fill** settings and change the **Face Hatch** to **Select hatch pattern type...** (Figure 26-38). In the **Hatch Pattern Type** dialog box, select **ANSI131** (Figure 26-39) and click **OK** to close the dialog box. Click **OK** to close the **Section Settings** dialog box also.

Figure 26-37 Specifying settings in the **Section Settings** dialog box

Figure 26-38 Specifying settings in the **Section Settings** dialog box

14. Back in the **Generate Section/Elevation** dialog box, click the **Create** button.
15. Click anywhere in the drawing area to specify an insertion point. Respond by pressing **<Enter↵>** to all other prompts. The 2D section created should look like Figure 26-40.

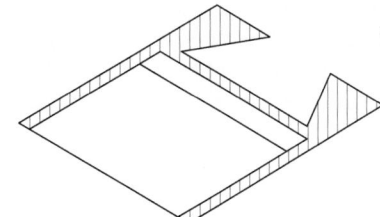

Figure 26-39   The **Hatch Pattern Type** dialog box

Figure 26-40   The resulting 2D section

16. Select the **Top** view and select the section object again.
17. With **ORTHO** mode activated, pull the grips located at the endpoints of the section object to get them closer to the 3D object (Figure 26-41).

TIP

Only one of the two endpoint grips can actually be used to stretch the section object.

18. Select the triangular grip located in the middle of the section object and stretch it downward. Try placing the section object close to the location shown in Figure 26-42.

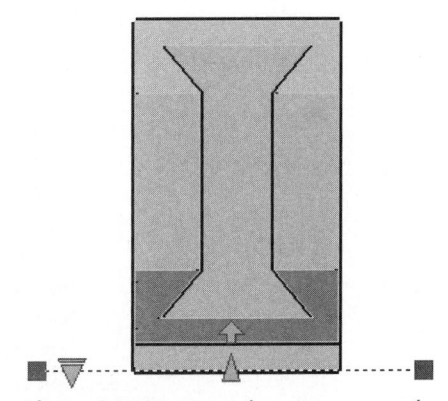

Figure 26-41   Using the grips to adjust the section object

Figure 26-42   Using the grips to move the section object

19. Select the **SE Isometric** viewing point.
20. Select the section object and right-click in the drawing area. Deselect **Activate live sectioning** in the shortcut menu to turn the sectioning effect off.
21. Invoke the **MOVE** command and move the section object from its midpoint to the center point of the bottom circular edge on the hole.
22. Turn **Activate live sectioning** on.

23. Invoke the **ROTATE** command and rotate the section object around its midpoint **90°** (Figure 26-43).
24. Select the section object and right-click to select **Add jog to section** from the shortcut menu. When prompted to specify a point, click on any point on the section object.
25. Select the **Top** view.
26. Select the section object and turn **Activate live sectioning** off.
27. Following in order the three operations shown in Figure 26-44, readjust the jogged section object.
28. Select the **SE Isometric** viewing point.
29. Select the section object and right-click in the drawing area. Select **Generate 2D/3D section...** from the shortcut menu.

Note:
The object snap automatically overrides to the nearest point when adding a jog. This allows you to actually specify a point on the section object.

Figure 26-43   The isometric view   **Figure 26-44**   Procedure to adjust the jogged section object from the top view

30. In the **Generate Section/Elevation** dialog box, select **3D Section** and click on the **Section Settings...** button. Under **Intersection Fill**, set the **Face Hatch** as **Predefined/ANSI131**, similar to what you did previously for the 2D section. When finished, close the **Section Settings** window by clicking **OK**.
31. Under **Destination**, select **Export to a file**, and click on the browse button (**...**).
32. In the **Browse for Drawing File** dialog box, type **Exercise 26-2** as the **File name**, and look for the folder where you have the other drawings. Click the **Save** button to close the dialog box. Then go back into the **Generate Section/Elevation** dialog box and click the **Create** button to generate the file.
33. Select the section object and turn **Activate live sectioning** on. Press **<Esc>** to unselect the section object.
34. Select the section object once again. Click on the arrowlike grid located inside the cylindrical hole (Figure 26-45). This action will switch the sectioned side.
35. Unselect the section object and invoke the **3DORBIT** command to inspect the other side of the 3D model (Figure 26-46).
36. **SAVE** the drawing.

Note:
Unlike 3D sections created inside the same drawing, 3D sections exported as independent drawing files are not generated as blocks.

Note:
Using jogged section objects can produce effects similar to these obtained using boundary section objects.

Figure 26-45   After activating live sectioning

Figure 26-46   Inspecting the opposite side of the sectioned object

CREATING VIEWS USING THE FLATSHOT COMMAND

The **FLATSHOT** command allows you to create projected views in a very simple way: It gener-ates a block by projecting the current view onto the current *XY* plane. Any existing 3D solid, sur-face, or region is included in the projected block.

For example, if you select the **Right** view, the *XY* plane automatically aligns with the **Right** plane. Thus, the projected block will correspond to the **Right** view and will be placed in the **Right** plane, which is where the current *XY* plane is.

Just as with the **SECTIONPLANE** command, you can specify different scale factors along the three axes in the **FLATSHOT** command. You can also select the rotation of the block generated.

Unlike the **SECTIONPLANE** command, **FLATSHOT** enables you to control the behavior of obscured lines. Many drawings contain standard projected views and sections, in which case you can use both commands jointly.

Exercise 26-2: Creating 2D Drawing Views in Paper Space Using the **FLATSHOT** and the **SECTIONPLANE** Commands

1. **OPEN** the file *Exercise 26-2* in the student data files.
2. **SAVE** it **AS** *Exercise 26-2 solved*.
3. Select the **Top** view.
4. Invoke the **FLATSHOT** command to open the **Flatshot** dialog box.
5. Under **Obscured lines**, select the **HIDDEN** linetype and select the color **Green**. Make sure that **Show** is checked and click the **Create** button (Figure 26-47).

To access student data files, go to www.pearsondesigncentral.com.

FLATSHOT	
Ribbon: **Solid Editing panel**	
Command Line	flatshot

> **TIP** To select the **HIDDEN** linetype, you must first load from the **Select Linetype** dialog box. You open this box by selecting **Other...** from the **Linetype** drop-down list.

6. Click in any empty spot of the drawing area to specify the insertion point. Respond by pressing **<Enter↵>** to all other prompts. The projected block created should look like Figure 26-48.
7. Select the **Front** view.
8. Invoke the **FLATSHOT** command and click the **Create** button in the **Flatshot** dialog box.
9. As in the previous projection, click anywhere in the drawing area to specify the insertion point. Press **<Enter↵>** to accept all other prompts (Figure 26-49).
10. Select the **SE Isometric** viewing point.
11. Right-click in the drawing area and select **Cut** from the shortcut menu. When prompted, select the block projected onto the front plane and press **<Enter↵>** to end the selection.
12. Select the **World** UCS.

Figure 26-47   The **Flatshot** dialog box

Figure 26-48   A projected block created with the **FLATSHOT** operation

13. Right-click in the drawing area to select **Paste** from the shortcut menu. Click in an empty spot to insert the block from the clipboard (Figure 26-50).

Figure 26-49   The front-projected block created with the **FLATSHOT** operation

Figure 26-50   The front-projected block pasted in the XY plane of the WCS

14. Invoke the **FLATSHOT** command. In the **Flatshot** dialog box, uncheck the **Show** checkbox under **Obscured lines** and click the **Create** button.
15. Click anywhere in the drawing area and press **<Enter.┘>** to accept all other prompts (Figure 26-51).
16. Invoke the **SECTIONPLANE** command and respond to the prompts as follows:

```
Select face or any point to locate section line or [Draw section/
Orthographic]: o ┘
```

`Align section to: [Front/bAck/Top/Bot-`
`tom/Left/Right] Top:` *r* ↵

17. Select the section object created and right-click to select **Generate 2D/3D section...** from the shortcut menu.

18. In the **Section Settings** palette, make the following changes:

   • Under **Intersection Fill**, set the **Face Hatch** as **Predefined/ANSI131**.
   • Under **Background Lines**, set **Hidden Line** to **No**.
   • Under **Cut-away Geometry**, set both **Show** and **Hidden Lines** to **No**.
   • Under **Curve Tangency Lines**, set **Show** to **No**.

19. Click **OK** to close the **Section Settings** dialog box.

20. Click **Create** to generate the section block. Click anywhere in the drawing area to specify an insertion point. Respond by pressing **<Enter↵>** to all other prompts.

21. **ERASE** the section object.

22. Select the **Top** view. The objects should look like Figure 26-52 in your own arrangement.

> **Note:**
> A section object with **Live sectioning** activated is placed in the middle of the 3D solid.

Figure 26-51   The isometric-projected block created with the **FLATSHOT** operation

Figure 26-52   All drawing views seen from the **Top** view

23. **ROTATE** the block projected onto the Top plane −90° about any point on it.

24. **MOVE** the projected blocks to space them out, if needed (Figure 26-53).

25. Click the **Layout1** tab to switch to paper space.

26. Right-click on top of the **Layout1** tab and select **From template...**

27. In the **Select Template From File** dialog box, browse for the file named **TB-Imperial.dwt** in the student data files. Select the file and click the **Open** button.

28. In the **Insert Layout(s)** dialog box, select **ANSI A (11 × 8.5)** and click **OK** (Figure 26-54).

> **Note:**
> The new Layout tab named **ANSI A (11 × 8.5)** is added to the drawing.

To access student data files, go to www.pearsondesigncentral.com.

Figure 26-53   The drawing views after they are relocated

Figure 26-54   The **Insert Layout(s)** dialog box

29. Click the **ANSI A (11 × 8.5)** Layout tab. It contains a title block and a page already prepared with no viewports.
30. Invoke the **VPORTS** command to open the **Viewports** dialog box. In the **New Viewports** tab select **Four: Equal**, select **2D** under **Setup**, and click **OK**. When prompted for the first and opposite corners, click two points diagonally inside the title block, to place the four viewports (Figure 26-55).
31. Double-click inside the top-right viewport to activate it.
32. **ZOOM** and **PAN** to center the block containing the **Top** view in the viewport.
33. Locate the **Viewport** toolbar and select the scale **1:2** from its drop-down list window (Figure 26-56).

Note:
The cut-and-paste procedure you used allowed you to locate all the blocks containing the drawing views in the same plane. This procedure allowed you to use the same viewing point in every viewport. You could have avoided the cutting-and-pasting process, however, by using a different approach. You could have changed the viewing point through the active viewport so the viewing plane was located parallel to the plane containing the projected block. For example, to show the block projected onto the front plane, you could select the Front orthographic view through the viewport.

TIP   When a viewport is active, any **ZOOM** operation, including the ones with the mouse wheel, will cause the view to zoom in and out. This will affect the current scale.

34. Click inside another viewport to make it active. Repeat the same procedure with the other three viewports to locate each corresponding view. When you are finished, the 2D drawing should look like Figure 26-57. The isometric view does not need to be shown to any specific scale.

Figure 26-55   Four viewports are created

Figure 26-56   After adjusting the scale and the view in the top-left viewport

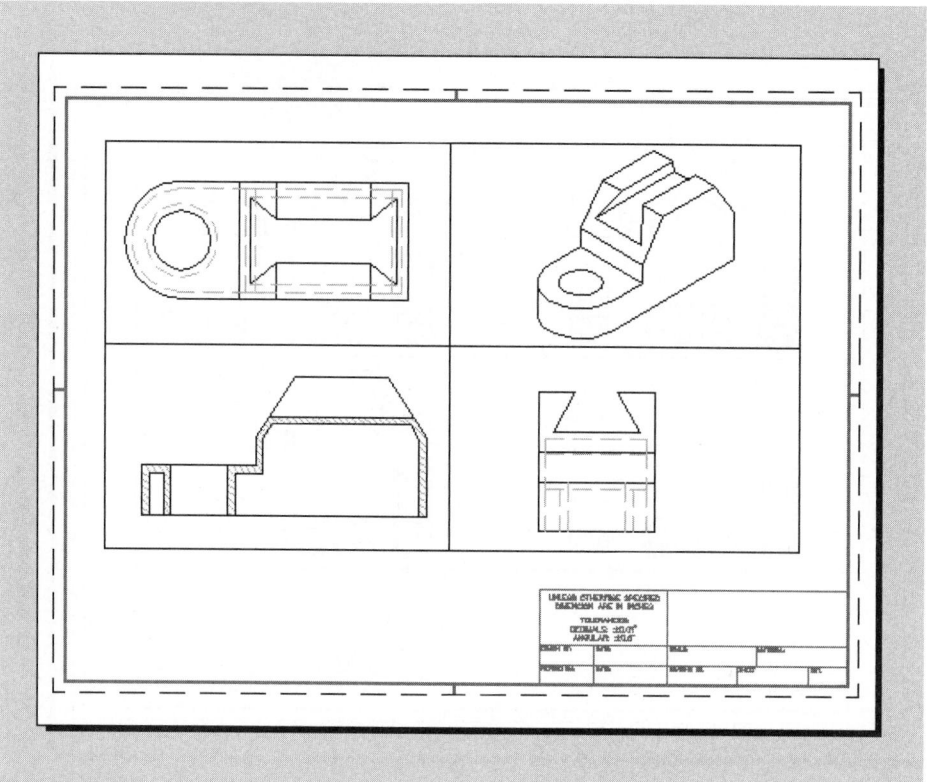

Figure 26-57   After adjusting all viewports

35. Double-click outside the viewports to deactivate them, or return to paper mode.
36. **MOVE** the viewport containing the top projected block from a point on the block to a point on the block of the viewport below (Figure 26-58).
37. With **ORTHO** mode activated, **MOVE** the viewport back up, maintaining the vertical alignment (Figure 26-59).
38. Repeat the same procedure to align the viewport showing the right view.
39. Select all viewports and set the **Display locked** property to **Yes** in the **Properties** palette (Figure 26-60).
40. Create a new layer named *VP*. Assign the layer to all viewport objects, and then turn it off. This will hide all the viewport objects (Figure 26-61).
41. Place the dimensions on top of the paper. When you are finished, the drawing will look like Figure 26-62.
42. Open the **Page Setup** dialog box for the current Layout. Select your printing device and the **monochrome.ctb** plot style. Close the dialog box by clicking **OK**.
43. Invoke the **PREVIEW** command and **PLOT** the drawing.
44. **SAVE** the drawing.

> **Note:**
> In this procedure, the drawing views are not aligned. You can align them by using the **Align** option of the **MVSETUP** command, or by simply moving the viewports around. Anyhow, it is not the viewports that need to be aligned, but rather the drawing views.

> **Note:**
> You can place the dimensions either inside the model space or on top of the paper space. AutoCAD corrects the measurement scale factor when placing dimensions on views that are not scaled 1 : 1.

Figure 26-58   The viewport is moved, snapping to points on the objects located in the model space

Figure 26-59   The viewport is moved back upward orthogonally

PLACING DIMENSIONS IN THE 3D SPACE

An elaborate drawing document that includes all the views and drafting standards often is not necessary. Instead, you can provide a quick isometric view with the proper dimensions, which might enable others to understand the drawing better. Using isometric views of 3D sections will enhance technical documents even more by enabling you to provide details and dimensions of the inside geometry.

Figure 26-60   The **Properties** palette

Figure 26-61   After turning the viewport's assigned layer off

Figure 26-63 shows a dimensioned isometric view (a) versus the standard drawing views displayed on the right (b).

Placing dimensions on 3D objects is really simple. Because the dimensions are always placed in the current *XY* plane, the UCS must be aligned beforehand with the face where the dimensions are to be placed.

When you place a dimension in the 3D space, the control grips at the origin of the extension lines are located at the points you specify. The rest of the dimension, however, is always placed in the current *XY* plane. In an orthographic view, this effect is not noticeable and the

Figure 26-62
Dimensions placed in paper space

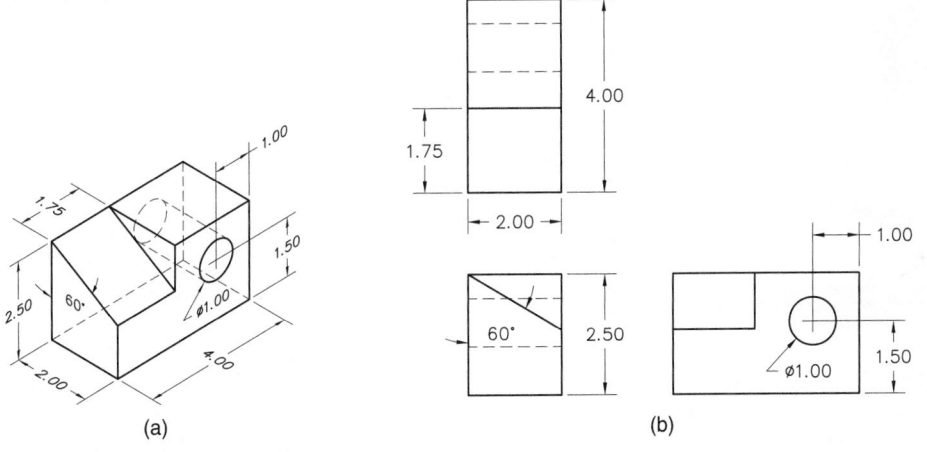

(a)   (b)

Figure 26-63   A dimensioned isometric view (a) can be used instead of the standard drawing views (b)

dimension appears to be completely contained in a plane. But from a nonorthographic viewing point, the dimension must be placed using the correct UCS to look right. Figure 26-64 shows the difference between placing a dimension in the 3D space using the incorrect and the correct UCS.

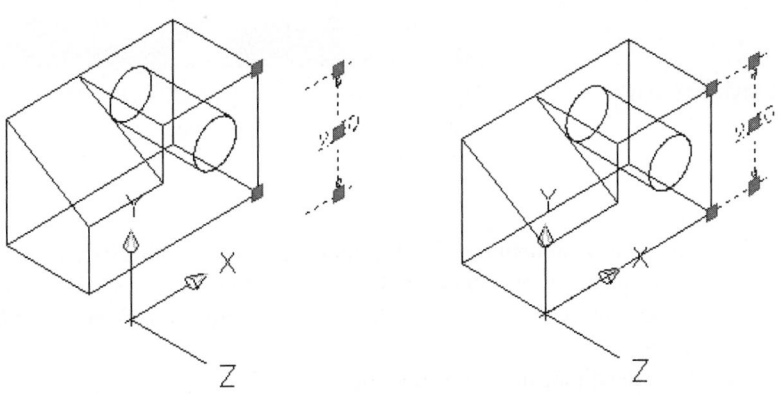

Figure 26-64   The UCS must be properly aligned before placing a dimension in the 3D space

Exercise 26-3: Placing Dimensions in the 3D Space and Setting up the Page in Paper Space

To access student data
files, go to
www.pearsondesigncentral.com.

1. **OPEN** the file *Exercise 26-3* you saved in **Exercise 26-1** by creating a 3D section. You can also open this file in the student data files if you did not complete the exercise.
2. **SAVE** the drawing **AS *Exercise 26-3 solved***.
3. Select the **SE Isometric** viewing point.
4. Open the **Visual Styles Manager** palette. Select the **2D Wireframe** visual style by clicking on its sample image and make the following changes (Figure 26-65):

   • Set **Contour lines** to **0**
   • Set **Draw true silhouettes** to **Yes**
   • Set **Solid smoothness** to **8**

5. Close the **Visual Styles Manager** palette and invoke the **REGEN** command.
6. Set the UCS icon to show up at its origin, rather than at the lower-left corner of the display. You can do so by checking the **Origin** option in the **View** drop-down menu, as shown in Figure 26-66.

Figure 26-65   The **Visual Styles Manager** palette

Figure 26-66   Accessing the UCS icon's **Origin** option from the **View** enhanced drop-down menu

7. Open the **Dimension Style Manager**. Click on the **Modify** button and set the **Precision** to two places in the **Primary Units** tab. Change other settings, such as the **Text Style** and **Colors**, to your liking. When finished, close the **Dimension Style Manager** dialog box.
8. Place the dimensions shown in Figure 26-67.

Figure 26-67   First dimensions placed

9. Select the **Right** UCS.
10. Place the UCS origin at the endpoint shown in Figure 26-68.
11. Place the dimensions shown in Figure 26-69.
12. Relocate the UCS origin to any point on the opposite face and place the dimensions shown in Figure 26-70.
13. Continue changing and relocating the UCS to place the rest of the dimensions. When you are finished, the dimensioned 3D section should look like Figure 26-71. Use the **3D Orbit** tool, if needed.

Note:
As long as you align the UCS with the plane in which you want to place the dimension, you can use any point to locate its origin.

Figure 26-68   The UCS is relocated

Figure 26-69   Other dimensions added in the new UCS

14. Click the **Layout1** tab to switch to paper space.
15. **OPEN** the file *TB-Imperial* in the student data files. It contains a title block drawn in the layout (Figure 26-72).
16. Right-click in the drawing area and select **Copy** from the shortcut menu. This will invoke the **COPYCLIP** command. When prompted, select all the objects forming the title block by using a selection window. Press **<Enter.⏎>** to end the selection.
17. **CLOSE** the *TB-Imperial* drawing file.
18. Once you are back in *Exercise 26-2*, right-click in the drawing area and select **Paste** from the shortcut menu. Specify a point that approximately centers the title block on the paper (Figure 26-73).
19. Right-click on top of the **Layout1** tab and select **Page Setup Manager....**

To access student data files, go to www.pearsondesigncentral.com.

Figure 26-70   More dimensions added after changing the UCS

Figure 26-71   After placing all the dimensions

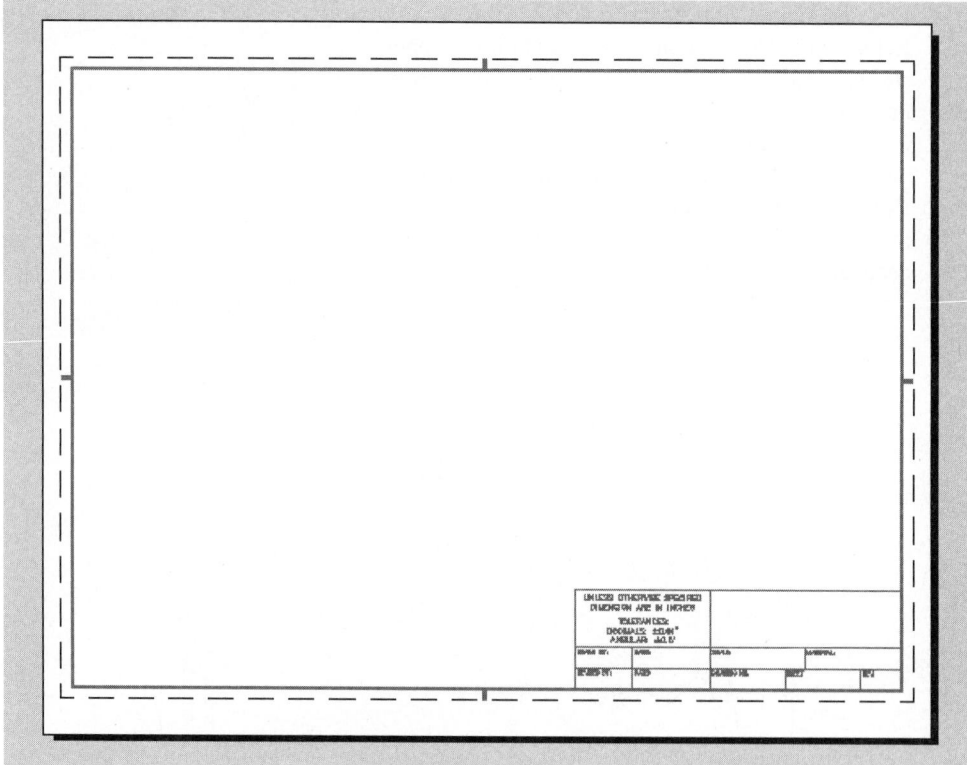

Figure 26-72   Title block contained in the drawing file

20. **Click on the Modify...** button to open the **Page Setup – Layout1** dialog box. Make the following changes:
    - Under **Printer/Plotter**, select your device.
    - Under **Plot style table**, select **monochrome.ctb**.
    - Under **Paper size**, select **Letter** or **8.50 × 11.00**.
    - Under **Drawing orientation**, select **Landscape**.
    - Under **Plot area**, select **Window**. When prompted to specify the first corner, select one of the corners in the main rectangle. Then select the diagonally opposite one.
    - Under **Plot offset**, check the **Center the plot** checkbox.
    - Make sure the **Scale** reads **1:1**. Click **OK** to close the **Page Setup – Layout1** dialog box.

21. Close the **Page Setup Manager** dialog box. The title block should now be perfectly centered on the paper (Figure 26-74).

Figure 26-73   Title block pasted into Layout1

Figure 26-74   The title block is perfectly centered on the paper

PREVIEW	
Standard Toolbar	
Pull-down Menu	File/Plot Preview
Command Line	preview

22. Open the **Layer Properties Manager** dialog box and create a new layer named *VIEWPORT*. Change its color to **Green**, and click on its **Plotter** icon to prevent it from being plotted. Click **OK** to close the **Layer Properties Manager** dialog box.
23. Apply the *VIEWPORT* layer to the viewport.
24. Double-click inside the viewport to make it active. **ZOOM** and **PAN** with the mouse wheel to set the isometric view to a proper size and location.
25. Double-click outside the viewport to deactivate it.
26. Select the viewport and right-click to display the shortcut menu. Set **Display Locked** to **Yes** and **Shade plot** to **Hidden**.
27. Invoke the **PREVIEW** command. It should look like Figure 26-75.
28. **PLOT** the drawing and then **SAVE** it.

Figure 26-75   The plot preview

EXPLODED ASSEMBLY DRAWINGS

Exploded 3D isometric views are commonly used for assembly instruction, product presentation, and many other purposes. They not only clearly demonstrate how to put the parts together but also provide a professional way to present a product design.

The AutoCAD program does not possess any special tools to produce assemblies or exploded views. To create exploded views, simply space the 3D objects that form the assembly out in strategic directions and then place centerlines to show the assembling traces.

Exercise 26-4: Creating Exploded Drawing Views

To access student data files, go to www.pearsondesigncentral.com.

1. **OPEN** the drawing *Exercise 26-4* in the student data files. It contains the assembly of several 3D solids.
2. **SAVE** the drawing **AS *Exercise 26-4 solved***.
3. Select the view named **Exploded View** from the drop-down list located in the **View** panel of the Ribbon (Figure 26-76).
4. Invoke the **HIDE** command. The 3D model should look like Figure 26-77.

Figure 26-76   The drop-down list located in the **View** panel of the Ribbon

Figure 26-77   Assembly contained in the drawing file

5. Invoke the **REGEN** command. Select the **Front** UCS.
6. **MOVE** the wrench and the set screw orthogonally down **4″**.
7. **MOVE** the wrench orthogonally down **2″**.
8. Invoke the **HIDE** command. The 3D model should look like Figure 26-78.
9. **MOVE** the wrench, the set screw, and the bracket **20″** along the positive *X*-axis.
10. **MOVE** the four socket head screws **6.5″** along the negative *Y*-axis. The 3D model should look like Figure 26-79.

Figure 26-78   The wrench is moved orthogonally down

Figure 26-79   The four socket screws are moved orthogonally down

11. First, load the **Center** linetype into the drawing and then set it current in the drop-down list on the **Properties** toolbar. The next object created will have this property.

12. Draw all the highlighted polylines shown in Figure 26-80. Snap to center points to locate all the polylines properly. For the polyline that shows the dovetail connection, just draw a short line going from the midpoint of the bottom edge in the direction of the *X*-axis.

Figure 26-80   After placing the assembly trails.

13. Click the **Layout1** tab to switch to paper space. It contains the same title block as in the previous exercise.

14. Double-click inside the viewport to make it active.

15. Select the view named **Exploded View** from the drop-down list located in the **View** toolbar, as you did in step 3.

16. **ZOOM** and **PAN** with the mouse wheel to set the view to the proper size.

17. Double-click outside the viewport to deactivate it.

18. Select the viewport and right-click to display the shortcut menu. Set **Display Locked** to **Yes**. Display the shortcut menu again and set the **Shade plot** to **Hidden**.

19. Invoke the **PREVIEW** command. The result should look like Figure 26-81.

20. **PLOT** the drawing and then **SAVE** it.

3D exploded assembly drawings are very important technical documents. They constitute a strong bridge for communicating special instructions in the fabrication process. Products that require end-user assembly are better accepted when you provide quality exploded assembly drawings to accompany them. Whether you use these techniques in your current job position or in your own business, perfecting this skill will enable you to provide technical documents with a higher level of professionalism.

Figure 26-81   The plot preview

CREATING DRAWING VIEWS IN PAPER SPACE

CREATING VIEWS IN PAPER SPACE WITH THE **SOLPROF** COMMAND—

The **SOLPROF** command enables you to extract the profile (edges and silhouettes) of the 3D solids you select, according to the viewing point on the viewport. This command can be invoked only from paper space and requires you to select the 3D solids through an active viewport.

This command generates either one or two anonymous blocks (blocks that cannot be inserted or edited).

By answering **Yes** or **No** to the command's prompts, you can alter three different aspects of the results:

1. You can create a single block or create separate blocks for the visible lines and the hidden or occulted lines. This option also creates either a single layer or two layers, one for each block.

2. You can create blocks that contain the profile projected onto a plane that is parallel to the current viewing plane and goes though the origin, or you can extract the edges and create blocks as 3D wireframes.

3. You may choose to include the tangential edges in the blocks or not.

For example, responding **Yes** to these three questions creates two projected blocks without including the tangential edges: one for the visible edges and silhouettes, and another one for the occulted edges and silhouettes. Each block will have its own layer assigned to it.

Note:
Having a separate layer for each block enables you to change the linetype and color for the entire block at any time.

Exercise 26-5: Generating the Drawing Views in Paper Space Using the **SOLPROF** Command

1. **OPEN** either *Exercise 23-8* or *Exercise 23-10* as completed in Chapter 23.
2. **SAVE** it **AS** *Exercise 26-5*.
3. Select the **SW Isometric** viewpoint.
4. Select the **World** UCS.
5. Make sure all the checkboxes concerning **Layout elements** in the **Display** tab of the **Options** dialog box are checked (Figure 26-82). Click **OK** to close the dialog box.
6. Click on the **Layout1** tab. Click the **Close** button to close the **Page Setup Manager** dialog box. The paper should be displayed with a single viewport that shows the current view in the model space (Figure 26-83).
7. **ERASE** the viewport. Without the viewport, you will see only an empty paper.
8. Invoke the **VPORTS** command to open the **Viewports** dialog box (Figure 26-84). In the **New Viewports** tab, select **Four: Equal** from the list. Select **3D** under **Setup**, and specify a value of **0.5** for the **Viewport Spacing**. Click **OK** to close the dialog box. When prompted for the first and opposite corners, click two points diagonally where the four viewports can fit. When you are finished, the layout should look like Figure 26-85.
9. Double-click inside the viewport located on the top left. It becomes activated as shown in Figure 26-86.
10. Locate the **Viewports** toolbar (Figure 26-87). The scale drop-down list of the **Viewport** toolbar shows the actual scale factor for the current active viewport.
11. Click on the drop-down list arrow and select the scale **1:2** (Figure 26-88).
12. Click inside any other viewport to make it active and change its scale factor to the **1:2** scale. Repeat the same procedure for the two other viewports containing orthographic

Note: The **Page Setup** dialog box is automatically opened the first time you enter a layout whenever the **Show Page Setup Manager for new layouts** option is enabled.

Figure 26-82   Layout elements settings located in the **Display** tab of the **Options** dialog box

Figure 26-83   Default viewport when entering a layout

Figure 26-84   The **Viewports** dialog box

views. If needed, **PAN** the view inside the viewport containing the isometric view to show it entirely.

13. When you are finished, double-click on any area outside the viewports or click the **MODEL** button in the status bar. The scaled viewports should look like Figure 26-89.

Note:
Besides clicking inside, another way to make another viewport active is to press <Ctrl> and <R> repeatedly. This method is especially useful when trying to activate a viewport that is completely contained inside another viewport.

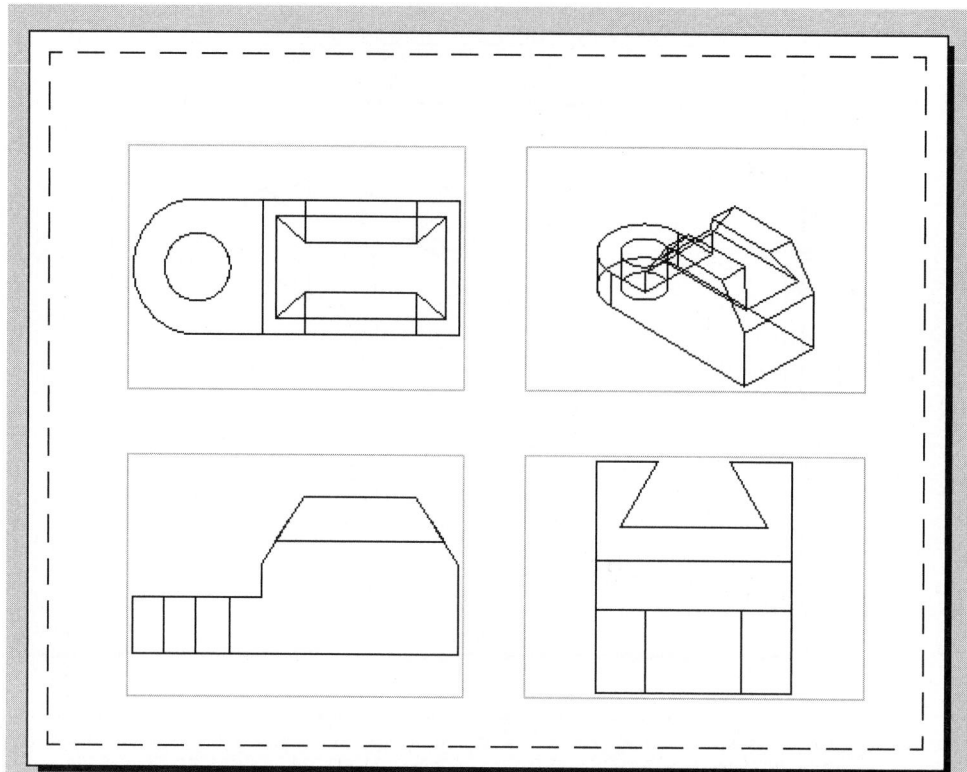

Figure 26-85   The resulting viewport arrangement

Figure 26-86   The top-left viewport is activated

Figure 26-87   The **Viewports** toolbar

Figure 26-88   The scale drop-down list in the **Viewports** toolbar

Figure 26-89   After setting the scale of the viewports

TIP   Depending on the size of the viewport, the 3D solid may or may not fit inside it. If the 3D solid does not fit, you can select the viewport object by clicking on it, and stretch it by grabbing its grips. This operation will not change the scale factor.

14. Double-click again inside the viewport that contains the **SE Isometric** view to make it active. Select the **SW Isometric** view. The view updates to the new viewing point (Figure 26-90).

Figure 26-90   Changing the viewing point through a viewport

15. Double-click outside the viewports to deactivate any one that is active. Select the four viewports and right-click to show the shortcut menu. Select **Yes** for the **Display Locked** option.
16. **Double-click** inside the top-left viewport to activate it.
17. Invoke the **SOLPROF** command and respond to the prompts as follows:

    Select objects: *Select the 3D solid through the active viewport.*

    Select objects: ↵ *(To end the selection)*

    Display hidden profile lines on separate layer? [Yes/No] <Y>: ↵ *(To accept the default)*

    Project profile lines onto a plane? [Yes/No] <Y>: ↵ *(To accept the default)*

    Delete tangential edges? [Yes/No] <Y>: ↵ *(To accept the default)*

18. Activate one by one the three remaining viewports, except the one containing the isometric view, and invoke the **SOLPROF** command to create the projected profiles. Respond **Yes** to all the prompts for each viewport.
19. Double-click outside the viewports to deactivate any one that is activated.

Note:
When you create several viewports using one of the viewport configurations, the views are automatically aligned with each other. Such alignment, however, can be noticed only between viewports whose views are related, and whose scale factor is the same. For example, if you create two viewports using the **Two: Horizontal** configuration, and you show the Top and Front views on the viewports, the views should end up aligned after selecting the same scale. This advantageous characteristic can save you the time required to align the views manually. You can lose this alignment, however, by performing operations that displace the center of the view, such as **PAN, ZOOM WINDOW**, or using the mouse wheel while a viewport is active.

SOLPROF	
Ribbon: Modeling panel	
Pull-down Menu	Draw/ Modeling/ Setup/ Profile
Command Line	solprof

20. Switch to model space by clicking on the **Model** tab.
21. Switch back to paper space by clicking on the **Layout1** tab.
22. Invoke the **VPMAX** command by double-clicking on the bottom-left viewport's border.
23. Invoke the **3DORBIT** command and rotate the viewing point (Figure 26-91).
24. Right-click and select **Minimize Viewport** to go back to **Layout1**.
25. Load the **HIDDEN** linetype into the drawing.
26. Open the **Layer Properties Manager** dialog box. Create two new layers named *Viewport* and *3DSolid*.
27. Select all the **PH-** layers. Change their linetype to **HIDDEN**. Give these layers a color different from that of the **PV-** layers. See Figure 26-92 as a guide. Click **OK** to close the **Layer Properties Manager** dialog box.

> **Note:**
> Any modification you perform in the model space will be shown through the viewports. There are three ways to access the model space.
> 1. Click the **Model** tab to go back into the model space.
> 2. Through an active viewport, you can use the **3D Orbit** tool and do any modification. This is not recommended, however, because all the settings regarding scale as well as the alignment will be lost, regardless of whether or not the viewport is locked.
> 3. Maximize a viewport.

Figure 26-91   Using the **3D Orbit** tool through a maximized viewport

> **Note:**
> In model space, you will see the different projected blocks created through each viewport for the selected 3D solid.

> **Note:**
> The advantage of using the maximized viewing mode is that you will see only the layers that are thawed in this particular viewport. In addition, the scale and alignment of the viewport remain unchanged.

TIP   The **HIDDEN** linetype can be loaded directly from the **Layers Properties Manager** window.

28. Maximize the viewport that shows the Top view.
29. Invoke the **3DORBIT** command to change the viewing point.
30. Assign the *3DSolid* layer to the 3D solid object. In the drop-down **Layer Control** window located in the **Layers** panel of the Ribbon, **Freeze** the *3DSolid* layer for the current viewport (third icon) (Figure 26-93). Click **OK** to close the warning.

Figure 26-92   List of layers contained in the **Layer Properties Manager** dialog box

Figure 26-93   The **Layer Control** drop-down list located on the **Layers** panel of the Ribbon

31. Right-click and select **Minimize Viewport** to go back to **Layout1**.
32. Activate one by one the viewports containing the Front and Right views to **Freeze** the *3DSolid* layer in each one. After deactivating the last active viewport, the 2D drawing should look like Figure 26-94.
33. Set the **LTSCALE** system variable to **0.5**.
34. Select the viewport that contains the isometric view. Right-click in the drawing area to display the shortcut menu and set **Shade plot** to **Hidden**.
35. Select the four viewports and change their layer to the *Viewport* layer.
36. **MOVE** all the viewports up to make some room for a title block.

Note:
The six new layers that start with PV- and PH- have been created automatically. They separate the visible and hidden projected blocks for each viewport. The digits following the dash stand for the viewport's handle ID, which can be obtained by invoking the **LIST** command after selecting the specific viewport.

TIP   At this point, if you need to **MOVE** the viewports around, you should move two at a time in an orthogonal direction to avoid losing the alignment between the views.

Figure 26-94   The viewports showing the projected objects

37. In the **Layer control** drop-down window, turn the *Viewport* layer off. The drawing should look like Figure 26-95.

38. This time you will create a simple title block yourself. Draw the objects shown in Figure 26-96 anywhere in the gray area to represent the title block.

Figure 26-95   After turning the *Viewport* layer off

Figure 26-96   A representative title block created in paper space

39. With **ORTHO** mode off, **MOVE** the title block into the drawing sheet so that all the drawing views fit well inside it. Do not be concerned about centering the title block with the paper, but rather center it with the drawing views (Figure 26-97).

Figure 26-97   The title block moved to the paper area

40. Point to the **Layout1** tab and right-click on it. Select **Page Setup Manager....** On the **Page Setup Manager** dialog box, select ***Layout1*** and click the **Modify...** button.

   • Under **Printer/Plotter**, select your printing device, or any virtual printer if you do not have one installed.

   • Select **monochrome.ctb** from the **Plot Style table** drop-down list.

   • Select **8.5 × 11″** or **Letter** for **Paper size**.

   • Select **Landscape** for **Drawing orientation**.

   • Select **1:1** for **Plot scale**

   • Under the plot area, select the **Window** button and specify the two diagonal corners on the border of the title block by snapping to its endpoints. When you return to the dialog box, check the **Center the plot** box (Figure 26-98).

   • Click **OK** to close the **Page Setup** dialog box. Close the **Page Setup Manager** dialog box. The drawing should look like Figure 26-99.

Figure 26-98   The **Page Setup** dialog box

Figure 26-99   After centering the title block in the paper area

41. Place dimensions and centerlines. Figure 26-100 shows the **Plot Preview** that appears just before you send the plot to the printer.

42. **SAVE** the drawing.

Figure 26-100   The plot preview after placing the dimensions

CREATING VIEWS AND SECTIONS WITH THE SOLVIEW AND SOLDRAW COMMANDS

The AutoCAD program provides many tools to generate drawing views in both paper space and model space. These tools can be combined to accomplish specific tasks. In this topic, you will learn the most sophisticated way to obtain drawing views in paper space: using the **SOLVIEW** and **SOLDRAW** commands jointly.

This pair of commands works together in a prepare–resolve process. The **SOLVIEW** command creates a special type of floating viewport, which is then resolved and processed with the **SOLDRAW** command. The **SOLDRAW** command generates the view projections according to the type of view, using different layers for visible, hidden, and hatch objects.

The **SOLVIEW** command can be invoked only in paper space. It allows you to create one or more special viewports within the same operation. For each viewport, you can specify the type of view it will contain. Depending on the option selected, you can create viewports that contain the following views:

Note:
Viewports created by the standard procedure are not recognized by the **SOLDRAW** command.

   UCS: Parallel to the *XY* plane of the **Current, World**, or any **Named** UCS. This is the only option you can use to specify the first viewport (Figure 26-101).

Using the **Front** or the **Top** UCS is the best choice for creating the first view with the **SOLDRAW** command. This view can be used as the Top or Plan view, and to place any other view relative to it.

   Ortho: Creates the corresponding Front, Back, Right, or Left orthographic projection of any other view specified, always perpendicular to it. Figure 26-102 shows the four

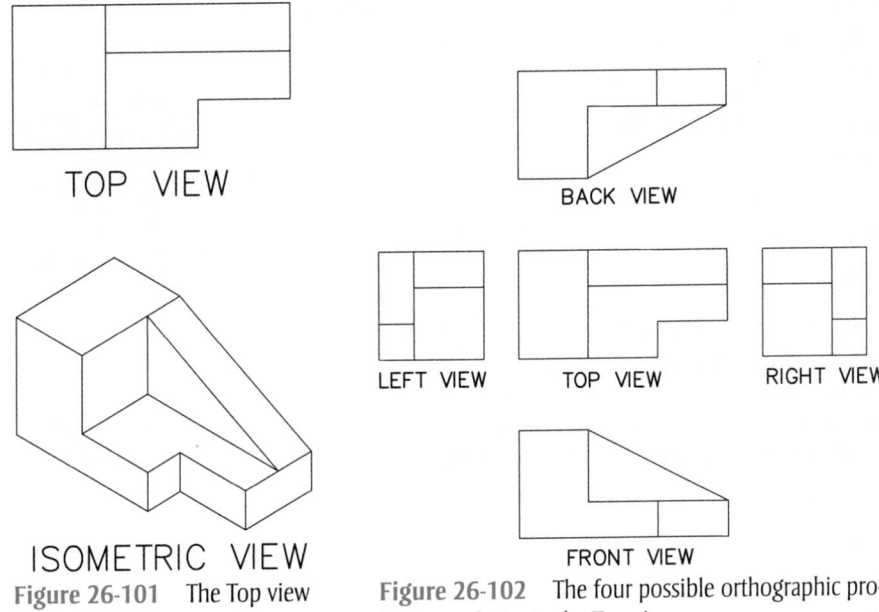

Figure 26-101   The Top view of the object shown in the isometric view can be the first view generated

Figure 26-102   The four possible orthographic projections relative to the Top view

possible orthographic projections of the Top view after it has been resolved with the **SOLDRAW** command.

TIP   You can create orthographic projections from other orthographic views to obtain different alignments.

Auxiliary: Perpendicular to the specified view as viewed from a plane you specify with two points. Figure 26-103 shows an auxiliary view after it has been resolved with the **SOLDRAW** command. The dotted lines are added for illustration purposes.

Section: Creates section views perpendicular to the specified view through a plane you specify with two points. Figure 26-104 shows a section view after it has been resolved with the **SOLDRAW** command. The dotted lines are added for illustration purposes.

Figure 26-103   An auxiliary view relative to the Front view

Figure 26-104   A section view relative to the Front view

The first special viewport generated with the **SOLVIEW** command requires you to respond to a set of prompts, which include requests for the following information:

1. Type of view (UCS only)
2. Scale
3. Center point
4. Two diagonal points to locate the viewport's corners
5. Name

Note:
You must enter all the required information; otherwise, the AutoCAD program will create a regular floating viewport.

For any subsequent viewport you must specify additional information, depending on the type of view created. For example, you must specify the first and second points of an inclined plane for an auxiliary view.

The **SOLVIEW** operation creates the following set of layers along with each viewport:

- *Name*-DIM
- *Name*-HAT (only for section views)
- *Name*-HID
- *Name*-VIS

The last three layers are automatically assigned to the objects by the **SOLDRAW** operation. The -DIM layer can be assigned to dimensions or used at your convenience.

Exercise 26-6: Generating Drawing Views and Sections in Paper Space Using the **SOLVIEW** and **SOLDRAW** Commands

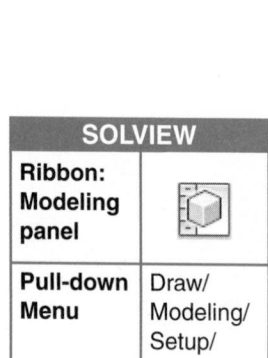

SOLVIEW	
Ribbon: Modeling panel	
Pull-down Menu	Draw/ Modeling/ Setup/ View
Command Line	solview

You will use the same 3D solid object as in a previous exercise. Thus you will be able to focus on the operations used in this procedure, and compare both methods efficiently.

1. **OPEN** either *Exercise 23-8* or *Exercise 23-10* as completed in Chapter 23.
2. **SAVE** it **AS** *Exercise 26-6*.
3. Select the **SW Isometric** viewpoint.
4. Select the **World** UCS.
5. Click on the **Layout1** tab to switch to paper space. Close the **Page Setup** dialog box if it opens automatically.
6. **DELETE** the viewport that the AutoCAD program automatically creates for you to completely clear the paper.
7. Invoke the **SOLVIEW** command. Respond to the prompts as follows:

Note:
A temporary active viewport that covers the entire sheet is created. You will reduce its size in the next step.

```
Enter an option [Ucs/Ortho/Auxiliary/ Section]: u
Enter an option [Named/World/?/Current] <Current>: ↵ (To accept
the current UCS (World))
Enter view scale <1.0000>: 0.5 ↵ (For a 1:2 scale)
Specify view center: Click in the upper-
left side of the paper (Figure 26-105).
Specify view center <specify
viewport>: Click inside the viewport
to relocate its center. You can click
as many times as needed. When you are
finished, press <Enter>.
Specify first corner of viewport:
Click to the left and over the view.
Specify opposite corner of view-
port: Click to the right and below
the view (Figure 26-106).
Enter view name: TopView ↵
```

Note:
Entering the view name is the end of the cycle for the first view. Pressing <Enter> now will exit the command. You will continue with a second cycle to create a section view.

Figure 26-105 First point to be specified in the **SOLVIEW** operation

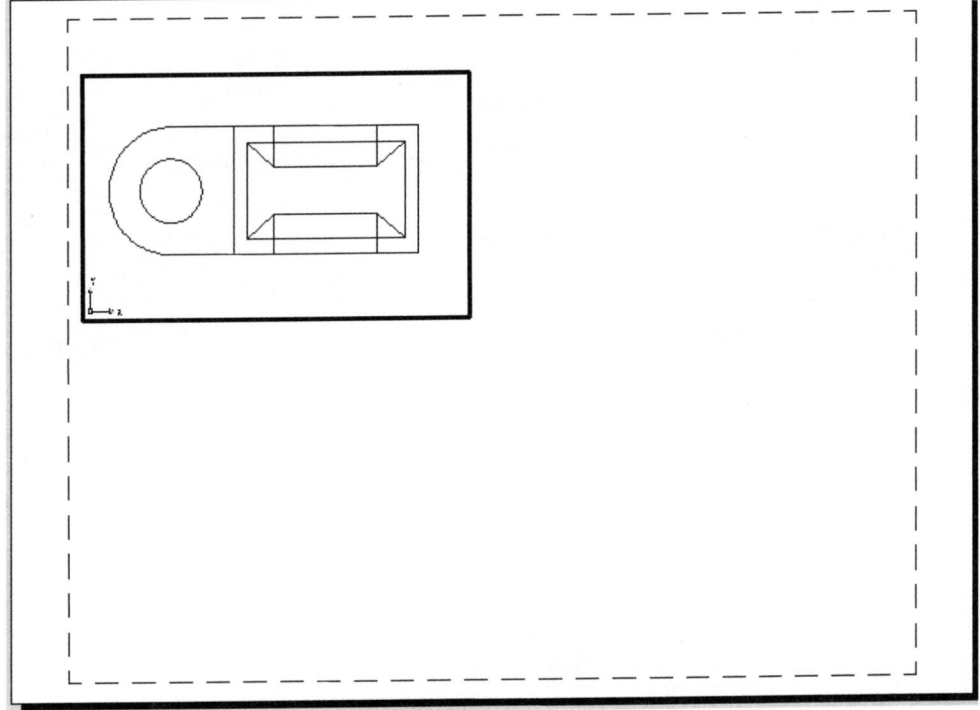

Figure 26-106 After specifying the viewport's two corners

```
Enter an option [Ucs/Ortho/Auxiliary/Section]: S ↵
Specify first point of cutting plane: Snap to the center point
shown in Figure 26-107.
```

TIP The AutoCAD program turns the object snap off at this stage of the command. You must select the **Center point** snap tool directly.

```
Specify second point of cutting plane: Snap to the midpoint.
Specify side to view from: Click on any empty place inside the
viewport and below the 3D model.
Enter view scale <0.5000>: ↵ (To accept the value)
```

Figure 26-107   Points to be specified for the section view

Specify view center: *Click below the viewport to locate the new view.*

Specify view center <specify viewport>: *Click to relocate the view center as many times as needed. When you are finished, press <Enter ⏎>.*

Specify first corner of viewport: *Click to the left and over the new view.*

Specify opposite corner of viewport: *Click to the right and below the new view (Figure 26-108).*

Enter view name: *SectionView* ⏎

Note:
Entering the view name is the end of the second cycle for the second view. You will continue with a third cycle to create an orthographic view.

Figure 26-108   After completing the section view

Enter an option [Ucs/Ortho/Auxiliary/ Section]: *o ↵*

Specify side of viewport to project: *Snap to the midpoint of the right border of the viewport that contains the Front view.*

Specify view center: *Click to the right of the viewport.*

Specify view center <specify viewport>: *Click to relocate the view center as many times as needed. When you are finished, press <Enter>.*

Specify first corner of viewport: *Click to the left and over the new view.*

Specify opposite corner of viewport: *Click to the right and below the new view.*

Enter view name: *RightView ↵*

Enter an option [Ucs/Ortho/Auxiliary/Section]: *↵(To exit the command) The drawing views should look like Figure 26-109.*

> **Note:**
> For the **Ortho** option, the Auto-CAD program turns on the midpoint object snap only.

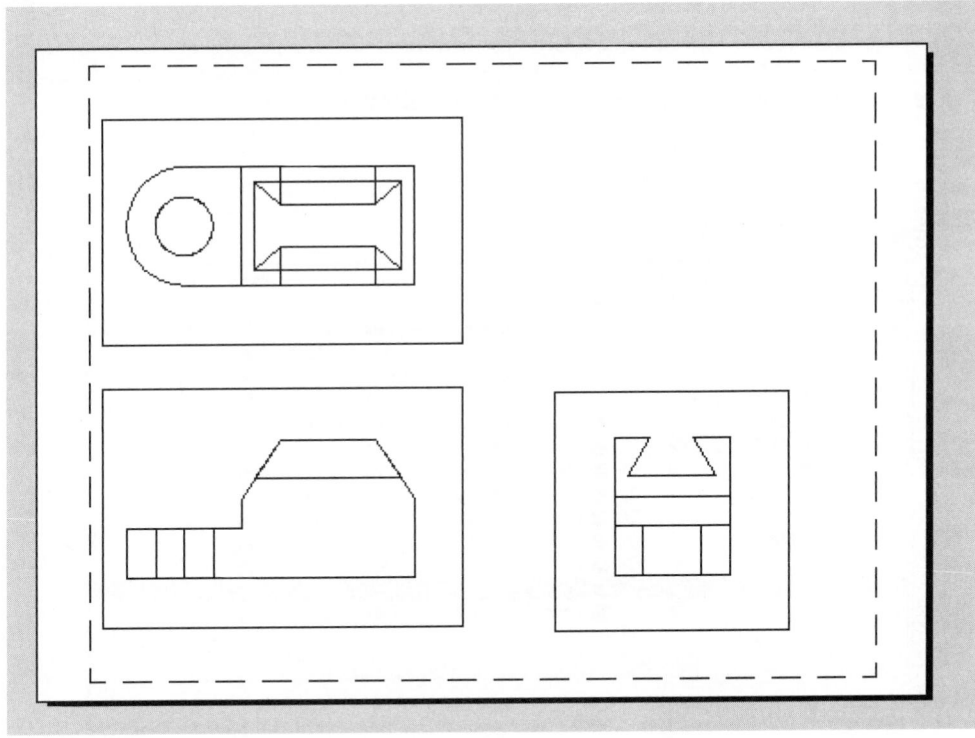

Figure 26-109   The viewport containing the Front view is created

8. Invoke the **SOLDRAW** command. When prompted, select the three viewports and press <Enter.↵> to end the selection. The AutoCAD program processes the projected objects and assigns the corresponding layers (Figure 26-110).

9. Open the **Layer Properties Manager** dialog box and perform the following operations:

   - Create a new layer named *3DSolid* (Figure 26-111).
   - Select all the **-VIS** layers and change their color to any other one.
   - Select all the **-HID** layers and change their linetype to **HIDDEN**. (This linetype can be loaded from the **Layer Properties Manager** directly.)

> **Note:**
> The AutoCAD program creates a set of layers for each of the views. The section view generates an additional layer for the hatch entity. An additional layer named VPORTS is also created and assigned to the viewports.

SOLDRAW	
Ribbon: Modeling panel	
Pull-down Menu	Draw/ Modeling/ Setup/ Drawing
Command Line	soldraw

Figure 26-110   The viewports are resolved with the **SOLDRAW** operation

Figure 26-111   The **Layer Properties Manager** dialog box

10. Change the **LTSCALE** system variable to **0.5**.
11. Select the three viewports and right-click in the drawing area to display the shortcut menu. Set their **Display Lock** property to **Yes**.
12. **MOVE** the viewports up to make room for a title block. If needed, continue moving the views orthogonally without losing the alignment between them.
13. Draw the objects shown in Figure 26-112 anywhere in the gray area to represent the title block.
14. Turn **ORTHO** mode off and **MOVE** the title block to the paper so that all the drawing views fit inside.
15. Double-click on the border of the viewport that contains the section view to maximize it.

Figure 26-112   A representative title block drawn in the gray area

16. Double-click on the hatch to open the **Hatch Edit** dialog box. Set its scale to **2** and click **OK** to close the dialog box.
17. Right-click in the drawing area and select **Minimize Viewport** from the shortcut menu.
18. Select the three viewports. Look at the **Layer control** drop-down window to make sure the *VPORTS* layer is assigned to them.
19. In the **Layer control** drop-down window, set the **0 Layer** as current and then turn the *VPORTS* layer off. The drawing should look like Figure 26-113.

Figure 26-113   After turning the *VPORTS* layer off

20. Right-click on the **Layout1** tab to access the **Page Setup Manager** dialog box. Select ***Layout1*** and click the **Modify ...** button.
   • Under **Printer/Plotter**, make a selection, or select any virtual printer if you do not have one installed.
   • Select **monochrome.ctb** for the **Plot Style table**.

- Select **8.5 × 11″** or **Letter** for **Paper size**.
- Select **Landscape** for **Drawing orientation**.
- Select **1:1** for **Plot scale**.
- Under the plot area, select the **Window** button and specify the two diagonal corners of the title block by snapping to its endpoints. After you return to the dialog box, check the **Center the plot** box.
- Click **OK** to close the **Page Setup** dialog box. The drawing should look like Figure 26-114.

Figure 26-114   After setting up the page

21. Create a new viewport in the upper-right corner of the paper, using the **–VPORTS** command.
22. Double-click inside the new viewport to activate it.
23. Select the **SW Isometric** viewing point.
24. Double-click outside the paper to deactivate the viewport.

TIP   You do not necessarily need to create the 3D views by using one of the automated ways of creating views, nor do you have to project them onto a plane.

25. Select the new viewport, and right-click in the drawing area and set the **Shade plot** to **Hidden** from the shortcut menu. Display the shortcut menu again and set the **Display Locked** property to **Yes**.
26. Assign the *VPORTS* layer to the new viewport.
27. Place dimensions and centerlines. Figure 26-115 shows the plot preview that appears just before you send the plot to the printer.
28. **SAVE** the drawing.

Figure 26-115 The plot preview right before it is sent to the printer

The preparation of engineering drawings for complex objects using the traditional 2D methods demands a high level of experience and concentration to avoid mistakes. Generating 2D drawings from an existing 3D model, on the other hand, not only is a faster approach, but also guarantees reliable accuracy. Your proper use of the techniques and procedures related to this important task along with your ability to generate 3D models will demonstrate special skills in the production of technical documents.

PUBLISHING AND PROTOTYPING

CREATING DWF FILES USING THE PUBLISH AND 3DDWF COMMANDS

With the AutoCAD software, you can create DWFx (Design Web Format; the "x" stands for the DWFx ePlot [XPS compatible plotter used]) files that contain different 3D models and layouts. DWFx files open with the Autodesk® Design Review software, which is free and can be downloaded from the Autodesk® website. The Autodesk® Design Review software is also included with the standard installation of the AutoCAD software.

Creating DWFx files allows you to communicate your ideas and projects to people who do not use AutoCAD. Such files allow them to observe, analyze, and plot your 3D models and 2D drawings using the Autodesk® Design Review software (Figure 26-116).

The **PUBLISH** command enables you to create DWFx files that include the model space and the layout content of several DWG files. The layouts can be included only as 2D drawings. You can choose, however, whether the model space content is included as a 2D drawing or a 3D model. Invoking the **PUBLISH** command opens the **Publish** dialog box (Figure 26-117).

Figure 26-116   The **Autodesk® Design Review** window

By default, the models and layouts of all the DWG files opened are included as individual sheets to publish. You can remove any selected sheet by clicking the **Remove Sheets** button or by pressing the **<Del>** key. You can also bring in another DWG file by clicking the **Add Sheets** button. You can click the **Page Setup/3D DWF** drop-down list of one of the model sheets to specify whether the content in the model space will be included as a 2D drawing or a 3D model (Figure 26-118). This flexibility allows you to generate DWFx files that contain both 2D drawings and 3D models. It is more convenient, however, to generate DWF files that contain a single 3D model that is independent from all the 2D drawing sheets.

Clicking on the **Publish Options...** button will open the **Publish Options** palette, where you can modify other details about the DWF file. For example, you can

Note:
To initialize a particular layout sheet, you must first open the **Page Setup Manager** or the **Plot** dialog box at least once inside this particular layout. You would perform the same procedure to initialize a model space sheet.

Figure 26-117   The **Publish** dialog box

Figure 26-118   The **Page Setup/3D DWF** drop-down list in the **Publish** dialog box

set up a **Password** so that your file can be seen only by those whom you authorize (Figure 26-119). The default **Location** or path where the DWF file will be saved is also changed in the **Publish Options** palette. Clicking on the **Publish** button will start the process by which the DWF file is generated.

On the other hand, the **3DDWF** and the **EXPORT** commands are used only to generate 3D DWF files of the model space content of a particular drawing file. Invoking these two commands opens the **Export 3D DWF** and the **Export Data** dialog boxes, respectively, where you can select a **Name** and **Path** for the 3D DWF files (Figures 26-120 and 26-121). In the **Export Data** dialog box, you must select **3D DWF (*.dwf)** as the file type.

The advantage of using the **3DDWF** and the **EXPORT** commands is that you can select specific objects in the model space to be included in the **3D DWF** file. You do so by selecting the

Figure 26-119   The **Publish Options** palette

Figure 26-120   The **Export 3D DWF** dialog box

Selected model space objects option in the **3D DWF Publish** dialog box and then clicking the **Select Objects** button. You can also specify whether the objects will be shown with the material applied by checking the **Publish with Materials** option.

FOR MORE DETAILS   See Chapter 27 for more information about applying materials.

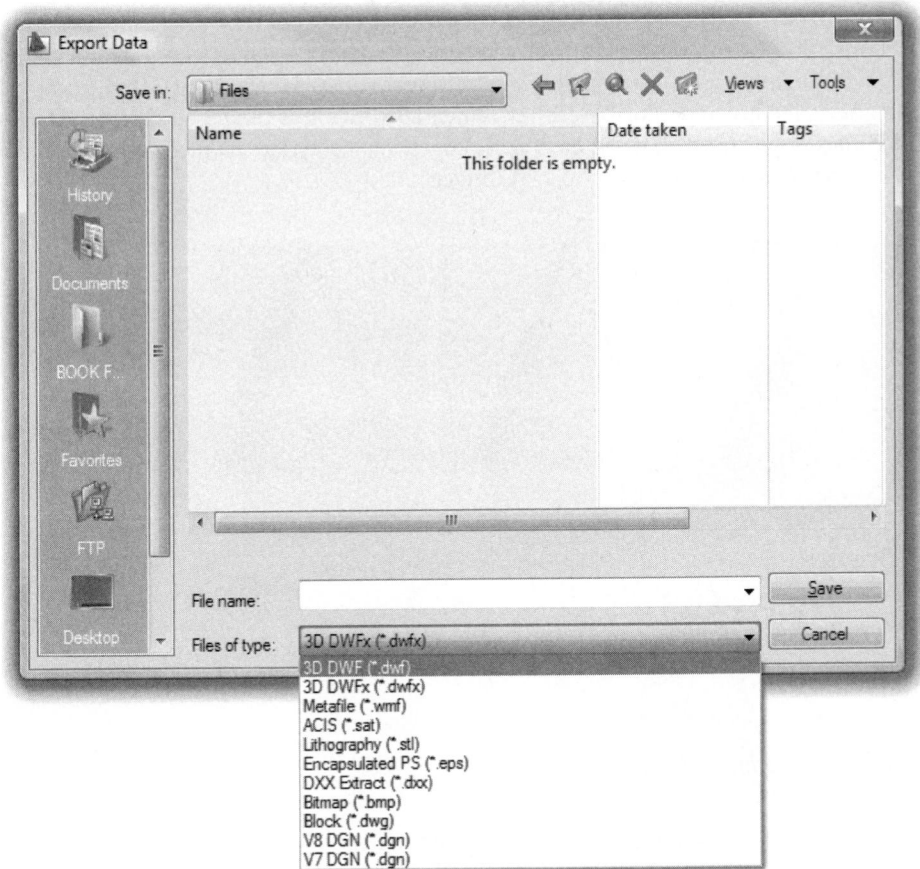

Figure 26-121   **3D DWF (*.dwf)** must be selected in the **Export Data** dialog box

You open the **3D DWF Publish** dialog box by selecting **Options...** from the **Tools** drop-down menu in either the **Export 3D DWF** or the **Export Data** dialog box (Figure 26-122).

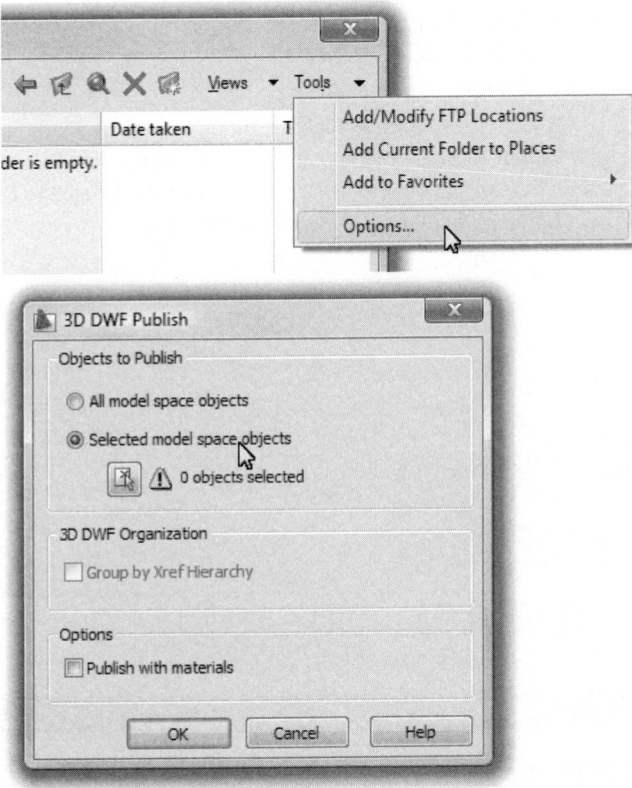

Figure 26-122   The **3D DWF Publish** dialog box; accessing **Options...** from the **Tools** drop-down menu

The **3DDWFPREC** system variable controls the smoothness of the 3D objects included in the DWF file. The value of this variable can be set between **2** and **6**. Higher values result in a better quality, but they also increase the file size (Figure 26-123). The **DISPSILH** system variable also affects the generation of DWF files. When **DISPSILH** is turned on (**1**), the 3D content of DWF files is generated showing the **Facets** edges. Including the 3D model objects in the DWF files as 2D content will have the opposite effect.

3DDWFPREC = 2   3DDWFPREC = 6   3DDWFPREC = 5
DISPSILH = 0   DISPSILH = 0   DISPSILH = 1

3DDWFPREC = 5   3DDWFPREC = 5
DISPSILH = 0   DISPSILH = 1

Figure 26-123   The **3DDWFPREC** system variable controls the smoothness of the DWF objects

Exercise 26-7: Creating DWF Files That Contain Multiple 2D Drawings Using the **PUBLISH** Command

1. **CLOSE** any drawing you might have opened.
2. **OPEN** the following drawings:

   - *Bench-Vise* from Chapter 25
   - *Exercise 26-2 solved*
   - *Exercise 26-3 solved*

3. Switch to the *Bench-Vise* file though the thumbnail previews displayed by clicking on the **Quick View Drawings** button on the status bar (Figure 26-124).
4. Click on **Layout1** to switch to paper space. Close the **Page Setup Manager** if it opens up.
5. **ERASE** the default viewport in the layout.

Figure 26-124   Switching to the *Bench-Vise* by clicking its thumbnail icon; these icons are displayed on the **Quick View Drawings** button on the status bar

6. Invoke the **VPORTS** command and create four equal viewports using a **3D** setup. Define the viewport spacing as **0**. When prompted, specify two points diagonally close to the corners of the paper. The layout should look like Figure 26-125.

Figure 26-125   The initial 3D setup of the four viewports

7. Double-click inside one of the viewports that show an orthographic view. Set the scale to **1:2** in the **Viewports** toolbar drop-down list.

TIP   Avoid making any **ZOOM** or **PAN** operations, especially with the wheel mouse, while a viewport is active to keep the views correctly aligned.

8. Activate the other two viewports that contain orthographic views to set the same scale factor. When you are finished, double-click outside the viewports to get back to paper space.
9. Select all the viewports to expose their grips. Then select common grips and stretch the viewports so the drawing views are shown in their entirety. **MOVE** the viewports around without losing the alignment, and separate them if necessary. The views' layout should look like Figure 26-126.
10. Select all the viewports. Set the **Shade Plot** to **Hidden** through the shortcut menu or in the **Properties** palette.
11. Create a new layer, apply it to the viewports, and turn it off to hide the viewports.
12. Open the **Page Setup** window for Layout1. Select **monochrome.ctb** as the plot style and close the **Page Setup** window.
13. Place the main dimensions in the orthographic views (Figure 26-127).
14. In the *Bench-Vise* drawing file, click the **Model** tab to switch to model space. Right-click on the **Model** tab and select **Page Setup Manager....** Click **Modify...** to open the **Page Setup – Model** dialog box.

Figure 26-126   After the viewports are adjusted

Figure 26-127   Main dimensions placed in the orthographic views

15. Select a plotter, and select **monochrome.ctb** as the plot style. Under **Plot scale**, check **Fit to paper**. Under **Plot area**, select **Window** and click on the **Window** button. When prompted, specify two points that enclose the 3D model in the drawing area.

16. Under **Shaded viewport options**, select the **Hidden** shade plot. Close the **Page Setup – Model** window by clicking **OK**. Close the **Page Setup Manager...** dialog box as well.

17. Repeat the previous three steps in the *Exercise 26-3 solved* drawing file to define aspects of the published sheet for the model space content.

18. Set the **3DDWFPREC** system variable to **4** and the **DISPSILH** system variable to **1** in each drawing file.

19. **SAVE** each drawing file.

20. Invoke the **PUBLISH** command from any of the three drawing files. In the **Publish** dialog box, select **DWF file** under **Publish to** and remove the following sheets:

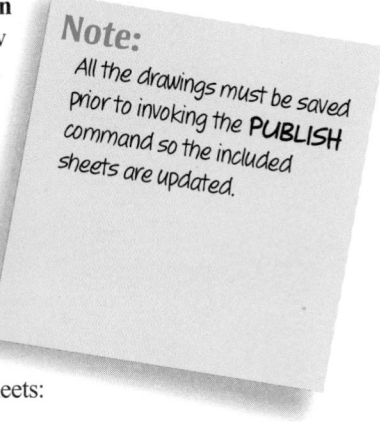

Note:
All the drawings must be saved prior to invoking the **PUBLISH** command so the included sheets are updated.

- **Bench-Vise-Layout2**
- **Exercise 26-2 solved-Model**
- **Exercise 26-2 solved-Layout1**
- **Exercise 26-2 solved-Layout2**
- **Exercise 26-3-solved-Layout2**

PUBLISH	
Standard Toolbar	
Ribbon: Output panel	
Pull-down Menu	File/ Publish...
Command Line	publish

TIP To remove a sheet you can either use the **Remove Sheet** button, or right-click on the sheet and select **Remove.** You can also select the sheet and press <Del>. To select multiple sheets, press and hold <Ctrl>.

21. After you remove the sheets, the **Publish** dialog box should contain only the sheets shown in Figure 26-128. Click the **Publish Options...** button to open the **Publish Options** dialog box. Under **General DWF options** make sure that **DWF type** is set to **Multi-sheet DWF** (Figure 26-129). Click **OK** to close the **Publish Options** dialog box.

Figure 26-128   These sheets should be contained in the **Publish** dialog box

Figure 26-129   The **Publish Options** dialog box

22. Click the **Publish** button. In the **Select DWF File** dialog box, look for where you have other exercise drawing files, and type **My Projects** as the file name. Click the **Select** button to generate the DWF file. Click **No** to close the **Save Sheet List** dialog box in case it opens up.

23. Wait a few minutes and open Windows Explorer. Look for the DWF file you just created. Right-click on the file and select **Open** with the **Autodesk DWF Application** if you are using Windows XP®, or select the file and choose **Open–Autodesk DWF Application** from the top Ribbon if you are using Windows Vista® (Figure 26-130).

Figure 26-130   Opening the DWF file with **Autodesk DWF Application** from Windows Explorer

TIP The **Plot/Publish** animated icon in the lower-right corner of the AutoCAD display will indicate when the publishing job has been completed.

24. The **Contents** window of the **Autodesk Design Review** window should contain five thumbnail icons (Figure 26-131). Click on each thumbnail icon to view its content.

Figure 26-131 The **Autodesk Design Review** window

Exercise 26-8: Creating DWF Files of 3D Objects Using the **3DDWF** Command

1. **OPEN** the *Bench-Vise* drawing from Chapter 25 if it is closed.
2. Click on the **Model** tab to switch to model space.
3. Set the **3DWDFPREC** system variable to **5**, the **DISPSILH** variable to **0**, and the **ISOLINES** variable to **4**.

3DDWF	
Standard Toolbar	
Command Line	3ddwf

4. Invoke the **REGEN** command and **SAVE** the drawing.
5. Invoke the **3DDWF** command to open the **Export 3D DWF** dialog box. Type **Main Body Subassembly** as the file name and look for the location where you saved the DWF file in the previous exercise (Figure 26-132).

Figure 26-132   The **Export 3D DWF** dialog box

6. In the **Export 3D DWF** dialog box, click on **Tools/Options…** to open the **3D DWF Publish** dialog box. Under **Objects to Publish** select **Selected model space objects** and click the button located right below this setting (Figure 26-133).

Figure 26-133   The **3D DWF Publish** dialog box

7. When prompted, select the *Main Body* and the other six components associated with it, including the two *Screws*. When you are finished, press **<Enter↵>** to return to the **3D DWF Publish** dialog box, and click **OK** to close it.

8. Click the **Save** button to start the process.

9. Click **Yes** to the inquiry: **Would you like to view it now**?

10. This will open the **Main Body Subassembly.dwf** file in the **Autodesk Design Review** application (Figure 26-134).

11. In the **Autodesk Design Review** window, click on the flyout button next to the 3D orbiting tools and select **Front Top Right** (Figure 26-135).

> **Note:**
> The **Autodesk Design Review** contains many other easy-to-use tools that allow you to move and rotate individual parts. You can also create cross sections to see the interior of 3D objects. For more information about using the **Autodesk Design Review**, see its help menu.

Figure 26-134   The **Autodesk Design Review** window

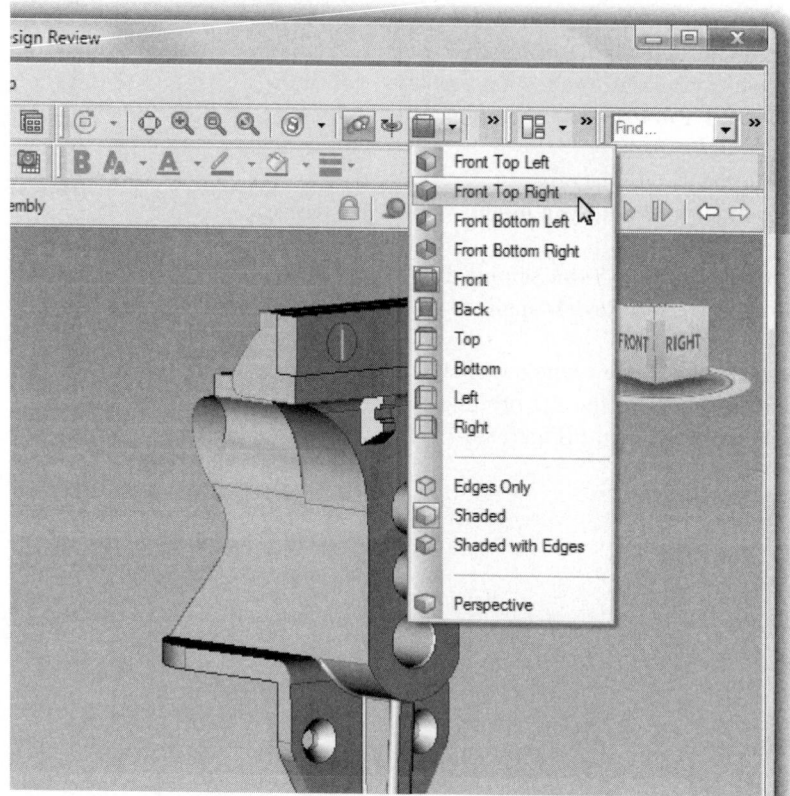

Figure 26-135   Selecting the **Front Top Right** option in the **Autodesk Design Review** window

12. Right-click on the viewing area and click on the **Select** tool at the very top of the short-cut menu. Select the *Main Body.* Right-click again and select **Transparent** from the shortcut menu. The 3D model should look like Figure 26-136.

RAPID PROTOTYPING

Rapid prototyping is a modern process of creating prototypes. Rapid prototyping employs different technologies such as *stereolithography* (SLA), *selective laser sintering* (SLS), *fused deposition modeling* (FDM), *3D printing,* and *PolyJet.* Selecting the appropriate technology depends on factors such as accuracy, strength, smoothness, and cost.

Stereolithography is one of the most cost-effective technologies commonly used to obtain rapid prototypes. In this process, a computer program extracts a set of parallel cross sections every 0.008″ to 0.004″ throughout the 3D model. A laser beam then re-creates the entire area covered by the cross sections on the surface of a liquid resin, solidifying it. A platform carries the solidified layer and submerges it to a depth equal to the distance between the cross sections, allowing more liquid resin to set on top of the solidified layer. Next, the laser beam solidifies the second layer of liquid, adhering it to the first layer. When the last layer is solidified, the platform moves all the way up and the process is completed.

The promptness, accuracy, and cost effectiveness of rapid prototyping technologies have made it increasingly accepted. Many companies even allow you to upload the **STL** file, obtain an instant electronic quote, and order the service.

You can use the **EXPORT** or the **STLOUT** command to create **STL** files from a 3D solid and request a rapid prototype via the Internet. **STL** files must be created from a single 3D solid that lies in the positive octant; that is, the *X, Y,* and *Z* coordinates must be positive for any point of the 3D solid.

Figure 26-136 Using the **Transparent** mode to view the objects in the **Autodesk Design Review** window

The cost of a rapid prototype depends mostly on the 3D solid's volume. You can use the **MASSPROP** command to obtain not only the volume, but also other engineering information of a 3D solid or a region, such as the centroid and the moment of inertia.

CHAPTER SUMMARY

Even the most expert drafters and designers sometimes make mistakes when they undertake the projecting of drawing views of complex objects. After going through this chapter, you should have learned something very important: Anyone able to create a 3D model does not have to worry much about creating drawing views that contain errors.

As you have also learned, the AutoCAD program contains several procedures from which you can automatically obtain professional drawing views that are free of errors. You can use the technique that best suits your type of work, or you might prefer to use several of them together.

In this chapter you reviewed the paper space concept and set up the viewports to create 2D drawings the correct way. You also learned how to create the increasingly accepted DWF files using different procedures, which can expand your design communication efforts without any limitations.

CHAPTER TEST QUESTIONS

Multiple Choice

1. Right-clicking on a paper space tab exposes a shortcut menu. Which of the following is not part of this menu list?
   a. **Viewports**
   b. **Rename**
   c. **Page Setup Manager...**
   d. **New layout**

2. Which of the following operations cannot be performed by clicking on the icons of the **Viewports** toolbar?
   a. Convert objects to viewport
   b. Specify a hidden shade plot
   c. Create a single rectangular viewport
   d. Set the scale on an active viewport

3. Which of the following properties of viewports must be changed to avoid losing the scale and alignment of the views by mistake?
   a. Layer
   b. Display locked
   c. Shade plot
   d. Maximize

4. Which of the following options cannot be used to create a section object?
   a. Orthographic
   b. Specifying two points
   c. Normal to a vector
   d. Selecting a planar face

5. Which of the following operations cannot be selected through the section object's shortcut menu?
   a. Change the type of section object
   b. Activate live sectioning
   c. Change the section object settings
   d. Create 2D/3D sections

6. Placing dimensions on top of a 3D object is a practical way of providing technical information. What is the most important consideration when performing this task?
   a. Changing the layers
   b. Selecting an orthographic view
   c. Relocating the UCS
   d. Rotating the object in the 3D space

7. Which of the following is impossible to obtain with the **SOLPROF** command?
   a. A block containing both the projected visible and hidden lines
   b. A block containing only the projected visible lines
   c. A section view of the 3D solid
   d. A 3D wireframe

8. Which of the following is necessary to obtain an STL file?
   a. No points of the 3D solid can have negative X, Y, or Z coordinates.
   b. The hidden lines must be turned off.
   c. Only one 3D solid must exist in the drawing.

9. Which of the following views cannot be created with the **SOLVIEW** command after a first viewport is created?
   a. Orthographic
   b. Auxiliary
   c. Isometric
   d. Section

10. Which of the following mass properties of a 3D solid cannot be obtained with the **MASSPROP** command?
    a. Volume
    b. Moment of inertia
    c. Surface area
    d. Bounding box

Matching

a. **SOLDRAW**
b. Paper space
c. **SOLVIEW**
d. **PUBLISH**
e. Floating viewports
f. **VPMAX**
g. **SOLPROF**
h. **FLATSHOT**
i. **3DDWF**
j. Section object

1. Extracts the profile of the selected 3D solids
2. Temporarily slices 3D objects and creates sections
3. Generates profiles and sections of the views
4. An infinite 2D space
5. Generates DWF files of selected 3D objects
6. Creates views projected onto the current XY plane
7. Objects that allow you to see the model space through them
8. Generates DWF files of 3D models and 2D drawings
9. Maximizes a viewport
10. Creates a special type of viewport

CHAPTER TUTORIALS

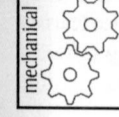

Tutorial 26-1: The Drawing of the Main Body

In this tutorial you will generate the drawing of the *Main Body* 3D model, created in Chapter 25. The projected drawing views will be created using the **SOLVIEW** and the **SOLDRAW** commands.

Color	Lineweight	Use in Drawing
White (7)	0.35 mm	Visible edges
Cyan (4)	0.15 mm	Hidden edges
Yellow (2)	0.20 mm	Dimension text Notes
Red (1)	0.10 mm	Dimension lines Centerlines Hatches Small texts
Magenta (6)	0.50 mm	Section lines Titles

For this tutorial, you will now create a **Pen Style Table** file to specify the **Lineweight** values for the colors shown in the following chart.

1. **OPEN** the *Main Body* drawing.
2. **SAVE** it **AS** *Tutorial 26-1*.
3. Open the **Plot** dialog box. Select **New...** from the **Plot style table (pen assignment)** drop-down list to create a new **.ctb** file.
4. In the **Begin** step, select **Start from scratch** and click **Next**. Name the file **MyColorStyle** and click **Next**.
5. In the **Finish** step, check only **Use this plot style for the current drawing** and click **Finish**.
6. Make sure that **MyColorStyle.ctb** appears as the current **Plot style table** and click on the **Edit** button to change the properties of the colors that you will use.
7. In the **From View** tab of the **Plot Style Table Editor**, select all the colors under **Plot styles** and change their **Color** to **Black** under **Properties**. To select all the colors, select the first one, then scroll to the last color and select it while holding the **<Shift>** key down. After setting the plot color, perform the following individual changes:

   - Select **Color 1** and change its **Lineweight** property to **0.1000 mm**.
   - Select **Color 2** and change its **Lineweight** property to **0.2000 mm**.
   - Select **Color 4** and change its **Lineweight** property to **0.1500 mm**.
   - Select **Color 6** and change its **Lineweight** property to **0.5000 mm**.
   - Select **Color 7** and change its **Lineweight** property to **0.3500 mm**.

8. Click the **Save & Close** button to return to the **Plot** dialog box.
9. Click on the **Colors...** button located in the **Display** tab of the **Options** dialog box to open the **Drawing Window Colors** dialog box.
10. Under **Context**, select **Sheet/layout**. Under **Interface element**, select **Uniform Background**. Under **Color**, select **Black** (Figure 26-137).
11. Click **Apply & Close** to close the **Drawing Window Colors** dialog box. Click **OK** to close the **Options** dialog box.

Note:
The set of colors that you will use with this tutorial makes a better contrast with a black display background. Next, you will change the background color of the paper in the **Options** dialog box.

Note:
When you change the background color, it will be shown in any other drawing you open. You can always change the background color to white again. You can also restore the default colors by clicking the **Restore** button on the **Drawing Window Colors** dialog box after you finish this tutorial.

Figure 26-137   The **Drawing Window Colors** dialog box

12. Open the **Layer Properties Manager** and create a new layer named **3D Model**. Select the **Green** color for the new layer. Close the **Layer Properties Manager** and assign the layer **3D Model** to the 3D solid. Set the **Color** property of the 3D solid as **ByLayer**.

13. Make sure **UCSORTHO** is set to **1** and select the **Top** view.

14. Click on the **Layout1** tab to switch to paper space.

15. Depending on the options settings, the **Page Setup Manager** may or may not open automatically the first time you access **Layout1**. If the **Page Setup Manager** does not open, right-click on the **Layout1** tab to open it from the shortcut menu.

16. Select **Layout1** and click the **Modify...** button to enter the **Page Setup** dialog box. Select your printing device from the list and select **MyColorStyle.ctb** as the plot style. Click **OK** to close the dialog box. Close the **Page Setup Manager** window.

17. **DELETE** the viewport that the AutoCAD program automatically creates to clean up the sheet of paper.

18. Invoke the **SOLVIEW** command and respond to the prompts as follows:

    Enter an option [Ucs/Ortho/Auxiliary/Section]: *u* ↵

    Enter an option [Named/World/?/Current] <Current>: ↵
    (To accept the current UCS World))

    Enter view scale <1.0000>: *0.5* ↵ *(For a 1:2 scale)*

    Specify view center: *Click in the lower-left side of the sheet.*

If you are not sure about which scale you can use so that all the views fit properly in the specific paper size, just specify any scale value, trying to make your best guess. It can later be changed in the **Scale** drop-down list of the **Viewports** toolbar.

Specify view center <specify viewport>: *Click to relocate the view center as many times as needed. When finished, press <Enter⏎>.*

Specify first corner of viewport: *Click to the left and over the view.*

Specify opposite corner of viewport: *Click to the right and below the view (Figure 26-138).*

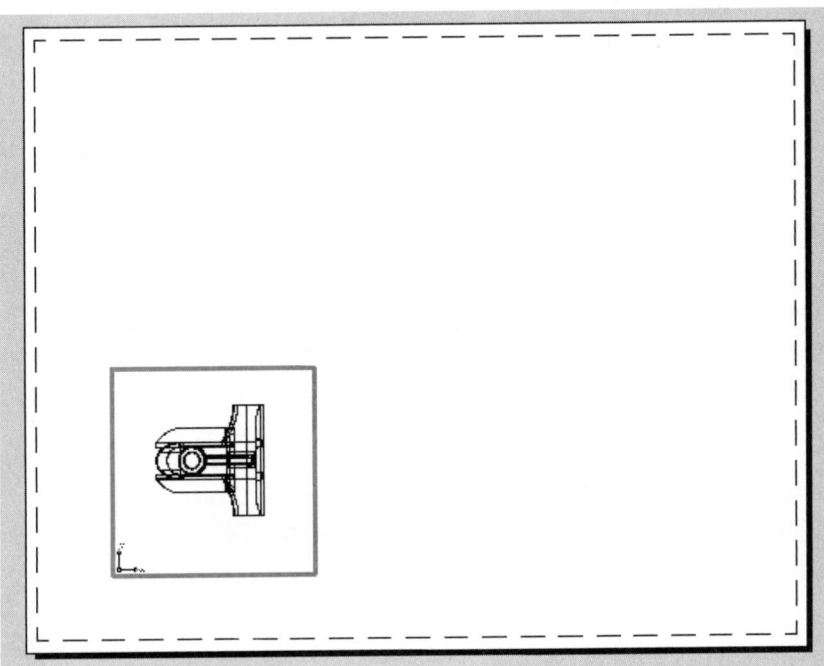

Figure 26-138   After completing the first viewport with the **SOLVIEW** operation

Do not use the mouse wheel during the entire process of the **SOLVIEW** command. Zooming with the mouse wheel will alter the view scale. Then, when you reset the scale to the correct factor, the alignment of the drawing view with respect to the other view will be lost. To achieve the alignment again, you will have to move the views manually.

Enter view name: *TopView ⏎*

Enter an option [Ucs/Ortho/Auxiliary/Section]: *s ⏎*

Specify first point of cutting plane: *Select the midpoint on the left; see Figure 26-139.*

Specify second point of cutting plane: *Specify the midpoint on the right.*

Specify side to view from: *Click on an empty place inside the viewport and below the 3D model.*

Enter view scale <0.5000>: *⏎ (To accept the value)*

Note:
This is the end of the cycle. If you press <Enter⏎> now you will exit the **SOLVIEW** command.

Figure 26-139   Points to be specified for the section view

TIP   Because the AutoCAD program turns OSNAP mode off at this stage of the command, you must specify the midpoint snap by selecting this object snap directly.

Specify view center: *Specify a point by clicking above the Top view.*

Specify view center <specify viewport>: *Click to relocate the view center as many times as needed. When finished, press <Enter↵>.*

Specify first corner of viewport: *Click to the left and over the new view.*

Specify opposite corner of viewport: *Click to the right and below the new view. The drawing views should look like Figure 26-140.*

Enter view name: *SectionA ↵*

Enter an option [Ucs/Ortho/Auxiliary/ Section]: *o ↵ (To create a third view, using the orthographic option)*

Specify side of viewport to project: *Snap to the midpoint of the right border of the viewport that contains the "SectionA" view.*

Specify view center: *Specify a point by clicking to the right of the "SectionA" view.*

Specify view center <specify viewport>: *Click to relocate the view center as many times as needed. When finished, press <Enter↵>.*

Specify first corner of viewport: *Click to the left and over the new view.*

Note: The two points in Figure 26-139 establish the location of the sectioning plane.

Note: For the **Ortho** option, the Auto-CAD program turns on the **Midpoint** Object Snap only.

Figure 26-140   After completing the section view

Specify opposite corner of viewport: *Click to the right and below the new view. The drawing views should look like Figure 26-141.*

Figure 26-141   After completing the third view

```
Enter view name: SideView ↵
Enter an option [Ucs/Ortho/Auxiliary/Section]: ↵ (To exit
the command)
```

19. Open the **Layer Manager** dialog box. As you can see, the AutoCAD program has created a set of layers for each view. You will change some properties of these layers before using the **SOLDRAW** command. Use Figure 26-142 along with the information below.

   • Change the color of layers ending with **-HID** to **Cyan** (4).
   • Change the color of layers ending with **-DIM** and **-HAT** to **Red** (1).
   • The color of layers ending with **-VIS** should stay as **White** (7).
   • Change the linetype of layers ending with **-HID** to **HIDDEN**.

Figure 26-142   The **Layer Manager** dialog box

TIP   To use the **HIDDEN** linetype, you must first load it to the drawing. You can do so directly from the **Layer Properties Manager**.

20. Set the **LTSCALE** system variable to **0.4**.
21. Invoke the **SOLDRAW** command. When prompted, select the three viewports and press **<Enter>** to end the selection.
22. Select the three viewports and assign them the layer *VPORT*.
23. With the viewports still selected, right-click on the drawing area and set the **Display locked** attribute to **Yes** in the shortcut menu.
24. With ORTHO mode activated, **MOVE** the viewports around to a desired location without losing their alignment.
25. Set **Layer 0** as current and turn the *VPORTS* layer off to hide the viewports.
26. Open the **Dimension Style Manager** dialog box and click on **New...** to create a new dimension style. Under **New Style**

Note: The AutoCAD program processes the projected objects and assigns layers accordingly in each viewport with the **SOLDRAW** operation.

Name: type **Mechanical Style** and then click **Continue**. In the **Modify Dimension Style** dialog box, change the following parameters:

- Click the **Text** tab. Click the **...** button near **Text Style** to open the **Text Style** dialog box. Select **romans.shx** from the **Fonts** drop-down list and click **Apply**. Click **Close** to return to the **Modify Dimension Style** dialog box. Under **Text Alignment** select **Aligned with dimension line**.
- Click the **Lines** tab. Change both the **Dimension lines** and the **Extension lines** to **Red** (1).
- Click the **Primary Units** tab and set the **Precision** to two decimal places (0.00).
- Click the **Fit** tab and set the overall scale value to **0.45** under **Scale for dimension features**. Click **OK** to close the **Modify Dimension Style** dialog box.
- In the **Dimension Style Manager** click on **New...** again while **Mechanical Style** is selected. Select **Radius dimensions** under **Use for:**. Click **Continue** to open the **Modify Dimension Style** dialog box. Click the **Text** tab and select **Horizontal** under **Text Alignment**. Click **OK** to return to the **Dimension Style Manager** dialog box.
- Repeat the previous operation to create substyles for **Diameter dimension** and **Angular dimension**.
- Before closing the **Dimension Style Manager**, set **Mechanical Style** as the current style by selecting it and then clicking on the **Set Current** button.

27. Create a new viewport in the lower-right corner of the paper using the **VPORTS** command or the icon on the **Viewports** toolbar.
28. Double-click inside the new viewport to activate it.
29. Select the **SW Isometric** viewing point.
30. **ZOOM** in or out to set a proper scale factor (not necessarily a standard scale factor).
31. Double-click outside the paper to deactivate the active viewport.
32. Select the viewport you just created and right-click in the paper area. Set the **Display Locked** attribute to **Yes** from the shortcut menu. Expose the same shortcut menu again and set the **Shade plot** to **Hidden**.
33. Change the layer of the new viewport to the *VPORT* Layer. Click **OK** to close the warning message, if it is displayed.
34. Open the *TB-Imperial* drawing in the student data files.
35. Copy the entire title block located in the **ANSI A (11 × 8.5)** layout to the clipboard using the **COPYCLIP** command. **CLOSE** the drawing without saving it.
36. Go back to **Layout1** of *Tutorial 26-1*. Right-click in the paper area and select **Paste as Block** from the shortcut menu. When prompted, specify a point anywhere. Then **MOVE** the block so that all the views fit inside. The drawing should look like Figure 26-143.
37. Right-click on the **Layout1** tab to access the **Page Setup** dialog box for this layout through the **Page Setup Manager** window.
38. In the **Page Setup** dialog box, select **Window** under **Plot area**. When prompted, specify the two diagonal corners by snapping to the endpoints on the title block.
39. In the **Page setup** dialog box, check the **enter the plot** checkbox. Make sure the scale is **1:1** and click **OK** to close the dialog box.
40. Set **Layer 0** as current and add some dimensions to the drawing views.
41. **EXPLODE** the title block and fill in the fields using *Text* or *Mtext* objects.

To access student data files, go to www.pearsondesigncentral.com.

TIP You can still move the viewport around, if needed, by turning its layer on first. When you move a viewport that contains dimensions, you should move the dimensions along with the viewport.

Figure 26-143   After pasting the title block in the layout

42. Create the **Detail I** view. Figure 26-144 shows the finished document after it has been printed.

Figure 26-144   The final drawing document with dimensions

> **TIP**
>
> You can create a detail view by drawing a circle in the drawing area and then converting it into a viewport. You can then activate the viewport and freeze the layers you do not need. The scale of the viewport that contains the detail view is typically two, four, or eight times bigger than the scale of the view you are magnifying.

43. **SAVE** the drawing.
44. Create a **DWF** file of this layout only using the **PUBLISH** command.

Tutorial 26-2: A 3D Exploded View of the Bench Vise

1. **OPEN** the **Bench-Vise** drawing file as it was finished in Chapter 25.
2. **SAVE** the drawing **AS Tutorial 26-2**.
3. Select the **Isometric SE** viewing point.
4. Select the **Front** UCS.
5. With **ORTHO** mode on, **MOVE** the following nine components **3.5″** along the positive *X*-axis (Figure 26-145).

   - the two *Guides*
   - the *Moving Jaw*
   - the *Aluminum Block* located on the *Moving Jaw*
   - the two *Screws* located on the *Moving Jaw*
   - the *Main Bolt*
   - the *Pin*
   - the *Handle* located on the *Main Bolt*

Figure 26-145   The first set of components is moved

6. **MOVE** the following seven components **3″** along the positive *X*-axis (Figure 26-146).

   - the *Moving Jaw*
   - the *Aluminum Block* located on the *Moving Jaw*

Figure 26-146   The second set of components is moved

- the two *Screws* located on the *Moving Jaw*
- the *Main Bolt*
- the *Pin*
- the *Handle* located on the *Main Bolt*

7. **MOVE** the following three components, **6″** along the positive *X*-axis (Figure 26-147).

- the *Main Bolt*
- the *Pin*
- the *Handle* located on the *Main Bolt*

8. **MOVE** the *Pin* **1.5″** along the negative *Y*-axis.

Figure 26-147   The third set of components is moved

9. **Move** the following three components **3″** along the negative Y-axis.
   * the *Fastening Bolt*
   * the *Pressing Plate*
   * the *Handle* located on the *Fastening Bolt*

10. **MOVE** the *Fastening Bolt* and its *Handle* **1″** along the negative Y-axis (Figure 26-148).

Figure 26-148   The fourth set of components is moved

11. **MOVE** the *Aluminum Block* located on the *Moving Jaw* and its two *Screws* **1″** along the negative X-axis.
12. **MOVE** the two *Screws* you just moved **1″** along the negative X-axis (Figure 26-149).

Figure 26-149   The two screws are moved

13. **MOVE** the *Aluminum Block* located on the *Main Body* and its two *Screws* **1″** along the positive X-axis.

14. **MOVE** the two *Screws* you just moved **1″** along the positive *X*-axis as well (Figure 26-150).

Figure 26-150   The other two screws are moved

15. Set **Center** as the only Object Snap mode active in the **Object Snap** tab of the **Drafting Settings** dialog box (Figure 26-151).

Figure 26-151   The **Drafting Settings** dialog box

16. Using a different color, draw nine polylines to show the assembly traces. Snap to the farthestmost center points to place the polylines.
17. Set the **LTSCALE** system variable to **0.4**.
18. Load the **CENTER** linetype into the drawing and change the **Linetype** of the polylines to **CENTER**. The 3D model should look now like Figure 26-152.

Figure 26-152   The completed
3D model

19. Select the **World** UCS.
20. **MOVE** all the objects from the bottom circular edge of the *Fastening Bolt* to the origin **0,0,0**.
21. **MOVE** all the objects again from any base point to the relative destination point **@4,4,0**.

Note:
You have just generated the *STL* file of the *Main Body*. This file can be used to request an instant quote and a rapid prototyping service via the Internet. The rapid prototype would look like Figure 26-153 if the service requested was a stereolithography process.

Figure 26-153   Rapid prototype of the *Main Body* generated by the stereolithography process

22. Double-click the mouse wheel in the drawing area to fit the objects in the display.
23. Invoke the **EXPORT** command through the **File** drop-down menu.
24. In the **Export data** dialog box, select **Lithography (*.stl)** as the file type. Type **Main Body** for the file name and select the folder in which you want the file to be saved.
25. Click **Save** to create the STL file. When prompted, select the *Main Body* and press **<Enter.⏎>**.
26. **OPEN** the file *TB-Imperial* and click on the **ANSI B (17 × 11)** layout.
27. Invoke the **COPYCLIP** command by right-clicking in the drawing area and selecting **Copy** from the shortcut menu. When prompted, select all the objects and press **<Enter.⏎>** to finish the command.
28. **CLOSE** the file *TB-Imperial*.
29. Go back to the *Tutorial 26-2* file and click on the **Layout2** tab to switch to paper space. Close the **Page Setup Manager** window if necessary and **ERASE** the existing default viewport.
30. **PASTE** the objects from the clipboard into **Layout2**. Specify any point as the insertion point by clicking on the drawing area.
31. Access the **Page Setup - Layout2** dialog box through the **Page Setup Manager** window. Select your plotter device and select the **monochrome.ctb** plot style table. Select the **ANSI expand B (17.00 × 11.00 Inches)** paper (Figure 26-154).
32. Select **Window** under the plot area and specify two diagonal endpoints on the title block's main rectangle. Return to the **Page Setup** dialog box and select the **Center the plot** checkbox. Close the **Page Setup** and the **Page Setup manager ...** dialog boxes.

Figure 26-154   The **Page Setup** dialog box for **Layout2**

33. Create a new viewport that encloses the entire paper.

TIP When you need a single viewport, create it outside the printable area to prevent its border from being plotted.

34. Activate the viewport. **ZOOM** and **PAN** with the mouse wheel to obtain a desired view.
35. Turn on the **Display Locked** property of the viewport, and change its **Shade plot** to **Hidden**. Access these settings through the **Properties** palette or through the shortcut menu.
36. **PLOT** the drawing. After being plotted, the drawing should look like Figure 26-155.
37. **SAVE** your drawing.

Figure 26-155   The completed drawing

CHAPTER PROJECTS

Project 26-1: Isometric Drawing of a Valve with Dimensions in the 3D Space

OPEN the drawing *Tutorial 23-3* that you developed in Chapter 23 and **SAVE** it **AS** *Project 26-1*. With the **FLATSHOT** command, obtain the top, front, and side orthographic views. Use a section object to generate the 3D section shown in Figure 26-156.

Use the three orthographic views and an Isometric view in which you show the 3D section to generate the 2D drawing in **Layout1**. Use one of the title blocks contained in the layouts of the *TB-Metric* drawing in the student data files.

To access student data files, go to www.pearsondesigncentral.com.

Figure 26-156   3D section to be generated using a section object

Project 26-2: Creating a Drawing of the Turning Bracket

OPEN the finished *Project 23-2* and **SAVE** it **AS** *Project 26-2*.

Using the **SOLVIEW** and **SOLDRAW** commands jointly, create the drawing document of the turning bracket. Include a section view to place the interior dimensions of the part.

Hints for the Project

Refer to *Project 23-2* for tips on which dimensions to place as well as on how to create section cuts and detail views.

Project 26-3: Extracting Elevations of the Community Recreational Hall 3D Solid Model

OPEN the drawing *Project 26-3* in the student data files and **SAVE** it **AS** *Project 26-3 solved*.

Select a top view of the 3D solid model of the community recreational hall and create the two elevations and two sections shown in Figure 26-157.

To access student data files, go to www.pearsondesigncentral.com.

Figure 26-157   Elevations and sections to be developed

Hints for the Project

Use the **FLATSHOT** command to create the elevations and the **SECTIONPLANE** command to create the sections.

Rendering and Other Presentations

27

Chapter
Objectives

- Use the Render Presets
- Learn how to obtain and save a rendered image
- Understand the use of lighting within the AutoCAD® program
- Create and modify the different types of lights
- Use existing materials from the tool palettes
- Create new materials using the materials templates
- Apply materials and textures to 3D objects
- Learn to create special effects such as transparency and reflection
- Learn to create materials containing bitmaps
- Create effects in 3D models using the visual styles
- Create computer animations that record 3D navigation operations
- Create computer animations using motion paths

INTRODUCTION

DEFINITION OF RENDERING

In CAD, *rendering* is the act of generating an image from a 3D model. The AutoCAD® program can render the following types of objects:

- 3D solids
- Surfaces
- Polygon meshes
- Regions
- 3D faces
- Thickened objects

Whether used for publicity purposes, or just to obtain a clearer idea of your design, rendering plays a necessary artistic role in the 3D modeling. In the past, this work was labor intensive because real artists had to touch up pictures of the product by hand to produce the proper images for catalogs. With the **Render** process you can create excellent quality images, which can then be used to illustrate catalogs or any other type of document. The commands and settings are in the **Light, Material**, and **Render** control panels of the Ribbon. The **Render** toolbar, and the **View/Render** drop-down menu provide access to these tools and settings as well (Figure 27-1).

Figure 27-1   The different locations of the **Render** commands and tools

SYSTEM VARIABLES AFFECTING THE SMOOTHNESS OF RENDERED OBJECTS

Before getting into the group of tools specifically related to the **Render** process, you should know that certain system variables studied earlier can improve the smoothness of rendered images. The **FACETRES** system variable, for example, controls the smoothness of the nonplanar faces of 3D solids and nonplanar surfaces. Increasing its value will improve the quality of the rendered images (Figure 27-2).

You can control the smoothness of polygon meshes by increasing the mesh density with the **SURFTAB1** and **SURFTAB2** system variables. The **SURFU** and **SURFV** variables control the

Figure 27-2   Increasing the value of the **FACETRES** system variable improves the smoothness of the non-planar faces of 3D solids and surfaces

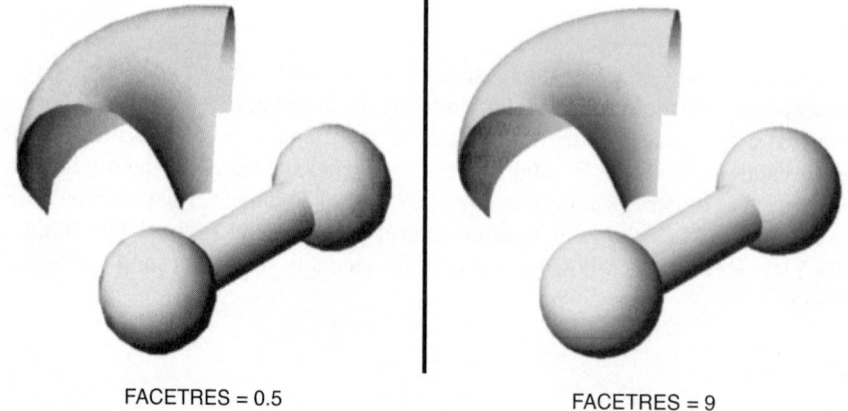

FACETRES = 0.5   FACETRES = 9

smoothness of polygon meshes that have been transformed by the **Smooth surface** operation of the **PEDIT** command. The **SPLINESEGS** system variable controls the smoothness of thickened objects.

THE BASICS OF RENDERING

OBTAINING A SIMPLE RENDERED IMAGE

Obtaining a rendered image is as simple as pressing a button. Simply invoking the **RENDER** command will generate a rendered image using the current Render Preset. Figure 27-3 shows the most basic rendered image in which no special elements have been used. Alternatively you can invoke the **RENDERCROP** command and specify a crop window to render instead of rendering the entire screen. Its icon is located next to the **RENDER** command icon in the **Render** control panel on the Ribbon.

RENDERCROP	
Ribbon : **Render** **Panel**	
Command **Line**	rendercrop

Figure 27-3   A basic rendered image without using any special elements

Using other **Render** elements such as lights, shadows, materials, and textures can improve the quality of your rendered images. Controlling settings regarding lighting effect and quality of the surfaces can also give you more realistic images (Figure 27-4).

As you will learn later, the number of settings involved in the rendering process is extremely large and to study every single one in depth could take a very long time. Experimenting with too many settings will probably cause you to spend an excessive amount of time trying to find the best image possible.

Still, the rendering process requires a lot of patience because trial and error in most cases is what will lead you to obtain the desired results. You can simplify the work substantially without sacrificing quality, however, by concentrating on the most important settings concerning the following aspects:

- Preparing the model
- Creating lights and specifying the shadows cast
- Creating and applying materials and textures
- Adjust mapping of materials using image files
- Selecting one of the Render Presets supplied with the program
- Defining a few other aspects such as destination and output size
- Creating the rendered image

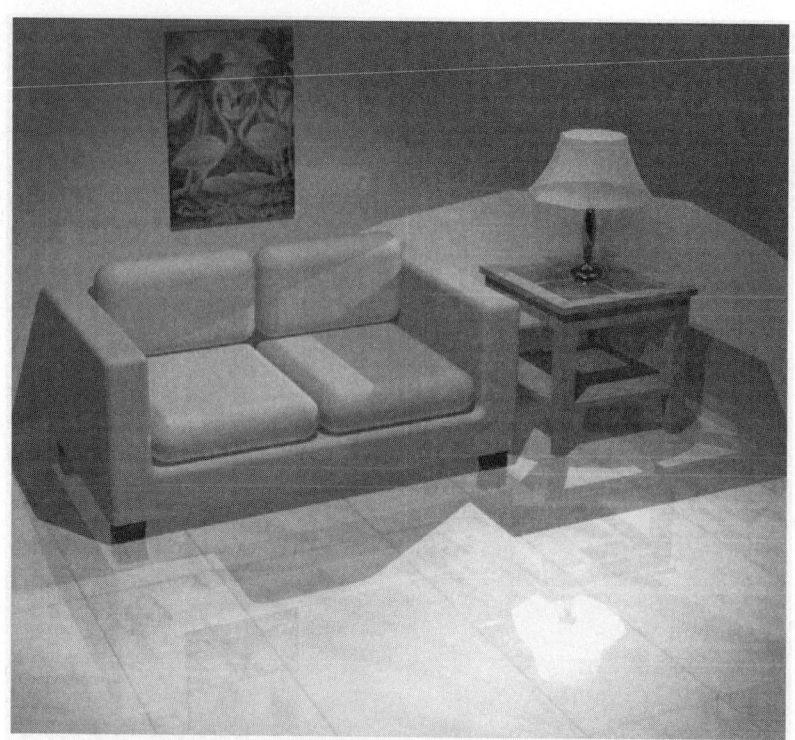

Figure 27-4 A rendered image in which elements and settings regarding this type of output have been used

Exercise 27-1: Creating a Basic Rendered Image

To access student data files, go to www.pearsondesigncentral.com.

RPREF	
Render Toolbar	
Ribbon: Render panel	
Pull-down Menu	View/ Render/ Advanced Settings...
Command Line	rpref

RENDER	
Render Toolbar	
Ribbon: Render panel	
Pull-down Menu	View/ Render/ Render
Command Line	render

1. **OPEN** *Exercise 27-1* in the student data files.
2. **SAVE** the drawing **AS** *Exercise 27-1 solved*.
3. Select **Render View** from the **Views** drop-down list located in the **Views** toolbar or in the **Navigate** control panel. This named view has been previously created to allow you to quickly change the viewing point to the one stored with it.
4. Open the **Viewports** dialog box. Select the **2D** setup and the **Two: Horizontal** to divide the display into two viewports that show the same view.
5. If needed, **ZOOM** into the corner of the room where furniture is located, in both viewports. Try to obtain a similar zoom factor for both viewports.

> **TIP** By using the **Scale** option of the **ZOOM** command, you can obtain the exact same zoom factor in two viewports by specifying the same scale factor in both viewports. For this exercise you can use a value between **1/7** and **1/9**.

6. Select **Medium** from the **Render Presets** drop-down list located in the **Render** panel of the Ribbon (Figure 27-5).
7. Invoke the **RPREF** command to open the **Advanced Render Settings** palette (Figure 27-6). Under **Render Context**, select **Viewport** as the **Destination**.
8. Click inside the bottom viewport to make it the active one.
9. Invoke the **RENDER** command using one of the methods shown in the grid.
10. Click inside the other viewport to make it the active one and select the **Realistic** visual style.
11. Select **No edges** from the **Edge** control flyout button located in the **Edge Effects** panel of the Ribbon (Figure 27-7). The two viewports should look like Figure 27-8.
12. **SAVE** the drawing.

> **Note:**
> Even though certain visual styles are also considered to be rendered images, the simplest rendered image obtained with a render process is of a superior quality. One reason is that the **Render** process uses different types of filters to eliminate the aliasing effect that makes the edges and silhouettes appear to be jagged or stepped.

Figure 27-6   The **Advanced Render Settings** palette

Figure 27-5 The **Render Presets** drop-down list

Figure 27-7   The **Edge** control flyout button located in the **Edge Effects** panel of the Ribbon

Figure 27-8   Comparison between a modified visual style (above) and a basic rendered image (below)

Realistic rendered images have a wide range of important uses, from providing visualized and conceived ideas to creating marketing images for catalogs. Demonstrated ability in producing rendered images increases job opportunities in organizations that value and require this skill.

USING RENDER PRESETS

Render Preset: A named collection of settings controlling the quality of the rendered image generated with the **RENDER** command.

A ***Render Preset*** is a named collection of settings that control the quality of the rendered image. You can use one of the **Standard Render Presets** (**Draft, Low, Medium, High**, and **Presentation**) that come with the AutoCAD program, or use your own **Custom Render Presets** from the **Render Presets** drop-down list. You can access this list from the **Render** panel of the Ribbon (Figure 27-9), or in the **Advanced Render Settings** palette (Figure 27-10), which opens when you invoke the **RPREF** command.

Figure 27-9   The **Render Presets** drop-down list located in the **Render** panel of the Ribbon

Figure 27-10   The **Render Presets** drop-down list located in the **Advanced Render Settings** palette

The **Render Presets Manager** dialog box (Figure 27-11) is the third way of accessing and setting one of the Render Presets current. The **Render Presets Manager** opens when you invoke the **RENDERPRESETS** command, or select **Manage Render Presets...** from the **Render Presets** drop-down list in the **Render** panel of the Ribbon. The **Render Presets Manager** dialog box is where you create **Custom Render Presets**. Clicking the **Create Copy** button will open the **Copy Render Preset** dialog box in which you can specify a name. You can create custom Render Presets by copying the current settings, or by copying any other selected Render Preset.

Each of the five **Standard Render Presets** contains specific rendering settings that, when used as a whole, enable you to obtain rendered images of different degrees of quality. Using the **Standard Render Presets** is a great way to start creating rendered images.

You can make temporary changes to the selected Render Preset in the **Advanced Render Preset** palette. An asterisk is added in front of the name of the Render Preset warning you of its nonoriginal condition (Figure 27-12).

Figure 27-11   The **Render Presets Manager** dialog box

Figure 27-12   Both the **Advanced Render Settings** palette and the **Render** panel indicate that the Render Preset has been modified

The **Standard Render Presets** cannot be permanently modified. The **Custom Render Presets**, however, can be modified permanently in the **Render Presets Manager**. To make the changes permanent, you have to click on the **Set Current** button while the render preset is selected (Figure 27-13).

THE RENDER CONTEXT

Render Context is a group of settings that determine the procedure used to input the render information as well as the type of output you will obtain. This is the only group of settings that is not stored with the Render Presets; rather, it is stored in the **Render Context** with the drawing (Figure 27-14).

Render Presets Manager

Render Presets

Current Settings (*MyPreset 2)
Standard Render Presets
— Draft
— Low
— Medium
— High
— Presentation
Custom Render Presets
— MyPreset 1
— MyPreset 2

Name	MyPreset 2
Description	
Thumbnail Image	

General	
Materials	
Apply materials	On
Texture filtering	On
Force 2-sided	On
Sampling	
Min samples	1
Max samples	4
Filter type	Gauss
Filter width	3.5000
Filter height	3.0000

Set Current

Create Copy

Delete

No thumbnail

OK   Cancel   Help

Figure 27-13   The changes made to the **Custom Render Presets** are not permanent until you click on the **Set Current** button

Figure 27-14   Render Context tools located in the **Advanced Render Settings** palette

Rendering Procedure

The **Rendering Procedure** setting allows you to change the way the AutoCAD program proceeds immediately after you invoke the **RENDER** command. The options are as follows:

View: This is the default procedure. When selected, it causes the entire view in the active viewport to be rendered.

Selected: This procedure enables you to select the objects that will be rendered.

Crop: This procedure allows you to render only a cropped window by specifying two points.

The rendering process takes a certain amount of time to produce the rendered image. The rendered area as well as the number of objects and their complexity are two important factors that, along with other render settings, determine the amount of time required. By using both the **Selected** and the **Crop** rendering procedures, you can reduce the time of the rendering process. The **Selected** procedure is particularly useful when testing the effects of a new material applied on a particular object because it does not require you to render the entire screen.

Rendering Destination

The **Destination** determines the type of output for the rendered image. The **Viewport** destination generates the rendered image in the currently active viewport. Using several viewports allows you to visually compare the effects before and after applying a specific setting.

When the **Window** destination is selected, invoking the **RENDER** command opens the **Render** window (Figure 27-15), where the rendered image is generated. As you generate other rendered images from the current model, they are added to the list in the **History** pane. This allows you to temporarily store the different rendered images that you have generated without having to save them.

Figure 27-15   The **Render** window

In the **Render** window you can perform the following operations (to access some of the operations you must right-click on the temporary image file):

- **ZOOM** and **PAN**
- Obtain information
- Save a file
- Delete a file whether or not it is saved
- Purge a file from the history list without deleting it, if it has been saved previously

Note:
You can close the **Render** window at any time without losing any of the temporarily stored image files listed in the **History** pane. Sending another rendered image will reopen the **Render** window. The RENDERWIN command may be used to open the **Render** window as well.

Saving a Rendered Image

You can use one of the following three procedures to save a rendered image:

- Save a temporary image file from the history list in the **Render** window.
- Render directly to a specified file when rendering to the **Render** window.

RENDERWIN	
Ribbon: Render panel	
Command Line	renderwin

• Save an image previously rendered to a viewport by using the **SAVEIMG** command.

As previously mentioned, you can save one of the temporary image files from the history list in the **Render** window; however, you can also choose to send a rendered image directly to a file when rendering to the **Render** window. This lists the file in the history instead of making it a temporary file. To do so, you must first enable this type of output in the **Render** panel of the Ribbon (Figure 27-16) and then click the browse **(...)** button to open the **Render Output File** dialog box (Figure 27-17), where you must specify the location, name, and type of file (BMP, PXC, TGA, TIF, JPEG, JPG, and PNG).

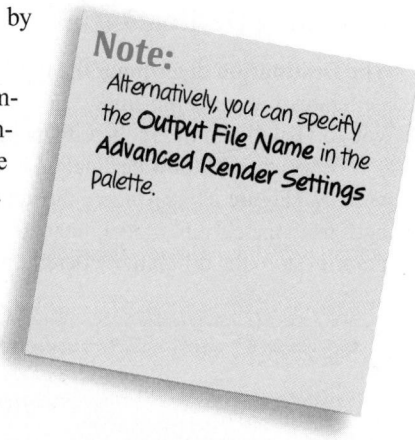

Note:
*Alternatively, you can specify the **Output File Name** in the Advanced Render Settings palette.*

(a)

(b)

Figure 27-16 (a) Enabling to save the file and (b) clicking the browse button to specify the location

Figure 27-17 The **Render Output File** dialog box

After you specify all the required information, clicking the **Save** button on the **Render Output File** dialog box will bring up another dialog box where you can select specific color and other imaging options depending on the type of file selected. Figure 27-18 shows the **Options** dialog box for three different image file formats.

You can also control the **Output Size** in pixels or the resolution of the rendered image in the **Advanced Render Settings** palette or in the **Render** control panel of the Ribbon. You can select one of four standard sizes from the **Output Size** drop-down list, which are based on a 4:3 aspect ratio, or select **Specify Output Size** to define your own size in the **Output Size** dialog box (Figure 27-19). Unlocking the **Image Aspect** will allow you to use a different ratio.

Figure 27-18   Options dialog box for three different image file formats

Figure 27-19   The **Output Size** dialog box

SAVEIMG	
Pull-down Menu	Tools/ Display Image/ Save...
Command Line	saveimg

When the file is sent to the viewport, on the other hand, it is not saved automatically, regardless of whether **Save rendering to file** is enabled or not. You can save the rendered image from a viewport only by using the **SAVEIMG** command. The output size is not as specified in the **Output Size** drop-down list either; it is controlled by the size of the viewport itself.

Exposure Type

This allows you to set the tone operator to either **Automatic** or **Logarithmic**. These two settings indicate that the tone operator used will either match the current viewport tone operator or will use a logarithmic exposure control. Owing to its direct relation to the light effect, this setting will also be discussed in the **Creating Illumination Effects** section in this chapter.

Exercise 27-2: Saving Rendered Images

1. **OPEN** *Exercise 27-1*.
2. **SAVE** it **AS** *Exercise 27-2*.
3. Invoke the **RPREF** command to open the **Advance Render Settings** palette. Under **Render Context**, select **Window** as the **Destination**. When finished, close the palette.
4. Select **Render View** from the **Views** drop-down list located in the **Views** toolbar or in the **3D Navigate** control panel.
5. Invoke the **RENDER** command.
6. In the **Render** panel of the Ribbon, enable saving the rendering to an image file directly. You can do so by clicking on the button shown highlighted (On) in Figure 27-20.
7. Click the browse **(...)** button to open the **Render Output File** dialog box. Select the location where you want to save the image file. Select the **TIF(*.tif)** file type and type in **FurnitureRenderA** as the file name.
8. Click the **Save** button. Click **OK** to close the **TIFF Image Options** dialog box and accept the defaults.
9. Invoke the **RENDER** command.
10. In the **Render** window, select the *Exercise 27-2-Temp000* temporary file from the history list. Select **Save** from the **File** drop-down menu to open the **Render Output File** dialog box. Select the same location as for the other image file, select the same type of file, and type **FurnitureRenderB** as the file name.
11. Click the **Save** button. Click **OK** to close the **TIFF Image Options** dialog box and accept the defaults.
12. Use Windows Explorer to browse for the image files in the location you specified. Right-click on one of the files and select **Open With** to use the image file using your favorite imaging program.
13. **SAVE** the drawing.

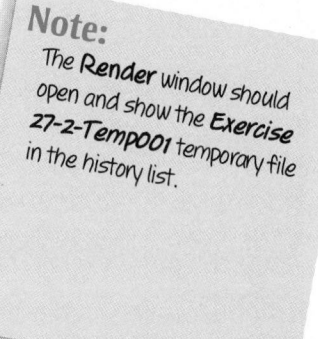

Note: The **Render** window should open and show the **Exercise 27-2-Temp001** temporary file in the history list.

Note: The **FurnitureRenderA** rendered image is added to the history list (Figure 27-21).

Note: The temporary image file becomes **FurnitureRenderB** after it it saved, and its icon changes to a folder with a checkmark.

Figure 27-20 Clicking on the button indicated allows rendering to an image file directly

Figure 27-21   The **Render** window. Two items are contained in the render history list

USING BACKGROUND AND FOG ENVIRONMENT

When rendering a scene such as the corner of the living room shown in the previous illustrations, you can cover the entire viewport by placing walls, floors, and other relatively large 3D objects. This allows you to control the total area of the rendered image.

When creating a rendered image of an isolated 3D object, you need not use other 3D objects to cover the entire viewport. You can achieve this purpose by simply changing the background environment associated with a named view.

Backgrounds are always associated with a defined Model View. The type of background can be specified in the **New View** dialog box (Figure 27-22), which opens when you click on the **New...** button in the **View Manager** dialog box, or it can be specified afterward in the **View Manager** dialog box for the selected Model View (Figure 27-23). Either way, you can choose from one of the following types of backgrounds:

> **Note:**
> The Sun & Sky type of background is available only when photometric lighting is enabled, that is, when the LIGHTINGUNITS is set to 1 or 2.

- Solid
- Gradient
- Image
- Sun & Sky

Figure 27-22 Selecting the type of background in the **New View** dialog box

Figure 27-23 Selecting the type of background for a defined Model View in the **View Manager** dialog box

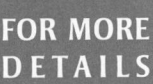

FOR MORE DETAILS   See the Photometric Lights section for more detail.

The **Solid** background override allows you to define a flat or single-color background. Clicking on the **Color**: window will open the **Select Color** window, where you can specify a color (Figure 27-24).

Gradient generates a two- or three-color gradient background. Each band color can be specified individually (Figure 27-25). You can specify a two-color gradient background by unselecting the **Three color** checkbox. You can also specify a **Rotation**: between –90° and 90°.

Figure 27-24   The **Background** dialog box for the **Solid** type

Figure 27-25   The **Background** dialog box for the **Gradient** type

Image enables you to browse and select an image file to be used as background (Figure 27-26). Clicking the **Adjust Image...** button opens the **Adjust Background Image** dialog box, where you can select one of three image positions (**Center, Stretch**, or **Tile**) (Figure 27-27). If you select the **Center** or **Tile** position, you can offset or scale the image to make specific adjustments. Keeping the **Maintain aspect ratio when scaling** option checked will prevent image distortion. Figure 27-28 shows examples of the three different types of background.

Sun & Sky is a more complex type of background. Selecting this background opens the **Adjust Sun & Sky Background** dialog box, where you can interactively adjust the many properties that define the simulated appearance of the sky and the sun (Figure 27-29). These properties are picked from the current settings of the Sun Properties.

FOR MORE DETAILS   See The Sun Light section for more detail on the Sun Properties.

Figure 27-26   The **Background** dialog box for the **Image** type

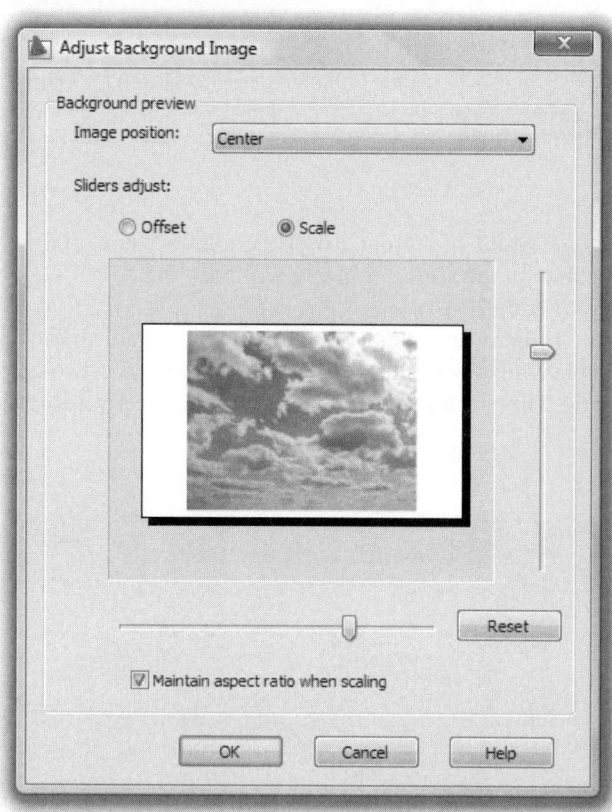

Figure 27-27   The **Adjust Background Image** dialog box

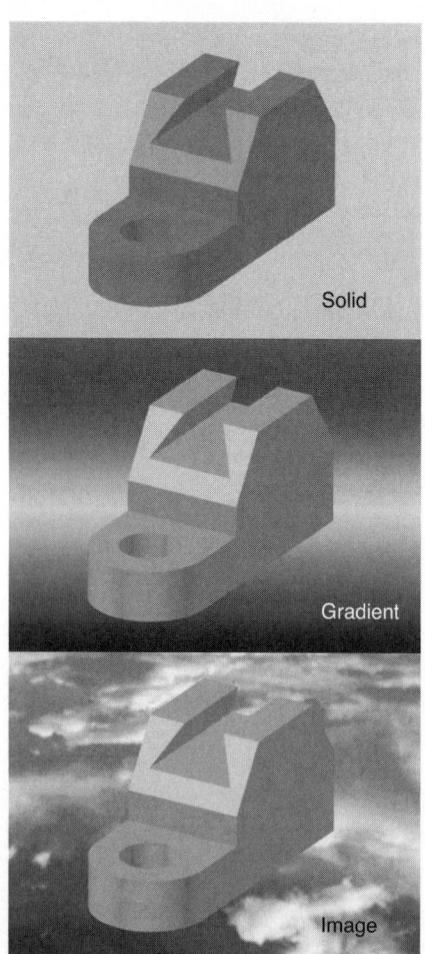

Figure 27-28   The three simple types of background

Figure 27-29   The **Adjust Sun & Sky Background** dialog box

The sky display can also be controlled in the **Sun** panel of the Ribbon (Figure 27-30); through its flyout button, you can choose among the following three settings:

- **Sky off**
- **Sky background**
- **Sky background and illumination**

The background is shown with the rendered image. But it is also shown when any visual style is selected (except **2D Wireframe**). You can turn the background off in a visual style individually through the **Visual Styles Manager** palette (Figure 27-31).

Another environmental effect can be created using the **FOG** command. When you invoke it, the **Render Environment** dialog box is displayed (Figure 27-32). In this dialog box you can turn

RENDERENVIRONMENT	
Render Toolbar	
Pull-down Menu	View/ Render/ Render Environment...
Command Line	Fog

Figure 27-31   The background can be turned off through the **Visual Styles Manager** palette

Figure 27-30   The **Sky** control flyout button, located in the **Sun** panel of the Ribbon

Figure 27-32   The **Render Environment** dialog box

the fog effect on and off. You can also set the distance from the camera at which the fog effect starts (**Near Distance**) and the distance from the camera at which the fog ends (**Far Distance**). By changing the **Near Fog Percentage** and **Far Fog Percentage**, you can control the intensity of the fog effect. Typically, the fog effect is higher at farther distances than at closer distances.

CREATING ILLUMINATION EFFECTS

OPTICAL PRINCIPLES OF LIGHT AND ITS PHOTOMETRIC QUANTITIES

Illumination is what allows us to see all objects around us. If there were no light, objects would not be visible at all, nor would their color, brightness, or any other properties. Shadows would not exist either.

Light is a very complex phenomenon, and its behavior is studied in optical physics. In essence, light is a form of energy that emanates or radiates from a source object in moving particles called *photons*. Depending on the medium through which the light travels and the type of light source, the energy of light, or its intensity, tends to decrease or attenuate as it gets farther from the object emitting it.

For materials of a certain transparency, light rays are divided into two portions when they reach an object's surface (incident rays). The rays reflected from the surface are called *reflected rays*. Those that penetrate the surface and get inside the object are called *refracted rays* (Figure 27-33). The angle between the incident rays and the surface normal is the same as the angle between the normal and the reflected rays. The refracted rays, on the other hand, change direction when they enter into another medium due to the differences in speed at which the rays travel in the two mediums.

How much of the light is reflected or refracted varies depending on the specific material properties of the object, as well as the angle of incidence of the light rays.

In the AutoCAD program you can create light sources that follow the same optical principles as real light sources. Using and combining different light sources enables you to control the illumination of the surfaces of 3D objects, which produces an infinite number of visual effects.

Light is a complex phenomenon. The simple inclusion of another 3D object may alter the illumination effect on preexisting objects. The intensity with which the surfaces are illuminated depends on how perpendicular they are to the light rays. The more perpendicular, the higher the illumination (Figure 27-34).

Photometry is the science that determines how the brightness of light is measured, as it is perceived by the human eye. Measurable values of light intensity, such as luminous intensity, luminous flux, and illuminance, are among the most important measured quantities in photometry.

Figure 27-33   Optical behavior of light rays striking a surface

Figure 27-34   Illumination effect increases as faces are located more perpendicular to the light rays

This diversification of measured quantities is due to the complexity of the illumination phenomenon itself, but all the quantities represent how bright and intense the light is.

Luminous intensity is a measurement of the power of the light emitted by a light source in a particular direction. For both systems, the customary and the International System of Units (SI), its value is measured in candelas (cd).

Luminous flux is a measurement of the total power of light emitted by a light source. For example, a 100-watt (W) incandescent lightbulb emits about 1,700 lumens (lm), which is its unit of measurement for both the customary and the SI systems. Manufacturers of lightbulbs and lamps usually specify this quantity for their products. From its value, one can tell how efficient a bulb is; for example, both a 60W incandescent bulb and a 15W compact fluorescent bulb emit approximately 900 lumens.

Illuminance measures the luminous flux arriving at a surface per unit area. This is the only one with different units. It is specified in lux in the SI system and in foot-candles in the customary system. One foot-candle is equal to 10.76 lux.

CREATING LIGHTS IN AutoCAD

Default Lighting

There are two different ways of illuminating the 3D model: using the *default lighting* or using user-created lights.

Default lighting provides light to the 3D model using two distant light sources. This illumination enables you to produce rendered images using a basic lighting setting, as well as to distinguish the faces in a rendered visual style.

You can make the default lighting use only one distant light source instead of two in a specific viewport by changing the **DEFAULTLIGHTINGTYPE** system variable value from the default **1** to **0**. Figure 27-35 shows the effect of changing this value on a rendered image that uses the default lighting.

Note:
The **LIGHT** command can be invoked only by typing its name in the command line.

default lighting: The default illumination provided by the AutoCAD program. It uses two distant light sources that follow the view direction.

DEFAULTLIGHTINGTYPE = 1

DEFAULTLIGHTINGTYPE = 0

Figure 27-35 The **DEFAULTLIGHTINGTYPE** system variable determines whether the default lighting uses two (above) or one distant light

Figure 27-36 The **LIGHT** command shortcut menu

Using the default lighting in rendered images gives very limited control over the illumination effects of the 3D model. You can create user-created lights (**Point** lights, **Spot** lights, **Web** lights, and **Distant** lights) by invoking the **LIGHT** command. Figure 27-36 shows these options within the command's shortcut menu.

User-created lights and the default lighting cannot be used at the same time. You can make AutoCAD turn off the default light automatically when user-created lights are added or turned on; this will reset the value of the **DEFAULTLIGHTING** system variable to **0**. All you have to do is select the choice that turns the default lighting off in the warning message that AutoCAD displays. This happens only when the **DEFAULTLIGHTING** system variable is set to **1** when you add a new light (Figure 27-37).

Figure 27-37 The AutoCAD program's warning

Photometric Lights

AutoCAD allows you to use and manipulate photometric properties of the lights in order to illuminate your scenes for more realistic rendered images. This allows you to use light sources with known real values of intensity, such as a 75W incandescent bulb or a 32W fluorescent lamp.

In order to use the **Photometric properties** of the lights [Figure 27-38(a)], the **LIGHTINGUNITS** system variable must be set to **1** to **2**. When its value is set to **0**, the photometric properties are not enabled. The only difference between setting this value to 1 or 2 is that AutoCAD uses different units of measurement for the illuminance—lux or foot-candle, respectively. You can set the **LIGHTIN-GUNITS** system variable in the **Lights** panel of the Ribbon [Figure 27-38(b)].

When the photometric lighting is enabled, the **LOGEXPBRIGHTNESS** system variable is also enabled to control the global brightness level of the drawing. You can also change the value of this system variable in the **Adjust Rendered Exposure** dialog box (Figure 27-39) by changing the **Brightness** value. Other illumination effects such as **Contrast** and **Mid tones** also can be adjusted in this dialog box. However, the most important feature of the **Adjust Rendered Exposure** dialog box is that you can interactively preview a sample of the future rendered image, which can save render processing time. You open the **Adjust Rendered Exposure** dialog box by invoking the **RENDEREXPOSURE** command by entering its name in the command prompt.

Any light (distant, spot, point, and web) can be adjusted using the photometric properties. Distant lights, however, may result in overexposure when the photometric properties are enabled, providing an unwanted result. AutoCAD displays the warning shown in Figure 27-40 if it intends to use distant lights when photometric properties are enabled.

From the **Tool Palettes**, you can access the **Photometric Lights** group of palettes, which contain many common lights used in real applications (Figure 27-41). Its type of light, color, and photometric characteristics are set to simulate the effects of the real light sources they represent.

(a)

(b)

Figure 27-38 (a) The **Photometric properties** located in the **Properties** palette and (b) the **LIGHTINGUNITS** system variable in the **Lights** panel of the Ribbon

Figure 27-39   Adjust Rendered Exposure dialog box

Distant Lights

Similar to daylight, a distant light emits parallel light rays that travel from infinity in the direction specified. Distant light reaches any object with the same intensity regardless of its location or relative distance. This type of light has no specific location, so no object can be located behind it.

Figure 27-40   Photometric distant light warning

Figure 27-41   The **Photometric Lights** group of **Tool Palettes**

DISTANTLIGHT	
Render Toolbar	
Ribbon: Lights panel	
Pull-down Menu	View/ Render/ Light/New Distant Light
Command Line	distantlight

LIGHTLIST	
Render Toolbar	
Ribbon: Lights panel	
Pull-down Menu	View/ Render/ Light/Light List...
Command Line	lightlist

To create a distant light, you can invoke either the **LIGHT** or the **DISTANTLIGHT** commands. In either case, you must define a vector direction by providing coordinate values or use the **Specify** option to specify two points:

Specify vector direction or [Specify] <0.0000,-0.0100,1.0000>:

The coordinates of the vector direction can be entered only through the command line. The direction is defined from the origin (0,0,0) to the specified coordinates. The **Specify** option enables you to specify two points using your pointing device: the direction from and the direction to.

Using a distant light allows you to control with precision the direction from which the light rays strike the objects' surfaces. It can also generate shadows whenever this setting is enabled. Figure 27-42 compares the lighting effect of a distant light with that of the AutoCAD program's default lighting.

Shadows, along with other properties, can be specified through the command line the moment the distant light is created. Figure 27-43 shows the command's options in its shortcut menu.

You can also change more easily the properties of a distant light after it has been created by accessing them in the **Properties** palette (Figure 27-44). Unlike point lights and spot lights, distant lights do not generate a glyph in 3D because they have no specific location. To access the properties of a distant light, you must select it from the **Lights in Model** palette (Figure 27-45), which opens when you invoke the **LIGHTLIST** command.

In the **Properties** palette, you can change the **Name** of the distant light, turn its **Status** on and off, and change its **Intensity factor** and **Color**. You can also control whether a particular light will cast **Shadows** or not; when this property is on, you can set specific details about the way the shadows are cast.

Note:
To delete a distant light, you can select it from the **Lights in Model** palette and then invoke the **ERASE** command or press the <Del> button.

Figure 27-42   Default lighting (above) versus using a distant light (below)

Figure 27-43   The **DIS-TANTLIGHT** command shortcut menu

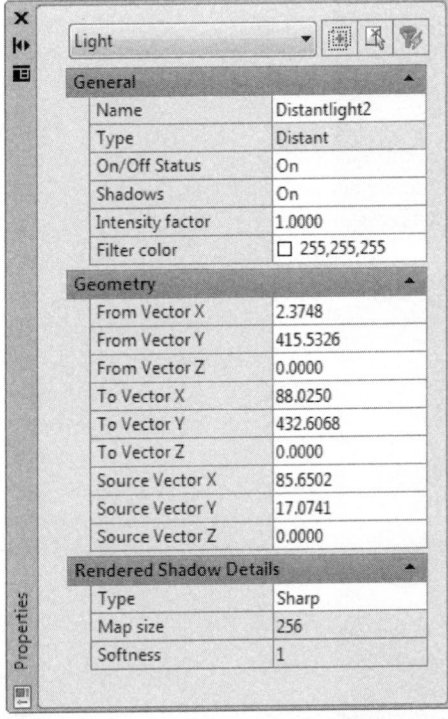

Figure 27-44   The **Properties** palette provides access to the **Distant Light** settings

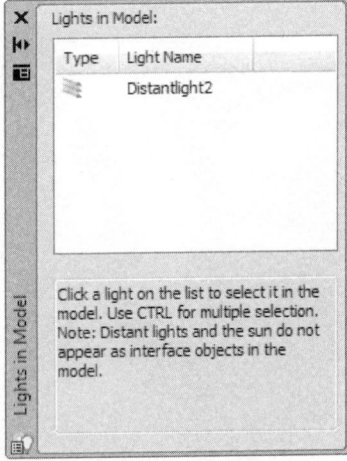

Figure 27-45   The **Lights in Model** palette

In general, lights can cast either ray-traced or map shadows. The main difference between these types of shadows is the way in which the area close to the border of the shadow is generated.

Ray-traced shadows are generated when an object blocks the light rays' traces in their path from a light source, and are more accurate than map shadows. They can generate high-quality shadows with a sharp, well-defined outline, and can transmit color from objects using materials of a certain transparency. Because they do not use a bitmap to be generated, no further adjustment has to be made to their resolution. Ray-traced shadows are the default type of shadow for any light source and are listed in the **Properties** palette as the **Sharp** type.

FOR MORE DETAILS	For more information about using a material and its transparency properties, see the section on using materials and textures in this chapter.

Selecting the **Soft** type of shadows in the **Properties** palette enables you to cast map shadows with a specific light. They cannot transmit color from objects that use transparent materials; however, they are the only way to generate shadows with soft edges. Figure 27-46 shows the difference between these shadows and the ray-traced shadows discussed above. You can adjust the **Map size** or resolution of the bitmap to improve the quality of the shadow. The **Softness** property is a measure of how much sharpness the shadow's contour loses.

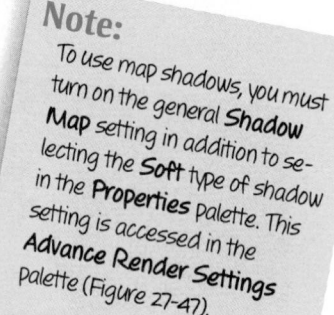

Note:
To use map shadows, you must turn on the general **Shadow Map** setting in addition to selecting the **Soft** type of shadow in the **Properties** palette. This setting is accessed in the **Advance Render Settings** palette (Figure 27-47).

Figure 27-46 Difference between **Sharp** (ray traced), shown above, and **Soft** (mapped) shadow, shown below

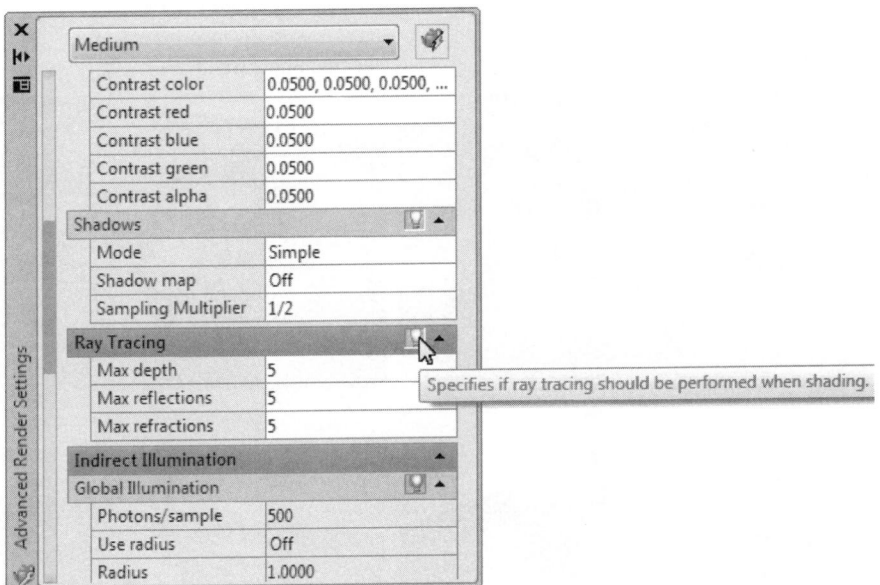

Figure 27-47 The **Advanced Render Settings** palette

In addition to controlling the effect of shadows for each light, you can also control their effect in each object by changing the **Shadow display** property in the **Properties** palette (Figure 27-48). By default, all objects are created with the property of casting and receiving shadows; however, you can change this property to **Casts shadows, Receives shadows**, or **Ignores shadows** for any object that can be rendered. Figure 27-49 shows the effect caused on the rendered image by modifying this property in the lamp base of the 3D model.

Point Lights

Similar to an incandescent lightbulb, a point light emits light beams from the source in all directions in the 3D space (Figure 27-50). Unlike a distant light, a point light has a specific location and generates a glyph, which allows you not only to select the light but also to perform operations such as **MOVE, ROTATE, COPY**, and **ERASE**.

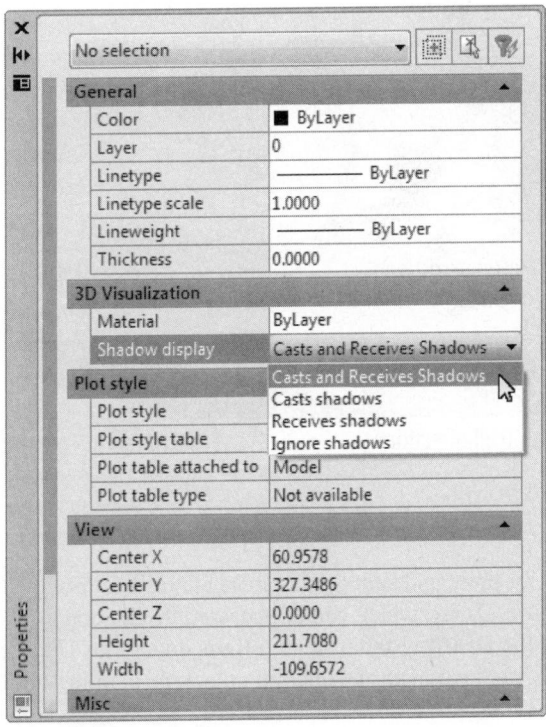

Figure 27-48 The **Shadow display** property in the **Properties** palette

Casts and Receives Shadows

Ignores Shadows

Casts Shadows Only

Receives Shadows Only

Figure 27-49   The four **Shadow display** options applied to the lamp base

Point Light Glyph

Figure 27-50   A point light emits light in all directions

POINTLIGHT	
Render Toolbar	
Ribbon: Lights panel	
Pull-down Menu:	View/ Render/ Light/New Point Light
Command Line	pointlight

The size and color of the glyph for point and spot lights can be controlled through the **Light Glyph Appearance** dialog box (Figure 27-51), which can be accessed by clicking on the **Lights Glyph Settings...** button located in the **Drafting** tab of the **Options** dialog box (Figure 27-52). You can turn off or on all the glyphs in the drawing by clicking the corresponding button in the **Lights** panel of the Ribbon (Figure 27-53).

Figure 27-51   The **Light Glyph Appearance** dialog box

Figure 27-52   The **Lights Glyph Settings...** button is located in the **Drafting** tab of the **Options** dialog box

Figure 27-53   The indicated button in the **Lights** panel of the Ribbon turns the light glyph off or on

To create a point light, you can invoke the **LIGHT** or the **POINTLIGHT** command. After specifying the location, you can modify the settings for shadows and other properties. Figure 27-54(a) shows the command's options in its shortcut menu when the photometric properties are not enabled. When the **Photometric Properties** are enabled, the shortcut menu also includes an option for these properties [Figure 27-54(b)].

Figure 27-54 The **POINTLIGHT** command shortcut menus with and without **Photometric Properties** enabled

(a)   (b)

As with distant lights, you can access these settings for point lights much more easily in the **Properties** palette (Figure 27-55), which can contain the **Photometric Properties** if they are enabled. You can select a point light to see its properties either by selecting its glyph or by selecting the light from the list in the **Lights in Model** palette.

In the **Properties** palette, you can change the **Name** of the point light. You can turn its **Status** on and off, change its **Intensity factor**, and change its **Color**.

Unlike distant lights, which are considered to always have the same intensity throughout the 3D space, the intensity of point and spot lights can diminish proportionally as their distance from the object increases. (This phenomenon is known as *attenuation*.) As a result, objects that appear farther from the light source will appear less illuminated.

Under the **Type** of attenuation in the **Properties** palette, you can set **Point** and **Spot** lights to have no attenuation by selecting **None**. By selecting **Inverse Linear** or **Inverse Square** you specify two different relationships between intensity and the distance.

Where P_1 is the location of the light, P_2 is the location of the object, and D is the distance between P_1 and P_2, the inverse linear attenuation can be expressed by:

Intensity @ P_2 = Intensity @ P_1/D

and the inverse square attenuation can be expressed by:

Intensity @ P_2 = Intensity @ P_1/D^2

The **Start limit offset** and **End limit offset** properties specify the distances from the source at which the light starts and ends, respectively. No light is cast beyond the end limit; this allows you to prevent certain objects from being illuminated by a specific light. Enabling the **Use limits** property allows you to control these two distances either by accessing the **Properties** palette or by pulling the glyph's grips (Figure 27-56).

Note: You can control the settings for shadows in the same manner as you can with the distance lights.

Note: When **Inverse Square** attenuation is selected, the intensity decreases much faster than with inverse linear attenuation as the distance increases. Usually, the use of attenuation requires higher values of intensity.

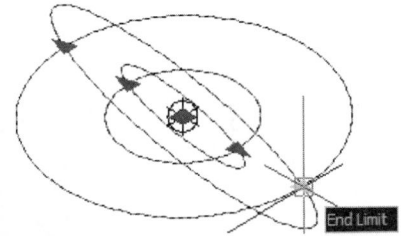

Figure 27-55   The **Properties** palette provides access to the Point Light settings; the photometric properties are available when **LIGHTINGUNITS** is set to **1** or **2**

Figure 27-56   The point light grips can be used to modify the **Start limit offset** and **End limit offset** values

When photometric lighting is enabled, that is, when **LIGHTINGUNITS** is set to **1** or **2**, the attenuation properties have no effect on the light. Photometric lights are defined by real values, including their own attenuation values.

You can control the intensity of photometric lights by changing the **Intensity factor** value on the **Properties** palette, just like you do with standard light. The **Lamp intensity** property, located under **Photometric properties**, is a better choice to set the intensity because it allows you to set real values; the **Lamp color** property allows you to select predetermined natural colors. Clicking on the buttons located inside the value fields of these two properties opens the **Lamp Intensity** and the **Lamp Color** dialog boxes, respectively; see Figure 27-57. In the **Lamp Intensity** dialog box, you can control the intensity of the light by specifying a value of **Intensity**, **Flux**, or **Illuminance**. In the **Lamp Color** dialog box, you can select from a group of standard colors such as Fluorescent, Incandescent, Xenon, Halogen, and so on.

> **Note:**
> Changing the **Intensity Factor** in the dialog box or in the **Properties** palette multiplies the photometric value.

Photometric lighting provides a more realistic illumination effect. Figure 27-58 shows the same point light with the standard lighting (top) and photometric lighting (bottom).

Spot Lights

Spot lights are probably the most common type of light used in rendered images. Resembling an actual spotlight or a flashlight, this type of light emits its light beams from the source in the form

Figure 27-57   The **Lamp Intensity** and **Lamp Color** dialog boxes

Figure 27-58   Ilumination effect created with a standard point light (top), and using photometric lighting (bottom)

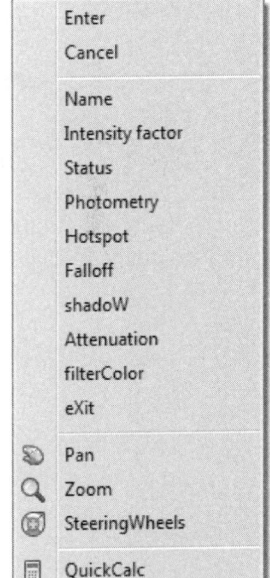

Figure 27-59   Spot lights emit light in the form of a cone

SPOTLIGHT	
Render Toolbar	
Ribbon: Lights panel	
Pull-down Menu	View/ Render/ Light/New Spotlight
Command Line	spotlight

of a cone (Figure 27-59). A spot light requires you to specify not only a source location but also a direction because you will be prompted to specify the target. This type of light also generates a glyph, which allows you to select it, perform operations such as **MOVE** and **ROTATE**, and modify some of its properties by pulling its grips.

To create a spot light, you can invoke the **LIGHT** or the **SPOTLIGHT** command. Alternatively, you can create a spot light using the **FREESPOT** command or the **Freespot** option of the **LIGHT** command. With these two options, you will not be prompted to specify a target, and the spot light will be automatically aligned with the *Z*-axis of the current UCS. The only difference between Spot lights and Freespot lights is that Freespot light does not have a specified target. Spot lights can be turned into Freespot (and vice versa) by changing the **Targeted** property in the **Properties** palette.

As with the other two types of light, you can specify the settings for the shadows and other properties after specifying the light's location and direction. Figure 27-60 shows the command's options in its shortcut menu. The **Properties** palette, as mentioned previously, gives you easier access to the same properties after the spot light has been created (Figure 27-61).

Hotspot angle and ***falloff angle*** are two new properties, inherent only to this type of light. Figure 27-62 shows the effect caused on the rendered image when different **Falloff** angle values are set in a spot light.

The cone of light emitted by a spot light is composed of two main conical volumes, each with different characteristics. An inner cone, called the *hotspot*, concentrates the light, without reducing its intensity as it gets farther from the cone's centerline. The outer conical volume surrounding the inner cone, called *falloff*, diminishes the light's intensity to zero as it gets farther from the centerline (Figure 27-63). The hotspot and falloff angles control how much the cones of light open. The value of the falloff angle cannot be set below that of the hotspot angle.

Note:
The settings for shadows and attenuation, as well as for start and end limit offset, are controlled in the same manner as with point lights.

Note:
The photometric properties of spot lights are controlled in the same manner as with point lights.

Enter
Cancel
Name
Intensity factor
Status
Photometry
Hotspot
Falloff
shadoW
Attenuation
filterColor
eXit
Pan
Zoom
SteeringWheels
QuickCalc

Figure 27-60   The **SPOTLIGHT** command shortcut menu

hotspot angle and falloff angle: The angles of the inner and outer cones defining the characteristics of the light rays emitted by a spot light.

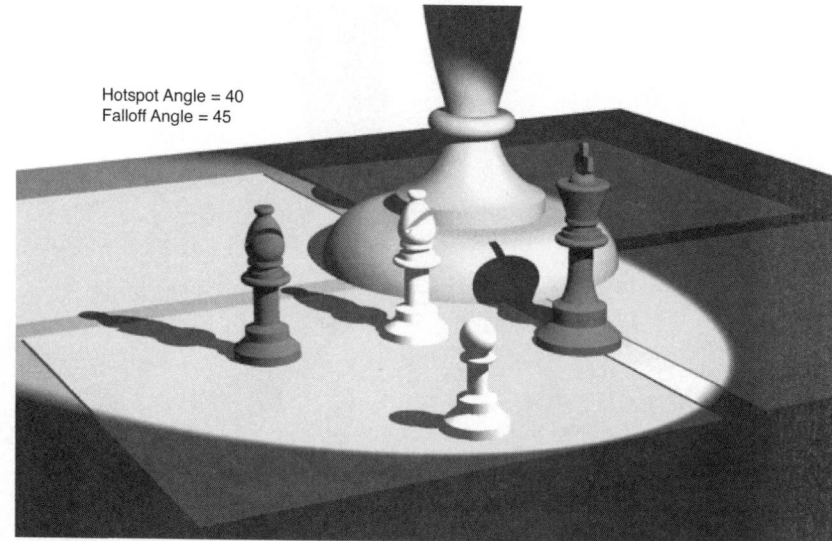

Hotspot Angle = 40
Falloff Angle = 45

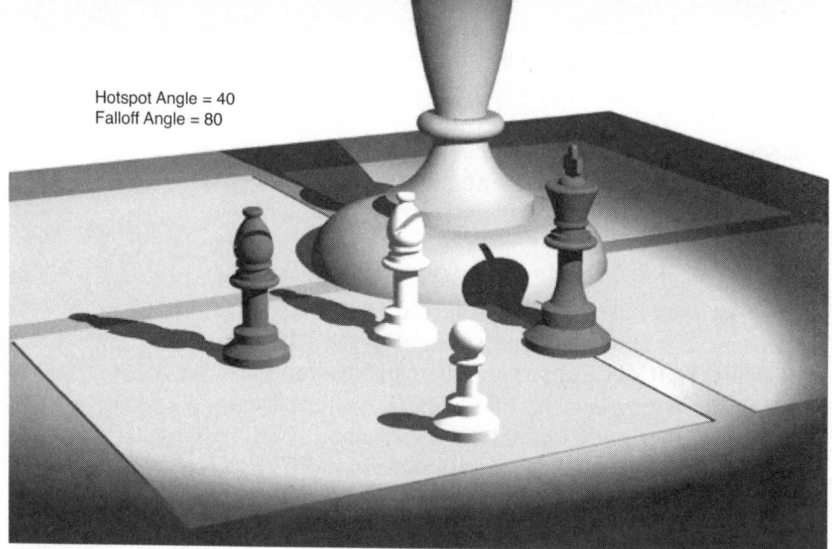

Hotspot Angle = 40
Falloff Angle = 80

Figure 27-61   The **Properties** palette provides access to the Spotlight settings

Figure 27-62   Effect of using different Falloff angle values in a spot light

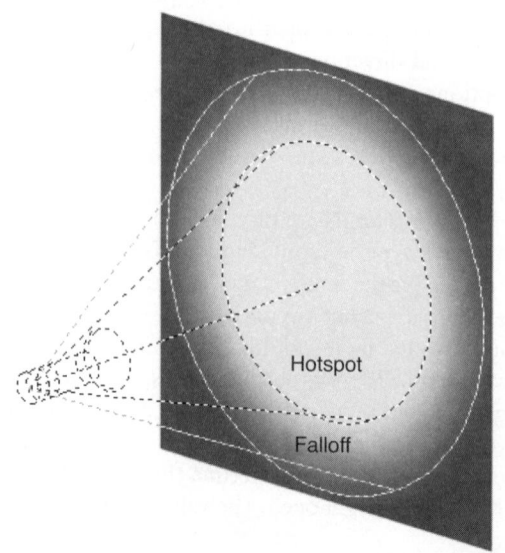

Hotspot

Falloff

Figure 27-63
Differentiation of areas illuminated by the hotspot and the falloff light zones

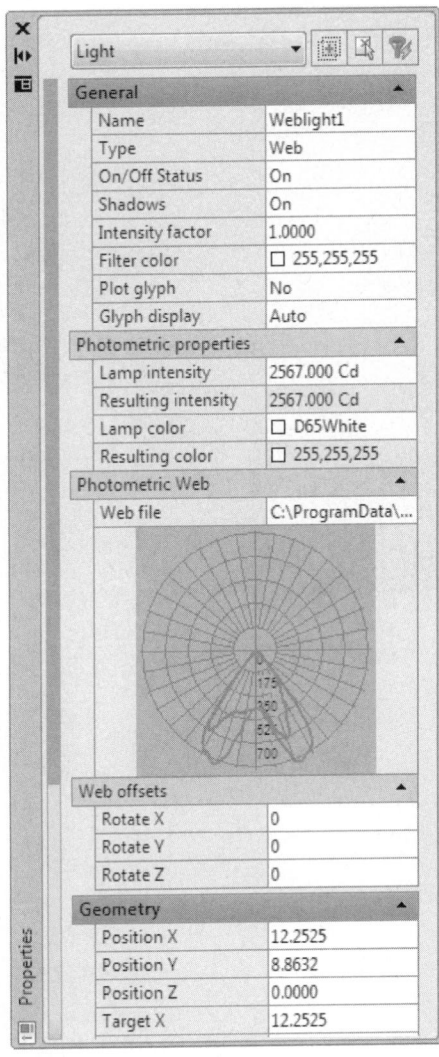

Figure 27-64   Properties palettes showing an isotropic and an anisotropic photometric web light

Web Lights

When the photometric properties are enabled, web lights offer a detailed 3D distribution of the intensity of the light emanating from the light source in all directions. When a web light is originally created, it provides an isotropic distribution of the light, which is represented as a sphere-shaped web. The effect of an isotropic web light is the same as the point light. The main purpose of a web light, however, is to show an anisotropic (nonuniform) light distribution. To do so, you must select one of the web files provided with the AutoCAD program. Figure 27-64 shows the **Properties** palette with the original web light on the left and with an anisotropic light distribution to the right.

Web files are created by using data provided by manufacturers of light and light fixtures. Depending on the web file you select, the light glyph will change to represent the photometric web according to its 3D light distribution.

Web lights are created by invoking either the **WEBLIGHT** or **FREEWEB** command, or you can also use the **LIGHT** command and select either of these options. Either of these commands can be invoked by entering its name in the command prompt. As with spot lights, Web lights are different from Freeweb lights because the Freeweb lights have no target location.

By using web lights, you can create more realistic illuminated scenes than with spot or point lights. Walls can be given a unique washed effect as they are hit with this type of photometric light (Figure 27-65).

Point, web, and spot lights can be transformed into one another by changing the **Type** property (Figure 27-66).

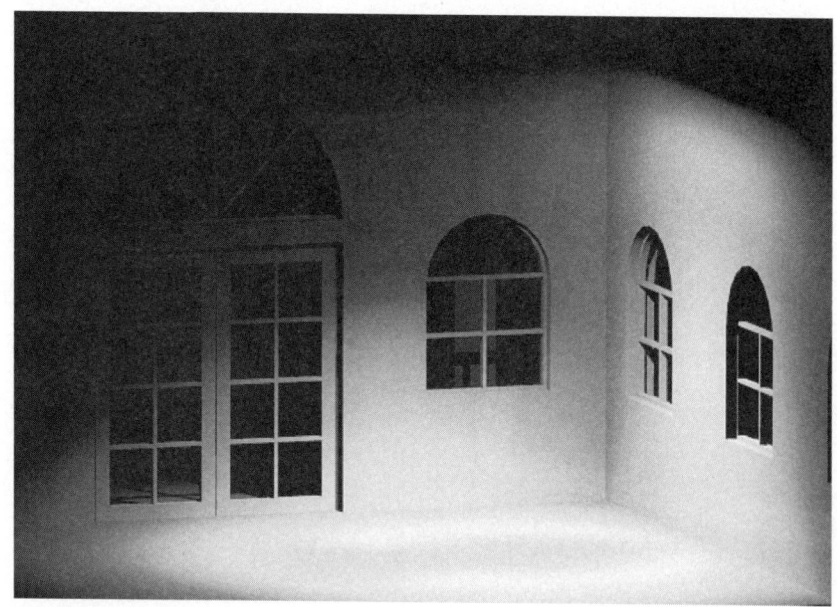

Figure 27-65 The illumination effects of an anisotropic web light

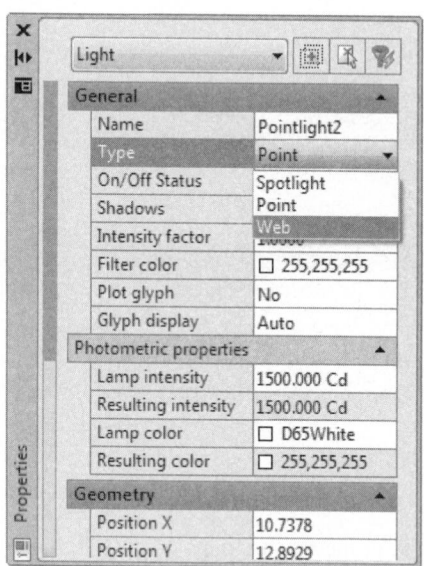

Figure 27-66 Point, web, and spot lights can be transformed into one another through the **Properties** palette

The Sun Light

The sun light behaves like any other distant light. It emits parallel light rays that travel from infinity in a specific direction, reaching any object with the same intensity. This special kind of distant light can be used to simulate the effect of the sunlight on your 3D model. Thus, it should be used for exterior environments only.

Like other distant lights, the sun does not place a glyph on the 3D model. It is not listed in the **Lights in Model** palette either. The properties of the sun are accessed in a special palette named **Sun Properties** rather than in the **Properties** palette (Figure 27-67). The **Sun Properties** palette is opened by invoking the **SUNPROPERTIES** command.

As with any other light, you can change the sun light's **Status** (on/off), **Intensity**, **Color**, and the effect of the shadows caused by its light rays. What really makes this particular light unique is the way in which its direction is specified. Simulating the presence of the real sun, the direction of the sun light is specified by its geographic location, the date, and the time of day rather than by an arbitrary vector direction.

The date and time can be changed in the **Sun Properties** palette. The **Geographic Location** dialog box allows you to determine the **Latitude** and **Longitude** of the sun light's direction by

SUNPROPERTIES	
Ribbon: **Sun panel**	
Pull-down Menu	View/ Render/ Light/Edit Sun Properties...
Command Line	sunproperties

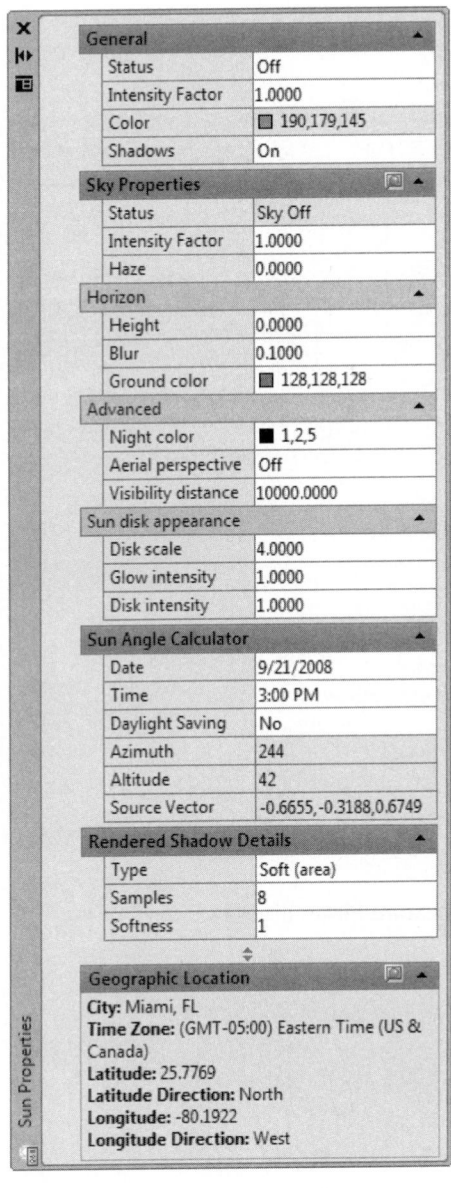

Figure 27-67   The **Sun Properties** palette

specifying its values directly (if you know such information) [Figure 27-68(a)]. Clicking on the **Use Map...** button opens the **Location Picker** dialog box, where you can easily select a location [Figure 27-68(b)]. You can open the **Geographic Location** dialog box by invoking the **GEOGRAPHICLOCATION** command or by clicking the button on the **Geographic Location** pane.

Under **Sun Angle Calculator** located in the **Properties** palette, you can control the direction in which the sun's light strikes the earth based on a particular geographic location. By modifying the **Date** and **Time**, you can change the incidence of the sun's light rays on your 3D model. The incidence is controlled by the **Azimuth** and **Altitude** angle settings. The **Azimuth** represents the angular position along the horizon. The **Azimuth** angle when the sun's light comes from the north (*Y*-axis) is zero, and its value is between 180° (clockwise) and –180° (counterclockwise). The **Altitude** represents the inclination of the horizon. Its values fall between –90° and 90° (Figure 27-69). Under **Sky Properties**, you can adjust the appearance of the sky and the sun.

GEOGRAPHIC LOCATION	
Ribbon: Sun panel	🌐
Pull-down Menu	View/ Render/ Light/ Geographic location...
Command Line	geographic-location

Exercise 27-3: Placing User-Created Lights

1. **OPEN** *Exercise 27-2*.
2. **SAVE** it **AS** *Exercise 27-3*.
3. Invoke the **RPREF** command to open the **Advanced Render Settings** palette. Under **Render Context**, select **Viewport** as the **Destination**.

Figure 27-68   (a) The **Geographic Location** dialog box and (b) the **Location Picker** dialog box

Figure 27-69   The azimuth and altitude angles

4. Make sure the **LIGHTINGUNITS** system variable is set to **2** and invoke the **LIGHT** command by typing its name in the command line.
5. Respond **Yes** to the **Viewport Lighting Mode** warning, and then enter **P** to specify a point light.
6. When prompted to specify the source location, snap to the top endpoint of the reference line located over the lamp base (Figure 27-70). Press **<Enter.↵>** to end the command.
7. Select **Render View** from the **Views** drop-down list located in the **Views** toolbar or in the **3D Navigate** control panel.
8. Invoke the **RENDER** command. The rendered image should look like Figure 27-71.

Figure 27-70   Location of the point light

Figure 27-71   The resulting rendered image

TIP   Using the **Medium** render preset should work OK with most computers. You can experiment with lower or higher levels of quality based on the properties of your equipment and the video adapter you have installed.

9. Invoke the **REGEN** command to regenerate the display.
10. Draw the line shown in Figure 27-72 between the two endpoints on the top of the walls.
11. Invoke the **WEBLIGHT** command by entering its full name in the command prompt. When prompted to specify a source location, snap to the midpoint of the line you just drew.
12. Snap to any point on the left front corner of the tabletop to specify the target location. Press **<Enter.↵>** to end the command.
13. Invoke the **LIGHTLIST** command by clicking its icon in the **Light** panel of the Ribbon. This will open the **Lights in Model** palette.
14. Open the **Properties** palette.

Note:
You can add some general illumination to the 3D model by using a direct light coming from the top.

TIP   When working with lights, it is a good idea to anchor both the **Lights in Model** and the **Properties** palettes, one below the other, on the right of the AutoCAD window (Figure 27-73).

Figure 27-72   Reference line

Figure 27-73   When working with lights, the **Lights in Model** and the **Properties** palettes can be anchored to the right for easier access

15. Select **Weblight2** from the **Lights in Model** palette to access its properties.
16. In the **Properties** palette, turn its **Shadows** property OFF. Under **Photometric properties**, set the **Lamp Intensity** to **800 Cd**.
17. Select **Render View** from the **Views** drop-down list located in the **Views** toolbar or in the **Navigate** panel.

18. Invoke the **RENDER** command. The rendered image should look like Figure 27-74.

19. Invoke the **REGEN** command to regenerate the display.

20. Invoke the **SPOTLIGHT** command by clicking on its icon in the **Light** panel of the Ribbon. When prompted to specify a source location, snap to the midpoint of the line you drew on top of the walls. Snap to the midpoint of the bottom front edge of the sofa for the target location.

21. Select the point light from the **Lights in Model** palette, and change its **Lamp Intensity** to **95 Cd** in the **Properties** palette.

22. Press the **<Esc>** key to unselect the point light. Then select the spot light by picking its glyph. In the **Properties** palette, change its **Lamp Intensity** to **800 Cd** and its **Falloff angle** value to **75**.

23. Select **Render View** from the **Views** drop-down list located in the **Views** toolbar or in the **Navigate** control panel.

24. Invoke the **RENDER** command. The rendered image should look like Figure 27-75.

25. Select **Weblight2** and change the Web file that controls the 3D anisotropic distribution of light. Experiment with different choices on your own.

26. **SAVE** the drawing.

Note:
Changing the **Lamp Intensity** of the web light and canceling its **Shadows** will cause this light to provide a soft general illumination to the 3D model without creating a mixture of shadows.

Figure 27-74   The resulting rendered image

Figure 27-75   The resulting rendered image after the specified settings are changed

MATERIALS AND TEXTURES

PURPOSE OF USING MATERIALS

Materials are used to provide properties such as shininess, translucency, and texture to the 3D objects in the model so they look like real objects when rendered. By applying materials you can simulate almost any property of the real-world objects. Similar to a layer, **Material** is a property inherent only to objects that can be rendered. The **Material** property can be handled in the **Properties** palette.

USING MATERIALS FROM THE TOOL PALETTES

Materials are created and stored in the **Materials** palette, which you can display by invoking the **MATERIALS** command. The top window (**Available Materials in Drawing**) displays sample images of any material available in the current drawing. Any new drawing starts off with a material named *Global*. This is the material we have been using throughout the exercises. The name of the selected material's icon is displayed in the drop-down list window below the icon's window. Also, hovering the mouse pointer over the icon displays a tooltip with the material's name (Figure 27-76).

MATERIALS	
Render Toolbar	
Ribbon: Materials panel	
Pull-down Menu	View/ Render/ Materi- als…
Command Line	materials

Figure 27-76   In the **Materials** palette, the tooltip description allows you to know the material's name

You can add other materials into the drawing either by creating them or by importing from the many materials stored by categorized palettes in the **Materials** and **Materials Library** groups of palettes. As you learned in a previous chapter, right-clicking on the vertical ribbon of the **Tool Palettes** shows a shortcut menu from which you can select one of the defined groups of palettes (Figure 27-77). You can select **Add to Current Drawing** from the shortcut menu that is displayed after you right-click on a particular material's icon (Figure 27-78). The sample image of the material added to the drawing is displayed in the **Materials** palette immediately. Alternatively, you can select **Copy** from the shortcut menu in the **Materials** palette and then right-click inside the sample images area in the **Materials** palette and select **Paste** (Figure 27-79). As with many other properties, pasting an AutoCAD object that has been copied to the clipboard from another drawing will also bring in any material that has been applied to that object.

In the reverse of this process, you can add any new material you create to a palette. You do this by selecting **Export to Active Tool Palette** or by dragging and dropping the material into the active palette directly.

Applying the Materials

After the materials are available in the drawing, you can apply them to the objects just as you assign a **Color** or a **Linetype** property. There are several methods you can use to do so. The **Materials** palette is probably the most frequently used. After you select the desired material, click on the **Apply Material** button, which is the second button from the right below the icon's pane. Double-clicking the material's icon will also activate this task. Then, you will be prompted to select the objects.

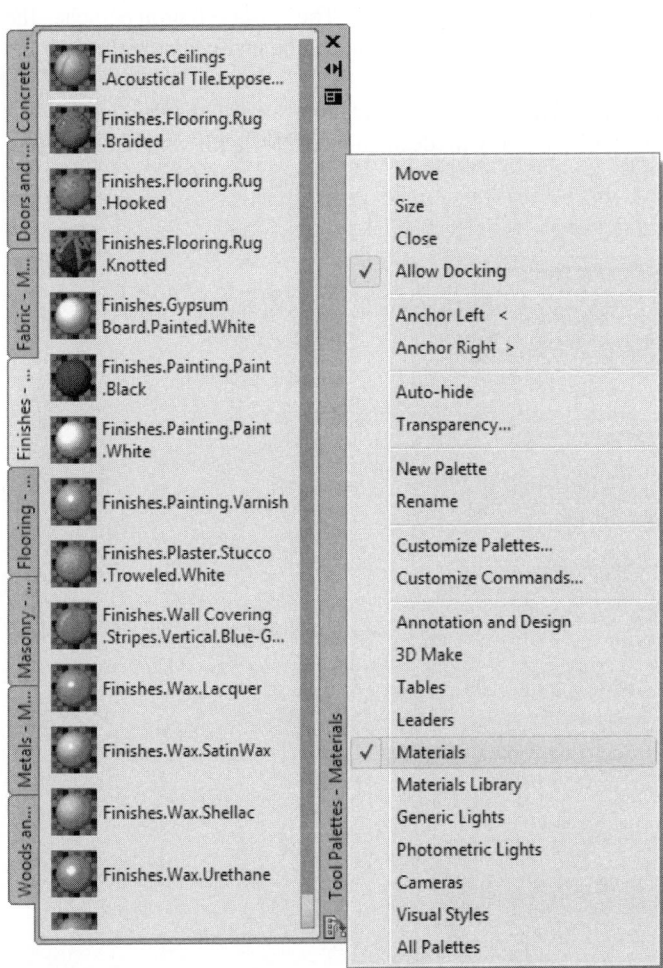

Figure 27-77   The **Materials** group of palettes can be selected in the **Tool Palettes** main shortcut menu

Figure 27-78   Shortcut menu displayed after right-clicking on a particular material in the **Tool Palettes**

Figure 27-79 Shortcut
menu displayed in the
Materials palette

Because **Material** is another property of objects, you can also use the **Properties** palette to change the material for selected objects (Figure 27-80). Objects that can be rendered are the only ones that possess this property.

Another way of applying a material is by linking it to a specific layer. Invoking the **MATERIALATTACH** command will display the **Material Attachment Options** dialog box, allowing you to drag a material from the list on the left and drop it over the layer. This creates a linkage similarly to linking a linetype to a layer (Figure 27-81). The **<Del>** button detaches the material from the layer. The **MATERIALATTACH** command can be invoked only through the command line.

Materials are shown after the rendered image is processed. You can also display them by selecting the **Realistic** visual style, which is the only predefined visual style for which, by default, materials are enabled (Figure 27-82).

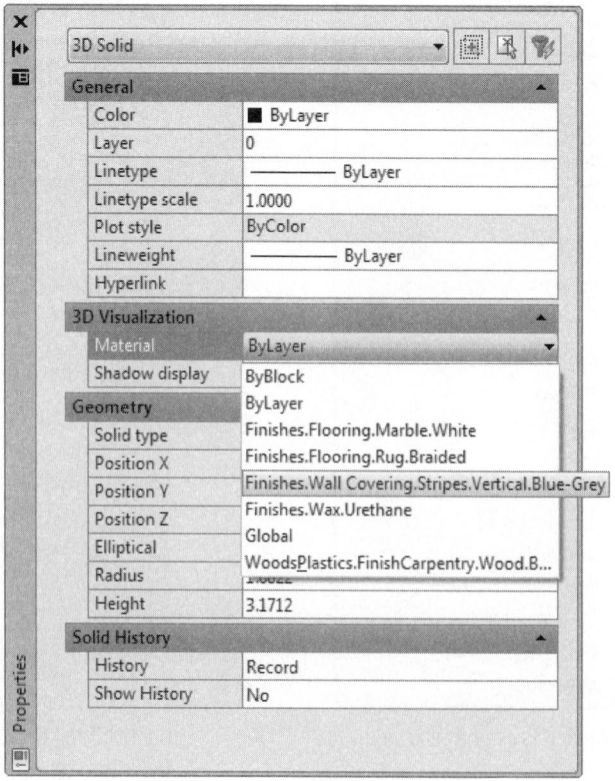

Figure 27-80 The **Properties** palette allows you to change the material for selected objects

Figure 27-81   The **Material Attachment Options** dialog box

Figure 27-82   Materials can be shown in both the rendered image and the **Conceptual** visual style

CREATING NEW MATERIALS AND TEXTURES

You can create a material by copying and modifying one of the materials existing in the current drawing. For example, a material named *Green Marble* would be copied as *Copy of Green Marble* in the sample images area. Then you can right-click on its sample image and select **Edit Name and Description...** to open the **Edit Name and Description** dialog box and change the material's name (Figure 27-83). You can also create a new material from scratch by clicking the corresponding button in the **Materials** palette. The **Create New Material** dialog box allows you to specify a name for the new material (Figure 27-84).

You can change the swatch geometry that is used to represent each material's sample image to a box, a cylinder, or a sphere by clicking the corresponding flyout button shown in Figure 27-85. A second flyout button allows you to change the illumination effect of the sample

Figure 27-83 The **Edit Name and Description** dialog box and the action that displays it

Figure 27-84 The **Create New Material** dialog box and the action that displays it

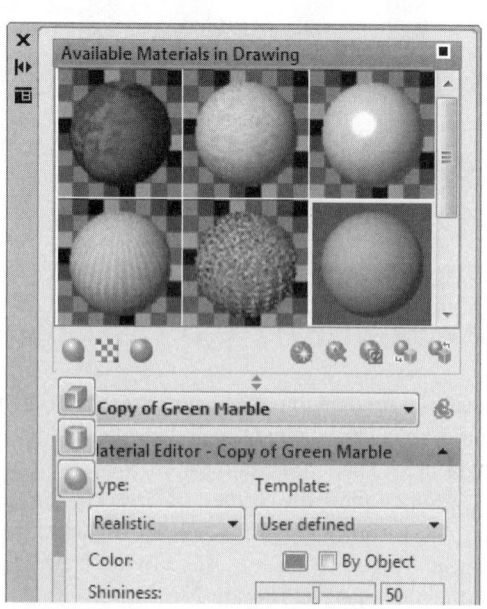

Figure 27-85 The **Swatch Geometry** and the **Preview Swatch Lighting Model** for the sample image can be changed in the flyout buttons

Figure 27-86   The size of the sample image can be changed or toggled to full size

image. You can also specify whether a material sample image uses a checkered underlay by clicking the button next to it. This allows you to determine how transparent the material is. You can also change the size of the sample images through the shortcut menu, or toggle the display mode to full size (Figure 27-86).

Specific properties for each particular material are controlled in the **Material Editor** area. The number of properties and initial settings for any material are first determined by *type* of material and the ***template*** it uses. New materials created from scratch always use the **Realistic** type. You can choose among four types of materials: **Realistic, Realistic Metal, Advanced**, and **Advanced Metal** (Figure 27-87). If you select the **Realistic** and **Realistic Metal** types of materials, you can also select one of the templates; by simply changing a material's template you can make a very close approach to the final material you intend to achieve. You change the material's template by selecting one from the drop-down list, after the material is selected (Figure 27-88).

template: Predefined collection of specific properties and property settings that gives a material a specific appearance.

The **Advanced** and **Advanced Metal** type of materials allow you to create special effects on materials. Selecting the **Advanced** type of material turns on all possible properties, thus allowing you to create materials with any characteristics. The **User defined** template of the **Realistic** type of materials is a simpler general version in which the reflection map as well as some of the colors' settings are not available. **Advanced Metal** and **Realistic Metal** types of materials turn off properties related to transparency, which are not supposed to belong to metals (Figure 27-89 and Figure 27-90).

Figure 27-87   You can choose from one of four types of materials

Figure 27-88   Templates available for the **Realistic** and **Realistic Metal** types of materials

Figure 27-89   Properties available for the **Advanced** and **Advanced Metal** templates

Figure 27-90   Properties available for the **Realistic** and **Realistic Metal** templates

Material's Colors

In general, you can control the effects of colors on a material using three options. **Diffuse** controls the general or main color of the material. You can use the same object's color by selecting the **By object** checkbox or specify another color independently. This is the most noticeable color. **Specular** controls the color of the areas that are more illuminated. **Ambient** sets the general ambient tone that is given to the main color. This is the least noticeable color effect.

The effects of all three colors can be controlled only when the **Advanced** type of material is used. By clicking on the **Lock** button, you can link either the **Specular** or the **Ambient** color to the **Diffuse** color. You can even link both and let the **Diffuse** color control all the color aspects (Figure 27-91). When the **Diffuse** and **Specular** colors are not linked, however, the surfaces appear to be shinier (Figure 27-92).

Controlling the Illumination Effects on the Object's Surfaces

The following properties affect in one way or another the effects of the incidence of light on materials:

- Shininess
- Refraction index
- Translucency
- Self-illumination

Shininess defines how reflective the material is. Using higher **Shininess** values accentuates the areas highlighted by the illumination, making them look smaller and with a more defined

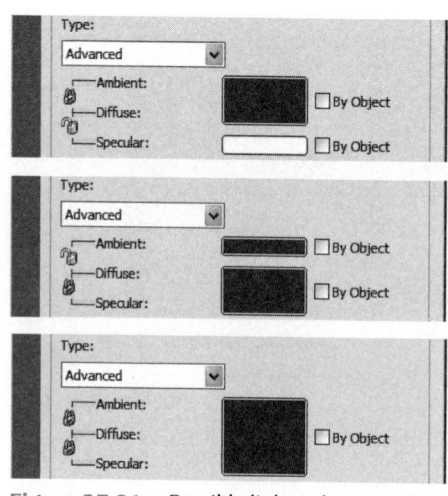

Figure 27-91   Possible linkage between the different materials' colors

Diffuse and Specular Colors Not Linked   Diffuse and Specular Colors Linked

Figure 27-92   Effects of linking the diffuse and specular colors

presence of the **Specular** color (Figure 27-93). High values of this property should be used in materials that will be applied to objects with smooth surfaces.

Refraction index refers to the ratio of the velocity of light in a vacuum to its velocity in a specified medium. Refraction is a property inherent only to materials that are not opaque because it refers to the portion of the light that goes into the objects. As the refraction index increases, light rays are bent more inside the objects, causing other objects seen through them to appear distorted (Figure 27-94). Materials with certain transparency or smaller opacity can properly show the different levels of refraction.

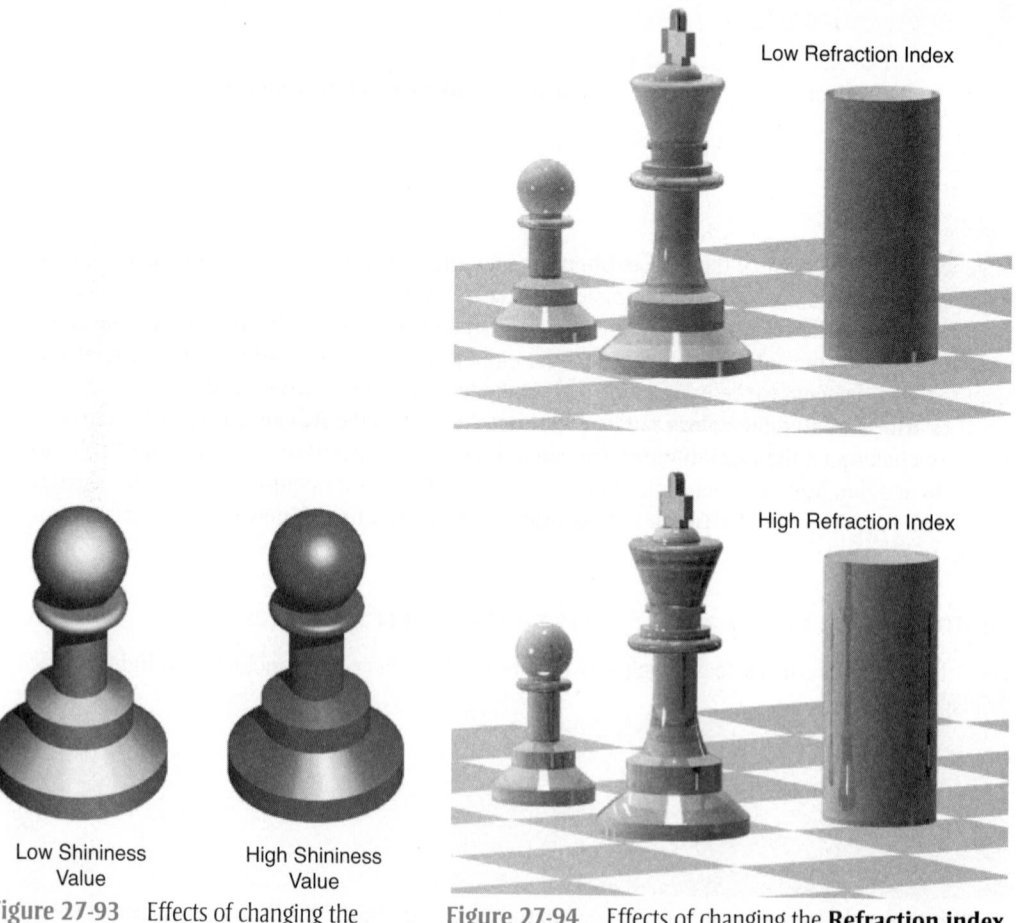

Low Refraction Index

High Refraction Index

Low Shininess Value   High Shininess Value

Figure 27-93   Effects of changing the **Shininess** value in a material

Figure 27-94   Effects of changing the **Refraction index** value in a material

Low Translucency

Minimal Self-Illumination

High Translucency

Some Self-Illumination

Figure 27-95   Effects of changing the **Translucency** value in a material

Figure 27-96   Effects of changing the **Self-illumination** value in a material

Translucency is a measurement of how much light enters and diffuses inside nonopaque objects (Figure 27-95).

The **Self-illumination** property controls brightness as well. Objects with self-illumination appear to be emitting light. Too high a value of self-illumination may cause the object not to be discernible (Figure 27-96). By selecting **Luminance**, you can specify photometric values for these properties.

Diffuse Maps

Other effects such as texture, roughness, reflection, and even transparency can be accurately defined by using an existing bitmap file. Valid formats are TGA, BMP, PNG, JFIF, TIFF, GIF, and PCX. You can use a bitmap file for the following four properties:

- **Diffuse maps**
- **Opacity**
- **Reflection**
- **Bump maps**

A diffuse map is the map most frequently used in a material. You can use the **Texture Map** option and attach a bitmap file or use one of the internal map types (**Checker, Marble, Noise, Speckle, Tiles, Waves**, or **Wood**) (Figure 27-97). Then you can apply the material with texture to cover the surfaces of the objects. You can also set the slide button on an intermediate value to allow the **Diffuse** color to blend with the bitmap file. When the slide button is completely to the right, the **Diffuse** color has no effect.

The main purpose of using a texture map is to create effects that can be represented by patterns of bitmaps, such as floor tiles, bricks, wallpapers, wood finishes, and metal finishes. You could even use a texture map to apply a specific color. The appearance achieved depends on the bitmap you use. The AutoCAD program comes with several images that you can use for this

Figure 27-97   The **Diffuse map** drop-down menu in the **Materials** palette

purpose. Other bitmaps can be purchased on the Internet, or you can simply take a picture with a digital camera of the spot you want to bring into your rendered image. Figure 27-98 shows some examples of effects you can achieve by using texture maps. Because you can stretch a single bitmap over a surface, you can also create effects such as wall pictures or labels.

To select a bitmap, you must click the **Select Image** button on the **Materials** palette to open the **Select Image File** dialog box (Figure 27-99), which allows you to browse, preview, and select

Figure 27-98   Four samples applied to the tabletop using texture maps

Figure 27-99   The **Select Image File** dialog box

Settings

Erase

Synchronization

Preview

Figure 27-100 Four new buttons and the slide bar appear after specifying a map

the bitmap. After you select the file or choose one of the internal map types, the **Select Image** button changes to the name of the file, and four new buttons, along with the slide bar, appear next to it (Figure 27-100).

The **Erase** button allows you to delete the current map information from the material. The next button controls whether or not the map is synchronized with the material. When the synchronization is enabled, changes in the setting of the map will affect the maps used in the material. When the synchronization is disabled, any changes in the setting of the map will affect only the current map; an AutoCAD warning is displayed to let you know this (Figure 27-101). Clicking the third button will open the corresponding **Map Preview** window (Figure 27-102). You can leave this window open while the **Materials** palette is open and check the **Auto Update** checkbox to visualize any changes you make to the particular map.

Figure 27-101 AutoCAD warning about the map desynchronization

Figure 27-102 The **Diffuse Map Preview**

The **Map Settings** button causes the entire **Materials** palette to switch from the **Material Editor** to the **Map Editor**, displaying the settings for this particular map instead of the settings of the material (Figure 27-103). You can switch from one map to another map at any time, or even back to the material's editor, through the drop-down list located below the sample images pane (Figure 27-104). You can control the same type of settings for the top-level material and for each map in particular. These settings are equally arranged in two panes: **Scaling & Tiling** and **Offset & Preview**.

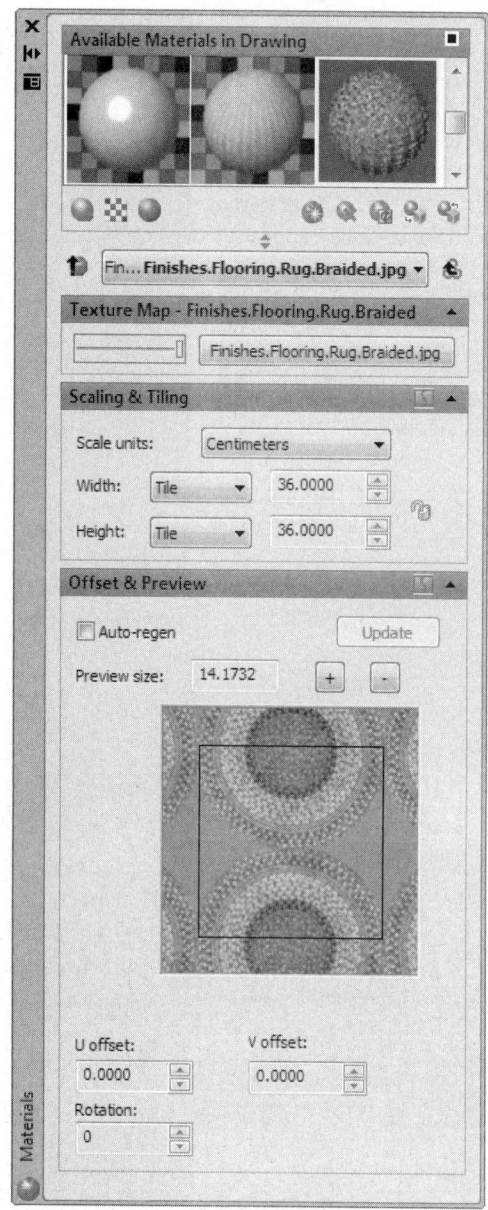

Figure 27-103   The **Map Editor**

Figure 27-104   The drop-down list allows easy access to the other maps and to the top-level material

After specifying the proper **Scale units**, the first thing you should do is select a proper **Preview size**. For example, the piece of lumber shown in Figure 27-105 would require a **Preview** size of around 8 × 8 units. Because you are using real **Scale units**, the preview shows how the bitmap is actually tiled in an area using a fixed scale or real-world scale. The size of the preview does not affect the mapping. You can then change the scale in the U and V directions independently in the **U Tile:** and **V Tile:** text boxes or by moving the slice buttons. Clicking on the lock icon will lock the U and V proportion. You can also specify the behavior of the tiling effect in the U and V directions independently (**None, Tile,** or **Mirror**). After you adjust the **Scale** to the new **Preview size**, the bitmap is easily mapped on the rendered image (Figure 27-106). You can also offset the image to locate a different area inside the 8 × 8 square, either inside the **U offset:** and **V offset:** text boxes, or by clicking

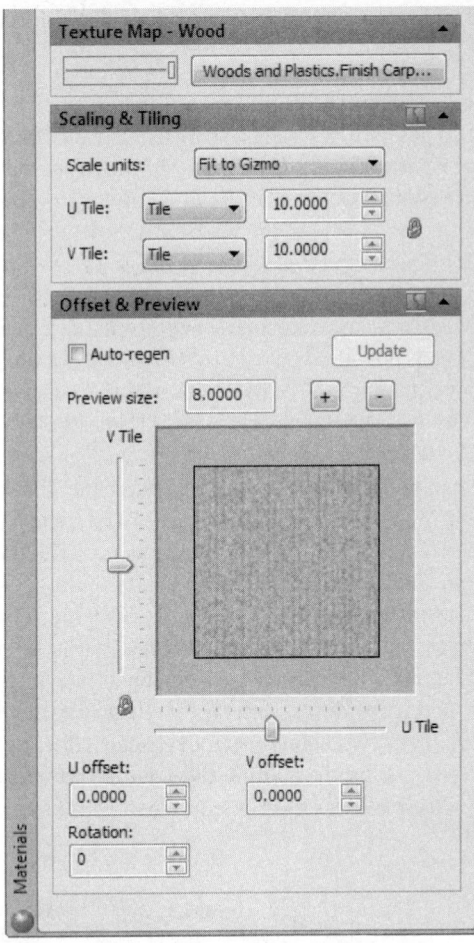

Figure 27-105   When using a particular **Scale unit**, the **Preview size** must be set correspondingly to the object size

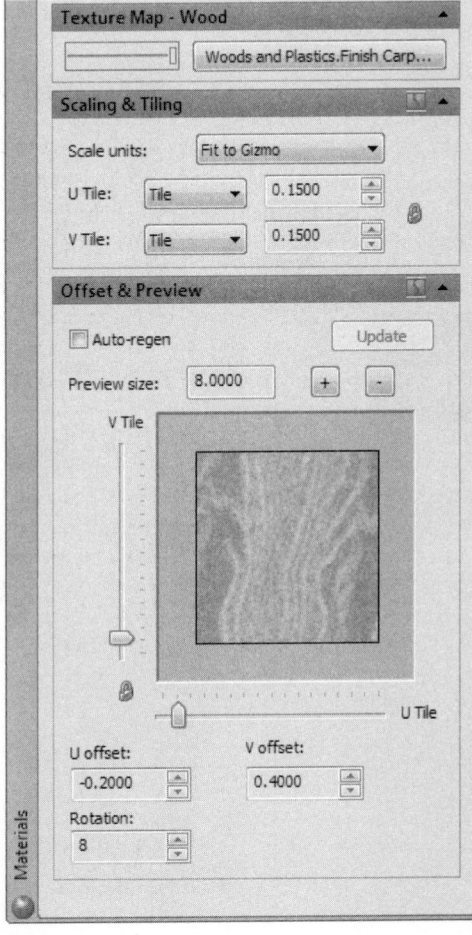

Figure 27-106   Result of adjusting the scale to the new preview size

and dragging inside the preview image. Specifying a rotation is also possible. You can do so by using the **Rotation:** text box, or by right-clicking and dragging inside the preview image.

When you use the **Fit to Gizmo** option under the **Scale units,** the square in the preview represents the tile that must be stretched to fit each face of the object. Setting this option as **1** will represent how the image will look in each face, which is more convenient. For this option, selecting the **Tile** options provides you with U × V number of tiled images to cover the faces. This option is especially useful for representing a defined pattern such as a chessboard. In Figure 27-107 an original image of 2 × 2 squares is used four times to fit the board (a region). When the **Tile** value of **U** and **V** is set to **1,** a single image will be stretched to cover a face. Pictures and other single images can be obtained with this option (Figure 27-108).

Besides the texture map created with image files, you can also use the other type of preset maps (**Checker, Marble, Noise, Speckle, Tiles, Waves,** and **Wood**). If you select any of these maps, clicking the **Map Settings** button displays the editor of this particular map inside the **Materials palette,** where you can adjust its appearance. Figure 27-109 shows, for instance, the **Wood** map editor. Each type of map is defined by its particular specific properties. As with texture maps, you can create a blended effect by using the **Slice** button. Particularly for the wood type of maps, the **Radial noise** and **Axial noise** control the randomness of the grain pattern along and across, respectively. The **Grain thickness** value determines how thick the wood rings are.

Note:
UN is a coordinate system that is used as a reference to define the bitmap's distances in two perpendicular directions, similar to the XY coordinate system. The UN coordinate system, however, is completely independent of the XY coordinate system. It moves and rotates with the bitmap.

Figure 27-107 The original image of 2 × 2 squares is repeated four times to fit the board

Figure 27-108   Pictures can be created with this option

Figure 27-109   The editor of the **Wood** diffuse map in the **Materials** palette

Opacity Maps

Opacity is a property that mostly affects the transparency effect on materials; it can help you accomplish two important functions. First, it determines how transparent a material is without using a bitmap file. The lower the value of the opacity, the more transparent will be the objects to which you apply the materials. The slide button is always present for **Realistic** and **Advanced** types of materials, to enable you to adjust their value at all times.

Second, **Opacity** enables you to assign different values of transparency to different areas on the same face. To achieve this effect, you must use a bitmap file. Images containing black-and-white areas are ideal for opacity purposes because black areas make the surface fully transparent and white areas make them fully opaque. Any other color would provide an intermediate opacity, depending on its grayscale value.

The bitmaps used to create opacity maps are selected and adjusted the same way as the bitmaps for texture maps. Unlike with texture maps, however, the **Diffuse** color is always present because the opacity map does not provide any color to the material.

Figure 27-110 The tabletop can be given the effect of having an engraved chessboard by using an opacity map

Original Bitmap

For example, by using an opacity map, you can give a tabletop the effect of being a pane of glass with a chessboard engraved on it (Figure 27-110). Another suitable use can be to create the effect of windows without really having them modeled.

Creating Landscapes

By using a texture map and its equivalent opacity map together, you can simulate the presence of other objects such as plants or people (Figure 27-111).

This effect is easily achieved; however, you must obtain or prepare the image files that correspond to both types of maps. The image to be attached to the texture map must contain the object in a black background. The corresponding image file to attach as the opacity map must be the same exact file with the shape of the object cropped (Figure 27-112).

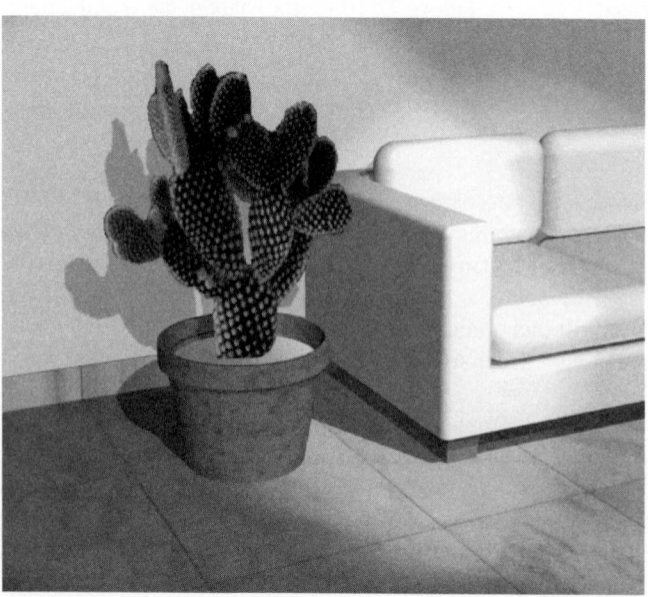

Figure 27-111 Landscape objects can be simulated by using a texture map and its equivalent opacity map together

Texture Map Image   Opacity Map Image

Figure 27-112   A texture map and its corresponding opacity map

You must create a new material using the **Advanced** template, then attach each image file to its corresponding type of map. You must set the same **Bitmap Scale** for both images in the **Adjust Bitmap** dialog box. Because the image should be stretched one time onto the 3D object, you should set the **Scale units** as **Fit to Gizmo** and set **U Tile** and **V Tile** both to **1** (Figure 27-113).

Figure 27-113   In the texture editors of both the **Diffuse** and **Opacity** maps, the **Scale units** must be set to **Fit to Gizmo** among other settings

The 3D object to which you apply the material for landscape purposes must be properly oriented to make the image appear as real as possible. If you need the landscape object to cast shadows, you can use very thin, extruded 3D solids or a surface like the one shown in Figure 27-114. You

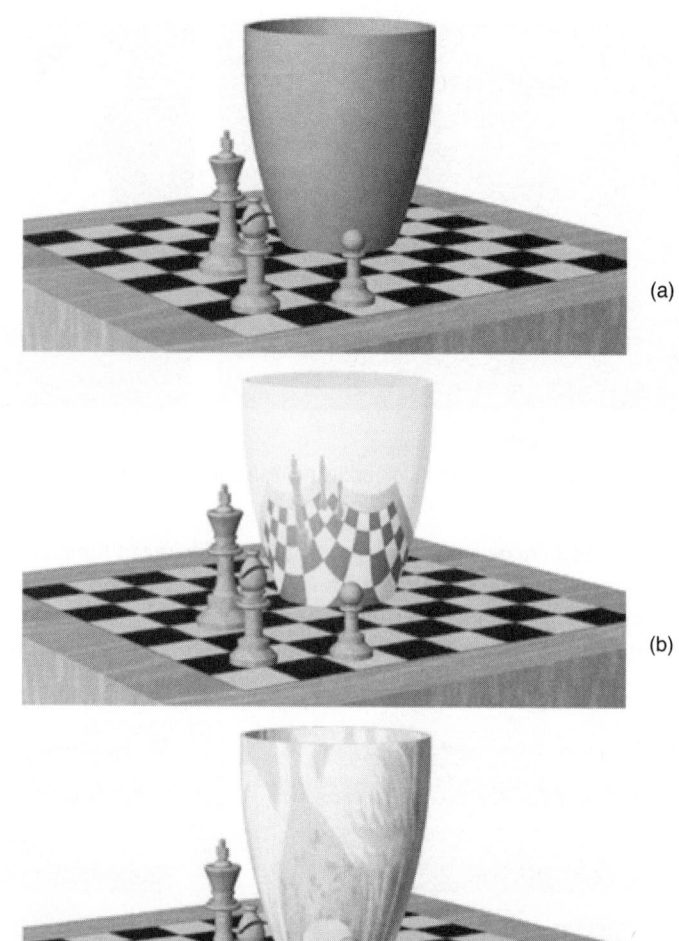

Figure 27-114   A surface is used to attach the material for landscape purposes

Figure 27-115   Effects of the **Reflection** property on a material: (a) no reflection; (b) reflection of its own environment; and (c) reflection of an attached image file

can use a simple imaging application such as Paint to prepare the image files. You can also use more sophisticated software, such as Adobe Photoshop®.

Reflection Maps

The **Reflection** property is available only for materials that use the **Advanced** and **Advanced Metal** templates. As with the **Opacity** property, you can use the **Reflection** property to control two effects. Without using a bitmap file, moving the slide button determines how reflective a material is.

Reflective objects normally reflect their own environment, which consists of the other objects around them. By using an image file with shiny materials, however, you can make the objects with this material attached reflect that image file instead of other objects. Figure 27-115(a) shows the rendered image with no **Reflection** property specified. In Figure 27-115(b), the rendered image shows the reflection of the object in its own environment. In Figure 27-115(c), the object reflects an attached bitmap instead.

Note:
The colors contained in a bitmap file used as a bump map do not affect the diffuse color of the material. Higher differences in their grayscale values, however, enhance the bumping effect.

Bump Maps

A bump map creates an embossed 3D texture in surfaces, giving them an appearance that is closer to that of the real objects. A bump map requires an image file to be selected. One example in which a bump map makes an outstanding difference is in brick and masonry walls (Figure 27-116). When used on wood, a bump map creates an antique or aged effect (Figure 27-117). Excellent results are usually achieved when the same bitmap file is used for both the texture map and the bump map.

No Bump Map

Using Bump Map

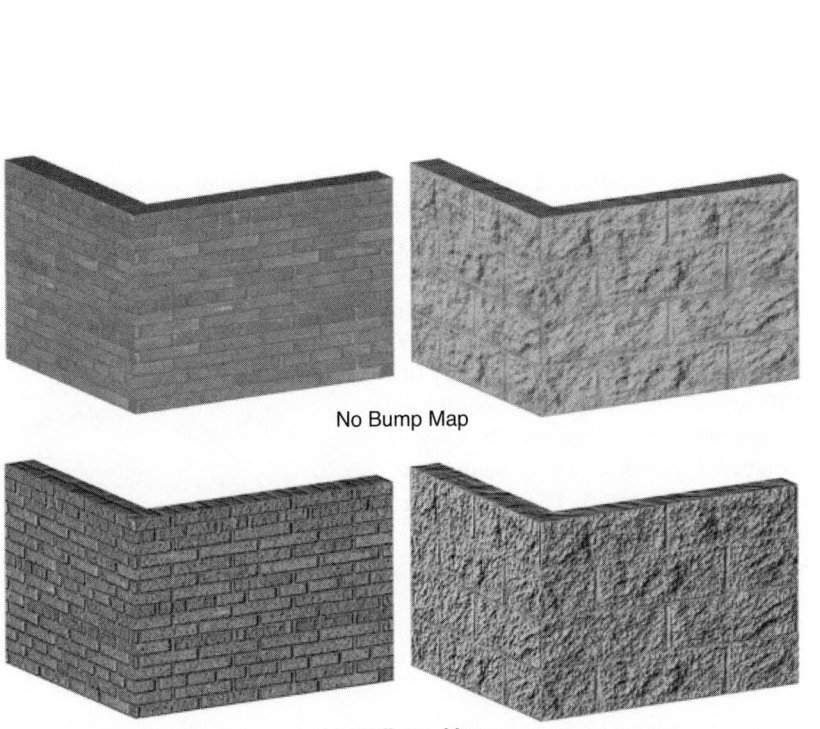

No Bump Map

Using Bump Map

Figure 27-116   Rendered image of a masonry wall with and without bump maps

Figure 27-117   Rendered image with and without bump maps attached to the woodlike material

Exercise 27-4: Using Materials

1. **OPEN** *Exercise 27-3*.
2. **SAVE** it **AS** *Exercise 27-4*.
3. Invoke the **MATERIALS** command to display the **Materials** palette.
4. Invoke the **TOOLPALETTES** command to open the **Tool Palettes**. Right-click on its blue ribbon and select the **Materials** group of palettes from the shortcut menu.
5. Click on the **Flooring** tab. Right-click on the **Finishes. Flooring.Marble.White** material sample icon and select **Add to Current Drawing** (Figure 27-118).
6. Close the **Tool Palettes**. The new material sample should show up in the **Materials** palette.

Note:
If the **Tool Palettes** is docked, the same shortcut menu will appear when you right-click on the double line bar at the top border.

7. Select the material you just brought into the drawing. Right-click on its sample image, and select **Edit Name and Description**. In the **Edit Name and Description** dialog box, change its name to **Marble Floor** and then click **OK**.

8. While the **Marble Floor** material is still selected, click on the swatch geometry flyout button and select the box as the sample image. Click on the checkered underlay button to turn the checkered underlay off.

9. Click the **Diffuse**: color box and select color **9** from the **Index Color** tab. Make sure the **By Object** checkbox is cleared. Scroll down to **Scaling & Tiling** and set both **U Tile** and **V Tile** to 4. Under **Scale units**, select **Fit to Gizmo**.

10. Click the **Apply material** button and select the 3D solid that represents the floor. Press **<Enter.↵>** to end the selection.

Note: The selected material shows a thick yellow outline around its sample image.

You can find information about any tool by placing the pointer over it and reading its brief description inside the **Description** box, located at the bottom of the palette.

11. Select **Render View** from the **Views** drop-down list located in the **Views** toolbar or in the **Navigate** control panel.

12. Invoke the **RENDER** command. The rendered image should look like Figure 27-119.

13. Invoke the **REGEN** command and open the **Materials** palette in case you have closed it. Create four new materials by clicking on the **New Material** button. Give the new materials the following names:

- Wood
- Brass
- Glass
- Canvas

Note: The rendered image can be created underneath the **Materials** palette. It is more convenient, however, to close or dock the **Materials** palette before invoking the **RENDER** command.

Figure 27-119   The resulting rendered image

14. Select the **Wood** material. Under **Diffuse map**, make sure **Texture Map** is selected from the drop-down list under **Map type** and click on the **Select Image** button. In the **Select Image File** dialog box, select the JPEG file named **Woods and Plastics.Finish Carpentry.Wood.Hickory** from the AutoCAD program's **Template** folder.

TIP

The AutoCAD program should automatically open the **Textures** folder containing the **Textures** bitmaps. If you are not taken to the **Textures** folder, you must manually browse to locate it. Because you do not want to spend time trying to locate this folder manually, you can find it using other procedures. One of them is performing a **Search** operation through Windows Explorer. Another fast way of locating this folder is as described below.

Close the **Select Image File** dialog box and open the **Options** dialog box. **Copy** the path corresponding to **Texture Maps Search Path** from the **Files** tab of the **Options** dialog box (Figure 27-120). The **Options** dialog box can be closed afterward.

Open the **Select Image File** dialog box again through the **Materials** palette, and simply **Paste** the path in the **File name:** box. After clicking the **Open** button, you should be taken to the **Textures** folder.

15. From the main drop-down list located under the material sample images, select **Diffuse Map: Woods and Plastics.Finish Carpentry.Wood.Hickory.jpg** to access the **Texture Map** editor for the **Diffuse Map** (Figure 27-121). Under the **Scaling & Tiling** section, set the **Scale units** as **None**, and set both **U Tile** and **V Tile** to **0.05**. Go back to the main material window by selecting **Wood** from the main drop-down list.

16. While the **Wood** material is still selected, select the box as **Swatch Geometry**. Click the **Apply Material** button and apply it to the 3D solid that represents the table base.

17. Click the **Indicate Materials in use** button to obtain information about which materials have been applied so far.

Note:
Materials that are currently in use show the AutoCAD drawing file icon in one of the corners.

Figure 27-120   The **Texture Maps Search Path** can be obtained from the **Files** tab of the **Options** dialog box

Figure 27-121   The main drop-down list for accessing the **Map Editor**

18. Select the **Brass** material. Select **Realistic Metal** as the type of material, and then select **Metal-Polished** as the template. Check the **By Object** option to use it as the **Diffuse** color.

19. With the **Brass** material still selected, click the **Checkered Underground** button. Apply this material to the 3D solid that represents the lamp base.

Figure 27-122   The sample images after clicking the **Checkered Underground** button

20. Click the **Indicate Materials in use** button. The sample images on the **Materials** palette should look like Figure 27-122.
21. Select the **Glass** material and click the **Checkered Underground** button.
22. Select the **By Object** option as the **Diffuse** color.
23. Move the **Shininess** slide button all the way to the right.
24. Move the **Refraction index** slide button to a value close to **2.00** or enter this value directly in the box.
25. Move the **Opacity** slide button to a value around **15**.
26. Apply this material to the 3D solid that represents the tabletop. **ZOOM** in as necessary and select the object by picking its edge.
27. Invoke the **RENDERCROP** command. When prompted, specify a window around the table to see how the new materials look so far (Figure 27-123).
28. Invoke the **REGEN** command. Select the **Canvas** material from the **Materials** palette and change its template to **Fabric**.
29. Select the **By Object** option as the **Diffuse** color.
30. Move the **Self-Illumination** slide button to a value around **20**.
31. Move the **Opacity** slide button to a value around **80**.
32. Apply this material to the eight polygon meshes that represent the lamp top.
33. Select **Render View** from the **Views** drop-down list located in the **Views** toolbar or in the **Navigate** control panel.
34. Invoke the **RENDER** command. The rendered image should look like Figure 27-124.

Figure 27-123   The resulting cropped rendered image   **Figure 27-124**   The resulting rendered image

35. Invoke the **REGEN** command. You will now create some reflection effects on the rendered image.
36. Select the **Marble Floor** material in the **Materials** palette and change its type of material to **Advanced**.
37. Set all three colors to be **By Object**.
38. Move the **Shininess** slide button to a value around **50**.
39. Move the **Reflection** slide button to a value around **26**.
40. Select the view named **Render View** from the drop-down menu in the **View** toolbar.
41. Invoke the **RENDER** command. The rendered image should look like Figure 27-125.
42. Invoke the **REGEN** command.
43. Select the **Right** UCS.
44. Using the **RECTANGLE** command, create a **20 × 28** rectangle. **EXTRUDE** the rectangle **1** unit.

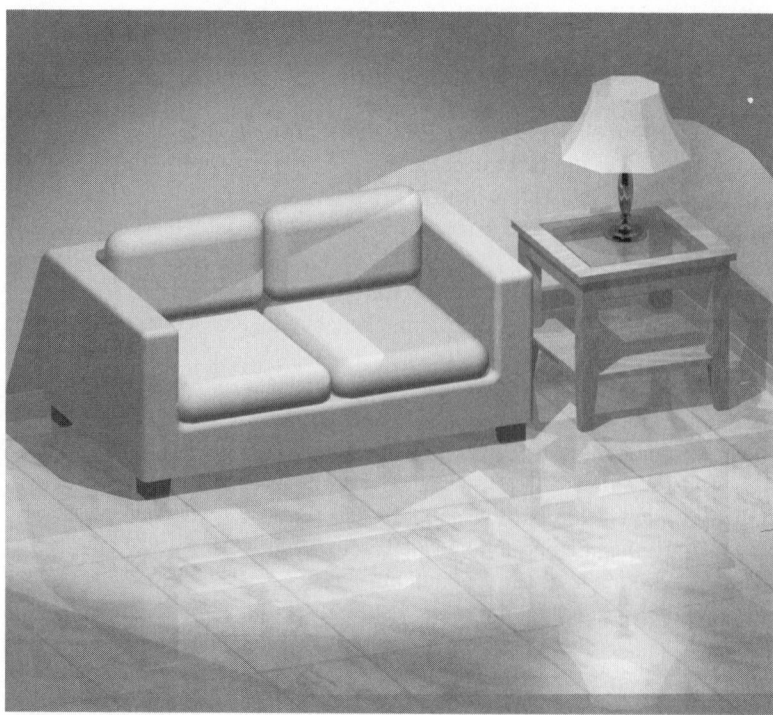

Figure 27-125   The resulting rendered image after changing the specified settings

45. **MOVE** the extruded 3D solid flush with the inside face of the wall, just above the sofa and centered with it (Figure 27-126).

TIP   You can relocate the extruded 3D solid using several **MOVE** operations, and select orthogonal views if necessary. Using **AutoTrack** might also be helpful.

Figure 27-126   After placing the extruded rectangle

46. Create a new material and name it **Picture**. Select the box **Geometry Swatch** for this material.
47. Click the **Diffuse**: color box and select color **254** from the **Index Color** tab. Leave the **By Object** checkbox unchecked.
48. Using Windows Explorer, **Copy** the *Flamingos* image file in the student data files and **Paste** it into the AutoCAD **Textures** folder, or into any other folder whose path you can remember.
49. Under **Diffuse map**, make sure **Texture Map** is selected from the drop-down list and click the **Select Image** button. Select the *Flamingos* image file from the location where you placed it. If you prefer, you can use any other picture.
50. Scroll down and select **Fit to Gizmo**. Set **U Tile** and **V Tile** both to **1**.
51. Apply the **Picture** material to the new 3D solid.
52. Select the view named **Render View** from the drop-down list on the **View** toolbar.
53. Set the **PERSPECTIVE** system variable to **1** by clicking the **Perspective Projection** icon in the **3D Navigate** panel of the Ribbon. This operation automatically switches to the **3D Wireframe** visual style, displaying a perspective view of the 3D model.
54. **ZOOM** and **PAN** as necessary. Invoke the **RENDER** command. The rendered image should look like Figure 27-127.
55. **SAVE** the drawing.

Note:
Remember that selecting an image file from a path different from that of the **Textures** folder will cause the AutoCAD program to search in this other folder the next time. So you will again have to relocate the **Textures** folder yourself. You can also create a backup copy of the entire **Textures** folder to another location and use it as your bitmap working folder. Then you can add, delete, or rename any file you want.

To access student data files, go to www.pearsondesigncentral.com.

Figure 27-127   The final rendered image

ADJUSTING MATERIALS' MAPS ON OBJECTS

MATERIALMAP	
Render Toolbar	
Ribbon: Materials panel	
Pull-down Menu	View/ Render/ Mapping/ ...
Command Line	materialmap

In addition to adjusting bitmaps for a specific material, you can also adjust the orientation at which an applied material is mapped to a specific object. This is achieved using the **MATERIALMAP** command. The primary use of this command is to change the method of wrapping the object with the material applied, so that its maps are properly shown. You can choose among **Box, Planar, Spherical**, and **Cylindrical** methods, as shown in the shortcut menu of the **MATERIALMAP** command (Figure 27-128). Although the 3D objects may not necessarily have the same shapes, there is always one that closely represents an object's overall look. Selecting this shape will improve the display of the material on the objects and faces in the rendered image. You can also use this tool to create specific effects.

Planar mapping maps the image onto the object as if it were projected in a single direction. Faces located more perpendicular to the projection display the image more clearly. This type of mapping is better applied on planar objects, especially regions.

Box mapping is the default mapping method when the materials are applied. It adjusts the mapping of the image as if it were projected onto the object perpendicularly from the six different faces of a box-shaped solid.

Cylindrical mapping maps the image as if it were projected onto the object perpendicularly from the cylindrical face of a cylinder-shaped solid. The image is wrapped only horizontally around the object.

Spherical mapping maps the image as if it were projected onto the object perpendicularly from the spherical face enclosing the object. As a result, the image is distorted both horizontally and vertically, with maximum compression at the two poles.

Selecting which mapping method to use depends on the shape of the object. But it is a good idea to try other choices as well (Figure 27-129).

As you try the different mapping methods, you will need to adjust the *UV* coordinate system used as a reference to define the bitmap. The scale at which the image is mapped onto the objects

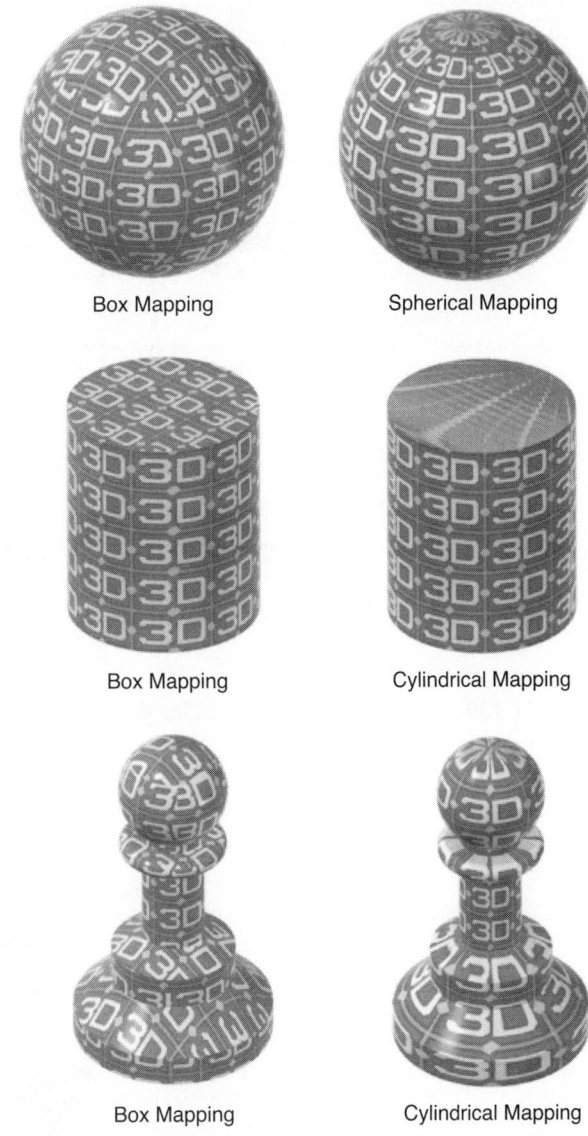

Box Mapping   Spherical Mapping

Box Mapping   Cylindrical Mapping

Box Mapping   Cylindrical Mapping

Enter
Cancel

Box
Planar
Spherical
Cylindrical
copY mapping to
Reset mapping

Pan
Zoom
SteeringWheels

QuickCalc

Figure 27-128   The **MATE-RIALMAP** command shortcut menu

Figure 27-129   Comparison of using different mapping methods on objects with different shapes

is affected by differences in how it projects on the faces. The *UV* coordinate system is adjusted in the **Adjust Bitmap** dialog box, which is accessed through the **Materials** palette.

You can make other adjustments by using the mapping grip tool that is displayed when a mapping method is applied to the object, along with an object that represents the type of mapping and its corresponding grips (Figure 27-130). You can switch between the move and rotate mapping grip tools for each mapping method.

The move mapping grip tool allows you to move the *UV* coordinates along one of the three axes or within one of the three planes (Figure 27-131). Clicking the corresponding element will constrain the movement to it. To constrain movement within a plane, you must click one of the squares between the axes. The rotate mapping grip tool allows you to rotate the *UV* coordinates in the direction of the selected ring (Figure 27-132). In addition to using the mapping grip tools, you can use the grips displayed on the objects that represent the type of mapping to perform other adjustments. Pulling a particular grip will stretch the image in this direction.

Among its options, the **MATERIALMAP** command allows you to **Reset** the mapping coordinates as well as to **Copy** mapping coordinates from one object to another. All the operations related to this command can be easily accessed through the **Materials** panel on the Ribbon (Figure 27-133).

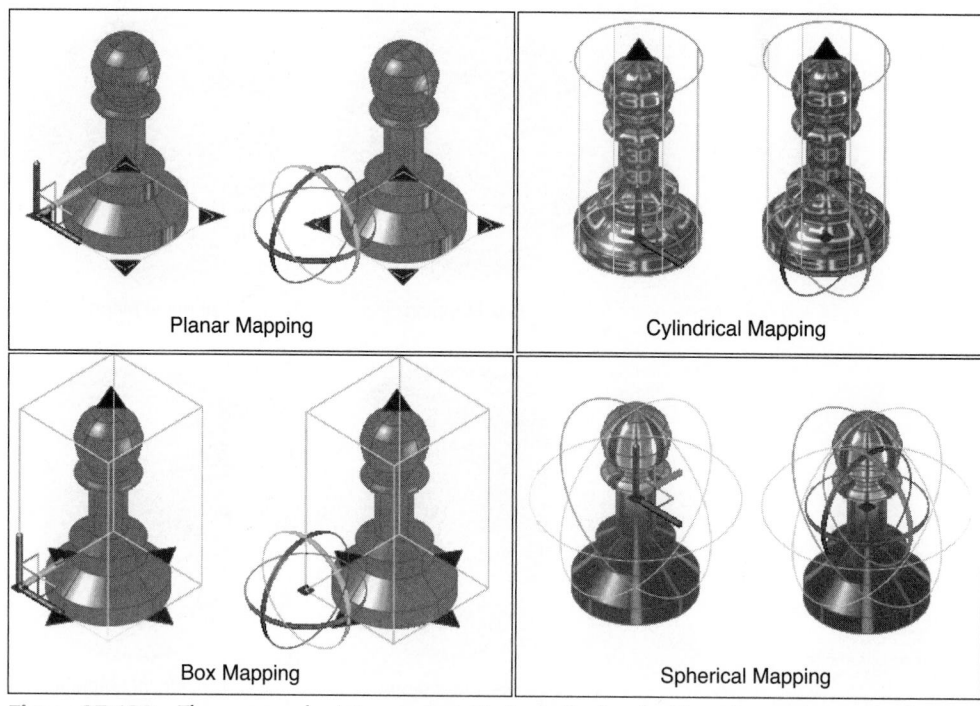

Figure 27-130   The move and rotate mapping grip tools displayed with each mapping method

Figure 27-131   Effects of using the move mapping grip tool on the material's mapping

Figure 27-132   Effects of using the rotate mapping grip tool on the material's mapping

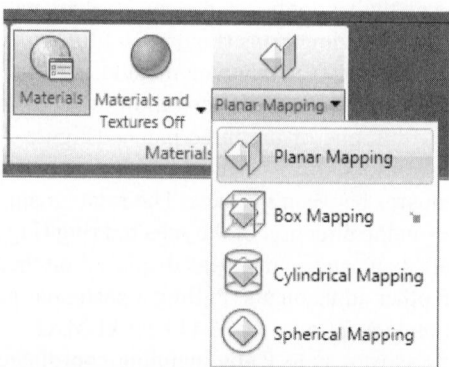

Figure 27-133   The **Materials Mapping** flyout icons located in the **Materials** panel on the Ribbon

ADVANCED USE OF VISUAL STYLES

CREATING AND MODIFYING VISUAL STYLES

In Chapter 1 you learned about the AutoCAD program's predefined visual styles. If you are using rendered visual styles (**Realistic** or **Conceptual**) to assist in the development of a 3D model, the predefined visual styles offer plenty of options. Visual styles can also be used, however, to create artistic representations of a 3D model (Figure 27-134).

Figure 27-134   Visual styles can be used to create pictorial illustrations

You can create and modify visual styles through the **Visual Styles Manager** palette. The sample images allow you to know which visual style is currently being used when you place a special icon on it. For instance, Figure 27-135 shows the five predefined visual styles; by looking at the sample images you can see that the **2D Wireframe** is currently in use. The predefined visual styles always show the AutoCAD's program icon on them.

To create a new visual style, you can perform one of the following operations:

- Right-click on a sample image and select **Copy**. Then right-click on an empty space of the panel and select **Paste**. You can also use a drag-and-drop operation while holding down the **<Ctrl>** key.

- Click on the **Create New Visual Style** button.

Clicking on the **Create New Visual Style** button will open the **Edit Name and Description** dialog box (Figure 27-136), where you can specify a name for the visual style. Right-clicking on any existing visual style and selecting **Edit Name and Description...** also will allow you to rename an existing visual style.

As with materials, you can export your own visual style to the **Tool Palettes** by clicking the corresponding button (the third button, going from left to right). This way you can make it available for other drawings (Figure 27-137).

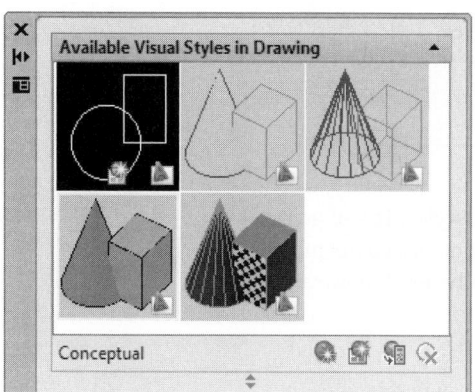

Figure 27-135   The five predefined visual styles

Figure 27-136   The **Edit Name and Description** dialog box

The settings that control the effects of a visual style are organized into three groups:

- Face settings
- Environment settings
- Edge settings

Face Settings

Face settings enable you to control visual properties that affect the display of faces. The **Face style** is the most important property because it defines whether the visual style displays as rendered or as a wireframe (Figure 27-138). **None** displays a wireframe 3D model. **Real** and **Warm-Cool** face styles display the 3D model rendered. **Real** uses dark and light colors, whereas **Warm-Cool** uses warm and cool colors.

Figure 27-137   A visual style exported to the tool palettes

Figure 27-138   The **Face style** drop-down list in the **Visual Styles Manager** dialog box

When **Real** or **Warm-Cool** face styles are selected, you can also select one of four face color modes (**Normal, Desaturate, Tint**, and **Monochrome**) (Figure 27-139). The last three color modes are a degradation of the **Normal** color mode, just as with many digital cameras. **Desaturate** simply softens or makes faint the color. Both **Tint** and **Monochrome** modes use the **Tint Color** specified below the **Face color mode** setting. **Tint** displays the objects in tones of the **Tint Color**, depending on how dark or light its normal color is. **Monochrome**, on the other hand, displays the 3D model in the **Tint Color** itself, affected only by the incidence of light. You can combine the **Real** and **Warm-Cool** styles with any of the face color modes and create eight different effects.

When the **Normal** color mode is selected, you can also choose to display the **Materials** or the **Materials and textures**. Any property that is defined by a bitmap attached to the material will not be displayed unless you select the **Materials and textures** mode.

Environment Settings

This group of settings controls the behavior of the shadows and the background. If the 3D model has any user-created lights, you can choose to turn off the default lighting and use the user-created lights. This will be noticeable only when one of the rendered face styles, **Real** or **Warm-Cool,** is selected.

You can use one of four modes for shadows: **Full shadows with ground plane, Full Shadows, Ground shadow**, and **Off** (Figure 27-140).

The **Ground shadow** is independent of any user-created lights. Its effect is as if the rays of a distant light were illuminating the objects in the direction of the negative *Z*-axis of the WCS (Figure 27-141). By default, the plane receiving the **Ground shadow** is located in the *XY* plane of the WCS. You can move this plane up or down parallel to it by changing the value of the **SHADOWPLANELOCATION** system variable. **Full shadows**, on the other hand, shows the shadows of any user-created light that is turned on (Figure 27-142). You can display both ground and full shadows by selecting **Full shadows with ground plane.**

Figure 27-139   The **Face color mode** drop-down list in the **Visual Styles Manager** dialog box

Figure 27-140   The **Shadow display** drop-down list in the **Visual Styles Manager** dialog box

Figure 27-141   Visual style using **Ground shadow**

Figure 27-142   Visual style using **Full shadows**

If you have specified a background with the **Background** dialog box, the **Background** setting determines whether it is turned on or off for a particular visual style.

Edge Settings

This group of settings controls the behavior of edges and silhouettes. In general, you can select one of three modes to display the edges: **Facet Edges, Isolines**, or **None** (Figure 27-143).

Figure 27-143   The Edge mode drop-down list in the **Visual Styles Manager** dialog box

Facet Edges

Isolines

None

Figure 27-144   Effect of selecting the **Edge** mode settings

None mode displays only the silhouette of the 3D objects. **Isolines** displays all the edges, including the tangential edges. **Facet Edges** displays all the edges and borders of the facets (Figure 27-144). You can control the **Width** and **Color** of the edges displayed in a particular mode. Because these settings cannot be changed in the **None** mode, you must change them prior to switching to this mode.

Depending on the particular viewing point, each edge of a 3D model can become one of the following types:

- **Fast Silhouette Edges**
- **Obscured Edges**
- **Intersection Edges**

Regardless of the current edges mode, you can control each category of edges independently. For example, turning on the **Fast Silhouette Edges** display mode will display the edges in a different way by delimiting the contours of the shaded areas (Figure 27-145).

Under **Edge Modifiers** you can control two other special visual effects for the edges in general: **Overhang, Jitter, Crease angle**, and **Halo gap %**. All edge modifiers are available in the **Facet Edges** mode. In the **Isolines** mode, however, only the **Overhang** and **Jitter** effects can be used.

The **Overhang** and **Jitter** effects give the impression of a drawing sketched by hand, which can be used to create accented presentations for both 3D models and 2D drawings (Figure 27-146).

Edges: None
Fast Silhouette Edges: No

Edges: None
Fast Silhouette Edges: Yes

Figure 27-145 Effect of turning **Fast Silhouette Edges** on and off

Figure 27-146 Effect of altering the **Overhang** and **Jitter** settings

To turn these effects on or off on a particular visual style, you must click on the buttons shown in Figure 27-147. **Crease angle** sets the maximum angle between two adjacent facets up to which its edges are not shown. As this value increases, fewer facet edges will be displayed. **Halo gap %** sets the gap displayed when an object is hidden by another object.

Note:
All the visual style settings can also be controlled from the **Visual Style** panel in the Ribbon. This is especially helpful when you need to create quick effects. You must be aware, however, that these changes will not be stored in any particular visual style; selecting another visual style will reset any changes.

Figure 27-147 Buttons that control whether the **Overhang** and **Jitter** are turned on or off on a visual style

CREATING ANIMATIONS

DEFINING COMPUTER ANIMATION

A computer *animation* generates and records successive positions of a 3D model, or frames, to create a video file that, when replayed, gives an illusion of movement. With the AutoCAD program, you can record, preview, and save an animation using one of two procedures:

- Using the **Animations** panel in the Ribbon
- Using the **Motion Path Animation** dialog box, displayed with the **ANIPATH** command

animation: A video file created by recording successive positions of the 3D model, giving the impression of movement when replayed.

Recording a 3D Navigation Scene

The display of a 3D model is defined by a default camera located between the viewer and the target. As you know, the viewing direction is always perpendicular to the viewing plane and defined by a vector from the camera position to the camera target. You can read and modify the camera and target locations in the **View** panel on the Ribbon (Figure 27-148).

Every time you **ZOOM, PAN,** or perform a **3D Orbit** operation, you change the location of the camera position and the camera target. Other operations such as **Adjust Distance** or **Swivel** modify either one or the other. The continuous change of these locations is precisely the meaning of *3D navigation,* which includes any of the following operations:

- **3DORBIT** (Constrained Orbit)
- **3DFORBIT** (Free Orbit)
- **3DCORBIT** (Continuous Orbit)

Figure 27-148   The actual coordinates of the camera and the target are displayed in the **View** panel of the Ribbon

- **3DSWIVEL** (Swivel)
- **3DDISTANCE** (Adjust Distance)
- **3DWALK** (Walk)
- **3DFLY** (Fly)
- **3DZOOM** (Zoom)
- **3DPAN** (Pan)

All 3D navigation commands can be found in the **3D Navigation** toolbar (Figure 27-149). After you invoke any of these commands, you can switch between them by simply pressing a number key between **1** and **9**, or you can right-click to select a mode from the shortcut menu (Figure 27-150). For example, after you invoke the **3DZOOM** command, pressing the key activates the **3DFORBIT** operation.

Figure 27-149   The **3D Navigation** toolbar   **Figure 27-150**   The **3D Navigation** shortcut menu

The **Record** button in the **Animations** panel on the Ribbon becomes available when any of the 3D navigation operations are activated (Figure 27-151). Whenever the recording mode is available, you can simply press the **Record** button to start recording the 3D navigation operations that you perform.

TIP

During a recording, you should switch between the 3D navigation modes only by pressing the corresponding number key or through the shortcut menu. The transition time is reduced greatly, however, when you use the number keys.

Figure 27-151 The **Record** and **Play** buttons in the **Animations** panel on the Ribbon

Anytime after you start recording, you can click the **Pause** button to temporarily stop recording. The **Play** button turns green as soon as you start the recording process. Pressing this button will also stop the recording and open the **Animation Preview** window (Figure 27-152). In the **Animation Preview** window, you can replay the animation. Press its **Record** button to continue recording, or click the **Save** button to create a video file. You can also move the slide button to view a specific frame of the animation. Closing the **Animation Preview** window will return you to the 3D navigation modes, where you can perform the same operations. The recording is discarded by exiting the 3D navigation mode.

Figure 27-152 The **Animation Preview** window

Before recording and saving your first animation, you should check the settings located in the **Animation Settings** dialog box (Figure 27-153). This box is displayed when you press the **Animation Settings** button in the **Animations** panel on the Ribbon.

You can select one of the visual styles from the list and one of the digital video formats supported for the video file output. AVI, MPG, and WMV files can be played in Windows Media Player, whereas MOV files can be played with the QuickTime player. The **Resolution** setting affects the size and quality of the video file. **Frame rate** controls the number of frames or pictures used per second; you can set this value between 1 and 60.

> **Note:**
> You can reduce the processing time by reducing the **Resolution** and the **Frame rate**, at the cost of losing quality. The length of the recording time, however, is what most increases the processing time.

Clicking the **Save** button in the **Animation Preview** window will open the **Save As** dialog box, where you can specify a location and a name for the video file (Figure 27-154). The **Animation Settings** dialog box can also be accessed from this window by clicking the **Animation settings...** button. After you click **Save**, the process of creating the video starts to run and the **Creating Video** window is displayed (Figure 27-155).

Figure 27-153   The **Animation Settings** dialog box

Figure 27-154   The **Save As** dialog box

3DWALK	
3D Naviga-tion Toolbar	👣
Ribbon: Anima-tions panel	
Pull-down Menu	View/ Walk and Fly/Walk
Command Line	3dwalk

Figure 27-155   The **Creating Video** window

Walking and Flying Through the 3D Model

The **Walk** and **Fly** modes are special 3D navigation modes that allow you to go through the model and turn around, as if you were playing a video game. These modes are available only in a perspective view.

When you switch to the **Walk** or **Fly** modes from another navigation mode, or invoke the **3DWALK** or **3DFLY** commands, special navigation instructions for these two modes are displayed in the help search window (Figure 27-156). After expanding it, this menu shows you how

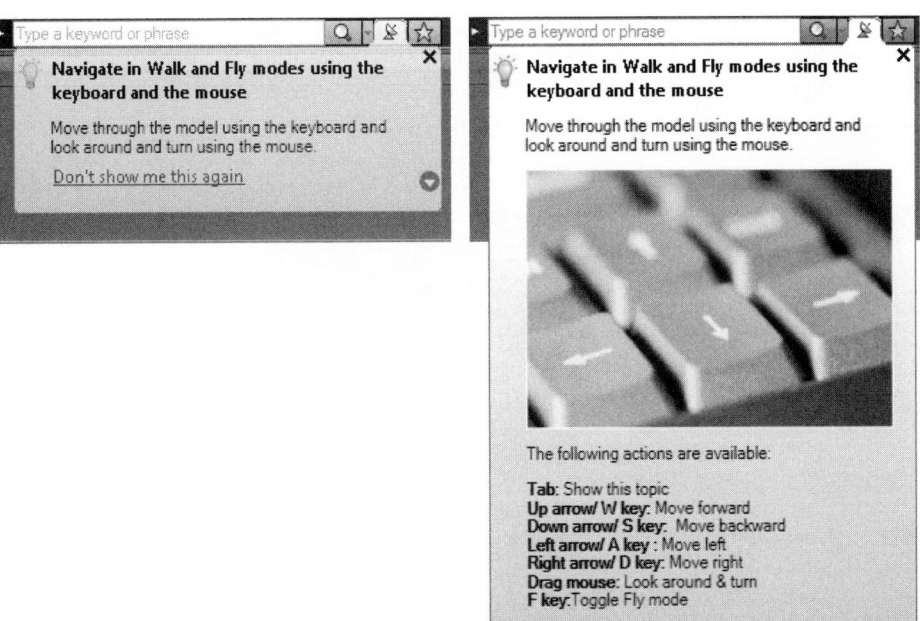

3DFLY	
3D Naviga-tion Toolbar	<image: airplane icon>
Ribbon: Anima-tions panel	
Pull-down Menu	View/ Walk and Fly/Fly
Command Line	3dfly

Figure 27-156   The 3D **Walk** and **Fly** navigation instructions

to use the keys and the mouse to move throughout the 3D model. You can make these instructions show up again by pressing the <Tab> key after it closes. You can toggle between **Walk** and **Fly** modes by pressing the corresponding number or the <F> key. The **Position Locator** window also opens in these navigation modes, displaying the top view of the 3D model (Figure 27-157). You can drag the position or the target indicator to relocate the view. You can also drag both indicators at the same time by clicking in an intermediate location.

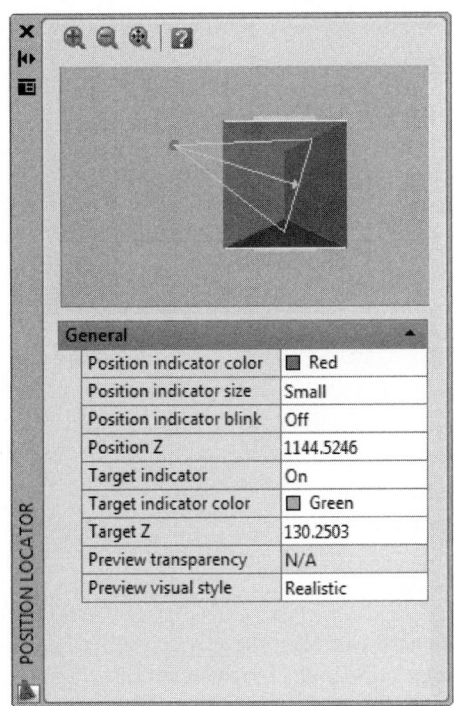

Figure 27-157   The **Position Locator** window

In the **Walk** mode, the camera position moves parallel to the *XY* plane of the WCS at the fixed distance of **5′** above it, regardless of the direction toward which the camera aims. The height of the camera target does not change either unless you drag the left mouse button, even when moving to the sides. Using this mode gives the impression that a person is carrying the camera or that you are actually walking though the 3D model. When the **Walk** mode is activated, the view automatically aligns itself to show the 3D model with the proper verticality and direction to simulate walking over the *XY* plane of the WCS (Figure 27-158).

Original Viewing Point

Figure 27-158   The view aligns itself when the **Walk** mode is activated

Viewing Point Before Starting the Walk-through

The **Fly** mode, on the other hand, does not restrict the camera position to any height, allowing you to move in any direction. In this mode, moving forward makes the camera fly from the camera position to the camera target. Even though the locations of the camera position and the camera target change, the direction does not change when you move forward or backward, unless you drag the mouse or move to the sides.

When either of these two modes is active, the shortcut menu displayed with a right-click provides access to the **Walk and Fly Settings** dialog box (Figure 27-159). In this dialog box, among other settings, you can change the speed at which the camera walks or flies through the model either by changing the distance between the steps (**Step size**) or by changing the number of **Steps per second**.

> **Note:**
> In the **Walk** and **Fly** 3D navigation modes, you can create walk-through and fly-through animations by using the same recording procedures that you use with any other 3D navigation mode.

motion paths: User-created routes through which the camera, the target, or both gradually move while the camera keeps its focus on the target.

ANIPATH	
Ribbon: Animations panel	🎞
Pull-down Menu	View/ Motion Path Animations...
Command Line	anipath

Recording Predefined Motion Path Scenes

You have previously learned to create animations in which the camera is directly controlled by the user operations. Using *motion paths* enables you to create animations in which the camera position and camera target gradually change their location according to a predefined **Path** or **Point**. These elements are defined in the **Motion Path Animation** dialog box (Figure 27-160), which opens when you invoke the **ANIPATH** command.

As with standard animations, you can control the video's format and resolution, as well as the visual style use. Because the animation is not created by user operations, you must also define its

Figure 27-159   The shortcut displayed when the 3D **Walk** and **Fly** navigation modes are activated and the **Walk and Fly Settings** dialog box

Figure 27-160   The **Motion Path Animation** dialog box

Duration. The total **Number of frames** is equal to the **Frame rate** times the **Duration**. After you set a **Frame rate**, you can specify either the **Number of frames** or the **Duration** (in seconds). The other value is automatically recalculated.

You can specify a point by snapping to the geometry of the 3D model. To define a path, select one of the following objects, previously created:

- Line
- Arc
- Ellipse (entire or trimmed)
- Circle
- Polyline
- 3D Polyline

You can specify a path for the camera and another one for the target, or you can combine a point with a path. In any case, you should try to keep this combination simple to achieve reasonable results. For example, making the camera move along a line whose midpoint is close to the target, defined as a *point*, can create the effect of approaching and leaving the target. Using two parallel lines, one for the camera and the other for the target, can simulate a straight walk-through or fly-through, depending on the location of the parallel lines.

> **Note:**
> You cannot select a point for both the camera and the target because this combination will cause no movement at all.

By selecting **Corner deceleration**, you can make the camera move more slowly when it reaches a corner of a path. Selecting **Reverse** makes the animation travel through the path in the opposite direction.

After you have specified everything, you can click the **Preview** button to open the **Animation Preview** window and watch the animation preview. You can also move the slide button to view a specific frame of the animation. After you close the **Animation Preview** window, you can click the **OK** button in the **Motion Path Animation** dialog box to save the video file.

Figure 27-161 shows the 3D model from which an animation has been recorded. It uses an arc as the motion path for the camera and a point for the target, as well as several positions of the camera along its motion path. The corresponding frame images of the video obtained are shown in Figure 27-162.

Figure 27-161 Position of the camera for different frame intervals as it moves along the motion path

Figure 27-162 The corresponding image for each frame recorded

Exercise 27-5: Animations—Recording 3D Navigation Operations

1. **OPEN** *Exercise 27-5* in the student data files.
2. **SAVE** it **AS** *Exercise 27-5 solved*.
3. Select the **Realistic** visual style.
4. Locate the **Animations** panel on the Ribbon.
5. Using the mouse wheel button, perform a **PAN** operation to center the 3D model in the display. Do not change the zoom factor.

    Next, you will record a scene in which you zoom into the 3D model by using a single smooth action. Click at the lower area of the screen and drag the pointer straight up slowly, just passing the middle of the screen. Then press **<1>** to start the **Constrained Orbit**. Without delay, click in the leftmost side of the screen about the middle and drag the pointer horizontally all the way to the right, at an intermediate speed. Between 12 and 16 seconds should elapse from the moment you click the **Record** button to the moment you click the **Play** button.

6. Invoke the **3DZOOM** command by typing the command in the command prompt window.
7. Click the **Record** button and without delay perform the operation you planned.
8. When finished, press the **Play** button. This operation stops the recording and opens the **Animation Preview** window.
9. Wait until the **Animation Preview** finishes playing, then click the black square button to save the video file (Figure 27-163).

To access student data files, go to www.pearsondesigncentral.com.

> **Note:**
> The **Record** button should turn red immediately after you invoke the **3DZOOM** command. Before you start recording you must plan the actions you will perform to avoid unnecessary delays.

Figure 27-163   The Animation Preview window

10. In the **Save As** dialog box, click the **Animation settings...** button to open the **Animation Settings** dialog box.
11. Select the **AVI** format and click **OK** to close the **Animation Settings** dialog box.
12. In the **Save As** dialog box, select a location for the video file and type **Hall-Navigation** as the file name. Click **Save** to close the dialog box and start the **Creating Video** process.
13. **SAVE** the drawing.
14. Use Windows Explorer to browse for the **Hall-Navigation** video file. Right-click on it, and select **Play**. It should open in Windows Media Player.

Exercise 27-6: Animations—Recording a Walk-through Operation

1. **OPEN** *Exercise 27-5 solved*.
2. **SAVE** the drawing **AS** *Exercise 27-6*.
3. Open the **Walk and Fly Settings** dialog box by invoking the **WALKFLYSETTINGS** command; the icon is located in the **Animations** panel on the Ribbon.
4. In the **Walk and Fly Settings** dialog box, set the **Step size** to **30** and the **Steps per second** to **3** [Figure 27-164(a)]. In the **View** panel of the Ribbon, set the **Z** coordinate of the **Camera Position** to **60** and press **<Enter.↵>** [Figure 27-164(b)].

(a)   (b)

Figure 27-164 (a) Setting the step size and the steps per second in the **Walk and Fly Settings** dialog box (b) Setting the **Z** coordinate of the camera position

5. Select the **Front** view.
6. Set the **PERSPECTIVE** system variable to **1** by entering its name in the command prompt window.
7. Click on the corresponding icon in the **3D Navigation** toolbar to invoke the **3DDISTANCE** command. Click and drag downward in the drawing area to see the 3D model farther. Press **<Esc>** to exit the command.
8. Click on the corresponding icon in the **Animations** panel to invoke the **3DWALK** command.
9. Close the **Walk and Fly—Change to Perspective View** warning by clicking the **Change** button.
10. Click the **X** button to close the **Position Locator** window.
11. Press the **<Up arrow>** key repeatedly or keep it pressed by intervals to approach the 3D model.
12. After you have gone through the 3D model, press the **<Down arrow>** key repeatedly to move out of the 3D model.
13. With the **3DWALK** command still active, click the **Record** button and repeat the same **Walk** operation. Enter the building, go through it, and then go back outside.
14. Immediately click the **Play** button to stop recording.
15. After the animation preview finishes playing, click the **Save** button.
16. Click the **Animation Settings...** button and select the **AVI** format in the **Animation Settings** dialog box.
17. Select a location for the video file and type **Hall-Walkthrough** in the **File name** field. Click **Save** to close the dialog box and start the **Create Video** process.

18. Continue performing **3D Walk** operations. Click and drag the left button to direct the camera up and down; drag it right and left to change the walk direction. At the same time use the arrow keys to walk forward, backward, or right and left.

19. Press the **<F>** key to switch to **Fly** mode. Click and drag the left button to change the direction in which the camera will fly forward. At the same time use the arrow keys to fly forward, backward, or right and left.

20. When finished, right-click in the drawing area and select **Exit**.

21. Select the **Parallel Projection** by setting the **PERSPECTIVE** system variable to **0**; enter its name in the command prompt window to do so.

22. Select the **SE Isometric** viewing point.

23. **SAVE** the drawing.

24. Using Windows Explorer, browse for the *Hall-Walkthrough* video file, right-click on it, and select **Play** to watch the animation.

Exercise 27-7: Recording a Motion Path Animation

1. **OPEN** *Exercise 27-5 solved*.
2. **SAVE** the drawing **AS** *Exercise 27-7*.
3. Select the **2D Wireframe** visual style.
4. Invoke the **3DORBIT** command to slightly change the viewing point.
5. Using a color that can be seen easily, draw the polyline highlighted in Figure 27-165. Snap to the three points shown.

Figure 27-165   Points to specify when creating the polyline

6. Offset the polyline outward **300″**.
7. With **ORTHO** mode on, **MOVE** the inner polyline 80″ and the outer polyline **120″** along the positive direction of the Z-axis.
8. Select the outer polyline and stretch the grip on its rightmost endpoint **300″** along the negative *Y*-axis. The two polylines should look like Figure 27-166.

Figure 27-166   After stretching the polyline

9. Select the **Realistic** visual style.
10. Invoke the **ANIPATH** command to display the **Motion Path Animation** dialog box.
11. Under **Camera**, select **Path** and click the **Select Path** button. Select the outer polyline.
12. In the **Path Name** dialog box, type *Outer Polyline* in the name field and click **OK**.
13. Under **Target**, select **Path** and click the **Select Path** button. Select the inner polyline.
14. In the **Path Name** dialog box, type *Inner Polyline* as the name and click **OK**.
15. Set the **Duration** to **6** seconds and change the format to **AVI** (Figure 27-167). The **Number of frames** setting should automatically change to **180**.

Figure 27-167   The **Motion Path Animation** dialog box

16. Click the **Preview** button to open the **Animation Preview** window.
17. After the preview stops, close the **Animation Preview** window.
18. In the **Motion Path Animation** dialog box, click **OK** to open the **Save As** dialog box.
19. Select a location for the video file and type **Hall-Motion Path** as the file name. Click **Save** to close the dialog box and start the **Creating Video** process.
20. **SAVE** the drawing.
21. Use Windows Explorer to browse for the *Hall-Motion Path* video file, right-click on it, and select **Play** to watch the animation.

Creating View Sequences with ShowMotion

With the ShowMotion tools, you can create animations that use different types of shots and transitions between them. It is a very simple tool to use, and you can use it to create professional presentations of the 3D models in model space or the drawings views in paper space.

Every time you create a new View in the **View Manager**, you are basically creating a new shot. The types of shots that can be created are **Still, Cinematic**, and **Recorded Walk** (Figure 27-168). You are required to enter a View or shot name; giving the shot a View Category allows you to define groups of shots that can later be played back together.

Figure 27-168   The **New View/Shot Properties** dialog box

In the **Shot Properties** tab, you can specify different parameters related to the behavior of this particular shot (Figure 27-169). You can select among eight different types of movements for the model space views: Zoom In, Zoom Out, Track Left, Track Right, Crank Up, Crank Down, Look, and Orbit. For paper space views, you can use only the Pan + Zoom type of movement. You can also set how long the shot movement will last by specifying the duration. Settings concerning the transition can also be specified here.

You can play back entire groups of categories or single shots throughout the thumbnail views displayed at the bottom center of the AutoCAD window. Such thumbnails along with the controls are displayed by invoking **NAVESMOTION** command. This command can be easily invoked using the icon located in the status bar. Let's say, for example, you have created four new views or shots: MyShot 1-1 and MyShot 1-2 under the category MyShotGroup 1, and MyShot 2-1 and MyShot 2-2 under the category MyShotGroup 2. Once the **NAVESMOTION** command is invoked, hovering the mouse pointer over one of the categories will show you a snapshot of all the shots contained on it (Figure 27-170). You can then click inside the category you want to play. Hovering the mouse pointer over one of the shots changes the thumbnail images of the shots for the particular corresponding category to a larger scale (Figure 27-171). Clicking inside one of these shots will cause it to play back by itself. You can use the ShowMotion controls to play back the shot or sequence of shots repeatedly in the form of a loop.

Figure 27-169 The **Shot Properties** tab of the **New View/Shot Properties** dialog box

Figure 27-170 The ShowMotion thumbnails focusing on the category for playback

Figure 27-171 The ShowMotion thumbnails focusing on the shots of a particular category for playback individually

Creating animations is a beneficial skill for many technical disciplines, especially architecture. Although animations are not a standard type of presentation yet, firms that have a strategic modernization policy have discovered the outstanding benefits that this particular skill can bring to their organizations.

CHAPTER SUMMARY

After completing this chapter you should be able to create illumination effects on a 3D model by placing and modifying the different types of lights. You should also be able to create different types of materials effects, using bitmaps to make the 3D objects resemble how they look in the real world.

All these skills should enable you to generate professional-quality rendered images. Such illustrations can be used to enhance the presentation of your designs or ideas.

Most render effects are defined by attaching and adjusting bitmap files. You can use the image files contained in AutoCAD's **Textures**

folder. But you can also create your own bitmap files by taking digital pictures of real objects. Most of the pictures will not even have to be edited.

Along with rendered images, you can also develop artistic illustrations by creating new visual styles. You can modify many settings that affect faces and edges to suit your presentation goal.

By creating animations, you can also generate video files for presentation purposes. Using motion paths will enable you to create very sophisticated video presentations for concept products and 3D architectural models.

CHAPTER TEST QUESTIONS

Multiple Choice

1. In which of the following cases is it impossible to create a rendered image from the 3D model?

   a. The 3D object has no material applied.
   b. The 3D model consists of a wireframe only.
   c. The 3D model contains no lights.
   d. The background has not been defined.

2. Which of the following cannot be used as a render procedure in the **Advanced Render Settings** palette?

   a. View
   b. Crop
   c. Fence
   d. Selected

3. For which of the following types of lights must you define both a location and a direction?

   a. Spot light
   b. Sun light
   c. Point light
   d. Direct light

4. Shadows are one of the key elements you need to control in a rendered image. In which of the following is it impossible to set aspects that specifically affect the way shadows are displayed?

   a. 3D objects
   b. Viewport
   c. Lights
   d. Render presets

5. Which of the following can be used to attach a material to a 3D object?

   a. Layers
   b. **Properties** palette

   c. **Materials** palette
   d. All of the above

6. Which of the following properties is the one that most affects the transparency effect on objects?

   a. Shininess
   b. Opacity
   c. Reflection
   d. Refraction index

7. When the **Walk** 3D navigation mode is activated, pressing the **<Up arrow>** key will make the camera:

   a. Move forward parallel to the *XY* plane
   b. Zoom into the 3D model
   c. Move in a direction toward the target
   d. None of the above

8. To create a material that, when applied to the 3D objects, displays specific areas of its surfaces as translucent after the rendering process, you must use a(n):

   a. Opacity map
   b. Reflection map
   c. Bump map
   d. Texture map

9. You can create animations in which:

   a. Only the camera moves
   b. Both the camera and the target move
   c. Only the target moves
   d. All of the above

Matching

a. **MATERIALATTACH**

b. Bump map

c. Render Presets

d. **RENDERCROP**

e. Attenuation

f. Desaturate

g. **RENDERWIN**

h. **RPREF**

i. Fly

j. **ANIPATH**

1. Creates motion path animations
2. One of the 3D navigation modes
3. Opens the **Render** window
4. One of the face color modes in the visual styles
5. Creates an embossed 3D texture in the surfaces
6. Renders a selected crop window
7. Opens the **Advanced Render** palette
8. Links a material to a specific layer
9. A named collection of render settings
10. Diminishing of light intensity over distance

CHAPTER TUTORIALS

Tutorial 27-1: The Bench-Vise Final Presentation

1. **OPEN** the *Bench-Vise* drawing created in Chapter 25.
2. **SAVE** the drawing **AS** *Tutorial 27-1*.
3. Select the **Top** UCS.
4. Select the **SE Isometric** viewing point.
5. Use the **PAN** command to make some room and create the **12 × 12 × 1** board using the **BOX** command (Figure 27-172).

Figure 27-172   After placing the 12 × 12 × 1 board

6. Select the **Front** view.
7. **MOVE** the board so that its top and right faces are placed flush with the faces of the *Main Body* (Figure 27-173).

Figure 27-173   Front view after moving the board

8. Using **AutoTrack, MOVE** the *Pressing Plate,* the *Fastening Bolt,* and the *Handle* orthogonally up or down so that the top of the *Pressing Plate* is placed flush with the bottom face of the board (Figure 27-174).
9. Select the **Top** view.
10. Using a tracking method, **MOVE** the board orthogonally in the negative *Y*-axis direction (down) to center it with the *Bench-Vise* (Figure 27-175).

Figure 27-174   The pressing plate and the other objects are placed flush with the bottom of the board

Figure 27-175   The board is centered with the bench vise

11. Select the **SE Isometric** viewing point.
12. Invoke the **MATERIALS** command to open the **Materials** palette.
13. Dock the **Materials** palette to the left of the AutoCAD window.
14. Click on the corresponding button to create a new material. Name it **board-mat**.
15. Select the **board-mat** material and select **Box** as the **Swatch Geometry** of the sample image.
16. Under **Diffuse map**, make sure **Texture map** appears in the drop-down list and click on the **Select Image** button to open the **Select Image File** dialog box.
17. Search for the **Textures** folder and select the image file named **Woods and Plastics.Finish Carpentry. Wood.Cherry**. Click the **Open** button to close the dialog box and insert the file.

> **FOR MORE DETAILS**   If you have trouble finding the **Textures** folder, refer to *Exercise 27-4* for tips on how to search for it.

18. Click on the **Settings** button to display only the map settings inside the **Materials** palette. Under **Scaling and Tiling**, set the units to **Fit to Gizmo**. Click the lock icon to link the **U Tile** and the **V Tile** values and specify a value of **0.250** for them (Figure 27-176). Click the **Home** button to go one level up to the material settings.
19. Under **Material Offset and Preview**, set the preview size to 1 and click the **Update** button. Click the **Apply Material** button. Select the board and press **<Enter↵>** to end the selection.
20. Create three more materials and name them **Steel, Cast Iron**, and **Alum**.
21. Select the **Steel** material sample image and turn on the **Checkered Underlay**. Select the **Realistic Metal** type, and then select the **Metal - Polished** template. Click the **Diffuse** color box and select color **253** from the **Index Color** tab. Click **OK** to close the **Select Color** window.
22. Apply this material to all the components of the *Bench-Vise,* except the *Main Body,* the *Moving Jaw,* and the two *Aluminum Blocks.* Use Figure 27-177 as a reference catalog for the components.

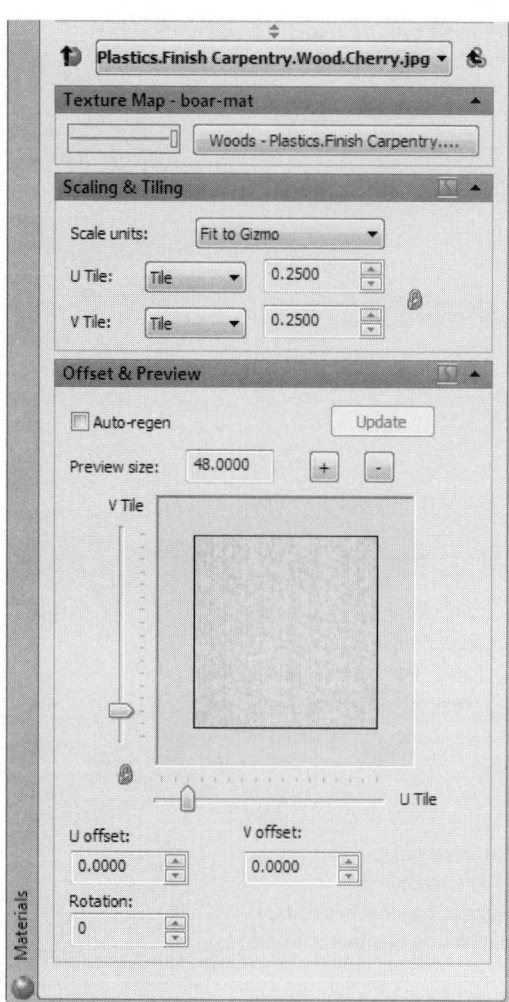

Figure 27-176   The controls for adjusting the **Texture Map** in the **Materials** palette

Figure 27-177   Component reference catalog

> **TIP** When you apply the material, you can select all the components using a selection window. Then you can use the **Remove Material** button to remove the selected material from the excluded components.

23. Select the **Alum** material and select the **Realistic** type for it. Click the **Diffuse** color box and select color **254** from the **Index Color** tab. Click **OK** to close the **Select Color** window.
24. Apply this material to the two *Aluminum Blocks*.
25. Select the **Cast Iron** material, select the **Realistic** type, then select the **Paint Flat** template. Click the **Diffuse** color box, and select color **147** from the **Index Color** tab. Click **OK** to close the **Select Color** window.
26. Set its **Shininess** value to **0**.
27. Scroll to **Bump Map** and click its **Select Image** button. Select the file **Metals.Ornamental Metals.Bronze. Satin.bump** from the **Bump** folder that is located inside the **Templates** folder.
28. Set the **Bump Map** slide button to a value between **100** and **150**.
29. Apply this material to the *Main Body* and the *Moving Jaw*.
30. Use the **3D Orbit** tool to select a view close to the one shown in Figure 27-178 and draw a line that runs from the endpoint of the board to the relative point **@6,2,10** (shown highlighted in the figure).
31. Invoke the **SPOTLIGHT** command. Click **Yes** to close the warning if it shows up. When prompted for the *source location,* snap to the top endpoint of the line. Snap to the top edge's midpoint on the furthermost *Aluminum Block* when prompted for the *target location.* Press **<Enter↵>** to end the command. The **Spotlight** glyph should be placed as shown in Figure 27-179, pointing in the direction indicated.

Figure 27-178   Line to be drawn as reference

Figure 27-179   Location and direction of the spot light

32. Select the **Spot** light and set its **Intensity factor** to **0.80** in the **Properties** palette.
33. Invoke the **DISTANTLIGHT** command. Click in an empty spot to specify the direction from, and then click on any point orthogonally below to specify the direction to. This will make the **Distant** light illuminate the 3D model in the negative *Z*-axis direction. Press **<Enter↵>** to end the command.
34. Open the **Lights in Model** window by invoking the **LIGHTLIST** command. Select the **Distantlight** from the **Lights in Model** window, and set its **Intensity factor** to **0.30** in the **Properties** palette. Turn its **Shadows** property off.
35. Set the **PERSPECTIVE** system variable to **1** to set the view in perspective mode.
36. Use the **Constrained 3D Orbit** and any other 3D navigation tool to adjust the final view to create the presentation of the *Bench-Vise.*

37. Invoke the **VIEW** command to open the **View Manager** dialog box. Click on the **New...** button. In the **New View** dialog box, type **Render View** in the **View name** field. Click **OK** to close the **New View** dialog box.
38. In the **View Manager** dialog box, select **Solid...** from the **Background override** drop-down list (Figure 27-180).

Figure 27-180   The **View Manager** dialog box

39. In the **Background** window, click on the **Color** box to open the **Select Color** dialog box. Select the color **255,255,255** in the **True Color** tab by moving the slide button all the way up. Click **OK** to close the **Select Color** dialog box, the **Background** window, and finally the **View Manager** dialog box.
40. Invoke the **RPREF** command to open the **Advanced Render Settings** palette. Select **View** under **Rendering Procedure** and **Viewport** under **Destination**.
41. Select **Render View** from the drop-down list located in the **View** toolbar or in the **3D Navigate** control panel.
42. Invoke the **RENDER** command. After the image is processed, it should look similar to the one in Figure 27-181.

Note:
To use the background you specified previously, you must select the **Named View** associated with it.

Figure 27-181   Final rendered image

43. **SAVE** the drawing.
44. Press the **<PrtScrn>** key to copy your entire screen to the clipboard. You can now open any imaging application such as Paint, paste the image from the clipboard, crop it, and save it for further uses or editing. This is another simple procedure for saving an image file.

Tutorial 27-2: Creating a Landscape Object

1. **OPEN** *Exercise 27-5* in the student data files.
2. **SAVE** it **AS** *Tutorial 27-2*.
3. Select the **SE Isometric** viewing point.
4. Select the **World** UCS.
5. Using the **3DORBIT** command, select a viewpoint similar to the one in Figure 27-182.

To access student data files, go to www.pearsondesigncentral.com.

Figure 27-182   View to be selected with the **3DORBIT** command

6. Open the **Materials** palette and create a new material. Name it *Palm*. Select the **Advanced** type for the **Palm** material. Turn **On** the **Checkered Underlay**.
7. Link the material's three colors so that only one **Color** box is shown by clicking the two **Lock** icons.
8. Move the **Shininess** slide button all the way to the right. Move the **Reflection** slide button located at the bottom all the way to the right (Figure 27-183).
9. Using Windows Explorer, **Copy** the image files **8tree14l** and **8tree14o** in the student data files and **Paste** them into another folder in your computer.
10. Under **Diffuse map**, select **Texture Map** from the drop-down list and click the **Select Image** button. In the **Select Image File** dialog box, select the **8tree14l** image file from the location where you previously copied it. Click **Open** to insert the file.
11. Under **Opacity** click the **Select Image** button and insert **8tree14o**.
12. Under **Diffuse map**, click the button located next to the button with the image file name. In the **Adjust Bitmap** dialog box, set both **U Tile** and **V Tile** to **1**. Under **Bitmap Scale**, select **Fit to Gizmo** and select **None** for the tiling option from the drop-down list for both tiles. Close the **Adjust Bitmap** dialog box by clicking the **Close** button.
13. Click the **Adjust scale...** button located under **Opacity**. In the **Adjust Bitmap** dialog box, repeat exactly the same settings you set for the diffuse map.
14. Select the **Front** UCS.
15. Using the **RECTANGLE** command, draw the **230 × 288** rectangle and **MOVE** it to the endpoint as shown in Figure 27-184.
16. Select the **World** UCS.
17. **ROTATE** the rectangle around the lower-left endpoint **30°**.
18. Place a copy of the rectangle on the midpoint of the same edge and **Scale** it down a factor of **0.75** based on its lower-left endpoint (Figure 27-185).
19. **Extrude** the rectangles to the new 3D solids.
20. In the **Materials** palette, select the **Palm** material and apply it to the two 3D solids.

To access student data files, go to www.pearsondesigncentral.com.

Figure 27-183   Settings to be specified in the **Materials** palette

Figure 27-184   Dimensions and location used to create the rectangle

Figure 27-185   After scaling down the copy of the rectangle

21. Select the **Global** material and set its **Diffuse** color **By Object**.
22. Set the **PERSPECTIVE** system variable to **1** to display a perspective view.
23. Open the **Advanced Render Settings** palette. Select **View** under **Rendering Procedure** and **Viewport** under **Destination**.
24. Open the **View Manager** dialog box. Click on the **New...** button and create a view named *Corner View*. Click **OK** to close the **New View** dialog box.
25. In the **View Manager** dialog box, select **Solid...** from the **Background override** drop-down list. Click the **Color** box In the **Background** window and select the color **255,255,255** in the **True Color** tab by moving the slide button all the way up. Click **OK** to close the **Select Color** dialog box, the **Background** window, and the **View Manager** dialog box.
26. Select **Corner View** from the drop-down list located in the **View** toolbar or in the **3D Navigate** panel.
27. Invoke the **RENDER** command. After you complete the render process, the image should look similar to the one in Figure 27-186.
28. **SAVE** the drawing.

Figure 27-186   The rendered image reveals the landscape objects

CHAPTER PROJECTS

Project 27-1: Enhancing the Hall with the Landscape Objects

OPEN the drawing *Tutorial 27-2* and **SAVE** it **AS** *Project 27-1*. Enhance the rendered image by applying materials with texture to represent a tiled roof and textured walls.

Use the sun light to create shadow effects. Create a thin 3D solid flush with the building base, big enough to receive the shadows of other objects in the 3D model. When finished, the rendered image should look similar to Figure 27-187.

Project 27-2: Two Options for Representing a Chessboard

OPEN *Exercise 27-1* in the student data files and copy the entire table into a new drawing. **SAVE** it **AS** *Project 27-2*. Create two different rendered images of the 3D model. In the first rendered image, make the tabletop look like an opaque chessboard. In the second one, make the tabletop look like a pane of glass with an engraved chessboard. The results should be similar to the ones in Figure 27-188.

To access student data files, go to www.pearsondesigncentral.com.

Figure 27-187   The final enhanced rendered image

Figure 27-188   Two different render effects are achieved by modifying the properties of the materials

Project 27-3: The Bench-Vise Motion Path Animation

OPEN the *Bench-Vise Presentation* drawing you developed in **Tutorial 27-1** and **SAVE** it **AS** *Project 27-3*. Create several motion path animations, using the **Realistic** visual style to show the materials.

Hints for the Project

Use a path for the camera and a point for the target, and vice versa.

Drafting Standards Overview

STANDARDS ORGANIZATIONS

Standards provide a basis for uniformity in engineering drawing. Many industries and governments can use these standards as a guideline to develop their documents. It is not the intent of recognized national standards organizations to prevent individual organizations from designing specific formats. The intent is to provide common engineering standards to aid the interchange of drawings between companies, government, and other users.

The following organizations are three leaders in drafting standards.

American National Standards Institute (ANSI)

ANSI has been a leader in the voluntary standards system of the United States. This organization has provided a forum for private and public sectors to collectively work together toward the development of national standards. Efforts to coordinate national standards date back to 1911. In 1916, the following agencies were instrumental in establishing a national body to oversee the development of national standards:

1. The American Institute of Electrical Engineers (now IEEE)
2. The American Society of Mechanical Engineers (ASME)
3. The American Society of Civil Engineers (ASCE)
4. The American Institute of Mining and Metallurgical Engineers (AIMME)
5. The American Society for Testing Materials (ASTM)

These organizations along with the U.S. Departments of War, Navy, and Commerce were the founders of the American Engineering Standards Committee (AESC). This organization led to the formation of the American National Standards Institute (ANSI) in 1969. Throughout its history, ANSI has continued to coordinate national and international efforts to approve voluntary standards. Over the past 85 years, this organization has maintained its strong ties with the original founding organizations and others to become one of the most highly regarded standards systems in the world.

Specific standards are revised periodically by a committee of industrial leaders who also serve as representatives of various industrial service organizations. For example, the vice president of engineering at Xerox Corporation might serve on the board of the American Society of Mechanical Engineers (ASME). These committee members revise such standards as Drawing Sheet Size and Format, Dimensioning and Tolerancing, and Line Conventions and Lettering. The standards should be readily available in the classroom so that students can develop engineering drawings that adhere to these standards. Specific standards need to be available for each content area—mechanical, electrical, or civil. The following is an example of some commonly used mechanical engineering standards.

American Society of Mechanical Engineers (ASME)

The American Society of Mechanical Engineers conducts one of the world's largest publishing operations to produce technical and engineering documents to establish standards. ASME documents are recognized worldwide for industrial and manufacturing codes and standards. Some of the popular documents on engineering standards include:

Y14.2M-1992 Line Conventions and Lettering

Y14.5.2-2000-2001 Certification of Geometric Dimensioning and Tolerancing

Y14.38-1999 Abbreviations and Acronyms

Y14.1-1980 (R1987) Drawing Sheet Size and Format
Y14.1M-1992 Metric Drawing Sheet Size and Format
Y14.3M-1994 Multiview and Sectional View Drawings

International Organization for Standardization (ISO)

The International Organization for Standardization is an organized network of the national standards institutes of 148 countries. It is a nongovernmental organization, but its members are not. ISO has a unique mission in acting as a bridge between business/industry and consumers/users. ISO has published more than 13,700 International Standards ranging from engineering drawing to medical devices. ISO is also responsible for providing a framework for quality management throughout the processes of producing and delivering products and services by implementing ISO 9000.

Some of the more commonly used ISO drawing standards are:

ISO 10135:1994

Technical drawings—Simplified representation of molded, cast, and forged parts

ISO 10209-1:1992

Technical product documentation—Vocabulary—Part 1: Terms relating to technical drawings: general and types of drawings

ISO 10209-2:1993

Technical product documentation—Vocabulary—Part 2: Terms relating to projection methods

Many companies, such as General Electric and General Motors, develop their own standards by incorporating the use of ANSI, ASME, and ISO criteria. In this way, national standards can be incorporated with company standards to meet specific requirements.

Text

Text can be inserted into the model space or into paper space layouts. When inserting text into a layout, the height of the text is equal to the printed or plotted size. Layouts are normally printed or plotted on a one-to-one scale. If the text height is inserted at 0.125 into the layout and printed at 1:1, the printed text height will be 0.125.

When text is entered into model space, consideration must be given to the drawing scale factor. See the following section for additional information about standard model space text heights.

Standard Text Heights

The typical standard height for text on a drawing is $\frac{1}{8}''$. Fractions need to be created $\frac{1}{4}''$ tall. These are general guidelines for text height. Text height should be increased or decreased based on individual situations.

To achieve these final printed and plotted text sizes, it is necessary to create the text within the Auto-CAD drawing at the correct size. The following table lists examples of the relationship between plot scale, sheet size, the model space drawing area, and text height.

	Sheet Size	Plot Scale	Scale Factor	Model Space Drawing Area	Text Height
Architect's Scale	12″ × 9″	1/8″ = 1′-0″	96	96′ × 72′	1′-0″
	24″ × 18″	1/2″ = 1′-0″	24	48′ × 36′	3″
Engineer's Scale (Civil)	18″ × 12″	1″ = 200′	2400	3600′ × 2400′	25′
	36″ × 24″	1″ = 50′	600	1800′ × 1200′	6.25′
Engineer's Scale (Mech.)	11″ × 8.5″	1″ = 2″	2	22″ × 17″	.25″
	34″ × 22″	1″ = 1.5″	1.5	51″ × 33″	3/16″
Metric Scale	279 mm × 216 mm	1 mm = 5 mm	5	1395 mm × 1080 mm	15.875 mm
	432 mm × 279 mm	1 mm = 20 mm	20	7620 mm × 5080 mm	63.5 mm

Notes and Locating Text on a Drawing

Notes and text are necessary to supplement a fully dimensioned engineering drawing. Notes should be clear and concise to avoid any misinterpretation. Notes are always lettered horizontally on the sheet and systematically organized. Do not place notes and text in crowded or busy locations on the drawing. Avoid placing notes in between orthographic views. Use only standard ANSI or ASME abbreviations with a note.

Notes are classified as General Notes or Local/Specific Notes.

General Notes

General notes apply to the entire drawing. General notes are typically placed in the lower right-hand corner of the drawing above or to the left of the title block. Title blocks may provide general information about the drawing such as tolerance, material, or treatment. General notes may be placed below the view to which the note applies.

Local/Specific Notes

Local notes provide specific detailed information. These notes are placed adjacent to the specific feature they describe. Local notes may be connected with a leader. The leader arrow or dot will touch the detail and end with a note.

Leaders

Leaders should be attached at the middle front of the first word of the note or after the last word of the note. Leaders to a circle should be developed radially. The slanted line of the leader should be aimed at the center of the circle or arc. A shoulder or horizontal line of the leader is optional. Leader lines should not cross each other. Refer to the following standard for additional information:

Y14.5.2-2000-2001 Certification of Geometric Dimensioning and Tolerancing

Sheet Layouts

A convenient code to identify American National Standard sheet sizes and forms suggested by the authors for title, parts or material list, and revision blocks, for use of instructors in making assignments, is shown here. All dimensions are in inches.

Three sizes of sheets are illustrated: Size A, Figure A-1, Size B, Figure A-5, and Size C, Figure A-6. Metric size sheets are not shown.

Eight forms of lettering arrangements are suggested, known as Forms 1, 2, 3, 4, 5, 6, 7, and 8, as shown below and on the next page. The total length of Forms 1, 2, 3, and 4 may be adjusted to fit Sizes A4, A3, and A2.

The term *layout* designates a sheet of certain size plus a certain arrangement of lettering. Thus Layout A–1 is a combination of Size A, Figure A-1, and Form 1, Figure A-2. Layout C–678 is a combination of Size C, Figure A-6, and Forms 6, 7, and 8, Figures A-9, A-10, and A-11. Layout A4–2 (adjusted) is a combination of Size A4 and Form 2, Figure A-3, adjusted to fit between the borders. Other combinations may be employed as assigned by the instructor.

Figure A-2   Form 1. Title block

Figure A-3   Form 2. Title block

Figure A-4   Form 3. Title block

Figure A-1   Size A sheet (8.50″ × 11.00″)

Figure A-5 Size B sheet (11.00″ × 17.00″)

Figure A-6 Size C sheet (17.00″ × 22.00″)

Figure A-7 Form 4. Title block

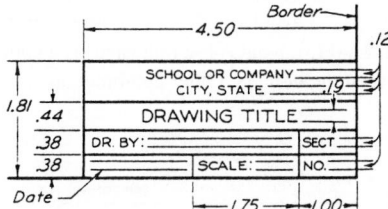

Figure A-8 Form 5. Title block

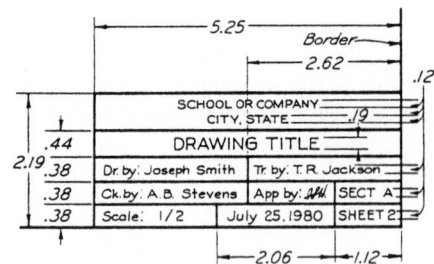

Figure A-9 Form 6. Title block

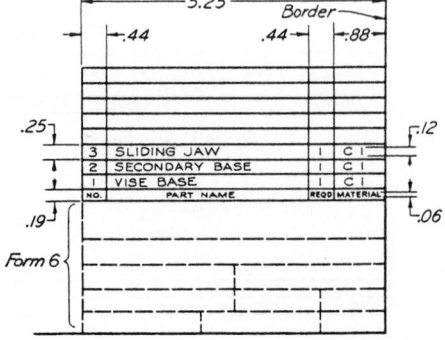

Figure A-10 Form 7. Parts list or material list

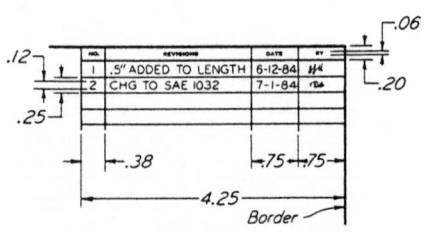

Figure A-11 Form 8. Revision block

DRAWING VIEWS

A drawing must contain as many views as needed to show most clearly the geometry of the objects and the possible ways of reproducing it. These views may include the three standard orthographic projected views, sections/elevations, auxiliary, details, or 3D views. There are two ways of showing the orthographic projected views; some engineering drawings show the corresponding symbol (Figure A-12):

- **Third Angle Projection:** The Front view is displayed at the lower left, the Top view is shown at the top, and the Right view is shown at the right. This method is primarily used in the United States and is based on the fact that the view you look at is placed on the same side as the one from which you are viewing it.

- **First Angle Projection:** The Front view is displayed at the upper left, the Top view is shown at the bottom, and the Right view is shown at the left. This method is primarily used for metric drawings and is based on the fact that the view you look at is placed on the side opposite from where you are viewing it.

 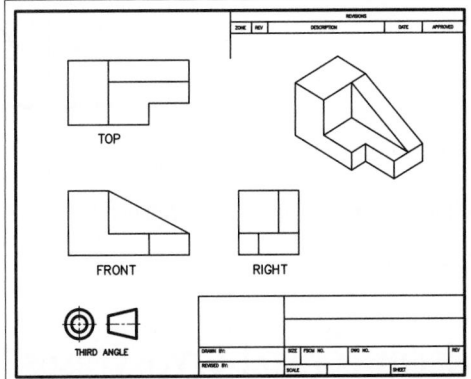

Figure A-12   The third and first angle projections are typically used to set up the drawing views in ANSI and ISO drawings, respectively

DIMENSIONS

The views of an object will describe the shape. The size of the object is described by the use of modern dimensioning techniques. It is important that an engineering drawing have accurate and functional dimensions.

Standard Feature Sizes

Figures A-13 and A-14 illustrate some common terms and distances to consider when dimensioning standard feature sizes.

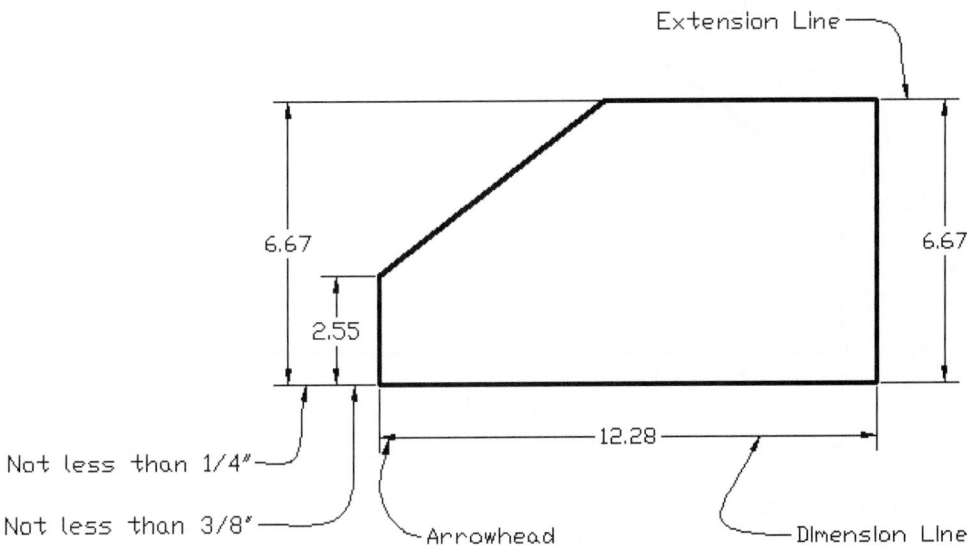

Figure A-13   Linear dimension features

(Angular Dimension)

34°

(Diameter Dimension)

⌀4.33

R3.00

(Radius Dimension)

3.84

(Locational Dimensions)

4.12

Figure A-14   Angular, radial, and diameter dimension features

Architectural Style versus Mechanical Style

Architectural Style

The architectural style of dimensioning has numbers placed on top of an unbroken dimension line. The dimension line typically ends with a slash, dot, or arrowhead. The numbers normally are designated with an inch (″) and foot (′) symbol (see Figure A-15).

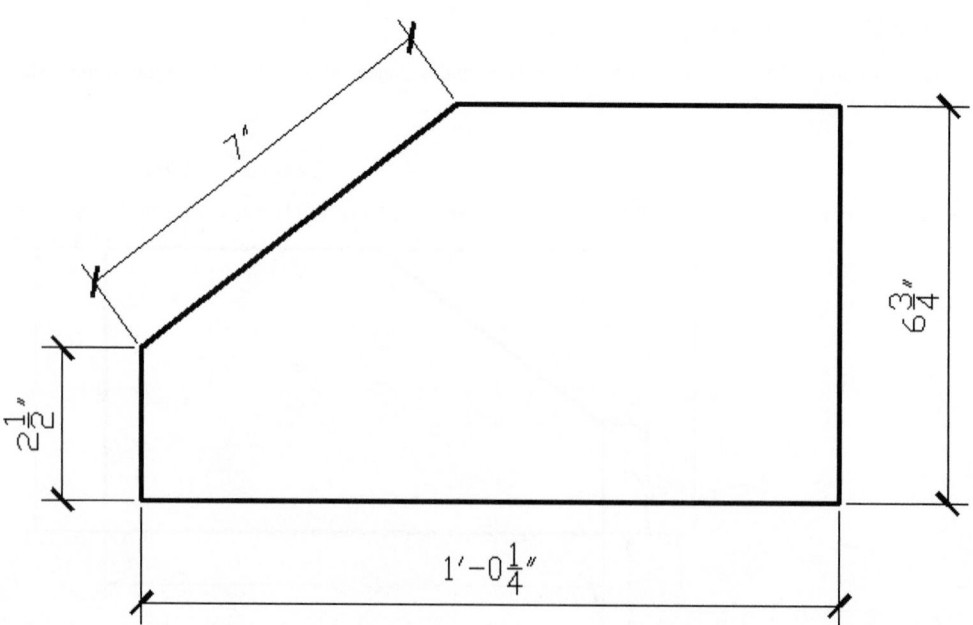

7″

$6\frac{3}{4}″$

$2\frac{1}{2}″$

$1′-0\frac{1}{4}″$

Figure A-15   Architectural dimension style

Mechanical Style

The mechanical style of dimensioning has numbers centered in the middle of a broken dimension line. The dimension line typically ends with an arrow.

There are two systems of reading dimensions on a drawing, the *unidirectional system* and the *aligned system.* In the unidirectional system, all the dimension figures and notes are lettered horizontally on the sheet. This is the preferred system of the American National Standards Institute. The mechanical style of dimensioning illustrates the unidirectional system. The unidirectional system is widely used because it is easy to read and interpret on large drawings. The unidirectional system is the standard default dimensioning system in AutoCAD.

The aligned system has all the dimension figures aligned with the dimension line. The architectural style of dimensioning illustrates the aligned system. Many of the dimension figures are horizontal on the sheet and some are aligned or turned. Any rotated figures are to be read from the right side of the sheet. Figures are not to be read from the right and left of the sheet. AutoCAD will dimension aligned figures after a few variables have been changed in the dimensioning environment (see Figure A-16).

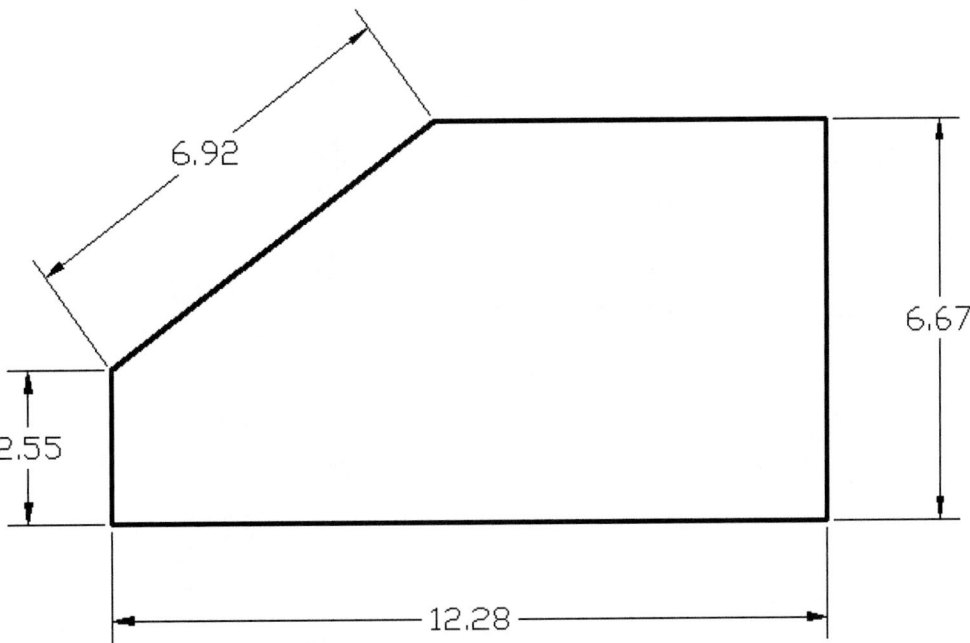

Figure A-16   Aligned dimensioning

Linetypes and Thicknesses

Linetypes that are used within AutoCAD should correspond with the standard ANSI Linetypes and thicknesses. Every line that is used on a technical drawing has a specific meaning and needs to be illustrated in a certain way. The American National Standards Institute has established the Line Convention and Lettering standard ANSI Y-14.2m-1992. This standard describes the size, application, and construction of various lines that are used in creating engineering drawings. Figure A-17 details various linetypes and their applications.

It should be noted that the line widths established in this illustration are approximate and the actual width is governed by the size and style of the drawing. Large drawings will need to have wider lines, and drawings that are reduced in size will need to have smaller line widths than specified in this illustration. The ANSI Y14.2M standard and this illustration should be used as a guide to produce crisp and legible engineering drawings from AutoCAD.

Linetypes are described in an AutoCAD file called ACAD.LIN. These linetypes should be loaded into the AutoCAD drawing file and assigned correct line weights that correspond with the ANSI standards. The AutoCAD command, LTSCALE, should be used to adjust the size of the linetypes to match the size of the drawing area in AutoCAD. Figure A-18 shows examples of AutoCAD's standard linetypes, which are defined in the ACAD.LIN file.

Figure A-17   Alphabet of lines (full-size)

STANDARD SHEET SIZES AND SCALES

The use of standard sheet sizes and the uniform location of the title block, revision block, and bill of material provide definite advantages for engineering drawings. These advantages include readability, handling, filing, and reproduction. As drawings are shared between organizations and companies, an advantage is realized when information is located in the same location on all drawings.

Standard sheet size also provides consistency between hand-drawn and printer/plotter-created engineering drawings. Drawings that are created on printers can use standard engineering sheet sizes of 8.5″ × 11″ or 17″ × 11″. Drawings that are created with plotters that use rolls of various media need to be trimmed to final standard size such as 17″ × 22″ or 22″ × 34″. International sheet sizes based on millimeters would need to be trimmed to final standard size such as 420 mm × 594 mm or 594 mm × 841 mm. (See Figure A-19.)

Continuous ————————
BORDER — · — · — · —
BORDER2 — · — · — · —
BORDERX2 — — · — — · —
CENTER — — · — — · —
CENTER2 —————————
CENTERX2 ———— — ——
DASHDOT — · — · — · —
DASHDOT2 —·—·—·—·—
DASHDOTX2 — · — · — ·
DASHED — — — — — —
DASHED2 ——————————
DASHEDX2 — — — — —
DIVIDE — · · — · · — · ·
DIVIDE2 —··—··—··—
DIVIDEX2 —— · · —— · ·

DOT ··················
DOT2 ··················
DOTX2 · · · · · · · · ·
HIDDEN ------------
HIDDEN2 ————————
HIDDENX2 — — — — —
PHANTOM ——— · · ———
PHANTOM2 —— · · —— · ·
PHANTOMX2 ——— — — ——
FENCELINE1 —o—o—o—o—
FENCELINE2 —□—□—□—□—
TRACKS +++++++++++++++
BATTING ⟨XXXXXXXXXX⟩
HOT_WATER_SUPPLY —■—■—■—■—
GAS_LINE —■—■—■—■—
ZIGZAG ∿∿∿∿∿∿∿

ACAD_ISO02W100 — — — —
ACAD_ISO03W100 — — — —
ACAD_ISO04W100 ——— · ———
ACAD_ISO05W100 ——— · · ——
ACAD_ISO06W100 —— · —— · —
ACAD_ISO07W100 · · · · · ·
ACAD_ISO08W100 ————————
ACAD_ISO09W100 ————————
ACAD_ISO10W100 — · — · — ·
ACAD_ISO11W100 —— · —— · —
ACAD_ISO12W100 — · · — · · —
ACAD_ISO13W100 —— · · —— ·
ACAD_ISO14W100 — · — · — ·
ACAD_ISO15W100 — · · — · · —

Figure A-18 Standard AutoCAD linetypes

Nearest International Size[a] (millimeters)	Standard U.S. Size[a] (inches)
A4 210 × 297	A 8.5 × 11.0
A3 297 × 420	B 11.0 × 17.0
A2 420 × 594	C 17.0 × 22.0
A1 594 × 841	D 22.0 × 34.0
A0 841 × 1189	E 34.0 × 44.0
[a] ANSI Y14.1m-1992.	

Figure A-19 Standard U.S. and metric paper sizes

STANDARD PLOT SCALES

Each drafting discipline has plot scales that are commonly used within that discipline. The following table lists standard plot scales for the mechanical, architectural, and civil engineering disciplines. These are preferred plot sales; other plot scales may be used as needed. In all cases, the plot scale should be clearly indicated on the drawing.

Mechanical Scale	Architectural Scale	Engineers' Scale
1:1	1/8″ = 1′-0″	1″ = 10′
1:2	¼″ = 1′-0″	1″ = 20′
1:4	½″ = 1′-0″	1″ = 30′
2:1	1″ = 1′-0″	1″ = 50′
4:1	1½″ = 1′-0″	1″ = 60′
10:1	3″ = 1′-0″	1″ = 100′

Specifying the Scale on a Drawing

For machine drawings, the scale indicates the ratio of the size of the drawn object to its actual size, irrespective of the unit of measurement used. The recommended practice is to letter full-size or 1:1; half-size or 1:2; and similarly for other reductions. Expansion or enlargement scales are given as 2:1 or 2:3; 3:1 or 3:3; 5:1 or 5:3; 10:1 or 10:3; and so on.

The various scale calibrations available on the metric scale and the engineers' scale provide almost unlimited scale ratios. The preferred metric scale ratios appear to be 1:1; 1:2; 1:5, 1:10, 1:20, 1:50, 1:100, and 1:200.

Map scales are indicated in terms of fractions, such as scale $\frac{1}{62500}$, or graphically, such as

400   0   400   800 Ft

STANDARD ANSI HATCH PATTERNS

Section Lining

Section-lining symbols (Figure A-20) have been used to indicate specific materials. These symbols represent general material types only, such as cast iron, brass, and steel. Now, however, because there are so many different types of materials, and each has so many subtypes, a general name or symbol is not enough. For example, there are hundreds of different kinds of steel. Since detailed specifications of material must be lettered in the form of a note or in the title strip, the general-purpose (cast-iron) section lining may be used for all materials on detail drawings (single parts).

Section-lining symbols may be used in assembly drawings in cases where it is desirable to distinguish different materials; otherwise, the general-purpose symbol is used for all parts.

CAD programs usually include a library that allows the user to select from a variety of section-lining patterns, making it easy to indicate various types of material rather than using the generic cast-iron symbol for all sectioned parts.

ANSI has standardized many section lines that are used for sectional drawing. AutoCAD uses the **HATCH** command to insert hatch patterns that are used to illustrate these section lines. The following table lists the ANSI section line with corresponding AutoCAD hatch pattern, as seen in Figure A-20.

Figure A-20 Symbols for section lining

Figure Number	ANSI Pattern Name	AutoCAD Hatch Pattern
A-20 (1)	Cast/General Use	ANSI 31
A-20 (2)	Steel	ANSI 32 or Steel
A-20 (3)	Bronze, brass, copper, etc.	ANSI 33
A-20 (4)	White metal, zinc, lead, etc.	ANSI 37
A-20 (5)	Magnesium, aluminum, etc.	ANSI 38 (include a material note)
A-20 (6)	Rubber, plastic, electrical insulation	ANSI 34
A-20 (7)	Cork, felt, fabric, leather, fiber	Cork
A-20 (8)	Sound insulation	Insulation (include a material note)
A-20 (9)	Thermal insulation	Insulation (include a material note)
A-20 (10)	Titanium/refractory material	
A-20 (11)	Electric windings, electromagnets, etc.	ANSI 37 (rotate 45°)
A-20 (12)	Concrete	AR-CONC
A-20 (13)	Marble, slate, glass, porcelain	Dash (rotate 45°)
A-20 (14)	Earth	Earth (rotate angle)
A-20 (15)	Rock	
A-20 (16)	Sand	AR-SAND
A-20 (17)	Water and other liquids	
A-20 (18)	Wood	

U.S. TO METRIC UNITS CONVERSIONS

AutoCAD provides some utilities for combining Metric and Imperial units within a single drawing. The following table lists standard U.S. (Imperial) units of measurements and their Metric conversions.

Length	
U.S. to Metric	**Metric to U.S.**
1 inch = 2.540 centimeters 1 foot = .305 meter 1 yard = .9l4 meter 1 mile = 1.609 kilometers	1 millimeter = .039 inch 1 centimeter = .394 inch 1 meter = 3.281 feet or 1.094 yards 1 kilometer = .621 mile
Area	
1 sq inch = 6.451 sq centimeters 1 sq foot = .093 sq meters 1 sq yard = .836 sq meters 1 acre = 4,046.873 sq meters	1 sq millimeter = .00155 sq inches 1 sq centimeter = .155 sq inches 1 sq meter = 10.764 sq feet or 1.196 sq yards 1 sq kilometer = .386 sq miles or 247.04 acres
Volume	
1 cu inch = 16.387 cu centimeters 1 cu foot = .028 cu meters 1 cu yard = .764 cu meters 1 quart = 0.946 liter 1 gallon = .003785 cu meters	1 cu centimeter = .061 cu inches 1 cu meter = 35.314 cu feet or 1.308 cu yards 1 liter = .2642 gallons 1 liter = 1.057 quarts 1 cu meter = 264.02 gallons
Weight	
1 ounce = 28.349 grams 1 pound = .454 kilogram 1 ton = .907 metric ton	1 gram = .035 ounce 1 kilogram = 2.205 pounds 1 metric ton = 1.102 tons
Velocity	
1 foot/second = .305 meter/second 1 mile/hour = .447 meter/hour	1 meter/second = 3.281 feet/second 1 kilometer/hour = .621 mile/hour
Acceleration	
$1 \text{ inch/second}^2 = .0254 \text{ meter/second}^2$ $1 \text{ foot/second}^2 = .305 \text{ meter/second}^2$	$1 \text{ meter/second}^2 = 3.278 \text{ feet/second}^2$
Force	
N (newton) = basic unit of force, kg-m/s^2. A mass of one kilogram (1 kg) exerts a gravitational force of 9.8 N (theoretically 9.80665 N) at mean sea level.	

Command Reference

Use the Help feature of AutoCAD for additional information about commands and their options.

Command	Description	Command	Description
3D	Creates 3D surfaced objects.	3DORBITCTR	Allows user selection of a center of rotation for the 3D Orbit view.
3DALIGN	Aligns objects with other objects in 2D and 3D environment.	3DPAN	Initiates interactive viewing of selected 3D objects and enables dragging the view.
3DARRAY	Copies objects in a rectangular or polar 3D array.		
3DCLIP	Opens the Adjust Clipping Planes window and starts the 3D Orbit view.	3DPOLY	Creates a polyline with 3D line segments.
		3DPRINT	Sends a 3D model to a 3D printing service.
3DCONFIG	Allows user to specify 3D graphics system configuration settings.	3DROTATE	Displays rotate grip tool in a 3D view and revolves objects around a base point.
-3DCONFIG	Provides a command line interface to 3D graphics system's configuration settings.	3DSCALE	In a 3D view, displays the 3D Scale gizmo to aid in resizing 3D objects.
3DCORBIT	Opens the 3D Orbit view and places selected objects in continuous orbit based on mouse click and drag direction and speed.	3DSIN	Starts import process for a 3D Studio file.
		3DSWIVEL	Initiates interactive viewing of selected 3D objects and moves the camera based on cursor movement.
3DDISTANCE	Opens the 3D Orbit view and allows user to move camera relative to object either increasing or decreasing object's apparent size without changing perspective.	3DWALK	Interactively changes view of a 3D drawing so that you appear to be walking through the model.
3DDWF	Displays Export 3D DWF dialog box.	3DZOOM	Initiates interactive viewing of selected 3D objects and allows zooming in or out.
3DFACE	Creates a three- or four-sided surface.		
3DFLY	Activates fly-through mode and enables you to navigate in any direction, including off *XY* plane.	ABOUT	Displays information about the software such as version number and the license agreement.
3DFORBIT	Controls interactive viewing of objects in 3D, using an unconstrained orbit.	ACISIN	Imports an SAT ACIS file into the drawing.
		ACISOUT	Exports an AutoCAD body, solid, or region to a SAT ACIS file.
3DMESH	Creates a free-form polygon mesh on an M×N grid.	ACTBASEPOINT	Inserts a base point in an action macro.
3DMOVE	Displays move grip tool in a 3D view and moves objects a specified distance in a specified direction.	ACTMANAGER	Manages action macro files.
		ACTRECORD	Starts the recording of an Action Macro.
3DORBIT	Allows interactive viewing of selected 3D objects by clicking and dragging the mouse.	ACTSTOP	Stops the recording of an Action Macro.
		-ACTSTOP	Stops the recording of an Action Macro.

Command	Description	Command	Description
ACTUSERINPUT	Requests a user input during playback.	ATTEDIT	Opens Edit Attributes dialog box, which permits editing of attribute values for a selected block.
ACTUSERMESSAGE	Inserts a message that will be viewed during playback.	ATTEXT	Opens Attribute Extraction dialog box, which permits informational text stored in blocks to be saved to a file.
-ACTUSERMESSAGE	Inserts a message that will be viewed during playback.		
ADCCLOSE	Closes DesignCenter window.		
ADCENTER	Opens DesignCenter window.	ATTIPEDIT	Changes the textual content of an attribute within a block.
ADCNAVIGATE	Loads a specified path or drawing file name into the tree view of DesignCenter.	ATTREDEF	Redefines an existing block and updates attribute definitions.
ADJUST	Adjusts the fade, contrast, and monochrome settings of the selected image or underlay (DWF, DWFx, PDF, or DGN).	ATTSYNC	Updates all occurrences of a specified block with the current attributes.
ALIGN	Aligns two objects in either 2D or 3D using one, two, or three pairs of source and destination points.	AUDIT	Finds and attempts to correct errors in a drawing.
		AUTOCONSTRAIN	Applies geometric constraints to a selection set of objects based on orientation of the objects relative to one another.
ALLPLAY	Plays all named views in current drawing.		
AMECONVERT	Converts Advanced Modeling Extension (AME) regions or solids to AutoCAD solid models.	AUTOPUBLISH	Publishes drawings to DWF, DWFx, or PDF files automatically to a specified location.
ANIPATH	Saves an animation along a path in a 3D model.	BACKGROUND	Reintroduction of Background Command.
ANNORESET	Resets the location of all scale representations for an annotative object to that of the current scale representation.	BACTION	Associates an action with a parameter in a dynamic block definition.
ANNOUPDATE	Updates existing annotative objects to match the current properties of their styles.	BACTIONBAR	Displays or hides action bars for a selection set of parameter objects.
APERTURE	Specifies size of the object snap target box.	BACTIONSET	Enables user to specify objects associated with an action in a dynamic block.
APPLOAD	Opens Load/Unload Applications dialog box.	BACTIONTOOL	Adds an action to a dynamic block.
ARC	Draws an arc based on specified points.	BASE	Sets the insertion base point coordinates of a drawing in the current UCS.
ARCHIVE	Opens the Archive Sheet Set dialog box, which packages the current sheet set files to be archived.	BASSOCIATE	Associates an action whose parameter has been removed with a new parameter in a dynamic block definition.
AREA	Calculates area and perimeter of specified objects or areas.	BATTMAN	Displays the Block Attribute Manager, which permits block attribute property edits.
ARRAY	Copies selected objects in either a rectangular or polar pattern.	BATTORDER	Controls order in which block attributes are listed when the block is inserted or edited.
ARX	Loads and unloads ObjectARX applications.		
ATTACH	Inserts an external reference, image, or underlay (DWF, DWFx, PDF, or DGN files) in the current drawing.	BAUTHORPALETTE	Opens Block Authoring Palettes window.
		BAUTHORPALETTECLOSE	Closes Block Authoring Palettes window.
ATTACHURL	Associates hyperlinks with selected objects or areas in a drawing.	BCLOSE	Closes the Block Editor.
		BCONSTRUCTION	Converts geometry into construction geometry.
ATTDEF	Opens the Attribute Definition dialog box.	BCPARAMETER	Applies constraint parameters to selected objects, or converts dimensional constraints to parameter constraints.
ATTDISP	Controls visibility of block attributes in a drawing.		

Command	Description	Command	Description
BCYCLEORDER	Displays Insertion Cycling Order dialog box allowing user to change the cycling order of grips in a dynamic block.	CHECKSTANDARDS	Compares the current drawing with a standards file and notes violations.
BEDIT	Opens the Edit Block Definition dialog box.	CHPROP	Enables changing the color, layer, linetype, linetype scale factor, lineweight, and thickness of a selected object.
BESETTINGS	Displays the Block Editor Settings dialog box.	CHSPACE	Moves objects from model space to paper space, or vice versa. (former Express Tool)
BGRIPSET	Controls number and position of grips for a parameter in a dynamic block.	CIRCLE	Draws a circle.
BHATCH	See HATCH.	CLASSICLAYER	Manages layer and layer properties.
BLIPMODE	Controls display of temporary marks associated with point selection.	CLEANSCREENOFF	Restores all toolbars and dockable windows cleared by the CLEANSCREENON command.
BLOCK	A group of reusable objects with flexible insert options.	CLEANSCREENON	Clears the screen of all toolbars and dockable windows.
BLOCKICON	Creates preview images for blocks displayed in DesignCenter.	CLIP	Crops a selected external reference, image, viewport, or underlay (DWF, DWFx, PDF, or DGN) to a specified boundary.
BLOOKUPTABLE	Displays Property Lookup Table dialog box.		
BMPOUT	Creates a bitmap file from selected objects.	CLOSE	Closes current active drawing.
BOUNDARY	Converts an enclosed area into a region or a polyline.	CLOSEALL	Closes all open drawings.
		COLOR	Specifies color for new objects.
BOX	Draws a solid 3-dimensional box.	COMMANDLINE	Restores the command line.
BPARAMETER	Adds a parameter to a dynamic block.	COMMANDLINEHIDE	Hides the command line.
		COMPILE	Compiles PostScript font and shape files.
BREAK	Splits the selected object into two parts.	CONE	Draws a 3D solid cone with a circular or elliptical base.
BREP	Removes history from 3D solid primitives and composite solids.	CONSTRAINTBAR	A toolbar-like UI element that displays the available geometric constraints on an object.
BROWSER	Launches the default Web browser.	CONSTRAINTSETTINGS	Controls the display of geometric constraints on constraint bars.
BSAVE	Saves changes to the current block definition and retains the same name.	CONVERT	Updates 2D polylines and associative hatches created in AutoCAD Release 13 or earlier.
BSAVEAS	Saves a copy of a block definition under a new name.	CONVERTCTB	Changes a color-dependent plot style table to a named plot style table.
BTABLE	Displays a dialog box to define variations of a block.		
BTESTBLOCK	Displays a window within the Block Editor to test a dynamic block.	CONVERTOLDLIGHTS	Converts lights created in previous releases to lights in AutoCAD 2010 format.
BVHIDE	Makes selected objects invisible in a visibility state.	CONVERTOLDMATERIALS	Converts materials created in previous releases to materials in AutoCAD 2010 format.
BVSHOW	Controls visibility of objects in a dynamic block.	CONVERTPSTYLES	Changes current drawing to either a named or color-dependent plot style.
BVSTATE	Manages visibility states in a dynamic block.		
CAL	Calculates mathematical and geometric expressions.	CONVTOSOLID	Converts polylines and circles with thickness to 3D solids.
		CONVTOSURFACE	Converts objects to surfaces.
CAMERA	Sets position of camera and target for viewing.	COPY	Creates copies of selected objects at a specified location.
CHAMFER	Draws an angled corner between two lines.	COPYBASE	Copies selected objects with a user-defined base point.
CHANGE	Changes the properties of selected objects.	COPYCLIP	Copies all selected objects to the Clipboard.

Command	Description	Command	Description
COPYHIST	Copies command line text to the Clipboard.	DELCONSTRAINT	Removes all geometric and dimensional constraints from a selection set of objects.
COPYLINK	Copies the current view to the Clipboard for inclusion in other OLE applications.	DETACHURL	Removes hyperlinks from selected objects.
COPYTOLAYER	Copies one or more objects to another layer. (former Express Tool)	DGNADJUST	Changes the display options of selected DGN underlays.
-COPYTOLAYER	Copies one or more objects to another layer. (command line version)	-DGNADJUST	Provides a command line interface to the DGN underlay display options.
CUI	Allows customization of workspaces, toolbars, menus, shortcut menus, and keyboard shortcuts.	DGNATTACH	Attaches a DGN underlay to the current drawing.
		-DGNATTACH	Attaches a DGN underlay to the current drawing from the command line.
CUIEXPORT	Exports customized settings.	DGNCLIP	Defines a clipping boundary for a selected DGN underlay.
CUIIMPORT	Imports customized settings.		
CUILOAD	Loads a CUIx file.	DGNEXPORT	Creates one or more DGN files from the current drawing. You will be able to attach DGN files with non-DGN extensions.
CUIUNLOAD	Unloads a CUIx file.		
CUSTOMIZE	Allows customization of tool palettes.		
CUTCLIP	Removes objects from the drawing and places them on the Clipboard.	-DGNEXPORT	Creates one or more DGN files from the current drawing from the command line.
CYLINDER	Draws a solid 3D cylinder with either a circular or elliptical cross section.	DGNIMPORT	Creates one or more DGN files from the current drawing. You will be able to attach DGN files with non-DGN extensions.
DASHBOARD	Opens Dashboard window.		
DASHBOARDCLOSE	Closes Dashboard window. Routed to the RIBBONCLOSE command.	-DGNIMPORT	Creates one or more DGN files from the current drawing from the command line.
DATAEXTRACTION	Exports object property, block attribute, and drawing information to a data extraction table or to an external file and specifies a data link to an Excel spreadsheet.	DGNLAYERS	Controls the display of layers in a DGN underlay.
		DGNMAPPING	Opens the DGN Mapping Setups Manager dialog.
DATALINK	Displays the Data Link Manager.	DIM and DIM1	Initiates Dimensioning mode. DIM1 allows user to execute a single dimensioning command before returning to the Command prompt.
DATALINKUPDATE	Updates data to or from an established external data link.		
DBCLOSE	Closes the dbConnect Manager and removes the dbConnect menu from the menu bar.	DIMALIGNED	Creates a linear dimension parallel to an angled edge.
DBCONNECT	Opens dbConnect Manager and adds dbConnect menu to the menu bar, establishing an interface with external database tables.	DIMANGULAR	Creates an angular dimension between two lines or three points.
		DIMARC	Creates an arc length dimension.
		DIMBASELINE	Creates a linear, angular, or ordinate dimension from a selected baseline.
DBLIST	Displays database information about drawing objects in the text window.	DIMBREAK	Adds or removes a dimension break.
DDEDIT	Enables editing of single-line text, dimension text, attribute definitions, and feature control frames.	DIMCENTER	Creates center marks or centerlines of circles and arcs.
		DIMCONSTRAINT	Applies dimensional constraints to selected objects or points on objects.
DDPTYPE	Specifies point display style and size.	DIMCONTINUE	Creates a chained linear, angular, or ordinate dimension.
DDVPOINT	Specification 3D viewing direction.	DIMDIAMETER	Creates diameter dimensions for circles and arcs, which include the diameter symbol.
DELAY	Specifies the length of a timed pause in a script.		

Command	Description	Command	Description
DIMDISASSOCIATE	Removes associativity from specified dimensions.	DWFFORMAT	Sets the default DWF format to the selected format to DWF or DWFx for the PUBLISH, 3DDWF, and EXPORT commands.
DIMEDIT	Edits dimension extension lines and text.		
DIMINSPECT	Creates or removes inspection dimensions.	DWFLAYERS	Controls the display of layers in a DWF underlay.
-DIMINSPECT	Provides a command line interface to create or remove inspection dimensions.	DWGPROPS	Sets and displays the properties of the current drawing.
DIMJOGGED	Creates a foreshortened radius dimension.	DXBIN	Imports Drawing Exchange Binary format files.
DIMJOGLINE	Adds or removes a jog line on a linear or aligned dimension.	EATTEDIT	Edits block attributes.
DIMLINEAR	Creates horizontal or vertical linear dimensions.	EATTEXT	Extracts block attribute data to a table or to an external file.
DIMORDINATE	Creates ordinate dimensions based on specified x and y data.	EDGE	Changes display visibility of 3D Face edges.
DIMOVERRIDE	Temporarily changes a dimension system variable without changing the dimension style.	EDGESURF	Creates a 3D mesh conforming to four selected edges.
DIMRADIUS	Creates a radius dimension for a circle or arc, which includes a radius symbol.	EDITSHOT	Opens the Edit View dialog box with the Shot Properties tab active.
DIMREASSOCIATE	Links selected dimensions to association points on objects.	ELEV	Sets elevation and extrusion thickness for new objects.
DIMREGEN	Updates the locations of associative dimensions.	ELLIPSE	Draws an ellipse or an elliptical arc.
DIMSPACE	Adjusts the spacing equally between parallel linear and angular dimensions.	ERASE	Removes selected objects.
		ETRANSMIT	Packages files for Internet transmission.
DIMSTYLE	Manages dimension styles.	EXPLODE	Breaks a selected compound object into component parts.
DIMTEDIT	Permits moving and rotating dimension text.	EXPORT	Saves object to other file formats.
DIST	Measures the distance and angle between two specified points.	EXPORTDWF	Creates a DWF file and allows you to set individual page setup overrides on a sheet-by-sheet basis.
DISTANTLIGHT	Creates a distant light.		
DIVIDE	Divides an object into evenly spaced segments marked by points.	EXPORTDWFX	Creates a DWFx file where you can set individual page setup overrides on a sheet-by-sheet basis.
DONUT	Draws filled rings and circles.		
DRAGMODE	Controls display of dragged objects.	EXPORTLAYOUT	Exports all visible objects from current layout to the model space of a new drawing.
DRAWINGRECOVERY	Displays list of files open during a system failure and offers options for recovery.	EXPORTPDF	Creates a PDF file where you can set individual page setup overrides on a sheet-by-sheet basis.
DRAWINGRECOVERYHIDE	Closes the Drawing Recovery Manager.		
DRAWORDER	Changes the draw order of drawing objects.	EXPORTTOAUTOCAD	Creates a new DWG file with all AEC objects exploded.
DSETTINGS	Sets snap, grid, polar tracking, object snap, and dynamic input.	-EXPORTTOUTOCAD	Provides a command line interface to creating a new DWG file with all AEC objects exploded.
DSVIEWER	Opens Aerial View window.		
DVIEW	Creates parallel projection or perspective views in 3D.	EXTEND	Extends selected object to meet a selected boundary edge.
DWFADJUST	Allows adjustment of a DWF underlay from the command line.		
DWFATTACH	Attaches a DWF underlay to current drawing.	EXTERNALREFERENCES	Displays External References palette.
DWFCLIP	Uses clipping boundaries to define a subregion of a DWF underlay.	EXTERNALREFERENCESCLOSE	Closes External References palette.

Command	Description	Command	Description
EXTRUDE	Creates a solid by extruding a cross-section to a specified height.	HYPERLINK	Attaches or modifies a hyperlink to a drawing object.
FIELD	Creates a multiline text object, which can be updated automatically when the field value changes.	HYPERLINKOPTIONS	Manages display of hyperlink properties.
		ID	Displays coordinates of selected point.
FILL	Controls the display of filled areas in hatches, 2D solids, and polylines.	IMAGE	Opens Image Manager.
		IMAGEADJUST	Controls image brightness, contrast, and fade values.
FILLET	Creates a rounded corner tangent to two objects with a specified radius.	IMAGEATTACH	Attaches image to drawing.
		IMAGECLIP	Creates clipping boundaries for images.
FILTER	Allows creation of a list of criteria for creating a selection set.	IMAGEFRAME	Controls image frame display and plotting.
FIND	Enables finding, selecting, and replacing specified text.	IMAGEQUALITY	Controls image display quality.
		IMPORT	Imports files from other applications.
FLATSHOT	Creates a 2D representation of all 3D objects in the current view.	IMPRESSION	Gives a CAD drawing a hand-drawn look by exporting it for rendering in Autodesk Impression.
FREEPOINT	Creates a target point light without a prompt for the target point.		
		IMPRINT	Imprints an edge on a 3D solid.
FREESPOT	Creates a free spotlight which is similar to a spotlight without a specified target.	INSERT	Places drawings or blocks into drawing.
		INSERTOBJ	Inserts a linked or embedded object.
FREEWEB	Creates a free web light which is similar to a web light without a specified target.	INTERFERE	Determines if two solid objects overlap.
GEOGRAPHICLOCATION	Specifies latitude and longitude of a location.	-INTERFERE	Highlights 3D solids that overlap. (command line version)
GEOMCONSTRAINT	Applies or persists geometric relationships between objects or points on objects.	INTERSECT	Creates a new solid from the area common to two or more solids or regions.
GOTOURL	Opens the file or Web page associated with a hyperlink in the drawing.	ISOPLANE	Selects active isometric plane.
		JOGSECTION	Adds a jogged segment to a section object.
GRADIENT	Fills a closed area with a gradient fill pattern.	JOIN	Combines similar objects into a single object.
GRAPHSCR	Closes the text window.	JPGOUT	Saves selected objects to a JPEG file format.
GRID	Displays a reference pattern of dots at user-specified spacing.	JUSTIFYTEXT	Changes the justification point of text.
GROUP	Creates and manages sets of grouped objects.	LAYCUR	Changes layer of selected objects to current layer. (former Express Tool)
HATCH	Creates a hatch pattern, solid fill, or gradient fill inside a closed area.	LAYDEL	Deletes layer of a selected object and all objects on layer, and purges layer from drawing. (former Express Tool)
HATCHEDIT	Changes existing hatches or fills.		
HELIX	Creates a 2D or 3D spiral.		
HELP	Displays explanation of concepts, commands, and procedures.	-LAYDEL	Deletes layer of a selected object and all objects on layer, and purges layer from drawing. (command line version)
HIDE	Regenerates model and suppresses hidden lines.		
HIDEPALETTES	Hides all currently displayed palettes such as the command line, DesignCenter, and properties, keeping track of their positions.	LAYER	Manages layers. The Layer Properties Manager dialog is a modeless dialog.
		LAYERCLOSE	Closes the Layer Properties Manager dialog from the command line.
HLSETTINGS	Controls hidden line display properties.	LAYERP	Undoes changes to layer settings.

Command	Description	Command	Description
LAYERPMODE	Controls tracking of layer setting changes.	LOAD	Loads shapes for use by the SHAPE command.
LAYERSTATE	Saves, restores, and manages named layer states.	LOFT	Creates a 3D solid or surface by lofting through a set of two or more curves.
LAYFRZ	Freezes layer of selected objects. (former Express Tool)	LOGFILEOFF	Closes the log file.
LAYISO	Isolates layer of selected objects so that all other layers are turned off. (former Express Tool)	LOGFILEON	Records contents of text window to a file.
		LTSCALE	Sets drawing linetype scale.
		LWEIGHT	Manages lineweights.
LAYLCK	Locks layer of selected objects. (former Express Tool)	MACROTRACE	Evaluates DIESEL expressions.
		MARKUP	Manages markup sets.
LAYMCH	Changes layer of a selected object to match destination layer. (former Express Tool)	MARKUPCLOSE	Closes Markup Set Manager.
		MASSPROP	Displays mass properties of solids and regions.
-LAYMCH	Changes layer of a selected object to match destination layer. (command line version)	MATCHCELL	Copies the properties of one table cell to other selected table cells.
LAYMCUR	Makes layer of a selected object current. (renamed AI_MOLC)	MATCHPROP	Copies the properties of one object to other selected objects.
LAYMRG	Merges selected layers onto a destination layer. (former Express Tool)	MATERIALATTACH	Attaches materials to objects by layer.
-LAYMRG	Merges selected layers onto a destination layer. (command line version)	MATERIALMAP	Displays a material mapper grip tool to adjust mapping on a face or an object.
LAYOFF	Turns off layer of selected object. (former Express Tool)	MATERIALS	Manages, applies, and modifies materials.
LAYON	Turns on all layers. (former Express Tool)	MATERIALSCLOSE	Closes Materials window.
		MEASURE	Marks segments of a specified length on an object.
LAYOUT	Manages drawing layout tabs.		
LAYOUTWIZARD	Starts layout wizard.	MEASUREGEOM	Measures the distance, radius, angle, area, and volume of selected objects or sequence of points.
LAYTHW	Thaws all layers. (former Express Tool)		
LAYTRANS	Converts drawing layers to specified standards.		
LAYULK	Unlocks layer of a selected object. (former Express Tool)	MENU	Loads a customizable XML-based file containing menus, toolbars, tool palettes, and other interface elements.
LAYUNISO	Turns on layers that were turned off with last LAYISO command. (former Express Tool)		
		MESH	Creates a 3D mesh primitive object such as a box, cone, cylinder, pyramid, sphere, wedge, or torus.
LAYVPI	Isolates an object's layer to the current viewport. (former Express Tool)		
LAYWALK	Dynamically displays layers in a drawing. (former Express Tool)	MESHCREASE	Sharpens the edges of selected mesh subobjects.
LEADER	Creates leader lines for notes and dimensions.	MESHOPTIONS	Displays the Mesh Tessellation Options dialog box, which controls default settings for converting existing objects to mesh objects.
LENGTHEN	Modifies object length.		
LIGHT	Controls lights in rendered scenes.		
LIGHTLIST	Opens Lights in Model window to add and modify lights.	MESHPRIMITIVEOPTIONS	Displays the Mesh Primitive Options dialog box, which sets the tessellation defaults for primitive mesh objects.
LIGHTLISTCLOSE	Closes Lights in Model window.		
LIMITS	Sets drawing size.	MESHREFINE	Multiplies the number of faces in selected mesh objects or faces.
LINE	Draws straight line segments.		
LINETYPE	Manages linetypes.		
LIST	Displays database information.	MESHSMOOTHLESS	Decreases the level of smoothness for mesh objects by one level.
LIVESECTION	Turns on live sectioning for a selected section object.		

Command	Description	Command	Description
MESHSMOOTHMORE	Increases the level of smoothness for mesh objects by one level.	OBJECTSCALE	Adds or deletes supported scales for annotative objects.
MESHSPLIT	Splits a mesh face into two faces.	-OBJECTSCALE	Provides a command line interface to add or delete supported scales for annotative objects.
MESHUNCREASE	Removes the crease from selected mesh faces, edges, or vertices.	OFFSET	Draws objects parallel to a specified object.
MINSERT	Inserts copies of a block in a rectangular array.	OLELINKS	Manages OLE (Object Linking and Embedding) links.
MIRROR	Creates a mirror image about an axis.	OLESCALE	Manages OLE (Object Linking and Embedding) object properties.
MIRROR3D	Creates a mirror image about a plane.	OOPS	Restores objects removed by the last ERASE command.
MLEADER	Creates a line that connects annotation to a feature.	OPEN	Opens a previously created drawing file.
MLEADERALIGN	Organizes selected multileaders along a specified line.	OPENDWFMARKUP	Opens a DWF or DWFx file that contains markups.
MLEADERCOLLECT	Organizes selected multileaders containing blocks as content into a group attached to a single leader line.	OPENSHEETSET	Opens a specified sheet set.
		OPTIONS	Controls AutoCAD settings.
MLEADEREDIT	Adds leader lines to, or removes leader lines from, a multileader object.	ORTHO	Limits cursor movement to horizontal and vertical directions while in drawing and editing commands.
MLEADERSTYLE	Defines a new multileader style.	OSNAP	Sets running object snaps.
MLEDIT	Modifies multiline vertices, breaks, and intersections.	PAGESETUP	Manages page layout, plotting device, paper size, and other layout settings.
MLINE	Creates multiple parallel lines.		
MLSTYLE	Controls multiline styles.	PAN	Moves drawing on screen without changing zoom factor.
MODEL	Enters model space.		
MOVE	Moves objects from one location to another.	PARAMETERS	Controls the associative parameters used in the drawing.
MREDO	Reverses multiple UNDO commands.	PARAMETERSCLOSE	Closes the Parameters Manager palette.
MSLIDE	Makes a slide file of current model viewport or layout.	PARTIALOAD	Loads additional components into a partially opened drawing.
MSPACE	Enters model space for active viewport in layout space.	PARTIALOPEN	Opens selected views and layers from a drawing file.
MTEDIT	Modifies multiline text.	PASTEASHYPERLINK	Pastes information from the Clipboard as a hyperlink.
MTEXT	Creates multiple lines of text as a single object.	PASTEBLOCK	Pastes objects from the Clipboard as a block.
MULTIPLE	Repeats the next command until you enter <Esc>.	PASTECLIP	Pastes data from the Clipboard.
MVIEW	Creates and manages layout viewports.	PASTEORIG	Pastes objects from the Clipboard retaining coordinate information from original drawing.
MVSETUP	Helps set up drawing views.		
NAVSMOTION	Displays the ShowMotion interface.	PASTESPEC	Sets file formats and linking options for pasted objects.
NAVSMOTIONCLOSE	Closes the ShowMotion interface.	PCINWIZARD	Opens wizard to import PCP and PC2 configuration file plot settings.
NAVSWHEEL	Displays the SteeringWheel.		
NAVVCUBE	Shows/hides the ViewCube.		
NETLOAD	Loads a .NET application.	PDFADJUST	Adjust the fade, contrast, and monochrome settings of a PDF underlay.
NEW	Starts a new drawing.		
NEWSHEETSET	Creates a new sheet set.		
NEWSHOT	Opens the New View dialog box with the Shot Properties tab active.	PDFATTACH	Insert a PDF file as an underlay into the current drawing.
NEWVIEW	Creates a named view with no motion.	PDFCLIP	Crops the display of a selected PDF underlay to a specified boundary.

Command	Description	Command	Description
PDFLAYERS	Controls the display of layers in a PDF underlay.	QUIT	Exits AutoCAD and prompts to save or discard changes.
PEDIT	Modifies polylines and 3D meshes.	QVDRAWING	Displays a two-level structure of preview images at the bottom of the application. The first level displays the images of open drawings and the second level displays the images for model space and layouts in a drawing.
PFACE	Creates a 3D mesh by entering vertices.		
PLAN	Creates a view looking down the current UCS Z-axis toward the origin.		
PLANESURF	Creates a planar surface.	QVDRAWINGCLOSE	Closes preview images of open drawings and layouts in a drawing.
PLINE	Creates a connected sequence of line and arc segments as a single object.		
PLOT	Prints a drawing to a plotter, printer, or file.	QVLAYOUT	Displays preview images of model space and layouts in a drawing.
PLOTSTAMP	Places information on corner of drawing and creates a log file.	QVLAYOUTCLOSE	Closes preview images of model space and layouts in a drawing.
PLOTSTYLE	Manages plot styles for new or selected objects.		
PLOTTERMANAGER	Adds or modifies a plotter configuration.	RAY	Creates a line extending to infinity in one direction.
PNGOUT	Saves to a Portable Network Graphics format file.	RECOVER	Repairs a damaged drawing.
		RECOVERALL	Repairs a damaged drawing and xrefs.
POINT	Draws a point.		
POINTLIGHT	Creates a point light.	RECTANG	Creates rectangles.
POLYGON	Draws regular polygons with up to 1024 sides.	REDEFINE	Restores AutoCAD commands previously changed by the UNDEFINE command.
POLYSOLID	Creates a 3D polysolid.		
PRESSPULL	Presses or pulls bounded areas.	REDO	Reverses the effects of a single UNDO command.
PREVIEW	Shows plot appearance.		
PROPERTIES	Used to view or change object properties.	REDRAW	Refreshes current viewport display.
PROPERTIESCLOSE	Closes Properties palette.	REDRAWALL	Refreshes display in all viewports.
PSETUPIN	Imports a page setup.		
PSPACE	Enters paper space.	REFCLOSE	Saves or discards changes made during in-place editing of an xref or block.
PUBLISH	Publishes drawings to DWF, DWFx, and PDF files, or to plotters.		
		REFEDIT	Selects a reference for editing.
PUBLISHTOWEB	Converts drawings to HTML pages.	REFSET	Modifies working set during in-place editing of a reference.
PURGE	Removes unused items from the drawing database.	REGEN	Regenerates the entire drawing and recomputes geometry for objects in the current viewport.
PYRAMID	Creates a 3D solid pyramid.		
QCCLOSE	Closes the QuickCalc calculator.		
QDIM	Quickly creates or edits a series of dimensions.	REGENALL	Regenerates and recomputes geometry for all viewports.
QLEADER	Quickly creates leader line and text.	REGENAUTO	Controls automatic regeneration of a drawing.
QNEW	Starts a new drawing from the default template file.	REGION	Creates a 2-dimensional area object from a closed shape or loop.
QSAVE	Saves the current drawing.		
QSELECT	Quickly creates a selection set based on filtering criteria.	REINIT	Reinitializes digitizer, digitizer input/output port, and program parameters file.
QTEXT	Controls text and attribute display and plotting.		
		RENAME	Changes object names.
QUICKCALC	Opens the QuickCalc calculator.	RENDER	Produces a realistically shaded view of a 3D model.
QUICKCUI	Displays the CUI editor in a collapsed state. Additional support for enhanced tooltips, quick access panel, and ribbons.	RENDERCROP	Selects a specific region in an image for rendering.
		RENDERENVIRONMENT	Provides visual cues for the apparent distance of objects.

Command	Description	Command	Description
RENDEREXPOSURE	Provides settings to interactively adjust the lighting global for the most recent rendered output.	SECTIONPLANETOBLOCK	Saves selected section planes as 2D or 3D blocks.
RENDERPRESETS	Specifies render presets, reusable rendering parameters for rendering an image.	SECURITYOPTIONS	Controls drawing security settings.
RENDERWIN	Displays Render Window without starting a render task.	SEEK	Opens a Web browser and displays the Autodesk Seek home page.
RESETBLOCK	Restores dynamic block references to the default value.	SELECT	Places objects in the Previous selection set.
RESUME	Restarts an interrupted script.	SEQUENCEPLAY	Plays the named views in one view category.
REVCLOUD	Creates a cloud-shaped polyline.		
REVERSE	Reverses the order of vertices of the selected lines, polylines, splines, and helixes.	SETBYLAYER	Changes property and ByBlock settings for selected objects to ByLayer.
REVOLVE	Creates a solid by revolving a closed 2-dimensional shape around an axis.	SETIDROPHANDLER	Sets i-drop content default type.
REVSURF	Creates a rotated surface about an axis.	SETVAR	Lists or changes system variable values.
RIBBON	Opens the Ribbon window.	SHADEMODE	Controls solid model shading.
RIBBONCLOSE	Closes the Ribbon window.	SHAPE	Inserts a shape into the current drawing.
ROTATE	Rotates selected objects around a specified base point.		
ROTATE3D	Rotates an object in a 3D coordinate system.	SHAREWITHSEEK	Uploads blocks or drawings to the Autodesk Seek Website.
RPREF	Controls rendering preferences.	SHEETSET	Opens the Sheet Set Manager.
RPREFCLOSE	Closes Advanced Render Settings palette, if it is displayed.	SHEETSETHIDE	Closes the Sheet Set Manager.
		SHELL	Allows execution of operating system commands within AutoCAD.
RSCRIPT	Creates a continuously running script.		
RULESURF	Creates a polygon mesh between two curves.	SHOWPALETTES	Restores the state of the display and position of palettes hidden by HIDEPALETTES. Press CTRL + SHIFT + H to switch between HIDEPALETTES and SHOWPALETTES.
SAVE	Saves a drawing.		
SAVEAS	Saves current drawing with options for renaming file, changing file type, or changing file location.		
		SIGVALIDATE	Displays digital signature information.
SAVEIMG	Saves a rendered image to a BMP, TGA, or TIFF file.	SKETCH	Draws a freehand line composed of segments.
SCALE	Proportionally enlarges or reduces objects relative to a base point.	SLICE	Divides a solid along a specified plane.
		SNAP	Limits cursor movement to specified intervals.
SCALELISTEDIT	Manages scales available for layout viewports, page layouts, and plotting.	SOLDRAW	Generates visible and hidden lines for viewports created with SOLVIEW.
SCALETEXT	Enlarges or reduces text objects while maintaining location.	SOLID	Creates 2D filled triangles and four-sided polygons.
SCRIPT	Executes a sequence of commands from a script file.	SOLIDEDIT	Edits faces and edges of 3D solid objects.
SECTION	Creates a cross-section through a solid.	SOLPROF	Creates a 2D profile of a 3D solid.
SECTIONPLANE	Creates a section object that acts as a cutting plane through a 3D object.	SOLVIEW	Creates orthographic, auxiliary, and sectional views of 3D solids.
SECTIONPLANEJOG	Adds a jogged segment to a section object.	SPACETRANS	Converts lengths between model space units and paper space units.
SECTIONPLANESETTINGS	Sets display options for the selected section plane.	SPELL	Checks spelling of selected objects in a drawing.
		SPHERE	Creates a solid sphere.

Command	Description	Command	Description
SPLINE	Creates a smooth curve fit to a sequence of points within a specified tolerance.	TOLERANCE	Adds geometric tolerances in feature control frames.
SPLINEDIT	Modifies splines or spline-fit polylines.	TOOLBAR	Manages toolbar display and customization.
SPOTLIGHT	Creates a spotlight.	TOOLPALETTES	Opens Tool Palettes window.
STANDARDS	Associates the current drawing with a Standards file.	TOOLPALETTESCLOSE	Closes Tool Palettes window.
		TORUS	Creates a donut-shaped solid.
STATUS	Displays drawing statistics, modes, and extents.	TPNAVIGATE	Displays a specified tool palette or palette group.
STLOUT	Stores solid data in a STL file format for stereo lithography.	TRACE	Creates solid lines.
		TRANSPARENCY	Controls transparency of background in images.
STRETCH	Stretches selected objects.		
STYLE	Manages text styles.	TRAYSETTINGS	Controls Status Bar tray content.
STYLESMANAGER	Manages plot styles.	TREESTAT	Displays information about a drawing's spatial index.
SUBTRACT	Creates composite solid or region by subtracting selected objects or regions.	TRIM	Removes part of an object at a selected cutting edge.
SUNPROPERTIES	Opens Sun palette and sets properties of the sun.	U	Undo.
		UCS	Creates and manages User Coordinate Systems.
SUNPROPERTIESCLOSE	Closes Sun Properties window.	UCSICON	Controls display and location of UCS icon.
SWEEP	Creates a 3D solid or surface by sweeping a 2D curve along a path.	UCSMAN	Manages defined User Coordinate Systems.
SYSWINDOWS	Arranges windows and icons when the application window is shared with external applications.	ULAYERS	Controls the display of layers in a DWF, DWFx, PDF, or DGN underlay.
TABLE	Creates an empty table in the drawing.	UNDEFINE	Allows an application-defined command to override an AutoCAD command.
TABLEDIT	Edits text in a selected table cell.	UNDO	Reverses previous commands.
TABLEEXPORT	Exports data from a table object in comma-separated file format.	UNION	Adds selected regions or solids.
		UNITS	Sets coordinate and angle display precision and formats.
TABLESTYLE	Sets the current table style. Creates, modifies, and deletes table styles.	UPDATEFIELD	Updates fields for selected items.
TABLET	Turns on and off, calibrates, and configures an attached digitizing tablet input device.	UPDATETHUMBSNOW	Updates thumbnail previews in the Sheet Set Manager.
TABSURF	Creates a surfaced polygon mesh by specifying a path curve and direction vector.	VBAIDE	Edits code, forms, and references for any loaded or embedded VBA projects in the current drawing.
TARGETPOINT	Creates a target point light.	VBALOAD	Loads a VBA (Visual Basic for Applications) project into the current work session.
TASKBAR	Controls drawing display mode on the Windows taskbar.		
TEXT	Creates a single line of user-entered text.	VBAMAN	Loads, unloads, saves, creates, embeds, and extracts VBA projects.
TEXTEDIT	Edits a dimensional constraint, dimension, or text object.	VBARUN	Runs a VBA macro.
TEXTSCR	Opens the command line in a separate window.	VBASTMT	Executes a Visual Basic complete instruction in the context of the current drawing on the AutoCAD command line.
TEXTTOFRONT	Brings text and/or dimensions in front of other drawing objects.		
THICKEN	Creates a 3D solid by thickening a surface.	VBAUNLOAD	Unloads a VBA (Visual Basic for Applications) project.
TIFOUT	Creates a TIFF file from selected objects.	VIEW	Saves and restores named views.
TIME	Displays drawing date and time statistics.	VIEWGO	Navigates to a named view.
		VIEWPLAY	Plays the ShowMotion animation for the named view.
TINSERT	Inserts a block in a table cell.		

Command	Description	Command	Description
VIEWPLOTDETAILS	Displays information about completed plot and publish jobs.	WEBLIGHT	Creates a web light.
VIEWRES	Sets resolution for objects in the current viewport.	WEDGE	Creates a 3D solid wedge.
VISUALSTYLES	Creates and modifies visual styles and applies a visual style to a viewport.	WHOHAS	Displays the current user's computer name, login ID, and full name (if available) and the date and time the drawing file was opened.
-VISUALSTYLES	Creates and modifies visual styles and applies a visual style to a viewport. (command line version).	WIPEOUT	Creates a polygonal area that covers existing objects with the current background color.
VISUALSTYLESCLOSE	Closes Visual Styles Manager dialog box.	WMFIN	Imports a Windows metafile as a block.
VLISP	Opens the Visual Lisp Console window to develop, test, and debug AutoLISP programs.	WMFOPTS	Sets options for the WMFIN command.
VPCLIP	Clips viewport objects and modifies viewport boundary.	WMFOUT	Saves selected objects to a Windows metafile format.
VPLAYER	Sets layer visibility within viewports. VPLAYER can now run in Model tab with a limited set of options.	WORKSPACE	Manages workspaces.
		WSSAVE	Saves a workspace scheme and settings.
VPMAX	Enlarges current viewport to full screen and switches to model space for editing.	WSSETTINGS	Sets workspace options.
		XATTACH	Attaches a drawing as an external reference to the current drawing.
VPMIN	Restores viewport to settings prior to maximizing.	XBIND	Adds specified xref-dependent named objects to the drawing.
VPOINT	Sets 3D viewing direction.	XCLIP	Defines an external reference display clipping boundary.
VPORTS	Creates viewports in model or paper space.	XEDGES	Creates wireframe geometry by extracting edges from a 3D solid or surface.
VSCURRENT	Sets visual style in current viewport.	XLINE	Creates a line that is infinite in both directions.
VSLIDE	Opens an image slide file for viewing in the current viewport.	XOPEN	Opens an external reference for editing in a new window.
		XPLODE	Disassembles a block into its component objects for editing.
VSSAVE	Saves a visual style.		
VTOPTIONS	Controls view transitions.	XREF	Manages external references.
WALKFLYSETTINGS	Specifies walk and fly settings.	ZOOM	Changes the magnification of objects in the current viewport.
WBLOCK	Saves a block to a new drawing file.		

Command Aliases

Command aliases are shortcuts for commands that you enter at the keyboard. *Note:* Command aliases beginning with a dash (-) suppress display of dialog box windows and force input entry from the command line.

Command	Alias	Command	Alias
3DARRAY	3A	DATALINKUPDATE	DLU
3DALIGN	3AL	DBCONNECT	DBC
3DFACE	3F	DDEDIT	ED
3DMOVE	3M	DDGRIPS	GR
3DORBIT	3DO, ORBIT	DDVPOINT	VP
3DPOLY	3P	DIMALIGNED	DAL
3DROTATE	3R	DIMANGULAR	DAN
3DWALK	3DNAVIGATE, 3DW	DIMARC	DAR
ADCENTER	ADC, DC, DCENTER	DIMBASELINE	DBA
ALIGN	AL	DIMCENTER	DCE
APPLOAD	AP	DIMCONTINUE	DCO
ARC	A	DIMDIAMETER	DDI
AREA	AA	DIMDISASSOCIATE	DDA
ARRAY	AR	DIMEDIT	DED
-ARRAY	-AR	DIMJOGGED	DJO, JOG
ATTDEF	ATT	DIMJOGLINE	DJL
-ATTDEF	-ATT	DIMLINEAR	DLI
ATTEDIT	ATE	DIMORDINATE	DOR
-ATTEDIT	-ATE, ATTE	DIMOVERRIDE	DOV
ATTIPE	ATI	DIMRADIUS	DRA
BACTION	AC	DIMREASSOCIATE	DRE
BLOCK	B	DIMSTYLE	D, DST
BCLOSE	BC	DIST	DI
BEDIT	BE	DIVIDE	DIV
BOUNDARY	BO	DONUT	DO
-BOUNDARY	-BO	DRAWINGRECOVERY	DRM
BPARAMETER	PARAM	DRAWORDER	DR
BREAK	BR	DSETTINGS	DS, SE
BSAVE	BS	DVIEW	DV
BVSTATE	VS	ELLIPSE	EL
CAMERA	CAM	ERASE	E
CHAMFER	CHA	EXPLODE	X
CHANGE	-CH	EXPORT	EXP
CHECKSTANDARDS	CHK	-EXPORTTOAUTOCAD	AECTOACAD
CIRCLE	C	EXTEND	EX
COLOR	COL, COLOUR	EXTERNALREFERENCES	ER
COMMANDLINE	CLI	EXTRUDE	EXT
COPY	CO, CP	FLATSHOT	FSHOT
CTABLESTYLE	CT	GEOGRAPHICLOCATION	GEO, NORTH, NORTHDIR
-BLOCK	-B	FILLET	F
CYLINDER	CYL	FILTER	FI
DATAEXTRACTION	DX	GRADIENT	GD
DATALINK	DL	GROUP	G

Command	Alias	Command	Alias
-GROUP	-G	POLYGON	POL
HATCH	BH, H	POLYSOLID	PSOLID
-HATCH	-H	PREVIEW	PRE
HATCHEDIT	HE	PROPERTIES	CH, MO, PR, PROPS
HIDE	HI	PROPERTIESCLOSE	PRCLOSE
IMAGE	IM	PSPACE	PS
-IMAGE	-IM	PUBLISHTOWEB	PTW
IMAGEADJUST	IAD	PURGE	PU
IMAGEATTACH	IAT	-PURGE	-PU
IMAGECLIP	ICL	PYRAMID	PYR
IMPORT	IMP	QLEADER	LE
INSERT	I	QUICKCALC	QC
-INSERT	-I	QUICKCUI	QCUI
INSERTOBJ	IO	QUIT	EXIT
INTERFERE	INF	RECTANG	REC
INTERSECT	IN	REDRAW	R
JOIN	J	REDRAWALL	RA
LAYER	LA	REGEN	RE
-LAYER	-LA	REGENALL	REA
-LAYOUT	LO	REGION	REG
LAYERSTATE	LAS	RENAME	REN
LAYERSTATE	LMAN	-RENAME	-REN
LENGTHEN	LEN	RENDER	RR
LINE	L	RENDERCROP	RC
LINETYPE	LT, LTYPE	RENDERENVIRONMENT	FOG
-LINETYPE	-LT, -LTYPE	RENDERPRESETS	RFILEOPT, RP
LIST	LI, LS, SHOWMAT	RENDERWIN	RENDSCR, RW
LTSCALE	LTS	REVOLVE	REV
LINEWEIGHT	LW, LWEIGHT	ROTATE	RO
MARKUP	MSM	RPREF	RPR
MATCHPROP	MA	SCALE	SC
MATERIALMAP	SETUV	SCRIPT	SCR
MATERIALS	FINISH, MAT, RMAT	SECTION	SEC
MEASURE	ME	SECTIONPLANE	SPLANE
MIRROR	MI	SETVAR	SET
MIRROR3D	3DMIRROR	SHADEMODE	SHA
MLEADER	MLD	SHEETSET	SSM
MLEADERALIGN	MLA	SLICE	SL
MLEADERCOLLECT	MLC	SNAP	SN
MLEADEREDIT	MLE	SOLID	SO
MLEADERSTYLE	MLS	SPELL	SP
MLINE	ML	SPLINE	SPL
MOVE	M	SPLINEDIT	SPE
MSPACE	MS	STANDARDS	STA
MTEXT	MT, T	STRETCH	S
-MTEXT	-T	STYLE	ST
MVIEW	MV	SUBTRACT	SU
OFFSET	O	TABLE	TB
OPTIONS	OP	TABLESTYLE	TS
OSNAP	OS	TABLET	TA
-OSNAP	-OS	TEXT	DT
PAN	P	THICKNESS	TH
-PAN	-P	TILEMODE	TI
-PARTIALOPEN	PARTIALOPEN	TOLERANCE	TOL
PASTESPEC	PA	TOOLBAR	TO
PEDIT	PE	TOOLPALETTES	TP
PLINE	PL	TORUS	TOR
PLOT	PRINT	TRIM	TR
POINT	PO	UCSMAN	UC
POINTLIGHT	FREEPOINT	VISUALSTYLES	VSM

Command	Alias	Command	Alias
-VISUALSTYLES	-VSM	WEDGE	WE
VSCURRENT	VS	XATTACH	XA
UNION	UNI	XBIND	XB
UNITS	UN	-XBIND	-XB
-UNITS	-UN	XCLIP	XC
VIEW	V	XLINE	XL
-VIEW	-V	XREF	XR
VPOINT	-VP	-XREF	-XR
WBLOCK	W	ZOOM	Z
-WBLOCK	-W		

System Variables

AutoCAD stores the values for its operating environment and some of its commands in system variables. System variables control how the commands work. They also set default colors, sizes, and values. They store information about the drawing and the software configuration. Some system variables can be changed by the user; others are read-only.

To see a list of all system variables and their current settings type **SETVAR** at the command line, type "?", and then "*".

Use AutoCAD's Help feature for additional information about system variables and their options.

Name	Description	Type	Storage Location	Initial Value
3DCONVERSIONMODE	Used to convert material and light definitions to the current product release.	Integer	Drawing	1
3DDWFPREC	Controls the precision of 3D DWF publishing.	Integer	Drawing	2
3DSELECTIONMODE	Controls the selection precedence of visually overlapping objects when using 3D visual styles.	Integer	User-settings	1
ACADLSPACDOC	Controls loading of acad.lsp file.	Integer	Registry	0
ACADPREFIX	Stores directory path.	String	Not-Saved	pathname
ACADVER	Stores AutoCAD version number.	String	Not-Saved	(Read-only)
ACISOUTVER	Controls ACIS version of SAT files created with ACISOUT command.	Integer	Not-Saved	70
ACTPATH	System variable that stores the paths where additional Action Scripts can be found.	String	Registry	" "
ACTRECORDSTATE	Specifies the current state of the Action Recorder.	Integer	Not-Saved	0
ACTRECPATH	System Variable that stores the path where the Action Scripts are saved.	String	Registry	pathname
ACTUI	Controls the type and level of user UI feedback provided during the playback and recording phase.	Bitcode	Registry	6
ADCSTATE	Indicates whether DesignCenter™ is active.	Integer	Not-Saved	varies
AFLAGS	Sets options for attributes.	Integer	Not-Saved	16
ANGBASE	Sets base angle relative to current UCS.	Real	Drawing	0.0000
ANGDIR	Sets direction of positive angle measurement.	Integer	Drawing	0
ANNOALLVISIBLE	Hides or displays annotative objects that do not support the current annotation scale.	Integer	Drawing	1

Name	Description	Type	Storage Location	Initial Value
ANNOAUTOSCALE	Updates annotative objects to support the annotation scale when the annotation scale is changed.	Integer	Registry	-4
ANNOTATIVEDWG	Specifies whether or not the drawing will behave as an annotative block when inserted into another drawing.	Integer	Drawing	0
APBOX	Controls display of AutoSnap™ aperture box.	Integer	Registry	0
APERTURE	Controls display size for object snap target box in pixels (1–50).	Integer	Registry	10
APSTATE	Stores a value that indicates whether the **Block Authoring Palettes** window is open in the block editor.	Integer	Not-saved	0
AREA	Stores last area computed by AREA command.	Real	Not-Saved	(Read-only)
ATTDIA	Controls whether INSERT command uses dialog box.	Integer	Registry	0
ATTIPE	Controls the display of the in-place editor used to create multiline attributes.	Integer	Registry	0
ATTMODE	Controls attribute display.	Integer	Drawing	1
ATTMULTI	Controls whether multiline attributes can be created.	Integer	Registry	1
ATTREQ	Controls whether INSERT command uses default attribute settings.	Integer	Registry	1
AUDITCTL	Controls writing of audit report files.	Integer	Registry	0
AUNITS	Sets angle units.	Integer	Drawing	0
AUPREC	Sets precision of angular units.	Integer	Drawing	0
AUTODWFPUBLISH	Controls whether the AutoPublish feature is on or off.	Bitcode	Registry	0
AUTOSNAP	Controls display of AutoSnap marker, tooltip, and magnet. Turns on and off polar and object snap tracking. Controls display of polar and object snap tracking tooltips.	Integer	Registry	63
BACKGROUNDPLOT	Controls background plotting.	Integer	Registry	2
BACKZ	Stores the back clipping plane offset (in drawing units) from the target plane for the current viewport.	Real	Drawing	0.0000
BACTIONBARMODE	Indicates whether the action bars or the legacy action objects are displayed in the Block Editor.	Integer	Registry	1
BACTIONCOLOR	Sets text color for Block Editor actions.	String	Registry	7
BACZ	Controls location of back clipping plane.	Real	Drawing	None
BCONSTATUSMODE	Turns the constraint display status on and off and controls the shading of objects based on their constraint level.	Integer	Not-Saved	0
BDEPENDENCYHIGHLIGHT	Controls highlighting of dependent objects when editing blocks.	Integer	Registry	1

Name	Description	Type	Storage Location	Initial Value
BGRIPOBJCOLOR	Sets grip color in Block Editor.	String	Registry	141
BGRIPOBJSIZE	Sets custom grip size in Block Editor relative to screen display (1–256).	Integer	Registry	8
BINDTYPE	Controls naming of xrefs when binding or editing in place.	Integer	Not-Saved	0
BLIPMODE	Controls display of marker blips.	Integer	Registry	0
BLOCKEDITLOCK	Controls opening Block Editor.	Integer	Registry	0
BLOCKEDITOR	Indicates whether Block Editor is open.	Integer	Not-Saved	0
BLOCKTESTWINDOW	Indicates whether or not a test block window is current.	Integer	Not-Saved	0
BPARAMETERCOLOR	Sets parameter color in Block Editor.	String	Registry	7
BPARAMETERFONT	Sets font for parameters and action in Block Editor.	String	Registry	Simplex.shx
BPARAMETERSIZE	Sets parameter and feature text size in Block Editor relative to screen display (1–256).	Integer	Registry	12
BTMARKDISPLAY	Controls display of value set markers.	Integer	Registry	1
BPTEXTHORIZONTAL	Forces the text displayed for action parameters and constraint parameters in the Block Editor to be horizontal.	Integer	Registry	1
BVMODE	Controls display of hidden objects in Block Editor.	Integer	Not-Saved	0
CALCINPUT	Controls evaluation of mathematical expressions and global constants in windows and dialog boxes.	Integer	Registry	1
CAMERADISPLAY	Toggle whether camera objects are displayed in the current drawing.	Integer	Drawing	0
CAMERAHEIGHT	Stores the default height for newly created camera objects.	Integer	Drawing	0
CANNOSCALE	Sets the name of the current annotation scale for the current space.	String	Drawing	1:1
CANNOSCALEVALUE	Returns the value to the current annotation scale.	Real	Drawing	1
CAPTURETHUMBNAILS	Controls whether thumbnails are generated for the Rewind tool when a view is changed by a navigation tool except ViewCube, SteeringWheel, and ShowMotion, and when to generate this type of thumbnail.	Integer	Registry	1
CCONSTRAINTFORM	Controls whether annotational or dynamic constraints are applied to objects.	Integer	Registry	0
CDATE	Reads calendar date and time.	Real	Not-Saved	(Read-only)
CECOLOR	Sets new object color.	String	Drawing	BYLAYER
CELTSCALE	Sets object linetype scaling factor relative to LTSCALE setting.	Real	Drawing	1.0000
CELTYPE	Sets new object linetype.	String	Drawing	BYLAYER
CELWEIGHT	Sets new object lineweight.	Integer	Drawing	-1
CENTERMT	Controls grip stretching of horizontally centered multiline text.	Switch	User-settings	0
CHAMFERA	Sets first chamfer distance.	Real	Drawing	0.0000

Name	Description	Type	Storage Location	Initial Value
CHAMFERB	Sets second chamfer distance.	Real	Drawing	0.0000
CHAMFERC	Sets chamfer length.	Real	Drawing	0.0000
CHAMFERD	Sets chamfer angle.	Real	Drawing	0.0000
CHAMMODE	Sets CHAMFER input method.	Integer	Not-Saved	0
CIRCLERAD	Sets circle radius default value.	Real	Not-Saved	0.0000
CLAYER	Sets current layer.	String	Drawing	0
CLEANSCREENSTATE	Stores a value that indicates whether the clean screen state is on or off.	Integer	Not-Saved	0
CLISTATE	Controls display of command window.	Integer	Not-Saved	1
CMATERIAL	Sets the material of new objects.	String	Drawing	BYLAYER
CMDACTIVE	Indicates whether ordinary command, transparent command, script, or dialog box is active.	Integer	Not-Saved	None
CMDDIA	Controls command dialog box display.	Integer	Registry	1
CMDECHO	Controls echoing of prompts and input during scripts.	Integer	Not-Saved	1
CMDINPUTHISTORYMAX	Sets maximum number of previous input values stored in command prompt.	Integer	Registry	20
CMDNAMES	Displays names of active and transparent commands.	String	Not-Saved	None
CMLEADERSTYLE	Sets the name of the current multileader style.	String	Drawing	STANDARD
CMLJUST	Specifies multiline justification.	Integer	Drawing	0
CMLSCALE	Controls multiline overall width.	Real	Drawing	1.0000 (Imperial) 20.0000 (metric)
CMLSTYLE	Sets multiline style.	String	Drawing	STANDARD
COMPASS	Controls display of 3D compass in current viewport.	Integer	Not-Saved	0
CONSTRAINTBARDISPLAY	Displays constraint bars for objects after you manually apply a constraint or autoconstrain them.	Bitcode	Registry	1
CONSTRAINTBARMODE	Controls the display of geometrical constraints on constraint bars.	Bitcode	Registry	4095
CONSTRAINTNAMEFORMAT	Controls the text format for dimensional constraints.	Integer	Registry	2
CONSTRAINTRELAX	Indicates whether constraints are enforced or relaxed when editing an object.	Integer	Not-Saved	0
CONSTRAINTSOLVEMODE	Controls constraint behavior when applying or editing constraints.	Bitcode	Registry	1
COORDS	Controls updating of coordinates on status line.	Integer	Registry	1
COPYMODE	Controls whether the COPY command repeats automatically.	Integer	Registry	0
CPLOTSTYLE	Controls new object plot style.	String	Drawing	Varies
CPROFILE	Displays current profile name.	String	Registry	(Read-only) <<Unnamed Profile>>
CROSSINGAREACOLOR	Controls the color of the selection area during crossing selection.	Integer	Registry	100
CSHADOW	Sets the shadow display property for a 3D object.	Integer	Drawing	0
CTAB	Stores name of current tab in drawing (model or layout).	String	Drawing	Varies

Name	Description	Type	Storage Location	Initial Value
CTABLESTYLE	Sets current table style name.	String	Drawing	STANDARD
CURSORSIZE	Sets crosshair size as percentage of screen size (1–100 percent).	Integer	Registry	5
CVPORT	Sets identification number of current viewport.	Integer	Drawing	2
DASHBOARDSTATE	Determines whether the Dashboard window is active or not.	Integer	Not-Saved	Varies
DATALINKNOTIFY	Controls the notification for updated or missing data links.	Integer	Registry	2
DATE	Stores current date and time in Modified Julian format.	Real	Not-Saved	Varies
DBCSTATE	Stores status of cbConnect Manager.	Integer	Drawing	(Read-only) 0
DBLCLKEDIT	Controls the double-click editing behavior in the drawing area. Double-click actions can be customized using the Customize User Interface (CUI) editor. The system variable can accept the values of On and Off in place of 1 and 0.	Integer	Registry	1
DBMOD	Indicates drawing modification status.	Integer	Not-Saved	(Read-only) 0
DCTCUST	Displays path and file name of current custom spelling dictionary.	String	Registry	Pathname
DCTMAIN	Displays file name of current main spelling dictionary.	String	Registry	Varies by country/region
DEFAULTGIZMO	Sets the 3D Move, 3D Rotate, or 3D Scale gizmo as the default during subobject selection.	Integer	Not-Saved	0
DEFAULTLIGHTING	Turns default lighting on and off.	Integer	Drawing	1
DEFAULTLIGHTINGTYPE	Specifies the type of default lighting.	Integer	Drawing	1
DEFLPLSTYLE	Specifies layer 0 default plot style.	String	Registry	Varies
DEFPLYSTYLE	Specifies new object default plot style.	String	Registry	None
DELOBJ	Controls whether source objects for new object creation are retained or deleted.	Integer	Registry	1
DEMANDLOAD	Specifies if and when to demand load certain applications.	Integer	Registry	3
DGNFRAME	Determines whether DGN underlay frames are visible or plotted in the current drawing.	Integer	Drawing	0
DGNIMPORTMAX	Controls the maximum number of elements translated during DGNIMPORT.	Real	Registry	10000000
DGNMAPPINGPATH	Stores the location of the DGNSetups.INI file, which stores the DGN mapping setups.	String	Registry	C:\Documents and Settings\ <username>\ Application Data\Autodesk\ AutoCAD\ R17.2\enu\ Support

Name	Description	Type	Storage Location	Initial Value
DGNOSNAP	Controls object snapping for geometry in DGN underlays.	Integer	Registry	1
DIASTAT	Specifies exit method for most recently used dialog box.	Integer	Not-Saved	None
DIMADEC	Controls angular dimension precision display.	Integer	Drawing	0
DIMALT	Controls display of dimension alternate units.	Switch	Drawing	OFF
DIMALTD	Controls precision of alternate units.	Integer	Drawing	2
DIMALTF	Controls multiplier for alternate units.	Real	Drawing	25.4
DIMALTRND	Rounds off alternate dimension units.	Real	Drawing	0.00
DIMALTTD	Sets tolerance value precision for alternate dimension units.	Integer	Drawing	2
DIMALTTZ	Controls tolerance value zero suppression.	Integer	Drawing	0
DIMALTU	Sets units format for alternate units of all secondary dimension styles except Angular.	Integer	Drawing	2
DIMALTZ	Controls alternate unit dimension value zero suppression.	Integer	Drawing	0
DIMANNO	Indicates whether or not the current dimension style is annotative.	Integer	Drawing	Based on current style
DIMAPOST	Specifies text prefix or suffix for alternate dimension values, except for angular dimensions.	String	Drawing	None
DIMARCSYM	Controls display of the arc symbol in an arc length dimension.	Integer	Drawing	0
DIMASO	Controls dimension object associativity. Obsolete— replaced by DIMASSOC.	Switch	Drawing	On
DIMASSOC	Controls dimension object associativity.	Integer	Drawing	2
DIMASZ	Controls dimension line and leader line arrowhead size.	Real	Drawing	0.1800
DIMATFIT	Controls spacing of dimension text and arrows when both will not fit between extension lines.	Integer	Drawing	3
DIMAUNIT	Sets angular dimension unit format.	Integer	Drawing	0
DIMAZIN	Suppresses angular dimension zeros.	Integer	Drawing	0
DIMBLK	Controls arrowhead style.	String	Drawing	None
DIMBLK1	Controls arrowhead style for first end of dimension line when DIMSAH is on.	String	Drawing	None
DIMBLK2	Controls arrowhead style for second end of dimension line when DIMSAH is on.	String	Drawing	None
DIMCEN	Controls drawing of circle and arc center marks or centerlines.	Real	Drawing	0.0900
DIMCLRD	Controls colors of dimension lines, arrowheads and leader lines.	Integer	Drawing	0
DIMCLRE	Controls colors of dimension extension lines.	Integer	Drawing	0

Name	Description	Type	Storage Location	Initial Value
DIMCLRT	Controls color of dimension text.	Integer	Drawing	0
DIMCONSTRAINTICON	Displays the lock icon next to the text for dimensional constraints.	Bitcode	Registry	3
DIMDEC	Sets precision of primary dimension units.	Integer	Drawing	4
DIMDLE	Sets dimension line extension beyond extension line for oblique line arrowhead style.	Real	Drawing	0.0000
DIMDLI	Controls dimension line spacing for baseline dimensions.	Real	Drawing	0.3800
DIMDSEP	Specifies decimal format dimension separator.	Single-character	Drawing	Decimal point
DIMEXE	Specifies distance extension line extends beyond dimension line.	Real	Drawing	0.1800
DIMEXO	Specifies extension line offset distance from origin points.	Real	Drawing	0.0625
DIMFIT	Preserves script integrity. Replaced by DIMATFIT and DIMTMOVE.	Integer	Drawing	3
DIMFRAC	Sets fraction format for architectural or fractional dimensions.	Integer	Drawing	0
DIMFXL	Sets the total length of the extension lines starting from the dimension line toward the dimension origin.	Real	Drawing	1
DIMFXLON	Controls whether extension lines are set to a fixed length.	Switch	Drawing	Off
DIMGAP	Sets distance around dimension text when text is between dimension lines.	Real	Drawing	0.0900
DIMJOGANG	Determines the angle of the transverse segment of the dimension line in a jogged radius dimension.	Real	Drawing	45° (90° Metric)
DIMJUST	Controls horizontal placement of dimension text.	Integer	Drawing	0
DIMLDRBLK	Specifies leader arrow type.	String	Drawing	None
DIMLFAC	Sets linear dimension measurement scale factor.	Real	Drawing	1.0000
DIMLIM	Generates dimension limits as default text.	Switch	Drawing	Off
DIMLTEX1	Sets the linetype of the first extension line.	String	Drawing	" "
DIMLTEX2	Sets the linetype of the second extension line.	String	Drawing	" "
DIMLTYPE	Sets the linetype of the dimension line.	String	Drawing	" "
DIMLUNIT	Sets units for all dimension types, except Angular.	Integer	Drawing	2
DIMLWD	Assigns dimension line lineweight.	Enum	Drawing	-2
DIMLWE	Assigns extension line lineweight.	Enum	Drawing	-2
DIMPOST	Specifies text prefix or suffix for dimension measurements.	String	Drawing	None
DIMRND	Sets rounding increment for dimension distances.	Real	Drawing	0.0000

Name	Description	Type	Storage Location	Initial Value
DIMSAH	Controls dimension line arrowhead display.	Switch	Drawing	Off
DIMSCALE	Sets overall dimensioning variable scale factor.	Real	Drawing	1.0000
DIMSD1	Controls first dimension line suppression.	Switch	Drawing	Off
DIMSD2	Controls second dimension line suppression.	Switch	Drawing	Off
DIMSE1	Controls first extension line suppression.	Switch	Drawing	Off
DIMSE2	Controls second extension line suppression.	Switch	Drawing	Off
DIMSHO	Preserves script integrity.	Switch	Drawing	On
DIMSOXD	Controls display of dimension lines outside extension lines.	Switch	Drawing	Off
DIMSTYLE	Stores name of current dimension style.	String	Drawing	(Read-only) STANDARD
DIMTAD	Controls vertical location of dimension text relative to dimension line.	Integer	Drawing	0
DIMTDEC	Sets precision of tolerance value display for primary dimension units.	Integer	Drawing	4
DIMTFAC	Specifies scale factor for fraction and tolerance value text relative to dimension text height.	Real	Drawing	1.0000
DIMTFILL	Controls the background of dimension text.	Integer	Drawing	0
DIMTFILLCLR	Sets the color for the text background in dimensions.	Integer	Drawing	0
DIMTIH	Controls dimension text position inside extension lines, except for ordinate dimensioning.	Switch	Drawing	On
DIMTIX	Positions dimension text between extension lines.	Switch	Drawing	Off
DIMTM	Sets lower tolerance limit for dimension text when DIMTOL or DIMLIM is on.	Real	Drawing	0.0000
DIMTMOVE	Sets dimension text movement rules.	Integer	Drawing	0
DIMTOFL	Controls drawing of dimension line between extension lines.	Switch	Drawing	Off
DIMTOH	Controls dimension text position outside extension lines.	Switch	Drawing	Off
DIMTOL	Adds tolerances to dimension text.	Switch	Drawing	Off
DIMTOLJ	Sets tolerance value vertical justification relative to nominal dimension text.	Integer	Drawing	1
DIMTP	Sets upper tolerance limit for dimension text when DIMTOL or DIMLIM is on.	Real	Drawing	0.0000
DIMTSZ	Specifies size of oblique line arrowhead style.	Real	Drawing	0.0000
DIMTVP	Controls vertical placement of dimension text relative to dimension line.	Real	Drawing	0.0000
DIMTXSTY	Specifies dimension text style.	String	Drawing	STANDARD
DIMTXT	Specifies dimension text height unless current text style has fixed height.	Real	Drawing	0.1800

Name	Description	Type	Storage Location	Initial Value
DIMTXTDIRECTION	Specifies the reading direction of the dimension text.	Integer	Drawing	0
DIMTZIN	Controls zero suppression in tolerance values.	Integer	Drawing	0
DIMUNIT	Obsolete—replaced by DIMLUNIT and DIMFRAC. Retained to preserve script integrity.	Integer	Drawing	2
DIMUPT	Controls options for dimension user-positioned text.	Switch	Drawing	Off
DIMZIN	Controls zero suppression in primary dimension unit values.	Integer	Drawing	0
DISPSLIH	Controls silhouette curve display for solid objects in wireframe display mode.	Integer	Drawing	0
DISTANCE	Stores value computed by DIST command.	Real	Not-Saved	None
DIVMESHBOXHEIGHT	Sets the number of subdivisions for the height of a mesh box along the Z axis.	Integer	User-settings	3
DIVMESHBOXLENGTH	Sets the number of subdivisions for the length of a mesh box along the X axis.	Integer	User-settings	3
DIVMESHBOXWIDTH	Sets the number of subdivisions for the width of a mesh box along the Y axis.	Integer	User-settings	3
DIVMESHCONEAXIS	Sets the number of subdivisions around the perimeter of the mesh cone base.	Integer	User-settings	8
DIVMESHCONEBASE	Sets the number of subdivisions between the perimeter and the center point of the mesh cone base.	Integer	User-settings	3
DIVMESHCONEHEIGHT	Sets the number of subdivisions between the base and the point or top of the mesh cone.	Integer	User-settings	3
DIVMESHCYLAXIS	Sets the number of subdivisions around the perimeter of the mesh cylinder base.	Integer	User-settings	8
DIVMESHCYLBASE	Sets the number of subdivisions around the perimeter of the mesh cylinder base.	Integer	User-settings	3
DIVMESHCYLHEIGHT	Sets the number of subdivisions between the base and the top of the mesh cylinder.	Integer	User-settings	3
DIVMESHPYRBASE	Sets the number of radial subdivisions between the center of the mesh pyramid base and its perimeter.	Integer	User-settings	3
DIVMESHPYRHEIGHT	Sets the number of subdivisions between the base and the top of the mesh pyramid.	Integer	User-settings	3
DIVMESHPYRLENGTH	Sets the number of subdivisions along each dimension of a mesh pyramid base.	Integer	User-settings	3
DIVMESHSPHEREAXIS	Sets the number of radial subdivisions around the axis endpoint of the mesh sphere.	Integer	User-settings	12
DIVMESHSPHEREHEIGHT	Sets the number of subdivisions between the two axis endpoints of the mesh sphere.	Integer	User-settings	6

Name	Description	Type	Storage Location	Initial Value
DIVMESHTORUSPATH	Sets the number of subdivisions in the path that is swept by the profile of a mesh torus.	Integer	User-settings	8
DIVMESHTORUSECTION	Sets the number of subdivisions in the profile that sweeps the path of a mesh torus.	Integer	User-settings	8
DIVMESHWEDGEBASE	Sets the number of subdivisions between the midpoint of the perimeter of the triangular dimension of the mesh wedge.	Integer	User-settings	3
DIVMESHWEDGEHEIGHT	Sets the number of subdivisions for the height of the mesh wedge along the Z axis.	Integer	User-settings	3
DIVMESHWEDGELENGTH	Sets the number of subdivisions for the length of a mesh wedge along the X axis.	Integer	User-settings	4
DIVMESHWEDGESLOPE	Sets the number of subdivisions in the slope that extends from the apex of the wedge to the edge of the base.	Integer	User-settings	3
DIVMESHWEDGEWIDTH	Sets the number of subdivisions for the width of the mesh wedge along the Y axis.	Integer	User-settings	3
DONUTID	Sets default value for donut inside diameter.	Real	Not-Saved	0.5000
DONUTOD	Sets default value for donut outside diameter.	Real	Not-Saved	1.0000
DRAGMODE	Controls visibility of objects during dragging.	Integer	Registry	2
DRAGP1	Sets regen-drag input sampling rate.	Integer	Registry	10
DRAGP2	Sets fast-drag input sampling rate.	Integer	Registry	25
DRAGVS	Sets the visual style while creating 3D objects.	String	Drawing	Current visual style
DRAWORDERCTL	Controls draw order functionality	Integer	Drawing	3
DRSTATE	Controls Drawing Recovery window.	Integer	Not-Saved	Varies
DTEXTED	Controls user interface for editing text.	Integer	Registry	0
DWFFRAME	Determines whether the DWF frame is visible and if it will plot.	Integer	Drawing	2
DWFOSNAP	Determines whether object snapping is enabled for DWF underlays.	Integer	Registry	1
DWGCHECK	Checks drawings for problems when opening.	Integer	Registry	0
DWGCODEPAGE	Stores same value as SYSCODEPAGE (for compatibility reasons).	String	Drawing	(Read-only)
DWGNAME	Stores drawing name entered by user.	String	Not-Saved	Drawing.dwg
DWGPREFIX	Stores drive/directory prefix for drawing.	String	Not-Saved	(Read-only)
DWGTITLED	Indicates current drawing naming status.	Integer	Not-Saved	0
DXEVAL	Controls when data extraction tables are compared against the data source, and if the data is not current, displays an update notification.	Integer	Drawing	12

Name	Description	Type	Storage Location	Initial Value
DYNCONSTRAINTDISPLAY	Displays or hides dynamic constraints.	Integer	Registry	1
DYNDIGRIP	Controls dynamic dimension display during grip stretch editing.	Bitcode	Registry	31
DYNDIVIS	Controls number of dynamic dimensions displayed during grip stretch editing.	Integer	User-settings	1
DYNMODE	Turns Dynamic Input features on and off.	Integer	User-settings	3
DYNPICOORDS	Controls type of coordinate, relative or absolute, used for pointer input.	Switch	User-settings	0
DYNPIFORMAT	Controls type of coordinate, polar or Cartesian, used for pointer input.	Switch	User-settings	0
DYNPIVIS	Controls pointer input display.	Integer	User-settings	1
DYNPROMPT	Controls Dynamic Input tooltip prompt display.	Integer	User-settings	1
DYNTOOLTIPS	Controls which tooltips are impacted by tooltip appearance settings.	Switch	User-settings	0
EDGEMODE	Controls cutting and boundary edge behavior in TRIM and EXTEND commands.	Integer	Registry	0
ELEVATION	Stores current elevation of new objects relative to active UCS.	Real	Drawing	0.0000
ENTERPRISEMENU	Stores CUI file name including path.	String	Registry	(Read-only) "."
ERRNO	Displays error code number when AutoLISP function causes error detected by AutoCAD.	Integer	Not-Saved	(Read-only) 0
ERSTATE	Determines whether the External References window is inactive, active/visible, or active/auto-hidden.	Integer	Not-Saved	Varies
EXPERT	Controls display of selected warning prompts.	Integer	Not-Saved	0
EXPLMODE	Controls whether EXPLODE command supports nonuniformly scaled blocks.	Integer	Not-Saved	1
EXTMAX	Stores upper-right coordinates of drawing extents.	3D-point	Drawing	Varies
EXTMIN	Stores lower-left coordinates of drawing extents.	3D-point	Drawing	Varies
EXTNAMES	Sets named object name parameters.	Integer	Drawing	1
FACETERDEVNORMAL	Sets the maximum angle between the surface normal and contiguous mesh faces.	Real	User-settings	40
FACETRATIO	Controls faceting aspect ratio for cylindrical and conic ShapeManager solids.	Integer	Not-Saved	0
FACETRES	Adjusts smoothness of shaded and rendered objects and objects with hidden lines removed (0.01–10.0).	Real	Drawing	0.5
FACETERDEVSURFACE	Sets how closely the converted mesh object adheres to the original shape of the solid or surface.	Real	User-settings	0.001

Name	Description	Type	Storage Location	Initial Value
FACETERGRIDRATIO	Sets the maximum aspect ratio for the mesh subdivisions that are created for solids and surfaces converted to mesh.	Real	User-settings	0.0000
FACETERMAXEDGELENGTH	Sets the maximum length of edges for mesh objects that are created by conversion from solids and surfaces.	Real	User-settings	0.0000
FACETERMAXGRID	Sets the maximum number of U and V grid lines for solids and surfaces converted to mesh.	Integer	User-settings	4096
FACETERMESHTYPE	Sets the type of mesh to be created.	Integer	User-settings	0
FACETERMINUGRID	Sets the minimum number of U grid lines for solids and surfaces that are converted to mesh.	Integer	User-settings	0
FACETERMINVGRID	Sets the minimum number of V grid lines for solids and surfaces that are converted to mesh.	Integer	User-settings	0
FACETERPRIMITIVEMODE	Specifies whether smoothness settings for objects that are converted to mesh are derived from the Mesh Tessellation Options or the Mesh Primitive Options dialog box.	Bitcode	User-settings	1
FACETERSMOOTHLEV	Sets the default level of smoothness for objects that are converted to mesh.	Integer	User-settings	1
FIELDDISPLAY	Controls field background display.	Integer	Registry	1
FIELDEVAL	Controls timing of field updates.	Integer	Drawing	31
FILEDIA	Controls display of file navigation dialog boxes.	Integer	Registry	1
FILLETRAD	Stores current fillet radius.	Real	Drawing	0.0000
FILLMODE	Controls display of filled objects.	Integer	Drawing	1
FONTALT	Specifies alternate font used when specified font cannot be found.	String	Registry	simplex.shx
FONTMAP	Specifies font mapping file.	String	Registry	acad.fmp
FRAME	Turns the display of frames on and off for all external references; images; and DWF, DWFx, PDF, and DGN underlays.	Integer	Drawing	3
FRONTZ	Stores back clipping plane location.	Real	Drawing	None
FULLOPEN	Indicates whether drawing is partially open.	Integer	Not-Saved	(Read-only)
FULLPLOTPATH	Controls whether plot spooler is sent full path of drawing file.	Integer	Registry	1
GEOLATLONGFORMAT	Controls the format of the Latitude/Longitude representation in the drawing.	Integer	Drawing	0
GEOMARKERVISIBILITY	Controls the visibility of geographic markers.	Integer	Drawing	1
GRIDDISPLAY	Controls the display behavior and display limits of the grid.	Bitcode	Drawing	3
GRIDMAJOR	Controls the frequency of major grid lines compared to minor grid lines.	Integer	Drawing	5
GRIDMODE	Controls grid display.	Integer	Drawing	0
GRIDUNIT	Specifies the grid spacing (*X* and *Y*) for the current viewport.	2D-point	Drawing	0.500,0.500 (Imperial) or 10, 10 (Metric)

Name	Description	Type	Storage Location	Initial Value
GRIPSUBOBJMODE	Sets whether edge, face, or vertex grips are active upon initial selection.	Bitcode	User-settings	1
GRIPBLOCK	Controls block grip locations.	Integer	Registry	0
GRIPCOLOR	Controls the color of nonselected grips.		Registry	150
GRIPDYNCOLOR	Controls dynamic block custom grip color.	Integer	Registry	140
GRIPHOT	Controls the color of selected grips (drawn as filled boxes).	Integer	Registry	12
GRIPHOVER	Controls the color of hoover grips (drawn as filled boxes).	Integer	Registry	11
GRIPOBJLIMIT	Sets object number limit for selection set and suppresses grip display when limit is exceeded (1–32,767).	Integer	Registry	100
GRIPS	Turns grips on and off.	Integer	Registry	1
GRIPSIZE	Sets size of grip box in pixels (1–255).	Integer	Registry	5
GRIPTIPS	Controls display of grip tips.	Integer	Registry	1
GTAUTO	Controls whether or not grip tools display automatically when selecting objects in 3D space.	Integer	Registry	1
GTDEFAULT	Controls whether or not the 3DMOVE, 3DROTATE, and 3DSCALE commands start automatically when the MOVE, ROTATE, and SCALE commands (respectively) are started in a 3D view.	Integer	Registry	0
GTLOCATION	Sets the default location for grip tools.	Integer	Registry	0
HALOGAP	Sets size of gap to be displayed when an object is hidden by another.	Integer	Drawing	0
HANDLES	Preserves integrity of scripts. Handles are always on.	Integer	Drawing	(Read-only) ON
HIDEPRECISION	Controls hide and shade accuracy.	Integer	Not-Saved	0
HIDETEXT	Specifies whether text objects are included in HIDE command.	Integer	Drawing	1
HIDEXREFSCALES	Controls the display of Xref scales. 0—Xref scales are displayed, 1—Xref scales are hidden.	Integer	Registry	1
HIGHLIGHT	Controls object highlighting.	Integer	Not-saved	1
HPANG	Specifies hatch pattern angle.	Real	Not-saved	0
HPASSOC	Controls associativity of hatch patterns and gradient fills.	Integer	Registry	1
HPBOUND	Controls object type created by BHATCH and BOUNDARY commands.	Integer	Not-Saved	1
HPDOUBLE	Specifies hatch pattern doubling for user-created patterns.	Integer	Not-Saved	0
HPDRAWORDER	Controls draw order of hatches and fills.	Integer	Not-Saved	3
HPGAPTOL	Sets allowable gap in hatch boundary.	Real	Registry	0

Name	Description	Type	Storage Location	Initial Value
HPINHERIT	Controls how MATCHPROP copies hatch origin from source to destination object.	Integer	Drawing	0
HPMAXLINES	Controls the maximum number of hatch lines that will generate. Values can be set at a minimum of 100 and a maximum of 10,000,000.	Real	Registry	1000000
HPNAME	Creates default hatch pattern name.	String	Not-Saved	ANSI131
HPOBJWARNING	Sets number of hatch boundary objects that can be selected before triggering a warning message.	Integer	Registry	10000
HPORIGIN	Sets hatch origin point for new hatch objects.	2D-point	Drawing	0,0
HPORIGINMODE	Controls determination of default hatch origin point.	Integer	Registry	0
HPSCALE	Specifies hatch pattern scale factor.	Real	Not-Saved	1.0000
HPSEPARATE	Controls number of hatch objects created when HATCH operates on multiple closed boundaries.	Integer	Registry	0
HPSPACE	Specifies pattern line spacing for user-created hatch patterns.	Real	Not-saved	1.0000
HYPERLINKBASE	Specifies the path used for all relative hyperlinks in the drawing. If no value is specified, the drawing path is used for all relative hyperlinks.	String	Drawing	" "
IMAGEHLT	Controls highlighting of raster images.	Integer	Registry	0
IMPLIEDFACE	Controls the detection of implied faces.	Integer	Registry	1
INDEXCTL	Controls whether layer and spatial indexes are created and saved in drawing files.	Integer	Registry	0
INETLOCATION	Stores Internet location used by BROWSER command and Browse the Web dialog box.	String	Registry	http://www.autodesk.com
INPUTHISTORYMODE	Controls the content and location of the display of a history of user input.	Bitcode	Registry	15
INSBASE	Stores insertion base point set by BASE.	3D-point	Drawing	0.0000, 0.0000
INSNAME	Sets default block name for INSERT command.	String	Not-Saved	" "
INSUNITS	Specifies drawing units value for automatic scaling of blocks, images, or xrefs inserted or attached to a drawing.	Integer	Drawing	1
INSUNITSDEFSOURCE	Sets source content units value (0–20).	Integer	Registry	1
INSUNITSDEFTARGET	Sets target drawing units value (0–20).	Integer	Registry	1
INTELLIGENTUPDATE	Controls graphic refresh rate.	Integer	Registry	20
INTERFERECOLOR	Sets the color of interference objects.	Integer	Drawing	1
INTERFEREOBJVS	Sets the visual style for interference objects.	String	Drawing	Realistic
INTERFEREVPVS	Sets the visual style for the current viewport while using the INTERFERENCE command.	String	Drawing	Wireframe

Name	Description	Type	Storage Location	Initial Value
INTERSECTIONCOLOR	Sets color of intersection polylines.	Integer	Drawing	257
INTERSECTIONDISPLAY	Controls display of intersection polylines.	Switch	Drawing	Off
ISAVEBAK	Controls creation of backup files (BAK).	Integer	Registry	1
ISAVEPERCENT	Sets allowable amount of wasted space in a drawing file (0–100).	Integer	Registry	50
ISOLINES	Sets number of contour lines on surfaced objects (0–2047).	Integer	Drawing	4
LARGEOBJECTSUPPORT	Controls large object size limit support when you open and save drawings.	Integer	Registry	0
LASTANGLE	Stores end angle of last arc created.	Real	Not-Saved	(Read-only) 0
LASTPOINT	Stores last point entered.	3D-point	Not-Saved	0.0000, 0.0000
LASTPROMPT	Stores last string echoed to the command line.	String	Not-Saved	" "
LATITUDE	Specifies the latitude of the drawing model.	Real	Drawing	Varies
LAYEREVAL	Controls when the Unreconciled New Layer filter list in the Layer Properties Manager is evaluated for new layers.	Integer	Drawing	1
LAYEREVALCTL	Controls the overall unreconciled new layer filter list in the **Layer Properties Manager** dialog box, which is evaluated for new layers.	Integer	User-settings	1
LAYERFILTERALERT	Controls layer filters.	Integer	Registry	2
LAYERMANAGERSTATE	Returns a value indicating whether the **Layer Properties Manager** dialog box is open or closed.	Integer	Not-saved	Varies
LAYERNOTIFY	Specifies when an alert displays for new layers that have not yet been reconciled.	Bitcode	Drawing	15
LAYLOCKFADECTL	Controls the dimming for objects on locked layers.	Integer	Registry	50
LAYOUTREGENCTL	Controls display list updates in model and layout tabs.	Integer	Registry	2
LEGACYCTRLPICK	Specifies the keys for selection cycling and the behavior for <Ctrl> + left-click.	Integer	Registry	0
LENSLENGTH	Stores lens length used if perspective viewing.	Real	Drawing	(Read-only) 50.0000
LIGHTGLYPHDISPLAY	Controls whether light glyphs are displayed.	Integer	Drawing	1
LIGHTINGUNITS	Controls whether generic or photometric lights are used, and indicates the current lighting units.	Integer	Drawing	0
LIGHTLISTSTATE	Indicates whether the Lights in Model window is open or closed.	Integer	Not-Saved	0
LIGHTSINBLOCKS	Controls whether lights contained in blocks are used when rendering.	Integer	Drawing	0
LIMCHECK	Controls object creation outside grid limits.	Integer	Drawing	0
LIMMAX	Stores coordinates of upper-right grid limits.	2D-point	Drawing	12.0000, 9.0000

Name	Description	Type	Storage Location	Initial Value
LIMMIN	Stores coordinates of lower-left grid limits.	2D-point	Drawing	0.0000, 0.0000
LINEARBRIGHTNESS	Controls the global brightness level of the drawing in the standard lighting workflow.	Integer	Drawing	0
LINEARCONTRAST	Controls the global contrast level of the drawing in the standard lighting workflow.	Integer	Drawing	0
LOCALE	Returns code indicating current locale.	String	Not-Saved	(Read-only) " "
LOCALROOTPREFIX	Stores path to root folder where local customizable files installed.	String	Registry	(Read-only) "pathname"
LOCKUI	Locks position and size of toolbars and windows.	Bitcode	Registry	0
LOFTANG1	Sets the draft angle through the first cross-section in a loft operation.	Real	Drawing	90
LOFTANG2	Sets the draft angle through the last cross-section in a loft operation.	Real	Drawing	90
LOFTMAG1	Sets the magnitude of draft angle through the first cross-section in a loft operation.	Integer	Drawing	1
LOFTMAG2	Sets the magnitude of draft angle through the last cross-section in a loft operation.	Integer	Drawing	1
LOFTNORMALS	Controls the normals of a lofted object where it passes through cross-sections.	Integer	Drawing	1
LOFTPARAM	Controls the shape of lofted solids and surfaces.	Bitcode	Drawing	7
LOGEXPBRIGHTNESS	Controls the global brightness level of the drawing when using photometric lighting.	Real	Drawing	65.0
LOGEXPCONTRAST	Controls the global contrast level of the drawing when using photometric lighting.	Real	Drawing	50.0
LOGEXPDAYLIGHT	Controls if exterior daylight is used when using photometric lighting.	Integer	Drawing	2
LOGEXPHYSICALSCALE	Controls the relative brightness of self-illuminated materials in a photometric environment.	Integer	Drawing	2
LOGEXPMIDTONES	Controls the global midtones level of the drawing when using photometric lighting.	Real	Drawing	1.0
LOGFILEMODE	Controls creation of log file.	Integer	Registry	0
LOGFILENAME	Specifies path and name of log file for current drawing.	String	Drawing	(Read-only) Varies
LOGFILEPATH	Specifies path for log files for all session drawings.	String	Drawing	"c:\Documents and Settings\ username\ LocalSettings\ ApplicationData\ Autodesk\ application_ name\release_ number\ locale_code"
LOGINNAME	Displays user's name.	String	Not-Saved	" "
LONGITUDE	Specifies the longitude of the drawing model.	Real	Drawing	Varies

Name	Description	Type	Storage Location	Initial Value
LTSCALE	Sets global linetype scale factor.	Real	Drawing	1.0000
LUNITS	Sets linear unit type.	Integer	Drawing	2
LUPREC	Sets precision for all read-only linear units.	Integer	Drawing	4
LWDEFAULT	Sets default lineweight value.	Enum	Registry	25
LWDISPLAY	Controls lineweight display.	Integer	Drawing	0
LWUNITS	Sets lineweight display unit as inches or millimeters.	Integer	Registry	1
MATSTATE	Indicates whether the Materials window is open or closed.	Integer	Not-Saved	0
MAXACTVP	Sets maximum number of active layout viewports.	Integer	Drawing	64
MAXSORT	Sets maximum number of symbol or block names sorted by listing commands.	Integer	Registry	1000
MBUTTONPAN	Controls pointing device third button or wheel behavior.	Integer	Registry	1
MEASUREINIT	Sets default units, Imperial or Metric, for drawing started from scratch.	Integer	Registry	Varies by country/region
MEASUREMENT	Sets units, Imperial or Metric, for hatch patterns and linetype files.	Integer	Drawing	0
MENUBAR	Controls the display of the menu bar.	Integer	Registry	0
MENUCTL	Controls screen menu page switching.	Integer	Registry	1
MENUECHO	Sets menu echo and prompt control bits.	Integer	Not-Saved	0
MENUNAME	Stores customization file name and path.	String	Registry	(Read-only) "customization _file_name"
MESHTYPE	Controls the type of mesh that is created by REVSURF, TABSURF, RULESURF and EDGESURF.	Bitcode	Drawing	1
MIRRTEXT	Controls text mirroring.	Integer	Drawing	0
MLEADERSCALE	Sets the overall scale factor applied to multileader objects.	Real	Drawing	1.0000
MODEMACRO	Displays a text string on the status line.	String	Not-Saved	" "
MSLTSCALE	Scales linetypes displayed on the Model tab by the annotation scale.	Real	Drawing	1
MSMSTATE	Stores a value that indicates whether the Markup Set Manager is open or closed.	Integer	Not-Saved	0
MSOLESCALE	Controls scale of an OLE object pasted into model space.	Real	Drawing	1.0
MTEXTCOLUMN	Sets the default column setting for an mtext object.	Integer	Drawing	2
MTEXTED	Defines application for editing multiline text.	String	Registry	"Internal"
MTEXTFIXED	Obsolete.	Integer	Registry	0
MTEXTTOOLBAR	Controls the display of the In-Place Text Editor.	Integer	User-settings	2
MTJIGSTRING	Sets content of sample text for MTEXT command.	String	Registry	"abc"
MYDOCUMENTSPREFIX	Stores full path to My Documents folder for current user.	String	Registry	(Read-only) "pathname"
NAVSWHEELMODE	Mode of the SteeringWheel.	Integer	Registry	0
NAVSWHEELOPACITYBIG	Controls the opacity of the big SteeringWheels.	Integer	Registry	50

Name	Description	Type	Storage Location	Initial Value
NAVSWHEELOPACITYMINI	Controls the size of the mini SteeringWheels.	Integer	Registry	50
NAVSWHEELSIZEBIG	Specifies the size of the big Steering Wheels.	Integer	Registry	1
NAVSWHEELSIZEMINI	Specifies the size of the mini Steering Wheels.	Integer	Registry	1
NAVVCUBEDISPLAY	Controls the display of the ViewCube on the canvas when the 3D graphic system is active.	Integer	Drawing	1
NAVVCUBELOCATION	Controls the display location of the ViewCube.	Integer	Registry	0
NAVVCUBEORIENT	Controls whether the ViewCube always reflects the WCS.	Integer	Registry	1
NAVVCUBESIZE	Controls the display size of the ViewCube.	Integer	Registry	1
NAVVCUBOPACITY	Controls the opacity of ViewCube when it is inactive.	Integer	Registry	50
NEWTRANSIENTAPI	Controls which version of APIs are used for 2D and 3D objects.	Integer	Registry	1
NOMUTT	Controls message display.	Short	Not-Saved	0
NORTHDIRECTION	Specifies the angle of the Sun from north.	Real	Drawing	Varies
OBSCUREDCOLOR	Sets obscured line color.	Integer	Drawing	257
OBSCUREDLTYPE	Sets obscured line linetype.	Integer	Drawing	0
OFFSETDIST	Sets offset distance default value.	Real	Not-Saved	1.0000
OFFSETGAPTYPE	Controls polyline gaps when polyline is offset.	Integer	Registry	0
OLEFRAME	Controls OLE object frame display and plotting.	Integer	Drawing	2
OLEHIDE	Controls OLE object display and plotting.	Integer	Registry	0
OLEQUALITY	Sets OLE object default plot quality.	Integer	Registry	3
OLESTARTUP	Controls loading of OLE source applications.	Integer	Drawing	0
OPENPARTIAL	Controls whether visible objects in a layout display as a drawing is being opened.	Integer	Registry	1
OPMSTATE	Stores a value that indicates whether the Properties palette is open, closed, or hidden.	Integer	Not-Saved	0
ORTHOMODE	Controls Ortho mode.	Integer	Drawing	0
OSMODE	Sets running Object Snap modes using the following bitcodes.	Integer	Registry	4133
OSNAPCOORD	Controls conflicts between running object snaps and entered coordinates.	Integer	Registry	2
OSNAPNODELEGACY	Controls whether the Node object snap can be used to snap to multiline text objects.	Integer	Registry	0
OSNAPZ	Controls projection of object snaps.	Integer	Not-Saved	0
OSOPTIONS	Automatically suppresses object snaps on hatch objects and when using a dynamic UCS.	Bitcode	Registry	3
PALETTEOPAQUE	Controls window transparency.	Integer	Registry	0
PAPERUPDATE	Controls print warning dialog display.	Integer	Registry	0

Name	Description	Type	Storage Location	Initial Value
PARAMETERCOPYMODE	Controls how constraints and referenced variables are copied when replicating constrained geometry.	Integer	Registry	1
PARAMETERSSTATUS	Indicates whether the Parameters Manager palette is displayed or hidden.	Integer	Registry	0
PDFFRAME	Determines whether the PDF underlay frame is visible.	Integer	Drawing	1
PDFOSNAP	Determines whether object snapping is active for geometry in PDF underlays that are attached to the drawing.	Integer	Registry	1
PDMODE	Sets point object symbol.	Integer	Drawing	0
PDSIZE	Sets point object display size.	Real	Drawing	0.0000
PEDITACCEPT	Controls display of PEDIT prompt.	Integer	Registry	0
PELLIPSE	Controls ellipse type.	Integer	Drawing	0
PERIMETER	Stores last perimeter computed by AREA or LIST command.	Real	Not-Saved	0.0000
PERSPECTIVE	Specifies whether the current viewport displays a perspective working view.	Integer	Drawing	Varies
PERSPECTIVECLIP	Determines the location of eyepoint clipping. The value determines where the eyepoint clipping occurs as a percentage. Values can range between 0.01 and 10.0. If you select a small value, the z-values of objects will be compressed at the target view and beyond. If you select a value such as 0.5%, the clipping will appear very close to the eyepoint of the view. In some extreme cases, it might be appropriate to use 0.1%, but it is recommended to change the setting to a higher value such as 5%.	Real	User-settings	5
PFACEVMAX	Sets maximum vertices per face.	Integer	Not-Saved	(Read-only) 4
PICKADD	Controls object selection.	Integer	Registry	1
PICKAUTO	Controls automatic windowing for object selection.	Integer	Registry	1
PICKBOX	Sets object selection target height in pixels.	Integer	Registry	3
PICKDRAG	Controls selection window drawing method.	Integer	Registry	0
PICKFIRST	Controls object selection order.	Integer	Registry	1
PICKSTYLE	Controls group and associative hatch selection.	Integer	Registry	1
PLATFORM	Stores name of platform in use.	String	Not-Saved	(Read-only) Varies
PLINEGEN	Controls polyline linetype generation around vertices.	Integer	Drawing	0
PLINETYPE	Controls type of polyline.	Integer	Registry	2
PLINEWID	Stores default polyline width.	Real	Drawing	0.0000
PLOTOFFSET	Controls location of plot offset.	Integer	Registry	0
PLOTROTMODE	Controls plot orientation.	Integer	Registry	2
PLQUIET	Controls display of plot dialog boxes and nonfatal errors.	Integer	Registry	0

Name	Description	Type	Storage Location	Initial Value
POLARADDANG	Controls user-defined polar angles.	String	Registry	" "
POLARANG	Sets polar angle increment.	Real	Registry	90
POLARDIST	Sets polar snap increment.	Real	Registry	0.0000
POLARMODE	Controls polar and object snap tracking settings.	Integer	Registry	0
POLYSIDES	Sets POLYGON default side number (3–1024).	Integer	Not-Saved	4
POPUPS	Displays status of current display driver.	Integer	Not-Saved	(Read-only) 1
PREVIEWEFFECT	Specifies display method for previewing selection of objects.	Integer	Registry	2
PREVIEWFILTER	Controls object types included in selection previewing.	Bitcode	Registry	1
PREVIEWTYPE	Controls the view to use for generating the thumbnail when the drawing is saved.	Integer	Drawing	0
PRODUCT	Returns product name.	String	Not-Saved	(Read-only) "AutoCAD"
PROGRAM	Returns program name.	String	Not-Saved	(Read-only) "acad"
PROJECTNAME	Assigns project name to current drawing.	String	Drawing	" "
PROJMODE	Sets projection mode for trimming or extending.	Integer	Registry	1
PROXYGRAPHICS	Controls saving of proxy object images.	Integer	Drawing	1
PROXYNOTICE	Controls proxy warning display.	Integer	Registry	1
PROXYSHOW	Controls proxy object display.	Integer	Registry	1
PROXYWEBSEARCH	Controls checking for object enablers.	Integer	Registry	1
PSLTSCALE	Controls paper space linetype scaling.	Integer	Drawing	1
PSOLHEIGHT	Sets the default height for a swept solid object created with the POLYSOLID command.	Real	Drawing	4 (Imperial) or 80 (Metric)
PSOLWIDTH	Sets the default width for a swept solid object created with the POLYSOLID command.	Real	Registry	0.25 (Imperial) or 5 (Metric)
PSTYLEMODE	Controls plot style table type.	Integer	Drawing	(Read-only) 1
PSTYLEPOLICY	Controls association of color with plot style.	Integer	Registry	1
PSVPSCALE	Sets view scale factor for new viewports.	Real	Drawing	0
PUBLISHALLSHEETS	Controls how the Publish dialog list is populated.	Integer	Registry	1
PUBLISHCOLLATE	Controls whether sheets are published as a single job.	Integer	User-settings	1
PUBLISHHATCH	Controls whether hatch patterns published to DWF format are treated as a single object when they are opened in Autodesk Impression.	Integer	Registry	1
PUCSBASE	Stores UCS name defining origin and orientation of orthographic UCS settings in paper space.	String	Drawing	" "
QCSTATE	Activates QuickCalc calculator.	Integer	Not-Saved	(Read-only) Varies
QPLOCATION	Sets the location mode of Quick Properties panel.	Integer	Registry	0
QPMODE	Sets the on or off state of Quick Properties panel.	Integer	Registry	1

Name	Description	Type	Storage Location	Initial Value
QTEXTMODE	Controls text display.	Integer	Drawing	0
QVDRAWINGPIN	Controls the default display state of preview images of drawings.	Integer	Registry	0
QVLAYOUTPIN	Controls the default display state of preview images of model space and layouts in a drawing.	Integer	Registry	0
RASTERDPI	Controls paper size and plot scaling when converting from dimensional to dimensionless output devices (100–32,767).	Integer	Registry	300
RASTERPERCENT	Sets the maximum percentage of available virtual memory that is allowed for plotting a raster image.	Integer	Registry	20
RASTERPREVIEW	Controls creation of BMP preview images.	Integer	Registry	1
RASTERTHRESHOLD	Specifies a raster threshold in megabytes. If the plotted raster image exceeds this threshold, the availability of system memory is checked.	Integer	Registry	20
RECOVERYMODE	Controls recording of drawing recovery information after system failure.	Integer	Registry	2
REFEDITNAME	Displays name of edited reference.	String	Not-Saved	" "
REGENMODE	Controls automatic drawing regeneration.	Integer	Drawing	1
RE-INIT	Reinitializes digitizer, digitizer port, and acad.pgp file.	Integer	Not-Saved	0
REMEMBERFOLDERS	Controls default path stored in standard file selection dialog boxes.	Integer	Registry	1
RENDERPREFSSTATE	Stores a value that indicates whether the Advanced Render Settings palette is open.	Integer	Not-saved	0
RENDERUSERLIGHTS	Controls whether user-lights are translated during rendering.	Integer	Drawing	1
REPORTERROR	Controls reporting of errors to Autodesk.	Integer	Registry	1
RIBBONCONTEXTSELECT	Controls how ribbon contextual tabs are displayed when you single- or double-click an object.	Integer	User-settings	1
RIBBONCONTEXTSELLIM	Suppresses the display of ribbon contextual tabs when the selection set includes more than the specified number of objects.	Integer	User-settings	2500
RIBBONSELECTMODE	Determines whether a pick first selection set remains selected after a ribbon contextual tab is invoked and the command is completed.	Integer	User-setting	1
RIBBONSTATE	Determines whether the Ribbon window is active or not.	Integer	Not-saved	1
ROAMABLEROOTPREFIX	Stores path to folder where roamable customizable files are stored.	String	Registry	(Read-only) "pathname"
ROLLOVERTIPS	Controls the display of rollover tooltips in the application.	Integer	Registry	1

Name	Description	Type	Storage Location	Initial Value
RTDISPLAY	Controls raster image and OLE content display during Realtime ZOOM and PAN.	Integer	Registry	1
SAVEFIDELITY	Controls whether the drawing is saved with visual fidelity.	Bitcode	Registry	1
SAVEFILE	Saves name of current automatic save file.	String	Registry	(Read-only) "c:\Documents and Settings\ username\ LocalSettings\ TEMP\ Drawing1.dwg"
SAVEFILEPATH	Specifies path to directory for all automatic save files in current session.	String	Registry	"c:\Documents and Settings\ username\Local Settings\TEMP\"
SAVENAME	Stores file name and directory path for most recently saved drawing.	String	Not-Saved	(Read-only) " "
SAVETIME	Sets automatic save interval, in minutes.	Integer	Registry	10
SCREENBOXES	Stores number of boxes in screen menu area.	Integer	Not-Saved	(Read-only) 0
SCREENMODE	Indicates display state.	Integer	Not-Saved	(Read-only) 3
SCREENSIZE	Stores current viewport size in pixels.	2D-point	Not-Saved	(Read-only) Varies
SELECTIONANNODISPLAY	Controls whether alternate scale representations are temporarily displayed in a dimmed state when an annotative object is selected.	Integer	Registry	1
SELECTIONAREA	Controls display effects for selection areas.	Integer	Registry	1
SELECTIONAREAOPACITY	Controls selection area opacity during window and crossing selection (0–100).	Integer	Registry	25
SELECTIONPREVIEW	Controls selection previewing display.	Bitcode	Registry	3
SETBYLAYERMODE	Controls which properties are selected for SETBYLAYER.	Integer	User-settings	127
SHADEDGE	Controls edge shading in rendering.	Integer	Drawing	3
SHADEDIF	Sets ratio of diffuse reflective light to ambient light.	Integer	Drawing	70
SHADOWPLANELOCATION	Controls the location of an invisible ground plane used to display shadows.	Integer	Drawing	0
SHORTCUTMENU	Controls display of Default, Edit, and Command mode shortcut menus.	Integer	Registry	11
SHOWHIST	Controls the Show History property for solids in a drawing.	Integer	Drawing	1
SHOWLAYERUSAGE	Controls Layer Properties Manager layer icon display.	Integer	Registry	1
SHOWMOTIONPIN	Controls the default state for ShowMotion. The setting of this system variable is cross session.	Integer	Registry	1
SHPNAME	Sets default shape name.	String	Not-Saved	" "
SIGWARN	Controls digital signature warning.	Integer	Registry	1

Name	Description	Type	Storage Location	Initial Value
SKETCHIN	Sets SKETCH command record increment.	Real	Drawing	0.1000
SKPOLY	Sets SKETCH command to create lines or polylines.	Integer	Drawing	0
SMOOTHMESHCONVERT	Sets whether mesh objects that you convert to 3D solids or surfaces are smoothed or faceted, and whether their faces are merged.	Bitcode	User-settings	0
SMOOTHMESHGRID	Sets the maximum level of smoothness at which the underlying mesh facet grid is displayed on 3D mesh objects.	Integer	User-settings	3
SMOOTHMESHMAXFACE	Sets the maximum number of faces permitted for mesh objects.	Integer	User-settings	1000000
SMOOTHMESHMAXLEV	Sets the maximum smoothness level for mesh objects.	Integer	User-settings	4
SNAPANG	Sets snap and grid rotation angle for current viewport.	Real	Drawing	0
SNAPBASE	Sets snap and grid origin point for current viewport.	2D-point	Drawing	0.0000, 0.0000
SNAPISOPAIR	Controls isometric plane for current viewport.	Integer	Drawing	0
SNAPMODE	Turns Snap on and off.	Integer	Drawing	0
SNAPSTYLE	Sets snap style for current viewport.	Integer	Drawing	0
SNAPTYPE	Sets snap type for current viewport.	Integer	Registry	0
SNAPUNIT	Sets snap spacing for current viewport.	2D-point	Drawing	0.5000, 0.5000
SOLIDCHECK	Controls solid validation.	Integer	Not-Saved	1
SOLIDHIST	Controls the default History property setting for new and existing objects.	Integer	Drawing	1
SORTENTS	Controls object sorting in support of draw order for several operations.	Integer	Drawing	127
SPLFRAME	Controls spline and spline-fit polyline display.	Integer	Drawing	0
SPLINESEGS	Sets number of segments in each spline-fit polyline.	Integer	Drawing	8
SPLINETYPE	Sets curve type for spline-fit polylines.	Integer	Drawing	6
SSFOUND	Displays sheet set path and file name.	String	Not-Saved	(Read-only) " "
SSLOCATE	Controls opening of associated sheet sets when drawing is opened.	Integer	User-settings	1
SSMAUTOOPEN	Controls Sheet Set Manager display when drawing is opened.	Integer	User-settings	1
SSMPOLLTIME	Sets time interval for automatic refreshes of sheet set status data.	Integer	Registry	60
SSMSHEETSTATUS	Controls refreshing of sheet set status data.	Integer	Registry	2
SSMSTATE	Activates Sheet Set Manager.	Integer	Not-saved	(Read-only) Varies
STANDARDSVIOLATION	Controls standards violation notification.	Integer	Registry	2
STARTUP	Controls display of Create New Drawing dialog box.	Integer	Registry	0
STATUSBAR	Controls the display of the application and drawing status bars.	Integer	Registry	1

Name	Description	Type	Storage Location	Initial Value
STEPSIZE	Specifies the step size in current units when users are in Walk mode.	Real	Drawing	6.000
STEPSPERSEC	Specifies the number of steps taken per second when users are in Walk mode.	Real	Drawing	2
SUBOBJSELECTIONMODE	Filters whether a face, edge, orvertex is selected with <Ctrl>+<Click>.	Integer	Not-saved	0
SUNPROPERTIESSTATE	Indicates whether the Sun Properties window is open or closed.	Integer	Not-saved	0
SUNSTATUS	Controls whether the Sun is casting light in the viewport.	Integer	Drawing	1
SURFTAB1	Sets tabulation number for RULESURF and TABSURF commands and M mesh density for REVSURF and EDGESURF.	Integer	Drawing	6
SURFTAB2	Sets N mesh density for REVSURF and EDGESURF.	Integer	Drawing	6
SURFTYPE	Controls surface type for PEDIT smooth option.	Integer	Drawing	6
SURFU	Sets M surface density for PEDIT smooth.	Integer	Drawing	6
SURFV	Sets N surface density for PEDIT smooth.	Integer	Drawing	6
SYSCODEPAGE	Returns system code page.	String	Not-Saved	(Read-only) " "
TABLEINDICATOR	Controls row and column label display for table cell text editor.	Integer	User-Settings	1
TABLETOOLBAR	Controls the display of the Table toolbar.	Integer	Registry	2
TABMODE	Controls tablet use.	Integer	Not-Saved	0
TARGET	Stores location of target point for current viewport.	3D-point	Drawing	(Read-only) 0.0000, 0.0000
TBCUSTOMIZE	Controls customization of toolbars.	Switch	Registry	1
TDCREATE	Stores local time and date of drawing creation.	Real	Drawing	(Read-only) Varies
TDINDWG	Stores total drawing editing time.	Real	Drawing	(Read-only) Varies
TDUCREATE	Stores universal time and date of drawing creation.	Read	Drawing	(Read-only) Varies
TDUPDATE	Stores local time and date of last drawing update/save.	Real	Drawing	(Read-only) Varies
TDUSRTIMER	Stores user-elapsed timer.	Real	Drawing	(Read-only) Varies
TDUUPDATE	Stores universal time and date of last drawing update/save.	Real	Drawing	(Read-only) Varies
TEMPOVERRIDES	Controls temporary override keys.	Integer	Registry	1
TEMPREFIX	Contains directory name for temporary file placement.	String	Not-Saved	(Read-only) "c:\Documents and Settings \username\Local Settings\Temp\"
TEXTEVAL	Controls evaluation of text strings entered with TEXT or -TEXT.	Integer	Not-Saved	0
TEXTFILL	Controls TrueType font fill when plotting and rendering.	Integer	Registry	1
TEXTOUTPUTFILEFORMAT	Provides Unicode options for plot and text window log files.	Integer	Registry	0

Name	Description	Type	Storage Location	Initial Value
TEXTQLTY	Sets TrueType font outline resolution tessellation fineness for plotting and rendering (0–100).	Integer	Not-Saved	50
TEXTSIZE	Sets default text height for current style.	Real	Drawing	0.2000
TEXTSTYLE	Sets name of current text style.	String	Drawing	STANDARD
THICKNESS	Sets current 3D thickness.	Real	Drawing	0.0000
THUMBSIZE	Controls the display of the ViewCube on the canvas when the 3D graphic system is active.	Integer	Registry	1
TILEMODE	Makes Model tab or last layout tab active.	Integer	Drawing	1
TIMEZONE	Sets the time zone for a sun study.	Enum	Drawing	-8000
TOOLTIPMERGE	Combines drafting tooltips into a single tooltip. The appearance of the merged tooltip is controlled by the settings in the Tooltip Appearance dialog box.	Switch	User-settings	0
TOOLTIPS	Controls tooltip display.	Integer	Registry	1
TPSTATE	Indicates whether Tool Palettes window is active.	Integer	Not-Saved	(Read-only) Varies
TRACEWID	Sets default trace width.	Real	Drawing	0.0500
TRACKPATH	Controls polar and object snap tracking alignment path display.	Integer	Registry	0
TRAYICONS	Controls Status Bar tray display.	Integer	Registry	1
TRAYNOTIFY	Controls display of service notifications in Status Bar tray.	Integer	Registry	1
TRAYTIMEOUT	Controls display time for service notifications.	Integer	Registry	5
TREEDEPTH	Controls spatial index tree branches.	Integer	Drawing	3020
TREEMAX	Controls number of nodes in spatial index.	Integer	Registry	10000000
TRIMMODE	Controls trimming of chamfers and fillets.	Integer	Registry	1
TSPACEFAC	Controls multiline line spacing expressed as a factor of text height (.25–4.0).	Real	Not-Saved	1.0
TSPACETYPE	Controls multiline line spacing type.	Integer	Registry	1
TSTACKALIGN	Controls stacked text vertical alignment.	Integer	Drawing	1
TSTACKSIZE	Controls stacked text fraction height expressed as percentage of text height (25–125).	Integer	Drawing	70
UCSAXISANG	Stores default UCS rotation angle for $X, Y, Z,$ option of UCS command.	Integer	Registry	90
UCSBASE	Stores name of UCS that defines origin and orientation of orthographic UCS settings.	String	Drawing	WORLD
UCSDETECT	Controls whether dynamic UCS acquisition is active or not.	Integer	Drawing	1
UCSFOLLOW	Generates a plan view when UCS changes.	Integer	Drawing	0

Name	Description	Type	Storage Location	Initial Value
UCSICON	Controls UCS icon display.	Integer	Drawing	3
UCSNAME	Stores name of current coordinate system for current viewport in current space.	String	Drawing	(Read-only)
UCSORG	Stores origin point of current coordinate system for current viewport in current space.	3D-point	Drawing	(Read-only)
UCSORTHO	Determines whether related UCS is restored when an orthographic view is restored.	Integer	Registry	1
UCSVIEW	Determines whether current UCS is saved with named view.	Integer	Registry	1
UCSVP	Determines whether UCS in viewports remains fixed or changes to reflect the UCS of the current viewport.	Integer	Drawing	1
UCSXDIR	Stores X direction of current UCS for current viewport in current space.	3D-point	Drawing	(Read-only) 1.0000, 0.0000, 0.0000
UCSYDIR	Stores Y direction of current UCS for current viewport in current space.	3D-point	Drawing	(Read-only) 0.0000, 1.0000, 0.0000
UNDOCTL	Stores state of Auto, Control, and Group options of UNDO command.	Integer	Not-Saved	(Read-only) 21
UNDOMARKS	Stores number of marks set in UNDO command by Mark option.	Integer	Not-Saved	(Read-only) 0
UNITMODE	Controls unit display format.	Integer	Drawing	0
UOSNAP	Determines whether object snapping is active for geometry in DWF, DWFx, PDF, and DGN underlays that are attached to the drawing.	Integer	Registry	1
UPDATETHUMBNAIL	Controls Sheet Set Manager thumbnail preview updates.	Bitcode	Drawing	15
USERI1-5	Provides storage and retrieval of integer values.	Integer	Drawing	0
USERR1-5	Provides storage and retrieval or real numbers.	Real	Drawing	0.0000
USERS1-5	Provides storage and retrieval of text string data.	String	Not-Saved	" "
VIEWCTR	Stores current viewport center.	3D-point	Drawing	(Read-only) Varies
VIEWDIR	Stores current viewport viewing direction.	3D-vector	Drawing	(Read-only) None
VIEWMODE	Stores current viewport View mode.	Integer	Drawing	(Read-only)
VIEWSIZE	Stores current viewport view height.	Real	Drawing	(Read-only) Varies
VIEWTWIST	Stores current viewport twist angle.	Real	Drawing	(Read-only) 0
VISRETAIN	Controls x-ref dependent layer properties.	Integer	Drawing	1
VPLAYEROVERRIDES	Indicates if there are any layers with viewport (VP) property overrides for the current layout viewport.	Integer	Drawing	1

Name	Description	Type	Storage Location	Initial Value
VPLAYEROVERRIDESMODE	Controls whether layer property overrides associated with layout viewports are displayed and plotted.	Integer	Registry	1
VPMAXIMIZEDSTATE	Indicates whether viewport is maximized.	Integer	Not-Saved	(Read-only) 0
VPROTATEASSOC	Controls whether the view within a viewport is rotated with the viewport when the viewport is rotated.	Integer	User-settings	1
VSBACKGROUNDS	Controls whether backgrounds are displayed in the current viewport.	Integer	Drawing	1
VSEDGECOLOR	Sets the color of edges.	String	Drawing	7
VSEDGEJITTER	Controls the degree to which lines are made to appear as though sketched with a pencil.	String	Drawing	-2
VSEDGEOVERHANG	Makes lines extend beyond their intersection, for a hand-drawn effect.	Integer	Drawing	-6
VSEDGES	Controls the types of edges that are displayed in the viewport.	Integer	Drawing	1
VSEDGESMOOTH	Specifies the angle at which crease edges are displayed.	Integer	Drawing	1
VSFACECOLORMODE	Controls how the color of faces is calculated.	Integer	Drawing	0
VSFACEHIGHLIGHT	Controls the display of specular highlights on faces without materials in the current viewport. The range is -100 to 100. The higher the number, the larger the highlight. Objects with materials attached ignore the setting of VSFACEHIGHLIGHT when VSMATERIALMODE is on.	Integer	Drawing	-30
VSFACEOPACITY	Controls the transparency of faces in the current viewport. The range is -100 to 100. At 100, the face is completely opaque. At 0, the face is completely transparent. Negative values set the transparency level but turn off the effect in the drawing.	Integer	Drawing	-60
VSFACESTYLE	Controls how faces are displayed in the current viewport.	Integer	Drawing	1
VSHALOGAP	Sets the halo gap in the visual style applied to the current viewport.	Integer	Drawing	1
VSHIDEPRECISION	Controls the accuracy of hides and shades in the visual style applied to the current viewport.	Integer	Not-Saved	0
VSINTERSECTIONCOLOR	Specifies the color of intersection polylines in the visual style applied to the current viewport.	Integer	Drawing	7

Name	Description	Type	Storage Location	Initial Value
VSINTERSECTIONEDGES	Specifies the display of intersection edges in the visual style applied to the current viewport.	Switch	Drawing	0
VSINTERSECTIONLTYPE	Controls whether obscured lines are displayed in the current viewport and sets their linetype.	Integer	Drawing	1
VSISOONTOP	Displays isolines on top of shaded objects in the visual style applied to the current viewport.	Integer	Drawing	0
VSLIGHTINGQUALITY	Sets the lighting quality in the current viewport.	Integer	Drawing	1
VSMATERIALMODE	Controls the display of materials in the current viewport.	Integer	Drawing	0
VSMAX	Stores coordinate of upper-right corner of current viewport's virtual screen.	3D-point	Drawing	(Read-only) Varies
VSMIN	Stores coordinate of lower-left corner of current viewport's virtual screen.	3D-point	Drawing	(Read-only) Varies
VSMONOCOLOR	Sets the color for monochrome display of faces.	String	Drawing	255,255,255
VSOBSCUREDCOLOR	Specifies the color of obscured lines in the visual style applied to the current viewport.	String	Drawing	BYENTITY
VSOBSCUREDEDGES	Controls whether obscured (hidden) edges are displayed.	Integer	Drawing	1
VSOBSCUREDLTYPE	Specifies the linetype of obscured lines in the visual style applied to the current viewport.	Integer	Drawing	1
VSSHADOWS	Controls whether a visual style displays shadows.	Integer	Drawing	0
VSSILHEDGES	Controls display of silhouette curves of solid objects in the visual style applied to the current viewport.	Integer	Drawing	0
VSSILHWIDTH	Specifies the width in pixels for display of silhouette edges in the current viewport.	Integer	Drawing	5
VSSTATE	Stores a value that indicates whether the Visual Styles window is open.	Integer	Not-Saved	0
VTDURATION	Sets smooth view transition duration (0–5000).	Integer	Registry	750
VTENABLE	Controls use of smooth view transitions.	Integer	Registry	3
VTFPS	Sets smooth view transition minimum speed (1.0–30.0).	Real	Registry	7.0
WHIPARC	Controls circle and arc display smoothness.	Integer	Registry	0
WHIPTHREAD	Controls multithreaded processing.	Integer	Registry	1
WINDOWAREACOLOR	Controls the color of the transparent selection area during window selection. The valid range is 1 to 255. SELECTIONAREA must be on.	Integer	Registry	150
WMFBKGND	Controls background display of Windows metafile objects.	Integer	Not-Saved	Off

Name	Description	Type	Storage Location	Initial Value
WMFFORGND	Controls foreground color for Windows metafile objects.	Integer	Not-Saved	Off
WORLDUCS	Indicates whether UCS is same as WCS.	Integer	Not-Saved	(Read-only) 1
WORLDVIEW	Determines whether input to DVIEW, VPOINT, 3DORBIT is relative to WCS or current UCS.	Integer	Drawing	1
WRITESTAT	Indicates write status of drawing file.	Integer	Not-Saved	(Read-only) 1
WSCURRENT	Returns name of current workspace and sets workspace to current.	String	Not-Saved	AutoCAD Default
XCLIPFRAME	Controls xref clipping boundary visibility.	Integer	Drawing	0
XDWGFADECTL	Controls the dimming for all DWG xref objects.	Integer	Registry	70
XEDIT	Controls availability of in-place reference editing.	Integer	Drawing	1
XFADECTL	Controls fading intensity percentage for references edited in place (0–90).	Integer	Registry	50
XLOADCTL	Controls xref demand loading.	Integer	Registry	2
XLOADPATH	Creates path for storing temporary copies of demand-loaded xref files.	String	Registry	"pathname"
XREFCTL	Controls creation of external reference log files.	Integer	Registry	0
XREFNOTIFY	Controls notification for updated or missing xrefs.	Integer	Registry	2
XREFTTYPE	Controls default reference type when attaching or overlaying an xref.	Integer	Registry	0
ZOOMFACTOR	Controls magnification changes when mouse wheel moves (3–100).	Integer	Registry	60
ZOOMWHEEL	Allows users to toggle the behavior of mouse wheel zoom operations.	Integer	Registry	0

Express Tools

Express Tools are additional productivity tools originally developed by users and unsupported by Autodesk, which extend the power of AutoCAD's basic commands. They cover a wide range of functions. All Express Tools can be entered at the command line; some are accessible through the Express Tools ribbon, the Express pull-down menu and the Express toolbars.

Express Tools are automatically installed with a full software installation or a custom installation with the Express Tool option selected. To activate Express Tools, enter **EXPRESSTOOLS** at the command line to load the library of tools. If the Express menu is not present, enter **EXPRESSMENU** to display the menu.

Tool Name	Description	Ribbon	Command Line	Toolbar	Express Menu
ALIASEDIT	Creates, modifies, and deletes command aliases.	Express Tools	ALIASEDIT		Tools – Command Alias Editor
ALIGNSPACE	Adjusts a viewport's zoom factor and position based on model space and/or paper space alignment points.	Express Tools	ALIGNSPACE		Layout – Align Space
ARCTEXT	Aligns text with a specified arc.	Express Tools	ARCTEXT	Express Tools Text	Text – Arc Aligned Text
ATTIN	Imports block attribute values from an external file.	Express Tools	ATTIN		Blocks – Import Attribute Information
ATTOUT	Exports block attribute values to an external file.	Express Tools	ATTOUT		Blocks – Export Attribute Information
BCOUNT	Counts blocks.	Express Tools	BCOUNT		
BLOCK?	Lists objects in block.	Express Tools	BLOCK?		
BLOCKREPLACE	Replaces block with another.	Express Tools	BLOCKREPLACE		Blocks – Replace block with another block
BLOCKTOXREF	Replaces block with xref.	Express Tools	BLOCKTOXREF		Blocks – Convert block to xref
BREAKLINE	Draws a breakline.	Express Tools	BREAKLINE	Express Tools Standard	Draw – Break line Symbol
BSCALE	Scales blocks.	Express Tools	BSCALE		Blocks – Scale blocks
BURST	Explodes block and converts attribute values to text.	Express Tools	BURST	Express Tools Block	Blocks – Explode Attributes to Text
CDORDER	Arranges object draw order based on color number.	Express Tools	CDORDER		
CHURLS	Changes a URL.	Express Tools	CHURLS		Web – Change URLs
CLIPIT	Clips xrefs or images with curves or lines.	Express Tools	CLIPIT	Express Tools Block	Modify – Extended Clip
CLOSEALL	Closes all open drawings prompting to save changes.	Express Tools	CLOSEALL		File tools – Close All Drawings
COPYM	Copies objects with options for repeat, array, divide, and measure.	Express Tools	COPYM	Express Tools Standard	Modify – Multiple copy
DIMEX	Exports dimension style to an external file.	Express Tools	DIMEX		Dimension – Dimstyle Export

Tool Name	Description	Ribbon	Command Line	Toolbar	Express Menu
DIMIN	Imports named dimension styles to drawing.	Express Tools	DIMIN		Dimstyle – Import
DIMREASSOC	Restores dimension value to measured value.	Express Tools	DIMREASSOC		Dimension – Reset Dim Text Value
DUMPSHX	Converts SHX files to SHP files.	Express Tools	See Express Help. This is an Operating System command.		
DWGLOG	Useful in network environments; identifies user of drawing.	Express Tools	DWGLOG		
EDITTIME	Tracks active editing time.	Express Tools	EDITTIME		Tools – Dwg Editing Time
EXOFFSET	Enhanced offset command.	Express Tools	EXOFFSET		Modify – Extended Offset
EXPLAN	Enhanced plan command.	Express Tools	EXPLAN		Tools – Plan View
EXPRESS-MENU	Loads Express Tool menu and displays menu on menu bar.	Express Tools	EXPRESSMENU		
EXPRESS-TOOLS	Loads Express Tools libraries. Adds Express directory to search path. Enables Express menu.	Express Tools	EXPRESSTOOLS		
EXTRIM	Enhanced trim command. Extends cutting edge options.	Express Tools	EXTRIM		
FASTSELECT	Creates selection set from objects touching selected object.	Express Tools	FS	Express Tools Standard	Selection – Fast Select
FLATTEN	Creates 2D drawing from 3D object.	Express Tools	FLATTEN		
FULLSCREEN	Hides title and menu bars to maximize drawing area.	Express Tools	FULLSCREEN, FULLSCREENON, FULLSCREENOFF, FULLSCREENOP-TIONS		Tools – Full Screen AutoCAD
GATTE	Globally edits attribute values for selected block.	Express Tools	GATTE		
GETSEL	Creates temporary selection set.	Express Tools	GETSEL		Selection – Get Selection Set
IMAGEDIT	Launches image editing program.	Express Tools	IMAGEDIT		File tools – Image edit
JULIAN	Performs calendar conversions.	Express Tools	DATE		
LAYOUTMERGE	Merges selected layouts into one.	Express Tools	LAYOUTMERGE, - LAYOUTMERGE		Layout – Merge layout(s)
LSP	Displays AutoLISP commands.	Express Tools	LSP		
LSPSURF	Displays AutoLISP file contents.	Express Tools	LSPSURF		
MKLTYPE	Makes a linetype from selected objects.	Express Tools	MKLTYPE		Tools – Make Linetype
MKSHAPE	Makes an AutoCAD shape from selected objects.	Express Tools	MKSHAPE		Tools – Make Shape
MOCORO	Moves, copies, rotates, and scales with a single command.	Express Tools	MOCORO	Express Tools Standard	Modify – Move Copy Rotate
MOVEBAK	Changes storage location for BAK files.	Express Tools	MOVEBAK		
MPEDIT	Like PEDIT but with multiple polyline capabilities.	Express Tools	MPEDIT		

Tool Name	Description	Ribbon	Command Line	Toolbar	Express Menu
MSTRETCH	Allows more than one crossing window or polygon selection for a stretch operation.	Express Tools	MSTRETCH	Express Tools Standards	Modify – Multiple Object Stretch
NCOPY	Copies nested objects in an xref or block.	Express Tools	NCOPY	Express Tools Block	Blocks – Copy Nested Objects
OVERKILL	Removes duplicate objects and overlapping lines and arcs.	Express Tools	OVERKILL, - OVERKILL		
PLT2DWG	Imports HPGL files retaining colors.	Express Tools	PLT2DWG		File tools – Convert PLT to DWG
PROPULATE	Manages Drawing Properties data.	Express Tools	PROPULATE		File tools – Updates Drawing Properties data
PSBSCALE	Scales blocks relative to paper space.	Express Tools	PSBSCALE		Blocks – Paper space block scale
PSTSCALE	Scales model space text to correct height in paperspace.	Express Tools	PSTSCALE		Text – Paper space text height
QLATTACH	Attaches leader line to mtext, tolerance or a block.	Express Tools	QLATTACH		Dimension - Leader Tools – Attach Leader to Annotation
QLATTACHSET	Attaches leader lines to AutoCAD 13 objects.	Express Tools	QLATTACHSET		Dimension - Leader Tools – Global Attach Leader to Annotation
QLDEATACHSET	Globally detaches leaders from annotation objects.	Express Tools	QLDETACHSET		Dimension - Leader Tools – Detach Leaders from Annotation
QQUIT	Closes all open drawings and exits AutoCAD.	Express Tools	QQUIT		File tools – Quick ext
REDIR	Redefines file paths in xrefs, images, shapes, styles, and rtext.	Express Tools	REDIR		File tools – Path Substitution
REDIRMODE	Sets object types or REDIR command.	Express Tools	REDIRMODE, -REDIRMODE		
REPRULS	Find and replace function for URL addresses.	Express Tools	REPURLS		Web – Replace URLs
REVERT	Closes and reopens current drawing saving changes.	Express Tools	REVERT		File – Revert
RTEDIT	Edit remote text objects.	Express Tools	RTEDIT		
RTEXT	Creates reactive text.	Express Tools	RTEXT		Text – Remote Text
RTUCS	Rotates UCS dynamically.	Express Tools	RTUCS	Express Tools UCS	Tools – Realtime UCS
SAVEALL	Saves all open drawings keeping drawings open.	Express Tools	SAVEALL		File tools – Save All Drawings
SHOWURLS	Displays all embedded URLs for viewing or editing.	Express Tools	SHOWURLS	Express Tools Standard	Web – Show URLs
SHP2BLK	Converts existing shape to block.	Express Tools	SHP2BLK		Modify – Convert Shape to Block
SSX	Creates a selected set.	Express Tools	SSX		
SUPERHATCH	Extends HATCH command to permit use of additional types of hatch patterns.	Express Tools	SUPERHATCH	Express Tools Standard	Draw – Super Hatch
SYSVDLG	Manages system variable settings.	Express Tools	SYSVDLG		Tools – System Variable Editor
TCASE	Changes case of text.	Express Tools	TCASE, -TCASE		Text – Change text case
TCIRCLE	Encloses selected text with a circle, slot, or rectangle.	Express Tools	TCIRCLE		Text – Enclose Text with Object
TCOUNT	Adds numbering to text objects.	Express Tools	TCOUNT		Text – Automatic Text Numbering

Tool Name	Description	Ribbon	Command Line	Toolbar	Express Menu
TEXTFIT	Fits text to selected start and end points.	Express Tools	TEXTFIT	Express Tools Text	Text – Text Fit
TEXTMASK	Places a mask behind selected text.	Express Tools	TEXTMASK	Express Tools Text	Text – Text Mask
TEXTUNMASK	Removes mask created by TEXTMASK.	Express Tools	TEXTUNMASK		Text – Unmask Text
TFRAMES	Toggles frames for wipeout and image objects on and off.	Express Tools	TFRAMES	Express Tools Standard	
TJUST	Changes justification for text without moving text.	Express Tools	TJUST		Text – Justify Text
TORIENT	Adjusts rotated block text to horizontal or right-read.	Express Tools	TORIENT		Text – Orient Text
TREX	Combines TRIM and EXTEND commands.	Express Tools	TREX		
TSCALE	Scales text, mtext, attributes, and attribute definitions.	Express Tools	TSCALE		Text – Scale Text
TXT2MTXT	Converts TEXT or DTEXT objects to MTEXT.	Express Tools	TXT2MTXT		Text – Convert Text to Mtext
TXTEXP	Explodes text into lines and arcs.	Express Tools	TXTEXP	Express Tools Text	Text – Explode Text
VPSCALE	Displays viewport scale factor.	Express Tools	VPSCALE		Layout – List Viewport Scale
VPSYNC	Synchronizes one or more viewports with a master.	Express Tools	VPSYNC		Layout – Synchronize Viewports
XDLIST	Lists extended object data for selected object.	Express Tools	XDLIST		Tools – List Object Xdata
XLIST	Extends LIST command to nested objects in blocks or xrefs.	Express Tools	XLIST, -XLIST	Express Tools Block	Blocks – List Xref/ Block Objects
XDATA	Attaches extended object data to an object.	Express Tools	XDATA		Tools – Xdata Attachment

Glossary

absolute coordinate entry: The process of specifying a point by typing in a coordinate. The coordinate is measured from the origin or 0,0 point in the drawing.

acquired point: Object tracking feature used to locate a point as an intermediate location in order to locate temporary alignment paths. Acquired points show up as a small cross in the drawing. Some points are acquired by simply placing your cursor over key object definition points while other acquired points require selecting a point with your mouse.

animation: A video file created by recording successive positions of the 3D model, giving the impression of movement when replayed.

annotate: To add text, notes, and dimensions to a drawing to communicate a complete design by indicating materials, locations, distances, and other key information.

array: A circular or rectangular pattern of objects.

associativity: A link between drawing objects and dimension objects. Associative dimensions will update and follow the drawing objects to which they are linked.

attenuation: Proportional reduction of light intensity over distance. You can select three different attenuations for point lights and spot lights: **None, Inverse Linear**, and **Inverse Square**.

autosave: The practice of AutoCAD automatically saving your drawing at regular intervals. The default save interval is 10 minutes. Autosave files have a .5V$ file extension by default and are automatically deleted when the drawing is closed normally.

AutoTracking: AutoCAD feature that helps you to draw objects at specific angles or in specific relationships to other objects. When you turn on AutoTracking, temporary alignment paths help you create objects at precise positions and angles. Both orthogonal and polar tracking are available.

block attribute: A dynamic text-like object that can be included in a block definition to store alphanumeric data. Attribute values can be preset, specified when the block is inserted, or updated anytime during the life of a drawing. Attribute data can be automatically extracted from a drawing and output to an AutoCAD table or an external file.

block definition: A user-defined collection of drawing objects assigned a base point and a name that is stored centrally in a drawing. A block can be inserted in a drawing multiple times as a block reference. When a block definition is updated, all block references with the same name are automatically updated.

block reference: An instance of a block definition inserted in a drawing that references the central block definition drawing data. All that is stored with the block reference is an insertion point, scale, and rotation angle. All other data is derived from the block definition.

Boolean operations: Union, subtract, and intersect operations that are performed on regions and 3D solids. The term is also used in algebra to define logical operations (AND, OR, XOR, and NOT), which resemble the operations performed with this group of tools in the AutoCAD® program.

B-spline: An approximate spline curve also referred to as a nonuniform rational B-spline or NURBS curve.

building a selection set: The process of specifying the objects you wish to edit. You can add and remove objects to a selection set and reuse previous selection sets.

camera: An object that encapsulates the geometric definitions of a particular view. A model view is created with each camera, which allows you to quickly change the viewing point as defined by the camera.

cell: The box at the intersection of a table row and column that contains the table data or a formula. A cell is typically referenced using its column letter and row number separated with a colon. For example, the cell in column A and row 1 is referenced as A:1.

chamfer: To cut off a corner with a slight angle or bevel.

character set: The set of numeric codes used by a computer system to represent the characters (letters, numbers, punctuation, etc.) of a particular country or place. The most common character set in use today is ASCII (American Standard Code for Information Interchange).

color-dependent plot style: Plot style that is organized by the AutoCAD Color Index (ACI) number. Color-dependent plot styles are automatically assigned by the color of the AutoCAD object. All objects with the same color are assigned the same plot style settings. Color-dependent plot styles are stored in .CTB files.

command alias: An abbreviated definition of a command name that enables you to enter commands more quickly at the keyboard by entering the first one or two letters of the command name. Appendix C contains a complete list of the default AutoCAD command aliases.

composite 3D solids: 3D solids obtained by combining 3D solids using one of the three Boolean operations: UNION, SUBTRACT, or INTERSECT.

contour line: A line on a map that joins points of equal elevation. On a single contour line, all points have the same elevation. Contour lines are typically placed at designated vertical intervals to indicate elevation changes.

coordinate entry: The process of specifying point locations.

crossing box: A method of selecting objects in a selection set by specifying a rectangular area. Anything that touches the crossing box area is selected.

curve fit: The process of adding vertex points to a straight line segment polyline in order to create a smooth curve. Adding more points creates a smoother curve fit.

default lighting: The default illumination provided by the AutoCAD program. It uses two distant light sources that follow the view direction.

deferred point: Object Snap feature that allows you to "build" the Object Snap point using multiple point selection input by deferring the first point selected so that it can be used in conjunction with other point or object selections. For example, to find the intersection of two lines that don't physically intersect but that would intersect if they were extended in the same direction requires that you pick both lines. The first point selection is deferred while you pick the second line. Deferred point AutoMarkers are followed by an elllipsis (...), indicating that more information is needed.

defpoints: Points created when placing dimensions that define the measurement value of the dimension. AutoCAD measures the distance between the defpoints and uses the value as the default dimension text.

demand loading: Loading only the visible part of a referenced drawing. Others parts of the drawing are loaded only when necessary. AutoCAD uses demand loading to increase system performance when xrefs are used.

dimension style: A collection of dimension settings that control how dimension objects act and are displayed.

direct distance entry: The process of specifying a point by dragging the AutoCAD cursor to specify direction and typing in a distance.

drawing template: A drawing used as a starting point when creating a new drawing. Drawing templates can include title blocks, dimension styles, layer definitions, or any information found in a regular drawing. Drawing templates have a file extension of .DWT.

edit in place: Using the **REFEDIT** command to make changes to an externally referenced drawing. This allows you to make changes to one drawing from within another drawing.

facets: Edges or subdivisions of a 3D solid's nonplanar faces and nonplanar surfaces, produced by internal calculations of the AutoCAD program.

fillet: To round off an inside or outside corner at a specific radius.

floating viewport: Paper space viewport created in a drawing layout tab that can have almost any size and shape—including circles and polygons. Paper space viewports are referred to as "floating" because they can be modified using standard AutoCAD editing commands so that they can be moved, resized, and erased. Unlike model space tiled viewports, paper space floating viewports can overlap and have space in between them.

freeze/thaw: Hiding or displaying the contents of a drawing layer. Objects on a frozen layer are ignored by AutoCAD, are not shown in the drawing, and cannot be edited.

fuzz distance: Distance used to determine if polyline endpoints that are not connected can be connected by extending them, trimming them, or connecting them with a new polyline segment.

grips: Editing points that appear at key locations on drawing objects. Once grips are activated, you can directly modify drawing objects by selecting their grips.

hatch boundary: The edges of a hatched area. These edges can be closed objects (such as a circle or closed polyline) or a combination of objects that define a closed area.

hatch islands: Closed areas within a hatch boundary. You have the option of telling AutoCAD how to deal with island areas when creating hatch objects.

hatch patterns: The pattern used to fill a hatch boundary. Hatch patterns are defined in .pat files and also include solid and gradient fill patterns.

hatching: The process of filling in a closed area with a pattern. Hatching can consist of solid filled areas, gradient filled areas, or areas filled with patterns of lines.

helix: 2D or 3D spiral curve that coils around an axis, gradually growing horizontally, vertically, or in both directions. 2D spiral curves grow only horizontally.

history: Original 3D solids involved in the Boolean operations of a composite 3D solid. A composite 3D solid can be modified by modifying its history.

hotspot angle and falloff angle: The angles of the inner and outer cones defining the characteristics of the light rays emitted by a spot light. The intensity of light inside the inner cone is always the same, whereas that inside the outer cone diminishes in intensity from the hotspot angle to the falloff angle.

imaginary axis of revolution: The vector, defined by specifying any two points, about which the objects are revolved. Its direction is defined from the first point to the second point.

imaginary axis of rotation: An imaginary vector defined by specifying two points, or a direction vector and a point, about which the objects are rotated. It is the equivalent of the point in a 2D rotation.

imaginary mirror plane: Imaginary plane about which the selected object is copied to the opposite side as a mirror image. It is the equivalent of the mirror line in a 2D mirror operation.

imaginary sectioning plane: Imaginary plane that defines a section through 3D solids as it crosses these objects. To define a plane in the 3D space, it is necessary to specify one of the following: three points, another plane and a point, or a vector.

imaginary slicing plane: Imaginary plane with which 3D solid objects are cut. To define a plane in 3D space, it is necessary to specify one of the following: three points, another plane and a point, or a vector.

implied windowing: Feature that allows you to create a Window or a Crossing selection automatically by picking an empty space in a drawing to define the first corner point. The opposite corner point defines a Window selection if it is picked to the right of the first corner point and a Crossing selection if it is picked to the left.

isometric view: A pseudo-3D pictorial drawing in which three axes represent accurate measurements of the drawing model in order to show three sides of an object. Sometimes called 2 1/2D because three sides of an object are shown but the drawing is still only two-dimensional.

layers: A collection of object properties and display settings that are applied to objects.

layout: 2D page setups created in paper space that represents the paper size and what the drawing will look like when it is printed.

layout viewport: The user-defined window created in a paper space layout that allows you to view drawing information that resides in model space. Layout viewports are sometimes referred to as "floating" viewports because they can be moved, copied, and resized unlike the "tiled" viewports created in model space that are static and must abut each other.

LOFT: Operation in which a set of open or closed objects are connected through a blended smooth transition, creating 3D solids and surfaces.

model: The geometry (lines, circles, etc.) created in a drawing that defines the object or objects drawn. The graphical representation of the real-world object or part.

model view: A combination of geometric specifications that define a view plus additional elements such as UCS, layer snapshot, and visual style.

motion paths: User-created routes through which the camera, the target, or both gradually move while the camera keeps its focus on the target.

move grip tool: Editing tool that allows you to choose among six movements along one of the three axes and parallel to one of the three planes.

named plot style: Plot style that is organized by a user-defined name. Named plot styles can be assigned to AutoCAD layers or hard-coded to individual drawing objects. Named plot styles are stored in .STB files.

nested xref: An xref within an xref. This occurs when the drawing you are referencing contains a reference to another drawing. For example, you reference drawing A, and drawing A contains a reference to drawing B; drawing B is the nested xref.

nonplanar curve: A curve placed throughout the 3D space that is not completely contained in a plane. Helixes are examples of nonplanar curves.

objects: Graphical drawing elements, such as lines, arcs, circles, polylines, and text.

object snaps/osnaps: Geometric points on objects such as the endpoints or midpoint of a line or the center of an arc of a circle. Object snaps can be construction points on objects or calculated points such as a point of tangency, a perpendicular point, or the projected intersection of two drawing objects.

obscured lines: Edges or other objects that cannot be seen from the current viewing point because of their position relative to other objects. Obscured lines can be removed by invoking the **HIDE** command.

offset: To create a parallel copy of an object.

orthographic: 90° increments. When the ORTHO mode is turned on, AutoCAD locks the cursor movement to 0°, 90°, 180°, and 270° angles.

orthographic projection: The two-dimensional graphic representation of an object formed by the perpendicular intersections of lines drawn from points on the object to a plane of projection. Orthographic projection is a drafting technique commonly used to create multiple view drawings by creating one view, then projecting perpendicular lines from the complete view to create the other views. This approach limits the number of times you need to measure in your drawing, reducing errors and increasing productivity.

orthographic UCS: A particular type of reorientation of the WCS in which the *XY* plane aligns parallel to the imaginary orthographic viewing planes. The six orthographic UCS are predefined in the AutoCAD program, so you can quickly select them.

orthographic view: View in which objects are seen from a viewing point perpendicular to the orthographic imaginary planes. According to drafting standards, three orthographic views are used to describe the dimensions and shape of objects: Top, Front, and Right.

page setup: A collection of plot settings that are applied to a drawing layout. Page setups can be used and shared among multiple drawings.

pan: The process of moving your drawing from side to side in the display window so the location of the view changes without affecting the zoom scale.

parametric: Automated creation of a drawing based on a given set of dimensions referred to as *parameters*. These input parameters are applied against algorithms that create points, distances, and angles for the creation of drawing geometry. A simple example of creating a drawing parametrically is entering a width (X) and a height (Y) to create a rectangle.

parsec: A unit of astronomical length based on the distance from Earth at which stellar parallax is one second of arc and equal to 3.258 light-years, 3.086×10^{13} kilometers, or 1.918×10^{13} miles.

.PC3 file: Plotter configuration file used to store and manage printer/plotter settings. PC3 files control plot device settings such as port connections and output settings, media, graphics, physical pen configuration, custom properties, initialization strings, calibration, and user-defined paper sizes.

perspective view: View in which the 3D objects represented give the impression not only of height, width, and depth, but also of relative distance from the viewing point to the viewing target.

pickbox: Square box that replaces the cursor crosshairs whenever AutoCAD prompts you to *Select objects:*. It is used to pick objects in a drawing to create a selection set.

plot style: A collection of property settings defined in a plot style table that is applied when the drawing is plotted to control the appearance of the drawing objects on the printed drawing. Plot styles can be used to control line thickness, grayscale, screening, and other plot features.

plotting: The process of printing a drawing in AutoCAD. Plotting includes outputting your drawing to printers and plotters as well as various electronic file formats.

point: A one-dimensional object that is defined as a single coordinate in space. Points have no length or width, only a coordinate location. Points are referenced with the Node object snap.

point filters: A method of entering a point by which the *X, Y,* and *Z* coordinates are given in separate stages using any combination. The different stages can contain information about a single coordinate or the combination of any two coordinates.

polar tracking: A process where AutoCAD will lock the cursor movement to predefined angles. When the cursor gets close to one of these predefined angles, AutoCAD will lock onto that angle and display the angle measurement at the cursor.

polygon mesh: Surface object composed of individual three- or four-sided polygons joined one with the other. The mesh is organized by an N × M matrix. A polygon mesh can be either open or closed in either of the two directions.

predefined visual styles: Predefined collections of settings, saved as visual styles, that control the display of edges and faces of 3D objects. There are five predefined visual styles: **2D Wireframe, 3D Hidden, 3D Wireframe, Conceptual**, and **Realistic**.

printable area: The actual physical area that can be printed for the currently specified plotting device and paper size. Most printers cannot print to the very edge of the paper because of mechanical limitations.

properties: The settings that control how and where a drawing object is shown in the drawing. Some properties are common to all objects (layer, color, linetype, and lineweight) or specific to a particular type of drawing object (the radius of a circle or the endpoint of a line).

Render Preset: A named collection of settings controlling the quality of the rendered image generated with the **RENDER** command.

revision cloud: Continuous line made from arcs to resemble a cloud that is used to highlight markups and changes. Sometimes marked with a delta triangle indicating the revision number or letter.

Ribbon: A special palette that provides a single, compact placement for the tools and commands needed for a particular workspace. The Ribbon is made of tabs and panels that are totally customizable.

right-hand rule: Easy-to-understand reference that can be used to determine the positive and negative direction of the *X, Y,* and *Z* axes. To use the right-hand rule, you clench your right hand into a fist with your palm facing towards you and extend your thumb to the right, point your pointer finger straight up, and point your middle finger towards you. If your palm is the origin at 0,0,0, then your thumb represents positive *X*, your pointer finger represents positive *Y*, and your middle fingers represent positive *Z*.

rotation grip tool: Editing tool that enables you to choose among three directions of rotation that are aligned with the axes of the current UCS.

rubber band: A live preview of a drawing object as it is being drawn. The rubber-band preview allows you to see objects as they are being created.

scale factor: Multiplier that determines the size of annotation features such as text height, dimension features, and linetype appearance when a drawing is plotted or printed. The scale factor is typically the reciprocal of the plot scale or view scale.

section object: An AutoCAD entity that allows you to temporarily slice 3D objects and create 2D and 3D sections from them. Section objects are created with the **SECTIONPLANE** command.

selection set: One or more selected objects that are treated as one unit by an AutoCAD command. Objects in a selection set are typically highlighted (dashed).

ShapeManager: Modeler or engine used by the AutoCAD program to change the form and appearance of 3D solids. After each edit operation, the system checks whether the 3D solid is still a valid ShapeManager solid.

sheet sets: An organized and named collection of sheets created from multiple AutoCAD drawing files.

silhouette: Outline that defines the limit or profile of the curved faces of an object in the 3D space, causing it to look more real. Silhouettes are not physical edges.

spline: Nonplanar continuous curve that goes through a set of points specified anywhere in the 3D space. This object is created with the **SPLINE** command.

spline-fit polyline: Polylines and 3D polylines after they have been transformed by the **Spline** option of the **PEDIT** command. As the name implies, spline-fit polylines are not real splines, but approximations to them.

Standard Colors: Colors 1–9 of the AutoCAD Color Index.

subobject: Any face, edge, or vertex of a 3D solid. The original 3D solids of a composite 3D solid can be considered to be subobjects as well. Subobjects are selected by holding down the **<Ctrl>** key.

SWEEP: Operation in which open or closed planar objects are passed through a curve, creating 3D solids and surfaces.

system variable: A named setting maintained by AutoCAD that controls an aspect of a drawing or the drawing environment. Most system variables can be changed by entering the variable name at the command line, although some variables are read-only and cannot be changed.

3D Orbit: The most useful viewing tool for quickly selecting any viewing point. With this simple-to-use tool, you can look at the objects from virtually any point in the 3D space.

3D polyline: A curve placed in the 3D space that does not belong to a plane. It can contain only straight segments and cannot be filleted.

tapering midplane: The cross section in the 3D solid that does not change its original dimensions when the **Taper faces** operation is performed. In the argot of mold design, it is known as the *parting line*.

template: Predefined collection of specific properties and property settings that gives a material a specific appearance.

tiled viewport: Rectangular model space viewport. Model space viewports are referred to as "tiled" because multiple viewports in model space must abut each other with no overlap or space between them to create a tile pattern.

Tool Palettes: Customizable AutoCAD window that allows the user to organize tools and many other settings by palettes. You can add a tool by dragging objects into a palette. You can create a tool palette by right-clicking on the **Tool Palettes** title bar and selecting **New Palette**.

transparent command: A command that can be used without interrupting the currently active command. Most display commands can be used transparently so that you can pan and zoom in a drawing while simultaneously using the drawing and editing commands. Transparent commands are run by entering an apostrophe (') before the command name.

typeface: The style or design of a font. Other unique properties include size, boldness (line thickness), and obliqueness (an angle applied to the characters, not to be confused with an italic font).

underlay: A CAD file that is not directly modifiable by AutoCAD but is still displayed within a drawing and updated when the source data is changed. AutoCAD currently supports the display of DWF and DGN files as underlays.

unit block: A block or symbol drawn within a 1×1 unit square that is inserted in the drawing with different X and Y scales to achieve different final sizes.

User Coordinate System (UCS): A user-defined variation of the World Coordinate system. Variations in the coordinate system range from moving the default drawing origin (0,0,0) to another location to changing orientations for the X, Y, and Z axes. It is possible to rotate the WCS on any axis to create a UCS with a different two-dimensional XY plane—a technique commonly used to create multiview 3D drawings.

viewing point: The point in the 3D space that establishes the viewing direction of the user. The viewing direction is considered to be a vector from the viewing point to the origin of the coordinate system.

viewport: A window in the paper space environment that shows the view of the model space environment.

visual style: A collection of settings or modifiers that control the display of edges and shading of 3D objects. Visual styles can be created and modified in the **Visual Style Manager** palette.

working set: The group of objects selected for in-place editing using the **REFEDIT** command. Objects can be added to and removed from the working set using the **Refedit** toolbar during the in-place editing process.

workspaces: Specific arrangements of user interface elements, including their contents, properties, display status, and locations. Workspaces allow you to quickly switch between specific arrangements of menus, toolbars, and dockable windows, as well as many other settings previously specified.

World Coordinate System (WCS): The default coordinate system in AutoCAD upon which all objects and user coordinate systems are based.

xref: A drawing that is referenced by another drawing. The drawing references are updated when the source drawing is modified.

zooming: The process of moving around the drawing. Zooming in shows you a close-up view of a drawing area. Zooming out shows you a larger viewing area.

Index